PRICE GUIDE

January - April 2020

published by
Hagerty's Cars That Matter, LLC

ISBN 978-1-675-50117-7

HAGERTY PRICE GUIDE
Box 477
Great Falls, VA 22066-0477
(703) 759-9100
www.hagerty.com/valuationtools

For insurance information, call (877) 922-9701

Do not even think of using this book after April 30, 2020. The market moves and prices change; don't be left behind.

TABLE OF CONTENTS

"May you live in interesting times," goes the old curse, and these are indeed interesting times. Except in the higher end of the collector market, as you will read in the following pages of this, the first Hagerty Price Guide of 2020. The values have gone flat at the top end and life has become somewhat more predictable in the last couple of years. If that sounds like a bad thing, it isn't. Knowing roughly the price you'll pay for an item before you embark on a search for one is actually how markets work best for the buyer, and we think it bodes better for people who actually acquire classics to drive and enjoy rather than as assets to flip for a profit. And, as you probably know by now, we are all about the driving here at Hagerty.

The other thing you'll see—and we've been hammering on this point at Hagerty for some time now—is that the younger generations are becoming more active in the hobby. In 2019, more than half of the calls to our call centers were from Gen X or millennials. We have been anticipating this inflection point for some time, and though some older folks still think "the kids don't care about this stuff," our data is telling us differently. Also note the vehicles that the younger buyers are interested in. Of course, they want the cars that were hot in their youth, so 1980s and '90s cars are now transitioning from the realm of used daily drivers to collectible classics with strengthening values. But these buyers also love good old '60s muscle cars for the same reasons their elders did: they are fun, easy to work on, and timelessly cool.

Yes, these are interesting times, and for some of the best reasons: new collectors are coming into the market and, just as preceding generations did years ago, are redefining what a "classic" is. And they are creating new events such as Radwood, Luftgekühlt, and the Japanese Classic Car Show to celebrate them. Change is never easy, but it is inevitable, and I think these are changes we can all get behind as the next generations step up to receive their inheritance, which is our shared automotive experience.

McKeel Hagerty

Welcome to Book 41 of the Hagerty Price Guide. Now that 2019 is history, we know that in the classic car world, it won't be universally remembered for ever-rising values and exciting auction moments. In fact, we can best refer to 2019 as an interesting year for many changes in values. And you know what? That's just fine. Following the various changes in value is what we do. Gathering information from all possible sources is what we do as well.

Just ten years ago, the economies of many countries were recovering from the so-called Great Recession. Without getting into the details, there was a "flight to collectibles" starting in 2009, and prices of gems and jewelry, fine art, rare coins and many more collectibles were soon on the rise. With few stock market or real estate investments making good sense at the time, this capital infusion happened in collector cars as well. The effect of more money was, of course, sellers raising prices. It appears that, at least for now, those days are mostly over, and the book on the 2020 economy is yet to be written.

The final quarter of 2019 will also be remembered for some lackadaisical land-based auction results worldwide. Starting with a generally disappointing set of auction sales in Monterey, and continuing (with some bright spots here and there) through the final few days of the year.

We can expect continued awareness with car collectors interested in trading cars in the so-called virtual auction sites, the first and still biggest being Bring a Trailer. Hemming's has recently entered the field, and these will all be worth following in 2020 and beyond.

As a reminder, we publish three times per year, and all the information inside (plus trucks, motorcycles and more) are available online at Hagerty.com/vaulationtools.

The weather might not make this the best time of year for many of us to drive, but cleaning, fixing, finding parts for, or just hanging out with car friends are also ways to enjoy our shared interest in collector cars.

Enjoy the drive!

Dave Kinney
Publisher

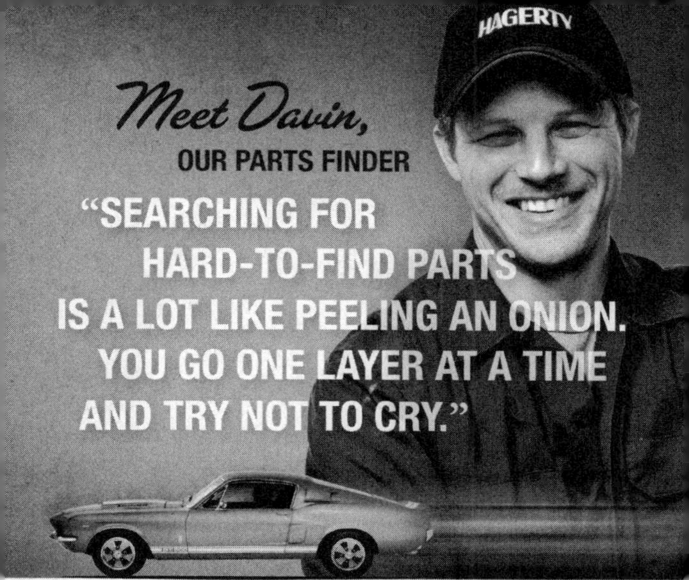

HAGERTY MARKET RATING

The Hagerty Market Rating uses a weighted algorithm to calculate the strength of the North American collector car market.

- The Hagerty Market Rating bounced back slightly from its 7-year low last month, growing nearly three-quarters of a point to 62.68. Last month excepted, though, this is still the lowest the rating has been since May 2012.
- And even though the overall rating is up month-over-month, most of its component ratings are down. The number of cars sold at auction is up slightly, but the median sale price at auction is at its lowest since May 2016. Activity on the private market, meanwhile, is at its lowest in over five years.
- The number of both mainstream and high-end vehicle owners who think that values are growing continues its downward trend that has lasted over a year. Both numbers are at their lowest point since they were first included in the Hagerty Market Rating a decade ago.
- With condition #3 (good) values down on average, the Hagerty Price Guide section of the rating is down as well.

Current Rating	62.68	All-time high:	71.95 (May 2015)
Five-Year High	71.95 (May 2015)	Five-Year Low	61.94 (Oct 2019)
1-Month Change	+0.74 (Oct 2019)	12-Month Change	-2.38 (Nov 2018)
36-Month Change	-3.85 (Nov 2016)	60-Month Change	-7.10 (Nov 2014)

**The Hagerty Market Rating is updated on the 15th of each month. The November update was the most current at the time of printing.*

Included below are some notable moves that occurred during the past four months. Percent change is based on the average value of all four conditions.

NOTABLE GAINS

1. 1991-98 Mercedes-Benz S320 .... +52%
2. 1964-67 Intermeccanica Vetta Ventura .... +46%
3. 1994-99 Ferrari F355 .... +46%
4. 2000-06 BMW M3 .... +41%
5. 1969-70 Shelby GT350 .... +31%

NOTABLE LOSSES

1. 1948-50 Packard Eight .... -37%
2. 1989-91 Chrysler TC by Maserati .... -25%
3. 1950-53 Aston Martin DB2 .... -23%
4. 1953-56 Packard Caribbean .... -21%
5. 1956-59 Ferrari 250 TdF .... -20%

INDICES

HAGERTY PRICE GUIDE publishes seven primary collector car indices that describe how various sectors of the market have performed over time. These seven indices, complete with commentary are on the following pages: *Blue Chip, British Cars, Ferrari, American Muscle Cars, Post-War German Collectible Cars, 1950s American Classics, Affordable Classics.*

BLUE CHIP INDEX

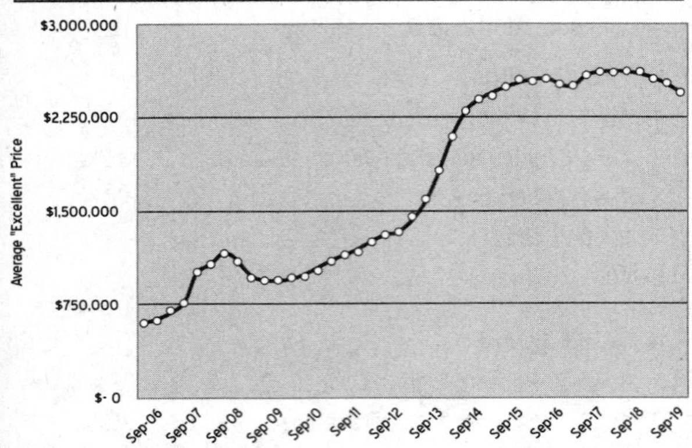

January was the third consecutive period of decline for Hagerty's Blue Chip index, dragging this group's level down 6 percent since January 2019. This is the single biggest 12-month slide since January 2010, though the price adjustment is more like a slow erosion than a sinkhole.

Upper echelon cars have faced headwinds for the last four years, and buyers at this level are increasingly selective with their purchases. Seven-figure cars with excellent history and specifications that are carefully represented are still acheiving steady prices, but any car with less than the best story is a tough sell at the moment. Several years in, owners are still coming to terms with this dynamic.

Five Blue Chip component cars fell more than 10 percent since September 2019, including the Aston Martin DB5, the Ferrari 275 GTB/4, the Jaguar D-Type, the Plymouth Hemi Cuda convertible, and the 1973 Porsche 911 Carrera RS. The Cuda excluded, most of these cars have historically seen strong interest among European buyers, and many of those buyers are hesitating due to unfavorable currency exchange rates and other macro-economic concerns.

BLUE CHIP INDEX

Index value:	409.6	All-time high:	438.8 (Sep 2018)
Five-year high:	438.8 (Sep 2018)	Five-year low:	400.5 (Jan 2015)
4-month change:	-3%	12-month change:	-6%
36-month change:	-3%	60-month change:	+2%
Component cars:	25	Gainers:	1
No change:	16	Losers:	8

1964 Alfa Romeo TZ-2	n/c
1965 Aston Martin DB5 coupe	-11%
1958 Bentley S1 Continental DHC	n/c
1960 BMW 507	n/c
1953 Chevrolet Corvette	-2%
1967 Chevrolet Corvette 427/435 conv	-5%
1958 Ferrari 250 GT California LWB Spyder	n/c
1963 Ferrari 250 GT California SWB Spyder	n/c
1968 Ferrari 275 GTB/4	-13%
1974 Iso Grifo SII coupe	+3%
1954 Jaguar D-type	n/c
1971 Lamborghini Miura SV	n/c
1954 Lancia Aurelia B24 Spider America	n/c
1957 Maserati 5000GT Frua coupe	n/c
1957 Mercedes-Benz 300SL Gullwing coupe	n/c
1963 Mercedes-Benz 300SL roadster	n/c
1970 Plymouth Hemi Cuda convertible	-15%
1958 Porsche 356A 1600 Super Speedster	n/c
1973 Porsche 911 Carrera RS Touring coupe	-12%
1957 Rolls-Royce Silver Cloud I Mulliner DHC	n/c
1963 Shelby Cobra 289 R&P	n/c
1966 Shelby Cobra 427 (CSX3300 - CSX3360)	n/c
1965 Shelby GT350	n/c
1969 Toyota 2000GT	n/c
1948 Tucker 48	-3%

INDEX OF BRITISH CARS

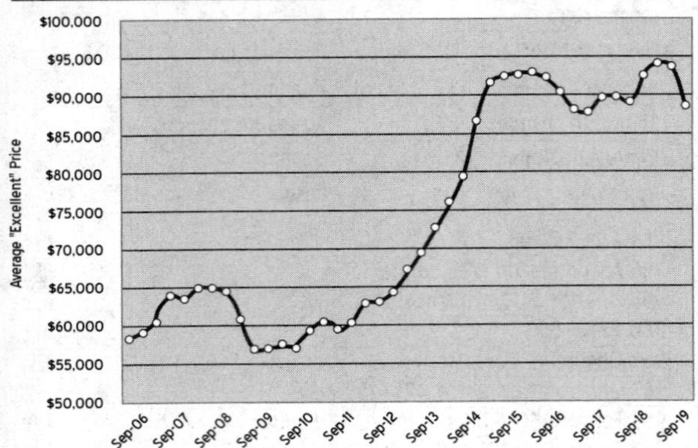

In May 2019, Hagerty's British Car Index hit an all-time high, but since September 2019 this sector has recorded a larger drop than any other index save for one. Half of this group's component cars recorded a loss over the past four months, and just one car—the 1972 Triumph TR6—recorded a gain. That increase was a minor 1 percent.

Outside the index, many 1950s Aston Martins recorded the biggest losses of any British cars, while the MG TD continued its gradual slide downward with a 7 percent loss and the Triumph GT6 continued its gradual climb upward with a 9 percent gain. Meanwhile, most bread-and-butter models from MG, Triumph and Austin-Healey were less volatile with either no change or minor movements up or down. We have noted in the past that the long-term outlook for British cars is uncertain since younger buyers in general still shy away from them. That still seems to be the case, but budget-conscious buyers looking for maximum fun and style per dollar should keep an eye on this segment.

INDEX OF BRITISH CARS

Index value:	152.0	All-time high:	161.1 (May 2019)
Five-year high:	161.1 (May 2019)	Five-year low:	148.7 (Jan 2015)
4-month change:	-6%	12-month change:	-4%
36-month change:	-2%	60-month change:	+2%
Component cars:	10	Gainers:	1
No change:	4	Losers:	5

Car	Change
1964 Austin-Healey 3000 Mk III BJ8 ph2	n/c
1956 Austin-Healey 100M BN2 Le Mans	n/c
1965 Jaguar E-type SI 4.2L convertible	-13%
1954 Jaguar XK120 roadster	-11%
1961 MGA 1600 roadster	-2%
1963 MGB Mk I	-1%
1955 MG TF-1500 roadster	-4%
1967 Sunbeam Tiger Mk II convertible	n/c
1962 Triumph TR3A roadster	n/c
1972 Triumph TR6 convertible	+1%

INDEX OF FERRARIS

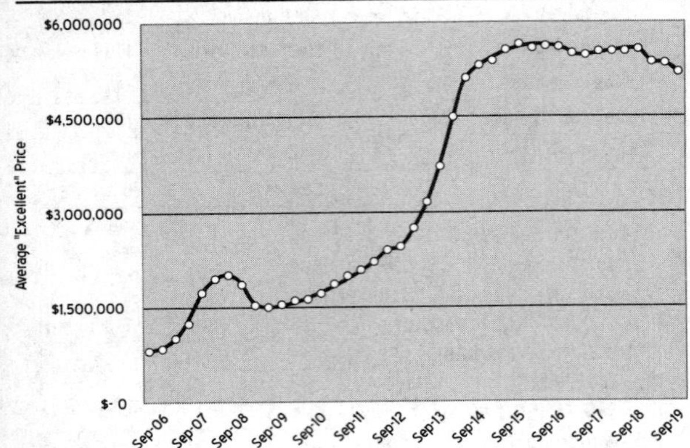

After a brief flat period over the summer, Hagerty's Ferrari Index fell 3 percent to close out 2019. This slip leaves the group 6 percent down year over year. More importantly, the index is now 2 percent below where it was five years ago, effectively rolling prices back to 2014 levels.

The biggest culprits in this period's change are the 250 GT SWB, which dropped 15 percent, and the 275 GTB/4, which fell 13 percent. Meanwhile, Daytona coupes and 246 Dinos both seem to have stabilized with two consecutive periods of unchanged prices.

The silver lining with Ferrari's downward trajectory, as many market observers are noting, is that it is unlikely to be long-lived. Name recognition and low production numbers should help insulate these cars in the long run, which means there are buying opportunities for those who intend to keep their cars for a while.

INDEX OF FERRARIS

Index value:	643.7	All-time high:	698.7 (Jan 2016)
Five-year high:	698.7 (Jan 2016)	Five-year low:	643.7 (Jan 2020)
4-month change:	-3%	12-month change:	-6%
36-month change:	-7%	60-month change:	-2%
Component cars:	13	Gainers:	0
No change:	8	Losers:	5

1957 Ferrari 410 Superamerica SIII coupe	n/c
1958 Ferrari 250 GT California Spyder LWB	n/c
1963 Ferrari 250 GT California Spyder SWB	n/c
1963 Ferrari 250 GT SWB	-15%
1960 Ferrari 250 GT PF coupe	-3%
1963 Ferrari 250 GT Lusso	n/c
1963 Ferrari 250 LM	n/c
1966 Ferrari 330 GT 2+2	-2%
1968 Ferrari 275 GTB/4	-13%
1968 Ferrari 330 GTC coupe	-6%
1972 Ferrari 365 GTS/4 "Daytona" Spyder	n/c
1972 Ferrari 365 GTB/4 "Daytona" coupe	n/c
1972 Ferrari 246 GTS Dino Spyder	n/c

INDEX OF MUSCLE CARS

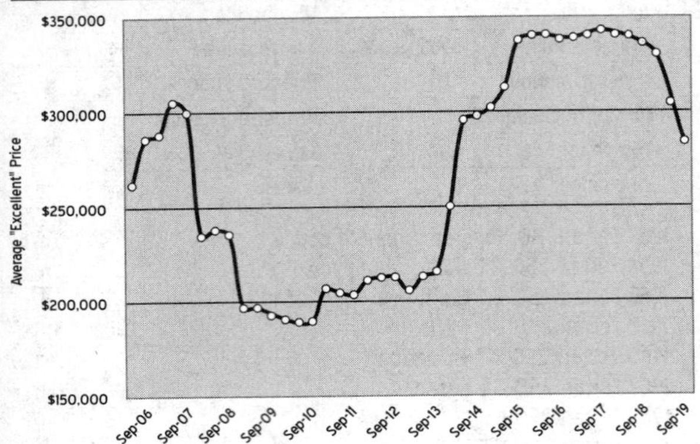

This time last year, Hagerty's Muscle Car Index was at an all-time high, but over the past four months it recorded the largest drop of any index for the second time in a row, falling 7 percent to a five-year low. While more than three-quarters of the index's component cars recorded no change at all, another large drop for the 1970 Hemi Cuda convertible (among the most valuable muscle cars of all) and a 4 percent decrease for the 1964 Impala SS were more than enough to pull the overall score down.

Values elsewhere in the classic muscle market either tracked straight or were slightly down. In recent years there hasn't been much appreciation in this segment, and certain top tier muscle cars like Hemi Cudas have stumbled. That said, the mass appeal of American muscle cars, particularly to younger enthusiasts, has kept values in this segment mostly firm. For more affordable and well-known models this trend should continue, but the outlook for more expensive and more obscure muscle cars is more uncertain.

INDEX OF MUSCLE CARS

Index value:	108.4	All-time high:	130.8 (Jan 2018)
Five-year high:	130.8 (Jan 2018)	Five-year low:	108.4 (Jan 2020)
4-month change:	-7%	12-month change:	-15%
36-month change:	-16%	60-month change:	-5%
Component cars:	15	Gainers:	0
No change:	12	Losers:	3

1969 AMC AMX 390/340	n/c
1970 Buick GS455 convertible	n/c
1964 Chevrolet Impala SS 409/425 convertible	-4%
1968 Chevrolet Camaro Yenko 427 coupe	n/c
1970 Chevrolet Chevelle SS 454 LS6 coupe	n/c
1969 Dodge Charger 426/425 Hemi 500 hardtop coupe	n/c
1969 Ford Mustang Boss 429/375 SportsRoof	n/c
1968 Mercury Cougar GTE 428/335 coupe	n/c
1970 Oldsmobile 4-4-2 W-30 coupe	n/c
1970 Plymouth Superbird 426/425 coupe	n/c
1970 Plymouth Hemi 'Cuda convertible	-15%
1970 Plymouth 'Cuda AAR coupe	-2%
1965 Pontiac LeMans GTO 389/360 Tri-Power convertible	n/c
1965 Shelby GT350	n/c
1968 Shelby GT500 KR convertible	n/c

INDEX OF GERMAN CARS

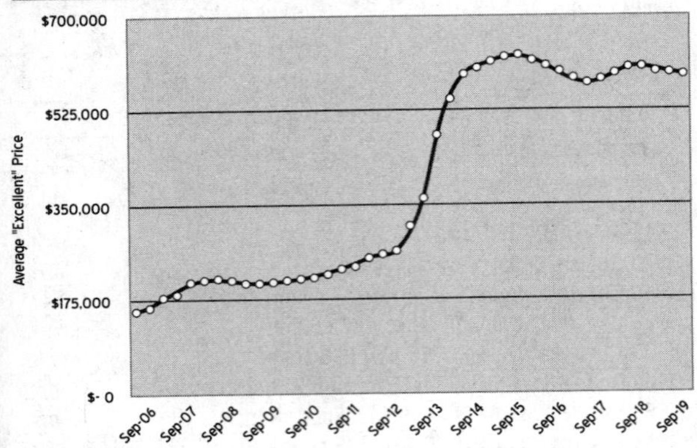

Hagerty's German Car Index remained steady for the past four months with a modest drop of 1 percent. Nearly three-quarters of the component cars recorded no movement at all. Three of them dropped, including previously red-hot Porsches like the 1973 911 Carrera RS Touring with a 12 percent decrease and the 1979 930, which continued its gradual slide with a 6 percent decrease. The only serious gain of any car in the index was for the Mercedes-Benz 280SL, which bounced back with a 17 percent surge after two years of continuous drops.

The most dynamic parts of the German car market are outside this index, particularly among newer and/or more affordable models. Volkswagens in particular had a strong showing, with every post-1952 Beetle recording significant gains along with Type 181 Things, Karmann Ghias and Sciroccos. Most Mercedes-Benz sedans from the 1980s and 1990s also recorded gains, as did BMWs of the same period. High build quality, clean styling, premium badges, and large and loyal fanbases for a low cost of entry continues to attract enthusiasts to these cars, and their prices are rising as a result.

INDEX OF GERMAN CARS

Index value:	380.8	All-time high:	405.1 (Jan 2016)
Five-year high:	405.1 (Jan 2016)	Five-year low:	380.8 (Jan 2020)
4-month change:	-1%	12-month change:	-3%
36-month change:	-1%	60-month change:	-2%
Component cars:	21	Gainers:	2
No change:	15	Losers:	4

1948 Porsche 356 Gmund coupe	n/c
1958 Porsche 356A 1600 Super Speedster	n/c
1956 Porsche 356A 1500 GS Carrera Speedster	n/c
1959 Porsche 356A Super coupe	n/c
1962 Porsche 356B Twin Grille S90 roadster	+3%
1965 Porsche 356C Super coupe	n/c
1967 Porsche 911S Targa	-3%
1972 Porsche 911S coupe	n/c
1973 Porsche 911 Carrera RS Touring coupe	-12%
1979 Porsche 930 Turbo Carrera coupe	-6%
1955 Mercedes-Benz 300Sc Cabriolet	-2%
1957 Mercedes-Benz 300SL Gullwing coupe	n/c
1962 Mercedes-Benz 190SL roadster	n/c
1963 Mercedes-Benz 300SL roadster	n/c
1970 Mercedes-Benz 280SE 3.5 convertible	n/c
1970 Mercedes-Benz 600 sedan	n/c
1971 Mercedes-Benz 280SL roadster	+17%
1973 BMW 3.0CSL "Batmobile"	n/c
1972-73 BMW 2002tii coupe	n/c
1959 BMW 507	n/c
1979-80 BMW M1	n/c

INDEX OF 1950s AMERICAN CLASSICS

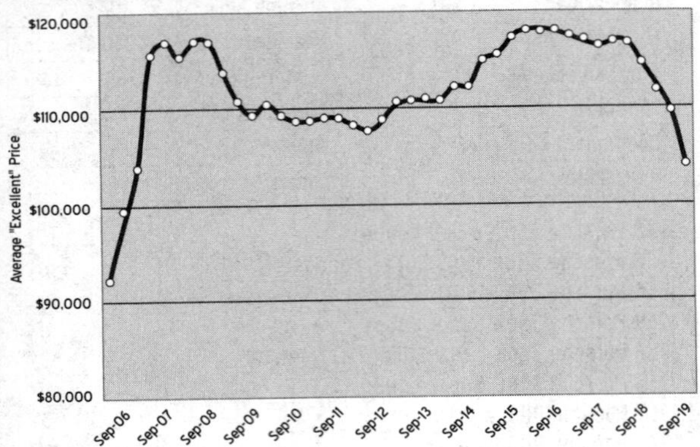

Postwar domestic cars are struggling to attract new enthusiasts, and many prices have been slipping as a result. The 1950s American Index continued its slide to close out 2019 with a 5 percent drop, and now sits at a 5-year low. While the 1954 Buick Skylark notched a significant gain of 5 percent, more than half the index's component cars recorded a serious loss. The 1955 Packard Caribbean took an especially serious blow with a 21 percent drop. The index's most expensive car, the 1953 Cadillac Eldorado, dropped 13 percent.

The wider 1950s American market is more of a mixed bag with some sizable growth seen for Hudson Hornets, Buick Specials and Pontiac Star Chiefs, but the index adequately represents a wider trend downward. No Studebakers or Packards in the Hagerty Price Guide grew in value, and many of them decreased anywhere from 2 percent to over 20 percent. The narrowing appeal of cars in this segment represents an opportunity for buyers, as well-kept older restorations and former show cars offer a lot of presence per dollar for enthusiasts who appreciate the chrome, excessive size and impossible-to-ignore style offered by many 1950s American cars.

INDEX OF 1950s AMERICAN CLASSICS

Index value:	112.9	**All-time high:**	128.0 (May 2016)
Five-year high:	128.0 (May 2016)	**Five-year low:**	112.9 (Jan 2020)
4-month change:	-5%	**12-month change:**	-9%
36-month change:	-12%	**60-month change:**	-7%
Component cars:	19	**Gainers:**	3
No change:	5	**Losers:**	11

1954 Buick Skylark sport convertible	+5%
1953 Cadillac Eldorado sport convertible	-13%
1958 Cadillac Eldorado Brougham sedan	-3%
1959 Cadillac Eldorado Biarritz convertible	n/c
1957 Chevrolet Bel Air convertible	+1%
1958 Chevrolet Bel Air Impala convertible	-5%
1957 Chrysler 300C convertible	-8%
1958 Chrysler 300D convertible	-8%
1959 Chrysler 300E convertible	-8%
1957 Ford Thunderbird convertible	-10%
1956 Ford Fairlane Victoria Sunliner conv	+2%
1957 Ford Fairlane 500 Skyliner retractable hardtop	-5%
1956 Continental Mk II coupe	n/c
1950 Oldsmobile Series 88 woody station wagon	n/c
1953 Oldsmobile Series 98 Fiesta conv	n/c
1957 Pontiac Bonneville convertible	-15%
1953 Hudson Hornet convertible	-3%
1955 Packard Caribbean convertible	-21%
1958 Studebaker Golden Hawk coupe	n/c

INDEX OF AFFORDABLE CLASSICS

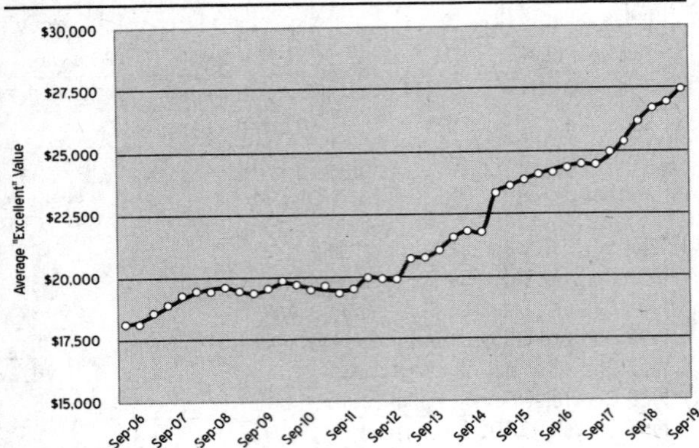

The Affordable Classics Index was the only one of Hagerty's seven primary indices to post any growth this past period, and it is currently perched at an all-time high. It is also the only index to show positive movement over the past 12 months, and one of only three indices sitting higher than it was five years ago. While most of the index's component cars tracked steady, the 1967 Volkswagen Beetle posted its third sizable increase in a row at 16 percent and the 1967 Karmann Ghia posted a more modest but still significant 4 percent.

Much of the heat in the market at the moment is for vintage trucks and SUVs as well as newer performance cars from Germany and Japan. While these vehicles appeal to different tastes, most of them are at the lower end of the price spectrum, so all the activity in this space has made Affordable Classics the brightest spot in the collector car market at the moment.

INDEX OF AFFORDABLE CLASSICS

Index value:	155.7	All-time high:	155.7 (Jan 2020)
Five-year high:	155.7 (Jan 2020)	Five-year low:	120.1 (Jan 2015)
4-month change:	+3%	12-month change:	+6%
36-month change:	+16%	60-month change:	+30%
Component cars:	13	Gainers:	4
No change:	8	Losers:	1

1969 AMC Javelin 343	n/c
1949 Buick Roadmaster Sedanette	+20%
1965 Chevrolet Corvair Monza convertible	n/c
1970 Chevrolet Camaro SS 350/300 coupe	n/c
1971 Datsun 240Z	n/c
1965 Ford Mustang GT coupe	n/c
1963 MGB Mk I	-1%
1972 Porsche 914 2.0 Targa	n/c
1962 Studebaker Lark convertible	n/c
1963 Studebaker Avanti R-1	n/c
1972 Triumph TR6 convertible	+1%
1967 Volkswagen Beetle Sedan	+16%
1967 Volkswagen Karmann Ghia coupe	+4%

HOW TO USE THIS GUIDE

Classify the vehicle. Use the printed guidelines for each condition and place the car in question in a #1 through #4 status.

Compare the car to others. Look at similar vehicles in the market. Do they have a better interior, more options, or fewer flaws? What is the asking price?

Clarify the claims of the seller. How many owners? Are there records of expenditures?

Consult with experts. Have a mechanical evaluation performed. Hire a qualified appraiser to value your purchase. Join a club that celebrates the brand or type of car. Participate in enthusiast internet chat rooms. Go to local and regional shows, as well as national events.

AND, KEEP IN MIND THAT:

HAGERTY PRICE GUIDE is a guide, not gospel. Use your senses; consult with experts in the field before making any buying or selling decisions.

Correct classification is paramount. Many sellers overrate the condition of their car; overeager buyers tend to do the same for potential purchases. Carefully look at and drive the vehicle, and evaluate its condition before purchase.

HAGERTY PRICE GUIDE reports on vehicles in four condition ratings. Fair (#4), Good (#3), Excellent (#2) and Concours (#1). We do not report values on cars in poor condition or parts cars.

HAGERTY PRICE GUIDE prices virtually all American cars assuming that the vehicle is equipped with the entry-level V8. All pricing additions assume equipment is from the factory.

Cars will always sell for prices above and below HAGERTY PRICE

GUIDE's price range for many reasons, including exceptional histories, extraordinarily beautiful or hideous coachwork, overheated market enthusiasm, a surfeit or dearth of buyers at the time of sale, cars being offered in incorrect venues and dozens more reasons.

It is very difficult to verify claims after multiple years and multiple owners. Many collector cars are sold with exempt or unknown miles. Use condition as a guideline, ask to see and get a copy of records. Additionally, restored cars could have had their odometers "zeroed" at restoration and cars that read in kilometers when new (or indeed all cars) could have replaced odometers.

CONDITION RATINGS

HAGERTY PRICE GUIDE reports on cars in four different conditions, #1 through #4.

#4 cars are "drivers" with some flaws visible to the naked eye. Examples of flaws that could be present on #4 cars include pitting or scratches on the chrome, a chip on the windshield, or a minor dent or chips in the paintwork. The paintwork might also have visible imperfections. You might find a split seam in a seat or a dash crack on the interior, the interior could be of a different type of material from original. No major parts are missing; however, components such as wheels might not be stock. A #4 car is often a deteriorated restoration. If too many flaws are present, it is no longer a #4 car. "Fair" is the one word that describes a #4 car.

#3 cars could possess some, but not all of the issues of a #4 car, but they will be balanced by other factors such as a fresh paint job or a new, correct interior. #3 cars drive and run well, but might have some incorrect parts. These cars are not used for daily transportation but are ready for a long tour without excuses, and the casual passerby will not find any visual flaws. "Good" is the one word description of a HAGERTY PRICE GUIDE #3.

#2 cars could win a local or regional show. They can be former #1 cars that have been driven or have aged. Seasoned observers will have to look closely for flaws, but will be able to find some not seen by the general public. The paint, chrome, glass and interior will all appear as excellent. No excessive smoke will be seen on startup, no unusual noises will emanate from the engine compartment. The vehicle will drive as a new car of its era would. The one word description for #2 cars is "excellent."

#1 vehicles in HAGERTY PRICE GUIDE are the best in the world. The visual image is of the best car, in the right colors, driving onto the lawn at the finest concours. Perfectly clean, the car has been groomed down to the tire treads. Painted and chromed surfaces are mirror-like. Dust and dirt are banned, and materials used are correct and superbly fitted. The one word description for #1 cars is "concours."

There are many cars in the market that are categorized below a condition #4. Even though HAGERTY PRICE GUIDE does not publish values for such cars, these definitions can help you properly classify what you are buying.

#5 cars are running examples with significant flaws and wear. Serious paint issues and rust may be present, interiors may be incomplete, and mechanicals are in need of attention before significant use. These cars may make good restoration candidates but are not suitable for prolonged use as they stand. "Poor" is the one word that describes a #5 car.

#6 cars are parts cars that are incomplete, not running, and severely compromised. Rot is persistent and interiors are worn to the point of being unusable. In rare and unusual cases these cars are sometimes restoration candidates, but mostly they serve to be the basis for a heavily modified car or to be a donor car for another project. "Parts" is the one word that describes a #6 car.

Year	Model	Body Style	4	3	2	1
1947	2-Litre	2dr Sdn	$7,200	$15,200	$20,500	$30,500
1948	2-Litre	2dr Sdn	$7,200	$15,200	$20,500	$29,500
1949	2-Litre	2dr Tourer	$24,000	$40,000	$54,000	$84,000
		2dr Bucklands Tourer	$26,000	$46,500	$75,000	$99,000
		4dr Tourer	$11,900	$21,900	$32,900	$47,000
		2dr Sdn	$7,200	$15,200	$20,500	$29,500
1950	2-Litre	2dr Tourer	$24,000	$40,000	$54,000	$84,000
		2dr Bucklands Tourer	$26,000	$46,500	$75,000	$99,000
		4dr Tourer	$11,900	$21,900	$32,900	$47,000
		2dr Sdn	$7,200	$15,200	$20,500	$29,500
1951	2-Litre	2dr Tourer	$24,000	$40,000	$54,000	$84,000
		2dr Bucklands Tourer	$26,000	$46,500	$75,000	$99,000
		4dr Tourer	$11,900	$21,900	$32,900	$47,000
		2dr Sdn	$7,200	$15,200	$20,500	$29,500
1952	2-Litre	2dr Tourer	$24,000	$40,000	$54,000	$84,000
		2dr Bucklands Tourer	$26,000	$46,500	$75,000	$99,000
		4dr Tourer	$12,000	$21,200	$31,900	$46,700
		2dr Sdn	$7,200	$15,200	$20,500	$29,500
		4dr Sdn	$3,000	$8,500	$14,900	$19,800
1953	Ace	2dr Rdstr	$195,000	$262,000	$351,000	$429,000
1953	Aceca	2dr Cpe	$88,000	$125,000	$175,000	$232,000
1953	2-Litre	2dr Tourer	$24,000	$40,000	$54,000	$84,000
		2dr Bucklands Tourer	$26,000	$46,500	$75,000	$99,000
		4dr Tourer	$12,000	$21,200	$31,900	$46,700
		2dr Sdn	$7,200	$15,200	$20,500	$29,500
		4dr Sdn	$3,000	$8,500	$14,900	$18,800
1954	Ace	2dr Rdstr	$195,000	$262,000	$351,000	$429,000
1954	Aceca	2dr Cpe	$88,000	$125,000	$175,000	$232,000
1954	2-Litre	4dr Tourer	$12,000	$21,200	$31,900	$46,700
		2dr Sdn	$7,200	$15,200	$20,500	$29,500
1955	Ace	2dr Rdstr	$195,000	$262,000	$351,000	$429,000
1955	Aceca	2dr Cpe	$88,000	$125,000	$175,000	$232,000
1955	2-Litre	4dr Tourer	$12,000	$21,200	$31,900	$46,700
		2dr Sdn	$7,200	$15,200	$20,500	$29,500
1956	Ace	2dr Rdstr	$195,000	$262,000	$351,000	$429,000
1956	Aceca	2dr Cpe	$88,000	$125,000	$175,000	$232,000
1956	2-Litre	2dr Sdn	$7,200	$15,200	$20,500	$29,500
		4dr Sdn	$3,000	$8,500	$14,900	$18,800
1957	Ace	2dr Rdstr	$195,000	$262,000	$351,000	$429,000
		2dr Bristol Rdstr	$247,000	$333,000	$426,000	$491,000
1957	Aceca	2dr Cpe	$88,000	$125,000	$175,000	$232,000
		2dr Bristol Cpe	$125,000	$168,000	$219,000	$297,000
1957	2-Litre	4dr Tourer	$12,000	$21,200	$31,900	$46,700
		4dr Sdn	$3,000	$8,500	$14,900	$18,800
1958	Ace	2dr Rdstr	$179,000	$246,000	$311,000	$389,000

AC

Year	Model	Body Style	4	3	2	1
		2dr Bristol Rdstr	$229,000	$317,000	$406,000	$471,000
1958	Aceca	2dr Cpe	$79,000	$115,000	$165,000	$207,000
		2dr Bristol Cpe	$125,000	$168,000	$219,000	$297,000
1958	2-Litre	4dr Tourer	$12,000	$21,200	$31,900	$46,700
		4dr Sdn	$3,000	$8,500	$14,900	$18,800
1959	Ace	2dr Rdstr	$179,000	$246,000	$311,000	$389,000
		2dr Bristol Rdstr	$229,000	$317,000	$426,000	$471,000
1959	Aceca	2dr Cpe	$79,000	$115,000	$165,000	$207,000
		2dr Bristol Cpe	$125,000	$168,000	$219,000	$297,000
1959	Greyhound	2dr Cpe	$68,000	$85,000	$110,000	$145,000
1960	Ace	2dr Rdstr	$179,000	$246,000	$311,000	$389,000
		2dr Bristol Rdstr	$229,000	$317,000	$406,000	$471,000
1960	Aceca	2dr Cpe	$79,000	$115,000	$165,000	$207,000
		2dr Bristol Cpe	$125,000	$168,000	$219,000	$297,000
1960	Greyhound	2dr Cpe	$68,000	$85,000	$110,000	$145,000
1961	Ace	2dr Rdstr	$179,000	$246,000	$311,000	$389,000
		2dr Bristol Rdstr	$229,000	$317,000	$406,000	$471,000
1961	Aceca	2dr Cpe	$79,000	$115,000	$165,000	$207,000
		2dr Bristol Cpe	$125,000	$168,000	$219,000	$297,000
1961	Greyhound	2dr Cpe	$68,000	$85,000	$110,000	$145,000
1962	Ace	2dr Rdstr	$179,000	$246,000	$311,000	$389,000
		2dr Bristol Rdstr	$229,000	$317,000	$426,000	$471,000
1962	Aceca	2dr Cpe	$79,000	$115,000	$165,000	$207,000
		2dr Bristol Cpe	$125,000	$168,000	$219,000	$297,000
1962	Greyhound	2dr Cpe	$68,000	$85,000	$110,000	$145,000
1963	Ace	2dr Rdstr	$179,000	$246,000	$311,000	$389,000
		2dr Bristol Rdstr	$229,000	$317,000	$406,000	$471,000
1963	Aceca	2dr Cpe	$79,000	$115,000	$165,000	$207,000
		2dr Bristol Cpe	$125,000	$168,000	$219,000	$297,000
1963	Greyhound	2dr Cpe	$68,000	$85,000	$110,000	$145,000
1964	Aceca	2dr Cpe	$79,000	$115,000	$165,000	$207,000
		2dr Bristol Cpe	$125,000	$168,000	$219,000	$297,000
1966	428	2dr Cpe	$112,000	$158,000	$204,000	$286,000
		2dr Conv	$132,000	$170,000	$225,000	$308,000
1967	428	2dr Cpe	$112,000	$158,000	$204,000	$286,000
		2dr Conv	$132,000	$170,000	$225,000	$308,000
1968	428	2dr Cpe	$112,000	$158,000	$204,000	$286,000
		2dr Conv	$132,000	$170,000	$225,000	$308,000
1969	428	2dr Cpe	$112,000	$158,000	$204,000	$286,000
		2dr Conv	$132,000	$170,000	$225,000	$308,000
1970	428	2dr Cpe	$112,000	$158,000	$204,000	$286,000
		2dr Conv	$132,000	$170,000	$225,000	$308,000
1971	428	2dr Cpe	$112,000	$158,000	$204,000	$286,000
		2dr Conv	$132,000	$170,000	$225,000	$308,000
1972	428	2dr Cpe	$112,000	$158,000	$204,000	$286,000
		2dr Conv	$132,000	$170,000	$225,000	$308,000
1973	428	2dr Cpe	$112,000	$158,000	$204,000	$286,000
		2dr Conv	$132,000	$170,000	$225,000	$308,000
1985	Mk IV	2dr Rdstr	$93,500	$114,000	$136,000	$172,000

ASA

Year	Model	Body Style	4	3	2	1
1962	AU 1000	2dr Bertone Cpe	$70,700	$98,900	$137,000	$179,000
		2dr Bertone Spyder	$94,500	$138,000	$174,000	$205,000
1963	AU 1000	2dr Bertone Cpe	$70,700	$98,900	$137,000	$179,000
		2dr Bertone Spyder	$94,500	$138,000	$174,000	$205,000
1964	AU 1000	2dr Bertone Cpe	$70,700	$98,900	$137,000	$179,000
		2dr Bertone Spyder	$94,500	$138,000	$174,000	$205,000
1965	AU 1000	2dr Bertone Cpe	$70,700	$98,900	$137,000	$179,000
		2dr Bertone Spyder	$94,500	$138,000	$174,000	$205,000
1966	AU 1000	2dr Bertone Cpe	$70,700	$98,900	$137,000	$179,000
		2dr Bertone Spyder	$94,500	$138,000	$174,000	$205,000
1967	AU 1000	2dr Bertone Cpe	$70,700	$98,900	$137,000	$179,000
		2dr Bertone Spyder	$94,500	$138,000	$174,000	$205,000

ATS

Year	Model	Body Style	4	3	2	1
1962	2500 GT	2dr Cpe	$895,000	$1.05 mil	$1.25 mil	$1.45 mil
1963	2500 GT	2dr Cpe	$895,000	$1.05 mil	$1.25 mil	$1.45 mil

Abarth

Year	Model	Body Style	4	3	2	1
1949	204A	Monoposto	$435,000	$540,000	$707,000	$882,000
1951	205A	2dr Vignale Cpe	$441,000	$560,000	$720,000	$910,000
1955	207A	2dr Boano Spider	$295,000	$420,000	$540,000	$680,000
1955	208A	2dr Boano Cpe	$262,000	$400,000	$510,000	$655,000
		2dr Boano Spider	$530,000	$610,000	$800,000	$990,000
1956	750	2dr Zagato SI Cpe	$122,000	$154,000	$185,000	$240,000
		2dr Zagato SII Cpe	$92,500	$123,000	$158,000	$205,000
1957	750	2dr Zagato SII Cpe	$92,500	$123,000	$158,000	$205,000
		2dr Zagato SIII Cpe	$75,000	$99,700	$138,000	$187,000
		2dr Zagato Spider	$40,400	$59,800	$75,600	$115,000
1958	750	2dr Zagato SIII Cpe	$75,000	$99,700	$138,000	$187,000
1959	750	2dr Zagato SIII Cpe	$75,000	$99,700	$138,000	$187,000
		2dr Allemano Spider	$42,400	$61,100	$76,300	$114,000
1959	750 Record Monza	2dr Cpe	$59,000	$88,200	$123,000	$158,000
		2dr GT Cpe	$87,000	$111,000	$143,000	$190,000
1959	2200	2dr Allemano 2+2 Cpe	$45,500	$64,700	$106,000	$144,000
		2dr Allemano Conv	$53,000	$85,500	$141,000	$195,000

Abarth

Year	Model	Body Style	4	3	2	1
1960	850	2dr Record Monza Cpe	$85,000	$110,000	$148,000	$192,000
1960	850 Scorpione	2dr Cpe	$19,400	$46,900	$66,700	$91,800
1960	2200	2dr Allemano Cpe 2+2	$45,500	$64,700	$106,000	$144,000
		2dr Allemano Conv	$53,000	$85,500	$141,000	$195,000
1961	750	2dr Scorpione Cpe	$12,700	$19,800	$32,900	$55,600
		2dr Sestiere Cpe	$35,700	$54,100	$68,600	$92,500
		2dr Riv Spider	$20,100	$27,900	$40,300	$62,700
1961	850	2dr Record Monza Cpe	$85,000	$110,000	$148,000	$192,000
1961	850 Scorpione	2dr Cpe	$19,400	$46,900	$66,700	$91,800
1961	1600	2dr Allemano Spider	$18,800	$28,500	$39,700	$55,900
1961	2400	2dr Ellena Cpe	$14,700	$23,300	$34,000	$58,600
1962	850	2dr Twin Cam Cpe	$11,000	$18,900	$32,300	$58,500
		2dr Allemano Scorpione Cpe	$15,000	$25,200	$37,500	$60,600
		2dr Record Monza Cpe	$48,500	$65,500	$99,600	$135,000
		2dr Allemano Riviera Spider	$14,800	$24,800	$35,700	$57,600
1962	AU 1000	2dr Cpe	$10,700	$15,400	$24,300	$44,200
		2dr Twin Cam Cpe	$14,500	$22,400	$35,900	$62,600
		2dr Allemano Scorpione Cpe	$21,700	$32,500	$50,400	$75,600
		2dr Allemano Riviera Spider	$14,700	$23,900	$34,300	$55,600
1962	1300	2dr SIMCA-Abarth Cpe	$52,400	$66,800	$87,900	$118,000
1962	1600	2dr Allemano Cpe	$13,400	$21,400	$27,300	$44,000
		2dr Spider	$16,400	$23,600	$31,100	$49,900
		2dr Allemano Spider	$18,800	$28,500	$39,700	$55,900
1962	2200	2dr Allemano Conv	$46,700	$75,500	$130,000	$171,000
1963	850	2dr TC Cpe	$11,000	$18,900	$32,300	$58,500
		2dr Allemano Scorpione Cpe	$15,000	$25,200	$37,500	$60,600
		2dr Record Monza Cpe	$48,500	$65,500	$99,600	$135,000
		2dr Allemano Riviera Spider	$14,800	$24,800	$35,700	$57,600
1963	AU 1000	2dr Cpe	$10,700	$15,400	$24,300	$44,200
		2dr TC Cpe	$15,300	$24,700	$39,500	$76,000
		2dr Allemano Scorpione Cpe	$21,700	$32,500	$50,400	$75,600
		2dr Allemano Riviera Spider	$14,700	$23,900	$34,300	$55,600

Year	Model	Body Style	4	3	2	1
1963	1300	2dr SIMCA-Abarth Cpe	$48,700	$60,400	$78,600	$101,000
1963	1600	2dr Allemano Cpe	$13,400	$21,400	$27,300	$44,000
		2dr Spider	$16,400	$23,600	$31,100	$49,900
		2dr Allemano Spider	$18,800	$28,500	$39,700	$55,900
1963	2000 GT	2dr SIMCA-Abarth Cpe	$99,500	$138,000	$182,000	$266,000
1963	2200	2dr Allemano Conv	$46,700	$75,500	$130,000	$171,000
1963	2400	2dr Allemano Cpe	$15,800	$26,200	$40,800	$57,500
1964	850	2dr TC Cpe	$11,000	$18,900	$32,300	$58,500
		2dr Allemano Scorpione Cpe	$15,000	$25,200	$37,500	$60,600
		2dr Record Monza Cpe	$48,500	$65,500	$99,600	$135,000
		2dr Allemano Riviera Spider	$14,800	$24,800	$35,700	$57,600
1964	AU 1000	2dr Cpe	$10,700	$15,400	$24,300	$44,200
		2dr TC Cpe	$15,300	$24,700	$39,500	$76,000
		2dr Allemano Scorpione Cpe	$21,700	$32,500	$50,400	$75,600
		2dr Allemano Riviera Spider	$14,700	$23,900	$34,300	$55,600
1964	1300	2dr SIMCA-Abarth Cpe	$48,700	$60,400	$78,600	$101,000
1964	1600	2dr Allemano Cpe	$13,400	$21,400	$27,300	$44,000
		2dr Allemano Spider	$18,800	$28,500	$39,700	$55,900
1964	2000 GT	2dr SIMCA-Abarth Cpe	$99,500	$138,000	$182,000	$266,000
1964	2200	2dr Allemano Conv	$46,700	$75,500	$130,000	$171,000
1964	2400	2dr Allemano Cpe	$15,800	$26,200	$40,800	$57,500
1965	850	2dr TC Cpe	$11,000	$18,900	$32,300	$58,500
		2dr Allemano Scorpione Cpe	$15,000	$25,200	$37,500	$60,600
		2dr Record Monza Cpe	$48,500	$65,500	$99,600	$135,000
		2dr Allemano Riviera Spider	$14,800	$24,800	$35,700	$57,600
1965	AU 1000	2dr Cpe	$10,700	$15,400	$24,300	$44,200
		2dr TC Cpe	$15,300	$24,700	$39,500	$76,000
		2dr Allemano Scorpione Cpe	$21,700	$32,500	$50,400	$75,600
		2dr Allemano Riviera Spider	$14,700	$23,900	$34,300	$55,600
1965	1600	2dr Allemano Cpe	$13,400	$21,400	$27,300	$44,000
		2dr Allemano Spider	$18,800	$28,500	$39,700	$55,900
1965	2200	2dr Allemano Conv	$46,700	$75,500	$130,000	$171,000
1965	2400	2dr Allemano Cpe	$15,800	$26,200	$40,800	$57,500
1966	850	2dr TC Cpe	$7,100	$11,000	$17,000	$25,200

Abarth

Year	Model	Body Style	4	3	2	1
1966	OT 1000	2dr Cpe	$11,500	$19,500	$25,400	$47,800
		2dr Spider	$19,200	$28,000	$36,500	$52,500
1966	AU 1000	2dr Bialbero Cpe	$29,300	$46,900	$61,600	$98,400
1966	1300	2dr SIMCA Cpe	$125,000	$171,000	$204,000	$265,000
1966	2000	2dr SIMCA Cpe	$141,000	$176,000	$229,000	$292,000
1967	AU 1000	2dr Cpe	$11,900	$14,700	$20,500	$33,200
		2dr OTS Cpe	$12,700	$19,100	$28,800	$47,000
		2dr OTR Cpe	$12,700	$19,100	$28,800	$47,000
		2dr Berlina Corsa Cpe	$12,100	$17,200	$27,200	$38,900
		2dr Spider	$13,900	$19,600	$26,900	$42,700
1967	OT 1000	2dr Cpe	$11,500	$19,500	$25,400	$47,800
		2dr Spider	$19,200	$28,000	$36,500	$52,500
1967	1300/124	2dr Cpe	$10,300	$15,600	$21,500	$31,600
1967	2000 OT	2dr Cpe	$14,400	$21,600	$28,200	$43,800
1968	AU 1000	2dr Cpe	$11,900	$14,700	$20,500	$33,200
		2dr ORS Cpe	$12,700	$19,100	$28,800	$47,000
		2dr OTR Cpe	$12,700	$19,100	$28,800	$47,000
		2dr Berlina Corsa Cpe	$12,100	$17,200	$27,200	$38,900
		2dr Spider	$13,900	$19,600	$26,900	$42,700
1968	OT 1000	2dr Cpe	$11,500	$19,500	$25,400	$47,800
		2dr Spider	$19,200	$28,000	$36,500	$52,500
1968	1300/124	2dr Cpe	$10,300	$15,600	$21,500	$31,600
1968	2000 OT	2dr Cpe	$14,400	$21,600	$28,200	$43,800
1969	AU 1000	2dr Cpe	$11,900	$14,700	$20,500	$33,200
		2dr OTS Cpe	$12,700	$19,100	$28,800	$47,000
		2dr OTR Cpe	$12,700	$19,100	$28,800	$47,000
		2dr Berlina Corsa Cpe	$12,100	$17,200	$27,200	$38,900
		2dr Spider	$13,900	$19,600	$26,900	$42,700
1969	OT 1000	2dr Cpe	$11,500	$19,500	$25,400	$47,800
		2dr Spider	$19,200	$28,000	$36,500	$52,500
1969	1300/124	2dr Cpe	$10,300	$15,600	$21,500	$31,600
1969	2000 OT	2dr Cpe	$14,400	$21,600	$28,200	$43,800

Acura

Year	Model	Body Style	4	3	2	1
1991	NSX	2dr Cpe	$33,800	$45,600	$66,400	$105,000 *-5% for auto.*
1992	NSX	2dr Cpe	$32,000	$43,600	$65,300	$103,000 *-5% for auto.*
1993	NSX	2dr Cpe	$28,800	$49,200	$70,400	$103,000 *-5% for auto.*
1994	NSX	2dr Cpe	$34,200	$52,400	$75,300	$115,000 *-5% for auto.*
1995	NSX	2dr Targa	$38,200	$59,700	$77,500	$117,000
1996	NSX	2dr Cpe	$38,200	$63,900	$82,100	$120,000

Acura

Year	Model	Body Style	4	3	2	1
		2dr Targa	$38,200	$62,200	$79,800	$120,000
1997	Integra	3dr Type-R Htchbk	$24,500	$35,000	$49,900	$76,000
1997	NSX	2dr 3.0L Cpe	$40,700	$53,500	$79,100	$109,000
		2dr 3.2L Cpe	$42,100	$54,900	$93,200	$113,000
		2dr 3.0L Targa	$39,200	$51,400	$77,400	$107,000
		2dr 3.2L Targa	$40,900	$52,500	$81,800	$110,000
1998	Integra	3dr Type-R Htchbk	$20,000	$29,000	$44,400	$69,000
1998	NSX	2dr 3.0L Cpe	$41,100	$55,600	$81,200	$110,000
		2dr 3.2L Cpe	$43,700	$57,200	$96,100	$117,000
		2dr 3.0L Targa	$40,300	$53,400	$79,600	$109,000
		2dr 3.2L Targa	$41,500	$54,700	$85,600	$113,000
1999	NSX	2dr 3.0L Cpe	$43,000	$56,800	$83,500	$111,000
		2dr 3.2L Cpe	$44,500	$58,500	$97,900	$118,000
		2dr 3.2L Zanardi Ed Cpe	$72,300	$84,800	$138,000	$172,000
		2dr 3.0L Targa	$41,400	$54,900	$81,900	$110,000
		2dr 3.2L Targa	$42,400	$56,300	$90,400	$116,000
2000	Integra	3dr Type-R Htchbk	$20,000	$29,000	$44,400	$69,000
2000	NSX	2dr 3.0L Cpe	$46,100	$60,600	$90,200	$114,000
		2dr 3.2L Cpe	$47,800	$62,400	$102,000	$120,000
2000	NSX-T	2dr 3.0L Targa	$43,400	$56,800	$85,500	$113,000
		2dr 3.2L Targa	$46,100	$58,100	$92,400	$117,000
2001	Integra	3dr Type-R Htchbk	$20,000	$29,000	$44,400	$69,000
2001	NSX	2dr 3.0L Cpe	$47,400	$61,900	$93,200	$116,000
		2dr 3.2L Cpe	$50,200	$63,900	$105,000	$121,000
2001	NSX-T	2dr 3.0L Targa	$45,400	$59,200	$90,300	$114,000
		2dr 3.2L Targa	$46,900	$60,200	$93,200	$118,000
2002	NSX-T	2dr 3.0L Targa	$49,300	$61,300	$90,000	$114,000
		2dr 3.2L Targa	$51,800	$61,800	$92,600	$118,000
2003	NSX-T	2dr 3.0L Targa	$50,500	$62,900	$91,800	$116,000
		2dr 3.2L Targa	$53,100	$63,000	$94,500	$121,000
2004	NSX-T	2dr 3.0L Targa	$55,400	$65,200	$95,200	$120,000
		2dr 3.2L Targa	$58,000	$64,500	$97,100	$122,000
2005	NSX-T	2dr 3.0L Targa	$60,600	$69,200	$101,000	$124,000
		2dr 3.2L Targa	$63,900	$71,500	$104,000	$128,000

Alfa Romeo

Year	Model	Body Style	4	3	2	1
1947	6C 2500	2dr SS Villa d'Este Cpe	$455,000	$544,000	$672,000	$845,000
		2dr Sport Cab	$261,000	$316,000	$383,000	$428,000
		2dr SS Cab	$316,000	$373,000	$488,000	$766,000
		2dr Villa d&'Este Cab	$518,000	$583,000	$711,000	$856,000
1948	6C 2500	2dr SS Cpe	$330,000	$412,000	$587,000	$774,000
		2dr Freccia d'Oro Sdn	$77,700	$117,000	$161,000	$225,000
		2dr Sport Cab	$261,000	$316,000	$383,000	$428,000
		2dr SS Cab	$316,000	$373,000	$488,000	$766,000

Alfa Romeo

Year	Model	Body Style	4	3	2	1
1949	6C 2500	2dr SS Cpe	$330,000	$412,000	$587,000	$774,000
		2dr SS Villa d'Este Cpe	$455,000	$544,000	$672,000	$845,000
		2dr Freccia d'Oro Sdn	$77,700	$117,000	$161,000	$225,000
		2dr Sport Cab	$261,000	$316,000	$383,000	$428,000
		2dr SS Cab	$316,000	$373,000	$488,000	$766,000
		2dr SS Villa d'Este Cab	$538,000	$635,000	$760,000	$835,000
1950	1900	4dr Berlina	$20,800	$33,600	$41,200	$62,600
1950	6C 2500	2dr SS Cpe	$334,000	$420,000	$595,000	$790,000
		2dr SS Villa d'Este Cpe	$455,000	$544,000	$672,000	$845,000
		2dr Freccia d'Oro Sdn	$77,700	$117,000	$161,000	$225,000
		2dr Sport Cab	$261,000	$316,000	$383,000	$428,000
		2dr SS Cab	$316,000	$373,000	$488,000	$766,000
		2dr Villa d'Este Cab	$518,000	$583,000	$711,000	$856,000
1951	1900	4dr Berlina	$20,800	$33,600	$41,200	$62,600
1951	1900C	2dr Sprint	$234,000	$312,000	$390,000	$537,000
		2dr Cab	$211,000	$285,000	$382,000	$484,000
1951	6C 2500	2dr SS Cpe	$334,000	$420,000	$595,000	$790,000
		2dr SS Villa d'Este Cpe	$455,000	$544,000	$672,000	$845,000
		2dr Freccia d'Oro Sdn	$77,700	$117,000	$161,000	$225,000
		2dr Sport Cab	$261,000	$316,000	$383,000	$428,000
		2dr SS Cab	$331,000	$405,000	$517,000	$786,000
		2dr Villa d'Este Cab	$518,000	$583,000	$711,000	$856,000
1952	1900	4dr Berlina	$20,800	$33,600	$41,200	$62,600
		4dr Berlina TI	$24,600	$32,900	$56,300	$79,700
1952	1900C	2dr Sprint	$234,000	$312,000	$390,000	$537,000
		2dr Cab	$211,000	$285,000	$382,000	$484,000
1952	1900L	2dr Cab	$171,000	$243,000	$325,000	$441,000
1952	6C 2500	2dr SS Cpe	$334,000	$420,000	$595,000	$790,000
		2dr SS Villa d'Este Cpe	$455,000	$544,000	$672,000	$845,000
		2dr Freccia d'Oro Sdn	$77,700	$117,000	$161,000	$225,000
		2dr Sport Cab	$261,000	$316,000	$383,000	$428,000
		2dr SS Cab	$331,000	$405,000	$517,000	$786,000
		2dr Villa d'Este Cab	$518,000	$583,000	$711,000	$856,000
1953	1900	4dr Berlina	$20,800	$33,600	$41,200	$62,600
		4dr Berlina TI	$24,600	$32,900	$56,300	$79,700
1953	1900C	2dr Sprint	$234,000	$312,000	$390,000	$537,000
		2dr Cab	$211,000	$285,000	$382,000	$484,000
1953	1900L	2dr Cab	$171,000	$243,000	$325,000	$441,000

Year	Model	Body Style	4	3	2	1
1954	Giulietta	2dr Sprint	$29,400	$47,800	$70,200	$110,000
1954	1900	4dr Berlina	$20,800	$33,600	$41,200	$62,600
		4dr Berlina Super	$21,600	$31,900	$47,300	$76,700
		4dr Berlina TI	$24,600	$32,900	$56,300	$79,700
		4dr Berlina TI Super	$32,400	$46,200	$70,500	$96,000
1954	1900L	2dr Cab	$171,000	$243,000	$325,000	$441,000
1955	Giulietta	2dr Sprint	$29,400	$47,800	$70,200	$110,000
		2dr Sprint Veloce	$44,000	$75,400	$133,000	$208,000
		4dr Berlina	$9,300	$14,500	$18,700	$25,600
		2dr Spider	$38,700	$62,600	$97,700	$132,000
1955	1900	2dr Primavera Cpe	$31,600	$47,800	$62,300	$81,200
		2dr SS Cpe	$168,000	$208,000	$338,000	$427,000
		Custom-bodied cars may be up to twice the value.				
		2dr SS Zagato Cpe	$750,000	$920,000	$1.1 mil	$1.35 mil
		4dr Berlina Super	$21,600	$31,900	$47,300	$76,700
		4dr Berlina TI Super	$32,400	$46,200	$70,500	$96,000
1956	Giulietta	2dr Sprint Veloce Alleggerita Cpe	$200,000	$304,000	$384,000	$486,000
		2dr Sprint	$29,400	$47,800	$70,200	$110,000
		2dr Sprint Veloce	$44,000	$75,400	$133,000	$208,000
		4dr Berlina	$9,400	$15,800	$22,600	$30,600
		2dr Spider	$38,700	$62,600	$97,700	$132,000
		2dr Spider Veloce	$75,400	$125,000	$161,000	$201,000
1956	1900	2dr Primavera Cpe	$31,600	$47,800	$62,300	$81,200
		2dr SS Cpe	$168,000	$208,000	$338,000	$427,000
		Custom-bodied cars may be up to twice the value.				
		2dr SS Zagato Cpe	$750,000	$920,000	$1.1 mil	$1.35 mil
		4dr Berlina Super	$21,600	$31,900	$47,300	$76,700
		4dr Berlina TI Super	$32,400	$46,200	$70,500	$96,000
1957	Giulietta	2dr Sprint	$28,100	$47,800	$63,600	$101,000
		2dr Sprint Veloce	$44,000	$75,400	$133,000	$208,000
		2dr Sprint SII	$40,000	$60,500	$83,800	$120,000
		2dr Sprint Speciale	$57,300	$101,000	$142,000	$196,000
		+50% for early low-nose cars (first 101 produced).				
		4dr Berlina	$9,400	$15,800	$22,600	$30,600
		2dr Spider	$36,300	$60,300	$95,300	$128,000
		2dr Spider Veloce	$75,400	$125,000	$161,000	$201,000
1957	1900	2dr Primavera Cpe	$31,600	$47,800	$62,300	$81,200
		2dr SS Cpe	$168,000	$208,000	$338,000	$427,000
		Custom-bodied cars may be up to twice the value.				
		2dr SS Zagato Cpe	$750,000	$920,000	$1.1 mil	$1.35 mil
		4dr Berlina Super	$21,600	$31,900	$47,300	$76,700

Alfa Romeo

Year	Model	Body Style	4	3	2	1
		4dr Berlina TI Super	$32,400	$46,200	$70,500	$96,000
1958	Giulietta	2dr Sprint	$28,100	$47,800	$63,600	$101,000
		2dr Sprint Veloce	$44,000	$75,400	$133,000	$208,000
		2dr Sprint SII	$40,000	$60,500	$83,800	$120,000
		2dr Sprint Speciale	$57,300	$101,000	$142,000	$196,000
		+50% for early low-nose cars (first 101 produced).				
		4dr Berlina	$9,400	$15,800	$22,600	$30,600
		2dr Spider	$36,300	$60,300	$95,300	$128,000
		2dr Spider Veloce	$75,400	$125,000	$161,000	$201,000
1958	1900	4dr Berlina Super	$21,600	$31,900	$47,300	$76,700
1958	2000	2dr Spider	$55,000	$84,200	$121,000	$187,000
1959	Giulietta	2dr Sprint	$28,100	$47,800	$63,600	$101,000
		2dr Sprint Veloce	$44,000	$75,400	$133,000	$208,000
		2dr Sprint Speciale	$57,300	$101,000	$142,000	$196,000
		+50% for early low-nose cars (first 101 produced).				
		4dr Berlina	$9,400	$15,800	$22,600	$30,600
		2dr Spider	$36,300	$60,300	$95,300	$128,000
		2dr Spider Veloce	$75,400	$125,000	$161,000	$201,000
1959	Giulietta Series 101	2dr Sprint	$16,800	$24,900	$36,100	$52,500
		2dr Veloce Cpe	$27,800	$39,800	$53,000	$74,700
		2dr Spider	$40,300	$55,600	$67,700	$89,300
		2dr Spider Veloce	$53,700	$78,400	$98,200	$120,000
1959	1900	4dr Berlina Super	$21,600	$31,900	$47,300	$76,700
1959	2000	4dr Berlina	$6,000	$9,100	$14,300	$19,100
		2dr Spider	$55,000	$84,200	$121,000	$187,000
1960	Giulietta	1290/80 2dr Sprint	$23,100	$39,500	$56,100	$77,400
		1290/91 2dr Sprint	$33,700	$52,500	$75,600	$126,000
		2dr Sprint Veloce	$34,700	$51,900	$74,300	$124,000
		4dr Berlina	$9,400	$15,800	$22,600	$30,600
		2dr Spider Veloce	$33,500	$56,100	$87,500	$132,000
1960	SZ-1	2dr Cpe	$305,000	$369,000	$430,000	$565,000
1960	2000	2dr Spider	$55,000	$84,200	$121,000	$187,000
1961	Giulietta	1290/80 2dr Sprint	$23,100	$39,500	$56,100	$77,400
		1290/91 2dr Sprint	$33,700	$52,500	$75,600	$126,000
		2dr Sprint Veloce	$34,700	$51,900	$74,300	$124,000
		4dr Berlina	$9,400	$15,800	$22,600	$30,600
		2dr Spider	$42,200	$68,200	$106,000	$144,000
		2dr Spider	$28,100	$43,400	$71,000	$97,600
		2dr Spider Veloce	$33,500	$56,100	$87,500	$132,000
1961	SZ-1	2dr Cpe	$305,000	$369,000	$430,000	$565,000
1961	SZ-2	2dr Cpe	$322,000	$382,000	$447,000	$590,000
1961	2000	4dr Berlina	$6,000	$9,100	$14,300	$19,100
		2dr Spider	$55,000	$84,200	$121,000	$187,000
1962	Giulietta	1290/80 2dr Sprint	$23,100	$39,500	$56,100	$77,400
		1290/91 2dr Sprint	$33,700	$52,500	$75,600	$126,000
		2dr Sprint Veloce	$34,700	$51,900	$74,300	$124,000

Year	Model	Body Style	4	3	2	1
		4dr Berlina				
			$9,400	$15,800	$22,600	$30,600
		1290/80 2dr Sprint	$28,100	$43,400	$71,000	$97,600
		1290/91 2dr Sprint	$42,200	$68,200	$106,000	$144,000
		2dr Spider Veloce	$33,500	$56,100	$87,500	$132,000
1962	SZ-2	2dr Cpe	$322,000	$382,000	$447,000	$590,000
1962	Giulia	2dr Sprint	$24,800	$36,500	$58,400	$95,100
		2dr Sprint Speciale	$53,800	$100,000	$134,000	$197,000
		4dr TI Super Berlina	$23,700	$35,400	$45,800	$64,200
		2dr Spider	$36,700	$50,600	$77,100	$111,000
		2dr Spider Veloce	$42,900	$61,300	$88,200	$125,000
1962	2600	2dr Sprint	$20,200	$29,700	$51,500	$88,200
		2dr Spider	$56,800	$79,700	$144,000	$193,000
		2dr Sprint Zagato	$111,000	$134,000	$181,000	$209,000
1963	Giulia	2dr Sprint	$24,800	$36,500	$58,400	$95,100
		2dr Sprint Speciale	$53,800	$100,000	$134,000	$197,000
		2dr Sprint GT	$23,500	$38,800	$53,100	$82,600
		4dr TI Super Berlina	$23,700	$35,400	$45,800	$64,200
		4dr Spr Berlina	$21,300	$31,100	$40,400	$54,100
		2dr Spider	$36,700	$50,600	$77,100	$111,000
		2dr Spider Veloce	$42,900	$61,300	$88,200	$125,000
1963	TZ-1	2dr Cpe	$880,000	$1.1 mil	$1.35 mil	$1.5 mil
1963	2600	2dr Sprint	$20,200	$29,700	$51,500	$88,200
		2dr Sprint Zagato	$111,000	$134,000	$181,000	$209,000
		2dr Spider	$56,800	$79,700	$144,000	$193,000
1964	Giulia	2dr Sprint	$24,800	$36,500	$58,400	$95,100
		2dr Sprint GT	$23,500	$38,800	$53,100	$82,600
		2dr GTC Conv	$50,600	$69,300	$96,800	$141,000
		2dr Spider	$36,700	$50,600	$77,100	$111,000
		2dr Spider Veloce	$42,900	$61,300	$88,200	$125,000
		2dr Sprint Speciale	$53,800	$100,000	$134,000	$197,000
		4dr TI Super Berlina	$23,700	$35,400	$45,800	$64,200
		4dr Spr Berlina	$21,300	$31,100	$42,500	$55,700
1964	2600	2dr Sprint	$20,200	$29,700	$51,500	$88,200
		2dr Sprint Zagato	$111,000	$134,000	$181,000	$209,000
		2dr Spider	$56,800	$79,700	$144,000	$193,000
1964	TZ-1	2dr Cpe	$880,000	$1.1 mil	$1.35 mil	$1.5 mil
1964	TZ-2	2dr Cpe	$2.1 mil	$2.6 mil	$3.1 mil	$3.35 mil
1965	Giulia	2dr Sprint GTA Cpe	$221,000	$320,000	$406,000	$487,000
			+40% for significant competition history.			
		2dr Sprint	$24,800	$36,500	$58,400	$95,100
		2dr Sprint GT	$23,500	$38,800	$53,100	$82,600

Alfa Romeo

Year	Model	Body Style	4	3	2	1
		2dr Sprint Speciale	$53,800	$100,000	$134,000	$197,000
		4dr TI Super Berlina	$23,700	$35,400	$45,800	$64,200
		4dr Spr Berlina	$22,200	$31,100	$44,100	$58,800
		2dr Spider	$36,700	$50,600	$77,100	$111,000
		2dr Spider Veloce	$42,900	$61,300	$88,200	$125,000
		2dr GTC Conv	$50,600	$69,300	$96,800	$141,000
1965	TZ-2	2dr Cpe	$2.1 mil	$2.6 mil	$3.1 mil	$3.35 mil
1965	2600	2dr Sprint	$20,200	$29,700	$51,500	$88,200
		2dr Sprint Zagato	$111,000	$134,000	$181,000	$209,000
		2dr Spider	$56,800	$79,700	$144,000	$193,000
1966	GT 1300 Jr	2dr Cpe	$12,200	$17,800	$24,600	$35,500
		2dr Zagato Cpe	$16,500	$26,600	$39,600	$62,400
1966	Giulia	2dr Sprint GTA Cpe	$221,000	$320,000	$406,000	$487,000
						+40% for significant competition history.
		2dr Sprint GT	$23,500	$38,800	$53,100	$82,600
		4dr Spr Berlina	$22,200	$31,700	$44,100	$58,800
		2dr Spider	$38,700	$53,100	$81,000	$117,000
		2dr GTC Conv	$50,600	$69,300	$96,800	$141,000
		2dr Duetto Spider	$19,400	$28,100	$39,900	$58,700
1966	2600	2dr Sprint	$20,200	$29,700	$51,500	$88,200
1966	4R Zagato	2dr Conv	$49,600	$68,700	$113,000	$155,000
1967	GT 1300 Jr	2dr Cpe	$12,200	$17,800	$24,600	$35,500
		2dr Zagato Cpe	$16,500	$26,600	$39,600	$62,400
1967	Giulia	2dr Sprint GTA Cpe	$221,000	$320,000	$406,000	$487,000
						+40% for significant competition history.
		2dr Sprint GTV	$24,900	$38,600	$59,500	$90,500
		4dr Spr Berlina	$22,200	$31,700	$44,100	$58,800
		2dr Duetto Spider	$19,400	$28,100	$39,900	$58,700
1967	2600	2dr Sprint	$20,200	$29,700	$51,500	$88,200
1967	4R Zagato	2dr Conv	$49,600	$68,700	$113,000	$155,000
1968	GT 1300 Jr	2dr Cpe	$12,200	$17,800	$24,600	$35,500
		2dr Zagato Cpe	$16,500	$26,600	$39,600	$62,400
1968	GTA 1300 Junior	2dr Cpe	$162,000	$188,000	$245,000	$305,000
1968	Giulia	4dr Spr Berlina	$22,200	$31,700	$44,100	$58,800
		2dr Sprint GTV	$24,900	$38,600	$59,500	$90,500
		2dr Duetto Spider	$19,400	$28,100	$39,900	$58,700
1968	1750 GTAm	2dr Cpe	$203,000	$288,000	$366,000	$439,000
						+40% for significant competition history.
1968	4R Zagato	2dr Conv	$49,600	$68,700	$113,000	$155,000
1968	2600	2dr Sprint	$20,200	$29,700	$51,500	$88,200
1969	GT 1300 Jr	2dr Cpe	$12,200	$17,800	$24,600	$35,500
		2dr Zagato Cpe	$16,500	$26,600	$39,600	$62,400
1969	GTA 1300 Junior	2dr Cpe	$162,000	$188,000	$245,000	$305,000
1969	Giulia	4dr Spr Berlina	$22,200	$31,700	$44,100	$58,800
1969	1750	2dr GTV Cpe	$23,700	$40,500	$83,100	$128,000
		4dr Berlina	$5,000	$7,400	$13,500	$24,700
		2dr Conv	$11,800	$19,500	$29,600	$50,800

Year	Model	Body Style	4	3	2	1
1969	1750 GTAm	2dr Cpe	$203,000	$288,000	$366,000	$439,000
				+40% for significant competition history.		
1970	GT 1300 Jr	2dr Cpe	$12,200	$17,800	$24,600	$35,500
		2dr Zagato Cpe	$16,500	$26,600	$39,600	$62,400
1970	GTA 1300 Junior	2dr Cpe	$162,000	$188,000	$245,000	$305,000
1970	Giulia	4dr Spr Berlina	$22,200	$31,700	$44,100	$58,800
1970	1750	2dr GTV Cpe	$23,700	$40,500	$83,100	$128,000
		4dr Berlina	$5,000	$7,400	$13,500	$24,700
		2dr Conv	$10,800	$16,500	$24,800	$43,900
1970	2000 GTAm	2dr Cpe	$221,000	$297,000	$390,000	$455,000
				+40% for significant competition history.		
1970	Montreal	2dr Cpe	$38,800	$55,000	$88,700	$120,000
1971	GT 1300 Jr	2dr Cpe	$12,200	$17,800	$24,600	$35,500
		2dr Zagato Cpe	$16,500	$26,600	$39,600	$62,400
1971	GTA 1300 Junior	2dr Cpe	$162,000	$188,000	$245,000	$305,000
1971	Giulia	4dr Spr Berlina	$22,200	$31,700	$44,100	$58,800
1971	1750	2dr GTV Cpe	$23,700	$40,500	$83,100	$128,000
		4dr Berlina	$5,000	$7,400	$13,500	$24,700
		2dr Conv	$10,800	$16,500	$24,800	$43,900
1971	2000	2dr Spider Veloce	$11,700	$16,900	$28,200	$45,600
1971	2000 GTAm	2dr Cpe	$221,000	$297,000	$390,000	$455,000
				+40% for significant competition history.		
1971	Montreal	2dr Cpe	$38,800	$55,000	$88,700	$120,000
1972	GT 1300 Jr	2dr Cpe	$12,200	$17,800	$24,600	$35,500
		2dr Zagato Cpe	$16,500	$26,600	$39,600	$62,400
1972	GTA 1300 Junior	2dr Cpe	$162,000	$188,000	$245,000	$305,000
1972	GT 1600 Jr	2dr Cpe	$13,300	$18,100	$25,800	$37,500
		2dr Zagato Cpe	$17,900	$33,700	$53,800	$78,500
1972	Giulia	4dr Spr Berlina	$22,200	$31,700	$44,100	$58,800
1972	1750	2dr GTV Cpe	$23,700	$40,500	$83,100	$128,000
		4dr Berlina	$5,000	$7,400	$13,500	$24,700
1972	2000	2dr GTV Cpe	$24,200	$41,800	$74,600	$119,000
		4dr Berlina	$6,100	$9,200	$14,200	$18,900
		4dr Berlina	$5,400	$8,000	$13,100	$22,300
		2dr Spider Veloce	$11,700	$16,900	$28,200	$45,600
1972	2000 GTAm	2dr Cpe	$221,000	$297,000	$390,000	$455,000
				+40% for significant competition history.		
1972	Montreal	2dr Cpe	$38,800	$55,000	$88,700	$120,000
1973	GT 1600 Jr	2dr Cpe	$13,300	$18,100	$25,800	$37,500
		2dr Zagato Cpe	$17,900	$33,700	$53,800	$78,500
1973	2000	2dr GTV Cpe	$24,200	$41,800	$74,600	$119,000
		4dr Berlina	$5,400	$8,000	$13,100	$22,300
		2dr Spider Veloce	$11,700	$16,900	$28,200	$45,600
1973	Montreal	2dr Cpe	$38,800	$55,000	$88,700	$120,000
1974	GT 1600 Jr	2dr Cpe	$13,300	$18,100	$25,800	$37,500
		2dr Zagato Cpe	$17,900	$33,700	$53,800	$78,500
1974	Alfetta	2dr GT Cpe	$4,500	$7,900	$15,500	$27,200
		4dr Berlina	$3,600	$5,200	$6,400	$14,800

Alfa Romeo

Year	Model	Body Style	4	3	2	1
1974	1750	2dr Spider Veloce	$11,700	$16,900	$28,200	$45,600
1974	2000	2dr GTV Cpe	$24,200	$41,800	$74,600	$119,000
		4dr Berlina	$5,400	$8,000	$13,100	$22,300
		2dr Spider Veloce	$11,700	$16,900	$28,200	$45,600
1974	Montreal	2dr Cpe	$38,800	$55,000	$88,700	$120,000
1975	GT 1600 Jr	2dr Cpe	$13,300	$18,100	$25,800	$37,500
		2dr Zagato Cpe	$17,900	$33,700	$53,800	$78,500
1975	Alfetta	2dr GT Cpe	$4,500	$7,900	$15,500	$27,200
		4dr Berlina	$3,600	$5,200	$6,400	$14,800
1975	2000	2dr Spider Veloce	$11,400	$16,600	$27,400	$44,300
1975	Montreal	2dr Cpe	$38,800	$55,000	$88,700	$120,000
1976	GT 1600 Jr	2dr Cpe	$13,300	$18,100	$25,800	$37,500
1976	Alfetta	2dr GT Cpe	$4,500	$7,900	$15,500	$27,200
		4dr Berlina	$3,600	$5,200	$6,400	$14,800
1976	GTV	2dr Cpe	$7,300	$11,900	$15,600	$22,500
1976	2000	2dr Spider Veloce	$11,400	$16,600	$27,400	$44,300
1976	Sport	4dr Sdn	$4,500	$6,800	$8,200	$10,600
1976	Spider	2dr Veloce	$6,800	$10,900	$15,500	$22,800
1976	Montreal	2dr Cpe	$38,800	$55,000	$88,700	$120,000
1977	Sport	4dr Sdn	$4,500	$6,800	$8,200	$10,600
1977	Spider	2dr Veloce	$6,800	$10,900	$15,500	$22,800
1977	GTV	2dr Cpe	$7,300	$11,900	$15,600	$22,500
1977	Montreal	2dr Cpe	$38,800	$55,000	$88,700	$120,000
1978	Sport	4dr Sdn	$4,500	$6,800	$8,200	$10,600
1978	Spider	2dr Veloce	$6,800	$10,900	$15,500	$22,800
1978	GTV	2dr Cpe	$7,300	$11,900	$15,600	$22,500
1979	Sport	4dr Sdn	$4,500	$6,800	$8,200	$10,600
1979	Spider	2dr Veloce	$6,800	$10,900	$15,500	$22,800
1979	GTV	2dr Cpe	$7,300	$11,900	$15,600	$22,500
1980	Spider	2dr Veloce	$7,500	$11,000	$15,700	$23,100
1981	Spider	2dr Veloce	$7,500	$11,000	$15,700	$23,100
1981	GTV-6	2dr Cpe	$5,700	$8,300	$13,100	$21,400
1982	Spider	2dr Veloce	$8,300	$14,300	$22,000	$28,900
1982	GTV-6	2dr Cpe	$5,700	$8,300	$13,100	$21,400
1983	Spider	2dr Veloce	$8,400	$14,700	$20,900	$28,200
1983	GTV-6	2dr Cpe	$5,700	$8,300	$13,100	$21,400
1984	Spider	2dr Veloce	$8,400	$14,700	$20,900	$28,200
1984	GTV-6	2dr Cpe	$8,400	$13,600	$18,200	$27,800
1985	Spider	2dr Veloce	$7,700	$11,300	$15,000	$22,800
		2dr Graduate	$5,800	$8,800	$12,400	$17,200
		2dr Quadrifoglio	$7,300	$11,900	$15,300	$21,300
1985	GTV-6	2dr Cpe	$8,400	$13,600	$18,200	$27,800
		Turbo 2dr Cpe	$12,800	$18,400	$26,600	$36,800
1986	Spider	2dr Veloce	$7,700	$11,300	$15,000	$22,800
		2dr Graduate	$5,800	$8,800	$12,400	$17,200
		2dr Quadrifoglio	$7,300	$11,900	$15,300	$21,300
1986	GTV-6	2dr Cpe	$8,400	$13,600	$18,200	$27,800
1987	Spider	2dr Veloce	$7,300	$11,600	$15,600	$22,600
		2dr Graduate	$6,600	$10,700	$14,000	$21,100

Year	Model	Body Style	4	3	2	1
		2dr Quadrifoglio	$7,700	$12,100	$14,400	$21,800
1987	Milano	4dr Platinum Sdn	$2,900	$4,700	$7,200	$11,700
1987	GTV-6	2dr Cpe	$8,400	$13,600	$18,200	$27,800
1988	Milano	4dr Platinum Sdn	$3,900	$6,400	$9,300	$13,000
		4dr Verde Sdn	$5,300	$9,700	$15,000	$23,400
1988	Spider	2dr Graduate	$7,200	$11,600	$15,300	$23,800
		2dr Veloce	$8,500	$13,800	$18,100	$26,700
		2dr Quadrifoglio	$7,100	$11,700	$15,300	$23,600
1989	Milano	4dr Platinum Sdn	$3,900	$6,400	$9,300	$13,000
		4dr Verde Sdn	$5,300	$9,700	$15,000	$23,400
1989	Spider	2dr Graduate	$7,200	$11,600	$15,300	$23,800
		2dr Veloce	$8,500	$13,800	$18,100	$26,700
		2dr Quadrifoglio	$7,100	$11,700	$15,300	$23,600
1990	Spider	2dr Graduate	$6,600	$10,600	$14,000	$21,800
		2dr Veloce	$6,800	$11,300	$18,600	$28,800
		2dr Quadrifoglio	$6,500	$10,800	$16,600	$25,600
1991	164	4dr Sdn	$4,400	$6,800	$9,500	$15,700
		4dr L Sdn	$4,800	$7,100	$9,900	$16,200
		4dr S Sdn	$5,600	$9,000	$12,200	$20,800
1991	Spider	2dr Conv	$9,600	$15,100	$21,100	$30,200
		2dr Veloce	$8,300	$14,200	$23,400	$35,300
1992	164	4dr Sdn	$4,400	$6,800	$9,500	$15,700
		4dr L Sdn	$4,800	$7,100	$9,900	$16,200
		4dr S Sdn	$5,600	$9,000	$12,200	$20,800
1992	Spider	2dr Conv	$9,600	$15,100	$21,100	$30,200
		2dr Veloce	$8,300	$14,200	$23,400	$35,300
1993	164	4dr Sdn	$4,400	$6,800	$9,500	$15,700
		4dr L Sdn	$4,800	$7,100	$9,900	$16,200
		4dr S Sdn	$5,500	$9,000	$12,200	$20,800
1993	Spider	2dr Conv	$9,600	$15,100	$21,100	$30,200
		2dr Veloce	$8,300	$14,200	$23,400	$35,300
		2dr Veloce Comm Ed Conv	$9,900	$15,400	$23,000	$33,200
1994	164	4dr L/S Sdn	$6,000	$7,600	$14,400	$22,800
1994	Spider	2dr Conv	$9,600	$15,100	$21,100	$30,200
		2dr Veloce	$8,300	$14,200	$23,400	$35,300
1995	164	4dr L/S Sdn	$6,000	$7,600	$14,400	$22,800
		4dr Quadrifoglio Sdn	$6,600	$11,200	$20,700	$32,700
1995	Spider	2dr Conv	$9,600	$15,100	$21,100	$30,200
		2dr Veloce	$8,300	$14,200	$23,400	$35,300
2008	8C	2dr Competizione Cpe	$180,000	$240,000	$330,000	$380,000
2009	8C	2dr Competizione Cpe	$180,000	$240,000	$330,000	$380,000
		2dr Spider Rdstr	$212,000	$283,000	$389,000	$448,000
2010	8C	2dr Spider Rdstr	$212,000	$283,000	$389,000	$448,000

Allard

Year	Model	Body Style	4	3	2	1
1946	K1	2dr Rdstr	$29,000	$66,500	$103,000	$139,000
						+5% for orig Mercury 239/95 engine.
1946	L-Type	2dr Rdstr	$23,500	$37,500	$62,000	$91,500
						+5% for orig Mercury 239/95 engine.
1947	K1	2dr Rdstr	$29,000	$66,500	$103,000	$139,000
						+5% for orig Mercury 239/95 engine.
1947	L-Type	2dr Rdstr	$23,500	$37,500	$62,000	$91,500
						+5% for orig Mercury 239/95 engine.
1947	M	2dr DHC	$23,500	$36,800	$63,000	$93,000
						+10% for orig 239/100 Mercury V8.
1948	K1	2dr Rdstr	$29,000	$66,500	$103,000	$139,000
						+5% for orig Mercury 239/95 engine.
1948	L-Type	2dr Rdstr	$23,500	$37,500	$62,000	$91,500
						+5% for orig Mercury 239/95 engine.
1948	M	2dr DHC	$23,500	$36,800	$63,000	$93,000
						+10% for orig 239/100 Mercury V8.
1949	K2	2dr Rdstr	$65,000	$85,000	$116,000	$150,000
						+5% for orig Mercury 239/100 engine.
1949	M	2dr DHC	$23,500	$36,800	$63,000	$93,000
						+10% for orig 239/100 Mercury V8.
1950	J2	2dr Rdstr	$135,000	$175,000	$260,000	$329,000
						+10% for orig Oldsmobile or Chrysler eng. +14% for orig Cadillac eng.
1950	K2	2dr Rdstr	$65,000	$85,000	$116,000	$150,000
						+5% for orig Mercury 239/100 engine.
1950	M	2dr DHC	$23,500	$36,800	$63,000	$93,000
						+10% for orig 239/100 Mercury V8.
1951	J2	2dr Rdstr	$135,000	$175,000	$260,000	$329,000
						+10% for orig Oldsmobile or Chrysler eng. +14% for orig Cadillac eng.
1951	K2	2dr Rdstr	$65,000	$85,000	$116,000	$150,000
						+5% for orig Mercury 239/100 engine.
1952	J2	2dr Rdstr	$135,000	$175,000	$260,000	$329,000
						+10% for orig Oldsmobile or Chrysler eng. +14% for orig Cadillac eng.
1952	J2X	2dr Rdstr	$165,000	$250,000	$331,000	$444,000
		2dr LeMans Rdstr	$260,000	$360,000	$420,000	$515,000
1952	K3	2dr Rdstr	$92,500	$114,000	$134,000	$187,000
						+8% for orig Chrysler eng. +12% for orig Cadillac eng. +5% for orig Mercury eng.
1952	Palm Beach	2dr Mk I 1.5 Rdstr	$35,600	$43,700	$69,000	$107,000
1953	J2R	2dr Rdstr	$119,000	$143,000	$195,000	$282,000
1953	J2X	2dr Rdstr	$165,000	$250,000	$331,000	$444,000
1953	K3	2dr Rdstr	$92,500	$114,000	$134,000	$187,000
						+8% for orig Chrysler eng. +12% for orig Cadillac eng. +5% for orig Mercury eng.
1953	Palm Beach	2dr Mk I 1.5 Rdstr	$35,600	$43,700	$69,000	$107,000
1954	K3	2dr Rdstr	$92,500	$114,000	$134,000	$187,000

Allard

Year	Model	Body Style	4	3	2	1
		+8% for orig Chrysler eng. +12% for orig Cadillac eng. +5% for orig Mercury eng.				
1954	Palm Beach	2dr Mk I 1.5 Rdstr	$35,600	$43,700	$69,000	$107,000
1954	J2X	2dr Rdstr	$165,000	$250,000	$331,000	$444,000
1955	K3	2dr Rdstr	$92,500	$114,000	$134,000	$187,000
		+8% for orig Chrysler eng. +12% for orig Cadillac eng. +5% for orig Mercury eng.				
1955	Palm Beach	2dr Mk I 1.5 Rdstr	$35,600	$43,700	$69,000	$107,000
1956	K3	2dr Rdstr	$92,500	$114,000	$134,000	$187,000
		+8% for orig Chrysler eng. +12% for orig Cadillac eng. +5% for orig Mercury eng.				
1956	Palm Beach	2dr Mk II 2.4 Rdstr	$45,900	$68,100	$97,700	$142,000
1957	Palm Beach	2dr Mk II 2.4 Rdstr	$45,900	$68,100	$97,700	$142,000
1958	Palm Beach	2dr Mk II 2.4 Rdstr	$45,900	$68,100	$97,700	$142,000
1959	Palm Beach	2dr Mk II 2.4 Rdstr	$45,900	$68,100	$97,700	$142,000

Allstate

Year	Model	Body Style	4	3	2	1
1952	Series 4	134/68 2dr Sdn	$5,600	$9,200	$14,800	$22,500
						+$500 for OD trans.
1952	Series 6	161/80 2dr Sdn	$7,800	$11,200	$19,000	$31,500
						+$500 for OD trans.
1953	Series 4	134/68 2dr Sdn	$5,600	$9,200	$14,800	$22,500
						+$500 for OD trans.
1953	Series 6	161/80 2dr Dlx Sdn	$7,800	$11,200	$19,000	$31,500
						+$500 for OD trans.

Alpine

Year	Model	Body Style	4	3	2	1
1958	A108	2dr Cpe	$47,500	$62,000	$92,500	$119,000
1959	A108	2dr Cpe	$47,500	$62,000	$92,500	$119,000
1960	A108	2dr Cpe	$47,500	$62,000	$92,500	$119,000
1961	A108	2dr Cpe	$47,500	$62,000	$92,500	$119,000
1962	A108	2dr Cpe	$47,500	$62,000	$92,500	$119,000
1962	A110	2dr Ltwt Cpe	$91,000	$134,000	$182,000	$224,000
			+$8,000 for 1600 eng. Significant competition history can greatly impact valuation.			
1963	GT4	2dr Cpe	$10,000	$15,300	$21,500	$32,500
1963	A108	2dr Cpe	$47,500	$62,000	$92,500	$119,000
1963	A110	2dr Cpe	$61,000	$84,000	$110,000	$150,000
		2dr Ltwt Cpe	$91,000	$134,000	$182,000	$224,000
			+$8,000 for 1600 eng. Significant competition history can greatly impact valuation.			

Alpine

Year	Model	Body Style	4	3	2	1
1964	GT4	2dr Cpe	$10,000	$15,300	$21,500	$32,500
1964	A108	2dr Cpe	$47,500	$62,000	$92,500	$119,000
1964	A110	2dr Cpe	$61,000	$84,000	$110,000	$150,000
		2dr Ltwt Cpe	$91,000	$134,000	$182,000	$224,000

+$8,000 for 1600 eng. Significant competition history can greatly impact valuation.

Year	Model	Body Style	4	3	2	1
1965	GT4	2dr Cpe	$10,000	$15,300	$21,500	$32,500
1965	A108	2dr Cpe	$47,500	$62,000	$92,500	$119,000
1965	A110	2dr Cpe	$61,000	$84,000	$110,000	$150,000
		2dr Ltwt Cpe	$91,000	$134,000	$182,000	$224,000

+$8,000 for 1600 eng. Significant competition history can greatly impact valuation.

Year	Model	Body Style	4	3	2	1
1966	GT4	2dr Cpe	$10,000	$15,300	$21,500	$32,500
1966	A110	2dr Cpe	$61,000	$84,000	$110,000	$150,000
		2dr Ltwt Cpe	$91,000	$134,000	$182,000	$224,000

+$8,000 for 1600 eng. Significant competition history can greatly impact valuation.

Year	Model	Body Style	4	3	2	1
1967	GT4	2dr Cpe	$10,000	$15,300	$21,500	$32,500
1967	A110	2dr Cpe	$61,000	$84,000	$110,000	$150,000
		2dr Ltwt Cpe	$91,000	$134,000	$182,000	$224,000

+$8,000 for 1600 eng. Significant competition history can greatly impact valuation.

Year	Model	Body Style	4	3	2	1
1968	GT4	2dr Cpe	$10,000	$15,300	$21,500	$32,500
1968	A110	2dr Cpe	$61,000	$84,000	$110,000	$150,000
		2dr Ltwt Cpe	$91,000	$134,000	$182,000	$224,000

+$8,000 for 1600 eng. Significant competition history can greatly impact valuation.

Year	Model	Body Style	4	3	2	1
1969	GT4	2dr Cpe	$10,000	$15,300	$21,500	$32,500
1969	A110	2dr Cpe	$61,000	$84,000	$110,000	$150,000
		2dr Ltwt Cpe	$91,000	$134,000	$182,000	$224,000

+$8,000 for 1600 eng. Significant competition history can greatly impact valuation.

Year	Model	Body Style	4	3	2	1
1970	GT4	2dr Cpe	$10,000	$15,300	$21,500	$32,500
1970	A110	2dr Cpe	$61,000	$84,000	$110,000	$150,000
		2dr Ltwt Cpe	$91,000	$134,000	$182,000	$224,000

+$8,000 for 1600 eng. Significant competition history can greatly impact valuation.

Year	Model	Body Style	4	3	2	1
1971	A110	2dr Cpe	$61,000	$84,000	$110,000	$150,000
		2dr Ltwt Cpe	$91,000	$134,000	$182,000	$224,000

+$8,000 for 1600 eng. Significant competition history can greatly impact valuation.

Year	Model	Body Style	4	3	2	1
1971	A310	2dr Cpe	$12,000	$17,600	$26,800	$40,400
1972	A110	2dr Cpe	$61,000	$84,000	$110,000	$150,000
		2dr Ltwt Cpe	$91,000	$134,000	$182,000	$224,000

+$8,000 for 1600 eng. Significant competition history can greatly impact valuation.

Year	Model	Body Style	4	3	2	1
1972	A310	2dr Cpe	$12,000	$17,600	$26,800	$40,400

Alpine

Year	Model	Body Style	4	3	2	1
1973	A110	2dr Cpe	$61,000	$84,000	$110,000	$150,000
		2dr Ltwt Cpe	$91,000	$134,000	$182,000	$224,000
			+$8,000 for 1600 eng. Significant competition history can greatly impact valuation.			
1973	A310	2dr Cpe	$12,000	$17,600	$26,800	$40,400
1974	A110	2dr Cpe	$61,000	$84,000	$110,000	$150,000
		2dr Ltwt Cpe	$91,000	$134,000	$182,000	$224,000
			+$8,000 for 1600 eng. Significant competition history can greatly impact valuation.			
1974	A310	2dr Cpe	$12,000	$17,600	$26,800	$40,400
1975	A110	2dr Cpe	$61,000	$84,000	$110,000	$150,000
		2dr Ltwt Cpe	$91,000	$134,000	$182,000	$224,000
			+$8,000 for 1600 eng. Significant competition history can greatly impact valuation.			
1975	A310	2dr Cpe	$12,000	$17,600	$26,800	$40,400
1976	A110	2dr Cpe	$61,000	$84,000	$110,000	$150,000
		2dr Ltwt Cpe	$91,000	$134,000	$182,000	$224,000
			+$8,000 for 1600 eng. Significant competition history can greatly impact valuation.			
1976	A310	2dr Cpe	$15,000	$22,000	$33,000	$52,500
1977	A110	2dr Cpe	$61,000	$84,000	$110,000	$150,000
		2dr Ltwt Cpe	$91,000	$134,000	$182,000	$224,000
			+$8,000 for 1600 eng. Significant competition history can greatly impact valuation.			
1977	A310	2dr Cpe	$15,000	$22,000	$33,000	$52,500
1978	A310	2dr Cpe	$15,000	$22,000	$33,000	$52,500
1979	A310	2dr Cpe	$15,000	$22,000	$33,000	$52,500
1980	A310	3dr Cpe	$15,000	$22,000	$33,000	$52,500
1981	A310	3dr Cpe	$15,000	$22,000	$33,000	$52,500
1982	A310	3dr Cpe	$15,000	$22,000	$33,000	$52,500
1983	A310	3dr Cpe	$15,000	$22,000	$33,000	$52,500
1984	A310	3dr Cpe	$15,000	$22,000	$33,000	$52,500
1985	A310	3dr Cpe	$15,000	$22,000	$33,000	$52,500

Alvis

Year	Model	Body Style	4	3	2	1
1947	TA14	4dr Sal	$4,300	$10,500	$16,900	$25,600
		2dr DHC	$8,200	$15,400	$23,400	$35,700
1948	TA14	4dr Sal	$4,300	$10,500	$16,900	$25,600
		2dr DHC	$8,200	$15,400	$23,400	$35,700
1948	TB14	2dr Rdstr	$14,000	$23,200	$31,900	$47,000
1949	TA14	4dr Sal	$4,300	$10,500	$16,900	$25,600
		2dr FHC	$8,200	$15,400	$23,400	$35,700
1949	TB14	2dr Rdstr	$14,000	$23,200	$31,900	$47,000
1950	TA21	2dr FHC	$11,200	$17,500	$29,300	$41,500
		4dr Sal	$4,700	$10,900	$17,300	$25,800
		2dr DHC	$20,100	$32,200	$48,800	$72,400

Alvis

Year	Model	Body Style	4	3	2	1
1950	TB21	2dr Tourer	$20,700	$32,600	$48,200	$67,300
1951	TA21	2dr FHC	$11,200	$17,500	$29,300	$41,500
		4dr Sdn	$4,300	$10,900	$17,300	$25,800
		2dr DHC	$20,100	$32,200	$48,800	$72,400
1951	TB21	2dr Tourer	$20,700	$32,600	$48,200	$67,300
1952	TA21	2dr FHC	$11,200	$17,500	$29,300	$41,500
		4dr Sdn	$4,300	$10,900	$17,300	$25,800
		2dr DHC	$20,100	$32,200	$48,800	$72,400
1952	TB21	2dr Tourer	$20,700	$32,600	$48,200	$67,300
1953	TA21	2dr FHC	$11,200	$17,500	$29,300	$41,500
		4dr Sdn	$4,300	$10,900	$17,300	$25,800
		2dr DHC	$20,100	$32,200	$48,800	$72,400
1953	TB21	2dr Tourer	$20,700	$32,600	$48,200	$67,300
1954	TC21/100	2dr FHC	$26,100	$36,600	$51,000	$70,300
		4dr Sal	$22,400	$33,900	$46,500	$61,000
		2dr DHC	$30,500	$45,800	$59,800	$76,000
1955	TC21/100	2dr FHC	$26,100	$36,600	$51,200	$70,300
		4dr Sal	$22,400	$34,000	$46,500	$61,000
		2dr DHC	$30,500	$45,800	$60,000	$76,000
1958	TD21	2dr SI FHC	$17,800	$25,400	$36,800	$55,300
		2dr SI DHC	$33,100	$50,300	$74,900	$113,000
1959	TD21	2dr SI FHC	$17,800	$25,400	$36,800	$55,300
		2dr SI DHC	$33,100	$50,300	$74,900	$113,000
1960	TD21	2dr SI DHC	$33,100	$50,300	$74,900	$113,000
1961	TD21	2dr SI FHC	$17,800	$25,400	$36,800	$55,300
		2dr SI DHC	$33,100	$50,300	$74,900	$113,000
1962	TD21	2dr SII FHC	$20,500	$31,000	$47,200	$68,000
		2dr SII DHC	$46,800	$61,600	$95,600	$136,000
1963	TD21	2dr SII DHC	$46,800	$61,600	$95,600	$136,000
1963	TE21	2dr Sdn	$24,100	$40,400	$54,900	$71,400
		2dr DHC	$59,800	$88,600	$121,000	$169,000
1964	TE21	2dr Sdn	$24,100	$40,400	$54,900	$71,400
		2dr DHC	$59,800	$88,600	$121,000	$169,000
1965	TE21	2dr Sdn	$24,100	$40,400	$54,900	$71,400
		2dr DHC	$59,800	$88,600	$121,000	$169,000
1966	TE21	2dr Sdn	$24,100	$40,400	$54,900	$71,400
		2dr DHC	$59,800	$88,600	$121,000	$169,000
1966	TF21	2dr DHC	$51,200	$75,500	$99,100	$138,000
1967	TF21	2dr DHC	$51,200	$75,500	$99,100	$138,000
1968	TF21	2dr DHC	$51,200	$75,500	$99,100	$138,000

American Motors

Year	Model	Body Style	4	3	2	1
1966	Marlin	287/198 2dr Fstbk	$8,500	$12,900	$16,900	$24,300
1967	Marlin	290/200 2dr Fstbk	$8,500	$12,900	$16,900	$24,300
1968	AMX	290/225 2dr Fstbk	$9,000	$15,700	$23,500	$35,500
		343/280 2dr Fstbk	$11,000	$18,000	$27,500	$41,800
		390/315 2dr Fstbk	$13,400	$25,500	$35,200	$46,500

American Motors

Year	Model	Body Style	4	3	2	1
			+20% for GO pkg. -20% for auto.			
1968	Javelin	343/280 2dr Fstbk	$7,400	$13,700	$17,900	$25,600
		343/280 2dr SST Fstbk	$8,800	$17,800	$22,200	$30,200
			-30% for 6-cyl. -20% for auto.			
1969	AMX	290/225 2dr Fstbk	$9,700	$17,100	$24,600	$35,800
		343/280 2dr Fstbk	$11,000	$18,300	$28,100	$43,000
		390/315 2dr Fstbk	$16,900	$27,300	$37,400	$53,000
		390/340 2dr SS Fstbk	$48,900	$67,800	$89,600	$118,000
			+25% for Big Bad pkg (exc SS). +20% for GO pkg (exc SS). -20% for auto.			
1969	Javelin	343/280 2dr Fstbk	$7,300	$13,600	$18,100	$26,200
		343/280 2dr SST Fstbk	$8,900	$17,200	$21,400	$29,300
		390/315 2dr SST Fstbk	$10,500	$20,000	$26,200	$36,500
			+10% for GO pkg. +30% for Mod pkg. -20% for auto.			
1969	SC/Rambler	390/315 2dr Hurst Hdtp Cpe	$29,200	$43,500	$55,500	$74,000
1970	Gremlin	232/145 2dr Sdn 2P	$3,800	$6,000	$9,600	$17,800
			-10% for 199/128 6-cyl.			
1970	AMX	360/290 2dr Fstbk	$11,000	$19,900	$26,500	$36,300
		390/325 2dr Fstbk	$19,100	$31,000	$42,400	$62,700
			+30% for Big Bad pkg. +10% for 4-spd. -20% for auto.			
1970	Javelin	360/245 2dr Fstbk	$7,300	$12,700	$18,300	$26,100
		360/290 2dr Fstbk	$7,700	$13,400	$20,200	$28,100
		390/325 2dr Fstbk	$10,700	$21,600	$27,700	$36,600
		390/325 2dr Trans Am Fstbk	$45,000	$66,000	$87,000	$125,000
			+15% for Mark Donohue. +10% for GO pkg. +25% for Big Bad pkg. -30% for 6-cyl. -20% for auto.			
1970	Rebel	390/340 2dr Machine Hdtp Cpe	$23,700	$36,000	$46,100	$69,300
1971	Gremlin	232/135 2dr Sdn 2P	$3,800	$6,000	$9,600	$17,800
		232/135 2dr X Sdn 4P	$6,000	$8,500	$13,100	$22,000
			+$150 for 258/150 6-cyl.			
1971	Javelin	360/285 2dr Fstbk	$6,700	$12,000	$15,700	$23,800
		360/285 2dr SST Fstbk	$8,100	$13,700	$18,100	$25,900
		401/330 2dr SST Fstbk	$8,500	$14,500	$19,800	$29,500
		360/285 2dr AMX Fstbk	$10,400	$18,000	$23,500	$33,200

American Motors

Year	Model	Body Style	4	3	2	1
		401/330 2dr AMX Fstbk	$10,700	$18,400	$24,600	$35,500
		+20% for GO pkg. -20% for auto.				
1972	Gremlin	232/100 2dr Sdn	$3,400	$5,700	$9,300	$15,800
		232/100 2dr X Sdn	$4,100	$6,500	$10,500	$17,400
		+$150 for 252/110 6-cyl. +30% for 304/150 V8.				
1972	Javelin	360/220 2dr SST Fstbk	$6,600	$12,400	$14,300	$19,200
		401/255 2dr SST Fstbk	$7,000	$12,600	$16,000	$22,000
		360/195 2dr AMX Fstbk	$8,100	$15,500	$18,800	$27,700
		401/255 2dr AMX Fstbk	$9,100	$18,200	$21,600	$30,000
		+30% for GO pkg. -30% for 6-cyl. -20% for auto.				
1973	Gremlin	232/100 2dr Sdn	$3,500	$5,900	$9,100	$14,800
		232/100 2dr X Sdn	$4,100	$6,500	$10,000	$17,000
		+20% for Levi's pkg. +$150 for 252/110 6-cyl. +30% for 304/150 V8.				
1973	Javelin	360/195 2dr Fstbk Cpe	$6,500	$11,300	$14,400	$18,900
		401/255 2dr Fstbk Cpe	$6,800	$12,500	$16,300	$25,200
		360/220 2dr AMX Fstbk Cpe	$8,200	$15,900	$19,600	$29,600
		401/255 2dr AMX Fstbk Cpe	$9,200	$18,200	$22,100	$31,000
		+30% for GO pkg. -30% for 6-cyl. -20% for auto.				
1974	Gremlin	232/100 2dr Sdn	$3,500	$5,900	$9,100	$14,800
		232/100 2dr X Sdn	$4,100	$6,500	$9,900	$16,800
		+20% for Levi's pkg. +10% for Rallye-X package. +$150 for 252/110 6-cyl. +30% for 304/150 V8.				
1974	Javelin	360/220 2dr Fstbk	$6,500	$11,500	$14,300	$19,100
		401/235 2dr Fstbk	$6,600	$12,000	$14,400	$20,400
		360/220 2dr AMX Fstbk	$7,700	$15,200	$18,700	$27,800
		401/235 2dr AMX Fstbk	$8,800	$18,000	$21,400	$30,100
		+30% for GO pkg. -30% for 6-cyl. -20% for auto.				
1975	Gremlin	232/100 2dr Sdn	$3,500	$5,900	$9,100	$14,800
		232/100 2dr X Sdn	$4,100	$6,500	$9,900	$16,800
		+20% for Levi's pkg. +10% for Rallye-X package. +$150 for 252/110 6-cyl. +30% for 304/150 V8.				
1975	Pacer	232/100 2dr Sdn	$2,400	$4,900	$9,100	$15,000
		232/100 2dr D/L Sdn	$3,100	$5,900	$10,800	$16,600

Year	Model	Body Style	4	3	2	1
		232/100 2dr X Sdn	$2,800	$5,400	$9,900	$15,400
1975	Matador	304/150 2dr Cpe	$2,000	$4,600	$7,600	$14,100
		304/150 2dr X Cpe	$2,800	$6,300	$8,700	$16,000
		+20% for Oleg Cassini. +10% for 360-c.i. V8. +20% for 401/255 V8. -20% for 6-cyl.				
1976	Gremlin	232/90 2dr Sdn	$3,500	$6,000	$9,200	$15,200
		304/120 2dr X Sdn	$4,300	$6,700	$10,300	$17,200
		+20% for Levi's pkg. +$150 for 252/110 6-cyl.				
1976	Pacer	232/90 2dr Sdn	$2,400	$4,900	$9,100	$15,000
		232/90 2dr X Sdn	$2,800	$5,400	$9,900	$15,400
		232/90 2dr D/L Sdn	$3,100	$5,900	$10,600	$16,300
		+20% for Bicentennial ed.				
1976	Matador	304/120 2dr Cpe	$2,000	$4,600	$7,500	$13,700
		+10% for Brougham pkg. +15% for Barcelona pkg. +10% for 360-c.i. V8. -20% for 6-cyl.				
1977	Gremlin	232/88 2dr X Sdn	$4,300	$6,800	$10,100	$17,000
		+20% for Levi's pkg. +25% for GT package. +$150 for 252/110 6-cyl. +30% for 304/150 V8. -20% for 4-cyl.				
1977	Pacer	232/88 2dr Sdn	$2,400	$4,900	$9,100	$15,000
		232/88 2dr Wgn	$2,400	$4,500	$9,100	$14,800
1977	Matador	304/126 2dr Cpe	$2,000	$4,600	$7,100	$13,500
		+10% for Brougham pkg. +10% for 360-c.i. V8. -20% for 6-cyl.				
1978	Gremlin	232/90 2dr Sdn	$3,800	$6,600	$10,500	$16,000
		258/120 2dr X Sdn	$4,300	$6,800	$10,700	$17,000
		+20% for Levi's pkg. +$150 for 252/110 6-cyl. +30% for 304/150 V8. -20% for 4-cyl.				
1978	Pacer	258/120 2dr D/L Htchbk	$2,700	$5,000	$9,400	$15,100
		258/120 2dr D/L Wgn	$2,700	$4,600	$9,000	$14,900
1978	Matador	360/140 2dr Hdtp Cpe	$2,000	$4,600	$7,200	$13,500
		+15% for Barcelona pkg. -20% for 6-cyl.				
1979	Pacer	258/110 2dr D/L Htchbk Cpe	$2,700	$5,000	$9,400	$15,100
		258/110 2dr D/L Wgn	$2,700	$4,600	$9,000	$14,900
		+15% for Limited pkg.				
1979	AMX	258/110 2dr Lftbk	$4,200	$6,600	$10,100	$17,000
		-30% for 6-cyl. -20% for auto.				
1980	Pacer	258/110 2dr D/L Htchbk Cpe	$3,100	$5,300	$9,300	$15,600
		258/110 2dr D/L Wgn	$3,000	$4,900	$9,200	$15,100
		+15% for Limited pkg.				

American Motors

Year	Model	Body Style	4	3	2	1
1980	AMX	258/110 2dr Lftbk	$3,800	$5,200	$8,400	$15,700

-30% for 6-cyl. -20% for auto.

Amphicar

Year	Model	Body Style	4	3	2	1
1961	Model 770	2dr Conv	$28,600	$46,600	$69,200	$89,900
1962	Model 770	2dr Conv	$28,600	$46,600	$69,200	$89,900
1963	Model 770	2dr Conv	$28,600	$46,600	$69,200	$89,900
1964	Model 770	2dr Conv	$28,600	$46,600	$69,200	$89,900
1965	Model 770	2dr Conv	$28,600	$46,600	$69,200	$89,900
1966	Model 770	2dr Conv	$28,600	$46,600	$69,200	$89,900
1967	Model 770	2dr Conv	$28,600	$46,600	$69,200	$89,900
1968	Model 770	2dr Conv	$28,600	$46,600	$69,200	$89,900

Apollo

Year	Model	Body Style	4	3	2	1
1962	3500GT	2dr Cpe	$89,000	$135,000	$170,000	$245,000
1963	3500GT	2dr Cpe	$89,000	$135,000	$170,000	$245,000
		2dr Conv	$150,000	$190,000	$270,000	$375,000
1964	5000GT	2dr Cpe	$100,000	$160,000	$215,000	$280,000
		2dr Conv	$120,000	$165,000	$240,000	$350,000
1965	5000GT	2dr Cpe	$100,000	$160,000	$215,000	$280,000
		2dr 2+2 Cpe	$55,000	$100,000	$140,000	$190,000
		2dr Conv	$120,000	$165,000	$240,000	$350,000

Arnolt-Bristol

Year	Model	Body Style	4	3	2	1
1954	Bolide	2dr Rdstr	$165,000	$240,000	$336,000	$395,000
1954	Deluxe	2dr Cpe	$249,000	$326,000	$382,000	$471,000
		2dr Rdstr	$230,000	$310,000	$356,000	$429,000
						+25% for all aluminum bodies.
1955	Bolide	2dr Rdstr	$165,000	$240,000	$336,000	$395,000
1955	Deluxe	2dr Cpe	$249,000	$326,000	$382,000	$471,000
		2dr Rdstr	$230,000	$310,000	$356,000	$429,000
						+25% for all aluminum bodies.
1956	Bolide	2dr Rdstr	$165,000	$240,000	$336,000	$395,000
1956	Deluxe	2dr Cpe	$249,000	$326,000	$382,000	$471,000
		2dr Rdstr	$230,000	$310,000	$356,000	$429,000
						+25% for all aluminum bodies.
1957	Bolide	2dr Rdstr	$165,000	$240,000	$336,000	$395,000
1957	Deluxe	2dr Cpe	$249,000	$326,000	$382,000	$471,000
		2dr Rdstr	$230,000	$310,000	$356,000	$429,000
						+25% for all aluminum bodies.
1958	Bolide	2dr Rdstr	$165,000	$240,000	$336,000	$395,000
1958	Deluxe	2dr Cpe	$249,000	$326,000	$382,000	$471,000
		2dr Rdstr	$230,000	$310,000	$356,000	$429,000

Arnolt-Bristol

Year	Model	Body Style	4	3	2	1
						+25% for all aluminum bodies.
1959	Bolide	2dr Rdstr	$165,000	$240,000	$336,000	$395,000
1959	Deluxe	2dr Cpe	$249,000	$326,000	$382,000	$471,000
		2dr Rdstr	$230,000	$310,000	$356,000	$429,000
						+25% for all aluminum bodies.
1960	Bolide	2dr Rdstr	$165,000	$240,000	$336,000	$395,000
1960	Deluxe	2dr Cpe	$249,000	$326,000	$382,000	$471,000
		2dr Rdstr	$230,000	$310,000	$356,000	$429,000
						+25% for all aluminum bodies.
1961	Bolide	2dr Rdstr	$165,000	$240,000	$336,000	$395,000
1961	Deluxe	2dr Cpe	$249,000	$326,000	$382,000	$471,000
		2dr Rdstr	$230,000	$310,000	$356,000	$429,000
						+25% for all aluminum bodies.

Arnolt-MG

Year	Model	Body Style	4	3	2	1
1953	Coupe	2dr FHC	$30,000	$40,500	$58,000	$81,500
1953	Convertible	2dr DHC	$53,200	$84,000	$126,000	$147,000
1954	Coupe	2dr FHC	$30,000	$40,500	$58,000	$81,500
1954	Convertible	2dr DHC	$53,200	$84,000	$126,000	$147,000

Aston Martin

Year	Model	Body Style	4	3	2	1
1950	DB2	2dr Cpe	$142,000	$205,000	$276,000	$374,000
		2dr DHC	$233,000	$310,000	$370,000	$486,000
1951	DB2	2dr Cpe	$142,000	$205,000	$276,000	$374,000
		2dr DHC	$233,000	$310,000	$370,000	$486,000
1952	DB2	2dr Cpe	$142,000	$205,000	$276,000	$374,000
		2dr DHC	$233,000	$310,000	$370,000	$486,000
1953	DB2	2dr DHC	$233,000	$310,000	$370,000	$486,000
		2dr Cpe	$142,000	$205,000	$276,000	$374,000
1953	DB2/4	2dr Mk I Sdn	$138,000	$191,000	$238,000	$296,000
		2dr Mk I DHC	$228,000	$285,000	$371,000	$435,000
1954	DB2/4	2dr Mk I Sdn	$138,000	$191,000	$238,000	$296,000
		2dr Mk I DHC	$228,000	$285,000	$371,000	$435,000
		2dr Bertone Spyder	$2.5 mil	$2.75 mil	$3.15 mil	$3.5 mil
						Pricing is for S/N LML502, LML505, LML507
1955	DB2/4	2dr Mk I Sdn	$138,000	$191,000	$238,000	$296,000
		2dr Mk I DHC	$228,000	$285,000	$371,000	$435,000
1956	DB2/4	2dr Mk II Sdn	$154,000	$223,000	$280,000	$340,000
		2dr Mk II DHC	$267,000	$311,000	$386,000	$476,000
1957	DB	2dr Mk III Ntchbk Cpe	$126,000	$146,000	$190,000	$273,000
		2dr Mk III Sal	$183,000	$229,000	$286,000	$368,000
		2dr Mk III DHC	$537,000	$664,000	$819,000	$975,000
1957	DB2/4	2dr Mk II Sdn	$154,000	$223,000	$280,000	$340,000

Aston Martin

Year	Model	Body Style	4	3	2	1
		2dr Mk II DHC	$267,000	$311,000	$386,000	$476,000
1958	DB	2dr Mk III Ntchbk Cpe	$126,000	$146,000	$190,000	$273,000
		2dr Mk III DHC	$537,000	$664,000	$819,000	$975,000
1958	DB4	2dr Sdn	$399,000	$501,000	$622,000	$778,000
1959	DB	2dr Mk III Sal	$183,000	$229,000	$286,000	$368,000
		2dr Mk III DHC	$537,000	$664,000	$819,000	$975,000
		2dr Mk III Ntchbk Cpe	$126,000	$146,000	$190,000	$273,000
1959	DB4	2dr Sdn	$399,000	$501,000	$622,000	$778,000
1960	DB4	2dr Sdn	$399,000	$501,000	$622,000	$778,000
		2dr GT Cpe	$2.3 mil	$2.65 mil	$3.25 mil	$3.75 mil
		2dr GT Ltwt Cpe	$2.65 mil	$2.95 mil	$3.5 mil	$4.25 mil
		2dr GT Zagato Cpe	$8.45 mil	$9.2 mil	$9.9 mil	$11 mil
1961	DB4	2dr Sdn	$399,000	$501,000	$622,000	$778,000
		2dr Vantage Conv	$870,000	$1.05 mil	$1.25 mil	$1.6 mil
		2dr Conv	$845,000	$1 mil	$1.15 mil	$1.5 mil
			+$50,000 for faired-in headlights.			
		2dr GT Cpe	$2.3 mil	$2.65 mil	$3.25 mil	$3.75 mil
		2dr GT Ltwt Cpe	$2.65 mil	$2.95 mil	$3.5 mil	$4.25 mil
		2dr GT Zagato Cpe	$8.45 mil	$9.2 mil	$9.9 mil	$11 mil
1962	DB4	2dr Sdn	$399,000	$501,000	$622,000	$778,000
		2dr Conv	$845,000	$1 mil	$1.15 mil	$1.5 mil
		2dr Vantage Conv	$870,000	$1.05 mil	$1.25 mil	$1.6 mil
			+$50,000 for faired-in headlights.			
		2dr GT Cpe	$2.3 mil	$2.6 mil	$3.25 mil	$3.75 mil
		2dr GT Ltwt Cpe	$2.65 mil	$2.95 mil	$3.5 mil	$4.25 mil
		2dr GT Zagato Cpe	$8.45 mil	$9.2 mil	$9.9 mil	$11 mil
1963	DB4	2dr Sdn	$365,000	$483,000	$598,000	$771,000
		2dr Conv	$845,000	$1 mil	$1.15 mil	$1.5 mil
		2dr Vantage Conv	$870,000	$1.05 mil	$1.25 mil	$1.6 mil
			+$50,000 for faired-in headlights.			
		2dr GT Cpe	$2.3 mil	$2.65 mil	$3.25 mil	$3.75 mil
		2dr GT Ltwt Cpe	$2.65 mil	$2.95 mil	$3.5 mil	$4.25 mil
1963	DB5	2dr Sal	$620,000	$800,000	$980,000	$1.25 mil
		2dr DHC	$900,000	$1.05 mil	$1.4 mil	$2.3 mil
			+$40,000 for factory a/c. -$50,000 for auto trans on coupe. -$100,000 for auto trans on convertible.			
1964	DB5	2dr Sal	$640,000	$820,000	$1.1 mil	$1.45 mil
		2dr Vantage Sal	$700,000	$845,000	$1.05 mil	$1.4 mil
		2dr DHC	$961,000	$1.1 mil	$1.55 mil	$2.6 mil
		2dr Vantage DHC	$950,000	$1.25 mil	$1.8 mil	$2.5 mil
			+$40,000 for factory a/c. -$50,000 for auto trans on coupe. -$100,000 for auto trans on convertible.			
1965	DB5	2dr Sal	$620,000	$800,000	$980,000	$1.25 mil
		2dr Vantage Sal	$700,000	$845,000	$1.05 mil	$1.4 mil

Year	Model	Body Style	4	3	2	1
		2dr Shtg Brk	$600,000	$725,000	$950,000	$1.3 mil
		2dr Vantage Shtg Brk	$700,000	$850,000	$1.1 mil	$1.45 mil
		2dr DHC	$901,000	$1.05 mil	$1.4 mil	$2.3 mil
		2dr Vantage DHC	$950,000	$1.25 mil	$1.8 mil	$2.5 mil
			+$40,000 for factory a/c. -$50,000 for auto trans on coupe. -$100,000 for auto trans on convertible.			
1965	DB6	2dr Mk I Sal	$219,000	$290,000	$375,000	$510,000
		2dr Mk I Vantage Sal	$282,000	$368,000	$452,000	$585,000
		2dr Mk I Short-Chassis Volante	$1.55 mil	$1.75 mil	$2.2 mil	$2.8 mil
			+$40,000 for factory a/c. -$50,000 for auto trans on coupe. -$100,000 for auto trans on convertible.			
1966	DB5	2dr Shtg Brk	$400,000	$485,000	$653,000	$790,000
		2dr Vantage Shtg Brk	$485,000	$575,000	$745,000	$875,000
			+$40,000 for factory a/c. -$50,000 for auto trans on coupe. -$100,000 for auto trans on convertible.			
1966	DB6	2dr Mk I Sal	$219,000	$290,000	$375,000	$510,000
		2dr Mk I Vantage Sal	$282,000	$368,000	$452,000	$585,000
		2dr Mk I Cnv	$421,000	$560,000	$990,000	$1.15 mil
		2dr Mk I Short-Chassis Volante	$1.55 mil	$1.75 mil	$2.2 mil	$2.8 mil
		2dr Mk I Vantage Cnv	$510,000	$695,000	$1.3 mil	$1.5 mil
			+$40,000 for factory a/c. -$50,000 for auto trans on coupe. -$100,000 for auto trans on convertible.			
1967	DB6	2dr Mk I Sal	$219,000	$290,000	$375,000	$510,000
		2dr Mk I Vantage Sal	$282,000	$368,000	$452,000	$585,000
		2dr Mk I Cnv	$421,000	$560,000	$990,000	$1.15 mil
		2dr Mk I Vantage Cnv	$510,000	$695,000	$1.3 mil	$1.5 mil
			+$40,000 for factory a/c. -$50,000 for auto trans on coupe. -$100,000 for auto trans on convertible.			
1968	DB6	2dr Mk I Sal	$219,000	$290,000	$375,000	$510,000
		2dr Mk I Vantage Sal	$282,000	$368,000	$452,000	$585,000
		2dr Mk I Cnv	$421,000	$560,000	$990,000	$1.15 mil
		2dr Mk I Vantage Cnv	$510,000	$695,000	$1.3 mil	$1.5 mil
			+$40,000 for factory a/c. -$50,000 for auto trans on coupe. -$100,000 for auto trans on convertible.			
1968	DBS	2dr Sal	$73,700	$112,000	$151,000	$228,000
			+$10,000 for factory a/c. -$15,000 for auto trans.			
1969	DB6	2dr Mk I Sal	$219,000	$290,000	$375,000	$510,000
		2dr Mk II Sal	$251,000	$320,000	$395,000	$521,000

Aston Martin

Year	Model	Body Style	4	3	2	1
		2dr Mk I Vantage Sal	$282,000	$368,000	$452,000	$585,000
		2dr Mk II Vantage Sal	$299,000	$389,000	$476,000	$610,000
		2dr Mk I Cnv	$421,000	$560,000	$990,000	$1.15 mil
		2dr Mk II Cnv	$1 mil	$1.15 mil	$1.3 mil	$1.6 mil
		2dr Mk I Vantage Cnv	$487,000	$626,000	$1.05 mil	$1.2 mil
		2dr Mk II Vantage Cnv	$1.1 mil	$1.2 mil	$1.4 mil	$1.75 mil
			+$40,000 for factory a/c. -$50,000 for auto trans on coupe. -$100,000 for auto trans on convertible.			
1969	DBS	2dr Sal	$73,700	$112,000	$151,000	$228,000
			+$10,000 for factory a/c. -$15,000 for auto trans.			
1970	DB6	2dr Mk II Sal	$251,000	$320,000	$395,000	$521,000
		2dr Mk II Vantage Sal	$299,000	$389,000	$476,000	$610,000
		2dr Mk II Cnv	$1 mil	$1.15 mil	$1.3 mil	$1.6 mil
		2dr Mk II Vantage Cnv	$1.1 mil	$1.2 mil	$1.4 mil	$1.75 mil
			+$40,000 for factory a/c. -$50,000 for auto trans on coupe. -$100,000 for auto trans on convertible.			
1970	DBS	2dr Vantage Cpe	$101,000	$138,000	$209,000	$278,000
			+$10,000 for factory a/c. -$15,000 for auto trans.			
1971	DBS	2dr Sal	$73,700	$112,000	$151,000	$228,000
			+$10,000 for factory a/c. -$15,000 for auto trans.			
1972	DBS	2dr Sal	$73,700	$112,000	$151,000	$228,000
			+$10,000 for factory a/c. -$15,000 for auto trans.			
		2dr Vantage Cpe	$108,000	$167,000	$226,000	$303,000
		2dr V8 Cpe	$106,000	$148,000	$219,000	$282,000
1973	AMV8	2dr Sal	$83,000	$122,000	$163,000	$202,000
1975	AMV8	2dr Sal	$66,600	$99,000	$139,000	$181,000
			-$10,000 for auto trans.			
1976	AMV8	2dr Sal	$66,600	$99,000	$139,000	$181,000
			-$10,000 for auto trans.			
1977	V8 Vantage	2dr Sal	$125,000	$185,000	$253,000	$318,000
			-$35,000 for U.S. "Cosmetic" V8 Vantage models.			
1977	AMV8	2dr Sal	$66,600	$99,000	$139,000	$181,000
			-$10,000 for auto trans.			
1977	Lagonda	4dr S2 Sdn	$25,900	$40,400	$64,500	$127,000
1978	V8 Vantage	2dr Sal	$125,000	$185,000	$253,000	$318,000
			-$35,000 for U.S. "Cosmetic" V8 Vantage models.			
1978	AMV8	2dr Sal	$58,200	$91,000	$128,000	$174,000
		2dr Volante	$106,000	$143,000	$230,000	$295,000
			-$10,000 for auto trans.			
1978	Lagonda	4dr S2 Sdn	$25,900	$40,400	$64,500	$127,000
1979	AMV8	2dr Sal	$88,100	$130,000	$173,000	$234,000

Year	Model	Body Style	4	3	2	1
		2dr Volante	$106,000	$143,000	$230,000	$295,000
		-$10,000 for auto trans.				
1979	V8 Vantage	2dr Sal	$119,000	$159,000	$217,000	$270,000
1979	Lagonda	4dr S2 Sdn	$25,900	$40,400	$64,500	$127,000
1980	V8	2dr Cpe	$102,000	$138,000	$197,000	$283,000
		2dr Vantage SII Cpe	$136,000	$188,000	$256,000	$321,000
		2dr Volante	$146,000	$195,000	$242,000	$338,000
		-$10,000 for auto trans. -$15,000 for black rubber 5-mph bumpers.				
1980	Lagonda	4dr S2 Sdn	$25,900	$40,400	$64,500	$127,000
1981	V8	2dr Cpe	$106,000	$147,000	$201,000	$283,000
		2dr Vantage SII Cpe	$136,000	$188,000	$256,000	$321,000
		2dr Volante	$146,000	$195,000	$242,000	$338,000
		-$10,000 for auto trans. -$15,000 for black rubber 5-mph bumpers.				
1981	Lagonda	4dr S2 Sdn	$25,900	$40,400	$64,500	$127,000
1982	V8	2dr Cpe	$102,000	$138,000	$197,000	$283,000
		2dr Vantage SII Cpe	$136,000	$188,000	$256,000	$321,000
		2dr Volante	$146,000	$195,000	$242,000	$338,000
		-$10,000 for auto trans. -$15,000 for black rubber 5-mph bumpers.				
1982	Lagonda	4dr S2 Sdn	$25,900	$40,400	$64,500	$127,000
1983	V8	2dr Cpe	$102,000	$138,000	$197,000	$283,000
		2dr Vantage SII Cpe	$136,000	$188,000	$256,000	$321,000
		2dr Volante	$146,000	$195,000	$242,000	$338,000
		-$10,000 for auto trans. -$15,000 for black rubber 5-mph bumpers.				
1983	Lagonda	4dr S2 Sdn	$25,900	$40,400	$64,500	$127,000
1984	V8	2dr Cpe	$102,000	$138,000	$197,000	$283,000
		2dr Vantage SII Cpe	$136,000	$188,000	$256,000	$321,000
		2dr Volante	$146,000	$195,000	$242,000	$338,000
		-$10,000 for auto trans. -$15,000 for black rubber 5-mph bumpers.				
1984	Lagonda	4dr S2 Sdn	$25,900	$40,400	$64,500	$127,000
1985	V8	2dr Cpe	$102,000	$138,000	$197,000	$283,000
		2dr Vantage SII Cpe	$136,000	$188,000	$256,000	$321,000
		2dr Volante	$146,000	$195,000	$242,000	$338,000
		-$10,000 for auto trans. -$15,000 for black rubber 5-mph bumpers.				
1985	Lagonda	4dr S2 Sdn	$25,900	$40,400	$64,500	$127,000
1986	V8	2dr Cpe	$97,000	$131,000	$172,000	$243,000
		2dr Vantage SIII Cpe	$168,000	$231,000	$297,000	$434,000
		2dr Zagato Cpe	$205,000	$300,000	$379,000	$517,000
		2dr Volante	$140,000	$175,000	$217,000	$308,000
		2dr Zagato Conv	$245,000	$341,000	$422,000	$537,000
		-$50,000 from Vantage prices for U.S. "Cosmetic" V8 Vantage models. -$15,000 for black rubber 5-mph bumpers. -$10,000 for auto trans.				

Aston Martin

Year	Model	Body Style	4	3	2	1
1986	Vantage Volante	2dr Conv	$272,000	$375,000	$460,000	$549,000
		-$50,000 for U.S. "Cosmetic" Vantage Volante. -$15,000 for black rubber 5-mph bumpers.				
1986	Lagonda	4dr S3 Sdn	$36,200	$54,300	$88,100	$143,000
1987	V8	2dr Vantage SIII Cpe	$168,000	$231,000	$297,000	$434,000
		2dr Zagato Cpe	$205,000	$300,000	$379,000	$517,000
		2dr Volante	$140,000	$175,000	$217,000	$308,000
		2dr Zagato Conv	$245,000	$341,000	$422,000	$537,000
		-$50,000 from Vantage prices for U.S. "Cosmetic" V8 Vantage models. -$15,000 for black rubber 5-mph bumpers. -$10,000 for auto trans.				
1987	Vantage Volante	2dr Conv	$272,000	$375,000	$460,000	$549,000
		-$50,000 for U.S. "Cosmetic" Vantage Volante. -$15,000 for black rubber 5-mph bumpers.				
1987	Lagonda	4dr S3 Sdn	$36,200	$54,300	$88,100	$143,000
1988	V8	2dr Vantage SIII Cpe	$168,000	$231,000	$297,000	$434,000
		2dr Zagato Cpe	$205,000	$300,000	$379,000	$517,000
		2dr Volante	$140,000	$175,000	$217,000	$308,000
		2dr Zagato Conv	$245,000	$341,000	$422,000	$537,000
		-$50,000 from Vantage prices for U.S. "Cosmetic" V8 Vantage models. -$15,000 for black rubber 5-mph bumpers. -$10,000 for auto trans.				
1988	Vantage Volante	2dr Conv	$272,000	$375,000	$460,000	$549,000
		-$50,000 for U.S. "Cosmetic" Vantage Volante. -$15,000 for black rubber 5-mph bumpers.				
1988	Lagonda	4dr S4 Sdn	$54,000	$79,100	$115,000	$161,000
1989	V8	2dr Vantage SIII Cpe	$166,000	$231,000	$296,000	$428,000
		2dr Zagato Cpe	$205,000	$300,000	$379,000	$517,000
		2dr Volante	$140,000	$175,000	$217,000	$308,000
		2dr Zagato Conv	$245,000	$341,000	$422,000	$537,000
		-$50,000 from Vantage prices for U.S. "Cosmetic" V8 Vantage models. -$15,000 for black rubber 5-mph bumpers. -$10,000 for auto trans.				
1989	Vantage Volante	2dr Conv	$272,000	$375,000	$460,000	$549,000
		-$50,000 for U.S. "Cosmetic" Vantage Volante. -$15,000 for black rubber 5-mph bumpers.				
1989	Lagonda	4dr S4 Sdn	$54,000	$79,100	$115,000	$161,000
1990	V8	2dr Zagato Cpe	$205,000	$300,000	$379,000	$517,000
		2dr Zagato Conv	$245,000	$341,000	$422,000	$537,000
1997	DB7	2dr Cpe	$17,200	$22,200	$31,100	$39,500
		2dr Conv	$16,300	$21,100	$29,500	$37,400
		+25% for 5-speed				
1998	DB7	2dr Cpe	$19,100	$24,000	$33,200	$42,400
		+25% for 5-speed				
		2dr Conv	$17,800	$22,100	$31,600	$39,100
		+10% for Neiman Marcus Edition convertible. +25% for 5-speed				
1999	DB7	2dr Cpe	$19,100	$24,000	$33,200	$42,400

Aston Martin

Year	Model	Body Style	4	3	2	1
						+25% for 5-speed
		2dr Vantage Cpe	$21,700	$26,600	$36,700	$46,300
						+25% for 6-speed
2000	DB7	2dr Vantage Conv	$19,600	$24,300	$34,100	$43,500
		2dr Vantage Cpe	$21,700	$26,600	$36,700	$46,300
						+25% for 6-speed
2001	DB7	2dr Vantage Cpe	$22,900	$28,900	$40,900	$51,700
		2dr Vantage Conv	$20,900	$25,600	$35,800	$46,100
						+25% for 6-speed
2002	DB7	2dr Vantage Cpe	$24,900	$31,400	$44,400	$57,200
		2dr Vantage Conv	$22,800	$28,700	$40,700	$52,000
						+25% for 6-speed
2002	Vanquish	2dr Cpe	$43,500	$54,000	$61,000	$72,500
2003	DB7	2dr Vantage Cpe	$27,000	$33,400	$46,700	$59,600
						+5% for Jubilee Ed. +25% for 6-speed
		2dr Zagato Cpe	$254,000	$280,000	$318,000	$375,000
		2dr Vantage Conv	$23,400	$29,200	$41,300	$53,000
						+5% for Jubilee Ed. +25% for 6-speed
2003	DB AR1	2dr Conv	$169,000	$222,000	$279,000	$396,000
2003	Vanquish	2dr Cpe	$46,000	$59,000	$66,000	$78,500
2004	Vanquish	2dr Cpe	$52,000	$64,000	$73,000	$89,500
2004	DB AR1	2dr Conv	$169,000	$222,000	$279,000	$396,000
2005	Vanquish	2dr S Cpe	$63,500	$72,000	$81,000	$98,500
2006	Vanquish	2dr S Cpe	$74,000	$85,000	$103,000	$117,000

Audi

Year	Model	Body Style	4	3	2	1
1983	GT	2dr Cpe	$3,600	$6,100	$9,700	$18,700
1983	Quattro	2dr Cpe	$15,000	$28,200	$46,800	$82,400
1984	GT	2dr Cpe	$3,600	$6,100	$9,700	$18,700
1984	Quattro	2dr Cpe	$15,000	$28,200	$46,800	$82,400
1985	GT	2dr Cpe	$3,600	$6,100	$9,700	$18,700
1985	Quattro	2dr Cpe	$15,000	$28,200	$46,800	$82,400
		3dr Turbo Spt Cpe	$265,000	$370,000	$440,000	$520,000
1986	GT	2dr Cpe	$3,600	$6,100	$9,700	$18,700
1986	Quattro	3dr Turbo Spt Cpe	$265,000	$370,000	$440,000	$520,000
1987	GT	2dr Cpe	$3,600	$6,100	$9,700	$18,700
2000	TT	2dr Cpe	$3,900	$6,100	$8,500	$15,300
		2dr Quattro Cpe	$4,900	$7,400	$11,200	$21,400
						-10% for auto trans on 4-cyl Quattro.
2001	TT	2dr Cpe	$3,900	$6,100	$8,500	$15,300
		2dr Quattro Cpe	$4,900	$7,400	$11,200	$21,400
		2dr Rdstr	$3,800	$6,000	$8,200	$15,000
		2dr Quattro Rdstr	$4,800	$7,300	$11,000	$21,000
						-10% for auto trans on 4-cyl Quattro.
2002	TT	2dr Cpe	$4,100	$6,400	$9,600	$18,400

Audi

Year	Model	Body Style	4	3	2	1
		2dr Quattro Cpe	$4,900	$7,900	$11,800	$23,500
		2dr Quattro Rdstr	$4,800	$7,800	$11,600	$23,000
		2dr Rdstr	$4,000	$6,300	$9,400	$18,000
			-10% for auto trans on 4-cyl Quattro.			
2003	TT	2dr Cpe	$4,400	$6,900	$9,800	$18,400
		2dr Quattro Cpe	$4,900	$7,900	$11,800	$23,500
		2dr Quattro Rdstr	$4,800	$7,800	$11,600	$23,000
		2dr Rdstr	$4,300	$6,800	$9,700	$18,000
			-10% for auto trans on 4-cyl Quattro.			
2004	TT	2dr 3.2 Quattro Cpe	$5,900	$8,400	$12,900	$23,500
		2dr Cpe	$4,600	$7,400	$10,300	$19,400
		2dr Quattro Cpe	$4,900	$7,900	$11,800	$23,500
		2dr Quattro Rdstr	$4,800	$7,800	$11,600	$23,000
		2dr Rdstr	$4,500	$7,300	$10,200	$19,000
		2dr 3.2 Quattro Rdstr	$5,800	$8,300	$12,600	$23,000
			-10% for auto trans on 4-cyl Quattro.			
2005	TT	2dr 3.2 Quattro Cpe	$5,900	$8,900	$13,400	$25,500
		2dr Cpe	$4,900	$7,700	$11,200	$21,400
		2dr Quattro Cpe	$5,100	$8,200	$12,300	$24,500
		2dr Quattro Rdstr	$5,000	$8,000	$12,100	$24,000
		2dr Rdstr	$4,800	$7,500	$11,000	$21,000
		2dr 3.2 Quattro Rdstr	$5,800	$8,800	$13,200	$25,000
			-10% for auto trans on 4-cyl Quattro.			
2006	TT	2dr 3.2 Quattro Cpe	$6,100	$9,200	$14,600	$28,600
		2dr Cpe	$4,900	$7,700	$11,800	$23,500
		2dr Quattro Cpe	$5,300	$8,500	$13,200	$27,500
		2dr Quattro Rdstr	$5,300	$8,500	$13,200	$27,500
		2dr Rdstr	$4,800	$7,500	$11,600	$23,000
		2dr 3.2 Quattro Rdstr	$6,000	$9,000	$14,300	$28,000
			-10% for auto trans on 4-cyl Quattro.			

Austin

Year	Model	Body Style	4	3	2	1
1949	A90	2dr Conv	$14,100	$21,900	$33,000	$44,000
1950	A90	2dr Atlantic Conv	$14,100	$21,900	$33,000	$44,000
1951	A90	2dr Atlantic Spt Sdn	$7,700	$12,600	$15,200	$23,100
		2dr Atlantic Conv	$14,100	$21,900	$33,000	$44,000
1959	Mini	2dr Sdn	$9,200	$13,300	$19,500	$24,800
1960	Mini	2dr Sdn	$9,200	$13,300	$19,500	$24,800
1961	Mini	2dr Sdn	$9,200	$13,300	$19,500	$24,800
1962	Mini	2dr Sdn	$9,200	$13,300	$19,500	$24,800

Austin

Year	Model	Body Style	4	3	2	1
		2dr Traveller Wgn	$12,800	$17,200	$21,800	$31,300
1963	Mini	2dr Sdn	$9,200	$13,300	$19,500	$24,800
		2dr Traveller Wgn	$12,800	$17,200	$21,800	$31,300
1963	Mini Cooper	2dr Sdn	$14,200	$18,400	$28,000	$42,000
1964	Mini Cooper	2dr Sdn	$14,200	$18,400	$27,400	$41,300
		2dr 1275S Sdn	$18,400	$26,400	$43,000	$60,000
1965	Mini Cooper	2dr 1275S Sdn	$18,400	$26,400	$43,000	$60,000
1966	Mini Cooper	2dr 1275S Sdn	$18,400	$26,400	$43,000	$60,000
1966	Mini Moke	Conv	$11,000	$18,500	$29,500	$39,500
1967	Mini Cooper	2dr 1275S Sdn	$18,400	$26,400	$43,000	$60,000

Austin-Healey

Year	Model	Body Style	4	3	2	1
1953	100-4	2dr BN1 Rdstr	$23,200	$38,300	$71,000	$121,000
1954	100-4	2dr BN1 Rdstr	$23,200	$38,300	$71,000	$121,000
1955	100-4	2dr BN1 Rdstr	$23,200	$38,300	$69,000	$120,000
1955	100	2dr M Rdstr	$56,000	$77,000	$124,000	$180,000
		2dr S Rdstr	$610,000	$825,000	$1 mil	$1.15 mil
1956	100-4	2dr BN2 Rdstr	$25,400	$38,800	$73,000	$122,000
1956	100	2dr M BN2 Le Mans Rdstr	$95,000	$140,000	$172,000	$250,000
1956	100-6	2dr BN4 Rdstr	$19,100	$31,500	$55,300	$103,000
					+$3,000 for factory hard top.	
1957	100-6	2dr BN4 Rdstr	$18,800	$30,500	$51,400	$100,000
					+$3,000 for factory hard top.	
1958	Sprite	2dr Mk I Bugeye Conv	$7,100	$12,800	$20,500	$32,500
1958	100-6	2dr BN4 Rdstr	$18,800	$30,500	$51,200	$100,000
		2dr BN6 Rdstr	$21,900	$32,600	$54,900	$103,000
					+$3,000 for factory hard top.	
1959	Sprite	2dr Mk I Bugeye Conv	$7,100	$12,800	$20,500	$32,500
1959	100-6	2dr BN4 Rdstr	$19,000	$31,900	$52,000	$100,000
		2dr BN6 Rdstr	$23,100	$35,800	$55,800	$103,000
					+$3,000 for factory hard top.	
1959	3000	2dr Mk I BN7 Rdstr	$26,000	$41,800	$77,300	$101,000
		2dr Mk I BT7 Rdstr	$20,900	$33,200	$61,900	$95,000
					+$3,000 for factory hard top.	
1960	Sprite	2dr Mk I Bugeye Conv	$7,100	$12,800	$20,500	$32,500
1960	3000	2dr Mk I BN7 Rdstr	$26,000	$41,800	$77,300	$101,000
		2dr Mk I BT7 Rdstr	$20,900	$33,200	$61,900	$95,000
					+$3,000 for factory hard top.	
1961	Sprite	2dr Mk II Conv	$4,000	$7,900	$12,900	$20,500
		2dr Mk II 1100 Rdstr	$4,800	$8,600	$13,100	$23,100

Austin-Healey

Year	Model	Body Style	4	3	2	1
1961	3000	2dr Mk II BN7 Rdstr	$28,700	$43,300	$77,300	$127,000
		2dr Mk II BT7 Rdstr	$19,000	$30,500	$58,700	$92,000
						+$3,000 for factory hard top.
1962	Sprite	2dr Mk II Conv	$4,100	$8,000	$13,000	$20,900
		2dr Mk II 1100 Rdstr	$4,700	$7,800	$12,900	$23,200
1962	3000	2dr Mk II BJ7 Conv	$26,600	$42,600	$76,500	$104,000
		2dr Mk II BJ7 Dlx Conv	$26,600	$42,600	$76,500	$104,000
		2dr Mk II BN7 Dlx Rdstr	$28,800	$43,400	$78,600	$127,000
		2dr Mk II BT7 Rdstr	$19,000	$30,500	$58,700	$92,000
						+$3,000 for factory hard top.
1963	Sprite	2dr Mk II Conv	$4,100	$8,000	$13,000	$20,900
1963	3000	2dr Mk II BJ7 Conv	$26,600	$42,800	$76,200	$104,000
		2dr Mk III BJ8 Rdstr	$23,600	$40,000	$77,000	$109,000
						+$3,000 for factory hard top.
1964	Sprite	2dr Mk III Conv	$3,100	$7,100	$11,000	$16,800
1964	3000	2dr Mk III BJ8 Rdstr	$23,600	$40,000	$72,000	$109,000
						+$3,000 for factory hard top.
1965	Sprite	2dr Mk III Conv	$3,100	$7,100	$11,000	$16,800
1965	3000	2dr Mk III BJ8 ph2 Conv	$31,600	$48,400	$78,500	$120,000
						+$3,000 for factory hard top.
1966	Sprite	2dr Mk III Conv	$3,100	$7,100	$11,000	$16,800
1966	3000	2dr Mk III BJ8 ph2 Conv	$31,600	$48,400	$78,500	$120,000
						+$3,000 for factory hard top.
1967	Sprite	2dr Mk III Conv	$3,100	$7,100	$11,000	$16,800
1967	3000	2dr Mk III BJ8 ph2 Conv	$31,600	$48,400	$78,500	$120,000
						+$3,000 for factory hard top.
1968	Sprite	2dr Mk IV Conv	$2,700	$6,100	$10,200	$14,400
1969	Sprite	2dr Mk IV Conv	$2,700	$6,100	$10,200	$14,400

Avanti

Year	Model	Body Style	4	3	2	1
1965	Avanti II	327/300 2dr Cpe	$8,500	$13,200	$23,000	$39,400
						+10% for a/c. +10% for 4-spd.
1966	Avanti II	327/300 2dr Cpe	$8,500	$13,200	$23,000	$39,400
						+10% for a/c. +10% for 4-spd.
1967	Avanti II	327/300 2dr Cpe	$8,500	$13,200	$23,000	$39,400
						+10% for a/c. +10% for 4-spd.
1968	Avanti II	327/300 2dr Cpe	$7,600	$13,000	$19,800	$37,900

Avanti

Year	Model	Body Style	4	3	2	1
					+10% for a/c. +10% for 4-spd.	
1969	Avanti II	350/300 2dr Cpe	$7,600	$13,000	$19,800	$37,900
					+10% for a/c. +10% for 4-spd.	
1970	Avanti II	350/300 2dr Cpe	$7,000	$11,700	$17,000	$27,200
1971	Avanti II	350/270 2dr Cpe	$7,000	$11,700	$17,000	$27,200
1972	Avanti II	350/270 2dr Cpe	$7,000	$11,700	$17,000	$27,200
1973	Avanti II	400/245 2dr Cpe	$7,000	$11,700	$17,000	$27,200
1974	Avanti II	400/180 2dr Cpe	$7,000	$11,700	$17,000	$27,200
1975	Avanti II	400/180 2dr Cpe	$6,800	$10,800	$16,700	$25,200
1976	Avanti II	400/175 2dr Cpe	$6,800	$10,800	$16,700	$25,200
1977	Avanti II	350/180 2dr Cpe	$6,800	$10,800	$16,700	$25,200
1978	Avanti II	350/180 2dr Cpe	$6,800	$10,800	$16,700	$25,200
1979	Avanti II	350/185 2dr Cpe	$6,800	$10,800	$16,700	$25,200
1980	Avanti II	350/190 2dr Cpe	$6,800	$10,800	$16,700	$25,200
1981	Avanti II	305/155 2dr Cpe	$6,800	$10,800	$16,700	$25,200
1982	Avanti II	305/155 2dr Cpe	$6,800	$10,800	$16,700	$25,200
1983	Avanti	305/190 2dr Cpe	$7,900	$13,400	$19,100	$26,700
		305/155 2dr Annv Cpe	$9,300	$15,700	$20,900	$29,500
1984	Avanti	305/190 2dr Cpe	$7,900	$13,600	$19,600	$30,200
		305/190 2dr Touring Cpe	$9,400	$15,800	$22,400	$33,000
1985	Avanti	305/155 2dr Cpe	$7,900	$14,300	$20,200	$31,000
		305/190 2dr 5-spd Cpe	$10,000	$16,000	$24,700	$37,100
		305/190 2dr Conv	$16,600	$30,000	$39,500	$56,500
1987	Avanti	305/185 2dr Cpe	$6,700	$11,400	$15,300	$23,000
		305/185 2dr LSC Cpe	$8,100	$12,100	$17,000	$23,600
		305/185 2dr Conv	$8,700	$14,500	$17,400	$27,200
1988	Avanti	305/155 2dr Cpe	$8,300	$13,300	$17,900	$26,200
		2dr LSC Cpe	$8,700	$13,500	$17,600	$26,700
		305/155 2dr Conv	$8,900	$14,600	$18,600	$31,800
1989	Avanti	305/155 2dr Cpe	$9,500	$13,600	$18,700	$26,800
		305/155 2dr Conv	$10,100	$15,100	$18,900	$32,100
1990	Avanti	305/170 4dr Sdn	$10,300	$16,500	$20,600	$38,000
1991	Avanti	305/170 2dr Conv	$10,200	$15,400	$19,100	$33,000
2001	Avanti	346/320 2dr Cpe	$11,600	$18,400	$26,600	$32,600
		346/320 2dr Conv	$14,500	$18,500	$28,300	$36,700
2002	Avanti	346/320 2dr Cpe	$11,800	$18,600	$27,300	$34,100
		346/320 2dr Conv	$14,700	$23,500	$30,600	$38,500
2003	Avanti	346/320 2dr Cpe	$11,800	$19,000	$28,000	$36,500
		346/320 2dr Conv	$15,800	$26,100	$32,200	$39,800

BMW

Year	Model	Body Style	4	3	2	1
1952	501	4dr Sdn	$15,100	$25,700	$34,900	$66,200
1953	501	4dr Sdn	$15,100	$25,700	$34,900	$66,200

BMW

Year	Model	Body Style	4	3	2	1
1954	501A	4dr Sdn	$15,100	$25,700	$34,900	$66,200
1954	501B	4dr Sdn	$15,600	$26,100	$36,800	$68,700
1954	502	4dr 2.6 Sdn	$17,300	$26,900	$38,600	$73,400
1955	Isetta	250 Cpe	$17,000	$24,600	$32,500	$50,700
1955	501	4dr Sdn	$18,900	$31,700	$47,300	$82,600
1955	501A	4dr Sdn	$15,100	$25,700	$34,900	$66,200
1955	501B	4dr Sdn	$15,600	$26,100	$36,800	$68,700
1955	502	4dr 2.6 Sdn	$17,300	$26,900	$38,600	$73,400
		4dr 3.2 Sdn	$17,800	$28,900	$49,200	$79,400
1956	Isetta	250 Cpe	$17,000	$24,600	$32,500	$50,700
		300 Cpe	$18,000	$27,600	$37,700	$57,200
1956	501	4dr Sdn	$18,900	$31,700	$47,300	$82,600
1956	501/3	4dr Sdn	$15,600	$27,300	$38,400	$68,800
1956	502	4dr 2.6 Sdn	$17,300	$26,900	$38,600	$73,400
		4dr 3.2 Sdn	$17,800	$28,900	$49,200	$79,400
1956	503	2dr FHC	$124,000	$200,000	$279,000	$357,000
		2dr DHC	$270,000	$350,000	$435,000	$605,000
		+$10,000 for sunroof on coupe. +$20,000 for knock-offs. +10% for floor shift.				
1956	507	2dr Rdstr	$1.65 mil	$1.85 mil	$2 mil	$2.35 mil
		+$75,000 for factory hard top. +$75,000 for original Rudge knock-offs.				
1957	502	4dr 2.6 Sdn	$17,700	$27,700	$39,800	$74,400
		4dr 3.2 Sdn	$19,000	$33,000	$55,900	$89,700
		4dr 3.2 Super Sdn	$26,600	$43,300	$70,200	$111,000
1957	Isetta	300 Cpe	$18,400	$28,100	$38,500	$58,300
1957	501	4dr Sdn	$18,900	$31,700	$47,300	$82,600
1957	501/3	4dr Sdn	$13,800	$27,300	$38,400	$68,800
1957	503	2dr FHC	$124,000	$200,000	$279,000	$357,000
		2dr DHC	$270,000	$350,000	$460,000	$605,000
		+$10,000 for sunroof on coupe. +$20,000 for knock-offs. +10% for floor shift.				
1957	507	2dr Rdstr	$1.8 mil	$1.9 mil	$2.1 mil	$2.4 mil
		+$75,000 for factory hard top. +$75,000 for original Rudge knock-offs.				
1958	502	4dr 2.6 Sdn	$17,700	$27,700	$39,800	$74,400
		4dr 3.2 Sdn	$19,600	$35,300	$57,100	$90,000
		4dr 3.2 Super Sdn	$28,200	$44,400	$71,600	$112,000
1958	Isetta	300 Cpe	$18,400	$28,100	$38,500	$58,300
		2dr 600 Sdn	$13,700	$21,700	$32,500	$47,800
1958	501	4dr Sdn	$18,900	$31,700	$47,300	$82,600
1958	501/3	4dr Sdn	$15,600	$27,300	$38,400	$68,800
1958	503	2dr FHC	$124,000	$200,000	$279,000	$357,000
		2dr DHC	$270,000	$350,000	$460,000	$605,000
		+$10,000 for sunroof on coupe. +$20,000 for knock-offs. +10% for floor shift.				
1958	507	2dr Rdstr	$1.8 mil	$1.9 mil	$2.1 mil	$2.55 mil
		+$75,000 for factory hard top. +$75,000 for original Rudge knock-offs.				
1959	Isetta	300 Cpe	$18,400	$28,100	$38,500	$58,300
		2dr 600 Sdn	$13,700	$21,700	$32,500	$47,800
1959	501	4dr Sdn	$21,100	$33,000	$49,500	$84,500
1959	502	4dr 2.6 Sdn	$17,900	$28,400	$40,900	$75,800
		4dr 3.2 Sdn	$20,300	$35,600	$57,800	$92,000

Year	Model	Body Style	4	3	2	1
		4dr 3.2 Super Sdn	$29,200	$45,400	$73,800	$114,000
1959	503	2dr FHC	$124,000	$200,000	$279,000	$357,000
		2dr DHC	$270,000	$350,000	$460,000	$605,000
		+$10,000 for sunroof on coupe. +$20,000 for knock-offs. +10% for floor shift.				
1959	507	2dr Rdstr	$1.9 mil	$2 mil	$2.2 mil	$2.55 mil
		+$75,000 for factory hard top. +$75,000 for original Rudge knock-offs. +$25,000 for factory disc brakes.				
1960	Isetta	300 Cpe	$18,400	$28,100	$38,500	$58,300
		2dr 600 Cpe	$13,700	$21,700	$32,500	$47,800
1960	502	4dr 2.6 Sdn	$16,000	$25,000	$39,800	$72,200
		4dr 3.2 Sdn	$20,100	$35,000	$56,200	$87,500
		4dr 3.2 Super Sdn	$28,900	$43,900	$71,600	$108,000
1960	503	2dr Cpe	$124,000	$200,000	$279,000	$357,000
		2dr Cab	$270,000	$350,000	$460,000	$605,000
		+$10,000 for sunroof on coupe. +$20,000 for knock-offs. +10% for floor shift.				
1961	Isetta	300 Cpe	$18,400	$28,100	$38,500	$58,300
		2dr 600 Cpe	$13,700	$21,700	$32,500	$47,800
1961	502	4dr 2.6 Sdn	$16,000	$25,000	$39,800	$72,200
		4dr 3.2 Sdn	$20,100	$35,000	$56,200	$87,500
		4dr 3.2 Super Sdn	$28,900	$43,900	$71,600	$108,000
1961	700	2dr Cpe	$5,800	$9,900	$17,200	$23,700
		2dr Sdn	$4,000	$7,700	$13,400	$17,600
1961	2600	4dr Sdn	$8,800	$16,100	$28,700	$50,800
1961	2600L	4dr Sdn	$9,400	$16,800	$29,100	$51,300
1961	3200L	4dr Sdn	$10,500	$22,600	$36,000	$54,400
1961	3200S	4dr Sdn	$11,200	$21,900	$35,500	$53,800
1962	Isetta	2dr 300 Cpe	$18,400	$28,100	$38,500	$58,300
		2dr 600 Cpe	$13,700	$21,700	$32,500	$47,800
1962	700	2dr Cpe	$5,800	$9,900	$17,200	$23,700
		2dr Sdn	$4,000	$7,700	$13,400	$17,600
1962	1500	4dr Sdn	$5,500	$7,600	$11,100	$19,500
1962	2600	4dr Sdn	$8,700	$15,800	$28,700	$48,600
1962	2600L	4dr Sdn	$9,300	$16,400	$29,200	$49,600
1962	3200S	4dr Sdn	$11,600	$22,300	$35,900	$53,900
1962	3200L	4dr Sdn	$12,400	$23,300	$36,800	$55,000
1962	3200CS	2dr Cpe	$41,600	$65,800	$98,000	$136,000
1963	700	2dr Cpe	$6,400	$10,700	$17,600	$24,000
		2dr Luxus LS Cpe	$7,300	$12,500	$20,100	$26,800
		2dr CS Cpe	$11,100	$15,500	$27,600	$39,000
		2dr Luxus Sdn	$4,300	$8,300	$14,900	$19,700
		2dr Luxus LS Sdn	$5,300	$9,400	$16,700	$21,600
		2dr Baur Conv	$9,500	$16,300	$29,600	$42,300
1963	1500	4dr Sdn	$5,800	$7,600	$11,400	$19,700
1963	1800	4dr Sdn	$6,100	$8,600	$13,100	$22,100
1963	2600L	4dr Sdn	$9,700	$17,500	$30,500	$51,800
1963	3200S	4dr Sdn	$12,600	$24,000	$37,700	$56,400
1963	3200L	4dr Sdn	$12,800	$27,000	$39,000	$57,100
1963	3200CS	2dr Cpe	$41,600	$65,800	$98,000	$136,000

BMW

Year	Model	Body Style	4	3	2	1
1964	700	2dr LS Cpe	$7,300	$12,500	$20,100	$26,800
		2dr CS Cpe	$11,400	$16,200	$27,700	$39,400
		2dr LS Sdn	$5,400	$9,700	$16,900	$21,600
1964	1500	4dr Sdn	$5,800	$7,600	$11,400	$19,700
1964	1600	4dr Sdn	$7,700	$11,300	$16,300	$27,900
1964	1800	4dr Sdn	$5,600	$7,800	$11,700	$19,700
1964	1800ti	4dr Sdn	$6,300	$9,300	$13,500	$21,800
1964	1800ti/SA	4dr Sdn	$24,900	$38,600	$51,400	$70,200
1964	3200CS	2dr Cpe	$41,600	$65,800	$98,000	$136,000
1965	700	2dr LS Cpe	$7,400	$12,800	$20,200	$27,300
		2dr LS Sdn	$5,500	$9,900	$17,200	$21,900
1965	1600	4dr Sdn	$7,700	$11,300	$16,300	$27,900
1965	1800	4dr Sdn	$5,600	$7,800	$11,700	$19,700
1965	1800ti	4dr Sdn	$6,300	$9,300	$13,500	$21,800
1965	1800ti/SA	4dr Sdn	$24,900	$38,600	$51,400	$70,200
1965	2000C	2dr Cpe	$11,300	$16,200	$23,500	$33,800
1965	2000CS	2dr Cpe	$17,900	$28,500	$40,400	$56,500
1965	3200CS	2dr Cpe	$47,000	$72,300	$114,000	$146,000
1966	1600	4dr Sdn	$7,700	$11,300	$16,300	$27,900
1966	1600-2	2dr Sdn	$9,400	$14,200	$22,100	$38,300
1966	1600ti	2dr Sdn	$10,500	$17,500	$28,200	$49,500
1966	1800	4dr Sdn	$6,200	$9,300	$14,000	$21,200
1966	1800ti	4dr Sdn	$6,600	$9,900	$14,400	$22,800
1966	1800ti/SA	4dr Sdn	$24,900	$38,600	$51,400	$70,200
1966	2000	4dr Sdn	$6,100	$9,600	$15,000	$24,400
1966	2000C	2dr Cpe	$11,900	$17,100	$25,500	$34,600
1966	2000ti	4dr Sdn	$6,400	$10,000	$15,800	$26,300
		4dr Luxus Sdn	$8,200	$12,600	$17,300	$28,000
1966	2000CS	2dr Cpe	$17,900	$28,500	$40,400	$56,500
1967	1600	2dr Conv	$17,400	$27,900	$38,500	$60,400
1967	1600-2	2dr Sdn	$9,400	$14,200	$22,100	$38,300
1967	1600ti	2dr Sdn	$10,500	$17,500	$28,200	$49,500
1967	1800	4dr Sdn	$6,200	$9,300	$14,000	$21,200
1967	1800ti	4dr Sdn	$6,600	$9,900	$14,400	$22,800
1967	1800ti/SA	4dr Sdn	$24,900	$38,600	$51,400	$70,200
1967	2000	4dr Sdn	$6,100	$9,600	$15,000	$24,400
1967	2000ti	4dr Sdn	$6,400	$10,000	$15,800	$26,300
		4dr Luxus Sdn	$8,200	$12,600	$17,300	$28,000
1967	2000C	2dr Cpe	$11,900	$17,100	$25,500	$34,600
1967	2000CS	2dr Cpe	$17,900	$28,500	$40,400	$56,500
1968	1600	2dr GT Cpe	$16,100	$25,100	$47,100	$74,100
1968	1800	4dr Sdn	$6,200	$9,300	$14,000	$21,200
1968	2000	4dr Sdn	$6,100	$9,700	$15,300	$25,200
1968	2002	2dr Sdn	$8,400	$14,100	$26,900	$41,100
1968	2800CS	2dr Cpe	$17,900	$33,300	$64,100	$112,000
1969	1600-2	2dr Sdn	$9,500	$14,900	$22,500	$38,800
1969	2000	4dr Sdn	$6,100	$9,700	$15,300	$25,200
1969	2002	2dr Sdn	$8,600	$14,300	$27,100	$41,400
1969	2500	4dr Sdn	$2,600	$5,900	$13,100	$22,600

Year	Model	Body Style	4	3	2	1
1969	2800	4dr Sdn	$3,600	$6,800	$14,100	$27,200
1969	2800CS	2dr Cpe	$17,900	$33,300	$64,100	$112,000
1970	1600-2	2dr Sdn	$9,500	$14,900	$22,500	$38,800
1970	2000	4dr Sdn	$6,100	$9,700	$15,300	$25,200
1970	2002	2dr Sdn	$8,600	$14,300	$27,100	$41,400
1970	2500	4dr Sdn	$2,600	$5,900	$13,100	$22,600
1970	2800	4dr Sdn	$3,600	$6,800	$14,100	$27,200
1970	2800CS	2dr Cpe	$17,900	$33,300	$64,100	$112,000
1971	1600-2	2dr Sdn	$9,900	$15,300	$23,000	$39,500
1971	2002	2dr Sdn	$8,600	$14,300	$27,100	$41,400
1971	2500	4dr Sdn	$2,600	$5,900	$13,100	$22,600
1971	2800	4dr Sdn	$3,600	$6,800	$14,100	$27,200
1971	2800CS	2dr Cpe	$17,900	$33,300	$64,100	$112,000
1971	3.0CSL	Dual Carb 2dr Cpe	$147,000	$188,000	$259,000	$329,000
1972	2002	2dr Sdn	$9,000	$16,500	$28,100	$46,800
						-15% for auto. +15% for sunroof.
1972	2002tii	2dr Sdn	$16,500	$30,000	$55,200	$85,200
						-15% for auto. +15% for sunroof.
1972	Bavaria	4dr Sdn	$3,800	$7,200	$15,000	$30,700
1972	3.0CS	2dr Cpe	$27,300	$55,000	$101,000	$130,000
						-25% for auto. +15% for sunroof.
1972	3.0CSL	2dr Cpe	$126,000	$157,000	$224,000	$293,000
		Dual Carb 2dr Cpe	$147,000	$188,000	$259,000	$329,000
1973	2002	2dr Sdn	$9,000	$16,500	$28,100	$46,800
		2dr Turbo Sdn	$52,200	$81,100	$152,000	$189,000
						-15% for auto. +15% for sunroof.
1973	2002tii	2dr Sdn	$16,500	$30,000	$55,200	$85,200
						-15% for auto. +15% for sunroof.
1973	Bavaria	4dr Sdn	$3,800	$7,200	$15,000	$30,700
1973	3.0CS	2dr Cpe	$27,300	$55,000	$101,000	$130,000
						-25% for auto. +15% for sunroof.
1973	3.0CSL	2dr Cpe	$126,000	$157,000	$224,000	$293,000
		2dr Batmobile Cpe	$147,000	$197,000	$292,000	$373,000
1974	2002	2dr Sdn	$8,700	$13,500	$23,000	$40,800
		2dr Turbo Sdn	$52,200	$81,100	$152,000	$189,000
						-15% for auto. +15% for sunroof.
1974	2002tii	2dr Sdn	$15,000	$27,000	$48,000	$77,700
						-15% for auto. +15% for sunroof.
1974	Bavaria	4dr Sdn	$3,500	$6,800	$14,700	$29,800
1974	3.0CS	2dr Cpe	$27,300	$47,500	$83,100	$116,000
						-25% for auto. +15% for sunroof.
1974	3.0CSi	2dr Cpe	$32,600	$51,000	$97,700	$129,000
						-25% for auto. +15% for sunroof.
1974	3.0CSL	2dr Batmobile Cpe	$160,000	$218,000	$320,000	$390,000
1975	2002	2dr Sdn	$8,400	$13,000	$22,800	$41,600

BMW

Year	Model	Body Style	4	3	2	1
						-25% for auto. +15% for sunroof.
1975	530i	4dr Sdn	$3,400	$6,000	$9,300	$20,600
1975	3.0Si	4dr Sdn	$3,500	$7,100	$10,300	$22,400
						-25% for auto. +15% for sunroof.
1975	3.0CSi	2dr Cpe	$32,600	$48,000	$90,900	$118,000
						-25% for auto. +15% for sunroof.
1975	3.0CSL	2dr Batmobile Cpe	$160,000	$218,000	$320,000	$390,000
1976	2002	2dr Sdn	$7,700	$11,600	$20,300	$37,500
						-25% for auto. +15% for sunroof.
1976	530i	4dr Sdn	$3,400	$6,000	$9,300	$20,600
1976	3.0Si	4dr Sdn	$3,500	$7,100	$10,300	$22,400
						-25% for auto. +15% for sunroof.
1977	320i	2dr Cpe	$4,300	$8,500	$12,100	$24,200
1977	530i	4dr Sdn	$3,400	$6,000	$9,300	$20,600
1977	630CSi	2dr Cpe	$4,600	$8,100	$15,600	$26,800
1978	320i	2dr Cpe	$4,300	$8,500	$12,100	$24,200
1978	530i	4dr Sdn	$3,400	$6,000	$9,300	$20,600
1978	633CSi	2dr Cpe	$5,200	$9,300	$17,400	$32,600
1978	635CSi	2dr Cpe	$9,700	$13,200	$19,800	$36,800
1978	733i	4dr Sdn	$3,400	$5,800	$12,300	$20,600
1979	320i	2dr Cpe	$4,300	$8,500	$12,100	$24,200
1979	633CSi	2dr Cpe	$5,200	$9,300	$17,400	$32,600
1979	733i	4dr Sdn	$3,400	$5,800	$12,300	$20,600
1979	M1	2dr Cpe	$380,000	$440,000	$510,000	$615,000
1980	320i	2dr Cpe	$4,000	$8,200	$11,400	$21,400
1980	633CSi	2dr Cpe	$5,200	$9,300	$17,400	$32,600
1980	733i	4dr Sdn	$3,400	$5,800	$12,300	$20,600
1980	M1	2dr Cpe	$380,000	$440,000	$510,000	$615,000
1981	320i	2dr Cpe	$4,000	$8,200	$11,400	$21,400
1981	633CSi	2dr Cpe	$5,200	$9,300	$17,400	$32,600
1981	733i	4dr Sdn	$3,400	$5,800	$12,300	$20,600
1981	M1	2dr Cpe	$380,000	$440,000	$510,000	$615,000
1982	320i	2dr Sdn	$4,000	$8,200	$11,400	$21,400
1983	320i	2dr Sdn	$4,000	$8,200	$11,400	$21,400
1984	325e	2dr Sdn	$3,000	$8,800	$12,700	$20,400
						-10% for auto.
1985	325e	2dr Sdn	$3,000	$8,800	$12,700	$20,400
						-10% for auto.
1986	325	2dr Sdn	$3,000	$8,800	$12,700	$20,400
		4dr Sdn	$2,500	$8,200	$11,700	$18,400
						-10% for auto.
1986	325e	4dr Sdn	$2,500	$8,200	$11,700	$18,400
						-10% for auto.
1986	325es	2dr Sdn	$3,000	$8,800	$12,700	$20,400
						-10% for auto.
1987	325	2dr Sdn	$3,000	$8,800	$12,700	$20,400

Year	Model	Body Style	4	3	2	1
		4dr Sdn	$2,500	$8,200	$11,700	$18,400
						-10% for auto.
1987	325e	4dr Sdn	$2,500	$8,200	$11,700	$18,400
						-10% for auto.
1987	325es	2dr Sdn	$3,000	$8,800	$12,700	$20,400
						-10% for auto.
1987	325is	2dr Sdn	$4,200	$12,600	$19,700	$29,900
						-10% for auto.
1987	325i	2dr Conv	$4,300	$12,100	$20,300	$31,300
		4dr Sdn	$3,900	$11,100	$17,300	$25,300
						-10% for auto.
1987	M6	2dr Cpe	$19,900	$32,400	$59,100	$96,100
1988	325	2dr Sdn	$3,000	$8,800	$12,700	$20,400
		4dr Sdn	$2,500	$8,200	$11,700	$18,400
						-10% for auto.
1988	325is	2dr Sdn	$4,200	$12,600	$19,700	$29,800
						-10% for auto.
1988	M3	2dr Cpe	$33,500	$56,000	$92,000	$139,000
1988	M5	4dr Sdn	$19,100	$40,100	$62,300	$98,900
1988	M6	2dr Cpe	$19,900	$32,400	$59,100	$96,100
1988	325i	2dr Conv	$4,300	$12,100	$20,300	$31,300
		4dr Sdn	$3,900	$11,100	$17,300	$25,300
						-10% for auto.
1988	325iX	2dr Sdn	$3,900	$11,600	$18,200	$26,800
						-10% for auto.
1989	325is	2dr Sdn	$4,200	$12,600	$19,700	$29,900
						-10% for auto.
1989	325iX	2dr Sdn	$3,900	$11,600	$18,200	$26,800
		4dr Sdn	$3,800	$10,800	$16,900	$23,900
						-10% for auto.
1989	Z1	2dr Conv	$30,600	$45,800	$67,800	$106,000
1989	M3	2dr Cpe	$33,500	$56,000	$92,000	$139,000
1989	M6	2dr Cpe	$19,900	$32,400	$59,100	$96,100
1989	325i	2dr Conv	$4,300	$12,100	$20,300	$31,300
		2dr Sdn	$4,200	$12,600	$19,700	$29,900
		4dr Sdn	$3,900	$11,100	$17,300	$25,300
						-10% for auto.
1990	325is	2dr Sdn	$4,200	$12,600	$19,700	$29,900
						-10% for auto.
1990	325iX	2dr Sdn	$3,900	$11,600	$18,200	$26,800
		4dr Sdn	$3,800	$10,300	$16,900	$23,900
						-10% for auto.
1990	Z1	2dr Conv	$30,600	$45,800	$67,800	$106,000
1990	M3	2dr Cpe	$33,500	$56,000	$92,000	$139,000
1990	325i	2dr Conv	$4,300	$12,100	$20,300	$31,300
		2dr Sdn	$4,200	$12,600	$19,700	$29,900

BMW

Year	Model	Body Style	4	3	2	1
		4dr Sdn	$3,900	$11,100	$17,300	$25,300
						-10% for auto.
1991	318i	2dr Conv	$3,900	$11,100	$17,300	$24,600
		4dr Sdn	$3,600	$10,300	$16,100	$21,400
						-10% for auto.
1991	318is	2dr Cpe	$4,000	$11,600	$17,900	$25,300
						-10% for auto.
1991	325is	2dr Sdn	$4,200	$12,100	$19,700	$29,900
						-10% for auto.
1991	325iX	2dr Sdn	$3,900	$11,100	$18,200	$26,800
		4dr Sdn	$3,800	$10,300	$16,900	$23,900
						-10% for auto.
1991	Z1	2dr Conv	$30,600	$45,800	$67,800	$106,000
1991	M3	2dr Cpe	$33,500	$56,000	$92,000	$139,000
1991	M5	4dr Sdn	$16,400	$27,600	$43,600	$72,600
1991	850i	2dr Cpe	$12,700	$29,900	$61,500	$86,900
						-20% for auto
1991	325i	2dr Conv	$4,300	$12,100	$20,300	$31,300
		2dr Sdn	$4,200	$12,600	$19,700	$29,900
		4dr Sdn	$3,900	$10,600	$17,300	$25,300
						-10% for auto.
1992	318i	2dr Conv	$3,900	$10,600	$17,300	$24,600
						-10% for auto.
1992	M5	4dr Sdn	$15,800	$26,400	$41,600	$70,800
1992	850i	2dr Cpe	$12,700	$29,900	$61,500	$86,900
						-20% for auto
1992	325i	2dr Conv	$4,300	$12,100	$20,300	$31,300
						-10% for auto.
1993	325i	2dr Conv	$4,300	$12,100	$20,300	$31,300
						-10% for auto.
1993	M5	4dr Sdn	$15,800	$26,400	$41,600	$70,800
1993	850Ci	2dr Cpe	$12,700	$22,500	$43,800	$63,100
1994	840Ci	2dr Cpe	$5,900	$14,600	$32,500	$42,200
1994	850Ci	2dr Cpe	$12,700	$22,500	$43,800	$63,100
1994	850CSi	2dr Cpe	$46,600	$92,400	$140,000	$237,000
1995	M3	2dr Cpe	$8,400	$19,200	$32,200	$46,600
						-15% for auto
1995	840Ci	2dr Cpe	$5,900	$14,600	$32,500	$42,200
1995	850Ci	2dr Cpe	$12,700	$22,500	$43,800	$63,100
1995	850CSi	2dr Cpe	$46,600	$92,400	$140,000	$237,000
1996	Z3	2dr Conv	$3,800	$6,600	$9,500	$14,200
			-15% for auto trans, +$2,000 for removable hardtop on convertible.			
1996	M3	2dr Cpe	$8,500	$19,300	$32,500	$47,100
						-15% for auto
1996	840Ci	2dr Cpe	$5,900	$14,600	$32,500	$42,200
1996	850Ci	2dr Cpe	$12,700	$22,500	$43,800	$63,100

Year	Model	Body Style	4	3	2	1
1997	Z3	2dr 2.8 Conv	$4,300	$7,600	$11,400	$20,900
		2dr Conv	$3,800	$6,600	$9,500	$14,200
		-15% for auto trans, +$2,000 for removable hardtop on convertible.				
1997	M3	2dr Cpe	$8,800	$19,900	$33,500	$47,700
		4dr Sdn	$6,900	$15,700	$28,000	$39,700
		-15% for auto				
1997	840Ci	2dr Cpe	$5,900	$14,600	$32,500	$42,200
1997	850Ci	2dr Cpe	$12,700	$22,500	$43,800	$63,100
1998	M Roadster	2dr Rdstr	$9,000	$13,500	$20,000	$32,000
		-15% for auto trans, +$2,000 for removable hardtop on convertible.				
1998	Z3	2dr 1.9 Conv	$3,800	$6,600	$9,500	$16,200
		2dr 2.8 Conv	$4,300	$7,600	$11,400	$20,900
		-15% for auto trans, +$2,000 for removable hardtop on convertible.				
1998	M3	2dr Cpe	$9,300	$20,200	$34,200	$48,800
		4dr Sdn	$7,200	$16,000	$28,600	$40,600
		2dr Conv	$6,900	$16,000	$26,100	$38,300
		-15% for auto				
1999	M Coupe	2dr Htchbk	$16,000	$25,500	$42,000	$54,700
1999	M Roadster	2dr Rdstr	$9,000	$13,500	$20,000	$32,000
		-15% for auto trans, +$2,000 for removable hardtop on convertible.				
1999	M3	2dr Cpe	$9,300	$20,600	$34,700	$49,000
		2dr Conv	$7,000	$16,200	$26,500	$38,600
		-15% for auto				
1999	Z3	2dr 2.3 Conv	$4,800	$8,100	$11,900	$20,900
		2dr 2.8 Conv	$6,200	$9,500	$14,200	$21,800
		-15% for auto trans, +$2,000 for removable hardtop on convertible.				
		2dr 2.8 Htchbk	$6,800	$9,600	$16,200	$24,300
2000	M Roadster	2dr Rdstr	$9,000	$13,500	$20,000	$32,000
		-15% for auto trans, +$2,000 for removable hardtop on convertible.				
2000	Z3	2dr 2.3 Conv	$4,800	$8,100	$11,900	$20,900
		2dr 2.8 Conv	$6,200	$9,500	$14,200	$21,800
		2dr 2.8 Htchbk	$6,800	$9,600	$16,200	$24,300
		-15% for auto trans, +$2,000 for removable hardtop on convertible.				
2000	M Coupe	2dr Htchbk	$17,100	$27,400	$45,400	$59,800
2000	Z8	2dr Rdstr	$110,000	$138,000	$177,000	$232,000
2000	M5	4dr Sdn	$12,100	$23,700	$42,300	$61,400
2001	Z3	2dr 2.5 Conv	$6,200	$9,500	$14,200	$21,800
		2dr 3.0 Conv	$7,100	$10,900	$16,600	$23,300
		2dr 3.0 Htchbk	$8,000	$13,600	$22,800	$28,800
		-15% for auto trans, +$2,000 for removable hardtop on convertible.				
2001	M Coupe	2dr Htchbk	$21,900	$34,900	$55,800	$84,700
2001	M Roadster	2dr Rdstr	$13,500	$17,100	$28,000	$40,000
		-15% for auto trans, +$2,000 for removable hardtop on convertible.				
2001	M3	2dr Cpe	$15,500	$23,100	$36,300	$49,800
		2dr Conv	$11,100	$18,900	$32,900	$51,700
		-25% for SMG.				

BMW

Year	Model	Body Style	4	3	2	1
2001	M5	4dr Sdn	$14,400	$28,300	$50,900	$74,000
2001	Z8	2dr Rdstr	$110,000	$138,000	$177,000	$232,000
2002	Z3	2dr 2.5 Conv	$4,800	$8,100	$11,900	$20,900
		2dr 3.0 Conv	$7,100	$10,900	$16,600	$23,300
		2dr 3.0 Htchbk	$8,000	$13,600	$22,800	$28,800
			-15% for auto trans, +$2,000 for removable hardtop on convertible.			
2002	M Coupe	2dr Htchbk	$27,500	$40,800	$66,100	$96,000
2002	M Roadster	2dr Rdstr	$13,500	$17,100	$28,000	$40,000
			-15% for auto trans, +$2,000 for removable hardtop on convertible.			
2002	M3	2dr Cpe	$15,500	$23,100	$36,300	$49,800
		2dr Conv	$11,100	$18,900	$32,900	$51,700
						-25% for SMG.
2002	M5	4dr Sdn	$17,500	$34,500	$62,100	$90,200
2002	Z8	2dr Rdstr	$110,000	$138,000	$177,000	$232,000
2003	M3	2dr Cpe	$15,500	$23,100	$36,300	$49,800
		2dr Conv	$11,100	$18,900	$32,900	$51,700
						-25% for SMG.
2003	M5	4dr Sdn	$19,700	$38,800	$69,800	$102,000
2003	Z8	2dr Rdstr	$110,000	$138,000	$177,000	$232,000
		2dr Alpina Rdstr	$132,000	$159,000	$219,000	$289,000
2004	M3	2dr Cpe	$21,500	$32,000	$48,600	$68,800
		2dr Conv	$15,300	$24,100	$38,900	$55,300
						-25% for SMG.
2005	M3	2dr Cpe	$21,500	$32,000	$48,600	$68,800
		2dr ZCP Cpe	$21,900	$35,200	$55,800	$73,300
		2dr Conv	$15,300	$24,100	$38,900	$55,300
						-25% for SMG.
2006	M3	2dr Cpe	$21,500	$32,000	$48,600	$68,800
		2dr ZCP Cpe	$21,900	$35,200	$55,800	$73,300
		2dr Conv	$15,300	$24,100	$38,900	$55,300
						-25% for SMG.

Beck

Year	Model	Body Style	4	3	2	1
1986	550	2dr Spyder	$17,700	$23,700	$34,600	$50,700
1987	550	2dr Spyder	$17,700	$23,700	$34,600	$50,700
1988	550	2dr Spyder	$17,700	$23,700	$34,600	$50,700
1989	550	2dr Spyder	$17,700	$23,700	$34,600	$50,700
1990	550	2dr Spyder	$17,700	$23,700	$34,600	$50,700
1991	550	2dr Spyder	$17,700	$23,700	$34,600	$50,700
1992	550	2dr Spyder	$17,700	$23,700	$34,600	$50,700
1993	550	2dr Spyder	$17,700	$23,700	$34,600	$50,700
1994	550	2dr Spyder	$17,700	$23,700	$34,600	$50,700
1995	550	2dr Spyder	$17,700	$23,700	$34,600	$50,700

Year	Model	Body Style	4	3	2	1
1946	Mk VI	2dr Cchblt FHC	$46,400	$56,300	$73,900	$98,200
		4dr Std Stl Sdn	$17,700	$24,700	$30,000	$45,300
		4dr Cchblt Sal	$28,600	$38,300	$51,200	$66,400
		2dr Cchblt DHC	$87,200	$113,000	$136,000	$173,000
1947	Mk VI	4dr Std Stl Sdn	$17,700	$24,700	$30,000	$45,300
		2dr Cchblt FHC	$46,400	$56,300	$73,900	$98,200
		4dr Cchblt Sal	$28,600	$38,300	$51,200	$66,400
		2dr Cchblt DHC	$87,000	$113,000	$136,000	$173,000
1948	Mk VI	4dr Std Stl Sdn	$17,700	$24,700	$30,000	$45,300
		2dr Cchblt FHC	$46,400	$56,300	$73,900	$98,200
		4dr Cchblt Sal	$28,600	$38,100	$51,200	$66,400
		2dr Cchblt DHC	$87,200	$113,000	$136,000	$173,000
1949	Mk VI	2dr Cchblt FHC	$46,400	$56,300	$73,900	$98,200
		4dr Std Stl Sdn	$17,700	$24,700	$29,800	$45,300
		4dr Cchblt Sal	$28,600	$38,300	$51,200	$66,400
		2dr Cchblt DHC	$87,200	$113,000	$136,000	$173,000
1950	Mk VI	2dr Cchblt FHC	$68,300	$84,600	$112,000	$130,000
		4dr Std Stl Sdn	$29,200	$36,400	$48,300	$61,100
		4dr Cchblt Sal	$37,000	$52,100	$78,600	$97,200
		2dr Cchblt DHC	$127,000	$150,000	$186,000	$214,000
						-30% for RHD.
1951	Mk VI	2dr Cchblt FHC	$68,300	$84,600	$112,000	$130,000
		4dr Std Stl Sdn	$29,200	$36,400	$48,300	$61,100
		4dr Cchblt Sal	$37,000	$52,100	$78,600	$97,200
		2dr Cchblt DHC	$127,000	$150,000	$186,000	$214,000
						-30% for RHD.
1952	Mk VI	2dr Cchblt FHC	$68,300	$84,600	$112,000	$130,000
		4dr Std Stl Sdn	$29,200	$36,400	$48,300	$61,100
		4dr Cchblt Sal	$37,000	$52,100	$78,600	$97,200
		2dr Cchblt DHC	$127,000	$150,000	$186,000	$214,000
						-30% for RHD.
1952	R-Type	2dr Cchblt FHC	$80,300	$111,000	$131,000	$158,000
		4dr Std Stl Sdn	$28,900	$37,900	$54,200	$72,500
		4dr Cchblt Sdn	$55,000	$67,900	$84,600	$108,000
		2dr Cchblt DHC	$136,000	$177,000	$209,000	$230,000
						-30% for RHD. -10% for man trans.
1952	R-Type Continental	2dr 4.6L Sdn	$950,000	$1.1 mil	$1.4 mil	$1.6 mil
						+20% for manual transmission, center floor shift
1953	R-Type	2dr Cchblt FHC	$80,300	$111,000	$131,000	$158,000
		4dr Std Stl Sdn	$28,800	$37,900	$54,200	$69,800
		4dr Cchblt Sdn	$55,000	$67,900	$84,600	$108,000
		2dr Cchblt DHC	$141,000	$186,000	$219,000	$234,000
						-30% for RHD. -10% for man trans.
1953	R-Type Continental	2dr 4.6L Sdn	$950,000	$1.1 mil	$1.4 mil	$1.6 mil
						+20% for manual transmission, center floor shift
1954	R-Type	2dr Cchblt FHC	$80,300	$111,000	$131,000	$158,000

Bentley

Year	Model	Body Style	4	3	2	1
		4dr Std Stl Sdn	$28,900	$37,900	$54,000	$69,800
		4dr Cchblt Sdn	$55,000	$67,900	$84,600	$108,000
		2dr Cchblt DHC	$141,000	$186,000	$219,000	$234,000
				-30% for RHD. -10% for man trans.		
1954	R-Type Continental	2dr 4.9L Sdn	$1.1 mil	$1.35 mil	$1.6 mil	$1.8 mil
				+20% for manual transmission, center floor shift		
1955	S1	2dr Cchblt FHC	$62,800	$84,200	$115,000	$140,000
		4dr Std Stl Sal	$22,200	$33,000	$44,200	$57,400
		4dr Cchblt Sal	$45,900	$59,900	$76,300	$94,600
		2dr Cchblt DHC	$243,000	$291,000	$341,000	$386,000
				-20% for no pwr strng. +10% for LWB.		
1955	S1 Continental	4dr Cchblt Flying Spur Sal	$180,000	$215,000	$260,000	$295,000
		2dr Cchblt DHC	$880,000	$975,000	$1.05 mil	$1.15 mil
		2dr HJM FHC	$450,000	$540,000	$630,000	$685,000
				+10% for factory a/c. -10% for no pwr steering (HJM).		
1955	R-Type	4dr Std Stl Sdn	$28,900	$37,900	$54,000	$69,800
		2dr Cchblt FHC	$78,800	$107,000	$127,000	$154,000
		4dr Cchblt Sdn	$55,000	$67,900	$84,600	$108,000
		2dr Cchblt DHC	$136,000	$177,000	$209,000	$230,000
				-30% for RHD. -10% for man trans.		
1955	R-Type Continental	2dr 4.9L Sdn	$1.1 mil	$1.35 mil	$1.6 mil	$1.8 mil
				+20% for manual transmission, center floor shift		
1956	S1	2dr Cchblt FHC	$67,500	$89,300	$123,000	$145,000
		4dr Std Stl Sal	$22,200	$33,000	$44,200	$57,400
		4dr Cchblt Sal	$45,900	$59,900	$76,200	$94,600
		2dr Cchblt DHC	$229,000	$275,000	$326,000	$374,000
				-20% for no pwr strng. +10% for LWB.		
1956	S1 Continental	2dr HJM FHC	$450,000	$540,000	$630,000	$685,000
		2dr Fstbk Cpe	$730,000	$940,000	$1.15 mil	$1.35 mil
		4dr Cchblt Flying Spur Sdn	$195,000	$231,000	$275,000	$315,000
				+10% for factory a/c. -20% for no pwr steering (HJM).		
		2dr Cchblt DHC	$880,000	$975,000	$1.05 mil	$1.15 mil
				+10% for factory a/c. -10% for no pwr steering (HJM).		
1957	S1	2dr Cchblt FHC	$78,900	$102,000	$137,000	$173,000
		4dr Std Stl Sal	$22,200	$33,000	$44,200	$57,400
		4dr Cchblt Sal	$48,300	$64,500	$79,100	$98,900
		2dr Cchblt DHC	$241,000	$296,000	$344,000	$384,000
				-20% for no pwr strng. +10% for LWB.		
1957	S1 Continental	2dr HJM FHC	$450,000	$540,000	$630,000	$685,000
		2dr Fstbk Cpe	$730,000	$940,000	$1.15 mil	$1.35 mil
		4dr Cchblt Flying Spur Sdn	$195,000	$231,000	$275,000	$315,000

Year	Model	Body Style	4	3	2	1
		2dr Cchblt DHC	$880,000	$975,000	$1.05 mil	$1.15 mil
		+10% for factory a/c. -20% for no pwr steering (HJM).				
1958	S1	2dr Cchblt FHC	$79,100	$102,000	$137,000	$173,000
		4dr Std Stl Sal	$22,200	$33,000	$44,100	$57,400
		4dr Cchblt Sal	$48,300	$64,500	$79,100	$98,900
		2dr Cchblt DHC	$241,000	$296,000	$344,000	$384,000
		-20% for no pwr strng. +10% for LWB.				
1958	S1 Continental	2dr HJM FHC	$451,000	$540,000	$630,000	$685,000
		2dr Fstbk Cpe	$800,000	$1 mil	$1.25 mil	$1.4 mil
		4dr Cchblt Flying Spur Sdn	$195,000	$231,000	$275,000	$315,000
		2dr Cchblt DHC	$880,000	$975,000	$1.05 mil	$1.15 mil
		+10% for factory a/c. -20% for no pwr steering (HJM).				
1959	S1	2dr Cchblt FHC	$79,100	$102,000	$137,000	$173,000
		4dr Std Stl Sal	$22,200	$33,000	$44,200	$57,400
		4dr Cchblt Sal	$48,300	$64,400	$79,100	$98,900
		2dr Cchblt DHC	$241,000	$296,000	$344,000	$384,000
		-20% for no pwr strng. +10% for LWB.				
1959	S1 Continental	2dr HJM FHC	$420,000	$510,000	$610,000	$660,000
		2dr Fstbk Cpe	$870,000	$1.1 mil	$1.35 mil	$1.6 mil
		4dr Cchblt Flying Spur Sdn	$195,000	$231,000	$275,000	$315,000
		2dr Cchblt DHC	$880,000	$975,000	$1.05 mil	$1.15 mil
		+10% for factory a/c. -20% for no pwr steering (HJM).				
1960	James Young	4dr Cchblt Sal	$46,700	$62,100	$82,800	$111,000
		4dr SCT100 Sal	$135,000	$172,000	$218,000	$252,000
1960	S2	4dr Std Stl Sal	$23,600	$33,100	$47,200	$66,200
		2dr Cchblt DHC	$234,000	$273,000	$314,000	$360,000
1960	S2 Continental	2dr HJM FHC	$365,000	$424,000	$457,000	$497,000
		4dr Flying Spur JY Sdn	$291,000	$331,000	$358,000	$376,000
		4dr Flying Spur HJM Sdn	$200,000	$237,000	$286,000	$345,000
		2dr PW DHC	$147,000	$198,000	$218,000	$265,000
		+10% for LWB. +10% for factory air.				
1961	James Young	4dr Cchblt Sal	$46,700	$62,100	$82,800	$111,000
		4dr SCT100 Sal	$135,000	$172,000	$218,000	$252,000
1961	S2	4dr Std Stl Sal	$23,600	$33,300	$47,200	$66,200
		4dr LWB Sdn	$26,800	$40,000	$63,800	$77,900
		2dr Cchblt DHC	$234,000	$273,000	$314,000	$360,000
1961	S2 Continental	2dr HJM FHC	$365,000	$424,000	$457,000	$497,000
		4dr Flying Spur JY Sdn	$291,000	$331,000	$358,000	$376,000
		4dr Flying Spur HJM Sdn	$213,000	$258,000	$300,000	$353,000

Bentley

Year	Model	Body Style	4	3	2	1
		2dr PW DHC	$147,000	$198,000	$218,000	$265,000
						+10% for LWB. +10% for factory air.
1962	James Young	4dr Cchblt Sal	$46,700	$62,100	$82,800	$111,000
		4dr SCT100 Sal	$135,000	$172,000	$218,000	$252,000
1962	S2	4dr Std Stl Sal	$23,400	$33,300	$47,000	$66,200
		4dr LWB Sdn	$26,800	$40,000	$63,800	$77,900
		2dr Cchblt DHC	$234,000	$273,000	$314,000	$360,000
1962	S2 Continental	2dr HJM FHC	$356,000	$418,000	$452,000	$493,000
		4dr Flying Spur JY Sdn	$291,000	$331,000	$358,000	$376,000
		4dr Flying Spur HJM Sdn	$213,000	$258,000	$300,000	$353,000
		2dr PW DHC	$148,000	$200,000	$220,000	$269,000
						+10% for LWB. +10% for factory air.
1963	S3	4dr Sdn	$40,500	$54,800	$78,600	$94,900
		4dr LWB Sdn	$51,600	$70,000	$90,000	$113,000
		2dr DHC	$311,000	$338,000	$386,000	$440,000
						1 built, RHD.
1963	S3 Continental	2dr PW FHC	$104,000	$132,000	$163,000	$200,000
		2dr HJM FHC	$673,000	$737,000	$786,000	$859,000
		4dr Flying Spur Sdn	$275,000	$319,000	$370,000	$425,000
		2dr PW DHC	$175,000	$208,000	$273,000	$314,000
1964	S3	4dr Sdn	$40,400	$54,800	$78,600	$94,900
		4dr LWB Sdn	$51,600	$70,000	$90,000	$113,000
		2dr DHC	$311,000	$338,000	$386,000	$440,000
						1 built, RHD.
1964	S3 Continental	2dr PW FHC	$104,000	$132,000	$163,000	$200,000
		2dr HJM FHC	$673,000	$737,000	$786,000	$859,000
		4dr Flying Spur Sdn	$275,000	$319,000	$370,000	$425,000
		2dr PW DHC	$175,000	$208,000	$273,000	$314,000
1965	S3	4dr Sdn	$39,300	$52,800	$76,300	$93,000
		4dr LWB Sdn	$47,000	$64,600	$85,700	$101,000
		2dr DHC	$311,000	$338,000	$386,000	$440,000
						1 built, RHD.
1965	S3 Continental	2dr PW FHC	$104,000	$132,000	$163,000	$200,000
		2dr HJM FHC	$673,000	$737,000	$786,000	$859,000
		4dr Flying Spur Sdn	$275,000	$319,000	$370,000	$425,000
		2dr PW DHC	$175,000	$208,000	$273,000	$314,000
1966	T1	2dr JY FHC	$15,000	$23,600	$33,400	$46,900
		2dr MPW FHC	$24,000	$33,800	$43,500	$54,300
		4dr Sdn	$12,300	$16,900	$23,500	$33,800
		2dr PW DHC	$28,800	$39,800	$51,700	$67,000

Bentley

Year	Model	Body Style	4	3	2	1
1967	T1	2dr JY FHC	$15,200	$23,600	$33,400	$46,900
		2dr MPW FHC	$24,000	$33,800	$43,500	$54,300
		4dr Sdn	$12,300	$16,900	$23,500	$33,800
		2dr PW DHC	$28,800	$39,600	$51,700	$67,000
1968	T1	2dr JY FHC	$15,200	$23,600	$33,400	$46,900
		2dr MPW FHC	$24,000	$33,800	$43,500	$54,300
		4dr Sdn	$12,300	$16,900	$23,400	$33,800
		2dr PW DHC	$28,800	$39,800	$51,700	$67,000
1969	T1	2dr JY FHC	$15,200	$23,600	$33,400	$46,900
		2dr MPW FHC	$24,000	$33,800	$43,500	$54,300
		4dr Sdn	$12,300	$16,900	$23,500	$33,800
		2dr PW DHC	$28,800	$39,700	$51,700	$67,000
1970	T1	2dr MPW FHC	$26,000	$35,600	$45,800	$60,200
		4dr Sdn	$12,300	$18,300	$24,400	$35,600
		2dr PW DHC	$30,900	$39,400	$53,800	$69,000
1971	T1	2dr MPW FHC	$26,000	$35,600	$45,800	$60,200
		4dr Sdn	$12,300	$18,300	$24,400	$35,600
		2dr PW DHC	$30,900	$39,400	$53,800	$69,000
1972	T1	2dr MPW FHC	$26,000	$35,600	$45,800	$60,200
		4dr Sdn	$12,300	$18,300	$24,400	$35,600
		2dr PW DHC	$30,900	$39,400	$53,800	$69,000
1973	T1	2dr MPW FHC	$26,000	$35,600	$45,800	$60,200
		4dr Sdn	$12,300	$18,300	$24,400	$35,600
		2dr PW DHC	$30,900	$39,400	$53,300	$68,000
1974	T1	2dr MPW FHC	$26,000	$35,600	$45,800	$60,200
		4dr Sdn	$12,300	$18,300	$24,400	$35,600
		2dr PW DHC	$30,900	$39,400	$53,800	$69,000
1975	T1	4dr Sdn	$11,600	$17,500	$23,500	$34,800
1975	Corniche	2dr Cpe	$26,500	$42,700	$50,400	$62,100
		2dr Conv	$33,800	$46,700	$55,800	$67,000
1976	T1	4dr Sdn	$11,600	$17,500	$23,500	$34,800
1976	Corniche	2dr Cpe	$26,500	$42,700	$50,400	$62,100
		2dr Conv	$33,800	$46,700	$55,800	$67,000
1977	T2	4dr Sdn	$12,000	$16,400	$24,100	$35,100
1977	Corniche	2dr Cpe	$26,500	$42,700	$50,400	$62,100
		2dr Conv	$33,800	$46,700	$55,800	$67,000
1978	T2	4dr Sdn	$12,000	$16,400	$24,100	$35,100
1978	Corniche	2dr Cpe	$26,500	$42,700	$50,400	$62,100
		2dr Conv	$33,800	$46,700	$55,800	$67,000
1979	T2	4dr Sdn	$12,000	$16,400	$24,100	$35,100
1979	Corniche	2dr Cpe	$25,500	$36,100	$50,900	$74,000
		2dr Conv	$35,800	$46,300	$56,800	$68,000
1980	T2	4dr Sdn	$12,000	$16,400	$24,100	$35,100
1980	Corniche	2dr Cpe	$25,500	$36,100	$50,900	$67,500
		2dr Conv	$40,000	$48,000	$58,000	$68,000
1981	Mulsanne	4dr Sdn	$7,800	$9,900	$15,400	$20,000
1981	Corniche	2dr Conv	$37,800	$42,300	$55,500	$70,000
1982	Mulsanne	4dr Sdn	$7,800	$9,900	$15,400	$20,000
		4dr Turbo Sdn	$9,800	$11,800	$16,800	$22,400

Bentley

Year	Model	Body Style	4	3	2	1
1982	Corniche	2dr Conv	$37,800	$42,300	$55,500	$70,000
1983	Mulsanne	4dr Sdn	$7,800	$9,900	$15,400	$20,000
		4dr Turbo Sdn	$9,800	$11,800	$16,800	$22,400
1983	Corniche	2dr Conv	$37,800	$42,300	$55,500	$70,000
1984	Mulsanne	4dr Sdn	$9,900	$11,300	$16,400	$21,700
1984	Continental	2dr Conv	$40,800	$49,300	$60,300	$77,500
1985	Mulsanne	2dr Sdn	$9,900	$11,300	$16,400	$21,700
1985	Continental	2dr Conv	$40,800	$49,200	$60,300	$77,500
1986	Mulsanne	4dr Sdn	$11,000	$12,900	$17,300	$22,100
1986	Continental	2dr Conv	$47,000	$54,800	$64,800	$83,500
1987	Mulsanne	4dr Sdn	$11,000	$12,900	$17,300	$22,100
1987	Continental	2dr Conv	$47,000	$58,000	$71,000	$96,000
1988	Eight	4dr Sdn	$9,900	$13,000	$16,700	$24,900
1988	Continental	2dr Conv	$54,000	$67,000	$83,500	$101,000
1988	Mulsanne	4dr S Sdn	$12,000	$14,900	$18,500	$22,600
1989	Eight	4dr Sdn	$10,100	$13,100	$17,000	$24,000
1989	Mulsanne S	4dr Sdn	$12,000	$14,900	$18,500	$22,600
1989	Turbo R	4dr Sdn	$10,600	$13,500	$18,700	$26,000
1989	Continental	2dr Conv	$58,000	$73,000	$92,000	$124,000
1990	Eight	4dr Sdn	$10,100	$13,100	$17,200	$24,000
1990	Mulsanne S	4dr Sdn	$12,000	$14,900	$18,500	$22,600
1990	Turbo R	4dr Sdn	$10,600	$13,500	$18,700	$26,000
1990	Continental	2dr Conv	$58,000	$73,000	$92,000	$124,000
1991	Eight	4dr Sdn	$10,100	$13,100	$17,000	$24,000
1991	Mulsanne S	4dr Sdn	$12,000	$14,900	$18,500	$22,600
1991	Turbo R	4dr Sdn	$10,600	$13,500	$18,700	$26,000
1991	Continental	2dr Conv	$58,000	$73,000	$92,000	$124,000
1992	Eight	4dr Sdn	$10,100	$14,200	$17,500	$24,900
1992	Mulsanne S	4dr Sdn	$10,000	$15,300	$18,900	$25,000
1992	Turbo R	4dr Sdn	$11,800	$15,300	$20,000	$26,900
1992	Turbo RL	4dr Sdn	$13,100	$18,000	$22,700	$29,900
1992	Continental	2dr Conv	$65,000	$92,000	$114,000	$133,000
1993	Brooklands	4dr Sdn	$13,300	$17,700	$22,100	$26,900
		4dr LWB Sdn	$13,800	$19,100	$25,300	$28,900
1993	Turbo R	4dr Sdn	$13,400	$17,700	$22,600	$30,000
1993	Turbo RL	4dr Sdn	$15,300	$19,100	$25,800	$32,700
1993	Continental	2dr R Cpe	$20,400	$26,600	$35,700	$42,000
		2dr Conv Cpe	$72,000	$99,000	$120,000	$138,000
1994	Brooklands	4dr Sdn	$14,300	$17,800	$22,200	$27,900
		4dr LWB Sdn	$15,100	$19,800	$24,400	$30,400
1994	Turbo R	4dr Sdn	$14,600	$19,200	$24,300	$31,700
1994	Turbo RL	4dr Sdn	$16,000	$20,700	$26,600	$33,900
1994	Continental	2dr R Cpe	$22,300	$28,000	$34,900	$43,000
		2dr Conv	$87,000	$112,000	$134,000	$152,000
1994	Continental S	2dr Cpe	$26,900	$33,400	$42,900	$49,000
1995	Continental	2dr Conv	$91,000	$116,000	$140,000	$160,000
2009	Brooklands	2dr Cpe	$112,000	$124,000	$145,000	$170,000
2010	Brooklands	2dr Cpe	$117,000	$128,000	$149,000	$172,000

Berkeley

Year	Model	Body Style	4	3	2	1
1956	B65	2dr Rdstr	$6,000	$9,600	$15,800	$21,200
1957	B65	2dr Rdstr	$6,000	$9,600	$15,800	$21,200
1958	SE328	2dr Rdstr	$5,900	$9,500	$15,600	$21,000
1958	Sports 492	2dr Rdstr	$7,200	$12,800	$18,900	$25,500
1959	T60	2dr Cpe	$4,500	$7,400	$11,300	$18,700
1959	Sports 492	2dr Rdstr	$7,200	$12,800	$18,900	$25,500
1959	B65	2dr Rdstr	$6,000	$9,600	$15,800	$21,200
1959	B95	2dr Rdstr	$7,500	$13,000	$19,600	$27,600
1959	B105	2dr Rdstr	$8,100	$13,300	$21,100	$28,700
1960	T60	2dr Cpe	$4,500	$7,400	$11,300	$18,700
1960	B65	2dr Rdstr	$6,000	$9,600	$15,800	$21,200

Bertone

Year	Model	Body Style	4	3	2	1
1983	X1/9	2dr Targa	$3,000	$5,900	$10,600	$20,300
1984	X1/9	2dr Targa	$3,000	$5,900	$10,600	$20,300
1985	X1/9	2dr Targa	$3,000	$5,900	$10,600	$20,300
1986	X1/9	2dr Targa	$3,000	$5,900	$10,600	$20,300
1987	X1/9	2dr Targa	$3,000	$5,900	$10,600	$20,300
1988	X1/9	2dr Targa	$3,000	$5,900	$10,600	$20,300
1989	X1/9	2dr Targa	$3,000	$5,900	$10,600	$20,300

Bitter

Year	Model	Body Style	4	3	2	1
1974	Diplomat CD	2dr Cpe	$9,500	$17,800	$26,300	$54,400
1975	Diplomat CD	2dr Cpe	$9,500	$17,800	$26,300	$54,400
1976	Diplomat CD	2dr Cpe	$9,500	$17,800	$26,300	$54,400
1977	Diplomat CD	2dr Cpe	$9,500	$17,800	$26,300	$54,400
1978	Diplomat CD	2dr Cpe	$9,500	$17,800	$26,300	$54,400
1979	Diplomat CD	2dr Cpe	$9,500	$17,800	$26,300	$54,400
1981	SC	2dr Cpe	$7,600	$14,100	$19,800	$35,500
					+$1,500 for 5-spd man.	
1982	SC	2dr Cpe	$7,600	$14,100	$19,800	$35,500
					+$1,500 for 5-spd man.	
1983	SC	2dr Cpe	$7,600	$14,100	$19,800	$35,500
					+$1,500 for 5-spd man.	
1984	SC	2dr Cpe	$7,600	$14,100	$19,800	$35,500
					+$1,500 for 5-spd man.	
		4dr Sdn	$6,200	$8,600	$14,100	$19,000
1985	SC	2dr Cpe	$7,500	$13,900	$19,200	$31,200
		2dr 3.9 Cpe	$9,600	$15,100	$20,300	$32,200
					+$1,500 for 5-spd man.	
		4dr Sdn	$6,200	$8,600	$14,100	$19,000
		2dr Conv	$9,900	$15,500	$26,500	$37,800
1986	SC	2dr Cpe	$7,500	$13,900	$19,200	$31,200
		2dr 3.9 Cpe	$9,600	$15,100	$20,300	$32,200

Bitter

Year	Model	Body Style	4	3	2	1
					+$1,500 for 5-spd man.	
		4dr Sdn	$6,200	$8,600	$14,100	$19,000
		2dr Conv	$9,900	$15,500	$26,500	$37,800

Bizzarrini

Year	Model	Body Style	4	3	2	1
1964	5300 GT Strada	2dr Cpe	$710,000	$795,000	$905,000	$1.2 mil
1965	5300 GT Strada	2dr Cpe	$710,000	$795,000	$905,000	$1.2 mil
1966	1900 Europa	2dr Cpe	$160,000	$190,000	$245,000	$325,000
1966	5300 GT Strada	2dr Cpe	$710,000	$795,000	$905,000	$1.2 mil
1966	5300 GT America	2dr Cpe	$600,000	$680,000	$740,000	$850,000
1967	1900 Europa	2dr Cpe	$160,000	$190,000	$245,000	$325,000
1967	5300 GT Strada	2dr Cpe	$710,000	$795,000	$905,000	$1.2 mil
1967	5300 GT America	2dr Cpe	$600,000	$680,000	$740,000	$850,000

Borgward

Year	Model	Body Style	4	3	2	1
1957	Isabella	2dr Cpe	$7,800	$16,500	$29,200	$40,400
1958	Isabella	2dr Cpe	$7,800	$16,500	$29,200	$40,400
1959	Isabella	2dr Cpe	$7,800	$16,500	$29,200	$40,400
1960	Isabella	2dr Cpe	$7,800	$16,500	$29,200	$40,400
1961	Isabella	2dr Cpe	$7,800	$16,500	$29,200	$40,400

Bricklin

Year	Model	Body Style	4	3	2	1
1974	SV-1	2dr Cpe	$6,800	$11,800	$20,600	$31,000
					+$1,500 for manual trans.	
1975	SV-1	2dr Cpe	$7,200	$13,300	$24,000	$34,900
					+$1,500 for manual trans.	
1976	SV-1	2dr Cpe	$7,200	$13,300	$24,000	$34,900
					+$1,500 for manual trans.	

Bristol

Year	Model	Body Style	4	3	2	1
1946	400	2dr Cpe	$30,000	$56,000	$80,000	$115,000
1947	400	2dr Sdn	$30,000	$56,000	$80,000	$115,000
1948	400	2dr Sdn	$30,000	$56,000	$80,000	$115,000
1949	400	2dr Sdn	$30,000	$56,000	$80,000	$115,000
1949	401	2dr Sdn	$24,000	$38,500	$62,000	$92,000
1949	402	2dr DHC	$151,000	$224,000	$314,000	$395,000
1950	400	2dr Sdn	$30,000	$56,000	$80,000	$115,000
1950	401	2dr Sdn	$24,000	$38,500	$62,000	$92,000
1950	402	2dr DHC	$151,000	$224,000	$314,000	$395,000
1951	401	2dr Sdn	$24,000	$38,500	$62,000	$92,000
1952	401	2dr Sdn	$24,000	$38,500	$62,000	$92,000

Year	Model	Body Style	4	3	2	1
1953	401	2dr Sdn	$24,000	$38,500	$62,000	$92,000
1953	403	2dr Sdn	$24,500	$40,500	$65,000	$99,000
1953	404	2dr FHC	$36,000	$57,000	$91,000	$130,000
1954	403	2dr Sdn	$24,500	$40,500	$65,000	$99,000
1954	404	2dr FHC	$36,000	$57,000	$91,000	$130,000
1954	405	4dr Sdn	$23,500	$39,000	$53,000	$80,000
		2dr DHC	$39,000	$54,000	$88,000	$145,000
1955	403	2dr Sdn	$24,500	$40,500	$65,000	$99,000
1955	404	2dr Cpe	$36,000	$57,000	$91,000	$130,000
1955	405	4dr Sdn	$23,500	$39,000	$53,000	$80,000
		2dr DHC	$39,000	$54,000	$88,000	$145,000
1956	405	4dr Sdn	$23,500	$39,000	$53,000	$80,000
		2dr DHC	$39,000	$54,000	$88,000	$145,000
1957	405	4dr Sdn	$23,500	$39,000	$53,000	$80,000
		2dr DHC	$39,000	$54,000	$88,000	$145,000
1958	405	4dr Sdn	$23,500	$39,000	$53,000	$80,000
		2dr DHC	$39,000	$54,000	$88,000	$145,000
1958	406	2dr Sdn	$23,000	$37,500	$50,000	$76,700
1959	406	2dr Sdn	$23,000	$37,500	$50,000	$76,700
1960	406	2dr Sdn	$23,000	$37,500	$50,000	$76,700
		2dr Zagato Sdn	$76,900	$126,000	$170,000	$218,000
1961	406	2dr Sdn	$23,000	$37,500	$50,000	$76,700
		2dr Zagato Sdn	$76,900	$126,000	$170,000	$218,000
1961	407	2dr Sdn	$28,400	$43,300	$59,500	$86,500
1962	407	2dr Sdn	$28,400	$43,300	$59,500	$86,500
1963	408	2dr Sdn	$27,800	$41,600	$56,600	$84,600
1964	407	2dr FHC	$28,400	$43,300	$59,500	$86,500
1964	408	2dr Sdn	$27,800	$41,600	$56,600	$84,600
1965	408	2dr Sdn	$27,800	$41,600	$56,600	$84,600
1965	409	2dr Sdn	$28,500	$42,500	$57,900	$85,300
1966	408	2dr Sdn	$27,800	$41,600	$56,600	$84,600
1966	409	2dr Sdn	$28,500	$42,500	$57,900	$85,300
1967	410	2dr Sdn	$28,700	$43,300	$58,700	$86,300
1968	410	2dr Sdn	$28,700	$43,300	$58,700	$86,300
1968	411	2dr SI Sdn	$32,400	$48,600	$69,300	$97,100
1969	410	2dr Sdn	$28,700	$43,300	$58,700	$86,300
1969	411	2dr SI Sdn	$32,400	$48,600	$69,300	$97,100
1970	411	2dr SI Sdn	$32,400	$48,600	$69,300	$97,100
1971	411	2dr SII Sdn	$32,400	$48,600	$69,300	$97,100
1972	411	2dr SIII Sdn	$28,800	$41,100	$54,900	$89,500
1973	411	2dr SIII Sdn	$28,800	$41,100	$54,900	$89,500
1974	411	2dr SIV Sdn	$28,800	$41,100	$54,900	$89,500
1975	411	2dr SIV Sdn	$28,800	$41,100	$54,900	$89,500
1976	411	2dr SV Sdn	$28,800	$41,100	$54,900	$89,500
1976	412	2dr DHC	$30,000	$45,300	$57,700	$92,300
1976	603	2dr FHC	$27,500	$39,900	$55,400	$90,000
1977	412	2dr DHC	$30,000	$45,300	$57,700	$92,300
1977	603	2dr FHC	$27,500	$39,900	$55,400	$90,000
1978	412	2dr DHC	$30,000	$45,300	$57,700	$92,300

Bristol

Year	Model	Body Style	4	3	2	1
1978	603	2dr FHC	$27,500	$39,900	$55,400	$90,000
1979	412	2dr DHC	$30,000	$45,300	$57,700	$92,300
1980	412	2dr DHC	$30,000	$45,300	$57,700	$92,300
1981	412	2dr DHC	$30,000	$45,300	$57,700	$92,300
1982	412	2dr DHC	$30,000	$45,300	$57,700	$92,300
1983	412	2dr DHC	$30,000	$45,300	$57,700	$92,300
1984	412	2dr DHC	$30,000	$45,300	$57,700	$92,300
1985	412	2dr DHC	$30,000	$45,300	$57,700	$92,300
1986	412	2dr DHC	$30,000	$45,300	$57,700	$92,300

Bugatti

Year	Model	Body Style	4	3	2	1
1949	101	2dr Cpe	$290,000	$345,000	$416,000	$488,000
		2dr Cab	$335,000	$388,000	$480,000	$550,000
1950	101	2dr Cpe	$290,000	$345,000	$416,000	$488,000
		2dr Cab	$335,000	$388,000	$480,000	$550,000
1951	101	2dr Cpe	$290,000	$345,000	$416,000	$488,000
		2dr Cab	$335,000	$388,000	$480,000	$550,000
1991	EB110	2dr GT Cpe	$550,000	$650,000	$775,000	$1 mil
1992	EB110	2dr GT Cpe	$550,000	$650,000	$775,000	$1 mil
		2dr SS Cpe	$770,000	$1.25 mil	$1.5 mil	$2.1 mil
1993	EB110	2dr GT Cpe	$550,000	$650,000	$775,000	$1 mil
		2dr SS Cpe	$770,000	$1.25 mil	$1.5 mil	$2.1 mil
1994	EB110	2dr GT Cpe	$550,000	$650,000	$775,000	$1 mil
		2dr SS Cpe	$770,000	$1.25 mil	$1.5 mil	$2.1 mil
1995	EB110	2dr GT Cpe	$550,000	$650,000	$775,000	$1 mil
		2dr SS Cpe	$770,000	$1.25 mil	$1.5 mil	$2.1 mil
2006	Veyron 16.4	2dr Cpe	$940,000	$1.1 mil	$1.35 mil	$1.7 mil
2007	Veyron 16.4	2dr Cpe	$940,000	$1.1 mil	$1.35 mil	$1.7 mil
2008	Veyron 16.4	2dr Cpe	$940,000	$1.1 mil	$1.35 mil	$1.7 mil

Buick

Year	Model	Body Style	4	3	2	1
1946	Special	248/110 2dr Model 46S Sdnt	$6,900	$10,400	$19,100	$35,800
		248/110 4dr Model 41 Sdn	$4,400	$7,700	$13,300	$21,600
1946	Super	248/110 2dr Model 56S Sdnt	$8,200	$13,100	$19,800	$36,200
		248/110 4dr Model 51 Sdn	$5,000	$8,100	$14,900	$20,900
		248/110 4dr Model 59 Est Wgn	$33,300	$46,300	$60,000	$98,000
		248/110 2dr Model 56C Conv Cpe	$12,500	$24,600	$53,100	$89,200
1946	Roadmaster	320/144 2dr Model 76S Sdnt	$9,200	$14,700	$22,600	$38,600
		320/144 4dr Model 71 Sdn	$5,700	$9,800	$17,800	$27,500

Year	Model	Body Style	4	3	2	1
		320/144 2dr Model 76C Conv Cpe	$15,000	$27,600	$74,500	$114,000
1947	Special	248/110 2dr Model 46S Sdnt	$6,900	$10,400	$19,100	$35,800
		248/110 4dr Model 41 Sdn	$4,400	$7,700	$13,300	$21,600
1947	Super	248/110 2dr Model 56S Sdnt	$8,200	$13,100	$19,800	$36,200
		248/110 4dr Model 51 Sdn	$5,000	$8,100	$14,900	$20,900
		248/110 4dr Model 59 Est Wgn	$33,300	$46,300	$60,000	$98,000
		248/110 2dr Model 56C Conv Cpe	$12,500	$24,600	$53,100	$89,200
1947	Roadmaster	320/144 2dr Model 76S Sdnt	$9,200	$14,700	$22,600	$38,600
		320/144 4dr Model 71 Sdn	$5,700	$9,800	$17,800	$27,500
		320/144 4dr Model 79 Est Wgn	$37,700	$54,000	$76,000	$111,000
		320/144 2dr Model 76C Conv Cpe	$15,000	$27,600	$74,500	$114,000
1948	Special	248/110 2dr Model 46S Sdnt	$6,900	$10,400	$19,100	$35,800
		248/110 4dr Model 41 Sdn	$4,400	$7,700	$13,300	$21,600
1948	Super	248/110 2dr Model 56S Sdnt	$8,200	$13,100	$19,800	$36,200
		248/110 4dr Model 51 Sdn	$5,000	$8,100	$14,900	$20,900
		248/110 4dr Model 59 Est Wgn	$33,300	$46,300	$60,000	$98,000
		248/110 2dr Model 56C Conv Cpe	$12,500	$24,600	$53,100	$89,200
1948	Roadmaster	320/144 2dr Model 76S Sdnt	$9,200	$14,700	$22,600	$38,600
		320/144 4dr Model 71 Sdn	$5,700	$9,800	$17,800	$27,500
		320/144 4dr Model 79 Est Wgn	$37,700	$49,100	$69,100	$111,000
		320/144 2dr Model 76C Conv Cpe	$15,000	$27,600	$74,500	$114,000
1949	Special	248/110 2dr Model 46S Sdnt	$7,500	$10,800	$21,900	$40,500
		248/110 4dr Model 41 Sdn	$4,100	$7,200	$12,300	$19,100
1949	Super	248/115 2dr Model 56S Sdnt	$8,400	$13,500	$20,600	$40,600

Buick

Year	Model	Body Style	4	3	2	1
		248/115 4dr Model 51 Sdn	$4,500	$7,500	$14,600	$20,700
		248/115 4dr Model 59 Est Wgn	$35,400	$52,500	$75,200	$111,000
		248/115 2dr Model 56C Conv Cpe	$16,000	$28,100	$63,600	$100,000
1949	Roadmaster	320/150 2dr Model 76S Sdnt	$8,300	$17,500	$25,600	$46,000
		320/150 4dr Model 71 Sdn	$5,300	$8,500	$16,800	$24,000
		320/150 4dr Model 79 Est Wgn	$39,900	$51,900	$72,900	$119,000
		320/150 2dr Model 76R Riv Hdtp	$15,700	$24,800	$38,900	$57,000
		320/150 2dr Model 76C Conv Cpe	$18,700	$32,300	$87,400	$117,000
1950	Special	248/115 2dr Model 46S Sdnt	$5,900	$9,800	$18,600	$34,400
		248/115 2dr Dlx Model 46D Sdnt	$6,700	$11,800	$20,000	$38,000
		248/115 4dr Model 41 Trbk Sdn	$3,700	$7,000	$12,600	$20,900
		248/115 4dr Dlx Model 41D Trbk Sdn	$4,300	$7,700	$14,900	$23,800
		248/115 2dr Model 46 Jtbck Cpe	$5,000	$8,600	$14,800	$23,400
1950	Super	263/124 2dr Model 56S Jtbck Sdnt	$7,500	$13,400	$22,100	$34,900
		263/124 4dr Model 51 Sdn	$4,000	$7,000	$14,700	$20,600
		263/124 4dr Model 59 Est Wgn	$36,000	$53,800	$76,700	$116,000
		263/124 2dr Model 56R Riv Hdtp	$8,400	$14,800	$24,200	$37,300
		263/124 4dr Model 52 Riv Sdn	$4,200	$7,300	$16,300	$23,100
		263/124 2dr Model 56C Conv	$13,600	$25,400	$55,500	$96,900
1950	Roadmaster	320/152 2dr Model 76S Jtbck Sdnt	$7,700	$13,400	$19,700	$32,700
		320/152 4dr Model 71 Trbk Sdn	$3,200	$5,400	$12,200	$19,700
		320/152 4dr Model 79 Est Wgn	$41,100	$54,900	$76,800	$121,000
		320/152 4dr Dlx Model 79R Est Wgn	$42,000	$55,900	$78,300	$127,000

Year	Model	Body Style	4	3	2	1
		320/152 2dr Model 75R Riv Hdtp	$14,900	$24,300	$37,200	$51,100
		320/152 2dr Dlx Model 76R Riv Hdtp	$16,300	$27,000	$41,000	$58,000
		320/152 4dr Model 72 Riv Sdn	$3,700	$6,300	$12,800	$19,300
		320/152 4dr Dlx Model 72R Riv Sdn	$5,100	$8,900	$14,900	$23,500
		320/152 2dr Model 76C Conv	$15,600	$28,600	$58,200	$106,000
1951	Special	263/120 2dr Model 46S Trbk Cpe	$4,800	$10,800	$17,800	$27,600
		263/120 2dr Dlx Model 48D Trbk Sdn	$4,800	$9,800	$15,800	$24,400
		263/120 4dr Model 41 Trbk Sdn	$3,000	$6,800	$12,300	$19,300
		263/120 4dr Dlx Model 41D Trbk Sdn	$4,100	$7,200	$13,600	$21,900
		263/120 2dr Model 45R Riv Hdtp	$6,700	$14,400	$23,000	$36,900
		263/128 2dr Model 46C Conv	$11,100	$20,300	$48,700	$84,500
1951	Super	263/124 2dr Model 56S Jtbck Sdnt	$6,400	$10,100	$17,500	$26,000
		263/124 4dr Model 51 Trbk Sdn	$4,100	$6,600	$14,400	$21,800
		263/124 4dr Model 59 Est Wgn	$34,100	$54,200	$76,200	$120,000
		263/124 2dr Model 56R Riv Hdtp	$7,500	$12,900	$21,600	$34,100
		263/124 4dr Model 52 Riv Sdn	$4,000	$7,300	$15,300	$21,900
		263/124 2dr Model 56C Conv	$12,600	$21,200	$54,500	$90,500
1951	Roadmaster	320/152 2dr Model 76R Riv Hdtp	$14,900	$22,600	$37,100	$47,900
		320/152 2dr Dlx Model 76MR Riv Hdtp	$14,900	$24,700	$38,900	$49,800
		320/152 4dr Model 79R Est Wgn	$40,700	$52,900	$76,200	$118,000
		320/152 4dr Model 72R Riv Sdn	$3,000	$5,200	$12,000	$18,700

Buick

Year	Model	Body Style	4	3	2	1
		320/152 2dr Model 76C Conv	$15,500	$28,700	$55,400	$103,000
1952	Special	263/120 2dr Model 46S Trbk Cpe	$5,000	$11,000	$18,300	$27,400
		263/120 2dr Dlx Model 48D Trbk Sdn	$4,700	$10,600	$16,800	$25,700
		263/120 4dr Model 41 Trbk Sdn	$3,400	$6,500	$12,300	$19,100
		263/120 4dr Dlx Model 41D Trbk Sdn	$4,000	$7,000	$13,200	$21,900
		263/120 2dr Model 45R Riv Hdtp	$6,600	$11,900	$20,400	$33,400
		263/120 2dr Model 46C Conv	$9,700	$19,300	$46,600	$82,600
1952	Super	263/124 4dr Model 59 Est Wgn	$33,900	$53,800	$75,200	$111,000
		263/124 2dr Model 56R Riv Hdtp	$7,500	$13,900	$21,800	$35,900
		263/124 4dr Model 52 Riv Sdn	$4,000	$5,400	$12,500	$19,400
		263/124 2dr Model 56C Conv	$12,000	$21,300	$54,100	$91,800
1952	Roadmaster	322/188 2dr Model 76R Riv Hdtp	$12,300	$21,500	$31,900	$43,800
		322/188 4dr Model 79R Est Wgn	$40,600	$52,100	$73,700	$112,000
		322/188 4dr Model 72R Riv Sdn	$3,100	$7,000	$14,700	$21,000
		322/188 2dr Model 76C Conv	$14,500	$27,300	$54,100	$99,100
1953	Special	263/125 2dr Dlx Model 48D Trbk Sdn	$5,200	$11,300	$18,000	$27,300
		263/125 4dr Dlx Model 41D Trbk Sdn	$3,400	$6,600	$12,300	$19,400
		263/125 2dr Model 45R Riv Hdtp	$6,700	$13,700	$22,200	$37,000
		263/125 2dr Model 46C Conv	$9,700	$12,000	$46,800	$83,100
1953	Super	322/164 2dr Model 56R Riv Hdtp	$7,000	$14,000	$23,500	$40,000
		322/164 4dr Model 59 Est Wgn	$33,800	$54,300	$75,400	$113,000
		322/164 4dr Model 52 Riv Sdn	$4,200	$9,300	$16,400	$24,800
		322/164 2dr Model 56C Conv	$12,100	$21,300	$53,900	$91,600

Year	Model	Body Style	4	3	2	1
1953	Roadmaster	322/188 2dr Model 76R Riv Hdtp	$12,100	$21,000	$32,500	$45,500
		322/188 4dr Model 79R Est Wgn	$39,000	$53,600	$75,200	$113,000
		322/188 4dr Model 72R Riv Sdn	$3,600	$5,600	$12,700	$19,800
		322/188 2dr Model 76C Conv	$16,800	$28,900	$65,200	$105,000
		322/188 2dr Model 76X Skylark Conv	$57,300	$92,900	$134,000	$171,000
1954	Special	264/143 2dr Dlx Model 48D Sdn	$9,200	$17,200	$22,900	$31,700
		264/143 4dr Dlx Model 41D Sdn	$5,100	$9,300	$16,000	$20,700
		264/143 4dr Model 49 Est Wgn	$8,300	$12,400	$22,000	$41,400
		264/143 2dr Model 46R Riv Hdtp	$10,500	$19,200	$27,000	$50,300
		264/143 2dr Model 46C Conv	$19,400	$36,100	$68,300	$103,000
1954	Century	322/195 2dr Model 66R Riv Hdtp	$8,500	$18,600	$29,400	$52,100
		322/195 4dr Model 61 Sdn	$3,800	$7,600	$15,000	$19,800
		322/195 4dr Model 69 Est Wgn	$6,500	$11,500	$19,700	$34,500
		322/195 2dr Model 66C Conv	$22,900	$41,500	$73,500	$108,000
1954	Super	322/177 2dr Model 56R Riv Hdtp	$8,300	$17,000	$27,100	$47,400
		322/177 4dr Model 52 Riv Sdn	$4,200	$8,500	$16,300	$20,800
		322/177 2dr Model 56C Conv	$23,500	$39,400	$69,500	$120,000
1954	Roadmaster	322/200 2dr Model 76R Riv Hdtp	$12,100	$21,300	$34,000	$60,300
		322/200 4dr Model 72R Riv Sdn	$4,200	$8,000	$14,800	$23,100
		322/200 2dr Model 76C Conv	$33,000	$56,100	$83,700	$126,000
1954	Skylark	322/200 2dr Model 100 Conv	$53,400	$91,400	$130,000	$172,000
1955	Special	322/188 2dr Model 48 Trbk Sdn	$9,500	$17,500	$23,800	$32,900
		322/188 4dr Model 41 Sdn	$5,400	$9,900	$16,600	$21,500
		322/188 4dr Model 49 Est Wgn	$8,500	$12,800	$23,000	$41,100
		322/188 2dr Model 46R Riv Hdtp	$10,800	$19,000	$28,800	$48,100

Buick

Year	Model	Body Style	4	3	2	1
		322/188 4dr Model 43 Riv Hdtp	$7,000	$13,100	$20,500	$30,100
		322/188 2dr Model 46C Conv	$25,100	$39,000	$75,600	$104,000
1955	Century	322/236 4dr Model 61 Sdn	$4,900	$10,300	$15,600	$23,800
		322/236 4dr Model 69 Est Wgn	$6,400	$11,500	$20,900	$36,500
		322/236 2dr Model 66R Riv Hdtp	$8,800	$19,700	$29,400	$49,700
		322/236 4dr Model 63 Riv Hdtp	$7,000	$13,800	$21,200	$34,900
		322/236 2dr Model 66C Conv	$23,000	$39,500	$71,900	$104,000
1955	Super	322/236 2dr Model 56R Riv Hdtp	$8,300	$17,500	$26,300	$44,000
		322/236 4dr Model 52 Sdn	$4,700	$7,900	$14,200	$20,900
		322/236 2dr Model 56C Conv	$23,700	$38,500	$67,800	$119,000
1955	Roadmaster	322/236 2dr Model 76R Riv Hdtp	$11,000	$21,200	$32,900	$56,900
		322/236 4dr Model 72 Sdn	$4,400	$8,900	$16,600	$21,800
		322/236 2dr Model 76C Conv	$31,100	$53,600	$81,600	$124,000
1956	Special	322/220 2dr Model 48 Sdn	$9,400	$17,600	$24,200	$33,000
		322/220 4dr Model 41 Sdn	$5,500	$10,200	$16,300	$21,600
		322/220 4dr Model 49 Est Wgn	$8,700	$13,000	$23,300	$41,300
		322/220 2dr Model 46R Riv Hdtp	$10,900	$19,000	$29,200	$47,800
		322/220 4dr Model 43 Riv Hdtp	$7,100	$12,900	$20,100	$29,900
		322/220 2dr Model 46C Conv	$27,000	$40,200	$76,800	$105,000
1956	Century	322/255 2dr Model 66R Riv Hdtp	$8,700	$19,700	$29,800	$49,700
		322/255 4dr Model 69 Est Wgn	$6,400	$11,500	$21,600	$37,600
		322/255 4dr Model 63 Riv Hdtp	$7,000	$14,500	$23,200	$38,000
		322/255 4dr Model 63D Riv Hdtp	$7,500	$15,600	$24,400	$40,200
		322/255 2dr Model 66C Conv	$23,600	$40,500	$77,100	$107,000

Year	Model	Body Style	4	3	2	1
1956	Super	322/255 2dr Model 56R Riv Hdtp	$8,300	$17,400	$26,300	$43,800
		322/255 4dr Model 52 Sdn	$4,600	$7,900	$14,400	$21,200
		322/255 4dr Model 53 Riv Hdtp	$7,800	$14,900	$23,300	$37,200
		322/255 2dr Model 56C Conv	$23,900	$39,800	$70,200	$120,000
1956	Roadmaster	322/255 2dr Model 76R Riv Hdtp	$11,500	$21,100	$34,100	$58,400
		322/255 4dr Model 72 Sdn	$4,500	$8,900	$16,900	$22,300
		322/255 4dr Model 73 Riv Hdtp	$7,900	$15,300	$23,600	$38,300
		322/255 2dr Model 76C Conv	$39,200	$57,900	$85,000	$128,000
1957	Special	364/250 2dr Model 48 Sdn	$6,700	$13,500	$20,800	$29,600
		364/250 4dr Model 41 Sdn	$4,000	$9,400	$14,400	$19,500
		364/250 4dr Model 49 Est Wgn	$5,500	$12,700	$20,600	$31,800
		364/250 2dr Model 46R Riv Hdtp	$8,000	$16,700	$24,700	$37,100
		364/250 4dr Model 43 Riv Hdtp	$5,500	$10,500	$18,600	$24,600
		364/250 4dr Model 49D Riv Est Wgn	$7,100	$16,300	$28,500	$43,200
		364/250 2dr Model 46C Conv	$21,200	$33,300	$61,400	$96,600
1957	Century	364/300 4dr Model 61 Sdn	$3,900	$8,100	$15,600	$22,200
		364/300 4dr Caballero Model 69 Est Wgn	$32,800	$57,500	$81,600	$111,000
		364/300 2dr Model 66R Riv Hdtp	$8,600	$20,100	$28,500	$43,200
		364/300 4dr Model 63 Riv Hdtp	$6,100	$13,100	$20,400	$30,400
		364/300 2dr Model 66C Conv	$22,700	$37,200	$70,700	$111,000
1957	Super	364/300 2dr Model 56R Riv Hdtp	$8,300	$18,000	$25,200	$39,300
		364/300 4dr Model 53 Riv Hdtp	$7,000	$14,900	$21,100	$32,300
		364/300 2dr Model 56C Conv	$26,200	$40,400	$71,700	$123,000
1957	Roadmaster	364/300 2dr Model 76R Riv Hdtp	$11,400	$21,400	$33,200	$55,200

Buick

Year	Model	Body Style	4	3	2	1
		364/300 2dr Model 75R Riv Hdtp	$12,000	$22,800	$35,500	$58,600
		364/300 4dr Model 73 Riv Hdtp	$7,700	$16,500	$23,400	$36,200
		364/300 4dr Model 75 Riv Hdtp	$7,700	$17,300	$24,200	$37,500
		364/300 2dr Model 76C Conv	$45,000	$63,100	$97,100	$157,000
1958	Special	364/250 2dr Model 48 Sdn	$6,400	$13,300	$20,000	$28,700
		364/250 4dr Model 41 Sdn	$3,600	$9,200	$13,900	$18,700
		364/250 4dr Model 49 Est Wgn	$5,200	$12,400	$19,800	$30,900
		364/250 2dr Model 46R Riv Hdtp	$7,300	$16,400	$23,800	$36,200
		364/250 4dr Model 43 Riv Hdtp	$5,000	$10,200	$17,600	$23,800
		364/250 4dr Model 49D Riv Est Wgn	$6,900	$15,900	$28,000	$42,000
		364/250 2dr Model 46C Conv	$19,100	$31,100	$64,300	$79,300
1958	Century	364/300 2dr Model 66R Riv Hdtp	$8,200	$19,100	$27,400	$41,800
		364/300 4dr Model 61 Sdn	$3,600	$7,800	$15,000	$21,200
		364/300 4dr Caballero Model 69 Est Wgn	$31,100	$53,600	$75,500	$98,600
		364/300 4dr Model 63 Riv Hdtp	$5,700	$12,400	$19,400	$29,000
		364/300 2dr Model 66C Conv	$21,300	$35,600	$66,100	$81,700
1958	Super	364/300 2dr Model 56R Riv Hdtp	$7,800	$16,800	$24,000	$37,200
		364/300 4dr Model 53 Riv Hdtp	$6,600	$14,300	$20,300	$30,900
1958	Roadmaster	364/300 2dr Model 75R Riv Hdtp	$10,700	$21,000	$32,200	$54,100
		364/300 4dr Model 75 Riv Hdtp	$7,200	$15,800	$22,000	$34,600
		364/300 2dr Model 75C Conv	$30,300	$50,200	$81,300	$127,000
1958	Limited	364/300 2dr Model 755 Riv Hdtp	$10,500	$20,500	$31,200	$49,700
		364/300 4dr Model 750 Riv Hdtp	$7,000	$15,100	$23,800	$37,000

Year	Model	Body Style	4	3	2	1
		364/300 2dr Model 756 Conv	$56,200	$78,900	$142,000	$225,000
1959	LeSabre	364/250 2dr Sdn	$4,600	$10,700	$15,100	$20,900
		364/250 4dr Sdn	$1,900	$6,200	$11,800	$17,000
		364/250 4dr Est Wgn	$4,700	$9,200	$16,100	$30,700
		364/250 2dr Hdtp	$5,600	$13,900	$17,700	$28,700
		364/250 4dr Hdtp	$3,700	$7,700	$13,000	$18,800
		364/250 2dr Conv	$20,600	$34,200	$67,500	$105,000
1959	Invicta	401/325 2dr Hdtp	$5,800	$12,500	$19,100	$30,000
		401/325 4dr Sdn	$3,000	$6,700	$11,800	$16,600
		401/325 4dr Est Wgn	$4,900	$9,000	$15,900	$32,100
		401/325 4dr Hdtp	$4,300	$6,900	$13,300	$18,400
		401/325 2dr Conv	$19,800	$31,000	$70,000	$104,000
1959	Electra	401/325 2dr Hdtp	$9,100	$15,500	$24,600	$35,900
		401/325 4dr Sdn	$3,300	$6,500	$12,300	$17,900
		401/325 4dr Hdtp	$4,000	$7,400	$13,700	$18,800
1959	Electra 225	401/325 4dr Hdtp	$4,400	$8,000	$14,200	$23,200
		401/325 4dr Riv Hdtp	$4,900	$9,300	$16,200	$25,400
		401/325 2dr Riv Conv	$24,100	$41,000	$74,600	$120,000
1960	LeSabre	364/250 2dr Sdn	$4,600	$10,600	$15,200	$20,500
		364/250 4dr Sdn	$2,200	$6,200	$11,800	$16,500
		364/250 4dr Est Wgn	$4,600	$9,000	$15,700	$29,500
		364/250 2dr Hdtp	$5,400	$13,400	$17,000	$26,600
		364/250 4dr Hdtp	$3,900	$7,900	$13,400	$18,500
		364/250 2dr Conv	$20,100	$33,100	$65,300	$99,300
1960	Invicta	401/325 2dr Hdtp	$5,700	$12,200	$18,700	$29,000
		401/325 4dr Sdn	$3,000	$6,700	$11,800	$16,400
		401/325 4dr Est Wgn	$4,700	$8,900	$15,600	$31,400
		401/325 4dr Hdtp	$4,300	$7,800	$13,000	$17,400
		401/325 2dr Conv	$19,500	$30,500	$64,600	$101,000
1960	Electra	401/325 2dr Hdtp	$9,000	$15,400	$24,100	$35,400
		401/325 4dr Sdn	$3,400	$6,400	$12,200	$17,500
		401/325 4dr Hdtp	$3,900	$7,300	$13,600	$18,200
1960	Electra 225	401/325 4dr Hdtp	$4,800	$8,500	$14,400	$23,600
		401/325 4dr Riv Hdtp	$4,900	$9,200	$16,300	$25,800
		401/325 2dr Conv	$27,000	$43,100	$77,700	$123,000
1961	Special	215/155 2dr Spt Cpe	$4,200	$7,000	$13,600	$20,700
		215/155 4dr Sdn	$2,400	$3,700	$9,000	$14,300
		215/155 4dr Stn Wgn 6P	$4,200	$6,800	$13,200	$19,100
1961	Special Deluxe	215/185 2dr Skylark Cpe	$4,700	$10,000	$19,500	$23,600
		215/155 4dr Sdn	$3,800	$5,500	$10,900	$16,300

Buick

Year	Model	Body Style	4	3	2	1
		215/155 4dr Wgn	$6,000	$8,400	$16,800	$21,200
1961	LeSabre	364/250 2dr Sdn	$4,500	$8,000	$13,500	$20,100
		364/250 4dr Sdn	$4,100	$5,400	$10,700	$16,500
		364/250 4dr Stn Wgn 6P	$6,400	$9,000	$17,700	$22,300
		364/250 2dr Hdtp	$5,400	$9,300	$14,400	$20,800
		364/250 4dr Hdtp	$5,000	$6,500	$12,300	$17,200
		364/250 2dr Conv	$9,500	$19,000	$30,700	$49,200
1961	Invicta	401/325 2dr Hdtp	$5,700	$11,300	$17,700	$25,800
		401/325 4dr Hdtp	$4,400	$8,700	$14,000	$18,800
		401/325 2dr Conv	$11,500	$22,900	$34,000	$53,300
1961	Electra	401/325 2dr Hdtp	$4,400	$8,600	$15,400	$23,200
		401/325 4dr Sdn	$3,000	$5,800	$10,700	$17,900
		401/325 4dr Hdtp	$3,300	$6,600	$11,800	$19,000
1961	Electra 225	401/325 4dr Riv Hdtp	$3,800	$8,400	$14,300	$23,000
		401/325 2dr Conv	$13,400	$22,700	$37,000	$53,000
1962	Special	215/155 2dr Cpe	$4,300	$8,000	$14,400	$21,600
		215/155 4dr Sdn	$2,800	$4,500	$11,000	$16,800
		215/155 4dr Stn Wgn	$4,700	$7,500	$13,500	$19,700
		215/155 2dr Conv	$7,400	$13,000	$24,000	$36,500
1962	Special Deluxe	215/155 4dr Sdn	$4,300	$5,800	$11,900	$16,800
		215/155 4dr Wgn	$6,700	$9,200	$17,600	$22,000
		215/155 2dr Conv	$9,200	$16,700	$28,100	$47,000
1962	Skylark	215/190 2dr Spt Cpe	$4,100	$7,800	$13,400	$20,200
		215/190 2dr Conv	$7,700	$13,800	$23,000	$36,800
1962	LeSabre	401/280 2dr Sdn	$4,200	$8,400	$13,800	$19,700
		401/280 4dr Sdn	$3,900	$5,200	$11,000	$16,000
		401/280 2dr Spt Cpe	$5,100	$9,400	$15,100	$22,400
		401/280 4dr Hdtp	$5,500	$6,500	$12,200	$17,000
1962	Invicta	401/325 2dr Wildcat Spt Cpe	$5,200	$9,800	$17,200	$28,100
		401/325 4dr Est Wgn	$4,200	$9,800	$15,200	$22,100
		401/325 2dr Hdtp	$5,600	$10,600	$17,300	$25,300
		401/325 4dr Hdtp	$4,400	$8,600	$16,100	$25,800
		401/325 2dr Conv	$8,500	$13,000	$28,200	$46,300
1962	Electra 225	401/325 2dr Spt Cpe	$6,200	$12,300	$20,500	$29,400
		401/325 4dr Sdn	$3,500	$7,600	$12,800	$20,700
		401/325 4dr Hdtp	$3,700	$8,400	$14,000	$22,400
		401/325 4dr Riv Hdtp	$4,100	$9,200	$15,600	$23,300
		401/325 2dr Conv	$12,300	$20,800	$33,200	$45,800
1963	Special	215/155 2dr Cpe	$4,000	$7,800	$13,500	$20,000
		215/155 4dr Sdn	$2,700	$3,800	$10,600	$14,800

Year	Model	Body Style	4	3	2	1
		215/155 4dr Stn Wgn	$4,300	$7,000	$12,800	$16,300
		215/155 2dr Conv	$7,100	$10,800	$22,800	$32,000
1963	Special Deluxe	215/155 4dr Sdn	$3,300	$6,400	$10,600	$16,500
		215/155 4dr Wgn	$4,600	$8,000	$13,500	$19,600
1963	Skylark	215/200 2dr Spt Cpe	$3,500	$7,800	$13,500	$19,800
		215/200 2dr Conv	$7,600	$15,700	$26,300	$34,200
1963	LeSabre	401/280 2dr Sdn	$4,000	$8,300	$13,800	$18,500
		401/280 4dr Sdn	$3,400	$4,800	$9,800	$15,000
		401/280 4dr Est Wgn	$3,900	$8,000	$13,900	$20,000
		401/280 2dr Spt Cpe	$5,100	$9,400	$15,100	$22,400
		401/280 2dr Conv	$7,700	$13,500	$30,000	$40,300
1963	Invicta	401/325 4dr Wgn	$4,300	$9,500	$14,900	$23,400
1963	Wildcat	401/325 2dr Spt Cpe	$5,600	$12,100	$20,800	$32,500
		401/325 4dr Hdtp	$4,200	$7,500	$14,400	$23,400
		401/325 2dr Conv	$6,700	$11,800	$25,800	$38,900
1963	Electra 225	401/325 4dr Sdn	$3,100	$7,500	$13,200	$20,200
		401/325 2dr Spt Cpe	$5,500	$10,500	$18,300	$27,500
		401/325 4dr Hdtp	$3,500	$8,100	$13,700	$21,500
		401/325 2dr Conv	$11,200	$15,500	$30,000	$43,600
1963	Riviera	401/325 2dr Spt Cpe	$8,900	$16,700	$27,100	$41,400
1964	Special	300/210 2dr Cpe	$3,600	$7,600	$12,700	$19,200
		300/210 4dr Sdn	$2,800	$4,000	$9,800	$13,400
		300/210 4dr Wgn	$4,300	$9,500	$14,900	$22,000
		300/210 2dr Conv	$7,200	$14,300	$25,000	$33,000
1964	Special Deluxe	300/210 2dr Cpe	$4,200	$8,300	$13,700	$20,300
		300/210 4dr Sdn	$3,300	$6,600	$10,800	$17,400
		300/210 4dr Wgn	$4,100	$9,100	$13,500	$20,500
1964	Skylark	300/210 2dr Spt Cpe	$3,900	$8,500	$14,900	$21,700
		300/210 4dr Sdn	$3,200	$6,800	$10,500	$17,200
		300/210 2dr Conv	$8,600	$15,300	$28,600	$37,900
1964	LeSabre	300/210 2dr Spt Cpe	$4,500	$10,600	$16,400	$26,800
		300/210 4dr Sdn	$3,000	$7,400	$11,400	$17,500
		401/325 4dr Est Wgn	$4,400	$10,200	$15,000	$25,000
		300/210 4dr Hdtp	$3,400	$8,800	$13,800	$19,500
		300/210 2dr Conv	$7,400	$14,200	$28,200	$38,000
1964	Wildcat	401/325 2dr Spt Cpe	$5,000	$12,600	$19,300	$32,000
		401/325 4dr Sdn	$3,500	$8,100	$13,000	$19,000
		401/325 2dr Conv	$7,100	$12,000	$22,000	$42,300

Buick

Year	Model	Body Style	4	3	2	1
1964	Electra 225	401/325 2dr Spt Cpe	$4,600	$11,200	$17,700	$30,500
		401/325 4dr Sdn	$3,400	$8,400	$12,800	$19,600
		401/325 4dr Hdtp	$3,500	$8,600	$13,100	$20,300
		401/325 2dr Conv	$10,500	$15,300	$27,600	$45,200
1964	Riviera	425/340 2dr Spt Cpe	$9,800	$18,400	$30,600	$46,200
1965	Special	300/210 2dr Cpe	$4,000	$7,700	$12,300	$18,200
		300/210 4dr Sdn	$2,800	$3,800	$9,200	$12,000
		300/210 4dr Dlx Sdn	$2,900	$3,900	$9,400	$12,200
		300/210 4dr Wgn	$3,500	$8,700	$14,400	$20,900
		300/210 4dr Dlx Wgn	$3,700	$9,000	$15,200	$22,200
		300/210 2dr Conv	$6,000	$13,400	$20,500	$29,400
1965	Skylark	300/210 2dr Cpe	$3,900	$8,200	$13,000	$19,100
		401/325 2dr GS Cpe	$8,000	$14,200	$22,300	$32,000
		300/210 4dr Sdn	$3,600	$6,500	$10,200	$15,300
		300/210 4dr Spt Wgn	$3,600	$9,000	$14,400	$21,000
		300/210 4dr Cstm Spt Wgn	$4,200	$10,100	$15,500	$23,300
		300/210 2dr Spt Cpe	$4,700	$9,200	$14,700	$21,000
		401/325 2dr GS Spt Cpe	$8,700	$15,800	$25,000	$37,500
		300/210 2dr Conv	$6,300	$14,500	$23,500	$35,200
		401/325 2dr GS Conv	$12,100	$19,900	$33,500	$54,500

-15% for 6-cyl on non-GS models.

Year	Model	Body Style	4	3	2	1
1965	LeSabre	300/210 2dr Spt Cpe	$4,400	$9,000	$14,500	$21,000
		300/210 2dr Cstm Spt Cpe	$4,600	$9,200	$15,000	$24,200
		300/210 4dr Sdn	$3,700	$7,200	$10,800	$15,600
		300/210 4dr Cstm Sdn	$3,800	$7,300	$10,800	$15,600
		300/210 4dr Hdtp	$4,600	$8,600	$12,800	$18,200
		300/210 4dr Cstm Hdtp	$4,700	$8,800	$13,100	$18,400
		300/210 2dr Cstm Conv	$6,100	$14,700	$23,000	$37,300
1965	Wildcat	401/325 2dr Spt Cpe	$4,400	$9,500	$15,100	$22,300
		401/325 2dr Dlx Spt Cpe	$4,500	$9,600	$15,700	$23,000
		401/325 2dr Cstm Spt Cpe	$4,500	$9,600	$16,200	$25,000
		401/325 4dr Sdn	$4,300	$7,800	$11,600	$16,300

Year	Model	Body Style	4	3	2	1
		401/325 4dr Dlx Sdn	$4,400	$8,100	$12,000	$16,700
		401/325 4dr Hdtp	$4,500	$8,100	$11,800	$17,000
		401/325 4dr Cstm Hdtp	$4,700	$8,400	$12,300	$17,100
		401/325 2dr Dlx Conv	$8,000	$15,400	$25,200	$39,600
		401/325 2dr Cstm Conv	$8,000	$16,300	$26,800	$40,700
1965	Electra 225	401/325 2dr Spt Cpe	$4,300	$9,000	$14,600	$21,100
		401/325 2dr Cstm Spt Cpe	$4,700	$9,600	$15,500	$24,000
		401/325 4dr Sdn	$4,600	$8,100	$12,100	$16,200
		401/325 4dr Cstm Sdn	$4,700	$8,200	$12,200	$16,300
		401/325 4dr Hdtp	$5,600	$9,500	$13,400	$18,700
		401/325 2dr Cstm Conv	$8,700	$16,100	$25,500	$44,000
1965	Riviera	401/325 2dr Spt Cpe	$9,000	$18,700	$28,500	$41,600
		425/360 2dr GS Spt Cpe	$22,500	$42,300	$70,400	$103,000
1966	Special	300/210 2dr Cpe	$3,600	$7,200	$11,700	$17,300
		300/210 2dr Dlx Cpe	$3,600	$7,400	$11,900	$17,500
		300/210 4dr Sdn	$2,600	$3,400	$8,200	$11,400
		300/210 4dr Dlx Sdn	$2,600	$3,400	$8,200	$11,400
		300/210 4dr Wgn	$3,500	$8,500	$14,300	$20,200
		300/210 4dr Dlx Wgn	$4,000	$9,100	$15,200	$22,000
		300/210 2dr Dlx Spt Cpe	$4,200	$9,600	$14,500	$21,400
		300/210 2dr Conv	$6,700	$12,700	$20,200	$28,500
1966	Skylark	300/210 2dr Cpe	$4,000	$8,100	$13,100	$18,800
		300/210 2dr Spt Cpe	$5,000	$9,700	$15,400	$22,300
		300/210 2dr Conv	$8,300	$16,100	$25,800	$43,800
						-15% for 6-cyl.
1966	Skylark Gran Sport	400/325 2dr Cpe	$8,600	$13,600	$21,100	$34,200
		400/325 2dr Spt Cpe	$10,300	$15,100	$23,300	$35,400
		400/325 2dr Conv	$11,500	$19,300	$37,900	$54,400
1966	Sportwagon	340/220 4dr Stn Wgn	$5,000	$9,300	$16,200	$24,800
		340/220 4dr Cstm Stn Wgn	$5,800	$10,600	$19,000	$28,800

Buick

Year	Model	Body Style	4	3	2	1
1966	LeSabre	340/220 2dr Spt Cpe	$3,400	$7,700	$12,600	$18,000
		340/220 2dr Cstm Spt Cpe	$3,800	$8,400	$13,800	$18,600
		340/220 2dr Cstm Conv	$7,400	$13,600	$21,700	$34,000
1966	Wildcat	401/325 2dr Spt Cpe	$3,400	$7,700	$12,500	$18,000
		401/325 2dr Cstm Spt Cpe	$3,500	$8,000	$13,500	$18,600
		401/325 2dr Conv	$8,600	$16,200	$25,100	$39,500
		401/325 2dr Cstm Conv	$9,400	$16,700	$25,500	$39,400
1966	Wildcat Gran Sport	425/340 2dr Spt Cpe	$8,700	$9,200	$15,800	$25,400
		425/340 2dr Cstm Spt Cpe	$6,400	$10,600	$18,100	$30,000
		425/340 2dr Conv	$8,700	$19,500	$32,100	$51,300
		425/340 2dr Cstm Conv	$12,700	$22,000	$35,400	$58,000
1966	Electra 225	401/325 2dr Spt Cpe	$4,500	$8,700	$14,600	$23,000
		401/325 2dr Cstm Spt Cpe	$5,700	$9,100	$15,200	$25,000
		401/325 2dr Cstm Conv	$8,500	$15,300	$25,300	$40,300
1966	Riviera	425/340 2dr Spt Cpe	$8,700	$15,200	$28,300	$42,300
		425/340 2dr GS Spt Cpe	$10,100	$17,700	$32,400	$49,300
1967	Special	300/210 2dr Cpe	$3,500	$7,000	$11,500	$17,000
		300/210 4dr Wgn	$3,500	$8,500	$14,300	$20,200
		300/210 4dr Dlx Wgn	$4,000	$9,100	$15,100	$22,100
						-15% for 6-cyl.
1967	Skylark	300/210 2dr Spt Cpe	$5,000	$9,700	$15,400	$22,300
		300/210 2dr Conv	$8,300	$16,100	$25,800	$43,800
1967	GS 340	340/260 2dr Spt Cpe	$10,400	$15,000	$23,200	$35,700
1967	GS 400	400/340 2dr Cpe	$11,300	$19,600	$32,000	$46,800
		400/340 2dr Spt Cpe	$12,500	$21,600	$37,500	$51,200
		400/340 2dr Conv	$15,600	$29,000	$41,600	$59,000
						-20% for auto.
1967	Sportwagon	340/220 4dr Stn Wgn	$5,600	$10,300	$18,500	$28,000
1967	LeSabre	340/220 2dr Spt Cpe	$3,600	$8,100	$12,600	$18,000

Year	Model	Body Style	4	3	2	1
		340/220 2dr Cstm Spt Cpe	$4,100	$8,700	$13,800	$19,800
		340/220 2dr Cstm Conv	$8,300	$15,600	$24,600	$38,300
1967	Wildcat	430/360 2dr Spt Cpe	$3,800	$8,100	$14,200	$22,400
		430/360 2dr Cstm Spt Cpe	$4,000	$8,400	$15,700	$25,500
		430/360 2dr Conv	$8,000	$15,200	$25,100	$39,500
		430/360 2dr Cstm Conv	$10,400	$18,800	$28,800	$44,500
1967	Electra 225	430/360 2dr Spt Cpe	$4,500	$8,700	$14,600	$23,000
		430/360 2dr Cstm Spt Cpe	$5,500	$9,100	$15,200	$24,900
		430/360 2dr Cstm Conv	$8,000	$15,200	$25,400	$40,800
1967	Riviera	430/360 2dr Spt Cpe	$8,700	$15,200	$28,300	$42,300
		430/360 2dr GS Spt Cpe	$10,100	$17,700	$32,400	$49,300
1968	Special Deluxe	350/230 2dr Cpe	$3,500	$7,300	$12,200	$18,400
		350/230 4dr Wgn	$3,300	$8,000	$13,200	$18,900
						-10% for 6-cyl.
1968	Skylark	350/230 2dr Spt Cpe	$4,100	$8,200	$12,700	$18,600
		350/230 2dr Cstm Spt Cpe	$4,400	$8,600	$13,400	$20,000
		350/230 2dr Cstm Conv	$7,500	$14,600	$23,800	$38,000
						-10% for 6-cyl.
1968	GS 350	350/280 2dr Spt Cpe	$9,700	$15,000	$24,000	$41,000
		350/280 2dr GS California Spt Cpe	$10,100	$15,400	$25,100	$42,200
1968	GS 400	400/340 2dr Conv	$17,500	$28,300	$44,100	$64,200
		400/340 2dr Spt Cpe	$13,600	$22,100	$31,100	$48,700
						-20% for auto.
1968	Sportwagon	350/230 4dr Wgn	$5,100	$9,400	$15,500	$23,600
1968	LeSabre	350/230 2dr Spt Cpe	$3,400	$7,400	$12,200	$17,600
		350/230 2dr Cstm Spt Cpe	$3,700	$8,000	$13,700	$19,200
		350/230 2dr Cstm Conv	$6,900	$15,000	$23,600	$36,300
1968	Wildcat	430/360 2dr Spt Cpe	$3,300	$7,700	$13,000	$18,700

Buick

Year	Model	Body Style	4	3	2	1
		430/360 2dr Cstm Spt Cpe	$4,500	$8,600	$14,000	$19,600
		430/360 2dr Cstm Conv	$8,800	$16,100	$27,800	$42,300
1968	Electra 225	430/360 2dr Spt Cpe	$4,300	$8,100	$13,800	$22,400
		430/360 2dr Cstm Spt Cpe	$5,100	$8,800	$14,900	$23,700
		430/360 2dr Cstm Conv	$6,100	$14,700	$24,500	$40,500
1968	Riviera	430/360 2dr Spt Cpe	$8,700	$15,200	$28,300	$42,300
		430/360 2dr GS Spt Cpe	$10,100	$17,700	$32,400	$49,300
1969	Special Deluxe	350/230 2dr Cpe	$3,500	$7,300	$11,500	$17,800
		350/230 4dr Wgn	$2,800	$7,600	$12,700	$18,200
						-10% for 6-cyl.
1969	Skylark	350/230 2dr Spt Cpe	$4,200	$8,400	$13,100	$19,100
		350/230 2dr Cstm Spt Cpe	$4,500	$9,000	$13,300	$20,100
		350/230 2dr Cstm Conv	$7,000	$14,700	$22,400	$37,000
						-10% for 6-cyl.
1969	GS 350	350/280 2dr Spt Cpe	$11,700	$16,700	$22,400	$31,800
1969	GS California	350/280 2dr Cpe	$12,100	$17,700	$25,200	$33,800
1969	GS 400	400/340 2dr Spt Cpe	$11,900	$17,900	$27,600	$38,600
		400/350 2dr Spt Cpe	$25,300	$36,700	$46,100	$67,700
		400/340 2dr Conv	$19,100	$31,900	$48,800	$71,500
		400/350 2dr Conv	$58,700	$79,700	$89,200	$107,000
						-20% for auto.
1969	Sportwagon	350/230 4dr Stn Wgn	$4,500	$8,500	$14,300	$22,100
1969	LeSabre	350/230 2dr Spt Cpe	$3,300	$7,200	$11,500	$17,100
		350/230 2dr Cstm Spt Cpe	$3,800	$8,600	$13,300	$20,100
		350/230 2dr Cstm Conv	$7,600	$15,800	$23,000	$35,500
1969	Wildcat	430/360 2dr Spt Cpe	$3,500	$7,900	$12,700	$18,400
		430/360 2dr Cstm Spt Cpe	$4,300	$9,100	$14,100	$20,500

Year	Model	Body Style	4	3	2	1
		430/360 2dr Cstm Conv	$8,400	$16,800	$25,100	$40,400
1969	Electra 225	430/360 2dr Spt Cpe	$4,000	$8,000	$13,300	$20,800
		430/360 2dr Cstm Spt Cpe	$4,300	$8,500	$13,900	$21,400
		430/360 2dr Cstm Conv	$7,800	$14,500	$24,100	$39,000
1969	Riviera	430/360 2dr Spt Cpe	$7,900	$13,700	$25,600	$39,300
		430/360 2dr GS Spt Cpe	$10,700	$18,500	$34,200	$52,100
1970	Skylark	350/260 2dr Sdn	$4,100	$8,100	$12,700	$18,800
		350/260 2dr 350 Spt Cpe	$4,400	$8,800	$13,400	$19,900
		350/260 2dr Cstm Spt Cpe	$4,500	$9,100	$13,800	$20,500
		350/260 2dr Cstm Conv	$7,100	$14,800	$22,600	$37,800
						-15% for 6-cyl.
1970	Sportwagon	350/260 4dr Stn Wgn	$3,800	$6,800	$11,100	$16,800
1970	GS	350/315 2dr Spt Cpe	$12,400	$18,300	$27,800	$44,600
		455/350 2dr 455 Spt Cpe	$16,000	$24,200	$40,800	$61,300
		455/360 2dr 455 Stage I Spt Cpe	$26,900	$45,500	$67,900	$102,000
		455/350 2dr 455 Conv	$21,100	$32,200	$49,300	$69,900
		455/360 2dr 455 Stage I Conv	$57,200	$104,000	$131,000	$162,000
						+20% for 4-spd. +10% for auto.
1970	GSX	455/350 2dr Spt Cpe	$46,400	$59,400	$97,900	$134,000
		455/360 2dr Stage I Spt Cpe	$93,500	$129,000	$163,000	$194,000
						+20% for 4-spd. +10% for auto.
1970	LeSabre	350/260 2dr Spt Cpe	$3,400	$7,500	$11,900	$18,000
		350/260 2dr Cstm Spt Cpe	$3,600	$7,700	$12,300	$18,800
		455/370 2dr Cstm 455 Spt Cpe	$4,500	$8,100	$13,400	$20,300
		350/260 2dr Cstm Conv	$7,200	$12,800	$20,100	$34,000
1970	Wildcat Custom	455/370 2dr Spt Cpe	$2,600	$5,300	$9,300	$13,000
		455/370 2dr Conv	$8,200	$16,800	$25,800	$35,600

Buick

Year	Model	Body Style	4	3	2	1
1970	Estate	455/370 4dr Stn Wgn	$4,200	$7,600	$12,500	$19,200
1970	Electra 225	455/370 2dr Spt Cpe	$3,500	$7,600	$12,000	$19,100
		455/370 2dr Cstm Spt Cpe	$4,100	$8,300	$12,900	$21,100
		455/370 2dr Cstm Conv	$7,700	$14,600	$20,100	$33,000
1970	Riviera	455/370 2dr Spt Cpe	$6,700	$11,800	$21,800	$33,000
		455/370 2dr GS Spt Cpe	$7,700	$16,000	$24,900	$37,700
1971	Skylark	350/230 2dr Sdn	$3,500	$7,200	$10,800	$14,500
		350/230 2dr Spt Cpe	$3,700	$7,400	$11,300	$15,000
		350/230 2dr Cstm Spt Cpe	$4,600	$8,900	$13,600	$18,700
		350/230 2dr Cstm Conv	$7,000	$13,500	$20,300	$30,000
						-15% for 6-cyl.
1971	Sportwagon	350/230 4dr Wgn	$4,000	$6,300	$10,200	$15,700
1971	GS	350/260 2dr Spt Cpe	$11,800	$17,700	$23,300	$36,700
		455/310 2dr 455 Spt Cpe	$13,600	$20,700	$31,700	$41,200
		455/345 2dr 455 Stage I Spt Cpe	$23,100	$36,100	$46,800	$64,700
		350/260 2dr Conv	$15,200	$20,900	$36,300	$50,500
		455/310 2dr 455 Conv	$15,300	$21,400	$39,000	$63,200
		455/345 2dr 455 Stage I Conv	$56,600	$80,200	$94,800	$117,000
					+20% for 4-spd.	+10% for auto.
1971	GSX	455/310 2dr Spt Cpe	$34,900	$55,300	$92,500	$122,000
		455/345 2dr Stage I Spt Cpe	$44,100	$90,700	$119,000	$144,000
					+20% for 4-spd.	+10% for auto.
1971	LeSabre	350/230 2dr Cstm Conv	$8,100	$12,100	$19,200	$28,200
1971	Estate	455/310 4dr Stn Wgn	$1,600	$5,400	$8,000	$13,600
1971	Electra 225	455/310 2dr Spt Cpe	$4,300	$7,600	$12,600	$18,700
		455/310 2dr Cstm Spt Cpe	$4,700	$8,000	$13,200	$19,800
1971	Riviera	455/310 2dr Spt Cpe	$8,300	$15,800	$25,100	$36,900

Year	Model	Body Style	4	3	2	1
		455/345 2dr GS Spt Cpe	$9,200	$17,300	$27,700	$40,800
1972	Skylark	350/155 2dr Cpe	$3,600	$5,800	$10,200	$13,600
		350/155 2dr Spt Cpe	$4,100	$8,000	$12,300	$16,500
		350/180 2dr 350 Spt Cpe	$5,700	$9,300	$12,700	$17,400
		350/155 2dr Cstm Spt Cpe	$4,800	$9,400	$14,200	$19,600
1972	Sportwagon	350/155 4dr Wgn	$4,000	$6,300	$10,200	$15,700
1972	GS	350/190 2dr Spt Cpe	$10,100	$13,600	$17,400	$28,300
		455/250 2dr 455 Spt Cpe	$11,700	$18,200	$25,600	$32,400
		455/270 2dr 455 Spt Cpe	$17,200	$23,300	$34,400	$49,400
		350/190 2dr Conv	$11,800	$16,900	$26,900	$40,200
		455/250 2dr 455 Conv	$15,400	$22,800	$36,200	$58,400
		455/270 2dr 455 Conv	$23,000	$40,900	$53,300	$98,300
						+20% for 4-spd. +10% for auto.
1972	GSX	455/270 2dr 455 Stage I Spt Cpe	$32,000	$51,200	$91,700	$123,000
						+20% for 4-spd. +10% for auto.
1972	LeSabre	350/180 2dr Cstm Conv	$8,000	$12,100	$16,300	$24,500
1972	Estate	455/225 4dr Stn Wgn	$1,600	$5,400	$8,000	$13,600
1972	Centurion	455/225 2dr Conv	$6,800	$9,900	$16,000	$25,200
1972	Electra 225	455/225 2dr Spt Cpe	$4,300	$7,600	$12,600	$18,700
		455/225 2dr Cstm Ltd Spt Cpe	$4,700	$8,000	$13,200	$19,800
1972	Riviera	455/250 2dr Spt Cpe	$8,400	$16,000	$25,500	$37,300
		455/260 2dr GS Spt Cpe	$9,300	$17,800	$28,200	$41,400
1973	Century	350/150 2dr Rgl Hdtp Cpe	$5,900	$9,700	$13,200	$18,400
		350/190 2dr Gran Sport Hdtp Cpe	$5,200	$9,200	$12,100	$17,500
		455/270 2dr Gran Sport 455 Stage I Hdtp Cpe	$9,100	$13,800	$18,200	$26,600
1973	Centurion	350/175 2dr Conv	$6,800	$9,900	$16,000	$25,200
1973	Riviera	455/250 2dr Hdtp Cpe	$8,700	$16,600	$26,400	$38,600
		455/260 2dr GS Hdtp Cpe	$9,700	$18,200	$29,100	$42,600

Buick

Year	Model	Body Style	4	3	2	1
1974	LeSabre	350/150 2dr Luxus Conv	$7,600	$12,200	$16,900	$23,900
1974	Riviera	455/210 2dr Hdtp Cpe	$3,600	$6,500	$9,400	$16,400
		455/245 2dr Hdtp Cpe	$5,800	$8,700	$11,800	$18,900
		455/245 2dr GS Hdtp Cpe	$5,900	$8,600	$11,100	$20,500
1975	LeSabre	350/165 2dr Cstm Conv	$7,800	$13,000	$17,600	$24,900
1975	Riviera	455/205 2dr Hdtp	$3,400	$5,900	$9,000	$14,900
1976	Skyhawk	231/105 2dr Free Spirit Htchbk Cpe	$1,500	$3,300	$5,400	$9,000
1976	Century	231/105 2dr Free Spirit Hdtp	$4,100	$5,900	$9,600	$16,400
1976	Riviera	455/205 2dr Hdtp Cpe	$3,400	$5,900	$9,000	$15,000
1977	Riviera	350/155 2dr Cpe	$2,100	$4,400	$6,400	$12,400
1978	Riviera	350/155 2dr Cpe	$2,000	$4,200	$6,200	$12,000
1979	Regal	305/155 2dr Ltd Cpe	$3,100	$5,500	$8,200	$10,300
1979	Riviera	350/155 2dr Ntchbk Cpe	$2,100	$3,900	$8,200	$12,200
1980	Regal	231/170 2dr Spt Cpe	$3,900	$6,400	$9,300	$12,500
1980	Riviera	350/160 2dr Cpe	$2,100	$3,900	$9,500	$13,800
1981	Regal	231/170 2dr Turbo Spt Cpe	$3,900	$6,400	$9,300	$12,500
1981	Riviera	307/140 2dr Cpe	$2,500	$4,200	$8,400	$12,600
		307/140 2dr T-Type Cpe	$3,000	$4,700	$10,400	$16,800
					-20% for non-turbo 6-cyl.	
1982	Regal	231/170 2dr Turbo Spt Cpe	$3,900	$6,100	$9,200	$12,400
1982	Riviera	307/140 2dr Cpe	$2,500	$4,200	$9,400	$15,100
		231/170 2dr T-Type Turbo Cpe	$3,200	$4,700	$11,300	$17,500
		307/140 2dr Conv	$5,400	$7,600	$15,000	$20,600
					-20% for non-turbo 6-cyl.	
1983	Regal	231/180 2dr T-Type Cpe	$6,400	$9,900	$17,200	$22,300
1983	Riviera	307/140 2dr Cpe	$2,500	$4,200	$9,400	$15,100
		231/180 2dr T-Type Turbo Cpe	$3,700	$5,300	$11,500	$18,200
		307/140 2dr Conv	$5,400	$7,600	$15,000	$20,600
		307/140 2dr XX Annv Ed Conv	$5,200	$9,600	$19,500	$24,300
					-20% for non-turbo 6-cyl.	
1984	Regal	231/200 2dr T-Type Cpe	$8,900	$12,600	$21,900	$28,400

Year	Model	Body Style	4	3	2	1
		231/200 2dr Grand National Cpe	$10,400	$14,100	$28,700	$39,900
1984	Riviera	307/140 2dr Cpe	$2,800	$4,300	$9,600	$15,200
		231/190 FI 2dr T-Type Cpe	$3,700	$5,100	$11,600	$18,100
		307/140 2dr Conv	$4,900	$7,300	$14,400	$19,300
						-10% for non-turbo 6-cyl.
1985	Regal	231/200 2dr T-Type Cpe	$8,900	$12,800	$23,100	$32,300
		231/200 2dr Grand National Cpe	$10,600	$13,900	$25,900	$35,800
1985	Riviera	307/140 2dr Cpe	$2,800	$4,200	$9,000	$13,600
		231/200 2dr T-Type Cpe	$3,700	$5,000	$11,000	$16,800
		307/140 2dr Conv	$4,900	$7,300	$14,400	$19,300
1986	Regal	231/235 2dr T-Type Cpe	$13,900	$17,900	$25,400	$36,300
		231/235 2dr Grand National Cpe	$15,500	$22,200	$35,700	$53,800
1986	Riviera	231/140 2dr Cpe	$2,400	$3,800	$6,800	$11,600
		231/140 2dr T-Type Cpe	$2,500	$4,100	$8,700	$14,400
1987	Regal	231/245 2dr T-Type Turbo Cpe	$14,500	$18,700	$25,800	$38,700
		231/245 2dr T-Type Turbo WE4 Cpe	$16,700	$19,800	$31,000	$46,300
		231/245 2dr T-Type Turbo Ltd Cpe	$16,600	$22,100	$30,000	$42,000
		231/245 2dr Grand National Cpe	$19,800	$28,900	$42,000	$57,000
		231/276 2dr GNX Cpe	$58,200	$85,100	$105,000	$131,000
1987	Riviera	231/150 2dr Cpe	$2,400	$4,000	$6,300	$11,000
		231/150 2dr T-Type Cpe	$2,600	$4,100	$7,000	$12,400
1988	Riviera	231/165 2dr Cpe	$2,300	$4,000	$6,400	$11,000
		231/165 2dr T-Type Cpe	$2,700	$4,300	$7,000	$12,400
1988	Reatta	231/165 2dr Cpe	$2,500	$3,300	$7,100	$10,000
1989	Riviera	231/165 2dr Cpe	$2,400	$3,900	$6,300	$9,700
1989	Reatta	231/165 2dr Cpe	$2,700	$3,600	$7,500	$10,800
1990	Riviera	231/165 FI 2dr Cpe	$2,400	$3,900	$6,300	$9,700
1990	Reatta	231/165 FI 2dr Cpe	$3,100	$4,200	$8,800	$12,100
		231/165 FI 2dr Ltd Dlr Spcl Ed Cpe	$3,300	$4,500	$9,800	$13,500
		231/165 FI 2dr Conv	$5,100	$6,500	$12,900	$21,400

Buick

Year	Model	Body Style	4	3	2	1
		231/165 FI 2dr Ltd Dlr Spcl Ed Conv	$6,700	$7,900	$16,400	$26,900
1991	Riviera	231/170 FI 2dr Cpe	$2,900	$4,400	$7,500	$11,900
1991	Reatta	231/170 FI 2dr Cpe	$3,300	$4,700	$9,400	$13,000
		231/170 FI 2dr Conv	$5,300	$7,400	$14,800	$23,600

Cadillac

Year	Model	Body Style	4	3	2	1
1946	Series 61	346/150 2dr Clb Cpe	$13,900	$24,100	$37,600	$49,500
		346/150 4dr Sdn	$10,000	$15,000	$22,000	$37,000
1946	Series 62	346/150 2dr Clb Cpe	$14,600	$25,800	$34,600	$53,000
		346/150 4dr Sdn	$10,700	$16,400	$23,900	$38,800
		346/150 2dr Conv	$43,800	$57,400	$89,700	$134,000
1946	Fleetwood 60 Special	346/150 4dr Trng Sdn	$23,500	$30,400	$39,600	$56,700
1946	Fleetwood Series 75	346/150 4dr Sdn 5P	$23,500	$33,900	$52,800	$74,300
		346/150 4dr Imp Sdn	$16,500	$28,600	$41,600	$73,300
		346/150 4dr Bus Sdn	$19,200	$33,500	$45,000	$79,400
					+$3,500 for division window.	
1947	Series 61	346/150 2dr Clb Cpe	$13,800	$24,300	$32,000	$49,600
		346/150 4dr Sdn	$10,300	$15,100	$22,300	$37,200
1947	Series 62	346/150 2dr Clb Cpe	$15,100	$26,200	$35,000	$53,500
		346/150 4dr Sdn	$10,900	$16,800	$24,200	$39,500
		346/150 2dr Conv	$44,000	$57,500	$89,700	$134,000
1947	Fleetwood 60 Special	346/150 4dr Trng Sdn	$24,500	$31,000	$39,900	$57,100
1947	Fleetwood Series 75	346/150 4dr Sdn 5P	$23,500	$34,000	$53,400	$75,000
		346/150 4dr Imp Sdn	$16,700	$28,800	$42,200	$73,800
		346/150 4dr Bus Sdn	$16,000	$27,100	$40,100	$71,400
		346/150 4dr Imp Bus Sdn	$19,500	$34,000	$45,400	$79,900
1948	Series 61	346/150 2dr Clb Cpe	$15,800	$26,900	$35,600	$55,400
		346/150 4dr Sdn	$9,200	$15,000	$20,300	$35,800

Year	Model	Body Style	4	3	2	1
1948	Series 62	346/150 2dr Clb Cpe	$18,700	$30,800	$45,300	$65,600
		346/150 4dr Sdn	$9,100	$15,300	$21,000	$37,400
		346/150 2dr Conv	$41,900	$54,300	$77,100	$104,000
1948	Fleetwood 60 Special	346/150 4dr Sdn	$18,000	$24,800	$40,100	$59,500
						+$3,500 for division window.
1948	Fleetwood Series 75	346/150 4dr Sdn 5P	$10,700	$17,600	$29,000	$40,400
		346/150 4dr Bus Sdn	$14,800	$25,100	$35,900	$61,500
		346/150 4dr Bus Sdn 9P	$17,100	$27,500	$38,900	$65,100
		346/150 4dr Imp Bus Sdn	$15,300	$26,700	$37,400	$63,300
						+$3,500 for division window.
1949	Series 61	331/160 2dr Clb Cpe	$15,800	$28,000	$36,800	$57,600
		331/160 4dr Trng Sdn	$9,500	$15,300	$21,400	$37,200
1949	Series 62	331/160 2dr Clb Cpe	$18,900	$32,000	$47,700	$67,800
		331/160 4dr Trng Sdn	$9,500	$16,100	$23,400	$41,600
		331/160 2dr Cpe de Ville Hdtp	$19,600	$36,200	$54,100	$78,700
		331/160 2dr Conv Cpe	$42,800	$55,900	$79,300	$112,000
1949	Fleetwood 60 Special	331/160 4dr Trng Sdn	$18,100	$25,600	$41,800	$62,500
1949	Fleetwood Series 75	331/160 4dr Sdn 7P	$11,300	$18,200	$30,200	$42,000
		331/160 4dr Imp Sdn	$16,500	$27,300	$38,400	$64,000
		331/160 4dr Bus Sdn 9P	$15,700	$25,600	$37,200	$60,900
		331/160 4dr Imp Bus Sdn	$17,500	$28,400	$40,000	$66,400
1950	Series 61	331/160 2dr Cpe	$13,300	$20,400	$28,100	$37,800
		331/160 4dr Sdn	$8,800	$12,700	$16,700	$23,300
1950	Series 62	331/160 2dr Clb Cpe	$16,300	$24,800	$36,200	$48,300
		331/160 4dr Sdn	$9,500	$14,000	$18,500	$28,100
		331/160 2dr Cpe de Ville Hdtp	$16,900	$25,600	$38,400	$50,800
		331/160 2dr Conv Cpe	$37,400	$50,200	$67,600	$88,200
1950	Fleetwood 60 Special	331/160 4dr Sdn	$12,500	$18,300	$31,600	$42,200

Cadillac

Year	Model	Body Style	4	3	2	1
1950	Fleetwood Series 75	331/160 4dr Sdn	$12,200	$18,300	$26,200	$32,900
		331/160 4dr Imp Sdn	$13,700	$19,800	$28,200	$36,100
		331/160 4dr Bus Sdn	$14,000	$20,500	$29,500	$38,400
1951	Series 61	331/160 2dr Cpe	$13,000	$20,000	$27,800	$37,100
		331/160 4dr Sdn	$8,700	$12,700	$16,800	$23,000
1951	Series 62	331/160 2dr Clb Cpe	$16,200	$24,900	$36,100	$48,100
		331/160 4dr Sdn	$9,500	$13,700	$18,100	$27,700
		331/160 2dr Cpe de Ville Hdtp	$17,300	$26,100	$39,800	$52,100
		331/160 2dr Conv Cpe	$37,400	$50,200	$67,600	$88,200
1951	Fleetwood 60 Special	331/160 4dr Sdn	$11,400	$17,200	$28,200	$38,500
1951	Fleetwood Series 75	331/160 4dr Sdn	$12,200	$18,200	$26,100	$33,000
		331/160 4dr Imp Sdn	$13,700	$19,800	$28,400	$36,000
		331/160 4dr Bus Sdn	$14,000	$20,900	$29,500	$38,400
1952	Series 62	331/190 2dr Clb Cpe	$13,000	$19,800	$28,100	$38,100
		331/190 4dr Sdn	$9,500	$13,800	$18,000	$27,300
		331/190 2dr Cpe de Ville Hdtp	$17,100	$25,800	$39,000	$51,200
		331/190 2dr Conv Cpe	$38,500	$51,800	$70,300	$91,600
1952	Fleetwood 60 Special	331/190 4dr Sdn	$11,800	$17,600	$28,900	$38,800
1952	Fleetwood Series 75	331/190 4dr Sdn	$12,600	$18,700	$26,800	$34,000
		331/190 4dr Imp Sdn	$14,000	$20,500	$28,800	$36,400
1953	Series 62	331/210 2dr Cpe	$13,800	$20,300	$29,100	$39,400
		331/210 4dr Sdn	$9,800	$14,100	$18,600	$24,600
		331/210 2dr Cpe de Ville Hdtp	$17,500	$26,600	$40,300	$52,900
		331/210 2dr Conv Cpe	$39,100	$52,300	$70,500	$92,000
					+20% for factory a/c.	
1953	Fleetwood 60 Special	331/210 4dr Sdn	$11,700	$17,500	$28,600	$38,600
1953	Fleetwood Series 75	331/210 4dr Sdn	$12,400	$18,300	$26,400	$33,700
		331/210 4dr Imp Sdn	$13,900	$20,100	$28,600	$36,300
1953	Eldorado	331/210 2dr Conv	$76,000	$106,000	$146,000	$224,000
					+20% for factory a/c.	

Year	Model	Body Style	4	3	2	1
1954	Series 62	331/230 2dr Cpe	$13,600	$20,300	$29,700	$46,600
		331/230 4dr Sdn	$10,400	$16,400	$21,600	$33,100
		331/230 2dr Cpe de Ville Hdtp	$16,500	$24,400	$36,700	$57,300
		331/230 2dr Conv Cpe	$45,000	$59,000	$81,400	$132,000
						+15% for factory a/c.
1954	Fleetwood 60 Special	331/230 4dr Sdn	$16,700	$23,900	$34,300	$46,400
1954	Fleetwood Series 75	331/230 4dr Sdn	$13,500	$19,700	$27,600	$34,800
		331/230 4dr Imp Sdn	$15,000	$21,100	$29,600	$37,400
1954	Eldorado	331/230 2dr Conv	$37,000	$58,500	$100,000	$152,000
						+15% for factory a/c.
1955	Series 62	331/250 2dr Cpe	$11,800	$18,000	$26,900	$41,800
		331/270 2dr Cpe	$12,900	$19,700	$28,900	$45,700
		331/250 4dr Sdn	$10,500	$16,600	$21,700	$33,000
		331/270 4dr Sdn	$11,400	$18,400	$24,200	$37,000
		331/250 2dr Cpe de Ville Hdtp	$15,500	$23,000	$33,900	$54,500
		331/270 2dr Cpe de Ville Hdtp	$17,000	$25,100	$37,400	$59,700
		331/250 2dr Conv	$45,100	$60,300	$86,300	$139,000
		331/270 2dr Conv	$49,400	$66,500	$99,500	$150,000
						+10% for factory a/c.
1955	Fleetwood 60 Special	331/250 4dr Sdn	$16,700	$24,100	$34,200	$42,100
1955	Fleetwood Series 75	331/250 4dr Sdn	$13,500	$19,700	$27,700	$34,700
		331/250 4dr Imp Sdn	$15,000	$21,200	$29,600	$37,400
1955	Eldorado	331/270 2dr Conv	$37,000	$54,400	$85,000	$120,000
						+10% for factory a/c.
1956	Series 62	365/285 2dr Cpe	$12,500	$19,600	$29,100	$46,300
		365/285 4dr Sdn	$10,900	$16,600	$23,100	$34,300
		365/285 2dr Cpe de Ville Hdtp	$16,200	$24,000	$35,500	$56,700
		365/285 4dr Sdn de Ville Hdtp	$11,300	$16,700	$23,600	$38,300
		365/285 2dr Conv	$41,200	$57,900	$83,500	$141,000
1956	Eldorado	365/305 2dr Seville Cpe	$18,900	$30,100	$45,600	$68,100
		365/305 2dr Biarritz Conv	$53,200	$94,900	$136,000	$195,000
						+10% for factory a/c.
1956	Fleetwood 60 Special	365/285 4dr Sdn	$17,100	$24,900	$35,500	$46,900
1956	Fleetwood Series 75	365/285 4dr Sdn	$13,700	$20,400	$28,400	$35,600

Cadillac

Year	Model	Body Style	4	3	2	1
		365/285 4dr Imp Sdn	$14,300	$21,200	$30,600	$37,800
1957	Series 62	365/300 2dr Hdtp	$11,300	$17,700	$25,000	$33,800
		365/300 2dr Cpe de Ville Hdtp	$13,700	$20,400	$27,600	$37,100
		365/300 4dr Hdtp	$12,100	$17,100	$26,100	$35,100
		365/300 4dr Sdn de Ville Hdtp	$13,600	$20,000	$30,100	$39,900
		365/300 2dr Conv Cpe	$37,300	$53,900	$74,200	$115,000
1957	Eldorado	365/300 2dr Seville Hdtp	$22,600	$35,700	$50,500	$74,700
		365/325 2dr Seville Hdtp	$24,600	$39,100	$56,000	$83,100
		365/325 4dr Brghm Sdn	$41,500	$60,200	$91,600	$119,000
		365/300 2dr Biarritz Conv	$48,700	$72,300	$118,000	$185,000
		365/325 2dr Biarritz Conv	$53,900	$78,600	$130,000	$202,000
		+10% for factory a/c on non-Brougham models. -$15,000 for missing vanity accessories on Brougham.				
1957	Fleetwood 60 Special	365/300 4dr Hdtp	$15,200	$21,600	$31,400	$41,300
		+10% for factory a/c.				
1957	Fleetwood Series 75	365/300 4dr Sdn	$13,700	$19,700	$28,200	$35,100
		365/300 4dr Imp Sdn	$15,300	$21,000	$29,800	$37,100
		+10% for factory a/c.				
1958	Series 62	365/335 2dr Cpe	$9,600	$15,100	$21,400	$28,900
		365/310 4dr Sdn	$13,800	$19,500	$29,800	$40,700
		365/335 4dr Sdn	$15,300	$21,200	$32,700	$45,000
		365/310 4dr Extnd Trnk Sdn	$9,900	$15,200	$24,300	$32,700
		365/335 4dr Extnd Trnk Sdn	$11,000	$16,800	$26,300	$35,600
		365/310 2dr Cpe de Ville Hdtp	$11,700	$18,400	$27,100	$34,100
		365/335 2dr Cpe de Ville Hdtp	$13,000	$20,200	$28,800	$38,200
		365/310 4dr Sdn de Ville Hdtp	$13,200	$17,200	$25,400	$32,700
		365/335 4dr Sdn de Ville Hdtp	$14,500	$18,600	$27,700	$36,200
		365/310 2dr Conv Cpe	$38,500	$51,800	$77,300	$130,000
		365/335 2dr Conv Cpe	$43,300	$59,300	$89,300	$147,000

Year	Model	Body Style	4	3	2	1
1958	Eldorado	365/335 2dr Seville Cpe	$25,000	$39,600	$59,900	$89,600
		365/335 4dr Brghm Sdn	$44,000	$68,200	$110,000	$146,000
		365/335 2dr Biarritz Conv	$62,300	$89,500	$129,000	$181,000
		+10% for factory a/c on non-Brougham models. -$15,000 for missing vanity accessories on Brougham.				
1958	Fleetwood 60 Special	365/310 4dr Sdn	$17,400	$24,800	$36,100	$45,800
		+10% for factory a/c.				
1958	Fleetwood Series 75	365/310 4dr Sdn	$16,300	$22,700	$30,600	$39,800
		365/310 4dr Imp Sdn	$17,500	$23,800	$32,800	$41,700
		+10% for factory a/c.				
1959	Series 62	390/325 2dr Hdtp Cpe	$20,300	$31,600	$43,000	$55,300
		390/325 4dr Hdtp 4W	$12,800	$18,800	$26,400	$33,400
		390/325 4dr Hdtp 6W	$11,900	$17,000	$24,000	$30,700
		390/325 2dr Conv	$80,400	$107,000	$142,000	$180,000
1959	Coupe de Ville	390/325 2dr Hdtp Cpe	$16,800	$26,000	$40,100	$57,100
		390/345 2dr Hdtp Cpe	$21,300	$34,800	$50,500	$67,900
		+10% for factory a/c.				
1959	Sedan de Ville	390/325 4dr Hdtp 4W	$12,900	$18,400	$26,300	$37,600
		+10% for factory a/c.				
1959	Eldorado	390/345 2dr Seville Hdtp Cpe	$34,300	$50,400	$70,500	$92,900
		390/345 4dr Brghm Hdtp Sdn	$68,800	$87,800	$124,000	$164,000
		390/345 2dr Biarritz Conv	$94,800	$121,000	$175,000	$254,000
		+10% for bucket seats on Biarritz.				
1959	Fleetwood 60 Special	390/325 4dr Hdtp Sdn	$17,900	$29,900	$58,200	$81,400
		+10% for factory a/c.				
1959	Fleetwood Series 75	390/345 4dr Imp Sdn	$13,400	$20,400	$28,900	$36,800
		390/325 4dr Imp Sdn	$12,200	$18,600	$26,100	$33,600
		390/325 4dr Limo	$11,500	$17,400	$24,700	$31,600
		390/345 4dr Limo	$12,700	$19,100	$27,200	$34,600

Cadillac

Year	Model	Body Style	4	3	2	1
			+10% for factory a/c. +20% for bucket seats.			
1960	Series 62	390/325 2dr Cpe	$15,900	$22,600	$34,400	$52,900
		390/345 4dr Hdtp 4W	$8,200	$11,700	$16,400	$20,900
		390/345 4dr Hdtp 6W	$8,500	$12,100	$17,300	$21,600
		390/325 2dr Conv	$34,000	$47,100	$62,900	$97,300
1960	DeVille	390/345 2dr Cpe	$18,000	$29,300	$48,700	$70,100
		390/345 4dr Hdtp 4W	$8,700	$13,800	$19,300	$27,100
		390/345 4dr Hdtp 6W	$8,900	$14,300	$20,000	$28,100
			+10% for factory a/c.			
1960	Eldorado	390/345 2dr Seville Cpe	$26,300	$38,500	$55,400	$74,600
		390/345 4dr Brghm Sdn	$46,800	$59,100	$84,100	$121,000
		390/345 2dr Biarritz Conv	$53,800	$72,800	$112,000	$161,000
			+10% for bucket seats on Biarritz.			
1960	Fleetwood 60 Special	390/325 4dr Sdn	$16,500	$25,300	$48,100	$71,000
			+10% for factory a/c.			
1960	Fleetwood Series 75	390/325 4dr Sdn	$10,800	$15,700	$22,300	$28,600
		390/345 4dr Sdn	$12,000	$17,500	$25,000	$32,000
		390/325 4dr Limo	$10,100	$14,800	$20,800	$26,500
		390/345 4dr Limo	$11,200	$16,700	$23,500	$29,700
			+10% for factory a/c.			
1961	Series 62	390/325 2dr Cpe	$9,600	$16,600	$23,800	$31,800
		390/325 4dr Hdtp 6W	$5,900	$10,600	$15,300	$20,500
		390/325 4dr Hdtp 4W	$6,700	$12,000	$17,100	$22,900
		390/325 2dr Conv	$23,200	$33,900	$48,800	$63,000
1961	DeVille	390/325 2dr Hdtp Cpe	$13,400	$21,100	$35,000	$50,400
		390/325 4dr Twn Sdn	$8,500	$13,200	$18,200	$25,900
		390/325 4dr Hdtp 4W	$8,300	$12,700	$17,600	$25,400
		390/325 4dr Hdtp 6W	$8,700	$13,600	$18,500	$26,500
		390/325 2dr Eldorado Biarritz Conv	$42,500	$64,900	$100,000	$139,000
			+10% for factory a/c.			
1961	Fleetwood 60 Special	390/325 4dr Sdn	$11,900	$21,300	$31,000	$43,200

Year	Model	Body Style	4	3	2	1
1961	Fleetwood Series 75	390/325 4dr Sdn	$11,000	$16,000	$21,700	$28,900
		390/325 4dr Imp Limo	$9,900	$14,700	$20,000	$25,700
1962	Series 62	390/325 2dr Cpe	$9,300	$14,600	$20,700	$27,800
		390/325 4dr Twn Sdn	$6,000	$10,900	$15,700	$21,000
		390/325 4dr Hdtp 4W	$6,300	$11,400	$16,600	$22,100
		390/325 4dr Hdtp 6W	$6,100	$11,200	$15,900	$21,300
		390/325 2dr Conv	$19,100	$30,600	$42,700	$56,100
1962	DeVille	390/325 2dr Cpe	$10,900	$17,300	$28,600	$41,000
		390/325 4dr Hdtp 4W	$9,400	$14,500	$20,400	$28,500
		390/325 4dr Hdtp 6W	$9,600	$14,600	$20,600	$28,900
		390/325 4dr Park Ave Sdn	$9,700	$14,600	$20,700	$29,200
						+10% for factory a/c.
1962	Eldorado	390/325 2dr Biarritz Conv	$27,700	$41,100	$61,500	$88,300
						+10% for factory a/c. +10% for bucket seats.
1962	Fleetwood 60 Special	390/325 4dr Sdn	$11,400	$21,500	$28,800	$41,200
1962	Fleetwood Series 75	390/325 4dr Sdn	$10,900	$16,400	$21,800	$28,900
		390/325 4dr Limo	$10,100	$16,000	$21,100	$25,800
1963	Series 62	390/325 2dr Cpe	$9,400	$14,700	$21,400	$28,500
		390/325 4dr Sdn 4W	$6,700	$12,000	$17,100	$22,900
		390/325 4dr Sdn 6W	$5,900	$10,600	$15,300	$20,500
		390/325 2dr Conv	$19,600	$31,400	$44,000	$58,400
1963	DeVille	390/325 2dr Cpe	$12,000	$18,000	$29,600	$42,900
		390/325 4dr Park Ave Sdn	$7,900	$12,500	$17,400	$24,500
		390/325 4dr Hdtp 4W	$9,000	$14,500	$20,100	$28,400
		390/325 4dr Hdtp 6W	$8,900	$14,300	$20,000	$28,100
						+10% for factory a/c.
1963	Eldorado	390/325 2dr Biarritz Conv	$27,700	$40,900	$61,200	$87,500
						+10% for factory a/c. +10% for bucket seats.
1963	Fleetwood 60 Special	390/325 4dr Hdtp Sdn	$11,600	$21,800	$29,600	$41,500
1963	Fleetwood Series 75	390/325 4dr Sdn	$11,100	$16,600	$22,300	$29,300

Cadillac

Year	Model	Body Style	4	3	2	1
		390/325 4dr Limo	$10,700	$17,200	$21,600	$27,100
1964	Series 62	429/340 2dr Cpe	$9,400	$14,700	$21,400	$28,500
		429/340 4dr Sdn 4W	$7,000	$12,000	$17,300	$23,100
		429/340 4dr Sdn 6W	$5,900	$10,600	$15,300	$20,500
1964	DeVille	429/340 2dr Cpe	$10,700	$17,000	$28,500	$40,700
		429/340 4dr Sdn 4W	$8,900	$14,300	$20,100	$28,100
		429/340 4dr Sdn 6W	$8,900	$14,300	$20,100	$28,100
		429/340 2dr Conv	$16,300	$26,500	$41,500	$57,700
						+10% for factory a/c.
1964	Eldorado	429/340 2dr Biarritz Spt Conv	$20,100	$28,600	$43,700	$62,500
						+10% for factory a/c. +10% for bucket seats.
1964	Fleetwood 60 Special	429/340 4dr Sdn	$11,800	$22,000	$29,500	$41,800
1964	Fleetwood Series 75	429/340 4dr Sdn	$10,900	$16,500	$22,300	$28,900
		429/340 4dr Limo	$10,600	$17,100	$21,400	$26,600
1965	Calais	429/340 2dr Cpe	$8,200	$13,900	$21,500	$36,800
		429/340 4dr Sdn	$5,400	$12,000	$17,300	$30,200
		429/340 4dr Hdtp Sdn	$5,100	$11,900	$16,400	$29,700
1965	DeVille	429/340 2dr Cpe	$7,000	$12,000	$17,600	$25,800
		429/340 4dr Sdn	$6,600	$11,400	$15,800	$22,500
		429/340 4dr Hdtp Sdn	$6,700	$11,500	$15,900	$22,600
		429/340 2dr Conv	$13,600	$24,500	$36,200	$55,400
1965	Fleetwood	429/340 4dr Sixty Spcl Sdn	$8,300	$15,900	$25,300	$39,100
		429/340 4dr Seventy Five Limo	$9,000	$16,500	$21,100	$26,200
		429/340 4dr Seventy Five Sdn	$9,000	$17,600	$21,700	$28,300
		429/340 2dr Eldorado Conv	$17,400	$30,300	$45,300	$64,500
						+10% for factory a/c.
1966	Calais	429/340 2dr Cpe	$6,900	$14,000	$21,600	$37,000
		429/340 4dr Sdn	$5,400	$12,000	$17,300	$30,200
		429/340 4dr Hdtp Sdn	$5,100	$11,900	$16,400	$29,700
1966	DeVille	429/340 2dr Cpe	$7,400	$12,300	$18,100	$27,800
		429/340 4dr Sdn	$6,700	$11,500	$15,900	$22,600
		429/340 4dr Hdtp Sdn	$6,800	$11,600	$16,000	$23,000
		429/340 2dr Conv	$13,000	$23,400	$34,900	$53,400
1966	Eldorado	429/340 2dr Conv	$20,300	$28,600	$44,800	$64,000

Year	Model	Body Style	4	3	2	1
1966	Fleetwood 60 Special	429/340 4dr Sdn	$8,400	$16,000	$25,500	$39,500
		429/340 4dr Brghm Sdn	$8,600	$16,400	$27,300	$43,900
1966	Fleetwood 75	429/340 4dr Sdn	$13,100	$19,800	$27,500	$35,800
		429/340 4dr Limo	$7,300	$14,300	$21,300	$25,300
1967	Calais	429/340 2dr Cpe	$7,800	$15,000	$23,600	$41,200
		429/340 4dr Sdn	$6,000	$12,500	$18,800	$35,100
		429/340 4dr Hdtp Sdn	$6,200	$12,800	$19,400	$35,700
1967	DeVille	429/340 2dr Cpe	$8,000	$13,300	$20,300	$30,700
		429/340 4dr Sdn	$7,100	$11,800	$17,900	$26,900
		429/340 4dr Hdtp Sdn	$7,300	$12,400	$18,000	$27,300
		429/340 2dr Conv	$12,200	$22,700	$34,200	$51,700
1967	Eldorado	429/340 2dr Cpe	$8,300	$15,100	$26,800	$43,500
1967	Fleetwood 60 Special	429/340 4dr Sdn	$8,100	$16,100	$25,600	$43,000
		429/340 4dr Brghm Sdn	$8,400	$16,700	$27,400	$47,800
1967	Fleetwood 75	429/340 4dr Sdn	$14,400	$21,100	$31,900	$42,700
		429/340 4dr Limo	$8,300	$15,800	$25,400	$32,000
1968	Calais	472/375 2dr Cpe	$7,500	$14,100	$22,600	$40,100
		472/375 4dr Hdtp Sdn	$5,900	$11,700	$18,500	$34,100
1968	DeVille	472/375 2dr Cpe	$7,700	$12,800	$19,600	$28,900
		472/375 4dr Sdn	$6,600	$10,900	$17,600	$25,600
		472/375 4dr Hdtp Sdn	$6,700	$11,200	$17,500	$25,300
		472/375 2dr Conv	$11,500	$20,700	$32,800	$50,600
1968	Eldorado	472/375 2dr Cpe	$6,600	$13,300	$23,700	$38,500
1968	Fleetwood 60 Special	472/375 4dr Sdn	$7,700	$15,400	$24,400	$40,900
		472/375 4dr Brghm Sdn	$7,900	$15,800	$26,100	$45,500
1968	Fleetwood 75	472/375 4dr Sdn	$13,400	$19,400	$30,100	$40,800
		472/375 4dr Limo	$7,600	$13,900	$23,200	$30,700
1969	Calais	472/375 2dr Cpe	$7,400	$14,000	$22,000	$39,200
		472/375 4dr Hdtp Sdn	$5,400	$11,100	$17,300	$32,900
1969	DeVille	472/375 2dr Cpe	$7,400	$12,400	$19,200	$27,900
		472/375 4dr Sdn	$6,200	$10,400	$16,700	$24,400
		472/375 4dr Hdtp Sdn	$6,400	$11,000	$16,800	$24,600
		472/375 2dr Conv	$10,000	$17,300	$26,200	$39,700
1969	Eldorado	472/375 2dr Hdtp Cpe	$6,200	$12,500	$22,600	$36,900

Cadillac

Year	Model	Body Style	4	3	2	1
1969	Fleetwood	472/375 4dr Sixty Spcl Sdn	$7,700	$15,400	$24,400	$40,900
		472/375 4dr Sixty Spcl Brghm Sdn	$7,900	$15,800	$26,100	$45,500
		472/375 4dr Seventy-Five Sdn	$10,600	$17,600	$25,200	$34,000
		472/375 4dr Seventy-Five Limo	$10,200	$16,800	$24,900	$33,200
1970	Calais	472/375 2dr Hdtp Cpe	$7,500	$14,100	$22,100	$39,300
		472/375 4dr Hdtp Sdn	$5,400	$11,100	$17,300	$32,700
1970	DeVille	472/375 2dr Cpe	$7,500	$12,600	$19,400	$28,600
		472/375 4dr Sdn	$6,200	$10,400	$16,700	$24,400
		472/375 4dr Hdtp Sdn	$6,400	$11,000	$16,800	$24,600
		472/375 2dr Conv	$10,900	$18,400	$28,900	$45,000
1970	Eldorado	500/400 2dr Cpe	$5,600	$10,500	$21,100	$29,800
1970	Fleetwood 60 Special	472/375 4dr Sdn	$8,400	$16,000	$25,500	$39,500
		472/375 4dr Brghm Sdn	$8,600	$16,400	$27,300	$43,900
1970	Fleetwood 75	472/375 4dr Sdn	$13,400	$19,400	$30,100	$40,700
		472/375 4dr Limo	$7,600	$14,000	$23,200	$30,800
1971	Calais	472/375 2dr Cpe	$7,300	$11,300	$17,500	$30,800
		472/375 4dr Sdn	$3,000	$4,900	$8,400	$16,400
						+$1,000 for sunroof.
1971	DeVille	472/375 2dr Cpe	$6,800	$11,200	$17,800	$23,700
		472/375 4dr Sdn	$4,400	$7,500	$12,600	$17,800
						+$1,000 for sunroof.
1971	Eldorado	500/365 2dr Hdtp Cpe	$4,800	$8,000	$14,700	$22,100
		500/365 2dr Conv	$6,400	$11,900	$26,100	$41,100
						+$1,000 for sunroof.
1971	Fleetwood 60 Special	472/375 4dr Brghm Sdn	$4,000	$6,500	$10,800	$15,400
						+$1,000 for sunroof.
1971	Fleetwood 75	472/375 4dr Sdn	$5,600	$8,800	$15,700	$23,600
		472/375 4dr Limo	$8,100	$10,700	$17,500	$24,800
						+$1,000 for sunroof.
1972	Calais	472/220 2dr Hdtp Cpe	$5,600	$9,000	$15,700	$29,200
		472/220 4dr Hdtp Sdn	$3,000	$4,900	$8,400	$16,600
						+$1,000 for sunroof.

Year	Model	Body Style	4	3	2	1
1972	DeVille	472/220 2dr Hdtp Cpe	$5,400	$9,500	$15,600	$21,300
		472/220 4dr Hdtp Sdn	$4,800	$8,100	$14,100	$20,000
						+$1,000 for sunroof.
1972	Eldorado	500/235 2dr Hdtp Cpe	$4,800	$8,000	$14,700	$22,100
		500/235 2dr Conv	$6,200	$11,400	$25,100	$39,400
						+$1,000 for sunroof.
1972	Fleetwood 60 Special	472/220 4dr Brghm Sdn	$3,900	$6,200	$10,500	$15,000
						+$1,000 for sunroof.
1972	Fleetwood	472/220 4dr 75 Sdn	$5,900	$9,000	$15,800	$24,000
		472/220 4dr 75 Limo	$8,000	$10,300	$17,100	$24,500
						+$1,000 for sunroof.
1973	Calais	472/220 2dr Hdtp Cpe	$4,300	$8,100	$14,500	$27,500
		472/220 4dr Hdtp Sdn	$2,700	$4,800	$7,700	$15,800
						+$1,000 for sunroof.
1973	DeVille	472/220 2dr Hdtp Cpe	$5,100	$6,400	$15,200	$21,100
		472/220 4dr Hdtp Sdn	$4,400	$7,300	$12,300	$17,600
						+$1,000 for sunroof.
1973	Eldorado	500/235 2dr Hdtp Cpe	$4,800	$8,000	$14,700	$22,100
		500/235 2dr Conv	$6,200	$11,400	$25,100	$39,400
		500/235 2dr Pace Car Conv	$10,600	$19,700	$35,900	$53,300
						+$1,000 for sunroof.
1973	Fleetwood 60 Special	472/220 4dr Brghm Sdn	$3,900	$6,200	$10,500	$15,000
						+$1,000 for sunroof.
1973	Fleetwood	472/220 4dr 75 Sdn	$5,600	$7,900	$14,600	$22,600
		472/220 4dr 75 Limo	$8,000	$10,200	$17,100	$23,900
						+$1,000 for sunroof.
1974	Calais	472/205 2dr Hdtp Cpe	$5,000	$8,800	$14,100	$24,000
		472/205 4dr Hdtp Sdn	$2,700	$4,800	$7,700	$15,800

Cadillac

Year	Model	Body Style	4	3	2	1
						+$1,000 for sunroof.
1974	DeVille	472/205 2dr Hdtp Cpe	$5,100	$6,400	$15,200	$21,100
		472/205 4dr Hdtp Sdn	$4,400	$7,300	$12,300	$17,600
						+$1,000 for sunroof.
1974	Eldorado	500/210 2dr Hdtp Cpe	$4,900	$8,200	$15,000	$22,600
		500/210 2dr Conv	$6,800	$12,500	$27,400	$43,000
						+$1,000 for sunroof.
1974	Fleetwood 60 Special	472/205 4dr Brghm Sdn	$3,700	$6,000	$10,200	$14,800
						+$1,000 for sunroof.
1974	Fleetwood	472/205 4dr 75 Sdn	$5,600	$7,900	$14,600	$22,600
		472/205 4dr 75 Limo	$8,000	$10,200	$17,100	$23,900
						+$1,000 for sunroof.
1975	Calais	500/190 2dr Hdtp Cpe	$4,900	$8,200	$13,800	$25,400
		500/190 4dr Hdtp Sdn	$3,100	$5,000	$8,400	$16,600
						+$1,000 for sunroof.
1975	DeVille	500/190 2dr Hdtp Cpe	$5,600	$9,700	$15,900	$21,600
		500/190 4dr Hdtp Sdn	$4,900	$7,700	$12,900	$18,300
						+$1,000 for sunroof.
1975	Eldorado	500/190 2dr Cpe	$5,300	$8,700	$16,200	$24,200
		500/190 2dr Conv	$7,100	$13,400	$28,700	$45,300
						+$1,000 for sunroof.
1975	Fleetwood 60 Special	500/190 4dr Brghm Sdn	$3,900	$6,400	$10,700	$15,300
		500/190 4dr Talis-man Sdn	$6,000	$8,500	$13,500	$20,300
						+$1,000 for sunroof.
1975	Fleetwood	500/190 4dr 75 Sdn	$6,600	$8,400	$15,700	$23,600
		500/190 4dr 75 Limo	$8,500	$10,800	$18,700	$24,700
						+$1,000 for sunroof.
1976	Seville	350/180 FI 4dr Sdn	$3,700	$7,100	$12,000	$17,800
						+$1,000 for sunroof.
1976	Calais	500/190 2dr Cpe	$4,800	$8,400	$14,100	$24,300
		500/190 4dr Sdn	$3,100	$5,000	$8,400	$16,400
						+$1,000 for sunroof.

Year	Model	Body Style	4	3	2	1
1976	DeVille	500/190 2dr Cpe	$5,600	$9,700	$15,900	$21,600
		500/190 4dr Sdn	$4,300	$6,600	$11,200	$15,900
						+$1,000 for sunroof.
1976	Eldorado	500/190 2dr Cpe	$5,400	$8,800	$16,400	$24,400
		500/190 2dr Conv	$10,100	$19,000	$39,400	$57,500
		500/190 2dr Bicentennial Ed Conv	$19,800	$33,700	$54,000	$77,300
						+$1,000 for sunroof.
1976	Fleetwood	500/190 4dr Brghm Sdn	$5,500	$7,500	$12,600	$23,700
		500/190 4dr Seventy Five Sdn	$6,600	$8,400	$15,700	$23,600
		500/190 4dr Talis-man Sdn	$8,100	$9,900	$14,700	$28,900
		500/190 4dr Seventy Five Limo	$8,500	$10,800	$18,700	$24,700
						+$1,000 for sunroof.
1977	Seville	350/180 FI 4dr Sdn	$3,700	$7,100	$12,000	$17,800
						+$1,000 for sunroof.
1977	DeVille	425/180 2dr Cpe	$4,300	$6,600	$13,400	$20,500
		425/180 4dr Sdn	$3,500	$5,300	$10,100	$15,800
						+$1,000 for sunroof.
1977	Eldorado	425/180 2dr Cpe	$4,800	$8,100	$14,800	$22,300
		425/180 2dr Biar-ritz Cpe	$6,600	$11,000	$21,000	$31,400
						+$1,000 for sunroof.
1977	Fleetwood	425/180 4dr Brghm Sdn	$4,100	$6,100	$9,500	$14,000
		425/180 4dr Limo	$3,500	$5,700	$10,800	$15,800
		425/180 4dr Fml Limo	$7,000	$9,000	$15,800	$21,300
						+$1,000 for sunroof.
1978	DeVille	425/180 2dr Cpe	$4,500	$7,000	$14,100	$22,300
		425/180 4dr Sdn	$3,900	$5,800	$11,100	$17,500
						+$1,000 for sunroof.
1978	Eldorado	425/180 2dr Cpe	$4,900	$8,300	$15,300	$22,800
		425/180 2dr Biar-ritz Cpe	$7,000	$11,700	$22,400	$33,500
						+$1,000 for sunroof.
1978	Seville	350/120 4dr Sdn	$3,800	$7,300	$12,200	$18,300
				+$4,000 for Elegante option. +$1,000 for sunroof.		
1978	Fleetwood	425/180 4dr Brghm Sdn	$4,200	$6,300	$9,700	$14,400
		425/180 4dr 75 Limo	$3,600	$5,900	$11,100	$16,300
		425/180 4dr 75 Fml Limo	$7,200	$9,300	$16,100	$21,900

Cadillac

Year	Model	Body Style	4	3	2	1
						+$1,000 for sunroof.
1979	Seville	350/170 FI 4dr Sdn	$3,900	$7,400	$12,400	$18,800
						+$4,000 for Elegante option.
1979	DeVille	425/180 2dr Cpe	$4,000	$6,200	$12,700	$19,800
		425/180 4dr Sdn	$3,000	$4,700	$9,000	$14,100
1979	Eldorado	350/170 FI 2dr Cpe	$4,000	$6,800	$13,000	$18,300
		350/170 FI 2dr d'Elegance Cpe	$4,300	$7,700	$13,900	$19,800
1979	Fleetwood	425/180 4dr Brghm Sdn	$3,500	$5,800	$7,700	$10,400
		425/180 4dr Limo	$3,400	$5,400	$9,000	$12,500
		425/180 4dr Fml Limo	$6,700	$8,500	$12,800	$15,800
1980	Seville	368/145 4dr Sdn	$2,400	$3,500	$9,200	$15,500
						+$1,500 for Elegante option.
1980	DeVille	368/150 2dr Cpe	$4,000	$6,100	$12,300	$19,000
		368/150 4dr Sdn	$2,800	$4,600	$8,900	$13,700
1980	Eldorado	368/145 2dr Cpe	$3,200	$6,000	$11,800	$16,900
		350/105 2dr Biarritz Cpe	$3,400	$7,100	$13,200	$18,800
1980	Fleetwood	368/150 2dr Brghm Cpe	$3,400	$6,300	$10,400	$14,900
		368/150 2dr Brghm d'Elegance Cpe	$3,600	$6,600	$10,500	$13,700
		368/150 4dr Brghm Sdn	$2,900	$4,200	$5,100	$7,100
		368/150 4dr Brghm d'Elegance Sdn	$3,200	$4,700	$5,800	$7,900
1981	Seville	368/140 4dr Sdn	$3,100	$4,100	$10,300	$18,800
						+$1,500 for Elegante option.
1981	DeVille	350/105 FI 2dr Cpe	$3,400	$5,400	$10,800	$16,800
		350/105 FI 4dr Sdn	$2,800	$4,500	$8,400	$13,000
1981	Eldorado	350/105 FI 2dr Cpe	$3,200	$6,000	$11,800	$16,900
1981	Fleetwood	368/140 2dr Brghm Cpe	$3,400	$6,300	$10,400	$14,900
		368/140 4dr Sdn	$3,000	$4,600	$5,800	$8,400
		368/140 4dr Brghm Sdn	$3,000	$4,200	$5,100	$7,100
		368/140 4dr Frml Sdn	$3,900	$5,300	$6,000	$9,300
						-20% for 6-cyl.
1982	Cimarron	112/88 4dr Sdn	$1,100	$1,600	$2,800	$6,100
						+$750 for 4-spd.
1982	Seville	249/125 4dr Sdn	$3,100	$4,100	$10,300	$18,800
						+$1,500 for Elegante option.
1982	DeVille	249/125 2dr Cpe	$3,400	$5,400	$10,800	$16,800

Year	Model	Body Style	4	3	2	1
		249/125 4dr Sdn	$2,800	$4,500	$8,400	$13,000
1982	Eldorado	249/125 2dr Cpe	$3,200	$6,000	$11,800	$16,900
1982	Fleetwood	249/125 2dr Brghm Cpe	$3,200	$6,200	$10,400	$14,800
		368/140 4dr Sdn	$2,800	$4,300	$5,600	$8,200
		249/125 4dr Brghm Sdn	$2,800	$4,000	$4,900	$7,000
		368/140 4dr Frml Sdn	$3,800	$5,200	$5,800	$9,000
1983	Cimarron	121/88 4dr Sdn	$1,100	$1,600	$2,800	$6,100
						+$750 for 4-spd.
1983	Seville	239/135 4dr Sdn	$3,100	$4,100	$10,300	$18,800
						+$1,500 for Elegante option.
1983	DeVille	239/135 2dr Cpe	$3,700	$5,700	$11,600	$17,800
		239/135 4dr Sdn	$2,800	$4,600	$8,700	$13,600
1983	Eldorado	239/135 2dr Cpe	$2,200	$4,900	$10,800	$16,300
1983	Fleetwood	239/135 2dr Brghm Cpe	$2,300	$5,400	$9,800	$14,600
		368/140 4dr Sdn	$1,900	$4,000	$5,600	$8,200
		239/135 4dr Brghm Sdn	$1,900	$3,900	$4,900	$7,000
		368/140 4dr Frml Sdn	$3,500	$5,200	$5,800	$9,000
1984	Cimarron	121/88 4dr Sdn	$1,100	$1,600	$2,800	$6,100
						+$750 for 4-spd.
1984	Seville	249/135 4dr Sdn	$3,100	$4,100	$10,300	$18,800
						+$1,500 for Elegante option.
1984	DeVille	249/135 2dr Cpe	$3,700	$5,700	$11,600	$17,800
		249/135 4dr Sdn	$2,800	$4,600	$8,700	$13,600
1984	Eldorado	249/135 2dr Cpe	$2,300	$4,900	$10,500	$16,300
		249/135 2dr Biarritz Conv	$1,700	$7,400	$16,400	$27,100
1984	Fleetwood	249/135 2dr Brghm Cpe	$2,300	$5,400	$9,800	$14,600
		249/135 4dr Sdn	$2,100	$4,400	$5,700	$8,700
		249/135 4dr Brghm Sdn	$1,800	$3,900	$4,900	$7,000
		368/140 4dr Frml Sdn	$2,300	$5,200	$6,200	$9,100
1985	Cimarron	173/125 4dr Sdn	$1,100	$1,600	$2,800	$6,100
						+$750 for 4-spd.
1985	Seville	249/135 4dr Sdn	$3,100	$4,100	$10,300	$18,800
						+$1,500 for Elegante option.
1985	DeVille	249/125 2dr Cpe	$3,100	$4,700	$7,700	$10,200
		249/125 4dr Sdn	$2,000	$3,400	$4,700	$6,500
1985	Eldorado	249/135 2dr Cpe	$2,200	$4,800	$11,100	$16,300
		249/135 2dr Biarritz Conv	$4,500	$7,300	$15,900	$26,000
1985	Fleetwood	249/125 2dr Cpe	$2,500	$5,600	$11,100	$15,800

Cadillac

Cadillac

Year	Model	Body Style	4	3	2	1
		249/135 2dr Brghm Cpe	$3,000	$5,900	$12,400	$16,800
		249/125 4dr Sdn	$2,500	$5,200	$7,900	$12,000
		249/135 4dr Brghm Sdn	$3,000	$6,000	$9,200	$13,000
		249/125 4dr Limo Fml Sdn	$2,700	$5,800	$8,200	$12,700
		249/125 4dr Limo Sdn	$2,600	$5,800	$8,200	$12,500
1986	Cimarron	173/125 4dr Sdn	$1,100	$1,600	$2,800	$6,100
						+$750 for 4-spd.
1986	Seville	249/140 FI 4dr Sdn	$1,400	$2,900	$4,400	$6,100
						+$1,000 for Elegante option.
1986	DeVille	249/140 FI 2dr Cpe	$2,500	$4,200	$6,500	$8,800
		249/140 FI 4dr Sdn	$1,900	$3,300	$3,800	$5,600
1986	Eldorado	249/140 FI 2dr Cpe	$2,200	$4,300	$8,100	$11,400
1986	Fleetwood	249/140 FI 2dr Cpe	$2,500	$5,500	$11,100	$15,500
		249/140 FI 4dr Sdn	$2,500	$5,200	$7,900	$11,700
		307/140 4dr Brghm Sdn	$3,000	$6,000	$9,200	$13,000
		249/140 FI 4dr Limo Sdn	$2,600	$5,800	$8,200	$12,500
		249/140 FI 4dr 75 Limo	$2,700	$5,800	$8,200	$12,700
1987	Cimarron	173/125 FI 4dr Sdn	$1,100	$1,600	$2,800	$6,100
						+$750 for 4-spd.
1987	Seville	249/130 4dr Sdn	$1,500	$2,900	$3,700	$5,400
						+$1,000 for Elegante option.
1987	DeVille	249/130 2dr Cpe	$2,500	$4,200	$6,500	$8,800
		249/130 4dr Sdn	$1,900	$3,300	$3,800	$5,600
1987	Eldorado	249/130 2dr Cpe	$2,100	$4,100	$7,800	$11,200
1987	Fleetwood	249/130 4dr d'Elegance Sdn	$2,500	$5,800	$8,200	$11,700
		249/130 4dr Sixty-Spcl Sdn	$2,600	$6,000	$8,700	$12,800
		249/130 4dr 75 Sdn	$2,600	$5,800	$8,200	$12,500
		249/130 4dr 75 Limo	$3,700	$6,800	$10,200	$16,000
1987	Allante	250/170 FI 2dr Conv	$2,700	$5,100	$8,700	$14,900
1988	Cimarron	173/125 FI 4dr Sdn	$1,300	$1,900	$3,300	$6,400
						+$750 for 5-spd.
1988	DeVille	273/155 FI 2dr Cpe	$2,200	$4,200	$6,300	$8,600
		273/155 FI 4dr Sdn	$1,500	$2,800	$3,700	$5,400
1988	Brougham	307/140 4dr Sdn	$2,000	$3,600	$4,700	$9,400

Year	Model	Body Style	4	3	2	1
1988	Seville	273/155 FI 4dr Sdn	$1,400	$2,800	$4,200	$5,900
		273/155 FI 4dr Trng Sdn	$2,000	$3,400	$4,800	$6,600
						+$1,000 for Elegante option.
1988	Eldorado	273/155 FI 2dr Cpe	$2,100	$3,800	$7,600	$10,800
1988	Fleetwood	273/155 FI 4dr d'Elegance Sdn	$2,500	$5,800	$8,200	$11,700
		273/155 FI 4dr Sixty-Spcl Sdn	$2,500	$5,900	$8,500	$12,700
1988	Allante	250/170 FI 2dr Conv	$2,700	$5,100	$8,700	$14,900
1989	DeVille	273/155 FI 2dr Cpe	$2,600	$4,400	$6,900	$10,000
		273/155 FI 4dr Sdn	$2,200	$4,300	$6,100	$9,400
1989	Brougham	307/140 4dr Sdn	$2,000	$3,800	$4,800	$9,600
1989	Seville	273/155 FI 4dr Sdn	$1,400	$2,800	$4,200	$5,900
		273/155 FI 4dr Trng Sdn	$2,000	$3,300	$4,700	$6,500
1989	Eldorado	273/155 FI 2dr Cpe	$2,100	$3,800	$7,600	$10,800
1989	Fleetwood	273/155 FI 2dr Cpe	$3,000	$6,000	$9,000	$13,500
		273/155 FI 4dr d'Elegance Sdn	$2,500	$5,800	$8,200	$11,700
		273/155 FI 4dr Sixty-Spcl Sdn	$2,500	$5,900	$8,500	$12,700
1989	Allante	273/200 FI 2dr Conv	$3,000	$5,600	$9,600	$15,700
1990	DeVille	275/180 FI 2dr Cpe	$1,900	$3,700	$5,700	$8,800
		275/180 FI 4dr Sdn	$1,700	$3,800	$5,100	$7,300
1990	Brougham	307/140 4dr Sdn	$1,600	$3,300	$4,400	$7,500
1990	Seville	275/180 FI 4dr Sdn	$1,200	$2,500	$3,800	$5,400
		275/180 FI 4dr Trng Sdn	$1,900	$3,100	$4,400	$6,100
1990	Eldorado	275/180 FI 2dr Cpe	$1,600	$3,600	$7,000	$9,900
1990	Fleetwood	275/180 FI 2dr Cpe	$2,400	$5,200	$7,900	$12,000
		275/180 FI 4dr Sdn	$2,500	$6,000	$9,600	$14,700
		275/180 FI 4dr Sixty-Spcl Sdn	$3,300	$6,300	$9,700	$15,500
1990	Allante	275/200 FI 2dr Conv	$3,100	$5,900	$10,100	$16,300
						+$1,000 for hard top.
1991	DeVille	300/200 FI 2dr Cpe	$1,900	$3,700	$5,700	$8,800
		300/200 FI 4dr Sdn	$1,700	$3,800	$5,100	$7,300
1991	Brougham	305/170 4dr Sdn	$2,100	$4,100	$5,800	$10,500
1991	Seville	300/200 FI 4dr Sdn	$1,200	$2,500	$3,800	$5,400

Cadillac

Year	Model	Body Style	4	3	2	1
		300/200 FI 4dr Trng Sdn	$1,900	$3,100	$4,400	$6,100
1991	Eldorado	300/200 FI 2dr Cpe	$1,600	$3,600	$7,000	$9,900
		300/200 FI 2dr Biarritz Cpe	$3,100	$4,700	$8,400	$11,200
1991	Fleetwood	300/200 FI 2dr Cpe	$2,400	$5,100	$7,800	$11,400
		300/200 FI 4dr Sdn	$2,500	$6,000	$9,600	$14,200
		300/200 FI 4dr Sixty-Spcl Sdn	$3,300	$6,300	$9,700	$15,500
1991	Allante	275/200 FI 2dr Conv	$3,100	$5,900	$10,100	$16,300
						+$1,000 for hard top.
1992	DeVille	300/200 2dr Cpe	$1,900	$3,700	$5,700	$8,800
		300/200 4dr Sdn	$1,700	$3,800	$5,100	$7,300
		300/200 4dr TS Sdn	$2,300	$4,300	$5,500	$7,900
1992	Seville	300/200 4dr Sdn	$1,200	$2,500	$3,800	$5,400
		300/200 4dr STS Sdn	$1,500	$2,900	$4,400	$6,200
1992	Eldorado	300/200 2dr Cpe	$1,800	$3,900	$7,500	$9,800
1992	Fleetwood	300/200 2dr Cpe	$2,400	$5,100	$7,800	$11,400
		300/200 4dr Sdn	$2,500	$6,000	$9,600	$14,200
		300/200 4dr Sixty-Spcl Sdn	$3,300	$6,300	$9,700	$15,500
1992	Allante	275/200 2dr Conv	$3,100	$5,900	$10,100	$16,300
						+$1,000 for hard top.
1993	DeVille	300/200 2dr Cpe	$1,900	$3,700	$5,700	$8,800
		300/200 4dr Sdn	$1,700	$3,800	$5,100	$7,500
		300/200 4dr Trng Sdn	$1,900	$3,600	$4,200	$6,100
1993	Seville	300/200 4dr Sdn	$1,200	$2,500	$3,800	$5,400
		279/295 4dr STS Sdn	$1,500	$2,900	$4,400	$6,200
1993	Eldorado	300/200 2dr Cpe	$1,800	$3,900	$7,500	$9,800
1993	Fleetwood	350/185 4dr Sdn	$1,700	$4,400	$7,100	$13,800
1993	Allante	279/295 2dr Conv	$3,600	$6,900	$11,900	$22,800
1994	Eldorado	279/270 2dr Cpe	$1,900	$4,000	$7,700	$10,100
1994	Fleetwood	350/260 4dr Sdn	$2,400	$6,100	$10,400	$21,000
1995	Eldorado	279/275 2dr Cpe	$1,900	$4,000	$7,700	$10,100
1995	Fleetwood	350/260 4dr Sdn	$2,400	$6,100	$10,400	$21,000
1996	Eldorado	279/275 2dr Cpe	$2,000	$4,100	$8,000	$10,400
1996	Fleetwood	350/260 4dr Sdn	$2,400	$6,100	$10,400	$21,000
1997	Eldorado	279/275 2dr Cpe	$2,000	$4,100	$8,000	$10,400
1998	Eldorado	279/275 2dr Cpe	$2,100	$4,200	$8,200	$10,700
1999	Eldorado	279/275 2dr Cpe	$2,100	$4,200	$8,200	$10,700
2000	Eldorado	279/275 2dr ESC Cpe	$2,300	$4,300	$8,400	$11,000

Cadillac

Year	Model	Body Style	4	3	2	1
2001	Eldorado	279/275 2dr ESC Cpe	$2,300	$4,300	$8,400	$11,000
2002	Eldorado	279/275 2dr ESC Cpe	$2,300	$4,300	$8,400	$11,000
2009	CTS-V	376/556 4dr Sdn	$23,000	$32,000	$43,000	$51,000
		-10% for auto trans, -15% for auto trans on Station Wagons.				
2010	CTS-V	376/556 4dr Sdn	$23,000	$32,000	$43,000	$51,000
		-10% for auto trans, -15% for auto trans on Station Wagons.				
2011	CTS-V	376/556 4dr Sdn	$23,000	$32,000	$43,000	$51,000
		376/556 2dr Cpe	$25,000	$36,000	$47,500	$55,000
		376/556 4dr Wgn	$38,000	$46,500	$62,000	$76,500
		-10% for auto trans, -15% for auto trans on Station Wagons.				
2012	CTS-V	376/556 4dr Sdn	$23,000	$32,000	$43,000	$51,000
		376/556 2dr Cpe	$25,000	$36,000	$47,500	$55,000
		376/556 4dr Wgn	$38,000	$46,500	$62,000	$76,500
		-10% for auto trans, -15% for auto trans on Station Wagons.				
2013	CTS-V	376/556 4dr Sdn	$23,000	$32,000	$43,000	$51,000
		376/556 2dr Cpe	$25,000	$36,000	$47,500	$55,000
		376/556 4dr Wgn	$38,000	$46,500	$62,000	$76,500
		-10% for auto trans, -15% for auto trans on Station Wagons.				
2014	CTS-V	376/556 4dr Sdn	$23,000	$32,000	$43,000	$51,000
		376/556 2dr Cpe	$25,000	$36,000	$47,500	$55,000
		376/556 4dr Wgn	$38,000	$46,500	$62,000	$76,500
		-10% for auto trans, -15% for auto trans on Station Wagons.				
2015	CTS-V	376/556 2dr Cpe	$25,000	$36,000	$47,500	$55,000
		-10% for auto trans, -15% for auto trans on Station Wagons.				

Checker

Year	Model	Body Style	4	3	2	1
1960	Superba	226/80 4dr Sdn	$5,700	$9,100	$13,000	$18,100
		226/80 4dr Spcl Sdn	$5,700	$9,100	$13,000	$18,100
		226/122 4dr Wgn	$7,700	$11,100	$14,100	$19,700
		226/122 4dr Spcl Wgn	$7,900	$11,300	$14,300	$19,900
1962	Marathon (A10)	226/80 4dr Sdn	$5,800	$9,100	$13,000	$18,100
		226/122 4dr Wgn	$7,500	$10,200	$13,000	$18,400
1962	Superba	226/80 4dr Sdn	$5,700	$9,100	$13,000	$18,100
		226/122 4dr Wgn	$7,700	$11,100	$14,100	$19,700
		+$3,500 for factory taxi option.				
1963	Marathon (A12)	226/141 4dr Sdn	$7,400	$11,600	$15,900	$22,700
		+$3,500 for factory taxi option.				
1964	Marathon (A12)	226/141 4dr Sdn	$7,400	$11,600	$15,900	$22,700
		+$3,500 for factory taxi option.				

Checker

Year	Model	Body Style	4	3	2	1
1965	Marathon (A12)	283/195 4dr Sdn	$7,400	$11,600	$15,900	$22,700
				+$3,500 for factory taxi option.		
1966	Marathon (A12)	327/250 4dr Sdn	$7,400	$11,600	$15,900	$22,700
				+$3,500 for factory taxi option.		
1967	Marathon (A12)	327/250 4dr Sdn	$7,400	$11,600	$15,900	$22,700
				+$3,500 for factory taxi option.		
1968	Marathon (A12)	327/250 4dr Sdn	$7,400	$11,600	$15,900	$22,700
		327/250 4dr Wgn	$9,500	$14,100	$17,400	$25,200
				+$3,500 for factory taxi option.		
1969	Marathon (A12)	327/235 4dr Sdn	$7,400	$11,600	$15,900	$22,700
		327/235 4dr Wgn	$9,500	$14,100	$17,400	$25,200
				+$3,500 for factory taxi option.		
1972	Marathon (A12)	250/145 4dr Sdn	$5,700	$9,100	$11,800	$16,600
		350/245 4dr Sdn	$7,000	$10,900	$14,100	$19,800
		350/245 4dr Wgn	$8,100	$11,300	$15,500	$21,600
1973	Marathon (A12)	250/100 4dr Sdn	$5,700	$9,100	$11,800	$16,600
		350/145 4dr Sdn	$7,000	$10,900	$14,100	$19,800
		350/145 4dr Wgn	$8,100	$11,300	$15,500	$21,600
1974	Marathon (A12)	250/100 4dr Sdn	$5,700	$9,100	$11,800	$16,600
		350/145 4dr Sdn	$7,000	$10,900	$14,100	$19,800
		350/145 4dr Wgn	$8,100	$11,300	$15,500	$21,600
1975	Marathon (A12)	250/100 4dr Sdn	$5,500	$8,600	$13,800	$19,300
		350/145 4dr Sdn	$6,500	$10,300	$16,500	$23,100
1976	Marathon (A12)	250/105 4dr Sdn	$5,500	$8,600	$13,800	$19,300
		350/145 4dr Sdn	$6,500	$10,300	$16,500	$23,100
1977	Marathon (A12)	250/110 4dr Sdn	$5,500	$8,600	$13,800	$19,300
		305/145 4dr Sdn	$6,500	$10,300	$16,500	$23,100
1978	Marathon (A12)	250/110 4dr Sdn	$5,500	$8,600	$13,800	$19,300
		305/145 4dr Sdn	$6,500	$10,300	$16,500	$23,100
1979	Marathon (A12)	250/110 4dr Sdn	$5,500	$8,600	$13,800	$19,300
		305/145 4dr Sdn	$6,500	$10,300	$16,500	$23,100
1980	Marathon (A12)	229/115 4dr Sdn	$5,500	$8,600	$13,800	$19,300
		267/120 4dr Sdn	$6,500	$10,300	$16,500	$23,100
				+$3,500 for factory taxi option.		

Checker

Year	Model	Body Style	4	3	2	1
1981	Marathon (A12)	229/110 4dr Sdn	$5,500	$8,600	$13,800	$19,300
						+$3,500 for factory taxi option.
		267/115 4dr Sdn	$6,500	$10,300	$16,500	$23,100
1982	Marathon (A12)	229/110 4dr Sdn	$5,500	$8,600	$13,800	$19,300
						+$3,500 for factory taxi option.
		267/115 4dr Sdn	$6,500	$10,300	$16,500	$23,100

Cheetah

Year	Model	Body Style	4	3	2	1
1965	GT	327/390 2dr Cpe	$420,000	$540,000	$685,000	$800,000

Chevrolet

Year	Model	Body Style	4	3	2	1
1946	Stylemaster	217/90 2dr Bus Cpe	$3,300	$8,900	$14,500	$22,600
		217/90 2dr Spt Cpe	$3,600	$9,000	$14,800	$22,800
		217/90 2dr Twn Sdn	$2,900	$6,500	$12,300	$19,600
		217/90 4dr Spt Sdn	$2,600	$5,700	$11,600	$15,700
1946	Fleetmaster	217/90 2dr Spt Cpe	$2,900	$8,400	$15,300	$24,400
		217/90 2dr Twn Sdn	$2,500	$7,500	$12,000	$19,000
		217/90 4dr Spt Sdn	$2,100	$6,400	$11,200	$16,200
		217/90 4dr Wgn	$21,500	$33,700	$58,900	$85,000
		217/90 2dr Cab	$9,900	$22,700	$48,300	$71,800
1946	Fleetline	217/90 2dr Aerosdn	$8,600	$16,700	$28,900	$40,400
		217/90 4dr Sptmstr Sdn	$3,600	$7,900	$17,700	$24,100
1947	Stylemaster	217/90 2dr Bus Cpe	$3,300	$8,900	$14,500	$22,600
		217/90 2dr Spt Cpe	$3,600	$9,000	$14,800	$22,800
		217/90 2dr Twn Sdn	$2,900	$6,500	$12,300	$19,600
		217/90 4dr Spt Sdn	$2,600	$5,700	$11,600	$15,700
1947	Fleetmaster	217/90 2dr Spt Cpe	$2,900	$8,400	$15,300	$24,400
		217/90 2dr Twn Sdn	$2,500	$7,500	$12,000	$19,000
		217/90 4dr Spt Sdn	$2,100	$6,400	$11,200	$16,200
		217/90 4dr Wgn	$21,500	$33,700	$58,900	$85,000

Chevrolet

Year	Model	Body Style	4	3	2	1
		217/90 2dr Cab	$9,900	$22,700	$48,300	$71,800
1947	Fleetline	217/90 2dr Aerosdn	$8,600	$16,700	$28,900	$40,400
		217/90 4dr Sptmstr Sdn	$3,600	$7,900	$17,700	$24,100
1948	Stylemaster	217/90 2dr Bus Cpe	$3,300	$8,900	$14,500	$22,600
		217/90 2dr Spt Cpe	$3,600	$9,000	$14,800	$22,800
		217/90 2dr Twn Sdn	$2,900	$6,500	$12,300	$19,600
		217/90 4dr Spt Sdn	$2,600	$5,700	$11,600	$15,700
1948	Fleetmaster	217/90 2dr Spt Cpe	$2,900	$8,400	$15,300	$24,400
		217/90 4dr Spt Sdn	$2,100	$6,400	$11,200	$16,200
		217/90 2dr Twn Sdn	$2,500	$7,500	$12,000	$19,000
		217/90 4dr Wgn	$21,500	$33,700	$58,900	$85,000
		217/90 2dr Cab	$9,900	$22,700	$48,300	$71,800
1948	Fleetline	217/90 2dr Aerosdn	$8,600	$16,700	$28,900	$40,400
		217/90 4dr Sptmstr Sdn	$3,600	$7,900	$17,700	$24,100
1949	Styleline	217/90 2dr Spcl Bus Cpe	$3,400	$8,300	$13,700	$19,300
		217/90 2dr Spcl Spt Cpe	$4,300	$9,700	$15,100	$22,700
		217/90 2dr Dlx Spt Cpe	$4,600	$10,100	$16,300	$25,300
		217/90 2dr Dlx Sdn	$3,400	$9,000	$14,400	$21,000
		217/90 4dr Spcl Sdn	$2,500	$7,000	$11,400	$16,400
		217/90 4dr Dlx Sdn	$2,200	$5,200	$9,100	$12,900
		217/90 4dr Dlx Stn Wgn	$33,100	$45,400	$73,500	$107,000
		217/90 4dr Dlx Wgn	$5,700	$14,600	$26,300	$39,600
		217/90 2dr Dlx Conv	$10,400	$20,400	$41,800	$56,700
1949	Fleetline	217/90 2dr Spcl Sdn	$3,600	$10,700	$14,800	$23,000
		217/90 2dr Dlx Sdn	$3,600	$6,200	$13,900	$21,600
		217/90 4dr Spcl Sdn	$3,000	$7,000	$10,500	$19,300
		217/90 4dr Dlx Sdn	$2,500	$7,000	$10,200	$15,100
1950	Styleline	216/92 2dr Spcl Bus Cpe	$3,700	$8,200	$14,100	$20,100

Year	Model	Body Style	4	3	2	1
		216/92 2dr Spcl Spt Cpe	$3,800	$9,500	$16,100	$23,800
		216/92 2dr Dlx Spt Cpe	$5,400	$10,900	$19,100	$26,700
		216/92 2dr Spcl Sdn	$4,700	$10,800	$16,500	$24,300
		216/92 2dr Dlx Sdn	$4,700	$10,800	$16,200	$21,800
		216/92 4dr Spcl Sdn	$3,100	$7,800	$13,200	$17,900
		216/92 4dr Dlx Sdn	$2,600	$7,300	$11,300	$15,100
		216/92 4dr Dlx Wgn	$5,100	$14,000	$23,200	$34,900
		216/92 2dr Dlx Bel Air Cpe	$8,100	$15,200	$24,600	$32,800
		216/92 2dr Dlx Conv	$11,400	$23,200	$45,500	$63,500
1950	Fleetline	216/92 2dr Spcl Sdn	$3,700	$10,900	$15,500	$24,700
		216/92 2dr Dlx Sdn	$3,600	$10,000	$14,700	$20,700
		216/92 4dr Spcl Sdn	$2,800	$8,400	$13,800	$19,600
		216/92 4dr Dlx Sdn	$2,500	$8,200	$11,800	$16,600
1951	Styleline	216/92 2dr Spcl Bus Cpe	$3,600	$8,400	$14,800	$20,400
		216/92 2dr Spcl Spt Cpe	$5,400	$11,400	$21,500	$28,600
		216/92 2dr Dlx Spt Cpe	$5,700	$11,700	$21,800	$30,900
		216/92 2dr Spcl Sdn	$4,100	$9,800	$15,800	$22,000
		216/92 2dr Dlx Sdn	$4,200	$9,900	$16,000	$22,000
		216/92 4dr Spcl Sdn	$3,000	$7,800	$12,000	$16,500
		216/92 4dr Dlx Sdn	$2,800	$7,000	$12,000	$17,800
		216/92 4dr Dlx Wgn	$6,200	$14,800	$25,100	$38,200
		216/92 2dr Dlx Bel Air Cpe	$9,900	$19,000	$29,300	$41,700
		216/92 2dr Dlx Conv	$12,500	$25,500	$49,100	$68,600
1951	Fleetline	216/92 2dr Spcl Sdn	$3,700	$10,800	$15,400	$24,200
		216/92 2dr Dlx Sdn	$4,400	$11,500	$16,200	$26,000
		216/92 4dr Spcl Sdn	$2,500	$8,400	$13,600	$19,900
		216/92 4dr Dlx Sdn	$2,900	$9,200	$14,500	$21,300

Chevrolet

Year	Model	Body Style	4	3	2	1
1952	Styleline	216/92 2dr Spcl Bus Cpe	$3,500	$7,900	$13,500	$20,000
		216/92 2dr Spcl Spt Cpe	$4,700	$9,700	$17,900	$25,900
		216/92 2dr Dlx Spt Cpe	$5,200	$10,400	$18,300	$27,000
		216/92 2dr Spcl Sdn	$4,400	$9,800	$16,200	$22,000
		216/92 2dr Dlx Sdn	$4,200	$9,000	$16,000	$21,900
		216/92 4dr Spcl Sdn	$3,100	$7,800	$11,900	$16,200
		216/92 4dr Dlx Sdn	$3,200	$7,900	$12,300	$16,300
		216/92 4dr Dlx Wgn	$6,200	$14,800	$25,100	$38,200
		216/92 2dr Dlx Bel Air Cpe	$6,800	$16,000	$24,000	$30,800
		216/92 2dr Dlx Conv	$12,200	$23,600	$46,100	$63,700
1952	Fleetline	216/92 2dr Dlx Sdn	$3,900	$10,000	$14,400	$22,800
1953	150	235/108 2dr Bus Cpe	$3,700	$7,500	$13,500	$19,600
		235/108 2dr Clb Cpe	$4,500	$8,800	$14,800	$21,000
		235/108 2dr Sdn	$2,800	$6,800	$10,400	$15,000
		235/108 4dr Sdn	$2,100	$6,000	$9,300	$13,300
		235/108 4dr Handyman Wgn	$6,100	$11,400	$21,500	$35,800
1953	210	235/108 2dr Clb Cpe	$4,200	$9,100	$15,800	$23,100
		235/108 2dr Sdn	$4,000	$9,500	$15,100	$21,400
		235/108 4dr Sdn	$2,900	$7,900	$12,900	$19,200
		235/108 4dr Handyman Wgn	$9,300	$18,000	$29,300	$46,900
		235/108 4dr Twnsmn Wgn	$9,400	$18,400	$30,100	$47,200
		235/108 2dr Spt Cpe	$8,700	$13,300	$21,300	$30,700
		235/108 2dr Conv	$9,400	$17,800	$35,700	$51,700
1953	Bel Air	235/108 2dr Sdn	$6,000	$15,600	$20,400	$27,500
		235/108 4dr Sdn	$3,800	$9,400	$14,700	$21,200
		235/108 2dr Spt Cpe	$9,600	$19,900	$29,600	$42,500
		235/108 2dr Conv	$12,100	$23,000	$42,200	$56,000
1953	Corvette	235/150 2dr Rdstr	$143,000	$189,000	$247,000	$335,000
1954	150	235/115 2dr Uty Sdn	$5,000	$10,600	$17,400	$23,300
		235/115 2dr Sdn	$3,200	$7,500	$11,200	$16,200
		235/115 4dr Sdn	$2,900	$6,600	$10,300	$14,800

Year	Model	Body Style	4	3	2	1
		235/115 4dr Handyman Wgn	$6,600	$10,400	$20,600	$33,600
1954	210	235/115 2dr Delray Clb Cpe	$4,900	$9,900	$15,600	$23,600
		235/115 2dr Sdn	$3,800	$8,500	$12,300	$17,900
		235/115 4dr Sdn	$3,100	$7,000	$11,000	$16,600
		235/115 4dr Handyman Wgn	$8,200	$10,800	$23,600	$34,800
1954	Bel Air	235/115 2dr Sdn	$6,000	$15,300	$20,300	$27,400
		235/115 4dr Sdn	$4,000	$10,400	$16,000	$23,400
		235/115 4dr Twnsmn Wgn	$8,500	$12,500	$25,300	$40,200
		235/115 2dr Spt Cpe	$9,300	$18,800	$28,400	$42,500
		235/115 2dr Conv	$12,200	$24,300	$44,300	$58,200
1954	Corvette	235/150 2dr Rdstr	$36,800	$57,100	$85,100	$131,000
		235/155 2dr Rdstr	$38,100	$60,400	$90,800	$138,000
1955	150	265/162 2dr Uty Sdn	$8,300	$11,200	$19,000	$30,000
		265/162 2dr Sdn	$12,400	$17,500	$26,600	$40,200
		265/162 4dr Sdn	$7,300	$10,900	$16,600	$25,100
		265/162 2dr Handyman Wgn	$7,100	$12,200	$18,000	$35,600

-20% for 6-cyl.

Year	Model	Body Style	4	3	2	1
1955	210	265/162 2dr Sdn	$12,000	$17,400	$24,300	$42,200
		265/162 2dr Delray Clb Cpe	$7,600	$12,200	$20,000	$27,000
		265/162 4dr Sdn	$7,400	$10,700	$14,700	$25,300
		265/162 2dr Handyman Wgn	$10,200	$17,200	$26,600	$43,500
		265/162 4dr Twnsmn Wgn	$8,200	$13,800	$21,300	$35,500
		265/162 2dr Spt Cpe	$8,600	$15,200	$23,500	$34,400

-20% for 6-cyl. +$2,500 for factory a/c.

Year	Model	Body Style	4	3	2	1
1955	Bel Air	265/162 2dr Sdn	$14,300	$25,500	$32,600	$45,600
		265/180 2dr Sdn	$17,500	$27,800	$39,500	$51,600
		265/162 4dr Sdn	$12,000	$15,700	$20,500	$26,500
		265/180 4dr Sdn	$12,200	$17,000	$21,500	$27,800
		265/180 2dr Nomad Wgn	$35,600	$49,900	$60,000	$86,400
		265/162 2dr Nomad Wgn	$34,600	$48,400	$58,200	$83,800
		265/162 4dr Beauville Wgn	$12,000	$17,800	$25,600	$38,400
		265/180 4dr Beauville Wgn	$12,300	$18,300	$26,500	$39,500
		265/162 2dr Spt Cpe	$18,000	$27,800	$38,200	$58,800

Chevrolet

Year	Model	Body Style	4	3	2	1
		265/180 2dr Spt Cpe	$18,000	$28,600	$39,300	$60,500
		265/162 2dr Conv	$27,500	$40,500	$59,500	$100,000
		265/180 2dr Conv	$35,000	$53,000	$82,000	$128,000
				-20% for 6-cyl. +$2,500 for factory a/c.		
1955	Corvette	235/155 2dr Rdstr	$37,500	$57,400	$86,200	$131,000
		265/195 2dr Rdstr	$60,100	$99,500	$139,000	$175,000
1956	150	265/162 2dr Uty Sdn	$8,700	$11,800	$20,000	$31,600
		265/205 2dr Uty Sdn	$9,100	$12,400	$21,000	$33,100
		265/162 2dr Sdn	$13,400	$18,900	$28,800	$43,500
		265/205 2dr Sdn	$14,100	$19,900	$30,300	$45,600
		265/162 4dr Sdn	$7,800	$11,600	$17,700	$26,700
		265/205 4dr Sdn	$8,300	$12,300	$18,500	$27,800
		265/162 2dr Handyman Wgn	$7,500	$12,800	$18,900	$37,500
		265/205 2dr Handyman Wgn	$7,900	$13,500	$19,900	$39,500
						-20% for 6-cyl.
1956	210	265/162 4dr Twnsmn Wgn	$8,300	$14,000	$21,700	$36,100
		265/205 4dr Twnsmn Wgn	$8,800	$15,000	$23,100	$38,500
		265/162 2dr Sdn	$12,400	$17,900	$25,000	$42,700
		265/205 2dr Sdn	$13,000	$18,900	$26,200	$44,800
		265/162 2dr Delray Clb Cpe	$11,800	$17,400	$23,800	$41,700
		265/205 2dr Delray Clb Cpe	$14,200	$20,900	$28,400	$49,900
		265/162 4dr Sdn	$8,100	$11,600	$16,200	$27,800
		265/205 4dr Sdn	$8,600	$12,200	$17,000	$29,300
		265/162 2dr Handyman Wgn	$9,700	$16,500	$25,500	$42,000
		265/205 2dr Handyman Wgn	$10,200	$17,400	$26,900	$44,600
		265/162 4dr Beauville Stn Wgn 9P	$9,100	$15,400	$23,400	$39,800
		265/205 4dr Beauville Stn Wgn 9P	$9,600	$16,200	$25,000	$41,800
		265/162 2dr Spt Cpe	$16,700	$25,200	$36,000	$44,300
		265/205 2dr Spt Cpe	$18,000	$27,400	$39,200	$48,200
		265/162 4dr Spt Sdn	$12,200	$18,000	$24,800	$39,300
		265/205 4dr Spt Sdn	$12,900	$19,000	$26,000	$41,300
						-20% for 6-cyl.

Year	Model	Body Style	4	3	2	1
1956	Bel Air	265/162 2dr Sdn	$16,200	$28,400	$36,400	$50,800
		265/205 2dr Sdn	$18,700	$30,000	$38,400	$53,600
		265/162 4dr Sdn	$8,600	$13,200	$20,800	$26,800
		265/205 4dr Sdn	$12,900	$16,200	$22,200	$29,100
		265/162 2dr Nomad Wgn	$29,100	$44,000	$53,200	$76,300
		265/205 2dr Nomad Wgn	$31,500	$47,900	$57,600	$82,700
		265/162 4dr Beauville Wgn	$12,800	$19,200	$27,400	$40,100
		265/205 4dr Beauville Wgn	$14,000	$21,000	$30,000	$43,500
		265/162 2dr Spt Cpe	$18,000	$27,900	$38,400	$59,000
		265/205 2dr Spt Cpe	$19,400	$30,100	$44,100	$63,800
		265/162 4dr Spt Sdn	$8,700	$12,700	$20,000	$33,900
		265/205 4dr Spt Sdn	$11,000	$16,100	$25,700	$40,100
		265/162 2dr Conv	$34,000	$46,700	$70,000	$111,000
		265/205 2dr Conv	$39,200	$57,500	$84,100	$144,000
						-20% for 6-cyl.
1956	Corvette	265/210 2dr Conv	$29,100	$39,700	$68,500	$99,800
		265/225 2dr Conv	$35,000	$50,600	$83,300	$133,000
		265/240 2dr Conv	$38,200	$59,800	$100,000	$148,000
			-15% for auto. +$1,025 for Wonderbar radio. +$450 for pwr wndws. +$2,900 for pwr top. +$4,050 for hard top.			
1957	150	283/185 2dr Uty Sdn	$9,600	$13,000	$22,000	$34,800
		283/245 2dr Uty Sdn	$10,100	$13,600	$22,600	$36,000
		283/250 FI 2dr Uty Sdn	$10,300	$13,900	$23,000	$36,600
		283/283 FI 2dr Uty Sdn	$12,800	$17,200	$28,700	$45,800
		283/185 2dr Sdn	$14,300	$20,200	$30,800	$46,500
		283/245 2dr Sdn	$15,000	$21,300	$32,400	$48,900
		283/250 FI 2dr Sdn	$15,300	$21,700	$33,000	$49,900
		283/283 FI 2dr Sdn	$17,300	$25,100	$40,000	$58,000
		283/185 4dr Sdn	$8,400	$12,600	$19,200	$29,000
		283/245 4dr Sdn	$8,800	$13,300	$20,200	$30,600
		283/250 FI 4dr Sdn	$9,000	$13,600	$20,700	$31,200
		283/283 FI 4dr Sdn	$10,600	$15,900	$24,300	$36,700
		283/185 2dr Handyman Wgn	$8,200	$13,900	$20,400	$40,600

Chevrolet

Year	Model	Body Style	4	3	2	1
		283/245 2dr Handyman Wgn	$8,400	$14,300	$21,000	$41,700
		283/250 FI 2dr Handyman Wgn	$8,600	$14,600	$21,600	$42,900
		283/283 FI 2dr Handyman Wgn	$10,200	$17,400	$25,700	$51,000
				-20% for 6-cyl. +15% for factory a/c.		
1957	210	265/162 2dr Sdn	$13,000	$18,700	$26,000	$44,800
		283/185 2dr Sdn	$19,100	$26,200	$33,500	$46,800
		283/245 2dr Sdn	$19,100	$26,500	$33,800	$47,200
		283/250 FI 2dr Sdn	$20,500	$29,600	$40,100	$54,700
		283/283 FI 2dr Sdn	$23,300	$32,500	$44,100	$60,100
		283/185 2dr Delray Clb Cpe	$20,200	$26,600	$33,500	$46,600
		283/245 2dr Delray Clb Cpe	$24,600	$32,500	$40,800	$57,100
		283/250 FI 2dr Delray Clb Cpe	$25,100	$33,300	$41,700	$58,400
		283/283 FI 2dr Delray Clb Cpe	$29,800	$39,900	$53,600	$75,800
		265/162 4dr Sdn	$8,300	$11,800	$16,400	$31,200
		283/185 4dr Sdn	$11,900	$16,500	$20,900	$32,400
		283/245 4dr Sdn	$12,100	$16,800	$21,200	$33,000
		283/250 FI 4dr Sdn	$14,000	$19,500	$26,400	$40,400
		283/283 FI 4dr Sdn	$15,400	$21,400	$29,000	$44,300
		265/162 2dr Handyman Wgn	$10,400	$17,800	$27,200	$50,100
		283/185 2dr Handyman Wgn	$12,400	$21,000	$32,200	$58,800
		283/245 2dr Handyman Wgn	$13,000	$22,000	$33,900	$62,000
		283/250 FI 2dr Handyman Wgn	$13,400	$22,500	$34,700	$63,600
		283/283 FI 2dr Handyman Wgn	$15,900	$27,200	$44,300	$82,000
		265/162 4dr Twnsmn Wgn	$8,300	$14,100	$21,800	$36,400
		283/185 4dr Twnsmn Wgn	$9,000	$15,300	$23,500	$42,900
		283/245 4dr Twnsmn Wgn	$10,000	$16,900	$26,000	$47,700
		283/250 FI 4dr Twnsmn Wgn	$10,300	$17,300	$26,700	$48,900
		283/283 FI 4dr Twnsmn Wgn	$12,200	$21,000	$34,100	$63,000
		283/185 4dr Beauville Wgn	$9,700	$16,600	$25,100	$46,800

Year	Model	Body Style	4	3	2	1
		283/245 4dr Beauville Wgn	$10,200	$17,400	$26,600	$48,700
		283/250 FI 4dr Beauville Wgn	$11,700	$19,900	$32,300	$59,600
		283/283 FI 4dr Beauville Wgn	$13,200	$22,500	$36,700	$67,700
		265/162 2dr Spt Cpe	$16,400	$24,600	$35,200	$47,200
		283/185 2dr Spt Cpe	$22,100	$33,600	$47,400	$58,200
		283/245 2dr Spt Cpe	$22,800	$34,600	$48,900	$60,000
		283/250 FI 2dr Spt Cpe	$24,800	$37,700	$58,100	$74,600
		283/283 FI 2dr Spt Cpe	$27,500	$41,900	$64,600	$82,900
		265/162 4dr Spt Sdn	$12,000	$17,200	$23,800	$37,300
		283/185 4dr Spt Sdn	$15,900	$23,500	$32,100	$51,400
		283/245 4dr Spt Sdn	$16,400	$24,200	$33,100	$53,000
		283/250 FI 4dr Spt Sdn	$18,200	$27,500	$40,300	$64,400
		283/283 FI 4dr Spt Sdn	$19,800	$29,900	$43,800	$70,000

-20% for 6-cyl. +15% for factory a/c.

Year	Model	Body Style	4	3	2	1
1957	Bel Air	265/162 2dr Sdn	$19,800	$30,700	$38,700	$55,100
		283/245 2dr Sdn	$24,200	$35,800	$45,300	$63,500
		283/250 FI 2dr Sdn	$28,900	$42,900	$54,600	$75,600
		283/283 FI 2dr Sdn	$28,800	$52,000	$75,300	$103,000
		265/162 4dr Sdn	$12,300	$16,300	$21,100	$27,100
		283/245 4dr Sdn	$13,700	$18,600	$24,000	$30,300
		283/250 FI 4dr Sdn	$15,600	$21,400	$28,500	$35,200
		283/283 FI 4dr Sdn	$17,200	$23,000	$31,400	$42,000
		265/162 2dr Nomad Wgn	$27,000	$47,500	$57,000	$84,800
		283/245 2dr Nomad Wgn	$32,000	$55,600	$67,000	$98,600
		283/250 FI 2dr Nomad Wgn	$36,500	$64,700	$78,300	$114,000
		283/283 FI 2dr Nomad Wgn	$37,900	$68,200	$90,100	$129,000
		265/162 4dr Twnsmn Wgn	$12,900	$19,400	$27,800	$41,400
		283/245 4dr Twnsmn Wgn	$18,800	$23,800	$30,800	$42,700

Chevrolet

Year	Model	Body Style	4	3	2	1
		283/250 FI 4dr Twnsmn Wgn	$19,800	$25,200	$32,100	$46,000
		283/283 FI 4dr Twnsmn Wgn	$22,800	$29,000	$37,200	$53,700
		265/162 2dr Spt Cpe	$21,600	$32,800	$44,300	$68,200
		283/245 2dr Spt Cpe	$25,800	$39,800	$53,200	$74,300
		283/250 FI 2dr Spt Cpe	$28,900	$42,700	$65,200	$81,400
		283/283 FI 2dr Spt Cpe	$30,400	$52,000	$71,200	$97,800
		265/162 4dr Spt Sdn	$18,000	$22,700	$28,400	$42,800
		283/245 4dr Spt Sdn	$23,600	$29,900	$41,500	$58,300
		283/250 FI 4dr Spt Sdn	$26,800	$35,900	$48,000	$66,900
		283/283 FI 4dr Spt Sdn	$27,000	$38,500	$51,700	$71,000
		265/162 2dr Conv	$32,100	$45,000	$64,800	$110,000
		283/245 2dr Conv	$36,600	$52,500	$77,000	$128,000
		283/250 FI 2dr Conv	$41,800	$58,300	$87,400	$140,000
		283/283 FI 2dr Conv	$48,500	$67,500	$102,000	$162,000
				-20% for 6-cyl. +15% for factory a/c.		
1957	Corvette	283/220 2dr Conv	$36,100	$50,700	$88,700	$130,000
		283/245 2dr Conv	$39,000	$62,400	$103,000	$153,000
		283/250 FI 2dr Conv	$45,400	$66,200	$125,000	$155,000
		283/270 2dr Conv	$43,900	$67,300	$112,000	$153,000
		283/283 FI 2dr Conv	$47,300	$71,000	$139,000	$187,000
			-10% for auto trans. +10% for 4-spd. +$1,025 for Wonderbar radio. +$450 for pwr wndws. +$2,900 for pwr top. +$4,050 for hard top.			
1958	Delray	283/185 2dr Uty Sdn	$7,000	$10,200	$13,900	$17,000
		283/270 2dr Uty Sdn	$8,000	$11,600	$16,000	$19,500
		348/250 2dr Uty Sdn	$9,700	$14,200	$19,400	$23,800
		348/280 2dr Uty Sdn	$10,200	$14,700	$20,100	$24,700
		348/315 2dr Uty Sdn	$10,900	$15,500	$21,500	$26,500
		283/185 2dr Sdn	$7,100	$10,300	$14,300	$19,000
		283/270 2dr Sdn	$8,200	$11,600	$16,100	$21,800
		348/250 2dr Sdn	$10,100	$14,100	$19,800	$26,700
		348/280 2dr Sdn	$10,400	$14,900	$20,400	$27,400
		348/315 2dr Sdn	$11,000	$15,600	$21,400	$29,500

Year	Model	Body Style	4	3	2	1
		283/185 4dr Sdn	$4,900	$7,200	$10,200	$14,700
		283/270 4dr Sdn	$5,600	$8,300	$11,700	$16,800
		348/250 4dr Sdn	$6,800	$10,200	$14,300	$20,500
		348/280 4dr Sdn	$6,900	$10,400	$14,700	$21,300
		348/315 4dr Sdn	$7,500	$11,200	$15,700	$22,700
				-20% for 6-cyl. +10% for factory a/c.		
1958	Yeoman	283/185 2dr Wgn	$10,300	$15,800	$22,400	$28,700
		283/270 2dr Wgn	$11,900	$18,300	$25,800	$33,000
		348/250 2dr Wgn	$14,400	$22,300	$31,300	$40,200
		348/280 2dr Wgn	$15,100	$22,900	$32,300	$41,600
		348/315 2dr Wgn	$16,100	$24,800	$34,300	$44,500
		283/185 4dr Wgn	$8,200	$11,800	$15,900	$21,100
		283/270 4dr Wgn	$9,300	$13,300	$18,600	$24,300
		348/250 4dr Wgn	$11,200	$16,200	$22,700	$29,700
		348/280 4dr Wgn	$11,900	$16,700	$23,500	$30,700
		348/315 4dr Wgn	$12,500	$18,100	$25,300	$32,900
				-20% for 6-cyl. +10% for factory a/c.		
1958	Biscayne	283/185 2dr Sdn	$9,200	$12,800	$18,100	$25,400
		283/270 2dr Sdn	$10,700	$14,700	$20,500	$29,300
		348/250 2dr Sdn	$13,100	$17,700	$25,200	$35,400
		348/280 2dr Sdn	$13,400	$18,400	$26,200	$36,500
		348/315 2dr Sdn	$14,600	$19,800	$28,100	$39,000
		283/185 4dr Sdn	$7,200	$9,500	$14,200	$18,800
		283/270 4dr Sdn	$8,200	$11,000	$16,200	$21,700
		348/250 4dr Sdn	$10,100	$13,200	$19,600	$26,400
		348/280 4dr Sdn	$10,400	$13,600	$20,400	$27,100
		348/315 4dr Sdn	$11,100	$14,700	$22,000	$29,300
				-20% for 6-cyl. +10% for factory a/c.		
1958	Brookwood	283/185 4dr Wgn	$8,300	$12,700	$20,600	$30,500
		283/270 4dr Wgn	$9,600	$14,500	$23,800	$34,900
		348/250 4dr Wgn	$11,600	$17,600	$28,800	$42,700
		348/280 4dr Wgn	$11,900	$18,300	$30,000	$44,200
		348/315 4dr Wgn	$13,000	$19,500	$32,000	$47,200
				-20% for 6-cyl. +10% for factory a/c.		
1958	Nomad	283/185 4dr Wgn	$13,100	$17,300	$23,400	$32,200
		283/270 4dr Wgn	$15,000	$20,100	$26,700	$37,300
		348/250 4dr Wgn	$18,400	$24,300	$32,100	$45,100
		348/280 4dr Wgn	$18,900	$25,200	$33,400	$46,700
		348/315 4dr Wgn	$19,600	$26,800	$35,700	$49,800
				-20% for 6-cyl. +10% for factory a/c.		
1958	Bel Air	283/185 2dr Sdn	$11,000	$13,800	$18,900	$25,500
		283/270 2dr Sdn	$12,700	$16,000	$21,600	$29,300
		348/250 2dr Sdn	$15,500	$19,400	$26,400	$35,700
		348/280 2dr Sdn	$16,100	$20,000	$27,500	$36,900
		348/315 2dr Sdn	$17,200	$21,500	$29,200	$39,500
		283/185 4dr Sdn	$6,600	$10,400	$13,500	$19,400
		283/270 4dr Sdn	$7,600	$11,900	$15,600	$22,300
		348/250 4dr Sdn	$9,300	$14,300	$18,900	$27,300
		348/280 4dr Sdn	$9,700	$14,900	$19,600	$28,300

Chevrolet

Year	Model	Body Style	4	3	2	1
		348/315 4dr Sdn	$10,200	$15,800	$21,000	$30,300
		283/185 2dr Spt Cpe	$16,000	$22,000	$32,000	$42,900
		283/270 2dr Spt Cpe	$17,700	$25,600	$36,700	$49,200
		348/250 2dr Spt Cpe	$20,900	$31,200	$44,500	$59,800
		348/280 2dr Spt Cpe	$22,000	$32,500	$46,700	$62,100
		348/315 2dr Spt Cpe	$23,600	$34,600	$49,300	$66,200
		283/185 2dr Impala Spt Cpe	$25,400	$32,700	$40,300	$52,600
		283/270 2dr Impala Spt Cpe	$26,400	$38,000	$57,300	$66,700
		283/290 FI 2dr Impala Spt Cpe	$33,600	$41,300	$67,600	$84,300
		348/250 2dr Impala Spt Cpe	$38,100	$46,600	$69,600	$81,000
		348/280 2dr Impala Spt Cpe	$40,200	$48,400	$71,800	$75,600
		348/315 2dr Impala Spt Cpe	$42,800	$52,400	$77,200	$88,400
		283/185 4dr Spt Sdn	$12,200	$17,100	$23,100	$34,200
		283/270 4dr Spt Sdn	$14,200	$19,400	$26,700	$39,400
		348/250 4dr Spt Sdn	$17,400	$23,800	$32,400	$47,900
		348/280 4dr Spt Sdn	$18,000	$24,900	$33,700	$49,600
		348/315 4dr Spt Sdn	$19,400	$26,600	$35,900	$53,100
		283/185 2dr Impala Conv	$31,300	$44,200	$63,600	$89,100
		283/270 2dr Impala Conv	$32,800	$46,900	$70,100	$104,000
		283/290 FI 2dr Impala Conv	$37,400	$52,800	$91,600	$139,000
		348/250 2dr Impala Conv	$42,000	$61,900	$86,200	$132,000
		348/315 2dr Impala Conv	$51,000	$75,900	$97,800	$149,000

-20% for 6-cyl. +10% for factory a/c.

Year	Model	Body Style	4	3	2	1
1958	Corvette	283/230 2dr Conv	$32,200	$46,800	$74,100	$111,000
		283/245 2dr Conv	$35,100	$55,600	$98,500	$147,000
		283/250 FI 2dr Conv	$39,800	$59,300	$113,000	$159,000
		283/270 2dr Conv	$38,000	$58,500	$101,000	$148,000
		283/290 FI 2dr Conv	$47,800	$84,000	$131,000	$166,000

Year	Model	Body Style	4	3	2	1
			-10% for auto trans. +10% for 4-spd. +25% for HD brakes and suspension. +$1,025 for Wonderbar radio. +$450 for pwr wndws. +$2,900 for pwr top. +$4,050 for hard top.			
1959	Biscayne	283/185 2dr Sdn	$6,800	$8,900	$14,800	$27,400
		283/230 2dr Sdn	$7,800	$10,200	$16,900	$31,200
		283/250 FI 2dr Sdn	$9,200	$11,900	$19,800	$36,500
		348/250 2dr Sdn	$9,500	$12,300	$20,500	$37,900
		348/280 2dr Sdn	$9,900	$12,800	$21,100	$39,200
		283/185 2dr Uty Sdn	$10,000	$12,900	$18,000	$25,200
		283/230 2dr Uty Sdn	$11,700	$14,800	$20,600	$28,800
		283/250 FI 2dr Uty Sdn	$13,500	$17,400	$24,400	$34,000
		348/250 2dr Uty Sdn	$14,200	$18,000	$25,300	$35,300
		348/280 2dr Uty Sdn	$14,600	$18,700	$26,200	$36,500
		283/185 4dr Sdn	$5,300	$8,400	$13,400	$18,000
		283/230 4dr Sdn	$5,800	$9,700	$15,500	$20,800
		283/250 FI 4dr Sdn	$6,900	$11,400	$18,000	$24,400
		348/250 4dr Sdn	$7,300	$11,800	$18,700	$25,300
		348/280 4dr Sdn	$7,400	$12,200	$19,400	$26,200
			-20% for 6-cyl. +10% for factory a/c.			
1959	Brookwood	283/185 2dr Wgn	$8,200	$14,400	$20,400	$31,300
		283/230 2dr Wgn	$9,400	$16,600	$23,500	$36,000
		283/250 FI 2dr Wgn	$11,000	$19,500	$27,800	$42,100
		348/250 2dr Wgn	$11,600	$20,200	$28,700	$43,600
		348/280 2dr Wgn	$11,900	$20,800	$29,700	$45,100
		283/185 4dr Wgn	$7,600	$12,400	$16,800	$24,900
		283/230 4dr Wgn	$8,700	$14,400	$19,400	$28,500
		283/250 FI 4dr Wgn	$10,200	$16,900	$22,800	$33,700
		348/250 4dr Wgn	$10,500	$17,500	$23,500	$34,800
		348/280 4dr Wgn	$10,900	$18,200	$24,500	$36,200
			-20% for 6-cyl. +10% for factory a/c.			
1959	Bel Air	283/185 2dr Sdn	$10,600	$13,700	$18,400	$23,400
		283/230 2dr Sdn	$12,100	$15,900	$21,300	$27,000
		283/250 FI 2dr Sdn	$14,200	$18,800	$24,900	$31,800
		348/250 2dr Sdn	$14,700	$19,400	$25,800	$32,800
		348/280 2dr Sdn	$15,300	$20,200	$26,700	$34,100
		283/185 4dr Sdn	$8,100	$10,300	$14,300	$18,600
		283/230 4dr Sdn	$9,100	$11,800	$16,400	$21,500
		283/250 FI 4dr Sdn	$10,800	$13,800	$19,400	$25,200
		348/250 4dr Sdn	$11,200	$14,300	$20,000	$26,100

Chevrolet

Year	Model	Body Style	4	3	2	1
		348/280 4dr Sdn	$11,500	$14,800	$20,800	$27,100
		283/185 2dr Hdtp Cpe	$16,700	$20,400	$26,600	$36,600
		283/230 2dr Hdtp Cpe	$19,200	$23,400	$30,700	$42,100
		283/250 FI 2dr Hdtp Cpe	$22,500	$27,500	$36,000	$49,400
		348/250 2dr Hdtp Cpe	$23,300	$28,500	$37,300	$51,200
		348/280 2dr Hdtp Cpe	$24,200	$29,500	$38,700	$53,000
		283/185 4dr Spt Sdn	$10,200	$12,800	$18,200	$25,300
		283/230 4dr Spt Sdn	$11,700	$14,700	$21,000	$29,100
		283/250 FI 4dr Spt Sdn	$13,800	$17,400	$24,500	$34,000
		348/250 4dr Spt Sdn	$14,300	$18,100	$25,400	$35,300
		348/280 4dr Spt Sdn	$14,700	$18,700	$26,300	$36,600
				-20% for 6-cyl. +10% for factory a/c.		
1959	Parkwood	283/185 4dr Wgn	$10,000	$13,700	$18,300	$24,800
		283/230 4dr Wgn	$11,500	$15,800	$21,100	$28,800
		283/250 FI 4dr Wgn	$13,500	$18,600	$24,700	$33,900
		348/250 4dr Wgn	$14,000	$19,200	$25,700	$35,000
		348/280 4dr Wgn	$14,500	$19,800	$26,600	$36,100
				-20% for 6-cyl. +10% for factory a/c.		
1959	Kingswood	283/185 4dr Wgn	$10,500	$13,800	$18,700	$26,100
		283/230 4dr Wgn	$12,000	$16,100	$21,600	$30,300
		283/250 FI 4dr Wgn	$14,200	$18,800	$25,400	$35,400
		348/250 4dr Wgn	$14,600	$19,500	$26,200	$36,600
		348/280 4dr Wgn	$15,200	$20,200	$27,200	$38,000
				-20% for 6-cyl. +10% for factory a/c.		
1959	Impala	283/185 4dr Sdn	$6,700	$10,400	$14,400	$20,300
		283/230 4dr Sdn	$7,800	$11,900	$16,400	$23,300
		283/250 FI 4dr Sdn	$9,500	$14,900	$20,500	$28,600
		348/250 4dr Sdn	$9,000	$13,900	$19,100	$27,500
		348/280 4dr Sdn	$9,800	$14,900	$20,900	$29,600
		283/185 2dr Spt Cpe	$21,100	$26,600	$39,800	$50,200
		283/230 2dr Spt Cpe	$24,100	$30,300	$46,800	$57,500
		283/250 FI 2dr Spt Cpe	$30,800	$40,800	$62,500	$79,700
		348/250 2dr Spt Cpe	$30,200	$38,100	$56,800	$73,100

Year	Model	Body Style	4	3	2	1
		348/280 2dr Spt Cpe	$33,400	$44,100	$66,400	$84,300
		283/185 4dr Spt Sdn	$11,300	$13,900	$18,900	$23,100
		283/230 4dr Spt Sdn	$13,100	$16,000	$21,800	$26,700
		283/250 FI 4dr Spt Sdn	$16,300	$19,800	$26,400	$32,200
		348/250 4dr Spt Sdn	$15,900	$18,900	$25,400	$31,400
		348/280 4dr Spt Sdn	$16,500	$20,300	$27,200	$33,400
		283/185 2dr Conv	$34,600	$52,600	$66,200	$82,600
		283/230 2dr Conv	$39,900	$60,700	$76,800	$94,100
		283/250 FI 2dr Conv	$52,400	$81,300	$108,000	$131,000
		348/250 2dr Conv	$51,300	$84,600	$102,000	$128,000
		348/280 2dr Conv	$57,800	$87,900	$125,000	$147,000
				-20% for 6-cyl. +10% for factory a/c.		
1959	Nomad	283/185 4dr Wgn	$12,700	$16,200	$24,600	$34,500
		283/230 4dr Wgn	$14,600	$18,000	$28,200	$39,600
		283/250 FI 4dr Wgn	$18,200	$21,400	$34,200	$48,800
		348/250 4dr Wgn	$17,600	$20,700	$33,100	$46,900
		348/280 4dr Wgn	$18,400	$21,400	$35,600	$49,900
				-20% for 6-cyl. +10% for factory a/c.		
1959	Corvette	283/230 2dr Conv	$28,000	$41,200	$84,600	$113,000
		283/245 2dr Conv	$32,900	$49,500	$86,600	$117,000
		283/250 FI 2dr Conv	$43,100	$64,600	$106,000	$147,000
		283/270 2dr Conv	$36,100	$56,600	$99,500	$146,000
		283/290 FI 2dr Conv	$47,300	$67,700	$116,000	$161,000
			-10% for auto trans. +10% for 4-spd. +25% for HD brakes and suspension. +$1,025 for Wonderbar radio. +$450 for pwr wndws. +$2,900 for pwr top. +$4,050 for hard top.			
1960	Corvair	140/80 2dr 500 Clb Cpe	$2,700	$4,400	$7,000	$9,300
		140/80 2dr 700 Clb Cpe	$2,700	$4,400	$7,100	$9,400
		140/95 2dr Monza 900 Clb Cpe	$3,900	$6,700	$9,800	$13,500
		140/80 4dr 500 Sdn	$2,100	$4,000	$6,600	$8,400
		140/80 4dr 700 Sdn	$2,200	$4,100	$6,700	$8,500
1960	Biscayne	283/170 2dr Sdn	$8,000	$10,200	$16,000	$20,500
		283/230 2dr Sdn	$9,200	$11,700	$18,100	$23,400
		348/250 2dr Sdn	$11,200	$14,300	$22,100	$28,300
		348/280 2dr Sdn	$11,700	$14,700	$23,000	$29,000

Chevrolet

Year	Model	Body Style	4	3	2	1
		348/305 2dr Sdn	$11,900	$15,100	$23,500	$29,600
		348/320 2dr Sdn	$12,000	$15,300	$23,900	$30,100
		348/335 2dr Sdn	$15,100	$18,200	$28,800	$37,800
		235/135 2dr Uty Sdn	$5,400	$7,300	$12,700	$18,000
		283/230 2dr Uty Sdn	$6,000	$8,400	$14,600	$20,800
		348/250 2dr Uty Sdn	$7,400	$10,200	$17,800	$25,300
		348/280 2dr Uty Sdn	$7,600	$10,700	$18,400	$26,300
		348/305 2dr Uty Sdn	$7,800	$10,900	$18,700	$26,800
		348/320 2dr Uty Sdn	$8,000	$11,000	$19,100	$27,000
		348/335 2dr Uty Sdn	$9,500	$13,200	$22,000	$32,200
		283/230 4dr Sdn	$4,800	$8,700	$13,300	$17,800
		348/250 4dr Sdn	$5,700	$10,700	$16,200	$21,700
		348/280 4dr Sdn	$5,900	$11,100	$16,800	$22,400
		348/305 4dr Sdn	$6,200	$11,200	$17,200	$23,000
		348/320 4dr Sdn	$6,300	$11,400	$17,300	$23,400
		348/335 4dr Sdn	$7,200	$12,900	$19,600	$26,300
		283/170 2dr Brookwood Wgn	$8,800	$12,200	$16,200	$23,800
		283/230 2dr Brookwood Wgn	$10,200	$14,100	$18,700	$27,100
		348/250 2dr Brookwood Wgn	$12,300	$17,300	$22,800	$33,300
		348/280 2dr Brookwood Wgn	$12,800	$17,800	$23,500	$34,500
		348/305 2dr Brookwood Wgn	$13,100	$18,300	$24,100	$35,200
		348/320 2dr Brookwood Wgn	$13,300	$18,500	$24,600	$35,600
		348/335 2dr Brookwood Wgn	$15,100	$20,900	$27,800	$40,300
		283/170 4dr Brookwood Wgn	$7,000	$9,700	$12,900	$18,700
		283/230 4dr Brookwood Wgn	$8,000	$10,900	$14,600	$21,300
		348/250 4dr Brookwood Wgn	$9,900	$13,300	$17,800	$25,900
		348/280 4dr Brookwood Wgn	$10,200	$14,000	$18,600	$26,600
		348/305 4dr Brookwood Wgn	$10,400	$14,300	$19,000	$27,200
		348/320 4dr Brookwood Wgn	$10,500	$14,400	$19,200	$27,800
		348/335 4dr Brookwood Wgn	$11,900	$16,500	$21,800	$31,600

Year	Model	Body Style	4	3	2	1
			-20% for 6-cyl. +$2,000 for factory a/c.			
1960	Bel Air	283/170 2dr Sdn	$7,400	$10,000	$14,400	$19,200
		283/230 2dr Sdn	$8,400	$11,400	$16,400	$22,100
		348/250 2dr Sdn	$10,400	$14,000	$20,100	$26,900
		348/280 2dr Sdn	$10,700	$14,400	$20,800	$27,700
		348/305 2dr Sdn	$10,900	$14,700	$21,300	$28,400
		348/320 2dr Sdn	$11,100	$15,000	$21,600	$28,800
		348/335 2dr Sdn	$15,800	$18,100	$26,000	$39,500
		283/170 4dr Sdn	$5,300	$7,700	$10,100	$13,000
		283/230 4dr Sdn	$6,100	$8,800	$11,600	$15,000
		348/250 4dr Sdn	$7,500	$10,700	$14,100	$18,200
		348/280 4dr Sdn	$7,800	$11,200	$14,400	$18,900
		348/305 4dr Sdn	$8,000	$11,400	$14,700	$19,300
		348/320 4dr Sdn	$8,100	$11,500	$15,000	$19,600
		348/335 4dr Sdn	$9,000	$13,100	$17,000	$22,100
		283/170 4dr Kingswood Stn Wgn 6P	$9,900	$12,600	$18,200	$25,600
		283/230 4dr Kingswood Stn Wgn 6P	$11,300	$14,600	$20,900	$29,700
		348/250 4dr Kingswood Stn Wgn 6P	$13,700	$17,900	$25,400	$35,900
		348/280 4dr Kingswood Stn Wgn 6P	$14,300	$18,600	$26,200	$37,200
		348/305 4dr Kingswood Stn Wgn 6P	$14,500	$18,900	$26,800	$37,900
		348/320 4dr Kingswood Stn Wgn 6P	$14,700	$19,200	$27,200	$38,700
		348/335 4dr Kingswood Stn Wgn 6P	$16,800	$21,700	$30,800	$43,800
		283/170 4dr Parkwood Stn Wgn 9P	$8,500	$11,600	$16,600	$24,100
		283/230 4dr Parkwood Stn Wgn 9P	$9,900	$13,400	$19,100	$27,700
		348/250 4dr Parkwood Stn Wgn 9P	$11,900	$16,400	$23,500	$33,800
		348/280 4dr Parkwood Stn Wgn 9P	$12,300	$17,000	$24,200	$34,800
		348/305 4dr Parkwood Stn Wgn 9P	$12,600	$17,400	$24,600	$35,500

Year	Model	Body Style	4	3	2	1
		348/320 4dr Parkwood Stn Wgn 9P	$12,800	$17,500	$25,000	$35,900
		348/335 4dr Parkwood Stn Wgn 9P	$14,500	$19,800	$28,400	$40,800
		283/170 2dr Spt Cpe	$12,100	$15,700	$21,200	$29,400
		283/230 2dr Spt Cpe	$14,000	$18,200	$24,400	$33,800
		348/250 2dr Spt Cpe	$17,100	$22,100	$29,500	$41,100
		348/280 2dr Spt Cpe	$17,700	$22,900	$30,700	$42,500
		348/305 2dr Spt Cpe	$18,000	$23,300	$31,300	$43,500
		348/320 2dr Spt Cpe	$18,300	$23,600	$31,900	$44,100
		348/335 2dr Spt Cpe	$22,500	$27,800	$40,400	$61,700
		283/170 4dr Spt Sdn	$7,900	$10,600	$15,300	$22,000
		283/230 4dr Spt Sdn	$9,000	$12,300	$17,500	$25,500
		348/250 4dr Spt Sdn	$10,900	$14,900	$21,500	$31,000
		348/280 4dr Spt Sdn	$11,300	$15,600	$22,200	$32,000
		348/305 4dr Spt Sdn	$11,500	$16,100	$22,600	$32,600
		348/320 4dr Spt Sdn	$11,700	$16,200	$23,100	$33,200
		348/335 4dr Spt Sdn	$13,300	$18,100	$26,000	$37,500
				-20% for 6-cyl. +$2,000 for factory a/c.		
1960	Impala	283/170 4dr Sdn	$8,700	$11,500	$14,200	$19,100
		283/230 4dr Sdn	$10,500	$13,400	$16,600	$22,000
		348/250 4dr Sdn	$12,900	$16,300	$20,500	$27,000
		348/280 4dr Sdn	$13,400	$16,700	$21,200	$27,900
		348/305 4dr Sdn	$13,700	$17,300	$21,700	$28,500
		348/320 4dr Sdn	$14,100	$17,600	$22,000	$28,800
		348/335 4dr Sdn	$16,000	$20,000	$24,600	$32,500
		283/170 4dr Nomad Wgn	$13,300	$16,500	$21,500	$30,800
		283/230 4dr Nomad Wgn	$16,100	$19,100	$24,600	$35,000
		348/250 4dr Nomad Wgn	$19,200	$23,300	$29,700	$42,800
		348/280 4dr Nomad Wgn	$19,400	$23,700	$31,500	$44,400
		348/305 4dr Nomad Wgn	$20,400	$25,000	$32,400	$45,400

Year	Model	Body Style	4	3	2	1
		348/320 4dr Nomad Wgn	$20,500	$25,900	$34,000	$48,700
		348/335 4dr Nomad Wgn	$23,700	$28,800	$39,700	$60,200
		283/170 2dr Spt Cpe	$15,600	$19,300	$27,200	$38,800
		283/230 2dr Spt Cpe	$17,700	$22,100	$31,400	$44,600
		348/250 2dr Spt Cpe	$22,700	$28,400	$40,200	$56,900
		348/280 2dr Spt Cpe	$23,600	$29,200	$41,600	$59,400
		348/305 2dr Spt Cpe	$24,100	$29,800	$42,900	$60,700
		348/320 2dr Spt Cpe	$24,400	$30,200	$43,700	$62,600
		348/335 2dr Spt Cpe	$27,900	$35,200	$51,100	$76,300
		283/170 4dr Spt Sdn	$10,500	$13,200	$17,100	$23,200
		283/230 4dr Spt Sdn	$12,000	$15,100	$19,800	$26,900
		348/250 4dr Spt Sdn	$14,600	$18,500	$24,200	$32,500
		348/280 4dr Spt Sdn	$15,300	$19,100	$24,800	$33,800
		348/305 4dr Spt Sdn	$15,700	$19,600	$25,300	$34,500
		348/320 4dr Spt Sdn	$15,900	$19,700	$25,700	$35,000
		348/335 4dr Spt Sdn	$17,800	$22,600	$29,100	$39,600
		283/170 2dr Conv	$29,000	$42,000	$49,400	$69,000
		283/230 2dr Conv	$35,300	$52,400	$62,200	$81,400
		348/250 2dr Conv	$44,200	$63,400	$75,000	$103,000
		348/280 2dr Conv	$48,300	$67,200	$82,700	$114,000
		348/305 2dr Conv	$50,200	$69,300	$85,900	$120,000
		348/320 2dr Conv	$52,500	$74,100	$88,200	$125,000
		348/335 2dr Conv	$54,200	$77,400	$94,800	$134,000

-20% for 6-cyl. +$2,000 for factory a/c.

Year	Model	Body Style	4	3	2	1
1960	Corvette	283/230 2dr Conv	$26,700	$44,000	$71,700	$107,000
		283/245 2dr Conv	$38,200	$56,400	$89,800	$131,000
		283/250 FI 2dr Conv	$41,700	$65,800	$112,000	$154,000
		283/270 2dr Conv	$40,200	$65,900	$112,000	$160,000
		283/290 FI 2dr Conv	$86,200	$102,000	$137,000	$178,000

-10% for auto trans. +10% for 4-spd. +25% for HD brakes and suspension. +$1,025 for Wonderbar radio. +$450 for pwr wndws. +$2,900 for pwr top. +$4,050 for hard top.

Chevrolet

Year	Model	Body Style	4	3	2	1
1961	Corvair	145/80 2dr 500 Clb Cpe	$2,700	$4,400	$7,000	$9,300
		145/80 2dr 700 Clb Cpe	$2,700	$4,400	$7,100	$9,400
		145/98 2dr Monza 900 Clb Cpe	$3,900	$6,700	$9,800	$13,700
		145/80 4dr 500 Sdn	$2,100	$4,000	$6,600	$8,400
		145/80 4dr 700 Sdn	$2,200	$4,100	$6,700	$8,500
		145/98 4dr Monza 900 Sdn	$2,600	$4,800	$7,100	$8,800
		145/80 4dr 500 Lakewood Wgn	$3,100	$5,900	$12,700	$17,300
		145/80 4dr 700 Lakewood Wgn	$3,500	$6,700	$13,000	$17,800
1961	Biscayne	283/170 2dr Sdn	$8,700	$9,900	$13,100	$17,700
		283/230 2dr Sdn	$10,100	$11,500	$15,100	$20,500
		348/250 2dr Sdn	$10,600	$11,900	$15,700	$21,300
		348/280 2dr Sdn	$11,500	$13,000	$17,000	$23,100
		348/305 2dr Sdn	$11,800	$13,100	$17,300	$23,400
		348/340 2dr Sdn	$12,000	$13,400	$17,700	$24,000
		348/350 2dr Sdn	$12,200	$13,600	$17,900	$24,300
		283/230 2dr Uty Sdn	$7,300	$12,100	$13,300	$19,000
		348/250 2dr Uty Sdn	$7,600	$12,500	$14,000	$19,800
		348/280 2dr Uty Sdn	$8,200	$13,700	$15,200	$21,500
		348/305 2dr Uty Sdn	$8,400	$13,800	$15,400	$21,700
		348/340 2dr Uty Sdn	$8,500	$14,200	$15,700	$22,300
		348/350 2dr Uty Sdn	$8,600	$14,300	$15,900	$22,600
		283/170 4dr Sdn	$8,100	$9,400	$11,900	$15,300
		283/230 4dr Sdn	$9,300	$11,000	$13,900	$17,700
		348/250 4dr Sdn	$9,700	$11,400	$14,300	$18,500
		348/280 4dr Sdn	$10,400	$12,200	$15,500	$20,000
		348/305 4dr Sdn	$10,600	$12,400	$15,700	$20,300
		348/340 4dr Sdn	$10,800	$12,700	$16,200	$20,700
		348/350 4dr Sdn	$11,000	$13,000	$16,400	$21,100
		283/170 4dr Brookwood Stn Wgn 6P	$9,200	$11,300	$15,400	$21,800
		283/230 4dr Brookwood Stn Wgn 6P	$10,600	$12,900	$17,800	$25,100
		348/250 4dr Brookwood Stn Wgn 6P	$11,000	$13,500	$18,600	$26,100

Year	Model	Body Style	4	3	2	1
		348/280 4dr Brookwood Stn Wgn 6P	$12,000	$14,500	$20,200	$28,300
		348/305 4dr Brookwood Stn Wgn 6P	$12,200	$14,800	$20,400	$28,800
		348/340 4dr Brookwood Stn Wgn 6P	$12,500	$15,200	$20,900	$29,500
		348/350 4dr Brookwood Stn Wgn 6P	$12,600	$15,400	$21,300	$29,900
			-20% for 6-cyl. +$2,000 for factory a/c.			
1961	Bel Air	283/170 2dr Sdn	$8,400	$10,700	$14,300	$19,600
		283/230 2dr Sdn	$9,600	$12,100	$16,500	$22,600
		348/250 2dr Sdn	$9,800	$12,300	$16,800	$22,900
		348/280 2dr Sdn	$10,800	$13,400	$18,200	$25,000
		348/305 2dr Sdn	$10,900	$13,600	$18,500	$25,400
		348/340 2dr Sdn	$11,200	$13,900	$18,900	$25,900
		348/350 2dr Sdn	$11,300	$14,100	$19,100	$26,400
		283/170 4dr Sdn	$5,500	$8,400	$11,100	$15,300
		283/230 4dr Sdn	$6,300	$9,600	$12,700	$17,700
		348/250 4dr Sdn	$6,600	$9,800	$12,900	$18,000
		348/280 4dr Sdn	$7,100	$10,800	$14,200	$19,600
		348/305 4dr Sdn	$7,200	$11,000	$14,500	$20,000
		348/340 4dr Sdn	$7,400	$11,200	$14,800	$20,400
		348/350 4dr Sdn	$7,500	$11,400	$15,000	$20,800
		283/170 4dr Parkwood Stn Wgn 6P	$9,000	$12,000	$16,200	$22,700
		283/230 4dr Parkwood Stn Wgn, 6-p.	$10,400	$13,800	$18,600	$26,000
		348/250 4dr Parkwood Stn Wgn 6P	$10,700	$14,100	$19,000	$26,600
		348/280 4dr Parkwood Stn Wgn 6P	$11,700	$15,500	$20,600	$28,900
		348/305 4dr Parkwood Stn Wgn 6P	$11,800	$15,700	$21,000	$29,300
		348/340 4dr Parkwood Stn Wgn 6P	$12,100	$16,100	$21,500	$30,100
		348/350 4dr Parkwood Stn Wgn 6P	$12,200	$16,300	$21,800	$30,500
		283/170 2dr Spt Cpe	$15,800	$18,800	$26,300	$37,100
		283/230 2dr Spt Cpe	$18,200	$21,700	$30,300	$42,600
		348/250 2dr Spt Cpe	$18,500	$22,100	$31,000	$43,500

Chevrolet

Year	Model	Body Style	4	3	2	1
		348/280 2dr Spt Cpe	$20,000	$24,100	$33,600	$47,300
		348/305 2dr Spt Cpe	$20,400	$24,400	$34,000	$48,100
		348/340 2dr Spt Cpe	$20,800	$24,900	$34,900	$49,200
		348/350 2dr Spt Cpe	$21,200	$25,200	$35,400	$49,800
		409/360 2dr Spt Cpe	$30,200	$36,000	$47,800	$65,700
		283/170 4dr Spt Sdn	$7,300	$9,900	$13,700	$19,700
		283/230 4dr Spt Sdn	$8,500	$11,500	$15,700	$22,600
		348/250 4dr Spt Sdn	$8,500	$11,700	$16,100	$23,000
		348/280 4dr Spt Sdn	$9,300	$12,700	$17,400	$25,000
		348/305 4dr Spt Sdn	$9,500	$12,900	$17,500	$25,400
		348/340 4dr Spt Sdn	$9,700	$13,200	$17,900	$25,900
		348/350 4dr Spt Sdn	$9,800	$13,400	$18,200	$26,400
		409/360 4dr Spt Sdn	$18,900	$24,500	$39,200	$55,900
				-20% for 6-cyl. +$2,000 for factory a/c.		
1961	Impala	283/170 2dr Sdn	$10,900	$13,700	$17,100	$24,300
		283/230 2dr Sdn	$12,600	$15,700	$19,500	$28,000
		348/250 2dr Sdn	$12,900	$16,300	$20,800	$29,700
		348/280 2dr Sdn	$13,900	$17,600	$23,100	$32,100
		348/305 2dr Sdn	$14,400	$18,100	$23,600	$33,000
		348/340 2dr Sdn	$14,700	$18,400	$24,200	$33,500
		348/350 2dr Sdn	$15,000	$18,700	$25,300	$35,900
		283/170 4dr Sdn	$8,500	$10,200	$14,600	$21,700
		283/230 4dr Sdn	$9,900	$11,700	$16,700	$25,000
		348/250 4dr Sdn	$10,000	$12,000	$17,700	$26,300
		348/280 4dr Sdn	$10,900	$13,100	$18,800	$28,400
		348/305 4dr Sdn	$11,100	$13,300	$19,200	$28,800
		348/340 4dr Sdn	$11,300	$13,600	$19,300	$29,000
		348/350 4dr Sdn	$11,500	$13,800	$19,700	$29,500
		283/170 4dr Nomad Stn Wgn 6P	$11,600	$14,300	$18,900	$27,400
		283/230 4dr Nomad Stn Wgn 6P	$13,600	$16,700	$21,900	$31,100
		348/250 4dr Nomad Stn Wgn 6P	$13,900	$17,300	$22,700	$33,000

Year	Model	Body Style	4	3	2	1
		348/280 4dr Nomad Stn Wgn 6P	$15,300	$18,500	$24,400	$35,400
		348/305 4dr Nomad Stn Wgn 6P	$15,600	$18,800	$25,200	$36,200
		348/340 4dr Nomad Stn Wgn 6P	$15,900	$19,300	$25,300	$36,700
		348/350 4dr Nomad Stn Wgn 6P	$16,100	$19,700	$25,700	$37,200
		348/350 4dr Nomad Stn Wgn 9P	$31,800	$41,200	$63,300	$84,900
		283/170 2dr Hdtp Cpe	$18,000	$22,700	$30,200	$43,600
		283/230 2dr Hdtp Cpe	$20,600	$26,000	$34,600	$50,100
		348/250 2dr Hdtp Cpe	$21,300	$27,000	$35,700	$52,800
		348/280 2dr Hdtp Cpe	$22,900	$29,200	$38,900	$56,900
		348/305 2dr Hdtp Cpe	$23,300	$29,700	$39,700	$57,500
		348/340 2dr Hdtp Cpe	$24,300	$30,500	$40,400	$59,900
		348/350 2dr Hdtp Cpe	$26,700	$31,800	$42,200	$63,400
		283/170 4dr Hdtp Sdn	$10,000	$12,700	$15,800	$22,300
		283/230 4dr Hdtp Sdn	$11,500	$14,600	$18,200	$25,500
		348/250 4dr Hdtp Sdn	$11,900	$15,200	$18,900	$26,800
		348/280 4dr Hdtp Sdn	$12,900	$16,500	$20,700	$28,700
		348/305 4dr Hdtp Sdn	$13,100	$16,700	$20,800	$29,200
		348/340 4dr Hdtp Sdn	$13,400	$17,000	$21,200	$29,600
		348/350 4dr Hdtp Sdn	$13,500	$17,400	$21,500	$30,100
		283/170 2dr Conv	$21,800	$27,400	$35,000	$51,200
		283/230 2dr Conv	$25,200	$31,600	$40,400	$58,800
		348/250 2dr Conv	$26,000	$32,400	$42,000	$61,000
		348/280 2dr Conv	$28,200	$35,200	$45,500	$66,200
		348/305 2dr Conv	$28,600	$35,800	$45,900	$67,200
		348/340 2dr Conv	$29,200	$36,500	$46,800	$68,400
		348/350 2dr Conv	$50,000	$77,700	$111,000	$168,000

-20% for 6-cyl. +$2,000 for factory a/c.

Chevrolet

Year	Model	Body Style	4	3	2	1
1961	Corvette	283/230 2dr Conv	$30,800	$47,700	$79,000	$108,000
		283/245 2dr Conv	$35,800	$55,700	$82,900	$110,000
		283/270 2dr Conv	$38,800	$61,700	$92,600	$122,000
		283/275 FI 2dr Conv	$41,000	$62,100	$94,500	$131,000
		283/315 FI 2dr Conv	$43,600	$79,700	$105,000	$150,000
		-10% for auto trans. +10% for 4-spd. +25% for HD brakes and suspension. +$1,025 for Wonderbar radio. +$450 for pwr wndws. +$2,900 for pwr top. +$4,050 for hard top.				
1962	Corvair	145/80 2dr 500 Clb Cpe	$2,700	$4,400	$7,100	$9,300
		145/80 2dr 700 Clb Cpe	$2,800	$4,500	$7,400	$9,700
		145/80 2dr Monza Clb Cpe	$3,800	$6,900	$11,500	$15,500
		145/150 2dr Monza Spyder Clb Cpe	$5,500	$8,900	$13,700	$19,400
		145/80 4dr 700 Sdn	$2,200	$4,200	$6,900	$8,700
		145/80 4dr Monza Sdn	$2,700	$4,900	$7,300	$9,000
		145/80 4dr 700 Wgn	$3,200	$6,400	$12,500	$17,800
		145/80 4dr Monza Wgn	$3,900	$7,400	$13,900	$18,600
		145/80 2dr Monza Conv	$6,600	$12,500	$16,000	$23,200
		145/150 2dr Monza Spyder Conv	$7,400	$13,600	$19,400	$27,300
1962	Chevy II	194/120 2dr 300 Sdn	$8,000	$10,000	$13,300	$16,300
		194/120 2dr Nova 400 Sdn	$9,300	$11,800	$16,200	$19,900
		194/120 4dr 300 Sdn	$5,100	$6,700	$7,500	$8,900
		194/120 4dr Nova 400 Sdn	$6,400	$8,300	$10,900	$13,800
		194/120 4dr 300 Wgn	$6,800	$8,500	$11,300	$14,600
		194/120 4dr Nova 400 Wgn	$6,500	$9,400	$12,500	$15,800
		194/120 2dr Nova 400 Spt Cpe	$11,400	$14,400	$19,800	$24,100
		194/120 2dr Nova 400 Conv	$13,700	$17,100	$23,100	$28,400
		-25% for 4-cyl.				
1962	Biscayne	283/170 2dr Sdn	$7,000	$9,900	$12,700	$17,300
		327/250 2dr Sdn	$8,000	$11,500	$14,600	$20,100

Year	Model	Body Style	4	3	2	1
		327/300 2dr Sdn	$8,300	$12,800	$16,300	$21,600
		409/380 2dr Sdn	$24,800	$38,000	$47,000	$59,900
		409/409 2dr Sdn	$29,000	$43,200	$55,000	$71,100
		283/170 4dr Sdn	$4,900	$7,000	$9,600	$14,600
		327/250 4dr Sdn	$5,400	$7,300	$10,500	$15,900
		327/300 4dr Sdn	$5,500	$7,400	$12,400	$18,100
		409/380 4dr Sdn	$23,400	$30,800	$40,300	$46,800
		409/409 4dr Sdn	$28,000	$36,300	$45,100	$52,700
		283/170 4dr Wgn	$8,700	$10,900	$15,300	$20,300
		327/250 4dr Wgn	$9,700	$11,400	$17,000	$22,400
		327/300 4dr Wgn	$10,400	$13,400	$19,000	$26,900
		409/380 4dr Wgn	$24,200	$35,500	$44,900	$56,000
		409/409 4dr Wgn	$27,200	$40,800	$51,000	$65,000

-20% for 6-cyl. +$2,000 for factory a/c.

Year	Model	Body Style	4	3	2	1
1962	Bel Air	283/170 2dr Sdn	$10,000	$13,200	$16,400	$20,700
		327/250 2dr Sdn	$11,000	$13,800	$17,900	$22,700
		327/300 2dr Sdn	$12,000	$15,700	$19,200	$24,500
		409/380 2dr Sdn	$24,700	$28,200	$38,900	$52,000
		409/409 2dr Sdn	$29,400	$46,100	$57,000	$69,200
		283/170 4dr Sdn	$5,500	$8,000	$11,700	$14,700
		327/250 4dr Sdn	$6,000	$8,500	$12,900	$16,200
		327/300 4dr Sdn	$6,900	$9,300	$14,100	$17,600
		409/380 4dr Sdn	$18,900	$25,400	$35,100	$45,200
		409/409 4dr Sdn	$22,100	$36,600	$46,700	$58,700
		283/170 4dr Stn Wgn 6P	$7,800	$12,300	$17,400	$22,500
		327/250 4dr Stn Wgn 6P	$8,500	$12,900	$19,000	$24,600
		327/300 4dr Stn Wgn 6P	$9,200	$14,400	$20,900	$26,800
		409/380 4dr Stn Wgn 6P	$23,500	$29,300	$40,300	$53,900
		409/409 4dr Stn Wgn 6P	$28,300	$33,100	$44,100	$60,100
		283/170 2dr Hdtp Cpe	$13,600	$19,400	$23,800	$31,100
		327/250 2dr Hdtp Cpe	$16,400	$22,300	$28,800	$38,200
		327/300 2dr Hdtp Cpe	$17,600	$25,100	$30,800	$41,100
		409/380 2dr Hdtp Cpe	$24,400	$30,400	$43,300	$56,800
		409/409 2dr Hdtp Cpe	$71,100	$82,800	$109,000	$152,000

-20% for 6-cyl. +$2,000 for factory a/c.

Year	Model	Body Style	4	3	2	1
1962	Impala	283/170 2dr Spt Cpe	$15,300	$19,100	$25,100	$34,700
		327/250 2dr Spt Cpe	$18,400	$22,200	$30,200	$42,700

Chevrolet

Year	Model	Body Style	4	3	2	1
		327/300 2dr Spt Cpe	$19,400	$23,800	$32,500	$45,700
		409/380 2dr Spt Cpe	$31,100	$36,900	$55,000	$75,000
		409/409 2dr Spt Cpe	$47,800	$77,700	$104,000	$119,000
		283/170 4dr Sdn	$9,100	$11,100	$14,900	$18,900
		327/250 4dr Sdn	$9,100	$11,700	$16,200	$20,900
		327/300 4dr Sdn	$9,200	$13,100	$17,100	$22,700
		409/380 4dr Sdn	$19,700	$27,300	$39,100	$54,300
		409/409 4dr Sdn	$27,100	$43,200	$56,800	$70,200
		283/170 4dr Stn Wgn 6P	$7,900	$11,500	$16,600	$27,000
		283/195 4dr Stn Wgn. 6-p.	$8,100	$11,800	$17,100	$27,800
		327/250 4dr Stn Wgn 6P	$8,300	$12,000	$18,300	$29,600
		327/300 4dr Stn Wgn 6P	$9,100	$13,500	$19,700	$32,100
		409/380 4dr Stn Wgn 6P	$25,700	$32,000	$42,800	$60,200
		409/409 4dr Stn Wgn 6P	$28,000	$33,700	$48,100	$70,700
		283/170 4dr Hdtp Sdn	$7,700	$11,500	$15,900	$21,400
		327/250 4dr Hdtp Sdn	$7,800	$12,100	$17,400	$23,700
		327/300 4dr Hdtp Sdn	$9,900	$13,200	$18,900	$25,300
		409/380 4dr Hdtp Sdn	$19,700	$27,300	$39,100	$54,300
		409/409 4dr Hdtp Sdn	$29,600	$45,200	$58,700	$72,900
		283/170 2dr Conv	$23,400	$29,600	$40,000	$54,900
		327/250 2dr Conv	$24,700	$31,200	$43,700	$60,600
		327/300 2dr Conv	$28,100	$35,500	$47,700	$64,900
		409/380 2dr Conv	$40,100	$52,600	$71,900	$106,000
		409/409 2dr Conv	$57,000	$84,400	$119,000	$158,000

+20% for SS. -20% for 6-cyl. +$2,000 for factory a/c.

Year	Model	Body Style	4	3	2	1
1962	Corvette	327/250 2dr Conv	$29,000	$49,800	$73,000	$91,900
		327/300 2dr Conv	$33,600	$54,300	$79,500	$98,900
		327/340 2dr Conv	$37,900	$57,700	$86,900	$117,000
		327/360 FI 2dr Conv	$41,900	$67,100	$103,000	$152,000

-10% for auto trans. +10% for 4-spd. +25% for HD brakes and suspension. +$1,025 for Wonderbar radio. +$450 for pwr wndws. +$2,900 for pwr top. +$4,050 for hard top.

Year	Model	Body Style	4	3	2	1
1963	Corvair	145/80 2dr 500 Clb Cpe	$2,700	$4,300	$7,100	$9,500

Year	Model	Body Style	4	3	2	1
		145/80 2dr 700 Clb Cpe	$2,700	$4,400	$7,300	$9,700
		145/150 2dr Monza Spyder Clb Cpe	$5,300	$8,800	$13,600	$19,500
		145/80 4dr 700 Sdn	$2,200	$4,100	$6,700	$8,700
		145/150 2dr Monza Spyder Conv	$8,100	$15,000	$21,700	$28,600
1963	Chevy II	194/120 2dr 300 Sdn	$8,000	$10,100	$13,400	$16,400
		194/120 4dr 300 Sdn	$5,100	$6,700	$7,500	$8,900
		194/120 4dr Nova 400 Sdn	$6,400	$8,300	$10,800	$16,300
		194/120 4dr 300 Wgn	$6,800	$8,400	$11,300	$14,700
		194/120 4dr Nova 400 Wgn	$6,500	$9,200	$12,500	$16,800
		194/120 2dr Nova 400 Spt Cpe	$10,100	$15,400	$22,200	$36,300
		194/120 2dr Nova 400 Conv	$13,500	$16,800	$24,200	$37,400
			-20% for 4-cyl. +10% for 4-spd. +20% for Super Sport.			
1963	Biscayne	283/195 2dr Sdn	$7,600	$9,500	$12,100	$16,400
		327/250 2dr Sdn	$9,500	$11,700	$15,000	$20,500
		327/300 2dr Sdn	$9,900	$12,100	$15,500	$21,200
		409/340 L33 2dr Sdn	$24,300	$35,200	$44,100	$57,200
		409/400 2dr Sdn	$27,200	$40,600	$51,700	$64,100
		409/425 2dr Sdn	$31,200	$43,500	$55,400	$68,500
		283/195 4dr Sdn	$6,000	$7,500	$9,800	$13,200
		327/250 4dr Sdn	$7,600	$9,300	$12,200	$16,300
		327/300 4dr Sdn	$7,900	$9,600	$12,800	$17,000
		409/340 L33 4dr Sdn	$21,600	$33,200	$40,900	$50,800
		409/400 4dr Sdn	$23,200	$37,100	$44,400	$56,500
		409/425 4dr Sdn	$29,700	$42,200	$49,300	$61,700
		283/195 4dr Wgn	$6,800	$9,200	$13,600	$20,200
		327/250 4dr Wgn	$8,600	$11,300	$16,800	$25,000
		327/300 4dr Wgn	$8,900	$11,700	$17,500	$26,000
		409/340 L33 4dr Wgn	$20,600	$31,300	$40,900	$54,000
		409/400 4dr Wgn	$24,000	$37,900	$50,000	$61,300
		409/425 4dr Wgn	$26,300	$39,300	$51,500	$63,200
				-20% for 6-cyl. +10% for 4-spd.		
1963	Bel Air	283/195 2dr Sdn	$14,800	$17,100	$22,000	$28,000
		327/250 2dr Sdn	$18,600	$21,100	$27,200	$34,800
		327/300 2dr Sdn	$19,400	$21,900	$28,300	$36,100

Chevrolet

Year	Model	Body Style	4	3	2	1
		409/340 L33 2dr Sdn	$19,400	$29,300	$41,200	$53,700
		409/400 2dr Sdn	$22,500	$34,300	$45,000	$58,300
		409/425 2dr Sdn	$30,400	$38,400	$46,900	$60,300
		283/195 4dr Sdn	$7,100	$8,700	$11,400	$15,200
		327/250 4dr Sdn	$9,000	$10,800	$14,200	$18,800
		327/300 4dr Sdn	$9,300	$11,200	$14,800	$19,700
		409/340 L33 4dr Sdn	$17,000	$24,700	$37,100	$47,000
		409/400 4dr Sdn	$21,000	$30,300	$43,200	$55,400
		409/425 4dr Sdn	$24,700	$35,600	$47,900	$59,100
		283/195 4dr Stn Wgn 6P	$8,700	$11,100	$15,500	$22,700
		327/250 4dr Stn Wgn 6P	$10,900	$13,400	$19,200	$27,900
		327/300 4dr Stn Wgn 6P	$11,300	$14,000	$20,000	$29,200
		409/340 L33 4dr Stn Wgn 6P	$21,100	$31,800	$43,200	$55,200
		409/400 4dr Stn Wgn 6P	$25,300	$36,500	$47,100	$58,000
		409/425 4dr Stn Wgn 6P	$26,100	$38,800	$49,800	$63,600

-20% for 6-cyl. +10% for 4-spd.

Year	Model	Body Style	4	3	2	1
1963	Impala	283/195 2dr Spt Cpe	$20,300	$24,100	$30,000	$41,000
		327/250 2dr Spt Cpe	$25,500	$29,500	$37,000	$50,800
		327/300 2dr Spt Cpe	$26,600	$32,300	$40,400	$52,900
		409/340 L33 2dr Spt Cpe	$24,100	$34,600	$50,400	$65,600
		409/400 2dr Spt Cpe	$29,300	$41,100	$55,600	$70,700
		409/425 2dr Spt Cpe	$42,400	$51,500	$63,700	$84,700
		283/195 2dr SS Spt Cpe	$23,900	$28,500	$35,100	$48,200
		327/250 2dr SS Spt Cpe	$30,000	$34,800	$43,400	$59,500
		327/300 2dr SS Spt Cpe	$31,000	$36,100	$45,200	$61,900
		409/340 L33 2dr SS Spt Cpe	$29,200	$41,700	$55,400	$70,300
		409/400 2dr SS Spt Cpe	$32,400	$46,300	$61,400	$78,000
		409/425 2dr SS Spt Cpe	$46,800	$58,100	$69,600	$94,800
		283/195 4dr Sdn	$9,200	$10,800	$14,200	$21,000
		327/250 4dr Sdn	$11,300	$13,300	$17,400	$26,000
		327/300 4dr Sdn	$11,800	$13,800	$18,100	$27,000

Year	Model	Body Style	4	3	2	1
		409/340 L33 4dr Sdn	$17,300	$24,800	$37,100	$51,100
		409/400 4dr Sdn	$18,700	$26,600	$42,000	$57,500
		409/425 4dr Sdn	$22,500	$30,700	$45,900	$61,400
		283/195 4dr Stn Wgn 6P	$8,900	$11,800	$17,400	$25,300
		327/250 4dr Stn Wgn 6P	$11,000	$14,400	$21,400	$31,200
		327/300 4dr Stn Wgn 6P	$11,400	$15,200	$22,600	$32,500
		409/340 L33 4dr Stn Wgn 6P	$20,700	$31,300	$44,600	$56,900
		409/400 4dr Stn Wgn 6P	$24,700	$35,500	$49,200	$61,800
		409/425 4dr Stn Wgn 6P	$27,400	$38,700	$52,000	$67,100
		283/195 4dr Spt Sdn	$12,700	$14,700	$18,100	$25,100
		327/250 4dr Spt Sdn	$16,100	$18,000	$22,600	$31,000
		327/300 4dr Spt Sdn	$16,600	$18,700	$23,400	$32,100
		409/340 L33 4dr Spt Sdn	$18,000	$25,900	$40,300	$54,300
		409/400 4dr Spt Sdn	$21,200	$29,300	$44,400	$60,400
		409/425 4dr Spt Sdn	$24,600	$33,800	$49,000	$65,600
		283/195 2dr Conv	$29,100	$36,300	$43,100	$62,400
		327/250 2dr Conv	$36,300	$44,200	$53,600	$77,200
		327/300 2dr Conv	$37,800	$46,100	$55,800	$80,500
		409/340 L33 2dr Conv	$34,100	$41,800	$55,400	$78,100
		409/400 2dr Conv	$37,400	$45,300	$58,500	$79,200
		409/425 2dr Conv	$50,700	$63,800	$96,900	$130,000
		427/430 2dr Z11 Lightweight Spt Cpe	$252,000	$279,000	$363,000	$441,000
						-20% for 6-cyl. +10% for 4-spd.
1963	Corvette	327/250 L30 2dr Splt-Wdw Cpe	$42,000	$56,000	$102,000	$147,000
		327/300 L75 2dr Splt-Wdw Cpe	$54,100	$80,500	$122,000	$165,000
		327/340 L79 2dr Splt-Wdw Cpe	$59,000	$92,100	$139,000	$183,000
		327/360 FI L84 2dr Splt-Wdw Cpe	$94,000	$124,000	$169,000	$235,000

Chevrolet

Year	Model	Body Style	4	3	2	1
		327/360 FI L84 2dr Z06 (small tank) Splt-Wdw Cpe	$168,000	$213,000	$304,000	$384,000
		327/360 FI L84 2dr Z06 (big tank) Splt-Wdw Cpe	$261,000	$386,000	$468,000	$681,000
		327/250 L30 2dr Conv	$29,500	$43,900	$65,500	$94,000
		327/300 L75 2dr Conv	$28,800	$42,700	$71,700	$96,100
		327/340 L79 2dr Conv	$34,200	$50,600	$84,200	$118,000
		327/360 FI L84 2dr Conv	$40,900	$59,500	$107,000	$152,000
		-10% for auto trans. -20% for 3-spd. +$500 for factory AM/FM radio. +$500 for pwr wndws. +$12,500 for a/c. +$3,700 for hard top. +$10,000 for knock-off wheels (exc Z06 Big Tank Cpe). +$2,500 for leather interior. +$2,500 for pwr strg.				
1964	Corvair	164/95 2dr 500 Clb Cpe	$2,700	$4,600	$7,300	$10,400
		164/95 2dr Monza Clb Cpe	$3,800	$7,300	$11,800	$16,800
		164/95 4dr 700 Sdn	$2,200	$4,400	$7,100	$9,100
		164/95 4dr Monza Sdn	$2,700	$4,800	$7,300	$9,400
		164/150 2dr Monza Spyder Cpe	$5,300	$9,200	$14,500	$20,200
		164/95 2dr Monza Conv	$6,800	$13,300	$17,900	$26,200
		164/150 2dr Monza Spyder Conv	$8,100	$13,800	$21,700	$28,600
1964	Chevy II	283/195 2dr 100 Sdn	$8,000	$9,900	$12,800	$16,000
		283/195 4dr 100 Sdn	$5,100	$6,400	$7,000	$8,600
		283/195 4dr 100 Wgn	$6,800	$8,400	$10,800	$14,300
		-15% for 6-cyl. +15% for 4-spd.				
1964	Nova	283/195 4dr Sdn	$6,400	$8,300	$10,300	$16,200
		283/195 4dr Wgn	$6,500	$9,100	$11,900	$16,500
		283/195 2dr Spt Cpe	$9,300	$11,500	$15,700	$25,300
		283/195 2dr SS Spt Cpe	$10,100	$12,800	$19,200	$33,300
		-15% for 6-cyl. +15% for 4-spd.				
1964	Chevelle	283/195 L32 2dr 300 Sdn	$6,900	$9,200	$11,700	$15,700

Year	Model	Body Style	4	3	2	1
		283/220 L77 2dr 300 Sdn	$7,200	$9,700	$12,300	$16,500
		327/250 L30 2dr 300 Sdn	$8,400	$10,400	$13,400	$17,300
		327/300 L74 2dr 300 Sdn	$8,600	$10,600	$13,000	$17,900
		283/195 L32 4dr 300 Sdn	$6,200	$6,700	$8,600	$10,700
		283/220 L77 4dr 300 Sdn	$6,400	$7,000	$8,900	$11,100
		327/250 L30 4dr 300 Sdn	$6,600	$7,400	$9,100	$11,600
		327/300 L74 4dr 300 Sdn	$6,900	$7,900	$9,700	$12,300
		283/195 L32 4dr Malibu Sdn	$6,700	$7,100	$9,000	$11,800
		283/220 L77 4dr Malibu Sdn	$6,900	$7,700	$9,700	$12,600
		327/250 L30 4dr Malibu Sdn	$7,700	$8,500	$10,300	$13,800
		327/300 L74 4dr Malibu Sdn	$7,900	$8,500	$11,300	$14,200
		283/195 L32 4dr 300 Wgn	$9,300	$11,100	$14,000	$19,900
		283/220 L77 4dr 300 Wgn	$9,800	$11,700	$14,700	$20,900
		327/250 L30 4dr 300 Wgn	$10,700	$12,900	$15,800	$22,500
		327/300 L74 4dr 300 Wgn	$11,200	$13,300	$16,400	$23,300
		283/195 L32 4dr Malibu Stn Wgn 6P	$11,000	$13,600	$17,800	$25,600
		283/220 L77 4dr Malibu Stn Wgn. 6-p.	$11,400	$14,100	$18,500	$26,600
		327/250 L30 4dr Malibu Stn Wgn 6P	$13,100	$16,000	$20,400	$28,900
		327/300 L74 4dr Malibu Stn Wgn 6P	$13,300	$16,800	$21,400	$30,500
		283/195 L32 2dr Malibu Spt Cpe	$12,000	$14,200	$19,400	$27,600
		283/220 L77 2dr Malibu Spt Cpe	$12,300	$15,400	$21,000	$30,500
		327/250 L30 2dr Malibu Spt Cpe	$15,400	$18,200	$22,600	$31,600
		327/300 L74 2dr Malibu Spt Cpe	$16,300	$19,100	$23,300	$32,100
		283/195 L32 2dr Malibu SS Spt Cpe	$19,400	$28,300	$34,800	$48,400

Chevrolet

Year	Model	Body Style	4	3	2	1
		283/220 L77 2dr Malibu SS Spt Cpe	$21,000	$30,600	$37,600	$52,300
		327/250 L30 2dr Malibu SS Spt Cpe	$22,600	$32,500	$39,100	$56,100
		327/300 L74 2dr Malibu SS Spt Cpe	$23,000	$33,700	$41,200	$58,400
		283/195 L32 2dr Malibu Conv	$16,300	$20,800	$27,600	$37,700
		283/220 L77 2dr Malibu Conv	$17,900	$22,000	$29,300	$40,700
		327/250 L30 2dr Malibu Conv	$18,300	$24,700	$30,700	$41,900
		327/300 L74 2dr Malibu Conv	$19,700	$25,900	$31,600	$44,000
		283/195 L32 2dr Malibu SS Conv	$27,600	$32,800	$40,400	$58,000
		283/220 L77 2dr Malibu SS Conv	$29,800	$35,400	$43,600	$62,600
		327/250 L30 2dr Malibu SS Conv	$32,400	$38,700	$47,200	$65,600
		327/300 L74 2dr Malibu SS Conv	$32,900	$38,800	$48,100	$66,100
				-20% for 6-cyl. +15% for 4-spd.		
1964	Biscayne	283/195 2dr Sdn	$7,500	$9,300	$13,600	$15,800
		327/250 L30 2dr Sdn	$8,900	$11,200	$16,600	$19,200
		327/300 L74 2dr Sdn	$9,300	$11,600	$17,400	$20,000
		409/340 L33 2dr Sdn	$26,200	$37,000	$46,000	$60,000
		409/400 L31 2dr Sdn	$28,000	$39,600	$49,200	$64,200
		409/425 L80 2dr Sdn	$33,700	$45,000	$57,100	$70,000
		283/195 4dr Sdn	$5,800	$7,200	$9,100	$11,500
		327/250 L30 4dr Sdn	$6,900	$8,800	$11,100	$13,700
		327/300 L74 4dr Sdn	$7,300	$9,200	$11,600	$14,300
		409/340 L33 4dr Sdn	$24,800	$33,000	$43,800	$54,100
		409/400 L31 4dr Sdn	$26,500	$35,300	$46,900	$57,900
		409/425 L80 4dr Sdn	$31,000	$43,300	$51,100	$64,000
		283/195 4dr Wgn	$6,500	$8,900	$12,600	$17,600
		327/250 L30 4dr Wgn	$7,800	$10,700	$15,400	$21,000
		327/300 L74 4dr Wgn	$8,200	$11,000	$16,000	$21,900

Year	Model	Body Style	4	3	2	1
		409/340 L33 4dr Wgn	$22,500	$32,700	$44,000	$58,100
		409/400 L31 4dr Wgn	$24,100	$35,000	$47,100	$62,200
		409/425 L80 4dr Wgn	$28,200	$42,000	$54,800	$66,400
				-20% for 6-cyl. +10% for 4-spd.		
1964	Bel Air	283/195 2dr Sdn	$14,200	$16,400	$20,600	$24,500
		327/250 L30 2dr Sdn	$17,000	$19,700	$24,600	$29,200
		327/300 L74 2dr Sdn	$17,800	$20,500	$25,800	$30,500
		409/340 L33 2dr Sdn	$18,700	$21,800	$27,100	$32,100
		409/400 L31 2dr Sdn	$21,700	$25,400	$31,600	$37,500
		409/425 L80 2dr Sdn	$24,700	$28,700	$35,800	$42,300
		283/195 4dr Sdn	$6,800	$8,400	$10,600	$13,100
		327/250 L30 4dr Sdn	$8,300	$10,200	$12,800	$15,600
		327/300 L74 4dr Sdn	$8,600	$10,600	$13,300	$16,300
		409/340 L33 4dr Sdn	$9,100	$11,200	$14,100	$18,500
		409/400 L31 4dr Sdn	$10,600	$13,000	$16,500	$21,400
		409/425 L80 4dr Sdn	$11,900	$14,700	$18,600	$23,900
		283/195 4dr Stn Wgn 6P	$8,300	$10,700	$14,400	$19,800
		327/250 L30 4dr Stn Wgn 6P	$9,900	$12,600	$17,500	$23,500
		327/300 L74 4dr Stn Wgn 6P	$10,500	$13,300	$18,200	$24,600
		409/340 L33 4dr Stn Wgn 6P	$11,000	$14,000	$19,200	$26,000
		409/400 L31 4dr Stn Wgn 6P	$12,900	$16,400	$22,300	$30,200
		409/425 L80 4dr Stn Wgn 6P	$14,500	$18,600	$25,200	$34,100
				-20% for 6-cyl. +10% for 4-spd.		
1964	Impala	283/195 L32 2dr Spt Cpe	$12,300	$18,000	$24,700	$35,800
		327/250 L30 2dr Spt Cpe	$14,600	$21,600	$29,900	$43,600
		327/300 L74 2dr Spt Cpe	$17,700	$24,500	$36,700	$50,300
		409/340 L33 2dr Spt Cpe	$25,200	$31,900	$43,100	$60,000

Chevrolet

Year	Model	Body Style	4	3	2	1
		409/400 L31 2dr Spt Cpe	$29,300	$35,700	$46,700	$66,300
		409/425 L80 2dr Spt Cpe	$31,100	$40,200	$50,200	$73,600
		283/195 L32 2dr SS Spt Cpe	$19,700	$29,700	$39,400	$63,000
		327/250 L30 2dr SS Spt Cpe	$24,100	$35,600	$47,600	$75,500
		327/300 L74 2dr SS Spt Cpe	$25,100	$37,200	$49,900	$78,700
		409/340 L33 2dr SS Spt Cpe	$31,200	$43,600	$58,000	$89,800
		409/400 L31 2dr SS Spt Cpe	$34,200	$47,900	$62,600	$98,900
		409/425 L80 2dr SS Spt Cpe	$41,100	$54,600	$69,900	$123,000
		283/195 L32 4dr Sdn	$5,900	$8,500	$11,400	$18,600
		327/250 L30 4dr Sdn	$7,200	$10,400	$13,900	$22,300
		327/300 L74 4dr Sdn	$7,600	$10,900	$14,400	$23,000
		409/340 L33 4dr Sdn	$10,200	$13,800	$18,800	$29,300
		409/400 L31 4dr Sdn	$11,300	$14,800	$20,200	$31,800
		409/425 L80 4dr Sdn	$14,400	$18,900	$27,000	$39,400
		283/195 L32 4dr Stn Wgn 6P	$8,200	$11,300	$15,300	$22,400
		327/250 L30 4dr Stn Wgn 6P	$9,800	$13,600	$18,400	$26,800
		327/300 L74 4dr Stn Wgn 6P	$10,300	$14,200	$19,300	$27,900
		409/340 L33 4dr Stn Wgn 6P	$12,200	$16,700	$23,200	$31,900
		409/400 L31 4dr Stn Wgn 6P	$13,400	$18,700	$26,600	$35,200
		409/425 L80 4dr Stn Wgn 6P	$15,200	$21,500	$29,400	$44,600
		283/195 L32 4dr Hdtp Sdn	$7,900	$11,100	$14,900	$21,800
		327/250 L30 4dr Hdtp Sdn	$9,400	$13,500	$17,900	$26,500
		327/300 L74 4dr Hdtp Sdn	$9,700	$13,900	$18,700	$27,600
		409/340 L33 4dr Hdtp Sdn	$11,800	$16,300	$22,400	$33,100
		409/400 L31 4dr Hdtp Sdn	$12,800	$18,200	$25,500	$36,900
		409/425 L80 4dr Hdtp Sdn	$17,100	$23,800	$31,500	$45,900

Year	Model	Body Style	4	3	2	1
		283/195 L32 2dr Conv	$19,300	$28,200	$37,300	$54,400
		327/250 L30 2dr Conv	$22,700	$33,000	$44,200	$66,100
		327/300 L74 2dr Conv	$23,900	$34,400	$46,100	$69,000
		409/340 L33 2dr Conv	$31,000	$44,100	$56,400	$84,200
		409/400 L31 2dr Conv	$38,300	$48,300	$61,500	$93,600
		409/425 L80 2dr Conv	$48,400	$58,300	$73,100	$115,000
		283/195 L32 2dr SS Conv	$22,500	$32,300	$43,000	$73,600
		327/250 L30 2dr SS Conv	$27,100	$38,600	$52,800	$88,300
		327/300 L74 2dr SS Conv	$28,300	$40,100	$58,500	$93,300
		409/340 L33 2dr SS Conv	$36,000	$51,000	$68,100	$115,000
		409/400 L31 2dr SS Conv	$38,900	$53,000	$73,100	$124,000
		409/425 L80 2dr SS Conv	$55,200	$64,100	$80,800	$156,000
						-15% for 6-cyl.
1964	Corvette	327/250 L30 2dr Cpe	$27,300	$40,800	$56,800	$74,100
		327/300 L75 2dr Cpe	$25,000	$36,200	$57,400	$82,300
		327/365 L76 2dr Cpe	$30,400	$45,500	$63,300	$83,300
		327/375 FI L84 2dr Cpe	$36,800	$52,000	$81,500	$102,000
		327/250 L30 2dr Conv	$26,300	$39,500	$56,600	$74,500
		327/300 L75 2dr Conv	$26,100	$39,800	$59,300	$77,300
		327/365 L76 2dr Conv	$28,100	$41,800	$60,100	$79,100
		327/375 FI L84 2dr Conv	$41,800	$62,300	$91,900	$118,000
						-10% for auto trans. -20% for 3-spd. +$250 for AM/FM radio. +$300 for pwr wndws. +$8,000 for a/c. +$3,700 for hard top. +$10,000 for knock-off wheels. +$7,000 for 36-gal tank. +$1,800 for leather. +$2,500 for pwr strg. +$1,500 for tele strng whl.
1965	Chevy II	283/195 L32 2dr 100 Sdn	$7,200	$9,200	$11,900	$17,100
		283/195 L32 4dr 100 Sdn	$4,800	$5,100	$6,000	$8,700
		283/195 L32 4dr 100 Wgn	$6,400	$9,000	$10,900	$15,700

Chevrolet

Year	Model	Body Style	4	3	2	1
					-15% for 6-cyl. +15% for 4-spd.	
1965	Corvair	164/95 2dr 500 Hdtp Cpe	$2,800	$4,600	$7,300	$12,800
		164/110 2dr Monza Spt Cpe	$4,100	$6,900	$10,800	$18,200
		164/180 2dr Corsa Spt Cpe	$4,700	$8,300	$14,500	$25,100
		164/95 4dr 500 Hdtp Sdn	$2,500	$4,000	$6,300	$10,000
		164/110 4dr Monza Spt Sdn	$2,800	$4,800	$7,400	$11,800
		164/110 2dr Monza Conv	$6,500	$12,500	$17,400	$30,300
		164/180 2dr Corsa Conv	$7,700	$14,300	$22,800	$37,100
1965	Nova	283/195 L32 2dr Spt Cpe	$8,900	$12,500	$17,400	$25,100
		283/195 L32 2dr SS Spt Cpe	$10,100	$14,800	$22,000	$32,200
		283/195 L32 4dr Sdn	$6,400	$8,900	$10,900	$15,700
		283/195 L32 4dr Wgn	$5,700	$7,600	$12,500	$18,000
					-15% for 6-cyl. +15% for 4-spd.	
1965	Chevelle	283/195 L32 2dr 300 Sdn	$6,200	$7,900	$10,900	$16,100
		283/220 L77 2dr 300 Sdn	$6,400	$8,200	$11,300	$16,700
		327/250 L30 2dr 300 Sdn	$6,500	$8,900	$12,100	$17,200
		327/300 L74 2dr 300 Sdn	$8,100	$11,100	$15,100	$21,500
		327/350 L79 2dr 300 Sdn	$7,600	$10,700	$17,000	$28,600
		283/195 L32 4dr 300 Sdn	$4,400	$5,600	$7,500	$10,700
		283/220 L77 4dr 300 Sdn	$4,500	$5,800	$7,700	$11,000
		327/250 L30 4dr 300 Sdn	$5,000	$6,300	$8,400	$11,600
		327/300 L74 4dr 300 Sdn	$5,200	$6,500	$8,700	$12,100
		327/350 L79 4dr 300 Sdn	$4,900	$6,500	$8,800	$12,700
		283/195 L32 4dr Malibu Sdn	$5,300	$6,500	$8,500	$11,800
		283/220 L77 4dr Malibu Sdn	$5,500	$7,000	$9,100	$12,700
		327/250 L30 4dr Malibu Sdn	$5,700	$7,900	$9,700	$13,900

Year	Model	Body Style	4	3	2	1
		327/300 L74 4dr Malibu Sdn	$6,400	$9,000	$11,100	$16,000
		327/350 L79 4dr Malibu Sdn	$7,500	$11,900	$19,600	$30,000
		283/195 L32 2dr 300 Wgn	$7,900	$11,900	$17,100	$22,400
		283/220 L77 2dr 300 Wgn	$8,200	$12,400	$17,900	$23,300
		327/250 L30 2dr 300 Wgn	$8,700	$14,300	$19,500	$25,500
		327/300 L74 2dr 300 Wgn	$12,500	$20,500	$24,600	$29,600
		327/350 L79 2dr 300 Wgn	$14,400	$21,400	$26,800	$33,400
		283/195 L32 4dr Malibu Wgn	$9,100	$13,800	$19,400	$26,400
		283/220 L77 4dr Malibu Wgn	$9,600	$14,500	$20,400	$27,700
		327/250 L30 4dr Malibu Wgn	$10,700	$16,500	$22,300	$29,700
		327/300 L74 4dr Malibu Wgn	$11,600	$17,800	$24,100	$32,100
		327/350 L79 4dr Malibu Wgn	$15,800	$22,300	$27,300	$36,900
		283/195 L32 2dr Malibu Spt Cpe	$8,900	$13,500	$18,500	$27,300
		283/220 L77 2dr Malibu Spt Cpe	$10,300	$15,200	$20,800	$31,200
		327/250 L30 2dr Malibu Spt Cpe	$11,900	$16,600	$22,000	$35,200
		327/300 L74 2dr Malibu Spt Cpe	$13,200	$17,900	$23,500	$36,700
		327/350 L79 2dr Malibu Spt Cpe	$14,300	$22,300	$32,100	$42,200
		283/195 L32 2dr Malibu SS Spt Cpe	$16,700	$23,400	$31,800	$48,200
		283/220 L77 2dr Malibu SS Spt Cpe	$17,400	$24,300	$33,100	$50,100
		327/250 L30 2dr Malibu SS Spt Cpe	$18,600	$26,200	$35,300	$52,800
		327/300 L74 2dr Malibu SS Spt Cpe	$19,700	$27,800	$37,400	$56,000
		327/350 L79 2dr Malibu SS Spt Cpe	$29,200	$39,200	$54,000	$79,600
		396/375 2dr Malibu SS 396 Spt Cpe	$120,000	$168,000	$237,000	$298,000
		283/195 L32 2dr Malibu Conv	$13,300	$18,400	$25,500	$38,900
		283/220 L77 2dr Malibu Conv	$15,500	$20,700	$28,600	$44,500

Chevrolet

Year	Model	Body Style	4	3	2	1
		327/250 L30 2dr Malibu Conv	$16,300	$22,700	$30,700	$46,200
		327/300 L74 2dr Malibu Conv	$17,900	$25,200	$33,200	$49,900
		327/350 L79 2dr Malibu Conv	$20,400	$27,900	$38,900	$55,700
		283/195 L32 2dr Malibu SS Conv	$21,100	$30,000	$39,400	$59,300
		283/220 L77 2dr Malibu SS Conv	$21,900	$31,200	$41,000	$61,700
		327/250 L30 2dr Malibu SS Conv	$23,800	$32,800	$42,900	$64,600
		327/300 L74 2dr Malibu SS Conv	$25,200	$34,800	$45,500	$68,500
		327/350 L79 2dr Malibu SS Conv	$34,600	$45,900	$61,400	$90,800

-30% for 6-cyl. +15% for 4-spd.

Year	Model	Body Style	4	3	2	1
1965	Biscayne	327/250 L30 2dr Sdn	$6,900	$11,900	$15,000	$22,400
		327/300 L74 2dr Sdn	$7,000	$12,600	$15,700	$23,500
		396/325 L35 2dr Sdn	$8,500	$15,000	$19,100	$28,600
		396/425 L78 2dr Sdn	$9,900	$17,200	$22,000	$33,300
		327/250 L30 4dr Sdn	$6,000	$8,400	$11,200	$16,700
		327/300 L74 4dr Sdn	$6,100	$8,800	$11,700	$17,400
		396/325 L35 4dr Sdn	$7,400	$10,800	$13,900	$21,200
		396/425 L78 4dr Sdn	$8,500	$12,400	$16,100	$24,200
		327/250 L30 4dr Wgn	$5,500	$8,900	$12,400	$19,300
		327/300 L74 4dr Wgn	$5,800	$9,300	$13,000	$20,300
		396/325 L35 4dr Wgn	$7,800	$12,500	$17,500	$27,000
		396/425 L78 4dr Wgn	$9,300	$14,700	$20,700	$32,300

-20% for 6-cyl. +10% for 4-spd. +10% for factory a/c.

Year	Model	Body Style	4	3	2	1
1965	Bel Air	283/195 2dr Sdn	$6,400	$10,800	$13,700	$20,500
		283/220 L77 2dr Sdn	$6,700	$11,200	$14,200	$21,300
		327/250 L30 2dr Sdn	$7,000	$12,000	$15,200	$22,600
		327/300 L74 2dr Sdn	$7,200	$12,700	$15,900	$23,900
		396/325 L35 2dr Sdn	$8,700	$15,200	$19,500	$28,800

Year	Model	Body Style	4	3	2	1
		396/425 L78 2dr Sdn	$10,200	$17,600	$22,800	$33,800
		283/195 4dr Sdn	$5,500	$7,800	$10,400	$15,300
		283/220 L77 4dr Sdn	$5,700	$8,100	$10,800	$15,900
		327/250 L30 4dr Sdn	$6,000	$8,600	$11,500	$17,000
		327/300 L74 4dr Sdn	$6,300	$8,900	$11,900	$17,600
		396/325 L35 4dr Sdn	$7,600	$11,000	$14,100	$21,700
		396/425 L78 4dr Sdn	$8,900	$13,100	$16,600	$24,900
		283/195 4dr Stn Wgn	$6,200	$9,100	$12,400	$18,800
		283/220 L77 4dr 2-Seat Stn Wgn	$6,400	$9,500	$12,900	$19,600
		327/250 L30 4dr Stn Wgn	$6,800	$10,200	$13,700	$20,700
		327/300 L74 4dr Stn Wgn	$7,000	$10,900	$13,900	$21,700
		396/325 L35 4dr Stn Wgn	$9,700	$14,200	$18,700	$29,000
		396/425 L78 4dr Stn Wgn	$12,100	$18,000	$24,100	$37,100

-15% for 6-cyl. +10% for 4-spd. +10% for factory a/c.

Year	Model	Body Style	4	3	2	1
1965	Impala	283/195 L32 2dr Hdtp Cpe	$8,500	$12,500	$16,800	$26,300
		283/220 L77 2dr Hdtp Cpe	$8,800	$13,000	$17,500	$27,400
		327/250 2dr Hdtp Cpe	$9,400	$13,600	$18,300	$29,000
		327/300 L74 2dr Hdtp Cpe	$9,800	$14,000	$19,500	$30,400
		396/325 L35 2dr Hdtp Cpe	$11,900	$17,400	$24,100	$37,200
		396/425 L78 2dr Hdtp Cpe	$15,000	$22,000	$30,100	$46,800
		409/340 L33 2dr Hdtp Cpe	$12,200	$17,800	$24,700	$37,700
		283/195 L32 2dr SS Spt Cpe	$13,300	$19,900	$27,400	$42,300
		283/220 L77 2dr SS Spt Cpe	$13,700	$20,500	$28,200	$43,600
		327/250 L30 2dr SS Spt Cpe	$14,800	$22,100	$30,000	$46,300
		327/300 L74 2dr SS Spt Cpe	$15,700	$23,200	$31,500	$48,400
		396/325 L35 2dr SS Spt Cpe	$18,700	$28,000	$39,000	$60,400

Chevrolet

Year	Model	Body Style	4	3	2	1
		396/425 L78 2dr SS Spt Cpe	$23,500	$35,200	$49,300	$76,000
		283/195 L32 4dr Sdn	$5,500	$8,000	$10,400	$16,300
		283/220 L77 4dr Sdn	$5,700	$8,300	$10,800	$17,000
		327/250 4dr Sdn	$6,100	$8,700	$11,400	$17,900
		327/300 L74 4dr Sdn	$6,400	$9,200	$11,900	$18,800
		396/325 L35 4dr Sdn	$7,700	$11,200	$14,700	$23,300
		396/425 L78 4dr Sdn	$9,500	$14,200	$18,600	$29,400
		409/340 L33 4dr Sdn	$8,000	$12,100	$15,200	$23,600
		283/195 L32 4dr Stn Wgn	$6,500	$9,500	$13,000	$20,200
		283/220 L77 4dr 2-Seat Stn Wgn	$6,800	$9,900	$13,500	$21,000
		327/250 L30 4dr Stn Wgn	$7,200	$10,700	$14,100	$22,300
		327/300 L74 4dr Stn Wgn	$7,500	$10,900	$14,800	$23,300
		396/325 L35 4dr Stn Wgn	$10,000	$14,700	$19,700	$31,400
		396/425 L78 4dr Stn Wgn	$16,400	$24,400	$33,100	$51,600
		283/195 L32 4dr Hdtp Sdn	$5,700	$8,200	$10,700	$17,300
		283/220 L77 4dr Hdtp Sdn	$5,900	$8,500	$11,100	$18,000
		327/250 L30 4dr Hdtp Sdn	$6,300	$8,900	$11,700	$18,900
		327/300 L74 4dr Hdtp Sdn	$6,600	$9,400	$12,300	$19,800
		396/325 L35 4dr Hdtp Sdn	$7,900	$11,500	$15,200	$24,800
		396/425 L78 4dr Hdtp Sdn	$9,800	$14,400	$19,200	$31,100
		409/340 L33 4dr Hdtp Sdn	$8,400	$12,400	$15,800	$25,000
		283/195 L32 4dr Caprice Hdtp Sdn	$8,500	$12,100	$16,300	$26,000
		327/250 4dr Caprice Hdtp Sdn	$9,200	$13,400	$18,000	$28,600
		327/300 L74 4dr Caprice Hdtp Sdn	$9,600	$14,300	$18,900	$29,900
		396/325 L35 4dr Caprice Hdtp Sdn	$11,800	$17,300	$23,400	$36,800
		396/425 L78 4dr Caprice Hdtp Sdn	$14,700	$21,600	$29,500	$46,300

Year	Model	Body Style	4	3	2	1
		283/195 L32 2dr Conv	$10,600	$15,700	$21,200	$33,800
		283/220 L77 2dr Conv	$11,000	$16,300	$22,000	$35,200
		327/250 L30 2dr Conv	$11,600	$17,400	$23,100	$37,300
		327/300 L74 2dr Conv	$12,100	$18,200	$24,100	$38,800
		396/325 L35 2dr Conv	$14,700	$22,000	$30,100	$48,200
		396/425 L78 2dr Conv	$18,500	$27,500	$37,500	$60,600
		409/340 L33 2dr Conv	$15,800	$23,600	$31,800	$51,800
		283/195 L32 2dr SS Conv	$17,100	$25,900	$34,100	$52,200
		283/220 L77 2dr SS Conv	$17,800	$26,900	$35,500	$54,300
		327/250 L30 2dr SS Conv	$18,700	$28,200	$37,300	$57,800
		327/300 L74 2dr SS Conv	$19,600	$29,500	$39,300	$59,900
		396/325 L35 2dr SS Conv	$23,900	$36,300	$48,000	$74,600
		396/425 L78 2dr SS Conv	$37,100	$56,200	$74,900	$109,000
		-15% for 6-cyl. +10% for 4-spd. +10% for factory a/c.				
1965	Corvette	327/250 L30 2dr Cpe	$31,400	$46,600	$61,900	$80,600
		327/300 L75 2dr Cpe	$32,900	$50,600	$68,600	$86,900
		327/350 L79 2dr Cpe	$33,300	$49,700	$69,200	$90,100
		327/365 L76 2dr Cpe	$39,700	$59,300	$76,600	$99,400
		327/375 FI L84 2dr Cpe	$49,900	$74,600	$104,000	$132,000
		396/425 L78 2dr Cpe	$53,900	$87,500	$124,000	$154,000
		327/250 L30 2dr Conv	$31,000	$46,300	$64,800	$83,000
		327/300 L75 2dr Conv	$30,600	$47,100	$65,200	$82,400
		327/350 L79 2dr Conv	$34,000	$49,800	$70,600	$91,900
		327/365 L76 2dr Conv	$39,200	$74,700	$104,000	$129,000
		396/425 L78 2dr Conv	$57,200	$95,400	$141,000	$176,000
		327/375 FI L84 2dr Conv	$48,200	$72,600	$103,000	$132,000

Chevrolet

Year	Model	Body Style	4	3	2	1
		-10% for auto trans. -20% for 3-spd. +$300 for pwr wndws. +$8,000 for a/c. +$3,700 for hard top. +$10,000 for knock-off wheels. +$3,500 for 36-gal tank. +$1,800 for leather. +$2,500 for pwr strg. +$2,000 for off-road exhaust. +$2,000 for side-mount exhaust. +$2,200 for teakwood strng whl. +$1,500 for tele strng whl. NOTE: A combination of options on 1965 Corvettes is often worth more than the sum of the preceding values. If you are spending more than you can afford to lose on one of these vehicles, it is prudent to consult a professional.				
1966	Corvair	164/110 2dr 500 Spt Cpe	$3,000	$4,800	$7,400	$12,600
		164/110 2dr Monza Spt Cpe	$4,300	$7,500	$11,900	$18,900
		164/180 2dr Corsa Spt Cpe	$4,700	$8,700	$14,400	$25,600
		164/160 2dr Yenko Stinger Cpe	$24,400	$36,000	$48,800	$77,600
		164/110 4dr Monza Hdtp Sdn	$2,500	$4,400	$7,200	$11,700
		164/110 2dr Monza Conv	$6,400	$10,800	$16,800	$30,900
		164/180 2dr Corsa Conv	$7,700	$13,800	$22,000	$35,600
1966	Chevy II	283/195 L32 2dr 100 Sdn	$7,000	$9,900	$14,100	$18,100
		283/220 L77 2dr 100 Sdn	$7,700	$10,900	$15,500	$19,900
		327/275 L30 2dr 100 Sdn	$13,300	$17,400	$21,200	$33,600
		327/350 L79 2dr 100 Sdn	$19,100	$26,000	$31,300	$45,400
		283/195 L32 4dr 100 Sdn	$5,000	$5,400	$6,500	$9,200
		283/220 L77 4dr 100 Sdn	$6,100	$6,600	$7,800	$11,000
		327/275 L30 4dr 100 Sdn	$7,800	$10,400	$12,600	$20,500
		327/350 L79 4dr 100 Sdn	$11,200	$15,600	$18,600	$27,600
		283/195 L32 4dr 100 Wgn	$6,400	$8,000	$9,400	$13,300
		283/220 L77 4dr 100 Wgn	$7,100	$8,900	$10,300	$14,600
		327/275 L30 4dr 100 Wgn	$7,200	$9,400	$10,800	$16,700
		327/350 L79 4dr 100 Wgn	$8,400	$12,000	$14,400	$21,000
						-15% for 6-cyl. +15% for 4-spd.
1966	Nova	283/195 L32 2dr Spt Cpe	$14,600	$18,800	$25,200	$36,000
		283/220 L77 2dr Spt Cpe	$15,200	$20,100	$27,700	$39,600

Year	Model	Body Style	4	3	2	1
		327/275 L30 2dr Spt Cpe	$17,700	$23,800	$30,000	$45,700
		327/350 L79 2dr Spt Cpe	$25,400	$35,800	$44,300	$61,700
		283/195 L32 2dr SS Spt Cpe	$19,000	$27,700	$39,700	$57,100
		283/220 L77 2dr SS Spt Cpe	$22,800	$33,200	$47,600	$68,500
		327/275 L30 2dr SS Spt Cpe	$26,100	$40,800	$64,400	$94,500
		327/350 L79 2dr SS Spt Cpe	$34,800	$54,400	$85,800	$126,000
		283/195 L32 4dr Sdn	$8,300	$10,700	$13,800	$20,500
		283/220 L77 4dr Sdn	$9,100	$11,700	$15,200	$22,600
		327/275 L30 4dr Sdn	$11,200	$15,000	$19,000	$30,600
		327/350 L79 4dr Sdn	$17,100	$24,000	$29,900	$44,100
		283/195 L32 4dr Wgn	$6,000	$7,800	$9,800	$14,500
		283/220 L77 4dr Wgn	$7,200	$9,100	$11,300	$16,700
		327/275 L30 4dr Wgn	$11,700	$15,800	$19,400	$31,100
		327/350 L79 4dr Wgn	$15,600	$21,100	$25,900	$41,400
						-15% for 6-cyl. +15% for 4-spd.
1966	Chevelle	283/195 L32 2dr 300 Sdn	$7,300	$10,000	$14,000	$20,300
		283/220 L77 2dr 300 Sdn	$8,400	$11,400	$16,100	$23,300
		327/275 L30 2dr 300 Sdn	$9,200	$13,200	$18,000	$27,100
		283/195 L32 4dr 300 Sdn	$5,200	$6,200	$8,400	$11,400
		283/220 L77 4dr 300 Sdn	$5,700	$6,800	$8,200	$12,500
		327/275 L30 4dr 300 Sdn	$6,200	$7,800	$10,400	$14,500
		283/195 L32 4dr 300 Dlx Wgn	$7,100	$11,700	$15,900	$20,800
		283/220 L77 4dr 300 Deluxe Wgn	$7,600	$12,400	$16,800	$22,000
		327/275 L30 4dr 300 Dlx Wgn	$9,000	$14,100	$19,100	$26,200
		283/195 L32 4dr Malibu Wgn	$9,200	$15,300	$20,600	$27,600
		283/220 L77 4dr Malibu Wgn	$10,100	$16,800	$22,700	$30,400

Chevrolet

Year	Model	Body Style	4	3	2	1
		327/275 L30 4dr Malibu Wgn	$11,900	$19,000	$25,500	$34,200
		283/195 L32 2dr Malibu Spt Cpe	$10,400	$14,500	$20,100	$29,800
		283/220 L77 2dr Malibu Spt Cpe	$12,200	$16,400	$22,800	$34,500
		327/275 L30 2dr Malibu Spt Cpe	$14,200	$19,700	$26,700	$44,300
		396/325 L35 2dr SS 396 Spt Cpe	$20,900	$29,800	$39,300	$58,400
		396/360 L34 2dr SS 396 Spt Cpe	$27,600	$38,700	$52,000	$76,100
		396/375 L78 2dr SS 396 Spt Cpe	$30,100	$40,900	$53,400	$91,600
		283/195 L32 4dr Malibu Spt Sdn	$6,000	$7,600	$10,000	$14,000
		283/220 L77 4dr Malibu Spt Sdn	$6,700	$8,300	$11,000	$15,400
		327/275 L30 4dr Malibu Spt Sdn	$6,800	$8,700	$12,000	$16,700
		283/195 L32 2dr Malibu Conv	$16,200	$23,200	$30,900	$46,700
		283/220 L77 2dr Malibu Conv	$19,000	$26,300	$35,100	$54,000
		327/275 L30 2dr Malibu Conv	$20,500	$27,500	$37,100	$59,800
		396/325 L35 2dr SS 396 Conv	$27,200	$37,100	$47,200	$76,500
		396/360 L34 2dr SS 396 Conv	$32,200	$45,000	$61,400	$99,600
		396/375 L78 2dr SS 396 Conv	$56,800	$87,100	$107,000	$129,000
						-50% for 6-cyl. +15% for 4-spd.
1966	Biscayne	283/195 L32 2dr Sdn	$6,100	$10,500	$13,700	$20,600
		283/220 L77 2dr Sdn	$6,200	$10,700	$14,000	$21,000
		327/275 L30 2dr Sdn	$6,800	$11,700	$15,000	$22,400
		396/325 L35 2dr Sdn	$7,800	$13,500	$17,800	$26,800
		427/390 L36 2dr Sdn	$10,900	$17,700	$24,200	$35,200
		427/425 L72 2dr Sdn	$21,000	$37,000	$56,000	$90,000
		283/195 L32 4dr Sdn	$5,200	$7,300	$10,000	$15,000
		283/220 L77 4dr Sdn	$5,500	$7,700	$10,500	$15,800
		327/275 L30 4dr Sdn	$5,800	$8,000	$11,200	$16,700

Year	Model	Body Style	4	3	2	1
		396/325 L35 4dr Sdn	$6,700	$9,400	$13,000	$19,700
		427/390 L36 4dr Sdn	$6,900	$9,500	$13,200	$20,000
		427/425 L72 4dr Sdn	$13,000	$18,500	$25,800	$40,700
		283/195 L32 4dr Wgn	$5,600	$8,100	$11,200	$17,500
		283/220 L77 4dr Wgn	$5,800	$8,300	$11,500	$18,000
		327/275 L30 4dr Wgn	$6,000	$8,800	$12,400	$19,200
		396/325 L35 4dr Wgn	$7,900	$11,700	$15,900	$25,100
		427/390 L36 4dr Wgn	$8,400	$12,600	$16,800	$27,100
		427/425 L72 4dr Wgn	$16,200	$22,000	$31,900	$51,300

-20% for 6-cyl. +10% for 4-spd.

Year	Model	Body Style	4	3	2	1
1966	Bel Air	283/195 L32 2dr Sdn	$6,300	$10,600	$13,900	$20,900
		283/220 L77 2dr Sdn	$6,400	$10,800	$14,200	$21,300
		327/275 L30 2dr Sdn	$7,000	$11,900	$15,100	$22,700
		396/325 L35 2dr Sdn	$8,000	$13,700	$18,000	$27,000
		427/390 L36 2dr Sdn	$11,200	$18,100	$24,500	$35,500
		427/425 L72 2dr Sdn	$20,800	$32,400	$46,900	$67,000
		283/195 L32 4dr Sdn	$5,400	$7,400	$10,000	$15,100
		283/220 L77 4dr Sdn	$5,800	$7,900	$10,700	$16,200
		327/275 L30 4dr Sdn	$6,000	$8,100	$11,300	$17,000
		396/325 L35 4dr Sdn	$6,900	$9,600	$13,200	$19,800
		427/390 L36 4dr Sdn	$7,100	$9,900	$13,700	$20,500
		427/425 L72 4dr Sdn	$13,100	$18,700	$25,700	$39,000
		283/195 L32 4dr Stn Wgn	$6,200	$9,200	$11,800	$18,700
		283/220 L77 4dr 2-Seat Stn Wgn	$6,400	$9,500	$12,200	$19,300
		327/275 L30 4dr Stn Wgn	$6,800	$10,200	$12,900	$20,500
		396/325 L35 4dr Stn Wgn	$8,600	$13,100	$16,700	$26,300

Chevrolet

Year	Model	Body Style	4	3	2	1
		427/390 L36 4dr Stn Wgn	$9,300	$14,000	$18,100	$28,800
		427/425 L72 4dr Stn Wgn	$18,400	$27,400	$35,000	$55,200
					-20% for 6-cyl. +10% for 4-spd.	
1966	Impala	283/195 L32 2dr Spt Cpe	$8,500	$12,300	$16,900	$25,900
		283/220 L77 2dr Spt Cpe	$8,800	$12,800	$17,600	$26,800
		327/275 L30 2dr Spt Cpe	$9,400	$13,600	$18,400	$28,500
		396/325 L35 2dr Spt Cpe	$10,900	$16,300	$22,200	$33,900
		427/390 L36 2dr Spt Cpe	$11,300	$18,400	$26,100	$37,300
		427/425 L72 2dr Spt Cpe	$20,800	$32,400	$47,100	$67,500
		283/220 L77 2dr SS Spt Cpe	$13,400	$20,200	$27,200	$42,300
		327/275 L30 2dr SS Spt Cpe	$14,700	$22,300	$29,800	$46,000
		396/325 L35 2dr SS Spt Cpe	$17,500	$26,300	$35,800	$55,500
		427/390 L36 2dr SS Spt Cpe	$17,700	$26,800	$36,300	$56,500
		427/425 L72 2dr SS Spt Cpe	$32,800	$49,600	$63,600	$96,200
		283/195 L32 4dr Sdn	$5,600	$7,600	$10,000	$15,600
		283/220 L77 4dr Sdn	$5,800	$7,900	$10,400	$16,200
		327/275 L30 4dr Sdn	$6,000	$8,400	$11,200	$17,400
		396/325 L35 4dr Sdn	$6,500	$9,900	$13,500	$20,700
		427/390 L36 4dr Sdn	$7,100	$10,100	$14,000	$21,000
		427/425 L72 4dr Sdn	$13,600	$18,900	$25,300	$38,500
		283/195 L32 4dr Stn Wgn	$6,300	$9,200	$12,500	$19,800
		283/220 L77 4dr 2-Seat Stn Wgn	$6,600	$9,600	$13,000	$20,600
		327/275 L30 4dr Stn Wgn	$6,900	$10,300	$13,900	$22,000
		396/325 L35 4dr Stn Wgn	$10,100	$14,900	$20,800	$32,600
		427/390 L36 4dr Stn Wgn	$14,100	$21,300	$27,200	$49,800
		427/425 L72 4dr Stn Wgn	$22,300	$32,900	$42,800	$71,200

Year	Model	Body Style	4	3	2	1
		283/195 L32 4dr Spt Sdn	$5,800	$8,100	$10,800	$16,800
		283/220 L77 4dr Spt Sdn	$6,000	$8,400	$11,200	$17,500
		327/275 L30 4dr Spt Sdn	$6,300	$8,800	$11,700	$18,400
		396/325 L35 4dr Spt Sdn	$7,000	$10,500	$14,200	$22,200
		427/390 L36 4dr Spt Sdn	$7,200	$10,500	$14,300	$22,400
		427/425 L72 4dr Spt Sdn	$13,700	$19,600	$25,800	$40,600
		283/195 L32 2dr Conv	$11,300	$16,900	$22,600	$35,000
		283/220 L77 2dr Conv	$11,800	$17,600	$23,500	$36,400
		327/275 L30 2dr Conv	$12,500	$18,700	$25,000	$38,500
		396/325 L35 2dr Conv	$14,900	$21,900	$30,100	$46,400
		427/390 L36 2dr Conv	$15,100	$22,300	$30,400	$47,300
		427/425 L72 2dr Conv	$28,100	$41,300	$54,400	$84,300
		283/220 L77 2dr SS Conv	$20,200	$30,300	$39,700	$58,500
		327/275 L30 2dr SS Conv	$22,300	$33,300	$43,500	$64,400
		396/325 L35 2dr SS Conv	$26,400	$39,500	$52,600	$77,800
		427/390 L36 2dr SS Conv	$28,200	$40,900	$54,500	$80,400
		427/425 L72 2dr SS Conv	$52,200	$75,600	$95,200	$136,000

-20% for 6-cyl. +10% for 4-spd.

Year	Model	Body Style	4	3	2	1
1966	Caprice	283/195 L32 2dr Cpe	$10,400	$13,800	$19,100	$27,600
		283/220 L77 2dr Cpe	$10,600	$14,100	$19,500	$28,200
		327/275 L30 2dr Cpe	$11,400	$15,200	$21,000	$30,600
		396/325 L35 2dr Cpe	$13,600	$18,700	$27,300	$39,900
		427/390 L36 2dr Cpe	$14,300	$20,000	$28,800	$43,400
		427/425 L72 2dr Cpe	$18,600	$25,800	$37,500	$57,000
		283/195 L32 4dr Stn Wgn	$6,400	$9,800	$13,400	$20,900
		283/220 L77 4dr 2-Seat Stn Wgn	$6,700	$10,300	$14,100	$21,900

Chevrolet

Year	Model	Body Style	4	3	2	1
		327/275 L30 4dr Stn Wgn	$7,100	$10,700	$14,700	$23,200
		396/325 L35 4dr Stn Wgn	$9,200	$14,400	$19,400	$30,600
		427/390 L36 4dr Stn Wgn	$9,900	$15,900	$21,300	$33,400
		427/425 L72 4dr Stn Wgn	$13,600	$20,900	$29,900	$44,400
		283/195 L32 4dr Hdtp Sdn	$7,400	$10,400	$14,000	$20,500
		283/220 L77 4dr Hdtp Sdn	$7,700	$10,800	$14,600	$21,300
		327/275 L30 4dr Hdtp Sdn	$8,200	$11,500	$15,200	$22,600
		396/325 L35 4dr Hdtp Sdn	$9,700	$13,700	$18,400	$27,200
		427/390 L36 4dr Hdtp Sdn	$9,800	$13,900	$18,700	$27,600
		427/425 L72 4dr Hdtp Sdn	$13,000	$18,400	$24,500	$36,100

-20% for 6-cyl. +10% for 4-spd.

Year	Model	Body Style	4	3	2	1
1966	Corvette	327/300 2dr Cpe	$31,400	$47,200	$64,300	$83,800
		327/350 L79 2dr Cpe	$32,200	$48,100	$67,000	$87,100
		427/390 L36 2dr Cpe	$40,600	$60,800	$89,900	$120,000
		427/425 L72 2dr Cpe	$42,800	$67,800	$94,500	$125,000
		327/300 2dr Conv	$31,700	$47,300	$67,300	$87,500
		327/350 L79 2dr Conv	$35,600	$52,200	$74,200	$96,500
		427/390 L36 2dr Conv	$45,200	$67,600	$93,600	$123,000
		427/425 L72 2dr Conv	$50,500	$77,500	$111,000	$142,000

-10% for auto trans. -20% for 3-spd. +$250 for pwr wndws. +$4,000 for a/c. +$3,700 for hard top. +$10,000 for knock-off wheels. +$5,000 for 36-gal tank. +$1,800 for leather. +$2,500 for pwr strg. +$2,000 for off-road exhaust. +$2,000 for side-mount exhaust. +$2,200 for teakwood strng whl. +$1,500 for tele strng whl. NOTE: A combination of options on 1966 Corvettes is often worth more than the sum of the preceding values. If you are spending more than you can afford to lose on one of these vehicles, it is prudent to consult a professional.

Year	Model	Body Style	4	3	2	1
1967	Corvair	164/95 2dr 500 Spt Cpe	$2,900	$4,800	$7,500	$12,700
		164/110 2dr Monza Spt Cpe	$4,400	$7,600	$11,800	$18,700
		164/95 4dr 500 Spt Sdn	$2,400	$4,100	$6,400	$10,300
		164/110 4dr Monza Spt Sdn	$3,000	$5,000	$7,700	$12,400

Year	Model	Body Style	4	3	2	1
		164/110 2dr Monza Conv	$6,700	$11,800	$16,900	$31,200
		164/160 2dr Yenko Stinger Cpe	$24,400	$36,000	$48,800	$77,600
1967	Chevy II	283/195 L32 2dr 100 Sdn	$6,700	$8,500	$9,700	$14,300
		327/275 L30 2dr 100 Sdn	$6,400	$8,800	$10,900	$16,100
		283/195 L32 4dr 100 Sdn	$4,800	$5,900	$7,000	$10,000
		327/275 L30 4dr 100 Sdn	$6,100	$7,600	$8,600	$12,000
		283/195 L32 4dr 100 Wgn	$6,700	$8,300	$9,700	$14,000
		327/275 L30 4dr 100 Wgn	$6,200	$8,600	$10,700	$15,700
					-20% for 6-cyl.	*+15% for 4-spd.*
1967	Nova	283/195 L32 2dr Spt Cpe	$15,100	$20,500	$26,200	$38,700
		327/275 L30 2dr Spt Cpe	$18,900	$23,500	$30,600	$49,700
		283/195 L32 2dr SS Spt Cpe	$20,300	$29,400	$39,000	$59,500
		327/275 L30 2dr SS Spt Cpe	$23,500	$30,400	$39,100	$66,800
		283/195 L32 4dr Sdn	$8,500	$11,200	$14,400	$21,400
		327/275 L30 4dr Sdn	$9,700	$13,800	$17,900	$25,900
		283/195 L32 4dr Wgn	$6,400	$8,400	$10,700	$16,000
		327/275 L30 4dr Wgn	$7,600	$10,200	$13,200	$19,600
					-15% for 6-cyl.	*+15% for 4-spd.*
1967	Camaro	327/210 LF7 2dr Spt Cpe	$14,600	$20,700	$27,500	$39,500
		327/275 L30 2dr Spt Cpe	$15,900	$22,200	$29,600	$42,600
		350/295 L48 2dr SS Spt Cpe	$19,200	$26,400	$35,000	$48,800
		396/325 L35 2dr SS Spt Cpe	$22,800	$34,700	$45,700	$64,700
		396/375 L78 2dr SS Spt Cpe	$28,900	$40,500	$54,500	$77,300
		302/290 2dr Z/28 Spt Cpe	$41,800	$52,000	$77,600	$101,000
		427/425 L72 2dr Yenko Spt Cpe	$257,000	$313,000	$378,000	$462,000
		327/210 LF7 2dr Conv	$16,700	$23,700	$32,000	$46,500

Chevrolet

Year	Model	Body Style	4	3	2	1
		327/275 L30 2dr Conv	$20,000	$29,000	$38,900	$52,300
		350/295 L48 2dr SS Conv	$22,200	$29,500	$38,500	$67,100
		396/325 L35 2dr SS Conv	$27,500	$38,000	$51,100	$80,000
		396/375 L78 2dr SS Conv	$33,400	$45,900	$59,700	$95,600
		350/295 L48 2dr Indy Pace Car Conv	$36,200	$47,500	$57,700	$90,700
		396/325 L35 2dr Indy Pace Car Conv	$39,900	$50,700	$63,600	$94,100
		396/375 L78 2dr Indy Pace Car Conv	$44,100	$60,200	$76,900	$108,000

+20% for RS pkg. +25% for RS pkg on factory SS and Z/28 cars. +20% for factory 4-spd (exc. Z/28 and Yenko). +10% for JL8 brakes. -30% for 6-cyl. -10% for 3-spd.

Year	Model	Body Style	4	3	2	1
1967	Chevelle	283/195 L32 2dr 300 Sdn	$7,600	$10,600	$15,100	$21,100
		327/275 L30 2dr 300 Sdn	$10,000	$13,300	$18,500	$27,400
		327/325 L79 2dr 300 Sdn	$19,200	$26,100	$33,600	$57,500
		283/195 L32 4dr 300 Sdn	$6,300	$7,700	$10,100	$13,700
		327/275 L30 4dr 300 Sdn	$6,900	$9,100	$12,000	$16,700
		327/325 L79 4dr 300 Sdn	$13,300	$18,100	$23,200	$34,100
		283/195 L32 4dr Malibu Sdn	$6,800	$8,500	$11,700	$16,100
		327/275 L30 4dr Malibu Sdn	$8,200	$10,700	$14,200	$19,500
		327/325 L79 4dr Malibu Sdn	$15,300	$20,600	$26,100	$37,600
		283/195 L32 4dr Malibu Wgn	$10,900	$16,600	$22,100	$28,800
		327/275 L30 4dr Malibu Wgn	$13,300	$19,900	$27,100	$34,100
		327/325 L79 4dr Malibu Wgn	$23,600	$30,900	$38,800	$63,800
		283/195 L32 2dr Malibu Spt Cpe	$11,400	$16,000	$22,500	$32,600
		327/275 L30 2dr Malibu Spt Cpe	$13,100	$18,300	$24,300	$36,300
		327/325 L79 2dr Malibu Spt Cpe	$21,600	$31,100	$38,800	$66,600
		396/325 L35 2dr SS 396 Spt Cpe	$31,500	$44,900	$52,500	$72,200

Year	Model	Body Style	4	3	2	1
		396/375 L78 2dr SS 396 Spt Cpe	$31,200	$41,900	$62,800	$94,500
		396/350 L34 2dr SS 396 Spt Cpe	$35,700	$49,300	$57,600	$77,700
		283/195 L32 4dr Malibu Spt Sdn	$6,900	$9,200	$12,300	$17,500
		327/275 L30 4dr Malibu Spt Sdn	$8,400	$11,400	$14,900	$22,000
		327/325 L79 4dr Malibu Spt Sdn	$15,500	$20,800	$26,300	$40,000
		283/195 L32 2dr Malibu Conv	$21,000	$28,900	$37,500	$55,700
		327/275 L30 2dr Malibu Conv	$20,600	$29,200	$37,200	$61,000
		327/325 L79 2dr Malibu Conv	$27,600	$37,400	$46,700	$78,700
		396/325 L35 2dr SS 396 Conv	$36,400	$53,100	$61,500	$88,300
		396/350 L34 2dr SS 396 Conv	$40,600	$63,100	$74,500	$95,900
		396/375 L78 2dr SS 396 Conv	$45,600	$74,400	$93,600	$117,000
				-50% for 6-cyl. +15% for 4-spd.		
1967	Biscayne	283/195 L32 2dr Sdn	$6,300	$10,900	$13,900	$21,300
		327/275 L30 2dr Sdn	$6,900	$12,000	$15,300	$23,500
		396/325 L35 2dr Sdn	$8,100	$13,900	$18,300	$27,900
		427/385 L36 2dr Sdn	$12,500	$19,100	$24,600	$36,800
		283/195 L32 4dr Sdn	$5,500	$7,600	$10,200	$15,300
		327/275 L30 4dr Sdn	$6,000	$8,500	$11,300	$17,000
		396/325 L35 4dr Sdn	$7,100	$9,900	$13,200	$20,100
		427/385 L36 4dr Sdn	$7,200	$10,000	$13,400	$20,300
		283/195 L32 4dr Wgn	$5,800	$8,400	$11,300	$17,600
		327/275 L30 4dr Wgn	$6,200	$9,200	$12,400	$19,400
		396/325 L35 4dr Wgn	$8,100	$12,000	$16,000	$25,200
		427/385 L36 4dr Wgn	$8,900	$12,900	$17,200	$27,000
				-20% for 6-cyl. +10% for 4-spd.		
1967	Bel Air	283/195 L32 2dr Sdn	$6,500	$11,100	$14,100	$21,500

Chevrolet

Year	Model	Body Style	4	3	2	1
		327/275 L30 2dr Sdn	$7,100	$12,200	$15,400	$23,900
		396/325 L35 2dr Sdn	$8,300	$14,100	$18,500	$28,600
		427/385 L36 2dr Sdn	$12,200	$18,800	$26,200	$38,700
		283/195 L32 4dr Sdn	$5,700	$7,800	$10,400	$15,500
		327/275 L30 4dr Sdn	$7,000	$8,600	$11,700	$17,200
		396/325 L35 4dr Sdn	$7,300	$10,200	$13,500	$20,200
		427/385 L36 4dr Sdn	$7,400	$10,500	$13,800	$20,700
		283/195 L32 4dr Stn Wgn	$6,300	$9,400	$12,100	$19,100
		327/275 L30 4dr Stn Wgn	$6,700	$10,400	$13,300	$20,900
		396/325 L35 4dr Stn Wgn	$8,900	$13,200	$17,100	$27,400
		427/385 L36 4dr Stn Wgn	$9,200	$14,000	$18,100	$29,100
				-20% for 6-cyl. +10% for 4-spd.		
1967	Impala	283/195 L32 2dr Spt Cpe	$8,900	$13,100	$17,600	$27,300
		327/275 L30 2dr Spt Cpe	$9,800	$14,400	$19,400	$30,000
		396/325 L35 2dr Spt Cpe	$11,400	$16,900	$23,300	$36,200
		427/385 L36 2dr Spt Cpe	$12,500	$19,300	$26,600	$39,500
		327/275 L30 2dr SS Spt Cpe	$15,800	$23,600	$31,100	$48,000
		396/325 L35 2dr SS Spt Cpe	$18,700	$27,900	$37,600	$58,100
		427/385 L36 2dr SS 427 Spt Cpe	$21,000	$32,000	$44,700	$69,100
		283/195 L32 4dr Sdn	$5,800	$7,900	$10,500	$16,500
		327/275 L30 4dr Sdn	$7,400	$8,700	$11,800	$18,200
		396/325 L35 4dr Sdn	$7,600	$10,300	$13,900	$21,900
		427/385 L36 4dr Sdn	$7,800	$10,700	$14,200	$22,500
		283/195 L32 4dr Stn Wgn	$6,500	$9,500	$13,000	$20,500
		327/275 L30 4dr Stn Wgn	$7,300	$10,400	$14,500	$22,700
		396/325 L35 4dr Stn Wgn	$9,900	$14,100	$19,600	$30,900

Year	Model	Body Style	4	3	2	1
		427/385 L36 4dr Stn Wgn	$12,900	$18,100	$25,000	$42,600
		283/195 L32 4dr Spt Sdn	$6,000	$8,300	$10,900	$17,400
		327/275 L30 4dr Spt Sdn	$7,400	$9,000	$12,200	$19,100
		396/325 L35 4dr Spt Sdn	$7,800	$10,900	$14,500	$23,000
		427/385 L36 4dr Spt Sdn	$8,100	$11,100	$14,800	$23,600
		283/195 L32 2dr Conv	$12,300	$18,200	$24,500	$37,800
		327/275 L30 2dr Conv	$13,300	$19,800	$27,100	$41,400
		396/325 L35 2dr Conv	$15,800	$23,600	$32,500	$50,000
		427/385 L36 2dr Conv	$16,300	$24,200	$33,400	$51,100
		327/275 L30 2dr SS Conv	$23,200	$33,100	$46,300	$69,200
		396/325 L35 2dr SS Conv	$27,300	$39,000	$55,800	$83,400
		427/385 L36 2dr SS 427 Conv	$35,000	$46,800	$68,700	$94,500
				-20% for 6-cyl. +10% for 4-spd.		
1967	Caprice	283/195 L32 2dr Hdtp Cpe	$9,900	$13,400	$18,300	$26,800
		327/275 L30 2dr Hdtp Cpe	$11,000	$14,800	$20,000	$29,500
		396/325 L35 2dr Hdtp Cpe	$13,200	$18,100	$25,900	$38,600
		427/385 L36 2dr Hdtp Cpe	$13,800	$19,200	$27,600	$41,900
		283/195 L32 4dr Hdtp Sdn	$6,400	$8,900	$11,900	$18,000
		327/275 L30 4dr Hdtp Sdn	$7,000	$9,600	$13,300	$19,800
		396/325 L35 4dr Hdtp Sdn	$8,400	$11,700	$16,000	$23,700
		427/385 L36 4dr Hdtp Sdn	$8,400	$11,800	$16,200	$24,200
		283/195 L32 4dr Stn Wgn	$6,400	$9,300	$12,600	$20,100
		327/275 L30 4dr Stn Wgn	$7,100	$10,300	$14,100	$22,100
		396/325 L35 4dr Stn Wgn	$9,400	$13,500	$18,600	$29,200
		427/385 L36 4dr Stn Wgn	$9,900	$14,500	$19,800	$31,000
				-20% for 6-cyl. +10% for 4-spd.		
1967	Corvette	327/300 2dr Cpe	$34,600	$55,000	$74,400	$95,200

Chevrolet

Year	Model	Body Style	4	3	2	1
		327/350 L79 2dr Cpe	$41,100	$61,400	$85,700	$111,000
		427/390 L36 2dr Cpe	$50,600	$75,700	$113,000	$146,000
		427/400 L68 2dr Cpe	$55,600	$88,000	$127,000	$165,000
		427/435 L71 2dr Cpe	$76,500	$99,800	$142,000	$197,000
		427/435 L89 2dr Cpe	$155,000	$210,000	$273,000	$340,000
		427/430 L88 2dr Cpe	$1.75 mil	$2.05 mil	$2.7 mil	$3.35 mil
		327/300 2dr Conv	$38,700	$57,800	$82,300	$107,000
		327/350 L79 2dr Conv	$41,600	$62,400	$88,700	$116,000
		427/390 L36 2dr Conv	$49,900	$74,000	$113,000	$148,000
		427/400 L68 2dr Conv	$59,900	$91,800	$130,000	$168,000
		427/435 L71 2dr Conv	$75,400	$111,000	$172,000	$238,000
		427/435 L89 2dr Conv	$230,000	$288,000	$347,000	$411,000
		427/430 L88 2dr Conv	$1.65 mil	$1.95 mil	$2.55 mil	$3.15 mil

-10% for auto trans. -20% for 3-spd. +$250 for pwr wndws. +$5,000 for a/c. +$3,700 for hard top. +$12,000 for bolt-on mag wheels. +$5,000 for 36-gal tank. +$1,800 for leather. +$2,500 for pwr strg. +$2,000 for off-road exhaust. +$2,000 for side-mount exhaust. +$1,000 for speed warning speedo. +$1,500 for headrest seats. +$1,500 for tele strng whl. NOTE: A combination of options on 1967 Corvettes is often worth more than the sum of the preceding values. If you are spending more than you can afford to lose on one of these vehicles, it is prudent to consult a professional.

Year	Model	Body Style	4	3	2	1
1968	Corvair	164/95 2dr 500 Spt Cpe	$3,700	$6,400	$9,800	$13,600
		164/110 2dr Monza Spt Cpe	$5,000	$8,800	$12,600	$18,800
		164/110 2dr Monza Conv	$11,400	$18,600	$23,600	$38,100
		164/160 2dr Yenko Stinger Hdtp Cpe	$24,400	$36,000	$48,800	$77,600
1968	Nova	350/295 L48 2dr SS Cpe	$16,000	$23,200	$29,500	$38,500
		307/200 L14 2dr Cpe	$10,500	$15,200	$19,600	$25,200
		396/325 L35 2dr SS Cpe	$24,700	$34,300	$47,300	$62,700
		307/200 L14 4dr Sdn	$5,800	$8,700	$11,100	$14,800

-20% for 6-cyl. +15% for 4-spd. +10% for factory a/c.

Year	Model	Body Style	4	3	2	1
1968	Camaro	327/210 LF7 2dr Spt Cpe	$15,800	$22,000	$27,600	$35,800
		327/275 L30 2dr Spt Cpe	$18,300	$24,400	$30,900	$41,000
		350/295 L48 2dr SS Spt Cpe	$20,600	$28,800	$37,100	$52,200
		396/325 L35 2dr SS Spt Cpe	$27,600	$38,000	$47,200	$65,400
		396/350 L34 2dr SS Spt Cpe	$31,000	$41,700	$51,300	$71,900
		396/375 L78 2dr SS Spt Cpe	$32,100	$44,000	$57,100	$79,400
		396/375 L89 2dr SS Spt Cpe	$65,000	$91,000	$109,000	$130,000
		302/290 2dr Z/28 Spt Cpe	$30,800	$41,800	$60,100	$83,000
		427/425 L72 2dr Yenko Spt Cpe	$250,000	$309,000	$374,000	$455,000
		327/210 LF7 2dr Conv	$18,700	$27,800	$35,500	$44,000
		327/275 L30 2dr Conv	$20,900	$29,000	$37,600	$53,300
		350/295 L48 2dr SS Conv	$24,900	$34,700	$44,000	$61,300
		396/325 L35 2dr SS Conv	$31,300	$43,000	$57,400	$72,000
		396/350 L34 2dr SS Conv	$35,100	$49,900	$62,200	$82,400
		396/375 L78 2dr SS Conv	$36,000	$53,600	$71,100	$88,900

+20% for RS pkg. +25% for RS pkg on factory SS and Z/28 cars. +20% for factory 4-spd (exc. Z/28 and Yenko). +10% for JL8 brakes. -30% for 6-cyl. -10% for 3-spd.

Year	Model	Body Style	4	3	2	1
1968	Chevelle	307/200 L14 2dr 300 Deluxe Cpe	$7,600	$10,100	$13,200	$17,500
		327/250 L73 2dr 300 Deluxe Cpe	$8,300	$10,900	$14,100	$19,200
		327/275 L30 2dr 300 Deluxe Cpe	$8,700	$11,400	$15,200	$21,300
		327/325 L79 2dr 300 Deluxe Cpe	$16,700	$22,600	$31,900	$44,500
		307/200 L14 4dr 300 Deluxe Sdn	$6,300	$7,900	$10,200	$13,700
		327/250 L73 4dr 300 Deluxe Sdn	$7,400	$9,100	$11,400	$14,800
		327/275 L30 4dr 300 Deluxe Sdn	$8,000	$10,800	$13,700	$18,000
		327/325 L79 4dr 300 Deluxe Sdn	$13,300	$17,500	$23,100	$32,100
		307/200 L14 4dr Malibu Sdn	$6,200	$8,300	$10,500	$14,600

Chevrolet

Year	Model	Body Style	4	3	2	1
		327/250 L73 4dr Malibu Sdn	$7,200	$9,500	$11,700	$15,500
		327/275 L30 4dr Malibu Sdn	$8,100	$10,800	$14,100	$18,600
		327/325 L79 4dr Malibu Sdn	$14,900	$20,000	$26,700	$32,500
		307/200 L14 4dr Malibu Wgn	$9,700	$12,600	$16,000	$21,500
		327/250 L73 4dr Malibu Wgn	$10,900	$14,100	$18,500	$24,100
		327/275 L30 4dr Malibu Wgn	$12,600	$17,000	$21,500	$28,500
		327/325 L79 4dr Malibu Wgn	$15,900	$21,200	$26,000	$33,800
		307/200 L14 2dr Malibu Spt Cpe	$10,500	$15,500	$20,800	$27,800
		327/250 L73 2dr Malibu Spt Cpe	$11,400	$16,300	$22,100	$29,900
		327/275 L30 2dr Malibu Spt Cpe	$13,900	$19,600	$25,300	$34,000
		327/325 L79 2dr Malibu Spt Cpe	$21,200	$29,500	$37,800	$49,800
		396/350 L34 2dr SS 396 Spt Cpe	$27,400	$37,000	$47,900	$63,800
		396/375 L78 2dr SS 396 Spt Cpe	$32,100	$41,500	$52,100	$74,200
		396/375 L89 2dr SS 396 Spt Cpe	$63,900	$88,500	$114,000	$138,000
		307/200 L14 4dr Malibu Spt Sdn	$7,200	$8,900	$11,500	$15,100
		327/250 L73 4dr Malibu Spt Sdn	$8,100	$10,600	$13,200	$16,700
		327/275 L30 4dr Malibu Spt Sdn	$9,300	$12,100	$15,600	$20,700
		327/325 L79 4dr Malibu Spt Sdn	$15,800	$20,800	$25,900	$33,100
		307/200 L14 2dr Malibu Conv	$19,700	$26,800	$34,500	$45,100
		327/250 L73 2dr Malibu Conv	$21,300	$29,000	$37,100	$49,600
		327/275 L30 2dr Malibu Conv	$23,100	$32,300	$40,200	$53,800
		327/325 L79 2dr Malibu Conv	$29,000	$39,600	$49,300	$60,000
		396/350 L34 2dr SS 396 Conv	$39,300	$53,800	$66,800	$79,600
		396/375 L78 2dr SS 396 Conv	$51,500	$79,500	$99,400	$123,000
		396/375 L89 2dr SS 396 Conv	$75,800	$103,000	$131,000	$181,000

-50% for 6-cyl. +15% for 4-spd.

Year	Model	Body Style	4	3	2	1
1968	Biscayne	307/200 L14 2dr Sdn	$6,800	$11,900	$14,500	$19,900
		327/250 L73 2dr Sdn	$7,600	$13,600	$16,700	$22,800
		327/275 L30 2dr Sdn	$7,900	$14,100	$17,600	$23,800
		396/325 L35 2dr Sdn	$8,100	$14,800	$18,400	$24,800
		427/385 L36 2dr Sdn	$13,400	$21,000	$27,200	$39,800
		427/425 L72 2dr Sdn	$19,000	$32,700	$44,600	$59,000
		307/200 L14 4dr Sdn	$5,600	$8,300	$10,500	$13,700
		327/250 L73 4dr Sdn	$6,200	$9,400	$12,000	$16,100
		327/275 L30 4dr Sdn	$6,600	$9,700	$12,400	$16,700
		396/325 L35 4dr Sdn	$6,800	$10,300	$12,800	$17,500
		427/385 L36 4dr Sdn	$7,600	$11,500	$14,400	$19,300
		427/425 L72 4dr Sdn	$12,300	$18,500	$23,600	$31,700
		307/200 L14 4dr Wgn	$5,800	$9,700	$11,800	$16,800
		327/250 L73 4dr Wgn	$6,700	$10,900	$13,200	$19,400
		327/275 L30 4dr Wgn	$7,000	$11,500	$13,800	$20,300
		396/325 L35 4dr Wgn	$8,000	$13,200	$15,900	$23,200
		427/385 L36 4dr Wgn	$9,300	$15,500	$18,700	$27,000

-20% for 6-cyl. +10% for factory a/c.

Year	Model	Body Style	4	3	2	1
1968	Bel Air	307/200 L14 2dr Sdn	$6,900	$12,100	$14,700	$20,000
		327/250 L73 2dr Sdn	$7,800	$13,700	$17,000	$23,100
		327/275 L30 2dr Sdn	$8,100	$14,400	$17,800	$24,000
		396/325 L35 2dr Sdn	$8,300	$15,000	$18,600	$25,000
		427/385 L36 2dr Sdn	$12,900	$21,000	$27,900	$39,100
		427/425 L72 2dr Sdn	$19,400	$32,900	$45,300	$60,400
		307/200 L14 4dr Sdn	$5,600	$8,400	$10,600	$13,900
		327/250 L73 4dr Sdn	$6,400	$9,600	$12,100	$16,200

Chevrolet

Year	Model	Body Style	4	3	2	1
		327/275 L30 4dr Sdn	$6,700	$9,800	$12,600	$17,000
		396/325 L35 4dr Sdn	$7,000	$10,500	$13,000	$17,800
		427/385 L36 4dr Sdn	$7,800	$11,800	$14,600	$19,600
		427/425 L72 4dr Sdn	$12,800	$18,900	$23,900	$32,100
		307/200 L14 4dr Stn Wgn	$5,900	$9,900	$12,000	$17,000
		327/250 L73 4dr Stn Wgn	$6,900	$11,100	$13,300	$19,500
		327/275 L30 4dr Stn Wgn	$7,200	$11,700	$14,000	$20,700
		396/325 L35 4dr Stn Wgn	$8,300	$13,400	$16,200	$23,700
		427/385 L36 4dr Stn Wgn	$9,500	$15,600	$18,900	$27,400
		4dr Stn Wgn	$13,500	$22,000	$26,700	$40,000
				-20% for 6-cyl. +10% for factory a/c.		
1968	Impala	307/200 L14 2dr Spt Cpe	$7,900	$12,200	$15,400	$22,100
		327/250 L73 2dr Spt Cpe	$8,300	$12,800	$16,300	$23,200
		327/275 L30 2dr Spt Cpe	$8,700	$13,400	$17,100	$24,100
		327/275 L30 2dr SS Spt Cpe	$14,800	$22,200	$28,200	$38,700
		396/325 L35 2dr SS Spt Cpe	$19,000	$29,100	$37,000	$51,400
		427/385 L36 2dr SS 427 Spt Cpe	$25,300	$37,300	$49,700	$67,800
		307/200 L14 4dr Sdn	$6,900	$10,900	$13,800	$18,900
		327/250 L73 4dr Sdn	$7,200	$11,400	$14,500	$19,800
		327/275 L30 4dr Sdn	$6,300	$9,900	$12,500	$17,300
		307/200 L14 4dr Stn Wgn	$7,000	$11,300	$14,200	$19,800
		327/250 L73 4dr 2-Seat Stn Wgn	$6,700	$10,800	$13,500	$18,900
		327/275 L30 4dr Stn Wgn	$7,400	$11,900	$14,900	$20,600
		307/200 L14 2dr Conv	$13,500	$20,400	$25,900	$35,600
		327/250 L73 2dr Conv	$14,200	$21,400	$27,200	$37,400
		327/275 L30 2dr Conv	$14,900	$22,400	$28,500	$38,800

Year	Model	Body Style	4	3	2	1
		327/275 L30 2dr SS Conv	$18,800	$28,200	$37,100	$54,000
		396/325 L35 2dr SS Conv	$21,900	$33,200	$47,600	$65,600
		427/385 L36 2dr SS 427 Conv	$30,300	$43,600	$63,400	$91,600

-15% for 6-cyl. +10% for factory a/c.

Year	Model	Body Style	4	3	2	1
1968	Caprice	307/200 L14 2dr Cpe	$9,700	$13,700	$17,600	$23,100
		327/250 L73 2dr Cpe	$11,000	$15,800	$21,600	$26,500
		327/275 L30 2dr Cpe	$11,500	$16,600	$21,200	$27,500
		396/325 L35 2dr Cpe	$12,000	$17,700	$24,000	$31,900
		427/385 L36 2dr Cpe	$14,100	$20,900	$28,400	$38,100
		427/425 L72 2dr Cpe	$16,100	$23,900	$32,200	$43,500
		307/200 L14 4dr Stn Wgn	$6,400	$10,400	$13,200	$18,400
		327/250 L73 4dr Stn Wgn	$7,300	$11,800	$15,200	$20,900
		327/275 L30 4dr Stn Wgn	$7,700	$12,400	$16,400	$22,800
		396/325 L35 4dr Stn Wgn	$8,900	$14,400	$18,200	$25,200
		427/385 L36 4dr Stn Wgn	$10,500	$16,900	$21,500	$30,200
		307/200 L14 4dr Hdtp Sdn	$7,000	$10,200	$13,300	$17,100
		327/250 L73 4dr Hdtp Sdn	$8,100	$11,800	$15,200	$19,900
		327/275 L30 4dr Hdtp Sdn	$8,500	$12,200	$15,800	$20,700
		396/325 L35 4dr Hdtp Sdn	$9,000	$13,100	$16,800	$22,000
		427/385 L36 4dr Hdtp Sdn	$10,000	$14,500	$18,900	$24,600
		427/425 L72 4dr Hdtp Sdn	$11,400	$16,800	$21,600	$28,100

-20% for 6-cyl. +10% for factory a/c.

Year	Model	Body Style	4	3	2	1
1968	Corvette	327/300 2dr Cpe	$10,800	$18,500	$32,900	$46,000
		327/350 L79 2dr Cpe	$12,400	$21,000	$36,700	$48,800
		427/390 L36 2dr Cpe	$16,400	$27,100	$47,500	$67,100
		427/400 L68 2dr Cpe	$16,800	$29,000	$49,500	$68,000
		427/435 L71 2dr Cpe	$20,900	$46,300	$66,300	$99,300

Chevrolet

Year	Model	Body Style	4	3	2	1
		427/435 L89 2dr Cpe	$66,700	$81,800	$123,000	$168,000
		427/430 L88 2dr Cpe	$290,000	$382,000	$476,000	$600,000
		327/300 2dr Conv	$13,500	$24,700	$39,600	$53,500
		327/350 L79 2dr Conv	$15,000	$26,800	$42,100	$62,000
		427/390 L36 2dr Conv	$16,100	$28,800	$51,200	$80,000
		427/400 L68 2dr Conv	$17,900	$33,300	$57,700	$82,100
		427/435 L71 2dr Conv	$25,000	$50,000	$74,100	$105,000
		427/435 L89 2dr Conv	$71,000	$91,200	$135,000	$195,000
		427/430 L88 2dr Conv	$356,000	$405,000	$546,000	$684,000
			-10% for auto trans. +10% for 4-spd. +$200 for pwr wndws. +$2,000 for a/c. +$2,200 for hard top. +$900 for leather. +$2,500 for pwr strg. +$1,500 for tele strng whl.			
1969	Corvair	164/95 2dr 500 Spt Cpe	$5,000	$9,200	$13,800	$21,200
		164/110 2dr Monza Spt Cpe	$6,300	$10,800	$16,500	$23,800
		164/110 2dr Monza Conv	$11,700	$18,600	$28,800	$41,400
1969	Nova	396/375 L89 2dr SS Cpe	$82,200	$115,000	$127,000	$152,000
		307/200 L14 2dr Cpe	$10,800	$15,400	$20,000	$25,500
		350/255 LM1 2dr Cpe	$12,300	$18,000	$23,100	$29,200
		396/350 L34 2dr SS Cpe	$30,400	$44,900	$58,500	$78,300
		396/375 L78 2dr SS Cpe	$38,900	$52,300	$67,500	$94,300
		427/425 L72 2dr Yenko Cpe	$253,000	$322,000	$399,000	$480,000
		307/200 L14 4dr Sdn	$6,100	$9,100	$11,500	$14,900
		350/255 LM1 4dr Sdn	$6,800	$10,500	$13,000	$17,000
			+15% for 4-spd exc Yenko. -20% for 6-cyl.			
1969	Camaro	307/200 L14 2dr Spt Cpe	$13,900	$22,700	$28,400	$36,000
		327/210 LF7 2dr Spt Cpe	$16,500	$24,800	$31,300	$39,500
		350/250 L65 2dr Spt Cpe	$19,000	$26,800	$34,100	$42,900
		350/255 LM1 2dr Spt Cpe	$18,100	$24,900	$33,000	$41,000

Year	Model	Body Style	4	3	2	1
		350/300 L48 2dr SS Spt Cpe	$23,200	$32,300	$39,000	$50,300
		396/325 L35 2dr SS Spt Cpe	$25,800	$35,900	$46,400	$59,100
		396/350 L34 2dr SS Spt Cpe	$29,400	$40,200	$53,000	$71,300
		396/375 L78 2dr SS Spt Cpe	$32,000	$42,700	$58,700	$79,900
		396/375 L89 2dr SS Spt Cpe	$68,000	$94,000	$111,000	$132,000
		302/290 2dr Z/28 Spt Cpe	$41,700	$55,400	$69,700	$88,100
		302/290 2dr Z/28 RS Spt Cpe	$46,300	$64,400	$77,900	$97,000
		427/425 L72 2dr Yenko Spt Cpe	$167,000	$210,000	$250,000	$335,000
		427/425 L72 2dr COPO Spt Cpe	$84,300	$114,000	$140,000	$200,000
		427/425 ZL1 2dr ZL1 Spt Cpe	$439,000	$510,000	$608,000	$712,000
		307/200 L14 2dr Conv	$17,200	$23,600	$29,000	$38,200
		327/210 LF7 2dr Conv	$21,100	$29,300	$36,500	$47,600
		350/250 L65 2dr Conv	$25,000	$35,000	$43,900	$57,000
		350/255 LM1 2dr Conv	$23,700	$32,400	$41,000	$51,300
		350/300 L48 2dr SS Conv	$26,400	$37,600	$46,900	$64,200
		396/325 L35 2dr SS Conv	$33,000	$44,500	$58,000	$70,900
		396/350 L34 2dr SS Conv	$35,800	$49,000	$63,000	$79,400
		396/375 L78 2dr SS Conv	$38,400	$52,000	$68,700	$86,700
		350/300 L48 2dr Indy Pace Car Conv	$35,600	$47,400	$59,500	$89,800
		396/325 L35 2dr Indy Pace Car Conv	$41,100	$51,400	$65,500	$96,400
		396/350 L34 2dr Indy Pace Car Conv	$43,000	$53,600	$85,600	$116,000
		396/375 L78 2dr Indy Pace Car Conv	$50,900	$69,100	$112,000	$145,000

+20% for RS pkg. +25% for RS pkg on factory SS cars. +20% for factory 4-spd (exc. Z/28 and Yenko). +10% for JL8 brakes. -30% for 6-cyl. -10% for 3-spd.

Chevrolet

Year	Model	Body Style	4	3	2	1
1969	Chevelle	307/200 L14 2dr 300 Deluxe Cpe	$8,000	$10,900	$13,400	$17,200
		350/250 L65 2dr 300 Deluxe Cpe	$8,600	$12,200	$15,500	$20,200
		350/255 LM1 2dr 300 Deluxe Cpe	$9,100	$12,800	$16,300	$21,300
		350/300 L48 2dr 300 Deluxe Cpe	$9,700	$13,300	$17,000	$22,200
		307/200 L14 4dr 300 Deluxe Sdn	$6,400	$8,700	$10,900	$13,800
		350/250 L65 4dr 300 Deluxe Sdn	$7,000	$9,200	$11,400	$14,700
		350/255 LM1 4dr 300 Deluxe Sdn	$7,100	$9,500	$11,600	$15,000
		350/300 L48 4dr 300 Deluxe Sdn	$8,200	$11,100	$14,200	$18,200
		307/200 L14 4dr Malibu Sdn	$6,600	$9,000	$11,300	$14,700
		350/255 LM1 4dr Malibu Sdn	$7,900	$9,900	$12,900	$17,000
		350/300 L48 4dr Malibu Sdn	$8,300	$10,900	$14,200	$18,600
		307/200 L14 4dr Cncrs 2-Seat Stn Wgn	$9,700	$13,000	$16,400	$21,600
		350/250 L65 4dr Concours 2-Seat Stn Wgn	$10,600	$13,900	$18,400	$24,100
		350/255 LM1 4dr Cncrs 2-Seat Stn Wgn	$10,800	$14,200	$18,800	$24,600
		350/300 L48 4dr Cncrs 2-Seat Stn Wgn	$12,500	$16,700	$21,400	$27,800
		307/200 L14 4dr Cncrs 3-Seat Stn Wgn	$9,700	$13,000	$16,400	$21,600
		350/250 L65 4dr Concours 3-Seat Stn Wgn	$10,500	$13,500	$18,000	$23,400
		350/255 LM1 4dr Cncrs 3-Seat Stn Wgn	$11,000	$14,200	$18,900	$24,600
		350/300 L48 4dr Cncrs 3-Seat Stn Wgn	$12,500	$16,800	$21,500	$27,800
		307/200 L14 2dr Malibu Spt Cpe	$9,400	$13,600	$17,400	$22,400
		350/250 L65 2dr Malibu Spt Cpe	$11,300	$15,700	$20,300	$26,900
		350/255 LM1 2dr Malibu Spt Cpe	$12,600	$17,400	$22,500	$29,900

Year	Model	Body Style	4	3	2	1
		350/300 L48 2dr Malibu Spt Cpe	$13,900	$18,900	$24,900	$32,500
		396/325 L35 2dr Malibu SS 396 Spt Cpe	$28,100	$41,800	$50,700	$67,500
		396/350 L34 2dr Malibu SS 396 Spt Cpe	$30,300	$44,800	$55,300	$72,100
		396/375 L78 2dr Malibu SS 396 Spt Cpe	$39,900	$58,300	$78,000	$110,000
		396/375 L89 2dr Malibu SS 396 Spt Cpe	$53,300	$70,800	$110,000	$163,000
		427/425 L72 2dr Yenko Spt Cpe	$169,000	$215,000	$245,000	$285,000
		307/200 L14 4dr Malibu Spt Sdn	$7,200	$9,600	$11,900	$15,300
		350/250 L65 4dr Malibu Spt Sdn	$7,700	$10,400	$13,100	$16,300
		350/255 LM1 4dr Malibu Spt Sdn	$8,100	$10,900	$13,800	$17,200
		350/300 L48 4dr Malibu Spt Sdn	$9,400	$12,600	$16,300	$21,800
		307/200 L14 2dr Malibu Conv	$20,200	$27,500	$34,900	$46,200
		350/250 L65 2dr Malibu Conv	$19,700	$28,200	$35,700	$47,500
		350/255 LM1 2dr Malibu Conv	$20,200	$28,800	$36,400	$48,500
		350/300 L48 2dr Malibu Conv	$22,500	$32,500	$45,000	$60,000
		396/325 L35 2dr Malibu SS 396 Conv	$37,500	$51,400	$67,200	$86,900
		396/350 L34 2dr Malibu SS 396 Conv	$39,000	$53,400	$68,100	$90,700
		396/375 L78 2dr Malibu SS 396 Conv	$61,200	$87,800	$119,000	$138,000
		396/375 L89 2dr Malibu SS 396 Conv	$72,800	$95,800	$130,000	$173,000

-50% for 6-cyl. +15% for 4-spd.

Year	Model	Body Style	4	3	2	1
1969	Biscayne	327/235 2dr Sdn	$6,800	$11,900	$14,500	$20,000
		350/255 LM1 2dr Sdn	$7,500	$13,100	$16,000	$22,000
		350/300 L48 2dr Sdn	$7,600	$13,600	$16,700	$22,800
		327/235 4dr Sdn	$5,500	$8,300	$10,500	$13,600

Chevrolet

Year	Model	Body Style	4	3	2	1
		350/255 LM1 4dr Sdn	$6,100	$9,100	$11,600	$15,000
		350/300 L48 4dr Sdn	$6,300	$9,400	$12,000	$15,900
		327/235 4dr Brookwood Wgn	$5,800	$9,700	$11,800	$16,600
		350/255 LM1 4dr Brookwood Wgn	$6,400	$10,700	$13,000	$18,300
		350/300 L48 4dr Brookwood Wgn	$6,700	$10,900	$13,300	$19,200
1969	Impala	327/235 2dr Spt Cpe	$7,400	$11,700	$15,100	$20,700
		350/250 L65 2dr Spt Cpe	$7,800	$12,300	$15,900	$21,700
		350/255 LM1 2dr Spt Cpe	$8,200	$12,900	$16,700	$22,800
		350/300 L48 2dr Spt Cpe	$8,600	$13,300	$17,200	$23,700
		427/390 L36 2dr SS 427 Spt Cpe	$24,200	$36,400	$48,700	$64,400
		327/235 4dr Sdn	$5,500	$8,700	$11,000	$14,900
		350/250 L65 4dr Sdn	$5,200	$8,300	$10,500	$14,200
		350/255 LM1 4dr Sdn	$5,800	$9,100	$11,600	$15,600
		350/300 L48 4dr Sdn	$5,900	$9,500	$11,900	$16,600
		327/235 4dr Kingswood Stn Wgn	$6,300	$9,600	$12,300	$17,900
		350/250 L65 4dr Kingswood 2-Seat Stn Wgn	$6,600	$10,100	$12,900	$18,800
		350/255 LM1 4dr Kingswood 2-Seat Stn Wgn	$6,900	$10,600	$13,500	$19,700
		350/300 L48 4dr Kingswood Stn Wgn	$7,200	$11,100	$14,300	$20,400
		327/235 4dr Spt Sdn	$6,300	$10,400	$13,100	$18,500
		350/250 L65 4dr Spt Sdn	$6,600	$10,900	$13,800	$19,400
		350/255 LM1 4dr Spt Sdn	$6,900	$11,400	$14,500	$20,300
		350/300 L48 4dr Spt Sdn	$7,200	$11,800	$15,200	$21,300
		327/235 2dr Conv	$12,300	$19,200	$24,600	$33,600
		350/250 L65 2dr Conv	$12,700	$19,800	$25,300	$34,600
		350/255 LM1 2dr Conv	$13,300	$20,800	$26,600	$36,300

Year	Model	Body Style	4	3	2	1
		350/300 L48 2dr Conv	$14,400	$21,900	$28,400	$38,400
		427/390 L36 2dr SS 427 Conv	$26,800	$40,200	$53,200	$70,700
						-20% for 6-cyl.
1969	Caprice	327/235 2dr Cpe	$8,500	$12,600	$16,000	$20,900
		350/250 L65 2dr Cpe	$8,900	$13,200	$16,800	$21,900
		350/255 LM1 2dr Cpe	$9,300	$13,900	$17,600	$23,000
		350/300 L48 2dr Cpe	$9,700	$14,200	$18,800	$24,100
		327/235 4dr Hdtp Sdn	$6,700	$9,900	$12,600	$16,500
		350/250 L65 4dr Hdtp Sdn	$7,000	$10,400	$13,200	$17,300
		350/255 LM1 4dr Hdtp Sdn	$7,400	$10,900	$13,900	$18,200
		350/300 L48 4dr Hdtp Sdn	$7,900	$11,500	$14,800	$19,200
		327/235 4dr Kingswood Estate Wgn	$6,300	$9,700	$12,100	$17,200
		350/250 L65 4dr Kingswood Estate Wgn	$6,600	$10,200	$12,700	$18,100
		350/255 LM1 4dr Kingswood Estate Wgn	$6,900	$10,700	$13,300	$19,000
		350/300 L48 4dr Kingswood Estate Wgn	$7,200	$11,100	$14,200	$19,800
						-20% for 6-cyl.
1969	Corvette	350/300 L48 2dr Cpe	$11,600	$20,600	$33,600	$46,200
		350/350 LT1 2dr Cpe	$12,300	$25,400	$38,700	$53,000
		427/390 L36 2dr Cpe	$13,700	$28,700	$46,800	$70,200
		427/400 L68 2dr Cpe	$16,900	$33,100	$51,900	$88,100
		427/435 L71 2dr Cpe	$19,500	$42,500	$64,900	$94,800
		427/435 L89 2dr Cpe	$49,500	$82,800	$113,000	$147,000
		427/430 L88 2dr Cpe	$304,000	$399,000	$494,000	$628,000
		427/425 ZL1 2dr Cpe	$898,000	$1.15 mil	$1.5 mil	$1.8 mil
		350/300 L48 2dr Conv	$14,300	$24,300	$39,400	$58,700

Chevrolet

Year	Model	Body Style	4	3	2	1
		350/350 LT1 2dr Conv	$16,700	$33,300	$49,000	$71,100
		427/390 L36 2dr Conv	$18,300	$33,400	$51,200	$91,800
		427/400 L68 2dr Conv	$20,400	$39,000	$67,500	$110,000
		427/435 L71 2dr Conv	$25,500	$47,300	$80,500	$130,000
		427/435 L89 2dr Conv	$65,300	$105,000	$141,000	$224,000
		427/430 L88 2dr Conv	$380,000	$488,000	$613,000	$725,000
		-10% for auto trans. +10% for 4-spd. +$200 for pwr wndws. +$2,000 for a/c. +$1,850 for hard top. +$900 for leather. +$2,500 for pwr strg. +$1,500 for tilt/tele strng whl.				
1970	Nova	307/200 2dr Cpe	$10,800	$15,000	$19,500	$24,400
		350/300 2dr SS Cpe	$24,200	$30,400	$36,400	$49,700
		396/350 2dr SS Cpe	$35,300	$49,200	$64,700	$79,500
		396/375 L78 2dr SS Cpe	$46,900	$63,500	$78,300	$95,400
		350/360 2dr Yenko Deuce Cpe	$65,000	$84,500	$109,000	$145,000
		307/200 4dr Sdn	$6,200	$9,000	$11,100	$14,300
		+15% for 4-spd. -20% for 6-cyl.				
1970	Camaro	307/200 2dr Spt Cpe	$11,500	$14,700	$17,700	$21,800
		350/250 L65 2dr Spt Cpe	$13,400	$17,500	$21,600	$28,400
		350/300 L48 2dr SS Spt Cpe	$18,600	$24,400	$34,200	$42,600
		396/350 L34 2dr SS Spt Cpe	$27,900	$37,700	$47,000	$58,400
		396/375 L78 2dr SS Spt Cpe	$28,900	$45,100	$62,700	$79,100
		350/360 2dr Z/28 Spt Cpe	$24,600	$38,300	$51,000	$59,500
		+15% for RS pkg. +20% for RS on Z/28 and SS models. +10% for 4-spd (exc Z/28). +15% for COPO spoiler. -30% for 6-cyl. -15% for 3-spd.				
1970	Chevelle	307/200 2dr Spt Cpe	$8,400	$12,300	$15,700	$20,000
		350/250 L65 2dr Spt Cpe	$9,600	$13,600	$18,800	$23,300
		350/300 L48 2dr Spt Cpe	$10,800	$15,400	$19,900	$25,200
		307/200 2dr Malibu Spt Cpe	$9,000	$12,900	$16,700	$20,800
		350/250 L65 2dr Malibu Spt Cpe	$9,900	$14,600	$19,300	$24,200

Year	Model	Body Style	4	3	2	1
		350/300 L48 2dr Malibu Spt Cpe	$13,300	$18,900	$24,500	$30,600
		396/350 L34 2dr SS 396 Spt Cpe	$43,400	$57,100	$71,600	$85,800
		396/375 L78 2dr SS 396 Spt Cpe	$45,000	$63,000	$79,300	$98,800
		396/375 L89 2dr SS 396 Spt Cpe	$45,800	$63,900	$77,700	$104,000
		454/360 LS5 2dr SS 454 Spt Cpe	$36,100	$49,000	$61,600	$77,700
		454/450 LS6 2dr SS 454 Spt Cpe	$65,200	$88,700	$127,000	$176,000
		307/200 4dr Sdn	$6,500	$9,000	$11,400	$14,200
		350/250 L65 4dr Sdn	$7,000	$9,600	$12,000	$15,300
		350/300 L48 4dr Sdn	$8,200	$11,200	$14,800	$18,800
		307/200 4dr Malibu Sdn	$7,600	$10,500	$13,100	$16,000
		350/250 L65 4dr Malibu Sdn	$7,900	$10,700	$13,800	$16,900
		350/300 L48 4dr Malibu Sdn	$8,400	$11,400	$14,900	$18,800
		307/200 4dr Cncrs Stn Wgn, 2-Seat	$10,000	$13,600	$18,500	$25,200
		350/250 L65 4dr Cncrs Stn Wgn, 2-Seat	$12,600	$16,200	$21,200	$28,700
		350/300 L48 4dr Cncrs Stn Wgn, 2-Seat	$13,700	$19,100	$25,500	$29,400
		307/200 4dr Malibu Spt Sdn	$7,700	$10,600	$13,300	$16,000
		350/250 L65 4dr Malibu Spt Sdn	$8,300	$11,100	$14,000	$17,600
		350/300 L48 4dr Malibu Spt Sdn	$9,900	$13,300	$17,600	$22,100
		307/200 2dr Malibu Conv	$20,600	$27,500	$36,300	$45,900
		350/250 L65 2dr Malibu Conv	$21,500	$29,500	$38,800	$48,800
		350/300 L48 2dr Malibu Conv	$23,800	$32,900	$42,600	$53,900
		396/350 L34 2dr SS 396 Conv	$74,600	$101,000	$122,000	$137,000
		396/375 L78 2dr SS 396 Conv	$85,700	$111,000	$128,000	$153,000
		396/375 L89 2dr SS 396 Conv	$92,700	$121,000	$144,000	$175,000
		454/360 LS5 2dr SS 454 Conv	$51,200	$70,100	$85,100	$107,000

Chevrolet

Year	Model	Body Style	4	3	2	1
		454/450 LS6 2dr SS 454 Conv	$123,000	$172,000	$244,000	$298,000
						-50% for 6-cyl. +15% for 4-spd.
1970	Monte Carlo	350/300 2dr Cpe	$10,200	$14,700	$22,100	$31,000
		454/360 2dr SS 454 Cpe	$15,500	$22,800	$34,300	$50,200
1970	Impala	350/250 2dr Spt Cpe	$7,400	$11,800	$14,900	$20,100
		350/250 4dr Sdn	$5,200	$7,700	$9,700	$13,400
		350/250 4dr Kingswood Stn Wgn, 2-Seat	$6,700	$10,900	$14,000	$19,800
		350/250 4dr Spt Sdn	$6,400	$10,000	$12,600	$17,500
		350/250 2dr Conv	$12,900	$19,500	$24,600	$33,400
						-20% for 6-cyl.
1970	Caprice	350/250 2dr Cpe	$8,600	$12,100	$15,500	$19,800
		350/250 4dr Kingswood Estate Stn Wgn, 2-Seat	$6,200	$9,300	$11,700	$15,700
		350/250 4dr Hdtp Sdn	$6,200	$9,100	$11,400	$14,800
						-20% for 6-cyl.
1970	Corvette	350/300 2dr Cpe	$15,100	$22,400	$38,700	$51,700
		350/350 LT1 2dr Cpe	$14,500	$23,400	$42,500	$58,500
		350/370 LT1 2dr Cpe	$23,900	$40,600	$62,900	$86,300
		454/390 LS5 2dr Cpe	$20,300	$36,300	$55,000	$75,200
		350/300 2dr Conv	$14,900	$26,100	$50,900	$68,900
		350/350 LT1 2dr Conv	$16,300	$28,000	$53,300	$73,100
		350/370 LT1 2dr Conv	$25,600	$41,100	$75,400	$119,000
		454/390 LS5 2dr Conv	$26,800	$41,900	$76,200	$126,000
						+$1,800 for close ratio 4-spd. -8% for auto trans. +$200 for pwr wndws. +$2,000 for a/c. +$1,850 for hard top. +$900 for custom interior (leather). +$2,500 for pwr strg. +$1,500 for tilt/tele strng whl.
1971	Nova	307/200 2dr Cpe	$10,500	$14,800	$18,600	$22,800
		350/270 2dr SS Cpe	$16,000	$22,300	$28,400	$34,600
						+15% for 4-spd.
		307/200 4dr Sdn	$6,100	$8,700	$10,800	$13,100
1971	Camaro	307/200 2dr Spt Cpe	$9,700	$14,300	$17,000	$20,800

Year	Model	Body Style	4	3	2	1
		350/245 L65 2dr Spt Cpe	$11,800	$16,800	$21,200	$27,700
		350/270 L48 2dr SS Spt Cpe	$15,900	$22,300	$27,400	$36,500
		396/300 LS3 2dr SS Spt Cpe	$26,000	$33,300	$41,900	$52,600
		350/330 LT1 2dr Z/28 Spt Cpe	$30,300	$37,900	$44,600	$56,500
			+15% for RS pkg. +20% for RS on Z/28 and SS models. +10% for 4-spd (exc Z/28). -30% for 6-cyl. -15% for 3-spd.			
1971	Chevelle	307/200 2dr Spt Cpe	$8,600	$11,900	$15,100	$17,800
		350/245 L65 2dr Spt Cpe	$9,100	$12,400	$16,100	$18,900
		350/270 L48 2dr Spt Cpe	$11,300	$16,500	$21,000	$25,500
		307/200 2dr Malibu Spt Cpe	$8,700	$12,500	$15,700	$19,300
		350/245 L65 2dr Malibu Spt Cpe	$10,900	$15,200	$18,900	$22,200
		350/270 L48 2dr Malibu Spt Cpe	$11,900	$16,800	$21,600	$25,800
		402/300 LS3 2dr SS Spt Cpe	$25,500	$34,900	$47,600	$57,800
		454/365 LS5 2dr SS Spt Cpe	$28,800	$45,900	$60,600	$80,400
		307/200 4dr Sdn	$6,400	$9,000	$11,100	$13,100
		350/245 L65 4dr Sdn	$6,600	$9,300	$11,200	$13,400
		350/270 L48 4dr Sdn	$8,100	$11,300	$14,700	$17,700
		307/200 4dr Malibu Sdn	$7,700	$10,700	$13,000	$15,500
		350/245 L65 4dr Malibu Sdn	$8,000	$11,200	$13,700	$16,300
		350/270 L48 4dr Malibu Sdn	$8,500	$12,000	$15,300	$18,400
		307/200 4dr Cncrs Stn Wgn, 2-Seat	$10,100	$13,600	$18,400	$25,200
		350/245 L65 4dr Cncrs Stn Wgn, 2-Seat	$12,500	$16,100	$22,400	$28,700
		350/270 L48 4dr Cncrs Stn Wgn, 2-Seat	$13,700	$19,300	$25,500	$29,400
		307/200 4dr Malibu Spt Sdn	$7,800	$10,800	$13,000	$15,500
		350/245 L65 4dr Malibu Spt Sdn	$8,300	$11,700	$14,500	$17,200

Chevrolet

Year	Model	Body Style	4	3	2	1
		350/270 L48 4dr Malibu Spt Sdn	$10,200	$13,900	$17,500	$21,600
		307/200 2dr Malibu Conv	$20,900	$28,800	$36,000	$43,000
		350/245 L65 2dr Malibu Conv	$22,200	$30,500	$38,200	$45,700
		350/270 L48 2dr Malibu Conv	$23,800	$32,800	$42,300	$50,600
		402/300 LS3 2dr SS Conv	$40,300	$50,400	$63,300	$76,300
		454/365 LS5 2dr SS Conv	$46,200	$66,900	$86,000	$105,000
					-50% for 6-cyl. +15% for 4-spd.	
1971	Monte Carlo	350/270 2dr Cpe	$10,200	$14,700	$22,100	$31,000
		454/365 2dr SS 454 Cpe	$15,300	$22,500	$33,900	$48,000
1971	Impala	350/245 2dr Spt Cpe	$6,800	$9,900	$12,700	$16,000
		350/270 2dr Spt Cpe	$6,900	$10,000	$12,900	$16,200
		400/255 2dr Spt Cpe	$11,700	$13,100	$14,800	$16,400
		402/300 2dr Spt Cpe	$11,900	$13,300	$15,000	$16,700
		454/365 2dr Spt Cpe	$12,100	$13,600	$15,300	$17,000
		350/245 4dr Sdn	$4,600	$6,600	$8,700	$10,600
		350/245 4dr Kingswood Stn Wgn	$5,500	$7,900	$10,000	$12,500
		350/245 4dr Spt Sdn	$5,900	$8,700	$11,100	$14,000
		350/245 2dr Conv	$12,000	$16,500	$21,700	$26,800
		350/270 2dr Conv	$12,200	$16,800	$22,100	$27,300
		400/255 2dr Conv	$12,400	$17,100	$22,500	$27,800
		402/300 2dr Conv	$16,900	$22,800	$32,700	$36,900
		454/365 2dr Conv	$18,800	$25,300	$36,300	$41,000
						-20% for 6-cyl.
1971	Caprice	402/300 2dr Cpe	$9,200	$13,100	$16,700	$20,500
		402/300 4dr Spt Sdn	$6,800	$9,600	$12,200	$15,400
		402/300 4dr Kingswood Estate Stn Wgn	$6,100	$8,400	$10,600	$12,900
1971	Corvette	350/270 2dr Cpe	$11,800	$17,700	$35,000	$46,800
		350/330 LT1 2dr Cpe	$15,800	$28,900	$45,800	$62,200

Year	Model	Body Style	4	3	2	1
		454/365 LS5 2dr Cpe	$15,200	$29,000	$45,400	$63,500
		454/425 LS6 2dr Cpe	$73,400	$106,000	$148,000	$204,000
		350/270 2dr Conv	$14,700	$25,500	$46,700	$68,000
		350/330 LT1 2dr Conv	$17,200	$33,400	$58,300	$86,700
		454/365 LS5 2dr Conv	$22,400	$38,000	$57,500	$98,600
		454/425 LS6 2dr Conv	$112,000	$139,000	$206,000	$267,000
		+$1,800 for close ratio 4-spd. -8% for auto trans. +$200 for pwr wndws. +$2,000 for a/c. +$1,850 for hard top. +$900 for custom interior (leather). +$2,500 for pwr strg. +$1,500 for tilt/tele strng whl.				
1972	Nova	307/130 2dr Cpe	$10,400	$14,800	$18,800	$23,800
		350/165 2dr Cpe	$13,800	$19,200	$24,500	$31,100
		350/200 2dr SS 350 Cpe	$15,900	$22,400	$28,500	$36,200
		307/130 4dr Sdn	$6,100	$8,800	$10,800	$13,800
		+15% for 4-spd.				
1972	Camaro	307/130 2dr Spt Cpe	$10,100	$13,900	$17,200	$22,700
		350/165 2dr Spt Cpe	$11,600	$16,500	$20,400	$26,600
		350/200 2dr SS Spt Cpe	$14,900	$20,700	$25,900	$33,200
		402/240 LS3 2dr SS Spt Cpe	$25,000	$35,000	$43,200	$53,700
		350/255 2dr Z/28 Spt Cpe	$23,700	$31,400	$44,100	$54,500
		+15% for RS pkg. +20% for RS on Z/28 and SS models. +10% for 4-spd (exc Z/28). -30% for 6-cyl. -15% for 3-spd.				
1972	Chevelle	307/130 2dr Spt Cpe	$8,600	$12,300	$15,100	$18,300
		350/165 L65 2dr Spt Cpe	$8,600	$12,500	$15,600	$18,900
		350/175 L48 2dr Spt Cpe	$11,800	$17,500	$21,900	$27,600
		307/130 2dr Malibu Spt Cpe	$8,900	$12,800	$15,500	$19,900
		350/165 L65 2dr Malibu Spt Cpe	$9,100	$14,500	$18,100	$24,500
		350/175 L48 2dr Malibu Spt Cpe	$11,600	$16,900	$21,100	$26,600
		350/165 L65 2dr SS Spt Cpe	$12,400	$20,300	$25,400	$34,300
		350/175 L48 2dr SS Spt Cpe	$16,500	$24,900	$31,900	$40,200

Chevrolet

Year	Model	Body Style	4	3	2	1
		402/240 LS3 2dr SS Spt Cpe	$26,000	$39,200	$49,100	$62,100
		454/270 LS5 2dr SS 454 Spt Cpe	$26,600	$42,500	$53,200	$69,200
		307/130 4dr Sdn	$6,600	$9,500	$11,000	$13,600
		350/165 L65 4dr Sdn	$6,700	$9,700	$11,200	$13,800
		350/175 L48 4dr Sdn	$8,100	$11,900	$14,500	$18,500
		307/130 4dr Malibu Sdn	$7,500	$10,900	$12,900	$15,700
		350/165 L65 4dr Malibu Sdn	$8,200	$11,700	$13,700	$17,300
		350/175 L48 4dr Malibu Sdn	$8,500	$12,000	$14,700	$19,000
		307/130 4dr Cncrs Stn Wgn, 2-Seat	$10,400	$14,900	$18,100	$21,200
		350/165 L65 4dr Cncrs Stn Wgn, 2-Seat	$13,000	$18,300	$20,600	$23,700
		350/175 L48 4dr Cncrs Stn Wgn, 2-Seat	$13,000	$18,300	$22,700	$28,000
		307/130 4dr Malibu Spt Sdn	$7,800	$11,100	$13,000	$16,000
		350/165 L65 4dr Malibu Spt Sdn	$8,000	$11,300	$13,800	$17,700
		350/175 L48 4dr Malibu Spt Sdn	$10,200	$14,200	$17,500	$22,200
		307/130 2dr Malibu Conv	$19,800	$27,600	$34,200	$43,100
		350/165 L65 2dr Malibu Conv	$21,000	$29,100	$35,800	$46,100
		350/175 L48 2dr Malibu Conv	$23,500	$33,000	$40,700	$51,900
		350/165 L65 2dr SS Conv	$28,400	$40,700	$50,200	$64,500
		350/175 L48 2dr SS Conv	$31,700	$46,200	$56,000	$71,700
		402/240 LS3 2dr SS Conv	$40,900	$56,300	$69,200	$81,900
		454/270 LS5 2dr SS 454 Conv	$42,500	$64,600	$76,800	$94,000
					-50% for 6-cyl. +15% for 4-spd.	
1972	Monte Carlo	350/165 2dr Cpe	$9,300	$13,300	$20,200	$26,300
		350/175 L48 2dr Cpe	$10,200	$14,700	$22,100	$31,000
		402/240 LS3 2dr Cpe	$12,100	$18,700	$25,200	$34,300

Year	Model	Body Style	4	3	2	1
		454/270 LS5 2dr Cpe	$14,000	$21,300	$28,900	$38,600
						-20% for 6-cyl.
1972	Caprice	400/170 2dr Cpe	$8,900	$13,000	$16,700	$21,200
		400/170 4dr Sdn	$6,600	$9,600	$12,100	$15,900
1972	Corvette	350/200 L48 2dr Cpe	$12,300	$19,000	$32,300	$42,100
		350/255 LT1 2dr Cpe	$22,000	$36,200	$53,700	$68,400
		454/270 LS5 2dr Cpe	$14,400	$28,100	$44,000	$57,900
		350/200 L48 2dr Conv	$13,800	$22,300	$37,000	$48,700
		350/255 LT1 2dr Conv	$20,600	$36,500	$54,700	$84,100
		454/270 LS5 2dr Conv	$21,700	$38,100	$52,300	$80,400
		+$1,000 for close ratio 4-spd. -8% for auto trans. +$200 for pwr wndws. +$7,000 for a/c on LT1. +$2,000 for a/c on all others. +$1,850 for hard top. +$900 for custom interior (leather). +$2,500 for pwr strg. +$1,500 for tilt/tele strng whl.				
1973	Nova	307/115 2dr Cpe	$5,200	$7,700	$9,900	$12,800
		307/115 2dr SS Cpe	$7,100	$10,400	$13,200	$17,100
1973	Camaro	307/115 2dr Spt Cpe	$8,900	$13,500	$16,600	$21,100
		350/145 L65 2dr Spt Cpe	$11,300	$15,900	$19,800	$25,800
		350/175 L48 2dr Spt Cpe	$11,800	$16,900	$20,600	$27,700
		350/245 2dr Z/28 Spt Cpe	$19,200	$27,000	$34,900	$45,700
		350/145 L65 2dr LT Spt Cpe	$11,900	$17,000	$21,100	$28,200
		350/175 L48 2dr LT Spt Cpe	$13,200	$18,700	$23,300	$30,100
		350/245 2dr Z/28 LT Spt Cpe	$21,600	$31,000	$37,500	$49,200
		+15% for RS pkg. +20% for RS on Z/28 models. +10% for 4-spd (exc Z/28). -30% for 6-cyl. -15% for 3-spd.				
1973	Chevelle	307/115 2dr Malibu Cpe	$6,200	$9,300	$11,400	$14,900
		350/145 L65 2dr Malibu Cpe	$7,200	$11,400	$14,400	$17,800
		350/175 L48 2dr Malibu Cpe	$8,200	$12,300	$16,500	$20,500
		454/245 LS4 2dr SS Cpe	$11,400	$17,300	$22,600	$26,900
		307/115 4dr Malibu Sdn	$5,000	$7,000	$8,500	$11,500

Chevrolet

Year	Model	Body Style	4	3	2	1
		350/145 L65 4dr Malibu Sdn	$5,500	$7,900	$9,800	$12,800
		350/175 L48 4dr Malibu Sdn	$6,300	$8,900	$11,400	$14,900
						-50% for 6-cyl. +15% for 4-spd.
1973	Monte Carlo	350/145 2dr Hdtp Cpe	$6,800	$10,500	$15,800	$21,300
		350/145 2dr Lan Hdtp Cpe	$7,000	$10,800	$16,600	$21,700
1973	Caprice Classic	400/150 2dr Conv	$10,200	$15,200	$19,600	$25,100
1973	Corvette	350/190 2dr Cpe	$9,700	$13,200	$23,900	$33,300
		350/250 L82 2dr Cpe	$11,200	$14,900	$27,200	$36,400
		454/275 LS4 2dr Cpe	$14,200	$18,100	$33,000	$45,800
		350/190 2dr Conv	$11,900	$16,300	$28,700	$42,700
		350/250 L82 2dr Conv	$14,600	$22,600	$34,400	$50,100
		454/275 LS4 2dr Conv	$16,700	$24,500	$36,200	$57,900
						+$500 for close ratio 4-spd. -8% for auto trans. +$200 for pwr wndws. +$2,000 for a/c. +$1,850 for hard top. +$2,500 for pwr strg. +$400 for alum whls. +$750 for tilt/tele strng whl.
1974	Nova	350/145 2dr Cpe	$5,300	$7,600	$9,900	$12,800
		350/145 2dr SS Cpe	$7,100	$10,500	$13,200	$17,100
1974	Camaro	350/145 L65 2dr Spt Cpe	$7,400	$11,900	$16,500	$21,800
		350/160 LM1 2dr Spt Cpe	$9,200	$13,700	$18,200	$24,100
		350/185 L48 2dr Spt Cpe	$10,500	$14,800	$20,100	$26,400
		350/245 2dr Z/28 Spt Cpe	$15,700	$21,900	$30,600	$38,400
		350/145 L65 2dr LT Spt Cpe	$10,900	$15,800	$21,100	$28,200
		350/160 LM1 2dr LT Spt Cpe	$12,200	$17,100	$22,200	$29,700
		350/185 L48 2dr LT Spt Cpe	$12,000	$17,300	$23,300	$30,900
		350/245 2dr Z/28 LT Spt Cpe	$17,000	$24,000	$32,100	$40,800
						+15% for RS pkg. +20% for RS on Z/28 models. +10% for 4-spd (exc Z/28). -30% for 6-cyl. -15% for 3-spd.
1974	Monte Carlo	350/145 2dr S Hdtp Cpe	$6,400	$10,300	$15,600	$21,300
		350/145 2dr Lan Hdtp Cpe	$6,800	$10,500	$16,100	$21,700

Year	Model	Body Style	4	3	2	1
1974	Caprice Classic	400/150 2dr Conv	$10,200	$15,200	$19,600	$25,100
1974	Corvette	350/195 L48 2dr Cpe	$6,000	$9,900	$19,100	$29,100
		350/250 L82 2dr Cpe	$7,400	$12,900	$20,900	$32,400
		454/270 LS4 2dr Cpe	$8,700	$13,500	$23,200	$35,400
		350/195 L48 2dr Conv	$7,700	$12,900	$25,000	$37,900
		350/250 L82 2dr Conv	$8,600	$13,400	$27,300	$44,200
		454/270 LS4 2dr Conv	$10,400	$18,400	$31,800	$47,700
		+$500 for close ratio 4-spd. -8% for auto trans. +$200 for pwr wndws. +$1,000 for a/c. +$1,850 for hard top. +$2,500 for pwr strg. +$500 for gymkhana suspension. +$750 for tilt/tele strng whl.				
1975	Vega	122/110 2dr Cosworth Cpe	$5,500	$10,000	$17,400	$28,200
1975	Nova	262/110 2dr SS Cpe	$6,200	$9,300	$11,400	$15,000
1975	Camaro	350/145 L65 2dr Spt Cpe	$6,700	$10,100	$13,500	$17,800
		350/155 LM1 2dr Spt Cpe	$7,800	$11,600	$15,400	$20,600
		350/145 L65 2dr LT Spt Cpe	$9,200	$13,300	$18,000	$24,100
		350/155 LM1 2dr LT Spt Cpe	$10,100	$14,700	$20,100	$26,400
		+15% for RS pkg. +10% for 4-spd. -30% for 6-cyl. -15% for 3-spd.				
1975	Caprice Classic	350/145 2dr Conv	$11,300	$16,700	$21,400	$27,600
1975	Corvette	350/165 L48 2dr Cpe	$5,200	$9,400	$14,200	$28,500
		350/205 L82 2dr Cpe	$6,400	$12,700	$17,800	$31,700
		350/165 L48 2dr Conv	$8,000	$13,300	$25,400	$40,100
		350/205 L82 2dr Conv	$9,400	$15,200	$27,800	$43,500
		+$500 for close ratio 4-spd. -8% for auto trans. +$200 for pwr wndws. +$1,000 for a/c. +$1,850 for hard top. +$2,500 for pwr strg. +$500 for gymkhana suspension. +$750 for tilt/tele strng whl.				
1976	Vega	122/110 2dr Cosworth Htchbk Cpe	$6,400	$10,400	$20,600	$32,800
1976	Nova	305/140 2dr SS Cpe	$6,400	$9,500	$11,800	$15,700
1976	Camaro	305/140 LG3 2dr Spt Cpe	$7,100	$10,300	$13,700	$18,000
		350/165 LM1 2dr Spt Cpe	$7,800	$11,500	$15,700	$20,700

Chevrolet

Year	Model	Body Style	4	3	2	1
		305/140 LG3 2dr LT Spt Cpe	$8,900	$13,300	$18,100	$23,600
		350/165 LM1 2dr LT Spt Cpe	$10,600	$14,800	$20,100	$27,200

+15% for RS pkg. +10% for 4-spd. -30% for 6-cyl. -15% for 3-spd.

Year	Model	Body Style	4	3	2	1
1976	Corvette	350/180 L48 2dr Cpe	$4,800	$7,800	$11,900	$22,200
		350/210 L82 2dr Cpe	$6,300	$9,200	$13,100	$24,600

+$500 for close ratio 4-spd. -8% for auto trans. +$200 for pwr wndws. +$1,000 for a/c. +$2,500 for pwr strg. +$400 for alum whls. +$500 for gymkhana suspension. +$750 for tilt/tele strng whl.

Year	Model	Body Style	4	3	2	1
1977	Camaro	305/145 LG3 2dr Spt Cpe	$5,100	$7,500	$10,100	$13,800
		350/170 LM1 2dr Spt Cpe	$5,700	$8,000	$10,900	$14,900
		305/145 LG3 2dr LT Spt Cpe	$6,200	$9,200	$12,300	$16,300
		350/170 LM1 2dr Z/28 Spt Cpe	$9,100	$13,500	$18,500	$25,500

+15% for RS pkg. +20% for RS on Z/28. +10% for 4-spd (exc Z/28). -30% for 6-cyl. -15% for 3-spd.

Year	Model	Body Style	4	3	2	1
1977	Corvette	350/180 L48 2dr Cpe	$5,200	$8,600	$12,700	$25,900
		350/210 L82 2dr Cpe	$5,900	$10,100	$16,700	$29,400

+$500 for close ratio 4-spd. -8% for auto trans. +$200 for pwr wndws. +$1,000 for a/c. +$400 for alum whls. +$500 for gym-khana suspension. +$750 for tilt/tele strng whl.

Year	Model	Body Style	4	3	2	1
1978	Camaro	350/185 2dr Z/28 Spt Cpe	$9,100	$14,700	$24,000	$33,100
		305/145 LG3 2dr Spt Cpe	$5,600	$7,900	$11,100	$14,900
		350/160 2dr Spt Cpe	$5,600	$8,600	$11,700	$15,700
		350/170 LM1 2dr Spt Cpe	$5,900	$9,100	$12,300	$16,500
		305/145 LG3 2dr LT Spt Cpe	$6,500	$10,000	$14,300	$18,200

+10% for RS. +15% for 4-spd (exc Z/28). +10% for t-tops. -30% for 6-cyl.

Year	Model	Body Style	4	3	2	1
1978	Corvette	350/185 L48 2dr Cpe	$4,800	$9,500	$13,400	$25,700
		350/220 L82 2dr Cpe	$6,300	$12,200	$16,900	$27,600
		350/185 L48 2dr Silver Annv Cpe	$7,700	$13,900	$20,800	$30,900
		350/220 L82 2dr Silver Annv Cpe	$8,500	$16,200	$23,000	$32,100
		350/185 L48 2dr Pace Car Cpe	$9,700	$18,600	$25,600	$52,300

Year	Model	Body Style	4	3	2	1
		350/220 L82 2dr Pace Car Cpe	$12,500	$21,500	$33,100	$58,800
		+$500 for close ratio 4-spd ($3,500 on Pace Car). -8% for auto trans. +$200 for pwr wndws. +$1,000 for a/c. +$400 for alum whls. +$500 for glass T-tops on base cpe. +$500 for gymkhana suspension. +$750 for tilt/tele strng whl.				
1979	Camaro	305/130 LG3 2dr Spt Cpe	$5,700	$7,900	$11,000	$15,000
		350/165 2dr Spt Cpe	$6,500	$9,500	$13,100	$17,400
		350/170 LM1 2dr Spt Cpe	$6,800	$10,000	$13,800	$18,300
		305/130 LG3 2dr Berlinetta Spt Cpe	$6,100	$9,200	$12,200	$16,300
		350/165 2dr Berlinetta Spt Cpe	$6,700	$10,100	$14,100	$18,700
		350/170 LM1 2dr Berlinetta Spt Cpe	$7,100	$10,600	$14,800	$19,700
		350/175 2dr Z/28 Spt Cpe	$9,800	$14,400	$23,900	$37,000
		+10% for RS. +15% for 4-spd (exc Z/28). +10% for t-tops. -30% for 6-cyl.				
1979	Corvette	350/195 2dr Cpe	$4,400	$10,600	$16,900	$28,600
		350/225 L82 2dr Cpe	$8,600	$13,700	$20,500	$31,500
		+$500 for close ratio 4-spd. -8% for auto trans. +$200 for pwr wndws. +$1,000 for a/c. +$400 for alum whls. +$500 for glass T-tops. +$500 for gymkhana suspension. +$750 for tilt/tele strng whl.				
1980	Camaro	267/120 2dr Spt Cpe	$5,000	$8,600	$9,700	$12,700
		305/155 LG4 2dr Spt Cpe	$6,400	$9,600	$12,900	$16,000
		267/120 2dr Berlinetta Spt Cpe	$5,900	$8,700	$11,300	$14,500
		305/155 LG4 2dr Berlinetta Spt Cpe	$6,900	$10,200	$13,800	$17,200
		305/165 LG4 2dr Z/28 Spt Cpe	$10,200	$14,500	$23,800	$31,400
		+10% for RS. +15% for 4-spd (exc Z/28). +10% for t-tops. -30% for 6-cyl.				
		350/190 LM1 2dr Z/28 Spt Cpe	$10,600	$15,600	$25,600	$34,600
1980	Corvette	350/190 L48 2dr Cpe	$5,400	$11,700	$17,600	$28,400
		350/230 L82 2dr Cpe	$7,000	$13,100	$19,400	$29,400
		+$500 for 4-spd. -8% for auto trans. +$400 for alum whls. +$500 for glass T-tops. +$500 for gymkhana suspension.				
1981	Camaro	267/115 2dr Spt Cpe	$4,700	$7,400	$9,900	$13,100

Chevrolet

Year	Model	Body Style	4	3	2	1
		305/150 2dr Spt Cpe	$5,700	$9,800	$13,300	$16,500
		267/115 2dr Berlinetta Spt Cpe	$5,200	$9,000	$11,500	$14,900
		305/150 2dr Berlinetta Spt Cpe	$6,600	$10,500	$14,300	$17,600
		305/165 2dr Z/28 Spt Cpe	$9,200	$15,400	$24,400	$32,100
		350/175 2dr Z/28 Spt Cpe	$10,800	$16,900	$26,400	$35,300
		-30% for 6-cyl. +10% for t-tops.				
1981	Corvette	350/190 2dr Cpe	$4,000	$11,000	$16,500	$26,900
		-8% for auto trans. +$500 for glass T-tops. +$500 for gymkhana suspension.				
1982	Camaro	305/145 2dr Spt Cpe	$3,200	$5,200	$7,100	$11,700
		305/145 2dr Berlinetta Spt Cpe	$3,800	$5,600	$7,700	$12,600
		305/145 2dr Z/28 Spt Cpe	$6,400	$9,700	$12,700	$21,000
		305/165 2dr Z/28 Spt Cpe	$7,200	$10,600	$14,600	$23,500
		-30% for 6-cyl. -50% for 4-cyl. +10% for t-tops.				
1982	Corvette	350/200 2dr Cpe	$6,800	$12,200	$18,100	$27,500
		350/200 2dr Collector Ed Cpe	$7,200	$11,100	$18,100	$30,400
		+$400 for alum whls on base cpe. +$500 for glass T-tops on base cpe. +$500 for gymkhana suspension.				
1983	Monte Carlo	305/150 2dr SS Cpe	$7,800	$11,600	$16,800	$23,000
		+5% for T-top.				
1983	Camaro	305/150 2dr Spt Cpe	$3,000	$5,100	$7,000	$11,300
		305/150 2dr Berlinetta Spt Cpe	$3,600	$5,600	$7,700	$12,500
		305/150 2dr Z/28 Spt Cpe	$5,900	$9,000	$11,900	$19,800
		305/175 2dr Z/28 Spt Cpe	$7,000	$10,200	$14,000	$22,800
		305/190 HO 2dr Z/28 Spt Cpe	$8,300	$11,600	$16,400	$25,400
		-30% for 6-cyl. -50% for 4-cyl. +10% for t-tops.				
1984	Monte Carlo	305/180 2dr SS Cpe	$8,100	$12,100	$17,500	$26,000
		+5% for T-top.				
1984	Camaro	305/150 2dr Spt Cpe	$3,100	$5,200	$7,100	$11,600
		305/150 2dr Berlinetta Spt Cpe	$3,600	$5,600	$7,700	$12,500

Year	Model	Body Style	4	3	2	1
		305/150 2dr Z/28 Spt Cpe	$6,100	$9,400	$12,000	$20,000
		305/190 HO 2dr Z/28 Spt Cpe	$7,600	$10,500	$14,900	$23,600
		-30% for 6-cyl. -50% for 4-cyl. +10% for t-tops.				
1984	Corvette	350/205 2dr Cpe	$3,500	$6,100	$12,100	$19,700
		+$500 for glass roof. +$500 for Z51 suspension pkg. -8% for auto trans.				
1985	Monte Carlo	305/180 2dr SS Cpe	$8,100	$12,100	$17,500	$26,000
		+5% for T-top.				
1985	Camaro	305/155 2dr Spt Cpe	$3,700	$5,600	$7,700	$12,600
		305/155 2dr Berlinetta Spt Cpe	$4,300	$6,200	$8,100	$13,400
		305/155 2dr Z/28 Spt Cpe	$6,200	$9,700	$13,000	$19,600
		305/215 2dr Z/28 Spt Cpe	$8,900	$12,000	$15,000	$22,900
		305/155 2dr IROC-Z Spt Cpe	$8,300	$11,800	$18,600	$24,200
		305/190 HO 2dr IROC-Z Spt Cpe	$9,000	$12,700	$19,400	$26,600
		305/215 2dr IROC-Z Spt Cpe	$10,800	$14,000	$21,300	$27,800
		-30% for 6-cyl. -50% for 4-cyl. +10% for t-tops.				
1985	Corvette	350/230 2dr Cpe	$3,500	$6,300	$12,300	$19,500
		+$500 for glass roof. +$500 for Z51 suspension pkg. -8% for auto trans.				
1986	Monte Carlo	305/180 2dr SS Aero Cpe	$9,300	$15,200	$20,100	$29,000
		305/180 2dr SS Cpe	$8,100	$12,100	$17,500	$26,000
		+5% for T-top.				
1986	Camaro	305/155 2dr Berlinetta Spt Cpe	$4,100	$5,900	$7,800	$12,800
		305/155 2dr Spt Cpe	$3,600	$5,200	$7,300	$11,800
		305/165 2dr IROC-Z Spt Cpe	$7,900	$11,200	$17,700	$23,300
		305/165 2dr Z/28 Spt Cpe	$6,500	$9,400	$12,500	$18,500
		305/190 2dr IROC-Z Spt Cpe	$10,700	$13,900	$21,000	$26,800
		305/190 2dr Z/28 Spt Cpe	$8,600	$11,600	$14,400	$22,200
		305/190 HO 2dr IROC-Z Spt Cpe	$10,100	$12,900	$19,300	$25,300
		305/190 HO 2dr Z/28 Spt Cpe	$7,400	$9,900	$13,100	$20,100
		-30% for 6-cyl. -50% for 4-cyl. +10% for t-tops.				

Chevrolet

Year	Model	Body Style	4	3	2	1
1986	Corvette	350/230 FI 2dr Cpe	$3,900	$6,200	$12,400	$19,400
		350/230 FI 2dr Malcolm Konner Cpe	$6,300	$8,800	$15,300	$24,000
		350/230 FI 2dr Conv	$4,700	$7,600	$16,700	$21,200
		+$500 for glass roof on cpe. +$500 for Z51 suspension pkg. -8% for auto trans.				
1987	Monte Carlo	305/180 2dr SS Aero Cpe	$9,300	$15,200	$20,100	$29,000
		305/180 2dr SS Cpe	$7,800	$11,600	$17,500	$26,000
		+5% for T-top.				
1987	Camaro	305/165 2dr Spt Cpe	$3,200	$4,100	$7,000	$10,800
		305/170 2dr Z/28 Spt Cpe	$8,500	$11,900	$15,500	$22,900
		305/190 2dr Z/28 Spt Cpe	$8,300	$11,600	$14,600	$23,100
		305/190 2dr IROC-Z Spt Cpe	$10,200	$14,600	$20,000	$27,600
		305/215 2dr IROC-Z Spt Cpe	$10,500	$14,100	$20,800	$29,700
		350/225 2dr IROC-Z Spt Cpe	$11,600	$15,500	$23,000	$32,900
		305/165 2dr Conv	$3,500	$5,700	$10,500	$14,600
		305/170 2dr Z/28 Conv	$7,400	$11,200	$14,600	$22,500
		305/190 2dr Z/28 Conv	$9,000	$11,900	$16,100	$24,000
		305/190 2dr IROC-Z Conv	$9,200	$13,500	$19,100	$26,600
		-30% for 6-cyl. +10% for t-tops.				
1987	Corvette	350/240 FI 2dr Cpe	$4,100	$6,600	$13,000	$20,600
		350/345 2dr Callaway Cpe	$8,400	$16,000	$23,500	$34,700
		350/240 FI 2dr Conv	$4,500	$8,300	$16,100	$23,000
		350/345 2dr Callaway Conv	$9,400	$19,900	$29,800	$37,100
		+$500 for glass roof on cpe. +$500 for Z51 suspension pkg. -8% for auto trans.				
1988	Monte Carlo	305/180 2dr SS Cpe	$7,700	$11,500	$17,000	$24,000
		+5% for T-top.				
1988	Camaro	305/170 2dr Spt Cpe	$3,200	$4,200	$7,200	$11,500
		305/170 2dr IROC-Z Spt Cpe	$9,800	$13,900	$19,600	$26,800

Year	Model	Body Style	4	3	2	1
		305/220 2dr IROC-Z Spt Cpe	$10,800	$14,800	$20,500	$28,700
		350/230 2dr IROC-Z Spt Cpe	$11,400	$15,400	$22,500	$29,700
		305/170 2dr Conv	$3,600	$6,300	$11,200	$14,700
		305/170 2dr IROC-Z Conv	$9,100	$13,100	$18,400	$25,300
		305/220 2dr IROC-Z Conv	$9,300	$13,900	$19,700	$27,200
						-30% for 6-cyl. +10% for t-tops.
1988	Corvette	350/245 FI 2dr Cpe	$3,400	$6,100	$12,200	$19,100
		350/245 FI 2dr 35th Annv Cpe	$7,000	$11,500	$25,300	$33,800
		350/382 2dr Callaway Cpe	$8,900	$18,300	$26,300	$39,600
		350/245 FI 2dr Conv	$4,200	$7,900	$16,200	$23,800
		350/382 2dr Callaway Conv	$10,100	$22,500	$31,700	$43,900
						+$500 for glass roof on cpe (exc 35th Anv). +$500 for Z51 suspension pkg. -8% for auto trans.
1989	Camaro	305/170 2dr RS Spt Cpe	$3,400	$4,400	$9,500	$15,100
		305/170 2dr IROC-Z Spt Cpe	$10,000	$13,900	$20,900	$30,100
		305/220 2dr IROC-Z Spt Cpe	$10,800	$14,800	$22,000	$32,000
		350/230 2dr IROC-Z Spt Cpe	$11,500	$15,500	$24,700	$33,000
		305/170 2dr RS Conv	$4,100	$6,500	$12,400	$17,500
		305/170 2dr IROC-Z Conv	$9,000	$13,100	$19,600	$28,100
		305/220 2dr IROC-Z Conv	$9,300	$13,900	$21,400	$30,600
						-30% for 6-cyl. +10% for t-tops.
1989	Corvette	350/245 FI 2dr Cpe	$4,400	$6,500	$13,000	$21,000
		350/382 2dr Callaway Cpe	$8,900	$20,500	$29,100	$41,600
		350/245 FI 2dr Conv	$4,800	$8,600	$17,000	$23,900
		350/382 2dr Callaway Conv	$11,500	$22,900	$34,500	$51,000
						+$500 for glass roof on cpe. +$1,000 for hard top on conv. +$500 for Z51 suspension pkg. -8% for auto trans.
1990	Camaro	305/170 2dr RS Spt Cpe	$3,400	$4,400	$9,100	$14,700
		305/210 2dr IROC-Z Spt Cpe	$10,200	$14,000	$21,200	$30,500

Chevrolet

Year	Model	Body Style	4	3	2	1
		305/230 2dr IROC-Z Spt Cpe	$10,800	$14,800	$22,000	$32,000
		350/245 2dr IROC-Z Spt Cpe	$11,500	$15,500	$24,700	$33,000
		305/170 2dr RS Conv	$4,200	$6,700	$12,500	$17,500
		305/210 2dr IROC-Z Conv	$9,200	$13,300	$19,700	$28,800
		305/230 2dr IROC-Z Conv	$9,300	$13,900	$21,400	$30,100
		-30% for 6-cyl. +10% for t-tops.				
1990	Corvette	350/245 2dr Cpe	$4,600	$7,300	$13,500	$22,000
		350/390 2dr Callaway Cpe	$11,200	$21,400	$30,700	$40,200
		350/375 2dr ZR-1 Cpe	$11,700	$18,900	$28,500	$41,000
		350/245 2dr Conv	$4,900	$9,100	$16,000	$24,400
		350/390 2dr Callaway Conv	$12,800	$24,000	$37,100	$48,400
		+$500 for glass roof on cpe. +$1,000 for hard top on conv. +$500 for Z51 suspension pkg. -10% for auto trans.				
1991	Camaro	305/170 2dr RS Spt Cpe	$3,200	$4,200	$8,800	$14,500
		305/205 2dr Z/28 Spt Cpe	$8,300	$10,500	$14,900	$23,000
		305/230 2dr Z/28 Spt Cpe	$8,800	$11,600	$16,000	$25,300
		350/245 2dr Z/28 Spt Cpe	$9,600	$12,600	$17,400	$26,600
		305/170 2dr RS Conv	$4,000	$6,400	$12,200	$17,200
		305/205 2dr Z/28 Conv	$8,000	$11,100	$15,100	$24,600
		305/230 2dr Z/28 Conv	$7,800	$11,200	$15,600	$24,800
		-30% for 6-cyl. +10% for t-tops.				
1991	Corvette	350/245 2dr Cpe	$4,500	$7,300	$13,400	$21,600
		350/375 2dr ZR-1 Cpe	$13,600	$16,600	$26,900	$39,700
		350/403 2dr Callaway Cpe	$11,700	$22,500	$23,200	$43,000
		350/245 2dr Conv	$6,100	$9,200	$17,600	$26,400
		350/403 2dr Callaway Conv	$14,000	$25,000	$38,800	$50,400
		+$500 for glass roof on cpe. +$1,000 for hard top on conv. -10% for auto trans.				
1992	Camaro	305/170 2dr RS Spt Cpe	$3,800	$4,900	$10,200	$16,800
		305/205 2dr Z/28 Spt Cpe	$9,900	$11,900	$16,700	$26,300

Year	Model	Body Style	4	3	2	1
		305/230 2dr Z/28 Spt Cpe	$10,700	$12,900	$18,000	$28,400
		350/245 2dr Z/28 Spt Cpe	$10,900	$14,700	$19,300	$29,600
		305/170 2dr RS Conv	$4,800	$7,800	$14,300	$20,200
		-30% for 6-cyl. +10% for Heritage Ed cpe. +25% for Heritage Ed on conv. +10% for t-tops.				
1992	Corvette	350/300 2dr Cpe	$4,600	$6,600	$13,700	$22,100
		350/375 2dr ZR-1 Cpe	$10,500	$16,200	$24,900	$34,100
		350/300 2dr Conv	$6,100	$9,000	$18,100	$26,200
		+$500 for glass roof on cpe. +$1,000 for hard top on conv. -10% for auto trans.				
1993	Camaro	207/160 2dr Spt Cpe	$2,600	$3,600	$4,900	$9,500
		350/275 2dr Z/28 Spt Cpe	$4,500	$7,400	$10,700	$18,300
		350/275 2dr Z/28 Indy Pace Car Spt Cpe	$7,600	$11,400	$14,400	$21,700
		-10% for auto. +10% for t-tops. +15% for Special Performance Pkg.				
1993	Corvette	350/300 2dr Cpe	$4,900	$9,100	$16,100	$25,500
		350/405 2dr ZR-1 Cpe	$12,800	$19,200	$27,800	$38,900
		350/300 2dr Conv	$6,300	$10,200	$21,200	$34,400
		+$3,000 for 40th Anv on base cpe. +$7,500 for 40th Annv on ZR-1. +$4,000 on conv. +$500 for glass roof on cpe. +$1,000 for hard top on conv. -10% for auto trans.				
1994	Impala	350/260 4dr SS Sdn	$9,500	$15,100	$21,200	$31,200
1994	Camaro	207/160 2dr Spt Cpe	$2,600	$3,600	$4,900	$9,500
		350/275 2dr Z/28 Spt Cpe	$4,500	$7,300	$10,500	$17,500
		207/160 2dr Conv	$4,900	$7,900	$10,500	$13,800
		350/275 2dr Z/28 Conv	$7,700	$11,400	$14,000	$20,800
		-10% for auto. +10% for t-tops. +15% for Special Performance Pkg.				
1994	Corvette	350/300 FI 2dr Cpe	$5,600	$8,200	$15,700	$25,600
		350/405 FI 2dr ZR-1 Cpe	$12,600	$18,700	$27,400	$38,500
		350/300 FI 2dr Conv	$6,900	$10,400	$20,100	$29,700
		+$500 for glass roof on cpe. +$1,000 for hard top on conv. -10% for auto trans.				
1995	Impala	350/260 4dr SS Sdn	$9,500	$15,100	$21,200	$31,200

Chevrolet

Year	Model	Body Style	4	3	2	1
1995	Camaro	207/160 2dr Spt Cpe	$2,600	$3,600	$4,800	$8,000
		350/275 2dr Z/28 Spt Cpe	$4,600	$6,900	$9,800	$17,200
		207/160 2dr Conv	$4,900	$7,900	$10,500	$13,800
		350/275 2dr Z/28 Conv	$7,800	$11,400	$13,800	$20,600
		-10% for auto. +10% for t-tops. +15% for Special Performance Pkg.				
1995	Corvette	350/300 FI 2dr Cpe	$6,000	$8,900	$16,300	$25,900
		350/405 FI 2dr ZR-1 Cpe	$15,200	$22,800	$31,200	$49,900
		350/300 FI 2dr Conv	$7,500	$10,500	$20,800	$31,300
		350/300 FI 2dr Indy Pace Car Conv	$11,000	$15,500	$25,200	$35,600
		+$500 for glass roof on cpe. +$1,000 for hard top on conv. -10% for auto trans.				
1996	Impala	350/275 4dr SS Sdn	$9,500	$15,100	$21,200	$31,200
1996	Camaro	231/200 2dr Spt Cpe	$2,700	$3,900	$5,200	$8,500
		231/200 2dr RS Spt Cpe	$3,000	$4,500	$5,600	$9,400
		350/285 2dr Z/28 Spt Cpe	$7,300	$9,800	$12,900	$17,800
		350/305 2dr SS Spt Cpe	$8,300	$11,900	$17,400	$24,200
		231/200 2dr Conv	$4,900	$7,200	$9,900	$12,400
		231/200 2dr RS Conv	$6,000	$7,700	$11,100	$13,600
		350/285 2dr Z/28 Conv	$8,800	$11,100	$14,100	$21,200
		350/305 2dr SS Conv	$9,000	$12,100	$19,700	$28,800
		-10% for auto. +10% for t-tops. +15% for Special Performance Pkg.				
1996	Corvette	350/300 FI 2dr Cpe	$6,000	$8,800	$16,800	$26,000
		350/330 2dr Cpe	$7,900	$10,700	$19,100	$28,100
		350/330 2dr GS Cpe	$15,000	$22,800	$34,000	$59,200
		350/300 FI 2dr Conv	$7,700	$10,800	$21,600	$33,900
		350/330 2dr Conv	$8,600	$11,400	$23,200	$35,900
		350/330 2dr GS Conv	$17,100	$25,000	$36,500	$62,000
		+$3,000 for Collector Ed on base cpe and conv. +$6,000 for Collector Ed on LT4. +$500 for glass roof on cpe. +$1,000 for hard top on conv. +$500 for Z51 suspension pkg. -10% for auto trans.				
1997	Camaro	231/200 2dr Cpe	$3,600	$5,400	$7,400	$11,900

Year	Model	Body Style	4	3	2	1
		231/200 2dr RS Cpe	$4,100	$6,100	$8,300	$13,100
		350/285 2dr Z/28 Cpe	$6,500	$9,100	$12,100	$19,300
		350/285 2dr Z/28 30th Annv Cpe	$8,300	$11,900	$14,500	$25,100
		350/305 2dr SS Cpe	$8,300	$11,900	$17,400	$23,000
		350/305 2dr SS 30th Annv Cpe	$9,900	$12,700	$16,500	$30,200
		350/330 2dr SS 30th Annv LT4 Cpe	$14,000	$22,400	$29,800	$41,400
		231/200 2dr Conv	$6,400	$8,900	$11,300	$15,300
		231/200 2dr RS Conv	$7,300	$9,700	$12,200	$16,600
		350/285 2dr Z/28 Conv	$10,100	$13,200	$16,100	$22,700
		350/285 2dr Z/28 30th Annv Conv	$10,100	$13,700	$19,500	$28,500
		350/305 2dr SS Conv	$9,000	$12,100	$19,700	$28,800
		350/305 2dr SS 30th Annv Conv	$13,600	$16,500	$23,200	$34,600
		-10% for auto. +10% for t-tops. +15% for Special Performance Pkg.				
1997	Corvette	346/345 2dr Cpe	$11,900	$16,300	$21,300	$24,900
		-10% for auto trans.				
1998	Camaro	231/200 2dr Cpe	$5,600	$7,400	$9,000	$12,000
		346/305 2dr Z/28 Cpe	$7,000	$9,200	$11,900	$16,000
		346/320 2dr SS Cpe	$11,000	$13,800	$18,100	$25,500
		231/200 2dr Conv	$6,800	$8,800	$10,800	$13,900
		346/305 2dr Z/28 Conv	$10,700	$14,500	$19,400	$22,200
		346/320 2dr SS Conv	$11,600	$15,300	$22,000	$27,800
		-10% for auto. +10% for t-tops. +15% for Special Performance Pkg.				
1998	Corvette	346/345 2dr Cpe	$11,900	$16,300	$21,300	$24,900
		346/345 2dr Conv	$12,900	$17,600	$23,100	$29,000
		346/345 2dr Indy Pace Car Conv	$18,400	$25,000	$31,200	$39,700
		-10% for auto trans.				
1999	Corvette	346/345 2dr Cpe	$11,900	$16,300	$21,300	$24,900
		346/345 2dr Conv	$12,900	$17,600	$23,100	$29,000
		-10% for auto trans.				
1999	Camaro	231/200 2dr Cpe	$6,300	$7,900	$9,700	$12,700
		346/305 2dr Z/28 Cpe	$6,900	$10,000	$12,700	$17,100

Chevrolet

Year	Model	Body Style	4	3	2	1
		346/320 2dr SS Cpe	$12,000	$14,900	$18,100	$25,500
		231/200 2dr Conv	$7,500	$9,700	$11,600	$14,900
		346/305 2dr Z/28 Conv	$11,500	$15,600	$21,000	$23,800
		346/320 2dr SS Conv	$12,400	$16,800	$22,000	$27,400
-10% for auto. +10% for t-tops. +15% for Special Performance Pkg.						
2000	Corvette	346/345 2dr Cpe	$11,900	$16,300	$21,300	$24,900
		346/345 2dr Conv	$12,900	$17,600	$23,100	$29,000
-10% for auto trans.						
2000	Camaro	231/200 2dr Cpe	$6,600	$8,800	$10,800	$13,500
		346/305 2dr Z/28 Cpe	$10,300	$11,100	$17,100	$21,500
		346/320 2dr SS Cpe	$12,500	$15,500	$19,900	$26,100
		231/200 2dr Conv	$9,600	$10,300	$12,300	$16,200
		346/305 2dr Z/28 Conv	$12,000	$16,400	$21,400	$25,400
		346/320 2dr SS Conv	$12,700	$17,200	$22,300	$28,300
-10% for auto. +10% for t-tops. +15% for Special Performance Pkg.						
2001	Corvette	346/350 2dr Cpe	$11,700	$16,800	$20,400	$25,500
		346/350 2dr Conv	$14,300	$20,400	$23,000	$28,600
		346/385 2dr Z06 Hdtp Cpe	$18,000	$22,500	$27,200	$34,800
-10% for auto trans.						
2001	Camaro	231/200 2dr Cpe	$6,900	$9,400	$11,300	$14,300
		231/205 2dr RS Cpe	$7,300	$9,800	$13,000	$15,500
		346/310 2dr Z/28 Cpe	$7,300	$10,800	$16,600	$22,600
		346/325 2dr SS Cpe	$9,300	$13,500	$21,500	$27,900
		231/200 2dr Conv	$9,900	$10,800	$13,500	$18,400
		231/205 2dr RS Conv	$10,300	$11,300	$14,600	$19,600
		346/310 2dr Z/28 Conv	$12,200	$16,800	$22,000	$25,900
		346/325 2dr SS Conv	$13,500	$17,900	$24,400	$29,300
-10% for auto. +10% for t-tops. +15% for Special Performance Pkg.						
2002	Corvette	346/350 2dr Cpe	$11,700	$16,800	$20,400	$25,500
		346/350 2dr Conv	$14,300	$20,400	$23,000	$28,600
		346/405 2dr Z06 Hdtp Cpe	$18,000	$22,500	$27,200	$34,800
-10% for auto trans.						
2002	Camaro	231/200 2dr Spt Cpe	$6,600	$8,700	$11,400	$15,900

Year	Model	Body Style	4	3	2	1
		231/205 2dr RS Spt Cpe	$6,900	$9,100	$12,000	$17,000
		346/310 2dr Z/28 Spt Cpe	$6,900	$9,900	$16,000	$22,600
		346/325 2dr SS Spt Cpe	$8,000	$11,900	$20,700	$27,000
		346/325 2dr SS 35th Annv Spt Cpe	$9,300	$14,400	$22,600	$30,200
		231/200 2dr Conv	$9,000	$9,900	$13,200	$21,000
		231/205 2dr RS Conv	$9,500	$10,400	$14,100	$21,600
		346/310 2dr Z/28 Conv	$10,900	$14,900	$20,200	$26,100
		346/325 2dr SS Conv	$12,200	$16,600	$23,300	$32,400
		346/325 2dr SS 35th Annv Conv	$12,100	$16,800	$24,000	$34,300
		-10% for auto. +10% for t-tops. +15% for Special Performance Pkg.				
2003	Corvette	346/350 2dr Cpe	$11,700	$16,800	$20,400	$25,500
		346/350 2dr Conv	$14,300	$20,400	$23,000	$28,600
		346/405 2dr Z06 Hdtp Cpe	$18,000	$22,500	$27,200	$34,800
		346/350 2dr 50th Annv Cpe	$17,500	$22,800	$29,800	$35,100
		346/350 2dr 50th Annv Conv	$19,800	$25,500	$32,800	$39,600
		346/350 2dr 50th Annv Pace Car Conv	$19,800	$26,400	$33,000	$41,700
		-10% for auto trans.				
2004	Corvette	346/350 2dr Cpe	$11,700	$16,800	$20,400	$25,500
		346/350 2dr Conv	$14,300	$20,400	$23,000	$28,600
		346/350 2dr Comm Ed Cpe	$15,400	$20,500	$24,000	$28,000
		346/350 2dr Comm Ed Conv	$16,700	$22,000	$26,000	$32,000
		346/405 2dr Z06 Hdtp Cpe	$18,000	$22,500	$27,200	$34,800
		346/405 2dr Z06 Comm Ed Hdtp Cpe	$19,700	$26,000	$33,600	$39,100
		-10% for auto trans.				
2005	Corvette	364/400 2dr Cpe	$13,000	$18,000	$23,500	$26,000
		364/400 2dr Conv	$15,000	$20,000	$27,000	$31,000
		-15% for auto trans.				
2006	Corvette	364/400 2dr Cpe	$13,000	$18,000	$23,500	$26,000
		427/505 2dr Z06 Cpe	$27,000	$36,000	$45,000	$62,000

Chevrolet

Year	Model	Body Style	4	3	2	1
		364/400 2dr Conv	$15,000	$20,000	$27,000	$31,000
						-10% for auto trans.
2007	Corvette	364/400 2dr Cpe	$13,000	$18,000	$23,500	$26,000
		427/505 2dr Z06 Cpe	$27,000	$36,000	$45,000	$62,000
		427/505 2dr Z06 Ron Fellows Ed Cpe	$29,700	$39,600	$49,500	$63,500
		364/400 2dr Conv	$15,000	$20,000	$27,000	$31,000
		364/400 2dr Indy Pace Car Conv	$17,000	$23,000	$30,000	$36,000
						-10% for auto trans.
2008	Corvette	376/430 2dr Cpe	$16,500	$20,000	$27,000	$32,000
		376/430 2dr Indy Pace Car Cpe	$19,500	$23,000	$31,000	$36,000
		427/505 2dr Z06 Cpe	$27,000	$36,000	$45,000	$62,000
		427/505 2dr 427 Limited Ed Z06 Cpe	$29,700	$39,600	$49,500	$63,600
		376/430 2dr Conv	$19,000	$23,000	$30,000	$35,000
		376/430 2dr Indy Pace Car Conv	$21,000	$26,500	$34,500	$38,000
						-10% for auto trans.
2009	Corvette	376/430 2dr Cpe	$16,500	$20,000	$27,000	$32,000
		376/430 2dr GT1 Championship Conv	$21,900	$26,500	$34,500	$40,300
		376/430 2dr GT1 Championship Cpe	$19,000	$23,000	$31,100	$36,800
		427/505 2dr Z06 Cpe	$27,000	$36,000	$45,000	$62,000
		427/505 2dr Z06 GT1 Championship Cpe	$32,400	$43,200	$54,000	$74,400
		376/638 2dr ZR1 Cpe	$47,000	$55,000	$65,000	$76,000
		376/430 2dr Conv	$19,000	$23,000	$30,000	$35,000
						-10% for auto trans.
2010	Camaro	376/400 2dr SS Cpe	$11,000	$15,000	$21,000	$32,000
		376/400 2dr Indy Pace Car Cpe	$12,700	$17,300	$24,200	$36,800
				-20% for 6-cyl, +5% for 2SS, +10% for Transformers Edition, +10% for Hot Wheels Edition, +10% for manual trans on SS, +15% for 1LE, +30% for COPO when ordered with all available engines.			
2010	Corvette	376/430 2dr Cpe	$16,500	$20,000	$27,000	$32,000

Year	Model	Body Style	4	3	2	1
		376/430 2dr Grand Sport Cpe	$23,000	$30,000	$38,000	$49,900
		427/505 2dr Z06 Cpe	$27,000	$36,000	$45,000	$62,000
		376/638 2dr ZR1 Cpe	$47,000	$55,000	$65,000	$76,000
		376/430 2dr Conv	$19,000	$23,000	$30,000	$35,000
		376/430 2dr Grand Sport Conv	$26,500	$36,000	$44,000	$53,000
		-10% for auto trans.				
2011	Camaro	376/400 2dr SS Conv	$13,000	$17,500	$24,000	$36,800
		376/400 2dr SS Cpe	$11,000	$15,000	$21,000	$32,000
		376/400 2dr Indy Pace Car Conv	$15,000	$20,100	$27,600	$42,300
		-20% for 6-cyl, +5% for 2SS, +10% for Transformers Edition, +10% for Hot Wheels Edition, +10% for manual trans on SS, +15% for 1LE, +30% for COPO when ordered with all available engines.				
2011	Corvette	376/430 2dr Cpe	$16,500	$20,000	$27,000	$32,000
		376/430 2dr Grand Sport Cpe	$23,000	$30,000	$38,000	$49,900
		427/505 2dr Z06 Cpe	$27,000	$36,000	$45,000	$62,000
		427/505 2dr Z06 Carbon Edition Cpe	$31,100	$41,400	$51,800	$71,300
		376/638 2dr ZR1 Cpe	$47,000	$55,000	$65,000	$76,000
		376/430 2dr Conv	$19,000	$23,000	$30,000	$35,000
		376/430 2dr Grand Sport Conv	$26,500	$36,000	$44,000	$53,000
		-10% for auto trans.				
2012	Camaro	376/400 2dr SS Cpe	$11,000	$15,000	$21,000	$32,000
		376/400 2dr 45th Anniv Cpe	$12,100	$16,500	$23,100	$35,200
		376/580 2dr ZL1 Cpe	$22,500	$32,000	$39,900	$45,000
		2dr COPO Cpe	$50,000	$75,000	$95,000	$120,000
		376/400 2dr 45th Anniv Conv	$14,300	$19,300	$26,400	$40,500
		-20% for 6-cyl, +5% for 2SS, +10% for Transformers Edition, +10% for Hot Wheels Edition, +10% for manual trans on SS, +15% for 1LE, +30% for COPO when ordered with all available engines.				
2012	Corvette	376/430 2dr Cpe	$16,500	$20,000	$27,000	$32,000
		376/430 2dr Centennial Ed Cpe	$18,200	$22,000	$29,700	$35,200

Chevrolet

Year	Model	Body Style	4	3	2	1
		376/430 2dr Grand Sport Cpe	$23,000	$30,000	$38,000	$49,900
		376/430 2dr Grand Sport Centennial Ed Cpe	$25,300	$33,000	$41,800	$54,900
		427/505 2dr Z06 Cpe	$27,000	$36,000	$45,000	$62,000
		427/505 2dr Z06 Centennial Ed Cpe	$29,700	$39,600	$49,500	$68,200
		376/638 2dr ZR1 Cpe	$47,000	$55,000	$65,000	$76,000
		376/638 2dr ZR1 Centennial Ed Cpe	$51,700	$60,500	$71,500	$88,000
		376/430 2dr Conv	$19,000	$23,000	$30,000	$35,000
		376/430 2dr Centennial Ed Conv	$20,900	$25,300	$33,000	$38,500
		376/430 2dr Grand Sport Conv	$26,500	$36,000	$44,000	$53,000
		376/430 2dr Grand Sport Centennial Ed Conv	$29,200	$39,600	$48,400	$58,300
		-10% for auto trans.				
2013	Camaro	376/400 2dr SS Cpe	$11,000	$15,000	$21,000	$32,000
		376/580 2dr ZL1 Cpe	$22,500	$32,000	$39,900	$45,000
		2dr COPO Cpe	$50,000	$75,000	$95,000	$120,000
		376/400 2dr SS Conv	$13,000	$17,500	$24,000	$36,000
		376/580 2dr ZL1 Conv	$25,000	$35,000	$44,500	$50,000
		-20% for 6-cyl, +5% for 2SS, +10% for Transformers Edition, +10% for Hot Wheels Edition, +10% for manual trans on SS, +15% for 1LE, +30% for COPO when ordered with all available engines.				
2013	Corvette	376/430 2dr Cpe	$16,500	$20,000	$27,000	$32,000
		376/430 2dr 60th Anniv Cpe	$19,000	$23,000	$31,100	$36,800
		376/430 2dr Grand Sport Cpe	$23,000	$30,000	$38,000	$49,900
		376/430 2dr Grand Sport 60th Anniv Cpe	$26,500	$34,500	$43,700	$57,400
		427/505 2dr Z06 Cpe	$27,000	$36,000	$45,000	$62,000
		427/505 2dr Z06 60th Anniv Cpe	$31,100	$41,400	$51,800	$71,300
		376/638 2dr ZR1 Cpe	$47,000	$55,000	$65,000	$76,000

Year	Model	Body Style	4	3	2	1
		376/638 2dr ZR1 60th Anniv Cpe	$54,100	$63,300	$74,800	$92,000
		376/430 2dr Conv	$19,000	$23,000	$30,000	$35,000
		376/430 2dr 60th Anniv Conv	$21,900	$26,500	$34,500	$40,300
		376/430 2dr Grand Sport Conv	$26,500	$36,000	$44,000	$53,000
		376/430 2dr Grand Sport 60th Anniv Conv	$30,500	$41,400	$50,600	$61,000
		427/505 2dr 427 Collector Edition Conv	$45,000	$51,000	$55,000	$61,000
		427/505 2dr 427 Collector Ed 60th Anniv Conv	$51,800	$58,700	$63,300	$70,200

-10% for auto trans.

Year	Model	Body Style	4	3	2	1
2014	SS	376/415 4dr Sdn	$24,000	$32,000	$40,000	$45,000
2014	Camaro	376/400 2dr SS Cpe	$11,000	$15,000	$21,000	$32,000
		376/580 2dr ZL1 Cpe	$22,500	$32,000	$39,900	$45,000
		427/505 2dr Z/28 Cpe	$36,000	$39,900	$46,000	$54,000
		2dr COPO Cpe	$50,000	$75,000	$95,000	$120,000
		376/400 2dr SS Conv	$13,000	$17,500	$24,000	$36,800
		376/580 2dr ZL1 Conv	$25,000	$35,000	$44,500	$50,000

-20% for 6-cyl, +5% for 2SS, +10% for Transformers Edition, +10% for Hot Wheels Edition, +10% for manual trans on SS, +15% for 1LE, +30% for COPO when ordered with all available engines.

Year	Model	Body Style	4	3	2	1
2015	SS	376/415 4dr Sdn	$26,000	$35,500	$42,000	$47,000

+15% for manual trans.

Year	Model	Body Style	4	3	2	1
2015	Camaro	376/400 2dr SS Cpe	$11,000	$15,000	$21,000	$32,000
		376/580 2dr ZL1 Cpe	$22,500	$32,000	$39,900	$45,000
		427/505 2dr Z/28 Cpe	$36,000	$39,900	$46,000	$54,000
		2dr COPO Cpe	$50,000	$75,000	$95,000	$120,000
		376/400 2dr SS Conv	$13,000	$17,500	$24,000	$36,800
		376/580 2dr ZL1 Conv	$25,000	$35,000	$44,500	$50,000

-20% for 6-cyl, +5% for 2SS, +10% for Transformers Edition, +10% for Hot Wheels Edition, +10% for manual trans on SS, +15% for 1LE, +30% for COPO when ordered with all available engines.

Year	Model	Body Style	4	3	2	1
2016	SS	376/415 4dr Sdn	$28,000	$35,500	$42,000	$47,000

+15% for manual trans.

Chevrolet

Year	Model	Body Style	4	3	2	1
2017	SS	376/415 4dr Sdn	$29,000	$35,500	$42,000	$47,000

+15% for manual trans.

Chrysler

Year	Model	Body Style	4	3	2	1
1946	Royal	250.6/114 2dr Cpe	$6,900	$9,800	$15,400	$20,700
		250.6/114 2dr Clb Cpe	$7,000	$10,900	$16,800	$23,600
		250.6/114 4dr Sdn	$4,500	$6,800	$11,500	$20,000
1946	Windsor	250.6/114 2dr Cpe	$7,900	$12,400	$19,600	$26,000
		250.6/114 2dr Clb Cpe	$8,200	$12,900	$19,500	$28,200
		250.6/114 4dr Sdn	$5,800	$8,600	$14,900	$23,100
		250.6/114 2dr Conv	$15,400	$23,900	$44,100	$60,700
1946	Saratoga	323.5/135 2dr Cpe	$8,200	$12,900	$19,600	$27,500
		323.5/135 2dr Clb Cpe	$8,800	$13,700	$21,200	$29,800
		323.5/135 4dr Sdn	$5,500	$7,900	$13,400	$21,300
1946	New Yorker	323.5/135 2dr Cpe	$12,300	$17,500	$28,400	$35,700
		323.5/135 2dr Clb Cpe	$13,000	$18,700	$32,100	$41,600
		323.5/135 4dr Sdn	$8,200	$12,300	$21,200	$28,900
		323.5/135 2dr Conv	$25,400	$36,200	$63,500	$91,600
1946	Town & Country	323.5/135 4dr Sdn	$36,300	$65,200	$93,800	$138,000
		323.5/135 2dr Conv	$44,100	$78,300	$112,000	$182,000
1947	Royal	250.6/114 2dr Cpe	$6,900	$9,800	$15,400	$20,700
		250.6/114 2dr Clb Cpe	$7,000	$10,900	$16,800	$23,600
		250.6/114 4dr Sdn	$4,500	$6,800	$11,500	$20,000
1947	Windsor	250.6/114 2dr Cpe	$7,900	$12,400	$19,600	$26,000
		250.6/114 2dr Clb Cpe	$8,200	$12,900	$19,500	$28,200
		250.6/114 4dr Sdn	$5,800	$8,600	$14,900	$23,100
		250.6/114 2dr Conv	$15,400	$23,900	$44,100	$60,700
1947	Saratoga	323.5/135 2dr Cpe	$8,200	$12,900	$19,600	$27,500
		323.5/135 2dr Clb Cpe	$8,800	$13,700	$21,200	$29,800
		323.5/135 4dr Sdn	$5,500	$7,900	$13,400	$21,300
1947	New Yorker	323.5/135 2dr Cpe	$12,300	$17,500	$28,400	$35,700
		323.5/135 2dr Clb Cpe	$13,000	$18,700	$32,100	$41,600
		323.5/135 4dr Sdn	$8,200	$12,300	$21,200	$28,900
		323.5/135 2dr Conv	$25,400	$36,200	$63,500	$91,600

Year	Model	Body Style	4	3	2	1
1947	Town & Country	250.6/114 4dr Sdn	$36,300	$65,200	$93,800	$138,000
		323.5/135 2dr Conv	$44,100	$78,300	$112,000	$182,000
1948	Royal	250.6/114 2dr Cpe	$6,900	$9,800	$15,400	$20,700
		250.6/114 2dr Clb Cpe	$7,000	$10,900	$16,800	$23,600
		250.6/114 4dr Sdn	$4,500	$6,800	$11,500	$20,000
1948	Windsor	250.6/114 2dr Cpe	$7,900	$12,400	$19,600	$26,000
		250.6/114 2dr Clb Cpe	$8,200	$12,900	$19,500	$28,200
		250.6/114 4dr Sdn	$5,800	$8,600	$14,900	$23,100
		250.6/114 2dr Conv	$15,400	$23,900	$44,100	$60,700
1948	Saratoga	323.5/135 2dr Cpe	$8,200	$12,900	$19,600	$27,500
		323.5/135 2dr Clb Cpe	$8,800	$13,700	$21,200	$29,800
		323.5/135 4dr Sdn	$5,500	$7,900	$13,400	$21,300
1948	New Yorker	323.5/135 2dr Cpe	$12,300	$17,500	$28,400	$35,700
		323.5/135 2dr Town & Country Cpe	$54,300	$87,000	$122,000	$189,000
		323.5/135 2dr Clb Cpe	$13,000	$18,700	$32,100	$41,600
		323.5/135 4dr Sdn	$8,200	$12,300	$21,200	$28,900
		323.5/135 2dr Conv	$23,500	$33,500	$58,800	$84,800
1948	Town & Country	323.5/135 2dr Conv	$39,200	$74,900	$104,000	$175,000
1949	Royal	250/116 2dr Clb Cpe	$6,700	$10,000	$15,200	$20,100
		250/116 4dr Sdn	$4,200	$6,200	$10,400	$13,700
1949	Windsor	250/116 2dr Clb Cpe	$6,900	$10,200	$16,500	$22,600
		250.6/114 4dr Sdn	$4,500	$7,300	$11,600	$16,700
		250.6/114 2dr Conv	$12,500	$21,000	$39,200	$55,800
1949	Saratoga	323.5/135 2dr Clb Cpe	$8,300	$12,200	$19,900	$25,800
		323.5/135 4dr Sdn	$4,200	$6,700	$11,900	$17,700
1949	New Yorker	323.5/135 2dr Clb Cpe	$9,200	$13,700	$22,700	$29,600
		323.5/135 4dr Sdn	$6,600	$9,600	$16,500	$21,500
		323.5/135 2dr Conv	$18,800	$29,500	$54,000	$74,800
1949	Town & Country	323.5/135 2dr Conv	$35,600	$72,500	$99,600	$151,000
1949	Crown Imperial	323.5/135 4dr Sdn	$5,600	$8,800	$15,400	$23,100
1950	Royal	250/116 2dr Clb Cpe	$6,100	$9,400	$14,600	$19,700

Chrysler

Year	Model	Body Style	4	3	2	1
		250/116 4dr Sdn	$3,600	$5,700	$10,200	$13,700
		250/116 4dr Wgn	$9,700	$14,500	$20,900	$32,600
		250/116 4dr Town & Country Wgn	$31,100	$43,100	$55,400	$98,900
1950	Windsor	250/116 2dr Clb Cpe	$7,000	$10,400	$16,800	$22,200
		250/116 4dr Sdn	$4,600	$7,400	$11,900	$15,700
		250/116 2dr Newport Hdtp	$5,600	$9,400	$16,200	$26,400
		250/116 2dr Conv	$14,100	$21,600	$41,600	$54,700
1950	Saratoga	324/135 2dr Clb Cpe	$8,100	$12,700	$20,100	$27,200
		324/135 4dr Sdn	$4,300	$7,200	$12,500	$17,700
1950	New Yorker	324/135 2dr Clb Cpe	$10,000	$13,900	$22,900	$30,000
		324/135 4dr Sdn	$4,800	$7,500	$12,600	$18,500
		324/135 4dr Imp Sdn	$5,800	$10,100	$16,300	$22,100
		324/135 2dr Newport Hdtp	$7,600	$12,600	$19,700	$24,700
		324/135 2dr Conv	$22,500	$32,300	$56,200	$74,800
1950	Town & Country	324/135 2dr Newport Hdtp	$22,600	$32,400	$49,800	$91,400
1950	Crown Imperial	324/135 4dr Sdn	$6,600	$12,500	$18,000	$28,400
1951	Windsor	250/116 2dr Clb Cpe	$7,000	$10,400	$16,700	$23,500
		250/116 4dr Sdn	$5,500	$9,000	$13,700	$17,900
		250/116 2dr Conv	$12,200	$20,200	$36,700	$52,300
1951	Windsor DeLuxe	250/116 2dr Newport Hdtp	$7,100	$10,800	$17,400	$25,000
1951	Saratoga	331/180 2dr Clb Cpe	$8,700	$12,900	$19,200	$26,900
		331/180 4dr Sdn	$6,400	$9,800	$14,600	$20,200
		331/180 4dr Town & Country Wgn	$11,700	$17,600	$25,800	$31,200
1951	New Yorker	331/180 2dr Clb Cpe	$8,500	$13,000	$20,800	$28,000
		331/180 4dr Sdn	$5,900	$9,500	$15,800	$23,400
		331/180 4dr Town & Country Wgn	$11,300	$17,400	$26,800	$46,200
		331/180 2dr Newport Hdtp	$9,900	$13,600	$23,300	$33,600
		331/180 2dr Conv	$21,100	$32,900	$56,000	$73,900
1951	Imperial	331/180 2dr Clb Cpe	$7,700	$12,100	$20,700	$31,900
		331/180 4dr Sdn	$5,500	$8,500	$14,100	$21,400
		331/180 2dr Conv	$19,100	$28,600	$61,000	$94,200
1951	Crown Imperial	331/180 4dr Sdn	$5,900	$9,300	$18,100	$24,100
1952	Windsor	265/119 2dr Clb Cpe	$6,900	$10,100	$16,900	$22,500

Year	Model	Body Style	4	3	2	1
		265/119 4dr Sdn	$5,200	$8,200	$13,400	$17,700
		265/119 2dr Conv	$12,800	$20,500	$37,900	$59,300
1952	Saratoga	331/180 2dr Clb Cpe	$8,500	$12,900	$19,400	$25,600
		331/180 4dr Sdn	$6,300	$9,800	$14,400	$19,500
		331/180 4dr Town & Country Wgn	$12,100	$17,600	$25,800	$37,700
1952	New Yorker	331/180 2dr New-port Hdtp	$8,500	$13,200	$21,600	$28,600
		331/180 4dr Sdn	$5,300	$8,700	$15,200	$21,800
		331/180 4dr Town & Country Wgn	$11,800	$18,300	$27,700	$49,300
		331/180 2dr Conv	$19,100	$29,900	$52,900	$74,200
1952	Imperial	331/180 2dr Clb Cpe	$6,800	$10,500	$18,300	$26,300
		331/180 4dr Sdn	$5,100	$8,200	$14,000	$19,100
1952	Crown Imperial	331/180 4dr Sdn	$5,700	$8,900	$15,800	$22,200
1953	Windsor	265/119 2dr Clb Cpe	$6,800	$10,200	$16,800	$23,500
1953	Windsor DeLuxe	265/119 4dr Sdn	$5,000	$8,000	$13,200	$17,700
		265/119 2dr Newport Hdtp	$7,000	$10,700	$17,500	$25,000
		265/119 2dr Conv	$13,700	$21,000	$38,100	$59,200
1953	New Yorker	331/180 2dr Clb Cpe	$8,800	$13,000	$20,900	$27,800
		331/180 4dr Sdn 6P	$6,200	$9,500	$15,600	$21,200
		331/180 4dr Town & Country Wgn	$12,500	$18,400	$28,900	$50,300
		331/180 2dr Newport Hdtp	$10,300	$14,600	$23,200	$31,300
1953	Custom Imperial	331/180 2dr Newport Hdtp	$11,700	$17,100	$27,600	$36,500
		331/180 4dr Sdn	$5,400	$8,000	$13,100	$19,100
1953	Crown Imperial	331/180 4dr Sdn	$5,400	$8,300	$13,700	$20,400
1954	Windsor DeLuxe	265/119 4dr Sdn	$5,100	$8,100	$13,100	$17,800
		265/119 2dr Newport Hdtp	$6,900	$10,500	$17,200	$23,700
		265/119 2dr Conv	$13,400	$20,800	$39,200	$60,600
1954	New Yorker	331/195 2dr Clb Cpe	$8,600	$13,000	$20,800	$28,300
		331/195 2dr Newport Hdtp	$9,800	$14,200	$22,900	$31,000
		331/195 4dr Town & Country Wgn	$13,200	$18,800	$31,000	$51,500
1954	New Yorker DeLuxe	331/235 4dr Sdn	$6,700	$10,500	$15,400	$21,800
		331/235 2dr Conv	$26,600	$39,600	$57,500	$76,200

Chrysler

Year	Model	Body Style	4	3	2	1
1954	Custom Imperial	331/235 4dr Sdn	$5,400	$8,300	$13,200	$20,500
		331/235 2dr Newport Hdtp	$12,000	$17,300	$27,600	$38,500
1954	Crown Imperial	331/235 4dr Sdn	$5,400	$8,500	$15,400	$26,000

From 1955 to 1970, Imperial was marketed as a separate make.

Year	Model	Body Style	4	3	2	1
1955	Windsor DeLuxe	301/188 2dr Conv	$28,500	$40,000	$63,600	$88,200
		301/188 2dr Nassau Hdtp	$13,900	$20,400	$29,600	$40,300
		301/188 4dr Newport Hdtp	$15,300	$22,700	$32,900	$42,700
		301/188 4dr Sdn	$10,500	$14,900	$20,700	$27,200
1955	New Yorker DeLuxe	331/250 2dr Newport Hdtp	$16,700	$23,200	$36,500	$53,500
		331/250 2dr St. Regis Hdtp	$19,900	$28,200	$41,700	$63,600
		331/250 4dr Sdn	$12,700	$17,300	$27,000	$35,000
		331/250 4dr Town & Country Wgn	$13,700	$20,300	$30,900	$40,900
		331/250 2dr Conv	$34,300	$52,900	$83,900	$124,000
1955	C-300	331/300 2dr Hdtp	$27,500	$41,400	$76,300	$120,000
1956	Windsor	331/225 2dr Nassau Hdtp	$13,600	$20,000	$29,500	$37,900
		331/225 4dr Sdn	$9,600	$14,800	$20,600	$27,200
		331/225 4dr Newport Hdtp	$14,700	$21,900	$31,800	$41,100
		331/225 2dr Conv	$27,700	$39,800	$60,500	$83,200
1956	New Yorker	354/280 2dr St. Regis Hdtp	$20,400	$29,500	$42,500	$64,100
		354/280 2dr Newport Hdtp	$16,900	$25,500	$39,800	$56,700
		354/280 4dr Newport Hdtp	$12,400	$18,400	$25,800	$35,100
		354/280 4dr Town & Country Wgn	$13,500	$20,000	$31,000	$41,200
		354/280 2dr Conv	$33,800	$50,100	$82,600	$121,000
1956	300B	354/340 2dr Hdtp	$30,100	$45,400	$70,800	$114,000

+10% for factory a/c.

Year	Model	Body Style	4	3	2	1
1957	Windsor	354/285 4dr Sdn	$11,300	$17,200	$21,500	$28,800
		354/285 2dr Hdtp	$16,800	$25,000	$36,300	$46,000
1957	Saratoga	354/295 2dr Hdtp	$19,100	$28,200	$41,400	$52,800
		354/295 4dr Sdn	$12,600	$18,700	$24,100	$32,400
		354/295 4dr Hdtp	$13,400	$20,300	$28,900	$36,400
1957	New Yorker	392/325 2dr Hdtp	$20,700	$30,300	$45,800	$60,800
		392/325 4dr Hdtp	$13,900	$21,500	$29,400	$40,900
		392/325 4dr Sdn	$12,700	$19,000	$25,700	$35,600

Year	Model	Body Style	4	3	2	1
		392/325 4dr Town & Country Wgn	$16,300	$24,300	$37,700	$49,600
		392/325 2dr Conv	$38,900	$52,300	$78,600	$102,000
1957	300C	392/375 2dr Hdtp	$25,500	$37,200	$57,600	$77,000
		392/375 2dr Conv	$73,400	$101,000	$128,000	$163,000
						+10% for factory a/c.
1958	Windsor	354/290 2dr Hdtp	$16,700	$24,900	$36,200	$46,000
		354/290 4dr Sdn	$11,000	$17,200	$22,800	$29,400
1958	Saratoga	354/310 2dr Hdtp	$19,100	$28,200	$41,400	$52,800
		354/310 4dr Sdn	$12,700	$18,800	$25,100	$30,900
		354/310 4dr Hdtp	$15,900	$23,000	$36,700	$44,100
1958	New Yorker	392/345 2dr Hdtp	$21,000	$31,300	$48,000	$63,000
		392/345 4dr Sdn	$13,600	$20,400	$26,800	$35,800
		392/345 4dr Town & Country Stn Wgn	$16,300	$24,300	$37,900	$50,000
		392/345 4dr Hdtp	$15,600	$23,200	$35,700	$45,500
		392/345 2dr Conv	$39,600	$54,700	$80,600	$109,000
1958	300D	392/380 2dr Hdtp Cpe	$26,200	$37,800	$57,900	$87,700
		392/380 2dr Conv	$83,000	$105,000	$135,000	$172,000
						+10% for factory a/c.
1959	Windsor	383/305 2dr Hdtp	$16,700	$25,000	$36,200	$46,000
		383/305 4dr Sdn	$11,300	$17,300	$24,900	$31,800
		383/305 2dr Conv	$31,200	$40,400	$54,000	$70,200
1959	Saratoga	383/325 2dr Hdtp	$19,000	$28,200	$41,300	$52,800
		383/325 4dr Sdn	$12,500	$18,700	$27,200	$34,500
		383/325 4dr Hdtp	$14,600	$22,000	$30,900	$40,200
1959	New Yorker	413/350 2dr Hdtp	$20,900	$31,200	$48,000	$63,100
		413/350 4dr Sdn	$13,400	$19,900	$28,500	$36,500
		413/350 4dr Town & Country Stn Wgn	$16,700	$24,700	$37,900	$52,500
		413/350 4dr Hdtp	$15,700	$22,500	$31,800	$44,200
		413/350 2dr Conv	$40,000	$54,700	$81,500	$110,000
1959	300E	413/380 2dr Hdtp	$26,900	$43,100	$59,600	$89,100
		413/380 2dr Conv	$85,000	$113,000	$138,000	$181,000
						+10% for factory a/c.
1960	Windsor	383/305 2dr Hdtp Cpe	$13,800	$20,600	$34,000	$42,300
		383/305 4dr Sdn	$7,000	$10,600	$16,200	$20,600
		383/305 4dr Hdtp Sdn	$11,300	$17,000	$25,900	$32,500
		383/305 2dr Conv	$24,100	$36,900	$59,000	$79,800
1960	Saratoga	383/325 2dr Hdtp Cpe	$14,000	$20,500	$30,400	$37,800
		383/325 4dr Sdn	$8,000	$11,900	$17,800	$22,500
		383/325 4dr Hdtp Sdn	$10,300	$15,300	$22,700	$28,800

Chrysler

Year	Model	Body Style	4	3	2	1
1960	New Yorker	413/350 2dr Hdtp Cpe	$17,700	$26,400	$39,700	$49,900
		413/350 4dr Sdn	$9,100	$15,400	$25,200	$31,900
		413/350 4dr Town & Country Stn Wgn	$16,800	$28,000	$41,800	$56,200
		413/350 4dr Hdtp Sdn	$11,000	$18,400	$30,300	$38,200
		413/350 2dr Conv	$32,600	$44,500	$70,200	$90,600
1960	300F	413/375 2dr Hdtp Cpe	$32,600	$47,900	$73,900	$93,600
		413/375 2dr Conv	$89,000	$112,000	$153,000	$192,000
						+10% for factory a/c.
1961	Newport	361/265 2dr Hdtp Cpe	$12,600	$18,600	$27,500	$34,200
		361/265 4dr Sdn	$7,600	$11,300	$16,700	$21,100
		361/265 4dr Hdtp Sdn	$8,900	$13,100	$19,400	$24,500
		361/265 2dr Conv	$23,400	$35,100	$52,900	$66,900
1961	Windsor	383/305 2dr Hdtp Cpe	$14,400	$24,300	$36,800	$44,100
		383/305 4dr Sdn	$9,200	$13,500	$21,100	$26,600
		383/305 4dr Hdtp Sdn	$11,700	$17,600	$27,200	$34,500
1961	New Yorker	413/350 2dr Hdtp Cpe	$17,600	$26,300	$39,100	$49,200
		413/350 4dr Sdn	$8,800	$14,700	$24,000	$30,400
		413/350 4dr Town & Country Stn Wgn	$16,300	$25,700	$38,600	$49,100
		413/350 4dr Hdtp Sdn	$9,900	$16,600	$27,500	$34,700
		413/350 2dr Conv	$31,600	$43,100	$67,200	$86,800
1961	300G	413/375 2dr Hdtp Cpe	$28,300	$43,500	$69,700	$90,100
		413/375 2dr Conv	$72,400	$89,200	$135,000	$180,000
						+10% for factory a/c.
1962	Newport	361/265 2dr Hdtp Cpe	$5,300	$8,100	$12,300	$15,200
		361/265 4dr Sdn	$4,100	$6,000	$8,800	$13,600
		361/265 4dr Hdtp Sdn	$4,400	$6,800	$10,100	$14,100
		361/265 2dr Conv	$13,200	$19,300	$29,800	$37,500
1962	New Yorker	413/340 4dr Sdn	$4,000	$7,100	$10,900	$15,000
		413/340 4dr Town & Country Stn Wgn	$4,600	$7,600	$12,400	$18,600
		413/340 4dr Hdtp Sdn	$4,200	$7,500	$12,200	$16,200
1962	300	383/305 2dr Hdtp Cpe	$5,300	$8,100	$12,400	$15,800

Year	Model	Body Style	4	3	2	1
		383/305 4dr Hdtp Sdn	$3,800	$7,000	$9,800	$12,400
		383/305 2dr Conv	$8,700	$16,000	$27,400	$37,300
						+10% for factory a/c.
1962	300H	413/380 2dr Hdtp Cpe	$16,400	$24,800	$37,200	$53,000
		413/405 2dr Hdtp Cpe	$22,400	$32,600	$44,700	$58,400
		413/380 2dr Conv	$37,400	$54,500	$79,600	$97,800
		413/405 2dr Conv	$47,200	$62,600	$85,100	$118,000
						+10% for factory a/c.
1963	Newport	361/265 2dr Hdtp Cpe	$5,300	$8,000	$12,100	$14,600
		361/265 4dr Sdn	$3,900	$5,900	$8,800	$10,800
		361/265 4dr Hdtp Sdn	$4,300	$6,600	$9,800	$12,100
		361/265 2dr Conv	$13,200	$19,500	$30,000	$37,500
1963	300	383/305 2dr Hdtp Cpe	$5,400	$8,200	$12,600	$16,000
		383/305 2dr Pace Setter Hdtp Cpe	$10,900	$16,000	$24,400	$30,400
		383/305 4dr Hdtp Sdn	$4,600	$7,200	$10,000	$12,600
		383/305 2dr Conv	$8,800	$14,800	$24,700	$33,300
		383/305 2dr Pace Setter Conv	$14,200	$20,500	$37,100	$48,100
						+10% for factory a/c.
1963	New Yorker	413/340 4dr Sdn	$4,200	$7,500	$12,600	$16,800
		413/340 4dr Town & Country Stn Wgn	$5,200	$9,100	$14,800	$28,000
		413/340 4dr Hdtp Sdn	$4,100	$6,800	$12,200	$15,600
1963	300J	413/390 2dr Hdtp Cpe	$11,300	$16,700	$25,800	$32,900
						+10% for factory a/c.
1964	Newport	361/265 2dr Hdtp Cpe	$5,100	$7,900	$12,000	$14,600
		361/265 4dr Sdn	$3,600	$5,600	$8,200	$10,600
		361/265 4dr Hdtp Sdn	$4,000	$6,300	$9,500	$11,700
		361/265 2dr Conv	$14,400	$21,600	$33,300	$41,700
1964	300	383/305 2dr Hdtp Cpe	$5,300	$8,000	$12,300	$15,400
		383/305 4dr Hdtp Sdn	$4,100	$6,600	$9,500	$12,200
		383/305 2dr Conv	$9,500	$17,000	$28,700	$39,300
1964	New Yorker	413/340 4dr Sdn	$3,900	$6,500	$11,100	$14,100

Chrysler

Year	Model	Body Style	4	3	2	1
		413/340 4dr Town & Country Stn Wgn	$5,500	$9,700	$16,600	$30,600
		413/340 4dr Hdtp Sdn	$4,400	$7,700	$12,900	$16,500
1964	300K	413/360 2dr Hdtp Cpe	$10,900	$15,600	$23,400	$31,600
		413/390 2dr Hdtp Cpe	$12,500	$18,700	$27,500	$35,200
		413/360 2dr Conv	$16,700	$23,900	$39,000	$53,200
		413/390 2dr Conv	$20,100	$29,700	$46,500	$62,300
						+10% for factory a/c.
1965	Newport	383/270 2dr Hdtp Cpe	$4,400	$7,100	$11,200	$18,000
		383/315 2dr Hdtp Cpe	$5,300	$8,800	$13,000	$20,400
		383/270 4dr Sdn	$3,800	$5,800	$8,500	$10,800
		383/315 4dr Sdn	$4,600	$6,900	$10,100	$13,000
		383/270 4dr Town & Country Stn Wgn	$4,700	$7,700	$11,200	$14,300
		383/315 4dr Town & Country Stn Wgn	$5,600	$9,100	$13,400	$16,900
		383/270 4dr Hdtp Sdn	$3,500	$5,400	$8,100	$10,300
		383/315 4dr Hdtp Sdn	$4,200	$6,400	$9,800	$12,400
		383/270 2dr Conv	$10,500	$16,700	$26,400	$33,200
		383/315 2dr Conv	$12,600	$20,000	$31,600	$39,900
1965	300	383/315 2dr Hdtp Cpe	$5,600	$8,600	$13,400	$18,700
		413/360 2dr Hdtp Cpe	$6,200	$9,200	$14,900	$21,400
		383/315 4dr Hdtp Sdn	$3,700	$5,800	$8,900	$11,500
		413/360 4dr Hdtp Sdn	$4,000	$6,500	$10,100	$12,400
		383/315 2dr Conv	$8,700	$15,500	$26,200	$37,000
		413/360 2dr Conv	$10,100	$17,600	$29,500	$42,400
1965	New Yorker	413/340 2dr Hdtp Cpe	$6,200	$9,700	$15,400	$22,300
		413/360 2dr Hdtp Cpe	$6,800	$10,600	$17,000	$24,700
		413/340 4dr Hdtp Sdn	$4,800	$7,500	$11,800	$15,800
		413/360 4dr Hdtp Sdn	$5,100	$8,300	$12,900	$17,400
1965	300L	413/360 2dr Hdtp Cpe	$8,900	$12,600	$19,400	$24,800
		413/360 2dr Conv	$16,200	$24,200	$38,700	$49,700

Year	Model	Body Style	4	3	2	1
1966	Newport	383/270 2dr Hdtp Cpe	$4,400	$7,100	$11,200	$18,000
		383/270 4dr Sdn	$3,800	$5,800	$8,600	$10,900
		383/325 4dr Sdn	$4,600	$6,900	$10,200	$13,000
		383/270 4dr Town & Country Stn Wgn	$5,000	$7,800	$11,200	$14,300
		383/325 4dr Town & Country Stn Wgn	$5,900	$9,200	$13,400	$16,900
		383/270 4dr Hdtp Sdn	$3,500	$5,400	$8,100	$10,300
		383/325 4dr Hdtp Sdn	$4,200	$6,400	$9,800	$12,400
		383/270 2dr Conv	$11,100	$17,000	$24,600	$31,700
		383/325 2dr Conv	$13,300	$20,300	$29,500	$37,900
1966	300	383/325 2dr Hdtp Cpe	$6,100	$9,300	$13,800	$19,900
		383/325 4dr Hdtp Sdn	$3,800	$6,000	$9,200	$11,700
		383/325 2dr Conv	$8,800	$15,000	$26,100	$37,200
1966	New Yorker	440/350 2dr Hdtp Cpe	$6,200	$9,600	$15,300	$21,900
		440/350 4dr Hdtp Sdn	$4,800	$7,100	$11,500	$14,700
1967	Newport	383/270 2dr Hdtp Cpe	$4,400	$7,100	$11,200	$18,000
		383/270 4dr Sdn	$3,800	$5,700	$8,500	$10,700
		383/270 4dr Town & Country Stn Wgn	$5,600	$8,400	$12,000	$14,500
		383/270 4dr Hdtp Sdn	$3,500	$5,300	$8,000	$10,100
		383/270 2dr Conv	$11,600	$17,300	$24,700	$31,300
1967	300	440/350 2dr Hdtp Cpe	$6,700	$9,700	$14,200	$20,300
		440/350 4dr Hdtp Sdn	$4,000	$6,200	$9,300	$11,400
		440/350 2dr Conv	$9,000	$16,800	$27,300	$37,900
1967	New Yorker	440/350 2dr Hdtp Cpe	$6,600	$9,800	$15,400	$21,900
		440/350 4dr Hdtp Sdn	$4,900	$7,300	$11,600	$14,600
1968	Newport	383/290 2dr Hdtp Cpe	$4,500	$7,200	$11,600	$18,200
		440/375 2dr Hdtp Cpe	$5,200	$8,500	$12,700	$19,400
		383/290 4dr Sdn	$3,900	$5,700	$8,500	$10,700
		440/375 4dr Sdn	$4,600	$6,500	$9,700	$12,300

Chrysler

Year	Model	Body Style	4	3	2	1
		383/290 4dr Town & Country Stn Wgn	$4,800	$7,300	$11,000	$16,100
		440/375 4dr Town & Country Stn Wgn	$5,500	$8,500	$12,500	$18,500
		383/290 4dr Hdtp Sdn	$3,600	$5,400	$8,200	$10,300
		440/375 4dr Hdtp Sdn	$4,300	$6,600	$9,600	$11,700
		383/290 2dr Conv	$11,400	$17,200	$25,200	$31,800
		440/375 2dr Conv	$13,300	$19,800	$28,400	$36,500
1968	300	440/350 2dr Hdtp Cpe	$6,400	$9,600	$14,100	$20,700
		440/375 2dr Hdtp Cpe	$7,300	$11,100	$16,200	$23,200
		440/350 4dr Hdtp Sdn	$3,800	$5,700	$8,600	$10,700
		440/375 4dr Hdtp Sdn	$4,500	$6,600	$10,000	$12,300
		440/350 2dr Conv	$10,900	$17,500	$27,600	$38,000
		440/375 2dr Conv	$11,200	$19,700	$31,500	$43,600
1968	New Yorker	440/350 2dr Hdtp Cpe	$6,300	$9,700	$15,300	$21,700
		440/375 2dr Hdtp Cpe	$7,100	$11,100	$17,600	$25,300
		440/350 4dr Hdtp Sdn	$5,300	$7,700	$11,700	$14,600
		440/375 4dr Hdtp Sdn	$6,300	$8,700	$13,600	$17,000
1969	Newport	383/290 2dr Hdtp Cpe	$4,600	$6,800	$9,800	$11,900
		440/375 2dr Hdtp Cpe	$5,400	$7,900	$11,200	$13,600
		383/290 4dr Sdn	$2,800	$3,700	$5,600	$6,900
		440/375 4dr Sdn	$3,200	$4,400	$6,500	$7,900
		383/290 4dr Hdtp Sdn	$3,700	$5,400	$8,300	$10,200
		440/375 4dr Hdtp Sdn	$4,400	$6,200	$9,500	$11,800
		383/290 2dr Conv	$5,900	$8,500	$12,600	$16,000
		440/375 2dr Conv	$6,700	$9,800	$14,600	$18,500
1969	Town & Country	383/290 4dr Stn Wgn	$4,800	$7,600	$11,200	$15,200
		440/350 4dr Stn Wgn	$5,600	$8,500	$12,800	$17,700
1969	300	440/350 2dr Hdtp Cpe	$6,600	$9,500	$14,100	$17,700
		440/375 2dr Hdtp Cpe	$7,600	$10,800	$16,100	$20,200

Year	Model	Body Style	4	3	2	1
		440/350 4dr Hdtp Sdn	$4,600	$6,900	$10,100	$12,500
		440/375 4dr Hdtp Sdn	$5,200	$8,000	$11,700	$14,700
		440/350 2dr Conv	$10,300	$17,900	$28,100	$38,700
		440/375 2dr Conv	$11,900	$20,900	$32,100	$43,600
1969	New Yorker	440/350 2dr Hdtp Cpe	$6,500	$10,300	$14,000	$17,500
		440/375 2dr Hdtp Cpe	$7,500	$11,800	$16,100	$20,200
		440/350 4dr Sdn	$3,600	$5,900	$8,400	$10,200
		440/375 4dr Sdn	$4,300	$6,800	$9,600	$11,800
		440/350 4dr Hdtp Sdn	$3,700	$6,200	$9,100	$11,300
		440/375 4dr Hdtp Sdn	$4,400	$7,000	$10,400	$13,000
1970	Newport	383/290 2dr Hdtp Cpe	$4,000	$6,100	$9,200	$11,400
		440/375 2dr Hdtp Cpe	$4,600	$7,100	$10,600	$13,200
		383/290 4dr Sdn	$2,700	$3,600	$5,400	$6,900
		440/375 4dr Sdn	$3,100	$4,100	$6,300	$7,900
		383/290 4dr Hdtp Sdn	$3,100	$4,300	$6,700	$8,200
		440/375 4dr Hdtp Sdn	$3,600	$4,900	$7,700	$9,500
		383/290 2dr Conv	$6,000	$8,500	$12,600	$16,000
		440/375 2dr Conv	$6,700	$9,900	$14,600	$18,500
1970	Town & Country	440/375 4dr Stn Wgn	$5,600	$8,500	$12,800	$18,100
		383/290 4dr Stn Wgn	$4,800	$7,600	$11,200	$15,700
1970	300	440/350 2dr Hdtp Cpe	$6,500	$9,300	$14,100	$17,700
		440/375 2dr Hdtp Cpe	$7,700	$10,500	$16,200	$20,200
		440/375 2dr Hurst Hdtp Cpe	$19,600	$26,700	$39,800	$50,400
		440/350 4dr Hdtp Sdn	$4,800	$7,000	$10,000	$12,500
		440/375 4dr Hdtp Sdn	$5,500	$8,100	$11,500	$14,400
		440/350 2dr Conv	$10,300	$17,700	$27,600	$37,900
		440/375 2dr Conv	$12,000	$20,200	$31,500	$43,500
1970	New Yorker	440/350 2dr Hdtp Cpe	$5,900	$9,200	$12,600	$15,800
		440/375 2dr Hdtp Cpe	$6,900	$10,600	$14,700	$18,300
		440/350 4dr Sdn	$3,600	$5,800	$8,300	$10,200

Chrysler

Year	Model	Body Style	4	3	2	1
		440/375 4dr Sdn	$4,300	$6,700	$9,500	$11,800
		440/350 4dr Hdtp Sdn	$3,500	$5,800	$8,700	$10,900
		440/375 4dr Hdtp Sdn	$4,200	$6,800	$10,000	$12,600
1981	Imperial	318/140 2dr Cpe	$2,500	$5,300	$8,200	$16,600
		+$3,000 for Frank Sinatra Edition.				
1982	Imperial	318/140 2dr Cpe	$2,500	$5,300	$8,200	$16,600
		+$3,000 for Frank Sinatra Edition				
1983	Imperial	318/140 2dr Cpe	$2,500	$5,300	$8,200	$16,600
1989	TC by Maserati	181/141 2dr Conv	$1,900	$3,500	$7,400	$10,700
1990	TC by Maserati	181/141 2dr Conv	$1,900	$3,500	$7,400	$10,700
1991	TC by Maserati	181/141 2dr Conv	$1,900	$3,500	$7,400	$10,700
2001	Prowler	215/253 2dr Conv	$17,800	$24,700	$37,700	$48,300
2002	Prowler	215/253 2dr Conv	$17,800	$24,700	$37,700	$48,300

Chrysler Ghia

Year	Model	Body Style	4	3	2	1
1952	d'Elegance	331/180 2dr Cpe	$655,000	$752,000	$930,000	$1.2 mil
1952	Special	331/180 2dr Cpe	$757,000	$930,000	$1 mil	$1.35 mil
1953	Thomas Special	331/180 2dr Cpe	$375,000	$490,000	$625,000	$775,000
1954	GS-1	331/235 2dr Cpe	$226,000	$344,000	$418,000	$587,000

Cisitalia

Year	Model	Body Style	4	3	2	1
1946	D46	Monoposto	$411,000	$498,000	$592,000	$775,000
1947	D46	Monoposto	$411,000	$498,000	$592,000	$775,000
1947	202	2dr Gran Sport Spt Cpe	$340,000	$435,000	$520,000	$633,000
		2dr Gran Sport Spt Conv	$274,000	$330,000	$428,000	$585,000
		2dr MM Spyder	$490,000	$580,000	$695,000	$860,000
1948	202	2dr Gran Sport Spt Cpe	$340,000	$435,000	$520,000	$633,000
		2dr Gran Sport Spt Conv	$274,000	$330,000	$428,000	$585,000
		2dr MM Spyder	$490,000	$580,000	$695,000	$850,000
1949	202 Gran Sport	2dr Cpe	$340,000	$435,000	$520,000	$633,000
		2dr Conv	$274,000	$330,000	$428,000	$585,000
1950	202 Gran Sport	2dr Cpe	$340,000	$435,000	$520,000	$633,000
		2dr Conv	$274,000	$330,000	$428,000	$585,000
1951	202 Gran Sport	2dr Cpe	$340,000	$435,000	$520,000	$633,000
		2dr Conv	$274,000	$330,000	$428,000	$585,000
1952	202 Gran Sport	2dr Cpe	$340,000	$435,000	$520,000	$633,000

Cisitalia

Year	Model	Body Style	4	3	2	1
		2dr Conv	$274,000	$330,000	$428,000	$585,000

Citroen

Year	Model	Body Style	4	3	2	1
1945	Traction Avant	4dr Sdn	$8,100	$16,600	$29,900	$44,100
		4dr 6-cyl. Sdn	$10,600	$20,300	$36,300	$54,700
1946	Traction Avant	4dr 11 Legere Sdn	$8,100	$16,600	$29,900	$44,100
1947	Traction Avant	4dr 11 Normale Sdn	$8,100	$16,600	$29,900	$44,100
		4dr 11 Legere Sdn	$10,600	$20,300	$36,300	$54,700
1948	Traction Avant	4dr 11 Normale Sdn	$8,100	$16,600	$29,900	$44,100
		4dr 11 Legere Sdn	$10,600	$20,300	$36,300	$54,700
1949	2CV	4dr Sdn	$7,500	$17,200	$31,200	$41,700
1949	Traction Avant	4dr 11 Normale Sdn	$8,100	$16,600	$29,900	$44,100
		4dr 11 Legere Sdn	$10,600	$20,300	$36,300	$54,700
1950	2CV	4dr Sdn	$6,000	$13,800	$24,600	$37,300
1950	Traction Avant	4dr Sdn	$8,100	$16,600	$29,900	$44,100
		4dr 6-cyl. Sdn	$10,600	$20,300	$36,300	$54,700
1951	2CV	4dr Sdn	$6,000	$13,800	$24,600	$37,300
1951	Traction Avant	4dr Sdn	$8,100	$16,600	$29,900	$44,100
		4dr 6-cyl. Sdn	$10,600	$20,300	$36,300	$54,700
1952	2CV	4dr Sdn	$6,000	$13,800	$24,600	$37,300
1952	Traction Avant	4dr Sdn	$8,100	$16,600	$29,900	$44,100
		4dr 6-cyl. Sdn	$10,600	$20,300	$36,300	$54,700
1953	2CV	4dr Sdn	$6,000	$13,800	$24,600	$37,300
1953	Traction Avant	4dr Sdn	$8,100	$16,600	$29,900	$44,100
		4dr 6-cyl. Sdn	$10,600	$20,300	$36,300	$54,700
1954	2CV	4dr Sdn	$6,000	$13,800	$24,600	$37,300
1954	Traction Avant	4dr Sdn	$8,100	$16,600	$29,900	$44,100
		4dr 6-cyl. Sdn	$10,600	$20,300	$36,300	$54,700
1955	Traction Avant	4dr 11 D Familiale Sdn	$8,100	$16,600	$29,900	$44,100
		4dr 11 D Normale Sdn	$10,600	$20,300	$36,300	$54,700
1955	DS19	4dr Sdn	$8,000	$19,000	$34,700	$66,500
1956	Traction Avant	4dr Sdn	$8,100	$16,600	$29,900	$44,100
		4dr 6-cyl. Sdn	$10,600	$20,300	$36,300	$54,700
1956	DS19	4dr Sdn	$8,000	$19,000	$34,700	$66,500
1957	Traction Avant	4dr Sdn	$8,100	$16,600	$29,900	$44,100
		4dr 6-cyl. Sdn	$10,600	$20,300	$36,300	$54,700
1957	DS19	4dr Sdn	$8,000	$19,000	$34,700	$66,500
1958	DS19	4dr Sdn	$8,000	$19,000	$34,700	$66,500
1959	DS19	4dr Sdn	$8,000	$19,000	$34,700	$66,500
1960	2CV	4dr Sdn	$6,000	$13,800	$24,600	$37,300
		2dr Sahara Cpe	$38,500	$64,200	$93,100	$135,000
1960	DS19	4dr Wgn	$6,900	$17,700	$30,000	$56,100

Citroen

Year	Model	Body Style	4	3	2	1
1961	2CV	4dr Sdn	$6,000	$13,800	$24,600	$37,300
		4dr Sahara Sdn	$38,500	$64,200	$93,100	$135,000
1961	DS19	4dr Sdn	$7,600	$18,300	$33,100	$60,000
		4dr Wgn	$6,900	$17,700	$30,000	$56,100
		2dr Chapron Cab	$96,800	$138,000	$206,000	$268,000
1962	2CV	4dr Sdn	$6,000	$13,800	$24,600	$37,300
		4dr Sahara Sdn	$38,500	$64,200	$93,100	$135,000
1962	DS19	4dr Sdn	$7,600	$18,300	$33,100	$60,000
		4dr Wgn	$6,900	$17,700	$30,000	$56,100
		2dr Chapron Cab	$96,800	$138,000	$206,000	$268,000
1963	2CV	4dr Sdn	$6,000	$13,800	$24,600	$37,300
		4dr Sahara Sdn	$38,500	$64,200	$93,100	$135,000
1963	DS19	4dr Sdn	$7,600	$18,300	$33,100	$60,000
		4dr Wgn	$6,900	$17,700	$30,000	$56,100
		2dr Chapron Cab	$96,800	$138,000	$206,000	$268,000
1964	2CV	4dr Sdn	$6,000	$13,800	$24,600	$37,300
		4dr Sahara Sdn	$38,500	$64,200	$93,100	$135,000
1964	DS19	4dr Sdn	$7,600	$18,300	$33,100	$60,000
		4dr Wgn	$6,900	$17,700	$30,000	$56,100
		2dr Chapron Cab	$96,800	$138,000	$206,000	$268,000
1965	2CV	4dr Sdn	$6,000	$13,800	$24,600	$37,300
		4dr Sahara Sdn	$38,500	$64,200	$93,100	$135,000
1965	DS19	4dr Sdn	$7,600	$18,300	$33,100	$60,000
		4dr Wgn	$6,900	$17,700	$30,000	$56,100
		2dr Chapron Cab	$96,800	$138,000	$206,000	$268,000
1965	DS21	4dr Sdn	$9,800	$21,300	$39,200	$71,900
		4dr Wgn	$8,700	$19,400	$33,300	$61,400
		2dr Chapron Cab	$116,000	$148,000	$228,000	$290,000
1966	2CV	4dr Sdn	$6,000	$13,800	$24,600	$37,300
		4dr Sahara Sdn	$38,500	$64,200	$93,100	$135,000
1966	DS19	4dr Sdn	$7,600	$18,300	$33,100	$60,000
		4dr Wgn	$6,900	$17,700	$30,000	$56,100
1966	DS21	4dr Sdn	$9,800	$21,300	$39,200	$71,900
		4dr Wgn	$8,700	$19,400	$33,300	$61,400
		2dr Chapron Cab	$116,000	$148,000	$228,000	$290,000
1967	2CV	4dr Sdn	$6,000	$13,800	$24,600	$37,300
		4dr Sahara Sdn	$38,500	$64,200	$93,100	$135,000
1967	DS19	4dr Wgn	$6,900	$17,700	$30,000	$56,100
		4dr Sdn	$7,600	$18,300	$33,100	$60,000
1967	DS21	4dr Sdn	$9,800	$21,300	$39,200	$71,900
		4dr Wgn	$8,700	$19,400	$33,300	$61,400
		2dr Chapron Cab	$116,000	$148,000	$228,000	$290,000
1968	2CV	4dr Sahara Sdn	$38,500	$64,200	$93,100	$135,000
1968	DS20	4dr Sdn	$7,600	$15,500	$24,800	$43,200
		4dr Wgn	$6,700	$14,900	$23,600	$38,400
		2dr Chapron Cab	$107,000	$135,000	$211,000	$278,000
1968	DS21	4dr Sdn	$9,800	$21,300	$39,200	$71,900
		4dr Wgn	$8,700	$19,400	$33,300	$61,400
		2dr Chapron Cab	$116,000	$148,000	$228,000	$290,000

Citroen

Year	Model	Body Style	4	3	2	1
1969	2CV	4dr Sahara Sdn	$38,500	$64,200	$93,100	$135,000
1969	DS20	4dr Sdn	$7,600	$15,500	$24,800	$43,200
		4dr Wgn	$6,700	$14,900	$23,600	$38,400
		2dr Chapron Cab	$107,000	$135,000	$211,000	$278,000
1969	DS21	4dr Sdn	$9,800	$21,300	$39,200	$71,900
		4dr Wgn	$8,700	$19,400	$33,300	$61,400
		2dr Chapron Cab	$116,000	$148,000	$228,000	$290,000
1970	DS20	4dr Sdn	$7,600	$15,500	$24,800	$43,200
		4dr Wgn	$6,700	$14,900	$23,600	$38,400
		2dr Chapron Cab	$107,000	$135,000	$211,000	$278,000
1970	DS21	4dr Sdn	$9,800	$21,300	$39,200	$71,900
		4dr Wgn	$8,700	$19,400	$33,300	$61,400
		2dr Chapron Cab	$116,000	$148,000	$228,000	$290,000
1970	Mehari	2dr PU	$7,900	$14,000	$21,600	$34,500
1971	DS20	4dr Sdn	$7,600	$15,500	$24,800	$43,200
		4dr Wgn	$6,700	$14,900	$23,600	$38,400
		2dr Chapron Cab	$107,000	$135,000	$211,000	$278,000
1971	DS21	4dr Sdn	$9,800	$21,300	$39,200	$71,900
		4dr Wgn	$8,700	$19,400	$33,300	$61,400
		2dr Chapron Cab	$116,000	$148,000	$228,000	$290,000
1972	DS20	4dr Sdn	$7,600	$15,500	$24,800	$43,200
		4dr Wgn	$6,700	$14,900	$23,600	$38,400
		2dr Chapron Cab	$107,000	$135,000	$211,000	$278,000
1972	DS21	4dr Sdn	$9,800	$21,300	$39,200	$71,900
		4dr Wgn	$8,700	$19,400	$33,300	$61,400
		2dr Chapron Cab	$116,000	$148,000	$228,000	$290,000
1973	DS20	4dr Sdn	$7,600	$15,500	$24,800	$43,200
		4dr Wgn	$6,700	$14,900	$23,600	$38,400
		2dr Chapron Cab	$107,000	$135,000	$211,000	$278,000
1973	SM	2dr Cpe	$16,800	$35,900	$66,000	$98,000
				-15% for auto. -10% for US version.		
1974	SM	2dr Cpe	$16,800	$35,900	$66,000	$98,000
				-15% for auto. -10% for US version.		
1975	SM	2dr Cpe	$16,800	$35,900	$66,000	$98,000
				-15% for auto. -10% for US version.		

Clenet

Year	Model	Body Style	4	3	2	1
1977	SI	351/135 2dr Rdstr	$17,600	$23,700	$30,600	$40,400
1978	SI	351/135 2dr Rdstr	$17,600	$23,700	$30,600	$40,400
1979	SI	351/135 2dr Rdstr	$17,600	$23,700	$30,600	$40,400
1979	SIII	351/135 2dr Cab	$17,700	$26,500	$35,600	$43,400
1980	SII	302/130 2dr Cab	$17,700	$26,500	$35,600	$43,400
1981	SII	302/130 2dr Cab	$17,700	$26,500	$35,600	$43,400
1982	SII	2dr Cab	$17,700	$26,500	$35,600	$43,400
1982	SIII	2dr Cpe	$20,200	$25,500	$33,500	$40,900
		2dr Lanlet Cpe	$23,100	$29,700	$33,500	$46,800
1983	SIII	2dr Cpe	$20,200	$25,500	$33,500	$40,900

Clenet

Year	Model	Body Style	4	3	2	1
		2dr Lanlet Cpe	$23,100	$29,300	$38,100	$46,300
		2dr Cab	$17,400	$25,700	$32,900	$40,800
1984	SIII	2dr Cpe	$20,200	$25,500	$33,200	$40,300
		2dr Lanlet Cpe	$23,100	$29,300	$38,100	$46,300
		2dr Cab	$17,400	$25,700	$32,900	$40,800
1985	SII	302/165 2dr Cab	$17,400	$25,800	$33,100	$41,200
1985	SIII	2dr Cpe	$20,200	$25,500	$33,200	$40,300
		2dr Lanlet Cpe	$23,100	$29,300	$38,100	$46,300
1986	SII	2dr Cab	$17,400	$25,800	$33,100	$41,200
1986	SIII	2dr Cpe	$20,200	$25,500	$33,200	$40,300
		2dr Lanlet Cpe	$23,100	$29,300	$38,100	$46,300

Clipper

Year	Model	Body Style	4	3	2	1
1956	Deluxe	352/240 2dr Spr Panama Hdtp	$5,700	$13,800	$20,200	$40,600
		352/240 4dr Sdn	$3,200	$6,900	$9,500	$17,700
		352/240 4dr Spr Sdn	$3,300	$7,200	$10,000	$17,900
1956	Custom	352/275 2dr Constellation Hdtp Cpe	$5,700	$14,400	$20,800	$41,000
		352/275 4dr Sdn	$4,300	$8,300	$11,400	$19,300

Connaught

Year	Model	Body Style	4	3	2	1
1948	L2	2dr Rdstr	$62,300	$78,000	$110,000	$145,000
1949	L2	2dr Rdstr	$62,300	$78,000	$110,000	$145,000
1950	L3	2dr Rdstr	$78,300	$106,000	$132,000	$170,000
1951	L3	2dr Rdstr	$78,300	$106,000	$132,000	$170,000
1952	L3	2dr Rdstr	$78,300	$106,000	$132,000	$170,000
1953	L3	2dr Rdstr	$78,300	$106,000	$132,000	$170,000

Continental

Year	Model	Body Style	4	3	2	1
1956	Mark II	368/285 2dr Spt Cpe	$28,600	$51,500	$115,000	$184,000
						+10% for factory a/c.
1957	Mark II	368/300 2dr Spt Cpe	$28,600	$51,500	$115,000	$184,000
						+10% for factory a/c.
1958	Mark III	430/375 2dr Spt Cpe	$11,900	$17,200	$28,900	$41,300
		430/375 4dr Sdn	$6,600	$9,700	$16,200	$24,000
		430/375 4dr Lan Sdn	$7,100	$10,700	$18,000	$27,100
		430/375 2dr Conv	$25,800	$40,600	$71,500	$88,600
						+10% for factory a/c.

Corbin

Year	Model	Body Style	4	3	2	1
1999	Sparrow	Jelly Bean Cpe	$4,200	$6,000	$8,500	$12,300
		Pizza Butt Cpe	$4,600	$6,600	$8,800	$12,800
2000	Sparrow	Jelly Bean Cpe	$4,200	$6,000	$8,500	$12,300
		Pizza Butt Cpe	$4,600	$6,600	$8,800	$12,800
2001	Sparrow	Pizza Butt Cpe	$4,600	$6,600	$8,800	$12,800
		Jelly Bean Cpe	$4,200	$6,000	$8,500	$12,300
2002	Sparrow	Pizza Butt Cpe	$4,600	$6,600	$8,800	$12,800
		Jelly Bean Cpe	$4,200	$6,000	$8,500	$12,300

Cord

Year	Model	Body Style	4	3	2	1
1964	8/10 Sportsman	164/110 2dr Conv	$9,000	$14,100	$17,900	$29,200
1965	8/10 Sportsman	164/110 2dr Conv	$9,000	$14,100	$17,900	$29,200
1966	8/10 Sportsman	164/110 2dr Conv	$9,000	$14,100	$17,900	$29,200
1968	Royale	440/350 2dr Conv	$11,300	$15,900	$19,900	$32,300
1968	Warrior	302/220 2dr Conv	$9,700	$13,800	$18,700	$30,100
1969	Royale	440/350 2dr Conv	$11,300	$15,900	$19,900	$32,300
1969	Warrior	302/220 2dr Conv	$9,700	$13,800	$18,700	$30,100
1970	Royale	440/350 2dr Conv	$11,300	$15,900	$19,900	$32,300
1970	Warrior	302/220 2dr Conv	$9,700	$13,800	$18,700	$30,100

Crosley

Year	Model	Body Style	4	3	2	1
1946	CC	44/26.5 2dr Sdn	$3,900	$5,900	$8,600	$14,500
		44/26.5 2dr Conv	$5,100	$7,700	$13,200	$21,100
1947	CC	44/26.5 2dr Sdn	$3,900	$5,900	$8,600	$14,500
		44/26.5 2dr Conv	$5,100	$7,700	$13,200	$21,100
1948	CC	44/26.5 2dr Sdn	$3,900	$5,900	$9,100	$16,300
		44/26.5 2dr Wgn	$4,300	$6,200	$14,000	$21,100
		44/26.5 2dr Conv	$5,400	$8,300	$14,600	$23,900
1949	CD	44/26.5 2dr Sdn	$3,900	$5,900	$9,500	$16,200
		44/26.5 2dr Wgn	$4,400	$6,300	$14,200	$21,400
		44/26.5 2dr Conv	$5,500	$8,400	$14,800	$24,500
1949	Hot Shot	44/26.5 2dr Rdstr	$8,300	$11,600	$20,200	$28,000
1950	CD	44/26.5 2dr Conv Sdn	$5,800	$8,200	$14,200	$25,100
		44/26.5 2dr Sdn	$3,900	$5,900	$9,400	$15,900
		44/26.5 2dr Super Conv Sdn	$7,000	$9,300	$15,500	$26,100
		44/26.5 2dr Super Sdn	$4,400	$6,700	$10,300	$16,900
		44/26.5 2dr Super Wgn	$5,600	$8,400	$16,200	$23,900
		44/26.5 2dr Wgn	$4,800	$6,400	$13,600	$20,200
1950	Hot Shot	44/26.5 2dr Rdstr	$7,600	$11,400	$19,700	$30,900
1951	Hot Shot	44/26.5 2dr Rdstr	$7,600	$11,400	$19,700	$30,900

Crosley

Year	Model	Body Style	4	3	2	1
1951	CD	44/26.5 2dr Sdn	$3,900	$5,800	$9,400	$16,000
		44/26.5 2dr Spr Sdn	$4,300	$6,700	$10,500	$16,900
		44/26.5 2dr Wgn	$4,500	$6,300	$13,600	$20,400
		44/26.5 2dr Spr Wgn	$5,100	$8,400	$16,400	$23,900
		44/26.5 2dr Conv	$5,700	$8,400	$14,900	$25,300
		44/26.5 2dr Spr Conv	$7,000	$9,600	$16,200	$26,100
1952	Hot Shot	44/26.5 2dr Rdstr	$7,600	$11,400	$19,700	$30,900
1952	CD	44/26.5 2dr Sdn	$3,800	$5,900	$9,400	$16,100
		44/26.5 2dr Spr Sdn	$4,400	$6,700	$10,300	$16,900
		44/26.5 2dr Wgn	$4,400	$6,300	$13,600	$20,400
		44/26.5 2dr Spr Wgn	$5,300	$8,400	$16,400	$23,700
		44/26.5 2dr Conv	$5,600	$8,600	$14,900	$25,300
		44/26.5 2dr Spr Conv	$7,000	$9,600	$15,900	$26,100

Cunningham

Prices on all Cunninghams are for legitimate cars only, and value is greatly influenced by race history. Fourteen or more chassis were never factory completed; prices on these cars are significantly reduced.

Year	Model	Body Style	4	3	2	1
1951	C2	2dr Rdstr	$948,000	$1.1 mil	$1.3 mil	$1.5 mil
1952	C3	2dr Vignale Cpe	$550,000	$712,000	$955,000	$1.1 mil
		2dr Vignale Rdstr	$690,000	$850,000	$1.05 mil	$1.3 mil

DKW

Year	Model	Body Style	4	3	2	1
1963	F11	2dr Cpe	$5,000	$9,000	$13,400	$22,600
1963	F12	2dr Cpe	$5,300	$9,800	$15,300	$26,300
		2dr Conv	$12,400	$19,100	$27,000	$37,200
1964	F11	2dr Cpe	$5,000	$9,000	$13,400	$22,600
1964	F12	2dr Cpe	$5,300	$9,800	$15,300	$26,300
		2dr Conv	$12,400	$19,100	$27,000	$37,200
1965	F11	2dr Cpe	$5,000	$9,000	$13,400	$22,600
1965	F12	2dr Cpe	$5,300	$9,800	$15,300	$26,300
		2dr Conv	$12,400	$19,100	$27,000	$37,200

Daimler

Year	Model	Body Style	4	3	2	1
1959	SP250	2dr Dart Conv	$21,000	$37,500	$55,000	$83,000
1960	SP250	2dr Dart Conv	$21,000	$37,500	$55,000	$83,000
1961	SP250	2dr Dart Conv	$21,000	$37,500	$55,000	$83,000
1962	SP250	2dr Dart Conv	$21,000	$37,500	$55,000	$83,000

Daimler

Year	Model	Body Style	4	3	2	1
1963	SP250	2dr Dart Conv	$21,000	$37,500	$55,000	$83,000
1964	SP250	2dr Dart Conv	$21,000	$37,500	$55,000	$83,000

Datsun

Year	Model	Body Style	4	3	2	1
1958	Fair Lady	2dr Conv	$5,200	$10,100	$25,100	$44,800
1959	Fair Lady	2dr Conv	$5,200	$10,100	$25,100	$44,800
1960	Fair Lady	2dr Rdstr	$5,200	$10,100	$25,100	$44,800
1961	Fair Lady	2dr Conv	$5,200	$10,100	$25,100	$44,800
1962	1500	2dr Conv	$5,200	$10,100	$25,100	$44,800
1963	1500	2dr Conv	$7,000	$11,200	$26,700	$48,100
1964	1500	2dr Conv	$7,000	$11,200	$26,700	$48,100
1965	1500	2dr Conv	$7,000	$11,200	$26,700	$48,100
1966	1600	2dr Conv	$7,400	$13,700	$30,900	$51,300
1967	1600	2dr Conv	$7,400	$13,700	$30,900	$51,300
1967	2000	2dr Conv	$17,800	$24,700	$45,700	$68,800
1968	1600	2dr Conv	$7,400	$13,300	$29,300	$48,800
1968	2000	2dr Conv	$8,100	$16,100	$37,900	$54,400
1968	510	2dr Sdn	$5,600	$10,400	$16,900	$32,100
		4dr Sdn	$2,600	$6,300	$13,000	$21,300
		4dr Wgn	$3,600	$7,400	$11,500	$19,600
1969	1600	2dr Conv	$7,200	$12,800	$27,100	$48,000
1969	2000	2dr Conv	$8,100	$16,100	$37,900	$54,400
1969	510	2dr Sdn	$5,600	$10,400	$16,900	$32,100
		4dr Sdn	$2,600	$6,300	$13,000	$21,300
		4dr Wgn	$3,600	$7,400	$11,500	$19,600
1970	1600	2dr Conv	$7,200	$12,800	$27,100	$48,000
1970	2000	2dr Conv	$8,100	$16,100	$37,900	$54,400
1970	510	2dr Sdn	$5,600	$10,400	$16,900	$32,100
		4dr Sdn	$2,600	$6,300	$13,000	$21,300
		4dr Wgn	$3,600	$7,400	$11,500	$19,600
1970	240Z	2dr Cpe	$8,900	$20,600	$38,700	$64,400
						-15% for auto trans.
1971	510	2dr Sdn	$5,600	$10,400	$16,900	$32,100
		4dr Sdn	$2,600	$6,300	$13,000	$21,300
1971	240Z	2dr Cpe	$7,900	$18,200	$38,300	$61,900
						-15% for auto trans.
1972	510	2dr Sdn	$5,600	$10,400	$16,900	$32,100
		4dr Sdn	$2,600	$6,300	$13,000	$21,300
1972	240Z	2dr Cpe	$7,900	$18,200	$38,300	$61,900
						-15% for auto trans.
1973	510	2dr Sdn	$5,600	$10,400	$16,900	$32,100
1973	240Z	2dr Cpe	$7,900	$18,200	$38,300	$61,900
						-15% for auto trans.
1974	260Z	2dr Cpe	$5,700	$11,100	$25,600	$48,200
		2dr 2+2 Cpe	$4,200	$7,600	$17,600	$34,300

+15% for early small bumper models. -15% for auto trans.

Datsun

Year	Model	Body Style	4	3	2	1
1975	280Z	2dr Cpe	$5,400	$10,700	$27,400	$51,800
		2dr 2+2 Cpe	$3,400	$6,800	$17,700	$35,400
					-15% for auto trans.	
1976	280Z	2dr Cpe	$5,400	$10,700	$27,400	$51,800
		2dr 2+2 Cpe	$3,400	$6,800	$17,700	$35,400
					-15% for auto trans.	
1977	280Z	2dr Cpe	$5,400	$10,700	$27,400	$51,800
		2dr 2+2 Cpe	$3,400	$6,800	$17,700	$35,400
					-15% for auto trans.	
1978	280Z	2dr Cpe	$5,400	$10,700	$27,400	$51,800
		2dr 2+2 Cpe	$3,400	$6,800	$17,700	$35,400
					-15% for auto trans.	
1979	280ZX	2dr Cpe	$3,700	$6,600	$15,200	$26,400
		2dr Grand Luxury 2+2 Cpe	$2,800	$5,100	$11,200	$19,000
1980	280ZX	2dr Dlx Cpe	$3,700	$6,600	$15,200	$26,400
		2dr Grand Luxury 2+2 Cpe	$2,800	$5,100	$11,200	$19,000
1981	280ZX	2dr Grand Luxury 2+2 Cpe	$2,800	$5,100	$11,200	$19,000
		2dr Dlx Cpe	$3,900	$5,800	$11,800	$19,400
		2dr Turbo Cpe	$5,500	$7,900	$17,900	$28,600
1982	280ZX	2dr 2+2 Cpe	$2,800	$5,100	$11,200	$19,000
		2dr Cpe	$3,900	$5,800	$13,000	$23,300
		2dr Turbo Cpe	$5,500	$7,900	$17,900	$28,600
1983	280ZX	2dr 2+2 Cpe	$2,800	$5,100	$11,200	$19,000
		2dr Turbo 2+2 Cpe	$4,600	$6,500	$14,800	$21,400
		2dr Cpe	$3,900	$5,800	$13,000	$23,300
		2dr Turbo Cpe	$5,500	$7,900	$17,900	$28,600
1984	300ZX	2dr Htchbk	$4,200	$5,800	$10,100	$18,300
		2dr Turbo Htchbk	$5,800	$8,300	$14,100	$24,500
		2dr 50th Annv Turbo Htchbk	$6,600	$9,900	$18,300	$25,800
					-15% for auto trans.	

Davis

Year	Model	Body Style	4	3	2	1
1948	D-2	133/46 2dr Divan Cpe	$29,500	$44,600	$79,700	$125,000
1948	494X	133/46 2dr Conv	$18,000	$31,200	$47,300	$72,100

DeSoto

Year	Model	Body Style	4	3	2	1
1946	Deluxe	237/109 2dr Cpe	$8,900	$12,800	$20,100	$28,900
		237/109 2dr Clb Cpe	$8,400	$15,300	$20,500	$27,800
		237/109 2dr Sdn	$5,200	$8,000	$11,300	$17,700

Year	Model	Body Style	4	3	2	1
		237/109 4dr Sdn	$3,500	$5,200	$8,800	$12,500
1946	Custom	237/109 2dr Clb Cpe	$12,600	$19,000	$28,400	$38,200
		237/109 4dr Sdn	$4,200	$5,600	$9,700	$13,800
		237/109 2dr Brghm Sdn	$6,100	$9,900	$14,100	$22,000
		237/109 4dr Sdn 7P	$5,300	$6,800	$11,200	$17,000
		237/109 4dr Sbrbn Sdn	$11,700	$24,500	$33,500	$42,800
		237/109 4dr Limo	$6,800	$9,500	$13,800	$22,300
		237/109 2dr Conv Cpe	$17,800	$32,100	$45,200	$67,200
1947	Deluxe	237/109 2dr Cpe	$8,900	$12,700	$20,100	$29,000
		237/109 2dr Clb Cpe	$8,400	$15,300	$20,500	$27,800
		237/109 2dr Sdn	$5,200	$8,000	$11,500	$17,800
		237/109 4dr Sdn	$3,500	$5,300	$8,800	$12,400
1947	Custom	237/109 2dr Clb Cpe	$12,600	$19,000	$28,400	$38,200
		237/109 4dr Sdn 6P	$4,200	$5,600	$9,700	$13,700
		237/109 2dr Brghm Sdn	$6,100	$10,000	$14,200	$22,000
		237/109 4dr Sdn 7P	$5,400	$6,900	$11,100	$17,000
		237/109 4dr Sbrbn Sdn	$11,700	$24,500	$33,500	$42,800
		237/109 4dr Limo	$6,800	$9,500	$13,800	$22,300
		237/109 2dr Conv Cpe	$17,800	$32,100	$45,200	$67,200
1948	Deluxe	237/109 2dr Cpe	$8,900	$12,700	$20,100	$29,000
		237/109 2dr Clb Cpe	$8,400	$15,300	$20,500	$27,800
		237/109 2dr Sdn	$5,200	$8,000	$11,500	$17,800
		237/109 4dr Sdn	$3,500	$5,300	$8,800	$12,400
1948	Custom	237/109 2dr Clb Cpe	$12,600	$19,000	$28,400	$38,200
		237/109 4dr Sdn 7P	$4,200	$5,600	$9,700	$13,700
		237/109 4dr LWB Sdn	$5,400	$6,900	$11,100	$17,000
		237/109 4dr Sbrbn Sdn 9P	$11,700	$24,500	$33,500	$42,800
		237/109 2dr Brghm Sdn	$6,100	$9,900	$14,300	$22,000
		237/109 4dr Limo	$6,800	$9,500	$13,800	$22,300
		237/109 2dr Conv Cpe	$17,800	$32,100	$45,200	$67,200
1949	Deluxe	237/112 2dr Clb Cpe	$5,500	$10,200	$13,800	$18,400
		237/112 4dr Sdn	$3,300	$7,200	$11,300	$16,400

DeSoto

Year	Model	Body Style	4	3	2	1
		237/112 4dr Carry-All Sdn	$3,700	$6,700	$10,700	$14,600
		237/112 4dr Wgn	$24,900	$40,200	$62,200	$82,200
1949	Custom	237/112 2dr Clb Cpe	$6,800	$10,500	$14,700	$19,200
		237/112 4dr Sdn 6P	$3,000	$7,400	$11,600	$16,800
		237/112 4dr Sdn 8P	$3,000	$7,000	$11,200	$16,200
		237/112 4dr Sbrbn Stn Wgn 9P	$7,500	$13,600	$18,700	$23,200
		237/112 2dr Conv Cpe	$19,600	$30,800	$48,800	$73,200
1950	Deluxe	237/112 2dr Clb Cpe	$5,500	$10,200	$13,800	$18,400
		237/112 4dr Sdn 6P	$3,300	$7,300	$13,300	$16,300
		237/112 4dr Carry-All Sdn	$3,800	$7,000	$11,100	$14,800
1950	Custom	237/112 2dr Clb Cpe	$6,800	$10,500	$14,700	$19,200
		237/112 4dr Sdn	$3,200	$7,200	$11,200	$16,300
		237/112 4dr Sdn 8P	$3,100	$7,000	$11,700	$16,600
		237/112 4dr Sbrbn Sdn 9P	$4,200	$7,700	$13,300	$20,100
		237/112 4dr Wgn	$39,800	$62,100	$90,900	$126,000
		237/112 4dr Stn Wgn	$14,200	$24,700	$30,700	$39,700
		237/112 2dr Sptsmn Hdtp Cpe	$8,400	$12,800	$17,300	$24,000
		237/112 2dr Conv	$20,400	$31,900	$51,200	$76,000
1951	Deluxe	250/116 2dr Clb Cpe	$5,500	$10,200	$13,800	$18,400
		250/116 4dr Sdn	$3,300	$7,200	$11,300	$16,500
		250/116 4dr Sdn 8P	$3,200	$7,100	$11,100	$13,900
		250/116 4dr Carry-All Sdn	$3,900	$7,100	$11,200	$14,900
1951	Custom	250/116 2dr Clb Cpe	$6,800	$10,600	$14,700	$19,200
		250/116 4dr Sdn	$3,200	$7,200	$11,200	$16,400
		250/116 4dr Sdn 8P	$3,100	$7,000	$11,600	$16,800
		250/116 4dr Sbrbn Sdn 9P	$4,200	$7,700	$13,300	$20,100
		250/116 4dr Wgn	$13,700	$23,000	$29,100	$38,300
		250/116 2dr Sptsmn Hdtp Cpe	$8,400	$12,600	$17,400	$24,300
		250/116 2dr Conv	$20,700	$33,900	$53,000	$77,300
1952	Deluxe	250/116 2dr Clb Cpe	$5,600	$10,500	$14,100	$19,400
		250/116 4dr Sdn	$3,400	$7,300	$11,500	$17,200

Year	Model	Body Style	4	3	2	1
		250/116 4dr Sdn 8P	$3,300	$7,400	$11,700	$14,500
		250/116 4dr Carry-All Sdn	$4,000	$7,200	$11,300	$15,700
1952	Custom	250/116 2dr Clb Cpe	$7,000	$10,800	$16,000	$19,800
		250/116 4dr Sdn	$3,200	$7,400	$11,300	$17,200
		250/116 4dr Sdn 8P	$3,200	$7,000	$11,800	$17,500
		250/116 4dr Sdn 9P	$4,200	$7,700	$13,300	$20,100
		250/116 4dr Wgn	$14,100	$23,300	$30,100	$41,100
		250/116 2dr Sptsmn Hdtp Cpe	$8,400	$12,800	$17,700	$25,600
		250/116 2dr Conv	$21,600	$35,600	$53,600	$78,800
1952	Firedome	276/160 2dr Clb Cpe	$15,400	$20,900	$31,400	$40,400
		276/160 4dr Sdn	$4,600	$8,600	$13,300	$19,300
		276/160 4dr Sdn 8P	$3,800	$7,700	$12,700	$19,200
		276/160 4dr Wgn	$12,800	$18,600	$31,400	$50,600
		276/160 2dr Sptsmn Hdtp Cpe	$18,400	$27,900	$45,300	$59,000
		276/160 2dr Conv	$25,200	$35,900	$58,400	$85,500
						+15% for factory a/c.
1953	Powermaster	250/116 2dr Clb Cpe	$6,000	$8,900	$13,100	$15,700
		250/116 4dr Sdn 6P	$3,000	$6,800	$10,700	$15,200
		250/116 4dr Wgn	$14,200	$25,600	$32,800	$42,600
		250/116 2dr Sptsmn Hdtp Cpe	$9,600	$14,000	$21,400	$32,400
1953	Firedome	276/160 2dr Clb Cpe	$16,300	$23,500	$33,900	$44,700
		276/160 4dr Sdn 6P	$5,200	$8,800	$15,900	$20,700
		276/160 4dr Wgn	$14,000	$19,300	$33,500	$53,800
		276/160 2dr Sptsmn Hdtp Cpe	$18,800	$30,200	$46,100	$61,700
		276/160 2dr Conv	$25,300	$39,000	$57,700	$86,100
						+15% for factory a/c.
1954	Powermaster	250/116 2dr Clb Cpe	$6,300	$9,100	$12,800	$15,300
		250/116 4dr Sdn 6P	$3,000	$6,500	$10,700	$15,200
		250/116 4dr Wgn	$14,200	$25,600	$32,800	$42,500
		250/116 2dr Sptsmn Hdtp Cpe	$9,500	$13,700	$21,400	$32,300
1954	Firedome	276/170 2dr Clb Cpe	$16,400	$23,100	$33,400	$43,900

DeSoto

Year	Model	Body Style	4	3	2	1
		276/170 4dr Sdn 6P	$5,100	$9,100	$16,100	$20,900
		276/170 4dr Coronado Sdn	$5,200	$9,600	$16,800	$21,200
		276/170 4dr Wgn	$14,000	$19,800	$33,600	$52,400
		276/170 2dr Sptsmn Hdtp Cpe	$19,100	$30,200	$46,300	$62,300
		276/170 2dr Conv	$25,400	$39,200	$58,800	$88,100
						+15% for factory a/c.
1955	Firedome	291/185 2dr Spcl Hdtp Cpe	$10,700	$17,300	$24,000	$34,200
		291/185 2dr Sptsmn Hdtp Cpe	$10,200	$16,400	$25,100	$36,300
		291/185 4dr Sdn	$3,300	$8,400	$13,300	$17,800
		291/185 2dr Conv	$43,800	$59,600	$93,800	$139,000
						+15% for factory a/c.
1955	Fireflite	291/200 2dr Sptsmn Hdtp Cpe	$10,000	$16,100	$25,300	$36,100
		291/200 4dr Sdn	$3,700	$8,400	$12,100	$16,800
		291/200 4dr Coronado Sdn	$5,400	$9,000	$15,300	$20,200
		291/200 2dr Conv	$38,300	$59,000	$94,800	$155,000
						+15% for factory a/c.
1956	Firedome	330/230 2dr Seville Hdtp Cpe	$8,500	$16,600	$22,700	$33,900
		330/230 2dr Sptsmn Hdtp Cpe	$9,300	$19,800	$29,100	$44,400
		330/230 4dr Sdn	$5,200	$11,000	$15,900	$19,700
		330/230 4dr Wgn	$11,000	$19,100	$30,500	$46,700
		330/230 4dr Seville Hdtp Sdn	$6,000	$12,300	$16,700	$20,800
		330/230 4dr Sptsmn Hdtp Sdn	$8,100	$15,300	$20,400	$27,400
		330/230 2dr Conv	$46,400	$59,800	$98,000	$142,000
						+15% for factory a/c.
1956	Fireflite	330/255 2dr Sptsmn Hdtp Cpe	$14,200	$22,300	$34,300	$54,200
		330/255 4dr Sdn	$5,200	$10,300	$14,400	$18,100
		330/255 4dr Sptsmn Hdtp Sdn	$7,700	$13,200	$17,400	$24,000
		330/255 2dr Conv	$36,700	$51,600	$88,000	$136,000
		330/255 2dr Pacesetter Conv	$40,200	$57,500	$94,800	$151,000
						+15% for factory a/c.
1956	Adventurer	341/320 2dr Hdtp Cpe	$27,200	$35,500	$58,300	$86,700
1957	Firesweep	325/245 2dr Sptsmn Hdtp Cpe	$12,500	$26,100	$35,000	$54,400
		325/245 4dr Sdn	$6,400	$10,500	$14,800	$18,200

Year	Model	Body Style	4	3	2	1
		325/245 4dr Sptsmn Hdtp Sdn	$8,400	$13,200	$17,000	$21,900
		325/245 4dr Shopper Stn Wgn 6P	$12,700	$23,000	$33,300	$43,500
		325/245 4dr Explorer Stn Wgn 9P	$15,100	$29,200	$36,600	$45,900
						+15% for factory a/c.
1957	Firedome	341/270 2dr Sptsmn Hdtp Cpe	$15,100	$26,500	$36,800	$57,800
		341/270 4dr Sdn	$8,100	$12,100	$16,500	$20,900
		341/270 4dr Sptsmn Hdtp Sdn	$10,100	$14,500	$19,700	$24,300
		341/270 2dr Conv	$41,200	$57,400	$86,800	$139,000
						+15% for factory a/c.
1957	Fireflite	341/295 2dr Sptsmn Hdtp Cpe	$15,100	$25,200	$33,500	$52,100
		341/295 4dr Sdn	$7,200	$11,600	$15,100	$19,700
		341/295 4dr Shopper Stn Wgn 6P	$13,200	$23,700	$34,700	$48,900
		341/295 4dr Explorer Stn Wgn 9P	$15,500	$27,000	$37,000	$50,100
		341/295 4dr Sptsmn Hdtp Sdn	$9,700	$13,300	$17,500	$25,700
		341/295 2dr Conv	$41,500	$56,900	$92,900	$153,000
						+15% for factory a/c.
1957	Adventurer	345/345 2dr Hdtp Cpe	$24,600	$33,700	$54,000	$69,500
		345/345 2dr Conv	$107,000	$149,000	$218,000	$294,000
						+15% for factory a/c. +$3,000 for swivel front seats.
1958	Firesweep	350/280 2dr Sptsmn Hdtp Cpe	$11,900	$24,900	$34,800	$53,000
		350/280 4dr Sdn	$6,400	$10,500	$14,800	$18,200
		350/280 4dr Shopper Wgn	$12,700	$22,800	$33,600	$43,400
		350/280 4dr Explorer Wgn	$15,100	$29,200	$36,600	$45,900
		350/280 4dr Sptsmn Hdtp Sdn	$8,400	$13,200	$17,000	$21,900
		350/280 2dr Conv	$42,500	$60,100	$95,800	$159,000
						+15% for factory a/c.
1958	Fireflite	361/305 2dr Sptsmn Hdtp Cpe	$15,300	$25,100	$35,700	$52,300
		361/305 4dr Sdn	$7,200	$11,600	$15,100	$19,700
		361/305 4dr Shopper Wgn	$13,000	$23,600	$33,900	$48,800

DeSoto

Year	Model	Body Style	4	3	2	1
		361/305 4dr Explorer Wgn	$15,500	$27,000	$37,000	$50,100
		361/305 2dr Conv	$41,700	$66,500	$112,000	$162,000
						+15% for factory a/c.
1958	Firedome	361/295 2dr Sptsmn Hdtp Cpe	$15,100	$26,500	$37,600	$57,300
		361/295 4dr Sdn	$8,100	$12,100	$16,500	$20,900
		361/295 4dr Sptsmn Hdtp Sdn	$10,100	$14,500	$19,700	$24,300
		361/295 2dr Conv	$55,400	$77,900	$126,000	$178,000
						+15% for factory a/c.
1958	Adventurer	361/345 2dr Hdtp Cpe	$23,900	$32,800	$57,300	$72,700
		361/345 2dr Conv	$105,000	$148,000	$208,000	$264,000
			+15% for factory a/c. +$3,000 for swivel front seats.			
1959	Firesweep	361/290 2dr Sptsmn Hdtp Cpe	$12,000	$24,700	$32,600	$51,800
		361/290 4dr Sdn	$6,400	$10,400	$14,700	$17,700
		361/290 4dr Shopper Wgn	$12,700	$22,900	$32,800	$42,300
		361/290 4dr Explorer Wgn	$14,900	$28,900	$36,900	$45,400
		361/290 4dr Sptsmn Hdtp Sdn	$8,300	$13,400	$16,800	$21,500
		361/290 2dr Conv	$46,100	$64,500	$97,100	$154,000
						+15% for factory a/c.
1959	Firedome	383/305 2dr Sptsmn Hdtp Cpe	$14,900	$26,100	$36,500	$56,300
		383/305 4dr Sdn	$8,000	$12,000	$16,300	$20,500
		383/305 4dr Sptsmn Hdtp Sdn	$10,000	$14,400	$19,500	$24,000
		383/305 2dr Conv	$47,100	$65,200	$98,900	$161,000
						+15% for factory a/c.
1959	Fireflite	383/325 2dr Sptsmn Hdtp Cpe	$14,900	$24,900	$34,000	$51,100
		383/325 4dr Sdn	$7,100	$11,600	$14,700	$19,300
		383/325 4dr Shopper Wgn	$12,900	$22,900	$33,100	$47,500
		383/325 4dr Explorer Wgn	$15,300	$26,900	$36,300	$48,500
		383/325 4dr Sptsmn Hdtp Sdn	$9,700	$13,600	$16,700	$24,700
		383/325 2dr Conv	$47,300	$67,600	$113,000	$164,000
						+15% for factory a/c.
1959	Adventurer	383/350 2dr Hdtp Cpe	$23,100	$31,400	$50,500	$69,300
		383/350 2dr Conv	$101,000	$143,000	$200,000	$259,000
			+15% for factory a/c. +$3,000 for swivel front seats.			
1960	Fireflite	361/295 2dr Hdtp	$9,000	$19,200	$22,600	$34,500

DeSoto

Year	Model	Body Style	4	3	2	1
		361/295 4dr Sdn	$5,100	$9,800	$14,100	$17,000
		361/295 4dr Hdtp	$6,900	$11,800	$14,400	$18,000
1960	Adventurer	383/305 2dr Hdtp	$14,200	$21,800	$33,500	$45,400
		383/305 4dr Sdn	$4,900	$10,100	$13,300	$17,600
		383/305 4dr Hdtp	$6,200	$12,400	$18,200	$26,900
				+15% for factory a/c. +$3,000 for swivel front seats.		
1961	Adventurer	361/265 2dr Hdtp Cpe	$13,000	$19,500	$34,600	$52,300
		361/265 4dr Hdtp Sdn	$5,900	$11,300	$15,500	$23,200
						+15% for factory a/c.

DeTomaso

Year	Model	Body Style	4	3	2	1
1967	Vallelunga	2dr Cpe	$200,000	$245,000	$300,000	$390,000
1967	Mangusta	2dr 302 Cpe	$160,000	$195,000	$220,000	$290,000
		2dr Cpe	$182,000	$210,000	$240,000	$310,000
						-10% for 2-headlights.
1968	Mangusta	2dr 302 Cpe	$160,000	$195,000	$220,000	$290,000
		2dr Cpe	$182,000	$210,000	$240,000	$310,000
						-10% for 2-headlights.
1969	Mangusta	2dr 302 Cpe	$160,000	$195,000	$220,000	$290,000
		2dr Cpe	$182,000	$210,000	$240,000	$310,000
						-10% for 2-headlights.
1970	Mangusta	2dr 302 Cpe	$160,000	$195,000	$220,000	$290,000
		2dr Cpe	$182,000	$210,000	$240,000	$310,000
						-10% for 2-headlights.
1970	Pantera	2dr Cpe	$56,000	$71,000	$97,000	$125,000
1971	Deauville	4dr Sdn	$26,400	$38,200	$46,600	$59,500
						+10% for manual trans.
1971	Pantera	2dr Cpe	$56,000	$71,000	$97,000	$125,000
1972	Deauville	4dr Sdn	$26,400	$38,200	$46,600	$59,500
						+10% for manual trans.
1972	Pantera	2dr Cpe	$56,000	$71,000	$97,000	$125,000
1973	Pantera L	2dr Cpe	$65,000	$80,000	$100,000	$130,000
		2dr GTS Cpe	$84,000	$108,000	$129,000	$165,000
1973	Deauville	4dr Sdn	$26,400	$38,200	$46,600	$59,500
						+10% for manual trans.
1974	Deauville	4dr Sdn	$26,400	$38,200	$46,600	$59,500
						+10% for manual trans.
1974	Pantera L	2dr Cpe	$65,000	$80,000	$100,000	$130,000
		2dr GTS Cpe	$84,000	$108,000	$129,000	$165,000
1975	Deauville	4dr Sdn	$26,400	$38,200	$46,600	$59,500
						+10% for manual trans.
1976	Deauville	4dr Sdn	$26,400	$38,200	$46,600	$59,500
						+10% for manual trans.

DeTomaso

Year	Model	Body Style	4	3	2	1
1977	Deauville	4dr Sdn	$26,400	$38,200	$46,600	$59,500
						+10% for manual trans.
1978	Deauville	4dr Sdn	$26,400	$38,200	$46,600	$59,500
						+10% for manual trans.
1979	Deauville	4dr Sdn	$26,400	$38,200	$46,600	$59,500
						+10% for manual trans.
1980	Deauville	4dr Sdn	$26,400	$38,200	$46,600	$59,500
						+10% for manual trans.
1981	Deauville	4dr Sdn	$26,400	$38,200	$46,600	$59,500
						+10% for manual trans.
1981	Pantera	2dr GT Cpe	$70,000	$87,000	$108,000	$137,000
1982	Deauville	4dr Sdn	$26,400	$38,200	$46,600	$59,500
						+10% for manual trans.
1982	Pantera	2dr GT Cpe	$70,000	$87,000	$108,000	$137,000
1983	Deauville	4dr Sdn	$26,400	$38,200	$46,600	$59,500
						+10% for manual trans.
1983	Pantera	2dr GT Cpe	$70,000	$87,000	$108,000	$137,000
1984	Deauville	4dr Sdn	$26,400	$38,200	$46,600	$59,500
						+10% for manual trans.
1984	Pantera	2dr GT Cpe	$71,000	$90,000	$114,000	$142,000
1985	Longchamp	2dr GTS Cpe	$25,900	$37,600	$50,500	$72,300
						-25% for auto trans.
1985	Deauville	4dr Sdn	$26,400	$38,200	$46,600	$59,500
						+10% for manual trans.
1985	Pantera	2dr GT Cpe	$71,000	$90,000	$114,000	$142,000
1986	Pantera	2dr GT Cpe	$76,800	$96,000	$122,000	$150,000
1987	Pantera	2dr GT Cpe	$76,800	$96,000	$122,000	$150,000
1988	Pantera	2dr GT Cpe	$76,800	$96,000	$122,000	$150,000
1989	Pantera	2dr GT Cpe	$80,000	$102,000	$127,000	$160,000

Delage

Year	Model	Body Style	4	3	2	1
						Body style is everything on postwar Delages. Pay less for ugly, pay more for pretty.
1946	D6	2dr Cab	$217,000	$272,000	$355,000	$405,000
		2dr Figoni & Falaschi Cab	$280,000	$322,000	$475,000	$655,000
1947	D6	2dr Cab	$223,000	$277,000	$368,000	$425,000
		2dr Figoni & Falaschi Cab	$280,000	$322,000	$475,000	$655,000
1948	D6	2dr Cab	$217,000	$272,000	$355,000	$405,000
		2dr Figoni & Falaschi Cab	$280,000	$322,000	$475,000	$655,000
1949	D6	2dr Cab	$223,000	$277,000	$368,000	$425,000
		2dr F&F Cab	$266,000	$309,000	$449,000	$605,000
1950	D6	2dr Cab	$217,000	$272,000	$355,000	$405,000

Delage

Year	Model	Body Style	4	3	2	1
		2dr F&F Cab	$280,000	$322,000	$475,000	$655,000
1951	D6	2dr Cab	$223,000	$277,000	$368,000	$425,000
		2dr F&F Cab	$266,000	$309,000	$449,000	$605,000
1952	D6	2dr Cab	$223,000	$277,000	$368,000	$425,000
		2dr F&F Cab	$280,000	$322,000	$475,000	$655,000
1953	D6	2dr Cab	$223,000	$277,000	$368,000	$425,000
		2dr F&F Cab	$266,000	$309,000	$449,000	$605,000

Delahaye

Year	Model	Body Style	4	3	2	1

All Delahayes are valued by coach builder. Many will be worth less than these prices; many will exceed these prices.

Year	Model	Body Style	4	3	2	1
1948	135	2dr Cab	$134,000	$209,000	$282,000	$365,000
1948	135M	2dr Cpe	$74,900	$104,000	$141,000	$193,000
		2dr Cab	$205,000	$282,000	$372,000	$510,000
1948	135MS	2dr Cpe	$90,000	$129,000	$187,000	$249,000
		2dr Cab	$222,000	$298,000	$391,000	$525,000
1948	148L	4dr Berline	$29,200	$41,500	$69,200	$97,600
1948	175	2dr Cpe	$68,000	$96,200	$135,000	$181,000
		2dr Cab	$206,000	$262,000	$360,000	$492,000
1949	135	2dr Cab	$134,000	$209,000	$282,000	$365,000
1949	135M	2dr Cpe	$74,900	$104,000	$141,000	$193,000
		2dr Cab	$205,000	$282,000	$372,000	$510,000
1949	135MS	2dr Cpe	$90,000	$129,000	$187,000	$249,000
		2dr Cab	$222,000	$298,000	$391,000	$525,000
1949	148L	4dr Sdn	$29,200	$41,500	$69,200	$97,600
1949	175	2dr Cpe	$68,000	$96,200	$135,000	$181,000
		2dr Cab	$206,000	$262,000	$360,000	$492,000
1950	135	2dr Cab	$134,000	$209,000	$282,000	$365,000
1950	135M	2dr Cpe	$74,900	$104,000	$141,000	$193,000
		2dr Cab	$205,000	$282,000	$372,000	$510,000
1950	135MS	2dr Cpe	$90,000	$129,000	$187,000	$249,000
		2dr Cab	$222,000	$298,000	$391,000	$525,000
1950	148L	4dr Sdn	$29,200	$41,500	$69,200	$97,600
1950	175	2dr Cpe	$68,000	$96,200	$135,000	$181,000
		2dr Cab	$206,000	$262,000	$360,000	$492,000
1951	235	2dr Cpe	$71,000	$99,000	$138,000	$187,000
		2dr Cab	$160,000	$224,000	$289,000	$365,000
1951	235M	2dr Cpe	$78,800	$109,000	$151,000	$198,000
		2dr Cab	$216,000	$287,000	$389,000	$520,000
1951	235MS	2dr Cab	$240,000	$312,000	$410,000	$540,000
1952	235	2dr Cpe	$71,000	$99,000	$138,000	$187,000
		2dr Cab	$160,000	$224,000	$289,000	$365,000
1952	235M	2dr Cpe	$78,800	$109,000	$151,000	$198,000
		2dr Cab	$216,000	$287,000	$389,000	$520,000
1952	235MS	2dr Cab	$240,000	$312,000	$410,000	$540,000
1953	235	2dr Cpe	$71,000	$99,000	$138,000	$187,000
		2dr Cab	$160,000	$224,000	$289,000	$365,000

Delahaye

Year	Model	Body Style	4	3	2	1
1953	235M	2dr Cpe	$78,800	$109,000	$151,000	$198,000
		2dr Cab	$216,000	$287,000	$389,000	$520,000
1953	235MS	2dr Cab	$240,000	$312,000	$410,000	$540,000
1954	235	2dr Cpe	$71,000	$99,000	$138,000	$187,000
		2dr Cab	$160,000	$224,000	$289,000	$365,000
1954	235M	2dr Cpe	$78,800	$109,000	$151,000	$198,000
		2dr Cab	$216,000	$287,000	$389,000	$520,000
1954	235MS	2dr Cab	$240,000	$312,000	$410,000	$540,000

Delorean

Year	Model	Body Style	4	3	2	1
1981	DMC-12	2dr Cpe	$20,600	$31,300	$45,500	$63,200
						-5% for auto.
1982	DMC-12	2dr Cpe	$20,600	$31,300	$45,500	$63,200
						-5% for auto.
1983	DMC-12	2dr Cpe	$20,600	$31,300	$45,500	$63,200
		2dr Gold Ed Cpe	$66,000	$87,000	$114,000	$185,000
						-5% for auto.

Denzel

Year	Model	Body Style	4	3	2	1
1957	WD Super 1300	2dr Cpe	$242,000	$281,000	$336,000	$404,000
		2dr Rdstr	$280,000	$345,000	$420,000	$510,000
1957	WD International 1500	2dr Rdstr	$293,000	$360,000	$441,000	$525,000
1958	WD Super 1300	2dr Cpe	$242,000	$281,000	$336,000	$404,000
		2dr Rdstr	$280,000	$345,000	$420,000	$510,000
1958	WD International 1500	2dr Rdstr	$293,000	$360,000	$441,000	$525,000
1959	WD Super 1300	2dr Cpe	$242,000	$281,000	$336,000	$404,000
		2dr Rdstr	$280,000	$345,000	$420,000	$510,000
1959	WD International 1500	2dr Rdstr	$293,000	$360,000	$441,000	$525,000

Deutsch-Bonnet

Year	Model	Body Style	4	3	2	1
1955	HBR5	2dr Cpe	$34,000	$53,600	$88,400	$103,000
1956	HBR5	2dr Cpe	$34,000	$53,600	$88,400	$103,000
1957	HBR5	2dr Cpe	$34,000	$53,600	$88,400	$103,000
1958	HBR5	2dr Cpe	$34,000	$53,600	$88,400	$103,000
1959	HBR5	2dr Cpe	$34,000	$53,600	$88,400	$103,000

Devin

Year	Model	Body Style	4	3	2	1
1957	SS	2dr Rdstr	$193,000	$232,000	$298,000	$340,000
1958	SS	283/220 2dr Rdstr	$193,000	$232,000	$298,000	$340,000

Devin

Year	Model	Body Style	4	3	2	1
1959	SS	283/220 2dr Rdstr	$193,000	$232,000	$298,000	$340,000
1960	SS	283/220 2dr Rdstr	$193,000	$232,000	$298,000	$340,000
1961	SS	283/220 2dr Rdstr	$193,000	$232,000	$298,000	$340,000
1962	SS	2dr Rdstr	$193,000	$232,000	$298,000	$340,000

Dodge

Year	Model	Body Style	4	3	2	1
1946	Deluxe	230/102 2dr Cpe	$4,700	$7,600	$12,400	$17,100
		230/102 2dr Sdn	$3,000	$5,200	$8,900	$12,000
		230/102 4dr Sdn	$4,000	$6,600	$11,300	$15,500
1946	Custom	230/102 2dr Clb Cpe	$5,200	$8,100	$12,800	$17,700
		230/102 4dr Sdn	$3,200	$5,600	$9,400	$12,400
		230/102 2dr Conv	$11,900	$19,100	$30,600	$43,300
1947	Deluxe	230/102 2dr Cpe	$4,700	$7,600	$12,400	$17,100
		230/102 2dr Sdn	$4,300	$6,800	$11,600	$15,600
		230/102 4dr Sdn	$2,900	$5,100	$8,700	$12,000
1947	Custom	230/102 2dr Clb Cpe	$5,200	$8,100	$12,800	$17,700
		230/102 4dr Sdn 6P	$3,200	$5,600	$9,400	$12,400
		230/102 2dr Conv	$11,900	$19,100	$30,600	$43,300
1948	Deluxe	230/102 2dr Cpe	$4,700	$7,600	$12,400	$17,100
		230/102 2dr Sdn	$4,300	$6,800	$11,600	$15,600
		230/102 4dr Sdn	$2,900	$5,100	$8,700	$12,000
1948	Custom	230/102 2dr Clb Cpe	$5,200	$8,100	$12,800	$17,700
		230/102 2dr Conv	$11,900	$19,100	$30,600	$43,300
1949	Deluxe	230/102 2dr Cpe	$5,400	$8,300	$13,300	$17,500
		230/102 2dr Sdn	$4,900	$7,700	$13,100	$16,400
		230/102 4dr Sdn	$2,700	$5,100	$8,800	$11,800
1949	Custom	2dr Clb Cpe	$5,900	$8,500	$14,000	$18,100
		4dr Sdn	$3,400	$5,600	$9,100	$12,700
		2dr Conv	$11,400	$18,200	$29,000	$40,700
1949	Wayfarer	230/103 2dr Bus Cpe	$3,700	$7,100	$11,300	$15,800
		230/103 2dr Sdn	$2,800	$5,400	$9,300	$13,000
		230/103 2dr Rdstr	$11,400	$17,200	$30,200	$46,500
1949	Meadowbrook	230/103 4dr Sdn	$1,800	$4,400	$7,900	$11,200
1949	Coronet	230/103 2dr Clb Cpe	$3,800	$7,000	$11,600	$16,400
		230/103 4dr Sdn	$2,200	$5,000	$8,700	$12,600
		230/103 4dr Wgn	$50,300	$65,500	$74,900	$95,000
		230/103 2dr Conv	$10,900	$14,900	$28,000	$44,300
1950	Wayfarer	230/103 2dr Cpe	$3,700	$7,100	$11,300	$15,800
		230/103 2dr Sdn	$2,900	$5,600	$9,600	$13,400
		230/103 2dr Rdstr	$11,200	$17,400	$30,100	$46,500
1950	Meadowbrook	230/103 4dr Sdn	$1,800	$4,400	$7,900	$11,200

Dodge

Year	Model	Body Style	4	3	2	1
1950	Coronet	230/103 2dr Clb Cpe	$3,800	$7,000	$12,200	$16,500
		230/103 4dr Sdn	$2,200	$5,000	$8,700	$12,600
		230/103 4dr Wgn	$50,300	$65,500	$74,900	$95,000
		230/103 4dr Sierra Wgn	$4,200	$7,700	$14,100	$19,400
		230/103 2dr Conv	$10,900	$14,900	$25,900	$45,900
1951	Wayfarer	230/103 2dr Cpe	$4,200	$7,300	$11,600	$16,000
		230/103 2dr Sdn	$3,800	$6,500	$10,800	$14,700
		230/103 2dr Sportabout Rdstr	$12,300	$18,000	$30,800	$49,400
1951	Meadowbrook	230/103 4dr Sdn	$2,200	$4,800	$8,200	$12,200
1951	Coronet	230/103 2dr Clb Cpe	$4,200	$7,700	$13,000	$17,300
		230/103 4dr Sdn	$2,300	$5,400	$9,000	$13,100
		230/103 4dr Sierra Wgn	$4,700	$8,100	$14,300	$18,800
		230/103 2dr Conv	$12,000	$15,400	$29,800	$49,400
1952	Wayfarer	230/103 2dr Cpe	$4,200	$7,300	$11,600	$16,000
		230/103 2dr Sdn	$3,700	$6,300	$10,500	$14,300
		230/103 2dr Rdstr	$12,300	$18,000	$30,800	$49,400
1952	Meadowbrook	230/103 4dr Sdn	$2,200	$4,800	$8,200	$12,200
1952	Coronet	230/103 2dr Clb Cpe	$4,200	$7,700	$13,000	$17,300
		230/103 4dr Sdn	$2,300	$5,400	$9,000	$13,100
		230/103 4dr Sierra Wgn	$4,700	$8,100	$14,300	$18,800
		230/103 2dr Conv	$12,000	$15,400	$29,800	$49,400
1953	Meadowbrook	230/103 2dr Spcl Clb Cpe	$3,700	$6,300	$10,100	$14,000
		230/103 4dr Sdn	$2,500	$4,800	$7,800	$10,300
						-10% for 6-cyl.
1953	Coronet	241/140 2dr Clb Cpe	$4,000	$6,500	$10,500	$15,200
		241/140 4dr Sdn	$2,000	$4,500	$8,000	$11,700
		241/140 4dr Sierra Wgn	$5,400	$8,500	$15,100	$20,000
		241/140 2dr Conv	$8,800	$12,100	$28,200	$48,700
						-10% for 6-cyl.
1954	Meadowbrook	240/140 2dr Clb Cpe	$3,600	$6,300	$10,200	$13,700
		240/140 4dr Sdn	$2,100	$4,300	$7,100	$9,600
						-10% for 6-cyl.
1954	Coronet	241/150 2dr Clb Cpe	$3,500	$6,300	$10,500	$14,500
		241/150 4dr Sdn	$2,000	$4,300	$8,200	$10,600
		241/150 4dr Sierra Stn Wgn, 6-p.	$5,500	$8,500	$15,200	$19,900

Year	Model	Body Style	4	3	2	1
						-10% for 6-cyl.
1954	Royal	241/150 2dr Clb Cpe	$4,500	$7,500	$11,300	$16,400
		241/150 2dr Spt Cpe	$6,400	$11,200	$17,900	$25,500
		241/150 4dr Sdn	$2,600	$5,300	$9,000	$11,700
		241/150 2dr Conv	$13,100	$18,100	$37,500	$51,100
		241/150 2dr Pace Car Conv	$16,200	$22,300	$41,600	$62,700
1955	Coronet	270/175 2dr Sdn	$5,400	$8,300	$14,300	$24,200
		270/183 2dr Sdn	$5,600	$8,600	$15,000	$25,500
		270/193 2dr Sdn	$5,800	$9,100	$15,700	$26,700
		270/175 4dr Sdn	$3,400	$5,800	$9,700	$13,400
		270/183 4dr Sdn	$3,800	$6,400	$10,700	$14,900
		270/193 4dr Sdn	$4,000	$6,800	$11,400	$15,500
		270/175 4dr Sierra Stn Wgn 6P	$7,000	$11,700	$23,600	$31,300
		270/183 4dr Sierra Stn Wgn 6P	$7,400	$12,500	$25,300	$32,900
		270/193 4dr Sierra Stn Wgn 6P	$7,700	$13,000	$26,500	$34,400
		270/175 2dr Lancer Hdtp Cpe	$5,900	$8,800	$15,600	$27,600
		270/183 2dr Lancer Hdtp Cpe	$6,200	$9,500	$16,300	$29,000
		270/193 2dr Lancer Hdtp Cpe	$6,500	$9,800	$17,200	$30,400
				+20% for factory a/c. -10% for 6-cyl.		
1955	Royal	270/175 2dr Lancer Hdtp Cpe	$7,100	$10,800	$18,100	$35,700
		270/183 2dr Lancer Hdtp Cpe	$7,500	$11,300	$19,200	$37,400
		270/193 2dr Lancer Hdtp Cpe	$8,000	$11,900	$19,900	$39,000
		270/175 4dr Sdn	$4,500	$6,400	$10,500	$17,300
		270/183 4dr Sdn	$4,700	$6,700	$11,000	$18,200
		270/193 4dr Sdn	$4,900	$7,000	$11,600	$19,000
		270/175 4dr Sierra Stn Wgn 6P	$8,300	$13,200	$24,900	$33,800
		270/183 4dr Sierra Stn Wgn 6P	$8,800	$14,100	$26,500	$35,700
		270/193 4dr Sierra Stn Wgn 6P	$9,200	$14,700	$27,500	$37,400
			+20% for factory a/c. -10% for 6-cyl. +25% for La Femme Lancer.			
1955	Custom Royal	270/183 2dr Lancer Hdtp Cpe	$7,600	$11,700	$19,600	$39,000
		270/193 2dr Lancer Hdtp Cpe	$7,900	$12,200	$20,500	$40,800
		270/183 4dr Sdn	$5,200	$6,700	$11,400	$18,500

Dodge

Year	Model	Body Style	4	3	2	1
		270/193 4dr Sdn	$5,300	$7,100	$12,400	$20,300
		270/183 2dr Lancer Conv	$21,200	$32,300	$57,000	$76,300
		270/193 2dr Lancer Conv	$22,600	$34,500	$59,200	$82,000
		+20% for factory a/c. -10% for 6-cyl.				
1956	Coronet	270/189 2dr Clb Sdn	$5,500	$8,500	$15,400	$26,700
		315/230 2dr Clb Sdn	$6,500	$10,100	$18,600	$32,300
		270/189 4dr Sdn	$3,400	$6,000	$9,900	$13,200
		315/260 4dr Sdn	$4,400	$7,500	$12,500	$17,100
		270/189 4dr Sierra Stn Wgn 6P	$7,400	$12,400	$24,500	$31,400
		270/189 2dr Lancer Hdtp Cpe	$5,700	$8,800	$15,300	$26,800
		315/260 2dr Lancer Hdtp Cpe	$8,500	$13,400	$22,300	$36,700
		270/189 4dr Lancer Hdtp Sdn	$3,700	$6,200	$10,200	$14,000
		315/260 4dr Lancer Hdtp Sdn	$4,800	$7,800	$12,800	$17,500
		270/189 2dr Conv	$19,100	$28,100	$48,200	$65,400
		315/260 2dr Conv	$25,200	$36,300	$66,600	$86,200
		+20% for factory a/c. -10% for 6-cyl.				
1956	Royal	315/218 2dr Lancer Hdtp Cpe	$6,600	$10,500	$18,100	$36,900
		315/260 2dr Lancer Hdtp Cpe	$8,000	$12,600	$21,400	$42,200
		315/218 4dr Sdn	$4,700	$7,500	$11,900	$17,300
		315/260 4dr Sdn	$6,100	$9,400	$15,000	$21,800
		315/218 4dr Cstm Sierra Stn Wgn 6P	$7,800	$13,200	$26,500	$33,100
		315/260 4dr Cstm Sierra Stn Wgn 6P	$9,500	$15,900	$31,600	$40,200
		315/218 4dr Lancer Hdtp Sdn	$5,000	$8,100	$12,500	$19,400
		315/260 4dr Lancer Hdtp Sdn	$6,500	$10,200	$15,700	$24,600
		+20% for factory a/c. +25% for La Femme Lancer. +10% for Texan Lancer. -10% for 6-cyl.				
1956	Custom Royal	315/230 2dr Lancer Hdtp Cpe	$7,100	$11,100	$18,600	$36,800
		2dr D-500 Lancer Hdtp Cpe	$8,600	$13,300	$23,800	$44,600
		315/230 4dr Sdn	$4,700	$6,400	$11,000	$18,200
		4dr D-500 Sdn	$5,900	$7,900	$13,900	$22,900
		315/230 4dr Lancer Hdtp Sdn	$5,100	$6,700	$11,800	$19,400

Year	Model	Body Style	4	3	2	1
		4dr D-500 Lancer Hdtp Sdn	$6,500	$8,500	$14,800	$24,300
		315/230 2dr Lancer Conv	$21,200	$30,900	$50,600	$71,500
		315/260 2dr Lancer Conv	$25,900	$37,200	$67,500	$89,000
				+20% for factory a/c. -10% for 6-cyl.		
1957	Coronet	325/245 2dr Clb Sdn	$9,200	$16,100	$24,800	$33,900
		354/285 2dr Clb Sdn	$11,600	$20,200	$31,100	$42,300
		354/340 2dr Clb Sdn	$12,800	$21,800	$33,600	$45,800
		325/245 4dr Sdn	$6,200	$9,500	$14,900	$18,500
		354/285 4dr Sdn	$8,200	$12,500	$19,700	$24,300
		325/245 2dr Lancer Hdtp Cpe	$10,400	$17,900	$26,900	$36,800
		354/285 2dr Lancer Hdtp Cpe	$13,000	$22,400	$33,200	$46,300
		325/245 4dr Lancer Hdtp Sdn	$7,100	$10,300	$15,800	$19,800
		354/285 4dr Lancer Hdtp Sdn	$9,600	$13,700	$20,800	$26,200
		325/245 2dr Lancer Conv	$15,900	$23,900	$44,000	$69,100
		354/285 2dr Lancer Conv	$19,900	$29,900	$55,000	$87,000
		354/340 2dr Lancer Conv	$21,600	$32,600	$59,600	$93,500
				+20% for factory a/c. -10% for 6-cyl.		
1957	Royal	325/245 2dr Lancer Hdtp Cpe	$10,900	$18,500	$27,800	$38,000
		354/285 2dr Lancer Hdtp Cpe	$14,100	$23,000	$34,900	$47,200
		325/245 4dr Sdn	$6,400	$10,000	$15,300	$19,000
		354/285 4dr Sdn	$8,600	$13,300	$20,200	$25,100
		325/245 4dr Cstm Sierra Stn Wgn 6P	$6,800	$10,900	$19,700	$26,200
		354/285 4dr Cstm Sierra Stn Wgn 6P	$8,700	$13,800	$24,600	$32,600
		325/245 4dr Lancer Hdtp Sdn	$7,100	$10,500	$16,100	$20,200
		354/285 4dr Lancer Hdtp Sdn	$9,800	$14,000	$21,100	$26,700
				+20% for factory a/c. -10% for 6-cyl.		
1957	Custom Royal	325/260 2dr Lancer Hdtp Cpe	$11,000	$18,800	$28,900	$41,300

Dodge

Year	Model	Body Style	4	3	2	1
		354/285 2dr Lancer Hdtp Cpe	$14,500	$25,100	$37,200	$51,900
		325/260 4dr Sdn	$6,500	$10,700	$16,000	$20,800
		354/285 4dr Sdn	$8,800	$14,200	$21,100	$27,400
		325/260 4dr Lancer Hdtp Sdn	$7,600	$11,400	$16,900	$22,700
		354/285 4dr Lancer Hdtp Sdn	$10,200	$15,200	$22,200	$30,000
		325/260 2dr Lancer Conv	$18,700	$28,100	$53,900	$78,200
		354/285 2dr Lancer Conv	$33,700	$45,100	$78,300	$113,000
				+20% for factory a/c. -10% for 6-cyl.		
1958	Coronet	325/252 2dr Clb Sdn	$9,800	$16,900	$25,500	$33,900
		350/295 2dr Clb Sdn	$12,200	$21,200	$31,900	$42,300
		361/333 FI 2dr Clb Sdn	$13,600	$24,100	$35,100	$47,000
		325/252 4dr Sdn	$6,100	$9,600	$14,900	$18,600
		350/295 4dr Sdn	$8,200	$12,600	$19,700	$24,400
		361/333 FI 4dr Sdn	$8,800	$13,600	$21,300	$26,200
		325/252 2dr Lancer Hdtp Cpe	$11,500	$19,700	$30,400	$39,700
		361/333 FI 2dr Lancer Hdtp Cpe	$15,400	$26,600	$40,800	$53,000
		325/252 4dr Lancer Hdtp Sdn	$6,900	$10,300	$15,800	$19,800
		350/295 4dr Lancer Hdtp Sdn	$10,200	$14,700	$22,500	$28,400
		361/305 4dr Lancer Hdtp Sdn	$9,400	$13,700	$20,800	$26,200
		325/252 2dr Lancer Conv	$16,600	$25,200	$44,100	$72,800
		361/333 FI 2dr Lancer Conv	$22,500	$34,200	$59,700	$98,300
				+20% for factory a/c. -10% for 6-cyl.		
1958	Royal	325/265 2dr Lancer Hdtp Cpe	$12,800	$19,800	$31,100	$41,800
		361/320 2dr Lancer Hdtp Cpe	$15,000	$26,200	$38,500	$52,300
		361/333 FI 2dr Lancer Hdtp Cpe	$16,400	$27,900	$40,900	$56,700
		325/265 4dr Sdn	$6,500	$10,000	$15,500	$19,100
		361/305 4dr Sdn	$8,500	$13,400	$20,200	$25,100
		361/333 FI 4dr Sdn	$9,100	$14,300	$21,900	$27,200
		325/265 4dr Lancer Hdtp Sdn	$7,100	$10,500	$16,100	$20,200
		361/320 4dr Lancer Hdtp Sdn	$9,600	$14,000	$21,100	$26,700

Year	Model	Body Style	4	3	2	1
		361/333 FI 4dr Lancer Hdtp Sdn	$10,300	$15,000	$22,800	$28,800

+20% for factory a/c. -10% for 6-cyl.

Year	Model	Body Style	4	3	2	1
1958	Custom Sierra	350/295 4dr Stn Wgn 6P	$6,900	$11,000	$19,600	$24,000
		361/305 4dr Stn Wgn 6P	$8,600	$13,600	$24,600	$29,900
		361/333 FI 4dr Stn Wgn. 6-p.	$9,400	$14,800	$26,500	$32,200

+20% for factory a/c. -10% for 6-cyl.

Year	Model	Body Style	4	3	2	1
1958	Custom Royal	350/295 4dr Rgl Lancer Hdtp Cpe	$8,100	$12,300	$17,900	$24,300
		361/305 4dr Regal Lancer Hdtp Cpe	$10,800	$16,300	$23,700	$32,200
		361/333 FI 4dr Regal Lancer Hdtp Cpe	$11,600	$17,600	$25,400	$34,700
		350/295 2dr Lancer Hdtp Cpe	$14,900	$25,300	$39,200	$63,900
		361/320 2dr Lancer Hdtp Cpe	$16,400	$27,600	$41,800	$67,400
		361/333 FI 2dr Lancer Hdtp Cpe	$17,900	$30,100	$46,500	$72,400
		350/295 4dr Sdn	$6,600	$10,700	$16,000	$20,800
		361/305 4dr Sdn	$8,600	$14,200	$21,200	$27,500
		361/333 FI 4dr Sdn	$9,400	$15,300	$22,700	$29,600
		350/295 4dr Lancer Hdtp Sdn	$7,600	$11,400	$16,900	$22,700
		361/320 4dr Lancer Hdtp Sdn	$10,100	$15,200	$22,200	$30,000
		361/333 FI 4dr Lancer Hdtp Sdn	$11,000	$16,400	$24,000	$32,300
		350/295 2dr Lancer Conv	$20,400	$31,000	$53,500	$88,000
		361/333 FI 2dr Lancer Conv	$38,400	$54,000	$96,800	$145,000

+20% for factory a/c. -10% for 6-cyl.

Year	Model	Body Style	4	3	2	1
1959	Coronet	326/255 2dr Clb Sdn	$10,400	$17,700	$27,200	$36,100
		383/320 2dr Clb Sdn	$13,100	$22,000	$33,900	$45,000
		383/345 2dr Clb Sdn	$14,100	$23,800	$36,600	$48,600
		326/255 4dr Sdn	$6,200	$9,500	$14,900	$18,500
		383/320 4dr Sdn	$8,100	$12,500	$19,700	$24,300
		383/345 4dr Sdn	$8,900	$13,600	$21,300	$26,200
		326/255 2dr Lancer Hdtp Cpe	$11,800	$20,300	$31,200	$41,900
		383/320 2dr Lancer Hdtp Cpe	$14,400	$24,900	$37,300	$50,200

Dodge

Year	Model	Body Style	4	3	2	1
		383/345 2dr Lancer Hdtp Cpe	$15,700	$26,400	$40,500	$54,100
		326/255 4dr Lancer Hdtp Sdn	$7,100	$10,300	$15,800	$19,800
		383/320 4dr Lancer Hdtp Sdn	$10,200	$14,700	$22,500	$28,400
		383/345 4dr Lancer Hdtp Sdn	$10,200	$14,700	$22,500	$28,400
		326/255 2dr Lancer Conv	$17,600	$26,700	$52,000	$75,500
		383/320 2dr Lancer Conv	$22,000	$33,300	$64,900	$94,700
		383/345 2dr Lancer Conv	$23,500	$36,000	$70,300	$102,000
		+20% for factory a/c. +5% for swivel bucket seats. -10% for 6-cyl.				
1959	Sierra	383/345 4dr Stn Wgn 6P	$9,400	$14,800	$26,500	$32,000
		+20% for factory a/c. +5% for swivel bucket seats. -10% for 6-cyl.				
1959	Royal	361/305 2dr Lancer Hdtp Cpe	$14,200	$21,800	$32,500	$43,400
		383/320 2dr Lancer Hdtp Cpe	$16,000	$28,400	$40,200	$54,400
		383/345 2dr Lancer Hdtp Cpe	$16,700	$29,800	$42,300	$60,600
		361/305 4dr Sdn	$6,400	$10,000	$15,300	$19,000
		383/320 4dr Sdn	$8,500	$13,300	$20,200	$25,100
		383/345 4dr Sdn	$9,100	$14,300	$22,000	$27,300
		4dr Wgn	$6,800	$10,900	$19,600	$23,900
		4dr D-500 Wgn	$8,600	$13,600	$24,500	$29,900
		361/305 4dr Lancer Hdtp Sdn	$7,100	$10,500	$16,100	$20,200
		383/320 4dr Lancer Hdtp Sdn	$9,600	$14,000	$21,100	$26,700
		383/345 4dr Lancer Hdtp Sdn	$10,300	$15,000	$22,800	$28,800
		+20% for factory a/c. +5% for swivel bucket seats. -10% for 6-cyl.				
1959	Custom Royal	361/305 2dr Lancer Hdtp Cpe	$16,100	$27,700	$42,100	$65,100
		383/320 2dr Lancer Hdtp Cpe	$17,000	$28,700	$43,100	$70,400
		383/345 2dr Lancer Hdtp Cpe	$18,600	$31,200	$49,500	$75,500
		361/305 4dr Sdn	$6,600	$10,700	$16,000	$20,900
		383/320 4dr Sdn	$8,800	$14,200	$21,200	$27,500
		383/345 4dr Sdn	$9,400	$15,400	$22,700	$29,600
		361/305 4dr Lancer Hdtp Sdn	$7,600	$11,400	$16,900	$22,700
		383/320 4dr Lancer Hdtp Sdn	$10,100	$15,200	$22,200	$30,000

Year	Model	Body Style	4	3	2	1
		383/345 4dr Lancer Hdtp Sdn	$10,900	$16,400	$24,000	$32,300
		361/333 FI 2dr Lancer Conv	$37,900	$51,600	$92,400	$132,000
		383/345 2dr Lancer Conv	$46,000	$66,900	$114,000	$161,000
		+20% for factory a/c. +5% for swivel bucket seats. -10% for 6-cyl.				
1960	Dart	318/255 2dr Seneca Sdn	$6,000	$11,100	$14,700	$23,600
		318/230 4dr Seneca Sdn	$3,800	$7,500	$9,200	$16,400
		318/255 4dr Seneca Sdn	$4,300	$8,400	$10,500	$18,700
		318/255 4dr Pioneer Sdn	$5,100	$9,700	$12,100	$21,600
		318/255 4dr Phoenix Sdn	$4,100	$8,100	$10,100	$18,000
		318/255 4dr Seneca Wgn	$6,600	$9,900	$13,400	$22,200
		318/230 4dr Pioneer Stn Wgn 9P	$7,900	$11,900	$16,300	$26,600
		318/255 2dr Pioneer Hdtp Cpe	$7,200	$13,400	$17,700	$28,800
		318/255 2dr Phoenix Conv	$11,500	$22,100	$30,500	$41,600
		361/310 2dr Phoenix Conv	$12,000	$23,000	$31,700	$43,400
		383/330 2dr Phoenix Conv	$23,400	$35,500	$58,500	$80,800
		+10% for factory a/c. +10% for swivel bucket seats. -10% for 6-cyl.				
1960	Matador	361/295 2dr Hdtp	$5,400	$7,700	$10,200	$14,200
		361/295 4dr Sdn	$3,900	$6,300	$8,200	$11,000
		361/295 4dr Stn Wgn 6P	$6,300	$8,600	$11,700	$16,400
		383/330 4dr Stn Wgn 6P	$6,800	$9,400	$12,800	$17,700
		361/295 4dr Stn Wgn 9P	$5,700	$7,800	$10,600	$14,800
		+10% for factory a/c. +10% for swivel bucket seats. -10% for 6-cyl.				
1960	Polara	383/325 2dr Hdtp	$7,800	$19,100	$30,700	$41,800
		383/325 4dr Sdn	$6,300	$13,900	$23,200	$32,500
		383/325 4dr Stn Wgn 6P	$7,800	$20,700	$33,200	$44,300
		383/325 2dr Conv	$28,600	$46,200	$61,400	$82,600
		+10% for factory a/c. +10% for swivel bucket seats. -10% for 6-cyl.				
1961	Lancer	170/101 2dr 170 Sdn	$4,700	$8,000	$10,300	$17,300
		225/195 2dr 170 Sdn	$6,000	$10,100	$13,000	$21,700

Dodge

Year	Model	Body Style	4	3	2	1
		170/101 4dr 170 Sdn	$3,200	$6,100	$7,400	$14,000
		225/145 4dr 170 Sdn	$3,700	$7,000	$8,500	$16,100
		225/195 4dr 170 Sdn	$4,000	$7,600	$9,300	$17,600
		170/101 4dr 170 Wgn	$4,800	$7,000	$9,700	$16,500
		225/145 4dr 170 Wgn	$5,600	$8,100	$11,100	$19,100
		225/195 4dr 170 Wgn	$6,100	$8,800	$12,100	$20,700
1961	Dart	361/305 2dr Seneca Sdn	$11,500	$21,300	$29,000	$37,300
		383/325 2dr Seneca Sdn	$13,100	$23,700	$32,400	$41,600
		318/230 2dr Pioneer Sdn	$4,500	$8,400	$10,900	$17,300
		361/265 2dr Pioneer Sdn	$5,500	$9,900	$13,000	$21,200
		318/230 4dr Seneca Sdn	$3,000	$6,100	$7,600	$14,100
		318/230 4dr Pioneer Sdn	$3,000	$6,100	$7,600	$14,100
		361/265 4dr Pioneer Sdn	$3,600	$7,300	$9,100	$17,000
		361/305 4dr Phoenix Sdn	$3,900	$7,900	$9,900	$18,400
		383/325 4dr Phoenix Sdn	$4,400	$8,800	$11,100	$20,600
		318/230 4dr Seneca Wgn	$5,000	$7,600	$10,600	$17,300
		318/230 4dr Pioneer Stn Wgn 6P	$5,000	$7,600	$10,600	$17,300
		361/265 4dr Pioneer Stn Wgn 6P	$6,000	$9,100	$12,800	$20,800
		361/305 4dr Pioneer Stn Wgn 9P	$6,600	$9,800	$14,000	$22,700
		383/325 4dr Pioneer Stn Wgn 9P	$7,300	$11,000	$15,500	$25,200
		361/305 2dr Pioneer Hdtp Cpe	$6,000	$10,800	$14,200	$23,400
		383/325 2dr Pioneer Hdtp Cpe	$6,600	$12,000	$15,800	$25,100
		318/230 2dr Phoenix Conv	$9,300	$17,100	$23,900	$31,100
		361/265 2dr Phoenix Conv	$11,100	$20,500	$28,700	$37,400

Year	Model	Body Style	4	3	2	1
						-5% for 225/145 slant six.
1961	Polara	361/265 2dr Hdtp Cpe	$6,600	$18,000	$28,700	$38,200
		383/330 2dr Hdtp Cpe	$8,100	$20,600	$32,000	$42,700
		361/265 4dr Sdn	$6,000	$13,100	$22,800	$31,600
		383/330 4dr Sdn	$6,500	$14,300	$24,600	$33,900
		361/265 4dr Stn Wgn 6P	$6,700	$19,600	$30,900	$40,800
		383/330 4dr Stn Wgn 6P	$8,200	$22,500	$34,500	$45,700
		361/265 2dr Conv	$27,900	$45,900	$60,500	$77,200
		383/330 2dr Conv	$30,500	$49,200	$65,200	$84,500
						+10% for factory a/c.
1962	Lancer	170/101 4dr 170 Sdn	$5,500	$8,700	$11,000	$15,300
		225/195 4dr 170 Sdn	$6,800	$10,800	$13,900	$19,300
		170/101 4dr 170 Wgn	$5,800	$9,200	$11,800	$16,200
		225/195 4dr 170 Wgn	$7,200	$11,600	$14,800	$20,400
		170/101 2dr GT Hdtp Cpe	$8,300	$10,900	$14,500	$21,300
		225/195 2dr GT Hdtp Cpe	$9,600	$12,500	$18,100	$26,800
1962	Dart	318/230 2dr Sdn	$7,800	$10,600	$14,100	$19,600
		318/230 4dr Sdn	$5,800	$9,200	$12,100	$15,700
		318/230 4dr Wgn	$6,000	$9,600	$12,500	$16,400
		318/230 2dr 440 Conv	$8,800	$16,800	$23,200	$30,500
						-5% for 225-c.i. slant six.
1962	Polara 500	361/305 2dr Hdtp Cpe	$6,600	$9,100	$14,000	$21,000
		413/410 Max Wedge 2dr Hdtp Cpe	$8,700	$11,900	$18,200	$27,500
		413/420 Max Wedge 2dr Hdtp Cpe	$10,100	$13,800	$21,100	$31,700
		361/305 4dr Hdtp Sdn	$6,400	$7,200	$9,000	$13,000
		413/410 Max Wedge 4dr Hdtp Sdn	$8,500	$9,300	$11,800	$16,800
		413/420 Max Wedge 4dr Hdtp Sdn	$9,800	$10,800	$13,600	$19,500
		361/305 2dr Conv	$13,900	$19,300	$28,700	$42,400
		413/410 Max Wedge 2dr Conv	$19,700	$29,000	$42,100	$66,300

Dodge

Year	Model	Body Style	4	3	2	1
		413/420 Max Wedge 2dr Conv	$22,800	$32,700	$48,100	$73,700
				-20% for 6-cyl. +10% for factory a/c.		
1962	Custom 880	361/265 2dr Hdtp Cpe	$6,600	$9,200	$13,600	$18,500
		361/265 4dr Sdn	$7,000	$8,900	$13,100	$17,100
		361/265 4dr Stn Wgn 6P	$7,100	$11,800	$15,300	$21,600
		361/265 2dr Conv	$13,600	$18,800	$27,800	$37,600
				-20% for 6-cyl. +10% for factory a/c.		
1963	Dart	225/145 2dr 270 Sdn	$5,300	$7,800	$11,500	$15,400
		225/145 2dr 270 Conv	$6,200	$8,600	$13,400	$18,200
		225/145 2dr GT Conv	$8,600	$12,400	$18,800	$25,700
				-20% for 170-c.i. slant six. +10% for factory a/c.		
1963	Polara	383/305 2dr Hdtp Cpe	$5,800	$8,200	$11,800	$18,400
		383/330 2dr Hdtp Cpe	$6,900	$9,700	$14,000	$21,700
		383/305 2dr Conv	$11,000	$15,400	$22,500	$34,000
		383/330 2dr Conv	$12,800	$18,000	$26,500	$40,200
		383/305 2dr 500 Conv	$13,400	$18,700	$27,300	$41,200
		383/330 2dr 500 Conv	$15,900	$22,000	$32,300	$48,700
				+10% for factory a/c.		
1963	Custom 880	361/265 2dr Cpe	$6,600	$9,200	$13,600	$18,500
		361/265 2dr Conv	$13,600	$18,800	$27,500	$37,200
				+10% for factory a/c.		
1964	Dart	225/145 2dr 270 Sdn	$5,300	$7,800	$11,500	$15,400
		273/180 2dr 270 Sdn	$6,100	$8,700	$13,200	$17,600
		225/145 2dr GT Hdtp Cpe	$6,800	$9,700	$15,200	$20,500
		273/180 2dr GT Hdtp Cpe	$7,800	$10,900	$17,300	$23,200
		225/145 2dr 270 Conv	$6,300	$8,700	$13,800	$18,300
		273/180 2dr 270 Conv	$7,400	$10,200	$15,800	$21,200
		225/145 2dr GT Conv	$8,600	$12,400	$18,800	$25,600
		273/180 2dr GT Conv	$10,000	$14,300	$21,800	$29,600
				-20% for 170-c.i. slant six. +10% for factory a/c.		

Year	Model	Body Style	4	3	2	1
1964	Polara	318/230 2dr Hdtp Cpe	$5,400	$7,600	$11,200	$17,200
		361/265 2dr Hdtp Cpe	$6,800	$9,500	$14,100	$21,600
		383/305 2dr Hdtp Cpe	$6,000	$8,400	$12,200	$18,900
		383/330 2dr Hdtp Cpe	$7,100	$9,900	$14,700	$22,600
		318/230 2dr Conv	$10,400	$14,200	$21,100	$31,900
		361/265 2dr Conv	$12,800	$17,700	$26,400	$39,800
		383/305 2dr Conv	$11,400	$15,700	$23,200	$35,100
		383/330 2dr Conv	$13,300	$18,500	$27,300	$41,400
		318/230 2dr 500 Conv	$12,200	$17,000	$24,900	$37,500
		361/265 2dr 500 Conv	$15,300	$21,200	$31,200	$47,000
		383/305 2dr 500 Conv	$13,400	$18,700	$27,300	$41,200
		383/330 2dr 500 Conv	$15,900	$22,000	$32,300	$48,700

-20% for 6-cyl. +10% for a/c.

Year	Model	Body Style	4	3	2	1
1964	Custom 880	361/265 2dr Hdtp Cpe	$6,900	$9,500	$14,200	$19,100
		383/305 2dr Hdtp Cpe	$7,500	$10,500	$15,600	$21,100
		383/330 2dr Hdtp Cpe	$9,100	$12,400	$18,400	$25,000
		361/265 2dr Conv	$13,100	$18,200	$26,800	$36,000
		383/305 2dr Conv	$14,500	$20,000	$29,300	$39,600
		383/330 2dr Conv	$16,900	$23,500	$34,700	$46,600

+10% for factory a/c.

Year	Model	Body Style	4	3	2	1
1965	Dart	225/145 2dr 270 Sdn	$5,400	$7,800	$11,800	$15,600
		273/180 2dr 270 Sdn	$6,200	$8,700	$13,500	$17,800
		225/145 2dr GT Hdtp Cpe	$7,200	$10,400	$16,300	$21,800
		273/180 2dr GT Hdtp Cpe	$8,400	$11,800	$18,400	$24,700
		225/145 2dr 270 Conv	$6,500	$9,100	$14,400	$19,300
		273/180 2dr 270 Conv	$7,600	$10,500	$16,800	$22,300
		225/145 2dr GT Conv	$9,400	$13,300	$20,600	$27,600
		273/180 2dr GT Conv	$10,800	$15,500	$23,900	$32,000

-20% for 170-c.i. slant six. +10% for factory a/c.

Year	Model	Body Style	4	3	2	1
1965	Coronet	318/230 2dr Sdn	$6,200	$8,300	$12,400	$17,100
		361/265 2dr Sdn	$7,700	$10,600	$15,500	$21,600

Dodge

Year	Model	Body Style	4	3	2	1
		426/365 2dr Sdn	$9,500	$13,300	$20,300	$28,400
		426/415 Hemi 2dr Sdn	$10,900	$15,600	$23,800	$33,700
		426/425 Hemi 2dr Sdn	$13,200	$18,300	$27,600	$38,900
		318/230 2dr 440 Hdtp Cpe	$9,600	$13,000	$19,300	$26,100
		361/265 2dr 440 Hdtp Cpe	$11,900	$16,500	$24,300	$32,900
		383/330 2dr 440 Hdtp Cpe	$11,500	$15,700	$23,200	$31,500
		426/365 2dr 440 Hdtp Cpe	$14,300	$20,600	$31,400	$43,300
		426/415 Hemi 2dr 440 Hdtp Cpe	$16,300	$24,200	$36,800	$50,800
		426/425 Hemi 2dr 440 Hdtp Cpe	$19,100	$28,000	$42,800	$59,000
		318/230 2dr 500 Cpe	$10,300	$14,000	$20,600	$28,100
		361/265 2dr 500 Cpe	$12,800	$17,600	$25,800	$35,300
		383/330 2dr 500 Cpe	$12,200	$16,800	$24,900	$33,800
		426/365 2dr 500 Cpe	$14,400	$21,900	$33,600	$46,400
		426/415 Hemi 2dr 500 Cpe	$17,600	$25,800	$39,200	$54,600
		426/425 Hemi 2dr 500 Cpe	$20,400	$29,900	$45,500	$63,100
		318/230 2dr 440 Conv	$13,400	$17,500	$27,000	$37,200
		361/265 2dr 440 Conv	$16,800	$23,400	$35,600	$46,500
		383/330 2dr 440 Conv	$16,100	$22,400	$33,300	$44,600
		426/365 2dr 440 Conv	$20,200	$29,500	$44,700	$61,400
		426/415 Hemi 2dr 440 Conv	$24,200	$35,500	$54,100	$74,200
		426/425 Hemi 2dr 440 Conv	$28,200	$41,100	$62,900	$86,200
		318/230 2dr 500 Conv	$16,400	$22,700	$33,700	$45,700
		361/265 2dr 500 Conv	$20,500	$28,400	$42,200	$57,000
		383/330 2dr 500 Conv	$19,800	$27,300	$40,300	$54,800
		426/365 2dr 500 Conv	$24,600	$35,700	$54,500	$75,400
		426/415 Hemi 2dr 500 Conv	$29,600	$43,000	$65,900	$91,100

Year	Model	Body Style	4	3	2	1
		426/425 Hemi 2dr 500 Conv	$34,500	$50,200	$76,700	$106,000

-20% for 6-cyl. +15% for 4-spd. +10% for factory a/c.

Year	Model	Body Style	4	3	2	1
1965	Polara	2dr Conv	$10,800	$15,300	$25,300	$34,700
		383/315 2dr Conv	$13,400	$18,400	$30,300	$41,800
		413/340 2dr Conv	$14,200	$19,500	$32,200	$44,100
		426/365 2dr Conv	$16,800	$23,200	$38,000	$52,100
		426/415 Hemi 2dr Conv	$19,900	$27,600	$45,400	$62,100
		426/425 Hemi 2dr Conv	$22,800	$31,500	$51,800	$71,000

-20% for 6-cyl. +10% for factory a/c.

Year	Model	Body Style	4	3	2	1
1965	Custom 880	383/270 2dr Hdtp Cpe	$7,200	$10,000	$14,900	$20,100
		383/315 2dr Hdtp Cpe	$8,800	$12,000	$17,800	$24,100
		413/340 2dr Hdtp Cpe	$9,300	$12,800	$18,900	$25,600
		426/365 2dr Hdtp Cpe	$11,000	$15,100	$22,400	$30,200
		426/415 Hemi 2dr Hdtp Cpe	$12,900	$17,700	$26,600	$35,800
		426/425 Hemi 2dr Hdtp Cpe	$15,000	$20,900	$30,900	$41,600
		383/315 4dr Hdtp Sdn	$8,800	$12,300	$18,000	$24,400
		426/425 Hemi 4dr Hdtp Sdn	$12,600	$17,500	$26,100	$35,200
		361/265 2dr Conv	$16,700	$23,000	$34,000	$45,500
		383/270 2dr Conv	$13,300	$18,400	$27,100	$36,400
		383/315 2dr Conv	$16,000	$22,100	$32,500	$43,600
		413/340 2dr Conv	$17,000	$23,200	$34,500	$46,200
		426/365 2dr Conv	$20,000	$27,600	$41,700	$56,600
		426/415 Hemi 2dr Conv	$26,700	$35,600	$53,400	$69,600
		426/425 Hemi 2dr Conv	$29,300	$45,000	$63,000	$82,300

-20% for 6-cyl. +10% for factory a/c.

Year	Model	Body Style	4	3	2	1
1965	Monaco	383/315 2dr Hdtp Cpe	$9,000	$12,400	$18,600	$25,000
		413/340 2dr Hdtp Cpe	$9,600	$13,200	$19,700	$26,600
		426/365 2dr Hdtp Cpe	$11,300	$15,600	$23,300	$31,400
		426/415 Hemi 2dr Hdtp Cpe	$13,300	$18,400	$27,600	$37,200
		426/425 Hemi 2dr Hdtp Cpe	$15,500	$21,500	$32,100	$43,300

-20% for 6-cyl. +10% for factory a/c.

Dodge

Year	Model	Body Style	4	3	2	1
1966	Dart	273/180 2dr 170 Sdn	$6,000	$8,400	$12,700	$16,800
		273/235 2dr 170 Sdn	$6,600	$9,100	$14,000	$18,600
		273/180 2dr GT Hdtp Cpe	$9,700	$13,500	$20,900	$27,900
		273/235 2dr GT Hdtp Cpe	$10,700	$14,800	$23,000	$30,600
		273/180 2dr 270 Conv	$9,700	$13,300	$20,500	$27,600
		273/235 2dr 270 Conv	$10,500	$14,700	$22,500	$30,300
		273/180 2dr GT Conv	$12,700	$18,000	$27,400	$37,200
		273/235 2dr GT Conv	$14,000	$19,800	$30,200	$40,900
		-20% for 170-c.i. slant six. +10% for factory a/c.				
1966	Coronet	273/180 2dr Sdn	$6,600	$9,000	$13,000	$17,800
		318/230 2dr Sdn	$7,700	$10,200	$14,600	$20,000
		361/265 2dr Sdn	$8,200	$10,400	$14,900	$20,200
		383/325 2dr Sdn	$8,500	$10,600	$15,100	$20,400
		426/425 Hemi 2dr Sdn	$47,900	$68,800	$88,700	$105,000
		273/180 2dr 440 Hdtp Cpe	$9,300	$12,600	$18,900	$25,500
		318/230 2dr 440 Hdtp Cpe	$11,600	$14,100	$21,000	$28,200
		361/265 2dr 440 Hdtp Cpe	$11,600	$14,400	$21,200	$28,500
		383/325 2dr 440 Hdtp Cpe	$11,800	$14,600	$21,600	$28,900
		273/180 2dr 500 Hdtp Cpe	$10,100	$13,700	$20,200	$27,400
		318/230 2dr 500 Hdtp Cpe	$10,400	$13,900	$20,500	$27,700
		361/265 2dr 500 Hdtp Cpe	$12,100	$15,400	$22,500	$30,300
		383/325 2dr 500 Hdtp Cpe	$13,100	$16,200	$24,900	$31,300
		273/180 2dr 440 Conv	$13,700	$18,400	$27,300	$35,900
		318/230 2dr 440 Conv	$14,000	$19,100	$27,700	$36,300
		361/265 2dr 440 Conv	$16,800	$20,800	$31,000	$39,500
		383/325 2dr 440 Conv	$18,200	$21,400	$33,000	$42,000
		273/180 2dr 500 Conv	$15,900	$21,900	$33,000	$44,100
		318/230 2dr 500 Conv	$16,300	$22,600	$33,900	$45,300

Year	Model	Body Style	4	3	2	1
		361/265 2dr 500 Conv	$17,500	$24,000	$35,300	$47,900
		383/325 2dr 500 Conv	$19,100	$25,500	$37,800	$49,800
			-20% for 6-cyl. +15% for 4-spd. +10% for factory a/c.			
1966	Charger	318/230 2dr Fstbk	$13,100	$18,800	$26,500	$36,900
		361/265 2dr Fstbk	$16,100	$22,700	$33,900	$44,700
		383/325 2dr Fstbk	$17,600	$24,500	$37,000	$50,200
		426/425 Hemi 2dr Fstbk	$46,300	$56,200	$81,000	$107,000
			-20% for 6-cyl. +15% for 4-spd. -10% for auto. +10% for factory a/c.			
1966	Polara	383/270 2dr Hdtp Cpe	$6,400	$8,900	$14,500	$20,100
		383/325 2dr Hdtp Cpe	$8,500	$11,500	$18,900	$26,200
		440/350 2dr Hdtp Cpe	$8,200	$11,200	$18,700	$25,300
		383/270 2dr 500 Hdtp Cpe	$7,600	$10,500	$17,200	$24,000
		383/325 2dr 500 Hdtp Cpe	$10,000	$13,700	$22,500	$31,100
		440/350 2dr 500 Hdtp Cpe	$9,700	$13,100	$21,700	$30,100
		383/270 2dr Conv	$9,200	$12,600	$21,000	$28,800
		383/325 2dr Conv	$12,000	$16,400	$27,200	$37,300
		440/350 2dr Conv	$11,500	$15,800	$26,300	$36,000
		383/270 2dr 500 Conv	$11,100	$14,900	$24,800	$34,000
		383/325 2dr 500 Conv	$14,300	$19,400	$32,300	$44,100
		440/350 2dr 500 Conv	$13,900	$18,700	$31,100	$42,600
			+10% for factory a/c.			
1966	Monaco	383/325 2dr Hdtp Cpe	$8,000	$10,900	$16,000	$21,700
		440/350 2dr Hdtp Cpe	$12,100	$16,300	$24,100	$32,500
		383/325 2dr 500 Hdtp Cpe	$8,300	$11,400	$16,700	$22,800
		440/350 2dr 500 Hdtp Cpe	$12,600	$17,000	$25,200	$34,100
			+10% for factory a/c.			
1967	Dart	225/145 2dr Sdn	$7,200	$10,200	$14,400	$17,800
		273/180 2dr Sdn	$7,900	$11,100	$15,800	$19,800
		225/145 2dr GT Hdtp Cpe	$11,700	$16,500	$23,800	$29,800
		273/180 2dr GT Hdtp Cpe	$13,000	$18,100	$26,100	$32,600

Dodge

Year	Model	Body Style	4	3	2	1
		383/325 2dr GTS Hdtp Cpe	$13,900	$19,400	$28,500	$37,600
		225/145 2dr GT Conv	$15,800	$22,700	$32,700	$41,200
		273/180 2dr GT Conv	$17,100	$24,900	$36,000	$45,400
		-20% for 170-c.i. slant six. +20% for 4-spd. +10% for factory a/c.				
1967	Coronet	273/180 2dr Dlx Sdn	$5,900	$8,500	$12,500	$17,200
		318/230 2dr Dlx Sdn	$7,200	$10,700	$15,500	$21,500
		383/325 2dr Dlx Sdn	$7,300	$10,900	$15,800	$21,800
		273/180 2dr 440 Hdtp Cpe	$8,300	$11,900	$17,700	$24,200
		318/230 2dr 440 Hdtp Cpe	$10,300	$14,800	$21,900	$29,900
		383/325 2dr 440 Hdtp Cpe	$10,500	$15,000	$22,300	$30,300
		273/180 2dr 500 Hdtp Cpe	$9,200	$13,000	$18,900	$25,800
		318/230 2dr 500 Hdtp Cpe	$11,300	$16,100	$23,500	$32,000
		383/325 2dr 500 Hdtp Cpe	$11,500	$16,300	$23,800	$32,400
		426/425 Hemi 2dr R/T Hdtp Cpe	$62,000	$82,400	$98,300	$124,000
		440/375 2dr R/T Hdtp Cpe	$17,000	$23,600	$35,100	$50,000
		273/180 2dr 440 Conv	$12,600	$18,000	$26,600	$35,900
		318/230 2dr 440 Conv	$15,600	$22,400	$33,000	$44,500
		383/325 2dr 440 Conv	$15,900	$22,700	$33,500	$45,300
		273/180 2dr 500 Conv	$14,300	$20,800	$30,900	$41,300
		318/230 2dr 500 Conv	$17,700	$26,000	$38,100	$51,000
		383/325 2dr 500 Conv	$18,200	$26,400	$39,000	$52,000
		426/425 Hemi 2dr R/T Conv	$74,700	$125,000	$155,000	$205,000
		440/375 2dr R/T Conv	$19,600	$28,900	$42,400	$58,400
		-20% for 6-cyl. +20% for 4-spd. -10% for auto. +10% for factory a/c. Colors can make an astonishing difference in both value and salability.				
1967	Charger	318/230 2dr Fstbk	$11,200	$17,700	$25,900	$35,800
		383/325 2dr Fstbk	$15,700	$22,200	$33,100	$43,000
		426/425 Hemi 2dr Fstbk	$53,900	$68,000	$88,000	$122,000

Year	Model	Body Style	4	3	2	1
		440/375 2dr Fstbk	$18,500	$26,800	$37,400	$57,100
		-20% for 6-cyl. +20% for 4-spd. -10% for auto. +10% for factory a/c. Colors can make an astonishing difference in both value and salability.				
1967	Polara	383/325 2dr Hdtp Cpe	$7,200	$10,500	$17,000	$22,800
		426/425 Hemi 2dr Hdtp Cpe	$10,800	$15,700	$25,500	$34,000
		440/375 2dr Hdtp Cpe	$9,300	$13,500	$21,800	$29,100
		383/325 2dr 500 Hdtp Cpe	$8,600	$12,100	$19,600	$26,600
		426/425 Hemi 2dr 500 Hdtp Cpe	$12,700	$17,900	$29,500	$39,600
		440/375 2dr 500 Hdtp Cpe	$10,800	$15,400	$25,300	$33,900
		383/325 2dr Conv	$10,400	$14,800	$24,100	$32,000
		426/425 Hemi 2dr Conv	$15,600	$22,200	$36,200	$48,100
		440/375 2dr Conv	$13,200	$18,900	$30,700	$41,100
		383/325 2dr 500 Conv	$11,000	$15,700	$25,700	$34,400
		426/425 Hemi 2dr 500 Conv	$16,900	$24,200	$39,400	$51,600
		440/375 2dr 500 Conv	$14,000	$20,200	$32,800	$44,100
		+20% for 4-spd.				
1967	Monaco	426/425 Hemi 2dr Hdtp Cpe	$15,100	$19,700	$28,700	$38,600
		440/375 2dr Hdtp Cpe	$11,700	$16,600	$24,200	$32,600
		426/425 Hemi 2dr 500 Hdtp Cpe	$15,700	$20,400	$30,000	$40,300
		440/375 2dr 500 Hdtp Cpe	$12,000	$17,200	$25,400	$34,100
		+20% for 4-spd.				
1968	Dart	225/145 2dr Sdn	$6,900	$9,900	$13,400	$17,200
		273/190 2dr Sdn	$7,600	$10,900	$14,700	$19,000
		225/145 2dr GT Hdtp Cpe	$11,700	$16,500	$22,700	$29,300
		273/190 2dr GT Hdtp Cpe	$12,700	$17,800	$24,600	$31,500
		383/330 2dr GTS Hdtp Cpe	$14,200	$20,100	$29,600	$39,500
		440/375 2dr GSS Hdtp Cpe	$102,000	$114,000	$126,000	$167,000
		225/145 2dr GT Conv	$15,800	$22,700	$31,300	$40,200
		273/190 2dr GT Conv	$17,100	$24,900	$34,500	$44,100

Dodge

Year	Model	Body Style	4	3	2	1
		383/330 2dr GTS Conv	$18,800	$26,600	$37,400	$47,900
						-20% for 225-c.i. slant six.
1968	Coronet	225/145 2dr Dlx Cpe	$5,800	$8,400	$11,800	$16,100
		273/190 2dr Dlx Cpe	$6,400	$9,500	$13,100	$17,600
		383/335 2dr Spr Bee Cpe	$20,200	$29,100	$42,000	$56,200
		426/425 Hemi 2dr Spr Bee Cpe	$52,200	$71,300	$88,600	$118,000
		225/145 2dr 440 Hdtp Cpe	$8,400	$11,800	$17,100	$22,900
		273/190 2dr 440 Hdtp Cpe	$9,300	$13,000	$18,700	$25,100
		318/230 2dr 500 Hdtp Cpe	$9,100	$13,000	$18,600	$25,000
		383/330 2dr 500 Hdtp Cpe	$9,900	$14,200	$20,400	$27,600
		426/425 Hemi 2dr R/T Hdtp Cpe	$65,100	$85,500	$99,700	$132,000
		440/375 2dr R/T Hdtp Cpe	$16,000	$25,100	$37,000	$52,700
		318/230 2dr 500 Conv	$14,300	$20,600	$29,800	$39,300
		383/330 2dr 500 Conv	$17,100	$24,800	$35,500	$47,300
		426/425 Hemi 2dr R/T Conv	$90,100	$126,000	$151,000	$195,000
		440/375 2dr R/T Conv	$28,200	$42,800	$62,300	$78,600
		For base cpe and 440 hdtp cpe: +20% for 4-spd. -10% for auto. -20% for 6-cyl. Colors can make an astonishing difference in both value and salability.				
1968	Charger	318/230 2dr Hdtp Cpe	$15,900	$22,700	$33,400	$45,700
		383/290 2dr Hdtp Cpe	$19,700	$25,500	$36,100	$50,100
		383/330 2dr Hdtp Cpe	$21,900	$28,300	$40,300	$55,000
		426/425 Hemi 2dr R/T Hdtp Cpe	$85,600	$104,000	$149,000	$197,000
		440/375 2dr R/T Hdtp Cpe	$37,300	$50,700	$73,800	$95,700
		+20% for 4-spd. -10% for auto. Colors can make an astonishing difference in both value and salability.				
1968	Polara	318/230 2dr Hdtp Cpe	$6,000	$8,600	$13,700	$18,300
		440/375 2dr Hdtp Cpe	$9,500	$13,700	$21,800	$29,200
		318/230 2dr 500 Hdtp Cpe	$6,700	$9,400	$15,000	$20,000

Year	Model	Body Style	4	3	2	1
		440/375 2dr 500 Hdtp Cpe	$10,400	$15,000	$23,900	$31,800
		318/230 2dr Conv	$8,400	$12,000	$19,600	$25,400
		440/375 2dr Conv	$13,300	$19,100	$31,200	$40,600
		318/230 2dr 500 Conv	$8,500	$12,200	$19,900	$25,700
		440/375 2dr 500 Conv	$13,600	$19,400	$31,700	$41,100
1968	Monaco	383/290 2dr Hdtp Cpe	$7,400	$10,500	$15,000	$20,000
		440/375 2dr Hdtp Cpe	$11,700	$16,700	$23,900	$31,800
		383/290 2dr 500 Hdtp Cpe	$7,400	$10,700	$15,200	$20,300
		440/375 2dr 500 Hdtp Cpe	$11,700	$17,100	$24,200	$32,300
1969	Dart	2dr Hdtp Cpe	$5,700	$8,200	$10,900	$14,200
		273/190 2dr Swinger Hdtp Cpe	$7,200	$10,100	$14,100	$19,300
		225/145 2dr Cstm Hdtp Cpe	$6,000	$8,900	$12,300	$15,900
		273/190 2dr Cstm Hdtp Cpe	$6,600	$9,900	$13,600	$17,400
		225/145 2dr GT Hdtp Cpe	$13,300	$18,900	$25,900	$32,800
		273/190 2dr GT Hdtp Cpe	$14,500	$21,000	$28,400	$36,100
		340/275 HiPo 2dr GTS Hdtp Cpe	$19,200	$27,100	$32,300	$43,300
		383/330 2dr GTS Hdtp Cpe	$22,200	$32,400	$38,900	$50,000
		440/375 2dr GTS Hdtp Cpe	$30,200	$49,000	$64,000	$81,500
		340/275 HiPo 2dr Swinger 340 Hdtp Cpe	$14,200	$19,800	$31,100	$47,600
		225/145 2dr GT Conv	$16,500	$23,900	$33,400	$42,000
		273/190 2dr GT Conv	$18,100	$26,200	$36,700	$46,300
		340/275 HiPo 2dr GTS Conv	$22,200	$33,900	$52,000	$64,400
		383/330 2dr GTS Conv	$29,100	$41,700	$58,300	$73,500
		-20% for 225-c.i. slant six. +15% for 4-spd.				
1969	Coronet	318/230 2dr Dlx Cpe	$4,400	$6,500	$9,200	$11,800
		383/290 2dr Dlx Cpe	$5,300	$7,900	$11,000	$14,400
		383/330 2dr Dlx Cpe	$5,800	$8,500	$12,100	$15,700

Dodge

Year	Model	Body Style	4	3	2	1
		318/230 4dr 440 Sdn	$4,500	$6,700	$9,300	$11,800
		383/290 4dr 440 Sdn	$5,400	$8,000	$11,100	$14,400
		383/330 4dr 440 Sdn	$5,900	$8,700	$12,200	$15,700
		318/230 2dr 440 Hdtp Cpe	$9,800	$14,200	$20,600	$27,200
		383/290 2dr 440 Hdtp Cpe	$11,800	$17,200	$24,600	$32,400
		383/330 2dr 440 Hdtp Cpe	$12,700	$18,600	$26,700	$35,100
		318/230 2dr 500 Hdtp Cpe	$10,100	$14,500	$21,000	$28,000
		383/290 2dr 500 Hdtp Cpe	$12,200	$17,500	$25,100	$33,500
		383/330 2dr 500 Hdtp Cpe	$13,100	$19,100	$27,500	$36,300
		426/425 Hemi 2dr R/T Hdtp Cpe	$71,800	$93,900	$122,000	$151,000
		440/375 2dr R/T Hdtp Cpe	$25,100	$40,200	$50,200	$63,100
		383/335 2dr Spr Bee Hdtp Cpe	$23,400	$32,200	$40,400	$51,800
		426/425 Hemi 2dr Spr Bee Hdtp Cpe	$62,300	$80,700	$112,000	$142,000
		440/390 2dr Spr Bee Hdtp Cpe	$46,300	$65,300	$79,800	$125,000
		318/230 2dr 500 Conv	$14,600	$21,200	$30,600	$39,900
		383/290 2dr 500 Conv	$17,500	$25,600	$36,800	$48,100
		383/330 2dr 500 Conv	$19,000	$27,500	$39,900	$52,000
		440/375 2dr R/T Conv	$37,400	$50,900	$65,800	$81,600

+15% for 4-spd. Colors can make an astonishing difference in both value and salability. Note: 440/390 Super Bee was a mid-model year introduction.

Year	Model	Body Style	4	3	2	1
1969	Charger	318/230 2dr Hdtp Cpe	$20,000	$29,200	$42,800	$55,700
		383/290 2dr Hdtp Cpe	$23,100	$33,700	$49,600	$66,600
		383/330 2dr Hdtp Cpe	$26,300	$38,100	$56,200	$74,100
		426/425 Hemi 2dr 500 Hdtp Cpe	$111,000	$139,000	$189,000	$263,000
		440/375 2dr 500 Hdtp Cpe	$31,900	$46,000	$64,500	$90,000
		426/425 Hemi 2dr R/T Hdtp Cpe	$89,400	$107,000	$154,000	$201,000

Year	Model	Body Style	4	3	2	1
		440/375 2dr R/T Hdtp Cpe	$36,400	$49,500	$71,800	$92,600
		426/425 Hemi 2dr Daytona Hdtp Cpe	$347,000	$445,000	$567,000	$830,000
		440/375 2dr Daytona Hdtp Cpe	$128,000	$167,000	$236,000	$296,000

For base cpe and 500 models: -20% for slant six. For base cpe, 500, and R/T: +15% for SE pkg. For all Chargers: +20% for 4-spd. -10% for auto. Colors can make an astonishing difference in both value and salability.

Year	Model	Body Style	4	3	2	1
1969	Polara	318/230 2dr Hdtp Cpe	$4,800	$7,300	$10,800	$14,200
		383/290 2dr Hdtp Cpe	$5,900	$8,800	$13,100	$17,100
		383/330 2dr Hdtp Cpe	$6,400	$9,600	$14,200	$18,500
		440/375 2dr Hdtp Cpe	$7,200	$10,600	$15,900	$20,700
		318/230 2dr 500 Hdtp Cpe	$5,800	$8,600	$12,900	$16,500
		383/290 2dr 500 Hdtp Cpe	$7,000	$10,300	$15,400	$19,900
		383/330 2dr 500 Hdtp Cpe	$7,600	$11,100	$16,800	$21,500
		440/375 2dr 500 Hdtp Cpe	$8,400	$12,400	$18,600	$24,000
		318/230 2dr Conv	$7,000	$10,000	$15,300	$19,600
		383/290 2dr Conv	$8,400	$12,300	$18,700	$26,400
		383/330 2dr Conv	$9,100	$13,400	$23,000	$35,400
		440/375 2dr Conv	$12,000	$18,000	$27,000	$38,400
		318/230 2dr 500 Conv	$9,100	$13,300	$20,200	$26,000
		383/290 2dr 500 Conv	$11,000	$15,900	$24,300	$31,400
		383/330 2dr 500 Conv	$11,800	$17,400	$26,400	$36,800
		440/375 2dr 500 Conv	$13,100	$19,200	$29,500	$41,600
1969	Monaco	383/290 2dr Hdtp Cpe	$7,200	$10,500	$15,200	$19,800
		383/330 2dr Hdtp Cpe	$7,700	$11,400	$16,500	$21,400
		440/375 2dr Hdtp Cpe	$8,600	$12,700	$18,400	$23,900
1970	Dart	318/230 2dr Swinger Hdtp Cpe	$8,300	$10,800	$14,800	$18,500
		318/230 2dr Cstm Hdtp Cpe	$6,900	$9,800	$13,100	$16,200
		340/275 2dr Swinger 340 Hdtp Cpe	$16,700	$22,300	$33,000	$44,200

Dodge

Year	Model	Body Style	4	3	2	1
1970	Challenger	318/230 2dr Hdtp Cpe	$14,500	$19,000	$29,900	$40,300
		340/275 2dr Hdtp Cpe	$17,000	$22,100	$35,000	$47,200
		383/290 2dr Hdtp Cpe	$15,900	$21,700	$37,000	$43,500
		383/335 2dr Hdtp Cpe	$16,800	$24,700	$38,200	$49,000
		318/230 2dr SE Hdtp Cpe	$14,500	$21,100	$30,600	$39,000
		383/290 2dr SE Hdtp Cpe	$17,200	$24,900	$36,400	$46,400
		383/335 2dr SE Hdtp Cpe	$17,900	$26,400	$40,900	$52,600
		383/335 2dr R/T Hdtp Cpe	$20,300	$29,500	$43,600	$60,400

+20% for Shaker hood. +15% for 4-spd. Colors can make an astonishing difference in both value and salability.

Year	Model	Body Style	4	3	2	1
		440/375 2dr R/T Hdtp Cpe	$22,300	$41,000	$62,700	$90,300

For Hemi cpe: -$57,000 for auto trans. For Hemi conv: -$150,000 for auto trans. +10% for 4-spd. Colors can make an astonishing difference in both value and salability.

Year	Model	Body Style	4	3	2	1
		440/390 2dr R/T Hdtp Cpe	$53,100	$78,300	$103,000	$135,000
		426/425 Hemi 2dr R/T Hdtp Cpe	$87,800	$115,000	$155,000	$224,000
		383/335 2dr R/T SE Hdtp Cpe	$21,600	$29,900	$46,000	$58,200
		340/290 2dr T/A Hdtp Cpe	$40,900	$58,200	$79,100	$106,000
		318/230 2dr Conv	$17,500	$25,400	$38,400	$56,800
		340/275 2dr Conv	$20,500	$29,700	$44,800	$66,500
		383/290 2dr Conv	$20,900	$30,200	$45,100	$66,900
		383/335 2dr Conv	$21,600	$30,900	$48,800	$71,700
		383/335 2dr R/T Conv	$49,500	$71,100	$90,600	$128,000
		440/375 2dr R/T Conv	$69,400	$99,600	$127,000	$179,000
		440/390 2dr R/T Conv	$94,900	$131,000	$170,000	$243,000
		426/425 Hemi 2dr R/T Conv	$432,000	$630,000	$926,000	$1.3 mil

+20% for Shaker hood. +15% for 4-spd. Colors can make an astonishing difference in both value and salability.

Year	Model	Body Style	4	3	2	1
1970	Charger	318/230 2dr Hdtp Cpe	$15,200	$22,100	$32,600	$42,400
		383/290 2dr Hdtp Cpe	$18,700	$27,300	$40,300	$53,200

Year	Model	Body Style	4	3	2	1
		383/335 2dr Hdtp Cpe	$21,300	$30,800	$45,600	$60,100
		318/230 2dr 500 Hdtp Cpe	$20,200	$29,400	$43,300	$56,000
		383/290 2dr 500 Hdtp Cpe	$23,300	$34,100	$51,000	$67,500
		383/335 2dr 500 Hdtp Cpe	$26,500	$38,500	$57,400	$75,600
		426/425 Hemi 2dr R/T Hdtp Cpe	$93,800	$131,000	$206,000	$244,000
		440/375 2dr R/T Hdtp Cpe	$34,400	$45,400	$69,700	$89,500
		440/390 2dr R/T Hdtp Cpe	$45,600	$59,300	$82,800	$109,000
			+15% for SE pkg on Charger 500. Colors can make an astonishing difference in both value and salability.			
1970	Coronet	318/230 2dr Dlx Sdn	$4,500	$6,800	$9,500	$12,500
		318/230 2dr 440 Hdtp Cpe	$8,300	$12,100	$17,300	$22,800
		318/230 2dr 500 Hdtp Cpe	$10,400	$15,100	$21,600	$28,500
		383/335 2dr Spr Bee Hdtp Cpe	$16,600	$24,200	$35,200	$46,800
		426/425 Hemi 2dr Spr Bee Hdtp Cpe	$49,000	$70,000	$86,200	$130,000
		440/390 2dr Spr Bee Hdtp Cpe	$35,100	$47,300	$65,100	$98,100
		426/425 Hemi 2dr R/T Hdtp Cpe	$47,900	$73,400	$92,900	$123,000
		440/375 2dr R/T Hdtp Cpe	$18,200	$27,300	$39,900	$52,600
		440/390 2dr R/T Hdtp Cpe	$45,500	$59,700	$77,900	$98,000
		318/230 2dr 500 Conv	$14,400	$20,900	$30,300	$39,300
		440/375 2dr R/T Conv	$22,600	$33,300	$49,400	$64,400
		440/390 2dr R/T Conv	$72,700	$85,900	$110,000	$129,000
						+10% for 4-spd.
1970	Polara	318/230 2dr Hdtp Cpe	$4,900	$7,400	$11,000	$14,500
		383/290 2dr Hdtp Cpe	$6,000	$9,000	$13,400	$17,400
		318/230 2dr Conv	$7,100	$10,300	$15,700	$20,000
		383/290 2dr Conv	$8,600	$12,500	$19,000	$27,000
1970	Monaco	383/290 4dr Hdtp Sdn	$3,900	$5,900	$8,400	$10,800
1971	Dart	318/230 2dr Demon Cpe	$6,300	$8,400	$11,200	$14,200

Dodge

Year	Model	Body Style	4	3	2	1
		340/275 HiPo 2dr Demon 340 Cpe	$15,300	$23,900	$32,800	$45,300
		318/230 2dr Hdtp Cpe	$5,000	$7,000	$9,100	$11,500
		318/230 2dr Swinger Hdtp Cpe	$7,800	$10,400	$13,900	$17,600
1971	Challenger	318/230 2dr Hdtp Cpe	$12,700	$18,300	$27,700	$34,700
		340/275 HiPo 2dr Hdtp Cpe	$14,700	$21,300	$32,400	$40,600
		383/275 2dr Hdtp Cpe	$14,700	$20,200	$28,500	$38,700
		383/300 2dr Hdtp Cpe	$15,000	$21,100	$31,300	$41,300
		383/300 2dr R/T Hdtp Cpe	$18,000	$24,200	$33,300	$43,600
		426/425 Hemi 2dr R/T Hdtp Cpe	$118,000	$154,000	$200,000	$254,000
		440/385 2dr R/T Hdtp Cpe	$48,900	$64,400	$83,200	$108,000
		318/230 2dr Conv	$21,500	$29,200	$44,000	$53,700
		340/275 HiPo 2dr Conv	$25,100	$34,200	$51,300	$62,800
		383/275 2dr Conv	$22,900	$32,700	$46,900	$58,900
		383/300 2dr Conv	$23,900	$34,600	$51,000	$63,700

+20% for Shaker hood. +15% for 4-spd. Colors can make an astonishing difference in both value and salability.

Year	Model	Body Style	4	3	2	1
1971	Charger	318/230 2dr Hdtp Cpe	$12,700	$17,700	$26,000	$34,000
		318/230 2dr 500 Hdtp Cpe	$13,200	$19,100	$27,500	$36,100
		383/300 2dr Spr Bee Hdtp Cpe	$17,300	$25,200	$38,600	$50,900
		426/425 Hemi 2dr Spr Bee Hdtp Cpe	$77,600	$109,000	$161,000	$188,000
		440/385 2dr Spr Bee Hdtp Cpe	$44,300	$56,600	$75,000	$87,600
		318/230 2dr SE Hdtp Cpe	$14,300	$20,400	$29,900	$38,700
		426/425 Hemi 2dr R/T Hdtp Cpe	$84,900	$118,000	$166,000	$198,000
		440/370 2dr R/T Hdtp Cpe	$21,700	$30,900	$48,100	$62,000
		440/385 2dr R/T Hdtp Cpe	$43,800	$57,300	$73,800	$87,000

Colors can make an astonishing difference in both value and salability.

Year	Model	Body Style	4	3	2	1
1971	Polara	318/230 2dr Hdtp Cpe	$2,800	$4,000	$6,200	$7,900
		383/275 2dr Hdtp Cpe	$3,200	$4,600	$7,100	$9,200

Year	Model	Body Style	4	3	2	1
		383/300 2dr Hdtp Cpe	$3,400	$4,800	$7,300	$9,500
1971	Monaco	383/275 2dr Hdtp Cpe	$3,500	$4,900	$7,300	$9,400
		383/300 2dr Hdtp Cpe	$3,600	$5,200	$7,600	$9,800
1972	Dart	2dr Cpe	$5,600	$7,400	$9,700	$12,200
		318/150 2dr Demon Cpe	$6,700	$9,000	$12,800	$16,900
		340/240 2dr Demon 340 Cpe	$12,200	$17,400	$25,000	$34,800
		318/150 2dr Hdtp Cpe	$5,100	$6,900	$9,000	$11,400
		318/150 2dr Swinger Hdtp Cpe	$7,900	$10,500	$14,000	$17,900
1972	Challenger	318/150 2dr Hdtp Cpe	$12,500	$20,000	$28,800	$39,300
		318/150 2dr Rallye Hdtp Cpe	$14,100	$20,500	$29,900	$42,400
				-20% for slant six (exc Rallye).		
1972	Charger	318/150 2dr Hdtp Cpe	$9,200	$13,200	$19,900	$26,000
		318/150 2dr SE Hdtp Cpe	$10,500	$14,800	$22,200	$29,400
					-20% for slant six.	
1972	Monaco	360/175 2dr Hdtp Cpe	$3,600	$5,300	$7,600	$10,000
1973	Dart	318/150 2dr Spt Cpe	$5,100	$6,900	$9,000	$11,500
		340/240 2dr 340 Spt Cpe	$5,700	$7,700	$10,200	$19,300
		318/150 2dr Swinger Hdtp Cpe	$5,400	$7,500	$10,000	$12,600
1973	Challenger	318/150 2dr Hdtp Cpe	$12,500	$20,500	$25,600	$36,700
		340/240 2dr Hdtp Cpe	$13,900	$22,100	$29,800	$43,300
		318/150 2dr Rallye Hdtp Cpe	$15,200	$23,700	$33,800	$49,800
1973	Charger	318/150 2dr Cpe	$8,200	$11,800	$17,500	$23,900
		340/240 2dr Cpe	$10,400	$15,200	$22,700	$31,000
		340/240 2dr Rallye Cpe	$8,900	$12,600	$18,700	$25,100
		318/150 2dr Hdtp Cpe	$8,100	$11,800	$17,400	$23,800
		340/240 2dr Hdtp Cpe	$10,700	$15,300	$22,800	$31,100
		340/240 2dr Rallye Hdtp Cpe	$11,300	$16,200	$24,200	$32,400
		318/150 2dr SE Hdtp Cpe	$8,400	$12,400	$18,200	$24,900

Dodge

Year	Model	Body Style	4	3	2	1
		340/240 2dr SE Hdtp Cpe	$11,300	$16,100	$24,100	$32,400
1973	Polara	318/150 2dr Hdtp Cpe	$3,100	$4,600	$6,900	$8,900
		318/150 2dr Cstm Hdtp Cpe	$3,300	$4,900	$7,300	$9,600
1973	Monaco	360/170 2dr Hdtp Cpe	$3,600	$5,400	$7,600	$10,100
1974	Dart	198/95 2dr Spt Cpe	$5,200	$7,400	$9,700	$12,300
		318/150 2dr Spt Cpe	$6,100	$8,400	$11,100	$14,200
		360/245 2dr 360 Spt Cpe	$6,100	$8,400	$11,600	$20,400
		225/105 2dr Swinger Spcl Hdtp Cpe	$4,200	$5,200	$7,000	$9,200
		318/150 2dr Swinger Spcl Hdtp Cpe	$4,700	$6,000	$8,300	$10,500
		198/95 2dr Swinger Hdtp Cpe	$4,300	$5,700	$7,600	$9,900
		318/150 2dr Swinger Hdtp Cpe	$4,800	$6,300	$8,900	$11,300
		225/105 2dr Spcl Ed Hdtp Cpe	$5,400	$7,500	$9,900	$12,400
		318/150 2dr Spcl Ed Hdtp Cpe	$6,300	$8,600	$11,200	$14,500
		225/105 2dr Convertriple Fstbk Cpe	$12,500	$23,800	$28,600	$33,600
1974	Challenger	318/150 2dr Hdtp Cpe	$10,800	$16,800	$24,600	$37,700
		360/245 2dr Hdtp Cpe	$14,400	$19,900	$28,200	$43,500
1974	Charger	318/150 2dr Cpe	$7,800	$10,100	$13,600	$19,400
		360/245 2dr Cpe	$9,200	$12,400	$17,800	$25,200
		440/275 2dr Cpe	$9,700	$13,100	$18,800	$25,300
		318/150 2dr Hdtp Cpe	$8,500	$11,200	$18,100	$22,200
		360/245 2dr Hdtp Cpe	$10,500	$13,900	$20,700	$27,200
		440/275 2dr Hdtp Cpe	$11,300	$14,900	$22,200	$29,000
		318/150 2dr SE Hdtp Cpe	$8,700	$11,600	$17,400	$23,300
		360/245 2dr SE Hdtp Cpe	$10,800	$14,600	$21,700	$29,000
		440/275 2dr SE Hdtp Cpe	$11,500	$15,600	$23,000	$30,800
1974	Monaco	360/180 2dr Hdtp Cpe	$2,900	$4,200	$6,100	$8,100

Year	Model	Body Style	4	3	2	1
		360/180 2dr Cstm Hdtp Cpe	$3,100	$4,700	$6,700	$8,600
1975	Dart	225/95 2dr Spt Cpe	$4,200	$5,700	$7,600	$10,000
		318/145 2dr Spt Cpe	$4,700	$6,300	$8,800	$11,400
		360/180 2dr 360 Sport Cpe	$4,500	$6,200	$8,700	$12,400
		360/230 2dr 360 Spt Cpe	$5,600	$7,700	$10,700	$16,600
		225/95 2dr Swinger Hdtp Cpe	$4,400	$5,900	$8,300	$11,000
		318/145 2dr Swinger Hdtp Cpe	$5,100	$6,900	$9,300	$12,400
		225/95 2dr SE Hdtp Cpe	$4,200	$5,200	$7,000	$9,100
		318/145 2dr SE Hdtp Cpe	$4,700	$6,000	$8,300	$10,400
1976	Dart	225/100 2dr Spt Cpe	$4,000	$5,600	$7,400	$9,700
		360/220 2dr Sport Cpe	$5,400	$7,500	$10,200	$12,900
		225/100 2dr Spirit of 76 Cpe	$5,200	$7,400	$9,200	$14,100
		318/150 2dr Spirit of 76 Cpe	$6,100	$8,400	$10,700	$16,400
		225/100 2dr Swinger Hdtp	$5,100	$6,300	$8,900	$11,600
		318/150 2dr Swinger Hdtp	$5,800	$7,400	$10,100	$13,300
1991	Stealth	181/164 2dr Htchbk	$1,800	$4,000	$5,900	$7,400
		181/222 2dr ES Htchbk	$2,300	$5,200	$7,800	$9,900
		181/222 2dr R/T Htchbk	$2,300	$5,200	$8,000	$10,200
		181/320 FI 2dr R/T Turbo Htchbk	$3,800	$9,200	$14,800	$21,400
1992	Stealth	181/164 2dr Htchbk	$1,800	$4,000	$5,900	$7,400
		181/222 2dr ES Htchbk	$2,300	$5,200	$7,800	$9,900
		181/222 2dr R/T Htchbk	$2,300	$5,200	$8,000	$10,200
		181/320 FI 2dr R/T Turbo Htchbk	$3,800	$9,200	$14,800	$21,400
1992	Viper	488/400 2dr RT/10 Rdstr	$22,200	$30,600	$44,700	$67,800
1993	Stealth	181/164 2dr Htchbk	$1,800	$4,000	$5,900	$7,400
		181/222 FI 2dr ES Htchbk	$2,300	$5,200	$7,800	$9,900
		181/222 FI 2dr R/T Htchbk	$2,300	$5,200	$8,000	$10,200

Dodge

Year	Model	Body Style	4	3	2	1
		181/320 FI 2dr R/T Turbo Htchbk	$3,800	$9,200	$14,800	$21,400
1993	Viper	488/400 2dr RT/10 Rdstr	$19,800	$27,400	$39,800	$59,000
1994	Stealth	181/164 2dr Htchbk	$2,500	$4,600	$7,100	$9,800
		181/222 2dr R/T Htchbk	$3,300	$6,100	$9,700	$13,400
		181/320 FI 2dr R/T Turbo Htchbk	$5,200	$10,900	$16,700	$28,300
1994	Viper	488/400 2dr RT/10 Rdstr	$19,800	$27,400	$39,800	$59,000
1995	Stealth	181/164 2dr Htchbk	$2,500	$4,600	$7,100	$9,800
		181/222 2dr R/T Htchbk	$3,300	$6,100	$9,700	$13,400
		181/320 FI 2dr R/T Turbo Htchbk	$5,200	$10,900	$16,700	$28,300
1995	Viper	488/400 2dr RT/10 Rdstr	$23,200	$29,700	$41,100	$60,400
1996	Stealth	181/164 2dr Htchbk	$2,500	$4,600	$7,100	$9,800
		181/222 2dr R/T Htchbk	$3,300	$6,100	$9,700	$13,400
		181/320 FI 2dr R/T Turbo Htchbk	$5,200	$10,900	$16,700	$28,300
1996	Viper	488/415 2dr GTS Cpe	$36,000	$42,600	$53,600	$68,300
		488/415 2dr RT/10 Conv	$21,900	$28,900	$39,100	$50,100
1997	Viper	488/450 2dr GTS Cpe	$35,800	$42,300	$53,400	$68,100
		488/450 2dr RT/10 Conv	$22,500	$29,800	$39,700	$50,400
1998	Viper	488/450 2dr GTS Cpe	$32,800	$39,200	$49,500	$61,900
		488/450 2dr RT/10 Conv	$26,300	$35,500	$43,900	$51,000
1999	Viper	488/450 2dr GTS Cpe	$33,700	$39,500	$49,600	$62,500
		488/450 2dr RT/10 Conv	$28,700	$36,500	$45,300	$51,300
2000	Viper	488/450 2dr GTS Cpe	$33,700	$40,000	$50,100	$64,000
		488/450 2dr RT/10 Conv	$28,700	$36,500	$45,300	$52,800
2001	Viper	488/450 2dr GTS Cpe	$35,900	$40,900	$51,100	$64,000
		488/450 2dr RT/10 Conv	$31,000	$37,300	$45,800	$53,300
2002	Viper	488/450 2dr GTS Cpe	$34,800	$40,100	$50,100	$64,500
		488/450 2dr RT/10 Conv	$31,100	$37,500	$46,000	$53,900

Year	Model	Body Style	4	3	2	1
2003	Viper	505/500 2dr SRT-10 Conv	$28,400	$35,400	$44,800	$55,000
			+8% for Copperhead Edition. +8% for Mamba Edition.			
2004	Viper	505/500 2dr SRT-10 Conv	$28,400	$35,400	$44,800	$55,000
			+8% for Copperhead Edition. +8% for Mamba Edition.			
2005	Magnum	345/340 4dr R/T AWD Wgn	$8,300	$11,100	$15,100	$20,800
		345/340 4dr R/T Wgn	$7,600	$10,100	$13,800	$18,900
2005	Viper	505/500 2dr SRT-10 Conv	$28,400	$35,400	$44,800	$55,000
			+8% for Copperhead Edition. +8% for Mamba Edition.			
2006	Magnum	345/340 4dr R/T AWD Wgn	$8,300	$11,100	$15,100	$20,800
		345/340 4dr R/T Wgn	$7,600	$10,100	$13,800	$18,900
		370/425 4dr SRT-8 Wgn	$12,500	$17,500	$23,400	$33,200
2006	Viper	505/510 2dr SRT-10 Conv	$28,400	$35,400	$44,800	$55,000
		505/510 2dr SRT-10 Cpe	$32,100	$40,400	$49,500	$64,200
			+8% for Copperhead Edition. +8% for Mamba Edition.			
2006	Charger	345/340 4dr R/T Sdn	$8,500	$11,400	$15,800	$21,200
			+5% for Road/Track Performance Group.			
		345/350 4dr Daytona R/T Sdn	$10,200	$13,700	$19,000	$25,000
		370/425 4dr SRT-8 Sdn	$12,900	$17,800	$24,000	$34,000
2007	Magnum	345/340 4dr R/T AWD Wgn	$8,300	$11,100	$15,100	$20,800
		345/340 4dr R/T Wgn	$7,600	$10,100	$13,800	$18,900
		370/425 4dr SRT-8 Wgn	$12,500	$17,500	$23,400	$33,200
2007	Charger	345/340 4dr R/T Sdn	$8,500	$11,400	$15,800	$21,200
			+5% for Road/Track Performance Group.			
		345/350 4dr Daytona R/T Sdn	$10,200	$13,700	$19,000	$25,000
		370/425 4dr SRT-8 Sdn	$12,900	$17,800	$24,000	$34,000
2008	Magnum	345/340 4dr R/T AWD Wgn	$8,300	$11,100	$15,100	$20,800
		345/340 4dr R/T Wgn	$7,600	$10,100	$13,800	$18,900
		370/425 4dr SRT-8 Wgn	$12,500	$17,500	$23,400	$33,200

Dodge

Year	Model	Body Style	4	3	2	1
2008	Charger	345/340 4dr R/T Sdn	$8,500	$11,400	$15,800	$21,200
		345/350 4dr Daytona R/T Sdn	$10,200	$13,700	$19,000	$25,000
		+5% for Road/Track Performance Group.				
		370/425 4dr SRT-8 Sdn	$12,900	$17,800	$24,000	$34,000
2008	Challenger	370/425 2dr SRT-8 Cpe	$14,000	$21,500	$27,500	$38,000
		+5% for special run High Impact colors. +5% for T/A or Shaker hood. +10% for manual trans.				
2009	Charger	345/368 4dr R/T Sdn	$8,900	$12,000	$16,600	$22,300
		+5% for Road/Track Performance Group.				
		345/372 4dr Daytona R/T Sdn	$10,700	$14,400	$20,000	$26,300
		370/425 4dr SRT-8 Sdn	$12,900	$17,800	$24,000	$34,000
		370/425 4dr SRT-8 Super Bee Sdn	$14,200	$19,900	$27,000	$38,000
2009	Challenger	345/372 2dr R/T Cpe	$8,000	$16,000	$20,000	$26,000
		370/425 2dr SRT-8 Cpe	$14,000	$21,500	$27,500	$38,000
		+5% for special run High Impact colors. +5% for T/A or Shaker hood. +10% for manual trans.				
2010	Charger	345/368 4dr R/T Sdn	$8,900	$12,000	$16,600	$22,300
		+5% for Road/Track Performance Group.				
		370/425 4dr SRT-8 Sdn	$12,900	$17,800	$24,000	$34,000
2010	Challenger	345/372 2dr R/T Cpe	$8,000	$16,000	$20,000	$26,000
		370/425 2dr SRT-8 Cpe	$14,000	$21,500	$27,500	$38,000
		+5% for special run High Impact colors, +5% for T/A or Shaker hood. +10% for manual trans.				
2011	Challenger	345/372 2dr R/T Cpe	$10,000	$18,000	$24,500	$30,000
		392/470 2dr SRT8 392 Cpe	$16,000	$25,000	$33,000	$40,000
		392/470 2dr SRT8 392 Inaugural Ed Cpe	$17,600	$27,500	$36,300	$44,000
		+5% for special run High Impact colors. +5% for T/A or Shaker hood. +10% for manual trans.				
2012	Challenger	345/375 2dr R/T Cpe	$10,000	$18,000	$24,500	$30,000

Year	Model	Body Style	4	3	2	1
		392/470 2dr SRT8 392 Cpe	$16,000	$25,000	$33,000	$40,000
		392/470 2dr SRT8 Yellow Jacket Cpe	$17,600	$27,500	$36,300	$44,000
		+5% for special run High Impact colors, +5% for T/A or Shaker hood, +10% for manual trans.				
2013	Challenger	345/375 2dr R/T Cpe	$10,000	$18,000	$24,500	$30,000
		392/470 2dr SRT8 392 Cpe	$16,000	$25,000	$33,000	$40,000
		+5% for special run High Impact colors, +5% for T/A or Shaker hood, +10% for manual trans.				
2014	Challenger	345/375 2dr R/T Cpe	$10,000	$18,000	$24,500	$30,000
		392/470 2dr SRT8 392 Cpe	$16,000	$25,000	$33,000	$40,000
		+5% for special run High Impact colors, +5% for T/A or Shaker hood, +10% for manual trans.				
2015	Challenger	376/707 2dr SRT Hellcat Cpe	$40,000	$51,000	$59,000	$70,000
		+5% for special run High Impact colors, +5% for T/A or Shaker hood, +10% for manual trans.				
2016	Challenger	376/707 2dr SRT Hellcat Cpe	$40,000	$51,000	$59,000	$70,000
		+5% for special run High Impact colors, +5% for T/A or Shaker hood, +10% for manual trans.				
2017	Challenger	376/707 2dr SRT Hellcat Cpe	$42,000	$52,000	$59,000	$70,000
		+5% for special run High Impact colors, +5% for T/A or Shaker hood, +10% for manual trans.				
2018	Challenger	376/707 2dr SRT Hellcat Cpe	$47,000	$54,000	$59,000	$70,000
		376/707 2dr SRT Hellcat Widebody Cpe	$56,000	$65,000	$69,400	$78,400
		376/840 2dr SRT Demon Cpe	$85,000	$100,000	$125,000	$145,000
		+5% for special run High Impact colors, +5% for T/A or Shaker hood, +10% for manual trans.				

Dual-Ghia

Year	Model	Body Style	4	3	2	1
1956	Wedge	315/230 2dr Conv	$173,000	$226,000	$342,000	$397,000
1956	Hemi	315/260 2dr Conv	$189,000	$269,000	$378,000	$439,000
1957	Wedge	315/230 2dr Conv	$173,000	$226,000	$342,000	$397,000
1957	Hemi	315/260 2dr Conv	$189,000	$269,000	$378,000	$439,000
1958	Wedge	315/230 2dr Conv	$173,000	$226,000	$342,000	$397,000
1958	Hemi	315/260 2dr Conv	$189,000	$269,000	$378,000	$439,000

Dual-Ghia

Year	Model	Body Style	4	3	2	1
1960	L6.4	383/335 2dr Cpe	$161,000	$244,000	$332,000	$450,000
1961	L6.4	383/335 2dr Cpe	$161,000	$244,000	$332,000	$450,000
1962	L6.4	383/335 2dr Cpe	$161,000	$244,000	$332,000	$450,000

Duesenberg II

Year	Model	Body Style	4	3	2	1
1978	LaGrande	4dr DC Phtn	$57,000	$96,800	$117,000	$164,000
1979	LaGrande	4dr DC Phtn	$57,000	$96,800	$117,000	$164,000
1980	LaGrande	4dr DC Phtn	$57,000	$96,800	$117,000	$164,000
1981	LaGrande	4dr DC Phtn	$57,000	$96,800	$117,000	$164,000
1982	LaGrande	4dr DC Phtn	$57,000	$96,800	$117,000	$164,000
1983	LaGrande	4dr DC Phtn	$57,000	$96,800	$117,000	$164,000
1984	LaGrande	4dr DC Phtn	$57,000	$96,800	$117,000	$164,000
1985	LaGrande	4dr DC Phtn	$57,000	$96,800	$117,000	$164,000
1986	LaGrande	4dr DC Phtn	$57,000	$96,800	$117,000	$164,000
1987	LaGrande	4dr DC Phtn	$57,000	$96,800	$117,000	$164,000
1988	LaGrande	4dr DC Phtn	$57,000	$96,800	$117,000	$164,000
1989	LaGrande	4dr DC Phtn	$57,000	$96,800	$117,000	$164,000
1990	LaGrande	4dr DC Phtn	$57,000	$96,800	$117,000	$164,000
1991	LaGrande	4dr DC Phtn	$57,000	$96,800	$117,000	$164,000
1992	LaGrande	4dr DC Phtn	$57,000	$96,800	$117,000	$164,000
1993	LaGrande	4dr DC Phtn	$57,000	$96,800	$117,000	$164,000
1994	LaGrande	4dr DC Phtn	$57,000	$96,800	$117,000	$164,000
1995	LaGrande	4dr DC Phtn	$57,000	$96,800	$117,000	$164,000
1996	LaGrande	4dr DC Phtn	$57,000	$96,800	$117,000	$164,000
1997	LaGrande	4dr DC Phtn	$57,000	$96,800	$117,000	$164,000
1998	LaGrande	4dr DC Phtn	$57,000	$96,800	$117,000	$164,000
1999	LaGrande	4dr DC Phtn	$57,000	$96,800	$117,000	$164,000
2000	LaGrande	4dr DC Phtn	$57,000	$96,800	$117,000	$164,000

Edsel

Year	Model	Body Style	4	3	2	1
1958	Citation	410/345 2dr Conv	$17,300	$37,400	$54,600	$74,100
					+15% for factory a/c.	
1958	Ranger	361/303 4dr Villager Stn Wgn 6P	$12,500	$20,200	$33,600	$49,800
					+15% for factory a/c.	
1958	Corsair	410/345 2dr Hdtp	$7,200	$11,500	$17,000	$28,800
		410/345 4dr Hdtp	$3,100	$6,100	$8,500	$16,200
					+15% for factory a/c.	
1959	Villager	332/225 4dr Stn Wgn 6P	$12,500	$20,200	$33,600	$49,800
					+15% for factory a/c.	
1959	Corsair	332/225 2dr Hdtp	$7,400	$12,400	$17,700	$29,700
		332/225 4dr Sdn	$4,600	$7,300	$11,000	$17,800
		332/225 2dr Conv	$16,900	$33,900	$50,900	$71,200
					+15% for factory a/c.	

Edsel

Year	Model	Body Style	4	3	2	1
1960	Villager	292/185 4dr Stn Wgn 6P	$14,000	$21,600	$35,700	$52,500

+15% for factory a/c.

Year	Model	Body Style	4	3	2	1
1960	Ranger	292/185 2dr Dlx Hdtp	$8,400	$13,200	$18,500	$31,100
		292/185 4dr Sdn	$4,900	$8,500	$13,300	$19,300
		292/185 2dr Conv	$29,800	$54,200	$74,700	$104,000

+15% for factory a/c.

Edwards

Year	Model	Body Style	4	3	2	1
1954	America	318/205 2dr Conv	$78,500	$115,000	$137,000	$185,000

Elva

Year	Model	Body Style	4	3	2	1
1958	Courier	2dr Mk I Rdstr	$15,000	$18,800	$35,000	$48,500
1959	Courier	2dr Mk I Rdstr	$15,000	$18,800	$35,000	$48,500
1960	Courier	2dr Mk I Rdstr	$15,000	$18,800	$35,000	$48,500
1961	Courier	2dr Mk I Rdstr	$15,000	$18,800	$35,000	$48,500
1962	Courier	2dr Mk II Cpe	$9,200	$14,500	$22,500	$30,000
		2dr Mk II Rdstr	$16,500	$21,200	$40,000	$56,500
1963	Courier	2dr Mk II Cpe	$9,200	$14,500	$22,500	$30,000
		2dr Mk II Rdstr	$16,500	$21,300	$40,000	$56,500
1964	Courier	2dr Mk II Cpe	$9,200	$14,600	$22,500	$30,000
		2dr Mk II Rdstr	$16,500	$21,200	$40,000	$56,500
1965	Courier	2dr Mk II Cpe	$9,200	$14,600	$22,500	$30,000
		2dr Mk II Rdstr	$16,500	$21,300	$40,000	$56,500
1966	Courier	2dr Mk II Cpe	$9,200	$14,500	$22,500	$30,000
		2dr Mk II Rdstr	$16,500	$21,200	$40,000	$56,500

Excalibur

Year	Model	Body Style	4	3	2	1
1965	SSK	327/300 2dr Rdstr	$36,700	$50,400	$73,200	$95,500
1966	SSK	327/300 2dr Rdstr	$35,200	$45,100	$66,700	$89,500
1967	SI	327/300 2dr Phtn	$16,800	$20,500	$34,600	$44,100
		327/300 2dr Rdstr	$30,000	$41,100	$53,100	$68,400

+10% for 4-spd.

Year	Model	Body Style	4	3	2	1
1968	SI	327/300 2dr Phtn	$16,800	$20,500	$34,600	$44,100
		327/300 2dr Rdstr	$30,000	$41,100	$53,100	$68,400

+10% for 4-spd.

Year	Model	Body Style	4	3	2	1
1969	SI	327/300 2dr Phtn	$16,800	$20,500	$34,600	$44,100
		327/300 2dr Rdstr	$30,000	$41,100	$53,100	$68,400

+10% for 4-spd.

Year	Model	Body Style	4	3	2	1
1970	SII	350/300 2dr Phtn	$16,900	$22,700	$35,300	$44,600

Excalibur

Year	Model	Body Style	4	3	2	1
		350/300 2dr Rdstr	$15,900	$21,400	$35,200	$53,000
					+10% for 4-spd.	+10% for a/c.
1971	SII	350/300 2dr Phtn	$16,900	$22,700	$35,300	$44,600
		350/300 2dr Rdstr	$15,900	$21,400	$35,200	$53,000
					+10% for 4-spd.	+10% for a/c.
1972	SII	454/365 2dr Phtn	$16,900	$22,700	$35,300	$44,600
		454/365 2dr Rdstr	$15,900	$21,400	$35,200	$53,000
					+10% for 4-spd.	+10% for a/c.
1973	SII	454/270 2dr Phtn	$16,900	$22,700	$35,300	$44,600
		454/270 2dr Rdstr	$15,900	$21,400	$35,200	$53,000
					+10% for 4-spd.	+10% for a/c.
1974	SII	454/275 2dr Phtn	$16,900	$22,700	$35,300	$44,600
		454/275 2dr Rdstr	$15,900	$21,400	$35,200	$53,000
					+10% for 4-spd.	+10% for a/c.
1975	SIII	454/215 2dr Phtn	$16,900	$22,000	$35,700	$46,900
		454/215 2dr Rdstr	$16,600	$20,900	$38,200	$55,500
1976	SIII	454/215 2dr Phtn	$16,900	$22,000	$35,700	$46,900
		454/215 2dr Rdstr	$16,600	$20,900	$38,200	$55,500
1977	SIII	454/215 2dr Phtn	$16,900	$22,000	$35,700	$46,900
		454/215 2dr Rdstr	$16,600	$20,900	$38,200	$55,500
1978	SIII	454/215 2dr Phtn	$16,900	$22,000	$35,700	$46,900
		454/215 2dr Rdstr	$16,600	$20,900	$38,200	$55,500
1979	SIII	454/215 2dr Phtn	$16,900	$22,000	$35,700	$46,900
		454/215 2dr Rdstr	$16,600	$20,900	$38,200	$55,500
1980	SIV	454/215 2dr Phtn	$17,700	$23,900	$38,500	$47,500
		454/215 2dr Rdstr	$20,900	$28,800	$44,800	$59,700
1981	SIV	305/155 2dr Phtn	$17,700	$23,900	$38,500	$47,500
		305/155 2dr Rdstr	$20,900	$28,800	$44,800	$59,700
1982	SIV	305/155 2dr Phtn	$17,700	$23,900	$38,500	$47,500
		305/155 2dr Rdstr	$20,900	$28,800	$44,800	$59,700
1983	SIV	305/155 2dr Phtn	$17,700	$23,900	$38,500	$47,500
		305/155 2dr Rdstr	$20,900	$28,800	$44,800	$59,700
1984	SIV	305/155 2dr Phtn	$17,700	$23,900	$38,500	$47,500
		305/155 2dr Rdstr	$20,900	$28,800	$44,800	$59,700
1985	Series V	305/155 2dr Phtn	$17,500	$24,900	$40,900	$49,000
		305/155 4dr Sdn	$16,800	$23,500	$35,200	$43,900
		305/155 2dr Rdstr	$20,400	$28,200	$44,100	$59,000
1986	Series V	305/155 2dr Phtn	$17,500	$24,900	$40,900	$49,000
		305/155 4dr Sdn	$16,800	$23,500	$35,200	$43,900
		305/155 2dr Rdstr	$20,400	$28,200	$44,100	$59,000
1987	Series V	305/170 2dr Phtn	$17,500	$24,900	$40,900	$49,000
		305/170 4dr Sdn	$16,800	$23,500	$35,200	$43,900
		305/170 2dr Rdstr	$20,400	$28,200	$44,100	$59,000
1988	Series V	305/170 2dr Phtn	$17,500	$24,900	$40,900	$49,000

Excalibur

Year	Model	Body Style	4	3	2	1
		305/170 4dr Sdn	$16,800	$23,500	$35,200	$43,900
		305/170 2dr Rdstr	$20,400	$28,200	$44,100	$59,000
1989	Series V	305/170 2dr Phtn	$17,500	$24,900	$40,900	$49,000
		305/170 4dr Sdn	$16,800	$23,500	$35,200	$43,900
		305/170 2dr Rdstr	$20,400	$28,200	$44,100	$59,000
1990	Series V	305/170 2dr Phtn	$17,500	$24,900	$40,900	$49,000
		305/170 4dr Sdn	$16,800	$23,500	$35,200	$43,900
		305/170 2dr Rdstr	$20,400	$28,200	$44,100	$59,000

Facel Vega

Year	Model	Body Style	4	3	2	1
1954	FV	2dr Cpe	$66,700	$110,000	$185,000	$286,000
		2dr Dual Carb Cpe	$85,100	$122,000	$203,000	$308,000
		+5% for factory a/c. +10% for Pont-a-Mousson 4-spd. +5% for wire wheels.				
1954	FV1	2dr Cpe	$68,500	$112,000	$187,000	$286,000
		2dr Dual Carb Cpe	$85,500	$123,000	$205,000	$310,000
		+5% for factory a/c. +10% for Pont-a-Mousson 4-spd. +5% for wire wheels.				
1954	FVS	2dr Cpe	$69,500	$113,000	$190,000	$288,000
		2dr Dual Carb Cpe	$87,000	$128,000	$206,000	$311,000
		+5% for factory a/c. +10% for Pont-a-Mousson 4-spd. +5% for wire wheels.				
1955	FV	2dr Cpe	$66,700	$110,000	$185,000	$286,000
		2dr Dual Carb Cpe	$85,100	$122,000	$203,000	$308,000
		+5% for factory a/c. +10% for Pont-a-Mousson 4-spd. +5% for wire wheels.				
1955	FV1	2dr Cpe	$68,500	$112,000	$187,000	$286,000
		2dr Dual Carb Cpe	$85,500	$123,000	$205,000	$310,000
		+5% for factory a/c. +10% for Pont-a-Mousson 4-spd. +5% for wire wheels.				
1955	FVS	2dr Cpe	$69,500	$113,000	$190,000	$288,000
		2dr Dual Carb Cpe	$87,000	$128,000	$206,000	$311,000
		+5% for factory a/c. +10% for Pont-a-Mousson 4-spd. +5% for wire wheels.				
1956	FVS	2dr Cpe	$69,500	$113,000	$190,000	$288,000
		2dr Dual Carb Cpe	$87,000	$128,000	$206,000	$311,000
		+5% for factory a/c. +10% for Pont-a-Mousson 4-spd. +5% for wire wheels.				
1957	FVS	2dr Cpe	$69,500	$113,000	$190,000	$288,000
		2dr Dual Carb Cpe	$87,000	$128,000	$206,000	$311,000
		+5% for factory a/c. +10% for Pont-a-Mousson 4-spd. +5% for wire wheels.				
1958	FVS	2dr Cpe	$69,500	$113,000	$190,000	$288,000
		2dr Dual Carb Cpe	$87,000	$128,000	$206,000	$311,000
		+5% for factory a/c. +10% for Pont-a-Mousson 4-spd. +5% for wire wheels.				

Facel Vega

Year	Model	Body Style	4	3	2	1
1958	Excellence	4dr Sdn	$96,000	$118,000	$182,000	$217,000
		4dr Dual Carb Sdn	$107,000	$128,000	$189,000	$238,000
		+5% for factory a/c. +10% for Pont-a-Mousson 4-spd. +5% for wire wheels.				
1959	Excellence	4dr Sdn	$96,000	$118,000	$182,000	$217,000
		4dr Dual Carb Sdn	$107,000	$128,000	$189,000	$238,000
		+5% for factory a/c. +10% for Pont-a-Mousson 4-spd. +5% for wire wheels.				
1959	HK500	2dr Cpe	$61,200	$99,000	$170,000	$270,000
		2dr Dual Carb Cpe	$77,800	$109,000	$189,000	$292,000
		+5% for factory a/c. +10% for Pont-a-Mousson 4-spd. +5% for wire wheels.				
1960	Facellia	2dr Dual Carb Cpe	$23,900	$32,000	$39,600	$49,200
		2dr Dual Carb Conv	$37,200	$44,800	$54,600	$70,700
		+5% for factory a/c. +5% for wire wheels. +$3,000 for hard top on conv.				
1960	HK500	2dr Dual Carb Cpe	$77,800	$109,000	$189,000	$292,000
		+5% for factory a/c. +10% for Pont-a-Mousson 4-spd. +5% for wire wheels.				
1961	Facellia	2dr Cpe	$21,000	$30,000	$36,800	$46,900
		2dr Dual Carb Cpe	$23,900	$32,000	$39,600	$49,200
		2dr DHC	$29,500	$40,000	$47,900	$60,600
		2dr Dual Carb Conv	$37,200	$44,800	$54,600	$70,700
		+5% for factory a/c. +5% for wire wheels. +$3,000 for hard top on conv.				
1961	Excellence	4dr Sdn	$96,000	$118,000	$182,000	$217,000
		4dr Dual Carb Sdn	$107,000	$128,000	$189,000	$238,000
		+5% for factory a/c. +10% for Pont-a-Mousson 4-spd. +5% for wire wheels.				
1961	HK500	2dr Cpe	$63,000	$102,000	$174,000	$273,000
		2dr Dual Carb Cpe	$79,600	$113,000	$191,000	$297,000
		+5% for factory a/c. +10% for Pont-a-Mousson 4-spd. +5% for wire wheels.				
1962	Facellia	2dr Cpe	$21,000	$30,000	$36,800	$46,900
		2dr Dual Carb Cpe	$23,900	$32,000	$39,600	$49,200
		2dr DHC	$29,500	$40,000	$47,900	$60,600
		2dr Dual Carb Conv	$37,200	$44,800	$54,600	$70,700
		+5% for factory a/c. +5% for wire wheels. +$3,000 for hard top on conv.				
1962	Facel II	2dr Cpe	$217,000	$235,000	$360,000	$447,000
		2dr Dual Carb Cpe	$263,000	$282,000	$387,000	$492,000
		+5% for factory a/c. +10% for Pont-a-Mousson 4-spd. +5% for wire wheels.				
1962	Excellence	4dr Sdn	$96,000	$118,000	$182,000	$217,000
		4dr Dual Carb Sdn	$107,000	$128,000	$189,000	$238,000
		+5% for factory a/c. +10% for Pont-a-Mousson 4-spd. +5% for wire wheels.				
1963	Facellia	2dr Dual Carb Cpe	$23,900	$32,000	$39,600	$49,200
		2dr Dual Carb Conv	$37,200	$44,800	$54,600	$70,700

Facel Vega

Year	Model	Body Style	4	3	2	1
		+5% for factory a/c. +5% for wire wheels. +$3,000 for hard top on conv.				
1963	Facel II	2dr Dual Carb Cpe	$263,000	$282,000	$387,000	$492,000
		+5% for factory a/c. +10% for Pont-a-Mousson 4-spd. +5% for wire wheels.				
1963	Excellence	4dr Dual Carb Sdn	$107,000	$128,000	$192,000	$238,000
		+5% for factory a/c. +10% for Pont-a-Mousson 4-spd. +5% for wire wheels.				
1964	Facellia	2dr Cpe	$21,000	$30,000	$36,800	$46,900
		2dr Dual Carb Cpe	$23,900	$32,000	$39,600	$49,200
		2dr DHC	$29,500	$40,000	$47,900	$60,600
		2dr Dual Carb Conv	$37,200	$44,800	$54,600	$70,700
		+5% for factory a/c. +5% for wire wheels. +$3,000 for hard top on conv.				
1964	Facel II	2dr Cpe	$217,000	$235,000	$360,000	$447,000
		2dr Dual Carb Cpe	$263,000	$282,000	$387,000	$492,000
		+5% for factory a/c. +10% for Pont-a-Mousson 4-spd. +5% for wire wheels.				
1964	Excellence	4dr Sdn	$96,000	$118,000	$182,000	$217,000
		4dr Dual Carb Sdn	$107,000	$128,000	$189,000	$238,000
		+5% for factory a/c. +10% for Pont-a-Mousson 4-spd. +5% for wire wheels.				

Ferrari

Year	Model	Body Style	4	3	2	1
1954	250 Europa	2dr Cpe	$1.4 mil	$1.55 mil	$1.7 mil	$1.8 mil
		2dr Cab	$2.6 mil	$2.9 mil	$3.1 mil	$3.6 mil
1955	250 Europa	2dr Cpe	$1.4 mil	$1.55 mil	$1.7 mil	$1.8 mil
1955	250 GT	2dr Boano Cpe	$670,000	$700,000	$730,000	$780,000
1955	410 Superamerica	2dr Cpe	$1.7 mil	$1.85 mil	$2.1 mil	$2.3 mil
1956	250 GT	2dr Boano Cpe	$670,000	$700,000	$730,000	$780,000
		2dr TdF Cpe	$6.8 mil	$7.4 mil	$8.2 mil	$8.9 mil
1956	410 Superamerica	2dr Cpe	$1.7 mil	$1.85 mil	$2.1 mil	$2.3 mil
1957	250 GT	2dr Boano Cpe	$670,000	$700,000	$730,000	$780,000
		2dr Ellena Cpe	$459,000	$505,000	$550,000	$610,000
		2dr TdF Cpe	$6.8 mil	$7.4 mil	$8.2 mil	$8.9 mil
1957	250 California	2dr LWB Spider	$9.7 mil	$10.3 mil	$11 mil	$11.5 mil
1957	250 TR	2dr Spider	$19.5 mil	$21 mil	$23 mil	$25 mil
1957	410 Superamerica	2dr SII Cpe	$1.95 mil	$2.1 mil	$2.3 mil	$2.45 mil
		2dr SIII Cpe (open HL)	$2.15 mil	$2.45 mil	$2.7 mil	$2.9 mil
		2dr SIII Cpe (closed HL)	$3.05 mil	$3.2 mil	$3.4 mil	$3.6 mil
1958	250 GT	2dr Cpe	$550,000	$620,000	$690,000	$725,000
		2dr Boano Cpe	$625,000	$655,000	$700,000	$730,000
		2dr Ellena Cpe	$450,000	$500,000	$545,000	$590,000
		2dr Boano Alloy Cpe	$1 mil	$1.1 mil	$1.25 mil	$1.4 mil
		2dr TdF Cpe	$6.8 mil	$7.4 mil	$8.1 mil	$8.4 mil

Ferrari

Year	Model	Body Style	4	3	2	1
		2dr Cab SI (open HL)	$4 mil	$4.3 mil	$4.75 mil	$5.1 mil
		2dr Cab SI (closed HL)	$6.2 mil	$6.6 mil	$7 mil	$7.5 mil
						+$50,000 for bumperettes. +$50,000 for side vents. +$50,000 for hard top.
1958	250 California	2dr LWB Spider (closed HL)	$11 mil	$12.4 mil	$13.6 mil	$14.9 mil
		2dr LWB Alloy Spider	$17 mil	$18.5 mil	$20.5 mil	$22.4 mil
1958	250 TR	2dr Rdstr	$19.5 mil	$21 mil	$23 mil	$25 mil
1958	410 Superamerica	2dr SII Cpe	$1.95 mil	$2.1 mil	$2.3 mil	$2.45 mil
		2dr SIII Cpe	$2.15 mil	$2.45 mil	$2.7 mil	$2.9 mil
1959	410 Superamerica	2dr SIII Cpe	$2.15 mil	$2.45 mil	$2.7 mil	$2.9 mil
1959	250 GT	2dr Cpe	$550,000	$620,000	$690,000	$725,000
		2dr SWB Cpe	$8 mil	$8.2 mil	$8.5 mil	$8.9 mil
		2dr TdF Cpe	$9 mil	$9.4 mil	$9.8 mil	$10.4 mil
		2dr Cab SI (open HL)	$4 mil	$4.3 mil	$4.75 mil	$5.1 mil
		2dr Cab SI (closed HL)	$6.2 mil	$6.6 mil	$7 mil	$7.5 mil
						+$50,000 for bumperettes. +$50,000 for side vents. +$50,000 for hard top.
1959	250 California	2dr LWB Spider (open HL)	$7.7 mil	$8.4 mil	$9.7 mil	$11.5 mil
		2dr LWB Spider (closed HL)	$11 mil	$12.4 mil	$13.6 mil	$14.9 mil
		2dr LWB Alloy Spider	$17 mil	$18.5 mil	$20.5 mil	$22.4 mil
1960	250 GT	2dr Cpe	$550,000	$620,000	$690,000	$725,000
		2dr SWB Cpe	$8 mil	$8.2 mil	$8.5 mil	$8.9 mil
		2dr SWB Alloy Cpe	$13.6 mil	$14.2 mil	$14.8 mil	$15.1 mil
1960	250 GTE	2dr Cpe 2+2	$320,000	$390,000	$455,000	$500,000
1960	250 California	2dr SWB Spider (open HL)	$9.9 mil	$11.2 mil	$12 mil	$12.5 mil
		2dr SWB Spider (closed HL)	$13.3 mil	$14.1 mil	$15.3 mil	$16.4 mil
		2dr SWB Alloy Spider	$17.9 mil	$19.5 mil	$21 mil	$23.7 mil
						+$50,000 for side vents. +$50,000 for hard top.
1960	250 SII	2dr Cab	$1.1 mil	$1.2 mil	$1.3 mil	$1.35 mil
						+$50,000 for hard top.
1960	400 Superamerica	2dr Cpe	$2.75 mil	$3 mil	$3.35 mil	$3.5 mil
						+$50,000 for factory hard top on cab. -10% for open headlights on cpe.
		2dr Cab (open HL)	$2.8 mil	$3.2 mil	$3.7 mil	$4 mil
		2dr Cab (closed HL)	$3.6 mil	$3.8 mil	$4 mil	$4.2 mil
						+$50,000 for factory hard top on cab.

Year	Model	Body Style	4	3	2	1
1961	250 GT	2dr SWB Cpe	$8 mil	$8.2 mil	$8.5 mil	$8.9 mil
		2dr SWB Alloy Cpe	$13.6 mil	$14.2 mil	$14.8 mil	$15.1 mil
1961	250 GTE	2dr Cpe 2+2	$320,000	$390,000	$455,000	$500,000
1961	250 California	2dr SWB Spider (open HL)	$9.9 mil	$11.2 mil	$12 mil	$12.5 mil
		2dr SWB Spider (closed HL)	$13.3 mil	$14.1 mil	$15.3 mil	$16.4 mil
		2dr SWB Alloy Spider	$17.9 mil	$19.5 mil	$21 mil	$23.7 mil
		+$50,000 for side vents. +$50,000 for hard top.				
1961	250 SII	2dr Cab	$1.1 mil	$1.2 mil	$1.3 mil	$1.35 mil
		+$50,000 for hard top.				
1961	400 Superamerica	2dr Cpe	$2.75 mil	$3 mil	$3.35 mil	$3.5 mil
		+$50,000 for factory hard top on cab. -10% for open headlights on cpe.				
		2dr Cab (open HL)	$2.8 mil	$3.2 mil	$3.7 mil	$4 mil
		2dr Cab (closed HL)	$3.6 mil	$3.8 mil	$4 mil	$4.2 mil
		+$50,000 for factory hard top on cab.				
1962	250 GT	2dr Lusso Cpe	$990,000	$1.1 mil	$1.25 mil	$1.4 mil
		2dr SWB Cpe	$8 mil	$8.2 mil	$8.5 mil	$8.9 mil
1962	250 GTE	2dr Cpe 2+2	$320,000	$390,000	$455,000	$500,000
1962	250 California	2dr SWB Spider (open HL)	$9.9 mil	$11.2 mil	$12 mil	$12.5 mil
		2dr SWB Spider (closed HL)	$13.3 mil	$14.1 mil	$15.3 mil	$16.4 mil
		2dr SWB Alloy Spider	$17.9 mil	$19.5 mil	$21 mil	$23.7 mil
		+$50,000 for side vents. +$50,000 for hard top.				
1962	250 SII	2dr Cab	$1.1 mil	$1.2 mil	$1.3 mil	$1.35 mil
		+$50,000 for hard top.				
1962	250 GTO	2dr SI Cpe	$50 mil	$56.5 mil	$64 mil	$68 mil
1962	GTO SII 330	2dr Cpe	$37 mil	$41 mil	$45 mil	$49 mil
1962	400 Superamerica	2dr Cpe	$2.8 mil	$3.1 mil	$3.3 mil	$3.5 mil
		+$50,000 for factory hard top on cab. -10% for open headlights on cpe.				
		2dr Cab (open HL)	$3 mil	$3.3 mil	$3.65 mil	$4 mil
		2dr Cab (closed HL)	$3.5 mil	$3.75 mil	$4 mil	$4.2 mil
		+$50,000 for factory hard top on cab.				
1963	250 GT	2dr Cab SII	$1 mil	$1.15 mil	$1.3 mil	$1.4 mil
		+$50,000 for hard top.				
		2dr Lusso Cpe	$990,000	$1.1 mil	$1.25 mil	$1.4 mil
		2dr SWB Cpe	$8 mil	$8.2 mil	$8.5 mil	$8.9 mil
1963	250 GTE	2dr Cpe 2+2	$320,000	$390,000	$455,000	$500,000
1963	250 California	2dr SWB Spider (open HL)	$9.9 mil	$11.2 mil	$12 mil	$12.5 mil
		2dr SWB Spider (closed HL)	$13.3 mil	$14.1 mil	$15.3 mil	$16.4 mil

Ferrari

Year	Model	Body Style	4	3	2	1
						+$50,000 for side vents. +$50,000 for hard top.
1963	250 LM	2dr Cpe	$16.8 mil	$18 mil	$19 mil	$21.1 mil
1963	250 GTO	2dr SI Cpe	$50 mil	$56.5 mil	$64 mil	$68 mil
1963	GTO SII 330	2dr Cpe	$37 mil	$40 mil	$45 mil	$49 mil
1963	330 LMB	2dr Cpe	$27 mil	$28.5 mil	$30 mil	$31.5 mil
1963	330 America	2dr 2+2 Cpe	$400,000	$460,000	$515,000	$540,000
1963	400 Superamerica	2dr Cpe	$2.8 mil	$3.1 mil	$3.3 mil	$3.5 mil
						+$50,000 for factory hard top on cab. -10% for open headlights on cpe.
		2dr Cab (open HL)	$3 mil	$3.3 mil	$3.65 mil	$4 mil
		2dr Cab (closed HL)	$3.5 mil	$3.75 mil	$4 mil	$4.2 mil
						+$50,000 for factory hard top on cab.
1964	250 GT	2dr Lusso Cpe	$990,000	$1.1 mil	$1.25 mil	$1.4 mil
1964	275 GTB	2dr Cpe	$1.55 mil	$1.7 mil	$1.8 mil	$1.95 mil
						+10% for 6-carb.
1964	275 GTS	2dr Spider	$1.1 mil	$1.4 mil	$1.45 mil	$1.55 mil
						+$50,000 for hard top.
1964	330 GT	2dr SI Cpe 2+2	$190,000	$214,000	$233,000	$265,000
						+$5,000 for 5-spd.
1964	330 America	2dr 2+2 Cpe	$400,000	$460,000	$515,000	$540,000
1964	400 Superamerica	2dr Cpe	$2.8 mil	$3.1 mil	$3.3 mil	$3.5 mil
						+$50,000 for factory hard top on cab. -10% for open headlights on cpe.
		2dr Cab (open HL)	$3 mil	$3.3 mil	$3.65 mil	$4 mil
		2dr Cab (closed HL)	$3.5 mil	$3.75 mil	$4 mil	$4.2 mil
						+$50,000 for factory hard top on cab.
1964	500 Superfast	2dr SI Cpe	$2.3 mil	$2.6 mil	$2.9 mil	$3.1 mil
						+$100,000 for a/c.
1964	250 LM	2dr Cpe	$16.8 mil	$18 mil	$19 mil	$21.1 mil
1964	250 GTO	2dr SII Cpe	$37 mil	$40 mil	$45 mil	$49 mil
1965	275 GTB	2dr Cpe	$1.55 mil	$1.7 mil	$1.8 mil	$1.95 mil
		2dr Alloy Cpe	$2.55 mil	$2.75 mil	$2.9 mil	$3.1 mil
						+10% for 6-carb.
1965	275 GTS	2dr Spider	$1.1 mil	$1.4 mil	$1.45 mil	$1.55 mil
						+$50,000 for hard top.
1965	330 GT	2dr SI Cpe 2+2	$190,000	$214,000	$233,000	$265,000
						+$5,000 for 5-spd.
1965	500 Superfast	2dr SI Cpe	$2.3 mil	$2.6 mil	$2.9 mil	$3.1 mil
						+$100,000 for a/c.
1965	250 LM	2dr Cpe	$16.8 mil	$18 mil	$19 mil	$21.1 mil
1966	275 GTB/2	2dr Longnose Cpe	$1.6 mil	$1.7 mil	$1.85 mil	$2 mil
		2dr Longnose Alloy Cpe	$2.1 mil	$2.25 mil	$2.35 mil	$2.5 mil
						+10% for torque tube. +10% for 6-carb.
1966	275 GTB/4	2dr Cpe	$1.75 mil	$1.95 mil	$2.1 mil	$2.25 mil
		2dr Alloy Cpe	$4.6 mil	$4.9 mil	$5.1 mil	$5.5 mil

Year	Model	Body Style	4	3	2	1
1966	275 GTS	2dr Spider	$1.1 mil	$1.4 mil	$1.45 mil	$1.55 mil
						+$50,000 for hard top.
1966	330 GTC	2dr Cpe	$500,000	$528,000	$570,000	$605,000
				-$5,000 w/o wires. +$50,000 for factory a/c.		
1966	330 GT	2dr SII Cpe 2+2	$205,000	$235,000	$260,000	$290,000
		+10% for factory a/c. +6% for pwr strng. +$12,500 Borrani wire wheels.				
1966	330 GTS	2dr Spider	$2 mil	$2.2 mil	$2.35 mil	$2.55 mil
		+$60,000 for factory a/c. +$50,000 for hard top. -$10,000 w/o wires.				
1966	365 California	2dr Spider	$3.7 mil	$3.85 mil	$4 mil	$4.1 mil
1966	500 Superfast	2dr SII Cpe	$2.6 mil	$2.8 mil	$3 mil	$3.2 mil
				+$75,000 for pwr strng. +10% for factory a/c.		
1967	Dino 206 GT	2dr Cpe	$515,000	$580,000	$623,000	$655,000
1967	275 GTB/4	2dr Cpe	$1.75 mil	$1.95 mil	$2.1 mil	$2.25 mil
		2dr Alloy Cpe	$4.6 mil	$4.9 mil	$5.1 mil	$5.5 mil
1967	275 GTS/4	2dr NART Spider	$19 mil	$20 mil	$21.5 mil	$22.8 mil
1967	330 GTC	2dr Cpe	$500,000	$528,000	$570,000	$605,000
				-$5,000 w/o wires. +$50,000 for factory a/c.		
1967	330 GT	2dr SII Cpe 2+2	$205,000	$235,000	$260,000	$290,000
		+10% for factory a/c. +6% for pwr strng. +$12,500 Borrani wire wheels.				
1967	330 GTS	2dr Spider	$2 mil	$2.2 mil	$2.35 mil	$2.55 mil
		+$60,000 for factory a/c. +$50,000 for hard top. -$10,000 w/o wires.				
1967	365 California	2dr Spider	$3.7 mil	$3.85 mil	$4 mil	$4.1 mil
1968	Dino 206 GT	2dr Cpe	$515,000	$580,000	$623,000	$655,000
1968	275 GTB/4	2dr Cpe	$1.75 mil	$1.95 mil	$2.1 mil	$2.25 mil
		2dr Alloy Cpe	$4.6 mil	$4.9 mil	$5.1 mil	$5.5 mil
1968	275 GTS/4	2dr NART Spider	$19 mil	$20 mil	$21.5 mil	$22.8 mil
1968	330 GTC	2dr Cpe	$500,000	$528,000	$570,000	$605,000
				-$5,000 w/o wires. +$50,000 for factory a/c.		
1968	330 GTS	2dr Spider	$2 mil	$2.2 mil	$2.35 mil	$2.55 mil
		+$60,000 for factory a/c. +$50,000 for hard top. -$10,000 w/o wires.				
1968	365 GTC	2dr Cpe	$575,000	$610,000	$645,000	$695,000
1968	365 GTB/4	2dr Daytona Cpe	$500,000	$530,000	$555,000	$585,000
		2dr Daytona Alloy Cpe	$805,000	$860,000	$917,000	$945,000
		2dr Daytona Cut Spyder	$360,000	$405,000	$430,000	$495,000
				+$8,000 for wire wheels. -$25,000 for no a/c.		
1968	365 GT	2dr Cpe 2+2	$158,000	$197,000	$228,000	$255,000
1968	365 GTS	2dr Spider	$2.2 mil	$2.5 mil	$2.6 mil	$2.85 mil
						+$50,000 for factory a/c.
1969	Dino 206 GT	2dr Cpe	$515,000	$580,000	$623,000	$655,000
1969	Dino 246 GT	2dr Cpe	$205,000	$245,000	$275,000	$315,000
				+$4,000 for pwr wndws. $4,000 for leather interior.		
1969	365 GTC	2dr Cpe	$575,000	$610,000	$645,000	$695,000
1969	365 GT	2dr Cpe 2+2	$158,000	$197,000	$228,000	$255,000

Ferrari

Year	Model	Body Style	4	3	2	1
1969	365 GTS	2dr Spider	$2.2 mil	$2.5 mil	$2.6 mil	$2.85 mil
						+$50,000 for factory a/c.
1969	365 GTB/4	2dr Daytona Cpe	$500,000	$530,000	$555,000	$585,000
		2dr Daytona Alloy Cpe	$805,000	$860,000	$917,000	$945,000
		2dr Daytona Cut Spyder	$360,000	$405,000	$430,000	$495,000
						+$8,000 for wire wheels. -$25,000 for no a/c.
1969	365 GTS/4	2dr Daytona Spider	$1.75 mil	$1.85 mil	$2 mil	$2.15 mil
						-$50,000 for no a/c.
1970	Dino 246 GT	2dr Cpe	$170,000	$210,000	$280,000	$310,000
1970	365 GTC	2dr Cpe	$575,000	$610,000	$645,000	$695,000
1970	365 GT	2dr Cpe 2+2	$211,000	$254,000	$292,000	$327,000
1970	365 GTB/4	2dr Daytona Cpe	$500,000	$530,000	$555,000	$585,000
		2dr Daytona Alloy Cpe	$805,000	$860,000	$917,000	$945,000
		2dr Daytona Cut Spyder	$350,000	$395,000	$440,000	$505,000
						+$8,000 for wire wheels. -$25,000 for no a/c.
1970	365 GTS/4	2dr Daytona Spider	$1.75 mil	$1.85 mil	$2 mil	$2.15 mil
						-$50,000 for no a/c.
1971	Dino 246 GT	2dr Cpe	$170,000	$210,000	$280,000	$310,000
1971	365 GTC/4	2dr Cpe	$180,000	$215,000	$242,000	$290,000
						+$8,000 for wire wheels.
1971	365 GT	2dr Cpe 2+2	$211,000	$254,000	$292,000	$327,000
1971	365 GTB/4	2dr Daytona Cpe	$500,000	$530,000	$555,000	$585,000
		2dr Daytona Cut Spyder	$350,000	$395,000	$440,000	$505,000
						+$8,000 for wire wheels. -$25,000 for no a/c.
1971	365 GTS/4	2dr Daytona Spider	$1.75 mil	$1.85 mil	$2 mil	$2.15 mil
						-$50,000 for no a/c.
1972	Dino 246 GT	2dr Cpe	$170,000	$210,000	$280,000	$310,000
1972	Dino 246 GTS	2dr Spider	$245,000	$284,000	$310,000	$340,000
						-20% for no a/c.
1972	365 GTC/4	2dr Cpe	$180,000	$215,000	$242,000	$290,000
						+$8,000 for wire wheels.
1972	365 GT4	2dr Cpe 2+2	$44,000	$55,000	$70,000	$95,000
1972	365 GTB/4	2dr Daytona Cpe	$500,000	$530,000	$555,000	$585,000
		2dr Daytona Cut Spyder	$350,000	$395,000	$440,000	$505,000
						+$8,000 for wire wheels. -$25,000 for no a/c.
1972	365 GTS/4	2dr Daytona Spider	$1.9 mil	$2 mil	$2.15 mil	$2.25 mil
						+$8,000 for wire wheels.
1973	Dino 246 GT	2dr Cpe	$170,000	$210,000	$280,000	$310,000
						+20% for factory a/c.
1973	Dino 246 GTS	2dr Spider	$245,000	$284,000	$310,000	$340,000

Year	Model	Body Style	4	3	2	1
		-20% for no a/c. +20% for flares and chairs. +5% for chairs no flares.				
1973	365 GT4	2dr Cpe 2+2	$44,000	$55,000	$70,000	$95,000
1973	365 GTB/4	2dr Daytona Cpe	$550,000	$595,000	$615,000	$640,000
		+$8,000 for wire wheels.				
		2dr Daytona Cut Spyder	$350,000	$395,000	$440,000	$505,000
		+$8,000 for wire wheels. -$25,000 for no a/c.				
1973	365 GTS/4	2dr Daytona Spider	$1.95 mil	$2.1 mil	$2.2 mil	$2.3 mil
		+$8,000 for wire wheels.				
1974	Dino 246 GTS	2dr Spider	$303,000	$320,000	$353,000	$375,000
		-20% for no a/c. +20% for flares and chairs. +5% for chairs no flares.				
1974	Dino 308 GT4	2dr 2+2 Cpe	$35,500	$48,500	$61,500	$79,500
		+$2,000 for sunroof.				
1974	365 GT4	2dr Cpe 2+2	$44,000	$55,000	$70,000	$95,000
1974	365 GT4 BB	2dr Cpe	$380,000	$445,000	$490,000	$510,000
1975	Dino 308 GT4	2dr 2+2 Cpe	$35,500	$48,500	$61,500	$79,500
		+$2,000 for sunroof.				
1975	365 GT4	2dr Cpe 2+2	$44,000	$55,000	$70,000	$95,000
1975	365 GT4 BB	2dr Cpe	$380,000	$445,000	$490,000	$510,000
1976	Dino 308 GT4	2dr 2+2 Cpe	$38,400	$51,000	$64,000	$82,000
		+$2,000 for sunroof.				
1976	308 GTB	2dr Cpe (fiberglass)	$108,000	$139,000	$167,000	$199,000
		+$30,000 for dry sump.				
		2dr Cpe (steel)	$45,000	$63,000	$109,000	$135,000
1976	400 GT	2dr Cpe	$24,000	$31,000	$38,000	$47,000
		+40% for 5-spd.				
1976	512 BB	2dr Cpe	$176,000	$208,000	$263,000	$290,000
1977	Dino 308 GT4	2dr 2+2 Cpe	$38,400	$51,000	$64,000	$82,000
		+$2,000 for sunroof.				
1977	308 GTB	2dr Cpe	$41,900	$58,500	$102,000	$123,000
		+10% for non-catalyst US-spec steel carbureted cars.				
1977	400 GT	2dr Cpe	$24,000	$31,000	$38,000	$47,000
		+40% for 5-spd.				
1977	512 BB	2dr Cpe	$176,000	$208,000	$263,000	$290,000
1978	Dino 308 GT4	2dr 2+2 Cpe	$39,500	$52,500	$70,500	$88,500
		+$2,000 for sunroof.				
1978	308 GTB	2dr Cpe	$38,000	$55,000	$97,900	$118,000
1978	308 GTS	2dr Spider	$28,800	$39,900	$71,000	$99,000
1978	400 GT	2dr Cpe	$24,000	$31,000	$38,000	$47,000
		+40% for 5-spd.				
1978	512 BB	2dr Cpe	$176,000	$208,000	$263,000	$290,000

Ferrari

Year	Model	Body Style	4	3	2	1
1979	Dino 308 GT4	2dr 2+2 Cpe	$41,500	$54,500	$72,500	$90,500
						+$3,500 for sunroof.
1979	308 GTB	2dr Cpe	$38,000	$55,000	$97,900	$118,000
1979	308 GTS	2dr Spider	$28,800	$39,900	$71,000	$99,000
1979	400 GT	2dr Cpe	$24,000	$31,000	$38,000	$47,000
						+40% for 5-spd.
1979	512 BB	2dr Cpe	$176,000	$208,000	$263,000	$290,000
1980	308 GTBi	2dr Cpe	$24,000	$31,000	$44,900	$55,000
1980	308 GTSi	2dr Spider	$21,500	$28,500	$40,000	$51,000
1980	Mondial	2dr 8 Cpe	$18,000	$23,500	$29,000	$38,000
1980	400i	2dr 2+2 Cpe	$22,000	$28,500	$34,900	$45,500
						+50% for 5-spd.
1980	512 BB	2dr Cpe	$176,000	$208,000	$263,000	$290,000
1981	308 GTBi	2dr Cpe	$24,000	$31,000	$44,900	$55,000
1981	308 GTSi	2dr Spider	$21,500	$28,500	$40,000	$51,000
1981	Mondial	2dr 8 Cpe	$18,000	$23,500	$29,000	$38,000
1981	400i	2dr 2+2 Cpe	$22,000	$28,500	$34,900	$45,500
						+50% for 5-spd.
1981	512 BB	2dr Cpe	$194,000	$218,000	$271,000	$305,000
1982	308 GTBi	2dr Cpe	$24,000	$31,000	$44,900	$55,000
1982	308 GTSi	2dr Spider	$21,500	$28,500	$40,000	$51,000
1982	Mondial	2dr 8 Cpe	$18,000	$23,500	$29,000	$40,000
1982	400i	2dr 2+2 Cpe	$22,000	$28,500	$34,900	$45,500
						+50% for 5-spd.
1982	512 BBi	2dr Cpe	$168,000	$205,000	$247,000	$289,000
1983	308 GTB	2dr QV Cpe	$33,000	$55,000	$70,000	$89,000
1983	308 GTS	2dr QV Spider	$28,000	$47,500	$63,500	$80,000
1983	Mondial	2dr QV 2+2 Cpe	$18,100	$25,000	$31,000	$41,000
		2dr QV 2+2 Cab	$16,000	$20,500	$29,100	$35,000
1983	400i	2dr 2+2 Cpe	$22,000	$28,500	$34,900	$45,500
						+50% for 5-spd.
1983	512 BBi	2dr Cpe	$170,000	$205,000	$248,000	$300,000
1984	308 GTB	2dr QV Cpe	$35,000	$58,000	$73,500	$97,000
1984	308 GTS	2dr QV Spider	$28,000	$47,500	$63,500	$80,000
1984	Mondial	2dr QV Cpe	$18,100	$25,000	$31,000	$40,000
		2dr 2+2 Cab	$16,000	$20,500	$29,100	$35,000
1984	400i	2dr 2+2 Cpe	$22,000	$28,500	$34,900	$45,500
						+50% for 5-spd.
1984	512 BBi	2dr Cpe	$184,000	$213,000	$252,000	$306,000
1984	Testarossa	2dr Cpe	$55,200	$70,600	$103,000	$115,000
1984	288 GTO	2dr Cpe	$1.9 mil	$2.1 mil	$2.35 mil	$2.75 mil
1985	308 GTB	2dr QV Cpe	$35,000	$58,000	$73,500	$97,000
1985	308 GTS	2dr QV Spider	$28,000	$47,500	$63,500	$80,000
1985	Mondial	2dr 2+2 Cab	$16,000	$20,500	$29,100	$35,000
		2dr QV Cpe	$18,100	$25,000	$31,000	$40,000
1985	400i	2dr 2+2 Cpe	$23,500	$30,000	$35,500	$46,000

Year	Model	Body Style	4	3	2	1
						+50% for 5-spd.
1985	412i	2dr 2+2 Cpe	$33,500	$40,000	$48,500	$60,000
						+40% for 5-spd.
1985	Testarossa	2dr Cpe	$56,000	$64,000	$95,000	$105,000
1985	288 GTO	2dr Cpe	$1.9 mil	$2.1 mil	$2.35 mil	$2.75 mil
1986	328 GTB	2dr Cpe	$40,000	$55,000	$91,500	$119,000
1986	328 GTS	2dr Spyder	$33,000	$45,000	$68,000	$88,500
1986	3.2 Mondial	2dr 2+2 Cpe	$17,500	$23,000	$30,500	$40,500
		2dr 2+2 Cab	$16,900	$22,600	$26,900	$35,300
1986	412i	2dr 2+2 Cpe	$33,500	$40,000	$48,500	$60,000
						+40% for 5-spd.
1986	Testarossa	2dr Cpe	$56,000	$64,000	$95,000	$105,000
1987	328 GTB	2dr Cpe	$40,000	$55,000	$91,500	$119,000
1987	328 GTS	2dr Spyder	$33,000	$45,000	$68,000	$88,500
1987	3.2 Mondial	2dr 2+2 Cpe	$17,500	$23,000	$30,500	$40,500
		2dr 2+2 Cab	$19,100	$24,900	$28,700	$37,300
1987	412i	2dr 2+2 Cpe	$33,500	$40,000	$48,500	$60,000
						+40% for 5-spd.
1987	Testarossa	2dr Cpe	$56,000	$64,000	$95,000	$105,000
1987	F40	2dr Cpe	$960,000	$1.2 mil	$1.35 mil	$1.6 mil
1988	328 GTB	2dr Cpe	$40,000	$55,000	$91,500	$119,000
						+10% for ABS.
1988	328 GTS	2dr Spider	$33,000	$45,000	$68,000	$88,500
						+10% for ABS.
1988	3.2 Mondial	2dr 2+2 Cpe	$18,800	$26,400	$33,300	$44,200
1988	412i	2dr 2+2 Cpe	$33,500	$40,000	$48,500	$60,000
						+40% for 5-spd.
1988	Testarossa	2dr Cpe	$56,000	$64,000	$95,000	$105,000
1988	F40	2dr Cpe	$960,000	$1.2 mil	$1.35 mil	$1.6 mil
1989	328 GTB	2dr Cpe	$40,000	$55,000	$91,500	$119,000
						+10% for ABS.
1989	328 GTS	2dr Spider	$33,000	$45,000	$68,000	$88,500
						+10% for ABS.
1989	Mondial	2dr T 2+2 Cpe	$24,000	$32,000	$38,900	$49,300
		2dr T 2+2 Cab	$22,000	$29,000	$36,500	$48,000
1989	348 tb	2dr Cpe	$36,500	$49,100	$60,300	$74,200
1989	348 ts	2dr Targa	$32,600	$42,800	$52,500	$62,400
1989	Testarossa	2dr Cpe	$59,000	$68,000	$100,000	$110,000
1989	F40	2dr Cpe	$960,000	$1.2 mil	$1.35 mil	$1.6 mil
1990	Mondial	2dr T 2+2 Cpe	$24,000	$32,000	$38,900	$49,300
		2dr T 2+2 Cab	$22,000	$29,000	$36,500	$48,000
1990	348 tb	2dr Cpe	$36,500	$49,100	$60,300	$74,200
1990	348 ts	2dr Targa	$32,600	$42,800	$52,500	$62,400
1990	Testarossa	2dr Cpe	$59,000	$68,000	$100,000	$110,000
1990	F40	2dr Cpe	$960,000	$1.2 mil	$1.35 mil	$1.6 mil
1991	Mondial	2dr T 2+2 Cpe	$24,000	$32,000	$38,900	$49,300
		2dr T 2+2 Cab	$22,000	$29,000	$36,500	$48,000

Ferrari

Year	Model	Body Style	4	3	2	1
1991	348 tb	2dr Cpe	$39,000	$51,400	$62,500	$76,800
1991	348 ts	2dr Targa	$35,300	$45,300	$55,100	$64,600
1991	Testarossa	2dr Cpe	$59,000	$68,000	$100,000	$110,000
1991	F40	2dr Cpe	$960,000	$1.2 mil	$1.35 mil	$1.6 mil
1992	Mondial	2dr T 2+2 Cpe	$25,800	$34,000	$40,900	$51,100
		2dr T 2+2 Cab	$25,000	$31,000	$38,500	$52,000
1992	348 tb	2dr Cpe	$41,300	$52,300	$63,400	$78,500
1992	348 ts	2dr Targa	$35,300	$45,300	$55,100	$64,600
1992	512 TR	2dr Cpe	$111,000	$134,000	$161,000	$187,000
1992	F40	2dr Cpe	$960,000	$1.2 mil	$1.35 mil	$1.6 mil
1993	Mondial	2dr T 2+2 Cpe	$26,500	$35,700	$42,000	$53,000
		2dr T 2+2 Cab	$25,000	$31,000	$38,500	$52,000
1993	348 tb	2dr Cpe	$41,300	$52,300	$63,400	$78,500
1993	348 ts	2dr Targa	$35,300	$45,300	$55,100	$64,600
		2dr Serie Speciale Targa	$44,400	$56,500	$67,900	$84,800
1993	348 GTS	2dr Spider	$43,600	$53,500	$65,100	$80,400
1993	512 TR	2dr Cpe	$118,000	$140,000	$165,000	$193,000
1994	348 tb	2dr Cpe	$42,200	$54,500	$64,200	$80,900
1994	348 ts	2dr Targa	$36,600	$46,800	$57,300	$65,700
		2dr Serie Speciale Targa	$44,400	$56,500	$67,900	$84,800
1994	348 GTS	2dr Spider	$43,600	$53,500	$65,100	$80,400
1994	512 TR	2dr Cpe	$118,000	$140,000	$165,000	$193,000
1995	348 GTS	2dr Spider	$43,600	$53,500	$65,100	$80,400
1995	F355	2dr Cpe	$41,700	$54,000	$67,300	$103,000
		2dr GTS Targa	$41,700	$54,000	$67,300	$103,000
		2dr Spider	$47,200	$63,100	$88,600	$129,000
						+20% for 6-spd.
1995	456 GT	2dr Cpe 2+2	$41,400	$53,800	$85,100	$99,700
			Lack of verifiable owner and service history can greatly affect value.			
1995	512 TR	2dr Cpe	$122,000	$150,000	$174,000	$205,000
1995	F512 M	2dr Cpe	$243,000	$320,000	$373,000	$405,000
1995	F50	2dr Cpe	$1.65 mil	$1.8 mil	$2.1 mil	$2.5 mil
1996	F355	2dr Cpe	$41,700	$54,000	$67,300	$103,000
		2dr GTS Targa	$41,700	$54,000	$67,300	$103,000
		2dr Spider	$47,200	$63,100	$88,600	$129,000
						+20% for 6-spd.
1996	456 GT	2dr Cpe 2+2	$41,400	$53,800	$85,100	$99,700
			Lack of verifiable owner and service history can greatly affect value.			
1996	456 GTA	2dr Cpe 2+2	$34,800	$39,000	$51,500	$62,000
			Lack of verifiable owner and service history can greatly affect value.			
1996	F512 M	2dr Cpe	$243,000	$320,000	$373,000	$405,000
1996	F50	2dr Cpe	$1.65 mil	$1.8 mil	$2.1 mil	$2.5 mil
1997	F355	2dr Cpe	$41,700	$54,000	$67,300	$103,000
		2dr GTS Targa	$41,700	$54,000	$67,300	$103,000
		2dr Spider	$47,200	$63,100	$88,600	$129,000
						+20% for 6-spd.

Year	Model	Body Style	4	3	2	1
1997	456 GT	2dr Cpe 2+2	$41,400	$53,800	$85,100	$99,700
			Lack of verifiable owner and service history can greatly affect value.			
1997	456 GTA	2dr Cpe 2+2	$34,800	$39,000	$51,500	$62,000
			Lack of verifiable owner and service history can greatly affect value.			
1997	550	2dr Maranello Cpe	$68,900	$88,700	$122,000	$146,000
			Lack of verifiable owner and service history can greatly affect value.			
1997	F50	2dr Cpe	$1.65 mil	$1.8 mil	$2.1 mil	$2.5 mil
1998	F355	2dr Cpe	$41,700	$54,000	$67,300	$103,000
		2dr GTS Targa	$41,700	$54,000	$67,300	$103,000
		2dr Spider	$47,200	$63,100	$88,600	$129,000
			+20% for 6-spd.			
1998	456 GTA	2dr Cpe 2+2	$39,500	$46,000	$57,500	$67,000
			Lack of verifiable owner and service history can greatly affect value.			
1998	550	2dr Maranello Cpe	$71,800	$93,800	$129,000	$153,000
			Lack of verifiable owner and service history can greatly affect value.			
1999	F355	2dr Cpe	$41,700	$54,000	$67,300	$103,000
		2dr GTS Targa	$41,700	$54,000	$67,300	$103,000
		2dr Spider	$47,200	$63,100	$88,600	$129,000
			+20% for 6-spd.			
1999	550	2dr Maranello Cpe	$74,600	$98,900	$136,000	$159,000
			Lack of verifiable owner and service history can greatly affect value.			
2000	360	2dr Cpe	$52,800	$61,400	$71,500	$80,600
			+$33% for 6-spd on cpe. Lack of verifiable owner and service history can greatly affect value.			
2000	550	2dr Maranello Cpe	$76,800	$102,000	$148,000	$168,000
			Lack of verifiable owner and service history can greatly affect value.			
2001	360	2dr Cpe	$52,800	$61,400	$71,500	$80,600
			+$33% for 6-spd on cpe. Lack of verifiable owner and service history can greatly affect value.			
		2dr Spider	$74,500	$87,600	$99,000	$116,000
		2dr Spider F1	$57,300	$67,600	$76,900	$85,300
			Lack of verifiable owner and service history can greatly affect value.			
2001	550	2dr Maranello Cpe	$82,500	$108,000	$155,000	$175,000
		2dr Barchetta Conv	$246,000	$292,000	$322,000	$349,000
			Lack of verifiable owner and service history can greatly affect value.			
2002	360	2dr Cpe	$57,800	$63,400	$77,300	$85,900
			+$33% for 6-spd on cpe. Lack of verifiable owner and service history can greatly affect value.			
		2dr Spider	$78,300	$93,100	$107,000	$123,000
		2dr Spider F1	$57,300	$67,600	$76,900	$85,300
			Lack of verifiable owner and service history can greatly affect value.			
2002	575M	2dr Maranello Cpe	$66,400	$84,000	$123,000	$143,000
			+$125,000 for 6-spd. Lack of verifiable owner and service history can greatly affect value.			
2003	360	2dr Cpe	$57,800	$63,400	$77,300	$85,900

Ferrari

Year	Model	Body Style	4	3	2	1
		+$33% for 6-spd on cpe. Lack of verifiable owner and service history can greatly affect value.				
		2dr Spider	$78,300	$93,100	$107,000	$123,000
		2dr Spider F1	$57,300	$67,600	$76,900	$85,300
		Lack of verifiable owner and service history can greatly affect value.				
2003	575M	2dr Maranello Cpe	$66,400	$84,000	$123,000	$143,000
		+$125,000 for 6-spd. Lack of verifiable owner and service history can greatly affect value.				
2003	Enzo	2dr Cpe	$2 mil	$2.4 mil	$2.8 mil	$3.1 mil
2004	Enzo	2dr Cpe	$2 mil	$2.4 mil	$2.8 mil	$3.1 mil
2004	360	2dr Cpe	$61,200	$69,800	$83,800	$91,800
		+$33% for 6-spd on cpe. Lack of verifiable owner and service history can greatly affect value.				
		2dr Challenge Stradale Cpe	$123,000	$144,000	$181,000	$235,000
		2dr Spider	$80,400	$93,600	$110,000	$128,000
		2dr Spider F1	$60,800	$71,500	$80,400	$94,100
		Lack of verifiable owner and service history can greatly affect value.				
2004	575M	2dr Maranello Cpe	$66,400	$84,000	$123,000	$143,000
		+$125,000 for 6-spd. Lack of verifiable owner and service history can greatly affect value.				
2005	360	2dr Cpe	$63,700	$73,300	$86,900	$100,000
		+$33% for 6-spd on cpe. Lack of verifiable owner and service history can greatly affect value.				
		2dr Spider F1	$64,700	$74,500	$86,200	$102,000
		Lack of verifiable owner and service history can greatly affect value.				
2005	F430	2dr Cpe	$77,000	$99,000	$106,000	$117,000
		2dr Spider Conv	$74,900	$92,000	$104,000	$114,000
		+$125,000 for manual trans.				
2005	612 Scaglietti	2dr Cpe	$68,400	$84,700	$92,200	$105,000
		+120% for manual trans.				
2005	575M	2dr Maranello Cpe	$66,400	$84,000	$123,000	$143,000
		+$125,000 for 6-spd. Lack of verifiable owner and service history can greatly affect value.				
2005	Superamerica	2dr Conv	$268,000	$321,000	$360,000	$388,000
		+$100,000 for 6-spd. Lack of verifiable owner and service history can greatly affect value.				
2006	F430	2dr Cpe	$80,000	$98,000	$109,000	$121,000
		2dr Challenge Cpe	$80,000	$91,000	$107,000	$137,000
		2dr Spider Conv	$80,000	$98,000	$108,000	$120,000
		+$125,000 for manual trans.				
2006	575M	2dr Maranello Cpe	$66,400	$84,000	$123,000	$143,000
		+$125,000 for 6-spd. Lack of verifiable owner and service history can greatly affect value.				
2006	612 Scaglietti	2dr Cpe	$88,000	$96,500	$112,000	$132,000
		+120% for manual trans.				

Year	Model	Body Style	4	3	2	1
2007	F430	2dr Cpe	$86,000	$103,000	$114,000	$128,000
		2dr Challenge Cpe	$83,500	$96,000	$118,000	$160,000
		2dr Spider Conv	$86,000	$107,000	$118,000	$136,000
						+$125,000 for manual trans.
2007	612 Scaglietti	2dr Cpe	$91,200	$101,000	$118,000	$139,000
						+120% for manual trans.
2007	599 GTB	2dr Fiorano Cpe	$97,000	$126,000	$152,000	$173,000
						+$150,000 for manual trans, +12% for HGTE package.
2008	F430	2dr Cpe	$92,000	$108,000	$123,000	$138,000
		2dr Challenge Cpe	$86,000	$100,000	$122,000	$164,000
		2dr Spider Conv	$92,000	$111,000	$122,000	$142,000
						+$125,000 for manual trans.
2008	430	2dr Scuderia Cpe	$181,000	$195,000	$207,000	$225,000
						+$125,000 for manual trans.
2008	612 Scaglietti	2dr Cpe	$96,500	$106,000	$121,000	$145,000
		2dr OTO Cpe	$123,000	$132,000	$148,000	$172,000
						+120% for manual trans.
2008	599 GTB	2dr Fiorano Cpe	$108,000	$134,000	$163,000	$184,000
						+$150,000 for manual trans, +12% got HGTE package.
2009	F430	2dr Cpe	$96,500	$113,000	$129,000	$146,000
		2dr Challenge Cpe	$86,000	$100,000	$122,000	$164,000
		2dr Spider Conv	$103,000	$117,000	$130,000	$156,000
						+$125,000 for manual trans.
2009	430	2dr Scuderia Cpe	$186,000	$211,000	$231,000	$268,000
		2dr Scuderia 16M Spider	$210,000	$229,000	$265,000	$350,000
						+$125,000 for manual trans.
2009	612 Scaglietti	2dr Cpe	$100,000	$110,000	$124,000	$151,000
		2dr OTO Cpe	$127,000	$137,000	$151,000	$177,000
						+120% for manual trans.
2009	599 GTB	2dr Fiorano Cpe	$117,000	$139,000	$170,000	$193,000
						+$150,000 for manual trans, +12% for HGTE package.
2010	458 Italia	2dr Cpe	$125,000	$139,000	$150,000	$168,000
2010	612 Scaglietti	2dr OTO Cpe	$113,000	$128,000	$148,000	$176,000
						+120% for manual trans.
2010	599 GTB	2dr Fiorano Cpe	$128,000	$152,000	$196,000	$214,000
						+$150,000 for manual trans, +12% for HGTE package.
2010	599 GTO	2dr Cpe	$600,000	$665,000	$730,000	$799,000
2011	FF	2dr Shtg Brk	$120,000	$147,000	$165,000	$189,000
2011	458 Italia	2dr Cpe	$138,000	$155,000	$179,000	$194,000
2011	458 Challenge	2dr Cpe	$110,000	$130,000	$148,000	$190,000
2011	599 GTB	2dr Fiorano Cpe	$128,000	$152,000	$196,000	$214,000
						+$150,000 for manual trans, +12% for HGTE package.
2011	599 GTO	2dr Cpe	$600,000	$665,000	$730,000	$799,000
2011	SA Aperta	2dr Spider	$1 mil	$1.25 mil	$1.35 mil	$1.5 mil
2012	FF	2dr Shtg Brk	$120,000	$147,000	$165,000	$189,000

Ferrari

Year	Model	Body Style	4	3	2	1
2012	458 Italia	2dr Cpe	$150,000	$169,000	$200,000	$220,000
2012	458 Challenge	2dr Cpe	$110,000	$130,000	$148,000	$190,000
2012	458 Spider	2dr Spider	$172,000	$199,000	$219,000	$248,000
2013	FF	2dr Shtg Brk	$120,000	$147,000	$165,000	$189,000
2013	458 Italia	2dr Cpe	$162,000	$178,000	$209,000	$227,000
2013	458 Spider	2dr Spider	$196,000	$211,000	$230,000	$256,000
2013	458 Challenge	2dr Cpe	$118,000	$130,000	$148,000	$190,000
2014	FF	2dr Shtg Brk	$120,000	$147,000	$165,000	$189,000
2014	458 Italia	2dr Cpe	$180,000	$190,000	$225,000	$245,000
2014	458 Challenge	2dr Cpe	$110,000	$130,000	$148,000	$190,000
2014	458 Speciale	2dr Cpe	$275,000	$299,000	$315,000	$350,000
2014	458 Spider	2dr Spider	$200,000	$214,000	$234,000	$263,000
2014	LaFerrari	2dr Cpe	$2.1 mil	$2.55 mil	$2.9 mil	$3.25 mil
2015	FF	2dr Shtg Brk	$120,000	$147,000	$165,000	$189,000
2015	458 Italia	2dr Cpe	$188,000	$200,000	$230,000	$249,000
2015	458 Speciale	2dr Cpe	$300,000	$337,000	$360,000	$389,000
		2dr A Spider	$546,000	$571,000	$630,000	$685,000
2015	458 Spider	2dr Spider	$206,000	$220,000	$237,000	$265,000
2015	LaFerrari	2dr Cpe	$2.1 mil	$2.55 mil	$2.9 mil	$3.25 mil
2016	458 Speciale	2dr Cpe	$309,000	$341,000	$375,000	$405,000
		2dr A Spider	$575,000	$600,000	$648,000	$700,000

Fiat

Year	Model	Body Style	4	3	2	1
1946	500 Topolino	2dr Cpe	$14,400	$22,600	$36,000	$57,000
1947	500	2dr Topolino Sdn	$14,400	$22,600	$36,000	$57,000
1948	500	2dr Topolino Cpe	$14,400	$22,600	$36,000	$57,000
1949	500 Topolino	2dr Cpe	$14,400	$22,600	$36,000	$57,000
		2dr Wgn	$15,400	$27,200	$38,200	$63,500
						+20% for woody Giardiniera.
1950	500 Topolino	2dr Cpe	$14,400	$22,600	$36,000	$57,000
		2dr Wgn	$15,400	$27,200	$38,200	$63,500
						+20% for woody Giardiniera.
1951	500 Topolino	2dr Cpe	$14,400	$22,600	$36,000	$57,000
		2dr Wgn	$15,400	$27,200	$38,200	$63,500
						+20% for woody Giardiniera.
1952	500 Topolino	2dr Cpe	$14,400	$22,600	$36,000	$57,000
		2dr Wgn	$15,400	$27,200	$38,200	$63,500
						+20% for woody Giardiniera.
1952	8V	2dr Rapi Cpe	$360,000	$422,000	$498,000	$640,000
		2dr Zagato Cpe	$790,000	$960,000	$1.5 mil	$1.9 mil
		2dr Cpe	$415,000	$505,000	$625,000	$750,000
1953	500 Topolino	2dr Cpe	$14,000	$20,400	$32,400	$50,400
		2dr Wgn	$15,400	$27,200	$36,900	$59,100
1953	8V	2dr Rapi Cpe	$360,000	$422,000	$498,000	$640,000
		2dr Zagato Cpe	$790,000	$960,000	$1.5 mil	$1.9 mil

Fiat

Year	Model	Body Style	4	3	2	1
		2dr Ghia Supersonic Cpe	$950,000	$1.1 mil	$1.65 mil	$2.1 mil
		2dr Cpe	$415,000	$505,000	$625,000	$750,000
1954	500 Topolino	2dr Cpe	$14,000	$20,400	$32,400	$50,400
		2dr Wgn	$15,400	$27,200	$36,900	$59,100
1954	8V	2dr Rapi Cpe	$360,000	$422,000	$498,000	$640,000
		2dr Zagato Cpe	$790,000	$960,000	$1.5 mil	$1.9 mil
		2dr Cpe	$415,000	$505,000	$625,000	$750,000
1955	500 Topolino	2dr Cpe	$14,000	$20,400	$32,400	$50,400
		2dr Wgn	$15,400	$27,200	$36,900	$59,100
1955	600	4dr Multipla Wgn	$20,300	$30,000	$41,800	$61,300
1955	1100TV	2dr Spider	$24,900	$36,200	$57,400	$93,600
1956	600	4dr Multipla Wgn	$20,300	$30,000	$41,800	$61,300
1956	1100TV	2dr Spider	$24,900	$36,200	$57,400	$93,600
1957	Nuova 500	2dr Cpe	$8,600	$16,700	$23,600	$34,800
1957	600	4dr Multipla Wgn	$20,300	$30,000	$41,800	$61,300
1957	1100TV	2dr Spider	$24,900	$36,200	$57,400	$93,600
1957	1200TV	2dr Spider	$30,800	$42,800	$63,600	$101,000
1958	Nuova 500	2dr Cpe	$8,600	$16,700	$23,600	$34,800
1958	600	4dr Multipla Wgn	$20,300	$30,000	$41,800	$61,300
1958	1200TV	2dr Spider	$30,800	$42,800	$64,600	$101,000
1959	500	2dr Jolly Sdn	$33,100	$44,600	$59,500	$98,100
1959	Nuova 500	2dr Cpe	$8,600	$16,700	$23,600	$34,800
1959	600	2dr Jolly Sdn	$34,400	$46,700	$61,000	$120,000
		4dr Multipla Wgn	$20,300	$30,000	$41,800	$61,300
1959	1200	2dr Spider	$11,300	$16,600	$22,500	$36,800
1959	1200TV	2dr Spider	$30,800	$42,800	$64,600	$101,000
1959	1500S	2dr OSCA Spider	$25,700	$32,300	$45,400	$69,600
1960	Nuova 500	2dr Cpe	$8,600	$16,700	$23,600	$34,800
1960	1200TV	2dr Spider	$30,800	$42,800	$64,600	$101,000
1960	1500S OSCA	2dr Spider	$25,500	$31,700	$44,500	$68,600
1961	500	2dr Jolly Sdn	$33,100	$44,600	$59,500	$98,100
1961	Nuova 500	2dr Cpe	$8,600	$16,700	$23,600	$34,800
1961	600	2dr Jolly Sdn	$34,400	$46,700	$61,000	$120,000
		4dr Multipla Wgn	$20,300	$30,000	$41,800	$61,300
1961	1200	2dr Spider	$11,300	$16,600	$22,500	$36,800
1961	1500S OSCA	2dr Spider	$25,500	$31,700	$44,500	$68,600
1961	2300S	2dr Cpe	$19,200	$30,400	$42,300	$61,000
1962	500	2dr Jolly Sdn	$33,100	$44,600	$59,500	$98,100
1962	Nuova 500	2dr Cpe	$8,600	$16,700	$23,600	$34,800
1962	600	2dr Jolly Sdn	$34,400	$46,700	$61,000	$120,000
1962	1200	2dr Spider	$11,300	$16,600	$22,500	$36,800
1962	1500S OSCA	2dr Spider	$25,500	$31,700	$44,500	$68,600
1962	1600S	2dr Spider	$15,500	$21,200	$31,600	$41,400
1962	2300S	2dr Cpe	$19,200	$30,400	$42,300	$61,000
1963	500	2dr Jolly Sdn	$33,100	$44,600	$59,500	$98,100
1963	Nuova 500	2dr Cpe	$8,600	$16,700	$23,600	$34,800
1963	600	2dr Jolly Sdn	$34,400	$46,700	$61,000	$120,000
1963	1500	2dr Spider	$15,200	$18,300	$30,600	$40,400

Fiat

Year	Model	Body Style	4	3	2	1
1963	1600S	2dr Spider	$15,500	$21,200	$31,600	$41,400
1963	2300S	2dr Cpe	$19,200	$30,400	$42,300	$61,000
1964	Nuova 500	2dr Cpe	$8,600	$16,700	$23,600	$34,800
1964	600	2dr Jolly Sdn	$34,400	$46,700	$61,000	$120,000
1964	1500	2dr Spider	$15,200	$18,300	$30,600	$40,400
1964	1600S	2dr Spider	$15,500	$21,200	$31,600	$41,400
1964	2300S	2dr Cpe	$19,200	$30,400	$42,300	$61,000
1965	Nuova 500	2dr Cpe	$8,600	$16,700	$23,600	$34,800
1965	1500	2dr Spider	$15,200	$18,300	$30,600	$40,400
1965	1600S	2dr Spider	$15,500	$21,200	$31,600	$41,400
1965	2300S	2dr Cpe	$19,200	$30,400	$42,300	$61,000
1966	Nuova 500	2dr Cpe	$8,600	$16,700	$23,600	$34,800
1966	124	2dr 1.4 Cpe	$2,500	$5,800	$9,600	$15,500
		2dr 1.4 Spider	$5,400	$11,900	$19,300	$34,500
1966	1500	2dr Spider	$15,200	$18,300	$30,600	$40,400
1966	1600S	2dr Spider	$15,500	$21,200	$31,600	$41,400
1966	2300S	2dr Cpe	$19,200	$30,400	$42,300	$61,000
1967	Nuova 500	2dr Cpe	$8,600	$16,700	$23,600	$34,800
1967	850	2dr Spider	$4,700	$8,600	$13,700	$22,700
1967	124	2dr 1.4 Cpe	$2,500	$5,800	$9,600	$15,500
		2dr 1.4 Spider	$5,400	$11,900	$19,300	$34,500
1967	2300S	2dr Cpe	$19,200	$30,400	$42,300	$61,000
1967	Dino	2dr 2.0 Cpe	$20,200	$30,000	$46,100	$71,500
		2dr 2.0 Spider	$61,400	$95,000	$121,000	$167,000
1968	Nuova 500	2dr Cpe	$8,600	$16,700	$23,600	$34,800
1968	Nuova 500L	2dr Cpe	$10,600	$18,800	$26,000	$36,000
1968	850	2dr Spider	$4,700	$8,600	$13,700	$22,700
1968	124	2dr Spt Cpe	$2,500	$5,800	$9,600	$15,500
		2dr Spider	$5,200	$11,800	$18,900	$29,900
1968	2300S	2dr Cpe	$19,200	$30,400	$42,300	$61,000
1968	Dino	2dr 2.0 Cpe	$20,200	$30,000	$46,100	$71,500
		2dr 2.0 Spider	$61,400	$95,000	$121,000	$167,000
1969	Nuova 500L	2dr Cpe	$10,600	$18,800	$26,000	$36,000
1969	850	2dr Spider	$4,700	$8,600	$13,700	$22,700
1969	124	2dr A Series Cpe	$2,500	$5,800	$9,600	$15,500
		2dr B Series Cpe	$2,200	$5,300	$8,600	$13,200
		2dr 1.4 Cpe	$2,500	$5,800	$9,600	$15,500
		2dr A Series Spider	$5,400	$11,900	$19,300	$34,500
		2dr B Series Spider	$4,700	$11,100	$18,300	$29,000
		2dr 1.4 Spider	$5,400	$11,900	$19,300	$34,500
1969	2300S	2dr Cpe	$19,200	$30,400	$42,300	$61,000
1969	Dino	2dr 2.4 Cpe	$25,100	$38,800	$53,300	$78,300
		2dr 2.4 Spider	$67,400	$103,000	$131,000	$182,000
1970	Nuova 500L	2dr Cpe	$10,600	$18,800	$26,000	$36,000
1970	850	2dr Spider	$4,700	$8,600	$13,700	$22,700
1970	124	2dr Spt Cpe	$2,200	$5,300	$8,600	$13,200
		2dr Spider	$4,600	$11,000	$17,900	$25,200

Year	Model	Body Style	4	3	2	1
1970	Dino	2dr 2.4 Cpe	$25,100	$38,800	$53,300	$78,300
		2dr 2.4 Spider	$67,400	$103,000	$131,000	$182,000
1971	Nuova 500L	2dr Cpe	$10,600	$18,800	$26,000	$36,000
1971	850	2dr Sport Spider	$4,700	$8,600	$13,700	$22,700
1971	124	2dr Spider	$4,700	$11,100	$18,000	$25,600
		2dr Spt Cpe	$2,200	$5,300	$8,600	$13,200
1971	Dino	2dr 2.4 Cpe	$25,100	$38,800	$53,300	$78,300
		2dr 2.4 Spider	$67,400	$103,000	$131,000	$182,000
1972	Nuova 500L	2dr Cpe	$10,600	$18,800	$26,000	$36,000
1972	850	2dr Spider	$4,700	$8,600	$13,700	$22,700
1972	124	2dr Spt Cpe	$2,200	$5,300	$8,600	$13,200
		2dr Abarth Rally Cpe	$12,800	$19,100	$28,700	$47,800
		2dr Spider	$4,700	$11,100	$18,000	$25,600
1972	X1/9	2dr 1300 Targa	$3,500	$6,300	$10,700	$21,800
1972	Dino	2dr 2.4 Cpe	$25,100	$38,800	$53,300	$78,300
		2dr 2.4 Spider	$67,400	$103,000	$131,000	$182,000
1973	850	2dr Spider	$4,700	$8,600	$13,700	$22,700
1973	124	2dr Spt Cpe	$2,200	$5,300	$8,600	$13,200
		2dr Abarth Rally Cpe	$12,800	$19,100	$28,700	$47,800
		2dr Spider	$4,700	$11,100	$18,000	$25,600
1973	X1/9	2dr 1300 Targa	$3,500	$6,300	$10,700	$21,800
1974	124	2dr Spt Cpe	$2,200	$5,300	$8,600	$13,200
		2dr Abarth Rally Cpe	$12,800	$19,100	$28,700	$47,800
		2dr Spider	$4,700	$11,100	$18,000	$25,600
1974	X1/9	2dr 1300 Targa	$3,500	$6,300	$10,700	$21,800
1975	124	2dr Abarth Rally Cpe	$12,800	$19,100	$28,700	$47,800
		2dr 1.8 Spider	$4,800	$11,300	$18,500	$29,700
1975	X1/9	2dr 1300 Targa	$3,500	$6,300	$10,700	$21,800
1976	124	2dr Abarth Rally Cpe	$12,800	$19,100	$28,700	$47,800
		2dr 1.8 Spider	$4,800	$11,300	$18,500	$29,700
1976	131 Abarth Rallye	2dr Cpe	$55,600	$73,500	$90,300	$125,000
1976	X1/9	2dr 1300 Targa	$3,500	$6,300	$10,700	$21,800
1977	124	2dr 1.8 Spider	$4,800	$11,300	$18,500	$29,700
1977	131 Abarth Rallye	2dr Cpe	$55,600	$73,500	$90,300	$125,000
1977	X1/9	2dr 1300 Targa	$3,500	$6,300	$10,700	$21,800
1978	124	2dr 1.8 Spider	$4,800	$11,300	$18,500	$29,700
1978	131 Abarth Rallye	2dr Cpe	$55,600	$73,500	$90,300	$125,000
1978	X1/9	2dr 1300 Targa	$3,500	$6,300	$10,700	$21,800
1979	2000	2dr Spider	$5,500	$12,500	$19,100	$31,900
1979	X1/9	2dr 1500 Targa	$3,800	$6,700	$11,100	$22,300
1980	2000	2dr Spider	$5,500	$12,500	$19,100	$31,900
1980	X1/9	2dr 1500 Targa	$3,800	$6,700	$11,100	$22,300
1981	2000	2dr Spider	$5,500	$12,500	$19,100	$31,900
1981	X1/9	2dr 1500 Targa	$3,800	$6,700	$11,100	$22,300
1982	X1/9	2dr 1500 Targa	$3,800	$6,700	$10,900	$22,300

Ford

Year	Model	Body Style	4	3	2	1
1946	Deluxe	239/100 2dr Cpe	$7,200	$13,700	$30,600	$40,400
		239/100 2dr Sdn	$5,200	$10,000	$18,500	$24,400
		239/100 4dr Sdn	$3,800	$7,500	$15,700	$20,000
						-10% for 6-cyl.
1946	Super Deluxe	239/100 2dr Cpe	$8,900	$16,300	$33,700	$43,100
		239/100 2dr Sdn	$6,500	$12,100	$23,300	$30,700
		239/100 4dr Sdn	$4,800	$9,400	$20,600	$25,800
		226/90 4dr Wdy Wgn	$51,200	$68,600	$83,100	$106,000
		239/100 4dr Wdy Wgn	$44,300	$62,400	$84,000	$94,400
		239/100 2dr Conv Clb Cpe	$14,400	$23,100	$49,800	$77,000
		239/100 2dr Sptsmn Conv	$97,200	$131,000	$173,000	$211,000
				For base cpe and sdn: -10% for 6-cyl.		
1947	Deluxe	239/100 2dr Cpe	$7,200	$13,700	$30,600	$40,400
		239/100 2dr Sdn	$5,200	$10,000	$18,500	$24,400
		239/100 4dr Sdn	$3,800	$7,500	$15,700	$20,000
						-10% for 6-cyl.
1947	Super Deluxe	239/100 2dr Cpe	$8,900	$16,300	$33,700	$43,100
		239/100 2dr Sdn	$6,500	$12,100	$23,300	$30,700
		239/100 4dr Sdn	$4,800	$9,400	$20,600	$25,800
		226/90 4dr Wdy Wgn	$51,200	$68,600	$83,100	$106,000
		239/100 4dr Wdy Wgn	$44,300	$62,400	$84,000	$94,400
		239/100 2dr Conv Clb Cpe	$14,400	$23,100	$44,800	$69,300
		239/100 2dr Sptsmn Conv	$97,200	$131,000	$173,000	$211,000
				For base cpe and sdn: -10% for 6-cyl.		
1948	Deluxe	239/100 2dr Cpe	$7,200	$13,700	$30,600	$40,400
		239/100 2dr Sdn	$5,200	$10,000	$18,500	$24,400
		239/100 4dr Sdn	$3,800	$7,500	$15,700	$20,000
						-10% for 6-cyl.
1948	Super Deluxe	239/100 2dr Cpe	$8,900	$16,300	$33,700	$43,100
		239/100 2dr Sdn	$6,500	$12,100	$23,300	$30,700
		239/100 4dr Sdn	$4,800	$9,400	$20,600	$25,800
		239/100 2dr Conv Clb Cpe	$14,400	$23,100	$44,800	$69,300
		226/95 4dr Wdy Wgn	$41,000	$54,900	$66,500	$84,800
		239/100 4dr Wdy Wgn	$55,400	$78,000	$105,000	$118,000
		239/100 2dr Sptsmn Conv	$97,200	$131,000	$173,000	$211,000

Year	Model	Body Style	4	3	2	1
				For base cpe and sdn: -10% for 6-cyl.		
1949	Deluxe	239/100 2dr Bus Cpe	$7,700	$12,700	$21,800	$32,800
		239/100 2dr Clb Cpe	$7,400	$13,500	$22,400	$33,200
		239/100 2dr Sdn	$6,500	$12,000	$19,100	$27,400
		239/100 4dr Sdn	$3,200	$6,900	$12,800	$18,300
						-10% for 6-cyl.
1949	Custom	239/100 2dr Clb Cpe	$7,300	$12,800	$21,300	$32,000
		239/100 2dr Sdn	$6,700	$12,600	$19,000	$27,000
		239/100 4dr Sdn	$3,100	$7,000	$12,500	$17,900
		239/100 2dr Wdy Wgn	$50,000	$68,400	$92,600	$109,000
		239/100 2dr Conv Clb Cpe	$12,200	$20,500	$43,900	$64,000
			For Club Cpe and sdns: -10% for 6-cyl. For Woody Wgn: -$10,000 for 6-cyl. For Club Conv: -$5,000 for 6-cyl.			
1950	Deluxe	239/100 2dr Bus Cpe	$7,100	$13,200	$22,600	$33,400
		239/100 2dr Tudor Sdn	$6,300	$11,900	$19,800	$27,800
		239/100 4dr Fordor Sdn	$2,700	$6,500	$12,100	$17,500
						-10% for 6-cyl.
1950	Custom Deluxe	239/100 2dr Crestliner Sdn	$8,600	$14,200	$24,800	$35,500
		239/100 2dr Clb Cpe	$7,400	$12,400	$22,200	$33,200
		239/100 2dr Tudor Sdn	$6,900	$12,300	$20,700	$28,500
		239/100 4dr Fordor Sdn	$3,700	$8,600	$12,200	$19,200
		239/100 2dr Ctry Sqr Wdy Wgn	$41,000	$56,400	$76,300	$99,800
		239/100 2dr Conv Clb Cpe	$12,500	$21,100	$47,300	$69,100
						-10% for 6-cyl.
1951	Deluxe	239/100 2dr Bus Cpe	$7,500	$13,100	$22,600	$33,000
		239/100 2dr Sdn	$6,300	$11,500	$17,800	$27,000
		239/100 4dr Sdn	$2,600	$6,800	$12,000	$18,000
						-10% for 6-cyl.
1951	Custom Deluxe	239/100 2dr Clb Cpe	$7,800	$12,800	$22,300	$33,200
		239/100 2dr Sdn	$6,900	$13,000	$20,900	$28,900
		239/100 4dr Sdn	$3,100	$7,100	$12,300	$18,200
		239/100 2dr Ctry Sqr Wdy Wgn	$41,000	$56,400	$76,300	$99,800

Ford

Year	Model	Body Style	4	3	2	1
		239/100 2dr Crestliner Sdn	$8,900	$13,900	$22,500	$32,900
		239/100 2dr Vic Hdtp	$9,000	$14,400	$26,000	$36,000
		239/100 2dr Conv	$12,200	$20,800	$43,500	$68,300
						-10% for 6-cyl.
1952	Mainline	239/110 2dr Bus Cpe	$5,700	$9,900	$18,700	$27,000
		239/110 2dr Sdn	$5,600	$9,400	$17,100	$23,000
		239/110 4dr Sdn	$3,700	$6,600	$11,000	$18,300
		239/110 2dr Rnch Wgn	$11,200	$18,900	$27,600	$42,000
						-10% for 6-cyl.
1952	Customline	239/110 2dr Clb Cpe	$6,400	$11,200	$20,300	$27,900
		239/110 2dr Sdn	$6,000	$9,800	$18,100	$23,200
		239/110 4dr Sdn	$3,900	$6,600	$11,900	$18,200
		239/110 4dr Ctry Sdn Wgn	$9,700	$16,500	$24,400	$40,000
						-10% for 6-cyl.
1952	Crestline	239/110 2dr Vic Hdtp	$7,100	$12,700	$23,900	$30,300
		239/110 4dr Ctry Sqr Wdy Wgn	$11,500	$19,100	$27,900	$41,700
		239/110 2dr Sunliner Conv	$17,300	$24,400	$40,700	$61,600
						-10% for 6-cyl.
1953	Mainline	239/110 2dr Bus Cpe	$5,700	$12,100	$18,900	$27,300
		239/110 2dr Sdn	$5,500	$9,500	$17,200	$23,100
		239/110 4dr Sdn	$3,800	$6,500	$11,100	$18,600
		239/110 2dr Rnch Wgn	$12,000	$19,400	$28,900	$43,200
						-10% for 6-cyl.
1953	Customline	239/110 2dr Clb Cpe	$6,500	$11,200	$20,400	$28,100
		239/110 2dr Sdn	$6,000	$9,700	$17,300	$22,400
		239/110 4dr Sdn	$4,000	$6,700	$12,000	$18,300
		239/110 4dr Ctry Sdn Wgn	$11,100	$17,100	$28,400	$40,400
						-10% for 6-cyl.
1953	Crestline	239/110 2dr Vic Hdtp	$7,000	$12,400	$22,600	$30,200
		239/110 4dr Ctry Sqr Wgn	$12,400	$20,300	$29,300	$42,400
		239/110 2dr Sunliner Conv	$17,500	$24,500	$40,800	$59,200
						-10% for 6-cyl.

Year	Model	Body Style	4	3	2	1
1954	Mainline	239/130 2dr Bus Cpe	$5,800	$9,900	$19,000	$27,200
		239/130 2dr Sdn	$5,400	$9,500	$16,100	$21,900
		239/130 4dr Sdn	$3,600	$6,500	$11,200	$18,500
		239/130 2dr Rnch Wgn	$12,800	$22,100	$30,400	$43,800
						-10% for 6-cyl.
1954	Customline	239/130 2dr Rnch Wgn	$13,500	$23,500	$31,600	$45,000
		239/130 2dr Clb Cpe	$6,300	$11,300	$20,300	$27,900
		239/130 2dr Sdn	$6,000	$9,500	$18,300	$23,300
		239/130 4dr Sdn	$4,000	$6,700	$11,800	$18,700
		239/130 4dr Ctry Sdn Wgn	$11,800	$20,900	$29,500	$42,000
						-10% for 6-cyl.
1954	Crestline	239/130 2dr Vic Hdtp	$7,200	$12,900	$24,200	$30,700
		239/130 4dr Sdn	$3,900	$6,100	$13,100	$20,000
		239/130 4dr Ctry Sqr Wgn	$13,500	$24,500	$31,200	$43,200
		239/130 2dr Skyliner Hdtp	$14,400	$19,500	$32,300	$41,600
		239/130 2dr Sunliner Conv	$16,200	$24,300	$40,900	$59,500
						-10% for 6-cyl.
1955	Mainline	272/162 2dr Bus Sdn	$4,800	$7,000	$12,400	$16,600
		272/162 2dr Sdn	$6,900	$10,700	$16,300	$22,300
						-20% for 6-cyl. +15% for factory a/c.
1955	Customline	272/162 2dr Sdn	$8,400	$13,800	$21,800	$30,700
		272/162 4dr Sdn	$6,100	$10,000	$17,600	$26,000
		272/162 2dr Rnch Wgn	$14,400	$24,300	$36,500	$51,700
		272/162 4dr Ctry Sdn Wgn	$12,800	$23,800	$34,200	$49,600
						-20% for 6-cyl. +15% for factory a/c.
1955	Fairlane	272/162 2dr Clb Sdn	$9,600	$16,500	$23,100	$32,600
		272/182 2dr Clb Sdn	$10,400	$18,100	$25,600	$36,000
		272/162 4dr Twn Sdn	$6,700	$10,900	$15,400	$21,200
		272/182 4dr Twn Sdn	$7,600	$12,400	$17,400	$24,500
		272/162 4dr Ctry Sqr Wgn	$18,100	$28,300	$43,100	$58,600
		272/162 2dr Vic Hdtp	$11,500	$18,800	$28,300	$37,900

Ford

Year	Model	Body Style	4	3	2	1
		272/182 2dr Vic Hdtp	$12,900	$20,600	$30,400	$41,800
		272/162 2dr Crwn Vic Hdtp	$13,500	$22,800	$32,600	$44,900
		272/182 2dr Crwn Vic Hdtp	$15,100	$24,800	$34,000	$45,900
		272/162 2dr Crwn Vic Skyliner Hdtp	$27,300	$42,900	$59,000	$82,600
		272/182 2dr Crwn Vic Skyliner Hdtp	$30,200	$46,400	$65,200	$90,500
		272/162 2dr Sunliner Conv	$25,000	$39,300	$54,600	$74,700
		272/182 2dr Sunliner Conv	$26,200	$42,700	$60,100	$79,900

-20% for 6-cyl. +15% for factory a/c.

Year	Model	Body Style	4	3	2	1
1955	Thunderbird	292/198 2dr Conv	$17,200	$27,200	$38,100	$62,600

Prices assume both hard and soft tops. -$6,000 for hard top only. -$4,000 for soft top only: deductions can never exceed 50% of condition #4 vehicle's value.

Year	Model	Body Style	4	3	2	1
1956	Mainline	272/173 2dr Sdn	$6,700	$11,300	$16,600	$23,300
		272/173 2dr Bus Sdn	$9,100	$14,800	$21,900	$30,000
		272/173 4dr Sdn	$4,400	$6,700	$12,500	$16,600
1956	Ranch Wagon	272/173 2dr Wgn	$14,600	$26,100	$37,200	$52,200

-20% for 6-cyl. +15% for factory a/c.

Year	Model	Body Style	4	3	2	1
1956	Customline	272/173 2dr Vic Cpe	$9,400	$15,300	$23,700	$32,600
		272/173 2dr Sdn	$6,700	$10,800	$17,100	$23,400
		272/173 4dr Sdn	$4,200	$6,700	$13,400	$17,900

-20% for 6-cyl. +15% for factory a/c.

Year	Model	Body Style	4	3	2	1
1956	Fairlane	312/215 2dr Ctry Sdn Hdtp Sdn	$9,500	$15,100	$21,500	$30,200
		312/225 2dr Ctry Sdn Hdtp Sdn	$10,000	$15,600	$22,300	$31,500
		292/200 2dr Clb Sdn	$8,800	$14,600	$21,400	$32,300
		312/215 2dr Clb Sdn	$9,700	$16,100	$23,800	$35,700
		312/225 2dr Clb Sdn	$10,100	$17,000	$24,400	$36,400
		272/173 4dr Twn Sdn	$6,800	$10,700	$15,600	$23,600
		312/215 4dr Twn Sdn	$7,600	$12,400	$17,300	$25,800
		312/225 4dr Twn Sdn	$8,300	$12,800	$18,000	$27,100
		272/173 4dr Ctry Sqr Wgn	$15,500	$26,900	$44,300	$65,800

Year	Model	Body Style	4	3	2	1
		292/200 2dr Pkln Wgn	$14,900	$23,500	$37,600	$55,000
		272/173 2dr Crwn Vic Hdtp Cpe	$15,200	$24,600	$33,700	$46,100
		312/215 2dr Crwn Vic Hdtp Cpe	$17,600	$28,000	$38,600	$53,300
		312/225 2dr Crwn Vic Hdtp Cpe	$18,300	$29,300	$40,100	$55,300
		272/173 2dr Crwn Vic Skyliner Cpe	$32,100	$47,300	$66,400	$92,900
		312/215 2dr Crwn Vic Skyliner Cpe	$36,900	$54,400	$76,100	$108,000
		312/225 2dr Crwn Vic Skyliner Cpe	$38,500	$56,500	$79,500	$112,000
		312/215 4dr Vic Hdtp Sdn	$7,500	$13,300	$17,900	$24,800
		312/225 4dr Vic Hdtp Sdn	$7,900	$13,700	$18,900	$26,000
		272/173 4dr Vic Sdn	$6,500	$11,400	$15,700	$22,000
		272/173 2dr Sunliner Conv	$24,800	$40,000	$59,900	$81,900
		312/215 2dr Sunliner Conv	$28,200	$46,400	$68,700	$94,100
		312/225 2dr Sunliner Conv	$29,500	$48,100	$75,100	$98,000
		-20% for 6-cyl. +15% for factory a/c.				
1956	Thunderbird	292/200 2dr Conv	$17,800	$30,700	$48,100	$68,700
		312/215 2dr Conv	$19,500	$34,300	$53,800	$76,900
		Prices assume both hard and soft tops. -$6,000 for hard top only. -$4,000 for soft top only; deductions can never exceed 50% of condition #4 vehicle's value.				
1957	Custom	272/190 2dr Bus Sdn	$7,400	$12,400	$17,700	$23,400
		312/245 2dr Bus Sdn	$8,900	$15,000	$21,300	$27,900
		312/270 2dr Bus Sdn	$10,100	$16,800	$23,900	$31,500
		312/300 2dr Bus Sdn	$12,000	$20,000	$28,300	$37,300
		272/190 2dr Sdn	$7,000	$11,400	$17,100	$22,200
		312/245 2dr Sdn	$8,400	$13,900	$20,500	$26,500
		312/270 2dr Sdn	$9,400	$15,500	$23,200	$29,800
		312/300 2dr Sdn	$11,200	$18,400	$27,500	$35,300
		272/190 4dr Sdn	$3,800	$6,800	$10,600	$19,300
		312/245 4dr Sdn	$4,600	$8,100	$13,000	$23,200
		312/270 4dr Sdn	$5,200	$9,000	$14,500	$26,000
		312/300 4dr Sdn	$6,100	$10,700	$17,100	$30,800
		-20% for 6-cyl. +15% for factory a/c.				

Ford

Year	Model	Body Style	4	3	2	1
1957	Custom 300	272/190 2dr Sdn	$8,700	$14,800	$21,300	$27,600
		312/245 2dr Sdn	$10,600	$17,900	$25,600	$32,900
		312/270 2dr Sdn	$11,900	$20,200	$28,700	$37,200
		312/300 2dr Sdn	$14,100	$24,000	$34,000	$43,900
		272/190 4dr Sdn	$5,100	$9,000	$13,600	$24,400
		312/245 4dr Sdn	$6,200	$10,700	$16,600	$29,300
		312/270 4dr Sdn	$6,900	$12,100	$18,500	$32,800
		312/300 4dr Sdn	$8,400	$14,300	$21,900	$38,800
				-20% for 6-cyl. +15% for factory a/c.		
1957	Fairlane	292/212 2dr Clb Sdn	$9,200	$15,100	$20,200	$30,800
		312/245 2dr Clb Sdn	$11,000	$18,400	$24,200	$36,600
		312/270 2dr Clb Sdn	$12,800	$20,900	$28,000	$42,100
		312/300 2dr Clb Sdn	$15,400	$26,000	$34,800	$52,600
		292/212 4dr Twn Sdn	$6,100	$10,100	$13,900	$20,600
		312/245 4dr Twn Sdn	$7,400	$12,300	$16,800	$24,900
		312/270 4dr Twn Sdn	$8,700	$14,100	$19,300	$28,700
		312/300 4dr Twn Sdn	$10,400	$17,500	$24,200	$35,800
		292/212 2dr Vic Clb Hdtp	$10,400	$16,400	$22,600	$31,100
		312/245 2dr Vic Clb Hdtp	$12,500	$19,700	$26,700	$37,300
		312/270 2dr Vic Clb Hdtp	$14,200	$23,200	$31,200	$43,200
		312/300 2dr Vic Hdtp	$20,500	$32,600	$44,900	$61,900
		292/212 4dr Vic Twn Hdtp	$6,800	$10,600	$14,700	$20,800
		312/245 4dr Vic Twn Hdtp	$8,000	$12,600	$17,600	$24,700
		312/270 4dr Vic Twn Hdtp	$9,100	$14,500	$20,300	$28,300
		312/300 4dr Vic Twn Hdtp	$11,400	$18,200	$25,600	$35,700
				-20% for 6-cyl. +15% for factory a/c.		
1957	Fairlane 500	312/245 2dr Clb Vic Hdtp	$16,000	$25,500	$35,500	$48,700
		292/212 2dr Clb Sdn	$11,300	$19,100	$31,800	$48,100
		312/245 2dr Clb Sdn	$14,300	$22,900	$38,000	$57,700
		312/270 2dr Clb Sdn	$15,200	$25,800	$44,300	$67,100

Year	Model	Body Style	4	3	2	1
		312/300 2dr Clb Sdn	$19,000	$32,200	$55,300	$83,600
		223/144 4dr Twn Sdn	$6,300	$10,300	$15,400	$22,500
		292/212 4dr Twn Sdn	$8,500	$14,600	$22,200	$32,700
		292/212 2dr Clb Vic Hdtp	$13,500	$21,700	$29,100	$40,400
		292/212 4dr Twn Vic Hdtp	$6,900	$11,100	$15,300	$21,700
		312/245 4dr Twn Vic Hdtp	$8,300	$13,200	$18,200	$26,100
		292/212 2dr Skyliner Rtrctble Hdtp	$23,200	$37,400	$55,500	$83,600
		312/245 2dr Skyliner Rtrctble Hdtp	$28,000	$44,400	$66,600	$101,000
		312/300 2dr Skyliner Rtrctble Hdtp	$40,300	$66,300	$96,900	$144,000
		292/212 2dr Sunliner Conv	$24,900	$42,500	$71,700	$97,200
		312/245 2dr Sunliner Conv	$32,400	$52,000	$87,600	$119,000
		-20% for 6-cyl. +15% for factory a/c.				
1957	Country Squire	292/212 4dr Wgn	$14,400	$23,800	$35,400	$54,800
		-20% for 6-cyl. +15% for factory a/c.				
1957	Thunderbird	292/212 2dr Conv	$18,400	$32,400	$48,900	$69,800
		312/245 2dr Conv	$31,400	$50,400	$87,300	$135,000
		312/270 2dr Conv	$53,400	$85,500	$132,000	$188,000
		312/300 2dr Conv	$67,000	$109,000	$166,000	$238,000
		Prices assume both hard and soft tops. -$6,000 for hard top only, -$4,000 for soft top only; deductions can never exceed 50% of condition #4 vehicle's value.				
1958	Custom 300	292/205 2dr Bus Sdn	$6,900	$11,100	$14,800	$20,100
		352/300 2dr Bus Sdn	$8,400	$13,400	$18,000	$24,000
		292/205 2dr Sdn	$4,700	$8,200	$10,800	$16,900
		352/300 2dr Sdn	$5,800	$9,800	$12,900	$20,200
		292/205 4dr Sdn	$3,800	$6,400	$8,500	$15,000
		352/300 4dr Sdn	$4,500	$7,700	$10,000	$18,200
		-20% for 6-cyl. +15% for factory a/c.				
1958	Ranch Wagon	332/240 2dr Wgn	$12,600	$17,400	$25,200	$40,400
		-20% for 6-cyl. +15% for factory a/c.				
1958	Fairlane	292/205 2dr Clb Sdn	$5,600	$8,900	$12,300	$17,200

Ford

Year	Model	Body Style	4	3	2	1
		332/265 2dr Clb Sdn	$6,200	$10,200	$13,400	$18,900
		352/300 2dr Clb Sdn	$6,700	$11,100	$14,600	$20,700
		292/205 4dr Twn Sdn	$4,000	$7,000	$9,600	$13,200
		332/265 4dr Twn Sdn	$4,700	$7,700	$10,400	$14,600
		352/300 4dr Twn Sdn	$4,900	$8,500	$11,200	$15,800
		292/205 2dr Clb Vic Hdtp	$7,600	$12,400	$17,300	$23,500
		332/265 2dr Clb Vic Hdtp	$8,400	$13,800	$19,000	$25,700
		352/300 2dr Clb Vic Hdtp	$9,100	$15,100	$20,600	$28,000
		292/205 4dr Twn Vic Hdtp	$4,200	$7,600	$9,400	$13,300
		332/265 4dr Twn Vic Hdtp	$4,900	$7,800	$10,400	$14,700
		352/300 4dr Twn Vic Hdtp	$5,000	$8,500	$11,400	$16,100
			-20% for 6-cyl. +15% for factory a/c.			
1958	Del Rio	332/240 4dr Rnch Wgn	$11,500	$14,500	$23,800	$34,200
			-20% for 6-cyl. +15% for factory a/c.			
1958	Fairlane 500	332/265 2dr Clb Sdn	$7,600	$12,200	$17,000	$23,100
		352/300 2dr Clb Sdn	$8,500	$13,500	$18,300	$25,100
		223/145 4dr Twn Sdn	$4,200	$7,100	$9,400	$13,300
		332/265 4dr Twn Sdn	$4,800	$7,800	$10,500	$14,700
		352/300 4dr Twn Sdn	$5,200	$8,500	$11,200	$15,900
		332/265 2dr Clb Vic Hdtp	$10,200	$16,500	$22,200	$30,700
		352/300 2dr Clb Vic Hdtp	$11,100	$18,000	$24,200	$33,500
		332/265 4dr Twn Vic Hdtp	$5,200	$8,600	$11,700	$16,400
		352/300 4dr Twn Vic Hdtp	$5,600	$9,500	$12,700	$18,000
		332/265 2dr Sunliner Conv	$22,900	$37,100	$57,600	$81,200
		352/300 2dr Sunliner Conv	$25,200	$40,800	$62,300	$87,400
		332/265 2dr Skyliner Rtrctble Hdtp	$17,600	$29,200	$50,500	$78,700

Year	Model	Body Style	4	3	2	1
		352/300 2dr Skyliner Rtrctble Hdtp	$19,400	$32,000	$54,600	$82,600
				-20% for 6-cyl. +15% for factory a/c.		
1958	Country Squire	332/240 4dr Wgn	$16,000	$21,600	$32,600	$51,100
				-20% for 6-cyl. +15% for factory a/c.		
1958	Thunderbird	352/300 2dr Cpe	$6,400	$12,400	$20,200	$33,300
		352/300 2dr Conv	$15,400	$25,100	$44,900	$60,300
					+10% for factory a/c.	
1959	Custom 300	292/200 2dr Bus Sdn	$8,500	$12,400	$16,600	$22,000
		352/300 2dr Bus Sdn	$10,100	$15,000	$19,800	$26,300
		292/200 2dr Tudor Sdn	$7,400	$11,300	$15,400	$21,800
		352/300 2dr Tudor Sdn	$8,900	$13,600	$18,300	$26,000
		292/200 4dr Fordor Sdn	$4,700	$8,200	$10,800	$15,000
		352/300 4dr Fordor Sdn	$5,800	$9,800	$12,900	$18,200
				+15% for factory a/c. -20% for 6-cyl.		
1959	Ranch Wagon	292/200 2dr Wgn	$6,400	$10,300	$13,400	$19,800
		332/225 2dr Wgn	$6,600	$10,700	$14,700	$20,100
		352/300 2dr Wgn	$7,400	$11,700	$16,000	$22,900
		292/200 4dr Wgn	$5,800	$9,600	$13,000	$18,500
		332/225 4dr Wgn	$6,100	$9,800	$13,700	$19,400
		352/300 4dr Wgn	$7,000	$11,200	$15,500	$22,500
				+15% for factory a/c. -20% for 6-cyl.		
1959	Fairlane	292/200 2dr Clb Sdn	$5,700	$9,300	$12,700	$17,600
		332/225 2dr Clb Sdn	$6,200	$9,700	$13,300	$18,400
		352/300 2dr Clb Sdn	$6,900	$11,200	$15,100	$21,000
		292/200 4dr Twn Sdn	$4,200	$7,000	$9,500	$13,200
		332/225 4dr Twn Sdn	$4,500	$7,400	$9,900	$14,200
		352/300 4dr Twn Sdn	$5,000	$8,300	$11,500	$16,000
				+15% for factory a/c. -20% for 6-cyl.		
1959	Country Sedan	292/200 4dr Stn Wgn 6P	$5,700	$9,500	$12,900	$18,500
		352/300 4dr Stn Wgn 6P	$6,900	$11,400	$15,400	$22,200

Ford

Year	Model	Body Style	4	3	2	1
		332/225 4dr Stn Wgn 9P	$6,100	$9,800	$13,500	$19,400
		+15% for factory a/c. -20% for 6-cyl.				
1959	Fairlane 500	292/200 2dr Clb Sdn	$6,700	$10,800	$15,200	$20,900
		332/225 2dr Clb Sdn	$7,000	$11,300	$15,900	$21,800
		352/300 2dr Clb Sdn	$8,100	$13,200	$18,000	$24,700
		292/200 4dr Twn Sdn	$4,500	$7,100	$9,500	$13,300
		352/300 4dr Twn Sdn	$5,300	$8,500	$11,400	$16,000
		332/225 4dr Twn Sdn	$4,700	$7,500	$9,900	$14,200
		292/200 2dr Clb Vic Hdtp	$5,100	$8,600	$11,500	$16,300
		332/225 2dr Clb Vic Hdtp	$5,300	$8,800	$12,300	$17,100
		352/300 2dr Clb Vic Hdtp	$6,200	$10,000	$14,300	$19,600
		292/200 4dr Twn Vic Hdtp	$4,600	$7,200	$9,800	$13,700
		332/225 4dr Twn Vic Hdtp	$4,800	$7,500	$10,300	$14,400
		352/300 4dr Twn Vic Hdtp	$5,400	$8,600	$11,500	$16,500
		+15% for factory a/c. -20% for 6-cyl.				
1959	Galaxie	292/200 2dr Clb Sdn	$4,200	$7,200	$9,600	$13,700
		352/300 2dr Clb Sdn	$5,100	$8,600	$11,400	$16,400
		292/200 4dr Twn Sdn	$4,100	$7,100	$9,500	$13,300
		352/300 4dr Twn Sdn	$5,000	$8,400	$11,300	$16,000
		292/200 4dr Ctry Sqr Wgn	$8,300	$13,500	$18,300	$25,700
		352/300 4dr Ctry Sqr Wgn	$10,000	$16,300	$22,000	$30,800
		292/200 2dr Clb Vic Hdtp	$7,400	$11,800	$16,700	$22,600
		352/300 2dr Clb Vic Hdtp	$8,800	$14,200	$19,800	$27,100
		292/200 4dr Twn Vic Hdtp	$4,500	$7,600	$10,000	$14,900
		352/300 4dr Twn Vic Hdtp	$5,400	$8,900	$11,900	$17,900
		292/200 2dr Sunliner Conv	$16,500	$26,700	$42,300	$61,700

Year	Model	Body Style	4	3	2	1
		352/300 2dr Sunliner Conv	$19,900	$32,000	$50,800	$73,600
		292/200 2dr Skyliner Rtrctble Hdtp	$18,600	$30,000	$47,800	$68,900
		352/300 2dr Skyliner Rtrctble Hdtp	$22,500	$36,500	$57,000	$82,300
				+15% for factory a/c. -20% for 6-cyl.		
1959	Thunderbird	352/300 2dr Cpe	$7,100	$13,400	$21,100	$34,600
		430/350 2dr Cpe	$8,000	$15,200	$22,900	$36,200
		352/300 2dr Conv	$17,500	$26,900	$48,200	$65,000
		430/350 2dr Conv	$21,400	$30,400	$51,200	$70,000
					+10% for factory a/c.	
1960	Falcon	144/90 2dr Sdn	$4,500	$7,800	$12,500	$19,100
		144/90 4dr Sdn	$3,200	$4,600	$12,100	$16,700
		144/90 2dr Wgn	$4,500	$7,700	$18,000	$29,300
		144/90 4dr Wgn	$3,800	$6,200	$10,300	$14,000
1960	Custom 300	292/185 2dr Clb Sdn	$6,100	$9,800	$13,200	$17,800
		292/185 4dr Twn Sdn	$4,100	$6,600	$9,200	$12,600
1960	Fairlane	292/185 2dr Bus Sdn	$10,400	$16,600	$22,900	$31,000
		352/235 2dr Bus Sdn	$11,400	$18,300	$25,200	$34,100
		352/300 2dr Bus Sdn	$12,400	$20,000	$27,400	$37,300
		352/360 2dr Bus Sdn	$14,500	$23,300	$31,900	$43,200
		292/185 2dr Clb Sdn	$4,300	$6,500	$8,300	$13,300
		352/235 2dr Clb Sdn	$4,800	$7,100	$9,300	$14,700
		352/300 2dr Clb Sdn	$5,200	$7,700	$10,100	$16,000
		352/360 2dr Clb Sdn	$6,000	$9,100	$11,600	$18,600
		292/185 4dr Twn Sdn	$3,600	$5,600	$7,200	$12,300
		352/235 4dr Twn Sdn	$3,900	$6,100	$7,900	$13,500
		352/300 4dr Twn Sdn	$4,300	$6,900	$8,600	$14,700
		352/360 4dr Twn Sdn	$5,100	$7,900	$10,100	$17,100
				+15% for factory a/c. -20% for 6-cyl.		
1960	Fairlane 500	292/185 2dr Clb Sdn	$4,600	$7,200	$9,300	$14,500

Ford

Year	Model	Body Style	4	3	2	1
		352/235 2dr Clb Sdn	$5,000	$7,900	$10,200	$16,100
		352/300 2dr Clb Sdn	$5,500	$8,600	$10,900	$17,500
		352/360 2dr Clb Sdn	$6,500	$10,200	$12,800	$20,400
		292/185 4dr Twn Sdn	$3,900	$5,900	$7,500	$13,000
		352/235 4dr Twn Sdn	$4,300	$6,700	$8,200	$14,200
		352/300 4dr Twn Sdn	$4,700	$7,200	$9,000	$15,600
		352/360 4dr Twn Sdn	$5,500	$8,400	$10,500	$18,200
				+15% for factory a/c. -20% for 6-cyl.		
1960	Ranch Wagon	292/185 4dr Wgn	$6,600	$9,900	$13,700	$19,000
		352/235 4dr Wgn	$7,500	$10,900	$14,900	$20,800
		352/300 4dr Wgn	$8,100	$11,700	$16,400	$22,800
		352/360 4dr Wgn	$9,400	$13,600	$19,200	$26,500
				+15% for factory a/c. -20% for 6-cyl.		
1960	Galaxie	292/185 2dr Clb Sdn	$12,700	$20,100	$27,900	$37,000
		352/300 2dr Clb Sdn	$15,300	$23,900	$33,200	$44,200
		352/360 2dr Clb Sdn	$17,700	$28,000	$38,800	$51,600
		292/185 4dr Twn Sdn	$3,000	$7,000	$9,400	$14,800
		352/300 4dr Twn Sdn	$3,500	$8,600	$11,300	$17,700
		352/360 4dr Twn Sdn	$4,100	$9,900	$13,200	$20,600
		292/185 2dr Strlnr Hdtp Cpe	$13,800	$21,700	$30,000	$40,200
		352/300 2dr Strlnr Hdtp Cpe	$16,500	$25,800	$35,900	$48,200
		352/360 2dr Strlnr Hdtp Cpe	$19,300	$30,200	$41,900	$56,200
		292/185 4dr Twn Vic Hdtp Sdn	$3,300	$7,500	$9,800	$15,200
		352/300 4dr Twn Vic Hdtp Sdn	$4,000	$9,100	$11,800	$18,300
		352/360 4dr Twn Vic Hdtp Sdn	$4,700	$10,400	$13,800	$21,200
		292/185 2dr Sunliner Conv	$14,900	$23,900	$33,800	$45,300
		352/300 2dr Sunliner Conv	$17,900	$28,600	$40,500	$54,300
		352/360 2dr Sunliner Conv	$20,900	$33,500	$47,200	$63,300

Year	Model	Body Style	4	3	2	1
				+15% for factory a/c. -20% for 6-cyl.		
1960	Country Sedan	292/185 4dr Stn Wgn 6P	$6,800	$10,200	$14,000	$20,400
		352/235 4dr Stn Wgn 6P	$7,800	$11,200	$15,200	$22,400
		352/300 4dr Stn Wgn 6P	$8,300	$12,200	$16,800	$24,500
		352/360 4dr Stn Wgn 6P	$9,800	$14,200	$19,700	$28,500
				+15% for factory a/c. -20% for 6-cyl.		
1960	Country Squire	292/185 4dr Stn Wgn 9P	$6,100	$9,100	$12,600	$17,400
		352/300 4dr Stn Wgn 9P	$7,300	$11,100	$15,200	$20,900
		352/360 4dr Stn Wgn 9P	$8,500	$12,700	$17,600	$24,300
				+15% for factory a/c. -20% for 6-cyl.		
1960	Thunderbird	352/300 2dr Cpe	$6,100	$12,500	$19,200	$26,700
		430/350 2dr Cpe	$7,500	$14,200	$21,800	$30,900
		352/300 2dr Conv	$21,900	$34,100	$49,700	$66,200
		430/350 2dr Conv	$22,800	$35,600	$51,700	$68,900
			+20% for factory sunroof on coupe. +10% for factory a/c.			
1961	Falcon	144/85 2dr Sdn	$4,800	$9,000	$18,100	$20,900
		144/85 2dr Futura Sdn	$6,400	$10,900	$15,600	$21,800
		144/85 4dr Sdn	$3,900	$5,600	$9,100	$16,600
		144/85 2dr Wgn	$5,400	$9,300	$13,800	$18,300
		144/85 4dr Wgn	$4,300	$7,100	$10,300	$13,800
				+15% for factory a/c. -20% for 6-cyl.		
1961	Fairlane	292/175 2dr Clb Sdn	$5,200	$8,500	$11,500	$15,500
		390/375 2dr Clb Sdn	$6,600	$10,700	$14,500	$19,500
		292/175 2dr 500 Clb Sdn	$5,600	$9,200	$12,400	$16,800
		390/375 2dr 500 Clb Sdn	$7,200	$11,300	$15,500	$21,000
		292/175 4dr Twn Sdn	$3,700	$6,600	$9,000	$13,300
		390/375 4dr Twn Sdn	$4,700	$8,200	$11,100	$16,700
		292/175 4dr 500 Twn Sdn	$4,100	$7,000	$9,400	$14,000
		390/375 4dr 500 Twn Sdn	$5,200	$8,700	$11,500	$17,500
				-20% for 6-cyl. +15% for factory a/c.		
1961	Ranch Wagon	292/175 4dr Wgn	$6,600	$9,900	$13,700	$19,000

Ford

Year	Model	Body Style	4	3	2	1
		390/375 4dr Wgn	$8,500	$12,300	$17,000	$23,800

-20% for 6-cyl. +15% for factory a/c.

Year	Model	Body Style	4	3	2	1
1961	Galaxie	292/175 2dr Clb Sdn	$6,600	$10,600	$17,000	$22,500
		352/220 2dr Clb Sdn	$7,500	$12,200	$19,500	$25,900
		390/300 2dr Clb Sdn	$7,800	$12,700	$20,400	$27,000
		390/375 2dr Clb Sdn	$8,100	$13,200	$21,200	$28,300
		292/175 4dr Twn Sdn	$3,400	$6,200	$10,900	$16,500
		352/220 4dr Twn Sdn	$3,900	$7,200	$12,400	$18,800
		390/300 4dr Twn Sdn	$4,100	$7,500	$13,000	$19,700
		390/375 4dr Twn Sdn	$4,300	$7,700	$13,600	$20,500
		292/175 2dr Clb Vic Hdtp Sdn	$6,800	$11,300	$17,500	$28,000
		352/220 2dr Clb Vic Hdtp Sdn	$7,800	$13,000	$20,200	$32,200
		390/300 2dr Clb Vic Hdtp Sdn	$8,100	$13,700	$21,000	$33,700
		390/375 2dr Clb Vic Hdtp Sdn	$8,500	$14,200	$21,900	$35,000
		292/175 2dr Strlnr Hdtp Cpe	$13,000	$20,500	$28,500	$38,000
		352/220 2dr Strlnr Hdtp Cpe	$14,800	$23,600	$32,800	$43,600
		390/300 2dr Strlnr Hdtp Cpe	$15,600	$24,500	$34,300	$45,500
		390/375 2dr Strlnr Hdtp Cpe	$16,200	$25,600	$35,600	$47,400
		292/175 4dr Twn Vic Hdtp Sdn	$3,700	$6,800	$11,400	$17,700
		352/220 4dr Twn Vic Hdtp Sdn	$4,300	$7,800	$13,100	$20,400
		390/300 4dr Twn Vic Hdtp Sdn	$4,500	$8,200	$13,700	$21,200
		390/375 4dr Twn Vic Hdtp Sdn	$4,700	$8,600	$14,300	$22,200
		292/175 2dr Sunliner Conv	$17,600	$27,300	$40,700	$54,400
		352/220 2dr Sunliner Conv	$20,200	$28,900	$46,700	$62,600
		390/300 2dr Sunliner Conv	$20,900	$30,900	$48,800	$65,200
		390/375 2dr Sunliner Conv	$22,100	$36,000	$50,800	$68,000

-20% for 6-cyl. +15% for factory a/c.

Year	Model	Body Style	4	3	2	1
1961	Country Sedan	292/175 4dr Stn Wgn 6P	$6,300	$9,400	$13,000	$18,500
		352/220 4dr Stn Wgn 6P	$7,400	$10,800	$14,800	$21,400
		390/375 4dr Stn Wgn 6P	$8,000	$11,700	$16,300	$23,200
				-20% for 6-cyl. +15% for factory a/c.		
1961	Country Squire	292/175 4dr Stn Wgn 6P	$6,200	$9,300	$12,700	$18,200
		352/220 4dr Stn Wgn 6P	$7,200	$10,700	$14,600	$20,900
		390/300 4dr Stn Wgn 6P	$7,600	$11,100	$15,300	$21,800
		390/375 4dr Stn Wgn 6P	$7,800	$11,500	$15,900	$22,800
				-20% for 6-cyl. +15% for factory a/c.		
1961	Thunderbird	390/300 2dr Cpe	$5,400	$10,300	$19,600	$28,600
		390/300 2dr Conv	$13,300	$23,400	$37,100	$47,300
		390/300 2dr Indy Pace Car Conv	$20,700	$39,700	$54,100	$70,700
					+10% for factory a/c.	
1962	Falcon	144/85 2dr Sdn	$5,600	$9,300	$13,200	$17,700
		144/85 2dr Futura Sdn	$6,600	$10,500	$15,500	$21,300
		144/85 4dr Sdn	$3,100	$4,700	$9,800	$14,500
		144/85 2dr Wgn	$5,400	$8,900	$12,200	$16,500
		144/85 4dr Wgn	$3,300	$4,800	$11,800	$13,800
		144/85 4dr Squire Wgn	$4,900	$8,500	$12,000	$15,800
1962	Fairlane	221/145 2dr Clb Sdn	$4,200	$6,700	$9,300	$12,500
		221/145 2dr 500 Clb Sdn	$4,300	$7,000	$9,900	$13,300
		221/145 4dr Twn Sdn	$3,500	$5,100	$7,600	$10,100
		221/145 4dr 500 Twn Sdn	$3,800	$5,300	$8,000	$10,900
		221/145 2dr 500 Spt Cpe	$4,900	$7,100	$10,300	$15,700
						-20% for 6-cyl.
1962	Galaxie	292/170 2dr Clb Sdn	$3,700	$5,900	$8,300	$11,200
		352/220 2dr Clb Sdn	$4,100	$6,500	$9,100	$12,200
		390/300 2dr Clb Sdn	$4,300	$6,800	$9,400	$12,800
		390/330 2dr Clb Sdn	$4,500	$7,000	$9,700	$13,400

Ford

Year	Model	Body Style	4	3	2	1
		406/385 2dr Clb Sdn	$5,400	$8,600	$11,800	$16,100
		406/405 2dr Clb Sdn	$7,300	$11,600	$15,800	$21,600
		292/170 2dr 500 Clb Sdn	$4,100	$6,700	$9,100	$12,200
		352/220 2dr 500 Clb Sdn	$4,500	$7,400	$9,900	$13,400
		390/300 2dr 500 Clb Sdn	$4,700	$7,700	$10,300	$14,000
		390/330 2dr 500 Clb Sdn	$5,000	$8,100	$10,800	$14,600
		406/385 2dr 500 Clb Sdn	$5,900	$9,800	$13,000	$17,500
		406/405 2dr 500 Clb Sdn	$8,000	$13,000	$17,600	$23,600
		292/170 4dr Twn Sdn	$2,800	$3,900	$6,300	$8,600
		352/220 4dr Twn Sdn	$3,100	$4,300	$6,900	$9,400
		390/300 4dr Twn Sdn	$3,200	$4,500	$7,200	$9,900
		390/330 4dr Twn Sdn	$3,300	$4,700	$7,500	$10,400
		406/385 4dr Twn Sdn	$4,000	$5,600	$9,200	$12,500
		406/405 4dr Twn Sdn	$5,400	$7,600	$12,200	$16,700
		292/170 4dr 500 Twn Sdn	$3,000	$4,100	$6,500	$9,000
		352/220 4dr 500 Twn Sdn	$3,200	$4,500	$7,100	$10,000
		390/300 4dr 500 Twn Sdn	$3,400	$4,700	$7,400	$10,500
		390/330 4dr 500 Twn Sdn	$3,500	$5,000	$7,700	$10,900
		406/385 4dr 500 Twn Sdn	$4,200	$5,900	$9,500	$13,100
		406/405 4dr 500 Twn Sdn	$5,700	$8,000	$12,600	$17,600
		292/170 2dr 500 Clb Vic Hdtp Sdn	$5,800	$9,200	$12,200	$16,600
		352/220 2dr 500 Clb Vic Hdtp Sdn	$6,400	$10,000	$13,500	$18,300
		390/300 2dr 500 Clb Vic Hdtp Sdn	$6,700	$10,400	$14,100	$19,200
		390/330 2dr 500 Clb Vic Hdtp Sdn	$6,800	$10,900	$14,700	$20,000
		406/385 2dr 500 Clb Vic Hdtp Sdn	$8,300	$13,100	$17,800	$23,900
		406/405 2dr 500 Clb Vic Hdtp Sdn	$11,400	$18,200	$28,700	$40,400

Year	Model	Body Style	4	3	2	1
		292/170 2dr 500 XL Clb Vic Hdtp Sdn	$9,400	$15,000	$20,700	$27,700
		352/220 2dr 500 XL Clb Vic Hdtp Sdn	$10,300	$16,600	$22,800	$30,600
		390/300 2dr 500 XL Clb Vic Hdtp Sdn	$10,800	$17,400	$23,800	$31,900
		390/330 2dr 500 XL Clb Vic Hdtp Sdn	$11,200	$18,100	$24,900	$33,200
		406/385 2dr 500 XL Clb Vic Hdtp Sdn	$13,500	$21,700	$30,000	$40,000
		406/405 2dr 500 XL Clb Vic Hdtp Sdn	$18,200	$29,300	$40,000	$53,700
		292/170 4dr 500 Twn Vic Hdtp Sdn	$3,300	$4,700	$7,200	$9,800
		352/220 4dr 500 Twn Vic Hdtp Sdn	$3,700	$5,100	$8,000	$10,900
		390/300 4dr 500 Twn Vic Hdtp Sdn	$3,800	$5,300	$8,500	$11,300
		390/330 4dr 500 Twn Vic Hdtp Sdn	$4,000	$5,700	$8,700	$11,800
		406/385 4dr 500 Twn Vic Hdtp Sdn	$4,900	$6,800	$10,500	$14,200
		406/405 4dr 500 Twn Vic Hdtp Sdn	$6,500	$9,200	$14,000	$19,100
		292/170 2dr 500 Sunliner Conv	$15,300	$24,700	$34,700	$46,600
		352/220 2dr 500 Sunliner Conv	$16,800	$27,200	$38,200	$51,300
		390/300 2dr 500 Sunliner Conv	$17,600	$28,400	$40,000	$53,600
		390/330 2dr 500 Sunliner Conv	$18,400	$29,500	$41,800	$55,900
		406/385 2dr 500 Sunliner Conv	$22,100	$35,600	$50,300	$67,300
		406/405 2dr 500 Sunliner Conv	$29,700	$48,000	$67,700	$90,600
		292/170 2dr 500 XL Sunliner Conv	$16,600	$27,300	$38,200	$51,200
		352/220 2dr 500 XL Sunliner Conv	$18,400	$29,900	$42,000	$56,200
		390/300 2dr 500 XL Sunliner Conv	$19,300	$31,200	$43,800	$58,900
		390/330 2dr 500 XL Sunliner Conv	$20,000	$32,700	$45,800	$61,500
		406/385 2dr 500 XL Sunliner Conv	$24,000	$39,200	$55,200	$73,900

Ford

Year	Model	Body Style	4	3	2	1
		406/405 2dr 500 XL Sunliner Conv	$32,400	$53,000	$74,300	$99,600
				-20% for 6-cyl. +15% for factory a/c.		
1962	Ranch Wagon	292/170 4dr Wgn	$5,400	$8,600	$11,800	$15,800
		352/220 4dr Wgn	$5,900	$9,500	$12,900	$17,300
		390/300 4dr Wgn	$6,300	$10,000	$13,500	$18,200
		390/330 4dr Wgn	$6,500	$10,400	$14,100	$18,900
		406/385 4dr Wgn	$7,100	$11,100	$15,300	$20,500
		406/405 4dr Wgn	$9,400	$15,100	$20,700	$27,700
				-20% for 6-cyl. +15% for factory a/c.		
1962	Country Sedan	292/170 4dr Stn Wgn 6P	$5,500	$8,700	$12,000	$16,100
		390/300 4dr Stn Wgn 6P	$6,400	$10,100	$13,700	$18,500
		390/330 4dr Stn Wgn 6P	$6,600	$10,500	$14,400	$19,300
		406/385 4dr Stn Wgn 6P	$7,300	$11,300	$15,600	$20,900
		406/405 4dr Stn Wgn 6P	$9,600	$15,300	$21,000	$28,200
		352/220 4dr Stn Wgn 9P	$6,000	$9,600	$13,200	$17,800
				-20% for 6-cyl. +15% for factory a/c.		
1962	Country Squire	292/170 4dr Stn Wgn 6P	$5,400	$8,600	$11,800	$15,800
		352/220 4dr Stn Wgn 6P	$5,900	$9,500	$12,900	$17,300
		390/300 4dr Stn Wgn 6P	$6,300	$10,000	$13,500	$18,200
		390/330 4dr Stn Wgn 6P	$6,500	$10,400	$14,100	$18,900
		406/385 4dr Stn Wgn 6P	$7,100	$11,100	$15,300	$20,500
		406/405 4dr Stn Wgn 6P	$9,400	$15,100	$20,700	$27,700
				-20% for 6-cyl. +15% for factory a/c.		
1962	Thunderbird	390/300 2dr Cpe	$4,300	$7,600	$18,200	$31,200
		390/300 2dr Lan Cpe	$5,900	$8,900	$22,400	$33,800
		390/300 2dr Conv	$15,900	$25,700	$42,300	$54,000
		390/300 2dr Spt Rdstr	$24,300	$34,300	$60,600	$83,700
					+10% for factory a/c.	
1962	Cortina	2dr Mk I Sdn	$6,200	$10,700	$18,300	$27,200
1963	Cortina	2dr Mk I Sdn	$6,200	$10,700	$18,300	$27,200
1963	Falcon	170/101 2dr Futura Spt Conv	$11,600	$19,800	$27,400	$36,300

Year	Model	Body Style	4	3	2	1
		144/85 2dr Sdn	$4,000	$7,900	$14,900	$21,600
		260/164 2dr Sdn	$4,800	$9,400	$15,600	$25,900
		144/85 2dr Futura Sdn	$5,700	$10,300	$15,300	$23,500
		260/164 2dr Futura Sdn	$7,000	$12,500	$17,400	$28,000
		260/164 2dr Futura Hdtp Sdn	$7,000	$12,700	$17,000	$23,800
		144/85 2dr Futura Spt Hdtp Sdn	$7,300	$13,300	$17,900	$24,000
		260/164 2dr Futura Spt Hdtp Sdn	$8,300	$15,900	$21,300	$28,700
		260/164 2dr Sprint Hdtp Sdn	$11,400	$19,000	$25,500	$33,600
		144/85 4dr Sdn	$3,400	$6,400	$11,400	$16,700
		260/164 4dr Sdn	$4,100	$7,500	$13,900	$19,900
		144/85 4dr Futura Sdn	$3,600	$6,900	$14,300	$19,000
		260/164 4dr Futura Sdn	$4,400	$8,200	$15,600	$22,800
		144/85 2dr Futura Hdtp Sdn	$5,800	$10,500	$14,200	$19,900
		144/85 2dr Wgn	$5,300	$9,200	$14,000	$19,200
		260/164 2dr Wgn	$6,500	$11,200	$16,800	$23,000
		144/85 2dr Dlx Wgn	$5,400	$10,300	$14,600	$20,100
		260/164 2dr Dlx Wgn	$6,700	$12,500	$17,500	$24,000
		144/85 4dr Wgn	$4,600	$7,800	$11,900	$16,300
		260/164 4dr Wgn	$5,300	$9,400	$14,200	$19,500
		144/85 4dr Dlx Wgn	$4,600	$8,300	$12,300	$17,000
		260/164 4dr Dlx Wgn	$5,400	$10,100	$14,600	$20,300
		144/85 4dr Squire Wgn	$4,800	$8,900	$12,900	$17,600
		260/164 4dr Squire Wgn	$5,800	$10,600	$15,500	$21,100
		144/85 2dr Futura Conv	$9,700	$16,800	$24,000	$32,300
		260/164 2dr Futura Conv	$11,500	$20,500	$28,800	$38,700
		260/164 2dr Sprint Conv	$12,900	$23,300	$32,100	$43,400
		260/164 2dr Futura Spt Conv	$14,100	$23,800	$33,100	$41,600
1963	Fairlane	221/145 2dr 500 Hdtp Cpe	$7,400	$11,700	$16,000	$21,200
		221/145 2dr 500 Spt Cpe	$7,400	$12,100	$16,400	$22,900

Ford

Year	Model	Body Style	4	3	2	1
		221/145 2dr Sdn	$4,300	$7,000	$10,000	$13,300
		221/145 4dr 500 Squire Wgn	$7,600	$12,200	$16,700	$22,200
		221/145 4dr Sdn	$3,600	$5,300	$7,400	$10,300
		289/271 2dr 500 Spt Cpe	$10,200	$16,200	$22,100	$31,100
		289/271 2dr Sdn	$5,900	$9,600	$13,500	$17,800
		289/271 2dr 500 Hdtp Cpe	$10,000	$15,900	$21,500	$28,800
		289/271 4dr Sdn	$4,900	$7,100	$10,300	$14,100
		221/145 2dr 500 Sdn	$4,400	$7,100	$10,200	$13,500
		289/271 2dr 500 Sdn	$6,000	$9,800	$13,800	$18,000
		221/145 4dr 500 Sdn	$4,200	$6,200	$8,300	$11,800
		289/271 4dr 500 Sdn	$5,700	$8,500	$11,400	$15,800
		221/145 4dr Rnch Wgn	$5,800	$9,300	$13,000	$17,200
		289/271 4dr Rnch Wgn	$7,800	$12,800	$17,500	$23,100
		221/145 4dr Cstm Rnch Wgn	$6,400	$10,500	$14,400	$19,100
		289/271 4dr Cstm Rnch Wgn	$8,900	$14,000	$19,200	$25,600
		289/271 4dr 500 Squire Wgn	$10,500	$16,300	$22,400	$30,000
1963	Galaxie	260/164 2dr 500 Hdtp Cpe	$7,400	$11,700	$16,100	$21,200
		260/164 2dr 500 Sdn	$6,400	$10,000	$13,600	$18,300
		260/164 2dr Sdn	$4,100	$6,700	$9,100	$12,200
		260/164 4dr 500 Country Squire Stn Wgn 6P	$6,500	$10,300	$13,800	$19,000
		260/164 4dr 500 Sdn	$3,500	$5,500	$7,700	$11,200
		260/164 4dr Ctry Sdn Stn Wgn 6P	$5,200	$8,400	$11,400	$15,300
		352/220 2dr 500 Hdtp Cpe	$8,100	$12,900	$17,700	$23,500
		352/220 2dr 500 Hdtp Sdn	$7,400	$11,700	$16,100	$21,300
		352/220 2dr 500 Sdn	$6,900	$11,100	$14,900	$20,200
		352/220 2dr 500 Sunliner Conv	$12,200	$19,700	$28,100	$37,300
		352/220 2dr 500 XL Fstbk	$10,600	$17,200	$23,800	$31,800
		352/220 2dr 500 XL Hdtp Cpe	$10,200	$16,500	$22,700	$30,400

Year	Model	Body Style	4	3	2	1
		352/220 2dr 500 XL Sunliner Conv	$15,900	$25,600	$36,200	$48,200
		352/220 2dr Sdn	$4,500	$7,400	$9,900	$13,400
		352/220 4dr 500 Country Squire Stn Wgn 6P	$7,200	$11,200	$15,200	$20,800
		352/220 4dr 500 Sdn	$3,900	$6,100	$8,600	$12,200
		352/220 4dr Sdn	$3,400	$5,900	$8,100	$11,300
		390/300 2dr 500 Hdtp Cpe	$8,500	$13,400	$18,500	$24,500
		390/300 2dr 500 Sdn	$7,300	$11,500	$15,800	$21,000
		390/300 4dr 500 Country Squire Stn Wgn 6P	$7,500	$11,700	$15,900	$21,800
		390/300 4dr 500 Sdn	$4,100	$6,400	$9,000	$12,800
		390/300 4dr Ctry Sdn Stn Wgn 6P	$5,900	$9,800	$13,200	$17,500
		390/330 2dr 500 Hdtp Cpe	$8,800	$14,100	$19,300	$25,600
		390/330 2dr 500 Sdn	$7,600	$12,100	$16,400	$22,000
		390/330 4dr 500 Country Squire Stn Wgn 6P	$7,700	$12,200	$16,600	$22,800
		390/330 4dr 500 Sdn	$4,200	$6,700	$9,400	$13,400
		390/330 4dr Ctry Sdn Stn Wgn 6P	$6,300	$10,200	$13,700	$18,300
		406/385 2dr 500 Hdtp Cpe	$10,600	$17,000	$23,200	$30,800
		406/385 2dr 500 Sdn	$9,100	$14,500	$19,800	$26,500
		406/385 4dr 500 Country Squire Stn Wgn 6P	$8,400	$13,300	$18,100	$24,700
		406/385 4dr 500 Sdn	$5,100	$8,000	$11,200	$16,100
		406/385 4dr Ctry Sdn Stn Wgn 6P	$6,900	$10,900	$14,900	$19,800
		406/405 2dr 500 Hdtp Cpe	$14,900	$23,600	$32,300	$44,700
		406/405 2dr 500 Sdn	$12,500	$19,700	$26,900	$36,400
		406/405 4dr 500 Country Squire Stn Wgn 6P	$11,300	$17,800	$24,300	$33,300
		406/405 4dr 500 Sdn	$7,000	$10,800	$15,100	$21,600

Ford

Year	Model	Body Style	4	3	2	1
		406/405 4dr Ctry Sdn Stn Wgn 6P	$9,100	$14,600	$20,200	$26,700
		427/410 2dr 500 Hdtp Cpe	$108,000	$133,000	$159,000	$218,000
		427/425 2dr 500 Hdtp Cpe	$118,000	$144,000	$168,000	$224,000
		390/300 2dr Sdn	$4,700	$7,700	$10,300	$14,000
		390/330 2dr Sdn	$5,000	$8,100	$10,800	$14,600
		406/385 2dr Sdn	$5,900	$9,800	$13,000	$17,500
		406/405 2dr Sdn	$8,400	$13,600	$18,900	$25,500
		260/164 4dr Sdn	$3,200	$5,300	$7,300	$10,400
		390/300 4dr Sdn	$3,600	$6,100	$8,600	$11,900
		390/330 4dr Sdn	$3,800	$6,400	$8,900	$12,300
		406/385 4dr Sdn	$4,600	$7,700	$10,500	$14,900
		406/405 4dr Sdn	$6,100	$10,500	$14,200	$20,000
		352/220 4dr Ctry Sdn Stn Wgn 6P	$5,700	$9,300	$12,600	$16,800
		260/164 2dr 500 XL Fstbk	$9,600	$15,700	$21,500	$28,900
		390/300 2dr 500 XL Fstbk	$11,100	$18,000	$24,800	$33,100
		390/330 2dr 500 XL Fstbk	$11,500	$18,800	$25,900	$34,600
		406/385 2dr 500 XL Fstbk	$13,900	$22,600	$31,100	$41,500
		406/405 2dr 500 XL Fstbk	$25,500	$36,200	$58,500	$72,500
		427/425 2dr 500 XL Fstbk	$44,200	$63,600	$77,500	$96,800
		260/164 2dr 500 Hdtp Sdn	$6,800	$10,700	$14,500	$19,400
		390/300 2dr 500 Hdtp Sdn	$7,700	$12,300	$16,700	$22,300
		390/330 2dr 500 Clb Vic Hdtp Sdn	$8,000	$12,800	$17,500	$23,400
		406/385 2dr 500 Clb Vic Hdtp Sdn	$9,600	$15,500	$21,100	$28,100
		406/405 2dr 500 Hdtp Sdn	$13,000	$20,800	$29,600	$42,300
		260/164 2dr 500 XL Hdtp Cpe	$9,300	$14,900	$20,600	$27,600
		390/300 2dr 500 XL Hdtp Cpe	$10,700	$17,300	$23,800	$31,800
		390/330 2dr 500 XL Hdtp Cpe	$11,100	$17,900	$24,800	$33,100
		390/340 2dr 500 XL Hdtp Cpe	$12,100	$19,400	$26,800	$35,900
		406/405 2dr 500 XL Hdtp Cpe	$18,000	$29,000	$39,800	$53,500
		260/164 4dr 500 XL Hdtp Sdn	$5,000	$7,500	$9,400	$13,500

Year	Model	Body Style	4	3	2	1
		390/300 4dr 500 XL Hdtp Sdn	$5,800	$8,600	$10,700	$15,500
		406/385 4dr 500 XL Hdtp Sdn	$7,300	$10,700	$13,400	$19,400
		406/405 4dr 500 XL Hdtp Sdn	$9,600	$14,500	$18,100	$26,200
		260/164 2dr 500 Sunliner Conv	$11,200	$18,000	$25,600	$33,900
		390/300 2dr 500 Sunliner Conv	$12,800	$20,700	$29,100	$39,000
		390/330 2dr 500 Sunliner Conv	$13,300	$21,600	$30,500	$40,600
		406/385 2dr 500 Sunliner Conv	$16,100	$26,000	$36,700	$48,900
		406/405 2dr 500 Sunliner Conv	$21,600	$34,700	$49,200	$65,700
		260/164 2dr 500 XL Sunliner Conv	$14,500	$23,400	$32,900	$43,800
		390/300 2dr 500 XL Sunliner Conv	$16,600	$26,800	$37,800	$50,300
		390/330 2dr 500 XL Sunliner Conv	$17,400	$28,000	$39,400	$52,600
		406/385 2dr 500 XL Sunliner Conv	$20,800	$33,500	$47,500	$63,200
		406/405 2dr 500 XL Sunliner Conv	$27,900	$45,400	$64,000	$85,300
				-20% for 6-cyl. +15% for factory a/c.		
1963	Thunderbird	390/300 2dr Cpe	$6,000	$11,200	$19,400	$31,600
		390/300 2dr Lan Cpe	$7,400	$11,600	$20,800	$34,500
		390/300 2dr Spt Rdstr	$26,400	$38,300	$62,000	$86,300
		390/340 2dr Spt Rdstr	$35,400	$51,200	$85,200	$121,000
		390/300 2dr Conv	$17,000	$26,700	$37,100	$54,700
		390/340 2dr Conv	$20,100	$31,500	$41,900	$66,800
					+10% for factory a/c.	
1963	GT40	2dr Prototype Cpe	$4.25 mil	$4.9 mil	$5.8 mil	$8 mil
		2dr Prototype Rdstr	$4.7 mil	$5.6 mil	$6.8 mil	$8.1 mil
		Note: For non-continuation GT40s, individual history and originality of chassis, body, and components dictate value more than condition.				
1964	Cortina	2dr Mk I Sdn	$6,200	$10,700	$18,300	$27,200
1964	Falcon	144/85 2dr Sdn	$4,600	$8,000	$10,800	$15,200
		260/164 2dr Sdn	$5,700	$10,500	$13,800	$21,300
		170/101 2dr Futura Sdn	$5,700	$9,800	$13,600	$19,000

Year	Model	Body Style	4	3	2	1
		260/164 2dr Futura Sdn	$6,900	$12,000	$16,000	$22,800
		144/85 4dr Sdn	$3,700	$6,100	$7,300	$12,100
		260/164 4dr Sdn	$4,500	$7,600	$9,200	$14,400
		170/101 4dr Futura Sdn	$4,300	$6,500	$8,600	$13,300
		260/164 4dr Futura Sdn	$5,000	$7,700	$9,400	$15,800
		260/164 2dr Wgn	$6,600	$11,700	$16,200	$23,200
		144/85 4dr Wgn	$4,900	$8,000	$11,100	$15,900
		260/164 4dr Wgn	$5,800	$9,600	$13,400	$19,100
		144/85 4dr Dlx Wgn	$5,000	$8,900	$12,600	$18,800
		260/164 4dr Dlx Wgn	$6,200	$10,700	$15,000	$22,400
		170/101 2dr Futura Hdtp Cpe	$6,900	$10,000	$13,900	$19,900
		260/164 2dr Futura Hdtp Cpe	$7,200	$12,200	$16,600	$23,700
		170/101 2dr Futura Spt Hdtp Cpe	$7,500	$13,600	$18,900	$26,000
		260/164 2dr Futura Spt Hdtp Cpe	$9,200	$16,300	$22,500	$31,200
		260/164 2dr Sprint Hdtp Cpe	$10,100	$18,100	$25,000	$34,600
		170/101 2dr Futura Conv	$10,300	$15,800	$22,700	$33,000
		260/164 2dr Futura Conv	$12,100	$19,100	$27,500	$39,200
		170/101 2dr Futura Spt Conv	$12,500	$19,600	$26,700	$39,100
		260/164 2dr Futura Spt Conv	$15,100	$23,600	$32,100	$41,900
		260/164 2dr Sprint Conv	$14,100	$22,800	$31,200	$43,200
1964	Fairlane	260/164 2dr Sdn	$4,300	$7,000	$9,900	$13,300
		289/271 2dr Sdn	$5,900	$9,600	$13,400	$17,800
		260/164 2dr 500 Sdn	$4,400	$7,100	$10,100	$13,500
		289/271 2dr 500 Sdn	$6,000	$9,800	$13,600	$18,000
		260/164 4dr Sdn	$3,300	$5,500	$7,300	$9,700
		289/271 4dr Sdn	$4,400	$7,400	$10,100	$13,300
		260/164 4dr 500 Sdn	$3,800	$6,000	$8,500	$10,500
		289/271 4dr 500 Sdn	$5,100	$8,300	$11,700	$14,400
		260/164 4dr Rnch Wgn	$4,700	$7,600	$10,500	$14,300

Year	Model	Body Style	4	3	2	1
		289/271 4dr Rnch Wgn	$6,400	$10,500	$14,300	$19,100
		260/164 4dr Cstm Rnch Wgn	$6,100	$9,800	$13,500	$17,800
		289/271 4dr Cstm Rnch Wgn	$8,400	$13,200	$18,200	$23,800
		260/164 2dr 500 Hdtp Cpe	$6,300	$10,000	$13,800	$18,100
		289/271 2dr 500 Hdtp Cpe	$8,800	$13,500	$18,600	$24,400
		260/164 2dr 500 Hdtp Spt Cpe	$7,600	$12,200	$16,700	$23,200
		289/271 2dr 500 Hdtp Spt Cpe	$10,300	$16,400	$22,400	$31,700
		427/425 2dr Thunderbolt Hdtp Cpe	$167,000	$204,000	$263,000	$309,000
1964	Custom	289/195 2dr Sdn	$4,400	$7,900	$10,700	$14,300
		352/250 2dr Sdn	$5,400	$8,700	$11,700	$15,800
		390/300 2dr Sdn	$4,900	$9,600	$12,700	$17,100
		289/195 2dr 500 Sdn	$5,500	$8,700	$11,200	$15,500
		352/250 2dr 500 Sdn	$6,600	$9,700	$12,400	$17,000
		390/300 2dr 500 Sdn	$6,000	$10,600	$13,500	$18,500
		289/195 4dr Sdn	$3,700	$5,100	$8,300	$12,300
		352/250 4dr Sdn	$4,400	$5,700	$9,200	$13,400
		390/300 4dr Sdn	$4,000	$6,100	$10,100	$14,600
		289/195 4dr 500 Sdn	$3,900	$5,600	$8,800	$13,000
		352/250 4dr 500 Sdn	$4,700	$6,100	$9,900	$14,300
		390/300 4dr 500 Sdn	$4,300	$6,700	$10,700	$15,600
						-20% for 6-cyl.
1964	Galaxie 500	289/195 2dr Sdn	$5,200	$8,600	$11,800	$15,600
		352/250 2dr Sdn	$5,800	$9,400	$12,800	$17,300
		390/300 2dr Sdn	$5,300	$8,600	$11,700	$15,800
		427/425 2dr Sdn	$29,700	$46,900	$64,900	$86,800
		427/425 2dr Lightweight Sdn	$139,000	$162,000	$194,000	$260,000
		289/195 4dr Sdn	$3,500	$6,400	$8,600	$12,400
		352/250 4dr Sdn	$4,200	$7,600	$10,200	$14,900
		390/300 4dr Sdn	$3,900	$7,000	$9,400	$13,700
		289/195 4dr Ctry Sqr Stn Wgn 6P	$5,600	$9,000	$12,200	$16,400
		352/250 4dr Ctry Sqr Stn Wgn 6P	$6,900	$10,800	$14,900	$20,600

Ford

Year	Model	Body Style	4	3	2	1
		390/300 4dr Ctry Sqr Stn Wgn 6P	$6,100	$9,900	$13,400	$18,200
		289/195 2dr Hdtp Cpe	$6,800	$10,900	$14,700	$20,300
		352/250 2dr Hdtp Cpe	$7,600	$12,200	$16,300	$22,000
		390/300 2dr Hdtp Cpe	$6,900	$11,200	$14,900	$20,200
		289/195 2dr XL Hdtp Cpe	$11,200	$17,700	$24,800	$32,900
		352/250 2dr XL Hdtp Cpe	$13,300	$21,200	$29,600	$39,400
		390/300 2dr XL Hdtp Cpe	$12,300	$19,400	$27,300	$36,200
		289/195 4dr Hdtp Sdn	$3,800	$6,900	$9,100	$12,800
		352/250 4dr Hdtp Sdn	$4,600	$8,500	$10,800	$15,300
		390/300 4dr Hdtp Sdn	$4,200	$7,600	$9,900	$14,100
		289/195 4dr XL Hdtp Sdn	$4,600	$7,400	$9,600	$13,900
		352/250 4dr XL Hdtp Sdn	$5,500	$8,900	$11,600	$16,700
		390/300 4dr XL Hdtp Sdn	$5,000	$8,200	$10,600	$15,200
		289/195 2dr Conv	$13,600	$22,000	$31,000	$41,500
		352/250 2dr Conv	$16,400	$26,500	$37,100	$49,900
		390/300 2dr Conv	$15,000	$24,300	$34,000	$45,600
		289/195 2dr XL Conv	$14,900	$24,300	$34,100	$45,400
		352/250 2dr XL Conv	$17,900	$29,200	$41,000	$54,600
		390/300 2dr XL Conv	$16,400	$26,700	$37,500	$50,000
						-20% for 6-cyl.
1964	Thunderbird	390/300 2dr Cpe	$4,600	$9,500	$15,200	$21,900
		390/300 2dr Lan Cpe	$6,100	$11,300	$17,400	$24,300
		390/300 2dr Conv	$14,100	$22,300	$34,900	$46,300
						+10% for factory a/c.
1965	Falcon	170/105 2dr Sdn	$4,700	$7,700	$13,200	$17,000
		289/200 2dr Sdn	$5,600	$9,100	$14,200	$17,600
		170/105 2dr Futura Sdn	$5,700	$9,300	$14,800	$20,800
		289/200 2dr Futura Sdn	$7,000	$11,200	$17,900	$24,800
		170/105 4dr Sdn	$3,700	$4,100	$8,000	$11,400

Year	Model	Body Style	4	3	2	1
		289/200 4dr Sdn	$4,700	$5,900	$11,800	$12,900
		170/105 4dr Futura Sdn	$4,500	$5,800	$12,200	$17,300
		289/200 4dr Futura Sdn	$5,300	$6,800	$14,500	$20,800
		200/120 2dr Wgn	$6,000	$9,600	$13,100	$19,200
		289/200 2dr Wgn	$7,100	$11,600	$15,500	$23,000
		200/120 4dr Wgn	$5,400	$8,500	$11,900	$16,100
		289/200 4dr Wgn	$6,200	$10,300	$14,100	$19,400
		170/105 2dr Futura Wgn	$5,900	$9,900	$13,300	$19,300
		170/105 4dr Futura Wgn	$5,500	$8,200	$10,800	$16,100
		289/200 4dr Futura Wgn	$6,700	$9,800	$13,100	$19,300
		200/120 4dr Squire Wgn	$5,600	$9,100	$12,500	$18,700
		289/200 4dr Squire Wgn	$6,800	$11,000	$15,000	$22,400
		170/105 2dr Futura Hdtp Cpe	$6,100	$9,900	$15,400	$20,600
		289/200 2dr Futura Hdtp Cpe	$7,400	$11,900	$17,900	$25,000
		289/200 2dr Sprint Hdtp Sdn	$10,000	$15,500	$21,400	$31,600
		170/105 2dr Futura Conv 5P	$10,400	$15,500	$23,800	$33,800
		289/200 2dr Futura Conv 5P	$13,600	$19,400	$28,300	$40,000
		200/120 2dr Futura Sprint Conv	$15,300	$23,200	$31,900	$44,700
1965	Mustang	260/164 2dr Cpe	$9,000	$15,100	$23,100	$27,400
		289/200 2dr Cpe	$9,700	$16,400	$23,700	$28,400
		289/210 2dr Cpe	$10,600	$17,900	$24,500	$32,700
		289/225 2dr Cpe	$11,500	$19,200	$26,300	$39,000
		289/271 2dr Cpe	$13,100	$23,400	$34,000	$47,500
		289/225 2dr GT Cpe	$13,600	$24,900	$37,200	$49,000
		289/271 2dr GT Cpe	$20,000	$36,500	$44,000	$56,500
		260/164 2dr Fstbk	$14,400	$26,600	$37,900	$46,600
		289/200 2dr Fstbk	$15,000	$29,000	$39,200	$48,300
		289/225 2dr Fstbk	$16,400	$31,300	$42,800	$58,300
		289/271 2dr Fstbk	$19,600	$32,400	$46,200	$63,100
		289/225 2dr GT Fstbk	$20,200	$32,800	$44,000	$61,100
		289/271 2dr GT Fstbk	$32,200	$44,200	$64,800	$86,200

Ford

Year	Model	Body Style	4	3	2	1
		289/200 2dr Conv	$18,900	$29,600	$37,600	$49,800
		260/164 2dr Conv	$16,100	$24,900	$36,800	$48,800
		289/210 2dr Conv	$20,000	$31,300	$39,000	$54,000
		289/225 2dr Conv	$20,900	$32,800	$42,100	$62,100
		289/271 2dr Conv	$24,600	$34,500	$44,300	$69,000
		289/225 2dr GT Conv	$26,700	$34,600	$44,700	$67,400
		289/271 2dr GT Conv	$48,300	$58,600	$69,900	$92,100
		+10% for 4-spd. -25% for 6-cyl. -10% for auto. +6% for a/c.				
1965	Fairlane	289/200 2dr Sdn	$4,700	$7,400	$10,400	$14,200
		289/225 2dr Sdn	$5,800	$9,100	$12,500	$17,000
		289/271 2dr Sdn	$6,500	$10,300	$13,900	$19,200
		289/200 2dr 500 Sdn	$4,700	$7,700	$10,500	$14,300
		289/225 2dr 500 Sdn	$5,800	$9,500	$12,600	$17,100
		289/271 2dr 500 Sdn	$6,500	$10,600	$14,100	$19,300
		289/200 4dr Sdn	$3,200	$5,000	$7,400	$10,100
		289/225 4dr Sdn	$3,900	$6,000	$9,100	$12,200
		289/271 4dr Sdn	$4,300	$6,700	$10,300	$13,800
		289/200 4dr 500 Sdn	$3,700	$5,400	$8,100	$10,700
		289/225 4dr 500 Sdn	$4,400	$6,500	$9,900	$13,000
		289/271 4dr 500 Sdn	$5,000	$7,300	$11,100	$14,500
		289/200 4dr Rnch Wgn	$4,400	$6,700	$10,000	$16,700
		289/225 4dr Rnch Wgn	$5,200	$7,900	$12,200	$20,000
		289/200 4dr 500 Custom Rnch Wgn	$4,800	$7,600	$11,200	$19,000
		289/225 4dr 500 Custom Rnch Wgn	$5,900	$9,100	$13,300	$22,800
		289/200 2dr 500 Hdtp Cpe	$8,200	$13,100	$17,900	$23,800
		289/225 2dr 500 Hdtp Cpe	$10,000	$15,600	$21,500	$28,700
		289/271 2dr 500 Hdtp Cpe	$11,200	$17,500	$24,200	$32,300
		289/200 2dr 500 Spt Cpe	$8,300	$12,900	$17,800	$25,000
		289/225 2dr 500 Spt Cpe	$10,000	$15,500	$21,300	$30,100
		289/271 2dr 500 Spt Cpe	$11,200	$17,400	$24,000	$34,000

Year	Model	Body Style	4	3	2	1
						-20% for 6-cyl.
1965	Custom	289/200 2dr Sdn	$4,200	$7,500	$9,400	$14,400
		352/250 2dr Sdn	$4,500	$8,200	$10,200	$15,800
		390/300 2dr Sdn	$4,600	$8,400	$10,300	$16,100
		390/330 2dr Sdn	$5,400	$9,600	$11,600	$18,000
		427/425 2dr Sdn	$42,600	$54,400	$65,400	$80,600
		289/200 2dr 500 Sdn	$4,700	$8,200	$10,200	$15,300
		352/250 2dr 500 Sdn	$5,300	$9,000	$11,000	$16,700
		390/300 2dr 500 Sdn	$5,400	$9,100	$11,200	$17,000
		390/330 2dr 500 Sdn	$6,000	$10,400	$12,800	$19,100
		427/425 2dr 500 Sdn	$47,800	$60,200	$71,300	$85,700
		289/200 4dr Sdn	$3,100	$5,300	$7,600	$12,600
		352/250 4dr Sdn	$3,400	$5,700	$8,200	$13,700
		390/300 4dr Sdn	$3,400	$5,800	$8,400	$14,000
		390/330 4dr Sdn	$3,900	$6,600	$9,700	$15,800
		427/425 4dr Sdn	$22,000	$30,000	$41,700	$46,600
		289/200 4dr 500 Sdn	$3,700	$6,200	$8,900	$14,000
		352/250 4dr 500 Sdn	$4,000	$6,700	$9,800	$15,300
		390/300 4dr 500 Sdn	$4,100	$6,800	$10,000	$15,600
		390/330 4dr 500 Sdn	$4,500	$7,700	$11,200	$17,500
		427/425 4dr 500 Sdn	$23,100	$31,400	$42,800	$47,800
						-20% for 6-cyl. +10% for 4-spd.
1965	Galaxie 500	289/200 4dr Ctry Sqr Wgn	$5,700	$9,400	$13,100	$19,100
		289/200 2dr Hdtp Cpe	$6,600	$10,300	$14,100	$19,100
		352/250 2dr Hdtp Cpe	$7,200	$11,300	$15,300	$20,700
		390/300 2dr Hdtp Cpe	$7,900	$12,100	$16,400	$22,200
		390/330 2dr Hdtp Cpe	$8,700	$13,500	$18,700	$25,300
		427/425 2dr Hdtp Cpe	$49,000	$64,300	$76,400	$91,800
		289/200 2dr XL Hdtp Cpe	$9,800	$15,300	$21,000	$28,400
		352/250 2dr XL Hdtp Cpe	$10,700	$16,700	$22,900	$30,900
		390/300 2dr XL Hdtp Cpe	$11,400	$17,800	$24,500	$33,100

Ford

Year	Model	Body Style	4	3	2	1
		390/330 2dr XL Hdtp Cpe	$13,000	$20,400	$28,600	$39,500
		427/425 2dr XL Hdtp Cpe	$54,800	$68,200	$81,500	$98,900
		289/200 2dr LTD Hdtp Cpe	$9,000	$13,800	$19,100	$25,900
		352/250 2dr LTD Hdtp Cpe	$9,700	$15,100	$20,700	$28,200
		390/300 2dr LTD Hdtp Cpe	$10,400	$16,100	$22,300	$30,100
		390/330 2dr LTD Hdtp Cpe	$11,800	$18,400	$25,400	$35,300
		427/425 2dr LTD Hdtp Cpe	$33,800	$45,300	$55,800	$67,100
		289/200 4dr Sdn	$3,800	$6,200	$8,800	$13,700
		352/250 4dr Sdn	$4,100	$6,700	$9,700	$15,000
		390/300 4dr Sdn	$4,200	$6,800	$9,800	$15,200
		390/330 4dr Sdn	$4,800	$7,800	$11,000	$17,200
		427/425 4dr Sdn	$35,800	$47,000	$61,500	$74,900
		289/200 4dr Ctry Sqr Stn Wgn 6P	$5,700	$9,400	$13,100	$19,100
		352/250 4dr Ctry Sqr Stn Wgn 6P	$6,300	$10,200	$14,300	$20,700
		390/300 4dr Ctry Sqr Stn Wgn 6P	$6,400	$10,400	$15,600	$23,100
		390/330 4dr Ctry Sqr Stn Wgn 6P	$7,200	$11,700	$17,300	$25,800
		289/200 4dr Hdtp Sdn	$4,300	$7,200	$9,600	$15,400
		352/250 4dr Hdtp Sdn	$4,800	$7,900	$10,400	$16,800
		390/300 4dr Hdtp Sdn	$4,800	$8,000	$10,600	$17,100
		390/330 4dr Hdtp Sdn	$5,400	$9,200	$12,000	$19,400
		427/425 4dr Hdtp Sdn	$28,100	$36,100	$47,900	$57,400
		289/200 4dr LTD Hdtp Sdn	$5,000	$8,400	$10,600	$16,900
		352/250 4dr LTD Hdtp Sdn	$5,400	$9,300	$11,600	$18,400
		390/300 4dr LTD Hdtp Sdn	$5,500	$9,500	$11,800	$18,800
		390/330 4dr LTD Hdtp Sdn	$6,300	$10,700	$13,200	$21,100
		427/425 4dr LTD Hdtp Sdn	$36,500	$44,300	$52,800	$62,100
		289/200 2dr Conv	$10,400	$16,700	$23,700	$32,000
		352/250 2dr Conv	$11,400	$18,300	$25,800	$34,800

Year	Model	Body Style	4	3	2	1
		390/300 2dr Conv	$12,300	$19,700	$27,800	$37,400
		390/330 2dr Conv	$14,000	$22,900	$31,800	$43,900
		427/425 2dr Conv	$80,000	$96,000	$108,000	$125,000
		289/200 2dr XL Conv	$11,000	$17,600	$24,700	$33,300
		352/250 2dr XL Conv	$12,000	$19,200	$26,900	$36,400
		390/300 2dr XL Conv	$12,800	$20,500	$29,000	$39,000
		390/330 2dr XL Conv	$14,700	$24,600	$36,400	$50,900
		427/425 2dr XL Conv	$92,100	$107,000	$121,000	$139,000
		-20% for 6-cyl. +10% for 4-spd.				
1965	Thunderbird	390/300 2dr Cpe	$4,800	$9,700	$15,100	$20,000
		390/300 2dr Lan Cpe	$5,900	$10,500	$16,300	$22,300
		390/300 2dr Conv	$14,500	$22,500	$37,000	$48,400
		+10% for factory a/c.				
1965	GT40	2dr Prototype Rdstr	$4.7 mil	$5.6 mil	$6.8 mil	$8.1 mil
		2dr Mk I Road Cpe	$2.9 mil	$3.8 mil	$4.5 mil	$5.25 mil
		2dr Mk I Race Cpe	$3.9 mil	$4.4 mil	$5.5 mil	$6.8 mil
		2dr Mk I Alan Mann Ltwt Cpe	$2.7 mil	$3.7 mil	$4.5 mil	$5.25 mil
		Note: For non-continuation GT40s, individual history and originality of chassis, body, and components dictate value more than condition.				
1965	Cortina	2dr Mk I Sdn	$6,200	$10,700	$18,300	$27,200
1966	Falcon	289/200 2dr Sdn	$5,100	$8,700	$11,700	$16,300
		170/105 2dr Futura Clb Cpe	$4,200	$6,800	$9,800	$13,700
		200/120 2dr Futura Clb Cpe	$5,200	$8,400	$11,900	$16,400
		289/200 2dr Futura Clb Cpe	$6,200	$10,000	$14,300	$19,600
		170/105 4dr Sdn	$3,800	$6,300	$8,200	$11,400
		289/200 4dr Sdn	$4,600	$7,500	$9,800	$13,600
		200/120 4dr Futura Sdn	$3,900	$6,000	$8,700	$11,800
		289/200 4dr Futura Sdn	$4,900	$7,200	$10,600	$14,000
		200/120 4dr Wgn	$4,900	$8,100	$10,900	$15,300
		289/200 4dr Wgn	$5,900	$9,700	$13,100	$18,400
		200/120 4dr Futura Wgn	$5,300	$8,500	$12,000	$16,700

Ford

Year	Model	Body Style	4	3	2	1
		289/200 4dr Futura Wgn	$6,400	$10,300	$14,400	$20,000
		200/120 2dr Futura Spt Cpe	$6,100	$9,000	$13,800	$19,000
		289/200 2dr Futura Spt Cpe	$7,200	$11,300	$16,600	$22,700
1966	Mustang	289/200 2dr Cpe	$9,000	$15,300	$22,200	$26,800
		289/225 2dr Cpe	$10,900	$19,500	$28,000	$36,900
		289/225 2dr GT Cpe	$12,900	$24,200	$37,500	$52,300
		289/271 2dr GT Cpe	$18,500	$30,700	$43,900	$59,900
		289/200 2dr Fstbk	$16,800	$30,000	$40,000	$47,300
		289/225 2dr Fstbk	$20,000	$33,500	$42,500	$53,800
		289/271 2dr Fstbk	$21,300	$33,900	$43,400	$61,700
		289/225 2dr GT Fstbk	$20,800	$34,700	$45,600	$61,100
		289/271 2dr GT Fstbk	$31,900	$42,500	$63,700	$84,000
		289/200 2dr Conv	$21,100	$29,500	$34,800	$51,200
		289/225 2dr Conv	$25,000	$34,300	$40,000	$58,800
		289/271 2dr Conv	$26,700	$38,300	$43,900	$65,300
		289/225 2dr GT Conv	$26,300	$36,000	$48,200	$70,400
		289/271 2dr GT Conv	$48,100	$60,200	$74,400	$101,000

+10% for 4-spd. -25% for 6-cyl. -10% for auto. +6% for a/c.

Year	Model	Body Style	4	3	2	1
1966	Fairlane	289/200 2dr Sdn	$5,400	$8,600	$12,100	$16,100
		390/265 2dr Sdn	$6,300	$10,100	$14,000	$18,400
		390/335 2dr Sdn	$7,100	$11,400	$15,700	$21,000
		289/200 2dr 500 Clb Cpe	$6,200	$9,900	$13,600	$18,000
		390/265 2dr 500 Clb Cpe	$7,200	$11,300	$15,600	$20,700
		390/335 2dr 500 Clb Cpe	$8,100	$12,800	$17,700	$23,300
		289/200 4dr Sdn	$3,700	$6,200	$7,700	$13,200
		390/265 4dr Sdn	$4,200	$7,100	$8,900	$15,200
		390/335 4dr Sdn	$4,900	$8,100	$10,200	$17,200
		289/200 4dr 500 Sdn	$4,100	$6,500	$8,100	$13,600
		390/265 4dr 500 Sdn	$4,800	$7,500	$9,500	$15,700
		390/335 4dr 500 Sdn	$5,400	$8,400	$10,800	$17,700
		289/200 4dr Wgn	$5,500	$9,000	$12,400	$16,600
		390/265 4dr Wgn	$6,400	$10,400	$14,300	$19,000
		390/335 4dr Wgn	$7,400	$11,700	$16,100	$21,400

Year	Model	Body Style	4	3	2	1
		289/200 4dr 500 Wgn	$5,900	$9,400	$12,900	$17,700
		390/265 4dr 500 Wgn	$6,900	$10,900	$14,900	$20,300
		390/335 4dr 500 Wgn	$7,900	$12,300	$16,900	$22,800
		289/200 4dr Squire Wgn	$5,900	$9,400	$12,900	$17,800
		390/265 4dr Squire Wgn	$6,900	$10,900	$14,900	$20,400
		390/335 4dr Squire Wgn	$7,900	$12,300	$16,900	$22,900
		289/200 2dr 500 Hdtp Cpe	$8,300	$12,800	$18,700	$24,600
		390/265 2dr 500 Hdtp Cpe	$9,500	$14,800	$21,500	$28,300
		390/335 2dr 500 Hdtp Cpe	$10,800	$16,700	$24,200	$32,200
		427/425 2dr 500 Hdtp Cpe	$44,600	$74,900	$114,000	$138,000
		390/335 2dr 500 GT Hdtp Cpe	$16,200	$25,800	$36,100	$47,500
		289/200 2dr 500 XL Hdtp Cpe	$10,900	$17,800	$24,500	$32,600
		390/265 2dr 500 XL Hdtp Cpe	$12,600	$20,400	$28,200	$37,400
		390/335 2dr 500 XL Hdtp Cpe	$14,200	$23,100	$31,800	$42,200
		390/335 2dr GT Hdtp Cpe	$18,200	$29,400	$40,700	$53,800
		289/200 2dr 500 Conv	$10,400	$16,900	$22,900	$30,700
		390/265 2dr 500 Conv	$11,900	$19,300	$26,500	$35,200
		390/335 2dr 500 Conv	$13,300	$21,800	$29,900	$39,800
		390/335 2dr 500 GT Conv	$19,400	$30,900	$42,600	$56,700
		289/200 2dr 500 XL Conv	$11,300	$18,200	$25,000	$33,300
		390/265 2dr 500 XL Conv	$12,900	$20,800	$28,800	$38,300
		390/335 2dr 500 XL Conv	$14,600	$23,600	$32,400	$43,000

-20% for 6-cyl.

Year	Model	Body Style	4	3	2	1
1966	Custom	289/200 2dr Sdn	$3,900	$6,300	$9,900	$15,400
		352/250 2dr Sdn	$4,100	$6,600	$10,400	$16,200
		427/425 2dr Sdn	$63,700	$73,500	$79,000	$86,400
		289/200 2dr 500 Sdn	$4,300	$6,700	$10,200	$16,000

Ford

Year	Model	Body Style	4	3	2	1
		352/250 2dr 500 Sdn	$4,500	$7,000	$10,700	$16,700
		427/425 2dr 500 Sdn	$69,000	$78,100	$84,900	$94,600
		289/200 4dr Sdn	$3,300	$6,000	$8,500	$14,000
		352/250 4dr Sdn	$3,600	$6,300	$9,100	$14,600
		427/425 4dr Sdn	$37,600	$51,200	$55,400	$64,600
		289/200 4dr 500 Sdn	$3,400	$6,300	$9,300	$14,500
		352/250 4dr 500 Sdn	$3,700	$6,600	$9,700	$15,300
		427/425 4dr 500 Sdn	$41,500	$54,300	$61,600	$72,300
						-20% for 6-cyl.
1966	Galaxie 500	390/315 2dr XL Hdtp Cpe	$11,000	$17,400	$24,000	$32,400
		289/200 2dr Hdtp Cpe	$5,700	$9,200	$12,500	$16,900
		352/250 2dr Hdtp Cpe	$6,000	$9,600	$13,100	$17,800
		390/315 2dr Hdtp Cpe	$6,600	$10,600	$14,400	$19,500
		427/425 2dr Hdtp Cpe	$59,500	$71,800	$80,800	$88,700
		289/200 2dr XL Hdtp Cpe	$9,500	$15,100	$20,700	$28,100
		352/250 2dr XL Hdtp Cpe	$9,900	$15,900	$21,900	$29,400
		427/425 2dr XL Hdtp Cpe	$72,100	$83,300	$89,700	$97,900
		289/200 2dr LTD Hdtp Cpe	$8,600	$13,600	$18,800	$25,500
		352/250 2dr LTD Hdtp Cpe	$9,100	$14,300	$19,800	$26,800
		390/315 2dr LTD Hdtp Cpe	$10,000	$15,800	$21,700	$29,500
		427/425 2dr LTD Hdtp Cpe	$78,100	$88,400	$96,200	$107,000
		289/200 4dr Sdn	$3,300	$6,500	$8,500	$10,300
		352/250 4dr Sdn	$3,600	$6,800	$9,100	$10,900
		390/315 4dr Sdn	$3,700	$7,100	$9,500	$11,400
		427/425 4dr Sdn	$32,300	$41,500	$50,000	$61,800
		289/200 4dr Ctry Sqr Stn Wgn 6P	$5,900	$8,800	$13,600	$20,500
		352/250 4dr Ctry Sqr Stn Wgn 6P	$6,300	$9,400	$14,400	$21,600
		390/315 4dr Ctry Sqr Stn Wgn 6P	$6,600	$9,800	$16,000	$24,500
		289/200 4dr Hdtp Sdn	$3,600	$6,900	$9,200	$11,000

Year	Model	Body Style	4	3	2	1
		352/250 4dr Hdtp Sdn	$3,800	$7,200	$9,600	$11,500
		390/315 4dr Hdtp Sdn	$3,900	$7,700	$10,100	$12,000
		427/425 4dr Hdtp Sdn	$40,600	$55,200	$59,800	$69,700
		289/200 4dr LTD Hdtp Sdn	$3,800	$7,500	$9,900	$12,600
		352/250 4dr LTD Hdtp Sdn	$4,000	$7,900	$10,400	$13,200
		390/315 4dr LTD Hdtp Sdn	$4,200	$8,200	$10,800	$13,800
		427/425 4dr LTD Hdtp Sdn	$44,800	$58,600	$66,400	$78,000
		289/200 2dr Conv	$10,000	$16,100	$22,000	$29,900
		352/250 2dr Conv	$10,400	$16,800	$23,200	$31,300
		390/315 2dr Conv	$11,700	$18,700	$25,700	$34,800
		427/425 2dr Conv	$77,000	$86,700	$96,900	$109,000
		289/200 2dr XL Conv	$10,300	$16,600	$23,000	$31,000
		352/250 2dr XL Conv	$10,900	$17,600	$24,200	$32,700
		390/315 2dr XL Conv	$12,000	$19,400	$26,900	$36,100
		427/425 2dr XL Conv	$82,100	$98,800	$108,000	$125,000

-20% for 6-cyl. +10% for 4-spd.

Year	Model	Body Style	4	3	2	1
		427/425 2dr 7-Litre Conv	$103,000	$118,000	$130,000	$147,000
		428/345 2dr 7-Litre Conv	$16,000	$24,200	$35,700	$52,500
		427/425 2dr 7-Litre Hdtp Cpe	$94,500	$108,000	$120,000	$130,000
		428/345 2dr 7-Litre Hdtp Cpe	$9,600	$15,900	$24,000	$34,600
1966	Thunderbird	390/315 2dr Hdtp Cpe	$5,000	$10,300	$14,500	$21,400
		428/345 2dr Hdtp Cpe	$6,400	$12,400	$16,800	$23,600
		390/315 2dr Hdtp Twn Cpe	$5,100	$10,200	$14,000	$19,700
		428/345 2dr Hdtp Twn Cpe	$5,700	$12,000	$15,200	$22,400
		390/315 2dr Lan Cpe	$8,300	$12,300	$16,500	$23,900
		428/345 2dr Lan Cpe	$7,500	$14,900	$18,500	$26,200
		390/315 2dr Conv	$15,000	$24,000	$37,500	$51,500
		428/345 2dr Conv	$16,200	$27,200	$40,000	$58,600

+10% for factory a/c.

Ford

Year	Model	Body Style	4	3	2	1
1966	GT40	2dr Mk I Road Cpe	$2.9 mil	$3.8 mil	$4.5 mil	$5.25 mil
		2dr Mk I Race Cpe	$3.9 mil	$4.4 mil	$5.5 mil	$6.8 mil
		2dr Mk I Alan Mann Ltwt Cpe	$2.75 mil	$3.7 mil	$4.5 mil	$5.25 mil
		2dr Mk II Alan Mann Ltwt Cpe	$3.9 mil	$5.5 mil	$6.25 mil	$7.5 mil
		2dr Mk II Cpe	$5.25 mil	$6 mil	$7.25 mil	$8.75 mil
		Note: For non-continuation GT40s, individual history and originality of chassis, body, and components dictate value more than condition.				
1966	Cortina	2dr Mk I Sdn	$6,200	$10,700	$18,300	$27,200
1967	Falcon	170/105 2dr Clb Cpe	$4,400	$7,300	$10,200	$14,200
		289/200 2dr Clb Cpe	$5,400	$8,900	$12,200	$16,900
		170/105 2dr Futura Clb Cpe	$5,200	$8,600	$11,800	$16,200
		289/200 2dr Futura Clb Cpe	$6,200	$10,300	$14,200	$19,400
		170/105 4dr Sdn	$3,000	$4,200	$6,900	$9,700
		289/200 4dr Sdn	$3,500	$5,000	$8,500	$11,600
		170/105 4dr Futura Sdn	$2,900	$4,300	$7,400	$10,500
		289/200 4dr Futura Sdn	$3,600	$5,400	$8,900	$12,600
		289/200 4dr Wgn	$5,800	$9,700	$13,000	$18,100
		200/120 4dr Futura Squire Wgn	$5,200	$8,600	$12,100	$16,600
		289/200 4dr Futura Squire Wgn	$6,300	$10,400	$14,500	$19,800
		200/120 2dr Futura Spt Cpe	$5,700	$8,900	$12,700	$17,100
		289/200 2dr Futura Spt Cpe	$6,900	$10,800	$15,100	$20,500
1967	Mustang	289/200 2dr Cpe	$10,800	$19,200	$23,900	$30,200
		289/225 2dr Cpe	$11,900	$21,000	$27,500	$34,100
		390/320 2dr Cpe	$13,700	$23,900	$32,100	$39,500
		289/200 2dr GT Cpe	$11,700	$20,400	$32,000	$38,000
		289/225 2dr GT Cpe	$13,100	$22,800	$34,000	$40,900
		289/271 2dr GT Cpe	$18,000	$30,800	$45,800	$51,300
		390/320 2dr GT Cpe	$21,200	$34,000	$48,300	$60,600
		289/200 2dr Fstbk	$14,100	$21,300	$36,100	$46,400
		289/225 2dr Fstbk	$14,900	$23,900	$38,400	$49,100
		390/320 2dr Fstbk	$16,900	$27,600	$43,200	$54,800

Year	Model	Body Style	4	3	2	1
		289/200 2dr GT Fstbk	$14,300	$24,000	$40,700	$49,300
		289/225 2dr GT Fstbk	$16,300	$26,100	$46,500	$57,100
		289/271 2dr GT Fstbk	$31,800	$41,500	$56,100	$65,700
		390/320 2dr GT Fstbk	$35,700	$53,000	$71,500	$81,700
		289/200 2dr Conv	$18,600	$25,400	$33,400	$45,800
		289/225 2dr Conv	$19,800	$28,700	$37,200	$48,700
		390/320 2dr Conv	$22,400	$32,400	$43,100	$55,200
		289/200 2dr GT Conv	$18,900	$28,400	$41,800	$50,700
		289/225 2dr GT Conv	$21,700	$31,200	$45,300	$57,200
		289/271 2dr GT Conv	$35,500	$51,000	$63,100	$72,400
		390/320 2dr GT Conv	$40,400	$55,100	$71,400	$82,700
		+10% for 4-spd. -10% for 6-cyl. -5% for auto. +6% for a/c.				
1967	Fairlane	289/200 2dr Sdn	$5,300	$8,500	$12,000	$15,900
		390/275 2dr Sdn	$6,200	$10,000	$13,900	$18,200
		390/320 2dr Sdn	$7,000	$11,300	$15,500	$20,800
		427/425 2dr Sdn	$18,700	$25,200	$39,300	$59,300
		289/200 2dr 500 Sdn	$6,300	$10,000	$13,800	$18,100
		390/275 2dr 500 Sdn	$7,400	$11,400	$15,700	$21,000
		390/320 2dr 500 Sdn	$8,200	$13,000	$17,800	$23,600
		289/200 4dr Sdn	$3,700	$5,000	$7,400	$12,700
		390/275 4dr Sdn	$4,200	$5,800	$8,500	$14,600
		390/320 4dr Sdn	$4,800	$6,600	$9,800	$16,500
		289/200 4dr 500 Sdn	$4,200	$5,200	$8,100	$13,400
		390/275 4dr 500 Sdn	$4,800	$6,100	$9,400	$15,400
		390/320 4dr 500 Sdn	$5,400	$6,800	$10,700	$17,400
		289/200 4dr Wgn	$5,800	$9,400	$13,000	$17,300
		390/275 4dr Wgn	$6,800	$11,000	$14,900	$19,800
		390/320 4dr Wgn	$7,800	$12,300	$16,900	$22,300
		427/425 4dr Wgn	$9,500	$15,000	$20,800	$27,600
		289/200 4dr 500 Wgn	$5,800	$9,300	$12,800	$17,000
		390/275 4dr 500 Wgn	$6,800	$10,800	$14,700	$19,500
		390/320 4dr 500 Wgn	$7,800	$12,200	$16,700	$22,000

Ford

Year	Model	Body Style	4	3	2	1
		289/200 4dr Squire Wgn	$5,300	$8,500	$12,000	$15,900
		390/275 4dr Squire Wgn	$6,200	$10,000	$13,900	$18,200
		390/320 4dr Squire Wgn	$7,000	$11,300	$15,500	$20,800
		289/200 2dr 500 Hdtp Cpe	$8,200	$13,400	$18,500	$24,300
		390/275 2dr 500 Hdtp Cpe	$9,400	$15,400	$21,300	$28,000
		390/320 2dr 500 Hdtp Cpe	$10,700	$17,300	$23,900	$31,900
		427/425 2dr 500 Hdtp Cpe	$25,400	$33,700	$47,800	$74,700
		289/200 2dr 500 XL Hdtp Cpe	$10,500	$17,000	$23,500	$31,300
		390/275 2dr 500 XL Hdtp Cpe	$12,100	$19,500	$27,000	$35,800
		390/320 2dr 500 XL Hdtp Cpe	$13,700	$22,000	$30,500	$40,400
		427/425 2dr 500 XL Hdtp Cpe	$34,100	$43,300	$68,000	$102,000
		289/200 2dr GT Hdtp Cpe	$14,200	$22,300	$31,100	$40,900
		390/275 2dr GT Hdtp Cpe	$16,400	$25,600	$35,700	$47,000
		390/320 2dr GT Hdtp Cpe	$18,400	$29,100	$40,300	$53,200
		289/200 2dr 500 Conv	$9,400	$15,500	$21,100	$27,900
		390/275 2dr 500 Conv	$10,900	$17,800	$24,200	$32,300
		390/320 2dr 500 Conv	$12,400	$20,000	$27,400	$36,400
		289/200 2dr 500 XL Conv	$11,100	$18,000	$24,600	$32,800
		390/275 2dr 500 XL Conv	$12,700	$20,600	$28,400	$37,700
		390/320 2dr 500 XL Conv	$14,300	$23,400	$32,000	$42,500
		289/200 2dr GT Conv	$15,400	$24,700	$34,000	$44,900
		390/275 2dr GT Conv	$17,700	$28,200	$39,000	$51,700
		390/320 2dr GT Conv	$19,900	$32,000	$44,100	$58,300
						-20% for 6-cyl.
1967	Custom	289/200 2dr Sdn	$4,900	$7,500	$10,300	$14,500
		390/315 2dr Sdn	$5,700	$8,700	$11,800	$16,700
		427/425 2dr Sdn	$7,900	$12,200	$16,400	$23,200
		428/345 2dr Sdn	$7,400	$11,500	$15,400	$21,700

Year	Model	Body Style	4	3	2	1
		289/200 2dr 500 Sdn	$5,300	$8,000	$10,700	$15,600
		390/315 2dr 500 Sdn	$6,000	$9,400	$12,400	$17,800
		427/425 2dr 500 Sdn	$8,400	$13,000	$17,100	$24,800
		428/345 2dr 500 Sdn	$8,000	$12,200	$16,100	$23,300
		289/200 4dr Sdn	$4,100	$5,500	$7,800	$10,900
		390/315 4dr Sdn	$4,700	$6,400	$9,100	$12,500
		427/425 4dr Sdn	$6,600	$8,800	$12,700	$17,400
		428/345 4dr Sdn	$6,200	$8,200	$11,900	$16,300
		289/200 4dr 500 Sdn	$4,400	$5,800	$8,200	$11,200
		390/315 4dr 500 Sdn	$5,200	$6,700	$9,700	$12,900
		427/425 4dr 500 Sdn	$7,200	$9,500	$13,300	$17,900
		428/345 4dr 500 Sdn	$6,700	$8,800	$12,600	$16,800
						-20% for 6-cyl.
1967	Galaxie 500	289/200 2dr Hdtp Cpe	$5,200	$8,500	$11,800	$15,700
		390/315 2dr Hdtp Cpe	$6,200	$10,400	$14,200	$19,000
		427/425 2dr Hdtp Cpe	$8,800	$14,400	$19,600	$26,400
		428/345 2dr Hdtp Cpe	$8,300	$13,500	$18,500	$24,900
		289/200 2dr XL Hdtp Cpe	$10,000	$16,100	$22,200	$29,800
		390/315 2dr XL Hdtp Cpe	$12,200	$19,400	$26,800	$36,000
		427/425 2dr XL Hdtp Cpe	$16,800	$26,900	$37,200	$50,000
		428/345 2dr XL Hdtp Cpe	$15,800	$25,200	$34,900	$46,900
		289/200 2dr LTD Hdtp Cpe	$7,900	$12,500	$17,200	$23,100
		390/315 2dr LTD Hdtp Cpe	$9,600	$15,000	$20,800	$27,900
		427/425 2dr LTD Hdtp Cpe	$13,100	$20,900	$29,000	$38,800
		428/345 2dr LTD Hdtp Cpe	$12,400	$19,500	$27,100	$36,500
		289/200 4dr Sdn	$4,400	$5,800	$8,300	$11,400
		390/315 4dr Sdn	$5,100	$6,600	$9,700	$13,100
		427/425 4dr Sdn	$7,200	$9,300	$13,400	$18,300
		428/345 4dr Sdn	$6,700	$8,600	$12,600	$17,100
		289/200 4dr LTD Sdn	$4,900	$6,300	$9,000	$12,400

Ford

Year	Model	Body Style	4	3	2	1
		390/315 4dr LTD Sdn	$5,600	$7,200	$10,300	$14,200
		427/425 4dr LTD Sdn	$7,900	$10,100	$14,300	$19,800
		428/345 4dr LTD Sdn	$7,500	$9,600	$13,400	$18,600
		390/315 4dr Ctry Sqr Stn Wgn 6P	$6,700	$10,200	$16,500	$25,200
		289/200 4dr Ctry Sqr Stn Wgn 6P	$5,800	$8,800	$13,500	$20,200
		427/425 4dr Ctry Sqr Stn Wgn 6P	$9,400	$14,300	$22,700	$34,400
		428/345 4dr Ctry Sqr Stn Wgn 6P	$8,900	$13,400	$21,300	$32,300
		289/200 4dr Hdtp Sdn	$4,900	$6,300	$8,600	$12,000
		390/315 4dr Hdtp Sdn	$5,600	$7,200	$10,000	$13,800
		427/425 4dr Hdtp Sdn	$7,900	$10,100	$13,900	$19,300
		428/345 4dr Hdtp Sdn	$7,500	$9,600	$13,100	$18,100
		289/200 4dr LTD Hdtp Sdn	$5,300	$6,900	$9,500	$13,000
		390/315 4dr LTD Hdtp Sdn	$6,000	$8,000	$10,900	$14,900
		427/425 4dr LTD Hdtp Sdn	$8,500	$11,200	$15,100	$20,800
		428/345 4dr LTD Hdtp Sdn	$8,100	$10,500	$14,200	$19,600
		289/200 2dr Conv	$8,100	$12,700	$17,600	$23,900
		390/315 2dr Conv	$9,800	$15,500	$21,500	$29,000
		427/425 2dr Conv	$13,500	$21,200	$29,500	$39,800
		428/345 2dr Conv	$12,800	$20,100	$28,000	$37,800
		289/200 2dr XL Conv	$9,700	$15,500	$21,400	$28,900
		390/315 2dr XL Conv	$11,800	$18,800	$26,000	$35,200
		427/425 2dr XL Conv	$16,200	$25,700	$35,700	$48,300
		428/345 2dr XL Conv	$15,400	$24,300	$33,800	$45,700
						-20% for 6-cyl.
1967	Thunderbird	390/315 2dr Hdtp Cpe	$4,700	$7,900	$12,800	$18,200
		428/345 2dr Hdtp Cpe	$5,100	$8,900	$14,400	$20,200
		390/315 2dr Lan Cpe	$5,000	$8,500	$13,700	$19,700

Year	Model	Body Style	4	3	2	1
		428/345 2dr Lan Cpe	$5,900	$9,800	$15,200	$21,400
		390/315 4dr Lan Sdn	$3,200	$5,600	$9,300	$16,300
		428/345 4dr Lan Sdn	$3,800	$6,400	$10,900	$18,900
						+10% for factory a/c.
1967	GT40	4727/310 2dr Mk III Cpe	$2.5 mil	$3 mil	$3.75 mil	$5 mil
		4727/507 2dr Mk IV Cpe	$3.2 mil	$3.9 mil	$5 mil	$6 mil
1968	Falcon	170/100 2dr Clb Cpe	$4,100	$6,800	$9,200	$12,700
		289/195 2dr Clb Cpe	$4,300	$7,100	$9,600	$13,400
		302/230 2dr Clb Cpe	$4,500	$7,500	$10,300	$14,100
		200/115 2dr Futura Clb Cpe	$5,100	$8,700	$11,100	$15,300
		289/195 2dr Futura Clb Cpe	$5,200	$9,300	$11,700	$16,000
		302/230 2dr Futura Clb Cpe	$5,600	$9,800	$12,200	$16,700
		170/100 4dr Sdn	$2,900	$5,000	$7,100	$9,500
		289/195 4dr Sdn	$3,200	$5,200	$7,600	$10,100
		302/230 4dr Sdn	$3,300	$5,400	$7,900	$10,600
		200/115 4dr Futura Sdn	$3,900	$5,700	$7,800	$9,500
		289/195 4dr Futura Sdn	$4,100	$6,000	$8,200	$10,100
		302/230 4dr Futura Sdn	$4,300	$6,200	$8,600	$10,500
		200/115 4dr Wgn	$4,300	$7,400	$10,200	$13,700
		289/195 4dr Wgn	$4,600	$7,800	$10,800	$14,500
		302/230 4dr Wgn	$4,900	$8,000	$11,300	$15,000
		200/115 4dr Futura Wgn	$5,000	$8,100	$11,300	$16,000
		289/195 4dr Futura Wgn	$5,200	$8,500	$11,900	$16,900
		302/230 4dr Futura Wgn	$5,600	$9,000	$12,500	$17,600
		200/115 2dr Futura Spt Cpe	$5,800	$8,400	$11,700	$15,800
		289/195 2dr Futura Spt Cpe	$6,100	$8,900	$12,300	$16,700
		302/230 2dr Futura Spt Cpe	$6,400	$9,300	$12,700	$17,400
1968	Mustang	289/195 2dr Cpe	$11,700	$19,500	$29,600	$37,500
		302/230 2dr Cpe	$12,300	$22,100	$31,100	$38,200
		390/325 2dr Cpe	$12,600	$23,300	$31,800	$38,600

Ford

Year	Model	Body Style	4	3	2	1
		302/230 2dr GT Cpe	$13,700	$25,900	$35,500	$40,400
		390/325 2dr GT Cpe	$22,500	$34,600	$49,900	$64,600
		428/335 CJ 2dr GT Cpe	$33,900	$44,600	$73,000	$87,600
		289/195 2dr California Special Cpe	$14,200	$23,700	$36,400	$41,500
		289/195 2dr High Country Special Cpe	$13,900	$21,600	$38,600	$43,500
		289/195 2dr Fstbk	$12,300	$18,500	$35,400	$46,200
		302/230 2dr Fstbk	$13,400	$19,600	$35,700	$46,900
		390/325 2dr Fstbk	$14,000	$20,100	$35,900	$47,300
		302/230 2dr GT Fstbk	$16,000	$22,300	$39,300	$50,000
		390/325 2dr GT Fstbk	$39,200	$55,700	$75,700	$86,900
		428/335 CJ 2dr GT Fstbk	$45,900	$62,700	$97,800	$126,000
		289/195 2dr Conv	$17,200	$22,400	$32,300	$45,300
		302/230 2dr Conv	$17,800	$25,000	$37,400	$48,200
		390/325 2dr Conv	$18,300	$26,300	$40,000	$49,600
		302/230 2dr GT Conv	$18,700	$27,700	$44,700	$54,100
		390/325 2dr GT Conv	$42,500	$55,600	$73,600	$91,400
		428/335 CJ 2dr GT Conv	$114,000	$135,000	$176,000	$226,000
			+10% for 4-spd.	*-10% for 6-cyl.*	*-5% for auto.*	*+6% for a/c.*
1968	Fairlane	289/195 2dr Hdtp Cpe	$7,000	$10,800	$15,200	$20,800
		289/195 4dr 500 Sdn	$4,500	$6,800	$10,000	$14,500
		289/195 4dr 500 Wgn	$6,300	$9,700	$13,500	$18,400
		289/195 4dr Sdn	$4,200	$6,500	$9,600	$13,800
		289/195 4dr Wgn	$5,900	$9,400	$12,800	$17,600
		302/210 2dr Hdtp Cpe	$7,500	$11,400	$16,000	$21,700
		390/265 2dr Hdtp Cpe	$7,900	$12,000	$16,700	$22,900
		390/325 2dr Hdtp Cpe	$8,500	$13,000	$18,200	$24,900
		289/195 2dr 500 Hdtp Cpe	$8,100	$12,500	$17,500	$23,500
		302/210 2dr 500 Hdtp Cpe	$8,500	$13,200	$18,300	$24,800

Year	Model	Body Style	4	3	2	1
		390/265 2dr 500 Hdtp Cpe	$8,800	$13,800	$19,100	$25,800
		390/325 2dr 500 Hdtp Cpe	$9,700	$15,100	$20,900	$28,000
		302/210 4dr Sdn	$4,400	$6,800	$10,100	$14,500
		390/265 4dr Sdn	$4,600	$7,100	$10,500	$15,200
		390/325 4dr Sdn	$5,100	$7,800	$11,500	$16,500
		302/210 4dr 500 Sdn	$4,800	$7,100	$10,500	$15,300
		390/265 4dr 500 Sdn	$5,000	$7,500	$11,000	$16,000
		390/325 4dr 500 Sdn	$5,400	$8,200	$12,000	$17,400
		302/210 4dr Wgn	$6,300	$9,800	$13,400	$18,400
		390/265 4dr Wgn	$6,600	$10,300	$14,100	$19,400
		390/325 4dr Wgn	$7,200	$11,200	$15,400	$21,000
		302/210 4dr 500 Wgn	$6,600	$10,200	$14,200	$19,400
		390/265 4dr 500 Wgn	$7,000	$10,700	$15,000	$20,200
		390/325 4dr 500 Wgn	$7,700	$11,600	$16,300	$22,100
		289/195 2dr 500 Fstbk	$7,500	$11,900	$16,300	$22,100
		302/210 2dr 500 Fstbk	$7,800	$12,400	$17,000	$23,100
		390/265 2dr 500 Fstbk	$8,200	$13,100	$17,900	$24,200
		390/325 2dr 500 Fstbk	$8,900	$14,300	$19,500	$26,300
		289/195 2dr 500 Conv	$7,200	$11,200	$15,400	$20,800
		302/210 2dr 500 Conv	$7,600	$11,700	$16,000	$21,900
		390/265 2dr 500 Conv	$7,800	$12,200	$16,700	$22,900
		390/325 2dr 500 Conv	$8,600	$13,400	$18,300	$24,800
						-20% for 6-cyl.
1968	Torino	302/210 2dr Hdtp Cpe	$6,200	$9,100	$15,200	$22,400
		302/210 2dr GT Hdtp Cpe	$9,200	$13,900	$20,200	$28,300
		427/390 2dr GT Hdtp Cpe	$13,700	$20,800	$30,500	$42,400
		302/210 4dr Sdn	$4,500	$5,600	$9,600	$13,900
		302/210 4dr Squire Wgn	$6,600	$10,100	$16,400	$23,100
		302/210 2dr GT Fstbk	$12,600	$18,600	$27,100	$37,900

Ford

Year	Model	Body Style	4	3	2	1
		427/390 2dr GT Fstbk	$18,900	$28,100	$40,700	$56,600
		302/210 2dr GT Conv	$12,600	$18,300	$26,700	$38,000
		427/390 2dr GT Conv	$18,800	$27,400	$39,900	$56,700
						-20% for 6-cyl.
1968	Custom	302/210 2dr Sdn	$4,300	$6,300	$9,300	$12,300
		390/265 2dr Sdn	$4,700	$6,900	$10,200	$13,500
		390/315 2dr Sdn	$5,000	$7,200	$10,600	$14,100
		302/210 2dr 500 Sdn	$4,700	$6,800	$9,800	$12,900
		390/265 2dr 500 Sdn	$5,300	$7,400	$10,700	$14,100
		390/315 2dr 500 Sdn	$5,500	$7,800	$11,200	$14,700
		302/210 4dr Sdn	$3,700	$5,500	$7,600	$10,600
		390/265 4dr Sdn	$4,000	$6,100	$8,300	$11,700
		390/315 4dr Sdn	$4,200	$6,400	$8,800	$12,300
		302/210 4dr 500 Sdn	$3,900	$5,600	$8,100	$11,200
		390/265 4dr 500 Sdn	$4,300	$6,200	$9,100	$12,300
		390/315 4dr 500 Sdn	$4,400	$6,500	$9,500	$12,900
						-20% for 6-cyl.
1968	Galaxie 500	302/210 2dr Hdtp Cpe	$4,900	$7,500	$10,100	$13,900
		390/265 2dr Hdtp Cpe	$5,700	$8,600	$11,700	$16,000
		390/315 2dr Hdtp Cpe	$5,900	$9,000	$12,200	$16,700
		302/210 2dr XL Fstbk	$7,100	$11,000	$15,100	$20,500
		390/265 2dr XL Fstbk	$8,300	$12,600	$17,400	$23,700
		390/315 2dr XL Fstbk	$8,600	$13,200	$18,200	$24,800
		302/210 4dr Sdn	$4,300	$5,400	$7,300	$9,800
		390/265 4dr Sdn	$4,800	$6,000	$8,000	$10,900
		390/315 4dr Sdn	$5,000	$6,300	$8,400	$11,400
		302/210 4dr Hdtp Sdn	$5,000	$6,200	$8,200	$10,300
		390/265 4dr Hdtp Sdn	$5,500	$6,800	$9,200	$11,400
		390/315 4dr Hdtp Sdn	$5,700	$7,100	$9,600	$11,900
		302/210 2dr Fstbk	$6,300	$9,700	$13,300	$17,900
		390/265 2dr Fstbk	$7,400	$11,200	$15,400	$20,700
		390/315 2dr Fstbk	$7,700	$11,800	$16,100	$21,600

Year	Model	Body Style	4	3	2	1
		302/210 2dr Conv	$8,000	$12,600	$17,200	$25,500
		390/265 2dr Conv	$9,300	$14,700	$20,000	$29,600
		390/315 2dr Conv	$9,700	$15,400	$20,800	$31,100
		302/210 2dr XL Conv	$10,200	$15,600	$21,200	$31,000
		390/265 2dr XL Conv	$11,900	$18,100	$24,600	$36,100
		390/315 2dr XL Conv	$12,400	$19,000	$25,700	$37,700
						-20% for 6-cyl.
1968	LTD	302/210 2dr Hdtp Cpe	$6,700	$10,400	$14,700	$19,500
		302/210 4dr Sdn	$4,600	$5,800	$7,700	$10,300
		390/315 4dr Ctry Sqr Stn Wgn 6P	$6,900	$10,600	$16,400	$23,600
		302/210 4dr Hdtp Sdn	$5,400	$6,700	$8,800	$11,100
		390/265 2dr Hdtp Cpe	$7,500	$11,500	$16,100	$21,500
		390/315 2dr Hdtp Cpe	$7,800	$12,000	$16,900	$22,400
		390/265 4dr Sdn	$5,100	$6,300	$8,400	$11,400
		390/315 4dr Sdn	$5,300	$6,600	$9,000	$11,900
		390/265 4dr Ctry Sqr Stn Wgn 6P	$6,600	$10,200	$15,800	$22,700
		390/265 4dr Hdtp Sdn	$5,900	$7,300	$9,700	$12,200
		390/315 4dr Hdtp Sdn	$6,300	$7,700	$10,200	$12,800
						-20% for 6-cyl.
1968	Thunderbird	429/360 2dr Hdtp Cpe	$5,000	$9,100	$13,800	$19,900
		429/360 2dr Lan Cpe	$5,600	$9,500	$14,500	$20,800
		429/360 4dr Lan Sdn	$3,200	$5,200	$9,300	$15,900
						-10% for bench seat. +10% for factory a/c.
1968	GT40	4727/310 2dr Mk III Cpe	$2.5 mil	$3 mil	$3.75 mil	$5 mil
		4727/507 2dr Mk IV Cpe	$3.2 mil	$3.9 mil	$5 mil	$6 mil
1968	Cortina	1298/57 2dr Mk II Sdn	$3,700	$7,600	$11,700	$17,000
1969	Falcon	170/100 2dr Clb Cpe	$3,500	$5,800	$8,000	$11,200
		302/220 2dr Clb Cpe	$3,700	$6,600	$9,100	$12,400
		200/115 2dr Futura Clb Cpe	$4,200	$6,800	$9,400	$13,300
		302/220 2dr Futura Clb Cpe	$4,700	$7,500	$10,500	$14,600

Ford

Year	Model	Body Style	4	3	2	1
		170/100 4dr Sdn	$3,000	$4,100	$6,100	$8,000
		302/220 4dr Sdn	$3,200	$4,600	$6,700	$8,700
		200/115 4dr Futura Sdn	$3,500	$4,400	$6,500	$8,400
		302/220 4dr Futura Sdn	$3,800	$5,000	$7,400	$9,400
		200/115 4dr Wgn	$4,000	$6,900	$9,300	$12,900
		302/220 4dr Wgn	$4,500	$7,500	$10,500	$14,200
		200/115 4dr Futura Wgn	$4,500	$7,400	$10,200	$14,600
		302/220 4dr Futura Wgn	$4,900	$8,200	$11,200	$16,100
		200/115 2dr Futura Spt Cpe	$4,500	$7,600	$10,800	$14,500
		302/220 2dr Futura Spt Cpe	$4,900	$8,400	$11,900	$15,900
1969	Mustang	302/220 2dr Cpe	$5,600	$9,900	$15,400	$21,800
		351/290 2dr Cpe	$6,300	$10,200	$16,700	$23,800
		302/220 2dr Grande Cpe	$7,400	$11,300	$18,700	$26,900
		351/250 2dr Grande Cpe	$8,000	$13,000	$20,500	$29,400
		351/290 2dr Grande Cpe	$8,600	$14,600	$22,300	$31,800
		351/250 2dr GT Cpe	$8,900	$16,000	$24,300	$34,600
		351/290 2dr GT Cpe	$9,900	$17,500	$26,800	$38,100
		302/220 2dr SprtsRf	$7,400	$12,400	$20,500	$29,800
		351/250 2dr SprtsRf	$8,100	$13,500	$21,600	$32,700
		351/290 2dr SprtsRf	$8,600	$14,600	$22,700	$35,300
		351/250 2dr GT SprtsRf	$9,700	$16,800	$26,400	$42,600
		351/290 2dr GT SprtsRf	$10,500	$18,400	$29,000	$47,000
		351/250 2dr Mach 1 SprtsRf	$26,900	$40,200	$49,100	$62,800
		351/290 2dr Mach 1 SprtsRf	$28,900	$42,900	$52,000	$67,100
		390/320 2dr Mach 1 SprtsRf	$30,700	$45,700	$54,800	$71,200
		428/335 CJ 2dr Mach 1 SprtsRf	$35,300	$52,500	$79,300	$93,600
		428/360 SCJ 2dr Mach 1 SprtsRf	$47,200	$76,300	$98,800	$130,000
		302/290 2dr Boss 302 SprtsRf	$42,400	$63,600	$88,800	$125,000

Year	Model	Body Style	4	3	2	1
		429/375 2dr Boss 429 SprtsRf	$142,000	$200,000	$301,000	$391,000
		302/220 2dr Conv	$11,900	$17,600	$28,100	$38,900
		351/250 2dr Conv	$12,600	$19,200	$30,300	$41,100
		351/290 2dr Conv	$13,400	$21,000	$32,800	$43,900
		351/250 2dr GT Conv	$16,200	$25,300	$41,400	$54,600
		351/290 2dr GT Conv	$17,200	$26,600	$43,800	$58,600
		428/335 CJ 2dr GT Conv	$56,700	$73,200	$88,900	$121,000
		428/360 SCJ 2dr GT Conv	$81,500	$106,000	$131,000	$165,000
		+10% for shaker hood exc on SCJ. -10% for 6-cyl. -5% for auto.				
1969	Fairlane	302/220 2dr Hdtp Cpe	$3,900	$6,000	$8,700	$11,600
		351/250 2dr Hdtp Cpe	$4,100	$6,400	$9,100	$12,200
		390/320 2dr Hdtp Cpe	$4,700	$7,200	$10,600	$14,000
		302/220 2dr 500 Hdtp Cpe	$5,500	$8,600	$12,400	$16,300
		351/250 2dr 500 Hdtp Cpe	$5,700	$9,000	$13,000	$17,000
		390/320 2dr 500 Hdtp Cpe	$6,600	$10,400	$14,800	$19,400
		428/360 SCJ 2dr 500 Hdtp Cpe	$23,100	$31,500	$38,800	$47,200
		302/220 4dr Sdn	$4,100	$5,200	$7,200	$9,000
		351/250 4dr Sdn	$4,300	$5,500	$7,600	$9,400
		390/320 4dr Sdn	$5,000	$6,300	$8,700	$10,900
		302/220 4dr 500 Sdn	$4,500	$5,900	$7,900	$9,500
		351/250 4dr 500 Sdn	$4,700	$6,200	$8,300	$10,100
		390/320 4dr 500 Sdn	$5,300	$7,000	$9,600	$11,600
		302/220 4dr Wgn	$3,900	$6,200	$8,700	$11,700
		351/250 4dr Wgn	$4,100	$6,500	$9,200	$12,300
		390/320 4dr Wgn	$4,700	$7,400	$10,600	$14,000
		302/220 4dr 500 Wgn	$4,700	$7,100	$10,200	$13,600
		351/250 4dr 500 Wgn	$4,900	$7,400	$10,700	$14,200
		390/320 4dr 500 Wgn	$5,600	$8,600	$12,200	$16,300
		302/220 2dr 500 SprtsRf	$5,600	$8,700	$12,400	$16,700
		351/250 2dr 500 SprtsRf	$6,000	$9,200	$13,100	$17,500

Ford

Year	Model	Body Style	4	3	2	1
		390/320 2dr 500 SprtsRf	$6,900	$10,500	$15,100	$19,900
		302/220 2dr 500 Conv	$7,800	$12,300	$17,300	$23,000
		351/250 2dr 500 Conv	$8,200	$13,000	$18,200	$24,100
		390/320 2dr 500 Conv	$9,400	$14,800	$20,700	$27,500
						-20% for 6-cyl.
1969	Torino	302/220 2dr Hdtp Cpe	$5,900	$8,900	$14,900	$20,800
		302/220 2dr GT Hdtp Cpe	$9,200	$13,600	$20,100	$27,700
		351/250 2dr GT Hdtp Cpe	$9,600	$14,300	$21,000	$28,900
		390/320 2dr GT Hdtp Cpe	$10,900	$16,300	$24,000	$33,100
		302/220 4dr Sdn	$4,500	$6,300	$8,100	$12,500
		302/220 4dr Squire Wgn	$5,900	$8,400	$12,800	$18,300
		302/220 2dr GT SprtsRf	$10,100	$15,200	$22,300	$30,400
		351/250 2dr GT SprtsRf	$10,500	$16,000	$23,500	$32,000
		390/320 2dr GT SprtsRf	$12,000	$18,100	$26,800	$36,600
		428/335 CJ 2dr Cobra SprtsRf	$28,800	$41,800	$64,300	$89,400
		302/220 2dr GT Conv	$12,000	$17,800	$26,400	$36,400
		351/250 2dr GT Conv	$12,500	$18,700	$27,800	$38,100
		390/320 2dr GT Conv	$14,100	$21,400	$31,500	$43,500
						-20% for 6-cyl.
1969	Talladega	428/335 CJ 2dr SprtsRf	$29,700	$50,800	$72,800	$93,500
1969	Custom	302/220 2dr Sdn	$3,400	$6,300	$8,500	$11,500
		351/250 2dr Sdn	$3,600	$6,600	$9,000	$12,100
		302/220 2dr 500 Sdn	$3,900	$6,800	$9,100	$12,000
		351/250 2dr 500 Sdn	$4,100	$7,100	$9,600	$12,700
		302/220 4dr Sdn	$3,200	$4,700	$7,000	$9,700
		351/250 4dr Sdn	$3,400	$4,900	$7,400	$10,200
		302/220 4dr 500 Sdn	$3,600	$5,200	$7,500	$10,200
		351/250 4dr 500 Sdn	$3,800	$5,500	$7,900	$10,800
		302/220 4dr Rnch Wgn	$3,800	$5,800	$8,200	$11,600

Year	Model	Body Style	4	3	2	1
		351/250 4dr Rnch Wgn	$4,000	$6,200	$8,700	$12,100
		302/220 4dr 500 Ranch Wagon Stn Wgn 6P	$5,600	$10,000	$12,200	$17,200
		351/250 4dr 500 Ranch Wagon Stn Wgn 6P	$5,900	$10,400	$12,900	$17,900
						-20% for 6-cyl.
1969	Galaxie 500	302/220 2dr Hdtp Cpe	$4,200	$6,400	$9,000	$12,100
		390/265 2dr Hdtp Cpe	$4,600	$7,100	$9,800	$13,300
		429/320 2dr Hdtp Cpe	$5,100	$7,700	$10,800	$14,400
		429/360 2dr Hdtp Cpe	$6,800	$10,400	$14,300	$19,300
		302/220 4dr Sdn	$3,900	$6,100	$8,000	$10,200
		390/265 4dr Sdn	$4,400	$6,700	$8,800	$11,200
		429/320 4dr Sdn	$4,800	$7,300	$9,700	$12,200
		429/360 4dr Sdn	$6,300	$9,800	$12,800	$16,100
		302/220 4dr Hdtp Sdn	$4,400	$6,800	$8,600	$11,000
		390/265 4dr Hdtp Sdn	$4,800	$7,500	$9,500	$12,100
		429/320 4dr Hdtp Sdn	$5,100	$8,100	$10,400	$13,200
		429/360 4dr Hdtp Sdn	$7,000	$11,000	$13,800	$17,500
		302/220 2dr SprtsRf	$5,000	$7,800	$11,100	$14,600
		390/265 2dr SprtsRf	$5,400	$8,600	$12,100	$16,000
		429/320 2dr SprtsRf	$6,000	$9,400	$13,300	$17,600
		429/360 2dr SprtsRf	$8,100	$12,600	$17,600	$23,400
		302/220 2dr XL SprtsRf	$5,900	$8,900	$12,800	$16,800
		390/265 2dr XL SprtsRf	$6,500	$9,800	$14,000	$18,500
		429/320 2dr XL SprtsRf	$7,100	$10,700	$15,300	$20,100
		429/360 2dr XL SprtsRf	$9,500	$14,300	$20,300	$27,000
		302/220 2dr Conv	$7,500	$11,800	$18,400	$23,800
		390/265 2dr Conv	$8,400	$12,900	$20,200	$26,300
		429/320 2dr Conv	$9,000	$14,100	$22,100	$28,700
		429/360 2dr Conv	$12,100	$18,700	$29,400	$38,300

Ford

Year	Model	Body Style	4	3	2	1
		302/220 2dr XL Conv	$8,600	$13,300	$20,400	$26,500
		390/265 2dr XL Conv	$9,300	$14,500	$22,500	$29,200
		429/320 2dr XL Conv	$10,200	$16,000	$24,600	$31,900
		429/360 2dr XL Conv	$13,600	$21,000	$32,700	$42,500
						-20% for 6-cyl.
1969	LTD	302/220 2dr Hdtp Cpe	$5,000	$8,000	$12,400	$16,400
		390/265 2dr Hdtp Cpe	$5,500	$8,700	$13,700	$18,100
		429/320 2dr Hdtp Cpe	$6,200	$9,600	$14,800	$19,700
		429/360 2dr Hdtp Cpe	$8,200	$12,700	$19,600	$26,300
		302/220 4dr Sdn	$4,500	$6,700	$8,900	$11,300
		390/265 4dr Sdn	$4,900	$7,300	$9,800	$12,500
		429/320 4dr Sdn	$5,300	$8,000	$10,700	$13,600
		429/360 4dr Sdn	$7,200	$10,800	$14,200	$18,000
		302/220 4dr Ctry Sqr Stn Wgn 6P	$8,600	$12,800	$18,000	$25,900
		390/265 4dr Ctry Sqr Stn Wgn 6P	$9,400	$14,100	$19,400	$28,500
		429/320 4dr Ctry Sqr Stn Wgn 6P	$10,300	$15,200	$21,100	$30,900
		429/360 4dr Ctry Sqr Stn Wgn 6P	$13,600	$19,600	$27,800	$41,000
		302/220 4dr Hdtp Sdn	$5,300	$7,600	$9,600	$12,200
		390/265 4dr Hdtp Sdn	$5,800	$8,400	$10,500	$13,500
		429/320 4dr Hdtp Sdn	$6,400	$9,300	$11,400	$14,600
		429/360 4dr Hdtp Sdn	$8,600	$12,300	$15,200	$19,400
						-20% for 6-cyl.
1969	Country Sedan	302/220 4dr Stn Wgn 6P	$4,800	$7,000	$9,900	$16,400
		390/265 4dr Stn Wgn 6P	$5,300	$7,700	$10,800	$18,000
		429/320 4dr Stn Wgn 6P	$5,700	$8,400	$11,900	$19,500
		429/360 4dr Stn Wgn 6P	$7,700	$11,300	$15,800	$26,100
						-20% for 6-cyl.
1969	Thunderbird	429/360 2dr Cpe	$5,800	$10,800	$15,600	$20,100
		429/360 2dr Lan Cpe	$6,600	$11,100	$16,600	$21,700

Year	Model	Body Style	4	3	2	1
		429/360 4dr Lan Sdn	$3,900	$6,500	$10,800	$16,700
				-10% for bench seat. +10% for factory a/c.		
1969	GT40	4727/310 2dr Mk III Cpe	$2.5 mil	$3 mil	$3.75 mil	$5 mil
1969	Cortina	1298/57 2dr Mk II Sdn	$3,700	$7,600	$11,700	$17,000
1970	Maverick	170/105 2dr Sdn	$3,300	$5,700	$9,000	$12,100
1970	Falcon	302/220 4dr Futura Wgn	$5,100	$8,300	$11,400	$16,900
		302/220 4dr Sdn	$3,700	$5,500	$7,700	$10,400
		302/220 4dr Wgn	$4,800	$7,600	$10,600	$13,900
		429/370 CJ 2dr Sdn	$7,500	$12,200	$16,100	$21,800
		429/375 SCJ 2dr Sdn	$7,500	$12,800	$16,900	$22,800
		429/375 SCJ 4dr Sdn	$6,600	$10,000	$14,200	$18,600
		429/375 SCJ 4dr Wgn	$8,700	$14,000	$19,100	$25,300
		302/220 2dr Sdn	$4,000	$6,700	$8,700	$12,200
		351/300 2dr Sdn	$4,400	$7,200	$9,500	$13,400
		429/360 2dr Sdn	$6,100	$9,800	$13,300	$17,900
		200/120 4dr Sdn	$3,300	$5,100	$7,000	$9,300
		351/300 4dr Sdn	$3,900	$6,100	$8,300	$11,200
		429/370 CJ 4dr Sdn	$5,400	$8,300	$11,800	$15,400
		200/120 4dr Futura Sdn	$3,600	$5,300	$7,600	$9,800
		302/220 4dr Futura Sdn	$3,900	$5,800	$8,300	$10,900
		200/120 4dr Wgn	$4,300	$7,000	$9,500	$12,700
		351/300 4dr Wgn	$5,300	$8,300	$11,600	$15,200
		429/370 CJ 4dr Wgn	$7,200	$11,700	$15,800	$21,000
		200/120 4dr Futura Wgn	$4,700	$7,500	$10,300	$15,400
		200/120 2dr Futura Clb Cpe	$4,200	$6,700	$9,200	$12,600
		302/220 2dr Futura Clb Cpe	$4,700	$7,300	$10,400	$13,900
1970	Mustang	302/220 2dr Cpe	$6,300	$10,400	$16,800	$24,900
		302/220 2dr Grande Cpe	$7,400	$11,100	$18,500	$26,600
		302/220 2dr SprtsRf	$8,200	$13,300	$22,500	$32,800
		351/250 2dr Mach 1 SprtsRf	$23,600	$32,300	$43,900	$59,900
		351/300 2dr Mach 1 SprtsRf	$25,900	$35,900	$48,300	$66,100

Ford

Year	Model	Body Style	4	3	2	1
		428/335 CJ 2dr Mach 1 SprtsRf	$34,700	$48,900	$76,600	$89,500
		428/360 SCJ 2dr Mach 1 SprtsRf	$42,300	$65,200	$89,900	$113,000
		302/290 2dr Boss 302 SprtsRf	$42,500	$63,500	$94,700	$124,000
		429/375 2dr Boss 429 SprtsRf	$135,000	$180,000	$311,000	$379,000
		302/220 2dr Conv	$11,800	$17,200	$29,300	$40,600
		428/335 CJ 2dr Conv	$62,600	$74,400	$87,700	$114,000
		428/360 SCJ 2dr Conv	$87,300	$114,000	$138,000	$151,000
					-10% for 6-cyl. -5% for auto.	
1970	Fairlane 500	302/220 2dr Hdtp Cpe	$5,100	$7,800	$10,800	$14,500
		351/300 2dr Hdtp Cpe	$6,100	$9,300	$13,000	$17,400
		429/360 2dr Hdtp Cpe	$7,700	$11,800	$16,200	$21,900
		429/370 2dr Hdtp Cpe	$8,100	$12,400	$17,200	$23,100
		429/375 2dr Hdtp Cpe	$8,200	$12,500	$17,400	$23,400
		302/220 4dr Wgn	$5,300	$8,000	$11,200	$14,900
		351/300 4dr Wgn	$6,400	$9,600	$13,400	$18,100
		429/360 4dr Wgn	$8,000	$12,100	$16,900	$22,500
		429/370 4dr Wgn	$8,500	$12,700	$17,900	$23,900
		429/375 4dr Wgn	$8,600	$13,000	$18,100	$24,200
		302/220 4dr Sdn	$3,900	$5,900	$7,700	$10,000
		351/300 4dr Sdn	$4,700	$7,000	$9,200	$11,900
		429/360 4dr Sdn	$5,900	$8,800	$11,600	$14,900
		429/370 4dr Sdn	$6,300	$9,300	$12,200	$15,900
		429/375 4dr Sdn	$6,400	$9,400	$12,400	$16,100
						-20% for 6-cyl.
1970	Torino	351/300 2dr Cobra SprtsRf	$31,100	$46,200	$65,900	$81,800
		429/375 2dr Cobra SprtsRf	$45,600	$66,500	$88,800	$104,000
		429/375 2dr GT SprtsRf	$17,600	$25,200	$39,800	$52,500
		429/375 2dr SprtsRf	$12,200	$16,400	$25,400	$36,200
		351/300 2dr Hdtp Cpe	$7,200	$10,500	$17,300	$24,800
		429/370 2dr Hdtp Cpe	$9,600	$13,900	$22,700	$32,300
		429/375 2dr Hdtp Cpe	$9,800	$14,300	$23,100	$33,100

Year	Model	Body Style	4	3	2	1
		351/300 2dr Brghm Hdtp Cpe	$7,200	$10,500	$17,400	$24,900
		429/370 2dr Brghm Hdtp Cpe	$9,600	$13,900	$22,900	$32,600
		429/375 2dr Brghm Hdtp Cpe	$9,800	$14,300	$23,200	$33,200
		351/300 4dr Sdn	$5,200	$7,200	$9,500	$14,700
		429/370 4dr Sdn	$6,700	$9,500	$12,400	$19,400
		429/375 4dr Sdn	$7,000	$9,700	$12,700	$19,800
		351/300 4dr Hdtp Sdn	$5,700	$7,800	$10,100	$15,200
		429/370 4dr Hdtp Sdn	$7,700	$10,200	$13,300	$20,200
		429/375 4dr Hdtp Sdn	$7,800	$10,400	$13,500	$20,500
		351/300 4dr Brghm Hdtp Sdn	$6,000	$8,000	$10,400	$15,400
		429/370 4dr Brghm Hdtp Sdn	$8,000	$10,500	$13,600	$20,500
		429/375 4dr Brghm Hdtp Sdn	$8,100	$10,700	$13,800	$20,800
		302/220 4dr Wgn	$5,900	$8,400	$12,600	$18,200
		351/300 4dr Wgn	$7,100	$10,000	$15,200	$21,800
		429/360 4dr Wgn	$9,400	$13,200	$19,800	$28,600
		351/300 2dr SprtsRf	$9,000	$12,200	$18,900	$27,100
		429/370 2dr SprtsRf	$12,000	$16,100	$24,900	$35,500
						-20% for 6-cyl.
		302/220 2dr GT SprtsRf	$8,700	$12,800	$19,700	$29,100
		351/250 2dr GT SprtsRf	$9,900	$14,600	$22,400	$33,000
		351/300 2dr GT SprtsRf	$11,600	$17,100	$26,400	$38,700
						-20% for 6-cyl.
		429/360 2dr GT SprtsRf	$13,400	$19,700	$29,900	$41,400
		429/370 2dr GT SprtsRf	$15,800	$23,200	$35,200	$48,600
		429/370 2dr Cobra SprtsRf	$41,200	$58,400	$82,600	$94,300
						-20% for 6-cyl.
		302/220 2dr GT Conv	$15,100	$21,600	$32,400	$44,500
		351/250 2dr GT Conv	$17,100	$24,500	$36,700	$50,300
		351/300 2dr GT Conv	$20,200	$28,800	$43,200	$59,200
		429/360 2dr GT Conv	$22,600	$32,400	$48,400	$66,200

Ford

Year	Model	Body Style	4	3	2	1
		429/370 2dr GT Conv	$26,600	$38,100	$57,000	$77,800
		429/375 2dr GT Conv	$27,100	$38,800	$58,000	$79,400
						-20% for 6-cyl.
1970	Galaxie 500	302/220 2dr Hdtp Cpe	$5,000	$7,500	$10,500	$13,700
		390/265 2dr Hdtp Cpe	$5,800	$8,600	$12,100	$15,900
		429/360 2dr Hdtp Cpe	$7,500	$11,200	$15,800	$20,800
		302/220 4dr Sdn	$3,700	$5,900	$7,800	$9,900
		390/265 4dr Sdn	$4,200	$6,800	$8,800	$11,300
		429/360 4dr Sdn	$5,500	$8,800	$11,600	$14,700
		351/250 4dr Ctry Sdn Stn Wgn	$4,600	$6,900	$10,400	$15,700
		390/265 4dr Ctry Sdn Stn Wgn	$5,200	$8,000	$11,900	$18,200
		429/360 4dr Ctry Sdn Stn Wgn	$6,800	$10,400	$15,600	$23,800
		302/220 4dr Hdtp Sdn	$4,200	$6,700	$8,400	$10,800
		390/265 4dr Hdtp Sdn	$4,800	$7,700	$9,700	$12,400
		429/360 4dr Hdtp Sdn	$6,400	$10,000	$12,700	$16,100
		302/220 2dr SprtsRf	$5,200	$7,800	$11,000	$14,500
		390/265 2dr SprtsRf	$6,000	$8,900	$12,700	$16,800
		429/360 2dr SprtsRf	$7,800	$11,700	$16,600	$22,000
		302/220 2dr XL SprtsRf	$5,900	$8,500	$11,800	$15,600
		390/265 2dr XL SprtsRf	$6,700	$9,800	$13,500	$18,100
		429/360 2dr XL SprtsRf	$8,700	$12,800	$17,700	$23,600
		302/220 2dr XL Conv	$9,000	$13,600	$19,000	$25,600
		390/265 2dr XL Conv	$10,400	$15,700	$21,900	$29,400
		429/360 2dr XL Conv	$13,700	$20,300	$28,600	$38,400
						-20% for 6-cyl.
1970	Thunderbird	429/360 2dr Cpe	$5,100	$9,700	$14,000	$19,800
		429/360 2dr Lan Cpe	$5,600	$10,000	$14,400	$20,200
		429/360 4dr Lan Sdn	$2,900	$5,600	$9,500	$15,900

Year	Model	Body Style	4	3	2	1
				-10% for bench seat. +10% for factory a/c.		
1970	Cortina	1298/57 2dr Mk II Sdn	$3,700	$7,600	$11,700	$17,000
1971	Maverick	170/100 2dr Grabber Cpe	$6,100	$9,700	$13,900	$17,800
1971	Mustang	302/210 2dr Cpe	$5,300	$8,900	$14,100	$17,900
		302/210 2dr Grande Cpe	$5,700	$9,600	$15,200	$21,900
		302/210 2dr SprtsRf	$6,100	$10,500	$17,400	$26,500
		302/210 2dr Mach 1 SprtsRf	$16,400	$24,600	$32,100	$43,900
		351/285 2dr Mach 1 SprtsRf	$18,100	$27,100	$35,500	$48,500
		429/370 2dr Mach 1 SprtsRf	$25,700	$37,100	$61,800	$76,500
		351/330 2dr Boss 351 SprtsRf	$40,200	$52,900	$77,300	$109,000
		302/210 2dr Conv	$10,500	$16,300	$25,000	$35,400
					-10% for 6-cyl. -5% for auto.	
1971	Torino	429/370 2dr 500 SprtsRf	$12,100	$16,100	$25,200	$36,000
		302/210 2dr Hdtp Cpe	$5,900	$8,800	$14,400	$20,600
		429/370 2dr Hdtp Cpe	$9,600	$14,200	$23,000	$32,900
		302/210 2dr 500 Hdtp Cpe	$5,900	$8,900	$14,500	$20,700
		429/370 2dr 500 Hdtp Cpe	$9,600	$14,400	$23,100	$33,000
		302/210 2dr Brghm Hdtp Cpe	$6,000	$9,000	$14,700	$20,900
		429/370 2dr Brghm Hdtp Cpe	$9,700	$14,500	$23,400	$33,400
		302/210 2dr 500 SprtsRf	$7,600	$10,000	$15,900	$22,600
		302/210 2dr GT SprtsRf	$9,300	$13,600	$20,700	$28,100
		351/240 2dr GT SprtsRf	$10,300	$15,000	$22,800	$31,000
		351/285 2dr GT SprtsRf	$11,200	$16,400	$24,800	$33,800
		429/370 2dr GT SprtsRf	$14,900	$21,900	$32,900	$44,900
		351/285 2dr Cobra SprtsRf	$21,300	$28,200	$47,100	$63,200
		429/370 2dr Cobra SprtsRf	$30,700	$44,000	$68,900	$85,600
		302/210 2dr GT Conv	$16,900	$24,100	$36,200	$49,400

Ford

Year	Model	Body Style	4	3	2	1
		351/240 2dr GT Conv	$18,600	$26,600	$39,800	$54,400
		351/285 2dr GT Conv	$20,300	$29,000	$43,400	$59,300
		429/370 2dr GT Conv	$26,700	$38,500	$57,900	$74,400
						-20% for 6-cyl.
1971	Galaxie 500	400/260 2dr Hdtp Cpe	$4,600	$7,000	$10,000	$13,200
		429/320 2dr Hdtp Cpe	$4,700	$7,100	$10,200	$13,300
		429/360 2dr Hdtp Cpe	$6,100	$9,200	$13,200	$17,400
		400/260 4dr Ctry Sdn Stn Wgn	$5,000	$8,000	$11,800	$18,000
		429/320 4dr Ctry Sdn Stn Wgn	$5,100	$8,100	$12,000	$18,300
		429/360 4dr Ctry Sdn Stn Wgn	$6,700	$10,400	$15,600	$23,800
						-20% for 6-cyl.
1971	LTD	351/240 2dr Conv	$5,600	$9,200	$14,400	$19,700
		400/260 2dr Conv	$6,400	$10,500	$16,600	$22,700
		429/320 2dr Conv	$6,600	$10,700	$16,900	$23,000
1971	Thunderbird	429/360 2dr Lan Cpe	$3,500	$11,300	$16,100	$22,400
		429/360 4dr Lan Sdn	$5,500	$6,600	$10,600	$17,600
				-10% for bench seat. +10% for factory a/c.		
1972	Maverick	170/82 2dr Grabber Sdn	$5,900	$9,400	$13,100	$16,800
1972	Mustang	302/141 2dr Cpe	$4,800	$7,000	$13,400	$16,800
		351/177 2dr Cpe	$5,400	$8,200	$15,800	$19,900
		351/266 CJ 2dr Cpe	$6,200	$9,200	$17,500	$21,900
		351/275 2dr Cpe	$6,400	$9,800	$18,300	$23,600
		302/141 2dr Grande Cpe	$5,100	$8,500	$14,100	$18,800
		351/177 2dr Grande Cpe	$6,300	$9,800	$17,100	$22,600
		351/266 CJ 2dr Grande Cpe	$6,600	$11,100	$19,000	$25,200
		351/275 2dr Grande Cpe	$7,200	$11,700	$20,100	$27,100
		302/141 2dr SprtsRf	$6,100	$9,400	$16,500	$25,300
		351/177 2dr SprtsRf	$7,300	$11,200	$20,000	$30,100
		351/266 CJ 2dr SprtsRf	$8,100	$11,800	$21,500	$32,500

Year	Model	Body Style	4	3	2	1
		351/275 2dr SprtsRf	$8,600	$13,000	$23,500	$35,000
		302/141 2dr Mach 1 SprtsRf	$12,700	$18,700	$25,800	$37,000
		351/177 2dr Mach 1 SprtsRf	$15,600	$22,300	$31,500	$45,000
		351/266 CJ 2dr Mach 1 SprtsRf	$16,800	$24,300	$33,600	$47,900
		351/275 2dr Mach 1 SprtsRf	$17,900	$25,900	$36,600	$51,600
		302/141 2dr Conv	$9,300	$13,600	$23,300	$34,200
		351/177 2dr Conv	$10,600	$17,500	$27,800	$41,400
		351/266 CJ 2dr Conv	$11,900	$19,100	$31,000	$44,800
		351/275 2dr Conv	$9,400	$14,800	$23,700	$35,300

-10% for 6-cyl.

Year	Model	Body Style	4	3	2	1
1972	Torino	302/140 2dr Hdtp Cpe	$5,100	$7,400	$11,200	$14,900

-20% for 6-cyl.

Year	Model	Body Style	4	3	2	1
1972	Gran Torino	302/140 2dr Hdtp Cpe	$4,600	$7,100	$10,700	$14,200
		351/161 2dr Hdtp Cpe	$4,800	$7,400	$11,200	$14,900
		351/248 CJ 2dr Hdtp Cpe	$5,900	$9,200	$13,800	$18,400
		400/168 2dr Hdtp Cpe	$5,500	$8,700	$13,000	$17,200
		429/205 2dr Hdtp Cpe	$5,700	$9,000	$13,400	$17,900
		302/140 2dr Sport Hdtp Cpe	$5,400	$8,400	$12,200	$16,600
		351/161 2dr Sport Hdtp Cpe	$5,700	$8,800	$12,800	$17,400
		351/248 CJ 2dr Sport Hdtp Cpe	$7,000	$10,700	$15,600	$21,500
		400/168 2dr Sport Hdtp Cpe	$6,600	$10,000	$14,700	$20,200
		429/205 2dr Sport Hdtp Cpe	$6,800	$10,400	$15,300	$21,000
		302/140 2dr Sport SprtsRf	$5,400	$8,500	$12,200	$16,900
		351/161 2dr Sport SprtsRf	$5,600	$9,000	$12,900	$17,500
		351/248 CJ 2dr Sport SprtsRf	$6,500	$10,300	$14,900	$20,800
		400/168 2dr Sport SprtsRf	$6,400	$10,300	$14,700	$20,400
		429/205 2dr Sport SprtsRf	$6,700	$10,700	$15,500	$21,400

-20% for 6-cyl. +10% for Rallye option pkg.

Ford

Year	Model	Body Style	4	3	2	1
1972	Galaxie 500	351/153 2dr Hdtp Cpe	$4,100	$6,200	$8,800	$11,500
		400/172 2dr Hdtp Cpe	$4,000	$6,000	$8,600	$11,000
		351/153 4dr Ctry Sdn Stn Wgn	$4,700	$7,200	$11,000	$16,500
		400/172 4dr Ctry Sdn Stn Wgn	$4,600	$7,000	$10,700	$16,000
		429/208 4dr Ctry Sdn Stn Wgn	$5,500	$8,600	$13,100	$19,700
						-20% for 6-cyl.
1972	LTD	351/153 2dr Conv	$6,900	$11,500	$17,900	$24,100
		400/172 2dr Conv	$6,600	$11,100	$17,200	$23,000
		429/208 2dr Conv	$7,000	$11,700	$18,400	$24,400
						-20% for 6-cyl.
1972	Thunderbird	429/212 2dr Cpe	$3,200	$6,600	$12,100	$17,100
		460/224 2dr Cpe	$4,000	$8,800	$12,700	$19,100
						+10% for factory a/c.
1973	Mustang	302/136 2dr Cpe	$4,800	$7,400	$14,400	$18,000
		351/168 2dr Cpe	$5,700	$8,800	$16,700	$21,500
		351/266 CJ 2dr Cpe	$6,800	$10,400	$19,500	$25,600
		302/136 2dr Grande Cpe	$5,200	$8,000	$13,300	$18,400
		351/168 2dr Grande Cpe	$6,300	$9,800	$16,200	$22,500
		351/264 2dr Grande Cpe	$7,100	$11,500	$18,800	$26,600
		302/136 2dr SprtsRf	$4,400	$9,600	$16,800	$23,500
		351/168 2dr SprtsRf	$6,000	$11,400	$20,000	$29,700
		351/266 CJ 2dr SprtsRf	$8,800	$13,200	$23,500	$34,200
		302/136 2dr Mach 1 SprtsRf	$13,000	$20,600	$25,600	$35,100
		351/168 2dr Mach 1 SprtsRf	$16,000	$24,900	$30,900	$42,600
		351/264 2dr Mach 1 SprtsRf	$18,600	$28,600	$36,400	$49,900
		302/136 2dr Conv	$10,000	$15,500	$22,900	$35,200
		351/168 2dr Conv	$11,800	$18,600	$27,500	$42,000
		351/266 CJ 2dr Conv	$13,900	$21,600	$32,800	$49,900
						-10% for 6-cyl.
1973	Torino	302/137 2dr Hdtp Cpe	$5,600	$8,300	$13,500	$18,900
						-20% for 6-cyl.

Year	Model	Body Style	4	3	2	1
1973	Gran Torino	302/137 2dr Hdtp Cpe	$4,700	$7,500	$10,900	$14,500
		302/137 2dr Brghm Hdtp Cpe	$5,600	$8,800	$13,000	$17,600
		302/137 2dr Sport Hdtp Cpe	$6,700	$10,500	$15,400	$22,300
		302/137 2dr Sport SprtsRf	$6,600	$10,400	$15,500	$21,100
						-20% for 6-cyl.
1973	Galaxie 500	351/158 2dr Hdtp Cpe	$4,000	$6,200	$9,000	$12,000
		400/168 2dr Hdtp Cpe	$4,400	$6,700	$9,800	$13,100
		429/201 2dr Hdtp Cpe	$5,200	$8,000	$11,700	$15,400
		460/202 2dr Hdtp Cpe	$5,300	$8,300	$12,100	$16,000
		460/274 2dr Hdtp Cpe	$6,400	$9,800	$14,300	$19,000
		400/167 4dr Ctry Sdn Stn Wgn	$4,700	$7,100	$11,100	$16,400
		429/198 4dr Ctry Sdn Stn Wgn	$5,400	$8,400	$13,000	$19,400
		460/198 4dr Ctry Sdn Stn Wgn	$5,600	$8,700	$13,600	$20,300
						-20% for 6-cyl.
1973	LTD	351/154 4dr Ctry Sqr Stn Wgn	$4,500	$7,000	$10,900	$16,200
						-20% for 6-cyl.
1973	Thunderbird	429/208 2dr Cpe	$3,500	$6,200	$9,700	$15,600
		460/208 2dr Cpe	$3,700	$7,000	$10,100	$16,900
						+10% for factory a/c.
1974	Mustang II	171/105 2dr Hdtp Cpe	$2,900	$3,900	$5,500	$9,400
		171/105 2dr Ghia Hdtp Cpe	$2,900	$4,000	$5,600	$9,600
		171/105 3dr Htchbk Cpe	$3,000	$4,100	$5,600	$9,400
		171/105 3dr Mach 1 Htchbk Cpe	$3,700	$5,000	$6,700	$10,200
						-20% for 4-cyl.
1974	Thunderbird	460/220 2dr Hdtp Cpe	$3,900	$7,200	$10,600	$17,100
1975	Mustang II	171/105 2dr Cpe	$2,600	$3,300	$4,400	$8,100
		302/140 2dr Cpe	$3,000	$4,000	$5,500	$10,300
		171/105 2dr Ghia Cpe	$2,500	$3,500	$5,000	$8,500
		302/140 2dr Ghia Cpe	$2,800	$4,200	$6,100	$10,600

Ford

Year	Model	Body Style	4	3	2	1
		171/105 3dr Htchbk Cpe	$2,600	$3,300	$4,500	$8,400
		302/140 3dr Htchbk Cpe	$3,000	$4,000	$5,600	$10,800
		171/105 3dr Mach 1 Htchbk Cpe	$3,200	$4,400	$5,700	$9,000
		302/140 3dr Mach 1 Htchbk Cpe	$4,100	$5,100	$6,700	$11,100
						-20% for 4-cyl.
1975	Thunderbird	460/218 2dr Hdtp Cpe	$3,600	$6,700	$9,800	$16,100
1976	Mustang II	171/103 3dr 2+2 Cpe	$2,500	$3,500	$5,000	$9,200
		302/134 3dr 2+2 Cpe	$2,600	$3,800	$5,600	$10,300
		171/103 3dr Cobra II 2+2 Cpe	$4,500	$7,600	$10,900	$15,000
		302/134 3dr Cobra II 2+2 Cpe	$5,000	$8,400	$12,200	$17,500
		171/103 3dr Mach 1 2+2 Cpe	$3,000	$4,300	$6,100	$9,500
		302/134 3dr Mach 1 2+2 Cpe	$3,600	$4,800	$6,400	$10,300
		171/103 2dr Hdtp	$2,400	$3,400	$4,900	$8,800
		302/134 2dr Hdtp	$2,600	$3,700	$5,400	$9,900
		171/103 2dr Ghia Hdtp	$2,500	$3,500	$5,300	$8,800
		302/134 2dr Ghia Hdtp	$2,800	$3,700	$6,000	$9,700
						+$500 for Stallion Pkg. -20% for 4-cyl.
1976	Thunderbird	460/202 2dr Hdtp	$3,300	$5,900	$10,200	$17,000
1977	Mustang II	171/93 3dr 2+2 Htchbk	$2,400	$3,500	$4,800	$8,300
		302/139 3dr 2+2 Htchbk	$2,600	$3,800	$5,600	$9,400
		171/93 3dr Mach 1 2+2 Htchbk	$2,800	$3,900	$5,600	$9,100
		302/139 3dr Mach 1 2+2 Htchbk	$2,900	$4,300	$6,200	$10,600
		171/93 3dr Cobra II 2+2 Htchbk	$4,800	$7,500	$10,200	$13,700
		302/139 3dr Cobra II 2+2 Htchbk	$5,500	$9,000	$12,400	$17,500
		171/93 2dr Hdtp	$2,400	$3,400	$4,900	$8,200
		302/139 2dr Hdtp	$2,600	$3,700	$5,400	$9,100
		171/93 2dr Ghia Hdtp	$2,500	$3,700	$5,700	$9,100
		302/139 2dr Ghia Hdtp	$2,800	$4,100	$6,100	$10,000
						+$250 for Sports Performance Pkg. -20% for 4-cyl.

Year	Model	Body Style	4	3	2	1
1977	Thunderbird	302/130 2dr Hdtp	$2,100	$4,100	$6,200	$12,600
		302/130 2dr Lan Hdtp	$2,500	$4,300	$7,700	$14,000
						+10% for factory a/c.
1978	Mustang II	171/90 3dr Htchbk Cpe	$2,600	$3,900	$5,400	$8,500
		302/139 3dr Htchbk Cpe	$2,900	$4,100	$6,100	$9,400
		171/90 3dr Cobra II Htchbk Cpe	$4,600	$7,700	$9,600	$14,000
		302/139 3dr Cobra II Htchbk Cpe	$4,800	$8,700	$11,400	$15,700
		302/139 3dr King Cobra Htchbk Cpe	$5,700	$9,000	$13,800	$21,500
		171/90 2dr Cpe	$2,600	$3,800	$5,200	$8,100
		302/139 2dr Cpe	$2,800	$4,100	$5,600	$9,100
		171/90 2dr Ghia Cpe	$2,500	$3,800	$4,600	$7,900
		302/139 2dr Ghia Cpe	$2,700	$4,200	$5,000	$8,600
						-20% for 4-cyl.
1978	Thunderbird	302/134 2dr Cpe	$2,200	$5,100	$8,100	$13,100
		302/134 2dr Lan Cpe	$2,500	$4,900	$8,300	$14,500
		302/134 2dr Diamond Jubilee Cpe	$3,000	$6,100	$10,900	$17,900
						+5% for T-tops. +10% for factory a/c.
1979	Mustang	302/140 3dr Htchbk Cpe	$2,200	$3,500	$6,900	$11,000
		302/140 3dr Indy Pace Car Htchbk Cpe	$6,600	$10,900	$16,800	$25,800
		302/140 3dr Cobra Htchbk Cpe	$5,500	$9,800	$13,800	$21,000
		302/140 2dr Cpe	$2,000	$3,300	$6,700	$10,300
		302/140 2dr Ghia Cpe	$2,400	$3,400	$6,700	$10,700
						-15% for I6. -20% for non-turbo 4-cyl.
1979	Thunderbird	302/133 2dr Cpe	$2,200	$4,400	$8,000	$13,200
		302/133 2dr Lan Cpe	$2,600	$4,500	$8,600	$14,900
		302/133 2dr Heritage Ed Cpe	$3,400	$6,400	$11,300	$18,300
						+5% for T-tops. +10% for factory a/c.
1980	Mustang	255/119 2dr Cpe	$2,600	$3,200	$6,400	$10,500

Ford

Year	Model	Body Style	4	3	2	1
		255/119 2dr Ghia Cpe	$2,600	$4,000	$7,100	$10,800
		255/119 3dr Htchbk Cpe	$2,300	$3,900	$6,500	$11,100
		255/119 3dr Ghia Htchbk Cpe	$2,600	$4,100	$7,100	$10,800
		255/119 3dr Cobra Htchbk Cpe	$5,800	$9,800	$14,500	$22,900
		-15% for I6. -20% for non-turbo 4-cyl.				
1980	Thunderbird	255/115 2dr Cpe	$1,900	$3,300	$6,800	$11,000
		302/131 2dr Cpe	$1,500	$2,700	$5,700	$10,000
		255/115 2dr Town Landau Cpe	$2,600	$4,500	$7,800	$12,500
		302/131 2dr Town Landau Cpe	$2,000	$3,400	$6,600	$10,900
		255/115 2dr Silver Annv Cpe	$3,000	$5,000	$8,900	$13,200
		302/131 2dr Silver Annv Cpe	$2,500	$4,000	$7,200	$12,000
		+10% for factory a/c.				
1981	Mustang	255/115 2dr Cpe	$2,300	$3,800	$7,100	$11,100
		255/115 2dr Ghia Cpe	$2,300	$4,100	$6,900	$11,100
		255/115 3dr Htchbk	$2,100	$3,500	$6,500	$9,900
		255/115 3dr Ghia Htchbk	$2,400	$3,500	$6,600	$10,400
		255/115 3dr Cobra Htchbk	$5,600	$8,900	$12,600	$19,900
		-15% for I6. -20% for non-turbo 4-cyl. +$500 for T-Roof.				
1981	Thunderbird	255/115 2dr Cpe	$2,300	$3,700	$6,900	$10,800
		302/130 2dr Cpe	$2,900	$4,100	$7,700	$12,300
		+10% for factory a/c. -10% for 6-cyl.				
1981	GT40	2dr Mk V Cont Cpe	$178,000	$228,000	$282,000	$355,000
		2dr Mk V Cont Rdstr	$216,000	$254,000	$327,000	$425,000
1982	Mustang	302/157 3dr 5.0 GT Htchbk	$3,200	$5,900	$11,800	$17,700
1982	Thunderbird	255/120 2dr Cpe	$2,200	$4,100	$7,600	$10,900
		+10% for factory a/c. -10% for 6-cyl.				
1982	GT40	2dr Mk V Cont Cpe	$178,000	$228,000	$282,000	$355,000
		2dr Mk V Cont Rdstr	$216,000	$254,000	$327,000	$425,000
1983	Mustang	302/175 3dr 5.0 GT Htchbk	$3,500	$6,500	$12,500	$20,300
		302/175 2dr 5.0 GT Conv	$4,500	$8,300	$16,000	$22,100

Year	Model	Body Style	4	3	2	1
1983	GT40	2dr Mk V Cont Cpe	$178,000	$228,000	$282,000	$355,000
		2dr Mk V Cont Rdstr	$216,000	$254,000	$327,000	$425,000
1984	Mustang	302/175 2dr 5.0 Cpe	$1,700	$3,100	$7,200	$11,700
		302/175 3dr 5.0 Htchbk	$1,700	$3,700	$7,400	$12,300
		302/175 3dr 5.0 GT Htchbk	$2,900	$5,400	$11,000	$18,000
		140/175 3dr SVO Htchbk	$4,800	$9,400	$14,300	$21,500
						-10% for auto.
		302/175 3dr Saleen Htchbk	$9,400	$15,300	$27,400	$34,300
		302/175 2dr 5.0 Conv	$2,700	$4,900	$11,600	$15,700
		302/175 2dr 5.0 GT Conv	$3,900	$7,300	$14,500	$19,900
						-10% for auto.
1984	GT40	2dr Mk V Cont Cpe	$178,000	$228,000	$282,000	$355,000
		2dr Mk V Cont Rdstr	$216,000	$254,000	$327,000	$425,000
1985	Mustang	302/210 2dr 5.0 Cpe	$2,100	$4,400	$8,000	$12,500
		302/210 3dr 5.0 Htchbk	$2,100	$4,500	$8,100	$12,700
		302/210 3dr 5.0 GT Htchbk	$4,200	$6,700	$12,000	$20,400
		140/205 3dr SVO Htchbk	$7,100	$12,600	$17,700	$28,900
				+15% for 20th Annv Pkg on GTs. -10% for auto.		
		302/210 3dr Saleen Htchbk	$10,400	$16,900	$28,800	$36,000
		302/210 2dr 5.0 Conv	$2,900	$5,100	$11,300	$15,900
		302/210 2dr 5.0 GT Conv	$5,800	$9,100	$17,700	$23,600
				+15% for 20th Annv Pkg on GTs. -10% for auto.		
		302/210 2dr Saleen Conv	$9,100	$16,000	$26,500	$33,800
1985	GT40	2dr Mk V Cont Cpe	$178,000	$228,000	$282,000	$355,000
		2dr Mk V Cont Rdstr	$216,000	$254,000	$327,000	$425,000
1986	Mustang	302/200 3dr 5.0 Htchbk	$1,900	$4,300	$7,600	$11,700
		302/200 3dr 5.0 GT Htchbk	$3,400	$6,000	$10,400	$17,200
		140/200 3dr SVO Htchbk	$6,400	$12,000	$16,600	$25,600

Ford

Year	Model	Body Style	4	3	2	1
		302/200 3dr Saleen Htchbk	$10,400	$16,900	$28,800	$36,000
		302/200 2dr 5.0 Conv	$3,100	$4,800	$11,500	$15,500
		302/200 2dr 5.0 GT Conv	$4,800	$7,900	$15,200	$19,700
		302/200 2dr Saleen Conv	$9,100	$16,000	$26,500	$33,800
1986	GT40	2dr Mk V Cont Cpe	$178,000	$228,000	$282,000	$355,000
		2dr Mk V Cont Rdstr	$216,000	$254,000	$327,000	$425,000
1987	Mustang	302/225 2dr 5.0 LX Cpe	$2,400	$3,900	$6,800	$11,500
		302/225 2dr Saleen Cpe	$8,900	$15,400	$25,800	$32,900
		302/225 3dr 5.0 LX Htchbk	$2,100	$4,600	$7,400	$12,600
		302/225 3dr 5.0 GT Htchbk	$3,800	$6,200	$9,800	$18,600
		302/225 3dr Saleen Htchbk	$10,400	$16,900	$28,800	$36,000
		302/225 2dr 5.0 LX Conv	$3,500	$5,100	$10,800	$15,600
		302/225 2dr 5.0 GT Conv	$5,700	$8,900	$15,800	$23,200
		302/225 2dr Saleen Conv	$9,100	$16,000	$26,500	$33,800
1987	GT40	2dr Mk V Cont Cpe	$178,000	$228,000	$282,000	$355,000
		2dr Mk V Cont Rdstr	$216,000	$254,000	$327,000	$425,000
1988	Mustang	302/225 2dr 5.0 LX Cpe	$2,600	$4,300	$7,500	$12,900
		302/225 2dr Saleen Cpe	$9,300	$16,200	$27,100	$34,500
		302/225 3dr 5.0 LX Htchbk	$2,500	$5,000	$7,600	$13,500
		302/225 3dr 5.0 GT Htchbk	$4,000	$6,400	$10,600	$19,800
		302/225 3dr Saleen Htchbk	$10,900	$17,700	$30,200	$37,800
		302/225 2dr 5.0 LX Conv	$3,700	$5,900	$11,700	$17,100
		302/225 2dr 5.0 GT Conv	$6,100	$9,000	$15,600	$22,700
		302/225 2dr Saleen Conv	$9,600	$16,800	$27,800	$35,500
1988	GT40	2dr Mk V Cont Cpe	$178,000	$228,000	$282,000	$355,000
		2dr Mk V Cont Rdstr	$216,000	$254,000	$327,000	$425,000
1989	Mustang	302/225 2dr 5.0 LX Cpe	$2,300	$5,200	$7,600	$13,000

Year	Model	Body Style	4	3	2	1
		302/225 2dr Saleen Cpe	$8,400	$14,700	$24,600	$31,300
		302/225 3dr 5.0 LX Htchbk	$2,500	$5,700	$8,400	$15,300
		302/225 3dr 5.0 GT Htchbk	$4,600	$7,100	$14,300	$22,400
		302/225 3dr Saleen Htchbk	$9,900	$16,100	$27,400	$34,300
		302/225 3dr Saleen SSC Htchbk	$20,300	$31,800	$43,600	$52,000
		302/225 2dr 5.0 LX Conv	$3,600	$5,900	$10,200	$16,100
		302/225 2dr 5.0 GT Conv	$5,800	$9,200	$16,700	$24,000
		302/225 2dr Saleen Conv	$8,700	$15,100	$25,200	$32,200
1989	Taurus	182/220 4dr SHO Sdn	$2,700	$4,400	$6,600	$13,300
1989	GT40	2dr Mk V Cont Cpe	$178,000	$228,000	$282,000	$355,000
		2dr Mk V Cont Rdstr	$216,000	$254,000	$327,000	$425,000
1990	Mustang	302/225 2dr 5.0 LX Cpe	$2,400	$5,700	$8,000	$14,000
		302/225 2dr Saleen Cpe	$8,900	$15,400	$25,800	$31,300
		302/225 3dr 5.0 LX Htchbk	$2,600	$6,100	$8,600	$15,100
		302/225 3dr 5.0 GT Htchbk	$3,700	$5,500	$11,300	$18,500
		302/225 3dr Saleen Htchbk	$10,400	$16,900	$28,800	$34,300
		3dr Saleen SC Htchbk	$25,000	$39,400	$54,700	$64,000
		302/225 2dr 5.0 LX Conv	$3,800	$6,400	$10,900	$17,200
		302/225 2dr LX 5.0 25th Annv Conv	$6,300	$10,000	$15,800	$27,900
		302/225 2dr 5.0 GT Conv	$4,700	$7,200	$11,900	$19,700
		302/225 2dr Saleen Conv	$9,100	$16,000	$26,500	$32,200
1990	Taurus	182/220 4dr SHO Sdn	$2,700	$4,400	$6,600	$13,300
1990	GT40	2dr Mk V Cont Cpe	$178,000	$228,000	$282,000	$355,000
		2dr Mk V Cont Rdstr	$216,000	$254,000	$327,000	$425,000
1991	Mustang	302/225 2dr 5.0 LX Cpe	$2,300	$6,100	$9,700	$14,800
		302/225 2dr Saleen Cpe	$8,600	$14,700	$24,600	$31,300

Year	Model	Body Style	4	3	2	1
		302/225 3dr 5.0 LX Htchbk	$2,400	$6,300	$10,100	$16,000
		302/225 3dr 5.0 GT Htchbk	$4,000	$7,400	$14,800	$20,400
		302/225 3dr Saleen Htchbk	$10,000	$16,100	$27,400	$34,300
		2dr Saleen SC Htchbk	$25,000	$39,500	$52,100	$64,000
		302/225 2dr 5.0 LX Conv	$3,800	$7,000	$13,000	$18,800
		302/225 2dr 5.0 GT Conv	$4,900	$9,200	$15,000	$21,700
		302/225 2dr Saleen Conv	$8,800	$15,200	$25,200	$32,200
1991	Taurus	182/220 4dr SHO Sdn	$2,700	$4,400	$6,600	$13,300
1991	GT40	2dr Mk V Cont Cpe	$178,000	$228,000	$282,000	$355,000
		2dr Mk V Cont Rdstr	$216,000	$254,000	$327,000	$425,000
1992	Mustang	302/225 2dr 5.0 LX Cpe	$2,300	$5,000	$7,300	$12,400
		302/225 3dr 5.0 LX Htchbk	$2,400	$5,100	$7,400	$12,500
		302/225 3dr 5.0 GT Htchbk	$4,700	$7,000	$13,400	$21,800
		302/225 3dr Saleen Htchbk	$10,100	$16,100	$27,400	$34,300
		302/225 2dr 5.0 LX Conv	$3,700	$6,600	$12,200	$21,400
		302/225 2dr 5.0 GT Conv	$5,900	$9,700	$16,000	$28,300
		302/225 2dr Saleen Conv	$8,900	$15,200	$25,200	$32,200
1992	Taurus	182/220 4dr SHO Sdn	$3,000	$4,900	$7,400	$13,600
1992	GT40	2dr Mk V Cont Cpe	$178,000	$228,000	$282,000	$355,000
		2dr Mk V Cont Rdstr	$216,000	$254,000	$327,000	$425,000
		2dr Mk II Holman Cont Cpe	$206,000	$238,000	$312,000	$406,000
1993	Mustang	302/205 2dr 5.0 LX Cpe	$3,200	$6,300	$10,000	$16,600
		302/205 2dr Saleen Cpe	$8,600	$14,700	$24,600	$31,300
		302/205 3dr 5.0 LX Htchbk	$3,600	$6,800	$10,600	$17,700
		302/205 3dr 5.0 GT Htchbk	$4,600	$7,500	$15,000	$22,700
		302/230 3dr 5.0 SVT Cobra Htchbk	$13,700	$21,400	$32,600	$51,300
		302/205 3dr Saleen Htchbk	$10,000	$16,100	$27,400	$34,300

Year	Model	Body Style	4	3	2	1
		2dr Saleen SC Htchbk	$26,300	$41,400	$54,700	$67,200
		302/230 3dr 5.0 SVT Cobra R Htchbk	$33,700	$49,200	$69,000	$95,000
		302/205 2dr 5.0 LX Conv	$4,900	$8,200	$16,400	$29,600
		302/205 2dr 5.0 GT Conv	$5,600	$9,300	$18,300	$33,800
		302/205 2dr Saleen Conv	$8,800	$15,200	$25,200	$32,200
		2dr Saleen SC Conv	$24,900	$39,800	$52,700	$65,200
1993	Taurus	195/220 4dr SHO Sdn	$3,000	$4,900	$7,400	$13,600
1993	GT40	2dr Mk V Cont Cpe	$178,000	$228,000	$282,000	$355,000
		2dr Mk V Cont Rdstr	$216,000	$254,000	$327,000	$425,000
		2dr Mk II Holman Cont Cpe	$206,000	$238,000	$312,000	$406,000
1994	Mustang	302/215 2dr GT Conv	$3,600	$7,300	$12,500	$25,300
		302/215 2dr GT Cpe	$2,700	$6,500	$11,100	$24,000
		302/240 2dr Indianapolis Pace Car Cobra Conv	$6,800	$10,000	$17,800	$37,300
		302/240 2dr SVT Cobra Cpe	$5,400	$8,400	$16,900	$33,700
						-5% for auto.
1994	Taurus	195/220 4dr SHO Sdn	$3,100	$5,100	$7,700	$13,900
1994	GT40	2dr Mk V Cont Cpe	$178,000	$228,000	$282,000	$355,000
		2dr Mk V Cont Rdstr	$216,000	$254,000	$327,000	$425,000
		2dr Mk II Holman Cont Cpe	$206,000	$238,000	$312,000	$406,000
1995	Mustang	302/215 2dr GT Conv	$3,600	$7,300	$12,500	$25,300
		302/215 2dr GT Cpe	$2,700	$6,500	$11,100	$24,000
		302/240 2dr SVT Cobra Conv	$5,900	$8,800	$16,000	$32,400
		302/240 2dr SVT Cobra Cpe	$5,400	$8,400	$16,900	$33,700
		351/300 FI 2dr SVT Cobra R Cpe	$9,700	$14,200	$19,600	$32,400
						-5% for auto.
1995	Taurus	195/220 4dr SHO Sdn	$3,100	$5,100	$7,700	$13,900
1995	GT40	2dr Mk V Cont Cpe	$178,000	$228,000	$282,000	$355,000

Ford

Year	Model	Body Style	4	3	2	1
		2dr Mk V Cont Rdstr	$216,000	$254,000	$327,000	$425,000
		2dr Mk II Holman Cont Cpe	$206,000	$238,000	$312,000	$406,000
1996	Mustang	281/215 2dr GT Conv	$3,600	$6,600	$11,300	$21,100
		281/215 2dr GT Cpe	$2,700	$5,900	$9,900	$20,000
		281/305 2dr SVT Cobra Conv	$7,600	$9,400	$15,300	$29,200
		281/305 2dr SVT Cobra Cpe	$7,300	$9,000	$16,100	$30,200
						-5% for auto.
1996	Taurus	207/224 4dr SHO Sdn	$3,000	$5,100	$7,900	$12,600
1996	GT40	2dr Mk V Cont Cpe	$178,000	$228,000	$282,000	$355,000
		2dr Mk V Cont Rdstr	$216,000	$254,000	$327,000	$425,000
		2dr Mk II Holman Cont Cpe	$206,000	$238,000	$312,000	$406,000
1997	Mustang	281/215 2dr GT Conv	$3,600	$6,600	$11,300	$21,100
		281/215 2dr GT Cpe	$2,700	$5,900	$9,900	$20,000
		281/305 2dr SVT Cobra Conv	$7,600	$9,400	$15,300	$29,200
		281/305 2dr SVT Cobra Cpe	$7,300	$9,000	$16,100	$30,200
						-5% for auto.
1997	Taurus	207/235 4dr SHO Sdn	$3,000	$5,100	$7,900	$12,600
1997	GT40	2dr Mk V Cont Cpe	$178,000	$228,000	$282,000	$355,000
		2dr Mk V Cont Rdstr	$216,000	$254,000	$327,000	$425,000
		2dr Mk II Holman Cont Cpe	$206,000	$238,000	$312,000	$406,000
1998	Mustang	281/225 2dr GT Conv	$4,100	$6,900	$11,800	$21,600
		281/225 2dr GT Cpe	$3,200	$6,200	$10,500	$20,600
		281/305 2dr SVT Cobra Conv	$7,600	$9,400	$15,300	$29,200
		281/305 2dr SVT Cobra Cpe	$7,300	$9,000	$16,100	$30,200
						-5% for auto.
1998	Taurus	207/235 4dr SHO Sdn	$3,000	$5,100	$7,900	$12,600
1998	GT40	2dr Mk V Cont Cpe	$178,000	$228,000	$282,000	$355,000
		2dr Mk V Cont Rdstr	$216,000	$254,000	$327,000	$425,000

Year	Model	Body Style	4	3	2	1
		2dr Mk II Holman Cont Cpe	$206,000	$238,000	$312,000	$406,000
1999	Mustang	281/260 2dr GT Conv	$4,900	$7,700	$13,000	$23,800
		281/260 2dr GT Cpe	$3,600	$6,900	$11,800	$22,700
		281/320 2dr Cobra SVT Conv	$6,800	$9,700	$14,800	$26,100
		281/320 2dr Cobra SVT Cpe	$7,300	$10,400	$16,700	$27,000
					+5% for 35th Anniversary.	
1999	Taurus	207/235 4dr SHO Sdn	$3,000	$5,100	$7,900	$12,600
1999	GT40	2dr Mk V Cont Cpe	$178,000	$228,000	$282,000	$355,000
		2dr Mk V Cont Rdstr	$216,000	$254,000	$327,000	$425,000
		2dr Mk II Holman Cont Cpe	$206,000	$238,000	$312,000	$406,000
2000	Mustang	281/260 2dr GT Conv	$4,900	$7,700	$13,000	$23,800
		281/260 2dr GT Cpe	$3,600	$6,900	$11,800	$22,700
		330/385 2dr Cobra R Cpe	$17,500	$21,600	$32,500	$64,800
						-5% for auto.
2000	GT40	2dr Mk V Cont Cpe	$178,000	$228,000	$282,000	$355,000
		2dr Mk V Cont Rdstr	$216,000	$254,000	$327,000	$425,000
		2dr Mk II Holman Cont Cpe	$206,000	$238,000	$312,000	$406,000
2001	Mustang	281/260 2dr GT Conv	$4,900	$7,700	$13,000	$23,800
		281/260 2dr GT Cpe	$3,600	$6,900	$11,800	$22,700
		281/265 2dr Bullitt Cpe	$7,800	$10,400	$23,200	$43,200
		281/320 2dr Cobra SVT Conv	$6,800	$9,700	$14,800	$26,100
		281/320 2dr Cobra SVT Cpe	$7,300	$10,400	$16,700	$27,000
						-5% for auto.
2001	GT40	2dr Mk V Cont Cpe	$178,000	$228,000	$282,000	$355,000
		2dr Mk V Cont Rdstr	$216,000	$254,000	$327,000	$425,000
		2dr Mk II Holman Cont Cpe	$206,000	$238,000	$312,000	$406,000
2002	Mustang	281/260 2dr GT Conv	$4,900	$7,700	$13,000	$23,800
						-5% for auto.

Ford

Year	Model	Body Style	4	3	2	1
		281/260 2dr GT Cpe	$3,600	$6,900	$11,800	$22,700
						-5% for auto
2002	Thunderbird	238/280 2dr Conv	$12,500	$16,300	$21,800	$31,700
		238/280 2dr Neiman Marcus Conv	$14,000	$18,600	$24,100	$33,100
2002	GT40	2dr Mk V Cont Cpe	$178,000	$228,000	$282,000	$355,000
		2dr Mk V Cont Rdstr	$216,000	$254,000	$327,000	$425,000
		2dr Mk II Holman Cont Cpe	$206,000	$238,000	$312,000	$406,000
2003	Mustang	281/260 2dr GT Conv	$4,900	$7,700	$13,000	$23,800
		281/260 2dr GT Cpe	$3,600	$6,900	$11,800	$22,700
		281/305 2dr Mach 1 Cpe	$7,500	$14,300	$19,400	$35,300
		281/390 2dr Cobra SVT Conv	$9,500	$14,100	$23,600	$37,000
		281/390 2dr Cobra SVT Cpe	$9,900	$14,800	$24,400	$38,000
						-5% for auto.
2003	Thunderbird	238/280 2dr Conv	$12,400	$14,500	$20,500	$31,100
						Plus 15% for Bond 007 Ed.
2003	GT40	2dr Mk V Cont Cpe	$178,000	$228,000	$282,000	$355,000
		2dr Mk V Cont Rdstr	$216,000	$254,000	$327,000	$425,000
		2dr Mk II Holman Cont Cpe	$206,000	$238,000	$312,000	$406,000
2004	Mustang	281/260 2dr GT Conv	$4,900	$7,700	$13,000	$23,800
		281/260 2dr GT Cpe	$3,600	$6,900	$11,800	$22,700
		281/305 2dr Mach 1 Cpe	$7,500	$14,300	$19,400	$35,300
		281/390 2dr Cobra SVT Conv	$9,500	$14,100	$21,900	$37,000
		281/390 2dr Cobra SVT Cpe	$9,900	$14,800	$22,700	$38,000
						-5% for auto.
2004	Thunderbird	240/280 2dr Conv	$14,100	$15,900	$19,700	$28,600
2004	GT40	2dr Mk V Cont Cpe	$178,000	$228,000	$282,000	$355,000
		2dr Mk V Cont Rdstr	$216,000	$254,000	$327,000	$425,000
		2dr Mk II Holman Cont Cpe	$206,000	$238,000	$312,000	$406,000

Year	Model	Body Style	4	3	2	1
2005	Thunderbird	240/280 2dr Conv	$15,700	$18,100	$23,000	$32,200
		240/280 2dr 50th Annv Conv	$17,000	$19,900	$24,900	$35,000
2005	GT	330/550 2dr Cpe	$196,000	$248,000	$313,000	$376,000
		+$4,000 for factory BBS wheels. +$3,000 for factory stripes. +$2,500 for McIntosh audiophile system. +$900 for painted calipers.				
2005	GT40	2dr Mk V Cont Cpe	$178,000	$228,000	$282,000	$355,000
		2dr Mk V Cont Rdstr	$216,000	$254,000	$327,000	$425,000
		2dr Mk II Holman Cont Cpe	$206,000	$238,000	$312,000	$406,000
2005	Mustang	281/300 2dr GT Cpe	$7,500	$9,700	$15,500	$22,000
		281/300 2dr GT Conv	$8,500	$11,500	$17,800	$25,000
		-15% for 6-cyl. -10% for auto trans. approximately -15% for Super Snakes with lower output.				
2006	GT	330/550 2dr Cpe	$199,000	$253,000	$319,000	$382,000
		330/550 2dr Heritage Cpe	$236,000	$283,000	$385,000	$450,000
		+$4,000 for factory BBS wheels. +$3,000 for factory stripes (exc. Heritage). +$2,500 for McIntosh audiophile system. +$900 for painted calipers.				
2006	GT40	2dr Mk V Cont Cpe	$178,000	$228,000	$282,000	$355,000
		2dr Mk V Cont Rdstr	$216,000	$254,000	$327,000	$425,000
		2dr Mk II Holman Cont Cpe	$206,000	$238,000	$312,000	$406,000
		2dr Mk IV Kar Kraft Cont Cpe	$210,000	$242,000	$322,000	$415,000
2006	Mustang	281/300 2dr GT Cpe	$7,500	$9,700	$15,500	$22,000
		281/325 2dr Shelby GT-H Cpe	$21,000	$26,000	$33,000	$44,000
		281/300 2dr GT Conv	$8,500	$11,500	$17,800	$25,000
		-15% for 6-cyl. -10% for auto trans. approximately -15% for Super Snakes with lower output.				
2007	GT40	2dr Mk V Cont Cpe	$178,000	$228,000	$282,000	$355,000
		2dr Mk V Cont Rdstr	$216,000	$254,000	$327,000	$425,000
		2dr Mk II Holman Cont Cpe	$206,000	$238,000	$312,000	$406,000
2007	Mustang	281/300 2dr GT Conv	$8,500	$11,500	$17,800	$25,000
		281/300 2dr GT Cpe	$7,500	$9,700	$15,500	$22,000
		281/319 2dr Shelby GT Cpe	$11,000	$14,500	$21,000	$29,000

Ford

Year	Model	Body Style	4	3	2	1
		330/500 2dr Shelby GT500 Cpe	$17,500	$25,000	$32,000	$41,000
		330/725 2dr Shelby GT500 Super Snake Cpe	$50,000	$52,000	$75,000	$90,000
		281/325 2dr Shelby GT-H Conv	$23,000	$30,000	$37,000	$46,500
		330/500 2dr Shelby GT500 Conv	$20,000	$28,000	$34,000	$45,000
		330/725 2dr Shelby GT500 Super Snake Conv	$63,000	$79,000	$95,000	$120,000

-15% for 6-cyl, -10% for auto trans, approximately -15% for Super Snakes with lower output.

Year	Model	Body Style	4	3	2	1
2008	GT40	2dr Mk V Cont Cpe	$178,000	$228,000	$282,000	$355,000
		2dr Mk V Cont Rdstr	$216,000	$254,000	$327,000	$425,000
		2dr Mk II Holman Cont Cpe	$206,000	$238,000	$312,000	$406,000
2008	Mustang	281/300 2dr GT Cpe	$7,500	$9,700	$15,500	$22,000
		281/315 2dr Bullitt Cpe	$9,900	$14,500	$20,000	$31,000
		330/500 2dr Shelby GT500 Cpe	$17,500	$25,000	$32,000	$41,000
		330/540 2dr Shelby GT500KR Cpe	$24,000	$39,000	$52,000	$63,000
		330/725 2dr Shelby GT500 Super Snake Cpe	$50,000	$62,000	$75,000	$90,000
		2dr Cobra Jet Cpe	$45,000	$58,000	$80,000	$100,000
		281/300 2dr GT Conv	$8,500	$11,500	$17,800	$25,000
		330/500 2dr Shelby GT500 Conv	$20,000	$28,000	$34,000	$45,000
		330/725 2dr Shelby GT500 Super Snake Conv	$63,000	$79,000	$95,000	$120,000

-15% for 6-cyl, -10% for auto trans, approximately -15% for Super Snakes with lower output.

Year	Model	Body Style	4	3	2	1
2009	GT40	2dr Mk V Cont Cpe	$178,000	$228,000	$282,000	$355,000
		2dr Mk V Cont Rdstr	$216,000	$254,000	$327,000	$425,000
		2dr Mk II Holman Cont Cpe	$206,000	$238,000	$312,000	$406,000

Year	Model	Body Style	4	3	2	1
2009	Mustang	281/300 2dr GT Cpe	$7,500	$9,700	$15,500	$22,000
		281/315 2dr Bullitt Cpe	$9,900	$14,500	$20,000	$31,000
		330/500 2dr Shelby GT500 Cpe	$17,500	$25,000	$32,000	$41,000
		330/540 2dr Shelby GT500KR Cpe	$24,000	$39,000	$52,000	$63,000
		330/725 2dr Shelby GT500 Super Snake Cpe	$50,000	$62,000	$75,000	$90,000
		281/300 2dr GT Conv	$8,500	$11,500	$17,800	$25,000
		330/500 2dr Shelby GT500 Conv	$20,000	$28,000	$34,000	$45,000
		330/725 2dr Shelby GT500 Super Snake Conv	$63,000	$79,000	$95,000	$120,000
			-15% for 6-cyl, -10% for auto trans, approximately -15% for Super Snakes with lower output.			
2010	Mustang	281/315 2dr GT Cpe	$9,500	$11,500	$17,800	$24,000
		2dr Cobra Jet Cpe	$45,000	$58,000	$80,000	$100,000
		330/540 2dr Shelby GT500 Cpe	$23,000	$29,500	$37,000	$45,000
		330/725 2dr Shelby GT500 Super Snake Cpe	$50,000	$62,000	$75,000	$90,000
		281/315 2dr GT Conv	$10,000	$12,900	$19,500	$26,500
		330/540 2dr Shelby GT500 Conv	$26,000	$33,000	$41,500	$50,000
		330/725 2dr Shelby GT500 Super Snake Conv	$63,000	$79,000	$95,000	$120,000
			-15% for 6-cyl, -10% for auto trans, approximately -15% for Super Snakes with lower output.			
2011	Mustang	302/412 2dr GT Cpe	$12,500	$17,900	$23,000	$29,000
		330/550 2dr Shelby GT500 Cpe	$23,000	$29,500	$37,000	$45,000
		330/800 2dr Shelby GT500 Super Snake Cpe	$50,000	$62,000	$75,000	$90,000
		302/412 2dr GT Conv	$14,000	$19,000	$26,500	$35,000

Ford

Year	Model	Body Style	4	3	2	1
		330/550 2dr Shelby GT500 Conv	$26,000	$33,000	$41,500	$50,000
		330/800 2dr Shelby GT500 Super Snake Conv	$63,000	$79,000	$95,000	$120,000

-15% for 6-cyl. -10% for auto trans, approximately -15% for Super Snakes with lower output.

Year	Model	Body Style	4	3	2	1
2012	Mustang	302/412 2dr GT Cpe	$12,500	$17,900	$23,000	$29,000
		302/444 2dr Boss 302 Cpe	$24,000	$29,000	$33,000	$38,000
		302/444 2dr Boss 302 Laguna Seca Cpe	$29,900	$34,000	$42,000	$50,000
		330/550 2dr Shelby GT500 Cpe	$23,000	$29,500	$37,000	$45,000
		330/800 2dr Shelby GT500 Super Snake Cpe	$50,000	$62,000	$75,000	$90,000
		2dr Cobra Jet Cpe	$45,000	$58,000	$80,000	$100,000
		302/412 2dr GT Conv	$14,000	$19,000	$26,500	$35,000
		330/550 2dr Shelby GT500 Conv	$26,000	$33,000	$41,500	$50,000
		330/800 2dr Shelby GT500 Super Snake Conv	$63,000	$79,000	$95,000	$120,000

-15% for 6-cyl. -10% for auto trans, approximately -15% for Super Snakes with lower output.

Year	Model	Body Style	4	3	2	1
2013	Mustang	302/420 2dr GT Cpe	$12,500	$17,900	$23,000	$29,000
		302/444 2dr Boss 302 Cpe	$24,000	$29,000	$33,000	$38,000
		302/444 2dr Boss 302 Laguna Seca Cpe	$29,900	$34,000	$42,000	$50,000
		351/650 2dr Shelby GT500 Cpe	$30,000	$38,500	$49,900	$57,000
		351/850 2dr Shelby GT500 Super Snake Cpe	$50,000	$62,000	$75,000	$90,000
		2dr Cobra Jet Cpe	$45,000	$58,000	$80,000	$100,000
		302/420 2dr GT Conv	$14,000	$19,000	$26,500	$35,000
		351/650 2dr Shelby GT500 Conv	$35,000	$42,500	$54,000	$63,000

Ford

Year	Model	Body Style	4	3	2	1
		351/850 2dr Shelby GT500 Super Snake Conv	$63,000	$79,000	$95,000	$120,000

-15% for 6-cyl, -10% for auto trans, approximately -15% for Super Snakes with lower output.

Year	Model	Body Style	4	3	2	1
2014	Mustang	302/420 2dr GT Cpe	$12,500	$17,900	$23,000	$29,000
		351/662 2dr Shelby GT500 Cpe	$30,000	$38,500	$49,900	$57,000
		351/850 2dr Shelby GT500 Super Snake Cpe	$50,000	$62,000	$75,000	$90,000
		2dr Cobra Jet Cpe	$45,000	$58,000	$80,000	$100,000
		302/420 2dr GT Conv	$14,000	$19,000	$26,500	$35,000
		351/662 2dr Shelby GT500 Conv	$35,000	$42,500	$54,000	$63,000
		351/850 2dr Shelby GT500 Super Snake Conv	$63,000	$79,000	$95,000	$120,000

-15% for 6-cyl, -10% for auto trans, approximately -15% for Super Snakes with lower output.

Frazer

Year	Model	Body Style	4	3	2	1
1947	Standard	226/100 4dr Sdn	$4,000	$8,400	$14,300	$25,500
1947	Manhattan	226/100 4dr Sdn	$5,500	$9,600	$15,800	$29,400
1948	Standard	226/100 4dr Sdn	$4,000	$8,400	$14,300	$25,500
1948	Manhattan	226/112 4dr Sdn	$5,500	$9,600	$15,800	$29,400
1949	Standard	226/112 4dr Sdn	$4,000	$8,400	$14,300	$25,500
1949	Manhattan	226/112 4dr Sdn	$5,500	$9,600	$15,800	$29,400
		226/112 4dr Conv	$17,300	$38,500	$57,500	$72,200
1950	Standard	226/112 4dr Sdn	$4,000	$8,400	$14,300	$25,500
1950	Manhattan	226/112 4dr Sdn	$5,500	$9,700	$15,900	$29,500
		226/112 4dr Conv	$17,300	$38,500	$57,500	$72,200
1951	Standard	226/115 4dr Sdn	$4,500	$8,700	$14,400	$25,600
1951	Manhattan	226/115 4dr Sdn	$5,500	$9,600	$15,800	$29,400
		226/115 4dr Conv	$17,300	$38,500	$57,500	$72,200
1951	Vagabond	226/115 4dr Uty Sdn	$5,200	$10,000	$15,600	$22,300

Frazer Nash

Year	Model	Body Style	4	3	2	1
1948	Mille Miglia	2dr Rdstr	$282,000	$326,000	$400,000	$470,000
1948	Le Mans	2dr Replica Mk I Rdstr	$585,000	$675,000	$750,000	$900,000

Frazer Nash

Year	Model	Body Style	4	3	2	1
1949	Mille Miglia	2dr Rdstr	$282,000	$326,000	$400,000	$470,000
1949	Le Mans	2dr Replica Mk I Rdstr	$585,000	$675,000	$750,000	$900,000
1950	Mille Miglia	2dr Rdstr	$282,000	$326,000	$400,000	$470,000
1950	Le Mans	2dr Replica Mk I Rdstr	$585,000	$675,000	$750,000	$900,000
1951	Mille Miglia	2dr Rdstr	$282,000	$326,000	$400,000	$470,000
1951	Le Mans	2dr Replica Mk I Rdstr	$585,000	$675,000	$750,000	$900,000
1952	Mille Miglia	2dr Rdstr	$282,000	$326,000	$400,000	$470,000
1952	Le Mans	2dr Replica Mk I Rdstr	$585,000	$675,000	$750,000	$900,000
1953	Le Mans	2dr Replica Mk II Rdstr	$585,000	$670,000	$735,000	$850,000

Ghia

Year	Model	Body Style	4	3	2	1
1962	1500	2dr Cpe	$18,600	$32,100	$55,600	$88,700
1963	1500	2dr Cpe	$18,600	$32,100	$55,600	$88,700
1964	1500	2dr Cpe	$18,600	$32,100	$55,600	$88,700
1965	1500	2dr Cpe	$18,600	$32,100	$55,600	$88,700
1966	1500	2dr Cpe	$18,600	$32,100	$55,600	$88,700
1966	450SS	2dr Conv	$60,600	$87,200	$135,000	$186,000
		+$10,000 for factory hard top. +$4,000 for wire wheels. +10% for manual trans.				
1967	1500	2dr Cpe	$18,600	$32,100	$55,600	$88,700
1967	450SS	2dr Conv	$60,600	$87,200	$135,000	$186,000
		+$10,000 for factory hard top. +$4,000 for wire wheels. +10% for manual trans.				

Ginetta

Year	Model	Body Style	4	3	2	1
1961	G4	2dr Rdstr	$17,000	$23,500	$38,500	$54,000
1962	G4	2dr Rdstr	$17,000	$23,500	$38,500	$54,000
1963	G4	2dr Rdstr	$17,000	$23,500	$38,500	$54,000
1964	G4	2dr Rdstr	$17,000	$23,500	$38,500	$54,000
1965	G4	2dr Rdstr	$17,000	$23,500	$38,500	$54,000
1966	G4	2dr Rdstr	$17,000	$23,500	$38,500	$54,000
1967	G4	2dr Rdstr	$17,000	$23,500	$38,500	$54,000
1967	G15	2dr Cpe	$4,700	$9,500	$15,900	$19,000
1968	G4	2dr Rdstr	$17,000	$23,500	$38,500	$54,000
1968	G15	2dr Cpe	$4,700	$9,500	$15,900	$19,000
1969	G4	2dr Rdstr	$17,000	$23,500	$38,500	$54,000
1969	G15	2dr Cpe	$4,700	$9,500	$15,900	$19,000
1970	G15	2dr Cpe	$4,700	$9,500	$15,900	$19,000
1971	G15	2dr Cpe	$4,700	$9,500	$15,900	$19,000
1972	G15	2dr Cpe	$4,700	$9,500	$15,900	$19,000
1973	G15	2dr Cpe	$4,700	$9,500	$15,900	$19,000
1974	G15	2dr Cpe	$4,700	$9,500	$15,900	$19,000

Glas

Year	Model	Body Style	4	3	2	1
1963	1700	4dr Sdn	$9,800	$15,500	$21,600	$33,700
1965	3000GT	2dr Cpe	$35,200	$48,500	$65,800	$90,500
1966	3000GT	2dr Cpe	$35,200	$48,500	$65,800	$90,500
1967	3000GT	2dr Cpe	$35,200	$48,500	$65,800	$90,500
1968	3000GT	2dr Cpe	$35,200	$48,500	$65,800	$90,500

Glassic

Year	Model	Body Style	4	3	2	1
1968	Model A	152/93 2dr Replica Rdstr	$4,700	$8,000	$11,900	$18,600
1969	Model A	196/111 2dr Replica Rdstr	$4,700	$8,000	$11,900	$18,600
1970	Model A	196/111 2dr Replica Rdstr	$4,700	$8,000	$11,900	$18,600
1971	Model A	196/111 2dr Replica Rdstr	$4,700	$8,000	$11,900	$18,600
1972	Model A	302/210 2dr Replica Rdstr	$5,400	$8,500	$13,300	$21,000
1973	Model A	302/210 2dr Replica Rdstr	$5,400	$8,500	$13,300	$21,000
1974	Model A	302/210 2dr Replica Rdstr	$5,400	$8,500	$13,300	$21,000

Glasspar

Year	Model	Body Style	4	3	2	1
1951	G2	2dr Rdstr	$35,000	$60,500	$94,600	$128,000
1952	G2	2dr Rdstr	$35,000	$60,500	$94,600	$128,000
1953	G2	2dr Rdstr	$35,000	$60,500	$94,600	$128,000
1954	G2	2dr Rdstr	$35,000	$60,500	$94,600	$128,000

Goggomobil

Year	Model	Body Style	4	3	2	1
1955	TS250	2dr Cpe	$11,000	$17,700	$27,300	$36,600
1955	T300	2dr Cpe	$11,400	$22,800	$31,900	$37,700
1955	TS300	2dr Cpe	$14,500	$22,500	$31,600	$38,900
1956	TS250	2dr Cpe	$11,000	$17,700	$27,300	$36,600
1956	T300	2dr Cpe	$11,400	$22,800	$31,900	$37,700
1956	TS300	2dr Cpe	$14,500	$22,500	$31,600	$38,900
1957	TS250	2dr Cpe	$11,000	$17,700	$27,300	$36,600
1957	T300	2dr Cpe	$11,400	$22,800	$31,900	$37,700
1957	TS300	2dr Cpe	$14,500	$22,500	$31,600	$38,900
1958	TS250	2dr Cpe	$11,000	$17,700	$27,300	$36,600
1958	T400	2dr Cpe	$16,400	$24,000	$34,100	$42,200
1958	TS400	2dr Cpe	$16,600	$24,100	$35,200	$46,900
1959	TS250	2dr Cpe	$11,000	$17,700	$27,300	$36,600
1959	T400	2dr Cpe	$16,400	$24,000	$34,100	$42,200
1959	TS400	2dr Cpe	$16,600	$24,100	$35,200	$46,900
1959	T700	2dr Cpe	$26,700	$30,800	$39,300	$49,900

Goggomobil

Year	Model	Body Style	4	3	2	1
1959	Dart	2dr Rdstr	$17,900	$24,700	$34,500	$46,400
1960	TS250	2dr Cpe	$11,000	$17,700	$27,300	$36,600
1960	TS400	2dr Cpe	$16,600	$24,100	$35,200	$46,900
1960	Dart	2dr Rdstr	$17,900	$24,700	$34,500	$46,400
1961	TS250	2dr Cpe	$11,000	$17,700	$27,300	$36,600
1961	T400	2dr Cpe	$16,400	$24,000	$34,100	$42,200
		2dr Conv	$18,100	$25,800	$36,200	$45,800
1961	TS400	2dr Cpe	$16,600	$24,100	$35,200	$46,900
1961	T700	2dr Cpe	$26,700	$30,800	$39,300	$49,900
		2dr Rdstr	$27,600	$34,300	$43,700	$52,600
1961	Dart	2dr Rdstr	$17,900	$24,700	$34,500	$46,400
1962	TS250	2dr Cpe	$11,000	$17,700	$27,300	$36,600
1962	Dart	2dr Rdstr	$17,900	$24,700	$34,500	$46,400
1963	TS250	2dr Cpe	$11,000	$17,700	$27,300	$36,600
1964	TS250	2dr Cpe	$11,000	$17,700	$27,300	$36,600
1965	TS250	2dr Cpe	$11,000	$17,700	$27,300	$36,600
1966	TS250	2dr Cpe	$11,000	$17,700	$27,300	$36,600
1967	TS250	2dr Cpe	$11,000	$17,700	$27,300	$36,600
1968	TS250	2dr Cpe	$11,000	$17,700	$27,300	$36,600
1969	TS250	2dr Cpe	$11,000	$17,700	$27,300	$36,600

Goliath

Year	Model	Body Style	4	3	2	1
1950	GP700	2dr Spt Cpe	$9,800	$14,800	$21,900	$32,500
		2dr Sdn	$3,200	$6,700	$11,000	$16,900
1951	GP700	2dr Spt Cpe	$9,800	$14,800	$21,900	$32,500
		2dr Sdn	$3,200	$6,700	$11,000	$16,900
1952	GP700	2dr Spt Cpe	$9,800	$14,800	$21,900	$32,500
		2dr Sdn	$3,200	$6,700	$11,000	$16,900
1953	GP700	2dr Spt Cpe	$9,800	$14,800	$21,900	$32,500
		2dr Sdn	$3,200	$6,700	$11,000	$16,900
1954	GP700	2dr Spt Cpe	$9,800	$14,800	$21,900	$32,500
		2dr Sdn	$3,200	$6,700	$11,000	$16,900
1955	GP700	2dr Spt Cpe	$9,800	$14,800	$21,900	$32,500
		2dr Sdn	$3,200	$6,700	$11,000	$16,900
1955	GP900	2dr Sdn	$3,500	$7,100	$12,000	$17,300
1956	GP700	2dr Spt Cpe	$9,800	$14,800	$21,900	$32,500
		2dr Sdn	$3,200	$6,700	$11,000	$16,900
1956	GP900	2dr Sdn	$3,500	$7,100	$12,000	$17,300
1957	GP700	2dr Cpe	$9,800	$14,800	$21,900	$32,500
		2dr Sdn	$3,200	$6,700	$11,000	$16,900
1957	GP900	2dr Sdn	$3,500	$7,100	$12,000	$17,300
1957	1100	2dr Sdn	$2,900	$6,200	$10,300	$16,000
		2dr Wgn	$4,000	$6,100	$9,400	$14,000
		2dr Conv	$6,400	$9,300	$13,200	$18,500
1958	1100	2dr Sdn	$2,900	$6,200	$10,300	$16,000
		2dr Wgn	$4,000	$6,100	$9,400	$14,000
		2dr Conv	$6,400	$9,300	$13,200	$18,500

Goliath

Year	Model	Body Style	4	3	2	1
1959	1100	2dr Sdn	$2,900	$6,200	$10,300	$16,000
		2dr Wgn	$4,000	$6,100	$9,400	$14,000
		2dr Conv	$6,400	$9,300	$13,200	$18,500

Gordon-Keeble

Year	Model	Body Style	4	3	2	1
1964	GK1	2dr Sdn	$40,600	$67,000	$99,400	$127,000
1965	GK1	2dr Sdn	$40,600	$67,000	$99,400	$127,000
1966	GK1	2dr Sdn	$40,600	$67,000	$99,400	$127,000
1967	GK1	2dr Sdn	$40,600	$67,000	$99,400	$127,000

Griffith

Year	Model	Body Style	4	3	2	1
1964	TVR 200	2dr Cpe	$62,800	$87,500	$113,000	$141,000
1965	TVR 200	2dr Cpe	$62,800	$87,500	$113,000	$141,000
1965	TVR 400	2dr Cpe	$69,000	$95,000	$128,000	$153,000
1966	TVR 400	2dr Cpe	$69,000	$95,000	$128,000	$153,000
1966	Intermeccanica GT	2dr Cpe	$43,000	$58,800	$92,400	$107,000
1967	Intermeccanica GT	2dr Cpe	$43,000	$58,800	$92,400	$107,000

Guanci

Year	Model	Body Style	4	3	2	1
1979	SJJ1 GT	2dr Cpe	$10,400	$18,900	$27,700	$39,900

HRG

Year	Model	Body Style	4	3	2	1
1946	1100	2dr Rdstr	$35,500	$52,500	$68,500	$90,000
1946	1500	2dr Rdstr	$52,400	$65,000	$92,500	$120,000
1947	1100	2dr Rdstr	$35,500	$52,500	$68,500	$90,000
1947	1500	2dr Rdstr	$52,400	$65,000	$92,500	$120,000
1947	1500 Aerodynamic	2dr Rdstr	$72,500	$108,000	$155,000	$185,000
1948	1100	2dr Rdstr	$35,500	$52,500	$68,500	$90,000
1948	1500	2dr Rdstr	$52,400	$65,000	$92,500	$120,000
1949	1100	2dr Rdstr	$35,500	$52,500	$68,500	$90,000
1949	1500	2dr Rdstr	$52,400	$65,000	$92,500	$120,000
1950	1100	2dr Rdstr	$35,500	$52,500	$68,500	$90,000
1950	1500	2dr Rdstr	$52,400	$65,000	$92,500	$120,000
1951	1500	2dr Rdstr	$52,400	$65,000	$92,500	$120,000
1952	1500	2dr Rdstr	$52,400	$65,000	$92,500	$120,000
1953	1500	2dr Rdstr	$52,400	$65,000	$92,500	$120,000
1954	1500	2dr Rdstr	$52,400	$65,000	$92,500	$120,000
1955	1500	2dr Rdstr	$52,400	$65,000	$92,500	$120,000
1955	1500 Twin Cam	2dr Rdstr	$105,000	$164,000	$215,000	$305,000
1956	1500	2dr Rdstr	$52,400	$65,000	$92,500	$120,000
1956	1500 Twin Cam	2dr Rdstr	$105,000	$164,000	$215,000	$305,000

Healey

Year	Model	Body Style	4	3	2	1
1946	Elliott	2dr Sal	$35,000	$53,000	$66,500	$73,500
1946	Westland	2dr Conv	$98,000	$132,000	$180,000	$215,000
1947	Elliott	2dr Sal	$35,000	$53,000	$66,500	$73,500
1947	Westland	2dr Conv	$98,000	$132,000	$180,000	$215,000
1948	Elliott	2dr Sal	$35,000	$53,000	$66,500	$73,500
1948	Westland	2dr Conv	$98,000	$132,000	$180,000	$215,000
1948	Silverstone	2dr Rdstr	$107,000	$138,000	$195,000	$265,000
1949	Elliott	2dr Sal	$35,000	$53,000	$66,500	$73,500
1949	Westland	2dr Conv	$98,000	$132,000	$180,000	$215,000
1949	Silverstone	2dr Rdstr	$107,000	$138,000	$195,000	$265,000
1950	Elliott	2dr Sal	$35,000	$53,000	$66,500	$73,500
1950	Westland	2dr Conv	$98,000	$132,000	$180,000	$215,000
1950	Silverstone	2dr Rdstr	$107,000	$138,000	$195,000	$265,000
1950	Tickford	4dr Sal	$19,700	$32,000	$44,700	$66,000
1950	Abbott	2dr Conv	$25,200	$42,500	$54,500	$70,000
1951	Tickford	4dr Sdn	$19,700	$32,000	$44,700	$66,000
1951	Abbott	2dr Conv	$25,200	$42,500	$54,500	$70,000
1952	Tickford	4dr Sdn	$19,700	$32,000	$44,700	$66,000
1952	Abbott	2dr Conv	$25,200	$42,500	$54,500	$70,000
1953	Tickford	4dr Sdn	$19,700	$32,000	$44,700	$66,000
1953	Abbott	2dr Conv	$25,200	$42,500	$54,500	$70,000
1954	Tickford	4dr Sdn	$19,700	$32,000	$44,700	$66,000
1954	Abbott	2dr Conv	$25,200	$42,500	$54,500	$70,000

Heinkel

Year	Model	Body Style	4	3	2	1
1956	Kabine	153 Cpe	$7,200	$13,100	$22,100	$38,900
		154 Cpe	$6,800	$10,600	$18,900	$33,900
1957	Kabine	153 Cpe	$7,200	$13,100	$22,100	$38,900
		154 Cpe	$6,800	$10,600	$18,900	$33,900
1958	Kabine	153 Cpe	$7,200	$13,100	$22,100	$38,900
		154 Cpe	$6,800	$10,600	$18,900	$33,900
1961	Trojan	Cpe	$7,900	$13,800	$25,900	$41,400
1962	Trojan	Cpe	$7,900	$13,800	$25,900	$41,400
1963	Trojan	Cpe	$7,900	$13,800	$25,900	$41,400
1964	Trojan	Cpe	$7,900	$13,800	$25,900	$41,400

Henry J

Year	Model	Body Style	4	3	2	1
1951	Standard	134/68 2dr Sdn	$5,600	$9,200	$14,800	$22,500
						+$500 for OD trans.
1951	Deluxe	161/80 2dr Sdn	$7,800	$11,200	$19,000	$31,500
						+$500 for OD trans.
1952	Vagabond	134/68 2dr Sdn	$5,600	$9,200	$14,800	$22,500
						+$500 for OD trans.
1952	Corsair	134/68 2dr Sdn	$5,600	$9,200	$14,800	$22,500
		161/80 2dr Dlx Sdn	$7,800	$11,200	$19,000	$31,500

Henry J

Year	Model	Body Style	4	3	2	1
						+$500 for OD trans.
1953	Corsair	134/68 2dr Sdn	$5,600	$9,200	$14,800	$22,500
		161/80 2dr Dlx Sdn	$7,800	$11,200	$19,000	$31,500
						+$500 for OD trans.
1954	Corsair	134/68 2dr Sdn	$5,600	$9,200	$14,800	$22,500
		161/80 2dr Dlx Sdn	$7,800	$11,200	$19,000	$31,500
						+$500 for OD trans.

Honda

Year	Model	Body Style	4	3	2	1
1964	S600	2dr Conv	$10,700	$18,400	$34,700	$49,500
1965	S600	2dr Cpe	$8,000	$14,700	$22,400	$31,400
		2dr Conv	$10,700	$18,400	$34,700	$49,500
1966	S600	2dr Cpe	$8,000	$14,700	$22,400	$31,400
		2dr Conv	$10,700	$18,400	$34,700	$49,500
1967	S800	2dr Cpe	$9,600	$17,200	$26,100	$34,800
		2dr SM Cpe	$9,800	$17,800	$28,200	$37,400
		2dr Conv	$10,500	$18,100	$34,000	$48,200
		2dr SM Conv	$12,300	$19,900	$35,700	$50,700
1968	S800	2dr Cpe	$9,600	$17,200	$26,100	$34,800
		2dr SM Cpe	$9,800	$17,800	$28,200	$37,400
		2dr Conv	$10,500	$18,100	$33,700	$48,500
		2dr SM Conv	$12,300	$19,900	$35,700	$50,700
1969	S800	2dr Cpe	$9,600	$17,200	$26,100	$34,800
		2dr SM Cpe	$9,800	$17,800	$28,200	$37,400
		2dr Conv	$10,500	$18,100	$33,700	$48,500
		2dr SM Conv	$12,300	$19,900	$35,700	$50,700
1970	S800	2dr Cpe	$9,600	$17,200	$26,100	$34,800
		2dr SM Cpe	$9,800	$17,800	$28,200	$37,400
		2dr Conv	$10,500	$18,100	$33,700	$48,500
		2dr SM Conv	$12,300	$19,900	$35,700	$50,700
1971	Z 600	2dr Cpe	$5,300	$8,600	$14,500	$22,000
1972	Z 600	2dr Cpe	$5,300	$8,600	$14,500	$22,000
2000	S2000	2dr Conv	$9,000	$15,300	$25,100	$47,400
2001	S2000	2dr Conv	$9,000	$15,300	$25,100	$47,400
2002	S2000	2dr Conv	$9,000	$15,300	$25,100	$47,400
2003	S2000	2dr Conv	$9,000	$15,300	$25,100	$47,400

Hudson

Year	Model	Body Style	4	3	2	1
1946	Super	212/102 2dr Cpe	$11,500	$19,300	$29,700	$45,000
		212/102 4dr Sdn	$8,400	$15,000	$23,600	$34,400
		212/102 2dr Conv Brghm	$16,200	$28,800	$47,700	$75,800
1946	Commodore	254/128 2dr Clb Cpe	$12,800	$25,800	$37,800	$56,400
		254/128 2dr Brghm	$29,100	$44,100	$63,700	$91,900

Hudson

Year	Model	Body Style	4	3	2	1
		254/128 2dr Conv Brghm	$7,300	$13,300	$24,700	$46,600
1947	Super	212/102 2dr Cpe	$11,500	$19,300	$29,700	$45,000
		212/102 4dr Sdn	$7,700	$13,800	$22,400	$32,700
		212/102 2dr Conv Brghm	$16,200	$28,800	$47,700	$75,800
1947	Commodore	254/128 2dr Clb Cpe	$12,800	$25,800	$37,800	$56,400
		254/128 4dr Sdn	$9,200	$17,300	$31,000	$52,600
		254/128 2dr Conv Brghm	$21,600	$34,600	$58,500	$92,000
1948	Super	262/121 2dr Cpe	$12,300	$21,000	$31,800	$46,800
		262/121 4dr Sdn	$8,200	$14,200	$23,200	$33,300
		262/121 2dr Conv	$19,200	$35,100	$57,900	$87,800
1948	Commodore	254/128 2dr Clb Cpe	$13,600	$28,000	$40,500	$58,500
		254/128 4dr Sdn	$10,700	$19,300	$31,600	$54,200
		254/128 2dr Conv Brghm	$21,000	$34,700	$60,800	$91,100
1949	Super	262/121 2dr Cpe	$12,300	$21,000	$31,800	$46,800
		262/121 4dr Sdn	$8,900	$15,400	$24,400	$35,100
		262/121 2dr Conv Brghm	$16,300	$29,800	$52,100	$79,000
1949	Commodore	254/128 2dr Clb Cpe	$13,600	$28,000	$40,500	$58,500
		254/128 4dr Sdn	$10,700	$19,300	$31,600	$54,200
		254/128 2dr Conv Brghm	$21,000	$34,700	$60,800	$91,100
1950	Super	262/123 2dr Clb Cpe	$11,400	$19,500	$32,000	$48,500
		254/128 2dr Clb Cpe	$12,300	$23,800	$36,400	$54,400
		262/123 4dr Sdn	$8,800	$14,600	$24,800	$38,800
		254/128 4dr Sdn	$9,800	$16,300	$28,200	$43,900
		262/123 2dr Conv Brghm	$16,300	$29,200	$54,200	$87,000
		254/128 2dr Conv Brghm	$19,600	$32,800	$59,200	$96,300
1951	Pacemaker Custom	232/112 2dr Cpe	$8,400	$13,900	$20,000	$33,800
		232/112 4dr Sdn	$7,700	$12,500	$21,500	$31,500
		232/112 2dr Conv Brghm	$26,700	$40,800	$59,400	$89,700
1951	Super-Six Custom	262/123 2dr Clb Cpe	$6,700	$9,500	$14,900	$23,000
		262/123 2dr Hl-lywd Hdtp	$5,800	$10,900	$18,200	$31,400
1951	Commodore Custom	262/123 2dr Clb Cpe	$7,300	$12,300	$20,700	$31,100
		262/123 4dr Sdn	$7,700	$11,400	$18,000	$27,800

Year	Model	Body Style	4	3	2	1
		262/123 2dr Hllywd Hdtp	$8,300	$14,600	$25,500	$38,400
		262/123 2dr Conv Brghm	$24,600	$40,600	$72,200	$116,000
1951	Hornet	308/145 2dr Clb Cpe	$11,800	$20,400	$31,400	$51,800
		308/145 4dr Sdn	$9,900	$15,700	$27,500	$38,600
		308/145 2dr Hllywd Hdtp	$15,600	$26,300	$41,900	$73,500
		308/145 2dr Conv Brghm	$42,900	$70,600	$99,900	$142,000
1952	Pacemaker	232/112 2dr Clb Cpe	$8,400	$13,900	$20,000	$33,800
		232/112 4dr Sdn	$7,700	$12,500	$21,500	$31,500
1952	Wasp	262/127 2dr Hllywd Hdtp	$9,700	$16,600	$28,500	$51,600
		262/127 4dr Sdn	$6,600	$10,700	$17,000	$25,600
		262/127 2dr Conv Brghm	$36,500	$59,500	$86,100	$121,000
1952	Commodore	262/127 2dr Hllywd Hdtp	$8,300	$14,600	$25,500	$38,000
		262/127 4dr Sdn	$7,700	$11,400	$18,000	$27,800
		262/127 2dr Conv Brghm	$24,500	$39,700	$74,400	$109,000
1952	Hornet	308/145 2dr Clb Cpe	$13,200	$21,000	$32,000	$53,600
		308/160 2dr Clb Cpe	$18,000	$28,500	$43,600	$72,900
		308/145 4dr Sdn	$9,900	$15,700	$27,500	$38,600
		308/160 4dr Sdn	$13,000	$19,100	$33,700	$47,200
		308/145 2dr Hllywd Hdtp	$15,600	$26,300	$41,900	$73,500
		308/160 2dr Hllywd Hdtp	$19,800	$32,100	$51,200	$89,900
		308/145 2dr Conv Brghm	$50,500	$81,200	$124,000	$166,000
		308/160 2dr Conv Brghm	$69,700	$106,000	$151,000	$198,000
1953	Jet	202/104 4dr Sdn	$8,100	$11,800	$18,000	$27,700
		202/114 4dr Sdn	$9,500	$14,200	$21,700	$33,000
1953	Super Jet	202/104 2dr Clb Sdn	$8,000	$11,700	$18,000	$25,800
		202/106 2dr Clb Sdn	$9,200	$14,200	$21,600	$31,000
1953	Wasp	232/112 2dr Clb Cpe	$7,700	$14,500	$23,600	$36,900
		232/112 4dr Sdn	$6,500	$10,400	$15,100	$23,500
1953	Super Wasp	262/127 2dr Clb Cpe	$9,000	$14,400	$20,700	$37,400
		262/127 4dr Sdn	$7,800	$11,700	$18,500	$28,100
		262/127 2dr Hllywd Hdtp	$7,600	$12,300	$19,000	$33,100

Hudson

Year	Model	Body Style	4	3	2	1
		262/127 2dr Conv Brghm	$38,400	$56,300	$74,900	$107,000
1953	Hornet	308/145 2dr Clb Cpe	$13,600	$22,200	$34,000	$54,700
		308/160 2dr Twin-H Clb Cpe	$18,000	$30,200	$55,600	$74,100
		308/145 4dr Sdn	$13,600	$21,500	$35,800	$46,300
		308/160 4dr Twin-H Sdn	$17,600	$26,800	$43,200	$55,200
		308/145 2dr Hllywd Hdtp	$13,200	$22,100	$35,000	$60,200
		308/160 2dr Twin-H Hllywd Hdtp	$19,800	$32,100	$62,000	$88,600
		308/145 2dr Conv Brghm	$49,800	$79,300	$122,000	$162,000
		308/160 2dr Twin-H Conv Brghm	$65,900	$104,000	$147,000	$195,000
1953	Italia	202/114 2dr Cpe	$198,000	$283,000	$449,000	$660,000
1954	Jet	202/104 2dr Family Clb Sdn	$10,900	$17,400	$28,300	$41,400
		202/104 4dr Sdn	$5,000	$9,500	$15,600	$25,500
		202/104 2dr Uty Sdn	$6,800	$13,500	$23,000	$32,100
1954	Super Jet	202/104 2dr Clb Sdn	$5,200	$10,400	$15,900	$22,100
		202/104 4dr Sdn	$4,800	$7,300	$11,000	$18,400
1954	Jet-Liner	202/104 2dr Clb Sdn	$5,200	$10,600	$16,100	$22,800
		202/104 4dr Sdn	$3,700	$6,800	$10,300	$17,100
1954	Wasp	232/126 2dr Clb Cpe	$5,800	$10,000	$14,600	$21,900
		232/126 4dr Sdn	$6,100	$9,300	$11,700	$19,100
1954	Super Wasp	262/149 2dr Clb Cpe	$8,400	$12,800	$18,100	$27,400
		262/149 2dr Conv Brghm	$34,100	$57,200	$67,200	$94,400
		262/149 2dr Hllywd Hdtp	$8,400	$16,100	$22,000	$29,200
		262/149 4dr Sdn	$7,500	$11,500	$14,800	$24,000
		262/140 2dr Clb Cpe	$5,800	$10,300	$14,800	$22,400
		262/140 4dr Sdn	$6,100	$9,500	$11,800	$19,700
		262/140 2dr Hllywd Hdtp	$6,000	$11,200	$15,200	$20,100
		262/140 2dr Conv Brghm	$26,900	$45,700	$53,800	$75,800
1954	Hornet	308/170 2dr Hllywd Hdtp	$15,700	$28,200	$38,900	$60,000
		308/160 2dr Clb Cpe	$8,700	$13,400	$20,100	$30,100

Hudson

Year	Model	Body Style	4	3	2	1
		308/160 4dr Sdn	$8,000	$13,500	$23,600	$30,100
		308/160 2dr Hllywd Hdtp	$11,400	$19,000	$25,900	$39,400
		308/160 2dr Conv Brghm	$38,200	$57,900	$75,100	$98,900
1955	Wasp	202/115 4dr Cstm Sdn	$5,900	$9,200	$11,600	$19,300
		202/120 4dr Spr Sdn	$5,900	$9,200	$11,600	$19,300
		202/115 2dr Cstm Hllywd Hdtp	$5,300	$9,600	$13,500	$19,600
1955	Hornet	320/208 2dr Cstm Hllywd Hdtp	$11,200	$19,000	$26,100	$39,500
		320/208 4dr Spr Sdn	$8,100	$13,500	$23,400	$30,100
						+15% for factory a/c.
1956	Wasp	202/120 4dr Spr Sdn	$5,400	$8,600	$11,500	$18,600
1956	Hornet	308/165 2dr Cstm Hllywd Hdtp	$8,500	$16,000	$24,100	$32,500
		308/165 4dr Cstm Sdn	$7,100	$12,700	$18,400	$25,000
						+15% for factory a/c.
1957	Hornet	327/255 2dr Spr Hllywd Hdtp	$11,500	$21,600	$31,300	$45,200
		327/255 4dr Spr Sdn	$7,800	$14,100	$19,500	$29,300
						+15% for factory a/c.

Imperial

Year	Model	Body Style	4	3	2	1
1955	Imperial	331/250 2dr Newport Hdtp	$16,800	$33,600	$54,500	$79,700
		331/250 4dr Sdn	$6,800	$12,200	$21,500	$32,900
1955	Crown Imperial	331/250 4dr Limo	$20,800	$36,100	$72,300	$114,000
1956	Imperial	354/280 2dr Sthmptn Hdtp	$13,800	$24,100	$43,600	$63,500
		354/280 4dr Sdn	$7,200	$13,600	$23,300	$35,600
		354/280 4dr Sthmptn Hdtp	$10,600	$18,400	$30,500	$49,000
1956	Crown Imperial	354/280 4dr Limo	$27,600	$49,500	$92,600	$143,000
1957	Imperial	392/325 2dr Sthmptn Hdtp	$12,900	$22,000	$38,200	$59,500
		392/325 4dr Sdn	$6,800	$12,500	$22,000	$33,500
		392/325 4dr Sthmptn Hdtp	$9,400	$16,100	$26,900	$43,300
1957	Imperial Crown	392/325 2dr Sthmptn Hdtp	$14,000	$24,900	$43,100	$64,500

Imperial

Year	Model	Body Style	4	3	2	1
		392/325 4dr Sdn	$7,900	$14,600	$25,600	$38,800
		392/325 4dr Sthmptn Hdtp	$9,800	$16,700	$27,800	$44,500
		392/325 4dr Ghia Limo	$47,200	$79,700	$131,000	$195,000
		392/325 2dr Conv	$32,600	$55,400	$92,500	$143,000
1957	Imperial LeBaron	392/325 4dr Sdn	$9,500	$16,700	$29,000	$44,600
		392/325 4dr Sthmptn Hdtp	$12,000	$20,300	$33,300	$53,200
1958	Imperial	392/345 2dr Sthmptn Hdtp	$10,000	$17,900	$32,200	$52,400
		392/345 4dr Sdn	$8,000	$14,300	$24,800	$37,000
		392/345 4dr Sthmptn Hdtp	$9,200	$16,000	$26,500	$41,500
1958	Imperial Crown	392/345 2dr Sthmptn Hdtp	$12,400	$23,600	$40,400	$61,200
		392/345 4dr Sdn	$9,200	$16,400	$28,000	$43,600
		392/345 4dr Sthmptn Hdtp	$10,200	$17,600	$29,500	$47,100
		392/345 4dr Ghia Limo	$47,500	$81,100	$135,000	$198,000
		392/345 2dr Conv	$38,900	$65,400	$95,600	$145,000
1958	Imperial LeBaron	392/345 4dr Sdn	$9,400	$16,500	$28,100	$43,700
		392/345 4dr Sthmptn Hdtp	$11,200	$19,300	$32,400	$51,600
1959	Imperial Custom	413/350 2dr Sthmptn Hdtp Cpe	$12,700	$22,600	$40,300	$59,000
		413/350 4dr Sdn	$6,900	$12,500	$21,000	$32,700
		413/350 4dr Sthmptn Hdtp Sdn	$8,700	$14,600	$23,000	$38,700
1959	Imperial Crown	413/350 2dr Sthmptn Hdtp	$15,100	$26,100	$45,500	$68,900
		413/350 4dr Sdn	$8,200	$15,100	$25,300	$40,100
		413/350 4dr Sthmptn Hdtp	$9,700	$16,900	$26,800	$43,300
		413/350 4dr Ghia Limo	$46,800	$81,100	$131,000	$197,000
		413/350 2dr Conv	$40,400	$67,300	$98,000	$149,000
1959	Imperial LeBaron	413/350 4dr Sdn	$8,100	$14,400	$25,000	$36,900
		413/350 4dr Sthmptn Hdtp	$9,900	$16,400	$27,100	$43,600
1960	Custom	413/350 2dr Sthmptn Hdtp	$9,200	$15,600	$26,800	$39,200
		413/350 4dr Sdn	$6,200	$10,900	$18,200	$28,500
		413/350 4dr Sthmptn Hdtp	$8,000	$13,900	$21,500	$29,900

Year	Model	Body Style	4	3	2	1
1960	Crown	413/350 4dr Ghia Limo	$29,700	$49,500	$91,200	$138,000
		413/350 2dr Sthmptn Hdtp	$11,300	$19,000	$31,500	$48,700
		413/350 4dr Sdn	$7,500	$13,300	$21,900	$34,100
		413/350 4dr Sthmptn Hdtp	$8,800	$15,200	$24,500	$39,500
		413/350 2dr Conv	$31,700	$52,800	$80,600	$124,000
1960	LeBaron	413/350 4dr Sdn	$7,800	$13,900	$23,500	$36,400
		413/350 4dr Sthmptn Hdtp	$10,300	$18,400	$30,700	$51,100
1961	Custom	413/350 2dr Sthmptn Hdtp Cpe	$8,500	$14,200	$26,600	$37,300
		413/350 4dr Sthmptn Hdtp Sdn	$6,200	$10,900	$18,000	$28,100
1961	Crown	413/350 2dr Sthmptn Hdtp Cpe	$9,500	$15,700	$28,800	$40,500
		413/350 4dr Sthmptn Hdtp Sdn	$6,900	$12,300	$19,600	$29,500
		413/350 4dr Ghia Limo	$29,700	$49,500	$91,200	$138,000
		413/350 2dr Conv	$25,800	$46,100	$74,900	$103,000
1961	LeBaron	413/350 4dr Sthmptn Hdtp Sdn	$7,400	$12,800	$20,700	$31,900
1962	Custom	413/340 2dr Sthmptn Hdtp Cpe	$7,900	$13,700	$25,800	$37,200
		413/340 4dr Sthmptn Hdtp Sdn	$5,800	$10,000	$16,800	$26,600
1962	Crown	413/340 2dr Sthmptn Hdtp Cpe	$8,400	$14,300	$27,100	$38,600
		413/340 4dr Sthmptn Hdtp Sdn	$6,500	$11,200	$18,800	$29,200
		413/340 2dr Conv	$25,800	$46,100	$74,900	$103,000
1962	LeBaron	413/340 4dr Sthmptn Hdtp Sdn	$6,800	$12,100	$20,200	$31,500
1963	Custom	413/340 2dr Sthmptn Hdtp Cpe	$8,000	$13,800	$25,800	$36,600
		413/340 4dr Sthmptn Hdtp Sdn	$5,800	$10,000	$16,800	$26,600
1963	Crown	413/340 2dr Sthmptn Hdtp Cpe	$8,500	$14,500	$26,700	$37,500
		413/340 4dr Sthmptn Hdtp Sdn	$6,500	$11,100	$18,000	$27,400
		413/340 2dr Conv	$25,800	$46,100	$74,900	$103,000
1963	LeBaron	413/340 4dr Sthmptn Hdtp Sdn	$6,300	$11,100	$19,000	$30,600

Imperial

Year	Model	Body Style	4	3	2	1
1964	Crown	413/340 2dr Hdtp Cpe	$5,800	$10,000	$16,100	$25,800
		413/340 4dr Hdtp Sdn	$4,900	$8,200	$13,600	$21,300
		413/340 2dr Conv	$10,800	$18,800	$30,200	$50,800
1964	LeBaron	413/340 4dr Hdtp Sdn	$5,700	$10,200	$16,200	$27,400
1965	Crown	413/340 4dr Ghia Limo	$15,600	$30,000	$42,400	$70,600
		413/340 2dr Hdtp Cpe	$5,600	$9,900	$16,000	$25,200
		413/340 4dr Hdtp Sdn	$4,800	$8,100	$13,500	$21,200
		413/340 2dr Conv	$10,700	$18,900	$30,100	$50,000
1965	LeBaron	413/340 4dr Hdtp Sdn	$5,500	$10,000	$16,000	$26,400
1966	Crown	440/350 2dr Hdtp Cpe	$5,600	$10,400	$16,000	$25,200
		440/350 4dr Hdtp Sdn	$5,300	$9,700	$15,200	$23,500
		440/350 2dr Conv	$13,200	$25,900	$39,200	$52,400
1966	LeBaron	440/350 4dr Hdtp Sdn	$6,700	$12,100	$18,200	$29,800
1967	Crown	440/350 4dr Sdn	$5,500	$9,900	$14,800	$22,700
		440/350 2dr Hdtp Cpe	$6,300	$11,500	$17,600	$27,100
		440/350 4dr Hdtp Sdn	$5,600	$10,200	$15,200	$23,400
		440/350 2dr Conv	$12,300	$23,500	$32,800	$47,600
1967	LeBaron	440/350 4dr Hdtp Sdn	$5,700	$10,600	$17,000	$27,700
1968	Crown	440/350 2dr Hdtp Cpe	$5,900	$11,100	$17,400	$27,100
		440/350 4dr Sdn	$4,900	$9,000	$14,200	$22,000
		440/350 4dr Hdtp Sdn	$5,100	$9,800	$15,000	$23,400
		440/350 2dr Conv	$12,300	$23,500	$32,800	$47,600
1968	LeBaron	440/350 4dr Hdtp Sdn	$5,500	$10,100	$15,900	$26,200
1969	Crown	440/350 2dr Hdtp Cpe	$4,500	$8,300	$13,500	$21,200
		440/350 4dr Sdn	$3,200	$5,600	$8,800	$13,800
		440/350 4dr Hdtp Sdn	$3,200	$5,700	$9,000	$14,800
1969	LeBaron	440/350 2dr Hdtp Cpe	$5,100	$9,200	$14,700	$23,500
		440/350 4dr Hdtp Sdn	$3,800	$6,800	$10,400	$17,000

Imperial

Year	Model	Body Style	4	3	2	1
1970	Crown	440/350 2dr Hdtp Cpe	$4,700	$8,300	$12,800	$19,900
		440/350 4dr Hdtp Sdn	$3,500	$6,000	$9,000	$13,800
1970	LeBaron	440/350 2dr Hdtp Cpe	$4,500	$8,800	$14,300	$22,700
		440/350 4dr Hdtp Sdn	$4,300	$8,200	$13,100	$21,600

Intermeccanica

Year	Model	Body Style	4	3	2	1
1964	Vetta Ventura	2dr Cpe	$75,000	$112,000	$164,000	$236,000
						-25% for auto.
1965	Vetta Ventura	2dr Cpe	$75,000	$112,000	$164,000	$236,000
						-25% for auto.
1966	Vetta Ventura	2dr Cpe	$75,000	$112,000	$164,000	$236,000
						-25% for auto.
1966	Griffith GT	2dr Cpe	$43,000	$58,800	$92,400	$107,000
1967	Vetta Ventura	2dr Cpe	$75,000	$112,000	$164,000	$236,000
						-25% for auto.
1967	Griffith GT	2dr Cpe	$43,000	$58,800	$92,400	$107,000
1967	Omega	2dr Cpe	$42,200	$53,200	$69,700	$96,500
1967	Torino	2dr Cpe	$38,500	$51,400	$68,800	$93,500
1967	Italia	2dr Cpe	$35,500	$47,400	$64,900	$85,900
		2dr Conv	$84,100	$110,000	$128,000	$169,000
1967	Murena	2dr Wgn	$17,900	$28,000	$45,200	$68,900
1968	Italia	2dr Cpe	$35,500	$47,400	$64,900	$85,900
		2dr Conv	$84,100	$110,000	$128,000	$169,000
1968	Murena	2dr Wgn	$17,900	$28,000	$45,200	$68,900
1969	Italia	2dr Cpe	$35,500	$47,400	$64,900	$85,900
		2dr Conv	$84,100	$110,000	$128,000	$169,000
1969	Murena	2dr Wgn	$17,900	$28,000	$45,200	$68,900
1970	Italia	2dr Cpe	$35,500	$47,400	$64,900	$85,900
		2dr Conv	$84,100	$110,000	$128,000	$169,000
1970	Murena	2dr Wgn	$17,900	$28,000	$45,200	$68,900
1971	Italia	2dr Cpe	$35,500	$47,400	$64,900	$85,900
		2dr Conv	$84,100	$110,000	$128,000	$169,000
1971	Murena	2dr Wgn	$17,900	$28,000	$45,200	$68,900
1971	Indra	2dr Ntchbk Cpe	$46,500	$61,100	$75,000	$88,200
		2dr Fstbk Cpe	$55,000	$71,800	$91,200	$120,000
		2dr Conv	$76,800	$97,200	$118,000	$136,000
						+15% for Ford 429-c.i. engine (1 factory built). -20% for Opel 2.8L engine.
1972	Italia	2dr Cpe	$35,500	$47,400	$64,900	$85,900
		2dr Conv	$84,100	$110,000	$128,000	$169,000
1972	Murena	2dr Wgn	$17,900	$28,000	$45,200	$68,900
1972	Indra	2dr Ntchbk Cpe	$46,500	$61,100	$75,000	$88,200
		2dr Fstbk Cpe	$55,000	$71,800	$91,200	$120,000
		2dr Conv	$74,600	$90,300	$106,000	$129,000

Intermeccanica

Year	Model	Body Style	4	3	2	1
		+15% for Ford 429-c.i. engine (1 factory built). -20% for Opel 2.8L engine.				
1973	Indra	2dr Ntchbk Cpe	$46,500	$61,100	$75,000	$88,200
		2dr Fstbk Cpe	$55,000	$71,800	$91,200	$120,000
		2dr Conv	$74,600	$90,300	$106,000	$129,000
		+15% for Ford 429-c.i. engine (1 factory built). -20% for Opel 2.8L engine.				
1974	Indra	2dr Ntchbk Cpe	$46,500	$61,100	$75,000	$88,200
		2dr Fstbk Cpe	$55,000	$71,800	$91,200	$120,000
		2dr Conv	$74,600	$91,000	$109,000	$132,000
		+15% for Ford 429-c.i. engine (1 factory built). -20% for Opel 2.8L engine.				

Iso

Year	Model	Body Style	4	3	2	1
1963	Rivolta	2dr IR 300 Cpe	$53,800	$67,000	$84,500	$104,000
		2dr IR 340 Cpe	$59,800	$78,900	$97,500	$111,000
		+$3,500 for wire wheels. +$3,500 for 5-spd. -$5,000 for auto. +$2,000 for sunroof. +$4,000 for factory a/c.				
1964	Rivolta	2dr IR 300 Cpe	$53,800	$67,000	$84,500	$104,000
		2dr IR 340 Cpe	$59,800	$78,900	$97,500	$111,000
		+$3,500 for wire wheels. +$3,500 for 5-spd. -$5,000 for auto. +$2,000 for sunroof. +$4,000 for factory a/c.				
1965	Rivolta	2dr IR 300 Cpe	$53,800	$67,000	$84,500	$104,000
		2dr IR 340 Cpe	$59,800	$78,900	$97,500	$111,000
		+$3,500 for wire wheels. +$3,500 for 5-spd. -$5,000 for auto. +$2,000 for sunroof. +$4,000 for factory a/c.				
1965	Grifo	2dr GL Cpe	$310,000	$361,000	$430,000	$495,000
		2dr GL Targa	$334,000	$417,000	$466,000	$539,000
		+$10,000 for 5-spd. -$25,000 for auto. +$10,000 for factory a/c. +$10,000 for factory covered headlights.				
1966	Rivolta	2dr IR 300 Cpe	$53,800	$67,000	$84,500	$104,000
		2dr IR 340 Cpe	$59,800	$78,900	$97,500	$111,000
		+$3,500 for wire wheels. +$3,500 for 5-spd. -$5,000 for auto. +$2,000 for sunroof. +$4,000 for factory a/c.				
1966	Grifo	2dr GL Cpe	$310,000	$361,000	$430,000	$495,000
		2dr GL Targa	$334,000	$417,000	$466,000	$539,000
		+$10,000 for 5-spd. -$25,000 for auto. +$10,000 for factory a/c. +$10,000 for factory covered headlights.				
1967	Rivolta	2dr IR 300 Cpe	$53,800	$67,000	$84,500	$104,000
		2dr IR 340 Cpe	$59,800	$78,900	$97,500	$111,000
		+$3,500 for wire wheels. +$3,500 for 5-spd. -$5,000 for auto. +$2,000 for sunroof. +$4,000 for factory a/c.				
1967	Grifo	2dr GL Cpe	$310,000	$361,000	$430,000	$495,000
		2dr GL Targa	$334,000	$417,000	$466,000	$539,000
		+$10,000 for 5-spd. -$25,000 for auto. +$10,000 for factory a/c. +$10,000 for factory covered headlights.				
1968	Rivolta	2dr IR 300 Cpe	$53,800	$67,000	$84,500	$104,000
		2dr IR 340 Cpe	$59,800	$78,900	$97,500	$111,000

Year	Model	Body Style	4	3	2	1
			+$3,500 for wire wheels. +$3,500 for 5-spd. -$5,000 for auto. +$2,000 for sunroof. +$4,000 for factory a/c.			
1968	Fidia	4dr Sdn	$25,400	$35,700	$48,800	$59,800
		4dr IR 340 Sdn	$28,100	$41,100	$51,700	$64,700
			+$3,500 for wire wheels. +$4,500 for factory a/c. +$4,000 for 5-spd. -$5,000 for auto.			
1968	Grifo	2dr GL Cpe	$310,000	$361,000	$430,000	$495,000
		2dr GL Targa	$334,000	$417,000	$466,000	$539,000
			+$10,000 for 5-spd. -$25,000 for auto. +$10,000 for factory a/c. +$10,000 for factory covered headlights.			
1969	Lele	2dr Cpe	$29,900	$39,600	$56,100	$69,700
			+$4,000 for wire wheels. +$1,500 for sunroof. -$5,000 for auto.			
1969	Rivolta	2dr IR 300 Cpe	$53,800	$67,000	$84,500	$104,000
		2dr IR 340 Cpe	$59,800	$78,900	$97,500	$111,000
			+$3,500 for wire wheels. +$3,500 for 5-spd. -$5,000 for auto. +$2,000 for sunroof. +$4,000 for factory a/c.			
1969	Fidia	4dr Sdn	$25,400	$35,700	$48,800	$59,800
			+$3,500 for wire wheels. +$4,500 for factory a/c. +$4,000 for 5-spd. -$5,000 for auto.			
1969	Grifo	2dr GL Cpe	$310,000	$361,000	$430,000	$495,000
		2dr GL Targa	$334,000	$417,000	$466,000	$539,000
			+$10,000 for 5-spd. -$25,000 for auto. +$10,000 for factory a/c. +$10,000 for factory covered headlights.			
1970	Lele	2dr Cpe	$29,900	$39,600	$56,100	$69,700
			+$4,000 for wire wheels. +$1,500 for sunroof. -$5,000 for auto.			
1970	Grifo	2dr IR9 Can Am Cpe	$355,000	$414,000	$492,000	$580,000
		2dr IR9 Can Am Targa	$373,000	$431,000	$503,000	$604,000
			-$25,000 for auto. +$10,000 for factory a/c. +$10,000 for 5-spd.			
1970	Rivolta	2dr IR 300 Cpe	$53,800	$67,000	$84,500	$104,000
		2dr IR 340 Cpe	$59,800	$78,900	$97,500	$111,000
			+$3,500 for wire wheels. +$3,500 for 5-spd. -$5,000 for auto. +$2,000 for sunroof. +$4,000 for factory a/c.			
1970	Fidia	4dr Sdn	$25,400	$35,700	$48,800	$59,800
			+$3,500 for wire wheels. +$4,500 for factory a/c. +$4,000 for 5-spd. -$5,000 for auto.			
1971	Lele	2dr Cpe	$29,900	$39,600	$56,100	$69,700
			+$4,000 for wire wheels. +$1,500 for sunroof. -$5,000 for auto.			
1971	Fidia	4dr Sdn	$25,400	$35,700	$48,800	$59,800
			+$3,500 for wire wheels. +$4,500 for factory a/c. +$4,000 for 5-spd. -$5,000 for auto.			
1971	Grifo	2dr IR9 Can Am Cpe	$355,000	$414,000	$492,000	$580,000
		2dr IR9 Can Am Targa	$373,000	$431,000	$503,000	$604,000

Iso

Year	Model	Body Style	4	3	2	1
			-$25,000 for auto. +$10,000 for factory a/c. +$10,000 for 5-spd.			
1972	Lele	2dr Cpe	$29,900	$39,600	$56,100	$69,700
			+$4,000 for wire wheels. +$1,500 for sunroof. -$5,000 for auto.			
1972	Fidia	4dr Sdn	$25,400	$35,700	$48,800	$59,800
			+$3,500 for wire wheels. +$4,500 for factory a/c. +$4,000 for 5-spd. -$5,000 for auto.			
1972	Grifo	2dr IR9 Can Am Cpe	$355,000	$414,000	$492,000	$580,000
		2dr IR9 Can Am Targa	$373,000	$431,000	$503,000	$604,000
			-$25,000 for auto. +$10,000 for factory a/c. +$10,000 for 5-spd.			
1973	Lele	2dr Cpe	$29,900	$39,600	$56,100	$69,700
		2dr Spt Cpe	$34,000	$46,500	$61,200	$74,800
			+$4,000 for wire wheels. +$1,500 for sunroof. -$5,000 for auto.			
1973	Fidia	4dr Sdn	$25,400	$35,700	$48,800	$59,800
			+$3,500 for wire wheels. +$4,500 for factory a/c. +$4,000 for 5-spd. -$5,000 for auto.			
1974	Lele	2dr Cpe	$29,900	$39,600	$56,100	$69,700
		2dr Spt Cpe	$34,000	$46,500	$61,200	$74,800
			+$4,000 for wire wheels. +$1,500 for sunroof. -$5,000 for auto.			
1974	Fidia	4dr Sdn	$25,400	$35,700	$48,800	$59,800
			+$3,500 for wire wheels. +$4,500 for factory a/c. +$4,000 for 5-spd. -$5,000 for auto.			

Jaguar

Year	Model	Body Style	4	3	2	1
1946	3.5 Litre	4dr Sdn	$10,000	$22,300	$42,500	$64,200
		2dr DHC	$44,500	$74,300	$126,000	$167,000
1947	3.5 Litre	4dr Sdn	$10,000	$22,300	$42,500	$64,200
		2dr DHC	$44,500	$74,300	$126,000	$167,000
1948	3.5 Litre	4dr Sdn	$10,000	$22,300	$42,500	$64,200
		2dr DHC	$44,500	$74,300	$126,000	$167,000
1949	Mark V	4dr 3.5 Sdn	$8,000	$16,500	$28,300	$47,400
		2dr 3.5 DHC	$31,700	$52,900	$106,000	$146,000
1949	XK 120	2dr Alloy Rdstr	$190,000	$212,000	$315,000	$385,000
1950	Mark V	4dr 2.5 Sdn	$8,000	$16,500	$28,300	$47,400
		2dr 3.5 DHC	$31,700	$52,900	$106,000	$146,000
1950	XK 120	2dr Rdstr	$64,000	$86,100	$125,000	$146,000
		2dr Alloy Rdstr	$183,000	$206,000	$308,000	$378,000
			+$2,500 for orig wire wheels on non-alloy.			
1951	Mark VII	4dr Sdn	$11,000	$15,300	$22,500	$39,900
1951	XK 120	2dr FHC	$51,900	$78,400	$107,000	$152,000
		2dr Rdstr	$62,000	$80,200	$123,000	$143,000
			+$2,500 for orig wire wheels.			
1952	Mark VII	4dr Sdn	$11,000	$15,300	$22,500	$39,900
1952	XK 120	2dr FHC	$51,900	$78,400	$107,000	$152,000

Year	Model	Body Style	4	3	2	1
		2dr Rdstr	$62,000	$80,200	$123,000	$143,000
				+$2,500 for orig wire wheels exc on SE/M.		
		2dr SE FHC	$53,400	$92,500	$112,000	$162,000
		2dr SE Rdstr	$63,700	$94,300	$128,000	$153,000
				+$2,500 for orig wire wheels exc on SE/M.		
1952	C-Type	2dr Rdstr	$2.7 mil	$3 mil	$4.3 mil	$5.8 mil
1953	Mark VII	4dr Sdn	$11,000	$15,300	$22,500	$39,900
1953	XK 120	2dr Rdstr	$61,800	$79,500	$123,000	$143,000
		2dr SE Rdstr	$63,700	$94,300	$128,000	$153,000
		2dr FHC	$53,100	$84,400	$110,000	$154,000
				+$2,500 for orig wire wheels exc on SE/M.		
		2dr SE FHC	$54,800	$100,000	$116,000	$164,000
		2dr DHC	$56,100	$83,400	$119,000	$153,000
				+$2,500 for orig wire wheels exc on SE/M.		
		2dr SE DHC	$58,000	$99,400	$124,000	$164,000
1953	C-Type	2dr Rdstr	$2.7 mil	$3 mil	$4.3 mil	$5.8 mil
1954	Mark VII	4dr Sdn	$11,000	$15,300	$22,500	$39,900
1954	XK 120	2dr FHC	$53,100	$84,400	$110,000	$154,000
				+$2,500 for orig wire wheels exc on SE/M.		
		2dr SE FHC	$54,800	$100,000	$116,000	$164,000
		2dr Rdstr	$61,800	$79,500	$123,000	$143,000
		2dr SE Rdstr	$63,700	$94,300	$128,000	$153,000
		2dr DHC	$56,100	$83,500	$119,000	$153,000
				+$2,500 for orig wire wheels exc on SE/M.		
		2dr SE DHC	$58,000	$99,400	$124,000	$164,000
1954	D-Type	2dr Rdstr	$2.9 mil	$3.7 mil	$5 mil	$9 mil
			Racing provenance can make for exceptional prices.			
1955	Mark VII	4dr Sdn	$10,300	$15,300	$21,100	$37,200
1955	XK 140	2dr FHC	$43,800	$60,800	$81,800	$123,000
		2dr MC FHC	$58,100	$72,500	$94,600	$142,000
		2dr Rdstr	$74,600	$89,400	$126,000	$163,000
		2dr MC Rdstr	$83,900	$107,000	$182,000	$232,000
		2dr DHC	$62,600	$78,100	$119,000	$163,000
		2dr MC DHC	$75,300	$92,200	$140,000	$195,000
				Note: the MC option is also referred to as SE.		
				+$6,000 for M option. -10% for auto.		
1955	D-Type	2dr Rdstr	$2.9 mil	$3.7 mil	$5 mil	$9 mil
			Racing provenance can make for exceptional prices.			
1956	2.4 Litre	4dr Sdn	$13,400	$17,400	$23,600	$36,700
1956	Mark VII	4dr Sdn	$10,300	$15,300	$21,100	$37,200
1956	XK 140	2dr FHC	$43,800	$60,800	$81,800	$123,000
		2dr MC FHC	$58,100	$72,500	$94,600	$142,000
		2dr Rdstr	$74,600	$89,400	$126,000	$163,000
		2dr MC Rdstr	$83,900	$109,000	$182,000	$232,000
		2dr DHC	$62,600	$78,100	$119,000	$163,000
		2dr MC DHC	$75,300	$92,200	$140,000	$195,000

Jaguar

Year	Model	Body Style	4	3	2	1
						Note: the MC option is also referred to as SE. +$6,000 for M option. -10% for auto.
1956	D-Type	2dr Rdstr	$2.9 mil	$3.7 mil	$5 mil	$9 mil
						Racing provenance can make for exceptional prices.
1957	2.4 Litre	4dr Sdn	$13,600	$17,600	$23,700	$36,800
1957	3.4 Litre	4dr Sdn	$18,600	$24,900	$43,900	$72,200
1957	Mark VIII	4dr Sdn	$15,400	$20,700	$34,300	$48,900
1957	XK 140	2dr FHC	$43,800	$60,800	$81,800	$123,000
		2dr MC FHC	$58,100	$72,500	$94,600	$142,000
		2dr Rdstr	$72,700	$88,200	$124,000	$162,000
		2dr MC Rdstr	$83,900	$109,000	$182,000	$231,000
		2dr DHC	$62,600	$78,100	$119,000	$163,000
		2dr MC DHC	$75,300	$92,200	$140,000	$195,000
						Note: the MC option is also referred to as SE. +$6,000 for M option. -10% for auto.
1957	D-Type	2dr Rdstr	$2.9 mil	$3.7 mil	$5 mil	$9 mil
						Racing provenance can make for exceptional prices.
1957	XKSS	2dr Rdstr	$7.8 mil	$8.6 mil	$9.75 mil	$12.5 mil
1958	3.4 Litre	4dr Sdn	$18,700	$25,300	$44,300	$72,700
1958	Mark VIII	4dr Sdn	$14,900	$20,000	$32,400	$45,600
1958	XK 150	2dr FHC	$37,300	$53,200	$76,500	$98,400
		2dr S FHC	$44,200	$60,100	$96,300	$120,000
		2dr 3.8L Cpe	$58,000	$84,700	$121,000	$166,000
		2dr Rdstr	$79,900	$108,000	$155,000	$193,000
		2dr S Rdstr	$130,000	$160,000	$206,000	$269,000
		2dr 3.8L Rdstr	$126,000	$168,000	$233,000	$303,000
		2dr DHC	$68,700	$95,800	$126,000	$176,000
		2dr S DHC	$101,000	$127,000	$174,000	$202,000
		2dr 3.8L DHC	$103,000	$148,000	$186,000	$269,000
						-10% for auto.
1959	3.4 Litre	4dr Sdn	$19,200	$26,600	$48,200	$76,300
1959	Mark IX	4dr Sdn	$14,800	$25,600	$39,400	$61,700
1959	XK 150	2dr FHC	$37,300	$53,200	$76,500	$102,000
		2dr S FHC	$44,400	$60,600	$97,400	$122,000
		2dr Rdstr	$77,400	$108,000	$153,000	$192,000
		2dr S Rdstr	$133,000	$163,000	$209,000	$273,000
		2dr DHC	$73,400	$102,000	$134,000	$184,000
		2dr S DHC	$98,600	$133,000	$177,000	$211,000
						-10% for auto.
1960	3.4 Litre	4dr Mk II Sdn	$19,600	$26,400	$47,200	$74,500
1960	Mark IX	4dr Sdn	$14,800	$25,600	$39,400	$61,700
1960	XK 150	2dr FHC	$37,100	$52,200	$76,500	$98,400
		2dr S FHC	$44,900	$60,500	$98,600	$119,000
		2dr Rdstr	$76,200	$105,000	$150,000	$196,000
		2dr S Rdstr	$115,000	$153,000	$210,000	$264,000
		2dr DHC	$69,400	$94,900	$132,000	$193,000
		2dr S DHC	$97,600	$127,000	$174,000	$202,000
						-10% for auto.

Year	Model	Body Style	4	3	2	1
1961	Mark II	4dr 3.8 Sdn	$19,200	$32,000	$56,800	$83,100
1961	Mark IX	4dr Sdn	$15,700	$26,200	$41,000	$64,400
1961	XK 150	2dr FHC	$38,100	$53,200	$77,700	$100,000
		2dr S FHC	$43,500	$60,700	$99,700	$121,000
		2dr 3.8L FHC	$63,800	$94,100	$122,000	$157,000
		2dr S 3.8L FHC	$77,400	$98,400	$132,000	$164,000
		2dr Rdstr	$77,400	$105,000	$161,000	$193,000
		2dr S Rdstr	$113,000	$153,000	$202,000	$252,000
		2dr 3.8L Rdstr	$221,000	$258,000	$308,000	$370,000
		2dr S 3.8L Rdstr	$166,000	$206,000	$281,000	$325,000
		2dr DHC	$71,700	$98,600	$130,000	$189,000
		2dr S DHC	$96,700	$130,000	$177,000	$208,000
		2dr 3.8L DHC	$132,000	$166,000	$198,000	$268,000
		2dr S 3.8L DHC	$161,000	$202,000	$247,000	$302,000
						-10% for auto.
1961	E-Type	2dr SI 3.8 Flt Flr Cpe	$72,700	$117,000	$178,000	$254,000
			+125% for outside bonnet locks and welded louvers.			
		2dr SI 3.8 Flt Flr Rdstr	$117,000	$181,000	$286,000	$385,000
		2dr SI Ltwt Rdstr	$4.4 mil	$5.1 mil	$7.8 mil	$11.5 mil
			+25% for outside bonnet locks and welded louvers.			
1962	Mark II	4dr 3.8 Sdn	$19,200	$32,000	$56,800	$83,100
1962	Mark X	4dr 3.8 Sdn	$8,800	$18,400	$27,100	$39,600
1962	E-Type	2dr SI 3.8 Cpe	$65,200	$84,500	$143,000	$206,000
			+25% for outside bonnet locks and welded louvers.			
		2dr SI 3.8 Flt Flr Cpe	$60,500	$104,000	$164,000	$238,000
			+125% for outside bonnet locks and welded louvers.			
		2dr SI Ltwt Rdstr	$4.4 mil	$5.1 mil	$7.8 mil	$11.5 mil
		2dr SI 3.8 Rdstr	$63,700	$104,000	$206,000	$284,000
		2dr SI 3.8 Flt Flr Rdstr	$110,000	$172,000	$275,000	$365,000
1963	Mark II	4dr 2.4 Sdn	$15,600	$24,300	$39,600	$76,900
1963	Mark X	4dr 3.8 Sdn	$10,100	$20,500	$29,200	$41,600
1963	E-Type	2dr SI 3.8 Cpe	$60,700	$84,800	$147,000	$208,000
		2dr SI 3.8 Rdstr	$59,800	$92,000	$186,000	$267,000
1964	Mark II	4dr Sdn	$19,800	$33,800	$60,500	$85,600
1964	Mark X	4dr 3.8 Sdn	$10,100	$20,500	$29,200	$41,600
1964	E-Type	2dr SI 3.8 Cpe	$60,800	$85,300	$147,000	$206,000
		2dr SI 3.8 Rdstr	$58,300	$90,400	$182,000	$263,000
1965	Mark II	4dr Sdn	$19,800	$33,800	$60,500	$85,600
1965	Mark X	4dr 4.2 Sdn	$10,000	$19,900	$27,900	$38,700
1965	E-Type	2dr SI 4.2 Cpe	$61,300	$98,900	$179,000	$247,000
		2dr SI 4.2 Cpe 2+2	$21,000	$38,700	$58,700	$86,900
		2dr SI 4.2 Rdstr	$69,400	$109,000	$232,000	$322,000
1966	Mark X	4dr 4.2 Sdn	$10,000	$19,900	$27,900	$38,700
1966	3.8	4dr Mk II Sdn	$18,200	$28,400	$59,100	$86,500
1966	E-Type	2dr SI 4.2 Cpe	$61,300	$98,900	$179,000	$247,000

Jaguar

Year	Model	Body Style	4	3	2	1
		2dr SI 4.2 Cpe 2+2	$21,000	$38,700	$58,700	$86,900
		2dr SI 4.2 Rdstr	$69,400	$109,000	$232,000	$322,000
1967	Mark X	4dr 4.2 Sdn	$10,000	$19,900	$27,900	$38,700
1967	3.8	4dr Mk II Sdn	$18,200	$28,400	$59,100	$86,500
1967	420	4dr Sdn	$9,900	$16,600	$21,100	$32,500
		4dr G Sdn	$13,000	$18,200	$29,700	$46,800
1967	E-Type	2dr SI 4.2 Cpe	$61,300	$98,900	$179,000	$247,000
		2dr SI 4.2 Cpe 2+2	$21,000	$38,700	$58,700	$86,900
		2dr SI 4.2 Rdstr	$69,400	$109,000	$232,000	$322,000
		2dr SI.5 Cpe	$27,400	$55,400	$75,500	$94,300
		2dr SI.5 Cpe 2+2	$24,700	$34,800	$50,100	$72,100
		2dr SI.5 Rdstr	$45,600	$72,700	$131,000	$177,000
				+10% for factory a/c. -10% for auto.		
1968	340	4dr Sdn	$12,100	$25,100	$40,700	$63,400
1968	420	4dr Sdn	$9,900	$16,600	$21,100	$32,500
		4dr G Sdn	$13,000	$18,200	$29,700	$46,800
1968	E-Type	2dr SI.5 Cpe	$32,300	$65,200	$90,000	$111,000
		2dr SII Cpe	$30,200	$50,400	$89,800	$113,000
		2dr SI.5 Cpe 2+2	$27,200	$38,400	$56,100	$80,100
		2dr SII Cpe 2+2	$22,000	$44,100	$56,700	$81,700
		2dr SI.5 Rdstr	$43,500	$69,300	$122,000	$165,000
		2dr SII Rdstr	$44,100	$75,600	$130,000	$181,000
				+10% for factory a/c. -10% for auto.		
1969	420	4dr G Sdn	$13,000	$18,200	$29,700	$46,800
1969	XJ6	4dr 4.2 Sdn	$4,700	$13,600	$24,900	$34,100
1969	E-Type	2dr SII Cpe	$30,200	$50,400	$89,800	$113,000
		2dr SII Cpe 2+2	$22,000	$44,100	$56,700	$81,700
		2dr SII Rdstr	$44,100	$75,000	$130,000	$181,000
				+10% for factory a/c. -10% for auto.		
1970	420	4dr G Sdn	$13,000	$18,200	$29,700	$46,800
1970	XJ	4dr Sdn	$4,700	$13,600	$24,900	$34,100
1970	E-Type	2dr SII Cpe	$30,200	$50,400	$89,800	$113,000
		2dr SII Cpe 2+2	$22,000	$44,100	$56,700	$81,700
		2dr SII Rdstr	$44,100	$75,000	$130,000	$181,000
				+10% for factory a/c. -10% for auto.		
1971	XJ	4dr Sdn	$4,000	$14,000	$22,800	$31,900
1971	E-Type	2dr SII Cpe	$30,200	$40,300	$82,900	$113,000
		2dr SII Rdstr	$41,800	$72,000	$126,000	$181,000
				+10% for factory a/c. -10% for auto.		
		2dr SIII Cpe 2+2	$27,600	$43,300	$59,600	$96,300
		2dr SIII Rdstr	$39,700	$57,400	$98,500	$148,000
			-15% for auto trans. +10% for a/c. +5% for wire wheels.			
1972	XJ-6	4dr Sdn	$3,500	$9,800	$17,700	$20,700
1972	E-Type	2dr SIII Cpe 2+2	$27,600	$43,300	$59,600	$96,300
		2dr SIII Rdstr	$39,700	$57,400	$115,000	$187,000
			-15% for auto trans. +10% for a/c. +5% for wire wheels.			
1973	XJ-6	4dr Sdn	$3,600	$9,800	$17,700	$20,700
1973	XJ-12	4dr Sdn	$4,500	$12,900	$22,300	$30,100

Year	Model	Body Style	4	3	2	1
1973	E-Type	2dr SIII Cpe 2+2	$27,600	$43,300	$59,600	$96,300
		2dr SIII Rdstr	$39,700	$57,400	$115,000	$187,000
		-15% for auto trans. +10% for a/c. +5% for wire wheels.				
1974	XJ-6	4dr Sdn	$5,700	$10,200	$17,700	$21,100
1974	XJ6L	4dr Sdn	$6,200	$11,000	$17,300	$22,700
1974	XJ-12	4dr Sdn	$5,500	$10,200	$16,600	$23,100
1974	XJ-12L	4dr Sdn	$6,000	$10,900	$17,600	$27,000
1974	E-Type	2dr SIII Rdstr	$39,700	$57,400	$115,000	$187,000
		-15% for auto trans. +10% for a/c. +5% for wire wheels.				
1975	XJ-6	2dr C Cpe	$7,300	$14,900	$25,600	$36,900
		4dr L Sdn	$5,700	$10,300	$17,700	$21,600
1975	XJ-12	2dr C Cpe	$9,000	$18,100	$27,300	$43,800
		4dr L Sdn	$6,400	$11,000	$18,000	$25,200
1976	XJ-6	2dr C Cpe	$7,300	$14,900	$25,600	$36,900
		4dr L Sdn	$5,700	$10,300	$17,800	$21,600
1976	XJ-12	2dr C Cpe	$9,000	$18,100	$27,300	$43,800
		4dr L Sdn	$6,400	$11,000	$18,000	$25,200
1976	XJ-S	2dr GT 2+2 Cpe	$6,200	$11,900	$24,400	$38,300
1977	XJ-6	2dr C Cpe	$7,300	$14,900	$25,600	$36,900
		4dr L Sdn	$5,700	$10,400	$17,700	$21,800
1977	XJ-12	4dr L Sdn	$6,400	$11,000	$18,000	$25,200
1977	XJ-S	2dr GT Cpe	$6,200	$11,900	$24,400	$38,300
1978	XJ-6	4dr L Sdn	$5,200	$9,900	$16,300	$20,700
1978	XJ-12L	4dr Sdn	$5,800	$10,700	$16,900	$26,200
1978	XJ-S	2dr GT Cpe	$6,200	$11,900	$24,400	$38,300
1979	XJ-6	4dr L Sdn	$2,900	$5,300	$10,700	$15,800
1979	XJ-12L	4dr Sdn	$5,800	$10,700	$16,900	$26,200
1979	XJ-S	2dr Cpe	$5,200	$10,300	$19,500	$34,300
1980	XJ-6	4dr Sdn	$3,600	$6,400	$12,200	$18,900
1980	XJ-S	2dr Cpe	$5,200	$10,300	$19,500	$34,300
1981	XJ-6	4dr Sdn	$3,600	$6,400	$12,200	$18,900
1981	XJ-S	2dr Cpe	$5,200	$10,300	$19,500	$34,300
1982	XJ-S	2dr Cpe	$5,200	$9,800	$17,800	$32,100
1982	XJ6	4dr Sdn	$3,600	$6,400	$12,200	$18,900
		4dr Vanden Plas Sdn	$3,700	$6,600	$12,500	$19,400
1983	XJ-S	2dr Cpe	$5,200	$9,800	$17,800	$32,100
1983	XJ6	4dr Sdn	$3,600	$6,400	$12,200	$18,900
		4dr Vanden Plas Sdn	$3,700	$6,600	$12,500	$19,400
1984	XJ-S	2dr Cpe	$5,200	$9,800	$17,800	$32,100
1984	XJ6	4dr Sdn	$3,600	$6,400	$12,200	$18,900
		4dr Vanden Plas Sdn	$3,700	$6,600	$12,500	$19,400
1985	XJ-S	2dr Cpe	$5,200	$9,800	$17,800	$32,100
1985	XJ6	4dr Sdn	$3,600	$6,400	$12,200	$18,900
		4dr Vanden Plas Sdn	$3,700	$6,600	$12,500	$19,400
1986	XJ-S	2dr Cpe	$5,200	$9,800	$17,800	$32,100

Jaguar

Year	Model	Body Style	4	3	2	1
1986	XJ6	4dr Sdn	$3,600	$6,400	$12,200	$18,900
		4dr Vanden Plas Sdn	$3,700	$6,600	$12,500	$19,400
1987	XJ-S	2dr Cpe	$5,200	$9,800	$17,800	$32,100
1987	XJ6	4dr Sdn	$3,600	$6,400	$12,200	$18,900
		4dr Vanden Plas Sdn	$3,700	$6,600	$12,500	$19,400
1988	XJ-S	2dr Cpe	$5,200	$9,800	$17,800	$32,100
1989	XJ-S	2dr Cpe	$5,200	$9,800	$17,800	$32,100
		2dr Conv	$8,600	$14,300	$27,500	$37,200
1990	XJ-S	2dr Cpe	$5,200	$9,800	$17,800	$32,100
		2dr Conv	$8,600	$14,300	$27,500	$37,200
1990	XJR-15	2dr Cpe	$330,000	$395,000	$476,000	$540,000
1991	XJ-S	2dr Conv	$7,200	$12,000	$23,100	$31,200
		2dr Cpe	$6,000	$11,300	$20,500	$36,900
1991	XJ 220	2dr Cpe	$320,000	$390,000	$461,000	$535,000
1991	XJR-15	2dr Cpe	$330,000	$395,000	$476,000	$540,000
1992	XJS	2dr Cpe	$6,000	$11,300	$20,500	$36,900
		2dr Conv	$7,500	$12,200	$23,000	$30,500
1992	XJ 220	2dr Cpe	$320,000	$390,000	$461,000	$535,000
1992	XJR-15	2dr Cpe	$330,000	$395,000	$476,000	$540,000
1993	XJS	5300/263 2dr Cpe	$6,000	$11,300	$20,500	$36,900
		5300/263 2dr Conv	$7,500	$12,200	$23,000	$30,500
		3980/245 2dr Cpe	$5,600	$10,700	$19,400	$35,100
		3980/245 2dr Conv	$7,100	$11,600	$21,800	$29,000
1993	XJ 220	2dr Cpe	$320,000	$390,000	$461,000	$535,000
1994	XJS	5300/263 2dr Cpe	$6,800	$12,900	$23,300	$42,100
		5300/263 2dr Conv	$8,700	$14,300	$27,000	$35,700
		3980/245 2dr Cpe	$6,100	$11,600	$21,200	$38,200
		3980/245 2dr Conv	$7,800	$12,600	$23,800	$31,600
1995	XJS	5994/301 2dr Cpe	$6,800	$12,900	$23,300	$42,100
		5994/301 2dr 2+2 Conv	$8,700	$14,300	$27,000	$35,700
		3980/245 2dr Cpe	$6,100	$11,600	$21,200	$38,200
		3980/245 2dr 2+2 Conv	$7,800	$12,600	$23,800	$31,600
1996	XJS	2dr 2+2 Conv	$7,800	$12,600	$23,800	$31,600
2000	XKR	2dr Conv	$11,200	$16,900	$20,700	$30,300
		2dr Cpe	$8,900	$13,400	$20,200	$28,400
2001	XKR	2dr Conv	$11,200	$16,900	$20,700	$30,300
		2dr Cpe	$8,900	$13,400	$20,200	$28,400
2002	XKR	2dr Conv	$11,200	$16,900	$20,700	$30,300
		2dr Cpe	$8,900	$13,400	$20,200	$28,400

Jaguar

Year	Model	Body Style	4	3	2	1
2003	XKR	2dr Conv	$12,000	$17,600	$21,500	$31,500
		2dr Cpe	$9,300	$14,000	$21,000	$29,500
2004	XKR	2dr Conv	$12,000	$17,600	$21,500	$31,500
		2dr Cpe	$9,300	$14,000	$21,000	$29,500
2005	XKR	2dr Conv	$12,000	$17,600	$21,500	$31,500
		2dr Cpe	$9,300	$14,000	$21,000	$29,500
2006	XKR	2dr Conv	$12,000	$17,600	$21,500	$31,500
		2dr Cpe	$9,300	$14,000	$21,000	$29,500

Jensen

Year	Model	Body Style	4	3	2	1
1954	541	2dr Cpe	$27,000	$52,000	$68,500	$92,000
1955	541	2dr Cpe	$27,000	$52,000	$68,500	$92,000
1956	541	2dr Cpe	$27,000	$52,000	$68,500	$92,000
1957	541	2dr Cpe	$27,000	$52,000	$68,500	$92,000
1958	541	2dr Cpe	$27,000	$52,000	$68,500	$92,000
1959	541	2dr Cpe	$27,000	$52,000	$68,500	$92,000
1960	541	2dr Cpe	$27,000	$52,000	$68,500	$92,000
1961	541	2dr Cpe	$27,000	$52,000	$68,500	$92,000
1962	541	2dr Cpe	$27,000	$52,000	$68,500	$92,000
1962	C-V8	2dr Mk I Cpe	$21,600	$37,200	$53,000	$75,000
1963	C-V8	2dr Mk II Cpe	$21,600	$37,200	$53,000	$75,000
1964	C-V8	2dr Mk II Cpe	$21,600	$37,200	$53,000	$75,000
1965	C-V8	2dr Mk II Cpe	$21,600	$37,200	$53,000	$75,000
1966	C-V8	2dr Mk III Cpe	$9,200	$18,900	$28,200	$44,000
1966	FF	2dr Cpe	$37,500	$67,900	$90,500	$138,000
1967	Interceptor	2dr I Cpe	$14,000	$31,000	$48,000	$65,000
1967	FF	2dr Cpe	$37,500	$67,900	$90,500	$138,000
1968	Interceptor	2dr I Cpe	$14,000	$31,000	$48,000	$65,000
1968	FF	2dr Cpe	$37,500	$67,900	$90,500	$138,000
1969	Interceptor	2dr I Cpe	$14,000	$31,000	$48,000	$65,000
1969	FF	2dr Cpe	$37,500	$67,900	$90,500	$138,000
1970	Interceptor	2dr II Cpe	$15,000	$32,000	$50,000	$65,000
1970	FF	2dr Cpe	$41,100	$71,700	$95,300	$145,000
1971	Interceptor	2dr II Cpe	$15,000	$32,000	$50,000	$65,000
1971	FF	2dr Cpe	$41,100	$71,700	$95,300	$145,000
1972	Interceptor	2dr III Cpe	$12,500	$32,000	$40,000	$63,000
1973	Interceptor	2dr III Cpe	$12,500	$32,000	$40,000	$63,000
1974	Interceptor	2dr III Cpe	$12,000	$32,000	$40,000	$60,000
		2dr III Conv	$30,000	$44,000	$75,000	$95,000
1975	Interceptor	2dr III Cpe	$12,000	$32,000	$40,000	$60,000
		2dr III Conv	$30,000	$44,000	$75,000	$95,000
1976	Interceptor	2dr III Cpe	$12,000	$32,000	$40,000	$60,000
		2dr III Conv	$30,000	$44,000	$75,000	$95,000

Jensen-Healey

Year	Model	Body Style	4	3	2	1
1972	Mk I	2dr Conv	$3,100	$6,400	$12,900	$22,600
					+$600 for factory hard top.	
1973	Mk I	2dr Conv	$3,100	$6,400	$12,900	$22,600
					+$600 for factory hard top.	
1974	Mk II	2dr Conv	$3,100	$6,400	$12,900	$22,600
					+$600 for factory hard top.	
1975	Mk II	2dr Conv	$3,100	$6,400	$12,900	$22,600
					+$600 for factory hard top.	
1976	GT	2dr Cpe	$5,000	$7,000	$12,500	$19,000

Jowett

Year	Model	Body Style	4	3	2	1
1947	Javelin	4dr Sdn	$5,200	$9,200	$12,900	$18,000
1948	Javelin	4dr Sdn	$5,200	$9,200	$12,900	$18,000
1949	Javelin	4dr Sdn	$5,200	$9,200	$12,900	$18,000
1950	Javelin	4dr Sdn	$5,200	$9,200	$12,900	$18,000
1950	Jupiter	2dr Rdstr	$15,800	$24,500	$34,400	$50,200
			Add more for coachbuilt cars; deduct for the ugly ones.			
1951	Javelin	4dr Sdn	$5,200	$9,200	$12,900	$18,000
1951	Jupiter	2dr Rdstr	$15,800	$24,500	$34,400	$50,200
			Add more for coachbuilt cars; deduct for the ugly ones.			
1952	Javelin	4dr Sdn	$5,200	$9,200	$12,900	$18,000
1952	Jupiter	2dr Rdstr	$15,800	$24,500	$34,400	$50,200
			Add more for coachbuilt cars; deduct for the ugly ones.			
1953	Javelin	4dr Sdn	$5,200	$9,200	$12,900	$18,000
1953	Jupiter	2dr Rdstr	$15,800	$24,500	$34,400	$50,200
			Add more for coachbuilt cars; deduct for the ugly ones.			
1953	R4 Jupiter	2dr Rdstr	$17,500	$28,300	$38,500	$53,100
1954	Javelin	4dr Sdn	$5,200	$9,200	$12,900	$18,000
1954	Jupiter	2dr Rdstr	$15,800	$24,500	$34,400	$50,200
			Add more for coachbuilt cars; deduct for the ugly ones.			

Kaiser

Year	Model	Body Style	4	3	2	1
1952	Manhattan	226/115 2dr Clb Cpe	$7,300	$16,000	$26,000	$36,700
		226/115 2dr Sdn	$5,700	$12,700	$22,700	$29,800
		226/115 4dr Sdn	$3,700	$9,500	$18,400	$26,000
1953	Manhattan	226/118 2dr Trvlr Clb Sdn	$5,200	$10,700	$19,200	$26,500
		226/118 4dr Trvlr Sdn	$3,700	$9,500	$18,400	$26,000
						+20% for supercharger.
1953	Dragon	226/118 4dr Sdn	$10,000	$15,100	$31,900	$41,900
1954	Manhattan	226/140 2dr Clb Sdn	$5,200	$10,700	$19,200	$26,500

Kaiser

Year	Model	Body Style	4	3	2	1
		2dr Clb Cpe	$7,300	$16,000	$26,000	$36,700
		226/140 4dr Sdn	$3,700	$9,500	$18,400	$26,000

+20% for supercharger.

Year	Model	Body Style	4	3	2	1
1954	Darrin	161/90 2dr Spt Conv	$50,000	$81,000	$114,000	$161,000
1955	Manhattan	226/140 2dr Clb Sdn	$5,500	$11,300	$19,200	$26,500
		226/140 4dr Sdn	$3,900	$10,000	$18,400	$26,000

+20% for supercharger.

Kurtis

Year	Model	Body Style	4	3	2	1
1949	Sports	2dr Conv	$58,000	$101,000	$146,000	$197,000
1950	Sports	2dr Conv	$58,000	$101,000	$146,000	$197,000
1953	500S	2dr Rdstr	$196,000	$270,000	$325,000	$405,000
1954	500M	331/250 2dr Rdstr	$97,000	$135,000	$178,000	$240,000
1954	500S	2dr Rdstr	$196,000	$270,000	$325,000	$405,000
1955	500M	331/250 2dr Rdstr	$79,000	$135,000	$178,000	$240,000
1955	500S	2dr Rdstr	$196,000	$270,000	$325,000	$405,000

Lagonda

Year	Model	Body Style	4	3	2	1
1948	2.6L	4dr Sdn	$11,600	$22,100	$34,500	$49,000
		2dr DHC	$40,000	$75,500	$100,000	$126,000
1949	2.6L	4dr Sdn	$11,600	$22,100	$34,500	$49,000
		2dr DHC	$40,000	$75,500	$100,000	$126,000
1950	2.6L	4dr Sdn	$11,600	$22,100	$34,500	$49,000
		2dr DHC	$40,000	$75,500	$100,000	$126,000
1951	2.6L	4dr Sdn	$11,600	$22,100	$34,500	$49,000
		2dr DHC	$40,000	$75,500	$100,000	$126,000
1952	2.6L	4dr Sdn	$11,600	$22,100	$34,500	$49,000
		2dr DHC	$40,000	$75,500	$100,000	$126,000
1953	2.6L	4dr Sdn	$11,600	$22,100	$34,500	$49,000
		2dr DHC	$40,000	$75,500	$100,000	$126,000
1954	3-Litre	4dr Sdn	$17,000	$32,000	$47,000	$61,000
		2dr DHC	$60,900	$99,000	$119,000	$145,000
1955	3-Litre	4dr Sdn	$17,000	$32,000	$47,000	$61,000
		2dr DHC	$60,900	$99,000	$119,000	$145,000
1956	3-Litre	4dr Sdn	$17,000	$32,000	$47,000	$61,000
		2dr DHC	$60,900	$99,000	$119,000	$145,000
1957	3-Litre	4dr Sdn	$17,000	$32,000	$47,000	$61,000
		2dr DHC	$60,900	$99,000	$119,000	$145,000
1958	3-Litre	4dr Sdn	$17,000	$32,000	$47,000	$61,000
		2dr DHC	$60,900	$99,000	$119,000	$145,000
1961	Rapide	4dr Sdn	$129,000	$185,000	$244,000	$288,000
1962	Rapide	4dr Sdn	$129,000	$185,000	$244,000	$288,000
1963	Rapide	4dr Sdn	$129,000	$185,000	$244,000	$288,000
1964	Rapide	4dr Sdn	$129,000	$185,000	$244,000	$288,000

Lamborghini

Year	Model	Body Style	4	3	2	1
1965	350 GT	2dr Cpe	$694,000	$719,000	$741,000	$785,000
1966	400 GT	2dr Cpe	$494,000	$548,000	$596,000	$617,000
		2dr Alloy Cpe	$594,000	$631,000	$667,000	$715,000
		2dr 2+2 Cpe	$328,000	$377,000	$409,000	$445,000
						+$10,000 for a/c on 2+2.
1966	Miura	2dr P400 Cpe	$710,000	$795,000	$857,000	$1 mil
1967	400 GT	2dr Cpe	$494,000	$548,000	$596,000	$617,000
		2dr Alloy Cpe	$594,000	$631,000	$667,000	$715,000
		2dr 2+2 Cpe	$328,000	$377,000	$409,000	$445,000
						+$10,000 for a/c on 2+2.
1967	Miura	2dr P400 Cpe	$740,000	$815,000	$880,000	$1 mil
1968	Islero	2dr 400 GT 2+2 Cpe	$140,000	$170,000	$207,000	$251,000
		2dr 400 GTS 2+2 Cpe	$151,000	$195,000	$230,000	$287,000
						+10% for factory a/c.
1968	400 GT	2dr 2+2 Cpe	$328,000	$377,000	$409,000	$445,000
						+$10,000 for a/c on 2+2.
1968	Espada	2dr 400 GT SI Cpe	$61,000	$80,000	$105,000	$124,000
1968	Miura	2dr P400 Cpe	$740,000	$815,000	$880,000	$1.1 mil
1969	Islero	2dr 400 GT 2+2 Cpe	$140,000	$170,000	$207,000	$251,000
						+10% for factory a/c.
1969	400 GT	2dr 2+2 Cpe	$328,000	$377,000	$409,000	$445,000
						+$10,000 for a/c on 2+2.
1969	Espada	2dr 400 GT SI Cpe	$61,000	$80,000	$105,000	$124,000
1969	Miura	2dr P400 Cpe	$740,000	$815,000	$880,000	$1.1 mil
		2dr P400 S Cpe	$1 mil	$1.1 mil	$1.2 mil	$1.45 mil
						+$25,000 for vented disc brakes. +10% for factory a/c.
1970	Espada	2dr 400 GTE SII Cpe	$46,000	$62,500	$83,000	$100,000
1970	Jarama	2dr 400 GT Cpe	$55,800	$67,500	$87,000	$101,000
						+10% for twin sunroof.
1970	Miura	2dr P400 S Cpe	$1 mil	$1.1 mil	$1.2 mil	$1.45 mil
						+$25,000 for vented disc brakes. +10% for factory a/c.
1971	Espada	2dr 400 GTE SII Cpe	$46,000	$62,500	$83,000	$100,000
1971	Jarama	2dr 400 GT Cpe	$55,800	$67,500	$87,000	$101,000
						+10% for twin sunroof.
1971	Miura	2dr P400 S Cpe	$1 mil	$1.1 mil	$1.2 mil	$1.45 mil
						+$25,000 for vented disc brakes. +10% for factory a/c.
		2dr P400 SV Cpe	$1.55 mil	$1.75 mil	$1.95 mil	$2.1 mil
						-10% w/o split sump. +10% for factory a/c.
1972	Espada	2dr 400 GTE SII Cpe	$46,000	$62,500	$83,000	$100,000
1972	Jarama	2dr 400 GT Cpe	$55,800	$67,500	$87,000	$101,000
						+10% for twin sunroof.

Year	Model	Body Style	4	3	2	1
1972	Miura	2dr P400 SV Cpe	$1.55 mil	$1.75 mil	$1.95 mil	$2.1 mil
						-10% w/o split sump. +10% for factory a/c.
1973	Espada	2dr 400 GTE SIII Cpe	$63,500	$87,000	$103,000	$117,000
						-$25,000 for auto trans. -$10,00 for no pwr strng.
1973	Urraco	2dr P250 Cpe	$32,000	$48,000	$61,000	$79,000
1973	Jarama	2dr 400 GT Cpe	$55,800	$67,500	$87,000	$101,000
						+10% for twin sunroof.
		2dr 400 GTS Cpe	$82,000	$100,000	$117,000	$140,000
						-$5,000 for no pwr strng.
1974	Espada	2dr 400 GTE SIII Cpe	$63,500	$87,000	$103,000	$117,000
						-$25,000 for auto trans. -$10,00 for no pwr strng.
1974	Jarama	2dr 400 GTS Cpe	$82,000	$100,000	$117,000	$140,000
						-$5,000 for no pwr strng.
1974	Urraco	2dr P250 Cpe	$32,000	$48,000	$61,000	$79,000
1974	Countach	2dr LP400 Cpe	$790,000	$880,000	$960,000	$1.25 mil
1975	Espada	2dr 400 GTE SIII Cpe	$63,500	$87,000	$103,000	$117,000
						-$25,000 for auto trans. -$10,00 for no pwr strng.
1975	Jarama	2dr 400 GTS Cpe	$82,000	$100,000	$117,000	$140,000
						-$5,000 for no pwr strng.
1975	Urraco	2dr P250 Cpe	$32,000	$48,000	$61,000	$79,000
1975	Countach	2dr LP400 Cpe	$790,000	$880,000	$960,000	$1.25 mil
1976	Espada	2dr 400 GTE SIII Cpe	$63,500	$87,000	$103,000	$117,000
						-$25,000 for auto trans. -$10,00 for no pwr strng.
1976	Jarama	2dr 400 GTS Cpe	$82,000	$100,000	$117,000	$140,000
						-$5,000 for no pwr strng.
1976	Urraco	2dr P250 Cpe	$32,000	$48,000	$61,000	$79,000
		2dr P300 Cpe	$49,000	$60,500	$80,000	$100,000
1976	Silhouette	2dr Cpe	$75,000	$100,000	$117,000	$140,000
1976	Countach	2dr LP400 Cpe	$540,000	$610,000	$640,000	$675,000
1977	Espada	2dr 400 GTE SIII Cpe	$74,500	$96,000	$110,000	$125,000
						-$25,000 for auto trans.
1977	Urraco	2dr P300 Cpe	$49,000	$60,500	$80,000	$100,000
1977	Silhouette	2dr Cpe	$75,000	$100,000	$117,000	$140,000
1977	Countach	2dr LP400S Cpe	$305,000	$355,000	$399,000	$425,000
1978	Countach	2dr LP400S Cpe	$305,000	$355,000	$399,000	$425,000
1979	Countach	2dr LP400S Cpe	$305,000	$355,000	$399,000	$425,000
1980	Countach	2dr LP400S Cpe	$305,000	$355,000	$399,000	$425,000
1981	Countach	2dr LP400S Cpe	$305,000	$355,000	$399,000	$425,000
1982	Jalpa	2dr P350 GTS Cpe	$37,000	$49,000	$68,500	$79,900
1982	Countach	2dr LP400S Cpe	$305,000	$355,000	$399,000	$425,000
		2dr LP500S Cpe	$295,000	$320,000	$365,000	$410,000
1983	Jalpa	2dr P350 GTS Cpe	$37,000	$49,000	$68,500	$79,900

Lamborghini

Year	Model	Body Style	4	3	2	1
1983	Countach	2dr LP500S Cpe	$295,000	$320,000	$365,000	$410,000
1984	Jalpa	2dr P350 GTS Cpe	$37,000	$49,000	$68,500	$79,900
1984	Countach	2dr LP500S Cpe	$295,000	$320,000	$365,000	$410,000
1985	Jalpa	2dr P350 GTS Cpe	$40,000	$51,000	$70,000	$82,000
1985	Countach	2dr LP500S Cpe	$296,000	$352,000	$375,000	$415,000
		2dr LP5000 QV Downdraft Cpe	$470,000	$500,000	$525,000	$565,000
		2dr LP5000 QV Cpe	$345,000	$400,000	$435,000	$470,000
1986	Jalpa	2dr P350 GTS Cpe	$41,500	$55,000	$77,500	$88,000
						+$1,500 for wing.
1986	Countach	2dr LP5000 QV Cpe	$345,000	$400,000	$435,000	$470,000
1987	Jalpa	2dr P350 GTS Cpe	$43,000	$59,000	$81,000	$95,000
						+10% for telephone dial wheels. +$1,500 for wing.
1987	Countach	2dr LP5000 QV Cpe	$345,000	$400,000	$435,000	$470,000
1988	Jalpa	2dr P350 GTS Cpe	$52,000	$69,500	$90,000	$104,000
1988	Countach	2dr LP5000 QV Cpe	$345,000	$400,000	$435,000	$470,000
		2dr Silver Annv Cpe	$220,000	$240,000	$265,000	$310,000
1989	Countach	2dr Silver Annv Cpe	$220,000	$240,000	$265,000	$310,000
1990	Diablo	2dr Cpe	$90,700	$114,000	$155,000	$209,000
1991	Diablo	2dr Cpe	$94,500	$117,000	$163,000	$216,000
1992	Diablo	2dr Cpe	$98,400	$120,000	$167,000	$219,000
1993	Diablo	2dr Cpe	$101,000	$124,000	$171,000	$225,000
		2dr VT Cpe	$100,000	$121,000	$167,000	$212,000
1994	Diablo	2dr VT Cpe	$102,000	$124,000	$170,000	$215,000
		2dr Cpe	$104,000	$127,000	$181,000	$230,000
1995	Diablo	2dr SV Cpe	$147,000	$178,000	$223,000	$273,000
		2dr VT Cpe	$105,000	$128,000	$175,000	$222,000
		2dr Cpe	$106,000	$130,000	$185,000	$234,000
		2dr VT Rdstr	$143,000	$171,000	$203,000	$251,000
1996	Diablo	2dr SV Cpe	$152,000	$182,000	$227,000	$292,000
		2dr VT Cpe	$109,000	$131,000	$178,000	$227,000
		2dr VT Rdstr	$147,000	$176,000	$207,000	$267,000
		2dr Cpe	$110,000	$133,000	$188,000	$241,000
1997	Diablo	2dr Cpe	$113,000	$138,000	$202,000	$276,000
		2dr SV Cpe	$162,000	$191,000	$249,000	$324,000
		2dr VT Cpe	$112,000	$133,000	$181,000	$232,000
		2dr VT Rdstr	$158,000	$184,000	$228,000	$296,000
1998	Diablo	2dr Cpe	$113,000	$138,000	$203,000	$278,000
		2dr SV Cpe	$162,000	$192,000	$252,000	$325,000
		2dr VT Cpe	$114,000	$134,000	$183,000	$234,000
		2dr VT Rdstr	$158,000	$184,000	$228,000	$296,000

Year	Model	Body Style	4	3	2	1
1945	Aprilia	4dr Sdn	$21,700	$28,300	$36,300	$49,300
1946	Ardea	4dr S1 Sdn	$10,200	$14,300	$21,900	$29,000
1946	Aprilia	4dr Sdn	$21,700	$28,300	$36,300	$49,300
1947	Ardea	4dr S1 Sdn	$10,200	$14,300	$21,900	$29,000
1947	Aprilia	4dr Sdn	$21,700	$28,300	$36,300	$49,300
1948	Ardea	4dr S3 Sdn	$11,400	$15,900	$23,700	$34,800
1948	Aprilia	4dr Sdn	$21,700	$28,300	$36,300	$49,300
1949	Ardea	4dr S3 Sdn	$11,400	$15,900	$23,700	$34,800
1949	Aprilia	4dr Sdn	$21,700	$28,300	$36,300	$49,300
1950	Ardea	4dr S4 Sdn	$11,400	$15,900	$23,700	$34,800
1950	Aurelia	4dr B10 Sdn	$15,900	$23,500	$29,500	$41,600
		2dr B50 Cab	$89,400	$124,000	$156,000	$190,000
1951	Ardea	4dr S4 Sdn	$11,400	$15,900	$23,700	$34,800
1951	Aurelia	2dr B20 GT S1 Cpe	$92,600	$142,000	$182,000	$282,000
		4dr B10 Sdn	$15,900	$23,500	$29,500	$41,600
		2dr B50 Cab	$89,400	$124,000	$156,000	$190,000
1952	Ardea	4dr S4 Sdn	$11,400	$15,900	$23,700	$34,800
1952	Aurelia	2dr B20 GT S1 Cpe	$92,600	$142,000	$182,000	$282,000
		4dr B10 Sdn	$15,900	$23,500	$29,500	$41,600
1953	Aurelia	2dr B20 GT S1 Cpe	$92,600	$142,000	$182,000	$282,000
		4dr B12 Sdn	$15,900	$23,500	$29,500	$41,600
1953	Appia	4dr S1 Sdn	$12,100	$16,000	$23,600	$29,200
1954	Appia	4dr S1 Sdn	$12,100	$16,000	$23,600	$29,200
1954	Aurelia	2dr B20 GT S3 Cpe	$92,600	$142,000	$182,000	$282,000
		4dr B12 Sdn	$15,900	$23,500	$29,500	$41,600
		2dr B24 Spider America	$926,000	$990,000	$1.4 mil	$1.9 mil
1955	Appia	4dr S1 Sdn	$12,100	$16,000	$23,600	$29,200
1955	Aurelia	2dr B20 GT S4 Cpe	$99,000	$159,000	$218,000	$313,000
		2dr B24 Spider America	$926,000	$990,000	$1.4 mil	$1.9 mil
1956	Appia	4dr S2 Sdn	$9,200	$12,400	$18,200	$24,400
1956	Aurelia	2dr B20 GT S4 Cpe	$99,000	$159,000	$218,000	$313,000
		2dr B24 Conv	$260,000	$339,000	$449,000	$504,000
1957	Appia	2dr S2 Zagato Cpe	$83,700	$115,000	$148,000	$208,000
		2dr S2 PF Cpe 2+2	$19,000	$29,000	$45,500	$66,200
		4dr S2 Sdn	$9,200	$12,400	$18,200	$24,400
1957	Aurelia	2dr B20 GT S5 Cpe	$93,600	$142,000	$187,000	$264,000
		2dr B24 Conv	$260,000	$339,000	$449,000	$504,000
1958	Appia	2dr S2 Zagato Cpe	$50,000	$65,000	$99,100	$157,000
		2dr S2 PF Cpe 2+2	$19,000	$29,000	$45,500	$66,200
		4dr S2 Sdn	$9,200	$12,400	$18,200	$24,400
		2dr S2 Vignale Conv	$21,500	$30,200	$49,500	$69,000
1958	Flaminia	4dr Sdn	$10,500	$14,000	$19,700	$27,800
1958	Aurelia	2dr B20 GT S6 Cpe	$93,600	$142,000	$187,000	$264,000
		2dr B24 Conv	$260,000	$339,000	$449,000	$504,000
1959	Appia	2dr S2 PF Cpe 2+2	$19,000	$29,000	$45,500	$66,200
		4dr S2 Sdn	$9,200	$12,400	$18,200	$24,400

Lancia

Year	Model	Body Style	4	3	2	1
		2dr S2 Zagato Conv	$50,000	$65,000	$99,100	$157,000
		2dr S3 Vignale Conv	$21,500	$30,200	$49,500	$69,000
1959	Flaminia	2dr PF Cpe	$17,400	$26,400	$36,500	$46,700
		2dr Spt Zagato Cpe	$202,000	$269,000	$355,000	$475,000
1959	Aurelia	2dr B24 Conv	$260,000	$339,000	$449,000	$504,000
1960	Appia	2dr S3 Cpe	$19,000	$29,000	$45,500	$66,200
		2dr Spt Zagato S3 Cpe	$30,800	$41,200	$57,500	$75,900
		2dr Vignale Conv	$21,500	$30,200	$49,500	$69,000
1960	Flaminia	2dr PF Cpe	$23,200	$34,100	$43,400	$58,000
		2dr Touring GT Cpe	$46,900	$60,500	$84,000	$113,000
		2dr Spt Zagato Cpe	$202,000	$269,000	$355,000	$475,000
		4dr Sdn	$10,500	$14,000	$19,700	$27,800
		2dr Touring GT Conv	$89,200	$118,000	$198,000	$229,000
1961	Appia	2dr S3 Cpe	$19,000	$29,000	$45,500	$66,200
		2dr Spt Zagato S3 Cpe	$30,800	$41,200	$57,500	$75,900
		2dr Vignale Conv	$21,500	$30,200	$49,500	$69,000
1961	Flavia	4dr 1500 Sdn	$4,500	$8,600	$13,800	$19,700
1961	Flaminia	2dr PF Cpe	$23,200	$34,100	$43,400	$58,000
		2dr Touring GT Cpe	$46,900	$60,500	$84,000	$113,000
		2dr Touring GTL Cpe	$35,300	$44,400	$62,100	$80,900
		2dr Spt Zagato Cpe	$202,000	$269,000	$355,000	$475,000
		2dr Touring GT Conv	$89,200	$118,000	$198,000	$229,000
		4dr Sdn	$10,500	$14,000	$19,700	$27,800
1962	Appia	2dr S3 Cpe	$19,000	$29,000	$45,500	$66,200
		2dr Spt Zagato S3 Cpe	$30,800	$41,200	$57,500	$75,900
		2dr Vignale Conv	$21,500	$30,200	$49,500	$69,000
1962	Flavia	4dr 1500 Sdn	$4,500	$8,600	$13,800	$19,700
		2dr 1500 Cpe	$18,900	$28,800	$41,600	$65,200
1962	Flaminia	2dr PF Cpe	$23,200	$34,100	$43,400	$58,000
		2dr Touring GT Cpe	$46,900	$60,500	$84,000	$113,000
		2dr Touring GTL Cpe	$35,300	$44,400	$62,100	$80,900
		2dr Spt Zagato Cpe	$132,000	$190,000	$242,000	$315,000
		4dr Sdn	$10,500	$14,000	$19,700	$27,800
		2dr Touring GT Conv	$89,200	$118,000	$198,000	$229,000

Year	Model	Body Style	4	3	2	1
1963	Appia	2dr S3 Cpe	$19,000	$29,000	$45,500	$66,200
		2dr Vignale Conv	$21,500	$30,200	$49,500	$69,000
1963	Fulvia	4dr S1 Sdn	$4,800	$6,800	$9,500	$13,700
1963	Flavia	2dr 1500 Cpe	$18,900	$28,800	$41,600	$65,200
		2dr Spt Zagato Cpe	$42,700	$56,800	$71,600	$91,100
		4dr 1500 Sdn	$4,500	$8,600	$13,800	$19,700
		2dr Vignale Conv	$25,400	$37,600	$54,800	$80,100
1963	Flaminia	2dr PF Cpe	$23,200	$34,100	$43,400	$58,000
		2dr Touring GT Cpe	$46,900	$60,500	$84,000	$113,000
		2dr Touring GTL Cpe	$35,300	$44,400	$62,100	$80,900
		2dr Spt Zagato Cpe	$132,000	$190,000	$242,000	$315,000
		2dr Touring GT Conv	$89,200	$118,000	$198,000	$229,000
1964	Flavia	2dr 1500 Cpe	$18,900	$28,800	$41,600	$65,200
		2dr Spt Zagato Cpe	$42,700	$56,800	$71,600	$91,100
		2dr Vignale Conv	$25,400	$37,600	$54,800	$80,100
		4dr 1500 Sdn	$4,500	$8,600	$13,800	$19,700
1964	Fulvia	4dr S1 Sdn	$4,800	$6,800	$9,500	$13,700
1964	Flaminia	2dr PF Cpe	$23,200	$34,100	$43,400	$58,000
		2dr Touring GT Cpe	$46,900	$60,500	$84,000	$113,000
		2dr Touring GTL Cpe	$35,300	$44,400	$62,100	$80,900
		2dr SS Zagato Cpe	$198,000	$272,000	$352,000	$473,000
		4dr Sdn	$10,500	$14,000	$19,700	$27,800
		2dr Touring GT Conv	$89,200	$118,000	$198,000	$229,000
1965	Fulvia	2dr 1.2 Cpe	$16,000	$20,400	$30,600	$45,900
		2dr 1.2HF Cpe	$24,400	$38,500	$53,200	$71,100
		2dr Spt Zagato Cpe	$30,200	$41,500	$57,300	$77,500
		4dr S1 Sdn	$4,800	$6,800	$9,500	$13,700
1965	Flavia	2dr 1500 Cpe	$18,900	$28,800	$41,600	$65,200
		2dr Spt Zagato Cpe	$42,700	$56,800	$71,600	$91,100
		4dr 1500 Sdn	$4,500	$8,600	$13,800	$19,700
		2dr Vignale Conv	$25,400	$37,600	$54,800	$80,100
1965	Flaminia	2dr PF Cpe	$23,200	$34,100	$43,400	$58,000
		2dr Touring GT Cpe	$46,900	$60,500	$84,000	$113,000
		2dr Touring GTL Cpe	$35,300	$44,400	$62,100	$80,900
		2dr SS Zagato Cpe	$198,000	$272,000	$352,000	$473,000
		4dr Sdn	$10,500	$14,000	$19,700	$27,800

Lancia

Year	Model	Body Style	4	3	2	1
		2dr Touring GT Conv	$89,200	$118,000	$198,000	$229,000
1966	Fulvia	2dr 1.2 Cpe	$16,000	$20,400	$30,600	$45,900
		2dr 1.2HF Cpe	$24,400	$38,500	$53,200	$71,100
		2dr Spt Zagato Cpe	$30,200	$41,500	$57,300	$77,500
		4dr SI Sdn	$4,800	$6,800	$9,500	$13,700
1966	Flavia	2dr 1500 Cpe	$18,900	$28,800	$41,600	$65,200
		2dr Spt Zagato Cpe	$42,700	$56,800	$71,600	$91,100
		4dr 1500 Sdn	$4,500	$8,600	$13,800	$19,700
		2dr Vignale Conv	$25,400	$37,600	$54,800	$80,100
1966	Flaminia	2dr PF Cpe	$23,200	$34,100	$43,400	$58,000
		2dr SS Zagato Cpe	$198,000	$272,000	$352,000	$473,000
		4dr Sdn	$10,500	$14,000	$19,700	$27,800
1967	Fulvia	2dr 1.2 Cpe	$16,000	$20,400	$30,600	$45,900
		2dr 1.2HF Cpe	$24,400	$38,500	$53,200	$71,100
		2dr 1.3 SI Cpe	$16,000	$20,400	$30,600	$45,900
		2dr 1.3HF Cpe	$33,800	$49,600	$67,400	$100,000
		2dr Spt Zagato 1.3 Cpe	$19,900	$27,800	$45,500	$64,000
		+15% for early all-alloy cars.				
		4dr SI Sdn	$4,800	$6,800	$9,500	$13,700
1967	Flavia	2dr 1500 Cpe	$18,900	$28,800	$41,600	$65,200
		2dr Spt Zagato Cpe	$42,700	$56,800	$71,600	$91,100
		4dr 1500 Sdn	$4,500	$8,600	$13,800	$19,700
		2dr Vignale Conv	$25,400	$37,600	$54,800	$80,100
1967	Flaminia	2dr PF Cpe	$23,200	$34,100	$43,400	$58,000
		2dr SS Zagato Cpe	$198,000	$272,000	$352,000	$473,000
		4dr Sdn	$10,500	$14,000	$19,700	$27,800
1968	Fulvia	2dr 1.2 Cpe	$16,000	$20,400	$30,600	$45,900
		2dr 1.3 SI Cpe	$16,000	$20,400	$30,600	$45,900
		2dr 1.3HF Cpe	$33,800	$49,600	$67,400	$100,000
		2dr Spt Zagato 1.3 Cpe	$19,900	$27,800	$45,500	$64,000
		+15% for early all-alloy cars.				
		2dr 1.6HF Fanalone Cpe	$76,700	$106,000	$139,000	$184,000
		Fakes abound: prices are for documented, genuine Fanalones. Documented Works racers start at about twice the price.				
		4dr SI Sdn	$4,800	$6,800	$9,500	$13,700
1968	Flavia	2dr 1500 Cpe	$18,900	$28,800	$41,600	$65,200
1968	Flaminia	4dr Sdn	$10,500	$14,000	$19,700	$27,800
1969	Flaminia	4dr Sdn	$10,500	$14,000	$19,700	$27,800
1969	Fulvia	4dr SI Sdn	$4,800	$6,800	$9,500	$13,700
		2dr 1.3 SI Cpe	$16,000	$20,400	$30,600	$45,900
		2dr 1.3HF Cpe	$33,800	$49,600	$67,400	$100,000

Year	Model	Body Style	4	3	2	1
		2dr Spt Zagato 1.3 Cpe	$19,900	$27,800	$45,500	$64,000
		+15% for early all-alloy cars.				
		2dr 1.6HF Fanalone Cpe	$76,700	$106,000	$139,000	$184,000
		Fakes abound; prices are for documented, genuine Fanalones. Documented Works racers start at about twice the price.				
		4dr S2 Sdn	$4,700	$6,900	$9,900	$15,500
1969	Flavia 2000	2dr Cpe	$22,600	$32,200	$53,600	$79,200
1970	Flaminia	4dr Sdn	$10,500	$14,000	$19,700	$27,800
1970	Fulvia	2dr 1.2 Cpe	$15,200	$19,800	$28,800	$40,500
		2dr 1.6HF Fanalone Cpe	$76,700	$106,000	$139,000	$184,000
		Fakes abound; prices are for documented, genuine Fanalones. Documented Works racers start at about twice the price.				
		4dr S2 Sdn	$4,700	$6,900	$9,900	$15,500
1970	Flavia 2000	2dr Cpe	$22,600	$32,200	$53,600	$79,200
1970	2000	4dr Sdn	$1,500	$3,500	$6,300	$10,100
1971	Fulvia	2dr 1.3 SI Cpe	$15,200	$19,800	$28,800	$40,500
		4dr S2 Sdn	$4,700	$6,900	$9,900	$15,500
1971	Flavia 2000	2dr Cpe	$22,600	$32,200	$53,600	$79,200
1971	2000	4dr Sdn	$1,500	$3,500	$6,300	$10,100
1972	Fulvia	2dr 1.2 Cpe	$15,200	$19,800	$28,800	$40,500
		2dr 1.6HF Lusso Cpe	$16,300	$24,700	$35,700	$61,100
		4dr S2 Sdn	$4,700	$6,900	$9,900	$15,500
1972	Flavia 2000	2dr Cpe	$22,600	$32,200	$53,600	$79,200
1972	2000	4dr Sdn	$1,500	$3,500	$6,300	$10,100
1972	Beta	4dr Sdn	$1,100	$3,400	$5,300	$7,400
1973	Fulvia	2dr 1.2 Cpe	$15,200	$19,800	$28,800	$40,500
		2dr 1.6HF Lusso Cpe	$16,300	$24,700	$35,700	$61,100
		4dr S2 Sdn	$4,700	$6,900	$9,900	$15,500
1973	Flavia 2000	2dr Cpe	$22,600	$32,200	$53,600	$79,200
1973	2000	4dr Sdn	$1,500	$3,500	$6,300	$10,100
1973	Beta	4dr Sdn	$1,100	$3,400	$5,300	$7,400
1974	Fulvia	2dr 1.3 SI Cpe	$15,200	$19,800	$28,800	$40,500
1974	2000	4dr Sdn	$1,500	$3,500	$6,300	$10,100
1974	Beta	4dr Sdn	$1,100	$3,400	$5,300	$7,400
		2dr Cpe	$2,100	$5,000	$7,000	$14,300
		4dr HPE Wgn	$1,600	$4,100	$6,800	$14,000
		2dr Zagato Spider	$3,500	$7,400	$13,600	$26,300
1974	Stratos	2dr HF Cpe	$388,000	$466,000	$527,000	$585,000
		Many Stradales have become Rally replicas; documented ex-works cars can be much higher.				
1974	Scorpion	2dr Cpe	$7,500	$11,200	$14,000	$18,200
1975	Fulvia	2dr 1.3 SI Cpe	$15,200	$19,800	$28,800	$40,500
1975	Beta	4dr Sdn	$1,100	$3,400	$5,300	$7,400
		2dr Cpe	$2,100	$5,000	$7,000	$14,300

Lancia

Year	Model	Body Style	4	3	2	1
		2dr HPE Wgn	$1,600	$4,100	$6,800	$14,000
		2dr Zagato Spider	$3,500	$7,400	$13,600	$26,300
1975	Stratos	2dr HF Cpe	$388,000	$466,000	$527,000	$585,000
			Many Stradales have become Rally replicas; documented ex-works cars can be much higher.			
1975	Scorpion	2dr Cpe	$7,500	$11,200	$14,000	$18,200
1976	Fulvia	2dr 1.3 SI Cpe	$15,200	$19,800	$28,800	$40,500
1976	Beta	4dr Sdn	$1,100	$3,400	$5,300	$7,400
		2dr Cpe	$2,100	$5,000	$7,000	$14,300
		2dr HPE Wgn	$1,600	$4,100	$6,800	$14,000
		2dr Zagato Spider	$3,500	$7,400	$13,600	$26,300
1976	Scorpion	2dr Cpe	$7,500	$11,200	$14,000	$18,200
1976	Gamma	4dr Sdn	$1,200	$2,400	$2,900	$3,900
		2dr Cpe	$6,800	$10,700	$12,800	$16,100
1977	Beta	4dr Sdn	$1,100	$3,400	$5,300	$7,400
		2dr Cpe	$2,100	$5,000	$7,000	$14,300
		4dr HPE Wgn	$1,600	$4,100	$6,800	$14,000
		2dr Zagato Spider	$3,500	$7,400	$13,600	$26,300
1977	Scorpion	2dr Cpe	$7,500	$11,200	$14,000	$18,200
1977	Gamma	4dr Sdn	$1,200	$2,400	$2,900	$3,900
		2dr Cpe	$6,800	$10,700	$12,800	$16,100
1978	Beta	4dr Sdn	$1,100	$3,400	$5,300	$7,400
		2dr Cpe	$2,100	$5,000	$7,000	$14,300
		4dr HPE Wgn	$1,600	$4,100	$6,800	$14,000
		2dr Zagato Spider	$3,500	$7,400	$13,600	$26,300
1978	Scorpion	2dr Cpe	$7,500	$11,200	$14,000	$18,200
1978	Gamma	4dr Sdn	$1,200	$2,400	$2,900	$3,900
		2dr Cpe	$6,800	$10,700	$12,800	$16,100
1979	Beta	4dr Sdn	$1,100	$3,400	$5,300	$7,400
		2dr Cpe	$2,100	$5,000	$7,000	$14,300
		2dr HPE Wgn	$1,600	$4,100	$6,800	$14,000
		2dr Zagato Spider	$2,900	$7,400	$13,600	$26,300
1979	Scorpion	2dr Cpe	$7,500	$11,200	$14,000	$18,200
1979	Gamma	4dr Sdn	$1,200	$2,400	$2,900	$3,900
		2dr Cpe	$6,800	$10,700	$12,800	$16,100
1980	Beta	4dr Sdn	$1,100	$3,400	$5,300	$7,400
		2dr Cpe	$2,100	$5,000	$7,000	$14,300
		4dr HPE Wgn	$1,600	$4,100	$6,800	$14,000
		2dr Zagato Spider	$3,500	$7,400	$13,600	$26,300
1980	Scorpion	2dr Cpe	$7,500	$11,200	$14,000	$18,200
1980	Gamma	4dr Sdn	$1,200	$2,400	$2,900	$3,900
		2dr Cpe	$6,800	$10,700	$12,800	$16,100
1981	Beta Zagato	2dr Spider	$2,900	$7,400	$13,600	$26,300
1981	Beta	2dr Cpe	$2,100	$5,000	$7,000	$15,100
		4dr Sdn	$1,100	$3,400	$5,300	$7,400
		2dr HPE Wgn	$1,600	$4,100	$6,800	$14,000
1981	Scorpion	2dr Cpe	$7,500	$11,200	$14,000	$18,200
1981	Gamma	4dr Sdn	$1,200	$2,400	$2,900	$3,900
		2dr Cpe	$6,800	$10,700	$12,800	$16,100

Year	Model	Body Style	4	3	2	1
1982	Beta	2dr Cpe	$2,100	$5,000	$7,000	$14,300
		2dr HPE Wgn	$1,600	$4,100	$6,800	$14,000
		2dr Zagato Spider	$3,500	$7,400	$13,600	$26,300
1982	Gamma	4dr Sdn	$1,200	$2,400	$2,900	$3,900
		2dr Cpe	$6,800	$10,700	$12,800	$16,100
1983	Beta	2dr Cpe	$2,100	$5,000	$7,000	$14,300
		2dr HPE Wgn	$1,600	$4,100	$6,800	$14,000
1983	Gamma	4dr Sdn	$1,200	$2,400	$2,900	$3,900
		2dr Cpe	$6,800	$10,700	$12,800	$16,100
1984	Beta	2dr Cpe	$2,100	$5,000	$7,000	$14,300
		2dr HPE Wgn	$1,600	$4,100	$6,800	$14,000
1984	Gamma	4dr Sdn	$1,200	$2,400	$2,900	$3,900
		2dr Cpe	$6,800	$10,700	$12,800	$16,100
1989	Delta	5dr HF Integrale 16v Htchbk	$29,000	$50,000	$74,000	$112,000
1990	Delta	5dr HF Integrale 16v Htchbk	$29,000	$50,000	$74,000	$112,000
1991	Delta	5dr HF Evoluzione I Htchbk	$32,000	$62,200	$92,100	$125,000
		Special edition colors such as Verde York, Gialla, Gialla Ferrari, Blu Lagos, and Bianco Perlato can be worth 1.5x base values. Rally or club themed special editions such as Dealers Collection, Martini 5 and 6, Club Italia, Final Edition, Lancia Club, and HiFi can be worth 2.0x base value or more.				
		5dr HF Integrale 16v Htchbk	$29,000	$50,000	$74,000	$112,000
1992	Delta	5dr HF Evoluzione I Htchbk	$32,000	$62,200	$92,100	$125,000
		Special edition colors such as Verde York, Gialla, Gialla Ferrari, Blu Lagos, and Bianco Perlato can be worth 1.5x base values. Rally or club themed special editions such as Dealers Collection, Martini 5 and 6, Club Italia, Final Edition, Lancia Club, and HiFi can be worth 2.0x base value or more.				
1993	Delta	5dr HF Evoluzione I Htchbk	$32,000	$62,200	$92,100	$125,000
		5dr HF Evoluzione II Htchbk	$37,000	$71,000	$104,000	$142,000
		Special edition colors such as Verde York, Gialla, Gialla Ferrari, Blu Lagos, and Bianco Perlato can be worth 1.5x base values. Rally or club themed special editions such as Dealers Collection, Martini 5 and 6, Club Italia, Final Edition, Lancia Club, and HiFi can be worth 2.0x base value or more.				
1994	Delta	5dr HF Evoluzione II Htchbk	$37,000	$71,000	$104,000	$142,000
		Special edition colors such as Verde York, Gialla, Gialla Ferrari, Blu Lagos, and Bianco Perlato can be worth 1.5x base values. Rally or club themed special editions such as Dealers Collection, Martini 5 and 6, Club Italia, Final Edition, Lancia Club, and HiFi can be worth 2.0x base value or more.				

Lea-Francis

Year	Model	Body Style	4	3	2	1
1946	Twelve	4dr Sal	$19,000	$26,300	$35,900	$44,800
1946	Fourteen	4dr Mk I Sal	$6,700	$11,800	$17,400	$22,000
1947	Twelve	4dr Mk II Sal	$25,400	$44,400	$54,900	$71,100
1947	Fourteen	4dr Mk II Sal	$6,700	$11,800	$17,400	$22,000
		4dr Mk III Sal	$24,400	$36,900	$51,600	$71,000
						+20% for LHD.
1948	14 HP	4dr Sal	$6,700	$11,800	$17,400	$22,000
		4dr Wgn	$19,000	$26,800	$35,900	$44,800
1948	14 HP Sports	2dr Conv	$24,700	$37,300	$52,700	$73,500
						+20% for LHD.
1949	14 HP	4dr Sal	$6,700	$11,800	$17,400	$22,000
		4dr Wgn	$19,000	$26,800	$35,900	$44,800
1949	14 HP Sports	2dr Conv	$24,700	$37,300	$52,700	$73,500
						+20% for LHD.
1949	2.5L Sports	2dr Conv	$33,700	$53,100	$80,000	$110,000
1950	14 HP	4dr Sal	$6,700	$11,800	$17,400	$22,000
		4dr Wgn	$19,000	$26,800	$35,900	$44,800
1950	2.5L Sports	2dr Conv	$33,700	$53,100	$80,000	$110,000
1951	14 HP	4dr Sal	$6,700	$11,800	$17,400	$22,000
		4dr Wgn	$19,000	$26,800	$35,900	$44,800
1951	2.5L Sports	2dr Conv	$33,700	$53,100	$80,000	$110,000
1952	14 HP	4dr Sal	$6,700	$11,800	$17,400	$22,000
		4dr Wgn	$19,000	$26,800	$35,900	$44,800
1952	2.5L Sports	2dr Conv	$33,700	$53,100	$80,000	$110,000
1953	14 HP	4dr Sal	$6,700	$11,800	$17,400	$22,000
		4dr Wgn	$19,000	$26,800	$35,900	$44,800
1953	2.5L Sports	2dr Conv	$33,700	$53,100	$80,000	$110,000
1954	14 HP	4dr Sal	$6,700	$11,800	$17,400	$22,000
1954	2.5L Sports	2dr Conv	$33,700	$53,100	$80,000	$110,000

Lincoln

Year	Model	Body Style	4	3	2	1
1946	Series 66H	305/130 2dr Clb Cpe	$12,400	$18,400	$34,500	$49,600
		305/130 4dr Sdn	$7,500	$11,300	$22,800	$33,400
		305/130 2dr Conv Cpe	$10,800	$16,900	$35,900	$57,900
1946	Continental	305/130 2dr Cpe	$11,700	$17,100	$31,900	$46,900
		305/130 2dr Cab	$12,200	$22,100	$49,000	$92,700
1947	Series 76H	292/125 2dr Clb Cpe	$12,400	$18,400	$34,500	$49,600
		292/125 4dr Sdn	$7,600	$11,200	$22,800	$33,400
		292/125 2dr Conv Cpe	$10,800	$16,900	$35,900	$57,900
1947	Continental	292/125 2dr Clb Cpe	$11,700	$17,100	$31,900	$46,900
		292/125 2dr Cab	$12,200	$22,100	$49,000	$92,700

Year	Model	Body Style	4	3	2	1
1948	Series 876H	292/120 2dr Clb Cpe	$13,800	$20,500	$36,300	$52,200
		292/120 4dr Sdn	$7,500	$11,200	$22,800	$33,400
		292/120 2dr Conv Cpe	$9,700	$15,200	$34,100	$55,000
1948	Continental	292/125 2dr Cpe	$11,700	$17,100	$31,900	$46,900
		292/125 2dr Cab	$12,200	$22,100	$49,000	$92,700
1949	Cosmopolitan	336.7/152 2dr Clb Cpe	$9,900	$14,700	$26,500	$38,400
		336.7/152 4dr Spt Sdn	$7,100	$14,400	$27,000	$38,100
		336.7/152 2dr Conv	$16,900	$25,100	$56,800	$71,700
1950	Cosmopolitan	336.7/152 2dr Clb Cpe	$9,900	$14,700	$26,500	$38,200
		336.7/152 4dr Spt Sdn	$7,100	$14,400	$27,000	$38,100
		336.7/152 2dr Capri Cpe	$9,100	$13,200	$25,600	$34,600
		336.7/152 2dr Conv	$17,700	$26,400	$59,600	$75,300
1951	Cosmopolitan	336.7/154 2dr Cpe	$10,400	$15,400	$28,000	$40,100
		336.7/154 2dr Capri Cpe	$9,200	$13,900	$25,100	$35,900
		336.7/154 4dr Spt Sdn	$7,500	$19,600	$36,900	$52,000
		336.7/154 2dr Conv	$17,700	$26,400	$59,600	$75,300
1952	Cosmopolitan	317.5/160 2dr Spt Cpe	$7,700	$11,600	$20,100	$28,600
		317.5/160 4dr Spt Sdn	$4,900	$8,700	$17,000	$24,300
1952	Capri	317.5/160 2dr Spt Cpe	$9,700	$14,700	$26,900	$44,600
		317.5/160 4dr Spt Sdn	$6,500	$9,200	$16,600	$24,200
		317.5/160 2dr Conv	$17,800	$24,200	$46,500	$71,800
1953	Cosmopolitan	318/205 2dr Spt Cpe	$7,900	$11,600	$20,100	$28,600
		318/205 4dr Spt Sdn	$4,900	$8,700	$17,000	$24,300
1953	Capri	318/205 2dr Spt Cpe	$9,700	$14,700	$26,900	$44,600
		318/205 4dr Spt Sdn	$6,400	$9,200	$16,600	$24,200
		318/205 2dr Conv	$17,800	$24,200	$46,500	$71,800

+20% for factory a/c. +5% for pwr strng.

Lincoln

Year	Model	Body Style	4	3	2	1
1954	Cosmopolitan	318/205 2dr Spt Cpe	$7,800	$11,600	$20,100	$28,600
		318/205 4dr Spt Sdn	$5,100	$9,200	$17,900	$25,600
1954	Capri	318/205 2dr Spt Cpe	$9,700	$14,700	$26,900	$44,600
		318/205 4dr Spt Sdn	$6,500	$9,100	$16,600	$24,200
		318/205 2dr Conv	$17,800	$24,200	$46,500	$71,800
				+20% for factory a/c. +5% for pwr strng.		
1955	Custom	341/225 2dr Spt Cpe	$9,100	$13,400	$21,000	$30,100
		341/225 4dr Spt Sdn	$6,700	$9,500	$14,800	$21,200
1955	Capri	341/225 2dr Spt Cpe	$10,900	$16,100	$28,500	$47,000
		341/225 4dr Sdn	$7,800	$11,000	$17,100	$24,800
		341/225 2dr Conv	$24,400	$34,700	$53,300	$73,100
				+20% for factory a/c. +5% for pwr strng.		
1956	Capri	368/285 2dr Hdtp Cpe	$10,800	$15,300	$25,700	$36,000
		368/285 4dr Sdn	$6,400	$9,100	$14,800	$21,400
1956	Premiere	368/285 2dr Hdtp Cpe	$11,200	$16,300	$28,800	$44,700
		368/285 4dr Sdn	$7,100	$9,800	$16,800	$25,500
		368/285 2dr Conv	$34,100	$53,500	$74,000	$101,000
1957	Capri	368/300 2dr Hdtp Cpe	$10,800	$15,300	$25,700	$36,000
		368/300 4dr Sdn	$6,400	$9,100	$14,800	$21,400
		368/300 4dr Lan Hdtp Sdn	$6,800	$9,600	$15,700	$22,400
1957	Premiere	368/300 2dr Hdtp Cpe	$11,200	$16,300	$28,800	$44,700
		368/300 4dr Hdtp Sdn	$7,100	$9,800	$16,800	$25,500
		368/300 4dr Lan Hdtp Sdn	$7,300	$10,200	$17,200	$26,200
		368/300 2dr Conv	$35,800	$55,700	$76,600	$105,000
1958	Capri	430/375 2dr Hdtp Cpe	$8,500	$11,700	$18,600	$26,800
		430/375 4dr Sdn	$6,800	$9,600	$14,900	$22,200
		430/375 4dr Lan Hdtp Sdn	$7,000	$9,900	$15,800	$23,200
1958	Premiere	430/375 2dr Hdtp Cpe	$8,300	$12,000	$21,000	$30,100
		430/375 4dr Sdn	$7,400	$10,600	$18,500	$26,200
		430/375 4dr Lan Hdtp Sdn	$7,600	$10,800	$18,400	$26,900
1959	Capri	430/350 2dr Hdtp Cpe	$8,500	$11,700	$18,400	$27,000
		430/350 4dr Sdn	$6,500	$9,100	$14,700	$21,400

Year	Model	Body Style	4	3	2	1
		430/350 4dr Lan Hdtp Sdn	$7,300	$10,100	$16,400	$23,700
1959	Premiere	430/350 2dr Cpe	$8,200	$12,000	$21,000	$30,100
		430/350 4dr Sdn	$7,300	$10,300	$17,500	$25,400
		430/350 4dr Lan Hdtp Sdn	$7,600	$10,800	$18,400	$26,400
1959	Continental Mk IV	430/350 2dr Cpe	$11,900	$17,400	$29,400	$42,600
		430/350 4dr Sdn	$8,300	$12,400	$20,600	$31,200
		430/350 4dr Town Car Fml Sdn	$9,500	$14,500	$26,400	$39,000
		430/350 4dr Lan Hdtp Sdn	$7,900	$11,300	$18,500	$27,700
		430/350 2dr Conv	$22,800	$37,100	$61,100	$81,900
						+10% for factory a/c.
1960	Lincoln Series	430/315 2dr Cpe	$9,000	$12,600	$21,000	$30,700
		430/315 4dr Sdn	$7,000	$9,800	$16,600	$24,200
		430/315 4dr Hdtp Sdn	$7,400	$10,800	$17,800	$26,400
1960	Premiere	430/315 2dr Hdtp Cpe	$8,200	$11,200	$19,200	$28,100
		430/315 4dr Sdn	$6,800	$9,700	$16,200	$23,400
		430/315 4dr Lan Hdtp Sdn	$7,100	$10,200	$16,900	$25,000
1960	Continental Mk V	430/315 2dr Cpe	$11,900	$17,400	$30,300	$47,700
		430/315 4dr Sdn	$8,000	$12,400	$21,300	$34,600
		430/315 4dr Town Car Sdn	$8,900	$14,000	$25,400	$42,400
		430/315 4dr Lan	$8,500	$13,500	$23,000	$37,400
		430/315 2dr Conv	$18,100	$32,400	$73,400	$106,000
						+10% for factory a/c.
1961	Continental	430/300 4dr Sdn	$7,700	$15,400	$27,300	$41,400
		430/300 4dr Conv	$17,800	$34,400	$62,000	$105,000
						+10% for factory a/c.
1962	Continental	430/300 4dr Sdn	$7,700	$15,500	$27,000	$41,700
		430/300 4dr Conv	$16,700	$34,000	$55,900	$99,200
						+10% for factory a/c.
1963	Continental	430/320 4dr Sdn	$7,800	$15,200	$27,000	$41,400
		430/320 4dr Conv	$15,700	$29,800	$50,900	$89,800
						+10% for factory a/c.

Lincoln

Year	Model	Body Style	4	3	2	1
1964	Continental	430/320 4dr Sdn	$7,400	$14,200	$24,800	$38,800
		430/320 4dr Conv	$15,700	$29,800	$50,900	$87,600
						+10% for factory a/c.
1965	Continental	430/320 4dr Sdn	$7,400	$14,300	$25,700	$40,400
		430/320 4dr Conv	$16,400	$30,300	$52,000	$84,800
						+10% for factory a/c.
1966	Continental	462/340 2dr Cpe	$8,600	$16,400	$27,400	$43,700
		462/340 4dr Sdn	$7,500	$14,800	$26,600	$41,100
		462/340 4dr Conv	$16,700	$31,300	$52,500	$84,000
						+10% for factory a/c.
1967	Continental	462/340 2dr Cpe	$8,600	$16,400	$27,500	$43,600
		462/340 4dr Sdn	$7,600	$14,800	$26,800	$41,200
		462/340 4dr Conv	$17,000	$34,600	$53,400	$87,900
						+10% for factory a/c.
1968	Continental	460/365 2dr Cpe	$7,000	$14,500	$26,200	$36,300
		460/365 4dr Sdn	$6,200	$12,500	$22,900	$38,600
						+10% for factory a/c.
1969	Continental	460/365 2dr Cpe	$7,400	$15,200	$27,400	$38,000
		460/365 4dr Sdn	$5,400	$10,800	$20,900	$36,000
1969	Continental Mk III	460/365 2dr Cpe	$4,800	$11,300	$20,200	$36,500
						+10% for factory a/c.
1970	Continental	460/365 2dr Cpe	$6,400	$11,500	$18,900	$29,200
		460/365 4dr Sdn	$4,800	$7,200	$15,300	$24,500
1970	Continental Mk III	460/365 2dr Cpe	$4,800	$11,500	$20,000	$36,700
1971	Continental	460/365 2dr Cpe	$4,600	$7,100	$13,900	$22,700
		460/365 4dr Sdn	$4,000	$6,100	$12,800	$21,400
1971	Continental Mk III	460/365 2dr Cpe	$4,800	$11,500	$20,000	$36,700
1972	Continental	460/212 2dr Cpe	$4,800	$7,400	$14,600	$23,900
		460/212 4dr Sdn	$4,200	$6,700	$13,600	$23,200
						+10% for Town Car pkg.
1972	Continental Mk IV	460/212 2dr Cpe	$5,400	$9,400	$15,100	$27,500
						+10% for Silver Mark pkg.
1973	Continental	460/208 2dr Cpe	$4,700	$7,300	$14,100	$23,100

Year	Model	Body Style	4	3	2	1
		460/208 4dr Sdn	$3,800	$6,300	$12,700	$21,700
					+10% for Town Car/Cpe pkg.	
1973	Continental Mk IV	460/208 2dr Cpe	$4,800	$7,700	$12,800	$23,000
					+10% for Silver Mark pkg.	
1974	Continental	460/215 2dr Cpe	$4,800	$7,700	$13,900	$23,100
		460/215 4dr Sdn	$4,000	$6,300	$12,800	$21,700
			+10% for Town Car/Coupe pkg. +10% for Silver Luxury pkg.			
1974	Continental Mk IV	460/220 2dr Cpe	$4,900	$8,000	$13,000	$23,300
		460/220 2dr Gold Luxury Cpe	$4,900	$8,600	$14,300	$27,100
					+10% for Silver Mark pkg.	
1975	Continental	460/206 2dr Cpe	$4,800	$7,700	$13,900	$23,100
		460/206 4dr Sdn	$4,000	$6,300	$12,800	$21,700
			+10% for Town Car/Coupe pkg. +10% for Silver Luxury pkg.			
1975	Continental Mk IV	460/194 2dr Cpe	$4,700	$7,600	$12,800	$23,900
		460/194 2dr Blue Diamond Ed Cpe	$4,700	$8,300	$14,200	$27,500
		460/194 2dr Lipstick and White Ed Cpe	$5,000	$8,700	$14,700	$28,800
1976	Continental	460/202 2dr Cpe	$4,700	$7,400	$14,000	$23,400
		460/202 4dr Sdn	$3,600	$5,800	$12,500	$21,300
					+10% for Town Car/Cpe pkg.	
1976	Continental Mk IV	460/202 2dr Cpe	$4,700	$7,700	$12,800	$22,700
		460/202 2dr Lipstick and White Ed Cpe	$4,700	$8,700	$14,100	$26,300
		460/202 2dr Bill Blass Ed Cpe	$5,100	$9,200	$14,500	$27,500
		460/202 2dr Cartier Ed Cpe	$5,100	$9,200	$14,400	$27,500
		460/202 2dr Givenchy Ed Cpe	$5,100	$9,200	$14,400	$27,500
		460/202 2dr Pucci Ed Cpe	$5,100	$9,200	$14,400	$27,500
1977	Versailles	302/122 4dr Sdn	$2,900	$4,600	$7,400	$11,600
1977	Continental	400/179 2dr Cpe	$4,800	$7,300	$14,200	$22,400
		400/179 4dr Sdn	$3,500	$5,900	$12,200	$20,700
1977	Continental Mk V	400/179 2dr Bill Blass Ed Cpe	$4,900	$8,500	$16,700	$33,300

Lincoln

Year	Model	Body Style	4	3	2	1
		+15% for Designer Series pkg (Blass, Cartier, Givenchy, or Pucci). +10% for Luxury Group pkg (Lipstick, Blue Diamond, Black Diamond Fire, etc.).				
1978	Versailles	302/133 4dr Sdn	$2,900	$4,600	$7,400	$11,600
1978	Continental	400/166 2dr Cpe	$4,700	$7,400	$13,700	$22,400
		400/166 4dr Sdn	$3,500	$5,800	$12,200	$20,700
		+10% for Town Car/Coupe pkg. +15% for Williamsburg Ed pkg.				
1978	Continental Mk V	400/166 2dr Cpe	$4,900	$8,700	$17,100	$34,600
		400/166 2dr Bill Blass Ed Cpe	$5,500	$9,900	$19,000	$38,200
		400/166 2dr Givenchy Ed Cpe	$5,500	$9,900	$19,000	$38,200
		400/166 2dr Cartier Ed Cpe	$5,500	$9,900	$19,000	$38,200
		400/166 2dr Pucci Ed Cpe	$5,500	$9,900	$19,000	$38,200
		400/166 2dr Diamond Jubilee Cpe	$5,300	$9,900	$18,500	$36,600
1979	Versailles	302/130 4dr Sdn	$3,000	$4,700	$7,500	$11,900
1979	Continental	400/159 2dr Cpe	$4,400	$7,000	$13,000	$21,100
		400/159 4dr Sdn	$3,500	$5,700	$11,900	$20,700
		+10% for Town Car/Coupe pkg. +15% for Williamsburg Ed pkg. +10% for Collector Series.				
1979	Continental Mk V	400/159 2dr Cpe	$4,500	$8,400	$17,000	$31,800
		400/159 2dr Bill Blass Ed Cpe	$5,100	$9,600	$18,100	$35,300
		400/159 2dr Givenchy Ed Cpe	$5,100	$9,600	$18,100	$35,300
		400/159 2dr Cartier Ed Cpe	$5,100	$9,600	$18,100	$35,300
		400/159 2dr Pucci Ed Cpe	$5,100	$9,600	$18,100	$35,300
		400/159 2dr Collector Series Cpe	$4,800	$9,000	$17,300	$33,700
1980	Versailles	302/132 4dr Sdn	$2,700	$4,200	$6,900	$10,800
1980	Continental	302/129 2dr Cpe	$4,600	$7,500	$11,400	$17,200
		302/129 4dr Sdn	$4,000	$6,000	$9,000	$13,900
1980	Continental Mk VI	302/129 2dr Cpe	$3,900	$6,000	$10,800	$17,200
		302/129 2dr Bill Blass Ed Cpe	$4,100	$6,500	$12,000	$18,800
		302/129 2dr Givenchy Ed Cpe	$4,100	$6,500	$12,000	$18,800
		302/129 2dr Cartier Ed Cpe	$4,100	$6,500	$12,000	$18,800

Year	Model	Body Style	4	3	2	1
		302/129 2dr Pucci Ed Cpe	$4,100	$6,500	$12,000	$18,800
		302/129 2dr Signature Series Cpe	$4,100	$6,500	$11,600	$18,400
		302/129 4dr Sdn	$3,400	$5,800	$10,500	$16,300
		302/129 4dr Signature Series Sdn	$3,900	$6,100	$11,400	$17,500
1981	Town Car	302/130 2dr Sdn	$1,100	$3,200	$5,400	$10,500
		302/130 4dr Sdn	$1,100	$2,700	$4,900	$9,100
1981	Continental Mk VI	302/130 2dr Cpe	$3,300	$5,500	$9,400	$15,300
		302/130 4dr Sdn	$2,500	$4,300	$7,900	$12,300
1982	Continental	302/131 4dr Sdn	$2,700	$5,400	$7,100	$12,800
1982	Continental Mk VI	302/134 2dr Cpe	$3,200	$5,100	$8,800	$14,600
		302/134 4dr Sdn	$2,300	$4,000	$7,300	$11,000
1982	Town Car	302/134 4dr Sdn	$1,100	$2,900	$4,900	$9,300
1983	Continental	302/130 4dr Sdn	$2,700	$5,400	$7,100	$12,800
1983	Town Car	302/130 4dr Sdn	$1,300	$3,000	$5,100	$9,400
1983	Continental Mk VI	302/130 2dr Cpe	$3,200	$5,200	$8,900	$14,600
		302/130 4dr Sdn	$2,300	$4,100	$7,500	$11,000
1984	Continental	302/140 4dr Sdn	$2,700	$5,400	$7,100	$12,800
1984	Continental Mk VII	302/140 2dr Cpe	$1,900	$4,500	$10,400	$16,400
		302/140 2dr LSC Cpe	$2,100	$4,900	$10,400	$16,400
1984	Town Car	302/140 4dr Sdn	$1,300	$2,900	$5,400	$10,000
1985	Continental	302/140 4dr Sdn	$2,700	$5,400	$7,100	$12,800
1985	Continental Mk VII	302/140 2dr Cpe	$1,900	$4,500	$10,400	$16,400
		302/180 2dr LSC Cpe	$2,100	$4,900	$10,400	$16,400
1985	Town Car	302/140 4dr Sdn	$1,300	$2,900	$5,400	$10,000
1986	Continental	302/150 4dr Sdn	$2,700	$5,400	$7,100	$12,800
1986	Continental Mk VII	302/150 2dr Cpe	$1,900	$4,500	$10,400	$16,400
1986	Town Car	302/150 4dr Sdn	$1,300	$3,300	$5,600	$10,500
1987	Mark VII	302/150 2dr Cpe	$1,800	$4,500	$7,800	$11,800
1987	Continental	302/150 4dr Sdn	$2,700	$5,400	$7,100	$12,800
1987	Town Car	302/150 4dr Sdn	$1,300	$3,300	$5,600	$10,500
1988	Mark VII	302/225 2dr LSC Cpe	$2,000	$4,900	$8,600	$12,900

Lincoln

Year	Model	Body Style	4	3	2	1
1988	Continental	232/140 4dr Sdn	$2,700	$4,100	$7,600	$11,800
1988	Town Car	302/150 4dr Sdn	$1,400	$3,400	$5,800	$11,500
1989	Mark VII	302/225 2dr LSC Cpe	$2,000	$4,900	$8,600	$12,900
1989	Continental	232/140 4dr Sdn	$2,500	$3,600	$7,500	$11,700
1989	Town Car	302/150 4dr Sdn	$1,200	$2,100	$4,500	$10,100
1990	Mark VII	302/225 2dr LSC Cpe	$2,000	$4,800	$8,400	$12,800
1990	Continental	232/140 4dr Sdn	$2,400	$3,500	$7,500	$11,700
1990	Town Car	302/150 4dr Sdn	$1,300	$3,600	$8,200	$16,700
1991	Mark VII	302/225 2dr LSC Cpe	$2,000	$4,800	$8,400	$12,300
1991	Continental	232/155 4dr Exec Sdn	$2,100	$3,400	$7,400	$11,200
		232/155 4dr Sig Sdn	$2,100	$3,500	$7,500	$11,600
1991	Town Car	281/190 4dr Sdn	$1,300	$3,600	$8,200	$16,700
1992	Mark VII	302/225 2dr LSC Cpe	$1,800	$4,400	$7,900	$11,800
1992	Continental	232/155 4dr Exec Sdn	$1,600	$2,900	$6,000	$10,400
		232/155 4dr Sig Sdn	$1,600	$3,000	$6,300	$10,800
1992	Town Car	281/190 4dr Exec Sdn	$1,200	$3,600	$8,200	$16,700
1993	Mark VIII	281/280 2dr Cpe	$2,300	$4,100	$9,600	$12,800
1993	Continental	232/160 4dr Exec Sdn	$1,500	$2,700	$6,000	$10,400
		232/160 4dr Sig Sdn	$1,600	$2,900	$6,300	$10,800
1993	Town Car	281/190 4dr Exec Sdn	$1,200	$3,600	$8,200	$16,700
1994	Mark VIII	281/280 2dr Cpe	$2,300	$4,100	$9,600	$12,900
1994	Continental	232/160 4dr Exec Sdn	$1,400	$2,400	$6,000	$10,400
		232/160 4dr Sig Sdn	$1,500	$2,600	$6,300	$10,800
1994	Town Car	281/210 4dr Exec Sdn	$1,300	$3,800	$8,300	$16,800

Lotus

Year	Model	Body Style	4	3	2	1
1956	Seven	2dr S1 Rdstr	$14,400	$22,000	$38,700	$60,000
1956	Eleven	2dr Rdstr	$57,000	$97,000	$145,000	$198,000
1957	Eleven	2dr Rdstr	$57,000	$97,000	$145,000	$198,000
1957	Seven	2dr S1 Rdstr	$14,400	$22,000	$38,700	$60,000
1957	Elite	2dr Cpe	$32,200	$60,000	$98,000	$132,000

Year	Model	Body Style	4	3	2	1
		+15% for Super. +10% for ZF gearbox. -10% for RHD or RHD conversion.				
1958	Seven	2dr S1 Rdstr	$14,400	$22,000	$38,700	$60,000
1958	Super Seven	2dr America Rdstr	$13,100	$21,200	$35,300	$58,500
1958	Eleven	2dr Rdstr	$57,000	$97,000	$145,000	$198,000
1958	Elite	2dr Cpe	$32,200	$60,000	$98,000	$132,000
		+15% for Super. +10% for ZF gearbox. -10% for RHD or RHD conversion.				
1959	Seven	2dr S1 Rdstr	$14,400	$22,000	$38,700	$60,000
1959	Super Seven	2dr America Rdstr	$13,100	$21,200	$35,300	$58,500
1959	Elite	2dr Cpe	$32,200	$60,000	$98,000	$132,000
		+15% for Super. +10% for ZF gearbox. -10% for RHD or RHD conversion.				
1960	Seven	2dr S1 Rdstr	$14,400	$22,000	$38,700	$60,000
1960	Super Seven	2dr America Rdstr	$13,100	$21,200	$35,300	$58,500
1960	Elite	2dr Cpe	$32,200	$60,000	$98,000	$132,000
		+15% for Super. +10% for ZF gearbox. -10% for RHD or RHD conversion.				
1961	Seven	2dr S2 Rdstr	$14,900	$23,000	$36,800	$49,500
		+20% for Cosworth. -20% for RHD.				
1961	Elite	2dr Cpe	$32,200	$60,000	$98,000	$132,000
		+15% for Super. +10% for ZF gearbox. -10% for RHD or RHD conversion.				
1962	Seven	2dr S2 Rdstr	$14,900	$23,000	$37,800	$50,500
		+20% for Cosworth. -20% for RHD.				
1962	Elite	2dr Cpe	$32,200	$60,000	$98,000	$132,000
		+15% for Super. +10% for ZF gearbox. -10% for RHD or RHD conversion.				
1962	Elan	2dr S1 DHC	$16,500	$27,700	$41,600	$49,000
		+10% for SE.				
1963	Seven	2dr S2 Rdstr	$14,900	$23,000	$37,800	$50,500
		+20% for Cosworth. -20% for RHD.				
1963	Elan	2dr S1 DHC	$16,500	$27,700	$41,600	$49,000
		+10% for SE.				
1963	Elite	2dr Cpe	$32,200	$60,000	$98,000	$132,000
		+15% for Super. +10% for ZF gearbox. -10% for RHD or RHD conversion.				
1963	Cortina	2dr Mk I Cpe	$31,000	$45,300	$78,000	$99,000
1964	Seven	2dr S2 Rdstr	$14,900	$23,000	$37,800	$50,500
		+20% for Cosworth. -20% for RHD.				
1964	Elan	2dr S1 DHC	$16,500	$27,700	$40,600	$49,000
		+10% for SE.				
1964	Cortina	2dr Mk I Cpe	$31,000	$45,300	$78,000	$99,000
1965	Seven	2dr S2 Rdstr	$14,900	$23,000	$37,800	$50,000
		+20% for Cosworth. -20% for RHD.				
1965	Cortina	2dr Mk I Cpe	$31,000	$45,300	$78,000	$99,000
1965	Elan	2dr S2 DHC	$17,500	$30,500	$43,000	$54,200
		+10% for SE.				
1966	Seven	2dr S2 Rdstr	$14,900	$23,000	$37,800	$50,500

Lotus

Year	Model	Body Style	4	3	2	1
						+20% for Cosworth. -20% for RHD.
1966	Elan	2dr S3 Cpe	$14,600	$23,000	$29,200	$32,000
		2dr S3 Rdstr	$17,600	$30,000	$41,400	$56,000
						+10% for SE.
1966	Cortina	2dr Mk I Cpe	$31,000	$45,200	$78,000	$99,000
1967	Seven	2dr S2 Rdstr	$14,900	$23,000	$37,800	$50,500
						+20% for Cosworth. -20% for RHD.
1967	Elan	2dr S3 Cpe	$14,600	$23,500	$29,200	$32,000
						+10% for SE.
		2dr Plus 2 Cpe	$9,600	$17,200	$31,100	$36,000
						+10% for S. +20% for S-130.
		2dr S3 DHC	$17,600	$29,500	$41,400	$56,000
						+10% for SE.
1967	Cortina	2dr Mk I Cpe	$31,000	$45,300	$78,000	$99,000
1967	Europa	2dr S1 Cpe	$9,000	$14,000	$23,000	$28,500
1968	Seven	2dr S2 Rdstr	$14,900	$23,000	$37,800	$50,500
						+20% for Cosworth. -20% for RHD.
		2dr S3 Rdstr	$15,500	$22,000	$37,700	$50,400
1968	Elan	2dr S3 Cpe	$14,600	$23,000	$29,200	$32,000
						+10% for SE.
		2dr Plus 2 Cpe	$9,600	$17,200	$31,100	$36,000
						+10% for S. +20% for S-130.
		2dr S4 Cpe	$12,600	$22,000	$28,400	$36,000
						+15% for SE on cpe.
		2dr S3 Rdstr	$17,600	$29,500	$41,400	$56,000
						+10% for SE.
		2dr S4 DHC	$15,900	$26,700	$34,500	$44,900
						+15% for SE on cpe.
1968	Cortina	2dr Mk II Cpe	$22,000	$29,300	$40,000	$60,000
1968	Europa	2dr S1 Cpe	$9,000	$14,000	$23,000	$28,500
		2dr S2 Cpe	$8,200	$12,100	$19,600	$28,300
1969	Seven	2dr S3 Rdstr	$15,500	$22,000	$37,700	$50,400
1969	Super Seven	2dr S4 Rdstr	$11,700	$17,200	$23,400	$31,500
1969	Elan	2dr S4 Cpe	$12,600	$22,000	$28,400	$36,000
						+15% for SE on cpe.
		2dr Plus 2 Cpe	$9,600	$17,200	$31,100	$36,000
						+10% for S. +20% for S-130.
		2dr S4 DHC	$15,900	$26,700	$34,500	$44,900
						+15% for SE on cpe.
1969	Cortina	2dr Mk II Cpe	$22,000	$29,300	$40,000	$60,000
1969	Europa	2dr S2 Cpe	$8,200	$12,100	$19,600	$28,300
1970	Seven	2dr S3 Rdstr	$15,500	$22,000	$37,700	$50,400
						+20% for twin cam.
1970	Super Seven	2dr S4 Rdstr	$11,700	$17,200	$23,400	$31,500
						+10% for twin cam.

Year	Model	Body Style	4	3	2	1
1970	Elan	2dr Plus 2 Cpe	$9,600	$17,200	$31,100	$36,000
		+10% for S. +20% for S-130.				
		2dr S4 Cpe	$12,600	$22,000	$28,400	$36,000
		2dr S4 DHC	$15,900	$26,700	$34,500	$44,900
		+15% for SE on cpe.				
1970	Cortina	2dr Mk II Cpe	$22,000	$29,300	$40,000	$60,000
1970	Europa	2dr S2 Cpe	$8,200	$12,100	$19,600	$28,300
1971	Super Seven	2dr S4 Rdstr	$11,700	$17,200	$23,400	$31,500
1971	Elan	2dr Plus 2 Cpe	$9,600	$17,200	$31,100	$36,000
		+10% for S. +20% for S-130.				
		2dr S4 Cpe	$12,600	$22,000	$28,400	$36,000
		+15% for SE on cpe.				
		2dr Sprint	$14,300	$22,700	$30,800	$40,400
		2dr S4 DHC	$15,900	$26,700	$34,500	$44,900
		+15% for SE on cpe.				
		2dr Sprint DHC	$20,300	$35,200	$45,300	$63,500
1971	Europa	2dr S2 Cpe	$8,200	$12,100	$19,600	$28,300
1972	Super Seven	2dr S4 Rdstr	$11,700	$17,200	$23,400	$31,500
1972	Elan	2dr Plus 2 Cpe	$9,600	$17,200	$31,100	$36,000
		+10% for S. +20% for S-130.				
		2dr Sprint	$14,300	$22,700	$30,800	$40,400
		2dr Sprint DHC	$20,300	$35,200	$45,300	$63,500
1972	Europa	2dr Twin Cam Cpe	$11,300	$17,100	$28,400	$37,900
		+10% for 5-spd. +10% for Special. +10% for JPS.				
1973	Super Seven	2dr S4 Rdstr	$11,700	$17,200	$23,400	$31,500
1973	Elan	2dr Plus 2 Cpe	$9,600	$17,200	$31,100	$36,000
		+10% for S. +20% for S-130.				
		2dr Sprint	$14,300	$22,700	$30,800	$40,400
		2dr Sprint DHC	$19,700	$33,500	$43,400	$60,400
1973	Europa	2dr Twin Cam Cpe	$11,300	$17,100	$28,400	$37,900
		+10% for 5-spd. +10% for Special. +10% for JPS.				
1974	Elan	2dr Plus 2 Cpe	$9,600	$17,200	$31,100	$36,000
		+10% for S. +20% for S-130.				
1974	Elite	2dr Type 75 Cpe	$4,300	$6,600	$9,400	$14,600
1974	Europa	2dr Twin Cam Cpe	$11,300	$17,100	$28,400	$37,900
		+10% for 5-spd. +10% for Special. +10% for JPS.				
1975	Elite	2dr Type 75 Cpe	$4,300	$6,600	$9,400	$14,600
1975	Eclat	2dr Cpe	$5,400	$7,700	$10,400	$15,900
1976	Elite	2dr Type 75 Cpe	$4,300	$6,600	$9,400	$14,600
1976	Eclat	2dr Cpe	$5,400	$7,700	$10,400	$15,900
1976	Esprit	2dr S1 Cpe	$13,500	$22,200	$37,000	$70,000
1977	Elite	2dr Type 75 Cpe	$4,300	$6,600	$9,400	$14,600
1977	Eclat	2dr Cpe	$5,400	$7,700	$10,400	$15,900
1977	Esprit	2dr S1 Cpe	$13,500	$22,200	$37,000	$62,000
1978	Elite	2dr Type 75 Cpe	$4,300	$6,600	$9,400	$14,600
1978	Eclat	2dr Cpe	$5,400	$7,700	$10,400	$15,900

Lotus

Year	Model	Body Style	4	3	2	1
1978	Esprit	2dr S2 Cpe	$10,100	$17,900	$26,600	$35,000
						+10% for JPS.
1979	Elite	2dr Type 75 Cpe	$4,300	$6,600	$9,400	$14,600
1979	Eclat	2dr Cpe	$5,400	$7,700	$10,400	$15,900
1979	Esprit	2dr S2 Cpe	$10,100	$17,900	$26,800	$35,000
						+10% for JPS.
1980	Elite	2dr Type 75 Cpe	$4,300	$6,600	$9,400	$14,600
1980	Eclat	2dr Cpe	$5,400	$7,700	$10,400	$15,900
1980	Esprit	2dr S2 Cpe	$10,100	$17,900	$26,600	$35,000
						+10% for JPS.
		2dr S2.2 Cpe	$10,800	$19,100	$28,100	$35,800
		2dr S2.2 Turbo Cpe	$11,800	$19,500	$31,400	$40,900
						+5% for Essex.
1981	Esprit	2dr S2.2 Cpe	$10,800	$19,100	$28,100	$35,800
		2dr S2.2 Turbo Cpe	$11,800	$19,500	$31,200	$40,900
						+5% for Essex.
1982	Esprit	2dr S2.2 Cpe	$10,800	$19,100	$28,100	$35,800
		2dr S2.2 Turbo Cpe	$11,800	$19,500	$31,200	$40,900
1983	Esprit	2dr S3 Turbo Cpe	$15,500	$22,700	$32,300	$46,400
		2dr S2.2 Cpe	$10,800	$19,100	$28,100	$35,800
		2dr S2.2 Turbo Cpe	$12,700	$17,900	$25,700	$38,900
		2dr S3 Cpe	$10,300	$18,500	$26,700	$34,900
1984	Esprit	2dr S2.2 Cpe	$10,800	$19,000	$27,800	$35,800
		2dr S3 Turbo Cpe	$15,500	$22,700	$32,300	$46,400
		2dr S2.2 Turbo Cpe	$13,800	$19,000	$26,400	$38,800
		2dr S3 Cpe	$10,300	$18,500	$26,700	$34,900
1985	Esprit	2dr S2.2 Cpe	$10,800	$19,000	$27,800	$35,800
		2dr S2.2 Turbo Cpe	$13,800	$19,000	$26,400	$38,800
		2dr S3 Cpe	$10,300	$18,500	$26,700	$34,900
		2dr S3 Turbo Cpe	$15,500	$22,700	$32,300	$46,400
1986	Esprit	2dr S2.2 Cpe	$10,800	$19,000	$27,800	$35,800
		2dr S2.2 Turbo Cpe	$13,800	$19,000	$26,400	$38,800
		2dr S3 Cpe	$10,300	$18,500	$26,400	$34,900
		2dr S3 Turbo Cpe	$16,400	$23,800	$33,000	$48,100
1987	Esprit	2dr S2.2 Cpe	$10,900	$19,100	$28,300	$36,500
		2dr S2.2 Turbo Cpe	$13,900	$19,100	$26,900	$39,500
		2dr S3 Cpe	$10,400	$18,600	$27,200	$35,600
		2dr S3 Turbo Cpe	$16,500	$23,900	$33,500	$48,800
1988	Esprit	2dr S3 Cpe	$12,300	$16,400	$23,900	$31,500
		2dr S3 Turbo Cpe	$16,500	$23,900	$33,500	$48,800
1989	Esprit	2dr S3 Cpe	$12,300	$16,400	$23,900	$31,500

Lotus

Year	Model	Body Style	4	3	2	1
		2dr S3 Turbo Cpe	$16,500	$23,900	$33,500	$48,800
		2dr Annv Turbo Cpe	$16,900	$24,800	$33,500	$49,600
1990	Esprit	2dr Turbo SE Cpe	$15,400	$21,400	$32,400	$45,800
1991	Elan	2dr M100 Rdstr	$8,500	$12,200	$17,500	$24,200
1991	Esprit	2dr Turbo SE Cpe	$15,800	$21,700	$32,200	$43,700
1992	Esprit	2dr Turbo SE Cpe	$16,100	$22,100	$33,400	$43,200
1993	Esprit	2dr Turbo SE Cpe	$16,600	$22,400	$33,900	$44,300
1994	Esprit	2dr S4 Turbo Cpe	$24,000	$29,700	$42,200	$63,000
1995	Esprit	2dr S4 Turbo Cpe	$24,000	$29,700	$42,200	$63,000
1996	Esprit	2dr S4 Turbo Cpe	$24,000	$29,700	$42,200	$63,000

MG

Year	Model	Body Style	4	3	2	1
1947	TC	2dr Rdstr	$13,000	$22,000	$39,200	$56,500
1947	YA	4dr Sdn	$6,200	$11,200	$20,100	$28,000
1948	TC	2dr Rdstr	$13,000	$22,000	$39,200	$56,500
1948	YA	4dr Sdn	$6,200	$11,200	$20,100	$28,000
1949	TC	2dr Rdstr	$13,000	$22,000	$39,200	$56,500
1949	YA	4dr Sdn	$6,200	$11,200	$20,100	$28,000
1950	TD	2dr Rdstr	$8,000	$14,600	$22,500	$36,000
1950	YT	4dr Sdn	$5,200	$10,600	$16,400	$26,800
		2dr Tourer	$11,600	$19,600	$32,200	$38,700
1951	TD	2dr Rdstr	$8,000	$14,600	$22,500	$36,000
1951	YB	4dr Sdn	$5,000	$10,100	$16,800	$25,400
1952	TD	2dr Rdstr	$8,000	$14,600	$22,500	$36,000
1953	TD	2dr Rdstr	$8,000	$14,600	$22,500	$36,000
1954	TF	2dr Rdstr	$13,000	$19,900	$33,900	$43,000
1955	Magnette	4dr Sdn	$6,200	$11,000	$20,000	$30,000
1955	TF	2dr Rdstr	$13,000	$19,900	$33,900	$43,000
		2dr 1500 Rdstr	$17,500	$25,800	$37,500	$56,000
1956	Magnette	4dr Sdn	$6,200	$11,000	$20,000	$30,000
1956	MGA	2dr Rdstr	$9,100	$19,000	$34,000	$47,400
1957	Magnette	4dr Sdn	$6,200	$11,000	$20,000	$30,000
1957	MGA	2dr Cpe	$7,900	$15,900	$25,900	$41,700
		2dr Rdstr	$9,100	$19,000	$34,000	$47,400
1958	Magnette	4dr Sdn	$6,200	$11,000	$20,000	$30,000
1958	MGA	2dr Cpe	$7,900	$15,900	$25,900	$41,700
		2dr Rdstr	$9,100	$19,000	$34,000	$47,400
1959	Magnette	4dr Mk III Sdn	$5,400	$9,500	$16,000	$25,000
1959	MGA	2dr Cpe	$7,900	$15,700	$25,900	$41,700
		2dr 1600 Mk I Cpe	$8,200	$15,400	$26,800	$37,400
		2dr Twin Cam Cpe	$14,500	$24,600	$43,200	$58,500
		2dr Rdstr	$9,700	$20,600	$36,400	$50,900
		2dr 1600 Mk I Rdstr	$8,900	$16,800	$29,900	$39,400
		2dr Twin Cam Rdstr	$18,200	$31,300	$53,300	$84,500

MG

Year	Model	Body Style	4	3	2	1
1960	Magnette	4dr Mk III Sdn	$5,400	$9,500	$16,000	$25,000
1960	MGA	2dr 1600 Mk I Cpe	$8,200	$15,400	$26,800	$37,400
		2dr Twin Cam Cpe	$14,500	$24,600	$43,200	$58,500
		2dr 1600 Mk I Rdstr	$8,900	$16,800	$29,900	$39,400
		2dr Twin Cam Rdstr	$18,200	$31,300	$53,300	$84,500
1961	Magnette	4dr Mk III Sdn	$5,400	$9,500	$16,000	$25,000
1961	MGA	2dr 1600 Mk I Cpe	$8,200	$15,400	$26,800	$37,400
		2dr 1600 Mk I Rdstr	$8,900	$16,800	$29,900	$39,400
1962	Magnette	4dr Mk IV Sdn	$5,400	$9,500	$16,200	$25,000
1962	Midget	2dr Mk I Conv	$2,900	$5,200	$10,700	$18,200
1962	MGA	2dr 1600 Mk I Cpe	$8,200	$15,400	$26,800	$37,400
		2dr 1600 Mk II Rdstr	$8,900	$16,800	$29,900	$39,400
1962	MGB	2dr Mk I Rdstr	$4,300	$9,700	$20,100	$30,300
1963	Magnette	4dr Mk IV Sdn	$5,400	$9,500	$16,200	$25,000
1963	Midget	2dr Mk I Conv	$2,900	$5,200	$10,700	$18,200
1963	MGB	2dr Mk I Rdstr	$4,300	$9,700	$20,100	$30,300
1964	Magnette	4dr Mk IV Sdn	$5,400	$9,500	$16,200	$25,000
1964	Midget	2dr Mk II Rdstr	$2,200	$4,700	$10,500	$18,200
1964	MGB	2dr Mk I Rdstr	$4,300	$9,700	$20,100	$30,100
1965	Magnette	4dr Mk IV Sdn	$5,400	$9,500	$16,200	$25,000
1965	Midget	2dr Mk II Rdstr	$2,200	$4,700	$10,500	$18,200
1965	MGB	2dr Mk I Rdstr	$4,300	$9,700	$19,800	$29,800
1966	Magnette	4dr Mk IV Sdn	$5,400	$9,500	$16,200	$25,000
1966	Midget	2dr Mk II Conv	$2,200	$4,700	$10,500	$18,200
1966	MGB	2dr GT Cpe	$3,100	$5,900	$15,300	$25,300
		2dr Mk I Rdstr	$4,300	$9,700	$19,800	$29,800
1967	Magnette	4dr Mk IV Sdn	$5,400	$9,500	$16,200	$25,000
1967	Midget	2dr Mk III Conv	$2,200	$4,100	$9,900	$16,000
1967	MGB	2dr GT Cpe	$3,100	$5,900	$15,300	$25,300
		2dr Mk I Rdstr	$4,000	$10,100	$20,100	$29,800
1968	Midget	2dr Mk III Conv	$2,200	$4,100	$9,900	$16,000
1968	MGB	2dr GT Cpe	$3,100	$6,000	$15,600	$24,300
		2dr Mk II Rdstr	$4,000	$8,500	$18,200	$26,300
1968	MGC	2dr GT Cpe	$6,200	$12,100	$21,900	$34,600
		2dr Rdstr	$7,400	$15,200	$32,800	$49,700
1969	Midget	2dr Mk III Conv	$2,200	$4,100	$9,900	$16,000
1969	MGB	2dr GT Cpe	$3,100	$6,000	$15,600	$24,300
		2dr Mk II Rdstr	$4,000	$8,500	$18,200	$26,300
1969	MGC	2dr GT Cpe	$6,200	$12,100	$21,900	$34,600
		2dr Rdstr	$7,400	$15,200	$32,800	$49,700
1970	Midget	2dr Mk III Conv	$2,200	$4,100	$9,900	$16,000
1970	MGB	2dr GT Cpe	$3,100	$6,200	$14,200	$21,200
		2dr Mk II Rdstr	$4,000	$8,900	$16,400	$26,500
1971	Midget	2dr Mk III Conv	$2,200	$4,100	$9,900	$16,000

MG

Year	Model	Body Style	4	3	2	1
1971	MGB	2dr GT Cpe	$3,100	$6,200	$14,200	$21,200
		2dr Mk II Rdstr	$4,000	$8,900	$16,400	$26,500
1972	Midget	2dr Mk III Conv	$2,200	$4,100	$9,900	$16,000
1972	MGB	2dr GT Cpe	$3,000	$6,100	$14,400	$21,200
		2dr Mk III Rdstr	$3,700	$8,700	$16,200	$26,800
1973	Midget	2dr Mk III Conv	$2,200	$4,100	$9,900	$16,000
1973	MGB	2dr GT Cpe	$3,000	$6,100	$14,400	$21,400
		2dr Mk III Rdstr	$3,700	$8,700	$16,200	$26,800
1974	Midget	2dr Mk III Conv	$2,200	$4,100	$9,900	$16,000
1974	MGB	2dr GT Cpe (rubber bump)	$2,700	$4,900	$13,300	$19,200
		2dr Mk III Rdstr (rubber bump)	$3,200	$7,500	$15,800	$20,700
1975	Midget	2dr Mk IV Rdstr	$2,300	$4,400	$8,900	$15,600
1975	MGB	2dr GT Cpe	$2,500	$4,500	$12,700	$18,300
		2dr Mk IV Rdstr	$2,900	$6,400	$14,900	$20,100
1976	Midget	2dr Mk IV Rdstr	$2,300	$4,400	$8,900	$15,600
1976	MGB	2dr GT Cpe	$2,400	$4,500	$12,700	$18,300
		2dr Mk IV Rdstr	$2,900	$6,400	$14,900	$20,100
1977	Midget	2dr Mk IV Rdstr	$2,300	$4,400	$8,900	$15,600
1977	MGB	2dr Mk IV Rdstr	$2,900	$6,400	$14,900	$20,100
1978	Midget	2dr Mk IV Conv	$2,300	$4,400	$8,900	$15,600
1978	MGB	2dr Mk IV Rdstr	$3,100	$6,500	$15,000	$21,200
1979	Midget	2dr Mk IV Conv	$2,300	$4,400	$8,900	$15,600
1979	MGB	2dr Mk IV Rdstr	$3,100	$6,500	$15,000	$21,200
						+$1,500 for Limited Edition.
1980	MGB	2dr Mk IV Rdstr	$3,300	$6,700	$16,100	$21,200
						+$1,500 for Limited Edition.

Marcos

Year	Model	Body Style	4	3	2	1
1964	GT	2dr 1800 Cpe	$10,400	$15,700	$23,900	$30,500
1965	Mini-Marcos	2dr Cpe	$5,200	$8,300	$13,900	$20,200
1965	GT	2dr 1800 Cpe	$10,400	$15,700	$23,900	$30,500
1966	Mini-Marcos	2dr Cpe	$5,200	$8,300	$13,900	$20,200
1966	1600	2dr Cpe	$10,400	$15,000	$23,200	$30,000
1966	GT	2dr 1800 Cpe	$10,400	$15,700	$23,900	$30,500
1967	Mini-Marcos	2dr Cpe	$5,200	$8,300	$13,900	$20,200
1967	1600	2dr Cpe	$10,400	$15,000	$23,200	$30,000
1968	Mini-Marcos	2dr Cpe	$5,200	$8,300	$13,900	$20,200
1968	1600	2dr Cpe	$10,400	$15,000	$23,200	$30,000
1968	3000GT	2dr Cpe	$13,500	$21,500	$30,200	$39,000
						-10% for auto trans.
1969	Mini-Marcos	2dr Cpe	$5,200	$8,300	$13,900	$20,200
1969	3000GT	2dr Cpe	$13,500	$21,500	$30,200	$39,000
						-10% for auto trans.
1970	Mini-Marcos	2dr Cpe	$5,200	$8,300	$13,900	$20,200

Marcos

Year	Model	Body Style	4	3	2	1
1971	Mini-Marcos	2dr Cpe	$5,200	$8,300	$13,900	$20,200
1972	Mini-Marcos	2dr Cpe	$5,200	$8,300	$13,900	$20,200
1973	Mini-Marcos	2dr Cpe	$5,200	$8,300	$13,900	$20,200
1974	Mini-Marcos	2dr Cpe	$5,200	$8,300	$13,900	$20,200

Maserati

Year	Model	Body Style	4	3	2	1
1957	3500GT	2dr Cpe	$165,000	$201,000	$235,000	$260,000
		2dr Vignale Spider	$645,000	$699,000	$725,000	$770,000
		For cpe: +$3,000 for pwr wndws. For Vignale Spider: +$35,000 for hard top. +$3,000 for pwr wndws. For all: +$10,000 for a/c. +$20,000 for wire wheels. +$20,000 for 5-spd.				
1957	5000GT	2dr Touring (gear/carbd) Cpe	$2.3 mil	$2.5 mil	$2.8 mil	$3 mil
		2dr Touring (chain/FI) Cpe	$1.3 mil	$1.5 mil	$1.75 mil	$2.1 mil
		+$25,000 for a/c. Add for one-off cars.				
1958	3500GT	2dr Cpe	$165,000	$201,000	$235,000	$260,000
		2dr Vignale Spider	$645,000	$699,000	$725,000	$770,000
		For cpe: +$3,000 for pwr wndws. For Vignale Spider: +$35,000 for hard top. +$3,000 for pwr wndws. For all: +$10,000 for a/c. +$20,000 for wire wheels. +$20,000 for 5-spd.				
1958	5000GT	2dr Touring (chain/FI) Cpe	$1.3 mil	$1.5 mil	$1.75 mil	$2.1 mil
		+$25,000 for a/c. Add for one-off cars.				
1959	3500GT	2dr Cpe	$165,000	$201,000	$235,000	$260,000
		2dr Vignale Spider	$645,000	$699,000	$725,000	$770,000
		For cpe: +$3,000 for pwr wndws. For Vignale Spider: +$35,000 for hard top. +$3,000 for pwr wndws. For all: +$10,000 for a/c. +$20,000 for wire wheels. +$20,000 for 5-spd.				
1959	5000GT	2dr Allemano Cpe	$1.15 mil	$1.25 mil	$1.5 mil	$1.7 mil
		2dr Frua Cpe	$1.9 mil	$2.1 mil	$2.5 mil	$2.8 mil
		2dr Touring (chain/FI) Cpe	$1.3 mil	$1.5 mil	$1.75 mil	$2.1 mil
		+$25,000 for a/c. Add for one-off cars.				
1960	3500GT	2dr Cpe	$165,000	$201,000	$235,000	$260,000
		2dr Vignale Spider	$645,000	$699,000	$725,000	$770,000
		For cpe: +$3,000 for pwr wndws. For Vignale Spider: +$35,000 for hard top. +$3,000 for pwr wndws. For all: +$10,000 for a/c. +$20,000 for wire wheels. +$20,000 for 5-spd.				
1960	5000GT	2dr Allemano Cpe	$1.15 mil	$1.25 mil	$1.5 mil	$1.7 mil
		2dr Frua Cpe	$1.9 mil	$2.1 mil	$2.5 mil	$2.8 mil
		2dr Touring (chain/FI) Cpe	$1.3 mil	$1.5 mil	$1.8 mil	$2.2 mil
		+$25,000 for a/c. Add for one-off cars.				
1961	3500GT	2dr Cpe	$174,000	$211,000	$249,000	$275,000
		2dr Vignale Spider	$645,000	$699,000	$725,000	$770,000

Year	Model	Body Style	4	3	2	1
		For cpe: +$3,000 for pwr wndws. For Vignale Spider: +$35,000 for hard top. +$3,000 for pwr wndws. For all: +$10,000 for a/c. +$20,000 for wire wheels. +$20,000 for 5-spd.				
1961	5000GT	2dr Allemano Cpe	$1.15 mil	$1.25 mil	$1.5 mil	$1.7 mil
		2dr Frua Cpe	$1.9 mil	$2.1 mil	$2.5 mil	$2.8 mil
		2dr Touring (chain/FI) Cpe	$1.3 mil	$1.5 mil	$1.8 mil	$2.1 mil
		+$25,000 for a/c. Add for one-off cars.				
1962	3500GT	2dr Cpe	$174,000	$211,000	$249,000	$275,000
		2dr Vignale Spider	$645,000	$699,000	$725,000	$770,000
		For cpe: +$3,000 for pwr wndws. For Vignale Spider: +$35,000 for hard top. +$3,000 for pwr wndws. For all: +$10,000 for a/c. +$20,000 for wire wheels. +$20,000 for 5-spd.				
1962	5000GT	2dr Allemano Cpe	$1.15 mil	$1.25 mil	$1.5 mil	$1.7 mil
		2dr Frua Cpe	$1.9 mil	$2.1 mil	$2.5 mil	$2.8 mil
		2dr Touring (chain/FI) Cpe	$1.3 mil	$1.5 mil	$1.8 mil	$2.1 mil
		+$25,000 for a/c. Add for one-off cars.				
1963	Sebring	2dr Cpe	$160,000	$200,000	$247,000	$285,000
		+$15,000 for wire wheels. +$10,000 for a/c. +$1,000 for pwr wndws. +10% for 3.7L.				
1963	3500GTi	2dr Cpe	$163,000	$199,000	$235,000	$279,000
		2dr Spyder	$660,000	$704,000	$730,000	$795,000
		+$15,000 for wire wheels. +$10,000 for a/c. +$25,000 for hard top on Spider.				
1963	5000GT	2dr Allemano Cpe	$1.15 mil	$1.25 mil	$1.5 mil	$1.7 mil
		2dr Frua Cpe	$1.9 mil	$2.1 mil	$2.5 mil	$2.8 mil
		2dr Touring (chain/FI) Cpe	$1.3 mil	$1.5 mil	$1.8 mil	$2.1 mil
		+$25,000 for a/c. Add for one-off cars.				
1963	Quattroporte	4dr Sdn	$23,600	$40,900	$53,300	$65,000
		+$3,500 for a/c. +$5,000 for wire wheels. -$5,000 for auto trans.				
1964	Mistral	2dr 3.5L Cpe	$130,000	$149,000	$195,000	$228,000
		2dr 3.5L Spyder	$559,000	$613,000	$665,000	$716,000
		For Spyder: +$30,000 for hard top. For all: +$20,000 for a/c. +$1,000 for pwr wndws.				
1964	Sebring	2dr Cpe	$160,000	$200,000	$247,000	$285,000
		+$15,000 for wire wheels. +$10,000 for a/c. +$1,000 for pwr wndws. +10% for 3.7L.				
1964	3500GTi	2dr Cpe	$163,000	$199,000	$235,000	$279,000
		2dr Spyder	$660,000	$704,000	$730,000	$795,000
		+$15,000 for wire wheels. +$10,000 for a/c. +$25,000 for hard top on Spider.				
1964	5000GT	2dr Allemano Cpe	$1.15 mil	$1.25 mil	$1.5 mil	$1.7 mil
		2dr Frua Cpe	$1.9 mil	$2.1 mil	$2.5 mil	$2.8 mil
		2dr Touring (chain/FI) Cpe	$1.3 mil	$1.5 mil	$1.8 mil	$2.1 mil
		+$25,000 for a/c. Add for one-off cars.				
1964	Quattroporte	4dr Sdn	$23,600	$40,900	$53,300	$65,000

Maserati

Year	Model	Body Style	4	3	2	1
		+$3,500 for a/c. +$5,000 for wire wheels. -$5,000 for auto trans.				
1965	Mistral	2dr 3.5L Cpe	$130,000	$149,000	$195,000	$228,000
		2dr Cpe	$152,000	$174,000	$219,000	$272,000
		+$20,000 for a/c. +$1,000 for pwr wndws. +$30,000 for hard top on Spyder.				
		2dr 3.5L Spyder	$559,000	$613,000	$665,000	$716,000
		For Spyder: +$30,000 for hard top. For all: +$20,000 for a/c. +$1,000 for pwr wndws.				
		2dr Spyder	$585,000	$636,000	$687,000	$762,000
		+$20,000 for a/c. +$1,000 for pwr wndws. +$30,000 for hard top on Spyder.				
1965	Sebring II	2dr Cpe	$194,000	$221,000	$250,000	$301,000
		2dr 4.0L Cpe	$205,000	$229,000	$274,000	$316,000
		+$15,000 for wire wheels. +10% for a/c.				
1965	3500GTi	2dr Cpe	$174,000	$205,000	$240,000	$290,000
		+$15,000 for wire wheels. +$10,000 for a/c.				
1965	Mexico	2dr 4.2 Cpe	$89,000	$106,000	$129,000	$150,000
		2dr 4.7 Cpe	$111,000	$143,000	$170,000	$193,000
		+10% for pwr steering. -25% for auto.				
1965	Quattroporte	4dr Sdn	$23,600	$40,900	$53,300	$65,000
		+$3,500 for a/c. +$5,000 for wire wheels. -$5,000 for auto trans.				
1966	Sebring II	2dr Cpe	$194,000	$221,000	$250,000	$301,000
		2dr 4.0L Cpe	$205,000	$229,000	$274,000	$316,000
		+$15,000 for wire wheels. +10% for a/c.				
1966	Mistral	2dr Cpe	$152,000	$174,000	$219,000	$272,000
		2dr 4.0L Cpe	$163,000	$209,000	$268,000	$330,000
		2dr Spyder	$596,000	$641,000	$694,000	$764,000
		2dr 4.0L Spyder	$627,000	$697,000	$762,000	$838,000
		+$20,000 for a/c. +$1,000 for pwr wndws. +$30,000 for hard top on Spyder.				
1966	Mexico	2dr 4.2 Cpe	$89,000	$106,000	$129,000	$150,000
		2dr 4.7 Cpe	$111,000	$143,000	$170,000	$193,000
		+10% for pwr steering. -25% for auto.				
1966	Quattroporte	4dr Sdn	$23,600	$40,900	$53,300	$65,000
		+$3,500 for a/c. +$5,000 for wire wheels. -$5,000 for auto trans.				
1967	Mistral	2dr Cpe	$152,000	$174,000	$219,000	$272,000
		2dr 4.0L Cpe	$163,000	$209,000	$268,000	$330,000
		2dr Spyder	$596,000	$641,000	$694,000	$764,000
		2dr 4.0L Spyder	$627,000	$697,000	$762,000	$838,000
		+$20,000 for a/c. +$1,000 for pwr wndws. +$30,000 for hard top on Spyder.				
1967	Ghibli	2dr Cpe	$169,000	$201,000	$220,000	$242,000
		+$7,500 for wire wheels. -30% for auto.				
1967	Mexico	2dr 4.2 Cpe	$89,000	$106,000	$129,000	$150,000
		2dr 4.7 Cpe	$111,000	$143,000	$170,000	$193,000
		+10% for pwr steering. -25% for auto.				
1967	Quattroporte	4dr Sdn	$26,700	$44,800	$56,000	$69,500
		+10% for pwr strng. +$8,000 for wire wheels. -$3,000 for no a/c. -25% for auto.				
1968	Mistral	2dr Cpe	$152,000	$174,000	$219,000	$272,000
		2dr 4.0L Cpe	$163,000	$209,000	$268,000	$330,000

Year	Model	Body Style	4	3	2	1
		2dr Spyder	$596,000	$641,000	$694,000	$764,000
		2dr 4.0L Spyder	$627,000	$697,000	$762,000	$838,000
		+$20,000 for a/c. +$1,000 for pwr wndws. +$30,000 for hard top on Spyder.				
1968	Ghibli	2dr Cpe	$163,000	$194,000	$217,000	$234,000
		+$7,500 for wire wheels. -30% for auto.				
1968	Mexico	2dr 4.7 Cpe	$111,000	$143,000	$170,000	$193,000
		+10% for pwr steering. -25% for auto.				
1968	Quattroporte	4dr Sdn	$26,700	$44,800	$56,000	$69,500
		+10% for pwr strng. +$8,000 for wire wheels. -$3,000 for no a/c. -25% for auto.				
1969	Indy	2dr 4.2 Cpe	$43,000	$54,500	$67,000	$85,000
		2dr 4.7 Cpe	$58,000	$78,500	$97,000	$115,000
		-30% for auto.				
1969	Mistral	2dr Cpe	$152,000	$174,000	$219,000	$272,000
		2dr 4.0L Cpe	$163,000	$209,000	$268,000	$330,000
		2dr Spyder	$596,000	$641,000	$694,000	$764,000
		2dr 4.0L Spyder	$627,000	$697,000	$762,000	$838,000
		+$20,000 for a/c. +$1,000 for pwr wndws. +$30,000 for hard top on Spyder.				
1969	Ghibli	2dr Cpe	$169,000	$201,000	$220,000	$242,000
		2dr Spyder	$644,000	$690,000	$745,000	$795,000
		2dr SS Spyder	$725,000	$770,000	$815,000	$875,000
		-10% for no pwr strng. +$7,500 for wire wheels. +$30,000 for hard top. -30% for auto.				
1969	Mexico	2dr 4.7 Cpe	$111,000	$143,000	$170,000	$193,000
		+10% for pwr steering. -25% for auto.				
1970	Indy	2dr 4.2 Cpe	$43,000	$54,500	$67,000	$86,000
		2dr 4.7 Cpe	$58,000	$78,500	$97,000	$115,000
		-30% for auto.				
1970	Mistral	2dr Cpe	$160,000	$188,000	$227,000	$284,000
		2dr 4.0L Cpe	$168,000	$214,000	$273,000	$335,000
		2dr Spyder	$592,000	$658,000	$738,000	$819,000
		2dr 4.0L Spyder	$640,000	$718,000	$783,000	$845,000
		+$30,000 for hard top on Spyder. +$20,000 for a/c. -25% for auto.				
1970	Ghibli	2dr Cpe	$169,000	$201,000	$220,000	$242,000
		2dr Spyder	$644,000	$690,000	$745,000	$795,000
		2dr SS Spyder	$725,000	$770,000	$815,000	$875,000
		-10% for no pwr strng. +$7,500 for wire wheels. +$30,000 for hard top. -30% for auto.				
1970	Mexico	2dr 4.7 Cpe	$111,000	$143,000	$170,000	$193,000
		+10% for pwr steering. -25% for auto.				
1971	Indy	2dr 4.7 Cpe	$58,000	$78,500	$97,000	$115,000
		-30% for auto.				
1971	Ghibli	2dr Cpe	$195,000	$220,000	$240,000	$259,000
		2dr SS Cpe	$215,000	$233,000	$250,000	$275,000
		+$30,000 for hard top on Spider. -30% for auto. +$7,500 for wire wheels.				
		2dr Spyder	$644,000	$690,000	$745,000	$795,000

Maserati

Year	Model	Body Style	4	3	2	1
		-10% for no pwr strng. +$7,500 for wire wheels. +$30,000 for hard top. -30% for auto.				
		2dr SS Spyder	$725,000	$770,000	$815,000	$875,000
		+$30,000 for hard top on Spider. -30% for auto. +$7,500 for wire wheels.				
1971	Bora	2dr Cpe	$80,000	$104,000	$129,000	$153,000
1971	Mexico	2dr 4.7 Cpe	$111,000	$143,000	$170,000	$193,000
		+10% for pwr steering. -25% for auto.				
1972	Indy	2dr 4.7 Cpe	$58,000	$78,500	$97,000	$115,000
		2dr 4.9 Cpe	$70,000	$96,000	$112,000	$134,000
		-30% for auto.				
1972	Merak	2dr Cpe	$30,000	$39,000	$50,000	$66,000
1972	Ghibli	2dr Cpe	$212,000	$230,000	$246,000	$270,000
		2dr SS Cpe	$220,000	$238,000	$265,000	$285,000
		+$30,000 for hard top on Spider. -30% for auto. +$7,500 for wire wheels.				
		2dr Spyder	$644,000	$690,000	$745,000	$795,000
		-10% for no pwr strng. +$7,500 for wire wheels. +$30,000 for hard top. -30% for auto.				
		2dr SS Spyder	$725,000	$770,000	$815,000	$875,000
		+$30,000 for hard top on Spider. -30% for auto. +$7,500 for wire wheels.				
1972	Bora	2dr Cpe	$80,000	$104,000	$129,000	$153,000
		2dr 4.9L Cpe	$109,000	$139,000	$160,000	$190,000
1972	Mexico	2dr 4.7 Cpe	$111,000	$143,000	$170,000	$193,000
		+10% for pwr steering. -25% for auto.				
1973	Indy	2dr 4.7 Cpe	$58,000	$78,500	$97,000	$115,000
		2dr 4.9 Cpe	$70,000	$96,000	$112,000	$134,000
		-30% for auto.				
1973	Merak	2dr Cpe	$30,000	$39,000	$50,000	$66,000
1973	Ghibli	2dr SS Cpe	$239,000	$258,000	$280,000	$310,000
		2dr SS Spyder	$725,000	$775,000	$830,000	$895,000
		+$30,000 for hard top on Spider. -30% for auto. +$7,500 for wire wheels.				
1973	Bora	2dr Cpe	$80,000	$104,000	$129,000	$153,000
		2dr 4.9L Cpe	$109,000	$139,000	$160,000	$190,000
1974	Merak	2dr Cpe	$30,000	$39,000	$50,000	$66,000
1974	Bora	2dr Cpe	$80,000	$104,000	$129,000	$153,000
		2dr 4.9L Cpe	$109,000	$139,000	$160,000	$190,000
1975	Merak	2dr Cpe	$30,000	$39,000	$50,000	$66,000
1975	Khamsin	2dr Cpe	$103,000	$134,000	$165,000	$197,000
		-25% for auto.				
1975	Bora	2dr 4.9L Cpe	$128,000	$149,000	$184,000	$190,000
1976	Merak	2dr Cpe	$30,000	$39,000	$50,000	$66,000
1976	Khamsin	2dr Cpe	$103,000	$134,000	$165,000	$200,000
		-25% for auto.				
1976	Bora	2dr 4.9L Cpe	$128,000	$149,000	$184,000	$190,000
1977	Khamsin	2dr Cpe	$116,000	$153,000	$185,000	$205,000
		-25% for auto.				
1977	Kyalami	2dr Cpe	$43,000	$56,000	$72,000	$90,000

Year	Model	Body Style	4	3	2	1
		2dr 4.9 Cpe	$60,000	$74,000	$89,000	$112,000
						-25% for auto.
1977	Bora	2dr 4.9L Cpe	$150,000	$187,000	$220,000	$270,000
1977	Merak	2dr SS Cpe	$46,000	$64,200	$75,000	$94,000
1978	Khamsin	2dr Cpe	$116,000	$153,000	$185,000	$205,000
						-25% for auto.
1978	Kyalami	2dr Cpe	$43,000	$56,000	$72,000	$90,000
		2dr 4.9 Cpe	$60,000	$74,000	$89,000	$112,000
						-25% for auto.
1978	Bora	2dr 4.9L Cpe	$180,000	$210,000	$252,000	$285,000
1978	Merak	2dr SS Cpe	$46,000	$64,200	$75,000	$94,000
1979	Khamsin	2dr Cpe	$112,000	$150,000	$185,000	$220,000
						-25% for auto.
1979	Kyalami	2dr Cpe	$43,000	$56,000	$72,000	$90,000
		2dr 4.9 Cpe	$60,000	$74,000	$89,000	$112,000
						-25% for auto.
1979	Quattroporte III	4dr Sdn	$7,700	$12,000	$23,700	$42,000
						+15% for 5-spd.
1979	Merak	2dr SS Cpe	$46,000	$64,200	$75,000	$94,000
1980	Merak	2dr SS Cpe	$47,000	$67,000	$78,500	$98,000
1980	Kyalami	2dr Cpe	$45,000	$65,000	$81,000	$97,000
		2dr 4.9 Cpe	$63,000	$79,000	$95,000	$121,000
						-25% for auto.
1980	Quattroporte III	4dr Sdn	$7,700	$12,000	$23,700	$42,000
						+15% for 5-spd.
1981	Merak	2dr SS Cpe	$47,000	$67,000	$78,500	$98,000
1981	Kyalami	2dr Cpe	$45,000	$65,000	$81,000	$97,000
		2dr 4.9 Cpe	$63,000	$79,000	$95,000	$121,000
						-25% for auto.
1981	Quattroporte III	2dr Sdn	$7,700	$12,000	$23,700	$42,000
						+15% for 5-spd.
1982	Quattroporte III	4dr Sdn	$7,700	$12,000	$23,700	$42,000
						+15% for 5-spd.
1983	Quattroporte III	4dr Sdn	$7,700	$12,000	$23,700	$42,000
						+15% for 5-spd.
1984	Biturbo	2dr Cpe	$2,000	$3,200	$5,600	$8,400
						-25% for auto.
1984	Quattroporte III	4dr Sdn	$7,700	$12,000	$23,700	$42,000
						+15% for 5-spd.
1985	Quattroporte III	4dr Sdn	$7,700	$12,000	$23,700	$42,000
						+15% for 5-spd.
1985	Biturbo	2dr Cpe	$2,000	$3,200	$5,600	$8,400
						-25% for auto.
1986	Quattroporte III	4dr Sdn	$7,700	$12,000	$23,700	$42,000
						+15% for 5-spd.

Maserati

Year	Model	Body Style	4	3	2	1
1986	425	4dr Sdn	$1,900	$2,800	$5,400	$8,300
						-25% for auto.
1986	Biturbo	2dr Spyder	$4,500	$6,500	$9,500	$16,500
						-25% for auto.
1987	Biturbo	2dr Cpe	$2,000	$3,400	$5,800	$8,600
		2dr Spyder	$4,500	$6,300	$9,200	$15,700
						-25% for auto on cpe.
1987	425	4dr Sdn	$1,600	$2,800	$4,100	$7,500
						-25% for auto.
1989	228	2dr Cpe	$4,200	$6,300	$7,800	$11,300
						-25% for auto.
1989	425	4dr Sdn	$1,800	$3,400	$4,600	$8,200
						-25% for auto.
1989	430	4dr Sdn	$2,300	$3,900	$5,500	$9,300
						-25% for auto.
1989	Zagato	2dr Spider	$6,300	$9,300	$12,900	$18,000
						-25% for auto.
1990	228	2dr Cpe	$4,200	$6,300	$7,800	$11,300
						-25% for auto.
1990	425	4dr Sdn	$1,800	$3,400	$4,600	$8,200
						-25% for auto.
1990	430	4dr Sdn	$2,300	$3,900	$5,500	$9,300
						-25% for auto.
1990	Zagato	2dr Spider	$6,300	$9,300	$12,900	$18,000
						-25% for auto.
1991	425	2dr Sdn	$1,700	$3,100	$4,500	$7,600
						-25% for auto.
1991	Biturbo	2dr Spyder	$6,000	$9,000	$12,500	$17,800
						-25% for auto.
1991	Zagato	2dr Spider	$6,400	$9,400	$13,000	$18,200
						-25% for auto.
1992	Zagato	2dr Spider	$7,000	$9,800	$13,400	$18,800
						-25% for auto.

Matra

Year	Model	Body Style	4	3	2	1
1965	Djet 5	2dr Cpe	$14,800	$22,600	$38,500	$60,000
1966	Djet 5	2dr Cpe	$14,800	$22,600	$38,500	$60,000
1968	530 LX	2dr Cpe	$6,800	$11,200	$17,400	$27,200
1969	530 LX	2dr Cpe	$6,800	$11,200	$17,400	$27,200
1970	530 LX	2dr Cpe	$6,800	$11,200	$17,400	$27,200
1971	530 LX	2dr Cpe	$6,800	$11,200	$17,400	$27,200
1972	530 LX	2dr Cpe	$6,800	$11,200	$17,400	$27,200
1973	530 LX	2dr Cpe	$6,800	$11,200	$17,400	$27,200
1973	Bagheera	2dr Cpe	$5,000	$9,700	$15,800	$26,000

Matra

Year	Model	Body Style	4	3	2	1
1974	Bagheera	2dr Cpe	$5,000	$9,700	$15,800	$26,000
1975	Bagheera	2dr Cpe	$5,000	$9,700	$15,800	$26,000
1976	Bagheera	2dr Cpe	$5,000	$9,700	$15,800	$26,000
1977	Bagheera	2dr Cpe	$5,000	$9,700	$15,800	$26,000
1978	Bagheera	2dr Cpe	$5,000	$9,700	$15,800	$26,000
1979	Bagheera	2dr Cpe	$5,000	$9,700	$15,800	$26,000
1980	Bagheera	2dr Cpe	$5,000	$9,700	$15,800	$26,000
1980	Murena	2dr Cpe	$5,900	$10,400	$16,800	$25,500
1981	Murena	2dr Cpe	$5,900	$10,400	$16,800	$25,500
1982	Murena	2dr Cpe	$5,900	$10,400	$16,800	$25,500
1983	Murena	2dr Cpe	$5,900	$10,400	$16,800	$25,500
1984	Murena	2dr Cpe	$5,900	$10,400	$16,800	$25,500

Mazda

Year	Model	Body Style	4	3	2	1
1967	Cosmo	2dr Cpe	$58,000	$71,300	$98,000	$138,000
1968	Cosmo	2dr Cpe	$58,000	$71,300	$98,000	$138,000
1969	Cosmo	2dr Cpe	$58,000	$71,300	$98,000	$138,000
1970	Cosmo	2dr Cpe	$58,000	$71,300	$98,000	$138,000
1971	Cosmo	2dr Cpe	$58,000	$71,300	$98,000	$138,000
1972	Cosmo	2dr Cpe	$58,000	$71,300	$98,000	$138,000
1979	RX-7	2dr GS Cpe	$3,800	$9,800	$17,400	$26,800
1980	RX-7	2dr GS Cpe	$3,800	$9,800	$17,400	$26,800
1981	RX-7	2dr Cpe	$3,700	$8,800	$16,400	$25,900
1982	RX-7	2dr Cpe	$3,700	$8,800	$16,400	$25,900
1983	RX-7	2dr Cpe	$3,700	$8,800	$16,400	$25,900
1984	RX-7	2dr Cpe	$3,500	$8,400	$15,900	$24,900
1985	RX-7	2dr Cpe	$3,500	$8,400	$15,900	$24,900
1986	RX-7	2dr Cpe	$3,100	$5,600	$11,000	$18,400
		2dr Turbo Cpe	$5,000	$10,000	$17,700	$29,600
1987	RX-7	2dr Cpe	$3,100	$5,600	$11,000	$18,400
		2dr Turbo Cpe	$5,000	$10,000	$17,700	$29,600
1988	RX-7	2dr Cpe	$3,100	$5,600	$11,000	$18,400
		2dr Turbo Cpe	$5,000	$10,000	$17,700	$29,600
		2dr Conv	$4,200	$7,200	$12,100	$22,000
1989	RX-7	2dr Cpe	$3,100	$5,500	$11,300	$18,900
		1308/182 2dr Turbo Cpe	$5,000	$10,000	$17,700	$29,600
		1308/200 2dr Turbo Cpe	$4,900	$9,400	$18,300	$30,600
		2dr Conv	$4,200	$7,200	$12,100	$22,000
1990	MX-5 Miata	2dr Conv	$4,400	$7,500	$14,800	$24,200
						-20% for auto.
1990	RX-7	2dr Cpe	$3,100	$5,500	$11,300	$18,900
		2dr Turbo Cpe	$4,900	$9,400	$18,300	$30,600
		2dr Conv	$4,200	$7,200	$12,100	$22,000
1991	MX-5 Miata	2dr Conv	$4,400	$7,500	$14,400	$23,100

+15% for Special Ed. -20% for auto.

Mazda

Year	Model	Body Style	4	3	2	1
1991	RX-7	2dr Cpe	$3,200	$5,800	$11,700	$19,500
		2dr Turbo Cpe	$4,900	$9,600	$19,000	$31,900
		2dr Conv	$4,200	$7,200	$12,100	$22,000
1992	MX-5 Miata	2dr Conv	$4,400	$7,500	$14,100	$23,100
			+15% for Black Special Ed. -20% for auto.			
1992	RX-7	2dr Cpe	$3,000	$5,500	$11,400	$20,100
1993	MX-5 Miata	2dr Conv	$4,200	$7,400	$14,100	$22,600
			+15% for Limited Ed. -20% for auto.			
1993	RX-7	2dr Cpe	$17,800	$27,400	$44,000	$64,400
1994	MX-5 Miata	2dr Conv	$4,200	$7,400	$14,100	$22,600
			+20% for M Ed. +15% for R Pkg. +15% for Limited Ed. -20% for auto.			
1994	RX-7	2dr Cpe	$17,800	$27,400	$44,000	$64,400
1995	MX-5 Miata	2dr Conv	$4,200	$7,800	$14,100	$22,600
			+20% for M Ed. +15% for Limited Ed. -20% for auto.			
1995	RX-7	2dr Cpe	$17,800	$27,400	$44,000	$64,400
1996	MX-5 Miata	2dr Conv	$4,700	$8,000	$14,300	$22,800
			+20% for M Ed. -20% for auto.			
1996	RX-7	2dr Cpe	$17,800	$27,400	$44,000	$64,400
1997	MX-5 Miata	2dr Conv	$4,700	$8,000	$14,300	$22,800
			+20% for M Ed. +20% for Touring Pkg. +25% for STO Pkg. +15% for R Pkg. -20% for auto.			
1999	MX-5 Miata	2dr 10th Anniversary Conv	$5,100	$7,600	$10,900	$17,800
		2dr Conv	$4,600	$7,200	$10,200	$16,200
			-20% for auto trans.			
2000	MX-5 Miata	2dr Conv	$4,600	$7,200	$10,200	$16,200
		2dr LS Conv	$4,800	$7,500	$10,800	$17,000
			-20% for auto trans.			
2001	MX-5 Miata	2dr Conv	$4,600	$7,200	$10,200	$16,200
		2dr LS Conv	$4,800	$7,500	$10,800	$17,000
			-20% for auto trans.			
2002	MX-5 Miata	2dr Conv	$4,600	$7,200	$10,200	$16,200
		2dr LS Conv	$4,800	$7,500	$10,800	$17,000
			-20% for auto trans.			
2003	MX-5 Miata	2dr Conv	$4,600	$7,200	$10,200	$16,200
		2dr LS Conv	$4,800	$7,500	$10,800	$17,000
			-20% for auto trans.			
2004	MAZDASPEED MX-5 Miata	2dr Conv	$6,600	$9,900	$13,800	$21,000
			-20% for auto trans.			
2004	MX-5 Miata	2dr Conv	$4,600	$6,500	$10,200	$16,200
		2dr LS Conv	$4,800	$6,800	$10,800	$17,000
			-20% for auto trans.			
2005	MAZDASPEED MX-5 Miata	2dr Conv	$6,600	$9,900	$13,800	$21,000
			-20% for auto trans.			

Mazda

Year	Model	Body Style	4	3	2	1
2005	MX-5 Miata	2dr Conv	$4,600	$6,500	$10,200	$16,200
		2dr LS Conv	$4,800	$7,500	$10,800	$17,000

-20% for auto trans.

McLaren

Year	Model	Body Style	4	3	2	1
1992	F1	2dr Cpe	$13.5 mil	$15.1 mil	$16.2 mil	$17.6 mil
1993	F1	2dr Cpe	$13.5 mil	$15.1 mil	$16.2 mil	$17.6 mil
1994	F1	2dr Cpe	$13.5 mil	$15.1 mil	$16.2 mil	$17.6 mil
1995	F1	2dr Cpe	$13.5 mil	$15.1 mil	$16.2 mil	$17.6 mil
1995	F1 LM	2dr Cpe	$16.5 mil	$19 mil	$21 mil	$23 mil
1996	F1	2dr Cpe	$13.5 mil	$15.1 mil	$16.2 mil	$17.6 mil
1997	F1	2dr Cpe	$13.5 mil	$15.1 mil	$16.2 mil	$17.6 mil
1998	F1	2dr Cpe	$13.5 mil	$15.1 mil	$16.2 mil	$17.6 mil
2014	P1	2dr Cpe	$1 mil	$1.2 mil	$1.4 mil	$1.65 mil
2015	P1	2dr Cpe	$1 mil	$1.2 mil	$1.4 mil	$1.65 mil

Mercedes-Benz

Year	Model	Body Style	4	3	2	1
1946	170V	4dr Sdn	$11,500	$19,900	$28,600	$44,500
1947	170V	4dr Sdn	$11,500	$19,900	$28,600	$44,500
1948	170V	4dr Sdn	$11,500	$19,900	$28,600	$44,500
1949	170V	4dr Sdn	$11,500	$19,900	$28,600	$44,500
1949	170D	4dr Sdn	$12,000	$19,600	$29,600	$42,400
1950	170V	4dr Sdn	$11,500	$19,900	$28,600	$44,500
1950	170D	4dr Sdn	$12,000	$19,600	$29,600	$42,400
1950	170S	4dr Sdn	$10,700	$16,700	$26,600	$39,900
		2dr Cab A	$40,900	$51,500	$84,000	$145,000
		2dr Cab B	$34,200	$44,900	$70,200	$126,000
1951	170D	4dr Sdn	$12,000	$19,600	$29,600	$42,400
1952	300	4dr Sdn	$16,000	$23,900	$39,100	$57,200
						+10% for fitted luggage.
1952	300S	2dr Cpe	$240,000	$320,000	$390,000	$435,000
		2dr Rdstr	$427,000	$480,000	$545,000	$610,000
		4dr Cab D	$442,000	$500,000	$560,000	$625,000
						+$10,000 for fitted luggage. +$10,000 for sunroof.
1953	170D	4dr Sdn	$12,000	$19,600	$29,600	$42,400
1953	170S	4dr Sdn	$10,700	$17,500	$26,600	$39,900
		2dr Cab	$33,900	$44,000	$69,200	$118,000
1953	220	2dr Cpe	$18,200	$31,200	$41,900	$58,500
		4dr Sdn	$14,700	$18,900	$29,200	$45,400
		2dr Cab B	$37,100	$59,000	$122,000	$165,000
						+10% for sunroof on cpe and sdn.
1953	300	4dr Sdn	$16,000	$23,900	$39,100	$57,200
						+$7,500 for fitted luggage on sdn.
		2dr Cab	$114,000	$130,000	$160,000	$193,000
1953	300S	2dr Cpe	$240,000	$320,000	$390,000	$435,000

Mercedes-Benz

Year	Model	Body Style	4	3	2	1
		2dr Rdstr	$427,000	$480,000	$545,000	$610,000
		2dr Cab	$442,000	$500,000	$560,000	$625,000
			+$10,000 for fitted luggage. +$10,000 for sunroof.			
1954	170S-D	4dr Sdn	$11,500	$19,000	$27,800	$41,100
1954	170S-V	4dr Sdn	$12,300	$20,000	$30,800	$42,900
1954	180	4dr Sdn	$8,300	$15,500	$22,900	$42,600
1954	180D	4dr Sdn	$8,900	$16,800	$24,200	$44,700
1954	220	2dr Cpe	$18,200	$31,200	$41,900	$58,500
		4dr Sdn	$14,700	$18,900	$29,200	$45,400
		2dr Cab	$57,500	$74,900	$138,000	$182,000
			+$5,000 for sunroof on cpe and sdn.			
1954	300	4dr Sdn	$16,700	$24,500	$39,400	$54,600
		4dr Cab	$115,000	$140,000	$162,000	$197,000
			+10% for sunroof on sdn.			
1954	300B	4dr Sdn	$15,300	$23,300	$35,200	$53,700
		4dr Cab	$130,000	$163,000	$197,000	$262,000
			+10% for sunroof on sdn.			
1954	300S	2dr Cpe	$240,000	$320,000	$390,000	$435,000
		2dr Rdstr	$440,000	$505,000	$560,000	$615,000
		2dr Cab	$450,000	$510,000	$565,000	$640,000
			+$10,000 for fitted luggage. +$15,000 for sunroof. +$5,000 for floor shift.			
1954	300SL	2dr Gullwing Cpe	$940,000	$1 mil	$1.1 mil	$1.3 mil
		2dr Alloy Gullwing Cpe	$4.2 mil	$5 mil	$6 mil	$6.9 mil
			+$50,000 for Rudge wheels. +$20,000 for fitted luggage. +$2,500 for Becker radio.			
1955	170S-D	4dr Sdn	$11,300	$18,600	$27,300	$40,300
1955	170S-V	4dr Sdn	$12,100	$19,600	$30,200	$42,100
1955	180	4dr Sdn	$8,300	$15,500	$22,900	$42,600
1955	180D	4dr Sdn	$8,900	$16,800	$24,200	$44,700
1955	190SL	2dr Conv	$49,400	$87,100	$131,000	$177,000
1955	220a	2dr Cpe	$26,000	$36,800	$49,100	$68,700
		4dr Sdn	$8,800	$13,600	$21,100	$31,600
		2dr Cab	$54,300	$74,600	$119,000	$167,000
			+10% for sunroof on cpe and sdn.			
1955	300B	4dr Sdn	$13,900	$19,000	$28,700	$44,800
		4dr Cab	$127,000	$150,000	$190,000	$248,000
			+10% for sunroof on sdn.			
1955	300Sc	2dr Cpe	$480,000	$530,000	$600,000	$685,000
		2dr Rdstr	$750,000	$810,000	$845,000	$975,000
		2dr Cab	$770,000	$830,000	$895,000	$975,000
			+$10,000 for fitted luggage. +$25,000 for sunroof in cpe.			
1955	300SL	2dr Gullwing Cpe	$965,000	$1.2 mil	$1.3 mil	$1.4 mil
		2dr Alloy Gullwing Cpe	$4.2 mil	$5 mil	$6 mil	$6.9 mil
			+$50,000 for Rudge wheels. +$20,000 for fitted luggage. +$2,500 for Becker radio.			

Year	Model	Body Style	4	3	2	1
1956	180	4dr Sdn	$8,600	$15,700	$22,700	$42,800
1956	180D	4dr Sdn	$9,000	$16,600	$24,300	$45,100
1956	190	4dr Sdn	$9,500	$14,900	$23,100	$35,400
1956	190SL	2dr Conv	$49,400	$87,100	$131,000	$177,000
1956	219	4dr Sdn	$10,300	$15,300	$20,800	$31,100
1956	220S	2dr Cpe	$16,600	$30,000	$46,900	$67,900
		4dr Sdn	$10,100	$14,400	$23,800	$39,900
		2dr Conv	$65,400	$91,800	$172,000	$248,000
1956	300C	4dr Sdn	$15,200	$22,600	$33,200	$55,400
		4dr Cab	$138,000	$153,000	$186,000	$293,000
1956	300Sc	2dr Cpe	$480,000	$530,000	$600,000	$685,000
		2dr Rdstr	$750,000	$810,000	$845,000	$975,000
		2dr Cab	$770,000	$830,000	$895,000	$975,000
		+$10,000 for fitted luggage. +$25,000 for sunroof in cpe.				
1956	300SL	2dr Gullwing Cpe	$950,000	$1.15 mil	$1.3 mil	$1.4 mil
		+$50,000 for Rudge wheels. +$20,000 for fitted luggage. +$2,500 for Becker radio.				
1957	180	4dr Sdn	$8,600	$15,700	$23,000	$43,100
1957	180D	4dr Sdn	$9,000	$16,300	$25,200	$45,400
1957	190	4dr Sdn	$9,600	$14,900	$22,900	$35,600
1957	190SL	2dr Conv	$49,400	$87,100	$131,000	$177,000
1957	219	4dr Sdn	$10,400	$15,700	$21,000	$31,400
1957	220S	2dr Cpe	$16,600	$30,000	$46,900	$67,900
		4dr Sdn	$10,100	$14,400	$23,200	$38,700
		2dr Conv	$65,400	$91,800	$172,000	$248,000
1957	300C	4dr Sdn	$15,500	$23,100	$34,500	$57,200
		4dr Cab	$138,000	$153,000	$186,000	$293,000
1957	300Sc	2dr Cpe	$510,000	$565,000	$630,000	$710,000
		4dr Sdn	$488,000	$540,000	$626,000	$769,000
		2dr Rdstr	$750,000	$810,000	$845,000	$975,000
		2dr Cab	$770,000	$830,000	$895,000	$975,000
		+$10,000 for fitted luggage. +$25,000 for sunroof in cpe.				
1957	300SL	2dr Gullwing Cpe	$1 mil	$1.3 mil	$1.4 mil	$1.55 mil
		2dr Rdstr	$835,000	$960,000	$1.1 mil	$1.25 mil
		+$50,000 for Rudge wheels on Gullwing. $100,000 for Rudge wheels on rdstr. +$20,000 for fitted luggage. +$60,000 for hard top on rdstr. +$2,500 for Becker radio.				
1958	180A	4dr Sdn	$7,900	$14,900	$22,900	$40,700
1958	180D	4dr Sdn	$8,900	$16,200	$25,300	$46,600
1958	190	4dr Sdn	$9,600	$14,700	$23,400	$36,300
1958	190D	4dr Sdn	$6,400	$12,200	$22,400	$33,600
1958	190SL	2dr Conv	$49,400	$87,100	$131,000	$177,000
1958	219	4dr Sdn	$10,400	$16,000	$22,800	$33,300
1958	220S	2dr Cpe	$17,000	$31,200	$47,900	$69,000
		4dr Sdn	$10,100	$14,400	$23,400	$39,200
		2dr Conv	$68,300	$93,600	$177,000	$253,000
1958	220SE	2dr Cpe	$17,900	$28,300	$50,600	$70,100
		4dr Sdn	$15,300	$19,900	$36,800	$53,200

Mercedes-Benz

Year	Model	Body Style	4	3	2	1
		2dr Cab	$113,000	$155,000	$194,000	$277,000
1958	300D	4dr Sdn	$18,900	$28,300	$51,600	$77,100
		4dr Cab	$119,000	$161,000	$192,000	$254,000
						+10% for sunroof on cpe.
1958	300SL	2dr Rdstr	$835,000	$960,000	$1.1 mil	$1.25 mil
			+$50,000 for Rudge wheels on Gullwing. $100,000 for Rudge wheels on rdstr. +$20,000 for fitted luggage. +$60,000 for hard top on rdstr. +$2,500 for Becker radio.			
1959	180A	4dr Sdn	$7,900	$14,900	$22,900	$40,700
1959	180D	4dr Sdn	$8,900	$16,200	$25,300	$46,600
1959	190	4dr Sdn	$9,600	$14,700	$23,400	$36,300
1959	190D	4dr Sdn	$6,400	$12,200	$22,400	$33,600
1959	190SL	2dr Conv	$49,400	$87,100	$131,000	$177,000
1959	219	4dr Sdn	$10,400	$16,000	$22,800	$33,300
1959	220S	2dr Cpe	$17,000	$31,200	$47,900	$69,000
		4dr Sdn	$10,100	$14,100	$23,400	$39,200
		2dr Conv	$68,300	$93,600	$177,000	$253,000
1959	220SE	2dr Cpe	$17,900	$28,300	$50,600	$70,100
		4dr Sdn	$15,300	$19,900	$36,800	$53,200
		2dr Cab	$113,000	$155,000	$194,000	$277,000
1959	300D	4dr Sdn	$18,900	$28,300	$51,600	$77,100
		4dr Cab	$119,000	$161,000	$192,000	$254,000
						+10% for sunroof on cpe.
1959	300SL	2dr Rdstr	$835,000	$960,000	$1.1 mil	$1.25 mil
			+$50,000 for Rudge wheels on Gullwing. $100,000 for Rudge wheels on rdstr. +$20,000 for fitted luggage. +$60,000 for hard top on rdstr. +$2,500 for Becker radio.			
1960	180B	4dr Sdn	$8,600	$14,900	$22,700	$40,300
1960	180Db	4dr Sdn	$9,100	$16,000	$24,900	$43,800
1960	190B	4dr Sdn	$9,100	$13,300	$21,000	$32,300
1960	190Db	4dr Sdn	$9,700	$14,300	$22,500	$34,300
1960	190SL	2dr Conv	$49,400	$87,100	$131,000	$177,000
1960	220B	4dr Sdn	$7,200	$9,700	$12,800	$19,700
1960	220Sb	4dr Sdn	$12,100	$17,400	$24,800	$41,600
1960	220SEb	2dr Cpe	$24,900	$37,100	$63,200	$85,900
		4dr Sdn	$15,500	$20,600	$36,600	$54,000
		2dr Conv	$138,000	$170,000	$207,000	$259,000
1960	300D	4dr Hdtp Sdn	$21,700	$29,900	$52,500	$78,100
		4dr Conv	$107,000	$147,000	$216,000	$280,000
						+10% for sunroof on sdn.
1960	300SE	2dr Cpe	$20,900	$37,300	$54,600	$82,700
						+10% for sunroof.
1960	300SL	2dr Rdstr	$915,000	$1 mil	$1.2 mil	$1.3 mil
			+$50,000 for Rudge wheels on Gullwing. $100,000 for Rudge wheels on rdstr. +$20,000 for fitted luggage. +$60,000 for hard top on rdstr. +$2,500 for Becker radio.			
1961	180B	4dr Sdn	$8,600	$15,100	$23,100	$39,800

Year	Model	Body Style	4	3	2	1
1961	180Db	4dr Sdn	$9,100	$16,300	$25,600	$43,700
1961	190B	4dr Sdn	$9,200	$13,400	$21,200	$32,100
1961	190Db	4dr Sdn	$9,800	$14,600	$22,800	$34,500
1961	190SL	2dr Conv	$49,400	$87,100	$131,000	$177,000
1961	220B	4dr Sdn	$7,200	$9,700	$12,900	$19,500
1961	220Sb	4dr Sdn	$12,200	$17,400	$25,300	$41,200
1961	220SEb	2dr Cpe	$22,400	$34,100	$61,300	$82,500
		4dr Sdn	$10,500	$17,400	$26,900	$43,800
		2dr Conv	$58,600	$78,500	$97,200	$162,000
1961	300D	4dr Hdtp Sdn	$22,100	$33,800	$55,400	$84,000
		4dr Conv	$131,000	$177,000	$245,000	$319,000
1961	300SE	4dr Cab	$25,000	$37,500	$54,000	$90,000
1961	300SL	2dr Rdstr	$990,000	$1.2 mil	$1.3 mil	$1.45 mil
		+$60,000 for hard top. +$20,000 for fitted luggage.				
1962	180C	4dr Sdn	$6,800	$12,300	$20,800	$30,600
1962	180Dc	4dr Sdn	$8,600	$14,500	$23,800	$38,700
1962	190C	4dr Sdn	$9,000	$11,600	$17,200	$24,500
1962	190Dc	4dr Sdn	$9,400	$12,600	$19,500	$26,300
1962	190SL	2dr Conv	$49,400	$87,100	$131,000	$177,000
1962	220B	4dr Sdn	$2,800	$6,200	$9,600	$13,000
1962	220Sb	4dr Sdn	$3,100	$7,400	$11,800	$22,300
1962	220SEb	2dr Cpe	$22,400	$34,100	$61,300	$82,500
		4dr Sdn	$5,900	$9,100	$14,800	$27,800
		2dr Cab	$59,200	$79,200	$97,800	$164,000
1962	300D	4dr Hdtp Sdn	$22,400	$34,100	$56,400	$85,600
		4dr Cab	$130,000	$174,000	$244,000	$318,000
1962	300SE	2dr Cab	$15,400	$24,300	$38,600	$56,400
		+10% for sunroof on cpe.				
1962	300SL	2dr Rdstr	$1 mil	$1.25 mil	$1.35 mil	$1.5 mil
		+$60,000 for hard top. +$20,000 for fitted luggage.				
1963	190C	4dr Sdn	$9,000	$11,600	$17,500	$24,100
1963	190Dc	4dr Sdn	$9,400	$12,600	$18,600	$25,900
1963	190SL	2dr Conv	$49,400	$87,100	$131,000	$177,000
1963	220B	4dr Sdn	$2,800	$6,200	$9,800	$12,800
1963	220Sb	4dr Sdn	$3,100	$7,400	$11,800	$22,300
1963	220SEb	2dr Cpe	$22,400	$34,100	$61,300	$82,500
		4dr Sdn	$3,800	$7,900	$14,100	$27,000
		2dr Cab	$56,500	$77,700	$96,600	$161,000
1963	230SL	2dr Conv	$26,400	$41,400	$61,200	$97,000
		+$4,500 for hard top. +10% for 4-spd. +15% for a/c.				
1963	300SE	2dr Cpe	$19,800	$35,400	$53,300	$85,300
		4dr Sdn	$12,500	$20,000	$28,800	$38,100
		+10% for sunroof on cpe and sdn.				
1963	300SL	2dr Rdstr	$1.2 mil	$1.35 mil	$1.45 mil	$1.6 mil
		+$50,000 for hard top. +$20,000 for fitted luggage.				
1964	190C	4dr Sdn	$8,900	$11,700	$16,600	$23,800
1964	190Dc	4dr Sdn	$9,300	$12,700	$18,200	$25,900
1964	220B	4dr Sdn	$2,900	$6,600	$9,200	$14,200

Mercedes-Benz

Year	Model	Body Style	4	3	2	1
1964	220Sb	4dr Sdn	$3,100	$7,500	$11,600	$22,600
1964	220SEb	2dr Cpe	$22,400	$34,100	$61,300	$82,500
		4dr Sdn	$3,900	$7,800	$13,600	$27,300
		2dr Cab	$55,800	$77,000	$93,300	$159,000
1964	230SL	2dr Conv	$26,400	$41,400	$61,200	$97,000
		+$4,500 for hard top. +10% for 4-spd. +15% for a/c.				
1964	300SE	4dr Sdn	$12,500	$20,000	$28,800	$38,100
		2dr Conv	$55,200	$106,000	$153,000	$260,000
1964	300SEL	4dr Sdn	$15,900	$22,900	$31,000	$43,600
1964	600	4dr Sdn	$50,300	$94,300	$155,000	$210,000
		4dr Pullman Limo	$71,600	$126,000	$204,000	$320,000
1965	190C	4dr Sdn	$8,900	$11,700	$16,600	$23,800
1965	190Dc	4dr Sdn	$9,300	$12,700	$18,200	$25,900
1965	220B	4dr Sdn	$2,900	$6,600	$9,200	$14,200
1965	220Sb	4dr Sdn	$3,100	$7,500	$11,600	$22,600
1965	220SEb	2dr Cpe	$22,400	$34,100	$61,300	$82,500
		4dr Sdn	$3,900	$7,800	$13,600	$27,300
		2dr Cab	$55,800	$77,000	$93,300	$159,000
1965	230SL	2dr Conv	$26,400	$41,400	$61,200	$97,000
		+$4,500 for hard top. +10% for 4-spd. +15% for a/c.				
1965	300SE	4dr Sdn	$12,500	$20,000	$28,800	$38,100
		2dr Cab	$55,200	$106,000	$153,000	$260,000
1965	300SEL	4dr Sdn	$15,900	$22,900	$31,000	$43,600
1965	600	4dr Sdn	$50,300	$94,300	$155,000	$210,000
		4dr Pullman Limo	$71,600	$126,000	$204,000	$320,000
1966	200	4dr Sdn	$3,300	$7,000	$10,400	$17,800
1966	200D	4dr Sdn	$7,100	$11,100	$17,100	$25,600
1966	220SE	2dr Cpe	$10,600	$15,300	$28,800	$44,400
		2dr Conv	$50,500	$66,600	$84,000	$138,000
1966	230	4dr Sdn	$7,100	$12,300	$18,100	$25,800
1966	230S	4dr Sdn	$7,900	$13,200	$18,500	$27,500
1966	230SL	2dr Conv	$26,400	$41,400	$61,200	$97,000
		+$4,500 for hard top. +10% for 4-spd. +15% for a/c.				
1966	250S	4dr Sdn	$6,500	$10,800	$14,800	$21,900
1966	250SE	2dr Cpe	$15,300	$32,000	$39,400	$68,200
		2dr Conv	$38,400	$61,200	$87,200	$145,000
1966	600	4dr Sdn	$50,300	$94,300	$155,000	$210,000
		4dr Pullman Limo	$71,600	$126,000	$204,000	$320,000
1967	200	4dr Sdn	$3,300	$7,000	$10,400	$17,800
1967	200D	4dr Sdn	$7,100	$11,100	$17,100	$25,600
1967	230	4dr Sdn	$7,100	$12,300	$18,100	$25,800
1967	230S	4dr Sdn	$7,900	$13,200	$18,500	$27,500
1967	230SL	2dr Conv	$26,400	$41,400	$61,200	$97,000
		+$4,500 for hard top. +10% for 4-spd. +15% for a/c.				
1967	250S	4dr Sdn	$6,500	$10,800	$14,800	$21,900
1967	250SE	2dr Cpe	$15,300	$32,000	$39,400	$68,200
		2dr Cab	$37,600	$59,000	$85,400	$143,000
1967	250SL	2dr Conv	$32,200	$44,400	$69,400	$117,000

Year	Model	Body Style	4	3	2	1
		+$4,500 for hard top. +10% for power steering. +10% for 4-spd. +15% for a/c.				
1967	300SE	2dr Cpe	$19,300	$34,200	$46,200	$79,000
		2dr Conv	$55,200	$106,000	$153,000	$260,000
1967	600	4dr Sdn	$50,300	$94,300	$155,000	$210,000
		4dr Pullman Limo	$71,600	$126,000	$204,000	$320,000
1968	220	4dr Sdn	$2,500	$5,600	$8,300	$11,500
1968	220D	4dr Sdn	$5,400	$8,800	$13,100	$20,300
1968	230	4dr Sdn	$6,400	$10,900	$15,500	$22,900
1968	250	4dr Sdn	$6,200	$10,400	$14,100	$21,100
1968	250SE	2dr Cpe	$15,300	$32,000	$39,400	$68,200
		2dr Cab	$37,600	$59,000	$85,400	$143,000
1968	280S	4dr Sdn	$9,200	$14,400	$18,000	$23,500
1968	280SE	2dr Cpe	$19,400	$30,100	$40,800	$58,000
		4dr Sdn	$13,000	$20,500	$28,900	$42,100
		2dr Conv	$50,300	$78,100	$105,000	$154,000
1968	280SEL	4dr Sdn	$13,900	$18,700	$28,400	$36,300
1968	280SL	2dr Conv	$32,900	$53,400	$85,900	$141,000
		+$4,500 for hard top. +10% for 4-spd. +15% for a/c.				
1968	600	4dr Sdn	$50,300	$94,300	$155,000	$210,000
		4dr Pullman Limo	$71,600	$126,000	$204,000	$320,000
1969	220	4dr Sdn	$2,500	$5,600	$8,300	$11,500
1969	220D	4dr Sdn	$5,400	$8,800	$13,100	$20,300
1969	230	4dr Sdn	$6,400	$10,900	$15,500	$22,900
1969	250	4dr Sdn	$6,200	$10,400	$14,100	$21,100
1969	280S	4dr Sdn	$9,200	$14,400	$18,000	$23,500
1969	280SE	2dr High Grille Cpe	$19,700	$30,200	$41,000	$57,800
		2dr Low Grille Cpe	$26,200	$35,500	$49,500	$62,900
		2dr 3.5 Cpe	$30,700	$63,200	$95,400	$125,000
		4dr Sdn	$13,000	$20,500	$28,900	$42,100
		2dr High Grille Conv	$61,200	$85,800	$109,000	$162,000
		2dr Low Grille Conv	$114,000	$136,000	$182,000	$244,000
		2dr 3.5 Cab	$139,000	$206,000	$285,000	$395,000
1969	280SL	2dr Conv	$32,900	$53,400	$85,900	$141,000
		+$4,500 for hard top. +10% for 4-spd. +17% for ZF 5-spd. +15% for a/c.				
1969	300SEL	4dr 2.8 Sdn	$12,400	$19,100	$26,200	$38,600
1969	600	4dr Sdn	$50,300	$94,300	$155,000	$210,000
		4dr Pullman Limo	$71,600	$126,000	$204,000	$320,000
1970	220	4dr Sdn	$2,400	$5,500	$8,000	$11,200
1970	220D	4dr Sdn	$5,300	$8,600	$13,000	$20,200
1970	250C	2dr Cpe	$5,200	$9,000	$13,700	$24,800
1970	250	4dr Sdn	$5,900	$10,100	$13,900	$20,900
1970	280S	4dr Sdn	$9,600	$14,600	$18,300	$23,800
1970	280SE	2dr 3.5 Cpe	$36,200	$73,200	$112,000	$149,000
		2dr 3.5 Cab	$148,000	$215,000	$301,000	$400,000
		2dr 2.8L Cpe	$26,800	$36,400	$50,200	$65,100
		4dr 2.8L Sdn	$15,600	$25,600	$30,300	$44,700

Mercedes-Benz

Year	Model	Body Style	4	3	2	1
		2dr 2.8L Conv	$139,000	$159,000	$209,000	$277,000
		+10% for sunroof on cpe. +15% for floor shift 4-spd.				
1970	280SL	2dr Conv	$34,200	$56,500	$90,300	$149,000
		+$4,500 for hard top. +10% for 4-spd. +17% for ZF 5-spd. +15% for a/c.				
1970	300SEL	4dr 3.5 Sdn	$15,000	$23,000	$32,800	$46,500
		4dr 6.3 Sdn	$22,000	$49,100	$67,400	$105,000
1970	600	4dr Sdn	$50,300	$94,300	$155,000	$210,000
		4dr Pullman Limo	$71,600	$126,000	$204,000	$320,000
1971	220	4dr Sdn	$2,400	$5,500	$8,000	$11,200
1971	220D	4dr Sdn	$5,200	$8,600	$12,600	$20,000
1971	250C	2dr 2.8 Cpe	$5,200	$9,000	$13,700	$24,800
1971	250	4dr 2.8 Sdn	$5,900	$10,100	$13,900	$20,900
1971	280S	4dr Sdn	$9,600	$14,600	$18,300	$23,800
1971	280SE	2dr 3.5 Cab	$155,000	$221,000	$309,000	$416,000
		2dr 3.5 Cpe	$38,700	$76,400	$125,000	$159,000
		+10% for sunroof on cpe. +15% for floor shift 4-spd.				
1971	280SL	2dr Conv	$38,500	$65,400	$105,000	$172,000
		+$4,500 for hard top. +10% for 4-spd. +17% for ZF 5-spd. +15% for a/c.				
1971	280SEL	4dr Sdn	$13,000	$18,400	$25,800	$34,100
		+10% for sunroof on cpe. +10% for floor shift on conv.				
1971	300SEL	4dr 3.5 Sdn	$15,000	$23,000	$32,800	$46,500
		4dr 6.3 Sdn	$22,000	$49,100	$67,400	$105,000
1971	600	4dr Sdn	$50,300	$94,300	$155,000	$210,000
		4dr Pullman Limo	$71,600	$126,000	$204,000	$320,000
1972	220	4dr Sdn	$2,400	$5,500	$8,300	$11,300
1972	220D	4dr Sdn	$5,200	$8,600	$12,600	$20,000
1972	250C	2dr 2.8 Cpe	$5,400	$9,300	$13,900	$25,000
1972	250	4dr 2.8 Sdn	$5,900	$10,100	$13,900	$20,900
1972	280SE	4dr Sdn	$7,500	$10,700	$16,300	$20,500
		4dr 4.5 Sdn	$9,500	$13,800	$21,000	$27,800
		+10% for sunroof. +10% for floor shift on 4.5 sdn.				
1972	280SEL	4dr 4.5 Sdn	$10,100	$15,600	$21,200	$30,800
1972	350SLC	2dr Cpe	$7,100	$13,400	$20,500	$34,400
1972	350SL	2dr Rdstr	$5,700	$13,100	$23,700	$36,500
1972	600	4dr Sdn	$50,300	$94,300	$155,000	$210,000
		4dr Pullman Limo	$71,600	$126,000	$204,000	$320,000
1973	220	4dr Sdn	$2,400	$5,500	$8,300	$11,300
1973	220D	4dr Sdn	$5,200	$8,600	$12,600	$20,000
1973	280	4dr Sdn	$3,800	$6,900	$10,900	$20,200
1973	280C	2dr Cpe	$4,600	$8,000	$14,600	$25,700
1973	280SE	4dr 4.5 Sdn	$8,900	$12,300	$17,900	$22,400
1973	280SEL	4dr Sdn	$9,400	$13,800	$19,500	$24,500
1973	300SEL	4dr Sdn	$16,300	$22,000	$27,600	$71,300
1973	450SLC	2dr Cpe	$6,800	$12,600	$21,800	$41,800
1973	450SE	4dr Sdn	$7,200	$11,600	$16,700	$22,500
1973	450SEL	4dr Sdn	$9,000	$14,500	$19,200	$28,400
1973	450SL	2dr Rdstr	$5,300	$14,900	$26,900	$36,700
1974	230.4	4dr Sdn	$5,100	$9,000	$12,500	$18,100

Mercedes-Benz

Year	Model	Body Style	4	3	2	1
1974	240D	4dr Sdn	$3,100	$6,800	$9,400	$13,200
1974	280	4dr Sdn	$3,800	$6,900	$10,900	$20,200
1974	280C	2dr Cpe	$4,600	$8,000	$14,600	$25,700
1974	450SLC	2dr Cpe	$6,800	$12,600	$21,800	$41,800
1974	450SE	4dr Sdn	$7,200	$11,300	$16,400	$22,200
1974	450SEL	4dr Sdn	$9,000	$14,500	$19,200	$28,400
1974	450SL	2dr Rdstr	$4,800	$12,400	$23,300	$33,300
1975	230	4dr Sdn	$5,100	$9,000	$12,500	$18,100
1975	240D	4dr Sdn	$3,100	$6,800	$9,400	$13,200
1975	280	4dr Sdn	$3,800	$6,900	$10,900	$20,200
1975	280C	2dr Cpe	$4,600	$8,000	$14,600	$25,700
1975	280S	4dr Sdn	$12,000	$17,400	$21,600	$28,100
1975	450SLC	2dr Cpe	$6,800	$12,600	$21,800	$41,800
1975	450SE	4dr Sdn	$7,200	$11,300	$16,400	$22,200
1975	450SEL	4dr Sdn	$9,000	$14,500	$19,200	$28,400
1975	450SL	2dr Rdstr	$4,800	$12,400	$23,300	$33,300
1976	230	4dr Sdn	$5,100	$9,000	$12,500	$18,100
1976	240D	4dr Sdn	$4,100	$9,100	$12,600	$17,600
1976	280	4dr Sdn	$3,800	$6,900	$10,900	$20,200
1976	280C	2dr Cpe	$4,600	$8,000	$14,600	$25,700
1976	280S	4dr Sdn	$12,000	$17,400	$21,600	$28,100
1976	450SLC	2dr Cpe	$6,800	$12,600	$21,800	$41,800
1976	450SE	4dr Sdn	$7,200	$11,300	$16,400	$22,200
1976	450SEL	4dr Sdn	$9,000	$14,500	$19,200	$28,400
1976	450SL	2dr Rdstr	$4,800	$12,400	$23,300	$33,300
1977	230	4dr Sdn	$4,500	$8,000	$10,900	$16,300
1977	240D	4dr Sdn	$6,900	$15,300	$21,300	$25,200
1977	280E	4dr Sdn	$4,000	$6,500	$8,800	$11,200
1977	280SE	4dr Sdn	$4,900	$7,400	$12,000	$16,300
1977	300D	4dr Lang Limo	$5,200	$8,500	$13,100	$21,300
1977	450SLC	2dr Cpe	$6,800	$12,600	$21,800	$41,800
1977	450SEL	4dr Sdn	$9,300	$15,600	$20,400	$29,100
		4dr 6.9 Sdn	$12,900	$24,400	$43,500	$67,200
1977	450SL	2dr Rdstr	$4,800	$12,400	$23,300	$33,300
1978	230	4dr Sdn	$4,500	$8,000	$10,900	$16,300
1978	240D	4dr Sdn	$6,900	$15,300	$21,300	$25,200
1978	280E	4dr Sdn	$4,000	$6,500	$8,800	$11,200
1978	280CE	2dr Cpe	$7,700	$12,000	$16,300	$22,500
1978	280SE	4dr Sdn	$4,900	$7,400	$12,000	$16,300
1978	300D	4dr Sdn	$5,600	$8,300	$13,900	$21,300
1978	300CD	2dr Cpe	$4,600	$6,000	$11,900	$19,400
1978	450SEL	4dr 6.9L Sdn	$12,900	$24,400	$43,500	$67,200
		4dr Sdn	$9,300	$15,600	$20,800	$29,700
1978	450SLC	2dr Cpe	$7,000	$13,300	$22,200	$43,400
1978	450SL	2dr Rdstr	$6,000	$14,000	$25,200	$35,300
1979	240D	4dr Sdn	$4,300	$9,100	$16,900	$23,300
1979	280E	4dr Sdn	$4,000	$6,500	$8,800	$11,200
1979	280CE	2dr Cpe	$7,700	$12,000	$16,300	$22,500
1979	280SE	4dr Sdn	$5,200	$7,800	$13,800	$17,400

Mercedes-Benz

Year	Model	Body Style	4	3	2	1
1979	300D	4dr Sdn	$5,200	$8,500	$13,100	$21,300
1979	300CD	2dr Cpe	$4,600	$6,000	$11,900	$19,400
1979	300TD	4dr Wgn	$6,900	$12,500	$24,300	$38,200
1979	450SLC	2dr Cpe	$6,300	$11,300	$20,500	$40,200
1979	450SEL	4dr 6.9L Sdn	$12,900	$24,400	$43,500	$67,200
		4dr Sdn	$6,200	$11,100	$18,800	$26,800
1979	450SL	2dr Rdstr	$4,700	$10,100	$19,300	$29,000
1979	300SD	4dr Sdn	$6,100	$10,100	$15,100	$26,900
1980	240D	4dr Sdn	$4,300	$9,100	$16,900	$23,300
1980	280E	4dr Sdn	$4,200	$6,600	$9,000	$11,500
1980	280CE	2dr Cpe	$8,100	$12,500	$16,900	$23,600
1980	280SE	4dr Sdn	$5,400	$8,000	$14,000	$17,800
1980	300D	4dr Sdn	$5,400	$8,700	$13,200	$21,900
1980	300CD	2dr Cpe	$4,600	$6,000	$12,200	$19,800
1980	300TD	4dr Wgn	$7,600	$15,300	$25,000	$39,100
1980	300SD	4dr Sdn	$6,200	$10,200	$15,200	$27,400
1980	450SEL	4dr Sdn	$5,900	$11,000	$18,600	$26,500
1980	450SLC	2dr Cpe	$4,700	$9,200	$18,100	$38,400
1980	450SL	2dr Rdstr	$4,600	$10,600	$19,800	$29,700
1981	240D	4dr Sdn	$4,300	$9,100	$16,800	$23,100
1981	280E	4dr Sdn	$4,200	$6,600	$8,500	$11,400
1981	280CE	2dr Cpe	$7,700	$12,100	$16,500	$23,000
1981	300CD	2dr Cpe	$4,600	$6,000	$12,100	$19,700
1981	300D	4dr Sdn	$5,400	$8,600	$13,100	$21,800
1981	300SD	4dr Sdn	$6,400	$10,200	$15,200	$27,400
1981	300TD	4dr Wgn	$7,800	$13,200	$26,100	$40,500
1981	380SLC	2dr Cpe	$5,200	$8,300	$14,600	$20,200
1981	380SEL	4dr Sdn	$7,500	$12,200	$22,900	$31,600
1981	380SL	2dr Rdstr	$5,900	$11,800	$21,800	$33,800
1982	240D	4dr Sdn	$4,300	$9,100	$16,800	$23,100
1982	300D	4dr Sdn	$5,400	$8,600	$13,100	$21,800
1982	300SD	4dr Sdn	$6,400	$10,200	$15,200	$27,400
1982	300TD	4dr Wgn	$7,800	$13,200	$26,100	$40,500
1982	300CD	2dr Cpe	$4,600	$6,000	$12,100	$19,700
1982	380SLC	2dr Cpe	$6,000	$8,200	$13,500	$18,000
1982	380SEL	4dr Sdn	$6,400	$11,700	$20,100	$28,800
1982	380SL	2dr Rdstr	$5,900	$11,800	$21,800	$33,800
1983	240D	4dr Sdn	$4,300	$9,100	$16,800	$23,100
1983	300CD	2dr Cpe	$5,400	$7,000	$14,200	$23,200
1983	300D	4dr Sdn	$5,200	$7,900	$12,500	$20,200
1983	300SD	4dr Sdn	$6,400	$10,200	$15,200	$27,400
1983	300TD	4dr Wgn	$7,800	$13,200	$26,100	$40,500
1983	380SEC	2dr Cpe	$5,000	$7,700	$15,600	$25,800
1983	380SEL	4dr Sdn	$6,400	$11,700	$20,100	$28,800
1983	380SL	2dr Rdstr	$5,900	$11,800	$21,800	$33,800
1984	190E	4dr Sdn	$3,400	$6,200	$7,700	$10,400
1984	190D	4dr Sdn	$1,800	$3,200	$5,600	$7,600
1984	300CD	2dr Cpe	$4,700	$7,000	$14,200	$23,200
1984	300D	4dr Sdn	$5,200	$7,500	$12,500	$20,200

Year	Model	Body Style	4	3	2	1
1984	300SD	4dr Sdn	$5,400	$8,600	$13,900	$25,800
1984	300TD	4dr Wgn	$7,800	$13,200	$26,100	$40,500
1984	380SE	4dr Sdn	$5,500	$8,000	$12,100	$19,600
1984	380SL	2dr Rdstr	$6,800	$13,000	$24,200	$38,100
1984	500SEC	2dr Cpe	$7,500	$10,200	$18,400	$41,500
1984	500SEL	4dr Sdn	$5,200	$8,900	$12,500	$24,800
1985	190E	4dr Sdn	$3,400	$6,200	$7,700	$10,400
1985	190D	4dr Sdn	$1,800	$3,200	$5,600	$7,600
1985	300CD	2dr Cpe	$4,700	$7,000	$14,200	$23,200
1985	300D	4dr Sdn	$5,200	$7,500	$12,500	$20,200
1985	300SD	4dr Sdn	$5,400	$8,600	$13,900	$25,800
1985	300TD	4dr Wgn	$7,800	$13,200	$26,100	$40,500
1985	380SE	4dr Sdn	$5,500	$8,000	$12,100	$19,600
1985	380SL	2dr Rdstr	$7,000	$13,400	$24,800	$38,100
1985	500SEC	2dr Cpe	$7,500	$10,200	$18,400	$41,500
1985	500SEL	4dr Sdn	$5,200	$8,900	$12,500	$24,800
1986	190E	4dr Sdn	$3,400	$6,200	$7,700	$10,400
		4dr 2.3 16v Sdn	$12,100	$19,600	$29,900	$44,100
						-20% for auto on 2.3 16v.
1986	190D	4dr Sdn	$2,000	$3,700	$6,000	$8,500
1986	300E	4dr Sdn	$3,700	$6,400	$11,100	$16,200
1986	300D	4dr Sdn	$4,500	$6,300	$7,800	$11,600
1986	300SDL	4dr Sdn	$5,200	$8,300	$12,100	$20,300
1986	420SEL	4dr Sdn	$4,300	$7,400	$12,200	$27,300
1986	560SEC	2dr Cpe	$9,000	$13,000	$29,500	$74,200
1986	560SEL	4dr Sdn	$6,700	$12,100	$21,200	$47,800
1986	560SL	2dr Rdstr	$8,200	$15,400	$45,600	$76,900
1987	190E	4dr 2.3 Sdn	$3,400	$6,200	$7,700	$10,400
		4dr 2.3 16v Sdn	$12,100	$19,600	$29,900	$44,100
						-20% for auto on 2.3 16v.
		4dr 2.6 Sdn	$2,500	$5,000	$8,100	$14,400
1987	190D	4dr 2.5 Sdn	$2,000	$3,700	$6,000	$8,500
		4dr 2.5 Turbo Sdn	$2,400	$4,200	$6,200	$9,500
1987	260E	4dr Sdn	$2,600	$3,700	$5,100	$7,200
1987	300E	4dr Sdn	$3,700	$6,400	$11,100	$16,200
1987	300D	4dr Sdn	$4,500	$6,300	$7,800	$11,600
1987	300SDL	4dr Sdn	$5,200	$8,300	$12,100	$20,300
1987	300TD	4dr Wgn	$6,100	$10,000	$12,600	$25,200
1987	420SEL	4dr Sdn	$4,300	$7,400	$12,200	$27,300
1987	560SEC	2dr Cpe	$9,000	$13,000	$29,500	$74,200
1987	560SEL	4dr Sdn	$6,700	$12,100	$21,200	$47,800
1987	560SL	2dr Rdstr	$8,200	$15,400	$45,600	$76,900
1988	190E	4dr 2.3 Sdn	$3,400	$6,200	$7,700	$10,400
		4dr 2.6 Sdn	$2,500	$5,000	$8,100	$14,400
1988	190D	4dr Sdn	$2,000	$3,700	$6,000	$8,500
1988	260E	4dr Sdn	$2,600	$3,700	$5,100	$7,200
1988	300CE	2dr Cpe	$3,600	$7,200	$12,600	$27,600
1988	300E	4dr Sdn	$3,700	$6,400	$11,100	$16,200

Mercedes-Benz

Year	Model	Body Style	4	3	2	1
1988	300SE	4dr Sdn	$4,400	$8,200	$12,400	$18,400
1988	300SEL	4dr Sdn	$5,800	$9,700	$14,000	$23,300
1988	300TE	4dr Wgn	$5,200	$8,600	$10,700	$16,400
1988	420SEL	4dr Sdn	$4,300	$7,400	$12,200	$27,300
1988	560SEC	2dr Cpe	$9,000	$13,000	$29,500	$74,200
1988	560SEL	4dr Sdn	$6,700	$12,100	$21,200	$47,800
1988	560SL	2dr Rdstr	$8,400	$16,300	$45,900	$77,000
1989	190E	4dr 2.6 Sdn	$3,200	$5,700	$9,900	$16,500
1989	190D	4dr Sdn	$2,200	$4,200	$6,600	$8,900
1989	260E	4dr Sdn	$2,600	$3,700	$5,100	$7,200
1989	300CE	2dr Cpe	$3,600	$7,200	$12,600	$27,600
1989	300E	4dr Sdn	$3,700	$6,400	$11,100	$16,200
1989	300SE	4dr Sdn	$4,400	$8,200	$12,400	$18,400
1989	300SEL	4dr Sdn	$5,800	$9,700	$14,000	$23,300
1989	300TE	4dr Wgn	$5,200	$8,600	$10,700	$16,400
1989	420SEL	4dr Sdn	$4,300	$7,400	$12,200	$27,300
1989	560SEC	2dr Cpe	$9,000	$13,000	$29,500	$74,200
1989	560SEL	4dr Sdn	$6,700	$12,100	$21,200	$47,800
1989	560SL	2dr Rdstr	$9,100	$18,400	$50,800	$83,900
1990	190E	4dr Sdn	$3,200	$5,600	$9,700	$16,200
1990	300CE	2dr Cpe	$4,300	$7,600	$15,200	$29,400
1990	300E	4dr 2.6 Sdn	$4,200	$6,200	$9,400	$13,500
		4dr Sdn	$4,400	$6,400	$10,500	$16,500
		4dr 4Matic Sdn	$4,000	$5,700	$7,500	$12,200
1990	300D	4dr 2.5 Sdn	$3,100	$4,400	$5,900	$8,500
1990	300SE	4dr Sdn	$4,400	$8,200	$12,400	$18,600
1990	300SEL	4dr Sdn	$6,000	$9,900	$14,500	$23,700
1990	300TE	4dr Wgn	$5,000	$8,300	$10,200	$15,900
		4dr 4Matic Wgn	$5,600	$9,600	$12,600	$19,500
1990	300SL	2dr Rdstr	$4,900	$8,200	$16,600	$24,900
1990	350SDL	4dr Sdn	$4,600	$6,200	$8,500	$13,100
1990	420SEL	4dr Sdn	$4,300	$7,400	$12,200	$27,300
1990	560SEC	2dr Cpe	$9,700	$13,200	$29,800	$76,400
1990	560SEL	4dr Sdn	$6,700	$12,100	$21,200	$47,800
1990	500SL	2dr Rdstr	$7,100	$11,800	$20,900	$36,900
1991	190E	4dr 2.3 Sdn	$3,400	$6,200	$7,700	$10,400
		4dr 2.6 Sdn	$3,400	$5,900	$10,400	$16,900
1991	300CE	2dr Cpe	$4,300	$7,600	$15,200	$29,400
1991	300E	4dr 2.6 Sdn	$4,200	$6,200	$9,400	$13,500
		4dr Sdn	$4,400	$6,400	$10,500	$16,500
		4dr 4Matic Sdn	$4,000	$5,700	$7,500	$12,200
1991	300D	4dr 2.5 Sdn	$3,200	$4,500	$6,000	$8,700
1991	300SE	4dr Sdn	$4,400	$8,200	$12,400	$18,600
1991	300TE	4dr Wgn	$5,000	$8,300	$10,200	$15,900
		4dr 4Matic Wgn	$5,600	$9,600	$12,600	$19,500
1991	300SEL	4dr Sdn	$5,800	$9,700	$14,000	$23,300
1991	300SL	2dr Rdstr	$5,100	$8,500	$17,700	$25,700
1991	350SDL	4dr Sdn	$4,600	$6,200	$8,500	$13,100
1991	420SEL	4dr Sdn	$4,300	$7,400	$12,200	$27,300

Year	Model	Body Style	4	3	2	1
1991	560SEC	2dr Cpe	$9,700	$13,200	$29,800	$76,400
1991	560SEL	4dr Sdn	$6,700	$12,100	$21,200	$47,800
1991	500SL	2dr Rdstr	$7,400	$12,000	$21,200	$37,300
1992	190E	4dr 2.3 Sdn	$3,400	$6,200	$7,700	$10,400
		4dr 2.6 Sdn	$3,400	$5,900	$10,400	$16,900
1992	300CE	2dr Cpe	$4,300	$7,600	$15,200	$29,400
1992	300E	4dr 2.6 Sdn	$4,200	$6,200	$9,400	$13,500
		4dr Sdn	$4,400	$6,400	$10,500	$16,500
		4dr 4Matic Sdn	$4,000	$5,700	$7,500	$12,200
1992	300SE	4dr Sdn	$3,000	$5,600	$7,900	$11,000
1992	300D	4dr 2.5 Sdn	$3,200	$4,500	$6,000	$8,700
1992	300SD	4dr Sdn	$3,700	$4,800	$6,200	$8,900
1992	300TE	4dr Wgn	$5,000	$8,300	$10,200	$15,900
		4dr 4Matic Wgn	$5,600	$9,600	$12,600	$19,500
1992	300SL	2dr Rdstr	$5,600	$9,200	$18,200	$26,100
1992	400E	4dr Sdn	$4,000	$6,600	$8,000	$9,700
1992	400SE	4dr Sdn	$5,400	$7,200	$8,300	$10,200
1992	500E	4dr Sdn	$19,300	$30,700	$53,200	$81,000
1992	560SEC	2dr Cpe	$9,700	$13,200	$29,800	$76,400
1992	500SEL	4dr Sdn	$7,500	$11,700	$16,400	$28,400
1992	500SL	2dr Rdstr	$7,600	$13,000	$22,000	$38,800
1992	600SEL	4dr Sdn	$6,300	$9,800	$12,500	$24,800
1993	190E	4dr 2.3 Sdn	$3,400	$6,200	$7,700	$10,400
		4dr 2.6 Sdn	$3,400	$5,900	$10,400	$16,900
1993	300CE	2dr Cpe	$4,600	$8,100	$15,800	$30,000
		2dr Conv	$6,900	$9,700	$17,200	$31,000
1993	300E	4dr 2.8 Sdn	$4,000	$5,600	$8,000	$11,000
		4dr Sdn	$5,200	$6,700	$12,300	$17,400
		4dr 4Matic Sdn	$5,100	$6,400	$9,200	$12,600
1993	300SE	4dr Sdn	$3,000	$5,600	$7,900	$11,000
1993	300D	4dr 2.5 Sdn	$3,200	$4,500	$6,000	$8,700
1993	300SD	4dr Sdn	$3,700	$4,800	$6,200	$8,900
1993	300TE	4dr Wgn	$5,100	$8,400	$10,500	$16,500
		4dr 4Matic Wgn	$5,700	$9,800	$12,900	$19,800
1993	300SL	2dr Rdstr	$5,600	$9,200	$18,200	$26,100
1993	400E	4dr Sdn	$4,000	$6,600	$8,000	$9,700
1993	400SEL	4dr Sdn	$5,600	$7,900	$9,100	$11,900
1993	500SEC	2dr Cpe	$6,200	$8,800	$10,800	$19,500
1993	500E	4dr Sdn	$19,300	$30,700	$53,200	$81,000
1993	500SEL	4dr Sdn	$6,600	$10,300	$14,400	$24,900
1993	500SL	2dr Rdstr	$7,600	$13,000	$22,000	$38,800
1993	600SEC	2dr Cpe	$6,800	$9,400	$12,600	$18,900
1993	600SEL	4dr Sdn	$6,300	$9,800	$12,500	$24,800
1993	600SL	2dr Rdstr	$8,200	$15,000	$25,100	$42,000
1994	C220	4dr Sdn	$1,900	$3,700	$4,900	$6,400
1994	C280	4dr Sdn	$3,200	$4,200	$5,800	$8,000
1994	E300	4dr Diesel Sdn	$3,200	$4,600	$6,000	$8,500
1994	E320	2dr Cpe	$5,000	$8,200	$16,500	$24,200
		4dr Sdn	$4,500	$6,000	$10,000	$19,000

Mercedes-Benz

Year	Model	Body Style	4	3	2	1
		4dr Wgn	$4,500	$7,300	$8,400	$12,600
		2dr Conv	$6,800	$10,800	$16,500	$25,000
1994	E420	4dr Sdn	$4,400	$7,400	$9,500	$14,000
1994	500E	4dr Sdn	$24,900	$39,500	$60,200	$88,900
1994	S350D	4dr Diesel Sdn	$3,400	$4,600	$6,000	$8,500
1994	S320	4dr Sdn	$4,700	$8,400	$12,300	$17,600
1994	S420	4dr Sdn	$6,400	$9,100	$13,400	$19,800
1994	S500	2dr Cpe	$6,500	$10,000	$13,900	$25,900
		4dr Sdn	$9,000	$12,200	$16,800	$24,400
1994	S600	2dr Cpe	$7,000	$10,600	$17,500	$32,900
		4dr Sdn	$8,800	$15,000	$21,000	$35,200
1994	SL320	2dr Rdstr	$3,800	$7,000	$15,700	$27,700
1994	SL500	2dr Rdstr	$6,600	$11,900	$23,800	$44,200
1994	SL600	2dr Rdstr	$6,700	$11,600	$23,500	$41,600
1995	C220	4dr Sdn	$1,900	$3,700	$4,900	$6,300
1995	C280	4dr Sdn	$3,200	$4,200	$5,800	$8,000
1995	C36 AMG	4dr Sdn	$6,800	$10,000	$14,100	$23,100
1995	E300	4dr Diesel Sdn	$3,200	$4,600	$6,000	$8,500
1995	E320	2dr Cpe	$5,000	$8,200	$16,500	$24,200
		4dr Sdn	$4,500	$6,000	$10,000	$19,000
		4dr Wgn	$4,600	$7,400	$8,500	$12,700
		2dr Conv	$6,800	$10,800	$16,500	$25,000
1995	E420	4dr Sdn	$4,400	$7,400	$9,500	$14,000
1995	E500	4dr Ltd Ed Sdn	$24,900	$39,500	$60,200	$88,900
1995	S350D	4dr Diesel Sdn	$3,400	$4,600	$6,000	$8,500
1995	S320	4dr Sdn	$4,700	$8,400	$12,500	$17,600
		4dr LWB Sdn	$5,000	$8,800	$13,100	$20,700
1995	S420	4dr Sdn	$6,600	$9,200	$13,500	$19,800
1995	S500	2dr Cpe	$6,500	$10,000	$13,900	$25,900
		4dr Sdn	$9,200	$12,400	$17,000	$24,800
1995	S600	2dr Cpe	$7,000	$10,600	$17,500	$32,900
		4dr Sdn	$9,000	$15,000	$21,000	$35,200
1995	SL320	2dr Rdstr	$3,800	$7,000	$15,700	$27,700
1995	SL500	2dr Rdstr	$6,600	$11,900	$23,800	$44,200
1995	SL600	2dr Rdstr	$6,700	$11,600	$23,500	$41,600
1996	C220	4dr Sdn	$1,900	$3,700	$4,900	$6,200
1996	C280	4dr Sdn	$3,200	$4,200	$5,600	$8,000
1996	C36 AMG	4dr Sdn	$6,800	$10,000	$14,100	$23,100
1996	E300	4dr Diesel Sdn	$3,500	$5,000	$6,600	$9,100
1996	E320	4dr Sdn	$3,200	$4,300	$5,800	$8,200
1996	E420	4dr Sdn	$4,100	$6,400	$8,100	$11,700
1996	S320	4dr Sdn	$4,700	$8,200	$12,300	$17,300
		4dr LWB Sdn	$5,000	$8,700	$12,900	$20,500
1996	S420	4dr Sdn	$6,400	$9,100	$13,400	$21,600
1996	S500	2dr Cpe	$6,600	$10,200	$14,300	$26,900
		4dr Sdn	$9,000	$12,300	$16,800	$25,200
1996	S600	2dr Cpe	$7,100	$10,800	$18,300	$35,200
		4dr Sdn	$8,800	$15,000	$21,000	$35,200
1996	SL320	2dr Rdstr	$3,700	$6,800	$15,500	$27,500

Year	Model	Body Style	4	3	2	1
1996	SL500	2dr Rdstr	$6,600	$11,900	$23,800	$44,200
1996	SL600	2dr Rdstr	$6,700	$11,600	$23,500	$41,600
1997	C230	4dr Sdn	$1,900	$3,900	$5,200	$6,800
1997	C280	4dr Sdn	$3,000	$4,300	$5,800	$8,600
1997	C36 AMG	4dr Sdn	$6,900	$10,200	$14,500	$23,600
1997	E300	4dr Diesel Sdn	$3,500	$5,000	$6,600	$9,100
1997	E320	4dr Sdn	$3,200	$4,500	$6,000	$8,500
1997	E420	4dr Sdn	$4,000	$6,500	$8,500	$12,300
1997	S320	4dr Sdn	$5,300	$8,500	$13,100	$19,900
		4dr LWB Sdn	$5,500	$9,300	$13,800	$22,300
1997	S420	4dr Sdn	$6,600	$9,800	$14,700	$23,700
1997	S500	2dr Cpe	$6,700	$10,600	$16,400	$29,400
		4dr Sdn	$9,300	$13,200	$18,000	$28,000
1997	S600	2dr Cpe	$7,300	$11,200	$19,200	$37,000
		4dr Sdn	$9,200	$15,400	$22,000	$38,200
1997	SL320	2dr Rdstr	$4,600	$7,400	$16,400	$28,800
1997	SL500	2dr Rdstr	$6,800	$13,000	$27,000	$51,200
1997	SL600	2dr Rdstr	$6,900	$13,900	$25,600	$48,000
1998	C230	4dr Sdn	$2,100	$4,100	$5,200	$7,200
1998	C280	4dr Sdn	$3,300	$4,700	$5,900	$8,900
1998	CLK320	2dr Cpe	$4,700	$6,700	$9,100	$11,800
1998	E300	4dr Diesel Sdn	$3,500	$5,200	$6,900	$9,200
1998	E320	4dr Sdn	$3,400	$4,800	$6,200	$8,900
		4dr 4Matic Sdn	$3,500	$5,200	$6,900	$9,400
		4dr Wgn	$5,300	$7,900	$11,100	$15,200
		4dr 4Matic Wgn	$5,600	$8,300	$11,700	$16,500
1998	E420	4dr Sdn	$5,900	$9,000	$10,600	$17,100
1998	S320	4dr Sdn	$5,300	$8,500	$13,100	$19,900
		4dr LWB Sdn	$5,500	$9,300	$13,800	$22,300
1998	S420	4dr Sdn	$6,600	$9,800	$14,700	$23,700
1998	S500	4dr Sdn	$9,300	$13,200	$18,000	$28,000
1998	S600	4dr Sdn	$9,200	$15,400	$22,000	$38,200
1998	CL500	2dr Cpe	$6,200	$9,000	$10,500	$15,400
1998	CL600	2dr Cpe	$6,400	$9,100	$11,100	$16,300
1998	SLK230	2dr Rdstr	$5,300	$7,900	$12,900	$19,700
1998	SL500	2dr Rdstr	$6,800	$13,000	$27,000	$51,200
1998	SL600	2dr Rdstr	$6,900	$13,900	$25,600	$48,000
1998	CLK GTR	2dr Cpe	$2.5 mil	$3 mil	$4 mil	$4.5 mil
1999	C230K	4dr Sdn	$2,900	$4,700	$6,000	$8,400
1999	C280	4dr Sdn	$3,300	$4,700	$5,900	$8,900
1999	C43 AMG	4dr Sdn	$7,400	$11,200	$16,900	$24,400
1999	CLK320	2dr Cpe	$5,100	$7,600	$9,400	$12,600
		2dr Conv	$5,900	$8,500	$11,200	$16,100
1999	CLK430	2dr Cpe	$5,700	$8,500	$10,400	$14,200
1999	E300	4dr Diesel Sdn	$3,500	$5,200	$6,900	$9,200
1999	E320	4dr Sdn	$3,400	$4,800	$6,200	$8,900
		4dr 4Matic AWD Sdn	$3,500	$5,200	$6,900	$9,400
		4dr Wgn	$5,300	$7,900	$11,100	$15,200

Mercedes-Benz

Year	Model	Body Style	4	3	2	1
		4dr 4Matic AWD Wgn	$5,600	$8,300	$11,700	$16,500
1999	E430	4dr Sdn	$6,800	$9,100	$10,900	$14,200
1999	E55	4dr AMG Sdn	$13,100	$20,700	$26,300	$36,400
1999	S320	4dr Sdn	$5,300	$8,500	$13,100	$19,900
		4dr LWB Sdn	$5,500	$9,300	$13,800	$22,300
1999	S420	4dr Sdn	$6,600	$9,800	$14,700	$23,700
1999	S500	4dr Sdn	$9,300	$13,200	$18,000	$28,000
1999	S600	4dr Sdn	$9,200	$15,400	$21,200	$36,800
1999	CL500	2dr Cpe	$6,200	$9,000	$10,500	$15,400
1999	CL600	2dr Cpe	$6,400	$9,100	$11,100	$16,300
1999	SLK230	2dr Rdstr	$5,300	$7,900	$12,900	$19,700
1999	SL500	2dr Rdstr	$7,000	$14,400	$27,900	$53,500
1999	SL600	2dr Rdstr	$7,200	$13,900	$26,000	$48,200
1999	CLK GTR	2dr Cpe	$2.5 mil	$3 mil	$4 mil	$4.5 mil
2000	E55	4dr AMG Sdn	$13,100	$20,700	$26,300	$36,400
2000	SLK 230	2dr Rdstr	$5,300	$7,900	$12,900	$19,700
2000	SL500	2dr Rdstr	$7,200	$14,700	$28,500	$54,800
2000	SL600	2dr Rdstr	$7,300	$14,100	$26,400	$49,000
2001	E55	4dr AMG Sdn	$13,100	$20,700	$26,300	$36,400
2001	SLK 230	2dr Rdstr	$5,300	$7,900	$12,900	$19,700
2001	SLK320	2dr Rdstr	$7,000	$10,300	$15,800	$24,100
2001	SL500	2dr Rdstr	$7,400	$15,000	$29,300	$56,200
2001	SL600	2dr Rdstr	$7,400	$14,400	$26,800	$49,700
2002	E55	4dr AMG Sdn	$13,100	$20,700	$26,300	$36,400
2002	SLK 230	2dr Rdstr	$5,300	$7,900	$12,900	$19,700
2002	SLK320	2dr Rdstr	$7,000	$10,300	$15,800	$24,100
2002	SLK32 AMG	2dr Kompressor Rdstr	$9,100	$14,300	$21,500	$32,600
2002	SL500	2dr Rdstr	$7,700	$15,300	$30,000	$57,600
2002	SL600	2dr Rdstr	$7,500	$14,600	$27,200	$50,400
2003	SLK 230	2dr Rdstr	$5,300	$7,900	$12,900	$19,700
2003	SLK320	2dr Rdstr	$7,000	$10,300	$15,800	$24,100
2003	SLK32 AMG	2dr Kompressor Rdstr	$9,100	$14,300	$21,500	$32,600
2003	SL500	2dr Rdstr	$11,400	$16,900	$25,300	$37,300
2003	SL55 AMG	2dr Rdstr	$13,600	$21,200	$31,300	$46,400
2004	SLK 230	2dr Rdstr	$5,300	$7,900	$12,900	$19,700
2004	SLK320	2dr Rdstr	$7,000	$10,300	$15,800	$24,100
2004	SLK32 AMG	2dr Kompressor Rdstr	$9,100	$14,300	$21,500	$32,600
2004	SL500	2dr Rdstr	$11,400	$16,900	$25,300	$37,300
2004	SL600	2dr Rdstr	$17,000	$24,500	$35,300	$50,700
2004	SL55 AMG	2dr Rdstr	$13,600	$21,200	$31,300	$46,400
2004	SLR McLaren	2dr Cpe	$174,000	$202,000	$221,000	$255,000
2005	SL500	2dr Rdstr	$11,400	$16,900	$25,300	$37,300
2005	SL600	2dr Rdstr	$17,000	$24,500	$35,300	$50,700
2005	SL55 AMG	2dr Rdstr	$13,600	$21,200	$31,300	$46,400
2005	SL65 AMG	2dr Rdstr	$22,200	$34,400	$49,300	$76,000

Mercedes-Benz

Year	Model	Body Style	4	3	2	1
2005	SLR McLaren	2dr Cpe	$174,000	$202,000	$221,000	$255,000
2006	SL500	2dr Rdstr	$11,400	$16,900	$25,300	$37,300
2006	SL600	2dr Rdstr	$17,000	$24,500	$35,300	$50,700
2006	SL55 AMG	2dr Rdstr	$13,600	$21,200	$31,300	$46,400
2006	SL65 AMG	2dr Rdstr	$22,200	$34,400	$49,300	$76,000
2006	SLR McLaren	2dr Cpe	$190,000	$231,000	$253,000	$299,000
		2dr 722 Ed Cpe	$320,000	$376,000	$445,000	$496,000
2007	SL550	2dr Rdstr	$16,600	$25,200	$35,100	$51,400
2007	SL600	2dr Rdstr	$17,000	$24,500	$35,300	$50,700
2007	SL55 AMG	2dr Rdstr	$13,600	$21,200	$31,300	$46,400
2007	SL65 AMG	2dr Rdstr	$22,200	$34,400	$49,300	$76,000
2007	SLR McLaren	2dr Cpe	$190,000	$231,000	$253,000	$299,000
		2dr 722 Ed Cpe	$320,000	$376,000	$445,000	$496,000
2008	SL550	2dr Rdstr	$16,600	$25,200	$35,100	$51,400
2008	SL600	2dr Rdstr	$17,000	$24,500	$35,300	$50,700
2008	SL55 AMG	2dr Rdstr	$13,600	$21,200	$31,300	$46,400
2008	SL65 AMG	2dr Rdstr	$22,200	$34,400	$49,300	$76,000
2008	SLR McLaren	2dr Conv	$227,000	$267,000	$310,000	$375,000
2009	SL550	2dr Conv	$16,600	$25,200	$35,100	$51,400
2009	SL600	2dr Conv	$17,000	$24,500	$35,300	$50,700
2009	SL63 AMG	2dr Conv	$24,300	$37,700	$54,800	$81,100
2009	SL65 AMG	2dr Conv	$22,200	$34,400	$49,300	$76,000
		2dr Black Series Conv	$84,300	$137,000	$205,000	$307,000
2009	SLR McLaren	2dr Conv	$242,000	$278,000	$329,000	$391,000
		2dr 722 S Conv	$572,000	$603,000	$675,000	$808,000
		2dr Stirling Moss Rdstr	$1.6 mil	$1.9 mil	$2.3 mil	$2.7 mil
2010	SL550	2dr Rdstr	$16,600	$25,200	$35,100	$51,400
2010	SL63 AMG	2dr Rdstr	$24,300	$37,700	$54,800	$81,100
2010	SL65 AMG	2dr Rdstr	$22,200	$34,400	$49,300	$76,000
2011	SL550	2dr Rdstr	$16,600	$25,200	$35,100	$51,400
2011	SL63 AMG	2dr Rdstr	$24,300	$37,700	$54,800	$81,100
2011	SL65 AMG	2dr Rdstr	$22,200	$34,400	$49,300	$76,000
2012	SL550	2dr Rdstr	$16,600	$25,200	$35,100	$51,400
2012	SL63 AMG	2dr Rdstr	$24,300	$37,700	$54,800	$81,100

Mercury

Year	Model	Body Style	4	3	2	1
1946	Series 69M	239/100 2dr Sdn Cpe	$12,500	$19,000	$29,600	$43,100
		239/100 4dr Twn Sdn	$8,800	$12,800	$21,300	$28,400
		239/100 4dr Wgn	$37,100	$64,600	$97,700	$126,000
		239/100 2dr Clb Conv	$16,600	$25,500	$54,900	$93,500
		239/100 2dr Sprtsmn Conv	$64,800	$130,000	$227,000	$297,000

Mercury

Year	Model	Body Style	4	3	2	1
1947	Series 79M	239/100 2dr Sdn Cpe	$12,500	$19,000	$29,600	$43,100
		239/100 4dr Twn Sdn	$8,800	$12,800	$21,300	$28,400
		239/100 4dr Wgn	$37,100	$64,600	$97,700	$126,000
		239/100 2dr Clb Conv	$16,600	$25,500	$54,900	$93,500
1948	Series 89M	239/100 2dr Sdn Cpe	$12,500	$19,000	$29,600	$43,100
		239/100 4dr Twn Sdn	$8,800	$14,100	$21,300	$28,400
		239/100 4dr Wgn	$35,200	$61,400	$97,700	$126,000
		239/100 2dr Clb Conv	$16,600	$25,500	$54,900	$93,500
1949	Series 9CM	255/110 2dr Cpe	$12,100	$22,800	$40,800	$53,600
		255/110 4dr Spt Sdn	$9,100	$14,700	$22,900	$31,400
		255/110 2dr Wgn	$33,800	$56,900	$90,400	$115,000
		255/110 2dr Conv	$20,800	$36,800	$83,400	$111,000
1950	Series 0CM	255/110 2dr Clb Cpe	$11,600	$21,000	$38,600	$51,800
		255/110 4dr Spt Sdn	$8,700	$14,000	$21,700	$29,800
		255/110 2dr Wgn	$35,600	$59,900	$90,400	$115,000
		255/110 2dr Cpe	$11,100	$18,500	$37,800	$49,000
		255/110 2dr Monterey Cpe	$12,300	$21,000	$41,100	$54,000
		255/110 2dr Conv	$20,800	$36,800	$83,400	$111,000
1951	Series 1CM	255/112 2dr Clb Cpe	$11,600	$19,200	$38,700	$51,800
		255/112 4dr Spt Sdn	$8,700	$12,700	$21,700	$29,800
		255/112 2dr Wgn	$33,800	$56,900	$90,400	$115,000
		255/112 2dr Monterey Cpe	$12,200	$20,800	$40,900	$53,700
		255/112 2dr Conv	$20,800	$36,800	$83,400	$111,000
1952	Custom	255/125 4dr Sdn	$5,800	$8,200	$13,300	$17,700
		255/125 4dr Stn Wgn 6P	$17,800	$26,600	$36,500	$57,700
		255/125 4dr Stn Wgn 8P	$16,600	$24,800	$37,000	$49,400
		255/125 2dr Spt Cpe	$10,300	$14,200	$21,800	$31,100
1952	Monterey	255/125 2dr Hdtp Cpe	$11,300	$15,600	$26,500	$37,800
		255/125 4dr Sdn	$5,800	$8,200	$14,200	$22,200
		255/125 2dr Conv	$18,100	$32,100	$75,800	$109,000
1953	Custom	255/125 4dr Sdn	$6,200	$8,400	$13,600	$17,900
		255/125 2dr Spt Cpe	$10,500	$14,200	$21,900	$31,200

Year	Model	Body Style	4	3	2	1
1953	Monterey	255/125 2dr Hdtp Cpe	$11,200	$15,600	$26,500	$37,800
		255/125 4dr Sdn	$6,000	$8,300	$14,200	$22,200
		255/125 4dr Wgn	$18,400	$27,300	$40,900	$54,800
		255/125 2dr Conv	$18,100	$32,100	$75,800	$109,000
1954	Custom	256/161 4dr Sdn	$6,200	$8,400	$13,900	$18,500
		256/161 2dr Spt Cpe	$10,500	$14,200	$22,200	$31,900
1954	Monterey	256/161 2dr Hdtp Cpe	$11,200	$15,600	$26,500	$37,800
		256/161 2dr Sun Valley Hdtp Cpe	$18,200	$33,000	$47,300	$64,500
		256/161 4dr Sdn	$6,100	$8,200	$14,200	$22,200
		256/161 4dr Wgn	$18,400	$27,300	$40,900	$54,800
		256/161 2dr Conv	$18,100	$32,100	$75,800	$109,000
1955	Custom	292/188 4dr Sdn	$5,400	$7,600	$13,000	$17,500
		292/188 4dr Wgn	$18,700	$27,400	$37,600	$59,100
		292/188 2dr Hdtp Cpe	$10,900	$14,600	$24,000	$33,600
1955	Monterey	292/188 2dr Hdtp Cpe	$11,500	$15,300	$23,800	$34,400
		292/188 4dr Sdn	$5,100	$7,300	$12,400	$17,200
		292/188 4dr Wgn	$19,700	$28,800	$42,100	$57,200
1955	Montclair	292/188 2dr Hdtp Cpe	$12,700	$16,500	$24,000	$34,300
		292/188 2dr Sun Valley Hdtp Cpe	$18,300	$36,200	$46,600	$74,700
		292/188 4dr Sdn	$6,200	$8,400	$12,800	$17,600
		292/188 2dr Conv	$22,800	$36,900	$65,300	$93,500
1956	Custom	312/210 4dr Wgn	$18,700	$27,400	$37,600	$59,100
		312/260 4dr Wgn	$23,100	$32,500	$45,300	$70,000
		312/210 2dr Hdtp Cpe	$11,000	$14,600	$24,000	$33,600
		312/260 2dr Hdtp Cpe	$13,800	$18,300	$28,700	$41,100
		312/210 4dr Hdtp Sdn	$5,500	$7,300	$13,000	$17,100
		312/260 4dr Hdtp Sdn	$6,900	$9,200	$16,200	$21,200
		312/210 2dr Conv	$17,800	$29,600	$60,600	$102,000
		312/260 2dr Conv	$22,500	$34,000	$80,400	$116,000
						+15% for factory a/c.
1956	Monterey	312/210 2dr Hdtp Cpe	$13,200	$18,000	$27,900	$39,800
		312/260 2dr Hdtp Cpe	$16,500	$22,500	$35,200	$49,900
		312/225 4dr Spt Sdn	$6,200	$8,500	$14,800	$20,200
		312/210 4dr Wgn	$19,700	$28,800	$42,100	$57,200
		312/260 4dr Wgn	$27,000	$41,800	$55,100	$68,800

Mercury

Year	Model	Body Style	4	3	2	1
		312/210 4dr Phtn Hdtp Sdn	$5,000	$7,000	$11,900	$16,200
		312/260 4dr Phtn Hdtp Sdn	$6,300	$8,600	$14,900	$20,200
						+15% for factory a/c.
1956	Montclair	312/210 2dr Hdtp Cpe	$12,800	$16,800	$24,300	$34,600
		312/260 2dr Hdtp Cpe	$15,900	$21,000	$30,400	$43,300
		312/260 4dr Spt Sdn	$7,900	$10,800	$16,100	$22,000
		312/260 4dr Phtn Hdtp Sdn	$8,400	$11,300	$16,900	$22,900
		312/260 2dr Conv	$36,500	$50,600	$87,600	$117,000
						+15% for factory a/c.
1957	Monterey	312/255 4dr Sdn	$5,500	$7,400	$11,200	$15,500
		368/290 4dr Sdn	$6,100	$8,200	$12,400	$16,900
		368/335 4dr Sdn	$6,400	$8,500	$12,900	$17,800
		312/255 2dr Phtn Cpe	$11,700	$15,100	$21,800	$31,400
		368/290 2dr Phtn Cpe	$12,900	$16,500	$23,900	$34,500
		368/335 2dr Phtn Cpe	$13,500	$17,300	$25,000	$36,000
		312/255 4dr Phtn Sdn	$5,800	$7,800	$12,300	$16,600
		368/290 4dr Phtn Sdn	$6,400	$8,600	$13,400	$18,300
		368/335 4dr Phtn Sdn	$6,600	$9,100	$14,000	$19,200
		368/290 2dr Conv	$23,100	$30,700	$47,500	$68,100
		368/335 2dr Conv	$24,200	$32,000	$49,700	$71,100
						+15% for factory a/c.
1957	Montclair	368/290 2dr Hdtp Cpe	$12,400	$16,100	$23,400	$33,400
		368/290 4dr Sdn	$6,500	$8,700	$13,400	$18,300
		368/290 4dr Hdtp Sdn	$6,500	$8,700	$13,400	$18,300
		368/290 2dr Conv	$20,700	$37,200	$62,400	$103,000
						+15% for factory a/c.
1957	Voyager	312/255 2dr Wgn	$15,100	$18,700	$24,500	$33,900
						+15% for factory a/c.
1957	Turnpike Cruiser	368/290 2dr Hdtp Cpe	$15,600	$25,500	$32,900	$44,500
		368/290 4dr Hdtp Sdn	$11,200	$15,900	$23,600	$32,400
		368/290 2dr Conv	$30,000	$44,000	$67,000	$108,000
		368/290 2dr Indy Pace Car Conv	$41,500	$57,700	$89,800	$135,000
						+15% for factory a/c.

Year	Model	Body Style	4	3	2	1
1957	Colony Park	312/255 4dr Wgn	$14,000	$17,300	$22,500	$30,600
						+15% for factory a/c.
1958	Monterey	383/330 4dr Sdn	$6,400	$8,600	$12,900	$17,900
		430/400 4dr Sdn	$7,100	$9,700	$14,500	$20,200
		383/330 2dr Phtn Cpe	$11,700	$15,400	$22,100	$31,900
		430/400 2dr Phtn Cpe	$15,100	$20,000	$28,700	$41,400
		383/330 4dr Phtn Sdn	$5,800	$7,700	$12,200	$16,300
		430/400 4dr Phtn Sdn	$7,600	$10,100	$15,800	$21,300
		383/330 2dr Conv	$21,300	$28,100	$43,400	$62,600
		430/400 2dr Conv	$27,800	$36,600	$56,400	$81,400
						+15% for factory a/c.
1958	Commuter	383/330 2dr Wgn	$15,300	$19,100	$25,100	$35,300
		383/330 4dr Stn Wgn 6P	$14,600	$18,000	$23,500	$32,000
						+15% for factory a/c.
1958	Montclair	383/330 2dr Phtn Cpe	$11,600	$15,200	$21,800	$31,400
		430/400 2dr Phtn Cpe	$15,000	$19,700	$28,300	$40,800
		383/330 2dr Turnpike Cruiser Hdtp Cpe	$16,400	$28,900	$34,000	$47,000
		430/400 2dr Turnpike Cruiser Hdtp Cpe	$18,600	$32,800	$38,300	$53,200
		383/330 4dr Sdn	$5,800	$7,800	$12,300	$16,700
		430/400 4dr Sdn	$7,700	$10,300	$15,800	$21,800
		383/330 4dr Phtn Sdn	$5,800	$7,800	$12,300	$16,700
		430/400 4dr Phtn Sdn	$7,600	$10,200	$15,800	$21,800
		383/330 4dr Turnpike Cruiser Hdtp Sdn	$10,200	$14,600	$21,600	$29,600
		430/400 4dr Turnpike Cruiser Hdtp Sdn	$11,300	$16,300	$24,600	$33,500
		383/330 2dr Conv	$17,500	$23,200	$33,400	$44,400
		430/400 2dr Conv	$22,600	$29,900	$43,600	$57,600
						+15% for factory a/c.
1958	Park Lane	430/360 2dr Hdtp Cpe	$20,600	$27,100	$38,500	$56,200

Mercury

Year	Model	Body Style	4	3	2	1
		430/400 2dr Hdtp Cpe	$23,300	$30,600	$43,400	$63,600
		430/360 4dr Hdtp Sdn	$14,500	$18,500	$27,900	$38,000
		430/400 4dr Hdtp Sdn	$16,400	$21,000	$31,500	$42,900
		430/360 2dr Conv	$30,700	$41,100	$69,700	$93,700
		430/400 2dr Conv	$31,600	$43,000	$73,300	$121,000
						+15% for factory a/c.
1958	Voyager	383/330 2dr Wgn	$15,200	$18,700	$24,600	$34,100
						+15% for factory a/c.
1959	Monterey	312/210 4dr Sdn	$5,700	$7,600	$11,500	$16,000
		383/280 4dr Sdn	$6,300	$8,400	$12,800	$17,400
		312/210 2dr Hdtp Cpe	$11,600	$15,500	$22,100	$31,900
		383/280 2dr Hdtp Cpe	$12,800	$17,000	$24,200	$35,100
		312/210 4dr Hdtp Sdn	$5,900	$7,900	$12,500	$16,800
		383/280 4dr Hdtp Sdn	$6,600	$8,800	$13,700	$18,500
		312/210 2dr Conv	$21,900	$29,200	$42,900	$62,400
		383/280 2dr Conv	$24,000	$32,100	$47,200	$68,700
						+15% for factory a/c.
1959	Montclair	383/322 2dr Hdtp Cpe	$11,500	$15,300	$21,800	$31,400
		383/322 4dr Sdn	$5,900	$8,000	$12,300	$16,700
		383/322 4dr Hdtp Sdn	$5,800	$7,900	$12,300	$16,700
						+15% for factory a/c.
1959	Park Lane	430/345 2dr Hdtp Cpe	$21,400	$28,300	$40,200	$58,600
		430/345 4dr Hdtp Sdn	$15,100	$19,400	$29,000	$39,600
		430/345 2dr Conv	$37,700	$47,300	$82,000	$143,000
						+15% for factory a/c.
1959	Country Cruiser	383/280 2dr Commuter Wgn	$14,800	$18,000	$24,000	$33,500
		383/280 4dr Commuter Wgn	$14,100	$17,500	$23,000	$31,400
		383/322 4dr Voyager Wgn	$14,100	$17,500	$23,000	$31,100
		383/322 4dr Colony Park Wgn	$14,100	$17,500	$22,800	$31,100
		430/345 4dr Colony Park Wgn	$16,800	$21,100	$27,300	$37,200
						+15% for factory a/c.
1960	Comet	144/90 2dr Sdn	$4,900	$7,200	$9,900	$14,600

Year	Model	Body Style	4	3	2	1
		144/90 4dr Sdn	$4,400	$6,400	$8,800	$13,100
		144/90 2dr Wgn	$5,500	$8,000	$11,200	$15,700
		144/90 4dr Wgn	$5,200	$7,500	$10,600	$15,000
						+15% for factory a/c.
1960	Monterey	312/205 2dr Sdn	$4,000	$5,700	$7,800	$10,600
		383/280 2dr Sdn	$4,400	$6,200	$8,700	$11,600
		312/205 2dr Hdtp Cpe	$4,900	$6,900	$9,700	$14,500
		383/280 2dr Hdtp Cpe	$5,400	$7,600	$10,600	$16,000
		312/205 4dr Hdtp Sdn	$4,100	$5,800	$8,400	$10,900
		383/280 4dr Hdtp Sdn	$4,600	$6,300	$9,300	$11,900
		312/205 2dr Conv	$9,600	$14,000	$19,200	$29,700
		383/280 2dr Conv	$10,700	$14,900	$21,200	$32,700
						+15% for factory a/c.
1960	Montclair	430/310 2dr Hdtp Cpe	$5,000	$7,200	$10,100	$14,800
		430/310 4dr Sdn	$3,600	$4,900	$7,100	$9,600
		430/310 4dr Hdtp Sdn	$3,700	$5,200	$7,200	$9,900
						+15% for factory a/c.
1960	Park Lane	430/310 2dr Hdtp Cpe	$5,900	$8,500	$12,000	$17,700
		430/310 4dr Hdtp Sdn	$5,100	$6,800	$9,700	$13,400
		430/310 2dr Conv	$32,700	$45,700	$79,200	$140,000
						+15% for factory a/c.
1960	Commuter	312/205 4dr Wgn	$4,500	$6,300	$9,000	$12,200
		383/280 4dr Wgn	$4,900	$6,900	$9,800	$13,300
						+15% for factory a/c.
1961	Comet	144/85 2dr Sdn	$4,900	$7,500	$10,600	$14,300
		144/85 2dr S-22 Sdn	$5,200	$8,000	$11,100	$14,500
		144/85 4dr Sdn	$3,900	$5,900	$8,900	$11,400
		144/85 2dr Wgn	$4,300	$6,300	$9,500	$12,800
		144/85 4dr Wgn	$4,100	$5,900	$9,400	$12,000
						+15% for factory a/c.
1961	Meteor	223/135 4dr 800 Sdn	$3,700	$5,100	$8,200	$9,800
		292/175 4dr 800 Sdn	$3,900	$5,400	$8,600	$10,400
		223/135 2dr 800 Hdtp Cpe	$4,500	$6,100	$9,100	$11,900
		292/175 2dr 800 Hdtp Cpe	$4,700	$6,400	$9,500	$12,500
						+15% for factory a/c.

Mercury

Year	Model	Body Style	4	3	2	1
1961	Colony Park	292/175 4dr Wgn	$14,400	$18,700	$25,500	$32,700
						+15% for factory a/c.
1961	Monterey	292/175 2dr Hdtp Cpe	$5,100	$7,100	$10,200	$13,200
		352/220 2dr Hdtp Cpe	$5,600	$7,800	$11,200	$14,600
		390/300 2dr Hdtp Cpe	$6,100	$8,400	$12,200	$15,800
		292/175 4dr Sdn	$4,100	$5,700	$8,500	$10,900
		352/220 4dr Sdn	$4,900	$6,800	$10,100	$13,000
		390/300 4dr Sdn	$4,100	$5,700	$8,500	$10,900
		292/175 4dr Hdtp Sdn	$4,300	$5,900	$8,700	$11,200
		352/220 4dr Hdtp Sdn	$4,700	$6,500	$9,600	$12,300
		390/300 4dr Hdtp Sdn	$5,100	$7,000	$10,400	$13,300
		292/175 2dr Conv	$9,400	$12,900	$18,800	$25,000
		352/220 2dr Conv	$10,300	$14,200	$20,700	$27,500
		390/300 2dr Conv	$11,400	$15,600	$22,800	$30,100
						+15% for factory a/c.
1961	Commuter	223/135 4dr Wgn	$14,300	$19,000	$26,100	$33,700
		292/175 4dr Wgn	$14,900	$20,000	$27,300	$35,200
						+15% for factory a/c.
1962	Comet	144/85 2dr Sdn	$5,700	$8,200	$11,400	$15,100
		144/85 2dr S-22 Sdn	$5,800	$8,500	$11,700	$16,300
		144/85 4dr Sdn	$4,900	$6,600	$9,600	$12,300
		144/85 2dr Wgn	$4,800	$6,600	$10,000	$13,300
		144/85 4dr Wgn	$4,700	$6,300	$9,600	$12,800
						+15% for factory a/c.
1962	Meteor	170/101 2dr Sdn	$4,500	$5,800	$8,800	$11,500
		221/145 2dr Sdn	$4,700	$6,100	$9,200	$12,000
		260/164 2dr Sdn	$5,100	$6,700	$10,100	$13,100
		170/101 2dr S-33 Sdn	$5,200	$6,800	$10,300	$13,500
		221/145 2dr S-33 Sdn	$5,400	$7,100	$10,800	$14,100
		260/164 2dr S-33 Sdn	$5,900	$7,900	$11,800	$15,500
		170/101 4dr Sdn	$4,200	$5,300	$8,200	$10,600
		221/145 4dr Sdn	$4,400	$5,600	$8,600	$11,100
		260/164 4dr Sdn	$4,800	$6,100	$9,400	$12,100
						+15% for factory a/c.
1962	Monterey	223/138 4dr Sdn	$4,100	$5,500	$8,300	$10,600
		292/170 4dr Sdn	$4,300	$5,800	$8,700	$11,100
		352/220 4dr Sdn	$4,700	$6,300	$9,500	$12,100

Year	Model	Body Style	4	3	2	1
		390/300 4dr Sdn	$5,100	$6,800	$10,300	$13,100
		390/330 4dr Sdn	$5,300	$7,100	$10,700	$13,600
		406/385 4dr Sdn	$5,900	$7,800	$11,900	$15,200
		406/405 4dr Sdn	$6,300	$8,400	$12,600	$16,300
		223/138 4dr Commuter Wgn	$15,500	$20,300	$27,800	$37,600
		223/138 4dr Colony Park Wgn	$15,200	$19,700	$26,700	$35,700
		223/138 2dr Hdtp Cpe	$5,100	$7,100	$10,200	$13,400
		292/170 2dr Hdtp Cpe	$5,300	$7,400	$10,700	$14,000
		352/220 2dr Hdtp Cpe	$5,800	$8,100	$11,600	$15,400
		390/300 2dr Hdtp Cpe	$6,300	$8,700	$12,700	$16,800
		390/330 2dr Hdtp Cpe	$6,600	$9,300	$13,100	$17,500
		406/385 2dr Hdtp Cpe	$7,800	$10,800	$15,500	$20,600
		406/405 2dr Hdtp Cpe	$8,200	$11,600	$16,700	$22,000
		390/300 2dr S-55 Hdtp Cpe	$6,000	$8,300	$12,000	$16,000
		390/330 2dr S-55 Hdtp Cpe	$7,800	$10,800	$15,500	$20,800
		406/385 2dr S-55 Hdtp Cpe	$9,400	$12,600	$18,600	$25,200
		406/405 2dr S-55 Hdtp Cpe	$9,900	$13,400	$19,800	$27,000
		223/138 4dr Hdtp Sdn	$4,400	$5,900	$8,900	$11,400
		292/170 4dr Hdtp Sdn	$4,600	$6,200	$9,300	$11,900
		352/220 4dr Hdtp Sdn	$5,000	$6,700	$10,200	$13,000
		390/300 4dr Hdtp Sdn	$5,500	$7,300	$11,000	$14,200
		390/330 4dr Hdtp Sdn	$5,700	$7,600	$11,500	$14,700
		406/385 4dr Hdtp Sdn	$6,300	$8,400	$12,700	$16,500
		406/405 4dr Hdtp Sdn	$6,800	$9,100	$13,700	$17,500
		390/300 2dr S-55 Conv	$11,700	$15,700	$23,400	$31,000
		390/330 2dr S-55 Conv	$15,100	$20,200	$30,400	$40,200
		406/385 2dr S-55 Conv	$17,000	$22,600	$33,800	$44,900
		406/405 2dr S-55 Conv	$18,100	$24,200	$36,000	$48,000

Mercury

Mercury

Year	Model	Body Style	4	3	2	1
						+15% for factory a/c.
1963	Comet	144/85 2dr Sdn	$5,600	$8,400	$11,900	$15,800
		170/101 2dr Sdn	$5,900	$8,800	$12,500	$16,500
		260/164 2dr Sdn	$6,100	$9,100	$13,000	$17,400
		144/85 4dr Sdn	$4,700	$6,500	$9,900	$12,600
		170/101 4dr Sdn	$4,900	$6,800	$10,400	$13,200
		260/164 4dr Sdn	$5,100	$7,200	$10,700	$14,000
		144/85 2dr Wgn	$4,600	$6,500	$10,200	$13,700
		170/101 2dr Wgn	$4,800	$6,900	$10,600	$14,300
		260/164 2dr Wgn	$5,000	$7,400	$11,200	$15,000
		144/85 4dr Wgn	$4,400	$6,400	$9,900	$12,900
		170/101 4dr Wgn	$4,600	$6,800	$10,300	$13,800
		260/164 4dr Wgn	$4,800	$7,000	$10,900	$14,200
		170/101 2dr S-22 Hdtp Cpe	$6,800	$9,700	$13,900	$18,300
		260/164 2dr S-22 Hdtp Cpe	$7,100	$10,200	$14,700	$19,100
		144/85 2dr Cstm Conv	$6,900	$10,400	$15,000	$19,200
		170/101 2dr Cstm Conv	$7,200	$10,900	$15,800	$20,200
		260/164 2dr Cstm Conv	$7,700	$11,400	$16,600	$21,100
		170/101 2dr S-22 Conv	$9,600	$13,000	$18,800	$24,700
		260/164 2dr S-22 Conv	$10,000	$13,500	$19,600	$26,000
						+15% for factory a/c.
1963	Meteor	200/116 2dr Sdn	$2,500	$3,600	$5,400	$7,000
		221/145 2dr Sdn	$2,600	$3,800	$5,700	$7,300
		260/164 2dr Sdn	$2,800	$4,000	$5,900	$7,800
		200/116 4dr Sdn	$4,000	$5,400	$8,400	$10,700
		221/145 4dr Sdn	$4,200	$5,700	$8,800	$11,200
		260/164 4dr Sdn	$4,400	$5,900	$9,200	$11,700
		200/116 4dr Wgn	$4,000	$5,400	$8,300	$10,700
		221/145 4dr Wgn	$4,100	$5,700	$8,700	$11,200
		260/164 4dr Wgn	$4,300	$5,900	$9,100	$11,700
		200/116 2dr S-33 Hdtp Cpe	$5,300	$7,400	$10,900	$14,300
		221/145 2dr S-33 Hdtp Cpe	$5,600	$7,800	$11,400	$15,000
		260/164 2dr S-33 Hdtp Cpe	$5,800	$8,100	$11,900	$15,600
						+15% for factory a/c.
1963	Monterey	390/250 2dr Sdn	$4,800	$6,600	$9,800	$12,900
		390/300 2dr Sdn	$6,000	$8,200	$12,200	$16,100
		390/330 2dr Sdn	$6,200	$8,600	$12,700	$16,800
		406/385 2dr Sdn	$7,000	$9,500	$14,100	$18,700
		406/405 2dr Sdn	$7,400	$10,200	$15,000	$19,900
		390/250 4dr Sdn	$4,000	$5,400	$8,200	$10,700

Year	Model	Body Style	4	3	2	1
		390/300 4dr Sdn	$5,000	$6,700	$10,200	$13,300
		390/330 4dr Sdn	$5,200	$7,000	$10,600	$13,800
		406/385 4dr Sdn	$5,800	$7,800	$11,800	$15,300
		406/405 4dr Sdn	$6,200	$8,300	$12,500	$16,500
		390/250 4dr Colony Park Stn Wgn 6P	$15,100	$19,800	$27,100	$36,100
		390/300 4dr Colony Park Stn Wgn 6P	$18,900	$24,800	$33,700	$45,100
		390/330 4dr Colony Park Stn Wgn 6P	$19,700	$25,700	$35,100	$46,800
		406/385 4dr Colony Park Stn Wgn 6P	$21,900	$28,700	$39,200	$52,300
		406/405 4dr Colony Park Stn Wgn 6P	$23,500	$30,800	$41,900	$55,900
		390/300 2dr S-55 Hdtp Cpe	$7,600	$10,300	$15,200	$20,300
		390/330 2dr S-55 Hdtp Cpe	$7,800	$10,600	$15,800	$21,000
		406/385 2dr S-55 Hdtp Cpe	$9,400	$12,500	$18,700	$25,000
		406/405 2dr S-55 Hdtp Cpe	$10,000	$13,400	$20,000	$26,700
		390/250 2dr Marauder Fstbk Cpe	$5,400	$7,400	$11,200	$14,700
		390/300 2dr Marauder Fstbk Cpe	$6,800	$9,200	$14,000	$18,400
		390/300 2dr S-55 Marauder Fstbk Cpe	$8,500	$12,100	$18,000	$23,500
		390/330 2dr S-55 Marauder Fstbk Cpe	$9,000	$12,500	$18,600	$24,500
		406/385 2dr S-55 Marauder Fstbk Cpe	$10,600	$15,000	$21,900	$28,900
		406/405 2dr S-55 Marauder Fstbk Cpe	$11,400	$16,000	$23,500	$30,900
		390/250 4dr Hdtp Sdn	$4,300	$5,800	$8,700	$11,400
		390/300 4dr Hdtp Sdn	$5,400	$7,200	$10,800	$14,100
		390/330 4dr Hdtp Sdn	$5,600	$7,500	$11,200	$14,700

Mercury

Year	Model	Body Style	4	3	2	1
		406/385 4dr Hdtp Sdn	$6,200	$8,400	$12,500	$16,500
		406/405 4dr Hdtp Sdn	$6,700	$8,900	$13,300	$17,600
		390/250 2dr Cstm Conv	$10,600	$14,400	$21,200	$27,800
		390/300 2dr Cstm Conv	$13,300	$17,800	$26,700	$34,700
		390/330 2dr Cstm Conv	$13,800	$18,500	$27,700	$36,200
		406/385 2dr Cstm Conv	$15,300	$20,700	$30,800	$40,300
		406/405 2dr Cstm Conv	$16,400	$22,100	$32,900	$43,000
		390/300 2dr S-55 Conv	$14,500	$19,300	$28,800	$38,100
		390/330 2dr S-55 Conv	$15,100	$20,000	$30,000	$39,600
		406/385 2dr S-55 Conv	$16,800	$22,500	$33,400	$44,300
		406/405 2dr S-55 Conv	$18,000	$23,900	$35,500	$47,200
						+15% for factory a/c.
1964	Comet	170/101 2dr 202 Sdn	$4,300	$5,900	$8,600	$11,400
		170/101 4dr 202 Sdn	$3,900	$5,400	$8,000	$10,300
		170/101 4dr 202 Wgn	$4,500	$6,100	$9,300	$12,400
						+15% for factory a/c.
1964	Comet Caliente	170/101 2dr Hdtp Cpe	$6,300	$9,300	$13,900	$17,100
		170/101 4dr Sdn	$5,900	$8,300	$12,500	$15,700
		170/101 2dr Conv	$10,000	$14,600	$21,000	$27,100
						+15% for factory a/c.
1964	Comet Cyclone	289/210 2dr Hdtp Cpe	$13,100	$17,600	$26,900	$36,500
		289/271 2dr Hdtp Cpe	$22,800	$39,300	$50,600	$76,000
						+15% for factory a/c.
1964	Monterey	390/250 2dr Sdn	$6,500	$9,000	$13,200	$17,400
		390/300 2dr Sdn	$8,100	$11,200	$16,600	$21,700
		390/330 2dr Sdn	$8,600	$11,700	$17,300	$22,600
		427/410 2dr Sdn	$10,800	$15,000	$22,000	$28,800
		427/425 2dr Sdn	$11,200	$15,400	$22,600	$29,700
		390/250 4dr Sdn	$3,800	$5,100	$7,900	$10,100
		390/300 4dr Sdn	$4,800	$6,400	$9,800	$12,500
		390/330 4dr Sdn	$4,900	$6,600	$10,200	$13,000
		427/410 4dr Sdn	$6,300	$8,400	$12,800	$16,500
		427/425 4dr Sdn	$6,500	$8,600	$13,200	$17,000

Year	Model	Body Style	4	3	2	1
		390/250 2dr Marauder Hdtp Cpe	$7,300	$10,000	$15,100	$20,000
		390/300 2dr Marauder Hdtp Cpe	$9,200	$12,600	$19,000	$25,100
		390/330 2dr Marauder Hdtp Cpe	$9,600	$13,000	$19,700	$26,000
		427/410 2dr Marauder Hdtp Cpe	$12,900	$17,600	$26,600	$35,100
		427/425 2dr Marauder Hdtp Cpe	$13,200	$18,200	$27,400	$36,100
		390/250 2dr Conv	$9,300	$12,400	$18,300	$24,000
		390/300 2dr Conv	$11,400	$15,600	$23,100	$30,100
		390/330 2dr Conv	$11,900	$16,200	$24,000	$31,200
		427/410 2dr Conv	$15,100	$20,400	$30,400	$39,600
		427/425 2dr Conv	$15,600	$21,000	$31,300	$40,700
					+15% for factory a/c.	
1964	Montclair	390/250 2dr Hdtp Cpe	$6,200	$8,500	$12,700	$16,400
		390/266 2dr Hdtp Cpe	$7,400	$10,200	$15,300	$19,600
		390/300 2dr Hdtp Cpe	$7,800	$10,600	$15,900	$20,500
		390/330 2dr Hdtp Cpe	$8,100	$11,100	$16,600	$21,300
		427/410 2dr Hdtp Cpe	$10,200	$14,100	$21,000	$27,100
		427/425 2dr Hdtp Cpe	$10,500	$14,600	$21,800	$27,900
		390/250 2dr Marauder Hdtp Cpe	$7,500	$10,200	$15,000	$19,900
		390/266 2dr Marauder Hdtp Cpe	$9,100	$12,200	$18,100	$24,000
		390/300 2dr Marauder Hdtp Cpe	$9,500	$12,900	$18,800	$25,000
		390/330 2dr Marauder Hdtp Cpe	$9,900	$13,400	$19,500	$26,100
		427/410 2dr Marauder Hdtp Cpe	$12,400	$16,800	$24,900	$33,000

Mercury

Year	Model	Body Style	4	3	2	1
		427/425 2dr Marauder Hdtp Cpe	$12,800	$17,300	$25,800	$34,000
		390/250 4dr Sdn	$4,700	$6,400	$9,400	$12,600
		390/266 4dr Sdn	$5,700	$7,600	$11,300	$15,100
		390/300 4dr Sdn	$5,900	$7,900	$11,800	$15,700
		390/330 4dr Sdn	$6,100	$8,300	$12,200	$16,400
		427/410 4dr Sdn	$7,700	$10,500	$15,500	$20,800
		427/425 4dr Sdn	$8,000	$10,900	$16,000	$21,400
						+15% for factory a/c.
1964	Parklane	390/300 2dr Hdtp Cpe	$6,800	$9,500	$15,100	$19,800
		390/330 2dr Hdtp Cpe	$7,100	$9,800	$15,800	$20,700
		427/410 2dr Hdtp Cpe	$9,000	$12,500	$19,900	$26,300
		427/425 2dr Hdtp Cpe	$9,300	$12,900	$20,600	$27,100
		390/300 4dr Sdn	$5,100	$6,700	$10,700	$13,900
		390/330 4dr Sdn	$5,300	$7,000	$11,100	$14,500
		427/410 4dr Sdn	$6,700	$8,900	$14,100	$18,400
		427/425 4dr Sdn	$6,900	$9,200	$14,500	$18,900
		390/300 2dr Conv	$11,600	$19,700	$31,600	$41,700
		390/330 2dr Conv	$12,000	$20,300	$32,700	$43,200
		427/410 2dr Conv	$15,300	$25,600	$41,500	$54,600
		427/425 2dr Conv	$15,800	$26,500	$42,800	$56,200
						+15% for factory a/c.
1965	Comet	200/120 2dr 202 Sdn	$4,400	$6,100	$8,800	$12,000
		200/120 4dr 202 Sdn	$4,100	$5,500	$8,100	$10,800
		200/120 4dr 202 Wgn	$4,500	$6,300	$9,500	$13,200
						+25% for 289/200 V8. +15% for factory a/c.
1965	Comet Caliente	200/120 2dr Hdtp Cpe	$6,600	$9,600	$13,300	$18,200
		200/120 4dr Sdn	$6,200	$8,900	$12,900	$17,600
		200/120 2dr Conv	$9,900	$14,100	$19,800	$26,800
						+25% for 289/200 V8. +15% for factory a/c.
1965	Comet Cyclone	289/225 2dr Hdtp Cpe	$19,900	$28,100	$42,500	$60,300
						+15% for factory a/c.
1965	Monterey	390/250 2dr Sdn	$6,500	$9,000	$13,200	$17,400
		390/300 2dr Sdn	$8,100	$11,200	$16,600	$21,700
		390/330 2dr Sdn	$8,600	$11,700	$17,300	$22,600
		427/425 2dr Sdn	$11,200	$15,400	$22,600	$29,700
		390/250 4dr Sdn	$3,900	$5,200	$8,000	$10,300
		390/300 4dr Sdn	$4,900	$6,500	$9,900	$12,800
		390/330 4dr Sdn	$5,100	$6,700	$10,300	$13,200

Year	Model	Body Style	4	3	2	1
		427/425 4dr Sdn	$6,600	$8,800	$13,400	$17,400
		390/330 2dr Marauder Fstbk Cpe	$9,300	$13,000	$19,100	$25,400
		390/300 2dr Marauder Hdtp Cpe	$9,000	$12,300	$18,400	$24,500
		390/300 4dr Marauder Hdtp Cpe	$8,100	$11,200	$16,900	$21,700
		390/330 4dr Marauder Hdtp Cpe	$8,400	$11,600	$17,500	$22,600
		390/250 2dr Conv	$10,900	$18,100	$28,500	$38,400
		390/300 2dr Conv	$13,500	$23,000	$35,900	$48,200
		390/330 2dr Conv	$14,000	$23,900	$37,200	$50,100
		427/425 2dr Conv	$18,400	$30,800	$48,700	$65,000
						+15% for factory a/c.
1965	Commuter	390/250 4dr Wgn	$16,300	$21,200	$29,100	$38,300
						+15% for factory a/c.
1965	Montclair	390/250 2dr Marauder Hdtp Cpe	$7,500	$10,300	$15,200	$20,200
		390/300 2dr Marauder Hdtp Cpe	$9,500	$13,100	$19,000	$25,400
		390/330 2dr Marauder Hdtp Cpe	$9,900	$13,600	$19,700	$26,500
		427/425 2dr Marauder Hdtp Cpe	$12,900	$17,500	$26,100	$34,500
		390/250 4dr Marauder Hdtp Sdn	$6,500	$9,000	$13,200	$18,000
		390/300 4dr Marauder Hdtp Sdn	$8,100	$11,300	$16,700	$22,500
		390/330 4dr Marauder Hdtp Sdn	$8,500	$11,700	$17,300	$23,500
		427/425 4dr Marauder Hdtp Sdn	$11,100	$15,500	$22,600	$30,700
						+15% for factory a/c.
1965	Colony Park	390/250 4dr Wgn	$13,900	$19,700	$27,200	$35,000
						+15% for factory a/c.
1965	Parklane	390/330 2dr Fstbk Cpe	$8,400	$11,300	$18,300	$24,400

Mercury

Year	Model	Body Style	4	3	2	1
		390/330 4dr Fstbk Cpe	$5,700	$7,900	$12,700	$16,700
		390/300 2dr Marauder Hdtp Cpe	$8,000	$10,900	$17,600	$23,500
		390/330 4dr Hdtp Sdn	$4,300	$5,600	$9,000	$11,800
		390/300 4dr Breezeway Hdtp Sdn	$5,300	$7,000	$11,200	$14,600
		390/330 4dr Breezeway Hdtp Sdn	$5,600	$7,200	$11,600	$15,200
		390/300 4dr Marauder Hdtp Sdn	$7,400	$10,200	$16,000	$20,800
		390/330 4dr Marauder Hdtp Sdn	$7,700	$10,600	$16,600	$21,600
		390/300 2dr Conv	$12,800	$21,200	$34,200	$46,100
		390/330 2dr Conv	$13,500	$22,100	$35,600	$47,800
		427/425 2dr Conv	$17,500	$28,900	$46,600	$62,600
						+15% for factory a/c.
1966	Comet	200/120 2dr 202 Sdn	$4,600	$6,400	$10,000	$13,400
		289/200 2dr 202 Sdn	$5,600	$7,400	$11,600	$15,500
		200/120 4dr 202 Sdn	$4,100	$5,800	$9,200	$12,100
		289/200 4dr 202 Sdn	$4,700	$6,600	$10,500	$13,800
						+15% for factory a/c.
1966	Comet Capri	200/120 2dr Hdtp Cpe	$5,900	$8,100	$12,200	$16,100
		289/200 2dr Hdtp Cpe	$6,700	$9,500	$14,000	$18,600
		200/120 4dr Sdn	$5,000	$6,900	$10,300	$13,500
		289/200 4dr Sdn	$5,900	$7,800	$11,800	$15,500
						+15% for factory a/c.
1966	Comet Caliente	200/120 2dr Hdtp Cpe	$6,600	$10,000	$14,300	$18,000
		289/200 2dr Hdtp Cpe	$7,700	$11,400	$16,500	$20,700
		200/120 4dr Sdn	$5,800	$8,600	$12,700	$16,100
		289/200 4dr Sdn	$6,700	$10,000	$14,500	$18,600
		200/120 2dr Conv	$10,900	$15,500	$22,200	$27,400
		289/200 2dr Conv	$12,500	$17,900	$25,500	$31,800
						+15% for factory a/c.

Year	Model	Body Style	4	3	2	1
1966	Comet Cyclone	289/200 2dr Hdtp Cpe	$7,800	$11,300	$15,900	$21,600
		390/265 2dr Hdtp Cpe	$10,100	$14,200	$20,800	$27,100
		390/275 2dr Hdtp Cpe	$10,200	$14,500	$21,600	$28,900
		390/335 2dr GT Hdtp Cpe	$12,000	$16,600	$22,900	$30,800
		289/200 2dr Conv	$12,900	$18,100	$24,900	$33,000
		390/265 2dr Conv	$15,200	$21,300	$30,500	$40,700
		390/275 2dr Conv	$15,800	$21,600	$31,300	$42,000
		390/335 2dr GT Conv	$16,800	$23,000	$32,700	$42,100
						+15% for factory a/c.
1966	Monterey	390/265 4dr Sdn	$3,800	$5,100	$7,800	$10,100
		390/275 4dr Sdn	$4,000	$5,400	$8,200	$10,600
		410/330 4dr Sdn	$4,800	$6,400	$9,700	$12,500
		428/345 4dr Sdn	$5,100	$6,900	$10,400	$13,500
		390/265 2dr Hdtp Cpe	$6,000	$8,400	$12,300	$16,400
		390/275 2dr Hdtp Cpe	$6,300	$8,800	$12,900	$17,200
		410/330 2dr Hdtp Cpe	$7,500	$10,500	$15,500	$20,400
		428/345 2dr Hdtp Cpe	$8,100	$11,300	$16,700	$22,000
		390/265 4dr Hdtp Sdn	$4,000	$5,400	$8,200	$10,700
		390/275 4dr Hdtp Sdn	$4,200	$5,700	$8,600	$11,200
		410/330 4dr Hdtp Sdn	$5,000	$6,700	$10,200	$13,300
		428/345 4dr Hdtp Sdn	$5,400	$7,300	$11,000	$14,300
		390/265 2dr Conv	$10,000	$16,800	$26,800	$35,600
		390/275 2dr Conv	$10,600	$17,700	$28,100	$37,800
		410/330 2dr Conv	$12,700	$21,200	$33,600	$44,800
		428/345 2dr Conv	$13,700	$23,000	$36,300	$48,500
						+15% for factory a/c.
1966	Commuter	390/265 4dr Wgn	$16,300	$21,200	$29,100	$38,300
						+15% for factory a/c.
1966	Montclair	390/265 2dr Hdtp Cpe	$6,100	$8,500	$12,500	$16,500
		390/275 2dr Hdtp Cpe	$6,400	$8,900	$13,100	$17,300
		410/330 2dr Hdtp Cpe	$7,600	$10,600	$15,800	$20,600
		428/345 2dr Hdtp Cpe	$8,200	$11,400	$17,000	$22,100

Mercury

Year	Model	Body Style	4	3	2	1
		390/265 4dr Hdtp Sdn	$4,400	$5,800	$8,800	$11,800
		390/275 4dr Hdtp Sdn	$4,600	$6,100	$9,200	$12,400
		410/330 4dr Hdtp Sdn	$5,500	$7,300	$11,000	$14,600
		428/345 4dr Hdtp Sdn	$6,000	$7,700	$11,800	$15,800
					+15% for factory a/c.	
1966	Colony Park	390/265 4dr Stn Wgn 6P	$13,900	$19,700	$27,000	$35,000
					+15% for factory a/c.	
1966	S-55	428/345 2dr Hdtp Cpe	$6,900	$9,800	$14,900	$20,700
		428/345 2dr Conv	$9,700	$15,000	$25,600	$34,500
					+15% for factory a/c.	
1966	Parklane	410/330 2dr Hdtp Cpe	$5,500	$7,700	$12,300	$16,400
		428/345 2dr Hdtp Cpe	$7,500	$10,400	$16,700	$22,000
		410/330 4dr Hdtp Sdn	$4,100	$5,400	$8,700	$11,300
		428/345 4dr Hdtp Sdn	$5,500	$7,300	$11,600	$15,100
		410/330 2dr Conv	$9,200	$15,300	$24,800	$33,200
		428/345 2dr Conv	$12,400	$20,900	$33,700	$44,800
					+15% for factory a/c.	
1967	Comet	200/120 2dr 202 Sdn	$4,600	$6,200	$10,000	$13,200
		289/200 2dr 202 Sdn	$5,100	$6,900	$11,000	$14,600
		200/120 4dr 202 Sdn	$4,000	$5,600	$9,000	$12,100
		289/200 4dr 202 Sdn	$4,400	$6,100	$10,000	$13,100
		289/200 4dr Voyager Wgn	$16,800	$21,500	$30,700	$39,700
		289/200 4dr Villager Wgn	$16,700	$20,900	$29,800	$38,100
					+15% for factory a/c.	
1967	Caliente	200/120 2dr Hdtp Cpe	$6,600	$9,900	$14,500	$20,900
		289/200 2dr Hdtp Cpe	$7,200	$11,000	$16,100	$23,100
		200/120 4dr Sdn	$5,500	$8,000	$12,300	$16,100
		289/200 4dr Sdn	$6,100	$8,800	$13,700	$17,700
		200/120 2dr Conv	$10,300	$15,300	$24,200	$32,100
		289/200 2dr Conv	$11,400	$16,800	$26,700	$35,300
					+15% for factory a/c.	

Year	Model	Body Style	4	3	2	1
1967	Cyclone	289/200 2dr Hdtp Cpe	$7,600	$10,800	$16,800	$23,300
		390/270 2dr Hdtp Cpe	$9,500	$13,500	$21,100	$29,200
		390/320 2dr GT Hdtp Cpe	$11,100	$15,500	$24,500	$33,800
		289/200 2dr Conv	$12,100	$16,600	$26,400	$36,100
		390/270 2dr Conv	$15,000	$20,600	$33,000	$45,300
		390/320 2dr GT Conv	$15,400	$21,400	$33,900	$47,100
						+15% for factory a/c.
1967	Cougar	289/200 2dr Hdtp Cpe	$8,500	$11,300	$18,200	$23,100
		289/225 2dr Hdtp Cpe	$9,700	$13,600	$20,700	$26,500
		390/320 2dr Hdtp Cpe	$11,600	$16,000	$25,000	$31,200
		390/320 2dr GT Hdtp Cpe	$13,900	$18,500	$27,600	$35,400
		289/200 2dr XR-7 Hdtp Cpe	$10,100	$13,800	$20,500	$26,300
		289/225 2dr XR-7 Hdtp Cpe	$11,800	$15,600	$23,700	$30,200
						+15% for factory a/c.
1967	Monterey	410/330 2dr Hdtp Cpe	$7,600	$10,600	$15,800	$20,500
		428/345 2dr Hdtp Cpe	$8,800	$12,200	$18,300	$23,600
		428/360 2dr Hdtp Cpe	$9,200	$12,800	$18,800	$24,800
		410/330 4dr Sdn	$4,600	$6,400	$9,600	$12,500
		428/345 4dr Sdn	$5,400	$7,400	$11,300	$14,500
		428/360 4dr Sdn	$5,600	$7,600	$11,800	$15,500
		410/330 2dr Conv	$12,600	$21,200	$33,600	$44,800
		428/345 2dr Conv	$14,700	$24,400	$38,700	$51,800
		428/360 2dr Conv	$15,500	$25,600	$39,700	$53,000
						+15% for factory a/c.
1967	Montclair	410/330 2dr Hdtp Cpe	$7,600	$10,700	$16,000	$20,600
		428/345 2dr Hdtp Cpe	$8,500	$12,100	$18,200	$23,600
		428/360 2dr Hdtp Cpe	$8,900	$12,500	$18,600	$24,100
		410/330 4dr Sdn	$5,400	$7,300	$11,000	$14,500
		428/345 4dr Sdn	$6,300	$8,300	$12,700	$17,200
		428/360 4dr Sdn	$6,500	$8,600	$13,300	$18,000
						+15% for factory a/c.
1967	Parklane	410/330 2dr Hdtp Cpe	$5,500	$7,700	$12,300	$16,400

Mercury

Year	Model	Body Style	4	3	2	1
		428/345 2dr Hdtp Cpe	$8,000	$11,200	$18,000	$23,800
		428/360 2dr Hdtp Cpe	$8,300	$11,800	$18,700	$24,600
		428/345 4dr Breezeway Sdn	$5,800	$7,700	$12,400	$16,300
		428/360 4dr Breezeway Sdn	$6,000	$8,200	$13,000	$16,900
		410/330 4dr Hdtp Sdn	$4,000	$5,400	$8,600	$11,200
		410/330 4dr Brghm Hdtp Sdn	$5,600	$7,700	$11,800	$15,700
		428/345 4dr Brghm Hdtp Sdn	$8,200	$11,200	$17,200	$23,100
		428/360 4dr Brghm Hdtp Sdn	$8,500	$11,600	$17,900	$23,900
		410/330 2dr Conv	$9,000	$15,300	$25,100	$33,400
		428/345 2dr Conv	$13,200	$22,100	$36,900	$48,000
		428/360 2dr Conv	$13,600	$22,900	$37,600	$50,000
						+15% for factory a/c.
1967	Marquis	410/330 2dr Hdtp Cpe	$5,800	$7,800	$12,200	$16,200
		428/345 2dr Hdtp Cpe	$8,300	$11,400	$17,800	$23,600
		428/360 2dr Hdtp Cpe	$8,700	$11,800	$18,500	$24,800
						+15% for factory a/c.
1968	Comet	200/115 2dr Hdtp Cpe	$4,200	$5,900	$8,800	$12,000
		302/210 2dr Hdtp Cpe	$4,600	$6,700	$9,700	$13,100
		302/230 2dr Hdtp Cpe	$5,000	$7,300	$10,500	$14,300
		390/265 2dr Hdtp Cpe	$4,900	$7,000	$10,100	$13,800
		390/335 2dr Hdtp Cpe	$5,900	$8,400	$12,200	$16,800
		427/390 2dr Hdtp Cpe	$6,500	$9,000	$13,100	$17,900
						+15% for factory a/c.
1968	Montego	302/210 2dr MX Conv	$10,700	$18,200	$27,900	$37,000
		302/230 2dr MX Conv	$11,600	$19,800	$30,300	$40,400
		390/265 2dr MX Conv	$11,200	$18,900	$29,100	$38,900
		390/335 2dr MX Conv	$13,700	$23,000	$35,200	$47,400
						+15% for factory a/c.

Year	Model	Body Style	4	3	2	1
1968	Cyclone	302/210 2dr Hdtp Cpe	$8,100	$11,400	$17,000	$23,300
		302/230 2dr Hdtp Cpe	$8,900	$12,400	$18,600	$25,500
		390/265 2dr Hdtp Cpe	$8,500	$11,900	$17,800	$24,300
		390/335 2dr Hdtp Cpe	$10,500	$14,500	$21,600	$29,800
		427/390 2dr Hdtp Cpe	$11,200	$15,700	$23,100	$31,900
		428/335 CJ 2dr Hdtp Cpe	$15,400	$21,300	$32,000	$44,400
		302/210 2dr GT Hdtp Cpe	$11,600	$16,300	$24,300	$34,000
		302/230 2dr GT Hdtp Cpe	$12,500	$17,700	$26,700	$37,000
		390/265 2dr GT Hdtp Cpe	$12,100	$17,100	$25,400	$35,400
		390/335 2dr GT Hdtp Cpe	$14,700	$20,700	$31,100	$43,300
		427/390 2dr GT Hdtp Cpe	$15,600	$22,200	$33,300	$46,300
		302/210 2dr Fstbk Cpe	$9,000	$12,900	$19,000	$26,600
		302/230 2dr Fstbk Cpe	$9,900	$14,100	$20,600	$29,000
		390/265 2dr Fstbk Cpe	$9,400	$13,500	$19,800	$27,800
		390/335 2dr Fstbk Cpe	$11,600	$16,400	$24,000	$33,800
		427/390 2dr Fstbk Cpe	$12,500	$17,500	$25,900	$36,300
		428/335 CJ 2dr Fstbk Cpe	$16,700	$23,700	$35,400	$49,300
		302/210 2dr GT Fstbk Cpe	$11,800	$16,500	$24,800	$34,500
		302/230 2dr GT Fstbk Cpe	$12,700	$17,800	$27,100	$37,700
		390/265 2dr GT Fstbk Cpe	$12,300	$17,100	$26,100	$36,100
		390/335 2dr GT Fstbk Cpe	$15,000	$20,900	$31,700	$44,000
		427/390 2dr GT Fstbk Cpe	$16,000	$22,400	$33,900	$47,100

+15% for factory a/c.

Year	Model	Body Style	4	3	2	1
1968	Cougar	302/210 2dr Hdtp Cpe	$9,500	$13,300	$18,900	$25,100
		302/230 2dr Hdtp Cpe	$11,700	$15,600	$22,800	$29,900
		390/280 2dr Hdtp Cpe	$12,300	$16,500	$24,200	$31,700

Mercury

Year	Model	Body Style	4	3	2	1
		390/325 2dr Hdtp Cpe	$13,500	$18,400	$26,300	$34,200
		428/335 2dr Hdtp Cpe	$14,100	$19,300	$27,400	$35,500
		427/390 2dr GT-E Hdtp Cpe	$82,200	$101,000	$120,000	$151,000
		428/335 2dr GT-E Hdtp Cpe	$54,000	$79,900	$108,000	$138,000
		302/210 2dr XR-7 Hdtp Cpe	$14,500	$19,700	$28,700	$37,100
		302/230 2dr XR-7 Hdtp Cpe	$17,500	$23,600	$34,500	$43,900
		390/265 2dr XR-7 Hdtp Cpe	$18,800	$25,700	$38,000	$48,400
		390/280 2dr XR-7 Hdtp Cpe	$19,600	$26,900	$38,700	$49,700
		390/325 2dr XR-7 Hdtp Cpe	$21,400	$29,600	$42,300	$55,000
		428/335 2dr XR-7 Hdtp Cpe	$25,900	$36,300	$49,900	$65,600
		302/210 2dr XR-7G Hdtp Cpe	$21,400	$28,600	$41,800	$54,300
		302/230 2dr XR-7G Hdtp Cpe	$25,600	$35,200	$49,500	$64,800
		390/265 2dr XR-7G Hdtp Cpe	$28,200	$38,900	$54,800	$71,300
		390/280 2dr XR-7G Hdtp Cpe	$28,500	$39,100	$56,600	$73,200
		390/325 2dr XR-7G Hdtp Cpe	$31,300	$43,200	$60,500	$78,400
		428/335 CJ 2dr XR-7G Hdtp Cpe	$36,300	$50,200	$71,000	$92,900

+15% for factory a/c.

Year	Model	Body Style	4	3	2	1
1968	Monterey	390/280 2dr Hdtp Cpe	$5,700	$8,100	$11,900	$15,700
		390/315 2dr Hdtp Cpe	$6,600	$9,200	$13,400	$17,900
		390/335 2dr Hdtp Cpe	$7,400	$10,400	$15,000	$19,900
		428/335 2dr Hdtp Cpe	$7,200	$9,900	$14,500	$19,200
		428/360 2dr Hdtp Cpe	$7,400	$10,400	$15,000	$19,900
		390/280 2dr Conv	$9,400	$15,900	$25,300	$33,700
		390/315 2dr Conv	$10,700	$18,100	$28,900	$38,800
		390/335 2dr Conv	$12,000	$20,400	$32,200	$43,400
		428/335 2dr Conv	$11,500	$19,700	$31,100	$41,900
		428/360 2dr Conv	$12,000	$20,400	$32,200	$43,400

+15% for factory a/c.

Year	Model	Body Style	4	3	2	1
1968	Montclair	390/265 2dr Hdtp Cpe	$5,300	$7,500	$11,000	$14,600

Year	Model	Body Style	4	3	2	1
		390/280 2dr Hdtp Cpe	$5,800	$8,200	$12,100	$16,100
		390/315 2dr Hdtp Cpe	$6,800	$9,300	$13,700	$18,200
		428/340 2dr Hdtp Cpe	$7,300	$10,100	$14,700	$19,600
		428/360 2dr Hdtp Cpe	$7,600	$10,500	$15,500	$20,300
						+15% for factory a/c.
1968	Parklane	390/335 2dr Hdtp Cpe	$6,500	$8,900	$14,400	$19,100
		428/335 2dr Hdtp Cpe	$7,100	$9,800	$15,800	$20,600
		428/360 2dr Hdtp Cpe	$7,400	$10,000	$16,300	$21,300
		390/335 2dr Conv	$8,900	$15,200	$25,100	$32,800
		428/335 2dr Conv	$9,500	$16,400	$27,000	$35,500
		428/360 2dr Conv	$9,900	$17,000	$28,000	$36,900
						+15% for factory a/c.
1968	Marquis	390/315 2dr Hdtp Cpe	$5,600	$7,900	$12,300	$16,200
		428/335 2dr Hdtp Cpe	$7,700	$10,700	$16,700	$21,700
		428/360 2dr Hdtp Cpe	$8,000	$11,100	$17,300	$22,600
						+15% for factory a/c.
1968	Colony Park	390/265 4dr Wgn	$15,100	$21,700	$28,600	$37,000
						+15% for factory a/c.
1969	Comet	302/220 2dr Spt Cpe	$5,900	$8,900	$13,400	$17,800
		351/250 2dr Spt Cpe	$6,100	$9,100	$13,600	$18,100
		351/290 2dr Spt Cpe	$6,800	$9,800	$14,700	$19,700
		390/320 2dr Spt Cpe	$7,600	$11,000	$16,600	$22,300
						+15% for factory a/c.
1969	Montego	250/155 2dr MX Conv	$8,600	$15,000	$23,300	$31,600
		302/220 2dr MX Conv	$9,000	$15,700	$24,400	$32,900
		351/250 2dr MX Conv	$9,100	$16,000	$25,000	$33,600
		351/290 2dr MX Conv	$10,000	$17,200	$27,000	$36,700
		390/320 2dr MX Conv	$11,200	$19,600	$30,600	$41,700
						+15% for factory a/c.

Mercury

Year	Model	Body Style	4	3	2	1
1969	Cyclone	302/220 2dr Fstbk Cpe	$8,400	$12,000	$17,800	$24,400
		351/250 2dr Fstbk Cpe	$8,600	$12,200	$18,100	$24,900
		351/290 2dr Fstbk Cpe	$9,300	$13,300	$19,600	$27,100
		390/320 2dr Fstbk Cpe	$10,500	$15,000	$22,100	$30,600
		429/360 2dr Fstbk Cpe	$10,600	$15,300	$22,300	$30,800
		302/220 2dr GT Fstbk Cpe	$9,800	$13,800	$20,700	$28,600
		351/250 2dr GT Fstbk Cpe	$10,000	$14,000	$21,200	$29,200
		351/290 2dr GT Fstbk Cpe	$10,900	$15,300	$22,900	$31,700
		390/320 2dr GT Fstbk Cpe	$12,300	$17,100	$26,000	$36,000
		429/360 2dr GT Fstbk Cpe	$12,400	$17,200	$26,100	$36,200
		428/335 CJ 2dr Spoiler II Hdtp Cpe	$18,600	$30,300	$44,200	$60,600
		428/335 CJ 2dr CJ Fstbk Cpe	$16,900	$23,900	$36,200	$50,100
						+15% for factory a/c.
1969	Cougar	351/250 2dr Hdtp Cpe	$8,600	$11,600	$16,800	$22,200
		351/290 2dr Hdtp Cpe	$9,900	$13,600	$19,500	$25,700
		390/320 2dr Hdtp Cpe	$11,400	$15,700	$22,500	$29,500
		428/335 CJ 2dr Hdtp Cpe	$13,800	$18,700	$27,100	$35,400
		351/250 2dr XR-7 Hdtp Cpe	$14,200	$19,000	$29,900	$39,400
		351/290 2dr XR-7 Hdtp Cpe	$16,100	$21,900	$35,300	$44,700
		390/320 2dr XR-7 Hdtp Cpe	$18,900	$26,500	$39,600	$51,500
		428/335 CJ 2dr XR-7 Hdtp Cpe	$25,200	$34,400	$53,300	$68,100
		302/290 2dr Eliminator Hdtp Cpe	$35,600	$61,800	$95,400	$123,000
		351/290 2dr Eliminator Hdtp Cpe	$16,000	$23,000	$34,200	$46,500
		390/320 2dr Eliminator Hdtp Cpe	$23,400	$32,800	$50,600	$60,000

Year	Model	Body Style	4	3	2	1
		428/335 CJ 2dr Eliminator Hdtp Cpe	$51,800	$77,900	$111,000	$154,000
		428/335 SCJ 2dr Eliminator Hdtp Cpe	$63,000	$88,700	$134,000	$187,000
		351/250 2dr Conv	$12,700	$17,400	$25,500	$32,700
		351/290 2dr Conv	$15,000	$20,300	$30,000	$38,500
		390/320 2dr Conv	$17,400	$23,500	$34,100	$43,300
		428/335 CJ 2dr Conv	$20,700	$27,700	$41,400	$53,400
		351/250 2dr XR-7 Conv	$18,100	$28,300	$44,600	$58,700
		351/290 2dr XR-7 Conv	$24,700	$32,300	$52,300	$68,500
		390/320 2dr XR-7 Conv	$28,600	$37,600	$59,800	$78,700
		428/335 CJ 2dr XR-7 Conv	$46,000	$57,800	$87,300	$115,000
						+15% for factory a/c.
1969	Monterey	390/280 2dr Hdtp Cpe	$5,100	$7,200	$10,700	$14,300
		390/320 2dr Hdtp Cpe	$5,300	$7,500	$11,200	$14,900
		428/335 2dr Hdtp Cpe	$6,500	$9,100	$13,500	$18,000
		429/360 2dr Hdtp Cpe	$5,800	$8,100	$12,100	$16,300
		390/280 2dr Conv	$9,800	$17,200	$26,700	$36,200
		390/320 2dr Conv	$10,100	$18,000	$27,800	$37,600
		428/335 2dr Conv	$12,400	$21,700	$33,400	$45,600
		429/360 2dr Conv	$11,000	$19,600	$30,000	$40,900
						+15% for factory a/c.
1969	Marauder	390/265 2dr Hdtp Cpe	$5,500	$7,700	$11,400	$14,900
		390/280 2dr Hdtp Cpe	$6,400	$8,900	$13,000	$17,100
		390/320 2dr Hdtp Cpe	$6,700	$9,300	$13,700	$17,800
		428/335 2dr Hdtp Cpe	$8,300	$11,500	$17,000	$22,000
		429/360 2dr Hdtp Cpe	$7,500	$10,300	$15,100	$19,800
		429/360 2dr X-100 Hdtp Cpe	$6,600	$9,500	$14,500	$18,600
						+15% for factory a/c.
1969	Marquis	429/320 2dr Conv	$9,800	$17,000	$26,000	$35,300
						+15% for factory a/c.
1970	Cyclone	429/375 SCJ 2dr Hdtp Cpe	$12,500	$17,600	$26,200	$36,000

Mercury

Year	Model	Body Style	4	3	2	1
		351/250 2dr GT Hdtp Cpe	$11,700	$16,400	$24,200	$34,000
		351/300 2dr GT Hdtp Cpe	$13,300	$18,400	$27,500	$38,600
		429/360 CJ 2dr GT Hdtp Cpe	$16,900	$23,600	$34,900	$48,800
		429/375 SCJ 2dr GT Hdtp Cpe	$16,400	$22,900	$34,000	$47,800
						-20% for 6-cyl. +10% for factory a/c.
1970	Cougar	351/250 2dr Hdtp Cpe	$9,100	$12,600	$17,300	$22,900
		351/300 2dr Hdtp Cpe	$11,900	$15,300	$22,300	$28,700
		428/335 CJ 2dr Hdtp Cpe	$15,000	$20,300	$27,000	$35,200
		351/250 2dr XR-7 Hdtp Cpe	$14,400	$19,900	$31,300	$40,700
		351/300 2dr XR-7 Hdtp Cpe	$18,900	$25,100	$41,100	$54,800
		428/335 CJ 2dr XR-7 Hdtp Cpe	$24,500	$34,400	$57,200	$73,600
		302/290 2dr Eliminator Hdtp Cpe	$41,700	$64,800	$88,300	$134,000
		351/300 2dr Eliminator Hdtp Cpe	$17,300	$22,800	$33,000	$43,300
		428/335 CJ 2dr Eliminator Hdtp Cpe	$55,100	$87,200	$125,000	$178,000
		351/250 2dr Conv	$14,400	$19,000	$27,000	$33,600
		351/300 2dr Conv	$18,100	$23,800	$33,100	$41,400
		428/335 CJ 2dr Conv	$22,300	$31,000	$41,700	$52,100
		351/250 2dr XR-7 Conv	$21,800	$29,600	$45,900	$61,400
		351/300 2dr XR-7 Conv	$27,800	$37,300	$57,400	$75,500
		428/335 CJ 2dr XR-7 Conv	$48,500	$62,700	$108,000	$144,000
						+10% for factory a/c.
1970	Monterey	390/265 2dr Conv	$7,900	$14,200	$21,800	$29,400
		429/320 2dr Conv	$10,300	$18,400	$28,500	$38,400
		429/360 CJ 2dr Conv	$11,000	$20,100	$30,900	$41,300
						+10% for factory a/c.
1970	Marauder	390/265 2dr Hdtp Cpe	$5,500	$7,700	$11,400	$14,900
		429/360 CJ 2dr Hdtp Cpe	$8,000	$11,200	$16,400	$21,300

Year	Model	Body Style	4	3	2	1
		429/360 CJ 2dr X-100 Hdtp Cpe	$9,500	$13,200	$20,500	$25,900
						+10% for factory a/c.
1970	Marquis	390/265 2dr Conv	$9,800	$17,000	$26,000	$35,600
		429/360 CJ 2dr Conv	$16,000	$29,500	$48,200	$64,500
						+10% for factory a/c.
1971	Capri	98/75 2dr 1600 Spt Cpe	$2,200	$4,000	$6,800	$9,600
						-15% for 1.6L 4-cyl.
1971	Comet	302/210 2dr Sdn	$4,400	$6,100	$9,300	$12,600
						-20% for 6-cyl. +10% for factory a/c.
1971	Cyclone	351/285 2dr Hdtp Cpe	$8,800	$12,200	$18,300	$25,100
		351/285 2dr GT Hdtp Cpe	$12,000	$16,200	$24,500	$34,000
		429/370 CJ 2dr GT Hdtp Cpe	$16,900	$23,600	$35,300	$48,800
						+10% for factory a/c.
1971	Cougar	351/240 2dr Hdtp Cpe	$8,700	$11,900	$17,700	$22,800
		351/285 2dr Hdtp Cpe	$5,100	$7,300	$12,800	$14,300
		429/370 CJ 2dr GT Hdtp Cpe	$20,800	$29,500	$43,500	$56,500
		351/240 2dr XR-7 Hdtp Cpe	$6,000	$8,500	$12,700	$16,400
		351/285 2dr XR-7 Hdtp Cpe	$6,900	$10,200	$14,800	$19,200
		351/240 2dr Conv	$4,700	$5,900	$9,000	$12,200
		351/285 2dr Conv	$10,600	$14,300	$21,000	$26,900
		351/240 2dr XR-7 Conv	$10,800	$14,500	$21,700	$27,700
		351/285 2dr XR-7 Conv	$12,400	$17,100	$25,700	$33,800
						+10% for factory a/c.
1972	Capri	1599/54 2dr Cpe	$2,200	$4,100	$6,800	$9,700
		2548/107 2dr V6 Cpe	$3,300	$5,500	$9,700	$18,500
						-15% for 1.6L 4-cyl.
1972	Comet	302/143 2dr Sdn	$4,400	$6,300	$9,500	$13,100
						-20% for 6-cyl. +10% for factory a/c.
1972	Cougar	351/164 2dr Hdtp Cpe	$4,800	$6,400	$8,900	$11,800
		351/262 2dr Hdtp Cpe	$5,900	$7,800	$11,700	$14,200
		351/266 CJ 2dr Hdtp Cpe	$6,600	$8,800	$13,200	$16,400

Mercury

Year	Model	Body Style	4	3	2	1
		351/164 2dr XR-7 Hdtp Cpe	$6,200	$9,200	$12,600	$15,700
		351/262 2dr XR-7 Hdtp Cpe	$7,600	$11,400	$15,600	$20,000
		351/266 CJ 2dr XR-7 Hdtp Cpe	$8,600	$12,700	$17,900	$22,100
		351/164 2dr Conv	$8,900	$12,700	$18,700	$23,100
		351/262 2dr Conv	$11,500	$16,000	$23,300	$28,600
		351/266 CJ 2dr Conv	$12,800	$17,900	$25,900	$32,300
		351/164 2dr XR-7 Conv	$12,100	$14,900	$22,500	$27,300
		351/262 2dr XR-7 Conv	$12,800	$18,200	$27,700	$34,700
		351/266 CJ 2dr XR-7 Conv	$14,200	$20,600	$31,800	$38,900
						+10% for factory a/c.
1972	Montego	302/140 2dr GT Hdtp Cpe	$5,800	$8,200	$12,000	$16,300
		351/161 2dr GT Hdtp Cpe	$7,100	$9,800	$14,400	$19,400
		351/248 CJ 2dr GT Hdtp Cpe	$8,500	$11,900	$17,600	$23,500
		400/168 2dr GT Hdtp Cpe	$6,800	$9,500	$13,800	$18,500
		429/205 2dr GT Hdtp Cpe	$7,600	$10,700	$15,700	$20,900
						+10% for factory a/c.
1973	Capri	122/85 2dr Cpe	$2,200	$4,000	$6,800	$9,700
		156/107 2dr V6 Cpe	$3,300	$5,500	$9,700	$18,500
1973	Cougar	351/168 2dr Hdtp Cpe	$4,700	$6,100	$9,200	$12,500
		351/264 2dr Hdtp Cpe	$6,000	$8,200	$12,600	$16,200
		351/168 2dr XR-7 Hdtp Cpe	$5,800	$8,300	$12,700	$15,800
		351/264 2dr XR-7 Hdtp Cpe	$7,900	$11,300	$16,900	$21,500
		351/168 2dr Conv	$8,300	$11,600	$18,000	$22,700
		351/264 2dr Conv	$11,300	$15,800	$23,800	$31,400
		351/168 2dr XR-7 Conv	$10,200	$14,100	$21,500	$27,300
		351/264 2dr XR-7 Conv	$13,900	$18,800	$25,700	$37,000
						+10% for factory a/c.
1974	Capri	1993/80 2dr Cpe	$2,200	$4,100	$6,600	$9,500
		2792/105 2dr V6 Cpe	$3,300	$5,500	$9,700	$18,500
1976	Capri II	2300/88 2dr Htchbk Cpe	$2,400	$4,700	$7,900	$13,000

Mercury

Year	Model	Body Style	4	3	2	1
		2795/109 2dr V6 Htchbk Cpe	$3,200	$6,300	$9,800	$15,400
		2300/88 2dr S Cpe	$2,800	$5,100	$8,100	$13,200
		2300/88 2dr Ghia Cpe	$2,800	$5,100	$8,100	$13,200
1977	Capri II	2300/92 3dr Htchbk Cpe	$2,300	$4,600	$7,600	$11,600
		2795/110 3dr Htchbk Cpe	$3,200	$6,300	$9,800	$15,400
		2300/92 3dr S Cpe	$2,900	$5,200	$8,200	$14,100
		2300/92 3dr Ghia Cpe	$2,900	$5,200	$8,200	$14,100
2003	Marauder	281/302 4dr Sdn	$11,600	$17,400	$22,100	$29,400
2004	Marauder	281/302 4dr Sdn	$11,600	$17,400	$22,100	$29,400

Merkur

Year	Model	Body Style	4	3	2	1
1985	XR4Ti	2dr Cpe	$1,600	$3,100	$4,600	$6,700
1986	XR4Ti	2dr Cpe	$1,600	$3,100	$4,600	$6,700
1987	XR4Ti	2dr Cpe	$1,600	$3,100	$4,600	$6,700
1988	XR4Ti	2dr Cpe	$1,400	$2,500	$3,800	$6,000
1988	Scorpio	4dr Sdn	$900	$1,600	$2,500	$4,400
1989	XR4Ti	2dr Cpe	$1,400	$2,500	$3,800	$6,000
1989	Scorpio	4dr Sdn	$900	$1,600	$2,500	$4,400

Messerschmitt

Year	Model	Body Style	4	3	2	1
1955	KR200	2dr Bubble Top	$26,000	$42,200	$56,500	$86,000
					+$2,000 for plexiglass roof.	
1956	KR200	2dr Bubble Top	$26,000	$42,200	$56,500	$86,000
					+$2,000 for plexiglass roof.	
1957	KR200	2dr Bubble Top	$26,000	$42,200	$56,500	$86,000
					+$2,000 for plexiglass roof.	
1958	KR200	2dr Bubble Top	$26,000	$42,200	$56,500	$86,000
					+$2,000 for plexiglass roof.	
1959	KR200	2dr Bubble Top	$26,000	$42,200	$56,500	$86,000
					+$2,000 for plexiglass roof.	
1960	KR200	2dr Bubble Top	$26,000	$42,200	$56,500	$86,000
					+$2,000 for plexiglass roof.	
1961	KR200	2dr Bubble Top	$26,000	$42,200	$56,500	$86,000
					+$2,000 for plexiglass roof.	
1962	KR200	2dr Bubble Top	$26,000	$42,200	$56,500	$86,000
					+$2,000 for plexiglass roof.	
1963	KR200	2dr Bubble Top	$26,000	$42,200	$56,500	$86,000

Messerschmitt

Year	Model	Body Style	4	3	2	1
						+$2,000 for plexiglass roof.
1964	KR200	2dr Bubble Top	$26,000	$42,200	$56,500	$86,000
						+$2,000 for plexiglass roof.

Metropolitan

Year	Model	Body Style	4	3	2	1
1955	1500	2dr SII Cpe	$5,400	$8,300	$15,800	$25,200
		2dr SII Conv	$7,700	$13,000	$25,800	$36,500
1956	1500	2dr SIII Cpe	$4,900	$8,100	$15,800	$25,300
		2dr SIII Conv	$7,000	$12,700	$25,200	$35,800
1957	1500	2dr SIII Cpe	$4,900	$8,100	$15,900	$25,300
		2dr SIII Conv	$7,000	$12,700	$25,200	$35,800
1958	1500	2dr SIII Conv	$7,000	$12,700	$25,200	$35,800
1959	1500	2dr SIV Conv	$7,000	$11,900	$23,200	$34,400
1960	1500	2dr SIV Conv	$7,000	$11,900	$23,200	$34,400
1961	1500	2dr SIV Conv	$7,000	$11,900	$23,200	$34,400
1962	1500	2dr SIV Conv	$7,000	$16,000	$23,200	$34,400

Mitsubishi

Year	Model	Body Style	4	3	2	1
1991	3000 GT	2dr Htchbk	$2,900	$6,400	$9,100	$11,800
		2dr SL Htchbk	$3,100	$6,900	$10,000	$12,900
		2dr VR4 Htchbk	$6,600	$14,300	$23,000	$31,000
1992	3000 GT	2dr Htchbk	$2,900	$6,400	$9,100	$11,800
		2dr SL Htchbk	$3,100	$6,900	$10,000	$12,900
		2dr VR4 Htchbk	$6,600	$14,300	$23,000	$31,000
1993	3000 GT	2dr Htchbk	$2,900	$6,400	$9,100	$11,800
		2dr SL Htchbk	$3,100	$6,900	$10,000	$12,900
		2dr VR4 Htchbk	$6,600	$14,300	$23,000	$31,000
1994	3000 GT	2dr Htchbk	$4,000	$7,500	$10,900	$15,700
		2dr SL Htchbk	$4,400	$8,200	$11,900	$17,000
		2dr VR4 Htchbk	$7,500	$13,900	$22,500	$40,300
1995	3000 GT	2dr Htchbk	$4,000	$7,500	$10,900	$15,700
		2dr SL Htchbk	$4,400	$8,200	$11,900	$17,000
		2dr Spyder SL	$5,800	$8,600	$15,200	$21,200
		2dr Spyder VR4	$10,500	$16,000	$27,700	$40,100
		2dr VR4 Htchbk	$7,500	$13,900	$22,500	$40,300
1996	3000 GT	2dr Htchbk	$4,000	$7,500	$10,900	$15,700
		2dr SL Htchbk	$4,400	$8,200	$11,900	$17,000
		2dr Spyder SL	$5,800	$8,600	$15,200	$21,200
		2dr Spyder VR4	$10,500	$16,000	$27,700	$40,100
		2dr VR4 Htchbk	$7,500	$13,900	$22,500	$40,300
1997	3000 GT	2dr Htchbk	$2,500	$5,400	$7,800	$10,100
		2dr SL Htchbk	$4,400	$8,200	$11,900	$17,000
		2dr VR4 Htchbk	$7,500	$13,900	$22,500	$40,300
1998	3000 GT	2dr Htchbk	$2,500	$5,400	$7,800	$10,100
		2dr SL Htchbk	$4,400	$8,300	$12,200	$17,300
		2dr VR4 Htchbk	$7,600	$14,200	$23,000	$41,200

Mitsubishi

Year	Model	Body Style	4	3	2	1
1999	3000 GT	2dr Htchbk	$2,500	$5,400	$7,800	$10,100
		2dr SL Htchbk	$4,400	$8,300	$12,200	$17,300
		2dr VR4 Htchbk	$7,700	$14,500	$23,400	$41,900

Mohs

Year	Model	Body Style	4	3	2	1
1967	Ostentatienne Model 68A	304/193 2dr Opera Sdn	$107,000	$160,000	$203,000	$312,000
1973	SafariKar	392/179 2dr Sdn	$94,000	$137,000	$194,000	$289,000

Monteverdi

Year	Model	Body Style	4	3	2	1
1967	375S	2dr Cpe	$164,000	$221,000	$266,000	$335,000
1968	375S	2dr Cpe	$164,000	$221,000	$266,000	$335,000
1968	375L	2dr 2+2 Cpe	$77,400	$115,000	$154,000	$268,000
1969	375S	2dr Cpe	$164,000	$221,000	$266,000	$335,000
1969	375L	2dr 2+2 Cpe	$77,400	$115,000	$154,000	$268,000
1969	375C	2dr Cab	$237,000	$299,000	$346,000	$451,000
1970	375S	2dr Cpe	$164,000	$221,000	$266,000	$335,000
1970	375L	2dr 2+2 Cpe	$77,400	$115,000	$154,000	$268,000
1970	375/4	4dr Sdn	$67,500	$107,000	$144,000	$203,000
1970	375C	2dr Cab	$237,000	$299,000	$346,000	$451,000
1970	Hai 450 SS	2dr Cpe	$505,000	$585,000	$669,000	$778,000
1971	375S	2dr Cpe	$164,000	$221,000	$266,000	$335,000
1971	375L	2dr 2+2 Cpe	$77,400	$115,000	$154,000	$268,000
1971	375/4	4dr Sdn	$67,500	$107,000	$144,000	$203,000
1971	375C	2dr Cab	$237,000	$299,000	$346,000	$451,000
1971	Hai 450 SS	2dr Cpe	$505,000	$585,000	$669,000	$778,000
1972	375S	2dr Cpe	$164,000	$221,000	$266,000	$335,000
1972	375L	2dr 2+2 Cpe	$77,400	$115,000	$154,000	$268,000
1972	375/4	4dr Sdn	$67,500	$107,000	$144,000	$203,000
1972	375C	2dr Cab	$237,000	$299,000	$346,000	$451,000
1972	Hai 450 SS	2dr Cpe	$505,000	$585,000	$669,000	$778,000
1973	375L	2dr 2+2 Cpe	$77,400	$115,000	$154,000	$268,000
1973	375/4	4dr Sdn	$67,500	$107,000	$144,000	$203,000
1973	375C	2dr Cab	$237,000	$299,000	$346,000	$451,000
1973	Hai 450 SS	2dr Cpe	$505,000	$585,000	$669,000	$778,000
1974	375L	2dr 2+2 Cpe	$77,400	$115,000	$154,000	$268,000
1974	375C	2dr Cab	$237,000	$299,000	$346,000	$451,000
1974	Hai 450 SS	2dr Cpe	$505,000	$585,000	$669,000	$778,000
1975	375L	2dr 2+2 Cpe	$77,400	$115,000	$154,000	$268,000
1975	375C	2dr Cab	$237,000	$299,000	$346,000	$451,000
1975	Hai 450 SS	2dr Cpe	$505,000	$585,000	$669,000	$778,000
1976	375L	2dr 2+2 Cpe	$77,400	$115,000	$154,000	$268,000
1976	375C	2dr Cab	$237,000	$299,000	$346,000	$451,000
1976	Hai 450 SS	2dr Cpe	$505,000	$585,000	$669,000	$778,000
1977	375L	2dr 2+2 Cpe	$77,400	$115,000	$154,000	$268,000

Monteverdi

Year	Model	Body Style	4	3	2	1
1977	375C	2dr Cab	$237,000	$299,000	$346,000	$451,000

Moretti

Year	Model	Body Style	4	3	2	1
1953	750 Grand Sport	2dr Cpe	$116,000	$155,000	$206,000	$252,000
			Significant coachwork can greatly enhance value.			
1954	750 Grand Sport	2dr Cpe	$116,000	$155,000	$206,000	$252,000
			Significant coachwork can greatly enhance value.			
1957	750 Tour du Monde	2dr Cpe	$15,500	$21,700	$33,000	$46,500
		2dr Spyder	$17,800	$28,900	$40,700	$55,500
1958	750 Tour du Monde	2dr Cpe	$15,500	$21,700	$33,000	$46,500
		2dr Spyder	$17,800	$28,900	$40,700	$55,500
1959	750 Tour du Monde	2dr Cpe	$15,500	$21,700	$33,000	$46,500
		2dr Spyder	$17,800	$28,900	$40,700	$55,500
1960	750 Tour du Monde	2dr Cpe	$15,500	$21,700	$33,000	$46,500
		2dr Spyder	$17,800	$28,900	$40,700	$55,500
1965	Sportiva	2dr Cpe	$13,600	$19,400	$28,900	$42,200
1966	Sportiva	2dr Cpe	$13,600	$19,400	$28,900	$42,200
1967	Sportiva	2dr Cpe	$13,600	$19,400	$28,900	$42,200

Morgan

Year	Model	Body Style	4	3	2	1
1949	4/4	2dr SI Rdstr	$21,800	$31,100	$46,400	$63,200
		2dr SI Rdstr 2+2	$17,400	$24,500	$38,500	$50,500
		2dr SI DHC	$20,400	$29,500	$41,100	$57,100
1950	4/4	2dr SI Rdstr	$21,800	$31,100	$46,400	$63,200
		2dr SI Rdstr 2+2	$17,400	$24,500	$38,500	$50,500
		2dr SI DHC	$20,400	$29,500	$41,100	$57,100
1951	Plus 4	2dr Rdstr	$18,200	$28,000	$43,200	$60,300
		2dr Rdstr 2+2	$13,200	$19,900	$30,900	$45,100
		2dr DHC	$18,500	$28,500	$42,200	$62,000
1951	4/4	2dr Rdstr	$21,800	$31,100	$46,400	$63,100
		2dr Rdstr 2+2	$17,400	$24,500	$38,500	$50,500
		2dr DHC	$20,500	$29,800	$41,200	$58,300
						-15% for Ford eng.
1952	Plus 4	2dr Rdstr	$18,200	$28,500	$43,600	$60,400
		2dr Rdstr 2+2	$13,200	$19,900	$30,900	$45,100
		2dr DHC	$18,500	$28,500	$42,200	$62,000
1952	4/4	2dr Rdstr	$22,000	$31,200	$46,500	$63,300
		2dr Rdstr 2+2	$17,400	$24,500	$38,500	$50,500
		2dr DHC	$20,700	$29,900	$41,000	$58,300
						-15% for Ford eng.
1953	Plus 4	2dr Rdstr	$18,600	$28,600	$44,200	$60,600
		2dr Rdstr 2+2	$13,200	$19,900	$30,900	$45,100

Year	Model	Body Style	4	3	2	1
		2dr DHC	$18,500	$28,500	$42,200	$62,000
1953	4/4	2dr Rdstr	$22,000	$31,200	$46,500	$63,300
		2dr Rdstr 2+2	$17,600	$24,600	$38,600	$50,700
		2dr DHC	$20,700	$29,900	$41,000	$58,300
						-15% for Ford eng.
1954	Plus 4	2dr Rdstr	$18,200	$28,500	$43,200	$60,300
		2dr Rdstr 2+2	$13,200	$19,900	$30,900	$45,100
		2dr DHC	$18,500	$28,500	$42,200	$62,000
1954	4/4	2dr Rdstr	$22,000	$31,200	$46,500	$63,300
		2dr Rdstr 2+2	$17,600	$24,600	$38,600	$50,700
		2dr DHC	$20,700	$29,900	$41,000	$58,300
						-15% for Ford eng.
1955	Plus 4	2dr Rdstr	$17,000	$27,300	$39,900	$58,800
		2dr Spr Sports Rdstr	$44,800	$67,800	$88,800	$120,000
		2dr Rdstr 2+2	$13,200	$19,900	$30,900	$45,100
		2dr DHC	$18,500	$28,500	$42,300	$62,000
1955	4/4	2dr SII Rdstr	$14,400	$21,900	$29,800	$45,900
1956	Plus 4	2dr Rdstr	$17,000	$27,300	$39,800	$58,800
		2dr Spr Sports Rdstr	$44,800	$67,800	$88,800	$120,000
		2dr Rdstr 2+2	$13,200	$19,900	$30,900	$45,100
		2dr DHC	$18,500	$28,500	$42,200	$62,000
1956	4/4	2dr SII Rdstr	$14,400	$21,900	$29,800	$45,900
1957	Plus 4	2dr Rdstr	$17,000	$27,300	$39,800	$58,800
		2dr Spr Sports Rdstr	$44,800	$67,800	$88,800	$120,000
		2dr Rdstr 2+2	$13,200	$19,900	$30,900	$45,100
		2dr DHC	$18,500	$28,500	$42,200	$62,000
1957	4/4	2dr SII Rdstr	$14,400	$21,900	$29,800	$45,900
1958	Plus 4	2dr Rdstr	$17,300	$27,500	$41,300	$60,900
		2dr Spr Sports Rdstr	$46,400	$69,700	$92,200	$123,000
		2dr Rdstr 2+2	$13,200	$19,900	$30,900	$45,100
		2dr DHC	$18,500	$28,500	$42,200	$62,000
1958	4/4	2dr SII Rdstr	$14,400	$22,000	$29,800	$45,900
1959	Plus 4	2dr Rdstr	$17,300	$27,500	$41,300	$60,900
		2dr Spr Sports Rdstr	$46,400	$69,700	$92,200	$123,000
		2dr Rdstr 2+2	$13,200	$19,900	$30,900	$45,100
		2dr DHC	$18,500	$28,500	$42,200	$62,000
1959	4/4	2dr SII Rdstr	$14,400	$22,000	$29,800	$45,900
1960	Plus 4	2dr Rdstr	$17,300	$27,500	$41,300	$60,900
		2dr Spr Sports Rdstr	$46,400	$69,700	$92,200	$123,000
		2dr Rdstr 2+2	$13,200	$19,900	$30,900	$45,100
		2dr DHC	$18,500	$28,500	$42,200	$62,000
1960	4/4	2dr SIII Rdstr	$16,200	$24,500	$32,800	$50,000
1961	Plus 4	2dr Rdstr	$17,300	$27,500	$41,300	$60,900

Morgan

Year	Model	Body Style	4	3	2	1
		2dr Spr Sports Rdstr	$46,400	$69,700	$92,200	$123,000
		2dr Rdstr 2+2	$13,200	$19,900	$30,900	$45,100
		2dr DHC	$18,500	$28,500	$42,200	$62,000
1961	4/4	2dr SIII Rdstr	$16,200	$24,500	$32,800	$50,000
		2dr SIV Rdstr	$18,000	$29,000	$35,900	$53,600
1962	Plus 4	2dr Rdstr	$18,900	$30,300	$45,000	$62,300
		2dr Spr Sports Rdstr	$46,400	$69,700	$92,200	$123,000
		2dr Rdstr 2+2	$14,500	$20,900	$31,900	$46,300
		2dr DHC	$18,500	$28,500	$42,200	$62,000
1962	4/4	2dr SIV Rdstr	$17,600	$28,000	$35,500	$54,500
1963	Plus 4	2dr Rdstr	$18,900	$30,300	$44,900	$62,300
		2dr Spr Sports Rdstr	$46,400	$69,700	$92,200	$123,000
		2dr Rdstr 2+2	$14,500	$20,900	$31,900	$46,300
		2dr DHC	$18,700	$29,200	$43,900	$64,300
1963	4/4	2dr SIV Rdstr	$17,600	$28,000	$35,600	$54,500
		2dr SV Rdstr	$15,900	$23,700	$32,100	$48,500
1964	4/4	2dr SV Rdstr	$15,900	$23,700	$32,100	$48,500
1965	Plus 4	2dr Plus 2 FHC	$74,000	$107,000	$139,000	$199,000
		2dr Rdstr	$19,100	$30,600	$45,400	$63,000
		2dr Spr Sports Rdstr	$45,400	$68,900	$90,200	$121,000
		2dr Rdstr 2+2	$14,500	$20,900	$31,900	$46,300
		2dr DHC	$18,700	$29,200	$43,900	$64,300
1965	4/4	2dr SV Rdstr	$15,900	$23,700	$32,100	$48,500
1966	Plus 4	2dr Plus 2 FHC	$74,000	$107,000	$139,000	$199,000
		2dr Rdstr	$19,100	$30,600	$45,400	$63,000
		2dr Spr Sports Rdstr	$45,400	$68,900	$90,200	$121,000
		2dr Rdstr 2+2	$14,500	$20,900	$31,900	$46,300
		2dr DHC	$18,700	$29,200	$43,900	$64,300
1966	4/4	2dr SV Rdstr	$15,900	$23,400	$31,700	$48,100
1967	Plus 4	2dr Plus 2 FHC	$74,000	$107,000	$139,000	$199,000
		2dr Rdstr	$19,100	$30,600	$45,400	$63,000
		2dr Spr Sports Rdstr	$45,400	$68,900	$90,200	$121,000
		2dr Rdstr 2+2	$14,500	$20,900	$31,900	$46,300
		2dr DHC	$18,700	$29,200	$43,900	$64,300
1967	4/4	2dr SV Rdstr	$15,900	$23,700	$32,100	$48,500
1968	Plus 4	2dr Rdstr	$19,100	$30,600	$45,400	$63,000
		2dr Spr Sports Rdstr	$46,600	$70,400	$93,700	$125,000
		2dr Rdstr 2+2	$15,500	$22,000	$32,900	$47,400
		2dr DHC	$18,700	$29,200	$43,900	$64,300
1968	Plus 8	2dr Rdstr	$17,500	$37,000	$65,200	$83,200
1968	4/4	2dr 1600 Rdstr	$19,000	$27,500	$39,900	$55,900
		2dr SV Rdstr	$16,600	$24,200	$33,100	$50,300
1969	Plus 4	2dr Rdstr	$19,100	$30,600	$45,400	$63,000

Year	Model	Body Style	4	3	2	1
		2dr Spr Sports Rdstr	$46,600	$70,400	$93,700	$125,000
		2dr Rdstr 2+2	$15,500	$22,000	$32,900	$47,400
		2dr DHC	$18,700	$29,200	$43,900	$64,300
1969	Plus 8	2dr Rdstr	$17,500	$37,000	$65,200	$84,200
1969	4/4	2dr SV Rdstr	$16,600	$24,200	$33,100	$50,300
		2dr 1600 Rdstr	$19,000	$27,700	$39,900	$55,900
1970	Plus 8	2dr Rdstr	$17,500	$37,000	$65,200	$84,200
1970	4/4	2dr 1600 Rdstr	$19,000	$27,900	$39,700	$55,900
1971	4/4	2dr 1600 Rdstr	$19,000	$27,900	$39,700	$55,900
1971	Plus 8	2dr Rdstr	$17,500	$37,000	$65,200	$84,200
1972	Plus 8	2dr Rdstr	$17,500	$37,000	$65,200	$84,200
1972	4/4	2dr 1600 Rdstr	$19,000	$27,900	$39,700	$55,900
1973	Plus 8	2dr Rdstr	$17,500	$37,000	$65,200	$84,200
1973	4/4	2dr 1600 Rdstr	$19,000	$27,900	$39,700	$55,900
1974	Plus 8	2dr Rdstr	$17,500	$37,000	$65,200	$84,200
1974	4/4	2dr 1600 Rdstr	$19,000	$28,100	$29,700	$55,900
1975	Plus 8	2dr Rdstr	$17,500	$37,000	$65,200	$84,200
1975	4/4	2dr 1600 Rdstr	$19,000	$27,900	$39,700	$55,900
1976	Plus 8	2dr Rdstr	$20,400	$40,500	$67,500	$87,200
1976	4/4	2dr 1600 Rdstr	$19,000	$27,900	$39,700	$55,900
1977	Plus 8	2dr Rdstr	$20,400	$40,500	$67,500	$87,200
			-10% for propane. +10% for Isis Imports turbocharger.			
1977	4/4	2dr 1600 Rdstr	$19,000	$28,100	$39,700	$55,900
1978	Plus 8	2dr Rdstr	$20,400	$40,500	$67,500	$87,200
			-10% for propane. +10% for Isis Imports turbocharger.			
1978	4/4	2dr 1600 Rdstr	$19,000	$28,100	$39,700	$55,900
1979	Plus 8	2dr Rdstr	$20,400	$40,500	$67,500	$87,200
			-10% for propane. +10% for Isis Imports turbocharger.			
1979	4/4	2dr 1600 Rdstr	$19,000	$27,900	$39,700	$55,900
1980	Plus 8	2dr Rdstr	$20,400	$40,500	$67,500	$87,200
			-10% for propane. +10% for Isis Imports turbocharger.			
1980	4/4	2dr 1600 Rdstr	$19,000	$27,900	$39,700	$55,900
1981	Plus 8	2dr Rdstr	$20,400	$40,500	$67,500	$87,200
			-10% for propane. +10% for Isis Imports turbocharger.			
1981	4/4	2dr 1600 Rdstr	$19,000	$27,900	$39,700	$55,900
1982	Plus 8	2dr Rdstr	$20,400	$40,500	$67,500	$87,200
			-10% for propane. +10% for Isis Imports turbocharger.			
1982	4/4	2dr 1600 Rdstr	$19,000	$27,500	$39,900	$55,900
1983	Plus 8	2dr Rdstr	$20,400	$40,500	$67,500	$87,200
			-10% for propane. +10% for Isis Imports turbocharger.			
1983	4/4	2dr 1600 Rdstr	$19,500	$29,400	$45,600	$62,900
1984	Plus 8	2dr Rdstr	$20,400	$40,500	$67,500	$87,200
			-10% for propane. +10% for Isis Imports turbocharger.			
1984	4/4	2dr 1600 Rdstr	$19,500	$29,400	$45,600	$62,900
1985	Plus 8	2dr Rdstr	$17,400	$35,800	$60,900	$81,200
			-10% for propane. +10% for Isis Imports turbocharger.			

Morgan

Year	Model	Body Style	4	3	2	1
1985	4/4	2dr 1600 Rdstr	$19,500	$29,400	$45,600	$62,900
1986	Plus 8	2dr Rdstr	$17,400	$35,800	$60,900	$81,200
			-10% for propane. +10% for Isis Imports turbocharger.			
1986	4/4	2dr 1600 Rdstr	$19,500	$29,400	$45,600	$62,900
1987	Plus 8	2dr Rdstr	$17,400	$35,800	$60,900	$81,200
			-10% for propane. +10% for Isis Imports turbocharger.			
1987	4/4	2dr 1600 Rdstr	$19,500	$29,400	$45,600	$62,900
1988	Plus 8	2dr Rdstr	$17,400	$35,800	$60,900	$81,200
			-10% for propane. +10% for Isis Imports turbocharger.			
1988	4/4	2dr 1600 Rdstr	$19,500	$29,400	$45,600	$62,900
1989	Plus 8	2dr Rdstr	$17,400	$35,800	$60,900	$81,200
			-10% for propane. +10% for Isis Imports turbocharger.			
1989	4/4	2dr 1600 Rdstr	$19,500	$29,400	$45,600	$62,900
1990	Plus 8	2dr Rdstr	$19,000	$38,900	$65,200	$83,200
			-10% for propane. +10% for Isis Imports turbocharger.			
1990	4/4	2dr 1600 Rdstr	$19,500	$29,400	$45,600	$62,900
1991	Plus 8	2dr Rdstr	$19,000	$38,900	$65,200	$83,200
			-10% for propane. +10% for Isis Imports turbocharger.			
1991	4/4	2dr 1600 Rdstr	$19,500	$29,400	$45,600	$62,900
1992	Plus 8	2dr Rdstr	$19,000	$38,900	$65,200	$83,200
			-10% for propane. +10% for Isis Imports turbocharger.			
1992	4/4	2dr 1600 Rdstr	$19,500	$29,400	$45,600	$62,900
1993	Plus 8	2dr Rdstr	$19,000	$38,900	$65,200	$83,200
			-10% for propane. +10% for Isis Imports turbocharger.			
1993	4/4	2dr 1800 Rdstr	$19,500	$29,400	$42,600	$60,700
1994	Plus 8	2dr Rdstr	$19,000	$38,900	$65,200	$83,200
			-10% for propane. +10% for Isis Imports turbocharger.			
1994	4/4	2dr 1800 Rdstr	$19,500	$29,400	$42,500	$60,700
1995	Plus 8	2dr Rdstr	$19,000	$38,900	$65,200	$83,200
			-10% for propane. +10% for Isis Imports turbocharger.			
1995	4/4	2dr 1800 Rdstr	$19,500	$29,400	$42,600	$60,700

Morris

Year	Model	Body Style	4	3	2	1
1948	Minor	2dr MM SI Sdn	$5,800	$7,800	$12,200	$17,000
		4dr MM SI Sdn	$3,600	$5,800	$9,000	$13,100
		2dr MM SI Tourer	$5,800	$8,600	$14,100	$19,400
1949	Minor	2dr MM SI Sdn	$5,800	$7,800	$12,200	$17,000
		4dr MM SI Sdn	$3,600	$5,800	$9,000	$13,100
		2dr MM SI Tourer	$5,800	$8,600	$14,100	$19,400
1950	Minor	2dr MM SI Sdn	$5,800	$7,800	$12,200	$17,000
		4dr MM SI Sdn	$3,600	$5,800	$9,000	$13,100
		2dr MM SI Tourer	$5,800	$8,600	$14,100	$19,400
1951	Minor	2dr MM SI Sdn	$5,800	$7,800	$12,200	$17,000
		4dr MM SI Sdn	$3,600	$5,800	$9,000	$13,100
		2dr MM SI Tourer	$5,800	$8,600	$14,100	$19,400

Year	Model	Body Style	4	3	2	1
1952	Minor	2dr MM SI Sdn	$5,800	$7,800	$12,200	$17,000
		2dr MM SII Sdn	$5,000	$8,300	$12,600	$17,700
		4dr MM SI Sdn	$3,600	$5,800	$9,000	$13,100
		4dr MM SII Sdn	$4,200	$6,200	$10,000	$13,900
		2dr MM SI Tourer	$5,800	$8,600	$14,100	$19,400
		2dr MM SII Tourer	$5,700	$8,700	$14,800	$19,800
1953	Minor	2dr MM SII Sdn	$5,500	$7,600	$13,100	$17,600
		4dr MM SII Sdn	$4,200	$6,200	$10,000	$13,900
		2dr MM SII Tourer	$5,700	$8,700	$14,800	$19,800
1954	Minor	2dr MM SII Sdn	$5,500	$7,600	$13,100	$17,600
		4dr MM SII Sdn	$4,200	$6,200	$10,000	$13,900
		2dr MM SII Tourer	$5,700	$8,700	$14,800	$19,800
1955	Minor	2dr MM SII Sdn	$5,200	$7,800	$12,400	$17,800
		2dr MM SII Tourer	$5,700	$8,700	$14,800	$19,800
		4dr MM SII Sdn	$4,200	$6,200	$10,000	$13,900
1956	Minor	2dr MM SII Sdn	$5,200	$7,900	$12,500	$15,700
		2dr 1000 Sdn	$5,700	$8,900	$14,400	$19,900
		4dr MM SII Sdn	$4,200	$6,300	$10,000	$13,900
		4dr 1000 Sdn	$4,800	$7,300	$11,400	$15,600
		2dr MM SII Tourer	$5,700	$8,900	$14,900	$19,900
		2dr 1000 Conv	$7,700	$11,400	$17,900	$25,200
1957	Minor	2dr 1000 Sdn	$5,700	$8,900	$14,400	$19,900
		4dr 1000 Sdn	$4,800	$7,300	$11,400	$15,600
		2dr 1000 Conv	$7,700	$11,400	$17,900	$25,200
1958	Minor	2dr 1000 Sdn	$5,700	$8,900	$14,400	$19,900
		4dr 1000 Sdn	$4,800	$7,300	$11,400	$15,600
		2dr 1000 Conv	$7,700	$11,400	$17,900	$25,200
1959	Mini Minor	2dr Sdn	$9,900	$13,800	$20,800	$28,300
1959	Minor	2dr 1000 Sdn	$5,700	$8,900	$14,400	$19,900
		4dr 1000 Sdn	$4,800	$7,300	$11,400	$15,600
		2dr 1000 Conv	$7,700	$11,400	$17,900	$25,200
1960	Mini Minor	2dr Sdn	$9,900	$13,800	$20,800	$28,300
1960	Minor	2dr 1000 Sdn	$5,700	$8,900	$14,400	$19,900
		4dr 1000 Sdn	$4,800	$7,300	$11,400	$15,600
		2dr 1000 Conv	$7,700	$11,400	$17,900	$25,200
1961	Mini Minor	2dr Sdn	$9,900	$13,800	$20,800	$28,300
1961	Minor	2dr 1000 Sdn	$5,700	$8,900	$14,400	$19,900
		4dr 1000 Sdn	$4,800	$7,300	$11,400	$15,600
		2dr 1000 Conv	$7,700	$11,400	$17,900	$25,200
1962	Mini Minor	2dr Sdn	$9,900	$13,800	$20,800	$28,300
1962	Minor	2dr 1000 Sdn	$5,700	$8,900	$14,400	$19,900
		4dr 1000 Sdn	$4,800	$7,300	$11,400	$15,600
		2dr 1000 Conv	$7,700	$11,400	$17,900	$25,200
1963	Mini Minor	2dr Sdn	$9,900	$13,800	$20,800	$28,300
1963	Minor	2dr 1000 Sdn	$5,700	$8,900	$14,400	$19,900
		4dr 1000 Sdn	$4,800	$7,300	$11,400	$15,600
		2dr 1000 Conv	$7,700	$11,400	$17,800	$25,200
1964	Mini Minor	2dr Sdn	$9,900	$13,800	$20,800	$28,300
1964	Minor	2dr 1000 Sdn	$5,700	$8,900	$14,400	$19,900
		4dr 1000 Sdn	$4,800	$7,300	$11,400	$15,500

Morris

Year	Model	Body Style	4	3	2	1
		2dr 1000 Conv	$7,700	$11,400	$17,900	$25,200
1965	Mini Minor	2dr Sdn	$9,900	$13,800	$20,800	$28,300
1965	Minor	2dr 1000 Sdn	$5,700	$8,900	$14,400	$19,900
		4dr 1000 Sdn	$4,800	$7,300	$11,400	$15,500
		2dr 1000 Conv	$7,700	$11,400	$17,900	$25,200
1966	Mini Minor	2dr Sdn	$9,900	$13,800	$20,800	$28,300
1966	Minor	2dr 1000 Sdn	$5,700	$8,900	$14,400	$19,900
		4dr 1000 Sdn	$4,800	$7,300	$11,400	$15,500
		2dr 1000 Conv	$7,700	$11,400	$17,900	$25,200
1967	Mini Minor	2dr Sdn	$9,900	$13,800	$20,800	$28,300
1967	Minor	2dr 1000 Sdn	$5,700	$8,900	$14,400	$19,900
		4dr 1000 Sdn	$4,800	$7,300	$11,400	$15,500
		2dr 1000 Conv	$7,700	$11,400	$17,900	$25,200
1968	Mini Minor	2dr Sdn	$9,900	$13,800	$20,800	$28,300
1968	Minor	2dr 1000 Sdn	$5,700	$8,900	$14,400	$19,900
		4dr 1000 Sdn	$4,800	$7,300	$11,400	$15,600
		2dr 1000 Conv	$7,700	$11,400	$17,900	$25,200
1969	Mini Minor	2dr Sdn	$9,900	$13,800	$20,800	$28,300
1969	Minor	2dr 1000 Sdn	$5,700	$8,900	$14,400	$19,900
		4dr 1000 Sdn	$4,800	$7,300	$11,400	$15,500
		2dr 1000 Conv	$7,700	$11,400	$17,900	$25,200
1970	Minor	2dr 1000 Sdn	$5,700	$8,900	$14,400	$19,900
		4dr 1000 Sdn	$4,800	$7,300	$11,400	$15,600
		2dr 1000 Conv	$7,700	$11,400	$17,900	$25,200
1971	Minor	2dr 1000 Sdn	$5,700	$8,900	$14,400	$19,900
		4dr 1000 Sdn	$4,800	$7,300	$11,400	$15,600
		2dr 1000 Conv	$7,700	$11,400	$17,900	$25,200

Muntz

Year	Model	Body Style	4	3	2	1
1951	Jet	336.7/154 2dr Conv	$51,000	$98,200	$143,000	$196,000
1952	Jet	336.7/154 2dr Conv	$51,000	$98,200	$143,000	$196,000
1953	Jet	337/218 2dr Conv	$51,000	$98,200	$143,000	$196,000
1954	Jet	337/218 2dr Conv	$51,000	$98,200	$143,000	$196,000

NSU

Year	Model	Body Style	4	3	2	1
1964	Wankel Spider	2dr Conv	$8,800	$18,800	$33,000	$46,700
1965	Wankel Spider	2dr Conv	$8,800	$18,800	$33,000	$46,700
1966	Wankel Spider	2dr Conv	$8,800	$18,800	$33,000	$46,700
1967	Ro80	4dr Sdn	$3,600	$8,100	$18,000	$27,900
1967	Wankel Spider	2dr Conv	$8,800	$18,800	$33,000	$46,700
1968	Ro80	4dr Sdn	$3,600	$8,200	$18,000	$27,900
1969	Ro80	4dr Sdn	$3,600	$8,200	$18,000	$27,900
1970	Ro80	4dr Sdn	$3,600	$8,200	$18,000	$27,900
1971	Ro80	4dr Sdn	$3,600	$8,200	$18,000	$27,900
1972	Ro80	4dr Sdn	$3,600	$8,200	$18,000	$27,900
1973	Ro80	4dr Sdn	$3,600	$8,200	$17,900	$27,900

NSU

Year	Model	Body Style	4	3	2	1
1974	Ro80	4dr Sdn	$3,600	$8,200	$17,900	$27,900
1975	Ro80	4dr Sdn	$3,600	$8,200	$17,900	$27,900
1976	Ro80	4dr Sdn	$3,600	$8,200	$17,900	$27,900

Nash

Year	Model	Body Style	4	3	2	1
1946	Ambassador	235/112 4dr Woody Sbrbn Sdn	$50,300	$63,300	$77,600	$113,000
1947	Ambassador	235/112 4dr Sbrbn Sdn	$53,000	$66,600	$81,700	$119,000
1948	Ambassador	235/112 2dr Cstm Cab	$35,500	$50,700	$73,400	$103,000
		235/112 4dr Spr Wdy Sbrbn Sdn	$53,000	$66,300	$81,900	$119,000
1950	Rambler	172/82 2dr Wgn	$16,100	$23,900	$32,000	$38,600
		172/82 2dr Conv	$16,100	$23,400	$31,500	$51,100
1951	Rambler	172/82 2dr Cstm Wgn	$16,100	$23,900	$32,000	$42,400
		172/82 2dr Cstm Conv Cpe	$16,100	$23,400	$31,500	$51,100
1952	Rambler	172/82 2dr Cstm Wgn	$16,100	$23,900	$32,000	$38,600
		172/82 2dr Cstm Conv	$16,100	$23,400	$31,500	$51,100
1953	Rambler	184/85 2dr Cstm Wgn	$14,400	$20,100	$25,400	$33,500
		184/85 2dr Cstm Crty Clb Hdtp	$7,200	$12,100	$18,100	$24,700
		184/85 2dr Cstm Conv	$14,900	$24,700	$32,500	$39,400
1954	Metropolitan	2dr Cpe	$5,100	$8,700	$16,300	$26,700
		2dr Conv	$8,100	$15,500	$26,400	$38,500
			Badged from the factory as Nash in 1954-55, Hudson in 1955, Metropolitan in 1956-62.			
1954	Rambler	184/85 2dr Spr Crty Clb Hdtp	$7,200	$12,100	$18,100	$24,700
		184/85 2dr Spr Sbrbn Wgn	$14,400	$20,100	$25,400	$33,500
		184/85 2dr Cstm Conv	$14,900	$24,700	$32,500	$39,400
1955	Metropolitan	2dr Cpe	$5,300	$8,100	$15,900	$25,400
		2dr Conv	$7,500	$12,700	$25,500	$35,600

Nash-Healey

Year	Model	Body Style	4	3	2	1
1951	Series 25	235/125 2dr Conv	$51,000	$71,000	$97,800	$131,000
1952	Series 25	235/125 2dr Conv	$54,500	$71,500	$106,000	$132,000
1953	Series 25	253/140 2dr Conv	$55,800	$74,400	$108,000	$135,000
1953	LeMans	253/140 2dr Hdtp	$38,900	$60,000	$90,000	$114,000

Nash-Healey

Year	Model	Body Style	4	3	2	1
1954	Series 25	253/140 2dr LeMans Hdtp	$38,900	$60,000	$90,000	$114,000

Nissan

Year	Model	Body Style	4	3	2	1
1985	300ZX	2dr 2+2 Htchbk	$4,100	$6,100	$9,400	$14,100
		2dr Turbo Htchbk	$6,500	$9,600	$20,700	$30,900
						-15% for Automatic
1986	300ZX	2dr Htchbk	$3,500	$5,900	$9,200	$12,700
		2dr Turbo Htchbk	$4,200	$6,700	$11,800	$16,800
						-15% for Automatic
1987	300ZX	2dr Htchbk	$3,400	$5,900	$9,200	$12,700
		2dr Turbo Htchbk	$4,300	$6,800	$11,900	$17,300
		2dr 2+2 Htchbk	$2,600	$5,400	$8,100	$10,000
						-15% for Automatic
1988	300ZX	2dr GS Htchbk	$3,400	$5,700	$8,600	$11,900
		2dr Turbo Htchbk	$4,700	$7,400	$13,400	$19,100
		2dr GS 2+2 Htchbk	$3,000	$5,700	$8,600	$10,100
						-15% for Automatic
1989	300ZX	2dr GS Htchbk	$3,500	$5,800	$9,200	$12,300
		2dr Turbo Htchbk	$4,700	$7,400	$13,400	$19,100
		2dr GS 2+2 Htchbk	$3,000	$5,500	$8,500	$10,100
						-15% for Automatic
1989	Skyline	2dr GT-R Cpe	$20,600	$34,900	$51,200	$96,800
1990	300ZX	2dr T-Roof	$5,400	$7,500	$12,100	$16,300
		2dr 2+2 T-Roof	$4,500	$7,000	$10,300	$13,800
		2dr Turbo T-Roof	$6,200	$16,500	$25,900	$52,400
						-15% for Automatic
1990	Skyline	2dr GT-R Cpe	$20,600	$34,900	$51,200	$96,800
1991	300ZX	2dr 2+2 T-Roof	$4,500	$7,000	$10,300	$13,800
		2dr T-Roof	$5,400	$7,200	$12,100	$16,300
		2dr Turbo T-Roof	$6,200	$16,500	$25,900	$52,400
						-15% for Automatic
1991	Skyline	2dr GT-R Cpe	$20,600	$34,900	$51,200	$96,800
1992	300ZX	2dr T-Roof	$5,400	$7,500	$11,500	$14,700
						-15% for Automatic
		2dr Turbo T-Roof	$6,200	$16,500	$25,900	$52,400
		2dr 2+2 T-Roof	$4,500	$7,000	$10,300	$13,800
						-15% for auto.
1992	Skyline	2dr GT-R Cpe	$20,600	$34,900	$51,200	$96,800
1993	300ZX	2dr 2+2 T-Roof	$4,500	$7,000	$10,300	$13,800
		2dr Conv	$4,500	$6,500	$9,800	$14,300
		2dr T-Roof	$5,400	$7,200	$12,100	$16,300
		2dr Turbo T-Roof	$6,200	$16,500	$25,900	$52,400
						-15% for auto.

Nissan

Year	Model	Body Style	4	3	2	1
1993	Skyline	2dr GT-R Cpe	$20,600	$34,900	$51,200	$96,800
1994	300ZX	2dr 2+2 T-Roof	$5,000	$6,900	$10,200	$12,700
		2dr Conv	$4,500	$6,500	$9,800	$14,300
		2dr T-Roof	$5,600	$7,500	$12,800	$16,900
		2dr Turbo T-Roof	$6,200	$16,500	$25,900	$52,400
						-15% for auto.
1995	300ZX	2dr 2+2 T-Roof	$5,000	$6,900	$10,200	$12,700
		2dr Conv	$4,800	$6,700	$10,400	$14,500
		2dr T-Roof	$5,600	$7,500	$12,800	$16,900
		2dr Turbo T-Roof	$6,200	$16,500	$25,900	$52,400
						-15% for auto.
1996	300ZX	2dr 2+2 T-Roof	$5,000	$6,900	$10,200	$12,700
		2dr Conv	$5,000	$6,900	$10,600	$14,900
		2dr T-Roof	$5,600	$7,500	$12,800	$16,900
		2dr Turbo Comm Ed T-Roof	$9,000	$18,700	$35,000	$69,800
		2dr Turbo T-Roof	$7,000	$18,300	$25,900	$61,700
		2dr Comm Ed 2+2 T-Roof	$7,300	$10,000	$14,800	$18,700
		2dr Comm Ed T-Roof	$8,200	$11,200	$17,100	$22,900
						-15% for auto.

OSCA

Year	Model	Body Style	4	3	2	1
1948	MT4	2dr Rdstr	$670,000	$810,000	$1 mil	$1.3 mil
1949	MT4	2dr Rdstr	$670,000	$810,000	$1 mil	$1.3 mil
1950	MT4	2dr Rdstr	$670,000	$810,000	$1 mil	$1.3 mil
1951	MT4	2dr Rdstr	$670,000	$810,000	$1 mil	$1.3 mil
1952	MT4	2dr Rdstr	$670,000	$810,000	$1 mil	$1.3 mil
1953	MT4	2dr Rdstr	$670,000	$810,000	$1 mil	$1.3 mil
1954	MT4	2dr Rdstr	$670,000	$810,000	$1 mil	$1.3 mil
1955	MT4	2dr Rdstr	$670,000	$810,000	$1 mil	$1.3 mil
1961	1600 GT	2dr Cpe	$148,000	$187,000	$236,000	$325,000
1961	1600 GTS	2dr Zagato Cpe	$198,000	$241,000	$329,000	$446,000
		2dr Zagato Dbl Bbl Cpe	$255,000	$328,000	$436,000	$645,000
1962	1600 GT	2dr Cpe	$148,000	$187,000	$236,000	$325,000
1962	1600 GTS	2dr Zagato Cpe	$198,000	$241,000	$329,000	$446,000
		2dr Zagato Dbl Bbl Cpe	$255,000	$328,000	$436,000	$645,000
1963	1600 GTS	2dr Zagato Cpe	$198,000	$241,000	$329,000	$446,000
		2dr Zagato Dbl Bbl Cpe	$255,000	$328,000	$436,000	$645,000
1964	1600 GT	2dr Cpe	$148,000	$187,000	$236,000	$325,000
1964	1600 GTS	2dr Zagato Cpe	$198,000	$241,000	$329,000	$446,000
		2dr Zagato Dbl Bbl Cpe	$255,000	$328,000	$436,000	$645,000

OSCA

Year	Model	Body Style	4	3	2	1
1965	1600 GT	2dr Cpe	$148,000	$187,000	$236,000	$325,000
1965	1600 GTS	2dr Zagato Cpe	$198,000	$241,000	$329,000	$446,000
		2dr Zagato Dbl Bbl Cpe	$255,000	$328,000	$436,000	$645,000
1966	1700	2dr Cpe	$70,200	$98,000	$131,000	$165,000
		2dr Rdstr	$81,500	$104,000	$135,000	$179,000
1967	1700	2dr Cpe	$70,200	$98,000	$131,000	$165,000
		2dr Rdstr	$81,500	$104,000	$135,000	$179,000

OSI

Year	Model	Body Style	4	3	2	1
1966	850	2dr Cpe	$7,200	$12,400	$17,300	$28,600
1966	1200	2dr Cpe	$10,000	$17,200	$29,200	$45,400

OTAS

Year	Model	Body Style	4	3	2	1
1968	Grand Prix	2dr Cpe	$10,200	$18,400	$32,200	$43,800
1969	Grand Prix	2dr Cpe	$10,200	$18,400	$32,200	$43,800
1970	Grand Prix	2dr Cpe	$10,200	$18,400	$32,200	$43,800
1971	Grand Prix	2dr Cpe	$10,200	$18,400	$32,200	$43,800
1972	Grand Prix	2dr Cpe	$10,200	$18,400	$32,200	$43,800

Oldsmobile

Year	Model	Body Style	4	3	2	1
1946	Series 66	238/100 2dr Spcl Clb Cpe	$6,600	$10,000	$15,300	$22,400
		238/100 4dr Spcl Sdn	$5,600	$8,000	$12,900	$19,000
		238/100 4dr Spcl Wgn	$40,700	$60,300	$85,600	$112,000
		238/100 2dr Spcl Conv	$14,300	$20,700	$36,900	$60,100
1946	Series 76	238/100 2dr Dynamic Cruiser Clb Sdn	$6,300	$9,600	$14,000	$20,600
		238/100 4dr Dynamic Cruiser Sdn	$5,800	$8,800	$13,600	$20,000
1946	Series 98	257/110 4dr Cstm 8 Cruiser Sdn	$6,100	$9,000	$14,000	$20,600
		257/110 2dr Cstm 8 Cruiser Conv	$17,800	$26,000	$46,300	$74,500
1947	Series 66	238/100 2dr Spcl Clb Cpe	$6,600	$10,000	$15,300	$22,400
		238/100 2dr Spcl Clb Sdn	$6,600	$9,500	$14,500	$21,300
		238/100 4dr Spcl Sdn	$5,600	$8,000	$12,900	$19,000

Year	Model	Body Style	4	3	2	1
		238/100 4dr Spcl Wgn	$40,700	$60,300	$85,600	$112,000
		238/100 2dr Spcl Conv	$14,300	$20,700	$36,900	$60,100
1947	Series 76	238/100 2dr Dynamic Cruiser Clb Sdn	$6,300	$9,600	$14,000	$20,600
		238/100 4dr Dynamic Cruiser Sdn	$5,800	$8,800	$13,600	$20,000
1947	Series 98	257/110 2dr Cstm Cruiser Clb Sdn	$6,600	$9,700	$14,300	$21,100
		257/110 4dr Cstm Cruiser Sdn	$6,100	$9,000	$14,000	$20,600
		257/110 2dr Cstm Cruiser Conv	$17,800	$26,000	$46,300	$74,500
1948	Series 66	238/100 2dr Dynamic Clb Cpe	$6,800	$10,400	$16,500	$24,600
		238/100 2dr Dynamic Clb Sdn	$6,800	$9,800	$15,700	$23,300
		238/100 4dr Dynamic Sdn	$5,600	$8,000	$12,900	$19,000
		238/100 4dr Dynamic Wgn	$42,800	$62,700	$92,400	$118,000
		238/100 2dr Dynamic Conv	$15,000	$21,700	$38,700	$63,100
1948	Series 76	238/100 2dr Dynamic Clb Sdn	$6,500	$9,900	$15,200	$22,600
		238/100 4dr Dynamic Sdn	$5,800	$8,800	$13,600	$20,000
1948	Series 98	257/115 2dr Futur-amic Clb Sdn	$6,700	$9,900	$15,600	$23,200
		257/115 4dr Futuramic Sdn	$6,100	$8,800	$14,300	$20,900
1949	Futuramic 76	257/105 2dr Clb Cpe	$7,200	$10,800	$17,800	$28,500
		257/105 2dr Sdn	$6,700	$9,800	$15,000	$21,700
		257/105 4dr Sdn	$5,800	$8,200	$13,600	$19,800
		257/105 4dr Twn Sdn	$5,700	$8,200	$13,500	$19,700
		257/105 4dr Dlx Wgn	$43,400	$63,900	$93,600	$119,000
		257/105 2dr Conv	$14,900	$24,000	$42,900	$66,800
1949	Futuramic 88	303/135 2dr Clb Cpe	$7,900	$11,900	$20,200	$31,900
		303/135 4dr Sdn	$6,300	$9,000	$14,900	$22,000
		303/135 4dr Twn Sdn	$5,600	$8,300	$13,600	$19,900
		303/135 4dr Dlx Wgn	$44,900	$64,600	$96,900	$122,000
		303/135 2dr Clb Sdn	$7,200	$10,700	$17,100	$25,300

Oldsmobile

Year	Model	Body Style	4	3	2	1
		303/135 2dr Conv	$18,300	$30,200	$54,500	$81,200
1949	Futuramic 98	303/135 2dr Clb Sdn	$8,500	$12,900	$20,600	$30,500
		303/135 4dr Sdn	$6,800	$9,900	$15,800	$23,300
1950	76	257/105 2dr Clb Cpe	$8,200	$12,900	$21,000	$32,700
		257/105 2dr Sdn	$6,300	$9,200	$14,100	$20,800
		257/105 4dr Wgn	$11,500	$17,700	$26,000	$36,300
		257/105 4dr Dlx Wgn	$43,100	$62,200	$92,300	$120,000
		257/105 2dr Clb Sdn	$6,300	$9,600	$15,100	$22,600
		257/105 4dr Sdn	$5,800	$8,100	$14,100	$20,400
		257/105 2dr Dlx Hol Cpe	$10,200	$16,900	$26,100	$37,700
		257/105 2dr Conv Cpe	$14,800	$23,900	$43,300	$67,200
1950	88	304/135 2dr Dlx Clb Cpe	$9,700	$15,100	$25,800	$40,200
		304/135 2dr Dlx Sdn	$7,500	$11,300	$17,000	$24,800
		304/135 4dr Dlx Sdn	$6,500	$9,500	$15,400	$22,700
		304/135 4dr Wgn	$12,900	$19,100	$29,000	$42,600
		304/135 4dr Dlx Wgn	$45,300	$65,700	$97,200	$124,000
		304/135 4dr Dlx Clb Sdn	$6,800	$9,900	$16,200	$23,900
		304/135 2dr Dlx Hol Cpe	$12,100	$19,900	$32,600	$46,900
		304/135 2dr Conv Cpe	$19,000	$31,800	$59,500	$90,100
1950	98	304/135 2dr Dlx Clb Sdn	$6,300	$9,600	$15,000	$22,500
		304/135 4dr Dlx Sdn	$5,900	$8,500	$14,200	$20,500
		304/135 4dr Dlx Twn Sdn	$6,400	$9,300	$15,400	$22,300
		304/135 2dr Dlx Hol Cpe	$11,600	$18,500	$30,300	$44,200
		304/135 2dr Dlx Conv Cpe	$18,400	$30,000	$55,300	$89,000
1951	88	304/135 2dr Sdn	$6,400	$9,600	$15,000	$21,800
		304/135 4dr Sdn	$5,600	$8,200	$13,600	$20,100
1951	Super 88	304/135 2dr Dlx Clb Cpe	$8,100	$12,400	$20,000	$31,600
		304/135 2dr Dlx Sdn	$6,500	$9,800	$15,200	$22,100
		304/135 4dr Dlx Sdn	$5,800	$8,500	$14,300	$21,100

Year	Model	Body Style	4	3	2	1
		304/135 2dr Dlx Hol Cpe	$10,900	$16,800	$24,600	$35,900
		304/135 2dr Dlx Conv Cpe	$16,500	$27,000	$48,100	$79,100
1951	98	304/135 2dr Hol Cpe	$9,500	$14,700	$24,000	$34,700
		304/135 4dr Dlx Hol Sdn	$5,900	$8,400	$14,300	$20,800
		304/135 2dr Dlx Conv Cpe	$17,000	$28,200	$52,700	$87,800
1952	Deluxe 88	304/145 2dr Sdn	$6,300	$9,500	$15,300	$23,400
		304/145 4dr Sdn	$5,800	$8,300	$14,000	$20,400
1952	Super 88	304/160 2dr Clb Cpe	$6,700	$10,600	$16,200	$24,700
		304/160 2dr Sdn	$6,600	$9,900	$15,500	$23,200
		304/160 4dr Sdn	$6,200	$8,900	$15,100	$22,000
		304/160 2dr Hol Cpe	$10,100	$15,200	$21,500	$32,100
		304/160 2dr Conv Cpe	$16,200	$27,000	$50,100	$83,400
1952	Ninety-Eight	304/160 2dr Hol Cpe	$9,700	$15,000	$23,200	$34,600
		304/160 4dr Sdn	$6,000	$8,800	$14,400	$21,300
		304/160 2dr Conv Cpe	$16,600	$27,800	$53,700	$87,400
1953	Deluxe 88	304/150 2dr Sdn	$6,000	$9,200	$14,400	$20,700
		304/150 4dr Sdn	$5,500	$8,000	$13,100	$19,300
1953	Super 88	304/165 2dr Sdn	$6,600	$9,800	$15,100	$22,300
		304/165 4dr Sdn	$6,100	$8,800	$14,600	$21,400
		304/165 2dr Hol Cpe	$9,900	$14,700	$21,000	$31,300
		304/165 2dr Conv Cpe	$17,600	$29,100	$51,300	$84,600
1953	Ninety-Eight	304/165 2dr Hol Cpe	$10,700	$16,100	$25,900	$37,900
		304/165 4dr Sdn	$5,600	$8,300	$13,500	$19,700
		304/165 2dr Conv Cpe	$16,500	$28,400	$54,400	$87,600
		304/165 2dr Fiesta Conv Cpe	$83,000	$109,000	$152,000	$208,000
					+10% for factory a/c.	
1954	88	324/170 2dr Sdn	$7,500	$11,300	$16,000	$23,500
		324/170 4dr Sdn	$6,400	$9,600	$13,500	$19,800
		324/170 2dr Hol Cpe	$10,300	$15,600	$21,800	$32,000
1954	Super 88	324/185 2dr Sdn	$6,900	$10,400	$14,800	$21,700
		324/185 4dr Sdn	$6,700	$10,100	$14,200	$20,800
		324/185 2dr Hol Cpe	$10,500	$15,900	$22,800	$33,300
		324/185 2dr Conv Cpe	$23,100	$32,300	$53,200	$77,400

Oldsmobile

Year	Model	Body Style	4	3	2	1
1954	Ninety-Eight	324/185 2dr Hol Cpe	$11,500	$17,300	$24,400	$35,600
		324/185 4dr Sdn	$6,600	$9,900	$14,000	$20,500
		324/185 2dr Starfire Conv	$31,500	$46,400	$68,600	$101,000
						+10% for factory a/c.
1955	88	324/185 2dr Sdn	$6,900	$10,600	$15,300	$22,700
		324/185 4dr Sdn	$6,300	$9,400	$13,200	$19,500
		324/185 2dr Hol Cpe	$10,300	$15,300	$21,400	$31,600
		324/185 4dr Hol Hdtp Sdn	$7,200	$11,200	$17,300	$25,800
1955	Super 88	324/202 2dr Sdn	$7,200	$10,900	$15,300	$22,500
		324/202 4dr Sdn	$6,800	$10,100	$14,200	$20,900
		324/202 2dr Hol Cpe	$11,100	$16,700	$25,200	$36,700
		324/202 4dr Hol Hdtp Sdn	$8,300	$12,900	$19,200	$28,800
		324/202 2dr Conv	$26,900	$42,400	$64,600	$94,000
1955	Series 98	324/202 2dr Hol Cpe	$11,600	$17,500	$24,600	$36,100
		324/202 4dr Sdn	$6,700	$10,000	$14,300	$20,800
		324/202 4dr Hol Hdtp Sdn	$6,900	$11,100	$16,600	$25,100
		324/202 2dr Conv	$30,300	$46,100	$67,200	$99,900
						+10% for factory a/c.
1956	Super 88	324/240 2dr Sdn	$7,500	$11,400	$15,900	$22,900
		324/240 4dr Sdn	$6,600	$9,800	$13,900	$20,000
		324/240 2dr Hol Cpe	$10,900	$16,500	$23,800	$34,500
		324/240 4dr Hol Sdn	$7,500	$11,600	$17,900	$27,400
		324/240 2dr Conv	$25,200	$39,800	$63,300	$92,400
1956	Ninety-Eight	324/240 2dr Hol Cpe	$11,800	$17,800	$25,200	$36,400
		324/240 4dr Sdn	$6,800	$10,300	$14,500	$21,000
		324/240 4dr Hol Sdn	$8,600	$13,700	$20,500	$31,000
		324/240 2dr Starfire Conv	$31,000	$47,400	$68,800	$100,000
1956	88	324/230 2dr Sdn	$7,300	$11,000	$15,700	$22,600
		324/230 4dr Sdn	$6,400	$9,600	$13,600	$19,800
		324/230 2dr Hol Cpe	$10,300	$15,300	$21,600	$31,500
		324/230 4dr Hol Sdn	$7,300	$11,400	$17,700	$26,800
1957	Golden Rocket 88	371/277 2dr Sdn	$6,500	$9,300	$13,300	$19,500
		371/300 2dr Sdn	$9,800	$13,900	$19,900	$29,300
		371/277 4dr Sdn	$6,300	$9,000	$12,800	$19,000

Year	Model	Body Style	4	3	2	1
		371/300 4dr Sdn	$9,400	$13,500	$19,200	$28,600
		371/277 4dr Fiesta Wgn	$24,900	$44,400	$61,700	$94,900
		371/300 4dr Fiesta Wgn	$33,900	$55,300	$74,800	$104,000
		371/277 2dr Hol Cpe	$10,400	$15,300	$24,000	$35,600
		371/300 2dr Hol Cpe	$16,900	$24,800	$37,200	$55,300
		371/277 4dr Hol Hdtp Sdn	$6,600	$9,500	$13,700	$19,800
		371/300 4dr Hol Hdtp Sdn	$9,800	$14,100	$20,200	$31,300
		371/277 2dr Conv	$22,800	$35,400	$50,600	$75,700
		371/300 2dr Conv	$29,600	$46,200	$66,500	$100,000
1957	Super 88	371/277 2dr Sdn	$7,000	$10,100	$14,500	$21,200
		371/300 2dr Sdn	$10,400	$15,000	$21,700	$31,700
		371/277 4dr Sdn	$6,400	$9,200	$13,100	$19,200
		371/300 4dr Sdn	$9,600	$13,800	$19,600	$28,900
		371/277 4dr Fiesta Wgn	$20,600	$29,800	$42,500	$61,900
		371/300 4dr Fiesta Wgn	$31,100	$44,900	$63,700	$92,900
		371/277 2dr Hol Cpe	$10,500	$15,400	$23,100	$34,400
		371/300 2dr Hol Cpe	$16,500	$24,600	$37,800	$59,100
		371/277 4dr Hol Hdtp Sdn	$6,800	$9,900	$14,300	$20,700
		371/300 4dr Hol Hdtp Sdn	$10,300	$14,900	$21,600	$33,600
		371/277 2dr Conv	$23,900	$37,300	$52,700	$79,100
		371/300 2dr Conv	$35,400	$58,000	$80,200	$118,000
1957	Starfire 98	371/277 2dr Hol Cpe	$13,000	$19,100	$28,100	$42,200
		371/300 2dr Hol Cpe	$20,400	$30,100	$43,400	$65,300
		371/277 4dr Sdn	$6,700	$9,800	$14,000	$20,500
		371/300 4dr Sdn	$10,100	$14,500	$20,900	$30,800
		371/277 4dr Hol Hdtp Sdn	$9,900	$14,900	$20,500	$32,700
		371/300 4dr Hol Hdtp Sdn	$12,900	$19,300	$27,300	$40,400
		371/277 2dr Conv	$27,500	$41,000	$60,200	$90,700
		371/300 2dr Conv	$44,800	$67,800	$104,000	$140,000
1958	Dynamic 88	371/265 2dr Sdn	$7,700	$11,300	$16,100	$23,600
		371/312 2dr Sdn	$9,600	$14,100	$20,000	$29,600
		371/265 4dr Sdn	$6,300	$8,900	$12,700	$18,600
		371/312 4dr Sdn	$7,900	$11,200	$15,900	$23,200

Oldsmobile

Year	Model	Body Style	4	3	2	1
		371/312 4dr Fiesta Wgn	$19,000	$27,100	$38,900	$56,700
		371/265 2dr Hol Cpe	$10,100	$14,800	$21,500	$32,800
		371/312 2dr Hol Cpe	$13,700	$19,000	$28,400	$42,900
		371/265 4dr Hol Sdn	$5,900	$8,600	$12,200	$17,900
		371/312 4dr Hol Sdn	$7,400	$10,700	$15,200	$22,200
		371/265 4dr Fiesta Hdtp Wgn	$15,100	$21,100	$30,200	$42,900
		371/265 2dr Conv	$18,400	$27,900	$40,200	$60,800
		371/312 2dr Conv	$25,500	$39,000	$56,000	$87,100
1958	Super 88	371/305 2dr Hol Cpe	$10,500	$15,700	$23,500	$35,000
		371/312 2dr Hol Cpe	$14,700	$20,900	$34,700	$52,800
		371/305 4dr Sdn	$6,800	$9,800	$14,000	$20,500
		371/312 4dr Sdn	$8,500	$12,300	$17,400	$25,700
		371/305 4dr Hol Hdtp Sdn	$7,300	$10,500	$15,100	$21,800
		371/312 4dr Hol Hdtp Sdn	$8,400	$12,600	$17,700	$28,900
		371/305 4dr Fiesta Wgn	$17,800	$25,600	$36,600	$53,200
		371/312 4dr Fiesta Wgn	$22,300	$32,000	$45,800	$66,500
		371/305 2dr Conv	$24,200	$37,800	$53,100	$81,100
		371/312 2dr Conv	$30,000	$47,400	$67,000	$94,500
1958	Ninety-Eight	371/305 2dr Hol Cpe	$11,600	$16,800	$25,200	$38,100
		371/312 2dr Hol Cpe	$14,200	$20,700	$31,700	$48,500
		371/305 4dr Sdn	$6,500	$9,300	$13,300	$19,500
		371/312 4dr Sdn	$8,100	$11,700	$16,500	$24,400
		371/305 4dr Hol Sdn	$6,900	$9,900	$14,200	$20,700
		371/312 4dr Hol Sdn	$8,200	$11,800	$16,800	$24,600
		371/305 2dr Conv	$29,000	$43,500	$65,300	$99,600
		371/312 2dr Conv	$39,500	$63,100	$89,700	$128,000
1959	Dynamic 88	371/270 2dr Sdn	$7,500	$10,800	$15,300	$22,000
		371/270 4dr Sdn	$5,100	$7,300	$10,400	$14,800
		371/270 4dr Fiesta Wgn	$10,100	$14,300	$20,200	$28,500
		371/270 2dr Hol Cpe	$7,600	$11,200	$17,100	$25,800
		371/270 4dr Hol Sdn	$5,400	$8,100	$12,600	$19,800

Year	Model	Body Style	4	3	2	1
		371/270 2dr Conv Cpe	$19,100	$30,000	$40,000	$61,200
1959	Super 88	394/315 2dr Hol Cpe	$8,200	$12,200	$18,300	$27,800
		394/315 4dr Sdn	$5,200	$7,400	$10,600	$15,000
		394/315 4dr Hol Sdn	$7,200	$10,600	$16,600	$26,300
		394/315 2dr Conv	$24,500	$39,300	$52,800	$73,500
		394/315 4dr Fiesta Wgn	$12,000	$17,600	$26,200	$36,300
1959	Ninety-Eight	394/315 2dr Hol Cpe	$9,200	$14,700	$20,700	$32,400
		394/315 4dr Sdn	$5,400	$7,600	$10,900	$15,500
		394/315 4dr Hol Sdn	$6,900	$10,400	$16,200	$25,500
		394/315 2dr Conv	$36,000	$50,600	$67,600	$93,600
1960	Dynamic 88	371/240 2dr Sdn	$7,100	$10,100	$14,500	$20,800
		371/240 4dr Sdn	$5,300	$7,600	$10,600	$15,400
		371/240 4dr Wgn	$7,900	$11,700	$16,500	$24,100
		371/240 2dr Hol Cpe	$6,800	$10,000	$15,600	$23,800
		371/240 4dr Hol Sdn	$4,400	$6,500	$10,200	$16,000
		371/240 2dr Conv	$15,800	$23,000	$32,500	$47,000
1960	Super 88	394/315 2dr Hol Cpe	$8,000	$11,600	$17,800	$26,800
		394/315 4dr Sdn	$5,500	$7,900	$11,000	$16,000
		394/315 4dr Wgn	$8,500	$12,600	$17,600	$25,800
		394/315 4dr Hol Sdn	$5,800	$9,100	$14,300	$22,900
		394/315 2dr Conv	$17,100	$24,700	$35,000	$51,000
1960	98	394/315 2dr Hol Cpe	$8,200	$12,300	$18,400	$27,900
		394/315 4dr Sdn	$5,800	$8,200	$11,500	$16,800
		394/315 4dr Hol Sdn	$5,700	$8,200	$13,300	$20,800
		394/315 2dr Conv	$17,900	$25,800	$36,700	$53,300
1961	F-85	215/155 2dr Clb Cpe	$4,000	$5,500	$7,900	$11,100
		215/155 4dr Dlx Stn Wgn	$4,500	$6,600	$9,200	$13,000
		215/185 2dr Cutlass Spt Cpe	$5,600	$8,200	$11,700	$16,100
1961	Dynamic 88	394/250 2dr Sdn	$4,400	$5,900	$8,600	$12,000
		394/250 4dr Sdn	$5,300	$7,800	$11,000	$15,300
		394/250 4dr Stn Wgn	$6,900	$10,400	$14,500	$20,100
		394/250 2dr Hol Cpe	$9,400	$12,400	$19,400	$28,100

Oldsmobile

Year	Model	Body Style	4	3	2	1
		394/250 4dr Hol Sdn	$4,400	$6,800	$10,000	$15,000
		394/250 2dr Conv	$16,700	$26,200	$34,800	$47,800
1961	Super 88	394/325 2dr Hol Cpe	$9,400	$12,700	$20,000	$28,700
		394/325 4dr Sdn	$4,300	$6,000	$8,600	$12,200
		394/325 4dr Stn Wgn	$7,300	$10,800	$15,000	$21,000
		394/325 4dr Hol Sdn	$5,400	$7,900	$11,600	$16,600
		394/325 2dr Conv	$15,900	$23,600	$33,100	$46,600
1961	Starfire	394/330 2dr Conv	$25,200	$34,300	$66,900	$88,800
1961	Ninety-Eight	394/325 2dr Hol Cpe	$10,500	$14,200	$22,400	$31,900
		394/325 4dr Spt Sdn	$4,300	$6,000	$8,600	$12,200
		394/325 4dr Twn Sdn	$3,700	$5,400	$7,700	$10,800
		394/325 4dr Hol Sdn	$5,800	$8,600	$12,500	$18,900
		394/325 2dr Conv	$16,600	$24,800	$34,600	$50,600
1962	F-85	215/155 2dr Clb Cpe	$3,900	$5,600	$8,000	$11,500
		215/155 4dr Sdn	$4,300	$5,900	$8,500	$12,200
		215/155 4dr Stn Wgn	$5,100	$7,400	$10,600	$14,500
		215/185 2dr Cutlass Cpe	$5,600	$8,300	$11,700	$16,200
		215/215 2dr Jetfire Cpe	$6,800	$10,000	$14,100	$19,600
		215/155 2dr Conv	$6,100	$8,800	$12,400	$17,800
		215/185 2dr Cutlass Conv	$9,700	$14,700	$20,300	$28,900
1962	Dynamic 88	394/280 2dr Hol Cpe	$9,200	$12,400	$19,700	$28,300
		394/280 4dr Sdn	$5,600	$7,900	$11,200	$15,700
		394/280 4dr Fiesta Stn Wgn	$5,500	$7,800	$11,200	$15,200
		394/280 4dr Hol Sdn	$4,000	$6,000	$8,800	$13,500
		394/280 2dr Conv	$13,500	$20,800	$28,400	$39,700
1962	Super 88	394/330 2dr Hol Cpe	$9,200	$12,400	$19,600	$28,200
1962	Starfire	394/345 2dr Cpe	$12,100	$17,400	$25,300	$35,300
		394/345 2dr Conv	$15,700	$23,100	$35,500	$49,400
1962	Ninety-Eight	394/330 2dr Hol Cpe	$10,100	$13,500	$21,500	$30,600
		394/330 4dr Sdn	$5,300	$7,600	$10,700	$14,700
		394/330 4dr Hol Sdn	$5,300	$7,600	$11,300	$16,200

Year	Model	Body Style	4	3	2	1
		394/330 4dr Twn Sdn	$5,200	$7,400	$10,300	$14,400
		394/330 2dr Conv	$12,500	$18,800	$26,000	$38,000
1963	F-85	215/155 2dr Cpe	$4,300	$6,100	$8,700	$12,400
		215/185 2dr Cutlass Cpe	$7,100	$10,800	$15,000	$21,100
		215/215 2dr Jetfire Hdtp Cpe	$10,500	$15,300	$22,400	$35,300
		215/185 2dr Cutlass Conv	$10,200	$15,200	$21,400	$30,200
1963	Dynamic 88	394/280 2dr Hol Cpe	$8,900	$11,800	$18,900	$27,500
		394/280 2dr Conv	$11,500	$17,300	$24,000	$33,800
1963	Super 88	394/330 2dr Hol Cpe	$8,900	$11,800	$18,900	$27,500
1963	Starfire	394/345 2dr Hol Cpe	$11,100	$16,300	$24,300	$35,000
		394/345 2dr Conv	$15,400	$22,800	$34,100	$48,300
1963	Ninety-Eight	394/330 2dr Hol Cpe	$10,200	$13,900	$21,700	$31,300
		394/345 2dr Cstm Spt Cpe	$6,500	$9,200	$13,100	$18,400
		394/330 2dr Conv	$12,400	$18,600	$25,800	$37,800
1964	Cutlass	330/290 2dr Cpe	$9,300	$13,600	$19,100	$26,800
		330/310 2dr 4-4-2 Cpe	$15,500	$23,600	$37,300	$50,800
		330/290 2dr Hol Cpe	$9,600	$14,100	$20,300	$28,700
		330/290 2dr Conv	$14,900	$22,500	$32,600	$48,300
		330/310 2dr 4-4-2 Conv	$21,100	$31,300	$45,700	$64,300
1964	Vista Cruiser	330/245 4dr Stn Wgn	$7,500	$10,400	$16,000	$27,800
1964	Jetstar 88	330/245 2dr Hol Cpe	$4,300	$6,200	$9,100	$13,200
		330/245 2dr Conv	$10,900	$16,500	$23,300	$32,500
1964	Jetstar I	394/345 2dr Spt Cpe	$6,500	$9,200	$13,200	$18,500
1964	Dynamic 88	394/280 2dr Hol Cpe	$7,400	$9,800	$15,000	$20,500
		394/280 2dr Conv	$11,300	$16,800	$23,800	$33,200
1964	Starfire	394/345 2dr Cpe	$9,600	$15,200	$21,300	$29,200
		394/345 2dr Conv	$14,800	$22,600	$32,100	$47,600
1964	Ninety-Eight	394/330 2dr Hol Cpe	$8,900	$11,800	$18,100	$25,300
		394/345 2dr Cstm Spt Cpe	$6,800	$9,800	$13,900	$19,600
		394/330 2dr Conv	$13,200	$20,100	$28,200	$40,600
1965	F-85	400/345 2dr 4-4-2 Clb Cpe	$15,800	$24,200	$37,300	$50,000

Oldsmobile

Year	Model	Body Style	4	3	2	1
1965	Cutlass	330/315 2dr Spt Cpe	$7,600	$11,300	$15,700	$22,100
		330/315 2dr Hol Cpe	$7,500	$11,200	$15,500	$21,900
		330/315 2dr Conv	$12,200	$18,400	$26,400	$39,700
		400/345 2dr 4-4-2 Conv	$21,700	$32,000	$46,400	$65,500
1965	Vista Cruiser	330/250 4dr Stn Wgn	$7,700	$11,000	$16,700	$29,100
1965	Jetstar 88	330/260 2dr Hol Cpe	$4,600	$6,600	$9,200	$13,100
		330/260 2dr Conv	$10,200	$15,200	$21,400	$30,400
1965	Jetstar I	425/370 2dr Spt Cpe	$5,700	$8,000	$11,600	$16,200
1965	Dynamic 88	425/300 2dr Hol Cpe	$4,800	$7,100	$10,000	$13,900
		425/300 2dr Conv	$10,100	$15,100	$21,400	$30,200
1965	Delta 88	425/300 2dr Hol Cpe	$5,400	$7,900	$12,000	$17,000
1965	Starfire	425/370 2dr Spt Cpe	$9,700	$14,100	$19,700	$28,000
		425/370 2dr Conv	$14,900	$22,700	$32,500	$48,300
1965	Series 98	425/360 2dr Spt Cpe	$6,300	$9,100	$13,000	$18,400
		425/360 2dr Conv	$11,000	$16,400	$23,300	$32,800
1966	Cutlass	330/310 2dr Spt Cpe	$6,600	$9,400	$13,300	$18,700
		400/350 2dr 4-4-2 Spt Cpe	$17,200	$25,800	$41,000	$54,100
		400/360 2dr 4-4-2 Spt Cpe	$25,400	$38,200	$60,800	$80,200
		330/310 2dr Hol Cpe	$7,500	$11,100	$15,400	$21,800
		330/310 2dr Conv	$11,400	$16,900	$24,500	$37,400
		400/350 2dr 4-4-2 Conv	$23,200	$34,600	$49,800	$69,800
		400/360 2dr 4-4-2 Conv	$34,400	$51,200	$73,800	$103,000
1966	Vista Cruiser	330/250 4dr Stn Wgn	$7,600	$10,900	$16,500	$28,700
1966	Jetstar 88	330/250 2dr Hol Cpe	$5,100	$7,300	$10,100	$14,500
1966	Dynamic 88	425/310 2dr Hol Cpe	$5,100	$7,300	$10,100	$14,500
		425/310 2dr Conv	$9,800	$14,200	$20,400	$28,700
1966	Delta 88	425/310 2dr Hol Cpe	$5,400	$7,800	$11,900	$17,100
		425/310 2dr Conv	$10,000	$14,700	$20,700	$29,800
1966	Starfire	425/375 2dr Cpe	$7,900	$12,500	$16,400	$24,300

Year	Model	Body Style	4	3	2	1
1966	Ninety-Eight	425/365 2dr Hol Cpe	$5,400	$7,800	$11,700	$15,900
		425/365 2dr Conv	$9,800	$14,500	$22,600	$33,600
1966	Toronado	425/385 2dr Spt Cpe	$8,100	$17,000	$29,600	$40,500
1967	Cutlass	330/250 2dr Hol Cpe	$7,100	$10,200	$14,300	$20,200
		330/250 2dr Conv	$11,600	$17,600	$25,300	$38,000
1967	Cutlass Supreme	330/320 2dr Cpe	$7,500	$11,300	$15,700	$22,600
		400/350 2dr 4-4-2 Spt Cpe	$18,600	$29,200	$41,400	$57,000
		400/350 W-30 2dr 4-4-2 Spt Cpe	$24,100	$37,800	$53,600	$73,900
		330/320 2dr Conv	$13,000	$20,500	$29,100	$44,600
		400/350 2dr 4-4-2 Conv	$23,000	$34,500	$48,200	$70,000
		400/350 W-30 2dr 4-4-2 Conv	$30,900	$46,500	$64,800	$94,200
1967	Vista Cruiser	330/250 4dr Wgn	$7,500	$10,700	$16,300	$28,600
1967	Delmont 88	425/300 2dr 425 Conv	$9,800	$14,300	$19,900	$28,700
1967	Delta 88	425/300 2dr Hol Cpe	$5,000	$7,600	$11,200	$16,400
		425/300 2dr Conv	$10,400	$15,300	$21,600	$30,700
1967	Ninety-Eight	425/365 2dr Hol Cpe	$5,400	$7,800	$11,700	$16,000
		425/365 2dr Conv	$9,400	$13,800	$21,500	$31,900
1967	Toronado	425/385 2dr Cpe	$7,300	$15,300	$27,000	$36,400
1968	Cutlass	350/250 2dr S Hol Cpe	$7,800	$11,400	$16,500	$23,000
		350/250 2dr S Conv	$12,000	$19,200	$24,900	$39,500
1968	4-4-2	400/325 2dr Spt Cpe	$16,900	$24,400	$35,700	$51,300
		455/390 2dr Hurst Cpe	$29,500	$53,600	$74,000	$101,000
		400/360 2dr W-30 Hol Cpe	$27,100	$40,200	$58,700	$85,800
		400/325 2dr Conv	$19,700	$30,000	$45,400	$74,200
		400/360 2dr W-30 Conv	$55,700	$74,300	$110,000	$155,000
1968	Vista Cruiser	350/250 4dr Stn Wgn	$5,200	$9,000	$12,100	$20,200
1968	Delmont 88	350/250 2dr Conv	$9,800	$14,300	$19,900	$28,700
1968	Delta 88	455/310 2dr Hol Cpe	$4,900	$7,200	$11,000	$16,000

Oldsmobile

Year	Model	Body Style	4	3	2	1
1968	Ninety-Eight	455/365 2dr Hol Cpe	$5,100	$7,700	$11,200	$15,600
		455/365 2dr Conv	$8,600	$12,500	$19,200	$28,800
1968	Toronado	455/375 2dr Cpe	$7,100	$15,100	$26,400	$35,600
1969	Cutlass	350/250 2dr Cpe	$8,100	$12,100	$17,400	$24,600
		350/250 2dr Conv	$12,300	$20,500	$26,400	$42,200
1969	4-4-2	400/350 2dr Spt Cpe	$16,800	$25,400	$38,200	$55,600
		400/360 2dr W-30 Spt Cpe	$30,800	$46,300	$68,300	$99,500
		350/325 2dr W-31 Spt Cpe	$24,200	$37,600	$55,800	$77,000
		455/380 2dr Hurst Hol Cpe	$30,500	$58,000	$79,000	$97,000
		400/350 2dr Conv	$20,700	$31,600	$50,000	$82,800
		400/360 2dr W-30 Conv	$71,600	$114,000	$135,000	$156,000
						+20% for 4-spd.
1969	Vista Cruiser	400/325 4dr Stn Wgn	$5,200	$9,000	$12,000	$20,000
1969	Delta 88	455/310 2dr Royale Hol Cpe	$4,900	$7,100	$11,000	$15,900
		350/250 2dr Conv	$8,100	$13,200	$18,500	$26,600
1969	Ninety-Eight	455/365 2dr Conv	$8,600	$12,500	$19,300	$28,700
1969	Toronado	455/375 2dr Cpe	$7,200	$15,200	$26,600	$35,900
1970	Cutlass	350/250 2dr S Spt Cpe	$8,100	$12,200	$17,600	$25,100
		350/310 2dr Rallye 350 Hol Cpe	$13,800	$21,000	$31,000	$42,600
1970	Cutlass Supreme	350/250 2dr Conv	$11,300	$16,400	$25,100	$40,200
1970	4-4-2	455/365 2dr Spt Cpe	$18,500	$28,300	$40,900	$64,400
		455/370 2dr W-30 Hol Cpe	$46,200	$70,800	$98,100	$119,000
		455/365 2dr Conv	$38,400	$62,700	$88,800	$132,000
		455/370 2dr W-30 Conv	$76,300	$114,000	$156,000	$218,000
						+30% for Indy 500 Pace Car pkg. +20% for 4-spd.
1970	Vista Cruiser	350/250 4dr Stn Wgn	$5,400	$9,000	$12,300	$20,400
1970	Delta 88	350/310 2dr Hol Cpe	$5,000	$7,100	$11,200	$16,100
		350/310 2dr Conv	$8,300	$13,500	$18,800	$29,100
1970	Ninety-Eight	455/365 2dr Conv	$8,000	$11,900	$18,200	$27,300
1970	Toronado	455/375 2dr Cpe	$5,900	$11,700	$18,300	$26,200

Year	Model	Body Style	4	3	2	1
1971	Cutlass	350/240 2dr S Hdtp Cpe	$7,000	$10,200	$14,500	$20,700
1971	Cutlass Supreme	350/260 2dr Hdtp Cpe	$7,800	$12,000	$16,600	$24,100
		455/320 2dr SX Hdtp Cpe	$10,000	$16,000	$21,300	$37,500
		350/260 2dr Conv	$10,900	$16,600	$23,900	$39,400
		455/320 2dr SX Conv	$13,900	$21,600	$29,800	$61,500
1971	4-4-2	455/340 2dr Hdtp Cpe	$21,800	$33,000	$50,200	$68,400
		455/350 2dr W-30 Cpe	$34,900	$49,300	$82,700	$94,800
		455/340 2dr Conv	$30,400	$44,600	$70,200	$112,000
		455/350 2dr W-30 Conv	$75,800	$120,000	$146,000	$179,000
						+20% for 4-spd.
1971	Vista Cruiser	350/240 4dr Stn Wgn	$5,200	$8,400	$12,000	$19,300
1971	Delta 88	455/280 2dr Royale Conv	$7,300	$11,300	$17,600	$27,200
1971	Toronado	455/350 2dr Hdtp Cpe	$4,800	$8,000	$11,600	$16,500
1972	Cutlass	350/180 2dr Hdtp Cpe	$6,000	$9,400	$12,700	$18,300
		350/180 2dr S Hdtp Cpe	$5,900	$9,100	$12,900	$18,400
		455/250 2dr 4-4-2 Hdtp Cpe	$14,700	$20,600	$31,000	$41,400
		455/300 2dr 4-4-2 W-30 Hdtp Cpe	$20,000	$30,100	$43,800	$61,300
		455/275 2dr Hurst/Olds Hdtp Cpe	$20,200	$32,700	$44,500	$63,900
		455/250 2dr 4-4-2 Conv	$20,700	$33,700	$44,200	$71,100
		455/300 2dr 4-4-2 W-30 Conv	$50,200	$74,200	$109,000	$154,000
						+20% for 4-spd.
1972	Cutlass Supreme	350/180 2dr Hdtp Cpe	$8,400	$13,000	$17,400	$24,900
		350/180 2dr Conv	$12,100	$18,100	$26,100	$41,700
						+20% for 4-spd.
1972	Vista Cruiser	350/160 4dr Wgn	$5,700	$9,300	$13,100	$21,600
1972	Delta 88	2dr Royale Conv	$7,900	$12,200	$19,500	$32,400
1972	Toronado	2dr Hdtp Cpe	$5,400	$8,000	$11,400	$16,200
1973	Cutlass	350/180 2dr 4-4-2 Cpe	$10,500	$16,000	$22,000	$35,100

Oldsmobile

Year	Model	Body Style	4	3	2	1
		455/250 2dr 4-4-2 Cpe	$10,900	$16,600	$22,800	$36,500
		455/270 2dr 4-4-2 Cpe	$11,200	$17,100	$23,500	$37,600
		455/270 2dr Hurst/Olds Cpe	$12,500	$20,100	$28,700	$42,000
		350/180 2dr Hdtp Cpe	$6,000	$8,900	$14,000	$21,100
1973	Vista Cruiser	455/275 4dr Stn Wgn	$5,700	$8,200	$11,700	$17,200
1973	Delta 88	350/180 2dr Royale Conv	$7,500	$11,600	$18,500	$30,900
1973	Toronado	455/250 2dr Hdtp Cpe	$5,000	$7,500	$10,600	$15,200
1974	Cutlass	350/180 2dr Hdtp Cpe	$5,400	$8,600	$12,000	$17,600
		455/230 2dr 4-4-2 Hdtp Cpe	$9,000	$14,000	$20,000	$28,000
		455/230 2dr Hurst/Olds Hdtp Cpe	$12,000	$17,500	$26,300	$36,400
						+10% for Pace Car
1974	Vista Cruiser	350/180 4dr Stn Wgn	$4,900	$6,800	$9,700	$14,400
1974	Delta 88	2dr Royale Conv	$7,700	$12,000	$19,000	$31,400
1974	Toronado	455/230 2dr Hdtp Cpe	$5,000	$7,500	$10,600	$14,900
1975	Cutlass	350/170 2dr Colonnade Hdtp Cpe	$5,500	$8,200	$11,500	$16,700
		350/170 2dr Hurst/Olds Hdtp Cpe	$9,500	$15,500	$22,100	$34,300
		455/190 2dr Hurst/Olds Hdtp Cpe	$10,400	$17,000	$24,500	$37,800
1975	Cutlass Supreme	350/170 4dr Vista Cruiser Stn Wgn	$4,900	$7,200	$10,200	$14,900
1975	Delta 88	350/170 2dr Royale Conv	$8,100	$13,300	$19,800	$33,800
1975	Toronado	455/215 2dr Cstm Hdtp Cpe	$4,600	$6,800	$9,500	$13,700
1976	Cutlass	350/155 2dr S Colonnade Hdtp Cpe	$4,900	$7,300	$10,700	$15,400
1976	Toronado	455/215 2dr Cstm Cpe	$4,600	$6,800	$9,500	$13,700
1977	Cutlass	403/185 2dr 4-4-2 Cpe	$6,000	$9,300	$13,700	$19,500
1977	Toronado	403/200 2dr Brghm Cpe	$4,600	$6,800	$9,500	$13,700

Oldsmobile

Year	Model	Body Style	4	3	2	1
		403/200 2dr XS Cpe	$5,300	$7,900	$11,200	$16,000
1978	Cutlass Salon	305/160 2dr 4-4-2 Cpe	$5,900	$9,200	$13,000	$19,600
1978	Toronado	403/190 2dr Brghm Cpe	$4,600	$6,800	$9,500	$13,700
		403/190 2dr XSR Cpe	$5,300	$8,000	$11,300	$16,000
1979	Cutlass	350/160 2dr 4-4-2 Cpe	$6,100	$9,500	$14,300	$20,900
		350/160 2dr Hurst/Olds Cpe	$7,500	$12,900	$15,800	$22,800
1979	Toronado	350/165 2dr Brghm Cpe	$4,400	$6,300	$9,100	$13,000
1980	Toronado	350/160 2dr Brghm Cpe	$4,200	$6,000	$8,800	$12,700
1983	Cutlass	307/180 2dr Hurst Cpe	$9,600	$16,100	$21,500	$32,400
1984	Cutlass Calais	307/180 2dr Hurst Cpe	$9,300	$15,900	$21,000	$32,000
1985	Cutlass	307/180 2dr 4-4-2 Cpe	$7,400	$13,100	$20,700	$30,700
1986	Toronado	231/140 2dr 20th Annv Cpe	$7,200	$12,300	$18,800	$37,500
					+10% for a/c. +10% for 4-spd.	
1986	Cutlass	307/180 2dr 4-4-2 Cpe	$7,400	$13,100	$20,700	$30,700
1987	Cutlass	307/170 2dr 4-4-2 Cpe	$7,400	$13,100	$20,700	$30,700

Opel

Year	Model	Body Style	4	3	2	1
1969	GT	2dr Cpe	$5,000	$9,900	$17,000	$26,800
1970	GT	2dr Cpe	$5,000	$9,900	$17,000	$26,800
1971	GT	2dr Cpe	$5,000	$9,900	$17,000	$26,800
1972	GT	2dr Cpe	$5,000	$9,900	$17,000	$26,800

Packard

Year	Model	Body Style	4	3	2	1
1946	Clipper Six	245/105 2dr Clb Sdn	$9,400	$16,200	$25,100	$43,300
		245/105 4dr Trng Sdn	$5,600	$9,100	$18,500	$28,500
1946	Clipper Eight	282/125 2dr Dlx Clb Sdn	$10,100	$19,000	$30,700	$49,300
		282/125 4dr Trng Sdn	$6,700	$10,200	$19,300	$34,300
		282/125 4dr Dlx Trng Sdn	$7,700	$11,600	$21,400	$37,300

Packard

Year	Model	Body Style	4	3	2	1
1946	Custom Super Clipper	356/165 4dr Trng Sdn	$8,200	$12,700	$23,300	$41,500
		356/165 2dr Clb Sdn	$13,700	$23,100	$37,000	$56,200
		356/165 4dr Sdn 7P	$9,800	$14,200	$25,000	$44,800
		356/165 4dr Limo 7P	$9,900	$17,600	$31,900	$55,400
1947	Clipper Six	245/105 2dr Clb Sdn	$9,400	$16,200	$25,500	$43,400
		245/105 4dr Trng Sdn	$5,600	$9,500	$18,500	$28,500
1947	Deluxe Clipper	282/125 2dr Clb Sdn	$10,100	$19,000	$30,700	$49,100
		282/125 4dr Trng Sdn	$8,500	$12,800	$23,700	$40,400
1947	Super Clipper	356/165 2dr Clb Sdn	$11,900	$22,500	$35,300	$55,700
		356/165 4dr Trng Sdn	$8,000	$12,100	$21,400	$38,100
1947	Custom Super Clipper	356/165 2dr Clb Sdn	$13,700	$23,100	$38,000	$56,600
		356/165 4dr Trng Sdn	$8,200	$12,700	$22,900	$41,100
		356/165 4dr Limo 8P	$9,900	$17,600	$31,700	$55,400
1948	Eight	288/130 2dr 22nd Srs Clb Sdn	$4,300	$6,900	$12,700	$25,400
		288/130 2dr Dlx-22nd Srs Clb Sdn	$4,500	$8,300	$14,300	$26,700
		288/130 4dr 22nd Srs Sta Sdn	$17,000	$26,100	$42,100	$53,400
		288/130 4dr 22nd Srs Trng Sdn	$3,600	$5,400	$12,000	$22,400
		288/130 4dr Dlx-22nd Srs Trng Sdn	$4,400	$6,300	$13,200	$24,800
1948	Super Eight	327/145 2dr 22nd Srs Clb Sdn	$5,400	$8,200	$16,900	$32,800
		327/145 4dr 22nd Srs Trng Sdn	$4,400	$6,400	$14,500	$26,700
		327/145 4dr Dlx LWB-22nd Srs Trng Sdn	$6,200	$9,700	$21,300	$38,000
		327/145 4dr LWB-22nd Srs Trng Sdn	$5,300	$8,000	$20,400	$36,200
		327/145 4dr Dlx LWB-22nd Srs Limo	$6,300	$11,600	$24,600	$37,400
		327/145 4dr LWB-22nd Srs Limo	$6,100	$9,200	$22,400	$36,000

Year	Model	Body Style	4	3	2	1
		327/145 2dr Vic-22nd Srs Conv	$17,100	$31,000	$47,700	$77,600
1948	Custom Eight	356/160 2dr 22nd Srs Clb Sdn	$6,300	$9,700	$18,900	$36,100
		356/160 4dr 22nd Srs Trng Sdn	$5,100	$8,200	$17,800	$32,700
		356/160 4dr LWB-22nd Srs Trng Sdn 7P	$5,700	$8,900	$23,400	$40,600
		356/160 4dr LWB-22nd Srs Limo	$6,800	$11,600	$25,400	$39,400
		356/160 2dr Vic-22nd Srs Conv	$20,100	$36,100	$57,200	$91,500
1949	Eight	288/135 2dr 22nd Srs Clb Sdn	$4,300	$6,900	$12,700	$25,400
		288/135 2dr Dlx-22nd Srs Clb Sdn	$4,500	$8,300	$14,300	$26,700
		288/135 2dr 23rd Srs Clb Sdn	$4,300	$7,300	$12,600	$25,000
		288/135 2dr Dlx-23rd Srs Clb Sdn	$4,900	$8,500	$13,800	$26,000
		288/135 4dr 22nd Srs Sta Sdn	$17,000	$26,100	$42,100	$53,400
		288/135 4dr 23rd Srs Sta Sdn	$16,800	$25,900	$41,900	$57,900
		288/135 4dr 22nd Srs Trng Sdn	$3,300	$5,200	$11,200	$21,300
		288/135 4dr Dlx-22nd Srs Trng Sdn	$4,200	$6,100	$12,600	$23,600
		288/135 4dr Dlx-23rd Srs Trng Sdn	$4,200	$6,300	$12,100	$23,100
		288/135 4dr 23rd Srs Trng Sdn	$3,100	$4,900	$10,900	$21,100
1949	Super Eight	327/150 2dr 22nd Srs Clb Sdn	$5,400	$8,200	$16,900	$32,800
		327/150 2dr Dlx-23rd Srs Clb Sdn	$5,700	$8,700	$17,100	$34,100
		327/150 2dr 23rd Srs Clb Sdn	$5,600	$8,500	$16,900	$32,200
		327/150 4dr 22nd Srs Sdn	$4,200	$6,200	$13,800	$25,300
		327/150 4dr Dlx-22nd Srs Trng Sdn	$6,200	$9,700	$21,300	$38,000
		327/150 4dr LWB-22nd Srs Trng Sdn	$5,100	$7,700	$19,500	$34,300
		327/150 4dr 23rd Srs Trng Sdn	$4,100	$6,300	$13,200	$24,900
		327/150 4dr Dlx-23rd Srs Trng Sdn	$5,100	$7,400	$14,400	$26,300
		327/150 4dr LWB-23rd Srs Trng Sdn	$5,200	$7,800	$18,900	$34,200

Packard

Year	Model	Body Style	4	3	2	1
		327/150 4dr 22nd Srs Limo	$5,700	$8,700	$21,400	$34,100
		327/150 4dr Dlx-22nd Srs Limo	$6,300	$11,600	$24,600	$37,400
		327/150 4dr 23rd Srs Limo	$6,300	$9,400	$21,700	$35,200
		327/150 2dr Vic-22nd Srs Conv	$17,100	$31,000	$47,700	$77,600
		327/150 2dr Vic-23rd Srs Conv	$18,000	$32,700	$51,200	$82,200
1949	Custom Eight	356/160 2dr 22nd Srs Clb Sdn	$6,300	$9,700	$18,900	$36,100
		356/160 4dr 22nd Srs Trng Sdn	$4,800	$7,800	$16,900	$31,200
		356/160 4dr LWB-22nd Srs Trng Sdn	$5,400	$8,500	$22,300	$38,500
		356/160 4dr 23rd Srs Trng Sdn	$4,900	$7,900	$16,400	$31,300
		356/160 4dr LWB-22nd Srs Limo	$6,500	$11,100	$24,100	$37,400
		356/160 2dr Vic-22nd Srs Conv	$20,100	$36,100	$57,200	$91,500
		356/160 2dr Vic-23rd Srs Conv	$20,100	$32,900	$49,600	$90,300
1950	Eight	288/135 2dr Clb Sdn	$4,300	$7,300	$12,600	$25,000
		288/135 2dr Dlx Clb Sdn	$5,000	$8,500	$13,800	$25,900
		288/135 4dr Sta Sdn	$16,800	$25,900	$41,900	$52,900
		288/135 4dr Trng Sdn	$3,100	$4,900	$10,900	$21,100
		288/135 4dr Dlx Trng Sdn	$4,200	$6,300	$12,100	$23,100
1950	Super	327/150 2dr Clb Sdn	$5,600	$8,500	$16,900	$32,200
		327/150 2dr Dlx Clb Sdn	$5,700	$8,700	$17,100	$34,100
		327/150 4dr Sdn 7P	$5,200	$7,800	$18,900	$34,200
		327/150 4dr Trng Sdn	$4,100	$6,300	$13,200	$24,900
		327/150 4dr Dlx Trng Sdn	$5,100	$7,400	$14,400	$26,300
		327/150 4dr Limo 7P	$6,300	$9,400	$21,800	$35,200
		327/150 2dr Vic Conv	$18,000	$32,600	$51,200	$82,200
1950	Custom	356/160 4dr Sdn	$4,800	$7,900	$16,400	$31,300
		356/160 2dr Vic Conv	$20,100	$32,900	$49,600	$90,300

Year	Model	Body Style	4	3	2	1
1951	200	288/135 2dr Bus Cpe	$3,900	$6,000	$9,500	$19,800
		288/135 4dr Clb Sdn	$3,300	$5,400	$9,100	$18,800
		288/135 4dr Dlx Clb Sdn	$3,800	$6,000	$9,400	$20,100
		288/135 4dr Trng Sdn	$2,900	$4,900	$7,600	$14,600
		288/135 4dr Dlx Trng Sdn	$3,200	$5,100	$8,000	$14,800
1951	250	327/150 2dr Mayfair Hdtp Cpe	$5,600	$8,500	$13,400	$25,100
		327/150 2dr Conv	$10,000	$13,600	$25,500	$45,000
1951	300	327/150 4dr Trng Sdn	$3,500	$5,900	$10,000	$19,700
1951	Patrician 400	327/155 4dr Trng Sdn	$3,500	$7,200	$11,300	$18,300
1952	200	288/135 4dr Clb Sdn	$3,300	$5,600	$10,400	$18,000
		288/135 4dr Dlx Clb Sdn	$3,800	$6,000	$9,900	$20,000
		288/135 4dr Trng Sdn	$2,900	$4,900	$7,600	$14,600
		288/135 4dr Dlx Trng Sdn	$3,200	$5,100	$8,000	$15,700
1952	250	327/150 2dr Mayfair Hdtp Cpe	$5,600	$8,800	$13,200	$25,000
		327/150 2dr Conv	$11,000	$15,400	$28,400	$48,700
1952	300	327/150 4dr Trng Sdn	$3,300	$6,000	$10,500	$20,300
1952	Patrician 400	327/155 4dr Trng Sdn	$3,800	$7,500	$11,500	$18,900
1953	Clipper	288/150 2dr Special Sptstr Cpe	$4,900	$7,700	$12,100	$24,200
		288/150 2dr Clb Sdn	$3,600	$5,500	$9,600	$21,000
		327/160 4dr Dlx Clb Sdn	$4,100	$6,200	$9,900	$21,000
		288/150 4dr Trng Sdn	$2,800	$5,000	$7,700	$15,800
		327/160 4dr Dlx Sdn	$3,200	$5,100	$8,300	$16,700
1953	Cavalier	327/180 4dr Sdn	$3,100	$5,100	$9,300	$20,600
1953	Mayfair	327/180 2dr Hdtp Cpe	$4,800	$7,200	$12,400	$25,700
		327/180 2dr Conv	$13,500	$19,100	$34,500	$58,400
1953	Patrician	327/180 4dr Sdn	$4,400	$8,600	$12,700	$21,000
		327/180 4dr Exec Fml Sdn	$7,200	$16,500	$23,100	$40,300
		327/180 4dr Corp Exec Sdn	$7,200	$16,500	$23,000	$40,300

Packard

Year	Model	Body Style	4	3	2	1
		327/180 4dr Corp Limo	$6,800	$16,500	$22,900	$39,200
1953	Caribbean	327/180 2dr Conv	$23,500	$44,000	$57,800	$78,100
1954	Standard 8	359/212 2dr Conv	$13,900	$19,000	$35,800	$60,600
1954	Clipper	288/150 4dr Spcl Clb Sdn	$3,600	$5,500	$8,800	$19,700
		327/165 4dr Dlx Clb Sdn	$3,900	$6,400	$10,500	$21,200
		327/165 4dr Spr Clb Sdn	$4,100	$7,200	$11,600	$22,500
		327/165 4dr Spr Sdn	$3,500	$7,000	$9,600	$18,300
		327/165 2dr Dlx Sptstr Cpe	$4,900	$7,700	$12,200	$24,500
		288/150 4dr Spcl Trng Sdn	$2,800	$4,800	$7,600	$15,300
		327/165 4dr Dlx Trng Sdn	$3,300	$6,200	$8,600	$16,700
		327/165 2dr Panama Hdtp Cpe	$5,300	$8,800	$14,300	$29,200
1954	Cavalier	327/185 4dr Sdn	$3,100	$5,300	$9,700	$21,100
1954	Pacific	359/212 2dr Hdtp Cpe	$5,900	$9,400	$16,200	$32,900
1954	Patrician	359/212 4dr Cstm Sdn	$4,400	$8,600	$12,700	$21,000
		359/212 4dr Corp Exec Sdn	$7,200	$16,500	$23,000	$40,300
		359/212 4dr Corp Limo	$6,800	$16,500	$22,900	$39,500
1954	Caribbean	359/212 2dr Conv	$26,500	$47,000	$62,300	$82,200
1955	400	352/260 2dr Hdtp Cpe	$6,300	$14,800	$25,200	$45,000
1955	Clipper	352/245 2dr Cstm Constellation Hdtp Cpe	$5,800	$14,700	$21,100	$43,200
		320/225 2dr Spr Panama Hdtp Cpe	$5,600	$13,600	$19,900	$42,300
		352/245 4dr Cstm Sdn	$4,400	$8,300	$11,600	$19,700
		320/225 4dr Dlx Sdn	$3,400	$6,900	$9,700	$18,000
		320/225 4dr Spr Sdn	$3,500	$7,200	$10,100	$18,300
1955	Caribbean	352/275 2dr Conv	$27,000	$49,800	$66,900	$82,200
1955	Packard	352/260 4dr Patrician Sdn	$4,900	$9,000	$13,500	$24,500
1956	Caribbean	374/310 2dr Hdtp Cpe	$5,800	$15,600	$23,800	$40,400
		374/310 2dr Conv	$29,500	$52,700	$72,300	$88,500
1956	Executive	352/275 2dr Hdtp Cpe	$6,700	$14,500	$20,300	$41,600

Packard

Year	Model	Body Style	4	3	2	1
		352/275 4dr Sdn	$3,300	$6,600	$10,300	$19,300
1956	Packard	374/290 2dr Four Hundred Hdtp Cpe	$7,200	$16,800	$30,100	$56,600
		374/290 4dr Patri-cian Sdn	$4,900	$9,000	$13,500	$24,500
1957	Clipper	289/275 4dr Sdn	$3,900	$8,000	$11,100	$19,000
		289/275 4dr Ctry Sdn Wgn	$14,000	$25,200	$38,600	$52,200
1958	Series 58L	289/225 2dr Hdtp Cpe	$10,300	$19,400	$30,000	$48,100
		289/225 4dr Sdn	$3,000	$6,000	$8,000	$14,500
		289/225 4dr Wgn	$5,000	$11,500	$19,100	$32,200
1958	Hawk	289/275 2dr Hdtp Cpe	$17,800	$30,300	$47,000	$71,800

Panoz

Year	Model	Body Style	4	3	2	1
1992	Roadster	302/205 2dr Rdstr	$20,900	$29,900	$36,900	$46,200
1993	Roadster	302/205 2dr Rdstr	$21,300	$30,500	$37,400	$46,600
1994	Roadster	302/205 2dr Rdstr	$21,800	$30,800	$37,700	$46,900
1995	Roadster	302/205 2dr Rdstr	$22,100	$31,600	$39,400	$47,600
1996	AIV	281/305 2dr Rdstr	$23,700	$32,700	$44,200	$50,800
1997	AIV	281/305 2dr Rdstr	$24,200	$34,900	$45,400	$52,000
1998	AIV	281/305 2dr Rdstr	$25,600	$35,600	$46,900	$55,200
1999	AIV	281/305 2dr Rdstr	$28,600	$37,500	$47,800	$59,900

Panther

Year	Model	Body Style	4	3	2	1
1972	J72	2dr Conv	$24,200	$34,700	$52,300	$69,500
1973	J72	2dr Conv	$24,200	$34,700	$52,300	$69,500
1974	J72	2dr Conv	$24,200	$34,700	$52,300	$69,500
1975	J72	2dr Conv	$24,200	$34,700	$52,300	$69,500
1976	J72	2dr Conv	$24,200	$34,700	$52,300	$69,500
1976	Lima	2dr SI Conv	$8,300	$10,500	$15,100	$20,300
1977	J72	2dr Conv	$24,200	$34,700	$52,300	$69,500
1977	Lima	2dr SI Conv	$8,300	$10,500	$15,100	$20,300
1978	J72	2dr Conv	$24,200	$34,700	$52,300	$69,500
1978	Lima	2dr SI Conv	$8,300	$10,500	$15,100	$20,300
1979	J72	2dr Conv	$24,200	$34,700	$52,300	$69,500
1979	Lima	2dr SI Conv	$8,300	$10,500	$15,100	$20,300
		2dr SII Conv	$11,600	$13,700	$19,800	$25,600
1979	DeVille	4dr Sdn	$28,400	$44,900	$62,900	$76,300
		2dr Conv	$40,400	$60,900	$83,300	$121,000
1980	J72	2dr Conv	$24,200	$34,700	$52,300	$69,500
1980	Lima	2dr SII Conv	$11,600	$13,700	$19,800	$25,600
1980	DeVille	4dr Sdn	$28,400	$44,900	$62,900	$76,300
		2dr Conv	$40,400	$60,900	$83,300	$121,000
1981	J72	2dr Conv	$24,200	$34,700	$52,300	$69,500

Panther

Year	Model	Body Style	4	3	2	1
1981	Kallista	2dr Conv	$12,800	$14,100	$18,500	$27,600
1981	DeVille	4dr Sdn	$28,400	$44,900	$62,900	$76,300
		2dr Conv	$40,400	$60,900	$83,300	$121,000
1982	Kallista	2dr Conv	$12,800	$14,100	$18,500	$27,600
1982	DeVille	4dr Sdn	$28,400	$44,900	$62,900	$76,300
		2dr Conv	$40,400	$60,900	$83,300	$121,000
1983	Kallista	2dr Conv	$12,800	$14,100	$18,500	$27,600
1983	DeVille	4dr Sdn	$28,400	$44,900	$62,900	$76,300
		2dr Conv	$40,400	$60,900	$83,300	$121,000
1984	Kallista	2dr Conv	$12,800	$14,100	$18,500	$27,600
1984	DeVille	4dr Sdn	$28,400	$44,900	$62,900	$76,300
		2dr Conv	$40,400	$60,900	$83,300	$121,000
1985	Kallista	2dr Conv	$12,800	$14,100	$18,500	$27,600
1985	DeVille	4dr Sdn	$28,400	$44,900	$62,900	$76,300
		2dr Conv	$40,400	$60,900	$83,300	$121,000
1986	Kallista	2dr Conv	$12,800	$14,100	$18,500	$27,600
1986	DeVille	4dr Sdn	$28,400	$44,900	$62,900	$76,300
		2dr Conv	$40,400	$60,900	$83,300	$121,000
1987	Kallista	2dr Conv	$12,800	$14,100	$18,500	$27,600
1987	DeVille	2dr Sdn	$28,400	$44,900	$62,900	$76,300
		2dr Conv	$40,400	$60,900	$83,300	$121,000
1988	Kallista	2dr Conv	$12,800	$14,100	$18,500	$27,600
1988	DeVille	4dr Sdn	$28,400	$44,900	$62,900	$76,300
		2dr Conv	$40,400	$60,900	$83,300	$121,000
1989	Kallista	2dr Conv	$12,800	$14,100	$18,500	$27,600
1989	DeVille	4dr Sdn	$28,400	$44,900	$62,900	$76,300
		2dr Conv	$40,400	$60,900	$83,300	$121,000
1990	Kallista	2dr Conv	$12,800	$14,100	$18,500	$27,600
1990	DeVille	4dr Sdn	$28,400	$44,900	$62,900	$76,300
		2dr Conv	$40,400	$60,900	$83,300	$121,000

Peerless

Year	Model	Body Style	4	3	2	1
1958	GT	2dr Ph1 Sdn	$14,000	$20,700	$37,700	$49,600
						-25% for RHD.
1959	GT	2dr Ph1 Sdn	$14,000	$20,700	$37,700	$49,600
		2dr Ph2 Sdn	$16,500	$27,400	$49,000	$53,500
						-25% for RHD.
1960	GT	2dr Ph2 Sdn	$16,500	$27,400	$49,000	$53,500
						-25% for RHD.

Pegaso

Year	Model	Body Style	4	3	2	1
1951	Z101	2dr Cpe	$425,000	$515,000	$607,000	$670,000
1951	Z102	2dr Flt Wndscrn Cpe	$690,000	$795,000	$890,000	$975,000

Year	Model	Body Style	4	3	2	1
		2dr Panoramica Cpe	$545,000	$705,000	$815,000	$903,000
		2dr Rdstr	$785,000	$980,000	$1.2 mil	$1.35 mil
		Z102 prices are dependent upon coachbuilder.				
1952	Z101	2dr Cpe	$425,000	$515,000	$607,000	$670,000
1952	Z102	2dr Flt Wndscrn Cpe	$690,000	$795,000	$890,000	$975,000
		2dr Panoramica Cpe	$545,000	$705,000	$815,000	$903,000
		2dr Rdstr	$785,000	$980,000	$1.2 mil	$1.35 mil
		Z102 prices are dependent upon coachbuilder.				
1953	Z102	2dr Flt Wndscrn Cpe	$690,000	$795,000	$890,000	$975,000
		2dr Panoramica Cpe	$545,000	$705,000	$815,000	$903,000
		2dr Rdstr	$785,000	$980,000	$1.2 mil	$1.35 mil
		Z102 prices are dependent upon coachbuilder.				
1954	Z102	2dr Flt Wndscrn Cpe	$690,000	$795,000	$890,000	$975,000
		2dr Panoramica Cpe	$545,000	$705,000	$815,000	$903,000
		2dr Rdstr	$785,000	$980,000	$1.2 mil	$1.35 mil
		Z102 prices are dependent upon coachbuilder.				
1955	Z102	2dr Flt Wndscrn Cpe	$690,000	$795,000	$890,000	$975,000
		2dr Panoramica Cpe	$545,000	$705,000	$815,000	$903,000
		2dr Rdstr	$785,000	$980,000	$1.2 mil	$1.35 mil
		Z102 prices are dependent upon coachbuilder.				
1955	Z103	2dr Cpe	$762,000	$878,000	$970,000	$1.15 mil
		2dr Rdstr	$960,000	$1.05 mil	$1.2 mil	$1.45 mil
1956	Z102	2dr Flt Wndscrn Cpe	$690,000	$795,000	$890,000	$975,000
		2dr Panoramica Cpe	$545,000	$705,000	$815,000	$903,000
		2dr Rdstr	$785,000	$980,000	$1.2 mil	$1.35 mil
		Z102 prices are dependent upon coachbuilder.				
1956	Z103	2dr Cpe	$762,000	$878,000	$970,000	$1.15 mil
		2dr Rdstr	$960,000	$1.05 mil	$1.2 mil	$1.45 mil
1957	Z102	2dr Flt Wndscrn Cpe	$690,000	$795,000	$890,000	$975,000
		2dr Panoramica Cpe	$545,000	$705,000	$815,000	$903,000
		2dr Rdstr	$785,000	$980,000	$1.2 mil	$1.35 mil
		Z102 prices are dependent upon coachbuilder.				
1957	Z103	2dr Cpe	$762,000	$878,000	$970,000	$1.15 mil
		2dr Rdstr	$960,000	$1.05 mil	$1.2 mil	$1.45 mil

Peugeot

Year	Model	Body Style	4	3	2	1
1948	203	4dr Sdn	$3,900	$7,300	$10,200	$16,300
		2dr Cab	$12,300	$19,300	$32,000	$59,900
		4dr Conv	$6,400	$8,000	$11,100	$19,700
1949	203	4dr Sdn	$3,900	$7,300	$10,200	$16,300
		2dr Cab	$12,300	$19,300	$32,000	$59,900
		4dr Conv	$6,400	$8,000	$11,100	$19,700
1950	203	4dr Sdn	$3,900	$7,300	$10,200	$16,300
		2dr Cab	$12,300	$19,300	$32,000	$59,900
		4dr Conv	$6,400	$8,000	$11,100	$19,700
1951	203	4dr Sdn	$3,900	$7,300	$10,200	$16,300
		2dr Cab	$12,300	$19,300	$32,000	$59,900
		4dr Conv	$6,400	$8,000	$11,100	$19,700
1952	203	4dr Sdn	$3,900	$7,300	$10,200	$16,300
		2dr Cab	$12,300	$19,300	$32,000	$59,900
		4dr Conv	$6,400	$8,000	$11,100	$19,700
1953	203	4dr Sdn	$3,900	$7,300	$10,200	$16,300
		2dr Cab	$12,300	$19,300	$32,000	$59,900
		4dr Conv	$6,400	$8,000	$11,100	$19,700
1954	203	4dr Sdn	$3,900	$7,300	$10,200	$16,300
		2dr Cab	$12,300	$19,300	$32,000	$59,900
		4dr Conv	$6,400	$8,000	$11,100	$19,700
1955	203	4dr Sdn	$3,900	$7,300	$10,200	$16,300
		2dr Cab	$12,300	$19,300	$32,000	$59,900
		4dr Conv	$6,400	$8,000	$11,100	$19,700
1955	403	4dr Sdn	$3,400	$6,800	$13,600	$22,300
1956	203	4dr Sdn	$3,900	$7,300	$10,200	$16,300
		2dr Cab	$12,300	$19,300	$32,000	$59,900
		4dr Conv	$6,400	$8,000	$11,100	$19,700
1956	403	4dr Sdn	$3,400	$6,800	$13,600	$22,300
1957	203	4dr Sdn	$3,900	$7,300	$10,200	$16,300
		2dr Cab	$12,300	$19,300	$32,000	$59,900
		4dr Conv	$6,400	$8,000	$11,100	$19,700
1957	403	4dr Sdn	$3,400	$6,800	$13,600	$22,300
		2dr Conv	$25,200	$35,600	$50,500	$88,500
1958	203	4dr Sdn	$3,900	$7,300	$10,200	$16,300
		2dr Cab	$12,300	$19,300	$32,000	$59,900
		4dr Conv	$6,400	$8,000	$11,100	$19,700
1958	403	4dr Sdn	$3,400	$6,800	$13,600	$22,300
		2dr Cab	$25,200	$35,600	$50,500	$88,500
1959	203	4dr Sdn	$3,900	$7,300	$10,200	$16,300
		2dr Cab	$12,300	$19,300	$32,000	$59,900
		4dr Conv	$6,400	$8,000	$11,100	$19,700
1959	403	4dr Sdn	$3,400	$6,800	$13,600	$22,300
		2dr Cab	$25,200	$35,600	$50,500	$88,500
1960	203	4dr Sdn	$3,900	$7,300	$10,200	$16,300
		2dr Cab	$12,300	$19,300	$32,000	$59,900
		4dr Conv	$6,400	$8,000	$11,100	$19,700
1960	403	4dr Sdn	$3,400	$6,800	$13,600	$22,300
		2dr Cab	$25,200	$35,600	$50,500	$88,500

Year	Model	Body Style	4	3	2	1
1961	403	4dr Sdn	$3,400	$6,800	$13,600	$22,300
		2dr Cab	$25,200	$35,600	$50,500	$88,500
1962	403	4dr Sdn	$3,400	$6,800	$13,600	$22,300
1962	404	2dr Cab	$18,800	$27,600	$43,300	$69,000
1963	403	4dr Sdn	$3,400	$6,800	$13,600	$22,300
1963	404	2dr Cab	$18,800	$27,600	$43,300	$69,000
1964	403	4dr Sdn	$3,400	$6,800	$13,600	$22,300
1964	404	2dr Cab	$18,800	$27,600	$43,300	$69,000
1965	403	4dr Sdn	$3,400	$6,800	$13,600	$22,300
1965	404	2dr Cab	$18,800	$27,600	$43,300	$69,000
1966	403	4dr Sdn	$3,400	$6,800	$13,600	$22,300
1966	404	2dr Cab	$18,800	$27,600	$43,300	$69,000
1967	304	2dr Cpe	$2,000	$4,500	$6,800	$8,900
		2dr Cab	$6,300	$9,600	$13,800	$17,100
1967	404	2dr Cab	$18,800	$27,600	$43,300	$69,000
1968	304	2dr Cpe	$2,000	$4,500	$6,800	$8,900
		2dr Cab	$6,300	$9,600	$13,800	$17,100
1968	404	2dr Cab	$18,800	$27,600	$43,300	$69,000
1969	304	2dr Cpe	$2,000	$4,500	$6,800	$8,900
		2dr Cab	$6,300	$9,600	$13,800	$17,100
1969	504	2dr Cab	$10,300	$16,000	$25,000	$38,900
1970	304	2dr Cpe	$2,000	$4,500	$6,800	$8,900
		2dr Cab	$6,300	$9,600	$13,800	$17,100
1970	504	2dr Cab	$10,300	$16,000	$25,000	$38,900
1971	304	2dr Cpe	$2,000	$4,500	$6,800	$8,900
		2dr Cab	$6,300	$9,600	$13,800	$17,100
1971	504	2dr Cab	$10,300	$16,000	$25,000	$38,900
1972	304	2dr Cpe	$2,000	$4,500	$6,800	$8,900
		2dr Cab	$6,300	$9,600	$13,800	$17,100
1972	504	2dr Cab	$10,300	$16,000	$25,000	$38,900
1973	304	2dr Cpe	$2,000	$4,500	$6,800	$8,900
		2dr Cab	$6,300	$9,600	$13,800	$17,100
1973	504	2dr Cab	$10,300	$16,000	$25,000	$38,900
1974	304	2dr Cpe	$2,000	$4,500	$6,800	$8,900
		2dr Cab	$6,300	$9,600	$13,800	$17,100
1974	504	2dr Cab	$10,300	$16,000	$25,000	$38,900
		2dr V6 Cab	$13,900	$23,100	$33,600	$48,400
1975	304	2dr Cpe	$2,000	$4,500	$6,800	$8,900
		2dr Cab	$6,300	$9,600	$13,800	$17,100
1975	504	2dr Cab	$10,300	$16,000	$25,000	$38,900
		2dr V6 Cab	$13,900	$23,100	$33,600	$48,400
1976	504	2dr Cab	$10,300	$16,000	$25,000	$38,900
		2dr V6 Cab	$13,900	$23,100	$33,600	$48,400
1977	504	2dr Cab	$10,300	$16,000	$25,000	$38,900
		2dr V6 Cab	$13,900	$23,100	$33,600	$48,400
1978	504	2dr Cab	$10,300	$16,000	$25,000	$38,900
		2dr V6 Cab	$13,900	$23,100	$33,600	$48,400
1979	504	2dr Cab	$10,300	$16,000	$25,000	$38,900
		2dr V6 Cab	$13,900	$23,100	$33,600	$48,400

Peugeot

Year	Model	Body Style	4	3	2	1
1980	504	2dr Cab	$10,300	$16,000	$25,000	$38,900
		2dr V6 Cab	$13,900	$23,100	$33,600	$48,400
1981	504	2dr Cab	$10,300	$16,000	$25,000	$38,900
		2dr V6 Cab	$13,900	$23,100	$33,600	$48,400
1982	504	2dr Cab	$10,300	$16,000	$25,000	$38,900
		2dr V6 Cab	$13,900	$23,100	$33,600	$48,400
1983	504	2dr Cab	$10,300	$16,000	$25,000	$38,900
		2dr V6 Cab	$13,900	$23,100	$33,600	$48,400

Pininfarina

Year	Model	Body Style	4	3	2	1
1983	Azzurra	2dr Conv	$7,400	$14,300	$23,300	$34,800
1984	Azzurra	2dr Conv	$7,400	$14,300	$23,300	$34,800
1985	Azzurra	2dr Conv	$7,300	$14,100	$22,900	$34,100

Playboy

Year	Model	Body Style	4	3	2	1
1947	Base	133/40 2dr Conv	$15,500	$26,000	$39,100	$56,400
1948	Base	91/40 2dr Conv	$15,500	$26,000	$39,100	$56,400
1949	Base	91/40 2dr Conv	$15,500	$26,000	$39,100	$56,400
1950	Base	91/40 2dr Conv	$15,500	$26,000	$39,100	$56,400
1951	Base	134/72 2dr Conv	$15,500	$26,000	$39,100	$56,400

Plymouth

Year	Model	Body Style	4	3	2	1
1946	Special Deluxe	218/95 2dr Clb Cpe	$4,100	$8,400	$20,300	$34,400
		218/95 4dr Sdn	$4,100	$7,200	$14,400	$19,100
		218/95 4dr Wgn	$36,300	$49,300	$73,700	$93,300
		218/95 2dr Conv	$12,200	$18,600	$36,500	$54,100
1947	P-15	218/95 2dr Dlx Cpe 3P	$4,100	$8,400	$20,300	$34,400
		218/95 4dr Dlx Sdn	$4,200	$7,300	$14,600	$19,700
		218/95 4dr Spcl Dlx Wgn	$36,300	$49,300	$73,700	$93,300
		218/95 2dr Spcl Dlx Conv Cpe	$12,200	$19,000	$38,500	$57,500
1948	P-15	218/95 2dr Dlx Clb Cpe	$4,100	$8,400	$20,300	$34,400
		218/95 4dr Dlx Sdn	$4,200	$7,300	$14,600	$19,700
		218/95 4dr Spcl Dlx Wgn	$36,300	$49,300	$73,700	$93,300
		218/95 2dr Spcl Dlx Conv Cpe	$12,200	$19,000	$38,500	$57,500
1949	P-15	218/97 2dr Dlx Cpe 3P	$3,800	$7,700	$20,200	$27,800

Year	Model	Body Style	4	3	2	1
		218/97 4dr Dlx Sdn	$3,700	$6,600	$14,200	$19,000
		218/97 4dr Spr Dlx Wgn	$36,500	$55,500	$72,700	$92,400
		218/97 2dr Spr Dlx Conv	$11,100	$16,600	$32,900	$48,300
1949	Deluxe	218/97 2dr P-18 Clb Cpe	$4,200	$8,100	$21,000	$29,400
		218/97 4dr P-18 Sdn	$3,500	$6,400	$12,500	$18,100
		218/97 2dr P-17 Sbrbn	$29,900	$46,500	$68,700	$89,000
1949	Special Deluxe	218/97 2dr P-18 Conv Cpe	$11,800	$17,800	$34,900	$51,000
1950	Deluxe	218/97 2dr Bus Cpe	$4,700	$8,900	$21,400	$29,800
		218/97 4dr Sdn	$4,000	$7,200	$12,300	$17,500
		218/97 4dr Sbrbn Stn Wgn	$29,900	$46,500	$68,700	$89,000
1950	Special Deluxe	218/97 2dr Conv Cpe	$16,700	$23,800	$37,800	$50,500
1951	Concord	218/97 2dr Sbrbn Wgn	$6,600	$9,100	$15,600	$25,500
		218/97 2dr Cpe 3P	$2,000	$3,400	$7,900	$12,300
		218/97 4dr Sdn	$1,500	$2,300	$4,900	$7,500
1951	Cambridge	218/97 2dr Clb Cpe	$2,200	$3,300	$8,200	$13,200
		218/97 4dr Sdn	$1,500	$2,200	$5,800	$8,300
1951	Cranbrook	218/97 2dr Clb Cpe	$3,600	$4,900	$8,900	$15,500
		218/97 2dr Belvedere Hdtp Cpe	$4,900	$7,000	$13,600	$21,700
		218/97 4dr Sdn	$3,300	$4,000	$7,200	$10,200
		218/97 2dr Conv Clb Cpe	$15,600	$22,200	$37,100	$50,000
1952	Concord	218/97 2dr Cpe 3P	$2,000	$3,400	$7,900	$12,300
		218/97 4dr Sdn	$1,500	$2,300	$4,900	$7,500
		218/97 2dr Savoy Wgn	$4,300	$6,400	$11,700	$18,600
1952	Cambridge	218/97 2dr Clb Cpe	$2,200	$3,300	$8,200	$13,200
		218/97 4dr Sdn	$1,500	$2,200	$5,800	$8,300
1952	Cranbrook	218/97 2dr Clb Cpe	$3,600	$4,900	$8,900	$15,500
		218/97 2dr Belvedere Hdtp Cpe	$4,900	$7,000	$13,600	$21,700
		218/97 4dr Sdn	$3,300	$4,000	$7,200	$10,200
		218/97 2dr Conv Clb Cpe	$15,600	$22,200	$37,100	$50,000
1953	Cambridge	218/100 2dr Clb Sdn	$3,200	$4,600	$9,300	$15,600
		218/100 4dr Sdn	$1,800	$2,400	$6,000	$8,500
		218/100 2dr Sbrbn Wgn	$4,400	$6,300	$10,300	$17,600
1953	Cranbrook	218/100 2dr Clb Cpe	$5,600	$7,000	$10,300	$16,700

Plymouth

Year	Model	Body Style	4	3	2	1
		218/100 2dr Belvedere Hdtp Cpe	$7,300	$10,100	$15,600	$23,200
		218/100 4dr Sdn	$3,400	$4,000	$7,300	$10,200
		218/100 2dr Savoy Wgn	$4,900	$6,800	$12,300	$20,700
		218/100 2dr Conv Clb Cpe	$15,900	$22,800	$37,400	$50,200
1954	Plaza	218/100 2dr Bus Cpe	$4,300	$6,300	$10,000	$16,700
		230/110 2dr Bus Cpe	$4,700	$6,900	$10,800	$18,300
		218/100 4dr Sdn	$2,800	$3,700	$6,400	$8,900
		230/110 4dr Sdn	$2,900	$4,000	$7,000	$9,800
		218/100 4dr Sbrbn Wgn	$4,600	$6,800	$10,800	$19,000
		230/110 4dr Sbrbn Wgn	$5,000	$7,400	$11,800	$20,900
1954	Savoy	218/100 2dr Clb Cpe	$4,800	$6,700	$12,200	$20,600
		218/100 4dr Sdn	$3,200	$4,300	$7,400	$10,100
		218/100 4dr Sbrbn Wgn	$5,000	$7,700	$11,400	$19,700
1954	Belvedere	230/110 2dr Spt Cpe	$6,100	$7,600	$12,200	$21,000
		230/110 4dr Sdn	$4,100	$5,200	$8,100	$11,000
		230/110 4dr Sbrbn Wgn	$5,700	$8,200	$12,800	$21,600
		230/110 2dr Conv Cpe	$17,600	$29,400	$40,200	$53,300
1955	Plaza	241/157 2dr Clb Sdn	$4,400	$6,800	$11,600	$19,600
		259/167 2dr Clb Sdn	$4,800	$7,500	$12,900	$21,600
		259/177 2dr Clb Sdn	$5,300	$8,100	$14,000	$23,500
		241/157 4dr Sdn	$2,900	$4,200	$7,200	$9,600
		259/167 4dr Sdn	$3,200	$4,600	$8,000	$10,500
		259/177 4dr Sdn	$3,500	$5,100	$8,600	$11,500
		241/157 4dr Sbrbn Wgn	$5,000	$7,600	$11,300	$19,700
		259/167 4dr Sbrbn Wgn	$5,500	$8,400	$12,400	$21,700
		259/177 4dr Sbrbn Wgn	$6,000	$9,100	$13,700	$23,600

+15% for factory a/c.

Year	Model	Body Style	4	3	2	1
1955	Savoy	241/157 2dr Clb Sdn	$4,300	$6,900	$12,800	$21,000
		241/157 4dr Sdn	$3,600	$4,200	$8,600	$11,700
1955	Belvedere	241/157 4dr Sdn	$4,100	$5,500	$8,600	$11,900
		259/167 4dr Sdn	$4,600	$6,100	$9,400	$13,100
		259/177 4dr Sdn	$4,900	$6,600	$10,200	$14,300

Year	Model	Body Style	4	3	2	1
		241/157 2dr Hdtp Cpe	$7,000	$9,900	$17,300	$26,700
		259/167 2dr Hdtp Cpe	$7,700	$10,900	$19,000	$29,400
		259/177 2dr Hdtp Cpe	$8,400	$11,900	$20,700	$32,000
		241/157 4dr Sbrbn Wgn	$6,200	$9,400	$17,000	$25,000
		259/167 4dr Sbrbn Wgn	$7,000	$10,200	$18,700	$27,500
		259/177 4dr Sbrbn Wgn	$7,500	$11,200	$20,400	$30,000
		241/157 2dr Conv	$20,300	$31,900	$45,700	$70,400
		259/167 2dr Conv	$22,300	$35,000	$50,200	$77,400
		259/177 2dr Conv	$24,500	$38,200	$54,900	$84,300
						+15% for factory a/c.
1956	Plaza	270/180 2dr Bus Cpe	$4,800	$7,300	$12,600	$21,100
		277/187 2dr Bus Cpe	$5,100	$7,600	$13,100	$22,100
		277/200 2dr Bus Cpe	$5,300	$7,900	$13,700	$23,000
		230/125 2dr Clb Sdn	$4,400	$6,600	$11,200	$19,200
		230/131 2dr Clb Sdn	$2,900	$4,000	$6,800	$9,500
		270/180 2dr Clb Sdn	$5,100	$7,500	$11,400	$19,900
		270/180 4dr Sdn	$3,200	$4,400	$7,500	$10,500
		277/187 4dr Sdn	$3,400	$4,700	$7,900	$10,900
		277/200 4dr Sdn	$3,500	$4,900	$8,300	$11,400
		270/180 4dr Dlx Sbrbn Wgn	$5,600	$8,300	$12,700	$21,900
		277/187 4dr Dlx Sbrbn Wgn	$5,900	$8,600	$13,200	$22,900
		277/200 4dr Dlx Sbrbn Wgn	$6,100	$9,000	$13,800	$23,900
						+15% for factory a/c.
1956	Savoy	230/125 2dr Clb Sdn	$6,000	$9,100	$14,400	$22,400
		230/125 4dr Sdn	$4,000	$4,500	$8,100	$11,300
		230/125 4dr Cstm Sbrbn Wgn	$5,500	$8,100	$12,600	$22,000
		230/125 2dr Hdtp Sdn	$6,700	$9,600	$17,800	$26,700
1956	Belvedere	230/125 4dr Sdn	$4,100	$5,400	$8,400	$11,600
		270/180 4dr Sdn	$4,600	$6,000	$9,200	$12,700
		277/187 4dr Sdn	$4,700	$6,300	$9,500	$13,300
		277/200 4dr Sdn	$4,900	$6,500	$9,900	$13,900
		230/125 4dr Spt Sbrbn Wgn	$6,200	$9,400	$17,000	$26,800

Plymouth

Year	Model	Body Style	4	3	2	1
		270/180 4dr Spt Sbrbn Wgn	$7,000	$10,200	$18,700	$29,500
		277/187 4dr Spt Sbrbn Wgn	$7,200	$10,700	$19,500	$30,800
		277/200 4dr Spt Sbrbn Wgn	$7,500	$11,200	$20,400	$32,100
		230/125 4dr Hdtp Sdn	$4,300	$5,700	$8,800	$13,000
		270/180 4dr Hdtp Sdn	$4,700	$6,300	$9,600	$14,300
		277/187 4dr Hdtp Sdn	$4,900	$6,600	$10,100	$15,000
		277/200 4dr Hdtp Sdn	$5,100	$6,800	$10,500	$15,600
		270/180 2dr Conv	$17,600	$25,700	$51,300	$79,700
		277/187 2dr Conv	$18,500	$27,100	$53,600	$83,500
		277/200 2dr Conv	$19,400	$28,200	$55,900	$87,100
						+15% for factory a/c.
1956	Fury	303/240 2dr Hdtp Cpe	$16,500	$23,200	$30,600	$48,100
		303/270 2dr Hdtp Cpe	$17,900	$25,800	$33,100	$51,400
						+20% for factory a/c.
1957	Plaza	277/197 2dr Cpe	$5,200	$9,200	$17,000	$22,800
		277/197 2dr Dlx Sbrbn Wgn	$6,900	$10,400	$16,300	$25,100
		277/197 4dr Sdn	$4,400	$7,300	$9,900	$14,600
		301/215 2dr Dlx Sbrbn Wgn	$7,600	$11,400	$17,900	$27,600
		301/235 2dr Dlx Sbrbn Wgn	$8,000	$12,000	$18,700	$28,900
		301/215 2dr Cpe	$5,700	$10,000	$18,700	$25,100
		301/235 2dr Cpe	$6,000	$10,500	$19,500	$26,200
		301/215 4dr Sdn	$4,800	$8,100	$10,800	$16,200
		301/235 4dr Sdn	$5,000	$8,400	$11,400	$16,900
						+15% for factory a/c.
1957	Savoy	301/215 2dr Clb Sdn	$9,200	$15,300	$20,800	$28,800
		301/215 4dr Cstm Sbrbn Wgn	$8,200	$12,400	$17,700	$27,100
		301/215 4dr Sdn	$7,600	$10,500	$15,100	$20,100
1957	Belvedere	230/132 4dr Sdn	$8,300	$11,500	$16,600	$22,500
		301/215 2dr Clb Sdn	$10,300	$16,500	$26,300	$35,300
		301/215 2dr Hdtp Cpe	$11,300	$18,100	$29,000	$38,800
		301/235 2dr Hdtp Cpe	$11,900	$18,900	$30,200	$40,500
		301/215 4dr Sdn	$9,100	$12,600	$18,200	$24,800
		301/235 4dr Sdn	$9,500	$13,200	$19,100	$25,800

Year	Model	Body Style	4	3	2	1
		301/235 2dr Clb Sdn	$8,600	$14,400	$23,600	$33,500
		301/215 4dr Hdtp Sdn	$9,500	$15,900	$25,900	$36,900
		301/235 4dr Hdtp Sdn	$10,000	$16,600	$27,100	$38,600
		301/215 4dr Spt Sbrbn Wgn	$9,500	$14,700	$22,500	$33,900
		301/235 4dr Spt Sbrbn Wgn	$9,900	$15,500	$23,500	$35,400
		230/132 2dr Clb Sdn	$24,200	$37,600	$56,700	$75,900
		301/215 2dr Conv	$24,000	$37,300	$59,200	$82,800
		301/235 2dr Conv	$25,100	$39,000	$61,800	$86,600
					+15% for factory a/c.	
1957	Fury	318/290 2dr Hdtp Cpe	$18,900	$28,300	$39,100	$63,200
					+20% for factory a/c.	
1958	Custom Suburban	350/305 4dr Stn Wgn, 6-p.	$9,200	$13,500	$18,400	$26,400
1958	DeLuxe Suburban	318/225 4dr Wgn	$8,100	$11,900	$17,300	$24,700
		350/305 4dr Wgn	$9,700	$14,300	$20,700	$29,600
		350/315 FI 4dr Wgn	$10,200	$14,900	$21,600	$30,900
					+10% for factory a/c.	
1958	Sport Suburban	318/225 4dr Stn Wgn, 6-p.	$8,600	$13,400	$20,700	$30,800
		350/305 4dr Stn Wgn, 6-p.	$10,300	$16,200	$24,900	$36,900
		350/315 FI 4dr Stn Wgn, 6-p.	$10,800	$16,900	$26,000	$38,500
					+10% for factory a/c.	
1958	Plaza	318/225 4dr Sdn	$4,400	$7,300	$15,100	$21,400
		318/250 4dr Sdn	$5,200	$9,200	$17,200	$23,000
		350/305 2dr Bus Cpe	$6,500	$10,900	$20,600	$27,600
		350/315 FI 2dr Bus Cpe	$6,800	$11,400	$21,600	$28,700
		350/305 4dr Sdn	$5,300	$8,700	$18,100	$25,700
		350/315 FI 4dr Sdn	$5,500	$9,100	$18,900	$26,700
					+10% for factory a/c.	
1958	Savoy	318/225 2dr Clb Sdn	$9,400	$15,600	$21,500	$30,300
		318/225 4dr Sdn	$7,500	$10,200	$16,100	$18,900
1958	Belvedere	318/225 2dr Hdtp	$10,300	$16,500	$26,300	$35,300
		318/225 4dr Hdtp	$8,600	$14,400	$21,500	$29,200
		318/225 4dr Sdn	$8,300	$11,500	$15,600	$21,600
		350/305 2dr Hdtp	$12,500	$19,700	$31,400	$42,400

Plymouth

Year	Model	Body Style	4	3	2	1
		350/315 FI 2dr Hdtp	$13,000	$20,500	$32,800	$44,100
		350/305 4dr Sdn	$10,000	$13,800	$18,700	$25,800
		350/315 FI 4dr Sdn	$10,300	$14,400	$19,500	$27,000
		350/305 4dr Hdtp	$10,300	$17,300	$25,700	$35,000
		350/315 FI 4dr Hdtp	$10,800	$18,100	$26,800	$36,500
		318/225 2dr Conv	$21,800	$33,800	$53,900	$75,200
		350/305 2dr Conv	$26,100	$40,600	$64,700	$90,400
		350/315 FI 2dr Conv	$27,200	$42,300	$67,400	$94,100
						+10% for factory a/c.
1958	Fury	318/290 2dr Hdtp Cpe	$19,800	$29,100	$40,400	$67,200
		350/305 2dr Hdtp Cpe	$23,200	$33,200	$46,700	$69,800
						+20% for factory a/c.
1959	Savoy	230/132 2dr Bus Cpe	$5,500	$8,100	$11,300	$16,700
		318/230 2dr Sdn	$5,200	$7,800	$10,900	$15,800
		318/230 4dr Sdn	$4,700	$7,200	$10,100	$14,600
		361/305 4dr Sdn	$6,500	$9,600	$13,700	$19,900
		361/305 2dr Sdn	$7,200	$10,400	$14,800	$21,400
						-20% for 6-cyl.
1959	Belvedere	318/230 2dr Hdtp	$10,000	$14,200	$20,200	$29,400
		318/230 4dr Hdtp	$5,000	$7,600	$10,500	$15,500
		318/230 4dr Sdn	$4,800	$7,200	$10,300	$14,800
		361/305 2dr Hdtp	$13,600	$19,300	$27,400	$39,700
		361/305 4dr Sdn	$6,700	$9,600	$13,800	$20,000
		361/305 4dr Hdtp	$6,900	$10,200	$14,300	$21,000
		318/230 2dr Conv	$15,200	$21,200	$30,900	$48,400
		361/305 2dr Conv	$20,600	$28,500	$41,800	$65,600
						-20% for 6-cyl.
1959	Suburban	318/230 2dr Cstm Wgn	$11,600	$16,400	$23,800	$34,300
		318/230 4dr Cstm Stn Wgn 6P	$10,400	$14,300	$20,300	$27,400
		318/230 4dr Sport Stn Wgn 6P	$11,100	$15,300	$23,100	$31,900
1959	Fury	318/230 2dr Hdtp	$11,700	$16,700	$23,500	$33,400
		318/230 4dr Sdn	$6,900	$9,900	$13,900	$20,100
		318/260 2dr Hdtp	$14,100	$20,000	$28,300	$41,800
		318/260 4dr Sdn	$8,500	$11,900	$16,900	$25,000
		361/305 2dr Hdtp	$15,900	$22,700	$31,900	$47,200
		361/305 4dr Sdn	$9,500	$13,300	$18,800	$27,800
						+20% for factory a/c. +7% for swivel bucket seats.
1959	Sport Fury	318/260 2dr Hdtp	$13,600	$19,600	$27,600	$41,200

Year	Model	Body Style	4	3	2	1
		361/305 2dr Hdtp	$15,500	$22,100	$31,100	$46,300
		318/260 2dr Conv	$25,600	$36,300	$50,500	$74,500
		361/305 2dr Conv	$35,600	$52,300	$85,100	$127,000
				+20% for factory a/c. +7% for swivel bucket seats.		
1960	Valiant	170/101 4dr V200 Sdn	$3,800	$7,200	$9,100	$16,300
		170/148 4dr V200 Sdn	$4,100	$7,900	$10,000	$18,100
		170/101 4dr V200 Stn Wgn 6P	$5,200	$8,100	$12,100	$18,900
		170/148 4dr V200 Stn Wgn 6P	$5,800	$8,700	$13,200	$20,700
1960	Savoy	318/230 2dr Sdn	$5,700	$8,400	$11,600	$16,800
		318/230 4dr Sdn	$5,400	$8,100	$11,100	$16,300
						-20% for 6-cyl.
1960	Belvedere	318/230 2dr Sdn	$5,700	$8,500	$11,800	$17,100
		318/230 4dr Sdn	$5,900	$8,600	$11,800	$17,200
		318/230 2dr Hdtp Cpe	$9,900	$13,900	$19,400	$28,400
						-20% for 6-cyl.
1960	Fury	318/230 2dr Hdtp Cpe	$10,000	$14,800	$19,600	$28,900
		361/305 2dr Hdtp Cpe	$13,000	$19,200	$27,200	$39,000
		383/330 2dr Hdtp Cpe	$13,600	$19,800	$28,100	$40,700
		318/230 4dr Hdtp Sdn	$7,900	$11,500	$16,100	$22,800
		361/305 4dr Hdtp Sdn	$10,300	$15,000	$21,100	$30,600
		383/330 4dr Hdtp Sdn	$10,800	$15,600	$21,800	$31,900
		318/230 2dr Conv	$25,100	$36,800	$51,300	$73,600
		361/305 2dr Conv	$32,800	$47,900	$66,400	$93,900
		383/330 2dr Conv	$35,800	$50,500	$71,700	$115,000
				+20% for factory a/c. +7% for swivel bucket seats.		
1961	Valiant	170/101 4dr V200 Sdn	$3,200	$6,500	$8,100	$14,700
		225/145 4dr V200 Sdn	$3,500	$7,100	$9,000	$16,200
		170/101 4dr V200 Wgn	$4,700	$7,300	$11,100	$18,800
		225/145 4dr V200 Wgn	$5,400	$8,200	$12,300	$20,500
		170/101 2dr V200 Hdtp Cpe	$4,800	$8,700	$11,300	$18,400
		225/145 2dr V200 Hdtp Cpe	$5,200	$9,400	$12,400	$20,200
1961	Belvedere	318/230 2dr Sdn	$5,500	$8,200	$11,200	$16,200
		361/305 2dr Sdn	$6,300	$9,500	$12,900	$18,800

Plymouth

Year	Model	Body Style	4	3	2	1
		383/325 2dr Sdn	$7,200	$10,600	$14,600	$21,200
		383/340 2dr Sdn	$8,900	$13,200	$18,300	$26,400
		413/350 2dr Sdn	$9,700	$14,300	$19,700	$28,700
		413/375 2dr Sdn	$12,400	$20,200	$25,400	$36,800
		318/230 4dr Sdn	$5,300	$7,800	$10,500	$15,100
		361/305 4dr Sdn	$6,100	$8,900	$12,100	$17,400
		383/325 4dr Sdn	$6,900	$10,100	$13,700	$19,800
		383/340 4dr Sdn	$8,600	$12,500	$16,900	$24,700
		413/350 4dr Sdn	$9,300	$13,500	$18,400	$26,800
		413/375 4dr Sdn	$12,000	$17,400	$23,700	$34,300
		318/230 2dr Hdtp Cpe	$7,100	$10,300	$13,900	$20,900
		361/305 2dr Hdtp Cpe	$8,200	$11,900	$16,000	$24,000
		383/325 2dr Hdtp Cpe	$9,200	$13,300	$18,100	$27,200
		383/340 2dr Hdtp Cpe	$11,600	$16,700	$22,500	$33,800
		413/350 2dr Hdtp Cpe	$12,400	$18,100	$24,400	$36,500
		413/375 2dr Hdtp Cpe	$16,000	$23,100	$31,400	$46,800
						-20% for 6-cyl.
1961	Fury	318/230 2dr Hdtp Cpe	$8,100	$12,100	$16,800	$23,500
		361/305 2dr Hdtp Cpe	$9,300	$13,900	$19,400	$27,200
		361/310 2dr Hdtp Cpe	$9,700	$14,500	$20,200	$28,300
		383/325 2dr Hdtp Cpe	$10,400	$15,700	$21,800	$30,600
		383/330 2dr Hdtp Cpe	$12,600	$19,200	$26,800	$37,300
		383/340 2dr Hdtp Cpe	$12,900	$19,600	$27,400	$38,100
		413/350 2dr Hdtp Cpe	$14,100	$21,200	$29,600	$41,100
		413/375 2dr Hdtp Cpe	$18,400	$28,200	$39,800	$57,600
		318/230 4dr Sdn	$4,800	$7,300	$10,100	$14,800
		361/305 4dr Sdn	$5,500	$8,400	$11,500	$17,100
		361/310 4dr Sdn	$5,700	$8,800	$12,100	$18,100
		383/325 4dr Sdn	$6,200	$9,400	$13,000	$19,700
		383/330 4dr Sdn	$7,700	$11,400	$16,000	$23,600
		383/340 4dr Sdn	$7,900	$11,800	$16,300	$24,200
		413/350 4dr Sdn	$8,400	$12,700	$17,600	$26,200
		413/375 4dr Sdn	$10,900	$16,700	$22,700	$33,700
		318/230 4dr Hdtp Sdn	$7,000	$10,600	$14,100	$21,100
		361/305 4dr Hdtp Sdn	$8,100	$12,200	$16,300	$24,200

Year	Model	Body Style	4	3	2	1
		361/310 4dr Hdtp Sdn	$8,400	$12,700	$16,900	$25,300
		383/325 4dr Hdtp Sdn	$9,000	$13,800	$18,500	$27,500
		383/330 4dr Hdtp Sdn	$11,000	$16,800	$22,400	$33,300
		383/340 4dr Hdtp Sdn	$11,300	$17,200	$23,000	$34,100
		413/350 4dr Hdtp Sdn	$12,200	$18,600	$24,800	$36,900
		413/375 4dr Hdtp Sdn	$15,700	$23,800	$31,900	$47,300
		318/230 2dr Conv	$20,300	$30,000	$42,100	$58,500
		361/305 2dr Conv	$24,300	$36,100	$50,500	$70,000
		383/325 2dr Conv	$26,300	$39,000	$54,600	$75,800
		383/330 2dr Conv	$32,200	$47,300	$66,500	$92,400
		383/340 2dr Conv	$33,000	$48,600	$68,100	$94,700
		413/350 2dr Conv	$35,600	$52,500	$73,600	$102,000
		413/375 2dr Conv	$45,600	$67,400	$94,000	$130,000
						-20% for 6-cyl.
1961	Suburban	318/230 4dr Cstm Stn Wgn 6P	$11,100	$14,200	$19,900	$31,600
1962	Valiant	170/101 2dr V200 Cpe	$7,500	$10,900	$14,000	$20,300
		225/145 2dr V200 Cpe	$8,200	$11,900	$15,500	$22,200
		170/101 4dr V200 Sdn	$5,700	$9,000	$11,600	$16,100
		225/145 4dr V200 Sdn	$6,400	$9,900	$12,700	$17,800
		170/101 4dr V200 Wgn	$6,100	$9,900	$12,300	$18,600
		225/145 4dr V200 Wgn	$6,700	$10,900	$13,500	$20,400
1962	Belvedere	318/230 2dr Sdn	$4,400	$6,400	$8,900	$13,000
		318/230 4dr Sdn	$4,300	$6,300	$8,400	$12,300
		318/260 2dr Hdtp Cpe	$6,900	$10,000	$12,600	$19,800
						-20% for 6-cyl.
1962	Fury	318/230 2dr Hdtp Cpe	$10,300	$15,000	$20,200	$27,800
		383/335 2dr Hdtp Cpe	$15,400	$22,600	$30,400	$41,500
		413/410 2dr Hdtp Cpe	$25,200	$37,100	$50,200	$67,300
		413/420 Max Wedge 2dr Hdtp Cpe	$44,300	$58,900	$78,100	$112,000
		318/230 4dr Sdn	$4,300	$6,300	$8,800	$12,900
		383/335 4dr Sdn	$6,500	$9,400	$13,100	$19,600
		413/410 4dr Sdn	$10,800	$15,700	$22,000	$32,600

Plymouth

Year	Model	Body Style	4	3	2	1
		413/420 Max Wedge 4dr Sdn	$19,500	$28,100	$39,600	$58,700
		318/230 4dr Hdtp Sdn	$5,900	$9,200	$12,500	$17,900
		383/335 4dr Hdtp Sdn	$9,000	$13,700	$19,000	$26,900
		413/410 4dr Hdtp Sdn	$14,900	$22,900	$31,500	$44,500
		413/420 Max Wedge 4dr Hdtp Sdn	$27,000	$41,300	$56,700	$80,200
		318/230 2dr Conv	$21,200	$31,800	$44,700	$62,900
		383/335 2dr Conv	$32,000	$47,700	$67,200	$94,400
		413/410 2dr Conv	$53,100	$79,500	$113,000	$153,000
		413/420 Max Wedge 2dr Conv	$91,200	$137,000	$192,000	$248,000
						-20% for 6-cyl.
1962	Sport Fury	361/305 2dr Hdtp Cpe	$10,900	$15,600	$21,900	$31,900
		383/335 2dr Hdtp Cpe	$16,500	$23,200	$32,800	$47,800
		413/410 2dr Hdtp Sdn	$27,300	$38,800	$54,700	$79,700
		361/305 2dr Conv	$25,100	$35,000	$52,300	$72,200
		383/335 2dr Conv	$37,700	$52,600	$78,500	$109,000
		413/410 2dr Conv	$62,900	$87,900	$131,000	$177,000
						-20% for 6-cyl.
1963	Valiant	170/101 2dr V200 Conv	$6,600	$9,600	$13,800	$20,000
		225/145 2dr V200 Conv	$7,200	$10,600	$15,100	$21,900
		170/101 2dr Signet Conv	$7,000	$10,600	$14,600	$21,200
		225/145 2dr Signet Conv	$7,700	$11,500	$16,100	$23,300
1963	Belvedere	318/230 2dr Sdn	$6,100	$8,700	$12,000	$18,000
		361/265 2dr Sdn	$7,700	$11,000	$15,100	$22,500
		383/330 2dr Sdn	$8,300	$11,700	$16,200	$24,200
		426/415 Max Wedge II 2dr Sdn	$16,700	$23,500	$32,700	$48,400
		426/425 Max Wedge II 2dr Sdn	$29,200	$41,100	$57,000	$84,700
		318/230 4dr Sdn	$4,600	$6,600	$9,200	$13,400
		361/265 4dr Sdn	$5,800	$8,200	$11,500	$17,000
		383/330 4dr Sdn	$6,200	$8,900	$12,400	$18,300
		426/415 Max Wedge II 4dr Sdn	$12,600	$17,800	$25,000	$36,500
		426/425 Max Wedge II 4dr Sdn	$22,000	$31,100	$43,600	$63,800
		318/230 4dr Stn Wgn 6P	$5,600	$8,300	$12,700	$18,400

Year	Model	Body Style	4	3	2	1
		361/265 4dr Stn Wgn 6P	$7,100	$10,400	$16,000	$23,000
		383/330 4dr Stn Wgn 6P	$7,700	$11,200	$17,200	$24,800
		426/415 Max Wedge II 4dr Stn Wgn 6P	$15,200	$22,400	$34,500	$49,600
		426/425 Max Wedge II 4dr Stn Wgn 6P	$26,800	$39,200	$60,300	$86,600
		318/230 2dr Hdtp Cpe	$7,000	$10,200	$14,000	$20,200
		361/265 2dr Hdtp Cpe	$8,700	$12,700	$17,600	$25,300
		383/330 2dr Hdtp Cpe	$9,400	$13,700	$19,000	$27,300
		426/415 Max Wedge II 2dr Hdtp Cpe	$18,900	$27,700	$38,100	$54,600
		426/425 Max Wedge II 2dr Hdtp Cpe	$33,000	$48,300	$66,500	$95,300
						-20% for 6-cyl.
1963	Fury	318/230 2dr Hdtp Cpe	$8,500	$13,100	$18,200	$25,900
		318/230 4dr Sdn	$4,800	$7,100	$9,800	$14,100
		318/230 4dr Stn Wgn 6P	$5,000	$7,600	$12,400	$18,400
		318/230 2dr Conv	$16,900	$25,200	$35,100	$50,200
1963	Sport Fury	318/230 2dr Hdtp Cpe	$10,300	$15,400	$20,800	$30,800
		361/265 2dr Hdtp Cpe	$12,800	$19,200	$26,200	$38,800
		383/330 2dr Hdtp Cpe	$13,900	$20,700	$28,200	$41,800
		426/415 Max Wedge II 2dr Hdtp Cpe	$27,200	$38,900	$53,000	$78,700
		426/425 Max Wedge II 2dr Hdtp Cpe	$48,900	$69,900	$95,200	$137,000
		318/230 2dr Conv	$23,300	$34,100	$47,500	$69,800
		361/265 2dr Conv	$29,100	$42,700	$59,300	$87,300
		383/330 2dr Conv	$31,400	$46,200	$64,000	$94,200
		426/415 Max Wedge II 2dr Conv	$61,500	$86,700	$114,000	$164,000
		426/425 Max Wedge II 2dr Conv	$106,000	$147,000	$208,000	$297,000
						-20% for 6-cyl.
1964	Valiant	170/101 2dr V200 Conv	$6,600	$9,600	$13,800	$20,000

Plymouth

Year	Model	Body Style	4	3	2	1
		225/145 2dr V200 Conv	$7,200	$10,600	$15,100	$21,900
		273/180 2dr V200 Conv	$7,700	$12,100	$16,500	$27,600
		170/101 2dr Signet Conv	$7,000	$10,600	$14,600	$21,200
		225/145 2dr Signet Conv	$7,700	$11,500	$16,100	$23,300
		273/180 2dr Signet Conv	$8,300	$13,300	$19,400	$27,600
1964	Barracuda	273/180 2dr Fstbk Cpe	$9,100	$14,000	$20,100	$28,300
					-20% for 6-cyl. +10% for 4-spd.	
1964	Belvedere	318/230 2dr Sdn	$4,600	$6,800	$9,400	$13,600
		361/265 2dr Sdn	$5,500	$8,100	$11,300	$16,300
		383/305 2dr Sdn	$5,800	$8,500	$11,700	$17,200
		383/330 2dr Sdn	$6,200	$9,100	$12,700	$18,600
		426/365 2dr Sdn	$11,600	$17,000	$23,600	$34,300
		426/415 Hemi 2dr Sdn	$14,300	$20,900	$29,100	$42,300
		426/425 Max Wedge III 2dr Sdn	$21,000	$30,500	$42,400	$61,700
		318/230 4dr Sdn	$4,500	$6,300	$9,000	$13,100
		361/265 4dr Sdn	$5,400	$7,500	$10,800	$15,700
		383/305 4dr Sdn	$5,600	$7,900	$11,200	$16,400
		383/330 4dr Sdn	$6,100	$8,500	$12,100	$17,900
		426/365 4dr Sdn	$11,400	$15,700	$22,600	$33,100
		426/415 Hemi 4dr Sdn	$14,000	$19,400	$27,900	$40,800
		426/425 Max Wedge III 4dr Sdn	$20,600	$28,200	$40,600	$59,500
		383/305 4dr Stn Wgn 6P	$6,700	$9,900	$15,700	$21,700
		383/330 4dr Stn Wgn 6P	$7,300	$10,600	$17,100	$23,400
		426/415 Hemi 4dr Stn Wgn 6P	$16,500	$24,300	$39,100	$53,700
		426/425 Max Wedge III 4dr Stn Wgn 6P	$24,200	$35,500	$57,000	$78,000
		318/230 4dr Stn Wgn 9P	$5,300	$7,900	$12,600	$17,400
		361/265 4dr Stn Wgn 9P	$6,500	$9,500	$15,100	$20,800
		426/415 Hemi 4dr Stn Wgn 9P	$13,400	$19,700	$31,700	$43,300
		318/230 2dr Hdtp Cpe	$7,000	$10,300	$14,500	$20,900
		361/265 2dr Hdtp Cpe	$8,400	$12,300	$17,500	$25,000

Year	Model	Body Style	4	3	2	1
		383/305 2dr Hdtp Cpe	$8,700	$12,900	$18,200	$26,200
		383/330 2dr Hdtp Cpe	$9,400	$13,900	$19,600	$28,200
		426/365 2dr Hdtp Cpe	$17,500	$25,800	$36,500	$52,300
		426/415 Hemi 2dr Hdtp Cpe	$25,400	$36,700	$50,500	$74,500
		426/425 Max Wedge III 2dr Hdtp Cpe	$37,500	$50,500	$77,400	$106,000
						-20% for 6-cyl.
1964	Fury	318/230 2dr Hdtp Cpe	$7,700	$11,400	$15,600	$22,700
		361/265 2dr Hdtp Cpe	$9,100	$13,600	$18,800	$27,400
		383/305 2dr Hdtp Cpe	$9,500	$14,200	$19,600	$28,500
		426/365 2dr Hdtp Cpe	$19,300	$28,500	$39,300	$56,900
		426/415 Hemi 2dr Hdtp Cpe	$23,800	$35,100	$48,500	$70,200
		426/425 Hemi 2dr Hdtp Cpe	$35,600	$52,800	$73,900	$108,000
		318/230 4dr Sdn	$4,900	$7,300	$10,100	$14,400
		361/265 4dr Sdn	$5,800	$8,700	$12,000	$17,600
		383/305 4dr Sdn	$6,000	$9,100	$12,500	$18,300
		426/365 4dr Sdn	$12,200	$18,200	$25,300	$36,500
		426/415 Hemi 4dr Sdn	$15,000	$22,300	$31,200	$45,000
		426/425 Hemi 4dr Sdn	$22,700	$33,600	$46,700	$67,600
		383/305 4dr Stn Wgn 6P	$6,300	$9,300	$15,900	$23,300
		426/415 Hemi 4dr Stn Wgn 6P	$15,300	$23,100	$39,500	$57,800
		426/425 Hemi 4dr Stn Wgn 6P	$23,200	$34,500	$59,300	$86,800
		361/265 4dr Stn Wgn 9P	$5,900	$8,900	$15,300	$22,400
		383/330 4dr Stn Wgn 9P	$6,800	$10,100	$17,200	$25,300
		426/365 4dr Stn Wgn 9P	$12,400	$18,700	$32,000	$46,800
		318/230 4dr Hdtp Sdn	$5,200	$8,100	$11,000	$16,100
		361/265 4dr Hdtp Sdn	$6,400	$9,800	$13,100	$19,500
		383/305 4dr Hdtp Sdn	$6,600	$10,200	$13,700	$20,300

Plymouth

Year	Model	Body Style	4	3	2	1
		426/365 4dr Hdtp Sdn	$13,200	$20,200	$27,600	$40,600
		426/415 Hemi 4dr Hdtp Sdn	$16,200	$24,900	$34,000	$50,000
		426/425 Hemi 4dr Hdtp Sdn	$24,600	$37,600	$50,900	$75,100
		318/230 2dr Conv	$19,200	$26,900	$38,500	$56,900
		361/265 2dr Conv	$23,100	$32,200	$46,300	$68,200
		383/305 2dr Conv	$24,000	$33,600	$48,000	$71,100
		426/365 2dr Conv	$48,000	$67,300	$96,000	$143,000
		426/415 Hemi 2dr Conv	$59,200	$84,300	$113,000	$170,000
		426/425 Hemi 2dr Conv	$89,800	$126,000	$173,000	$232,000
						-20% for 6-cyl.
1964	Sport Fury	318/230 2dr Hdtp Cpe	$8,900	$13,100	$18,500	$27,400
		426/415 Hemi 2dr Hdtp Cpe	$28,300	$40,100	$56,400	$83,000
		426/425 Hemi 2dr Hdtp Cpe	$24,100	$30,100	$38,300	$51,500
		318/230 2dr Conv	$22,600	$32,700	$46,000	$67,200
		426/415 Hemi 2dr Conv	$71,600	$99,800	$131,000	$198,000
		426/425 Hemi 2dr Conv	$35,800	$49,900	$70,100	$102,000
						+10% for 4-spd.
1965	Valiant	170/101 2dr V200 Conv	$6,900	$10,200	$14,200	$20,700
		225/145 2dr V200 Conv	$7,400	$11,100	$15,700	$22,700
		273/180 2dr V200 Conv	$8,400	$12,600	$18,200	$26,900
		170/101 2dr Signet Conv	$7,300	$11,100	$15,400	$22,100
		225/145 2dr Signet Conv	$8,000	$12,300	$17,000	$24,300
		273/180 2dr Signet Conv	$9,300	$14,500	$20,500	$34,300
1965	Barracuda	273/180 2dr Fstbk	$9,100	$14,000	$19,900	$28,400
		273/235 2dr Fstbk	$11,600	$17,500	$23,400	$34,700
		273/235 2dr Formula S Fstbk	$11,800	$16,700	$23,200	$35,200
						-20% or 6-cyl. +10% for 4-spd.
1965	Belvedere	273/180 2dr I Sdn	$4,500	$6,600	$9,200	$13,300
		426/365 2dr I Sdn	$9,100	$13,100	$18,400	$26,900
		426/415 Hemi 2dr I Sdn	$11,700	$16,800	$23,600	$34,500
		426/425 Hemi 2dr I Sdn	$17,900	$25,800	$36,400	$53,100

Year	Model	Body Style	4	3	2	1
		273/180 4dr I Sdn	$4,100	$6,100	$8,700	$12,400
		426/365 4dr I Sdn	$8,300	$12,100	$17,400	$25,000
		426/415 Hemi 4dr I Sdn	$10,600	$15,500	$22,200	$32,100
		426/425 Hemi 4dr I Sdn	$16,300	$23,800	$34,300	$49,400
		273/180 4dr II Sdn	$4,600	$6,600	$9,200	$13,400
		426/365 4dr II Sdn	$9,300	$13,100	$18,400	$27,100
		426/415 Hemi 4dr II Sdn	$11,900	$16,800	$23,600	$34,700
		426/425 Hemi 4dr II Sdn	$18,200	$25,800	$36,400	$53,500
		273/180 4dr II Stn Wgn 6P	$4,500	$6,600	$12,900	$19,100
		383/330 4dr II Stn Wgn 6P	$6,400	$9,200	$18,100	$26,800
		426/365 4dr II Stn Wgn 6P	$9,100	$13,100	$26,000	$38,100
		426/415 Hemi 4dr II Stn Wgn 6P	$11,700	$16,800	$33,200	$48,900
		426/425 Hemi 4dr II Stn Wgn 6P	$17,900	$25,800	$51,000	$75,300
		273/180 2dr II Hdtp Cpe	$8,500	$12,100	$16,700	$24,600
		426/365 2dr II Hdtp Cpe	$11,900	$17,000	$23,500	$34,500
		426/415 Hemi 2dr II Hdtp Cpe	$22,300	$32,500	$45,600	$66,800
		426/425 Hemi 2dr II Hdtp Cpe	$33,500	$47,600	$66,100	$97,300
		273/180 2dr II Conv	$10,900	$15,300	$21,000	$30,900
		426/365 2dr II Conv	$21,800	$30,400	$42,100	$61,800
		426/415 Hemi 2dr II Conv	$27,800	$38,800	$53,900	$79,300
		426/425 Hemi 2dr II Conv	$38,700	$53,000	$76,700	$111,000
						-20% for 6-cyl.
1965	Satellite	273/235 2dr Hdtp Cpe	$7,800	$11,600	$18,200	$27,400
		318/230 2dr Hdtp Cpe	$9,400	$12,800	$20,900	$29,700
		383/325 2dr Hdtp Cpe	$10,000	$14,500	$22,200	$33,200
		426/360 2dr Hdtp Cpe	$16,000	$22,400	$36,000	$51,100
		426/415 Hemi 2dr Hdtp Cpe	$23,000	$28,000	$45,200	$65,100

Plymouth

Year	Model	Body Style	4	3	2	1
		426/425 Hemi 2dr Hdtp Cpe	$31,100	$43,200	$68,500	$99,100
		273/235 2dr Conv	$13,800	$19,300	$29,800	$41,000
		318/230 2dr Conv	$14,400	$20,500	$32,700	$47,200
		383/325 2dr Conv	$15,500	$22,300	$35,100	$52,300
		426/360 2dr Conv	$24,600	$35,400	$52,600	$79,900
		426/415 Hemi 2dr Conv	$32,700	$45,000	$71,400	$101,000
		426/425 Hemi 2dr Conv	$51,600	$69,400	$111,000	$147,000
1965	Fury	318/230 2dr I Sdn	$4,000	$6,000	$9,200	$13,400
		383/270 2dr I Sdn	$4,600	$6,800	$10,700	$15,500
		426/365 2dr I Sdn	$8,000	$11,800	$18,500	$27,300
		318/230 2dr II Sdn	$3,900	$5,800	$8,900	$13,000
		383/270 2dr II Sdn	$4,400	$6,700	$10,300	$15,000
		426/365 2dr II Sdn	$7,600	$11,400	$17,900	$26,500
		318/230 2dr III Hdtp Cpe	$7,600	$11,300	$17,800	$25,800
		383/270 2dr III Hdtp Cpe	$8,700	$13,000	$20,400	$29,500
		426/365 2dr III Hdtp Cpe	$15,300	$23,000	$35,700	$51,400
		318/230 4dr III Hdtp Sdn	$4,500	$7,000	$10,700	$15,600
		318/230 2dr III Conv	$12,500	$18,100	$27,800	$40,500
		383/270 2dr III Conv	$14,400	$20,800	$32,000	$46,600
		426/365 2dr III Conv	$24,100	$34,300	$50,800	$74,500
						-20% for 6-cyl.
1965	Sport Fury	318/230 2dr Hdtp Cpe	$8,400	$12,200	$19,400	$28,400
		426/365 2dr Hdtp Cpe	$16,800	$24,500	$38,900	$56,800
		426/415 Hemi 2dr Hdtp Cpe	$33,800	$48,800	$77,800	$115,000
		426/425 Hemi 2dr Hdtp Cpe	$38,400	$55,600	$88,900	$131,000
		318/230 2dr Conv	$13,200	$18,900	$29,400	$42,700
		426/365 2dr Conv	$25,400	$36,100	$53,700	$77,600
		426/415 Hemi 2dr Conv	$52,700	$75,400	$113,000	$168,000
		426/425 Hemi 2dr Conv	$60,200	$86,100	$129,000	$193,000
						+15% for 4-spd.
1966	Valiant	170/101 2dr Signet Conv	$4,900	$7,300	$10,200	$15,300

Year	Model	Body Style	4	3	2	1
		225/145 2dr Signet Conv	$5,500	$8,200	$11,200	$16,900
		273/235 2dr Signet Conv	$9,500	$15,900	$21,100	$38,000
1966	Barracuda	273/180 2dr Fstbk	$9,900	$14,200	$20,100	$30,200
		273/235 2dr Fstbk	$12,000	$17,500	$23,600	$36,200
		273/235 2dr Form S Fstbk	$12,300	$17,300	$24,300	$36,800
					-30% or 6-cyl. +15% for 4-spd.	
1966	Belvedere I	318/230 2dr Sdn	$5,300	$7,600	$10,500	$15,800
		361/265 2dr Sdn	$5,800	$8,300	$11,400	$17,300
		383/325 2dr Sdn	$6,000	$8,600	$11,800	$18,000
		426/415 Hemi 2dr Sdn	$16,800	$22,600	$33,500	$54,600
		426/425 Hemi 2dr Sdn	$48,900	$63,500	$82,400	$103,000
		318/230 4dr Sdn	$5,100	$7,100	$10,200	$15,200
		361/265 4dr Sdn	$5,500	$7,800	$11,100	$16,500
		383/325 4dr Sdn	$5,700	$8,100	$11,500	$17,400
		426/415 Hemi 4dr Sdn	$13,600	$19,200	$27,400	$44,600
		426/425 Hemi 4dr Sdn	$17,400	$24,600	$35,100	$58,700
						-30% for 6-cyl.
1966	Belvedere II	273/180 2dr Hdtp Cpe	$10,500	$14,300	$20,700	$31,000
		318/230 2dr Hdtp Cpe	$12,300	$16,800	$23,700	$35,600
		361/265 2dr Hdtp Cpe	$13,400	$18,200	$25,800	$38,700
		383/325 2dr Hdtp Cpe	$13,900	$19,000	$27,400	$40,900
		426/415 Hemi 2dr Hdtp Cpe	$32,900	$44,800	$63,300	$95,400
		426/425 Hemi 2dr Hdtp Cpe	$47,300	$61,800	$80,100	$102,000
		318/230 4dr Sdn	$4,800	$6,800	$9,500	$14,400
		361/265 4dr Sdn	$5,300	$7,400	$10,500	$15,600
		383/325 4dr Sdn	$5,500	$7,700	$10,900	$16,300
		426/415 Hemi 4dr Sdn	$13,000	$18,200	$26,200	$40,000
		426/425 Hemi 4dr Sdn	$16,700	$23,500	$33,200	$49,900
		273/180 2dr Conv	$11,300	$15,200	$21,300	$31,800
		318/230 2dr Conv	$12,800	$17,400	$24,300	$36,600
		361/265 2dr Conv	$13,900	$18,900	$26,400	$39,700
		383/325 2dr Conv	$14,400	$21,000	$29,900	$45,800
		426/415 Hemi 2dr Conv	$34,000	$46,200	$65,500	$98,500
		426/425 Hemi 2dr Conv	$71,100	$99,500	$113,000	$147,000

Plymouth

Year	Model	Body Style	4	3	2	1
						-30% for 6-cyl.
1966	Satellite	273/180 2dr Hdtp Cpe	$10,200	$14,000	$21,700	$32,700
		318/230 2dr Hdtp Cpe	$11,400	$15,600	$25,200	$38,200
		383/325 2dr Hdtp Cpe	$12,900	$18,000	$28,900	$42,800
		426/425 Hemi 2dr Hdtp Cpe	$43,200	$64,600	$103,000	$129,000
		273/180 2dr Conv	$12,600	$17,600	$27,800	$41,500
		318/230 2dr Conv	$14,300	$20,000	$32,200	$47,900
		383/325 2dr Conv	$16,000	$22,600	$35,800	$53,100
		426/425 Hemi 2dr Conv	$47,700	$73,700	$111,000	$152,000
						-30% for 6-cyl.
1966	Fury III	318/230 2dr Hdtp Cpe	$8,500	$12,700	$18,200	$27,400
		383/325 2dr Hdtp Cpe	$11,100	$16,600	$23,600	$35,500
		440/365 2dr Hdtp Cpe	$12,700	$19,100	$27,400	$40,900
		318/230 2dr Conv	$12,600	$17,900	$25,800	$38,600
		383/325 2dr Conv	$16,500	$23,300	$33,600	$50,200
		440/365 2dr Conv	$19,000	$26,900	$38,800	$57,900
					-30% for 6-cyl.	-20% for auto.
1966	Sport Fury	318/230 2dr Hdtp Cpe	$9,100	$12,200	$19,600	$30,000
		383/325 2dr Hdtp Cpe	$11,700	$15,900	$25,500	$38,900
		440/365 2dr Hdtp Cpe	$13,500	$18,400	$29,500	$44,900
		318/230 2dr Conv	$13,100	$17,800	$28,700	$42,400
		383/325 2dr Conv	$17,000	$23,100	$37,400	$55,200
		440/365 2dr Conv	$19,600	$26,700	$43,200	$63,800
						-30% for 6-cyl.
1966	VIP	318/230 2dr Hdtp Cpe	$7,300	$11,000	$15,100	$21,800
		383/325 2dr Hdtp Cpe	$9,500	$14,200	$19,700	$28,300
		440/365 2dr Hdtp Cpe	$11,000	$16,500	$22,700	$32,600
		318/230 4dr Hdtp Sdn	$5,800	$8,100	$11,500	$17,200
		383/325 4dr Hdtp Sdn	$7,600	$10,700	$14,900	$22,300
		440/365 4dr Hdtp Sdn	$8,800	$12,300	$17,200	$25,900
						-30% for 6-cyl.
1967	Valiant	170/115 2dr 100 Sdn	$5,500	$7,800	$11,700	$16,800

Year	Model	Body Style	4	3	2	1
		225/145 2dr 100 Sdn	$6,000	$8,500	$12,900	$18,400
		273/180 2dr 100 Sdn	$6,300	$8,900	$13,500	$19,300
		170/115 4dr 100 Sdn	$3,400	$4,600	$6,600	$8,700
		225/145 4dr 100 Sdn	$3,700	$5,000	$7,200	$9,500
		273/180 4dr 100 Sdn	$3,900	$5,200	$7,500	$10,000
1967	Barracuda	273/180 2dr Hdtp Cpe	$9,600	$14,000	$21,500	$32,900
		383/280 2dr Hdtp Cpe	$12,500	$16,600	$24,700	$37,200
		273/180 2dr Fstbk	$10,900	$15,900	$23,500	$35,500
		383/280 2dr Fstbk	$13,600	$18,500	$27,600	$40,600
		273/235 2dr Form S Fstbk	$12,200	$16,900	$24,300	$38,500
		273/180 2dr Conv	$12,800	$20,900	$31,400	$45,200
		383/280 2dr Conv	$16,000	$26,100	$39,300	$56,500
					-30% for 6-cyl.	*+10% for 4-spd.*
1967	Belvedere I	273/180 2dr Sdn	$8,300	$11,500	$16,400	$24,400
		318/230 2dr Sdn	$9,600	$13,200	$18,800	$28,000
		383/270 2dr Sdn	$10,400	$14,400	$20,400	$30,400
		383/325 2dr Sdn	$10,700	$15,000	$21,300	$31,600
		426/425 Hemi 2dr Sdn	$46,600	$60,700	$78,800	$101,000
		273/180 4dr Sdn	$3,900	$5,600	$7,500	$11,600
		318/230 4dr Sdn	$4,500	$6,400	$8,600	$13,300
		383/270 4dr Sdn	$4,900	$7,000	$9,400	$14,500
		383/325 4dr Sdn	$5,100	$7,300	$9,800	$15,100
		426/425 Hemi 4dr Sdn	$15,600	$22,200	$30,000	$46,200
						-30% for 6-cyl.
1967	Belvedere II	273/180 2dr Hdtp Cpe	$9,200	$12,800	$18,200	$27,100
		318/230 2dr Hdtp Cpe	$10,600	$14,700	$20,900	$31,100
		383/270 2dr Hdtp Cpe	$11,500	$16,000	$22,700	$33,800
		383/325 2dr Hdtp Cpe	$12,900	$17,800	$26,500	$39,800
		426/425 Hemi 2dr Hdtp Cpe	$46,600	$60,700	$78,800	$103,000
		273/180 4dr Sdn	$4,100	$5,800	$7,900	$11,900
		318/230 4dr Sdn	$4,700	$6,700	$9,100	$13,700
		383/270 4dr Sdn	$5,100	$7,300	$9,900	$14,900
		383/325 4dr Sdn	$5,300	$7,500	$10,400	$15,500
		426/425 Hemi 4dr Sdn	$16,300	$23,000	$31,600	$47,500

Plymouth

Year	Model	Body Style	4	3	2	1
		273/180 2dr Conv	$12,000	$16,400	$22,900	$33,900
		318/230 2dr Conv	$13,800	$18,800	$26,300	$39,000
		383/270 2dr Conv	$15,000	$20,400	$28,600	$42,400
		383/325 2dr Conv	$15,600	$22,400	$30,600	$46,200
		426/425 Hemi 2dr Conv	$78,600	$102,000	$121,000	$155,000
						-30% for 6-cyl.
1967	Satellite	273/180 2dr Hdtp Cpe	$9,000	$12,800	$20,800	$31,100
		318/230 2dr Hdtp Cpe	$10,300	$14,800	$23,900	$35,800
		383/270 2dr Hdtp Cpe	$11,200	$16,000	$26,200	$38,900
		383/325 2dr Hdtp Cpe	$11,700	$16,600	$27,100	$40,500
		426/425 Hemi 2dr Hdtp Cpe	$36,100	$49,500	$80,600	$122,000
		273/180 2dr Conv	$11,900	$17,000	$27,600	$41,200
		318/230 2dr Conv	$13,600	$19,400	$31,700	$47,400
		383/270 2dr Conv	$14,800	$21,200	$34,400	$51,500
		383/325 2dr Conv	$15,500	$22,000	$35,900	$53,900
		426/425 Hemi 2dr Conv	$47,700	$65,600	$96,800	$142,000
						-30% for 6-cyl.
1967	GTX	426/425 Hemi 2dr Hdtp Cpe	$57,500	$79,800	$95,600	$122,000
		440/375 2dr Hdtp Cpe	$21,400	$32,800	$47,100	$68,400
		426/425 Hemi 2dr Conv	$111,000	$136,000	$169,000	$206,000
		440/375 2dr Conv	$27,100	$43,400	$62,000	$85,700
			+10% for 4-spd. Colors can make an astonishing difference in both value and salability.			
1967	Fury III	318/230 2dr Hdtp Cpe	$4,600	$6,700	$9,100	$14,000
		383/270 2dr Hdtp Cpe	$5,700	$8,300	$11,600	$17,700
		383/325 2dr Hdtp Cpe	$5,900	$8,600	$12,100	$18,400
		440/350 2dr Hdtp Cpe	$6,900	$10,200	$13,800	$21,300
		440/375 2dr Hdtp Cpe	$7,100	$10,500	$14,300	$22,000
		318/230 2dr Conv	$12,300	$17,500	$25,000	$37,300
		383/270 2dr Conv	$15,300	$21,900	$31,400	$46,700
		383/325 2dr Conv	$16,100	$22,700	$32,500	$48,400
		440/350 2dr Conv	$18,400	$26,300	$37,600	$56,000
		440/375 2dr Conv	$19,000	$27,200	$38,800	$57,800
						-30% for 6-cyl. -20% for auto.

Year	Model	Body Style	4	3	2	1
1967	Sport Fury	318/230 2dr Fstbk	$6,400	$8,700	$14,000	$21,300
		383/270 2dr Fstbk	$8,000	$11,000	$17,600	$26,700
		383/325 2dr Fstbk	$8,300	$11,300	$18,200	$27,700
		440/350 2dr Fstbk	$9,700	$13,100	$21,000	$32,000
		440/375 2dr Fstbk	$10,000	$13,500	$21,800	$33,100
		318/230 2dr Hdtp Cpe	$5,800	$7,800	$12,700	$19,500
		383/270 2dr Hdtp Cpe	$7,200	$10,000	$15,800	$24,400
		383/325 2dr Hdtp Cpe	$7,500	$10,400	$16,500	$25,400
		440/350 2dr Hdtp Cpe	$8,600	$11,900	$19,100	$29,200
		440/375 2dr Hdtp Cpe	$9,000	$12,200	$19,700	$30,300
		318/230 2dr Conv	$12,900	$17,300	$27,300	$41,500
		383/270 2dr Conv	$16,100	$21,600	$34,400	$52,000
		383/325 2dr Conv	$16,700	$22,500	$35,700	$54,100
		440/350 2dr Conv	$19,300	$26,000	$41,200	$62,300
		440/375 2dr Conv	$20,100	$26,900	$42,500	$64,500
						-30% for 6-cyl.
1967	VIP	318/230 2dr Hdtp Cpe	$8,000	$11,400	$16,100	$24,100
		383/270 2dr Hdtp Cpe	$10,000	$14,200	$20,200	$30,200
		383/325 2dr Hdtp Cpe	$10,400	$14,800	$21,000	$31,400
		440/350 2dr Hdtp Cpe	$11,900	$17,100	$24,200	$36,200
		440/375 2dr Hdtp Cpe	$12,300	$17,500	$25,100	$37,300
		318/230 4dr Hdtp Sdn	$7,200	$9,700	$13,700	$20,700
		383/270 4dr Hdtp Sdn	$8,900	$12,300	$17,200	$25,900
		383/325 4dr Hdtp Sdn	$9,300	$12,700	$17,900	$27,000
		440/350 4dr Hdtp Sdn	$10,700	$14,700	$20,700	$31,100
		440/375 4dr Hdtp Sdn	$11,100	$15,100	$21,300	$32,000
						-30% for 6-cyl.
1968	Valiant	170/115 2dr 100 Sdn	$5,500	$7,600	$11,400	$16,200
		225/145 2dr 100 Sdn	$5,700	$7,900	$11,900	$17,100
		273/190 2dr 100 Sdn	$6,000	$8,400	$12,500	$17,900

Plymouth

Year	Model	Body Style	4	3	2	1
		318/230 2dr 100 Sdn	$6,300	$8,700	$13,100	$18,700
		170/115 4dr 100 Sdn	$3,400	$4,600	$6,400	$8,600
		225/145 4dr 100 Sdn	$3,500	$4,800	$6,700	$9,000
		273/190 4dr 100 Sdn	$3,700	$5,100	$7,000	$9,500
		318/230 4dr 100 Sdn	$3,900	$5,300	$7,400	$9,900
1968	Barracuda	318/230 2dr Hdtp Cpe	$10,300	$14,400	$22,000	$33,800
		340/275 2dr Hdtp Cpe	$14,100	$18,600	$27,200	$39,300
		383/300 2dr Hdtp Cpe	$14,800	$19,900	$29,400	$44,400
		318/230 2dr Fstbk	$11,200	$16,400	$24,200	$36,600
		340/275 2dr Fstbk	$14,600	$20,400	$30,000	$42,800
		383/300 2dr Fstbk	$15,400	$21,500	$33,200	$45,600
		2dr Super Stock Fstbk	$99,700	$147,000	$200,000	$230,000
		318/230 2dr Conv	$13,800	$20,700	$29,400	$44,800
		340/275 2dr Conv	$17,600	$26,400	$36,000	$56,700
		383/300 2dr Conv	$18,900	$27,600	$39,000	$59,800

-30% for 6-cyl. +10% for 4-spd. Colors can make an astonishing difference in both value and salability.

Year	Model	Body Style	4	3	2	1
1968	Belvedere	273/190 2dr Cpe	$8,500	$11,700	$16,500	$24,600
		318/230 2dr Cpe	$9,700	$13,400	$19,000	$28,200
		273/190 4dr Sdn	$4,200	$5,800	$8,200	$12,300
		318/230 4dr Sdn	$4,800	$6,700	$9,400	$14,100

-30% for 6-cyl.

Year	Model	Body Style	4	3	2	1
1968	Satellite	273/190 2dr Hdtp Cpe	$9,000	$12,800	$20,400	$30,700
		383/290 2dr Hdtp Cpe	$10,700	$15,400	$24,400	$36,900
		383/330 2dr Hdtp Cpe	$12,100	$17,300	$27,600	$41,400
		273/190 4dr Sdn	$4,200	$6,000	$9,700	$14,500
		383/290 4dr Sdn	$5,100	$7,200	$11,700	$17,700
		383/330 4dr Sdn	$5,800	$8,100	$13,200	$19,900
		273/190 2dr Conv	$12,400	$17,600	$28,500	$41,900
		383/290 2dr Conv	$14,900	$21,200	$34,200	$50,300
		383/330 2dr Conv	$16,700	$23,800	$38,500	$56,900

-30% for 6-cyl.

Year	Model	Body Style	4	3	2	1
1968	Sport Satellite	318/230 2dr Hdtp Cpe	$8,700	$14,000	$22,100	$33,000
		383/290 2dr Hdtp Cpe	$10,400	$16,600	$26,700	$39,600

Year	Model	Body Style	4	3	2	1
		383/330 2dr Hdtp Cpe	$11,700	$18,700	$30,000	$44,500
		318/230 2dr Conv	$13,600	$19,400	$31,400	$46,400
		383/290 2dr Conv	$16,300	$23,400	$37,700	$55,900
		383/330 2dr Conv	$18,400	$26,300	$42,300	$62,900
						-30% for 6-cyl.
1968	GTX	426/425 Hemi 2dr Hdtp Cpe	$53,800	$75,300	$89,700	$114,000
		440/375 2dr Hdtp Cpe	$25,900	$40,200	$55,800	$80,800
		426/425 Hemi 2dr Conv	$116,000	$152,000	$194,000	$233,000
		440/375 2dr Conv	$29,100	$46,500	$66,600	$92,100
			+10% for 4-spd. Colors can make an astonishing difference in both value and salability.			
1968	Road Runner	383/335 2dr Cpe	$19,000	$29,300	$41,800	$61,000
		426/425 Hemi 2dr Cpe	$47,300	$67,900	$88,500	$135,000
		383/335 2dr Hdtp Cpe	$20,000	$30,900	$43,900	$64,000
		426/425 Hemi 2dr Hdtp Cpe	$48,100	$67,400	$86,500	$128,000
			+10% for 4-spd. Colors can make an astonishing difference in both value and salability.			
1968	Fury III	318/230 2dr Hdtp Cpe	$4,400	$6,500	$8,800	$13,400
		383/290 2dr Hdtp Cpe	$5,300	$7,700	$10,800	$16,100
		383/330 2dr Hdtp Cpe	$5,800	$8,400	$11,700	$17,700
		440/375 2dr Hdtp Cpe	$6,800	$10,200	$13,800	$21,000
		318/230 2dr Fstbk	$6,300	$8,800	$12,600	$19,100
		383/290 2dr Fstbk	$7,500	$10,800	$15,100	$22,800
		383/330 2dr Fstbk	$8,200	$11,700	$16,400	$24,800
		440/375 2dr Fstbk	$9,800	$13,800	$19,500	$29,400
		318/230 2dr Conv	$9,800	$14,000	$19,700	$29,400
		383/290 2dr Conv	$11,700	$16,900	$23,600	$35,300
		383/330 2dr Conv	$12,500	$18,200	$25,700	$38,200
		440/375 2dr Conv	$15,100	$21,700	$30,700	$45,600
					-30% for 6-cyl. -20% for auto.	
1968	Sport Fury	318/230 2dr Hdtp Cpe	$5,900	$8,000	$12,900	$19,500
		383/290 2dr Hdtp Cpe	$7,100	$9,800	$15,300	$23,400

Plymouth

Year	Model	Body Style	4	3	2	1
		383/330 2dr Hdtp Cpe	$7,700	$10,600	$16,700	$25,200
		440/375 2dr Hdtp Cpe	$9,300	$12,600	$19,900	$30,100
		318/230 2dr Fstbk Cpe	$6,800	$9,200	$14,400	$21,500
		383/290 2dr Fstbk Cpe	$8,000	$11,000	$17,200	$25,600
		383/330 2dr Fstbk Cpe	$8,600	$11,800	$18,700	$27,800
		440/375 2dr Fstbk Cpe	$10,400	$14,200	$22,300	$33,200
		318/230 2dr Conv	$11,600	$15,900	$24,500	$36,800
		383/290 2dr Conv	$14,000	$19,000	$29,400	$44,200
		383/330 2dr Conv	$15,300	$20,700	$32,000	$47,800
		440/375 2dr Conv	$18,000	$24,600	$38,000	$57,300
						-30% for 6-cyl.
1968	VIP	318/230 2dr Fstbk Cpe	$7,800	$10,900	$15,300	$23,100
		383/290 2dr Fstbk Cpe	$9,300	$13,000	$18,300	$27,600
		383/330 2dr Fstbk Cpe	$10,100	$14,100	$19,900	$29,900
		440/375 2dr Fstbk Cpe	$11,900	$16,900	$23,600	$35,700
		318/230 4dr Hdtp Sdn	$7,500	$10,200	$14,300	$21,600
		383/290 4dr Hdtp Sdn	$9,000	$12,300	$17,200	$25,800
		383/330 4dr Hdtp Sdn	$9,800	$13,200	$18,600	$27,800
		440/375 4dr Hdtp Sdn	$11,600	$15,800	$22,100	$33,200
						-20% for 6-cyl.
1969	Valiant	170/115 2dr 100 Sdn	$5,100	$7,100	$10,900	$15,300
		225/145 2dr 100 Sdn	$5,300	$7,400	$11,400	$16,000
		273/190 2dr 100 Sdn	$5,600	$7,800	$12,000	$16,900
		318/230 2dr 100 Sdn	$5,800	$8,100	$12,500	$17,600
		170/115 4dr 100 Sdn	$3,400	$4,600	$6,300	$8,600
		225/145 4dr 100 Sdn	$3,500	$4,800	$6,600	$9,000
		273/190 4dr 100 Sdn	$3,700	$5,100	$6,900	$9,500
		318/230 4dr 100 Sdn	$3,900	$5,200	$7,200	$9,800
1969	Barracuda	318/230 2dr Hdtp Cpe	$10,600	$14,800	$22,700	$34,800

Year	Model	Body Style	4	3	2	1
		383/330 2dr Hdtp Cpe	$15,200	$20,500	$30,300	$45,700
		340/275 HiPo 2dr Cuda 340 Hdtp Cpe	$12,600	$18,500	$27,100	$41,700
		383/330 2dr Cuda 383 Hdtp Cpe	$16,000	$21,500	$31,800	$48,000
		440/375 2dr Cuda 440 Hdtp Cpe	$23,900	$34,200	$48,800	$70,800
		318/230 2dr Fstbk	$11,500	$16,900	$24,900	$37,700
		383/330 2dr Fstbk	$15,900	$22,100	$34,200	$47,000
		340/275 HiPo 2dr Cuda 340 Fstbk	$13,800	$19,800	$29,400	$45,300
		383/330 2dr Cuda 383 Fstbk	$16,700	$23,200	$35,900	$49,400
		440/375 2dr Cuda 440 Fstbk	$29,300	$41,800	$59,800	$86,300
		318/230 2dr Conv	$14,500	$21,700	$30,900	$47,000
		340/275 2dr Conv	$16,500	$24,600	$35,700	$52,000
		383/330 2dr Conv	$21,500	$32,400	$46,800	$68,500
					-30% for 6-cyl. +10% for 4-spd.	
1969	Belvedere	318/230 2dr Cpe	$8,400	$11,500	$16,200	$24,300
		383/290 2dr Cpe	$10,000	$13,800	$19,400	$29,000
		383/330 2dr Cpe	$10,900	$14,900	$21,000	$31,400
		440/350 2dr Cpe	$12,500	$17,200	$24,300	$36,300
		440/375 2dr Cpe	$12,900	$17,800	$25,200	$37,500
		318/230 4dr Sdn	$4,400	$6,000	$8,600	$12,900
		383/290 4dr Sdn	$5,400	$7,200	$10,400	$15,500
		383/330 4dr Sdn	$5,800	$7,800	$11,300	$17,000
		440/350 4dr Sdn	$6,700	$9,000	$13,000	$19,600
		440/375 4dr Sdn	$6,900	$9,300	$13,400	$20,200
						-30% for 6-cyl.
1969	Satellite	318/230 2dr Hdtp Cpe	$8,500	$12,100	$19,500	$29,000
		383/290 2dr Hdtp Cpe	$10,200	$14,500	$23,300	$34,800
		383/330 2dr Hdtp Cpe	$11,000	$15,800	$25,200	$37,700
		318/230 2dr Conv	$12,000	$17,200	$27,900	$41,400
		383/290 2dr Conv	$14,400	$20,600	$33,500	$49,600
		383/330 2dr Conv	$15,700	$22,200	$36,300	$54,100
						-30% for 6-cyl.
1969	Sport Satellite	318/230 2dr Hdtp Cpe	$8,700	$13,800	$22,100	$32,400
		383/290 2dr Hdtp Cpe	$10,400	$16,500	$26,700	$38,900
		383/330 2dr Hdtp Cpe	$11,200	$17,800	$28,900	$42,100

Plymouth

Year	Model	Body Style	4	3	2	1
		318/230 2dr Conv	$12,900	$18,300	$29,600	$44,100
		383/290 2dr Conv	$15,500	$21,900	$35,400	$53,300
		383/330 2dr Conv	$16,700	$23,800	$38,500	$57,700
						-30% for 6-cyl.
1969	GTX	426/425 Hemi 2dr Hdtp Cpe	$55,100	$76,600	$91,800	$117,000
		440/375 2dr Hdtp Cpe	$26,300	$40,300	$57,600	$83,500
		426/425 Hemi 2dr Conv	$121,000	$158,000	$201,000	$242,000
		440/375 2dr Conv	$29,700	$47,500	$67,800	$93,700
			+10% for 4-spd. Colors can make an astonishing difference in both value and salability.			
1969	Road Runner	383/335 2dr Cpe	$21,400	$29,400	$42,600	$67,000
		426/425 Hemi 2dr Cpe	$63,700	$79,200	$111,000	$154,000
		440/390 2dr Cpe	$61,600	$76,800	$103,000	$134,000
		383/335 2dr Hdtp Cpe	$22,500	$30,900	$44,600	$70,200
		426/425 Hemi 2dr Hdtp Cpe	$60,400	$80,200	$112,000	$158,000
		440/390 2dr Hdtp Cpe	$62,800	$78,400	$105,000	$137,000
		383/335 2dr Conv	$28,100	$36,900	$65,000	$80,500
		426/425 Hemi 2dr Conv	$85,700	$113,000	$135,000	$188,000
			+10% for 4-spd. Colors can make an astonishing difference in both value and salability.			
1969	Fury III	318/230 2dr Hdtp Cpe	$4,500	$6,400	$9,000	$13,600
		383/290 2dr Hdtp Cpe	$5,400	$7,700	$11,000	$16,300
		383/330 2dr Hdtp Cpe	$5,900	$8,300	$11,900	$17,900
		440/375 2dr Hdtp Cpe	$6,900	$10,000	$14,100	$21,300
		318/230 2dr Conv	$9,900	$13,800	$19,600	$30,300
		383/290 2dr Conv	$11,800	$16,600	$23,500	$36,400
		383/330 2dr Conv	$12,700	$18,000	$25,600	$39,400
		440/375 2dr Conv	$15,200	$21,300	$30,500	$47,000
						-30% for 6-cyl.
1969	Sport Fury	318/230 2dr Hdtp Cpe	$7,100	$9,800	$13,600	$20,200
		383/290 2dr Hdtp Cpe	$8,600	$11,800	$16,400	$24,200
		383/330 2dr Hdtp Cpe	$9,300	$12,800	$17,700	$26,100
		440/375 2dr Hdtp Cpe	$11,100	$15,200	$21,000	$31,100

Year	Model	Body Style	4	3	2	1
		318/230 2dr Conv	$12,100	$16,900	$23,500	$35,300
		383/290 2dr Conv	$14,400	$20,200	$28,300	$42,300
		383/330 2dr Conv	$15,700	$22,000	$30,700	$45,900
		440/375 2dr Conv	$18,700	$26,100	$36,600	$55,000
						-30% for 6-cyl.
1969	VIP	318/230 2dr Hdtp Cpe	$7,300	$10,300	$14,400	$21,500
		383/290 2dr Hdtp Cpe	$8,700	$12,300	$17,300	$25,700
		383/330 2dr Hdtp Cpe	$9,400	$13,400	$18,700	$27,800
		440/375 2dr Hdtp Cpe	$11,200	$15,900	$22,300	$33,100
		318/230 4dr Hdtp Sdn	$5,100	$6,800	$9,700	$14,900
		383/290 4dr Hdtp Sdn	$6,100	$8,200	$11,700	$18,100
		383/330 4dr Hdtp Sdn	$6,600	$8,800	$12,700	$19,600
		440/375 4dr Hdtp Sdn	$8,000	$10,600	$15,100	$23,300
1970	Valiant	318/230 2dr Duster Cpe	$8,000	$11,000	$14,500	$19,700
		340/275 HiPo 2dr Duster 340 Cpe	$11,900	$20,700	$32,400	$49,200
		198/125 4dr Sdn	$4,200	$5,400	$7,200	$9,100
		225/145 4dr Sdn	$4,300	$5,600	$7,500	$9,500
		318/230 4dr Sdn	$4,700	$6,200	$8,100	$10,500
						-10% for 6-cyl on Duster.
1970	Barracuda	318/230 2dr Hdtp Cpe	$21,400	$27,400	$42,500	$51,700
		383/290 2dr Hdtp Cpe	$27,600	$38,600	$54,800	$64,700
		383/330 2dr Hdtp Cpe	$37,300	$44,400	$58,800	$72,800
		318/230 2dr Conv	$25,400	$34,900	$47,900	$63,600
		383/290 2dr Conv	$31,700	$41,800	$57,900	$77,600
		383/330 2dr Conv	$39,800	$48,700	$62,900	$86,400
						-30% for 6-cyl. +10% for 4-spd. +10% for Gran Coupe. Colors can make an astonishing difference in both value and salability.
1970	Cuda	383/335 2dr Hdtp Cpe	$35,700	$42,600	$58,800	$72,800
		426/425 Hemi 2dr Hdtp Cpe	$99,600	$155,000	$202,000	$243,000
		440/375 2dr Hdtp Cpe	$39,000	$59,400	$84,800	$109,000
		440/390 2dr Hdtp Cpe	$46,800	$71,300	$102,000	$130,000
		340/290 2dr AAR Hdtp Cpe	$39,500	$59,200	$83,300	$108,000

Plymouth

Year	Model	Body Style	4	3	2	1
		383/335 2dr Conv	$57,200	$68,200	$94,100	$117,000
		426/425 Hemi 2dr Conv	$900,000	$1.1 mil	$1.7 mil	$2 mil
		440/375 2dr Conv	$126,000	$164,000	$231,000	$282,000
		440/390 2dr Conv	$177,000	$231,000	$326,000	$398,000
		For Hemi cpe: -$57,000 for auto trans. For Hemi conv: -$150,000 for auto trans. +10% for 4-spd. Colors can make an astonishing difference in both value and salability.				
1970	Belvedere	318/230 2dr Cpe	$8,300	$11,300	$15,900	$24,000
		383/290 2dr Cpe	$10,000	$13,500	$19,000	$28,700
		383/330 2dr Cpe	$10,800	$14,600	$20,700	$31,100
		-30% for 6-cyl.				
1970	Road Runner	426/425 Hemi 2dr Superbird Hdtp Cpe	$183,000	$222,000	$304,000	$371,000
		383/335 2dr Cpe	$24,400	$33,600	$47,900	$70,300
		426/425 Hemi 2dr Cpe	$64,200	$82,700	$107,000	$137,000
		440/375 2dr Superbird Hdtp Cpe	$92,700	$126,000	$174,000	$237,000
		440/390 2dr Superbird Hdtp Cpe	$99,000	$143,000	$185,000	$261,000
		440/390 2dr Cpe	$61,200	$76,100	$102,000	$133,000
		383/335 2dr Hdtp Cpe	$25,900	$35,300	$50,400	$73,800
		426/425 Hemi 2dr Hdtp Cpe	$61,400	$81,100	$107,000	$140,000
		440/390 2dr Hdtp Cpe	$62,100	$78,100	$104,000	$136,000
		383/335 2dr Conv	$31,500	$39,900	$67,400	$82,600
		426/425 Hemi 2dr Conv	$118,000	$142,000	$176,000	$232,000
		440/390 2dr Conv	$80,000	$103,000	$119,000	$145,000
		+10% for 4-spd. Colors can make an astonishing difference in both value and salability.				
1970	Satellite	318/230 2dr Hdtp Cpe	$8,400	$12,300	$19,800	$29,300
		318/230 2dr Conv	$12,200	$17,600	$28,600	$42,300
		-30% for 6-cyl.				
1970	Sport Satellite	318/230 2dr Hdtp Cpe	$9,400	$14,000	$22,700	$33,500
		-30% for 6-cyl.				
1970	GTX	426/425 Hemi 2dr Hdtp Cpe	$53,800	$75,300	$89,700	$114,000
		440/375 2dr Hdtp Cpe	$26,300	$40,300	$57,600	$83,500

Year	Model	Body Style	4	3	2	1
		440/390 2dr Hdtp Cpe	$37,600	$62,200	$78,100	$93,800
		+10% for 4-spd. Colors can make an astonishing difference in both value and salability.				
1970	Fury III	318/230 2dr Hdtp Cpe	$4,600	$6,900	$9,400	$14,200
		318/230 4dr Hdtp Sdn	$4,500	$6,700	$9,400	$14,000
		318/230 2dr Conv	$10,600	$15,800	$23,600	$33,200
		-30% for 6-cyl.				
1970	Sport Fury	318/230 2dr Hdtp Cpe	$7,500	$10,600	$14,800	$21,700
		440/390 2dr GT Hdtp Cpe	$12,300	$17,100	$23,800	$35,300
1971	Valiant	318/230 2dr Scamp Hdtp Cpe	$5,500	$11,700	$15,600	$22,200
		198/125 4dr Sdn	$3,900	$5,200	$7,300	$9,400
		225/145 4dr Sdn	$4,000	$5,400	$7,600	$9,800
		318/230 4dr Sdn	$4,200	$5,700	$8,000	$10,400
1971	Duster	318/230 2dr Cpe	$7,900	$10,400	$13,600	$17,400
		318/230 2dr Twister Cpe	$9,500	$12,500	$17,900	$26,900
		340/275 HiPo 2dr 340 Cpe	$10,900	$21,200	$34,900	$50,900
		+10% for 4-spd. -20% for 6-cyl.				
1971	Barracuda	318/230 2dr Cpe	$21,400	$28,800	$39,600	$49,300
		383/275 2dr Cpe	$24,900	$34,600	$43,800	$57,600
		383/300 2dr Cpe	$29,300	$39,600	$51,100	$63,800
		318/230 2dr Conv	$24,900	$33,200	$46,800	$62,400
		383/275 2dr Conv	$30,500	$40,000	$50,600	$71,600
		383/300 2dr Conv	$34,700	$48,700	$59,900	$82,800
		+10% for 4-spd. +10% for Gran Coupe. Colors can make an astonishing difference in both value and salability.				
1971	Cuda	383/300 2dr Hdtp Cpe	$40,700	$48,500	$67,000	$83,700
		For Hemi cpe: -$57,000 for auto trans. For Hemi conv: -$150,000 for auto trans. +10% for 4-spd. Colors can make an astonishing difference in both value and salability.				
		426/425 Hemi 2dr Hdtp Cpe	$192,000	$264,000	$349,000	$439,000
		440/385 2dr Hdtp Cpe	$52,000	$79,300	$113,000	$145,000
		340/275 HiPo 2dr 340 Hdtp Cpe	$29,000	$39,100	$52,600	$65,700
		+10% for Gran Coupe. For Hemi cpe: -$57,000 for auto trans. For Hemi conv: -$150,000 for auto trans. For all: +10% for 4-spd. Colors can make an astonishing difference in both value and salability.				
		383/300 2dr Conv	$65,100	$77,600	$107,000	$134,000

Plymouth

Year	Model	Body Style	4	3	2	1
		For Hemi cpe: -$57,000 for auto trans. For Hemi conv: -$150,000 for auto trans. +10% for 4-spd. Colors can make an astonishing difference in both value and salability.				
		426/425 Hemi 2dr Conv	$1.25 mil	$1.7 mil	$2.1 mil	$2.6 mil
		440/385 2dr Conv	$254,000	$367,000	$632,000	$794,000
		340/275 HiPo 2dr 340 Conv	$49,700	$61,200	$89,000	$122,000
		+10% for Gran Coupe. For Hemi cpe: -$57,000 for auto trans. For Hemi conv: -$150,000 for auto trans. For all: +10% for 4-spd. Colors can make an astonishing difference in both value and salability.				
1971	Satellite	318/230 2dr Cpe	$6,800	$10,900	$15,800	$24,700
		383/275 2dr Cpe	$8,100	$13,000	$19,000	$29,700
		318/230 2dr Sebring Hdtp Cpe	$8,000	$13,200	$19,100	$28,300
		383/275 2dr Sebring Hdtp Cpe	$9,700	$15,900	$22,900	$34,000
		-20% for 6-cyl.				
1971	Road Runner	383/300 2dr Hdtp Cpe	$19,300	$26,300	$35,900	$45,600
		426/425 Hemi 2dr Hdtp Cpe	$65,500	$85,700	$101,000	$121,000
		440/385 2dr Hdtp Cpe	$44,400	$59,200	$74,500	$90,900
		+10% for 4-spd. Colors can make an astonishing difference in both value and salability.				
1971	GTX	426/425 Hemi 2dr Hdtp Cpe	$67,800	$98,000	$139,000	$175,000
		440/370 2dr Hdtp Cpe	$27,200	$41,700	$59,700	$86,600
		440/385 2dr Hdtp Cpe	$48,200	$67,100	$100,000	$116,000
		+10% for 4-spd. Colors can make an astonishing difference in both value and salability.				
1971	Fury III	318/230 2dr Hdtp Cpe	$4,500	$6,700	$9,400	$14,000
		318/230 2dr Fml Hdtp Cpe	$4,500	$6,700	$9,400	$14,000
1971	Sport Fury	318/230 2dr Hdtp Cpe	$7,400	$10,500	$14,800	$21,600
		318/230 2dr Fml Hdtp Cpe	$5,300	$7,500	$10,500	$15,700
1972	Valiant	318/150 2dr Scamp Hdtp Cpe	$5,200	$10,800	$14,200	$18,300
		198/100 4dr Sdn	$4,000	$5,100	$7,300	$9,100
		225/110 4dr Sdn	$4,100	$5,300	$7,600	$9,500
		318/150 4dr Sdn	$4,300	$5,500	$8,000	$9,900
1972	Duster	318/150 2dr Spt Cpe	$8,400	$11,000	$13,200	$16,400

Year	Model	Body Style	4	3	2	1
		318/150 2dr Twister Spt Cpe	$9,800	$12,900	$18,300	$25,000
		340/240 2dr 340 Spt Cpe	$11,100	$18,900	$29,800	$40,200
						+10% for 4-spd. -20% for 6-cyl.
1972	Barracuda	318/150 2dr Hdtp Cpe	$20,000	$27,400	$36,600	$42,800
		340/240 2dr Hdtp Cpe	$22,400	$30,000	$40,800	$47,600
						-20% for 6-cyl. +10% for 4-spd.
1972	Cuda	340/240 2dr Hdtp Cpe	$26,200	$36,700	$51,200	$61,100
						+10% for 4-spd.
1972	Satellite	318/150 2dr Cpe	$5,800	$9,800	$13,900	$21,700
		360/175 2dr Cpe	$11,100	$18,800	$26,400	$41,200
		400/190 2dr Cpe	$6,500	$11,000	$15,400	$24,100
		400/255 2dr Cpe	$7,400	$12,300	$17,500	$27,100
		318/150 2dr Sebring Hdtp Cpe	$7,700	$13,000	$18,500	$26,700
		340/240 2dr Sebring Hdtp Cpe	$14,800	$24,600	$35,100	$50,600
		400/190 2dr Sebring Hdtp Cpe	$8,600	$14,300	$20,600	$29,600
		400/255 2dr Sebring Hdtp Cpe	$9,700	$16,300	$24,300	$33,300
						-20% for 6-cyl.
1972	Road Runner	340/240 2dr Hdtp Cpe	$12,000	$17,700	$26,200	$36,500
		400/255 2dr Hdtp Cpe	$15,000	$21,100	$32,400	$44,200
		440/280 2dr GTX Hdtp Cpe	$20,400	$30,100	$43,000	$63,000
						+10% for 4-spd.
1972	Fury III	318/150 2dr Hdtp Cpe	$4,100	$6,200	$8,600	$13,500
		318/150 2dr Fml Hdtp Cpe	$4,300	$6,500	$8,900	$13,600
1972	Gran Fury	318/150 2dr Fml Hdtp Cpe	$5,200	$7,600	$10,500	$15,300
1973	Valiant	318/150 2dr Scamp Hdtp Cpe	$4,000	$8,100	$10,700	$16,700
		198/95 4dr Sdn	$3,700	$4,800	$6,400	$8,200
		318/150 4dr Sdn	$4,200	$5,400	$7,400	$9,300
1973	Duster	318/150 2dr Spt Cpe	$7,300	$9,800	$12,400	$15,600
		318/150 2dr Space Duster Spt Cpe	$8,100	$11,200	$15,900	$19,800
		318/150 2dr Gold Duster Spt Cpe	$9,100	$12,700	$17,300	$21,400

Plymouth

Year	Model	Body Style	4	3	2	1
		318/150 2dr Twister Spt Cpe	$9,400	$12,700	$18,100	$24,100
		340/240 2dr 340 Spt Cpe	$9,000	$17,400	$27,900	$36,300
						+10% for 4-spd. -20% for 6-cyl.
1973	Barracuda	318/150 2dr Hdtp Cpe	$17,000	$24,000	$33,600	$39,500
		340/240 2dr Hdtp Cpe	$22,200	$29,900	$39,900	$46,100
1973	Cuda	318/150 2dr Hdtp Cpe	$24,900	$35,900	$44,300	$54,800
						+10% for 4-spd.
1973	Satellite	318/150 2dr Cpe	$5,800	$9,400	$13,500	$19,600
		400/260 2dr Cpe	$7,400	$11,900	$16,800	$24,500
		318/150 2dr Sebring Hdtp Cpe	$7,400	$11,600	$16,600	$24,600
		400/260 2dr Sebring Hdtp Cpe	$9,400	$15,700	$23,500	$32,500
						-20% for 6-cyl.
1973	Road Runner	318/170 2dr Cpe	$12,700	$18,000	$26,000	$36,300
		400/260 2dr Cpe	$15,000	$21,800	$34,400	$48,100
		440/280 2dr GTX Hdtp Cpe	$21,400	$30,100	$44,100	$63,000
						+10% for 4-spd.
1974	Valiant	318/150 2dr Scamp Hdtp Cpe	$4,200	$8,600	$11,500	$18,200
		198/95 4dr Sdn	$3,400	$4,500	$6,100	$7,300
		318/150 4dr Sdn	$3,800	$5,100	$7,000	$8,400
1974	Duster	198/95 2dr Spt Cpe	$6,300	$8,700	$11,400	$15,500
		360/245 2dr 360 Spt Cpe	$7,900	$16,200	$23,600	$30,200
1974	Barracuda	318/150 2dr Hdtp Cpe	$17,200	$23,900	$33,400	$40,000
		360/245 2dr Hdtp Cpe	$22,500	$30,000	$40,000	$46,600
1974	Cuda	318/150 2dr Hdtp Cpe	$24,500	$36,400	$45,600	$61,000
						+10% for 4-spd.
1974	Satellite	318/150 2dr Cpe	$5,800	$9,300	$13,300	$19,500
		400/205 2dr Cpe	$6,900	$11,200	$15,900	$23,400
		318/150 2dr Sebring Hdtp Cpe	$6,200	$9,800	$14,000	$21,000
		400/205 2dr Sebring Hdtp Cpe	$7,600	$11,800	$17,300	$25,100
						-20% for 6-cyl.
1974	Road Runner	318/170 2dr Cpe	$12,500	$18,400	$24,800	$36,700
		400/250 2dr Cpe	$14,700	$21,400	$34,000	$46,700

Plymouth

Year	Model	Body Style	4	3	2	1
		440/275 2dr Cpe	$17,000	$25,000	$35,700	$48,000
						•15% for 4-spd.
1975	Valiant	225/95 2dr Scamp Hdtp	$4,100	$8,400	$10,600	$17,300
		225/95 4dr Sdn	$3,300	$4,300	$5,900	$7,200
1975	Duster	225/95 2dr Cpe	$6,200	$8,400	$11,000	$14,900
		360/230 2dr 360 Cpe	$7,400	$14,400	$21,500	$25,800
1975	Road Runner	318/150 2dr Hdtp	$12,200	$17,600	$24,900	$36,900
1976	Valiant	225/100 2dr Duster Cpe	$5,200	$8,000	$10,400	$14,000
		225/100 2dr Feather Duster Cpe	$5,500	$8,400	$11,600	$16,200
		360/220 2dr Duster 360 Cpe	$6,900	$12,900	$19,800	$21,700
		225/100 4dr Sdn	$3,200	$4,200	$5,300	$6,600
		225/100 2dr Scamp Hdtp	$4,300	$8,700	$10,600	$16,300
1997	Prowler	215/214 2dr Conv	$18,100	$24,500	$37,100	$47,100
1999	Prowler	215/253 2dr Conv	$16,800	$22,900	$35,000	$44,600
2000	Prowler	215/253 2dr Conv	$17,400	$23,700	$36,000	$46,400
2001	Prowler	215/253 2dr Conv	$17,800	$24,700	$37,700	$48,300

Prowler production continued from 2001-02 as Chryslers.

Pontiac

Year	Model	Body Style	4	3	2	1
1946	Torpedo	249/103 2dr Bus Cpe	$7,900	$11,200	$18,500	$26,600
		249/103 4dr Sdn	$4,500	$8,400	$13,400	$17,700
		249/103 2dr Conv	$13,200	$23,100	$45,100	$63,400
						-15% for 6-cyl.
1946	Streamliner	249/103 2dr Cpe	$8,800	$14,400	$25,200	$37,700
		249/103 4dr Sdn	$5,700	$8,700	$14,500	$19,200
		249/103 4dr Dlx Wdy Wgn	$56,200	$78,800	$97,200	$112,000

-15% for 6-cyl on cpe and sdn. -20% for 6-cyl on Woody wgn.

Year	Model	Body Style	4	3	2	1
1947	Torpedo	249/103 2dr Cpe	$8,100	$11,500	$19,100	$27,400
		4dr Sdn	$4,500	$8,400	$13,400	$17,700
		249/103 4dr Sdn	$6,000	$9,000	$14,500	$19,200
		249/103 2dr Conv	$13,200	$23,100	$45,100	$63,400
						-15% for 6-cyl.
1947	Streamliner	249/103 2dr Cpe	$8,800	$14,400	$25,200	$37,700
		249/103 4dr Sdn	$5,700	$8,700	$14,500	$19,200
		249/103 4dr Wdy Wgn	$56,200	$78,800	$97,200	$112,000

Pontiac

Year	Model	Body Style	4	3	2	1
1948	Torpedo	249/103 2dr Spt Cpe	$8,100	$11,500	$19,100	$27,400
		249/103 4dr Sdn	$4,500	$8,400	$13,400	$17,700
		249/103 2dr Conv	$13,200	$23,100	$45,100	$63,400
						-15% for 6-cyl.
1948	Streamliner	249/103 2dr Sdn Cpe	$8,800	$14,400	$25,200	$37,700
		249/103 4dr Sdn	$5,700	$8,700	$14,500	$19,200
		249/103 4dr Wdy Wgn	$56,200	$78,800	$97,200	$112,000
1949	Streamliner	249/103 2dr Sdn Cpe	$8,900	$13,000	$20,700	$28,200
		249/103 4dr Sdn	$5,600	$8,900	$14,600	$19,700
		249/103 4dr Wdy Wgn	$56,200	$78,800	$97,200	$112,000
		-15% for 6-cyl on cpe, sdn, and steel wgn. -20% for 6-cyl on Woody wgn.				
1949	Chieftain	249/103 2dr Bus Cpe	$8,800	$13,100	$21,000	$29,700
		249/103 4dr Sdn	$4,900	$7,600	$13,100	$17,800
						-15% for 6-cyl.
1950	Streamliner	268/108 2dr Cpe	$8,000	$10,400	$16,800	$25,200
		268/108 4dr Sdn	$4,200	$7,200	$11,900	$16,000
		268/108 4dr Wdy Wgn	$11,600	$21,200	$30,600	$43,500
		268/108 2dr Sdn Del	$6,300	$9,800	$13,700	$18,200
						-15% for 6-cyl.
1950	Chieftain	268/108 2dr Cpe	$8,400	$10,900	$19,300	$29,300
		268/108 4dr Sdn	$4,700	$7,600	$13,100	$17,800
		268/108 2dr Dlx Catalina	$8,400	$12,600	$21,100	$31,200
		268/108 2dr Dlx Conv Cpe	$11,400	$17,500	$33,900	$46,200
						-15% for 6-cyl.
1951	Streamliner	268/116 2dr Sdn Cpe	$8,200	$10,500	$17,200	$25,500
		268/116 4dr Wdy Wgn	$11,600	$21,200	$30,600	$43,500
						-15% for 6-cyl.
1951	Chieftain	268/116 2dr Sdn Cpe	$8,800	$11,300	$19,600	$29,700
		268/116 4dr Sdn	$4,800	$7,800	$13,400	$18,000
		268/116 2dr Dlx Catalina Hdtp	$8,400	$12,600	$21,500	$31,500
		268/116 2dr Dlx Conv	$11,800	$17,900	$34,900	$46,700
						-15% for 6-cyl.
1952	Chieftain	268/118 2dr Sdn	$8,000	$10,400	$18,400	$28,200

Year	Model	Body Style	4	3	2	1
		268/118 4dr Sdn	$4,400	$7,200	$12,500	$17,200
		268/118 4dr Wgn	$22,100	$32,800	$40,900	$68,200
		268/118 2dr Dlx Catalina Hdtp	$7,500	$11,700	$20,500	$29,900
		268/118 2dr Dlx Conv	$10,600	$16,100	$32,100	$44,100
						-15% for 6-cyl.
1953	Chieftain	268/118 2dr Spcl Sdn	$8,000	$10,400	$18,400	$28,200
		268/118 4dr Spcl Sdn	$4,400	$7,200	$12,500	$17,200
		268/118 4dr Spcl Stn Wgn 6P	$9,000	$12,200	$21,000	$32,300
		268/118 4dr Dlx Stn Wgn 6P	$22,100	$32,800	$40,900	$68,200
		268/118 2dr Dlx Catalina Hdtp	$7,500	$11,700	$20,500	$29,900
		268/118 2dr Dlx Conv	$10,600	$16,100	$32,000	$44,100
						-15% for 6-cyl.
1954	Chieftain	268/122 2dr Spcl Sdn	$8,000	$10,500	$18,400	$28,100
		268/122 4dr Spcl Sdn	$4,400	$7,200	$12,500	$17,200
		268/122 4dr Spcl Stn Wgn 6P	$9,200	$12,200	$21,000	$32,200
		268/122 2dr Dlx Catalina Hdtp	$7,600	$11,800	$20,200	$29,200
						-15% for 6-cyl. +15% for factory a/c.
1954	Star Chief	268/127 2dr Cstm Catalina Hdtp	$8,200	$12,700	$22,500	$35,200
		268/127 4dr Dlx Sdn	$5,100	$7,800	$13,200	$19,000
		268/127 2dr Dlx Conv	$11,600	$18,000	$35,300	$52,500
						+15% for factory a/c.
1955	Chieftain	287/173 2dr 860 Sdn	$8,900	$13,300	$23,900	$33,000
		287/173 4dr 860 Sdn	$6,600	$9,000	$13,600	$21,000
		287/173 4dr 860 Wgn	$9,100	$14,600	$25,600	$39,200
		287/173 2dr 870 Wgn	$23,400	$37,000	$57,900	$73,300
						+15% for factory a/c. +15% for Deluxe.
1955	Star Chief	287/180 2dr Cstm Catalina Hdtp	$10,600	$16,900	$29,600	$50,400
		287/180 4dr Dlx Sdn	$6,600	$9,800	$14,400	$22,000

Pontiac

Year	Model	Body Style	4	3	2	1
		287/180 4dr Cstm Sdn	$7,300	$11,200	$16,500	$24,300
		287/200 2dr Cstm Safari Wgn	$22,200	$41,300	$58,600	$81,600
		287/180 2dr Dlx Conv	$26,400	$40,200	$61,600	$82,300
		287/200 2dr Dlx Conv	$31,700	$46,600	$75,300	$98,800
						+15% for factory a/c.
1956	Chieftain	316/205 2dr 860 Sdn	$9,600	$13,700	$25,000	$36,000
		316/205 4dr 860 Sdn	$6,900	$9,400	$14,300	$21,500
		316/205 4dr 860 Wgn	$9,100	$14,900	$25,800	$40,000
		316/205 2dr 860 Catalina Hdtp Cpe	$10,300	$15,300	$27,000	$40,000
		316/205 4dr 860 Catalina Hdtp Sdn	$7,400	$9,700	$14,900	$22,300
						+15% for factory a/c. +15% for Deluxe.
1956	Star Chief	316/227 2dr Cstm Catalina Hdtp	$11,400	$19,000	$36,800	$52,000
		317/285 2dr Cstm Catalina Hdtp	$14,700	$24,400	$46,900	$60,500
		317/285 4dr Dlx Sdn	$9,700	$13,600	$22,400	$32,700
		316/227 2dr Cstm Safari Wgn	$20,600	$38,300	$51,900	$72,700
		317/285 2dr Cstm Safari Wgn	$26,000	$49,800	$67,400	$93,800
		316/227 4dr Cstm Catalina Hdtp	$8,000	$11,900	$18,100	$25,800
		317/285 4dr Cstm Catalina Hdtp	$10,300	$15,400	$23,500	$33,500
		316/227 2dr Dlx Conv	$31,900	$47,000	$66,900	$83,500
		317/285 2dr Dlx Conv	$40,700	$60,400	$84,400	$105,000
						+15% for factory a/c.
1957	Chieftain	347/252 2dr Sdn	$9,600	$13,900	$25,500	$36,600
		347/252 4dr Sdn	$7,000	$9,600	$14,600	$21,900
		347/252 2dr Catalina Cpe	$10,500	$16,400	$28,700	$43,500
		347/252 4dr Catalina Hdtp Sdn	$7,500	$9,900	$15,100	$22,700
						+15% for factory a/c.
1957	Super Chief	347/270 2dr Catalina Cpe	$9,900	$16,000	$27,000	$41,400
		347/270 4dr Sdn	$6,900	$9,800	$14,500	$22,600

Year	Model	Body Style	4	3	2	1
		347/270 4dr Catalina Hdtp Sdn	$7,400	$10,000	$15,200	$22,900
						+15% for factory a/c.
1957	Star Chief	347/270 2dr Cstm Catalina Hdtp	$11,400	$18,900	$37,400	$54,000
		347/290 2dr Cstm Catalina Hdtp	$16,800	$29,300	$53,000	$74,700
		347/317 FI 2dr Cstm Catalina Hdtp	$16,000	$26,700	$51,200	$68,900
		347/270 4dr Sdn	$7,600	$10,800	$17,300	$25,500
		347/290 4dr Sdn	$10,300	$14,400	$23,500	$34,600
		347/317 4dr Sdn	$10,600	$15,000	$24,400	$36,000
		347/270 4dr Cstm Catalina Hdtp	$8,100	$12,100	$18,500	$26,400
		347/290 4dr Cstm Catalina Hdtp	$10,700	$16,600	$25,000	$35,500
		347/317 FI 4dr Cstm Catalina Hdtp	$11,100	$17,100	$25,600	$36,800
		347/270 4dr Cstm Safari Wgn	$24,800	$37,700	$56,300	$84,500
		347/290 4dr Cstm Safari Wgn	$33,600	$50,200	$78,000	$114,000
		347/317 4dr Cstm Safari Wgn	$34,700	$52,600	$81,000	$117,000
		347/270 2dr Conv	$35,500	$53,100	$91,600	$131,000
		347/290 2dr Conv	$47,800	$71,700	$121,000	$174,000
		347/317 2dr Conv	$49,700	$74,500	$127,000	$182,000
						+15% for factory a/c.
1957	Bonneville	347/317 FI 2dr Conv	$61,200	$84,700	$115,000	$164,000
						+30% for factory a/c.
1958	Chieftain	370/270 2dr Sdn	$9,300	$13,200	$23,600	$33,900
		370/270 4dr Sdn	$6,900	$9,200	$13,700	$19,900
		370/270 2dr Catalina Hdtp Cpe	$9,200	$14,400	$24,700	$36,500
		370/270 4dr Catalina Hdtp Sdn	$6,900	$9,300	$14,900	$22,100
		370/270 2dr Conv	$29,600	$47,800	$68,300	$89,100
						+15% for factory a/c.
1958	Super Chief	370/285 2dr Catalina Hdtp Cpe	$8,900	$14,800	$25,500	$36,900
		370/285 4dr Sdn	$6,400	$9,200	$13,700	$22,800
		370/285 4dr Catalina Hdtp Sdn	$6,500	$9,200	$13,900	$19,900
						+15% for factory a/c.

Pontiac

Year	Model	Body Style	4	3	2	1
1958	Star Chief	370/285 2dr Catalina Hdtp Cpe	$8,900	$14,800	$24,100	$33,700
		370/285 4dr Sdn	$7,400	$9,600	$16,800	$22,200
		370/285 4dr Safari Wgn	$8,900	$15,000	$21,200	$36,600
		370/285 4dr Catalina Hdtp Sdn	$4,500	$9,000	$14,000	$19,900
			+15% for factory a/c. +10% for Golden Jubilee ed.			
1958	Bonneville	370/285 2dr Hdtp Cpe	$18,700	$30,700	$58,400	$87,300
		370/310 2dr Hdtp Cpe	$32,800	$49,100	$92,300	$149,000
		370/315 2dr Hdtp Cpe	$21,000	$34,200	$66,600	$94,600
		370/330 2dr Hdtp Cpe	$24,300	$40,400	$79,700	$116,000
		370/285 2dr Conv	$50,800	$80,300	$106,000	$129,000
		370/310 2dr Conv	$71,300	$110,000	$141,000	$173,000
		370/315 2dr Conv	$58,100	$88,800	$117,000	$140,000
		370/330 2dr Conv	$66,400	$104,000	$135,000	$166,000
						+10% for factory a/c.
1959	Catalina	389/215 2dr Spt Cpe	$5,800	$13,700	$22,100	$31,600
		389/260 2dr Spt Cpe	$6,500	$15,200	$24,400	$34,700
		389/280 2dr Spt Cpe	$7,500	$12,100	$17,200	$26,200
		389/315 2dr Spt Cpe	$7,300	$17,200	$27,700	$39,400
		389/260 4dr Sdn	$3,700	$7,100	$14,300	$21,900
		389/280 4dr Sdn	$3,400	$6,400	$13,000	$19,900
		389/315 4dr Sdn	$4,300	$8,100	$16,300	$24,900
		389/260 4dr Safari Stn Wgn 6P	$4,600	$8,200	$17,900	$26,100
		389/280 4dr Safari Stn Wgn 6P	$4,200	$7,500	$16,300	$23,600
		389/315 4dr Safari Stn Wgn 6P	$5,400	$9,300	$20,400	$29,600
		389/260 2dr Spt Sdn	$8,100	$13,200	$19,000	$28,700
		389/315 2dr Spt Sdn	$9,300	$15,200	$21,600	$32,700
		389/215 4dr Vista Hdtp Sdn	$4,000	$7,400	$15,200	$22,300
		389/260 4dr Vista Hdtp Sdn	$4,100	$7,400	$15,500	$23,400
		389/315 4dr Vista Hdtp Sdn	$4,700	$8,400	$17,700	$26,500
		389/260 2dr Conv Cpe	$19,700	$31,100	$56,500	$81,200

Year	Model	Body Style	4	3	2	1
		389/280 2dr Conv Cpe	$18,000	$28,200	$51,400	$73,900
		389/315 2dr Conv Cpe	$22,600	$35,300	$64,300	$92,200
						+10% for factory a/c.
1959	Star Chief	389/260 2dr Spt Sdn	$9,000	$16,300	$27,900	$39,900
		389/280 2dr Spt Sdn	$8,200	$14,700	$25,400	$36,200
		389/315 2dr Spt Sdn	$10,300	$18,500	$31,800	$45,300
		389/260 4dr Sdn	$3,800	$7,700	$14,200	$19,900
		389/280 4dr Sdn	$3,400	$6,900	$12,900	$18,100
		389/315 4dr Sdn	$4,400	$8,700	$16,200	$22,600
		389/215 4dr Vista Hdtp Sdn	$4,600	$7,500	$16,800	$23,900
		389/260 4dr Vista Hdtp Sdn	$5,200	$8,300	$18,600	$26,300
		389/315 4dr Vista Hdtp Sdn	$5,900	$9,400	$21,100	$30,000
						+10% for factory a/c.
1959	Bonneville	389/300 2dr Spt Cpe	$10,600	$23,200	$42,100	$58,700
		389/315 2dr Spt Cpe	$11,500	$24,700	$44,300	$62,100
		389/300 4dr Safari Wgn	$6,600	$10,700	$19,400	$27,200
		389/315 4dr Safari Wgn	$8,100	$13,600	$24,500	$34,200
		389/300 4dr Vista Hdtp Sdn	$6,500	$11,600	$20,200	$31,200
		389/315 4dr Vista Hdtp Sdn	$8,300	$14,400	$25,300	$37,100
		389/300 2dr Conv Cpe	$26,400	$37,200	$66,500	$91,200
		389/315 2dr Conv Cpe	$31,600	$43,200	$81,200	$116,000
						+10% for factory a/c.
1960	Catalina	389/283 2dr Spt Sdn	$7,900	$12,600	$17,500	$26,500
		389/303 2dr Spt Sdn	$9,400	$15,000	$20,900	$31,500
		389/315 2dr Spt Sdn	$9,900	$15,800	$22,000	$33,200
		389/283 4dr Sdn	$3,500	$6,600	$13,400	$20,000
		389/303 4dr Sdn	$4,400	$8,000	$16,000	$23,900
		389/315 4dr Sdn	$4,600	$8,400	$16,800	$25,200
		389/283 4dr Safari Stn Wgn 6P	$4,400	$7,700	$16,600	$23,900

Pontiac

Year	Model	Body Style	4	3	2	1
		389/303 4dr Safari Stn Wgn. 6-p.	$4,800	$8,500	$18,300	$26,300
		389/315 4dr Safari Stn Wgn 6P	$5,600	$9,700	$20,800	$30,000
		389/283 2dr Spt Cpe	$6,200	$14,400	$22,400	$32,100
		389/303 2dr Spt Cpe	$7,300	$17,100	$26,800	$38,100
		389/315 2dr Spt Cpe	$7,700	$18,000	$28,200	$40,100
		389/215 4dr Vista Hdtp Sdn	$3,800	$6,900	$14,300	$21,500
		389/283 4dr Vista Hdtp Sdn	$4,000	$7,200	$15,000	$22,600
		389/303 4dr Vista Hdtp Sdn	$4,600	$8,300	$17,000	$25,700
		389/315 4dr Vista Hdtp Sdn	$4,800	$8,700	$17,900	$27,000
		389/283 2dr Conv	$19,100	$29,600	$52,800	$75,500
		389/315 2dr Conv	$23,900	$37,000	$65,900	$94,300
		389/330 2dr Conv	$22,700	$35,200	$62,600	$89,600
						+10% for factory a/c.
1960	Ventura	389/283 2dr Spt Cpe	$8,200	$15,200	$25,600	$38,500
		389/315 2dr Spt Cpe	$12,400	$21,300	$36,700	$51,900
		389/283 4dr Vista Hdtp Sdn	$3,900	$8,900	$16,800	$26,700
		389/315 4dr Vista Hdtp Sdn	$5,000	$11,100	$21,000	$33,500
						+10% for factory a/c.
1960	Star Chief	389/215 2dr Spt Sdn	$8,500	$15,300	$26,000	$36,900
		389/315 2dr Spt Sdn	$10,700	$19,200	$32,400	$46,100
		389/283 4dr Sdn	$3,600	$7,200	$13,200	$18,200
		389/315 4dr Sdn	$3,600	$7,200	$13,200	$18,200
		389/283 4dr Vista Hdtp Sdn	$6,100	$9,800	$21,400	$30,400
		389/315 4dr Vista Hdtp Sdn	$6,100	$9,800	$21,400	$30,400
						+10% for factory a/c.
1960	Bonneville	389/315 2dr Spt Cpe	$13,300	$28,400	$48,400	$72,600
		389/303 4dr Cstm Safari Wgn	$7,000	$12,200	$20,700	$29,900
		389/315 4dr Cstm Safari Wgn	$8,800	$15,100	$26,200	$38,500
		389/303 4dr Vista Hdtp Sdn	$6,900	$11,900	$20,600	$34,500

Year	Model	Body Style	4	3	2	1
		389/315 4dr Vista Hdtp Sdn	$8,500	$14,800	$25,700	$38,800
		389/281 2dr Conv	$27,100	$39,600	$65,200	$94,000
		389/303 2dr Conv	$26,400	$35,600	$65,300	$96,000
		389/315 2dr Conv	$33,000	$44,500	$81,600	$120,000
						+10% for factory a/c.
1961	Catalina	389/267 2dr Spt Cpe	$5,200	$9,200	$16,900	$29,000
		389/287 2dr Spt Cpe	$5,700	$10,100	$18,600	$31,900
		389/303 2dr Spt Cpe	$6,300	$11,400	$20,700	$35,800
		389/318 2dr Spt Cpe	$7,000	$12,700	$23,000	$39,800
		389/333 2dr Spt Cpe	$7,900	$14,200	$26,000	$45,000
		389/348 2dr Spt Cpe	$8,300	$14,800	$27,100	$46,900
		421/405 2dr Spr Duty Ltwt Spt Cpe	$56,700	$90,900	$145,000	$215,000
		389/267 4dr Sdn	$2,100	$5,200	$9,200	$16,200
		389/287 4dr Sdn	$2,200	$5,500	$9,700	$17,000
		389/303 4dr Sdn	$2,400	$6,200	$10,900	$19,100
		389/318 4dr Sdn	$2,500	$6,500	$11,500	$20,100
		389/333 4dr Sdn	$2,600	$6,700	$12,000	$21,000
		389/348 4dr Sdn	$2,700	$7,000	$12,300	$21,800
		389/215 4dr Safari Stn Wgn 6P	$3,100	$6,500	$10,300	$17,500
		389/318 4dr Safari Stn Wgn 6P	$3,900	$8,200	$12,900	$21,800
		389/333 4dr Safari Stn Wgn 6P	$4,100	$8,500	$13,400	$22,600
		389/348 4dr Safari Stn Wgn 6P	$4,300	$8,900	$13,900	$23,500
		389/215 4dr Vista Hdtp Sdn	$4,000	$7,400	$12,800	$20,100
		389/318 4dr Vista Hdtp Sdn	$5,100	$9,300	$16,100	$25,500
		389/333 4dr Vista Hdtp Sdn	$5,300	$9,700	$16,700	$26,400
		389/348 4dr Vista Hdtp Sdn	$5,500	$10,100	$17,300	$27,400
		389/267 2dr Conv	$12,500	$18,800	$31,800	$46,100
		389/287 2dr Conv	$13,100	$19,700	$33,400	$48,400
		389/303 2dr Conv	$14,900	$22,200	$37,700	$54,600
		389/318 2dr Conv	$15,700	$23,400	$39,700	$57,500
		389/333 2dr Conv	$16,300	$24,300	$41,300	$59,900
		389/348 2dr Conv	$16,900	$25,300	$42,800	$62,200
						+10% for factory a/c.

Pontiac

Year	Model	Body Style	4	3	2	1
1961	Ventura	389/267 2dr Spt Cpe	$8,500	$13,200	$25,600	$36,600
		389/318 2dr Spt Cpe	$14,800	$23,200	$34,600	$49,600
		389/333 2dr Spt Cpe	$16,800	$27,100	$41,200	$55,500
		389/348 2dr Spt Cpe	$19,500	$28,500	$44,800	$66,600
		389/267 4dr Vista Hdtp Sdn	$4,200	$7,900	$14,400	$20,000
		389/318 4dr Vista Hdtp Sdn	$5,300	$10,100	$17,900	$25,300
		389/333 4dr Vista Hdtp Sdn	$5,500	$10,500	$18,700	$26,400
		389/348 4dr Vista Hdtp Sdn	$5,600	$10,800	$19,400	$27,300
						+10% for factory a/c.
1961	Star Chief	389/287 4dr Sdn	$3,100	$6,300	$10,100	$14,900
		389/318 4dr Sdn	$3,900	$7,800	$12,600	$18,600
		389/333 4dr Sdn	$4,100	$8,200	$13,200	$19,300
		389/348 4dr Sdn	$4,300	$8,500	$13,700	$20,000
		389/287 4dr Vista Hdtp Sdn	$4,000	$7,400	$11,800	$18,600
		389/318 4dr Vista Hdtp Sdn	$5,100	$9,300	$14,800	$23,300
		389/333 4dr Vista Hdtp Sdn	$5,300	$9,700	$15,400	$24,200
		389/348 4dr Vista Hdtp Sdn	$5,500	$10,100	$16,000	$25,400
						+10% for factory a/c.
1961	Bonneville	389/235 2dr Spt Cpe	$8,000	$14,200	$27,600	$39,200
		389/303 2dr Spt Cpe	$9,500	$16,800	$32,700	$46,600
		389/318 2dr Spt Cpe	$10,000	$17,700	$34,400	$49,000
		389/333 2dr Spt Cpe	$10,400	$18,500	$35,700	$51,000
		389/348 2dr Spt Cpe	$10,800	$19,300	$37,200	$52,900
		389/235 4dr Vista Hdtp Sdn	$5,100	$8,500	$16,600	$23,400
		389/303 4dr Vista Hdtp Sdn	$6,000	$10,100	$19,800	$28,000
		389/318 4dr Vista Hdtp Sdn	$6,300	$10,600	$20,800	$29,500
		389/333 4dr Vista Hdtp Sdn	$6,500	$11,000	$21,700	$30,700
		389/348 4dr Vista Hdtp Sdn	$6,800	$11,400	$22,400	$31,800
		389/235 2dr Conv	$14,800	$27,800	$50,100	$65,200

Year	Model	Body Style	4	3	2	1
		389/303 2dr Conv	$17,500	$33,100	$59,300	$77,600
		389/318 2dr Conv	$18,400	$34,800	$62,400	$81,700
		389/333 2dr Conv	$19,300	$36,100	$64,800	$84,900
		389/348 2dr Conv	$19,900	$37,500	$67,200	$88,200
					+10% for factory a/c.	
1961	Bonneville Safari	389/235 4dr Wgn	$4,800	$8,000	$13,000	$21,500
		389/318 4dr Wgn	$6,000	$10,100	$16,400	$27,100
		389/333 4dr Wgn	$6,200	$10,500	$16,900	$28,200
		389/348 4dr Wgn	$6,400	$10,800	$17,500	$29,300
					+10% for factory a/c.	
1962	Bonneville Safari	389/303 4dr Wgn	$4,400	$7,500	$15,200	$22,200
		389/318 4dr Wgn	$5,200	$8,700	$17,400	$25,800
		389/333 4dr Wgn	$5,300	$8,800	$17,700	$26,200
		389/348 4dr Wgn	$6,000	$10,300	$20,500	$30,200
					+10% for factory a/c.	
1962	Tempest	195/120 2dr Conv	$4,000	$7,800	$12,000	$19,300
		215/190 2dr Conv	$4,400	$8,600	$13,100	$21,200
1962	Catalina	389/267 2dr Spt Cpe	$4,900	$10,000	$20,200	$29,300
		389/303 2dr Spt Cpe	$5,800	$11,500	$23,600	$34,100
		389/318 2dr Spt Cpe	$6,300	$12,500	$25,600	$37,100
		389/333 2dr Spt Cpe	$7,000	$13,800	$28,300	$41,000
		389/348 2dr Spt Cpe	$7,800	$16,000	$32,800	$47,500
		421/405 2dr Spr Duty Cpe	$39,900	$55,000	$86,000	$113,000
		421/405 2dr Spr Duty Ltwt Cpe	$86,600	$123,000	$187,000	$248,000
		389/267 4dr Sdn	$3,000	$6,100	$11,600	$18,500
		389/303 4dr Sdn	$3,300	$6,600	$12,600	$20,000
		389/318 4dr Sdn	$3,500	$6,900	$13,300	$21,100
		389/333 4dr Sdn	$3,500	$7,100	$13,500	$21,500
		389/348 4dr Sdn	$4,100	$8,200	$15,700	$24,900
		389/267 4dr Safari Stn Wgn, 6-p.	$3,500	$6,400	$12,700	$18,800
		389/303 4dr Safari Stn Wgn, 6-p.	$3,900	$7,000	$14,000	$20,500
		389/318 4dr Safari Stn Wgn, 6-p.	$4,100	$7,400	$14,700	$21,600
		389/333 4dr Safari Stn Wgn, 6-p.	$4,100	$7,500	$14,900	$21,900

Pontiac

Year	Model	Body Style	4	3	2	1
		389/348 4dr Safari Stn Wgn 6P	$4,800	$8,700	$17,200	$25,500
		389/267 4dr Vista Hdtp Sdn	$3,500	$7,000	$14,500	$22,000
		389/303 4dr Vista Hdtp Sdn	$3,900	$7,700	$16,000	$24,200
		389/318 4dr Vista Hdtp Sdn	$4,100	$8,100	$16,800	$25,500
		389/333 4dr Vista Hdtp Sdn	$4,100	$8,200	$17,000	$25,900
		389/348 4dr Vista Hdtp Sdn	$4,800	$9,600	$19,700	$29,900
		389/267 2dr Conv	$10,400	$20,500	$33,900	$43,300
		389/303 2dr Conv	$11,400	$22,300	$37,200	$47,200
		389/318 2dr Conv	$12,000	$23,500	$39,200	$49,700
		389/333 2dr Conv	$12,300	$23,900	$39,700	$50,700
		389/348 2dr Conv	$14,300	$27,600	$45,800	$58,300

+10% for factory a/c. +5% for Ventura pkg.

Year	Model	Body Style	4	3	2	1
1962	Star Chief	389/283 4dr Sdn	$3,700	$6,800	$13,500	$20,200
		389/318 4dr Sdn	$4,300	$7,900	$15,600	$23,300
		389/333 4dr Sdn	$4,400	$8,000	$15,900	$23,700
		389/348 4dr Sdn	$5,200	$9,300	$18,300	$27,400
		389/283 4dr Vista Hdtp Sdn	$4,400	$7,100	$14,600	$21,700
		389/318 4dr Vista Hdtp Sdn	$5,100	$8,200	$16,900	$25,100
		389/333 4dr Vista Hdtp Sdn	$5,200	$8,400	$17,100	$25,600
		389/348 4dr Vista Hdtp Sdn	$5,900	$9,800	$19,800	$29,400

+10% for factory a/c.

Year	Model	Body Style	4	3	2	1
1962	Bonneville	389/303 2dr Spt Cpe	$7,700	$13,600	$24,900	$35,400
		389/318 2dr Spt Cpe	$9,800	$17,600	$31,600	$44,800
		389/333 2dr Spt Cpe	$10,100	$17,700	$32,100	$45,700
		389/348 2dr Spt Cpe	$11,600	$20,500	$36,900	$52,500
		389/303 4dr Vista Hdtp Sdn	$4,700	$8,000	$17,200	$25,300
		389/318 4dr Vista Hdtp Sdn	$5,500	$9,200	$19,800	$29,000
		389/333 4dr Vista Hdtp Sdn	$5,600	$9,400	$20,200	$29,500
		389/348 4dr Vista Hdtp Sdn	$6,400	$10,900	$23,200	$34,100
		389/303 2dr Conv	$15,100	$28,500	$48,200	$64,500
		389/318 2dr Conv	$17,500	$32,700	$55,500	$74,300
		389/333 2dr Conv	$17,700	$33,300	$56,500	$75,500
		389/348 2dr Conv	$20,400	$38,400	$65,100	$87,300

Year	Model	Body Style	4	3	2	1
						+10% for factory a/c.
1962	Grand Prix	389/303 2dr Spt Cpe	$10,100	$17,800	$32,800	$43,200
		389/318 2dr Spt Cpe	$11,500	$20,400	$37,700	$49,700
		389/333 2dr Spt Cpe	$11,700	$20,700	$38,300	$50,700
		389/348 2dr Spt Cpe	$13,700	$24,000	$44,300	$58,300
		421/405 2dr Spr Duty Spt Cpe	$98,600	$126,000	$185,000	$257,000
						+10% for factory a/c.
1963	Tempest	326/260 2dr Cpe	$4,100	$6,500	$12,600	$19,000
		326/260 2dr Spt Cpe	$4,500	$7,100	$14,600	$23,400
		326/260 2dr Conv	$8,000	$14,400	$23,500	$32,300
						-20% for 6-cyl. -25% for 4-cyl. +10% for factory a/c.
1963	LeMans	326/260 2dr Spt Cpe	$5,400	$8,200	$16,700	$26,400
		326/260 2dr Conv	$4,800	$7,800	$15,800	$22,300
						-20% for 6-cyl. +10% for factory a/c.
1963	Catalina	389/267 2dr Spt Cpe	$4,700	$8,000	$16,800	$28,200
		389/303 2dr Spt Cpe	$5,600	$9,700	$20,000	$33,600
		389/313 2dr Spt Cpe	$5,900	$10,200	$21,000	$35,400
		421/320 2dr Spt Cpe	$7,500	$11,400	$25,000	$44,300
		421/353 2dr Spt Cpe	$7,900	$12,000	$26,300	$46,600
		421/370 2dr Spt Cpe	$9,100	$17,200	$31,800	$60,500
		421/390 2dr Spt Cpe	$9,700	$17,800	$32,700	$63,300
		421/405 2dr Super Duty Spt Cpe	$43,200	$60,000	$93,500	$124,000
		421/405 2dr Super Duty Light-weight Spt Cpe	$95,000	$135,000	$205,000	$270,000
		389/267 2dr Spt Sdn	$2,100	$4,200	$8,200	$14,100
		389/303 2dr Spt Sdn	$2,400	$5,000	$9,700	$16,800
		389/313 2dr Spt Sdn	$2,500	$5,300	$10,200	$17,700
		421/320 2dr Spt Sdn	$2,500	$5,100	$9,900	$17,100

Pontiac

Year	Model	Body Style	4	3	2	1
		421/353 2dr Spt Sdn	$2,600	$5,400	$10,400	$18,000
		421/370 2dr Spt Sdn	$2,700	$5,700	$11,100	$18,900
		421/390 2dr Spt Sdn	$2,800	$6,000	$11,500	$19,600
		389/267 4dr Safari Stn Wgn 6P	$3,100	$5,600	$9,000	$16,200
		389/303 4dr Safari Stn Wgn. 6-p.	$3,400	$6,200	$9,900	$17,800
		389/313 4dr Safari Stn Wgn 6P	$3,900	$7,000	$11,200	$20,100
		421/320 4dr Safari Stn Wgn. 6-p.	$4,000	$7,100	$11,300	$20,300
		421/353 4dr Safari Stn Wgn 6P	$4,000	$7,100	$11,400	$20,400
		421/370 4dr Safari Stn Wgn 6P	$4,300	$7,500	$12,100	$21,700
		421/390 4dr Safari Stn Wgn 6P	$4,400	$7,800	$12,500	$22,600
		389/267 4dr Vista Hdtp Sdn	$4,000	$6,600	$11,600	$18,500
		389/303 4dr Vista Hdtp Sdn	$4,800	$7,900	$13,900	$21,900
		389/313 4dr Vista Hdtp Sdn	$5,100	$8,300	$14,600	$23,000
		421/320 4dr Vista Hdtp Sdn	$4,800	$8,000	$14,000	$22,100
		421/353 4dr Vista Hdtp Sdn	$5,100	$8,400	$14,700	$23,300
		421/370 4dr Vista Hdtp Sdn	$5,500	$9,000	$15,700	$24,900
		421/390 4dr Vista Hdtp Sdn	$5,600	$9,400	$16,400	$25,900
		389/267 2dr Conv	$8,600	$14,500	$24,700	$37,300
		389/303 2dr Conv	$10,400	$17,300	$29,400	$44,300
		389/313 2dr Conv	$10,900	$18,200	$30,900	$46,600
		421/320 2dr Conv	$12,500	$20,400	$34,300	$50,400
		421/353 2dr Conv	$13,200	$21,500	$36,100	$53,000
		421/370 2dr Conv	$14,000	$22,500	$38,300	$56,300
		421/390 2dr Conv	$14,500	$23,400	$39,800	$58,600
				+10% for factory a/c. +5% for Ventura pkg.		
1963	Star Chief	389/283 4dr Sdn	$3,000	$5,600	$9,200	$16,800
		389/313 4dr Sdn	$3,800	$7,000	$11,500	$20,900
		421/353 4dr Sdn	$3,900	$7,100	$11,700	$21,200
		421/370 4dr Sdn	$4,100	$7,500	$12,300	$22,600
		421/390 4dr Sdn	$4,300	$7,800	$12,800	$23,400
		389/283 4dr Vista Hdtp Sdn	$3,000	$5,800	$9,400	$17,700

Year	Model	Body Style	4	3	2	1
		389/313 4dr Vista Hdtp Sdn	$3,800	$7,200	$11,700	$22,000
		421/353 4dr Vista Hdtp Sdn	$3,900	$7,300	$11,900	$22,300
		421/370 4dr Vista Hdtp Sdn	$4,100	$7,800	$12,600	$23,800
		421/390 4dr Vista Hdtp Sdn	$4,300	$8,100	$13,100	$24,800
						+10% for factory a/c.
1963	Bonneville	389/303 2dr Spt Cpe	$5,500	$10,300	$21,100	$33,200
		389/313 2dr Spt Cpe	$6,800	$12,900	$26,500	$41,400
		421/320 2dr Spt Cpe	$7,200	$13,500	$28,100	$43,900
		421/353 2dr Spt Cpe	$7,600	$14,200	$29,600	$46,200
		421/370 2dr Spt Cpe	$7,900	$15,200	$31,700	$49,100
		421/390 2dr Spt Cpe	$8,100	$15,800	$32,700	$50,800
		389/303 4dr Safari Wgn	$3,800	$6,500	$12,000	$20,200
		389/313 4dr Safari Wgn	$4,300	$7,400	$13,500	$23,000
		421/320 4dr Safari Wgn	$4,800	$8,200	$15,000	$25,500
		421/353 4dr Safari Wgn	$4,900	$8,300	$15,300	$25,900
		421/370 4dr Safari Wgn	$5,300	$8,800	$16,300	$27,400
		421/390 4dr Safari Wgn	$5,500	$9,200	$16,900	$28,500
		389/303 4dr Vista Hdtp Sdn	$4,300	$7,400	$14,800	$22,100
		389/313 4dr Vista Hdtp Sdn	$5,000	$8,400	$16,700	$25,000
		421/320 4dr Vista Hdtp Sdn	$5,500	$9,300	$18,600	$27,800
		421/353 4dr Vista Hdtp Sdn	$5,600	$9,500	$18,900	$28,200
		421/370 4dr Vista Hdtp Sdn	$5,900	$10,200	$20,100	$30,100
		421/390 4dr Vista Hdtp Sdn	$6,100	$10,500	$20,900	$31,200
		389/303 2dr Conv	$10,600	$18,100	$32,900	$42,300
		389/313 2dr Conv	$11,900	$20,200	$37,100	$47,600
		421/320 2dr Conv	$13,200	$22,400	$41,200	$52,900
		421/353 2dr Conv	$13,400	$22,700	$41,800	$53,700
		421/370 2dr Conv	$14,400	$24,200	$44,600	$57,100
		421/390 2dr Conv	$14,800	$25,100	$46,200	$59,300

Pontiac

Year	Model	Body Style	4	3	2	1
						+10% for factory a/c.
1963	Grand Prix	389/303 2dr Spt Cpe	$8,000	$12,400	$23,800	$34,800
		389/313 2dr Spt Cpe	$10,000	$15,400	$29,700	$43,500
		421/320 2dr Spt Cpe	$10,200	$15,500	$29,800	$43,700
		421/353 2dr Spt Cpe	$10,300	$15,600	$30,100	$44,100
		421/370 2dr Spt Cpe	$10,800	$16,600	$32,100	$46,900
		421/390 2dr Spt Cpe	$11,200	$17,400	$33,300	$48,700
						+10% for factory a/c.
1964	Tempest	326/250 2dr Spt Cpe	$4,500	$7,100	$14,900	$23,700
1964	Tempest Custom	326/250 2dr Conv	$7,800	$14,300	$23,300	$32,000
						-20% for 6-cyl. +10% for factory a/c.
1964	LeMans	326/280 2dr Spt Cpe	$6,100	$10,300	$20,600	$29,100
		326/280 2dr Hdtp Cpe	$6,800	$10,700	$21,800	$34,400
		326/280 2dr Conv	$13,300	$22,200	$35,700	$49,900
						-20% for 6-cyl.
		389/325 2dr GTO Spt Cpe	$16,500	$26,200	$46,700	$63,600
		389/348 2dr GTO Spt Cpe	$30,700	$49,800	$93,200	$119,000
		389/325 2dr GTO Hdtp Cpe	$19,400	$30,600	$53,000	$69,900
		389/348 2dr GTO Hdtp Cpe	$33,200	$53,900	$96,500	$124,000
		389/325 2dr GTO Conv	$26,600	$42,500	$79,900	$113,000
		389/348 2dr GTO Conv	$45,400	$68,400	$125,000	$180,000
						+10% for factory a/c. +15% for factory 4-spd. -10% for auto.
1964	Catalina	389/267 2dr Spt Cpe	$3,200	$6,300	$10,700	$18,500
		389/283 2dr Spt Cpe	$3,200	$6,500	$10,900	$18,800
		389/303 2dr Spt Cpe	$3,500	$6,800	$11,500	$19,900
		389/306 2dr Spt Cpe	$3,500	$6,900	$11,800	$20,300
		389/330 2dr Spt Cpe	$5,900	$10,100	$21,100	$35,100
		421/320 2dr Spt Cpe	$7,800	$11,900	$26,400	$46,300

Year	Model	Body Style	4	3	2	1
		421/350 2dr Spt Cpe	$8,000	$12,300	$27,100	$47,700
		421/370 2dr Spt Cpe	$8,600	$13,200	$29,000	$51,500
		389/267 4dr Safari Stn Wgn 6P	$3,100	$5,600	$9,000	$16,200
		389/283 4dr Safari Stn Wgn, 6-p.	$3,200	$5,700	$9,200	$16,500
		389/303 4dr Safari Stn Wgn, 6-p.	$3,400	$6,100	$9,800	$17,600
		389/306 4dr Safari Stn Wgn 6P	$3,400	$6,200	$9,900	$17,800
		389/330 4dr Safari Stn Wgn 6P	$3,900	$6,900	$11,100	$19,900
		421/320 4dr Safari Stn Wgn 6P	$3,900	$7,000	$11,300	$20,300
		421/350 4dr Safari Stn Wgn 6P	$4,100	$7,200	$11,700	$20,900
		421/370 4dr Safari Stn Wgn 6P	$4,400	$7,800	$12,500	$22,600
		389/267 4dr Vista Hdtp Sdn	$4,000	$6,600	$11,600	$18,500
		389/283 4dr Vista Hdtp Sdn	$4,100	$6,800	$11,900	$19,100
		389/303 4dr Vista Hdtp Sdn	$4,300	$7,200	$12,500	$20,000
		389/306 4dr Vista Hdtp Sdn	$4,400	$7,300	$12,800	$20,400
		389/330 4dr Vista Hdtp Sdn	$5,000	$8,300	$14,400	$22,800
		421/320 4dr Vista Hdtp Sdn	$5,100	$8,400	$14,600	$23,200
		421/350 4dr Vista Hdtp Sdn	$5,200	$8,700	$15,100	$23,900
		421/370 4dr Vista Hdtp Sdn	$5,500	$9,400	$16,400	$25,800
		389/267 2dr Conv	$8,600	$14,400	$25,100	$38,300
		389/283 2dr Conv	$8,800	$14,700	$25,600	$39,100
		389/303 2dr Conv	$9,500	$15,800	$27,600	$42,200
		389/306 2dr Conv	$9,600	$16,000	$27,900	$42,600
		389/330 2dr Conv	$10,700	$18,000	$31,500	$47,900
		421/320 2dr Conv	$10,900	$18,300	$31,900	$48,700
		421/350 2dr Conv	$11,300	$18,900	$33,000	$50,300
		421/370 2dr Conv	$12,200	$20,200	$35,700	$54,300
		389/330 2dr 2+2 Spt Cpe	$12,600	$19,900	$34,100	$59,500
		421/320 2dr 2+2 Spt Cpe	$12,900	$20,300	$34,700	$60,400

Pontiac

Year	Model	Body Style	4	3	2	1
		421/350 2dr 2+2 Spt Cpe	$13,100	$20,900	$35,700	$62,400
		421/370 2dr 2+2 Spt Cpe	$14,100	$22,300	$38,300	$67,400
		389/330 2dr 2+2 Conv	$19,600	$35,600	$48,900	$75,600
		421/320 2dr 2+2 Conv	$20,000	$36,100	$49,600	$77,200
		421/350 2dr 2+2 Conv	$20,500	$37,400	$51,500	$79,500
		421/370 2dr 2+2 Conv	$22,300	$40,500	$54,900	$85,600
				+10% for factory a/c. +5% for Ventura pkg.		
1964	Star Chief	389/235 4dr Sdn	$3,000	$5,600	$9,200	$16,800
		389/330 4dr Sdn	$3,700	$6,900	$11,400	$20,700
		421/320 4dr Sdn	$3,800	$7,000	$11,600	$21,000
		421/350 4dr Sdn	$3,900	$7,200	$12,000	$21,700
		421/370 4dr Sdn	$4,200	$7,800	$12,800	$23,400
		389/235 4dr Vista Hdtp Sdn	$3,000	$5,800	$9,400	$17,700
		389/330 4dr Vista Hdtp Sdn	$3,700	$7,100	$11,600	$21,800
		421/320 4dr Vista Hdtp Sdn	$3,800	$7,300	$11,800	$22,200
		421/350 4dr Vista Hdtp Sdn	$3,900	$7,500	$12,100	$22,900
		421/370 4dr Vista Hdtp Sdn	$4,200	$8,100	$13,100	$24,700
						+10% for factory a/c.
1964	Bonneville	389/306 2dr Spt Cpe	$5,400	$10,300	$21,900	$33,600
		389/330 2dr Spt Cpe	$6,700	$12,800	$26,900	$41,600
		421/320 2dr Spt Cpe	$7,500	$14,200	$30,100	$46,400
		421/350 2dr Spt Cpe	$7,700	$14,600	$31,200	$48,000
		421/370 2dr Spt Cpe	$8,100	$15,800	$33,600	$51,500
		389/306 4dr Safari Wgn	$3,800	$6,500	$12,000	$20,200
		389/330 4dr Safari Wgn	$4,700	$8,100	$14,900	$25,100
		421/320 4dr Safari Wgn	$4,800	$8,200	$15,200	$25,600
		421/350 4dr Safari Wgn	$5,100	$8,500	$15,700	$26,400
		421/370 4dr Safari Wgn	$5,500	$9,200	$16,900	$28,400
		389/306 4dr Vista Hdtp Sdn	$4,300	$7,400	$14,800	$22,100

Year	Model	Body Style	4	3	2	1
		389/330 4dr Vista Hdtp Sdn	$5,500	$9,200	$18,400	$27,500
		421/320 4dr Vista Hdtp Sdn	$5,500	$9,400	$18,800	$27,900
		421/350 4dr Vista Hdtp Sdn	$5,600	$9,700	$19,400	$28,800
		421/370 4dr Vista Hdtp Sdn	$6,100	$10,500	$20,900	$31,100
		389/306 2dr Conv	$10,600	$18,300	$33,000	$43,300
		389/330 2dr Conv	$13,100	$22,500	$41,000	$53,600
		421/320 2dr Conv	$13,300	$22,800	$41,700	$54,300
		421/350 2dr Conv	$13,700	$23,500	$43,000	$56,100
		421/370 2dr Conv	$14,800	$25,400	$46,300	$60,500
						+10% for factory a/c.
1964	Grand Prix	389/303 2dr Spt Cpe	$8,500	$14,300	$25,400	$38,200
		389/306 2dr Spt Cpe	$8,700	$14,600	$26,000	$39,000
		389/330 2dr Spt Cpe	$10,600	$17,700	$31,500	$47,400
		421/320 2dr Spt Cpe	$10,700	$17,900	$31,900	$48,100
		421/350 2dr Spt Cpe	$11,100	$18,500	$33,000	$49,600
		421/370 2dr Spt Cpe	$12,000	$19,800	$35,500	$53,400
						+10% for factory a/c.
1965	Tempest	326/250 2dr Spt Cpe	$4,800	$7,800	$15,800	$25,600
		326/250 2dr Cstm Conv	$8,200	$15,300	$24,300	$32,800
						-20% for 6-cyl. +10% for factory a/c.
1965	Tempest Custom	326/250 2dr Hdtp Cpe	$4,600	$7,000	$15,000	$20,300
						-20% for 6-cyl. +10% for factory a/c.
1965	LeMans	326/250 2dr Spt Cpe	$5,500	$9,300	$17,300	$27,400
		326/250 2dr Hdtp Cpe	$5,700	$9,600	$18,800	$29,100
		326/250 2dr Conv	$10,600	$17,600	$28,700	$40,400
		389/335 2dr GTO Spt Cpe	$19,900	$30,100	$57,600	$70,200
		389/360 2dr GTO Spt Cpe	$28,600	$46,000	$91,100	$113,000
		389/335 2dr GTO Hdtp Cpe	$27,000	$37,400	$64,500	$85,400
		389/360 2dr GTO Hdtp Cpe	$37,600	$55,000	$103,000	$136,000
		389/335 2dr GTO Conv	$35,700	$54,200	$96,400	$138,000

Pontiac

Year	Model	Body Style	4	3	2	1
		389/360 2dr GTO Conv	$41,800	$62,600	$114,000	$152,000
		+15% for factory a/c. +15% for factory 4-spd. -10% for auto.				
1965	Catalina	389/290 2dr Spt Cpe	$2,500	$5,400	$9,100	$14,500
		421/376 2dr Spt Cpe	$7,100	$8,600	$15,000	$24,100
		389/290 2dr Conv	$7,500	$12,400	$20,600	$34,300
		421/376 2dr Conv	$12,700	$18,200	$31,100	$52,500
		421/376 2dr 2+2 Spt Cpe	$10,800	$20,500	$39,200	$54,400
		421/376 2dr 2+2 Conv	$19,400	$37,200	$57,100	$87,300
		+10% for factory a/c. +5% for Ventura pkg.				
1965	Bonneville	389/325 2dr Spt Cpe	$3,900	$6,100	$11,600	$18,700
		389/333 2dr Spt Cpe	$4,100	$6,400	$12,200	$19,600
		389/338 2dr Spt Cpe	$4,500	$7,000	$13,400	$21,600
		389/360 2dr Spt Cpe	$5,200	$8,100	$15,100	$24,500
		421/338 2dr Spt Cpe	$5,100	$7,900	$14,800	$24,000
		421/356 2dr Spt Cpe	$5,400	$8,300	$15,600	$25,300
		421/376 2dr Spt Cpe	$5,500	$8,500	$16,200	$26,200
		389/325 2dr Conv	$8,300	$15,600	$28,400	$40,400
		389/333 2dr Conv	$8,700	$16,400	$29,800	$42,400
		389/338 2dr Conv	$9,100	$17,200	$31,300	$44,500
		389/360 2dr Conv	$10,200	$18,800	$36,300	$51,600
		421/338 2dr Conv	$10,000	$18,400	$35,600	$50,600
		421/356 2dr Conv	$10,400	$19,200	$37,100	$52,700
		421/376 2dr Conv	$10,900	$20,000	$39,200	$56,200
		+10% for factory a/c.				
1965	Grand Prix	389/325 2dr Spt Cpe	$5,300	$10,500	$20,100	$32,600
		389/333 2dr Spt Cpe	$5,400	$10,700	$20,600	$33,200
		389/338 2dr Spt Cpe	$5,600	$11,200	$21,600	$34,900
		421/338 2dr Spt Cpe	$6,400	$12,800	$24,200	$36,900
		421/356 2dr Spt Cpe	$6,700	$13,400	$25,500	$38,700
		421/376 2dr Spt Cpe	$7,800	$15,700	$26,500	$41,900
		+10% for factory a/c.				

Year	Model	Body Style	4	3	2	1
1966	Tempest	326/250 2dr Spt Cpe	$5,000	$9,500	$18,000	$26,500
		326/250 4dr Wgn	$3,100	$6,500	$12,300	$18,800
				-20% for 6-cyl. +10% for factory a/c.		
1966	Tempest Custom	326/250 2dr Conv	$7,000	$12,500	$22,500	$32,000
1966	LeMans	326/250 2dr Spt Cpe	$6,500	$11,200	$22,300	$30,400
		326/250 2dr Hdtp Cpe	$7,000	$12,200	$22,700	$31,600
		326/250 4dr Hdtp Sdn	$3,600	$6,500	$11,800	$17,000
		326/250 2dr Conv	$12,500	$18,100	$30,600	$41,200
				-20% for 6-cyl. +10% for factory a/c.		
1966	GTO	389/360 2dr Hdtp Cpe	$24,000	$43,000	$63,000	$75,500
		389/335 2dr Cpe	$14,100	$25,500	$49,400	$59,400
		389/360 2dr Cpe	$21,100	$37,900	$56,000	$72,000
		389/335 2dr Hdtp Cpe	$14,900	$26,500	$52,900	$64,100
		389/335 2dr Conv	$26,100	$39,800	$73,300	$95,500
		389/360 2dr Conv	$40,800	$57,500	$102,000	$133,000
			+15% for factory a/c. +15% for factory 4-spd. -10% for auto. +10% for red inner fender liners.			
1966	Catalina	389/290 2dr Hdtp Cpe	$2,500	$5,400	$9,300	$14,800
		389/293 2dr Hdtp Cpe	$2,600	$5,500	$9,500	$15,100
		389/325 2dr Hdtp Cpe	$2,900	$6,200	$10,600	$17,100
		389/333 2dr Hdtp Cpe	$3,200	$6,800	$11,700	$18,800
		421/338 2dr Hdtp Cpe	$6,600	$9,800	$16,500	$23,600
		421/356 2dr Hdtp Cpe	$7,400	$11,200	$17,600	$26,500
		421/376 2dr Hdtp Cpe	$7,900	$13,000	$18,200	$28,200
		389/290 2dr Conv	$8,000	$13,400	$21,200	$36,700
		389/293 2dr Conv	$8,200	$13,700	$21,600	$37,400
		389/325 2dr Conv	$9,200	$15,300	$24,200	$42,200
		389/333 2dr Conv	$10,100	$16,800	$26,600	$46,400
		421/338 2dr Conv	$12,000	$18,100	$29,400	$51,000
		421/356 2dr Conv	$12,100	$18,300	$29,900	$51,800
		421/376 2dr Conv	$12,900	$19,700	$31,900	$55,500
		421/338 2dr 2+2 Hdtp Cpe	$10,700	$19,700	$36,800	$53,600
		421/356 2dr 2+2 Hdtp Cpe	$10,700	$19,800	$37,400	$54,500

Pontiac

Year	Model	Body Style	4	3	2	1
		421/376 2dr 2+2 Hdtp Cpe	$11,600	$21,000	$39,900	$58,500
		421/338 2dr 2+2 Conv	$20,300	$36,000	$58,200	$84,700
		421/356 2dr 2+2 Conv	$20,500	$36,500	$59,300	$86,100
		421/376 2dr 2+2 Conv	$22,100	$39,100	$63,600	$92,000
						+10% for factory a/c. +5% for Ventura pkg.
1966	Bonneville	389/325 2dr Hdtp Cpe	$4,600	$7,400	$12,100	$19,800
		389/333 2dr Conv	$9,600	$15,800	$30,500	$42,000
		389/333 2dr Hdtp Cpe	$5,100	$8,100	$13,300	$21,800
		421/338 2dr Hdtp Cpe	$6,100	$9,500	$15,600	$25,400
		421/356 2dr Hdtp Cpe	$6,300	$9,900	$16,200	$26,100
		421/376 2dr Hdtp Cpe	$6,600	$10,400	$17,000	$27,700
		389/325 2dr Conv	$8,700	$14,400	$27,700	$38,200
		421/338 2dr Conv	$11,900	$19,800	$38,000	$53,800
		421/356 2dr Conv	$12,400	$20,200	$39,100	$55,100
		421/376 2dr Conv	$13,000	$21,500	$41,800	$56,600
						+10% for factory a/c.
1966	Grand Prix	389/325 2dr Hdtp Cpe	$6,900	$13,100	$25,500	$37,000
		389/333 2dr Hdtp Cpe	$7,400	$14,100	$27,500	$39,600
		421/338 2dr Hdtp Cpe	$8,000	$14,900	$29,900	$42,000
						+10% for factory a/c.
1967	Tempest	326/250 4dr Wgn	$3,400	$6,700	$12,500	$19,100
						-20% for 6-cyl. +10% for factory a/c.
1967	Tempest Custom	326/250 2dr Conv	$7,100	$12,200	$23,900	$33,900
						-20% for 6-cyl. +10% for factory a/c.
1967	Firebird	326/250 2dr Hdtp Cpe	$7,400	$15,300	$28,500	$39,900
		326/285 2dr Hdtp Cpe	$8,300	$17,100	$29,300	$42,500
		400/325 2dr 400 Hdtp Cpe	$12,800	$17,700	$33,300	$47,900
		400/325 RA 2dr 400 Hdtp Cpe	$30,400	$46,200	$59,700	$73,200
		326/250 2dr Conv	$9,700	$17,700	$34,000	$45,600
		326/285 2dr Conv	$12,900	$19,900	$35,100	$47,900
		400/325 2dr 400 Conv	$18,500	$30,100	$43,700	$61,600

Year	Model	Body Style	4	3	2	1
		400/325 RA 2dr 400 Conv	$41,000	$58,000	$78,200	$107,000
						-30% for 6-cyl. +10% for factory a/c.
1967	LeMans	326/250 2dr Spt Cpe	$7,000	$12,200	$23,400	$32,300
		326/250 2dr Hdtp Cpe	$7,300	$13,300	$24,000	$33,400
		326/250 4dr Hdtp Sdn	$4,200	$7,200	$12,600	$18,100
		326/250 2dr Conv	$12,900	$18,800	$32,600	$43,100
1967	GTO	400/255 2dr Spt Cpe	$12,100	$21,800	$41,600	$53,900
		400/335 2dr Spt Cpe	$16,000	$30,600	$56,700	$71,600
		400/360 2dr Spt Cpe	$21,100	$40,400	$65,000	$94,500
		400/360 RA 2dr Spt Cpe	$35,300	$60,100	$76,900	$104,000
		400/255 2dr Hdtp Cpe	$15,200	$28,500	$50,100	$59,800
		400/335 2dr Hdtp Cpe	$20,400	$37,600	$66,800	$79,000
		400/360 2dr Hdtp Cpe	$27,000	$49,600	$85,000	$106,000
		400/360 RA 2dr Hdtp Cpe	$40,900	$70,800	$96,500	$120,000
		400/255 2dr Conv	$23,500	$38,000	$72,400	$94,300
		400/335 2dr Conv	$38,600	$53,400	$95,400	$123,000
		400/360 2dr Conv	$43,800	$60,500	$102,000	$139,000
		400/360 RA 2dr Conv	$63,400	$83,400	$117,000	$151,000
						+15% for factory a/c. +15% for factory 4-spd. -10% for auto.
1967	Grand Prix	400/350 2dr Hdtp Cpe	$6,500	$11,100	$22,000	$33,600
		428/360 2dr Hdtp Cpe	$9,100	$15,500	$30,700	$46,800
		428/376 2dr Hdtp Cpe	$11,100	$19,100	$37,800	$57,900
		400/350 2dr Conv	$13,900	$21,600	$39,900	$55,100
		428/360 2dr Conv	$16,400	$25,700	$48,400	$68,900
		428/376 2dr Conv	$18,900	$29,700	$54,600	$76,400
						+10% for factory a/c.
1967	Catalina	400/290 2dr Hdtp Cpe	$2,600	$5,700	$9,500	$15,200
		400/293 2dr Hdtp Cpe	$2,700	$5,800	$9,700	$15,500

Pontiac

Year	Model	Body Style	4	3	2	1
		400/325 2dr Hdtp Cpe	$3,000	$6,400	$10,700	$17,100
		400/333 2dr Hdtp Cpe	$3,200	$6,700	$11,200	$18,000
		400/376 2dr Hdtp Cpe	$3,200	$7,000	$11,700	$18,500
		428/360 2dr Hdtp Cpe	$3,300	$7,100	$11,900	$18,900
		428/376 2dr Hdtp Cpe	$3,700	$8,000	$13,200	$21,200
		400/290 2dr Conv	$8,200	$13,700	$21,700	$37,300
		400/293 2dr Conv	$8,400	$14,000	$22,100	$38,000
		400/325 2dr Conv	$8,800	$14,700	$23,200	$39,900
		400/333 2dr Conv	$9,200	$15,400	$24,400	$41,900
		400/376 2dr Conv	$10,000	$16,700	$26,100	$45,200
		428/360 2dr Conv	$10,300	$17,200	$26,900	$46,600
		428/376 2dr Conv	$11,500	$19,200	$30,200	$52,300
		400/290 2dr 2+2 Hdtp Cpe	$9,400	$15,600	$30,900	$46,700
		400/293 2dr 2+2 Hdtp Cpe	$9,600	$15,900	$31,500	$47,600
		400/325 2dr 2+2 Hdtp Cpe	$10,400	$17,200	$34,000	$51,400
		400/333 2dr 2+2 Hdtp Cpe	$10,900	$18,100	$35,700	$54,000
		400/376 2dr 2+2 Hdtp Cpe	$11,300	$19,400	$37,200	$56,800
		428/360 2dr 2+2 Hdtp Cpe	$11,600	$20,000	$38,400	$58,600
		428/376 2dr 2+2 Hdtp Cpe	$12,900	$21,900	$43,300	$65,500
		400/290 2dr 2+2 Conv	$17,400	$30,400	$49,200	$70,500
		400/293 2dr 2+2 Conv	$17,700	$31,000	$50,200	$71,900
		400/325 2dr 2+2 Conv	$18,900	$33,200	$53,700	$76,900
		400/333 2dr 2+2 Conv	$19,800	$34,900	$56,400	$80,700
		400/376 2dr 2+2 Conv	$21,300	$36,700	$59,800	$85,600
		428/360 2dr 2+2 Conv	$22,000	$37,800	$61,700	$88,200
		428/376 2dr 2+2 Conv	$24,700	$42,600	$68,900	$98,400
				+10% for factory a/c. +5% for Ventura pkg.		
1967	Bonneville	400/325 2dr Hdtp Cpe	$4,600	$7,200	$12,100	$19,500

Year	Model	Body Style	4	3	2	1
		400/333 2dr Hdtp Cpe	$4,800	$7,600	$12,700	$20,500
		428/360 2dr Hdtp Cpe	$6,400	$9,900	$16,600	$26,500
		428/376 2dr Hdtp Cpe	$7,000	$11,200	$18,700	$29,700
		400/325 2dr Conv	$8,900	$14,500	$28,200	$39,200
		400/333 2dr Conv	$9,300	$15,200	$29,600	$41,200
		428/360 2dr Conv	$12,400	$19,900	$38,400	$53,400
		428/376 2dr Conv	$13,700	$22,300	$43,000	$59,900
						+10% for factory a/c.
1968	Tempest Custom	350/265 2dr Cpe	$7,200	$13,900	$25,300	$35,600
		350/320 2dr Cpe	$8,300	$15,300	$27,000	$37,300
		400/330 2dr Cpe	$12,400	$17,200	$32,200	$43,900
		400/335 RA 2dr Cpe	$25,200	$38,700	$63,900	$88,300
		400/340 RA II 2dr Cpe	$37,500	$56,400	$81,800	$110,000
		350/265 2dr Conv	$10,100	$15,300	$31,700	$41,600
		350/320 2dr Conv	$12,000	$17,800	$33,100	$45,700
		400/330 2dr Conv	$16,800	$28,400	$38,000	$55,000
		400/335 RA 2dr Conv	$24,300	$53,700	$81,500	$103,000
		400/340 RA II 2dr Conv	$86,800	$129,000	$164,000	$213,000
						-30% for 6-cyl. +20% for 4-spd.
1968	Firebird	350/265 2dr Hdtp Cpe	$7,400	$16,200	$27,600	$38,800
		350/320 2dr Hdtp Cpe	$8,600	$17,800	$29,800	$40,600
		400/330 2dr 400 Hdtp Cpe	$14,500	$20,200	$39,800	$52,400
		400/340 RA II 2dr 400 Hdtp Cpe	$41,100	$60,900	$95,100	$128,000
		400/335 RA 2dr 400 Hdtp Cpe	$23,300	$35,900	$60,200	$83,000
		350/265 2dr Conv	$10,100	$18,900	$32,300	$42,400
		350/320 2dr Conv	$12,100	$20,500	$33,100	$45,700
		400/330 2dr 400 Conv	$18,100	$30,600	$43,700	$63,500
		400/340 RA II 2dr 400 Conv	$90,300	$134,000	$169,000	$215,000
		400/335 RA 2dr 400 Conv	$23,900	$52,200	$84,000	$105,000
1968	LeMans	350/265 2dr Spt Cpe	$3,700	$7,600	$14,800	$20,800
		350/265 2dr Hdtp Cpe	$4,200	$8,300	$15,800	$21,500

Pontiac

Year	Model	Body Style	4	3	2	1
		350/265 2dr Conv	$8,600	$14,800	$30,000	$41,200
		-20% for 6-cyl. +10% for factory a/c.				
1968	GTO	400/265 2dr Hdtp Cpe	$10,700	$18,300	$35,300	$46,600
		400/350 2dr Hdtp Cpe	$13,900	$23,600	$46,300	$61,900
		400/360 2dr Hdtp Cpe	$25,200	$36,900	$56,200	$71,800
		400/360 RA 2dr Hdtp Cpe	$25,300	$37,200	$58,100	$72,900
		400/366 RA II 2dr Hdtp Cpe	$28,700	$47,100	$79,300	$106,000
		400/360 2dr Conv	$22,600	$34,900	$68,600	$87,500
		400/265 2dr Conv	$13,800	$22,200	$46,300	$57,200
		400/350 2dr Conv	$18,700	$30,400	$62,000	$77,300
		400/360 RA 2dr Conv	$36,600	$50,000	$78,500	$97,900
		400/366 RA II 2dr Conv	$60,600	$79,100	$109,000	$139,000
		+10% for factory a/c. +15% for factory 4-spd. -10% for auto.				
1968	Grand Prix	400/265 2dr Hdtp Cpe	$7,200	$12,300	$24,000	$35,400
		400/350 2dr Hdtp Cpe	$8,100	$14,400	$28,200	$41,500
		428/375 2dr Hdtp Cpe	$9,900	$16,900	$30,800	$45,500
		428/390 2dr Hdtp Cpe	$11,200	$19,100	$35,200	$51,300
		+10% for factory a/c.				
1968	Catalina	400/340 2dr Conv	$5,900	$10,400	$19,900	$27,200
		428/375 2dr Conv	$6,100	$10,700	$20,800	$28,400
		428/390 2dr Conv	$6,400	$11,200	$21,700	$29,600
		+10% for factory a/c. +5% for Ventura pkg.				
1968	Bonneville	428/375 2dr Hdtp Cpe	$7,900	$9,500	$15,000	$25,000
		428/390 2dr Hdtp Cpe	$8,200	$10,100	$16,400	$26,300
		400/340 2dr Brghm Hdtp Cpe	$5,500	$8,500	$13,500	$21,800
		428/375 2dr Conv	$10,700	$18,700	$32,000	$49,400
		428/390 2dr Conv	$11,000	$19,600	$33,700	$51,900
		400/340 2dr Brghm Conv	$9,200	$15,700	$27,500	$42,700
		+10% for factory a/c.				
1969	Tempest	350/330 2dr Spt Cpe	$3,100	$6,600	$12,200	$16,700
		-20% for 6-cyl. +10% for factory a/c.				

Year	Model	Body Style	4	3	2	1
1969	Tempest Custom S	350/265 2dr Conv	$6,000	$11,700	$21,000	$29,600
			-20% for 6-cyl. +10% for factory a/c.			
1969	Firebird	350/265 2dr 350 Hdtp Cpe	$8,200	$18,000	$28,600	$42,300
		350/325 2dr H.O. Hdtp Cpe	$10,100	$18,500	$32,200	$45,300
		400/330 2dr 400 Hdtp Cpe	$14,400	$21,000	$38,700	$53,600
		400/335 RA III 2dr 400 H.O. Hdtp Cpe	$24,800	$37,000	$54,000	$69,800
		400/345 RA IV 2dr 400 Ram Air IV Hdtp Cpe	$92,700	$120,000	$147,000	$204,000
		400/335 RA III 2dr Trans Am Hdtp Cpe	$64,500	$93,000	$120,000	$161,000
		400/345 RA IV 2dr Trans Am Hdtp Cpe	$127,000	$170,000	$206,000	$262,000
		350/265 2dr 350 Conv	$9,600	$18,900	$33,100	$44,400
		350/325 2dr H.O. Conv	$11,300	$20,300	$34,300	$51,000
		400/330 2dr 400 Conv	$13,700	$27,900	$55,400	$63,400
		400/335 RA III 2dr 400 H.O. Conv	$37,500	$53,200	$73,500	$96,600
		400/345 RA IV 2dr 400 Ram Air IV Conv	$164,000	$205,000	$252,000	$316,000
		400/335 RA III 2dr Trans Am Conv	$637,000	$776,000	$924,000	$1.2 mil
			-30% for 6-cyl. +20% for 4-spd (exc T/A).			
1969	LeMans	350/265 2dr Spt Cpe	$3,700	$7,500	$14,800	$20,400
		350/265 2dr Hdtp Cpe	$4,900	$9,600	$17,300	$23,500
		350/265 2dr Conv	$8,600	$14,800	$30,000	$41,200
			-20% for 6-cyl. +10% for factory a/c.			
1969	GTO	400/350 2dr Cpe	$16,300	$30,000	$49,000	$67,200
		400/350 2dr Conv	$29,000	$35,000	$59,500	$81,700
		400/366 Ram Air III 2dr Cpe	$20,800	$34,400	$52,600	$73,400
		400/370 RA IV 2dr Cpe	$34,100	$55,200	$83,800	$118,000
		400/366 Ram Air III 2dr Judge Cpe	$38,900	$56,000	$75,000	$119,000

Pontiac

Year	Model	Body Style	4	3	2	1
		400/370 RA IV 2dr Judge Cpe	$76,000	$101,000	$148,000	$195,000
		400/366 Ram Air III 2dr Conv	$35,500	$46,900	$76,100	$94,400
		400/370 RA IV 2dr Conv	$92,500	$114,000	$142,000	$181,000
		400/366 Ram Air III 2dr Judge Conv	$106,000	$130,000	$179,000	$204,000
		400/370 RA IV 2dr Judge Conv	$371,000	$432,000	$495,000	$550,000

+15% for 4-spd. +10% for factory a/c. -10% for auto. -$150,000 for auto on RA IV Judge conv.

Year	Model	Body Style	4	3	2	1
1969	Grand Prix	400/350 2dr Model J Hdtp Cpe	$11,400	$16,200	$32,500	$42,000
		428/370 2dr Model SJ Hdtp Cpe	$13,800	$20,100	$36,800	$51,800
		428/390 2dr Model SJ Hdtp Cpe	$15,000	$24,200	$40,000	$56,400

+10% for factory a/c.

Year	Model	Body Style	4	3	2	1
1969	Catalina	400/290 2dr Conv	$5,200	$8,800	$17,100	$23,600
		428/360 2dr Conv	$6,100	$10,700	$20,600	$28,200
		428/390 2dr Conv	$6,600	$11,600	$22,200	$30,700

+10% for factory a/c. +5% for Ventura pkg.

Year	Model	Body Style	4	3	2	1
1969	Bonneville	400/265 2dr Hdtp Cpe	$4,600	$6,100	$11,200	$18,200
		428/360 2dr Hdtp Cpe	$5,900	$7,500	$14,000	$22,500
		428/390 2dr Hdtp Cpe	$6,300	$8,200	$15,500	$24,500
		428/360 2dr Conv	$10,400	$17,500	$30,100	$48,700
		428/390 2dr Conv	$12,500	$20,000	$35,800	$53,000

+10% for factory a/c.

Year	Model	Body Style	4	3	2	1
1970	Tempest	350/255 2dr Cpe	$3,100	$6,600	$12,200	$16,600
		350/255 2dr GT-37 Cpe	$4,200	$7,900	$15,300	$21,300
		400/265 2dr GT-37 Cpe	$5,200	$9,500	$17,700	$24,600
		400/330 2dr GT-37 Cpe	$5,600	$10,000	$19,000	$26,700

-20% for 6-cyl. +10% for factory a/c.

Year	Model	Body Style	4	3	2	1
1970	Firebird	350/255 2dr Hdtp Cpe	$6,400	$11,000	$19,900	$30,300
		350/255 2dr Esprit Hdtp Cpe	$7,100	$11,800	$23,900	$33,600
		400/265 2dr Esprit Hdtp Cpe	$7,500	$12,400	$25,100	$35,300
		400/330 2dr Esprit Hdtp Cpe	$8,900	$17,000	$29,300	$40,100

Year	Model	Body Style	4	3	2	1
		400/335 2dr Formula 400 Hdtp Cpe	$12,100	$23,600	$44,700	$62,000
		400/345 RA III 2dr Formula 400 Hdtp Cpe	$28,600	$41,500	$67,200	$84,700
		400/345 RA III 2dr Trans Am Hdtp Cpe	$25,100	$44,300	$74,800	$92,400
		400/370 RA IV 2dr Trans Am Hdtp Cpe	$115,000	$130,000	$175,000	$218,000
						-30% for 6-cyl.
1970	LeMans	350/255 2dr Spt Cpe	$4,200	$8,700	$16,300	$22,300
		350/255 2dr Hdtp Cpe	$4,900	$9,500	$17,100	$23,200
						-20% for 6-cyl. +10% for factory a/c.
1970	GTO	400/350 2dr Hdtp Cpe	$16,600	$26,400	$46,000	$62,500
		400/366 Ram Air III 2dr Hdtp Cpe	$21,000	$27,700	$50,500	$70,000
		400/370 RA IV 2dr Hdtp Cpe	$35,500	$60,100	$80,000	$107,000
		455/360 2dr Hdtp Cpe	$25,100	$31,300	$58,200	$80,000
		400/366 Ram Air III 2dr Judge Hdtp Cpe	$39,300	$54,500	$95,800	$114,000
		400/370 RA IV 2dr Judge Hdtp Cpe	$49,400	$78,500	$120,000	$150,000
		400/350 2dr Conv	$22,100	$33,600	$58,800	$76,300
		400/366 Ram Air III 2dr Conv	$32,100	$43,700	$70,800	$94,900
		400/370 RA IV 2dr Conv	$60,900	$79,600	$109,000	$138,000
		455/360 2dr Conv	$36,000	$48,200	$82,100	$122,000
		400/366 Ram Air III 2dr Judge Conv	$93,000	$102,000	$131,000	$161,000
		400/370 RA IV 2dr Judge Conv	$274,000	$339,000	$426,000	$509,000
						+15% for 4-spd. +10% for factory a/c. -10% for auto.
1970	Grand Prix	400/350 2dr Model J Hdtp Cpe	$11,200	$15,800	$31,800	$42,000
		455/370 2dr Model SJ Hdtp Cpe	$14,200	$22,800	$37,600	$53,800
						+10% for factory a/c.
1970	Catalina	400/265 2dr Conv	$5,900	$10,200	$19,300	$26,700

Pontiac

Year	Model	Body Style	4	3	2	1
		400/290 2dr Conv	$5,200	$8,700	$16,800	$23,200
		400/330 2dr Conv	$5,600	$9,300	$18,000	$24,800
		455/360 2dr Conv	$6,400	$11,000	$21,100	$28,900
		455/370 2dr Conv	$6,600	$11,500	$21,900	$30,200
				+10% for factory a/c. +5% for Ventura pkg.		
1970	Bonneville	455/360 2dr Hdtp Cpe	$4,900	$6,400	$12,100	$19,600
		455/370 2dr Hdtp Cpe	$6,500	$8,300	$15,800	$25,300
		455/360 2dr Conv	$7,200	$12,100	$20,900	$32,400
		455/370 2dr Conv	$9,500	$15,900	$27,200	$42,300
						+10% for factory a/c.
1971	T-37	350/250 2dr Cpe	$3,300	$6,400	$12,400	$17,400
		400/265 2dr Cpe	$4,200	$8,000	$15,500	$21,700
		400/300 2dr Cpe	$4,600	$8,900	$17,300	$24,100
		455/325 2dr Cpe	$4,800	$9,200	$18,200	$25,300
		455/335 2dr Cpe	$5,300	$10,700	$21,100	$33,900
				-20% for 6-cyl. +10% for factory a/c.		
1971	GT-37	350/250 2dr Hdtp Cpe	$4,200	$7,400	$14,300	$20,000
		400/265 2dr Hdtp Cpe	$4,800	$9,200	$17,800	$25,000
		400/300 2dr Hdtp Cpe	$5,100	$10,200	$19,900	$27,700
		455/325 2dr Hdtp Cpe	$5,900	$10,700	$20,900	$29,200
		455/335 2dr Hdtp Cpe	$8,200	$13,900	$26,000	$37,200
1971	Ventura II	250/145 2dr Cpe	$2,600	$6,400	$12,300	$18,500
				-20% for 6-cyl. +10% for factory a/c.		
1971	Firebird	350/250 2dr Hdtp Cpe	$5,900	$8,600	$18,200	$24,100
		350/250 2dr Esprit Hdtp Cpe	$6,500	$10,600	$19,900	$26,700
		400/265 2dr Esprit Hdtp Cpe	$8,600	$16,500	$27,500	$36,500
		350/250 2dr Formula 350 Hdtp Cpe	$8,600	$14,000	$23,800	$36,500
		400/300 2dr Formula 400 Hdtp Cpe	$13,900	$24,800	$43,600	$55,100
		455/325 2dr Formula 455 Hdtp Cpe	$15,800	$27,300	$54,900	$65,400
		455/335 2dr Formula 455 Hdtp Cpe	$17,500	$32,100	$58,900	$75,000

Year	Model	Body Style	4	3	2	1
		455/335 2dr Trans Am Hdtp Cpe	$23,300	$34,800	$64,200	$90,100
						-30% for 6-cyl.
1971	LeMans	400/300 2dr Cpe	$3,700	$7,500	$14,500	$20,100
		455/325 2dr Cpe	$3,900	$8,000	$15,300	$21,000
		455/335 2dr Cpe	$4,600	$9,400	$17,900	$24,600
		250/145 2dr Hdtp Cpe	$3,700	$7,900	$14,000	$19,100
		400/300 2dr Hdtp Cpe	$3,500	$7,400	$14,000	$18,600
		455/325 2dr Hdtp Cpe	$4,300	$9,100	$16,200	$21,700
		455/335 2dr Hdtp Cpe	$5,000	$10,800	$19,000	$25,500
		250/145 2dr Sport Hdtp Cpe	$2,900	$5,800	$11,900	$16,600
		350/250 2dr Sport Conv	$8,800	$13,000	$26,300	$37,700
		400/300 2dr Sport Conv	$9,800	$14,300	$29,000	$41,600
		455/325 2dr Sport Conv	$10,200	$14,900	$30,300	$43,600
				-20% for 6-cyl. +10% for factory a/c.		
1971	GTO	400/300 2dr Cpe	$13,900	$20,700	$38,900	$54,800
		455/325 2dr Cpe	$16,400	$27,700	$50,700	$69,400
		455/335 2dr Cpe	$19,400	$32,000	$57,600	$84,200
		455/335 2dr Judge Cpe	$41,100	$65,900	$100,000	$124,000
		400/300 2dr Conv	$26,100	$31,000	$56,700	$72,700
		455/325 2dr Conv	$29,700	$40,400	$65,500	$85,500
		455/335 2dr Conv	$39,800	$51,800	$81,600	$109,000
		455/335 2dr Judge Conv	$190,000	$251,000	$297,000	$361,000
		+15% for 4-spd (exc Judge conv). +10% for factory a/c. -10% for auto.				
1971	Grand Prix	400/300 2dr Model J Hdtp Cpe	$10,000	$15,500	$24,000	$34,000
						+10% for SJ pkg.
		455/325 2dr Model SJ Hdtp Cpe	$11,300	$18,000	$30,100	$40,800
1971	Grand Ville	455/325 2dr Conv	$4,500	$8,500	$16,500	$24,800
1972	Ventura II	250/110 2dr Cpe	$2,800	$6,700	$12,600	$18,900
				-20% for 6-cyl. +10% for factory a/c.		
1972	Firebird	350/160 2dr Hdtp Cpe	$6,200	$9,000	$18,800	$24,800
		350/160 2dr Esprit Hdtp Cpe	$6,800	$11,000	$20,200	$26,300
		350/175 2dr Esprit Hdtp Cpe	$6,600	$10,700	$19,600	$25,500

Pontiac

Year	Model	Body Style	4	3	2	1
		400/175 2dr Esprit Hdtp Cpe	$8,600	$16,900	$27,200	$34,400
		350/175 2dr Formula 350 Hdtp Cpe	$8,100	$14,300	$24,200	$34,300
		400/250 2dr Formula 400 Hdtp Cpe	$11,300	$20,600	$36,500	$47,300
		455/300 2dr Formula 455 Hdtp Cpe	$13,300	$23,200	$43,800	$52,600
		455/300 2dr Trans Am Hdtp Cpe	$23,200	$34,000	$63,900	$86,600
						-30% for 6-cyl.
1972	LeMans	250/110 2dr Cpe	$3,100	$6,800	$12,500	$17,100
		400/250 2dr GTO Cpe	$10,600	$16,500	$31,000	$46,200
		455/250 2dr GTO Cpe	$11,200	$17,900	$33,000	$49,100
		455/300 2dr GTO Cpe	$16,200	$24,700	$51,200	$69,800
						+10% for factory a/c. -10% for auto.
1972	Grand Prix	400/250 2dr Model J Hdtp Cpe	$9,800	$14,600	$23,700	$33,000
		455/250 2dr Model SJ Hdtp Cpe	$10,500	$17,600	$29,500	$39,200
1973	Firebird	350/175 2dr Hdtp Cpe	$5,800	$9,400	$16,900	$24,200
		350/150 2dr Esprit Hdtp Cpe	$6,000	$9,400	$18,100	$24,600
		350/175 2dr Formula 350 Hdtp Cpe	$7,000	$11,900	$21,500	$29,600
		400/230 2dr Formula 400 Hdtp Cpe	$7,900	$14,300	$26,800	$39,500
		455/310 2dr Formula 455 Hdtp Cpe	$64,000	$95,300	$122,000	$150,000
		455/250 2dr Trans Am Hdtp Cpe	$10,600	$20,500	$39,800	$55,100
		455/310 2dr Trans Am Hdtp Cpe	$97,700	$117,000	$159,000	$196,000
						-20% for auto trans. -30% for 6-cyl.
1973	LeMans	400/170 2dr Hdtp	$3,600	$6,100	$9,900	$15,600
		400/230 2dr GTO Hdtp	$6,300	$9,600	$15,100	$22,400
						+10% for factory a/c. -10% for auto.

Year	Model	Body Style	4	3	2	1
1973	Grand Am	400/170 2dr Hdtp	$5,100	$10,400	$16,900	$24,300
1973	Grand Ville	455/215 2dr Conv	$5,500	$9,500	$17,500	$26,800
1973	Grand Prix	455/250 2dr Hdtp Cpe	$5,100	$8,800	$15,700	$23,600
						-30% for 6-cyl.
1974	Ventura	350/200 2dr GTO Cpe	$6,300	$12,200	$20,200	$27,800
		350/200 2dr GTO Htchbk Cpe	$6,700	$13,500	$21,400	$29,200
						+10% for factory a/c. -10% for auto.
1974	Firebird	350/155 2dr Hdtp Cpe	$5,600	$8,700	$15,700	$23,400
		350/155 2dr Esprit Hdtp Cpe	$5,900	$9,200	$17,600	$23,800
		350/155 2dr Formula 350 Hdtp Cpe	$6,000	$12,300	$21,700	$29,400
		400/175 2dr Formula 400 Hdtp Cpe	$6,400	$12,900	$23,300	$31,400
		400/190 2dr Formula 400 Hdtp Cpe	$6,600	$13,500	$23,700	$32,400
		400/225 2dr Formula 400 Hdtp Cpe	$6,900	$13,900	$25,000	$33,800
		455/290 2dr Formula 455 Hdtp Cpe	$23,400	$37,000	$64,400	$81,200
		400/225 2dr Trans Am Hdtp Cpe	$9,300	$16,400	$30,800	$43,400
		455/250 2dr Trans Am Hdtp Cpe	$10,500	$18,300	$31,800	$47,800
		455/290 2dr Trans Am Hdtp Cpe	$47,100	$65,100	$82,400	$99,100
						-20% for auto trans. -30% for 6-cyl.
1974	LeMans	350/155 2dr Hdtp Cpe	$3,300	$5,800	$9,700	$15,000
1974	Grand Am	400/190 2dr Hdtp Cpe	$5,300	$10,400	$16,800	$23,900
1974	Grand Ville	455/215 2dr Conv	$5,700	$9,700	$17,700	$27,100
1974	Grand Prix	400/225 2dr Hdtp Cpe	$5,100	$8,800	$15,700	$23,600
1975	Firebird	350/155 2dr Hdtp Cpe	$4,400	$6,900	$12,700	$19,300
		350/155 2dr Esprit Hdtp Cpe	$5,300	$8,800	$13,900	$20,100

Pontiac

Year	Model	Body Style	4	3	2	1
		350/175 2dr Formula Hdtp Cpe	$6,200	$11,800	$19,800	$29,100
		400/185 2dr Trans Am Hdtp Cpe	$9,100	$17,300	$33,400	$48,300
		455/200 2dr Trans Am Hdtp Cpe	$11,000	$18,000	$34,300	$50,900
						-30% for 6-cyl.
1975	LeMans	400/185 2dr Colonnade Hdtp Cpe	$3,400	$5,900	$9,600	$15,300
1975	Grand Am	400/170 2dr Colonnade Hdtp Cpe	$5,300	$10,400	$16,800	$23,900
1975	Grand Ville	400/185 2dr Brghm Conv	$5,900	$9,900	$17,700	$30,400
1975	Grand Prix	400/185 2dr Hdtp Cpe	$4,900	$8,200	$15,300	$22,700
1976	LeMans	400/185 2dr Hdtp Cpe	$3,400	$5,900	$9,600	$15,300
1976	Firebird	350/160 2dr Hdtp Cpe	$4,400	$7,400	$12,800	$20,300
		350/160 2dr Esprit Hdtp Cpe	$5,300	$9,700	$14,400	$21,100
		350/160 2dr Formula 350 Hdtp Cpe	$6,100	$12,200	$20,600	$30,600
		400/185 2dr Formula 400 Hdtp Cpe	$7,500	$13,700	$25,300	$36,500
		400/185 2dr Trans Am Hdtp Cpe	$10,900	$20,800	$39,100	$55,200
		455/200 2dr Trans Am Hdtp Cpe	$12,000	$22,000	$40,200	$60,000
		400/185 2dr Trans Am Limited Ed Hdtp Cpe	$16,300	$27,300	$47,500	$73,200
		455/200 2dr Trans Am Limited Edition Hdtp Cpe	$17,900	$30,000	$52,300	$80,500
						-30% for 6-cyl.
1976	Grand Prix	400/185 2dr Hdtp Cpe	$4,300	$7,200	$14,000	$20,900
1977	LeMans	400/200 2dr Can Am Cpe	$6,800	$12,400	$21,100	$31,200
		403/185 2dr Can Am Cpe	$6,400	$11,200	$19,000	$28,100
1977	Firebird	305/145 2dr Hdtp Cpe	$4,200	$7,200	$13,200	$18,900
		350/170 2dr Hdtp Cpe	$4,300	$7,400	$13,600	$19,500

Year	Model	Body Style	4	3	2	1
		400/180 2dr Hdtp Cpe	$4,400	$7,500	$13,600	$20,900
		350/170 2dr Esprit Hdtp Cpe	$4,700	$9,100	$14,900	$23,100
		400/180 2dr Esprit Hdtp Cpe	$4,500	$7,900	$14,000	$21,200
		400/180 2dr Formula Hdtp Cpe	$7,700	$13,900	$22,200	$29,500
		400/200 2dr Trans Am Hdtp Cpe	$12,300	$19,300	$35,800	$47,700
		403/185 2dr Trans Am Hdtp Cpe	$10,400	$16,400	$30,500	$40,500
		400/200 2dr Trans Am Special Ed Y81 Hdtp Cpe	$18,100	$32,400	$50,100	$68,900
		400/200 2dr Trans Am Special Ed Y82 Hdtp Cpe	$20,100	$36,000	$54,600	$76,600
						-30% for 6-cyl.
1977	Grand Prix	350/170 2dr Cpe	$4,200	$6,900	$13,700	$19,400
1978	Firebird	305/145 2dr Hdtp Cpe	$4,100	$7,100	$12,900	$18,900
		350/160 2dr Hdtp Cpe	$4,200	$7,300	$13,200	$19,700
		350/170 2dr Hdtp Cpe	$4,300	$7,500	$13,600	$20,300
		350/170 2dr Esprit Hdtp Cpe	$4,700	$9,100	$14,500	$23,100
		400/180 2dr Formula Hdtp Cpe	$7,700	$14,000	$22,200	$29,500
		400/220 2dr Trans Am Hdtp Cpe	$11,800	$19,300	$35,800	$46,900
		403/185 2dr Trans Am Hdtp Cpe	$10,000	$16,400	$30,500	$39,900
		400/220 2dr Trans Am Special Ed Hdtp Cpe	$34,200	$49,900	$59,200	$72,900
						+15% 4-spd. -30% for 6-cyl.
1979	Firebird	350/170 2dr Hdtp Cpe	$4,800	$8,100	$14,400	$22,100
		301/135 2dr Esprit Hdtp Cpe	$3,700	$6,000	$12,400	$18,400
		301/150 2dr Esprit Hdtp Cpe	$4,100	$6,600	$13,600	$20,200
		350/165 2dr Esprit Hdtp Cpe	$5,300	$10,000	$15,200	$24,300
		301/150 2dr Esprit Red Bird Hdtp Cpe	$4,400	$6,800	$14,500	$21,400

Pontiac

Year	Model	Body Style	4	3	2	1
		350/170 2dr Formula Hdtp Cpe	$8,000	$14,000	$23,000	$31,300
		400/220 2dr Formula Hdtp Cpe	$14,500	$24,200	$43,600	$59,600
		301/150 2dr Trans Am Hdtp Cpe	$12,000	$19,500	$37,200	$54,600
		403/185 2dr Trans Am Hdtp Cpe	$12,700	$21,200	$38,200	$52,200
		400/220 2dr Trans Am Hdtp Cpe	$14,900	$22,500	$44,900	$61,400
		403/185 2dr 10th Annv Trans Am Hdtp Cpe	$16,000	$24,000	$44,700	$63,300
		400/220 2dr 10th Annv Trans Am Hdtp Cpe	$21,200	$33,600	$53,700	$75,900
		403/185 2dr Trans Am Special Ed Y84 Hdtp Cpe	$21,100	$29,400	$45,000	$60,700
		400/220 2dr Trans Am Special Ed Y84 Hdtp Cpe	$24,000	$32,000	$56,300	$75,800

-30% for 6-cyl.

Year	Model	Body Style	4	3	2	1
1980	Firebird	265/120 2dr Cpe	$5,300	$7,900	$12,700	$17,700
		265/120 2dr Esprit Cpe	$5,900	$8,700	$14,000	$20,200
		301/140 2dr Formula Cpe	$5,700	$8,700	$14,000	$20,100
		301/210 2dr Formula Cpe	$6,600	$11,300	$19,200	$25,800
		301/140 2dr Trans Am Cpe	$9,500	$16,000	$24,800	$40,800
		301/210 2dr Trans Am Cpe	$11,600	$19,600	$31,100	$49,400
		301/210 2dr Trans Am Daytona Pace Car Cpe	$12,300	$22,300	$36,400	$48,300
		301/210 2dr Trans Am Indy Pace Car Cpe	$12,300	$22,300	$36,400	$48,300
		301/210 2dr Trans Am Special Ed Y84 Cpe	$13,900	$22,100	$33,100	$48,100

-10% for 6-cyl. -15% for auto. +10% for Special Edition. +10% for T-tops. +11% for Red Bird. +7% for Yellow Bird. -10% for 305/145 V8 on Trans Am.

Year	Model	Body Style	4	3	2	1
1981	Firebird	265/120 2dr Cpe	$5,200	$7,400	$10,600	$17,100
		265/120 2dr Esprit Cpe	$5,400	$7,600	$11,100	$17,700
		265/120 2dr Formula Cpe	$6,000	$9,200	$16,800	$22,800

Year	Model	Body Style	4	3	2	1
		301/200 2dr Formula Turbo Cpe	$6,500	$10,900	$18,800	$25,700
		301/135 2dr Trans Am Cpe	$7,500	$13,600	$24,800	$38,200
		301/200 2dr Trans Am Daytona Pace Car Cpe	$10,900	$17,400	$34,800	$48,800
		301/200 2dr Trans Am Turbo Cpe	$9,500	$16,100	$28,100	$46,600
		-10% for 6-cyl. +10% for Special Edition. -10% for 305/145 V8 on Trans Am. +10% for T-tops. -15% for auto.				
1982	Firebird	305/145 2dr Cpe	$3,000	$4,000	$6,300	$10,600
		305/145 2dr S/E Cpe	$3,300	$4,600	$7,300	$11,900
		305/145 2dr Trans Am Cpe	$4,900	$7,200	$12,900	$19,100
		305/165 2dr Trans Am Cpe	$5,300	$8,100	$13,200	$20,400
		-10% for 6-cyl. -20% for 4-cyl. +10% for Recaro Pkg. +10% for T-tops. -15% for auto.				
1983	Firebird	305/150 2dr Cpe	$3,000	$4,000	$6,300	$10,600
		305/150 2dr S/E Cpe	$3,000	$4,400	$6,900	$11,300
		305/150 2dr Trans Am Cpe	$4,800	$6,900	$12,600	$18,800
		305/175 2dr Trans Am Cpe	$5,100	$8,000	$13,000	$19,900
		305/150 2dr Trans Am Daytona Pace Car Cpe	$5,900	$8,500	$13,400	$22,500
		305/175 2dr Trans Am Daytona Pace Car Cpe	$7,400	$9,700	$15,100	$24,000
		-10% for 6-cyl. -20% for 4-cyl. +10% for Recaro Pkg. +10% for T-tops. -15% for auto (exc Daytona LU5).				
1984	Fiero	151/92 2dr Cpe	$1,600	$3,000	$5,400	$7,900
		151/92 2dr SE Cpe	$1,900	$3,700	$6,700	$9,000
		151/92 2dr Indy Pace Car Cpe	$4,000	$6,400	$9,600	$13,800
1984	Firebird	305/150 2dr Cpe	$2,600	$3,700	$6,500	$11,000
		305/150 2dr S/E Cpe	$2,800	$4,400	$7,600	$12,300
		305/150 2dr Trans Am Cpe	$5,000	$7,200	$14,100	$21,100
		305/190 HO 2dr Trans Am Cpe	$5,500	$8,600	$14,600	$22,700
		-10% for 6-cyl. -20% for 4-cyl. +10% for Recaro Pkg. +10% for T-tops. +5% for Aero Pkg. -15% for auto.				
1985	Fiero	151/92 2dr Cpe	$1,600	$3,400	$5,700	$8,000
		151/92 2dr SE Cpe	$2,200	$4,500	$6,900	$9,500

Pontiac

Year	Model	Body Style	4	3	2	1
		173/130 FI 2dr GT Cpe	$2,700	$5,800	$8,400	$14,900
						-$1,000 for auto.
1985	Firebird	305/165 2dr Cpe	$2,800	$4,200	$6,700	$11,100
		305/165 2dr S/E Cpe	$3,300	$4,600	$7,900	$12,900
		305/190 HO 2dr Trans Am Cpe	$5,600	$8,800	$15,800	$22,900
		305/205 FI 2dr Trans Am Cpe	$6,100	$9,300	$15,900	$23,300
						-10% for 6-cyl. -20% for 4-cyl. +10% for Recaro Pkg. +10% for T-tops. +5% for Aero Pkg. -15% for auto.
1986	Fiero	151/92 2dr Cpe	$1,700	$3,500	$5,800	$8,300
		173/125 FI 2dr GT Cpe	$2,900	$5,900	$9,200	$15,100
		151/92 2dr SE Cpe	$2,400	$4,600	$7,000	$9,600
						-$1,000 for auto.
1986	Firebird	305/150 2dr Cpe	$3,000	$4,300	$6,800	$11,300
		305/150 2dr S/E Cpe	$3,500	$4,600	$8,200	$13,200
		305/205 FI 2dr Trans Am Cpe	$6,000	$9,300	$15,900	$26,500
						-10% for 6-cyl. -20% for 4-cyl. +10% for T-tops. -15% for auto.
1987	Fiero	151/98 2dr Cpe	$1,800	$3,600	$5,900	$8,500
		151/98 2dr SE Cpe	$2,400	$4,600	$7,200	$9,700
		173/125 2dr GT Cpe	$4,100	$6,000	$10,500	$16,400
						-$1,000 for auto.
1987	Firebird	2dr Formula Cpe	$5,500	$8,200	$13,500	$19,800
		350/210 FI 2dr Trans Am GTA Cpe	$6,800	$10,000	$17,800	$28,900
		305/165 FI 2dr Cpe	$2,600	$4,000	$6,400	$11,100
		305/165 FI 2dr Trans Am Cpe	$5,600	$8,400	$12,800	$22,300
						-10% for 6-cyl. -20% for 4-cyl. +10% for T-tops. -15% for auto.
1988	Fiero	151/98 2dr Cpe	$2,200	$3,700	$6,300	$8,700
		173/135 2dr Formula Cpe	$3,900	$6,400	$10,300	$17,000
		173/135 2dr GT Cpe	$4,800	$7,800	$12,700	$19,600
						-$1,000 for auto.
1988	Firebird	350/225 2dr Trans Am GTA Cpe	$7,200	$10,300	$17,000	$30,000
		305/170 FI 2dr Cpe	$3,500	$5,200	$7,200	$11,600
		305/215 2dr Formula Cpe	$5,500	$8,200	$13,500	$20,100

Year	Model	Body Style	4	3	2	1
		350/225 2dr Formula Cpe	$6,200	$9,300	$14,900	$22,600
		305/190 2dr Trans Am Cpe	$5,800	$8,800	$14,400	$27,000
			-10% for 6-cyl. +10% for T-tops. -15% for auto.			
1989	Firebird	305/225 FI 2dr Formula Cpe	$6,200	$9,400	$15,000	$22,600
		305/225 FI 2dr Trans Am Cpe	$7,200	$10,700	$16,200	$29,000
		350/235 FI 2dr Trans Am GTA Ntchbk Cpe	$11,200	$13,500	$21,700	$35,900
		350/235 FI 2dr Trans Am GTA Cpe	$9,600	$11,900	$18,600	$32,200
		231/250 2dr 20th Annv Trans Am GTA Indy Pace Car Cpe	$16,900	$25,300	$38,500	$48,900
			-10% for 6-cyl (exc Pace Car). -10% for 305/190 V8 on GTA. +10% for T-tops. -15% for auto.			
1990	Firebird	305/225 FI 2dr Formula Cpe	$6,700	$9,800	$14,900	$22,700
		305/170 2dr Trans Am Cpe	$6,900	$9,900	$16,100	$28,900
		305/225 FI 2dr Trans Am Cpe	$7,400	$11,300	$16,600	$29,800
		305/225 FI 2dr Trans Am GTA Cpe	$10,400	$13,000	$18,900	$32,400
		350/235 2dr Trans Am GTA Cpe	$10,800	$13,700	$19,500	$33,100
			-10% for 6-cyl. +10% for T-tops. -10% for auto (exc GTA).			
1991	Firebird	305/170 2dr Formula Cpe	$5,400	$8,600	$12,000	$18,000
		305/225 FI 2dr Formula Cpe	$7,000	$9,900	$14,600	$21,600
		305/225 FI 2dr Trans Am Cpe	$7,300	$10,800	$16,700	$28,900
		350/240 2dr Trans Am Cpe	$8,700	$12,100	$17,600	$30,700
		350/240 2dr Trans Am GTA Cpe	$10,000	$13,500	$19,800	$33,400
		350/350 2dr SLP Firehawk Cpe	$36,000	$50,000	$61,000	$97,500
		305/170 2dr Conv	$5,400	$7,200	$11,400	$13,400
		305/225 FI 2dr Formula Conv	$8,100	$11,100	$17,500	$23,200

Pontiac

Year	Model	Body Style	4	3	2	1
		350/240 2dr Formula Conv	$8,600	$12,100	$18,500	$25,200
		305/170 2dr Trans Am Conv	$9,100	$12,500	$19,400	$30,700
		305/225 FI 2dr Trans Am Conv	$9,200	$13,100	$20,400	$32,000
		350/240 2dr Trans Am Conv	$9,900	$14,300	$22,100	$34,200
		-10% for 6-cyl. +10% for T-tops. -10% for 305/225 V8 on GTA. -15% for auto.				
1992	Firebird	305/170 2dr Cpe	$3,800	$5,600	$7,800	$11,700
		305/170 2dr Formula Cpe	$5,600	$9,200	$12,200	$18,700
		305/225 FI 2dr Formula Cpe	$7,200	$10,400	$14,900	$21,800
		350/240 2dr Formula Cpe	$7,500	$11,100	$16,400	$23,100
		350/240 2dr Trans Am Cpe	$8,400	$12,100	$17,700	$30,700
		350/240 2dr Trans Am GTA Cpe	$10,500	$13,500	$20,500	$35,100
		350/350 2dr SLP Firehawk Cpe	$36,000	$50,000	$61,000	$97,500
		305/170 2dr Conv	$5,500	$7,800	$11,600	$13,600
		305/225 FI 2dr Formula Conv	$8,700	$12,100	$19,300	$25,800
		350/240 2dr Formula Conv	$9,500	$13,200	$20,400	$27,100
		305/225 FI 2dr Trans Am Conv	$9,200	$13,100	$19,600	$31,800
		350/240 2dr Trans Am Conv	$9,900	$14,900	$22,400	$35,200
		-10% for 6-cyl. +10% for T-tops. -10% for 305/205 V8 on GTA.				
1993	Firebird	207/160 2dr Cpe	$2,600	$3,600	$4,900	$9,500
		350/270 2dr Formula Cpe	$4,600	$6,700	$9,600	$16,200
		350/270 2dr Trans Am Cpe	$4,800	$7,200	$10,400	$17,900
		350/300 2dr SLP Firehawk Cpe	$11,700	$17,600	$22,000	$32,400
		-10% for auto trans.				
1994	Firebird	207/160 2dr Cpe	$2,600	$3,600	$4,900	$9,500
		207/160 2dr Conv	$4,900	$7,900	$10,600	$13,900
		350/275 2dr Formula Cpe	$4,600	$6,700	$9,600	$16,200
		350/275 2dr Formula Conv	$7,800	$10,600	$12,800	$19,100
		350/275 2dr Trans Am Cpe	$5,000	$7,500	$10,700	$17,900
		350/275 2dr Trans Am Conv	$8,600	$11,700	$14,200	$21,100

Year	Model	Body Style	4	3	2	1
		350/275 2dr Trans Am GT Cpe	$5,300	$7,900	$11,200	$18,700
		350/275 2dr Trans Am GT Conv	$9,000	$12,300	$14,900	$22,200
		350/275 2dr Trans Am 25th Annv Cpe	$9,300	$13,700	$18,500	$28,900
		350/275 2dr Trans Am 25th Annv Conv	$10,300	$15,400	$26,000	$33,000
		350/300 2dr SLP Firehawk Cpe	$11,700	$17,600	$22,000	$32,400
						-10% for auto trans.
1995	Firebird	231/200 2dr Cpe	$2,700	$3,900	$5,100	$8,500
		231/200 2dr Conv	$4,900	$7,200	$9,900	$12,500
		350/275 2dr Formula Cpe	$4,700	$6,400	$9,000	$16,100
		350/275 2dr Formula Conv	$8,800	$10,400	$13,100	$19,700
		350/275 2dr Trans Am Cpe	$5,100	$7,000	$10,000	$17,700
		350/275 2dr Trans Am Conv	$9,800	$11,400	$14,500	$21,700
		350/300 2dr SLP Firehawk Cpe	$11,700	$17,600	$22,000	$32,400
		350/300 2dr SLP Firehawk Conv	$15,100	$20,000	$24,100	$35,600
		350/300 2dr SLP Firehawk Comp T/A Cpe	$14,700	$22,800	$27,700	$36,400
						-10% for auto trans.
1996	Firebird	231/200 2dr Cpe	$2,700	$3,900	$5,100	$8,500
		231/200 2dr Conv	$4,900	$7,200	$9,900	$12,500
		350/285 2dr Formula Cpe	$6,500	$8,300	$11,200	$18,000
		350/285 2dr Formula Conv	$8,800	$10,600	$12,800	$19,100
		350/285 2dr Trans Am Cpe	$6,800	$8,700	$11,800	$18,900
		350/285 2dr Trans Am Conv	$9,300	$11,100	$13,500	$20,100
		350/305 2dr Formula WS6 Cpe	$9,100	$12,000	$17,800	$26,600
		350/305 2dr Trans Am WS6 Cpe	$9,500	$12,600	$18,800	$28,000
		350/310 2dr SLP Firehawk Cpe	$11,700	$17,600	$22,000	$32,400
		350/310 2dr SLP Firehawk Conv	$15,100	$20,000	$24,100	$35,600

Pontiac

Year	Model	Body Style	4	3	2	1
		350/310 2dr SLP Firehawk Comp T/A Cpe	$14,700	$22,800	$27,700	$36,400
						-10% for auto trans.
1997	Firebird	231/200 2dr Cpe	$3,600	$5,400	$7,400	$12,000
		231/200 2dr Conv	$6,400	$8,900	$11,400	$15,400
		350/285 2dr Formula Cpe	$6,500	$8,300	$11,200	$18,000
		350/285 2dr Formula Conv	$10,200	$12,400	$14,900	$21,100
		350/285 2dr Trans Am Cpe	$6,800	$8,700	$11,800	$18,900
		350/285 2dr Trans Am Conv	$10,700	$13,000	$15,700	$22,200
		350/305 2dr Formula WS6 Cpe	$9,100	$12,000	$17,800	$26,600
		350/305 2dr Formula WS6 Conv	$9,600	$12,300	$20,000	$29,300
		350/305 2dr Trans Am WS6 Cpe	$9,500	$12,600	$18,800	$28,000
		350/305 2dr Trans Am WS6 Conv	$10,100	$12,900	$21,000	$30,800
		350/310 2dr SLP Firehawk Cpe	$11,700	$17,600	$22,000	$32,400
		350/310 2dr SLP Firehawk Conv	$15,100	$20,000	$24,100	$35,600
		350/310 2dr SLP Firehawk Comp T/A Cpe	$14,700	$22,800	$27,700	$36,400
		350/330 2dr SLP Firehawk LT4 Cpe	$21,200	$33,000	$42,000	$58,900
						-10% for auto trans.
1998	Firebird	231/200 2dr Cpe	$5,600	$7,400	$9,000	$12,100
		231/200 2dr Conv	$6,800	$8,800	$10,900	$14,000
		346/305 2dr Formula Cpe	$7,600	$11,300	$16,900	$23,800
		346/305 2dr Trans Am Cpe	$7,600	$11,300	$16,900	$23,800
		346/305 2dr Trans Am Conv	$12,600	$17,300	$22,500	$26,700
		346/320 2dr Formula WS6 Cpe	$8,900	$13,100	$20,000	$28,700
		346/320 2dr Trans Am WS6 Cpe	$8,900	$13,100	$20,000	$28,700
		346/320 2dr Trans Am WS6 Conv	$14,500	$20,100	$26,700	$32,200
						-10% for auto trans.

Year	Model	Body Style	4	3	2	1
1999	Firebird	231/200 2dr Cpe	$6,300	$7,900	$9,700	$12,800
		231/200 2dr Conv	$7,400	$9,700	$11,700	$15,000
		346/305 2dr Formula Cpe	$7,600	$11,300	$16,900	$23,800
		346/305 2dr Trans Am Cpe	$7,800	$11,500	$17,200	$24,300
		346/305 2dr Trans Am Conv	$12,900	$17,600	$22,900	$27,200
		346/320 2dr Formula WS6 Cpe	$9,300	$13,700	$21,000	$31,000
		346/320 2dr Trans Am WS6 Cpe	$9,300	$13,700	$21,000	$31,000
		346/320 2dr Trans Am WS6 Conv	$15,200	$21,100	$28,000	$33,800
		346/320 2dr Trans Am 30th Annv Cpe	$15,900	$21,800	$28,500	$37,700
		346/320 2dr Trans Am 30th Annv Conv	$19,100	$26,200	$34,600	$45,500
		346/327 2dr Formula SLP Firehawk Cpe	$12,100	$16,800	$29,100	$37,500
		346/327 2dr Trans Am SLP Firehawk Cpe	$12,100	$16,800	$29,100	$37,500
		346/327 2dr Trans Am SLP Firehawk Conv	$17,300	$23,200	$32,700	$41,900
			-10% for auto trans. +10% without T-Top for Firehawk.			
2000	Firebird	231/200 2dr Cpe	$6,600	$8,800	$10,900	$13,600
		231/200 2dr Conv	$9,600	$10,400	$12,400	$16,300
		346/305 2dr Formula Cpe	$7,600	$11,300	$16,900	$23,800
		346/305 2dr Trans Am Cpe	$7,800	$11,500	$17,200	$24,300
		346/305 2dr Trans Am Conv	$12,900	$17,600	$22,900	$27,200
		346/320 2dr Formula WS6 Cpe	$9,300	$13,700	$21,000	$31,000
		346/320 2dr Trans Am WS6 Cpe	$9,300	$13,700	$21,000	$31,000
		346/320 2dr Trans Am WS6 Conv	$15,200	$21,100	$28,000	$33,800
		346/330 2dr Formula SLP Firehawk Cpe	$12,100	$16,800	$29,100	$37,500

Pontiac

Year	Model	Body Style	4	3	2	1
		346/330 2dr Trans Am SLP Firehawk Cpe	$12,100	$16,800	$29,100	$37,500
		346/330 2dr Trans Am SLP Firehawk Conv	$17,300	$23,200	$32,700	$41,900
		-10% for auto trans. +10% without T-Top for Firehawk.				
2001	Firebird	231/200 2dr Cpe	$6,900	$9,400	$11,400	$14,400
		-10% for auto trans. +10% without T-Top for Firehawk.				
		231/200 2dr Conv	$9,900	$10,900	$13,600	$18,500
		346/310 2dr Formula Cpe	$7,600	$11,300	$16,900	$23,800
		346/310 2dr Trans Am Cpe	$7,300	$10,800	$16,100	$22,800
		346/310 2dr Trans Am Conv	$12,100	$16,500	$21,600	$25,500
		346/325 2dr Trans Am WS6 Cpe	$9,300	$13,700	$21,000	$31,000
		346/325 2dr Trans Am WS6 Conv	$15,200	$21,100	$28,000	$33,800
		346/345 2dr Formula SLP Firehawk Cpe	$12,100	$16,800	$29,100	$37,500
		346/345 2dr Trans Am SLP Firehawk Cpe	$12,100	$16,800	$29,100	$37,500
		346/345 2dr Trans Am SLP Firehawk Conv	$17,300	$23,200	$32,700	$41,900
		-10% for auto trans. +10% without T-Top for Firehawk.				
2002	Firebird	231/200 2dr Cpe	$6,900	$9,400	$11,400	$14,400
		231/200 2dr Conv	$9,900	$10,900	$13,600	$18,500
		346/310 2dr Formula Cpe	$7,600	$11,300	$16,900	$23,800
		346/310 2dr Trans Am Cpe	$7,800	$11,500	$17,200	$24,300
		346/310 2dr Trans Am Conv	$12,900	$17,600	$22,900	$27,200
		346/325 2dr Trans Am WS6 Cpe	$9,300	$13,700	$21,000	$31,000
		346/325 2dr Trans Am WS6 Conv	$15,200	$21,100	$28,000	$33,800
		346/325 2dr Trans Am Collector Ed Cpe	$11,000	$17,500	$27,100	$35,000
		346/325 2dr Trans Am Collector Ed Conv	$13,800	$19,100	$29,400	$38,000
		346/345 2dr Formula SLP Firehawk Cpe	$12,100	$16,800	$29,100	$37,500

Year	Model	Body Style	4	3	2	1
		346/345 2dr Trans Am SLP Firehawk Cpe	$12,100	$16,800	$29,100	$37,500
		346/345 2dr Trans Am SLP Firehawk Conv	$17,300	$23,200	$32,700	$41,900
		-10% for auto trans. +10% without T-Top for Firehawk.				
2004	GTO	346/350 2dr Cpe	$10,900	$15,100	$19,500	$29,900
		-15% for auto trans.				
2005	GTO	364/400 2dr Cpe	$12,500	$18,900	$24,800	$34,700
		-15% for auto trans.				
2006	GTO	364/400 2dr Cpe	$12,500	$18,900	$24,800	$34,700
		-15% for auto trans.				
2006	Solstice	145/177 2dr Conv	$5,000	$7,900	$13,600	$20,000
		+$1,500 for hardtop with convertible. -15% for auto trans on GXP.				
2007	Solstice	145/177 2dr Conv	$5,100	$8,100	$14,000	$20,500
		122/260 2dr GXP Conv	$7,000	$11,000	$16,500	$27,000
		+$1,500 for hardtop with convertible. -15% for auto trans on GXP.				
2008	G8	364/361 4dr GT Sdn	$12,900	$17,400	$22,100	$28,700
2008	Solstice	145/172 2dr Conv	$5,100	$8,100	$14,000	$20,500
		122/260 2dr GXP Conv	$7,000	$11,000	$16,500	$27,000
		+$1,500 for hardtop with convertible. -15% for auto trans on GXP.				
2009	G8	364/361 4dr GT Sdn	$12,900	$17,400	$22,100	$28,700
		364/500 4dr GT SLP Firehawk SC Sdn	$31,500	$38,100	$47,800	$58,900
		376/415 4dr GXP Sdn	$22,800	$28,900	$34,500	$46,700
		376/500 4dr GXP SLP Firehawk SC Sdn	$31,500	$38,100	$47,800	$58,900
		+15% for 6-speed manual trans.				
2009	Solstice	145/172 2dr Conv	$5,100	$8,100	$14,000	$20,500
		145/172 2dr Street Edition Conv	$6,100	$8,700	$14,300	$21,500
		122/260 2dr GXP Conv	$7,000	$11,000	$16,500	$27,000
		145/172 2dr Cpe	$10,000	$13,500	$18,000	$25,500
		122/260 2dr GXP Cpe	$15,000	$23,700	$37,100	$44,900
		+$1,500 for hardtop with convertible. -15% for auto trans on GXP.				
2010	Solstice	145/172 2dr Conv	$5,700	$8,800	$15,300	$22,600
		122/260 2dr GXP Conv	$7,700	$12,100	$18,200	$29,700
		145/172 2dr Cpe	$11,000	$14,900	$19,800	$28,100

Pontiac

Year	Model	Body Style	4	3	2	1
		122/260 2dr GXP Cpe	$20,000	$30,900	$48,400	$58,100

+$1,500 for hardtop with convertible, -15% for auto trans on GXP.

Porsche

Year	Model	Body Style	4	3	2	1
1948	356	2dr Gmund Cpe	$800,000	$1 mil	$1.75 mil	$2.5 mil
		Equipment and history can make a tremendous difference in value on Gmund coupes.				
1949	356	2dr Gmund Cpe	$800,000	$1 mil	$1.75 mil	$2.5 mil
		Equipment and history can make a tremendous difference in value on Gmund coupes.				
1950	356	2dr Gmund Cpe	$800,000	$1 mil	$2 mil	$2.5 mil
		Equipment and history can make a tremendous difference in value on Gmund coupes.				
1951	356	2dr Cpe	$157,000	$240,000	$402,000	$629,000
		2dr 1500S Cpe	$167,000	$260,000	$440,000	$775,000
		2dr Cab	$160,000	$244,000	$418,000	$693,000
		2dr 1500S Cab	$175,000	$295,000	$515,000	$810,000
		+20% for 5-digit s/n.				
1952	356	2dr 1100 Cpe	$57,000	$77,000	$115,000	$192,000
		2dr 1500 Cpe	$90,000	$143,000	$248,000	$379,000
		2dr 1100 Cab	$101,000	$146,000	$242,000	$338,000
		2dr 1500 Cab	$127,000	$205,000	$302,000	$455,000
1953	356	2dr Cpe	$56,000	$76,000	$114,000	$184,000
		2dr 1500S Cpe	$80,000	$121,000	$205,000	$308,000
		2dr Cab	$100,000	$146,000	$237,000	$359,000
		2dr 1500S Cab	$117,000	$190,000	$251,000	$403,000
1954	356	2dr 1500 Cpe	$46,000	$59,300	$95,500	$173,000
		2dr 1500 Super Cpe	$64,300	$102,000	$151,000	$210,000
		2dr 1500 Cab	$57,000	$109,000	$175,000	$250,000
		2dr 1500 Super Cab	$94,800	$187,000	$250,000	$327,000
		2dr 1500 Spdstr	$201,000	$287,000	$384,000	$480,000
		2dr 1500 Super Spdstr	$242,000	$320,000	$452,000	$595,000
1955	356	2dr Cpe	$45,100	$58,500	$94,000	$170,000
		2dr 1500 Super Cpe	$64,300	$102,000	$151,000	$210,000
		2dr Cab	$56,700	$109,000	$171,000	$250,000
		2dr 1500 Super Cab	$95,000	$187,000	$251,000	$329,000
		2dr Spdstr	$201,000	$287,000	$383,000	$479,000
		2dr 1500 Super Spdstr	$242,000	$320,000	$450,000	$593,000
		2dr Carrera Spdstr	$900,000	$1 mil	$1.2 mil	$1.5 mil
1956	356A	2dr Cpe	$54,000	$80,000	$112,000	$168,000

Year	Model	Body Style	4	3	2	1
		2dr 1600 Super Cpe	$81,500	$119,000	$184,000	$252,000
		2dr 1500 GS Carrera Cpe	$299,000	$420,000	$615,000	$795,000
		2dr 1500 GS/GT Carrera Cpe	$399,000	$530,000	$720,000	$899,000
		2dr Cab	$72,800	$124,000	$179,000	$221,000
		2dr 1600 Super Cab	$110,000	$168,000	$225,000	$281,000
		2dr 1500 GS Carrera Cab	$579,000	$690,000	$805,000	$915,000
		2dr Spdstr	$212,000	$272,000	$370,000	$445,000
		2dr 1500 GS Carrera Spdstr	$900,000	$1 mil	$1.2 mil	$1.5 mil
		2dr 1500 GS/GT Carrera Spdstr	$1 mil	$1.2 mil	$1.5 mil	$1.85 mil
1957	356A	2dr Cpe	$54,000	$80,000	$112,000	$168,000
		2dr 1600 Super Cpe	$78,300	$117,000	$170,000	$222,000
		2dr 1500 GS Carrera Cpe	$299,000	$420,000	$615,000	$795,000
		2dr 1500 GS/GT Carrera Cpe	$399,000	$530,000	$720,000	$899,000
		2dr Cab	$81,500	$119,000	$185,000	$235,000
		2dr 1600 Super Cab	$110,000	$168,000	$225,000	$281,000
		2dr 1500 GS Carrera Cab	$810,000	$920,000	$1 mil	$1.2 mil
		2dr Spdstr	$212,000	$272,000	$370,000	$445,000
		2dr 1600 Super Spdstr	$228,000	$305,000	$415,000	$538,000
		2dr 1500 GS Carrera Spdstr	$1 mil	$1.2 mil	$1.3 mil	$1.65 mil
		2dr 1500 GS/GT Carrera Spdstr	$1 mil	$1.2 mil	$1.5 mil	$1.85 mil
1958	356A	2dr Cpe	$54,000	$80,000	$112,000	$168,000
		2dr 1600 Super Cpe	$78,300	$124,000	$180,000	$221,000
		2dr Carrera GS Cpe	$299,000	$420,000	$615,000	$795,000
		2dr GS/GT Carrera Cpe	$810,000	$979,000	$1.15 mil	$1.45 mil
		2dr Cab	$81,500	$119,000	$185,000	$252,000
		2dr 1600 Super Cab	$110,000	$168,000	$225,000	$281,000
		2dr Carrera GS Cab	$599,000	$821,000	$915,000	$1 mil
		2dr Spdstr	$212,000	$272,000	$370,000	$445,000
		2dr 1600 Super Spdstr	$228,000	$305,000	$415,000	$538,000

Porsche

Year	Model	Body Style	4	3	2	1
		2dr Carrera GS Spdstr	$900,000	$1 mil	$1.2 mil	$1.5 mil
		2dr GS/GT Carrera Spdstr	$810,000	$1.3 mil	$1.6 mil	$1.9 mil
1959	356A	2dr Cpe	$58,500	$89,200	$138,000	$189,000
		2dr 1600 Super Cpe	$81,500	$119,000	$182,000	$248,000
		2dr Carrera GS Cpe	$299,000	$420,000	$615,000	$795,000
		2dr GS/GT Carrera Cpe	$810,000	$979,000	$1.15 mil	$1.45 mil
		2dr Conv	$122,000	$175,000	$232,000	$305,000
			Two Conv Ds were equipped with Carrera engines from the factory and are worth considerably more.			
		2dr Cab	$81,500	$119,000	$185,000	$235,000
		2dr 1600 Super Cab	$110,000	$168,000	$225,000	$281,000
		2dr Carrera GS Cab	$599,000	$821,000	$915,000	$1 mil
		2dr Carrera GS Spdstr	$870,000	$1 mil	$1.15 mil	$1.35 mil
		2dr GS/GT Carrera Spdstr	$1 mil	$1.3 mil	$1.5 mil	$1.85 mil
1960	356B (T5)	2dr Cpe	$35,500	$55,000	$80,300	$113,000
		2dr 1600 Super Cpe	$38,200	$60,500	$84,700	$125,000
		2dr S90 Cpe	$54,000	$83,000	$115,000	$147,000
		2dr Rdstr	$69,000	$103,000	$172,000	$235,000
		2dr 1600 Super Rdstr	$79,000	$118,000	$199,000	$275,000
		2dr S90 Rdstr	$96,500	$142,000	$225,000	$298,000
		2dr Cab	$48,900	$66,700	$134,000	$182,000
		2dr 1600 Super Cab	$69,000	$105,000	$180,000	$235,000
		2dr S90 Cab	$91,500	$128,000	$199,000	$275,000
1961	356B (T5)	2dr Cpe	$35,500	$55,000	$80,300	$113,000
		2dr 1600 Super Cpe	$38,200	$60,500	$84,700	$125,000
		2dr S90 Cpe	$54,000	$83,000	$115,000	$147,000
		2dr Karmann Hdtp	$27,600	$36,500	$47,900	$65,000
		2dr Rdstr	$69,000	$103,000	$172,000	$235,000
		2dr 1600 Super Rdstr	$79,000	$118,000	$199,000	$275,000
		2dr S90 Rdstr	$96,500	$142,000	$225,000	$298,000
		2dr Cab	$48,900	$66,700	$134,000	$182,000
		2dr 1600 Super Cab	$69,000	$105,000	$180,000	$235,000
		2dr S90 Cab	$91,500	$128,000	$199,000	$275,000
1962	356B	2dr 1600 Super Rdstr	$96,500	$142,000	$225,000	$298,000

Year	Model	Body Style	4	3	2	1
		2dr 1600 Super Cpe	$47,000	$69,000	$98,900	$135,000
		2dr S90 Cpe	$61,000	$99,900	$133,000	$159,000
		2dr S90 Rdstr	$125,000	$181,000	$252,000	$319,000
		2dr 1600 Super Cab	$75,000	$111,000	$202,000	$274,000
		2dr S90 Cab	$91,500	$128,000	$199,000	$275,000
1962	Carrera	2dr 2 GS Cpe	$401,000	$515,000	$725,000	$915,000
		2dr 2 GS Cab	$792,000	$893,000	$1.1 mil	$1.2 mil
1963	356B (T6)	2dr Cpe	$40,000	$58,900	$92,000	$118,000
		2dr 1600 Super Cab	$66,800	$102,000	$172,000	$244,000
		2dr 1600 Super Cpe	$48,000	$70,200	$99,000	$138,000
		2dr Cab	$48,900	$66,700	$135,000	$177,000
1963	Carrera	2dr 2 GS Cpe	$401,000	$515,000	$725,000	$915,000
		2dr 2 GS Cab	$792,000	$893,000	$1.1 mil	$1.2 mil
1964	356C	2dr 1600 C Cpe	$48,500	$74,000	$108,000	$145,000
		2dr 1600 SC Cpe	$65,000	$110,000	$144,000	$176,000
		2dr 1600 C Cab	$58,300	$78,300	$113,000	$151,000
		2dr 1600 SC Cab	$90,100	$149,000	$210,000	$286,000
		+5% for sunroof on cpes. +$7,000 for hard top on cabs.				
1964	911	2dr Cpe	$165,000	$258,000	$398,000	$595,000
1964	Carrera 2	2dr GS Cpe	$420,000	$565,000	$762,000	$928,000
1965	356C	2dr Cpe	$48,500	$74,000	$108,000	$145,000
		2dr 1600 SC Cpe	$65,000	$110,000	$144,000	$176,000
		2dr Cab	$49,600	$76,100	$137,000	$185,000
		2dr 1600 SC Cab	$90,100	$149,000	$211,000	$282,000
		+5% for sunroof on cpes. +$7,000 for hard top on cabs.				
1965	911	2dr Cpe	$90,000	$142,000	$218,000	$300,000
		+10% for factory sunroof.				
1965	Carrera	2dr 2 GS Cpe	$420,000	$565,000	$762,000	$928,000
1966	912	2dr Cpe	$19,000	$32,500	$45,000	$73,000
		+10% for 5-spd.				
1966	911	2dr Cpe	$65,000	$90,000	$138,000	$199,000
		+10% for factory sunroof.				
1967	912	2dr Cpe	$19,000	$32,500	$45,000	$73,000
		2dr Targa	$25,000	$38,000	$54,200	$79,000
		+10% for 5-spd.				
1967	911	2dr Cpe	$41,000	$58,000	$97,000	$147,000
		2dr S Cpe	$125,000	$170,000	$239,000	$294,000
		2dr Targa	$38,000	$55,000	$95,000	$143,000
		2dr S Targa	$117,000	$159,000	$219,000	$278,000
		+10% for a/c. -10% for glass rear window on Targa. +10% for factory sunroof on coupe.				
1968	912	2dr Cpe	$17,500	$31,000	$43,500	$71,000
		+10% for 5-spd.				
		2dr Targa	$22,500	$35,500	$51,000	$76,500

Porsche

Year	Model	Body Style	4	3	2	1
			+10% for 5-spd. -10% for glass rear window on Targa.			
1968	911	2dr L Targa	$41,000	$63,200	$92,000	$133,000
		2dr Cpe	$39,000	$56,500	$81,000	$118,000
		2dr L Cpe	$44,500	$67,500	$96,500	$137,000
		2dr S Cpe	$108,000	$132,000	$178,000	$235,000
		2dr Targa	$31,000	$50,000	$76,000	$115,000
		2dr S Targa	$101,000	$120,000	$164,000	$218,000
			+10% for 5-spd. +10% for factory sunroof on coupe. +10% for a/c. -15% for Sportomatic. -10% for glass rear window on Targa.			
1969	912	2dr Cpe	$15,900	$27,500	$40,000	$59,000
		2dr Targa	$20,000	$33,000	$47,200	$71,000
			+10% for 5-spd. -10% for glass rear window on Targa.			
1969	911	2dr T Cpe	$26,000	$42,000	$65,000	$100,000
		2dr E Cpe	$40,000	$69,000	$88,000	$137,000
		2dr S Cpe	$87,000	$115,000	$162,000	$200,000
		2dr T Targa	$22,000	$38,500	$58,500	$84,000
		2dr E Targa	$35,000	$65,000	$83,500	$131,000
		2dr S Targa	$81,000	$109,000	$131,000	$182,000
			+10% for a/c. +10% for 5-speed. +10% for factory sunroof on coupe. -15% for Sportomatic. -10% for glass rear window on Targa.			
1970	914/4	2dr Targa	$8,200	$15,000	$32,000	$62,000
1970	914/6	2dr Targa	$39,000	$57,500	$82,000	$134,000
			+10% for factory a/c. +10% for 5-spd.			
1970	911	2dr T Cpe	$28,000	$45,000	$68,000	$106,000
		2dr E Cpe	$45,500	$75,000	$90,000	$140,000
		2dr S Cpe	$91,500	$120,000	$166,000	$209,000
		2dr T Targa	$27,000	$41,500	$60,000	$86,500
		2dr E Targa	$40,000	$71,500	$86,000	$134,000
		2dr S Targa	$81,000	$109,000	$121,000	$182,000
			+10% for a/c. +10% for 5-speed. +10% for factory sunroof on coupe. -15% for Sportomatic. -10% for glass rear window on Targa.			
1971	914/6	2dr Targa	$39,000	$57,500	$82,000	$134,000
			+10% for factory a/c. +10% for 5-spd.			
		2dr GT Targa	$163,000	$202,000	$250,000	$305,000
1971	911	2dr T Cpe	$31,500	$50,000	$72,000	$121,000
		2dr E Cpe	$45,500	$75,000	$90,000	$140,000
		2dr S Cpe	$91,500	$120,000	$166,000	$209,000
		2dr T Targa	$29,000	$46,500	$63,000	$92,000
		2dr E Targa	$40,000	$71,500	$86,000	$134,000
		2dr S Targa	$81,000	$109,000	$131,000	$182,000
			+10% for a/c. +10% for 5-speed. +10% for factory sunroof on coupe. -15% for Sportomatic. -10% for glass rear window on Targa.			
1972	914	2dr 1.7 Targa	$8,200	$15,000	$32,000	$62,000
		2dr 2.0 Targa	$12,500	$20,000	$41,000	$82,500
			+10% for factory a/c.			
1972	914/4	2dr Targa	$8,200	$15,000	$32,000	$62,000
1972	914/6	2dr Targa	$39,000	$57,500	$82,000	$134,000

Year	Model	Body Style	4	3	2	1
				+10% for factory a/c. +10% for 5-spd.		
1972	911	2dr T Cpe	$30,000	$48,000	$69,000	$109,000
		2dr E Cpe	$46,000	$76,500	$92,000	$144,000
		2dr S Cpe	$92,900	$122,000	$171,000	$249,000
		2dr T Targa	$26,000	$41,000	$61,500	$89,000
		2dr E Targa	$41,000	$72,900	$88,000	$135,000
		2dr S Targa	$82,500	$114,000	$151,000	$215,000
			+10% for a/c. +10% for 5-speed. +10% for factory sunroof on coupe. -15% for Sportomatic.			
1973	914	2dr 1.7 Targa	$8,200	$15,000	$32,000	$62,000
		2dr 2.0 Targa	$12,500	$20,000	$41,000	$82,500
					+10% for factory a/c.	
1973	911	2dr Carrera RS 2.7 Cpe	$290,000	$399,000	$525,000	$725,000
		2dr S Cpe	$92,900	$122,000	$171,000	$249,000
		2dr T Cpe	$30,000	$48,000	$69,000	$109,000
		2dr E Cpe	$46,000	$76,500	$92,000	$144,000
		2dr Carrera RS 2.7 Ltwt Cpe	$645,000	$715,000	$915,000	$1.25 mil
		2dr T Targa	$26,000	$41,000	$61,500	$89,000
		2dr E Targa	$41,000	$72,900	$88,000	$135,000
		2dr S Targa	$82,500	$114,000	$151,000	$215,000
			+10% for a/c. +10% for 5-speed. +10% for factory sunroof on coupe. -15% for Sportomatic.			
1974	914	2dr 1.8 Targa	$7,700	$14,000	$30,000	$62,000
		2dr 2.0 Targa	$12,500	$20,000	$41,000	$82,500
					+10% for factory a/c.	
1974	911	2dr Cpe	$18,000	$29,000	$46,000	$71,000
		2dr S Cpe	$21,000	$33,000	$52,000	$78,500
		2dr Carrera 2.7 Cpe	$26,000	$41,500	$69,900	$100,000
		2dr Targa	$16,900	$26,500	$43,000	$63,000
		2dr S Targa	$20,000	$31,000	$47,500	$73,000
		2dr Carrera 2.7 Targa	$24,000	$38,000	$62,000	$91,000
			+10% for a/c. +10% for 5-spd. +10% for bright greens, oranges, yellows and blues. +5% for factory sunroof on cpe.			
1975	914	2dr 1.8 Targa	$7,200	$12,500	$26,000	$51,500
		2dr 2.0 Targa	$11,000	$19,000	$37,300	$74,900
					+10% for factory a/c.	
1975	911	2dr S Cpe	$18,500	$27,500	$37,000	$52,000
		2dr S Annv Cpe	$19,000	$28,900	$39,000	$54,500
		2dr Carrera 2.7 Cpe	$21,000	$30,000	$50,000	$66,900
		2dr S Targa	$18,000	$26,000	$35,200	$50,200
		2dr S Annv Targa	$18,500	$27,200	$37,500	$52,900
		2dr Carrera 2.7 Targa	$19,500	$27,500	$48,000	$64,000

Porsche

Year	Model	Body Style	4	3	2	1
		+10% for a/c. +10% for 5-spd. +10% for bright greens, oranges, yellows and blues. +5% for factory sunroof on cpe.				
1976	914	2dr 2.0 Targa	$11,000	$19,000	$37,300	$74,900
		+10% for factory a/c.				
1976	912	2dr E Cpe	$15,000	$25,000	$37,900	$51,000
		+5% for factory sunroof.				
1976	911	2dr S Cpe	$18,500	$27,500	$37,000	$52,000
		+10% for a/c. +10% for factory sunroof. +10% for bright greens, oranges, yellows and blues.				
		2dr Carrera Turbo Cpe	$68,000	$128,000	$210,000	$289,000
		+10% for a/c. +10% for factory sunroof.				
		2dr S Targa	$18,000	$26,000	$35,200	$50,200
		+10% for a/c. +10% for factory sunroof. +10% for bright greens, oranges, yellows and blues.				
1977	924	2dr Cpe	$3,200	$6,000	$18,000	$25,000
		+15% for Martini Edition. +5% for Pasha interior. -15% for auto.				
1977	911	2dr S Cpe	$18,500	$27,500	$37,000	$52,000
		+10% for a/c. +10% for factory sunroof. +10% for bright greens, oranges, yellows and blues.				
		2dr Carrera Turbo Cpe	$55,000	$108,000	$152,000	$209,000
		+10% for a/c. +10% for factory sunroof. -10% for gray market cars.				
		2dr S Targa	$18,000	$26,000	$35,200	$50,200
		+10% for a/c. +10% for factory sunroof. +10% for bright greens, oranges, yellows and blues.				
1978	924	2dr Cpe	$3,300	$6,300	$19,500	$29,000
		+5% for Pasha interior. -15% for auto.				
1978	928	2dr Cpe	$8,000	$21,500	$46,000	$65,500
		-20% for auto.				
1978	911	2dr SC 3.0 Cpe	$23,500	$34,500	$52,800	$76,000
		+25% for extremely rare bright 1978-only colors like Apple Green, Fern Green, Continental Orange and Arrow Blue. +5% for original bright trim on coupes and brushed stainless Targa bar.				
		2dr Carrera Turbo Cpe	$47,000	$92,000	$134,000	$185,000
		+25% for extremely rare bright 1978-only colors like Apple Green, Fern Green, Continental Orange, Talbot Yellow and Arrow Blue. +5% for original bright trim on coupes and brushed stainless Targa bar.				
		2dr SC 3.0 Targa	$20,000	$38,000	$42,500	$68,000
		+25% for extremely rare bright 1978-only colors like Apple Green, Fern Green, Continental Orange and Arrow Blue. +5% for original bright trim on coupes and brushed stainless Targa bar.				
1979	924	2dr Cpe	$3,500	$6,600	$19,500	$29,000
		+5% for Sebring Edition. +5% for Pasha interior. -15% for auto.				
1979	928	2dr Cpe	$7,200	$20,000	$38,500	$60,000

Year	Model	Body Style	4	3	2	1
						-20% for auto.
1979	911	2dr SC 3.0 Cpe	$23,500	$34,500	$52,800	$76,000
						+5% for original bright trim on coupes and brushed stainless Targa bar.
		2dr Carrera Turbo Cpe	$47,000	$92,000	$134,000	$185,000
						+5% for original bright trim on coupes, -20% for gray market cars without EPA/DOT paperwork.
		2dr SC 3.0 Targa	$20,000	$38,000	$42,500	$68,000
						+5% for original bright trim on coupes and brushed stainless Targa bar.
1980	924	2dr Cpe	$3,300	$6,300	$19,500	$29,000
		2dr Turbo Cpe	$4,700	$10,300	$22,000	$36,000
						+5% for Pasha interior. -15% for auto.
1980	928	2dr Cpe	$6,900	$18,500	$32,000	$48,300
						-20% for auto. +5% for Pasha interior.
1980	911	2dr SC 3.0 Cpe	$23,500	$34,500	$52,800	$76,000
		2dr SC Weissach Cpe	$26,000	$40,000	$58,000	$78,500
		2dr SC 3.0 Targa	$20,000	$38,000	$42,500	$68,000
1981	924	2dr Cpe	$3,300	$6,300	$19,500	$29,000
		2dr Turbo Cpe	$4,700	$10,300	$22,000	$36,000
						+5% for Pasha interior. -15% for auto.
1981	928	2dr Cpe	$6,900	$18,500	$32,000	$48,300
						-20% for auto. +5% for Pasha interior.
1981	911	2dr SC 3.0 Cpe	$23,500	$34,500	$52,800	$76,000
		2dr SC Weissach Cpe	$26,000	$40,000	$58,000	$78,500
		2dr SC 3.0 Targa	$20,000	$38,000	$42,500	$68,000
1982	924	2dr Cpe	$3,300	$6,300	$19,500	$29,000
		2dr Turbo Cpe	$4,700	$10,300	$22,000	$36,000
						+5% for Pasha interior. -15% for auto.
1982	928	2dr Cpe	$6,900	$18,500	$32,000	$48,300
						-20% for auto. +5% for Pasha interior.
1982	911	2dr SC 3.0 Cpe	$23,500	$34,500	$52,800	$76,000
		2dr SC Weissach Cpe	$26,000	$40,000	$58,000	$78,500
		2dr SC 3.0 Targa	$20,000	$38,000	$42,500	$68,000
1983	944	2dr Cpe	$4,600	$8,800	$23,500	$36,900
1983	928	2dr S Cpe	$7,100	$19,500	$35,000	$51,500
						-20% for auto. +5% for Pasha interior.
1983	911	2dr SC 3.0 Cpe	$23,500	$34,500	$52,800	$76,000
		2dr SC 3.0 Targa	$20,000	$38,000	$42,500	$68,000
		2dr SC 3.0 Cab	$19,000	$27,000	$42,000	$59,000
1984	944	2dr Cpe	$3,600	$7,500	$19,000	$30,000
1984	928	2dr S Cpe	$7,100	$19,500	$35,000	$51,500
						-20% for auto. +5% for Pasha interior.
1984	911	2dr Carrera Cpe	$25,000	$38,500	$58,500	$80,000
		2dr Carrera Targa	$22,000	$32,000	$51,000	$68,500

Porsche

Year	Model	Body Style	4	3	2	1
		2dr Carrera Cab	$20,000	$34,000	$45,000	$62,000
						+25% for turbo look.
1985	944	2dr Cpe	$3,600	$7,500	$19,000	$30,000
1985	928	2dr S Cpe	$7,100	$19,500	$35,000	$51,500
						-20% for auto.
1985	911	2dr Carrera Cpe	$25,000	$38,500	$58,500	$80,000
						+25% for turbo look.
		2dr Carrera Targa	$22,000	$32,000	$51,000	$68,500
						+15% for 1987-only color Summer Yellow.
		2dr Carrera Cab	$20,000	$34,000	$45,000	$62,000
						+25% for turbo look.
1986	944	2dr Cpe	$3,600	$7,500	$19,000	$30,000
		2dr Turbo Cpe	$6,900	$14,000	$34,500	$50,000
1986	928	2dr S Cpe	$7,100	$19,500	$35,000	$51,500
						-20% for auto.
1986	911	2dr Carrera Cpe	$25,000	$38,500	$58,500	$80,000
						+25% for turbo look.
		2dr Carrera Targa	$22,000	$32,000	$51,000	$68,500
						+25% for factory Turbo look.
		2dr Carrera Cab	$20,000	$34,000	$45,000	$62,000
						+25% for turbo look.
		2dr Turbo 930 Cpe	$62,900	$114,000	$168,000	$234,000
		2dr Turbo 930 Targa	$54,000	$105,000	$147,000	$206,000
		2dr Turbo 930 Cab	$47,500	$92,000	$140,000	$197,000
						+30% for factory Slantnose. -20% for gray market cars without EPA/DOT paperwork. -10% for gray market cars with paperwork.
1986	959	2dr Komfort Cpe	$659,000	$825,000	$1 mil	$1.3 mil
		2dr Spt Cpe	$1.1 mil	$1.35 mil	$1.8 mil	$2.35 mil
1987	924	2dr S Cpe	$3,700	$8,000	$15,500	$31,000
						-15% for auto.
1987	944	2dr Cpe	$3,600	$7,500	$19,000	$30,000
		2dr S Cpe	$5,800	$9,000	$23,000	$33,000
		2dr Turbo Cpe	$6,900	$14,000	$34,500	$50,000
1987	928	2dr S4 Cpe	$14,000	$31,300	$40,500	$60,000
						-20% for auto.
1987	911	2dr Carrera Cpe	$30,000	$42,000	$68,000	$86,900
		2dr Carrera Targa	$23,500	$38,000	$56,000	$74,500
		2dr Carrera Cab	$21,000	$36,000	$51,500	$67,500
						+15% for 1987-only color Summer Yellow. +25% for turbo look.
		2dr Turbo 930 Cpe	$62,900	$114,000	$168,000	$234,000
		2dr Turbo 930 Targa	$54,000	$105,000	$147,000	$206,000

Year	Model	Body Style	4	3	2	1
		2dr Turbo 930 Cab	$47,500	$92,000	$140,000	$197,000
		+30% for factory Slantnose. -20% for gray market cars without EPA/DOT paperwork. -10% for gray market cars with paperwork.				
1987	959	2dr Komfort Cpe	$659,000	$825,000	$1 mil	$1.3 mil
		2dr Spt Cpe	$1.1 mil	$1.35 mil	$1.8 mil	$2.35 mil
1988	924	2dr S Cpe	$4,000	$8,500	$17,000	$35,000
		-15% for auto.				
1988	944	2dr Cpe	$3,600	$7,500	$19,000	$30,000
		2dr S Cpe	$2,800	$9,000	$23,000	$33,000
		2dr Turbo Cpe	$7,100	$15,500	$37,000	$51,500
		2dr S Turbo Cpe	$13,300	$20,900	$44,500	$70,000
1988	928	2dr S4 Cpe	$14,000	$31,300	$40,500	$60,000
		-20% for auto.				
1988	911	2dr Carrera Cpe	$30,000	$42,000	$68,000	$86,900
		2dr Carrera Targa	$23,500	$38,000	$56,000	$74,500
		2dr Carrera Cab	$21,000	$36,000	$51,500	$67,500
		+25% for turbo look.				
		2dr Turbo 930 Cpe	$62,900	$114,000	$168,000	$234,000
		2dr Turbo 930 Targa	$54,000	$105,000	$147,000	$206,000
		2dr Turbo 930 Cab	$47,500	$92,000	$140,000	$197,000
		+30% for factory Slantnose. -20% for gray market cars without EPA/DOT paperwork. -10% for gray market cars with paperwork.				
1988	959	2dr Komfort Cpe	$659,000	$825,000	$1 mil	$1.3 mil
		2dr Spt Cpe	$1.1 mil	$1.35 mil	$1.8 mil	$2.35 mil
1989	944	2dr Cpe	$4,600	$8,300	$21,500	$32,500
		2dr S2 Cpe	$9,000	$15,000	$33,000	$42,500
		2dr Turbo Cpe	$14,300	$21,900	$45,800	$71,900
1989	928	2dr GT Cpe	$17,000	$35,900	$48,300	$69,900
		2dr S4 Cpe	$14,000	$31,300	$40,500	$60,000
		-20% for auto.				
1989	911	2dr Carrera Cab	$22,000	$37,000	$52,900	$69,000
		+$1,500 for Anniversary models. +25% for turbo look.				
		2dr Carrera Spdstr	$120,000	$150,000	$245,000	$299,000
		+$1,500 for Anniversary models.				
		2dr Carrera Cpe	$30,000	$44,900	$70,000	$91,000
		+$1,500 for Anniversary models. +25% for turbo look.				
		2dr Carrera 4 Cpe	$25,000	$41,500	$61,000	$81,500
		+$1,500 for Anniversary models.				
		2dr Carrera Targa	$24,000	$39,500	$57,500	$78,900
		+$1,500 for Anniversary models. +25% for turbo look.				
		2dr Turbo 930 Cpe	$79,000	$160,000	$229,000	$289,000

Porsche

Year	Model	Body Style	4	3	2	1
		2dr Turbo 930 Targa	$63,900	$122,000	$169,000	$235,000
		2dr Turbo 930 Cab	$59,000	$111,000	$165,000	$240,000
		+30% for factory Slantnose. -20% for gray market cars without EPA/DOT paperwork. -10% for gray market cars with paperwork.				
1990	944	2dr S2 Cpe	$9,000	$15,000	$33,000	$42,500
		2dr S2 Cab	$7,000	$12,900	$22,200	$31,000
1990	928	2dr S4 Cpe	$14,000	$31,300	$40,500	$60,000
		2dr GT Cpe	$17,000	$35,900	$48,300	$69,900
		-20% for auto.				
1990	911	2dr Carrera 2 Cpe	$27,000	$46,000	$67,500	$85,500
		2dr Carrera 4 Cpe	$29,000	$48,000	$70,000	$89,900
		2dr Carrera 2 Targa	$22,000	$34,000	$47,900	$61,000
		2dr Carrera 4 Targa	$24,300	$37,300	$54,500	$67,900
		2dr Carrera 2 Cab	$20,300	$31,000	$45,500	$56,500
		2dr Carrera 4 Cab	$22,000	$32,300	$48,000	$61,500
		-10% for Tiptronic.				
1991	944	2dr S2 Cpe	$9,000	$15,000	$33,000	$42,500
		2dr S2 Cab	$7,000	$12,900	$22,200	$31,000
1991	928	2dr S4 Cpe	$14,000	$31,300	$40,500	$60,000
		2dr GT Cpe	$17,000	$35,900	$48,300	$69,900
		-20% for auto.				
1991	911	2dr Carrera 2 Cab	$20,300	$31,000	$45,500	$56,500
		2dr Carrera 2 Cpe	$27,000	$46,000	$67,500	$85,500
		2dr Carrera 4 Cpe	$29,000	$48,000	$70,000	$89,900
		2dr Turbo Cpe	$91,000	$146,000	$219,000	$282,000
		2dr Carrera 2 Targa	$22,000	$34,000	$47,900	$61,000
		2dr Carrera 4 Targa	$24,300	$37,300	$54,500	$67,900
		2dr Carrera 4 Cab	$22,000	$32,300	$48,000	$61,500
		-10% for Tiptronic.				
1992	968	2dr Cpe	$12,500	$22,500	$41,500	$60,000
		2dr Cab	$8,800	$16,100	$28,700	$39,800
		-15% for Tiptronic. +20% for Speed Yellow and Riviera Blue.				
1992	928	2dr GTS Cpe	$41,000	$65,800	$89,900	$126,000
		-20% for auto.				
1992	911	2dr Carrera RS Cpe	$120,000	$179,000	$235,000	$295,000
		2dr Carrera 2 Cpe	$27,000	$46,000	$67,500	$85,500
		2dr Carrera 4 Cpe	$29,000	$48,000	$70,000	$89,900
		2dr America Rdstr	$68,900	$102,000	$125,000	$141,000
		2dr Turbo Cpe	$91,000	$146,000	$219,000	$282,000
		2dr Turbo S Cpe	$325,000	$445,000	$596,000	$745,000
		2dr Carrera 2 Targa	$22,000	$34,000	$47,900	$61,000

Year	Model	Body Style	4	3	2	1
		2dr Carrera 4 Targa	$24,300	$37,300	$54,500	$67,900
		2dr Carrera 2 Cab	$20,300	$31,000	$45,500	$56,500
		2dr Carrera 4 Cab	$22,000	$32,300	$48,000	$61,500
						-10% for Tiptronic.
1993	968	2dr Cpe	$12,500	$22,500	$41,500	$60,000
		2dr Cab	$8,800	$16,100	$28,700	$39,800
						-15% for Tiptronic, +20% for Speed Yellow and Riviera Blue.
1993	928	2dr GTS Cpe	$41,000	$65,800	$89,900	$126,000
						-20% for auto.
1993	911	2dr Carrera 2 Cpe	$27,000	$46,000	$67,500	$85,500
		2dr Carrera RS 3.8 Cpe	$505,000	$600,000	$950,000	$1.55 mil
		2dr Carrera 4 Cpe	$29,000	$48,000	$70,000	$89,900
		2dr Turbo Cpe	$91,000	$146,000	$219,000	$282,000
		2dr Carrera 2 Targa	$22,000	$34,000	$47,900	$61,000
		2dr Carrera 4 Targa	$24,300	$37,300	$54,500	$67,900
		2dr Carrera 2 Cab	$20,300	$31,000	$45,500	$56,500
		2dr Carrera 4 Cab	$22,000	$32,300	$48,000	$61,500
		2dr America Rdstr	$66,000	$100,000	$122,000	$137,000
						-10% for Tiptronic.
1994	968	2dr Cpe	$12,500	$22,500	$41,500	$60,000
		2dr Cab	$8,800	$16,100	$28,700	$39,800
						-15% for Tiptronic, +20% for Speed Yellow and Riviera Blue.
1994	928	2dr GTS Cpe	$41,000	$65,800	$89,900	$126,000
						-20% for auto.
1994	911	2dr Carrera Cpe	$27,000	$46,000	$67,500	$85,500
		2dr RS America Cpe	$59,000	$77,500	$89,000	$121,000
		2dr Carrera Turbo Cpe	$130,000	$199,000	$268,000	$348,000
		2dr Carrera 4 Cpe	$29,000	$48,000	$70,000	$89,900
		2dr Carrera Cab	$20,300	$31,000	$45,500	$56,500
		2dr Carrera Spdstr	$145,000	$192,000	$270,000	$300,000
						-10% for Tiptronic.
1995	968	2dr Cpe	$13,000	$23,000	$42,900	$62,000
		2dr Conv	$8,800	$16,100	$28,700	$39,800
						-15% for Tiptronic, +20% for Speed Yellow and Riviera Blue.
1995	928	2dr GTS Cpe	$48,000	$76,000	$101,000	$151,000
						-20% for auto.
1995	911	2dr Carrera Cpe	$30,000	$45,900	$62,000	$77,900
		2dr Carrera RS Cpe	$249,000	$329,000	$472,000	$650,000
		2dr Turbo Cpe	$97,500	$144,000	$205,000	$253,000
		2dr GT2 Cpe	$695,000	$920,000	$1.1 mil	$1.35 mil
		2dr Carrera 4 Cpe	$36,500	$53,000	$68,500	$85,500

Porsche

Year	Model	Body Style	4	3	2	1
		2dr Carrera Cab	$25,000	$35,000	$51,000	$67,000
		2dr Turbo Cab	$93,500	$139,000	$201,000	$248,000
		2dr Carrera 4 Cab	$26,900	$36,900	$55,000	$68,900
						-15% for Tiptronic.
1996	911	2dr Carrera Cpe	$30,500	$46,500	$62,900	$78,800
		2dr Turbo Cpe	$97,500	$144,000	$205,000	$253,000
		2dr Carrera RS Cpe	$220,000	$325,000	$489,000	$675,000
		2dr GT2 Cpe	$695,000	$920,000	$1.1 mil	$1.35 mil
		2dr Carrera 4 Cpe	$37,000	$53,900	$69,500	$87,500
		2dr Carrera 4S Cpe	$60,000	$88,000	$123,000	$162,000
		2dr Carrera Targa	$29,000	$44,900	$59,000	$75,000
		2dr Carrera Cab	$25,000	$35,000	$51,000	$67,000
		2dr Carrera 4 Cab	$27,000	$37,500	$56,000	$70,000
						-15% for Tiptronic.
1997	Boxster	2dr Rdstr	$5,800	$9,200	$15,500	$24,000
1997	911	2dr Carrera Cpe	$30,500	$46,500	$62,900	$78,800
		2dr GT2 Cpe	$695,000	$920,000	$1.1 mil	$1.35 mil
		2dr Carrera S Cpe	$58,000	$79,000	$112,000	$138,000
		2dr Turbo Cpe	$97,500	$144,000	$205,000	$253,000
		2dr Turbo S Cpe	$195,000	$290,000	$398,000	$499,000
		2dr Carrera 4 Cpe	$37,000	$53,900	$69,500	$87,500
		2dr Carrera 4S Cpe	$60,000	$88,000	$123,000	$162,000
		2dr Carrera Targa	$29,000	$44,900	$59,000	$75,000
		2dr Carrera Cab	$25,000	$35,000	$51,000	$67,000
		2dr Carrera 4 Cab	$27,000	$37,500	$56,000	$70,000
						-15% for Tiptronic.
1998	Boxster	2dr Rdstr	$5,800	$9,200	$15,500	$24,000
1998	911	2dr Carrera S Cpe	$58,000	$79,000	$112,000	$138,000
		2dr Carrera 4S Cpe	$60,000	$88,000	$123,000	$162,000
		2dr GT2 Cpe	$695,000	$920,000	$1.1 mil	$1.35 mil
		2dr Turbo Cpe	$97,500	$144,000	$205,000	$253,000
		2dr Turbo S Cpe	$195,000	$290,000	$398,000	$499,000
		2dr Carrera Targa	$29,000	$44,900	$59,000	$75,000
						-15% for Tiptronic.
1999	Boxster	2dr Rdstr	$5,800	$9,200	$15,500	$24,000
1999	911	2dr Carrera Cpe	$14,000	$22,000	$29,000	$39,500
		2dr Carrera 4 Cpe	$14,500	$23,000	$30,000	$40,000
		2dr Carrera Cab	$10,500	$16,800	$24,000	$32,000
		2dr Carrera 4 Cab	$11,300	$17,900	$25,000	$33,300
						-15% for any non-turbo 996 without a documented intermediate shaft bearing remedy.
2000	Boxster	2dr Rdstr	$5,800	$9,200	$15,500	$24,000
		2dr S Rdstr	$7,400	$11,200	$17,900	$26,500
2000	911	2dr Carrera Cpe	$12,000	$20,500	$27,000	$38,000
		2dr Carrera 4 Cpe	$13,800	$22,900	$29,000	$39,300

Year	Model	Body Style	4	3	2	1
		2dr Carrera Cab	$10,500	$16,800	$24,000	$32,000
		2dr Carrera 4 Cab	$11,300	$17,900	$25,000	$33,300
		-15% for any non-turbo 996 without a documented intermediate shaft bearing remedy.				
2001	Boxster	2dr Rdstr	$5,800	$9,200	$15,500	$24,000
		2dr S Rdstr	$7,400	$11,200	$17,900	$26,500
2001	911	2dr Carrera Cpe	$12,000	$20,500	$27,000	$38,000
		2dr Carrera 4 Cpe	$13,800	$22,900	$29,000	$39,300
		2dr Turbo Cpe	$31,500	$39,500	$58,000	$75,000
		2dr Carrera Cab	$10,500	$16,800	$24,000	$32,000
		2dr Carrera 4 Cab	$11,300	$17,900	$25,000	$33,300
		-15% for any non-turbo 996 without a documented intermediate shaft bearing remedy. -15% for Tiptronic on Turbo.				
2002	Boxster	2dr Rdstr	$6,600	$10,200	$16,800	$25,300
		2dr S Rdstr	$8,400	$12,200	$19,000	$27,900
2002	911	2dr Carrera Cpe	$12,000	$20,500	$27,000	$38,000
		2dr Carrera 4S Cpe	$20,000	$28,500	$41,000	$53,000
		Turbo 2dr GT2 Cpe	$65,000	$88,800	$120,000	$162,000
		2dr Turbo X-50 Cpe	$31,500	$39,500	$58,000	$75,000
		2dr Turbo Cpe	$38,000	$46,000	$66,000	$82,000
		2dr Targa Cpe	$11,200	$18,900	$27,200	$37,500
		2dr Carrera Cab	$11,000	$16,500	$24,500	$34,500
		2dr Carrera 4 Cab	$12,000	$17,500	$25,500	$35,500
		-15% for any non-turbo 996 without a documented intermediate shaft bearing remedy. -15% for Tiptronic on Turbo.				
2003	Boxster	2dr Rdstr	$6,600	$10,200	$16,800	$25,300
		2dr S Rdstr	$8,400	$12,200	$19,000	$27,900
2003	911	2dr Carrera Cpe	$11,900	$19,700	$28,200	$38,500
		2dr Carrera 4S Cpe	$20,000	$28,500	$41,000	$53,000
		2dr Turbo Cpe	$31,500	$39,500	$58,000	$75,000
		2dr Turbo X-50 Cpe	$38,000	$46,000	$66,000	$82,000
		Turbo 2dr GT2 Cpe	$68,000	$90,000	$125,000	$166,000
		2dr Targa Cpe	$11,200	$18,900	$27,200	$37,500
		2dr Carrera Cab	$11,000	$16,500	$24,500	$34,500
		2dr Carrera 4 Cab	$12,000	$17,500	$25,500	$35,500
		-15% for any non-turbo 996 without a documented intermediate shaft bearing remedy. -15% for Tiptronic on Turbo.				
2004	Boxster	2dr Rdstr	$6,600	$10,200	$16,800	$25,300
		2dr S Rdstr	$8,400	$12,200	$19,000	$27,900
		2dr S 550 Spyder 50th Annv Ed Rdstr	$11,100	$15,600	$22,700	$32,400
2004	911	2dr Carrera Cpe	$13,500	$20,500	$30,000	$41,000

Porsche

Year	Model	Body Style	4	3	2	1
		2dr Carrera 4S Cpe	$20,000	$28,500	$41,000	$53,000
		2dr 40th Anniv Ed Cpe	$22,000	$32,500	$45,000	$64,000
		2dr Turbo Cpe	$31,500	$39,500	$58,000	$75,000
		Turbo 2dr GT2 Cpe	$68,000	$90,000	$125,000	$166,000
		2dr Turbo X-50 Cpe	$38,000	$46,000	$66,000	$82,000
		2dr GT3 Cpe	$47,000	$64,000	$90,500	$123,000
		2dr Targa Cpe	$13,000	$20,000	$28,500	$39,500
		2dr Carrera Cab	$12,000	$17,000	$25,000	$36,500
		2dr Carrera 4 Cab	$13,000	$18,000	$26,000	$37,500
		2dr Carrera 4S Cab	$17,500	$24,000	$34,000	$46,000
		2dr Turbo Cab	$32,100	$41,300	$52,000	$71,400
		2dr Turbo X-50 Cab	$33,200	$43,400	$55,000	$74,600

-15% for any non-turbo 996 without a documented intermediate shaft bearing remedy. -15% for Tiptronic on Turbo.

Year	Model	Body Style	4	3	2	1
2004	Carrera GT	2dr Cpe	$505,000	$650,000	$750,000	$985,000
2005	911	2dr Turbo Cpe	$31,500	$39,500	$58,000	$75,000
		2dr Turbo X-50 Cpe	$33,900	$43,500	$56,300	$76,500
		2dr Turbo S Cpe	$41,000	$53,000	$71,000	$89,800
		Turbo 2dr GT2 Cpe	$71,000	$93,500	$128,000	$170,000
		2dr GT3 Cpe	$48,200	$65,000	$89,500	$121,000
		2dr Turbo Cab	$32,700	$42,500	$53,900	$73,200
		2dr Turbo X-50 Cab	$33,200	$43,400	$55,000	$74,600
		2dr Turbo S Cab	$36,900	$44,900	$59,000	$79,000

-15% for any non-turbo 996 without a documented intermediate shaft bearing remedy. -15% for Tiptronic on Turbo.

Year	Model	Body Style	4	3	2	1
2005	Carrera GT	2dr Cpe	$505,000	$650,000	$750,000	$985,000
2006	Carrera GT	2dr Cpe	$505,000	$650,000	$750,000	$985,000
2007	Carrera GT	2dr Cpe	$505,000	$650,000	$750,000	$985,000
2014	918 Spyder	2dr Rdstr	$990,000	$1.1 mil	$1.2 mil	$1.4 mil
2015	918 Spyder	2dr Rdstr	$990,000	$1.1 mil	$1.2 mil	$1.4 mil
		2dr Weissach Rdstr	$1.1 mil	$1.35 mil	$1.5 mil	$1.65 mil

Puma

Year	Model	Body Style	4	3	2	1
1964	GT	2dr Cpe	$6,000	$9,500	$16,400	$27,900
1965	GT	2dr Cpe	$6,000	$9,500	$16,400	$27,900
1966	GT	2dr Cpe	$6,000	$9,500	$16,400	$27,900
1967	GT	2dr Cpe	$6,000	$9,500	$16,400	$27,900

Puma

Year	Model	Body Style	4	3	2	1
1968	GT	2dr Cpe	$6,000	$9,500	$16,400	$27,900
1969	GT	2dr Cpe	$6,000	$9,500	$16,400	$27,900
1970	GT	2dr Cpe	$6,000	$9,500	$16,400	$27,900
1971	GT	2dr Cpe	$6,000	$9,500	$16,400	$27,900
1972	GT	2dr Cpe	$6,000	$9,500	$16,400	$27,900
1972	GTS	2dr Conv	$6,500	$10,500	$17,400	$29,500
1973	GT	2dr Cpe	$6,000	$9,500	$16,400	$27,900
1973	GTS	2dr Conv	$6,500	$10,500	$17,400	$29,500
1974	GT	2dr Cpe	$6,000	$9,500	$16,400	$27,900
1974	GTS	2dr Conv	$6,500	$10,500	$17,400	$29,500
1975	GT	2dr Cpe	$6,000	$9,500	$16,400	$27,900
1975	GTS	2dr Conv	$6,500	$10,500	$17,400	$29,500
1976	GT	2dr Cpe	$6,000	$9,500	$16,400	$27,900
1976	GTS	2dr Conv	$6,500	$10,500	$17,400	$29,500
1977	GT	2dr Cpe	$6,000	$9,500	$16,400	$27,900
1977	GTS	2dr Conv	$6,500	$10,500	$17,400	$29,500
1978	GT	2dr Cpe	$6,000	$9,500	$16,400	$27,900
1978	GTS	2dr Conv	$6,500	$10,500	$17,400	$29,500
1979	GT	2dr Cpe	$6,000	$9,500	$16,400	$27,900
1979	GTS	2dr Conv	$6,500	$10,500	$17,400	$29,500
1980	GT	2dr Cpe	$6,000	$9,500	$16,400	$27,900
1980	GTS	2dr Conv	$6,500	$10,500	$17,400	$29,500
1980	GTC	2dr Cpe	$6,200	$10,000	$17,400	$27,700
		2dr Conv	$7,300	$12,000	$18,200	$30,900
1981	GT	2dr Cpe	$6,000	$9,500	$16,400	$27,900
1981	GTC	2dr Cpe	$6,200	$10,000	$17,400	$27,700
		2dr Conv	$7,300	$12,000	$18,200	$30,900
1982	GT	2dr Cpe	$6,000	$9,500	$16,400	$27,500
1982	GTC	2dr Cpe	$6,200	$10,000	$17,400	$27,700
		2dr Conv	$7,300	$12,000	$18,200	$30,900
1983	GT	2dr Cpe	$6,000	$9,500	$16,400	$27,500
1983	GTC	2dr Cpe	$6,200	$10,000	$17,400	$27,700
		2dr Conv	$7,300	$12,000	$18,200	$30,900
1984	GT	2dr Cpe	$6,000	$9,500	$16,400	$27,900
1984	GTC	2dr Cpe	$6,200	$10,000	$17,400	$27,700
		2dr Conv	$7,300	$12,000	$18,200	$30,900
1985	GT	2dr Cpe	$6,000	$9,500	$16,400	$27,500
1985	GTC	2dr Cpe	$6,200	$10,000	$17,400	$27,700
		2dr Conv	$7,300	$12,000	$18,200	$30,900

Qvale

Year	Model	Body Style	4	3	2	1
2000	Mangusta	2dr Conv	$13,200	$22,100	$30,000	$39,400
			+7% for 1 of 3 Tommy Bahama Ed cars. -20% for auto.			
2001	Mangusta	2dr Conv	$13,200	$22,100	$30,000	$39,400
			+7% for 1 of 3 Tommy Bahama Ed cars. -20% for auto.			

Rambler

Year	Model	Body Style	4	3	2	1
1965	Marlin	287/198 2dr Fstbk	$8,000	$12,300	$16,100	$23,100

Renault

Year	Model	Body Style	4	3	2	1
1954	Dauphine	4dr Sdn	$2,500	$4,100	$6,600	$11,100
1955	Dauphine	4dr Sdn	$2,500	$4,100	$6,600	$11,100
1956	Dauphine	4dr Sdn	$2,500	$4,100	$6,600	$11,100
1957	Dauphine	4dr Sdn	$2,500	$4,100	$6,600	$11,100
1958	Dauphine	4dr Sdn	$2,500	$4,100	$6,600	$11,100
		4dr Gordini Sdn	$4,900	$8,700	$14,100	$19,100
1959	Dauphine	4dr Sdn	$2,500	$4,100	$6,600	$11,100
		4dr Gordini Sdn	$4,900	$8,700	$14,100	$19,100
1960	Dauphine	4dr Sdn	$2,500	$4,100	$6,600	$11,100
		4dr Gordini Sdn	$4,900	$8,700	$14,100	$19,100
1961	Dauphine	4dr Sdn	$2,500	$4,100	$6,600	$11,100
		4dr Gordini Sdn	$4,900	$8,700	$14,100	$19,100
1962	Dauphine	4dr Sdn	$2,500	$4,100	$6,600	$11,100
		4dr Gordini Sdn	$4,900	$8,700	$14,100	$19,100
1963	Dauphine	4dr Sdn	$2,500	$4,100	$6,600	$11,100
		4dr Gordini Sdn	$4,900	$8,700	$14,100	$19,100
1964	Dauphine	4dr Gordini Sdn	$4,900	$8,700	$14,100	$19,100
1964	Caravelle	2dr Conv	$9,300	$15,000	$21,300	$30,200
1964	8 Gordini 1100	2dr Cpe	$5,600	$10,200	$18,900	$29,700
1965	Dauphine	4dr Gordini Sdn	$4,900	$8,700	$14,100	$19,100
1965	Caravelle	2dr Conv	$9,300	$15,000	$21,300	$30,200
1965	8 Gordini 1100	2dr Cpe	$5,600	$10,200	$18,900	$29,700
1966	Dauphine	4dr Gordini Sdn	$4,900	$8,700	$14,100	$19,100
1966	8 Gordini 1100	2dr Cpe	$5,600	$10,200	$18,900	$29,700
1967	Dauphine	4dr Gordini Sdn	$4,900	$8,700	$14,100	$19,100
1967	Caravelle	2dr Conv	$9,300	$15,000	$21,300	$30,200
1967	8 Gordini 1100	2dr Cpe	$5,600	$10,200	$18,900	$29,700
1967	8 Gordini 1300	2dr Cpe	$7,500	$13,600	$22,300	$41,400
1968	Caravelle	2dr Conv	$9,300	$15,000	$21,300	$30,200
1968	8 Gordini 1300	2dr Cpe	$7,500	$13,600	$22,300	$41,400
1969	Caravelle	2dr Conv	$9,300	$15,000	$21,300	$30,200
1969	8 Gordini 1300	2dr Cpe	$7,500	$13,600	$22,300	$41,400
1970	8 Gordini 1300	2dr Cpe	$7,500	$13,600	$22,300	$41,400
1982	Fuego	2dr Cpe	$800	$1,700	$3,800	$5,400
1983	Fuego	2dr Cpe	$800	$1,700	$3,800	$5,400
1983	R5	2dr Turbo 1 Htchbk	$55,000	$73,000	$98,000	$132,000
1984	Fuego	2dr Cpe	$800	$1,700	$3,800	$5,400
1984	R5	2dr Turbo 1 Htchbk	$55,000	$73,000	$98,000	$132,000
1985	Fuego	2dr Cpe	$800	$1,700	$3,800	$5,400
1985	R5	2dr Turbo 1 Htchbk	$54,500	$73,000	$98,000	$132,000
1986	R5	2dr Turbo 1 Htchbk	$55,000	$73,000	$98,000	$132,000

Replicar

Year	Model	Body Style	4	3	2	1
1976	Base	2dr Rdstr	$5,200	$8,300	$14,000	$20,600
		4dr Phtn	$4,500	$7,800	$12,700	$19,200
1977	Base	2dr Rdstr	$5,200	$8,300	$14,000	$20,600
		4dr Phtn	$4,500	$7,800	$12,700	$19,200
1978	Base	2dr Rdstr	$5,200	$8,300	$14,000	$20,600
		4dr Phtn	$4,500	$7,800	$12,700	$19,200
1979	Base	302/135 2dr Rdstr	$5,200	$8,300	$14,000	$20,600
		302/135 4dr Phtn	$4,500	$7,800	$12,700	$19,200
1980	Base	302/135 2dr Rdstr	$5,200	$8,300	$14,000	$20,600
		302/135 4dr Phtn	$4,500	$7,800	$12,700	$19,200
1981	Base	302/135 2dr Rdstr	$5,200	$8,300	$14,000	$20,600
		302/135 4dr Phtn	$4,500	$7,800	$12,700	$19,200

Riley

Year	Model	Body Style	4	3	2	1
1948	1 1/2-Litre	4dr Sal	$4,000	$8,000	$13,100	$17,600
1948	2.5L	4dr RMB Sdn	$5,200	$9,600	$15,600	$22,900
		2dr RMB Rdstr	$12,800	$20,700	$35,200	$57,200
		2dr RMB DHC	$9,400	$19,000	$30,300	$48,300
1949	1 1/2-Litre	4dr Sal	$4,000	$8,000	$13,100	$17,600
1949	2.5L	4dr RMB Sdn	$5,200	$9,600	$15,600	$22,900
		2dr RMB Rdstr	$12,800	$20,700	$35,200	$57,200
		2dr RMB DHC	$9,400	$19,000	$30,600	$48,300
1950	1 1/2-Litre	4dr Sal	$4,000	$8,000	$13,100	$17,600
1950	2.5L	4dr RMB Sdn	$5,200	$9,600	$15,600	$22,900
		2dr RMB Rdstr	$12,800	$20,700	$35,200	$57,200
		2dr RMB DHC	$9,400	$19,000	$30,600	$48,300
1951	1 1/2-Litre	4dr Sal	$4,000	$8,000	$13,100	$17,600
1951	2.5L	4dr RMB Sdn	$5,200	$9,600	$15,600	$22,900
		2dr RMB Rdstr	$12,800	$20,700	$35,200	$57,200
		2dr RMB DHC	$9,400	$19,000	$30,600	$48,300
1952	1 1/2-Litre	4dr Sal	$4,000	$8,000	$13,100	$17,600
1952	2.5L	4dr RMB Sdn	$5,200	$9,600	$15,600	$22,900
		2dr RMB Rdstr	$12,800	$20,700	$35,200	$57,200
		2dr RMB DHC	$9,400	$19,000	$30,300	$48,300
1953	1 1/2-Litre	4dr Sal	$4,000	$8,000	$13,100	$17,600
1953	2.5L	4dr RMF Sdn	$5,500	$10,000	$16,300	$24,800
		2dr RMF Rdstr	$13,500	$23,100	$36,900	$58,800
		2dr RMF DHC	$9,900	$20,200	$31,800	$51,000
1954	1 1/2-Litre	4dr Sal	$4,000	$8,000	$13,100	$17,600
1954	Pathfinder	4dr Sal	$2,500	$5,300	$9,000	$17,000
1955	Pathfinder	4dr Sal	$2,500	$5,300	$9,000	$17,000
1956	Pathfinder	4dr Sal	$2,500	$5,300	$9,000	$17,000
1957	Pathfinder	4dr Sal	$2,500	$5,300	$9,000	$17,000

Rolls-Royce

Year	Model	Body Style	4	3	2	1
1946	Silver Wraith	4dr JY Spt Sal	$43,000	$51,500	$77,900	$123,000

Rolls-Royce

Year	Model	Body Style	4	3	2	1
						+15% for auto.
		4dr F & W Sal	$18,400	$24,400	$35,600	$75,900
				+15% for auto through 1953, exc Dawns.		
1947	Silver Wraith	4dr PW Sal	$43,000	$51,500	$77,900	$123,000
		4dr PW Limo 7P	$18,400	$24,400	$35,600	$75,900
						+15% for auto.
1948	Silver Wraith	4dr Cchblt Sdn	$43,000	$51,500	$77,900	$123,000
						+15% for auto.
1949	Silver Dawn	4dr Sdn	$25,500	$38,300	$46,300	$60,200
1949	Silver Wraith	4dr Cchblt Sdn	$43,000	$51,500	$77,900	$123,000
						+15% for auto.
1950	Silver Dawn	4dr Sdn	$25,500	$38,300	$46,300	$60,200
1950	Silver Wraith	4dr Cchblt Sdn	$43,000	$51,500	$77,900	$123,000
						+15% for auto.
1950	Phantom IV	4dr Limo	$703,000	$800,000	$906,000	$1 mil
						+15% for auto.
1951	Silver Dawn	4dr Sdn	$37,400	$50,800	$59,700	$74,500
						-30% for RHD.
1951	Silver Wraith	4dr Cchblt Sdn	$84,400	$98,800	$117,000	$174,000
					+15% for auto. -30% for RHD.	
1951	Phantom IV	4dr Limo	$703,000	$800,000	$906,000	$1 mil
					+15% for auto. -30% for RHD.	
1952	Silver Dawn	4dr Sdn	$40,700	$54,500	$71,100	$90,600
		2dr PW Conv	$163,000	$218,000	$297,000	$353,000
						-30% for RHD.
1952	Silver Wraith	4dr Cchblt Sdn	$84,400	$98,800	$117,000	$174,000
					+15% for auto. -30% for RHD.	
1952	Phantom IV	4dr Limo	$703,000	$800,000	$906,000	$1 mil
					+15% for auto. -30% for RHD.	
1953	Silver Dawn	4dr Sdn	$42,200	$57,000	$73,800	$91,700
		2dr PW Conv	$185,000	$235,000	$316,000	$403,000
						-30% for RHD.
1953	Silver Wraith	4dr Cchblt Sdn	$94,300	$110,000	$128,000	$189,000
					+15% for auto. -30% for RHD.	
1953	Phantom IV	4dr Limo	$703,000	$800,000	$906,000	$1 mil
					+15% for auto. -30% for RHD.	
1954	Silver Dawn	4dr Sdn	$42,200	$57,000	$73,800	$91,700
		2dr PW Conv	$185,000	$235,000	$316,000	$403,000
						-30% for RHD.

Year	Model	Body Style	4	3	2	1
1954	Silver Wraith	4dr Cchblt Sdn	$95,200	$112,000	$130,000	$196,000
						-30% for RHD.
1954	Phantom IV	4dr Limo	$703,000	$800,000	$906,000	$1 mil
						-30% for RHD.
1955	Silver Wraith	4dr Cchblt Sdn	$95,200	$112,000	$130,000	$196,000
						-30% for RHD.
1955	Silver Dawn	4dr Sdn	$44,300	$58,600	$76,100	$93,100
		2dr PW Conv	$185,000	$235,000	$316,000	$403,000
						-30% for RHD.
1955	Silver Cloud I	4dr Std Stl Sdn	$23,000	$36,100	$52,300	$65,200
		4dr LWB Sdn	$31,600	$48,000	$58,300	$70,200
		2dr HJM DHC	$326,000	$397,000	$473,000	$546,000
			-30% for RHD. +7% for factory pwr strng. +10% for factory a/c.			
1955	Phantom IV	4dr Limo	$703,000	$800,000	$906,000	$1 mil
						-30% for RHD.
1956	Silver Cloud I	4dr Std Stl Sdn	$23,000	$36,100	$52,300	$65,200
		4dr LWB Sdn	$31,600	$48,000	$58,300	$70,200
		2dr HJM DHC	$326,000	$397,000	$473,000	$546,000
			-30% for RHD. +7% for factory pwr strng. +10% for factory a/c.			
1956	Silver Wraith	4dr Cchblt Sdn	$118,000	$150,000	$191,000	$324,000
						-30% for RHD.
1956	Phantom IV	4dr Limo	$703,000	$800,000	$906,000	$1 mil
						-30% for RHD.
1957	Silver Cloud I	4dr Std Stl Sdn	$27,600	$39,800	$56,600	$71,000
		4dr LWB Sdn	$35,700	$50,000	$62,600	$76,500
		2dr HJM DHC	$326,000	$397,000	$473,000	$546,000
			-30% for RHD. +7% for factory pwr strng. +10% for factory a/c.			
1957	Silver Wraith	4dr Cchblt Sdn	$118,000	$150,000	$191,000	$324,000
						-30% for RHD.
1958	Silver Cloud I	4dr Std Stl Sdn	$29,000	$44,100	$59,900	$72,900
		4dr LWB Sdn	$37,600	$52,400	$65,800	$78,200
		2dr HJM DHC	$326,000	$397,000	$473,000	$546,000
			-30% for RHD. +7% for factory pwr strng. +10% for factory a/c.			
1958	Silver Wraith	4dr Cchblt Sdn	$146,000	$186,000	$225,000	$392,000
						-30% for RHD.
1959	Silver Cloud I	4dr Std Stl Sdn	$32,700	$46,000	$61,100	$75,900
		4dr LWB Sdn	$40,100	$54,800	$70,200	$88,100

Rolls-Royce

Year	Model	Body Style	4	3	2	1
						-30% for RHD. +10% for factory a/c.
		2dr HJM DHC	$329,000	$400,000	$478,000	$551,000
						-30% for RHD. +7% for factory pwr strng. +10% for factory a/c.
1959	Silver Wraith	4dr Cchblt Sdn	$156,000	$202,000	$248,000	$405,000
						-30% for RHD.
1959	Phantom V	4dr JY Limo	$108,000	$123,000	$144,000	$187,000
		4dr PW Limo	$68,500	$80,400	$90,900	$106,000
		4dr HJM Limo	$73,800	$92,700	$105,000	$124,000
						-30% for RHD.
1960	Silver Cloud II	4dr Std Stl Sdn	$38,500	$52,400	$67,100	$81,200
		4dr LWB Sdn	$39,600	$57,800	$71,300	$87,300
		2dr HJM DHC	$320,000	$401,000	$450,000	$545,000
						-30% for RHD. +10% for factory a/c.
1960	Phantom V	4dr JY Limo	$108,000	$123,000	$144,000	$187,000
		4dr PW Limo	$68,500	$80,400	$90,900	$106,000
		4dr HJM Limo	$73,800	$92,700	$105,000	$124,000
						-30% for RHD.
1961	Silver Cloud II	4dr Std Stl Sdn	$41,100	$53,700	$69,200	$85,000
		4dr LWB Sdn	$43,200	$59,100	$74,600	$90,100
		2dr HJM DHC	$320,000	$401,000	$450,000	$545,000
						-30% for RHD. +10% for factory a/c.
1961	Phantom V	4dr JY Limo	$108,000	$128,000	$153,000	$191,000
		4dr PW Limo	$68,500	$80,400	$90,900	$106,000
		4dr HJM Limo	$74,300	$93,600	$108,000	$128,000
						-30% for RHD.
1962	Silver Cloud II	4dr Std Stl Sdn	$42,100	$54,300	$72,400	$87,100
		4dr LWB Sdn	$48,900	$63,400	$79,400	$93,800
		2dr HJM DHC	$320,000	$401,000	$450,000	$545,000
						-30% for RHD. +10% for factory a/c.
1962	Phantom V	4dr JY Limo	$108,000	$128,000	$153,000	$191,000
		4dr PW Limo	$70,400	$81,500	$95,700	$120,000
		4dr HJM Limo	$74,300	$93,600	$108,000	$128,000
						-30% for RHD.
1963	Silver Cloud III	4dr Std Stl Sdn	$50,300	$64,000	$96,200	$108,000
		4dr LWB Sdn	$58,600	$75,800	$108,000	$121,000
		2dr HJM DHC	$554,000	$622,000	$690,000	$757,000
						-30% for RHD. +10% for factory a/c.
1963	Phantom V	4dr JY Limo	$113,000	$133,000	$172,000	$215,000
		4dr HJM Limo	$75,800	$96,000	$115,000	$134,000
		4dr PW Limo	$70,400	$81,500	$95,700	$120,000
						-30% for RHD.

Year	Model	Body Style	4	3	2	1
1964	Silver Cloud III	4dr Std Stl Sdn	$51,800	$64,900	$97,300	$114,000
		4dr LWB Sdn	$58,600	$75,800	$108,000	$122,000
		2dr HJM DHC	$554,000	$622,000	$690,000	$757,000
			-30% for RHD. +10% for factory a/c.			
1964	Phantom V	4dr JY Limo	$116,000	$137,000	$172,000	$215,000
		4dr HJM Limo	$81,200	$104,000	$119,000	$139,000
		4dr PW Limo	$81,600	$98,500	$114,000	$129,000
			-30% for RHD.			
1965	Silver Shadow	4dr Sdn	$5,000	$8,600	$15,200	$34,000
		2dr MPW FHC	$21,300	$29,500	$37,100	$59,100
			-30% for RHD.			
1965	Silver Cloud III	4dr Std Stl Sdn	$58,600	$71,200	$102,000	$124,000
		4dr LWB Sdn	$64,600	$84,800	$116,000	$133,000
		2dr HJM DHC	$554,000	$622,000	$690,000	$757,000
			-30% for RHD. +10% for factory a/c.			
1965	Phantom V	4dr JY Limo	$116,000	$137,000	$172,000	$215,000
		4dr HJM Limo	$81,200	$104,000	$119,000	$139,000
		4dr PW Limo	$81,600	$98,500	$114,000	$129,000
			-30% for RHD.			
1966	Silver Shadow	4dr Sdn	$5,000	$8,600	$15,200	$34,000
		2dr MPW FHC	$21,300	$29,500	$37,100	$59,100
		2dr MPW DHC	$23,400	$32,500	$40,800	$64,900
			-30% for RHD.			
1966	Phantom V	4dr JY Limo	$122,000	$143,000	$182,000	$225,000
		4dr PW Limo	$81,600	$98,500	$114,000	$129,000
		4dr HJM Limo	$81,200	$104,000	$119,000	$139,000
			-30% for RHD.			
1967	Silver Shadow	4dr Sdn	$5,100	$8,700	$15,200	$34,000
		2dr MPW FHC	$21,700	$29,800	$37,100	$59,100
		2dr MPW DHC	$23,900	$32,800	$40,800	$64,900
			-30% for RHD.			
1967	Phantom V	4dr JY Limo	$134,000	$158,000	$201,000	$239,000
		4dr PW Limo	$83,300	$99,500	$114,000	$129,000
		4dr HJM Limo	$87,800	$110,000	$124,000	$148,000
			-30% for RHD.			
1968	Silver Shadow	4dr Std Stl Sdn	$5,100	$8,700	$15,200	$34,000
		2dr MPW FHC	$21,700	$29,800	$37,100	$59,100
		2dr MPW DHC	$23,900	$33,900	$42,500	$66,400
			-30% for RHD.			
1968	Phantom V	4dr JY Limo	$148,000	$167,000	$225,000	$278,000
		4dr PW Limo	$83,300	$99,500	$114,000	$129,000
		4dr HJM Limo	$94,000	$117,000	$134,000	$159,000
			-30% for RHD.			

Rolls-Royce

Year	Model	Body Style	4	3	2	1
1969	Silver Shadow	4dr Std Stl Sdn	$5,100	$8,700	$15,200	$34,000
		2dr MPW FHC	$21,700	$29,800	$37,100	$59,100
		2dr MPW DHC	$23,900	$33,900	$42,500	$66,400
						-30% for RHD.
1969	Phantom VI	4dr Limo	$100,000	$137,000	$187,000	$221,000
						-30% for RHD.
1970	Silver Shadow	4dr Std Stl Sdn	$5,100	$8,700	$15,200	$34,000
		2dr MPW FHC	$21,700	$29,800	$37,100	$59,100
		2dr MPW DHC	$23,900	$33,900	$42,500	$66,400
						-30% for RHD.
1970	Phantom VI	4dr Limo	$100,000	$137,000	$187,000	$221,000
						-30% for RHD.
1971	Silver Shadow	4dr Std Stl Sdn	$5,100	$8,700	$15,200	$34,000
		4dr LWB Sdn	$6,600	$11,100	$17,000	$33,800
						-30% for RHD.
1971	Corniche I	2dr FHC	$14,600	$23,800	$36,800	$48,800
		2dr DHC	$20,900	$30,700	$39,700	$52,700
						-30% for RHD.
1971	Phantom VI	4dr Limo	$104,000	$145,000	$193,000	$230,000
						-30% for RHD.
1972	Silver Shadow	4dr Std Stl Sdn	$5,100	$8,700	$15,200	$36,300
		4dr LWB Sdn	$6,600	$11,100	$17,000	$41,300
						-30% for RHD.
1972	Corniche I	2dr FHC	$14,600	$23,800	$36,800	$48,800
		2dr DHC	$20,900	$30,700	$39,700	$52,700
						-30% for RHD.
1972	Phantom VI	4dr Limo	$111,000	$152,000	$203,000	$242,000
						-30% for RHD.
1973	Silver Shadow	4dr Std Stl Sdn	$5,200	$9,600	$15,200	$36,300
		4dr LWB Sdn	$6,600	$11,100	$17,000	$41,300
						-30% for RHD.
1973	Corniche I	2dr FHC	$14,600	$23,800	$36,800	$48,800
		2dr FHC (rubber bump)	$9,700	$16,800	$27,700	$41,400
		2dr DHC	$20,900	$30,700	$39,700	$52,700
		2dr DHC (rubber bump)	$22,500	$31,700	$41,600	$55,100
						-30% for RHD.
1973	Phantom VI	4dr Limo	$118,000	$169,000	$209,000	$248,000
						-30% for RHD.
1974	Silver Shadow	4dr Std Stl Sdn	$5,200	$9,600	$15,200	$31,600

Year	Model	Body Style	4	3	2	1
		4dr LWB Sdn	$6,600	$11,100	$17,000	$33,800
						-30% for RHD.
1974	Corniche I	2dr FHC (rubber bump)	$9,700	$16,800	$27,700	$41,400
		2dr DHC (rubber bump)	$22,500	$31,700	$41,600	$55,100
						-30% for RHD.
1974	Phantom VI	4dr Limo	$120,000	$174,000	$217,000	$256,000
						-30% for RHD.
1975	Silver Shadow	4dr Std Stl Sdn	$5,200	$9,600	$15,200	$31,600
		4dr LWB Sdn	$6,600	$11,100	$17,000	$33,800
						-30% for RHD.
1975	Corniche I	2dr FHC (rubber bump)	$9,700	$16,800	$27,700	$41,400
		2dr DHC (rubber bump)	$22,500	$31,700	$41,600	$55,100
						-30% for RHD.
1975	Camargue	2dr Cpe	$22,400	$31,000	$40,000	$51,000
						-30% for RHD.
1975	Phantom VI	4dr Limo	$125,000	$182,000	$227,000	$260,000
						-30% for RHD.
1976	Silver Shadow II	4dr Std Stl Sdn	$6,300	$11,900	$16,900	$33,500
						-30% for RHD.
1976	Corniche I	2dr FHC	$17,500	$29,700	$41,100	$53,800
		2dr DHC	$22,500	$33,300	$43,800	$56,400
						-30% for RHD.
1976	Camargue	2dr Cpe	$24,000	$31,900	$42,500	$55,000
						-30% for RHD.
1976	Phantom VI	4dr Limo	$125,000	$182,000	$227,000	$260,000
						-30% for RHD.
1977	Silver Shadow II	4dr Sdn	$6,300	$11,900	$16,900	$33,500
						-30% for RHD.
1977	Corniche I	2dr FHC	$17,500	$29,700	$41,100	$53,800
		2dr DHC	$22,500	$33,300	$43,800	$56,400
						-30% for RHD.
1977	Camargue	2dr Cpe	$24,000	$31,900	$42,500	$55,000
						-30% for RHD.
1977	Silver Wraith II	4dr Sdn	$6,600	$12,400	$17,500	$35,000
						-30% for RHD.
1977	Phantom VI	4dr Limo	$125,000	$182,000	$227,000	$260,000
						-30% for RHD.
1978	Silver Shadow II	4dr Sdn	$6,300	$11,900	$16,900	$33,500
						-30% for RHD.
1978	Corniche I	2dr FHC	$17,500	$29,700	$41,100	$53,800

Rolls-Royce

Year	Model	Body Style	4	3	2	1
		2dr DHC	$22,500	$33,300	$43,800	$56,400
						-30% for RHD.
1978	Camargue	2dr Cpe	$22,400	$31,000	$40,000	$51,000
						-30% for RHD.
1978	Silver Wraith II	4dr Sdn	$6,600	$12,400	$17,500	$35,000
						-30% for RHD.
1978	Phantom VI	4dr Limo	$125,000	$182,000	$227,000	$260,000
						-30% for RHD.
1979	Silver Shadow II	4dr Sdn	$6,300	$11,900	$16,900	$33,500
						-30% for RHD.
1979	Corniche I	2dr FHC	$23,000	$35,900	$47,600	$64,800
		2dr DHC	$24,900	$34,000	$46,200	$53,800
						-30% for RHD.
1979	Camargue	2dr Cpe	$22,400	$31,000	$40,000	$51,000
						-30% for RHD.
1979	Silver Wraith II	4dr Sdn	$6,600	$12,400	$17,500	$35,000
						-30% for RHD.
1979	Phantom VI	4dr Limo	$125,000	$182,000	$227,000	$260,000
						-30% for RHD.
1980	Silver Shadow II	4dr Sdn	$6,700	$13,100	$20,500	$36,400
						-30% for RHD.
1980	Corniche I	2dr FHC	$23,700	$36,600	$48,400	$66,900
		2dr DHC	$25,700	$34,700	$47,000	$54,800
						-30% for RHD.
1980	Camargue	2dr Cpe	$24,000	$33,000	$44,000	$58,000
						-30% for RHD.
1980	Silver Wraith II	4dr Sdn	$7,400	$14,200	$23,400	$38,600
						-30% for RHD.
1980	Phantom VI	4dr Limo	$160,000	$202,000	$242,000	$281,000
						-30% for RHD.
1981	Corniche I	2dr DHC	$25,000	$34,300	$45,600	$55,000
						-30% for RHD.
1981	Camargue	2dr Cpe	$24,000	$33,000	$44,000	$58,000
						-30% for RHD.
1981	Silver Spirit	4dr Sdn	$6,100	$8,800	$13,300	$18,100
						-30% for RHD.
1981	Silver Spur	4dr Sdn	$6,800	$9,600	$14,400	$19,100
						-30% for RHD.
1981	Phantom VI	4dr Limo	$168,000	$207,000	$248,000	$292,000
						-30% for RHD.
1982	Corniche I	2dr DHC	$25,000	$34,300	$45,600	$55,000
						-30% for RHD.
1982	Camargue	2dr Cpe	$26,000	$35,000	$46,000	$58,000
						-30% for RHD.

Year	Model	Body Style	4	3	2	1
1982	Silver Spirit	4dr Sdn	$6,100	$8,800	$13,300	$18,100 -30% for RHD.
1982	Silver Spur	4dr Sdn	$6,800	$9,600	$14,400	$19,100 -30% for RHD.
1982	Phantom VI	4dr Limo	$168,000	$207,000	$248,000	$292,000 -30% for RHD.
1983	Corniche I	2dr DHC	$25,000	$34,300	$45,600	$55,000 -30% for RHD.
1983	Camargue	2dr Cpe	$26,000	$35,000	$46,000	$58,000 -30% for RHD.
1983	Silver Spirit	4dr Sdn	$6,100	$8,800	$13,300	$18,100 -30% for RHD.
1983	Silver Spur	4dr Sdn	$6,800	$9,600	$14,400	$19,100 -30% for RHD.
1983	Phantom VI	4dr Limo	$168,000	$207,000	$248,000	$292,000 -30% for RHD.
1984	Corniche I	2dr DHC	$25,000	$34,300	$45,600	$55,000 -30% for RHD.
1984	Camargue	2dr Cpe	$26,400	$35,300	$47,500	$62,000 -30% for RHD.
1984	Silver Spirit	4dr Sdn	$6,100	$9,000	$13,900	$21,700 -30% for RHD.
1984	Silver Spur	4dr Sdn	$6,900	$10,900	$16,500	$23,800 -30% for RHD.
1984	Phantom VI	4dr Limo	$174,000	$216,000	$256,000	$302,000 -30% for RHD.
1985	Corniche I	2dr DHC	$25,500	$34,800	$46,100	$56,000 -30% for RHD.
1985	Camargue	2dr Cpe	$26,400	$35,300	$47,500	$62,000 -30% for RHD.
1985	Silver Spirit	4dr Sdn	$6,100	$9,000	$13,900	$21,700 -30% for RHD.
1985	Silver Spur	4dr Sdn	$6,900	$10,900	$16,500	$23,800 -30% for RHD.
1985	Phantom VI	4dr Limo	$174,000	$216,000	$256,000	$302,000 -30% for RHD.
1986	Corniche I	2dr DHC	$25,500	$34,800	$46,100	$56,000 -30% for RHD.
1986	Camargue	2dr Cpe	$31,000	$42,000	$55,000	$67,500 -30% for RHD.
1986	Silver Spirit	4dr Sdn	$6,100	$9,000	$13,900	$21,700 -30% for RHD.
1986	Silver Spur	4dr Sdn	$6,900	$10,900	$16,500	$23,800 -30% for RHD.

Rolls-Royce

Year	Model	Body Style	4	3	2	1
1986	Phantom VI	4dr Limo	$174,000	$216,000	$256,000	$302,000
						-30% for RHD.
1987	Corniche I	2dr DHC	$27,000	$36,000	$48,000	$59,000
						-30% for RHD.
1987	Corniche II	2dr (S/Ns 20,000 and above) DHC	$47,000	$56,000	$69,000	$84,500
						-30% for RHD.
1987	Camargue	2dr Cpe	$39,000	$48,000	$67,000	$80,000
						-30% for RHD.
1987	Silver Spirit	4dr Sdn	$6,100	$9,000	$13,900	$21,700
		4dr (S/Ns 20,000 and above) Sdn	$7,800	$13,000	$16,600	$23,800
						-30% for RHD.
1987	Silver Spur	4dr Sdn	$6,900	$10,900	$16,500	$23,800
		4dr (S/Ns 20,000 and above) Sdn	$7,900	$13,300	$18,000	$24,900
						-30% for RHD.
1987	Phantom VI	4dr Limo	$181,000	$221,000	$268,000	$313,000
						-30% for RHD.
1988	Corniche II	2dr DHC	$47,000	$56,000	$69,000	$84,500
						-30% for RHD.
1988	Silver Spirit	4dr Sdn	$7,800	$13,000	$16,600	$23,800
						-30% for RHD.
1988	Silver Spur	4dr Sdn	$7,900	$13,300	$18,000	$24,900
						-30% for RHD.
1988	Phantom VI	4dr Limo	$181,000	$221,000	$268,000	$313,000
						-30% for RHD.
1989	Corniche III	2dr DHC	$53,000	$69,000	$89,000	$105,000
						-30% for RHD.
1989	Silver Spirit II	4dr Sdn	$9,400	$14,700	$21,700	$28,000
						-30% for RHD.
1989	Silver Spur	4dr Sdn	$9,800	$15,600	$22,900	$29,800
						-30% for RHD.
1989	Phantom VI	4dr Limo	$181,000	$221,000	$268,000	$313,000
						-30% for RHD.
1990	Corniche III	2dr DHC	$53,000	$69,000	$89,000	$105,000
						-30% for RHD.
1990	Silver Spirit II	4dr Sdn	$9,400	$14,700	$21,700	$28,000
						-30% for RHD.
1990	Silver Spur II	4dr Sdn	$9,800	$15,600	$22,900	$29,800
						-30% for RHD.
1990	Phantom VI	4dr Limo	$184,000	$226,000	$278,000	$322,000
						-30% for RHD.
1991	Corniche IV	2dr Sdn	$49,500	$63,400	$89,000	$112,000
						-30% for RHD.

Rolls-Royce

Year	Model	Body Style	4	3	2	1
1991	Silver Spirit II	4dr Sdn	$9,400	$14,700	$21,700	$28,000 -30% for RHD.
1991	Silver Spur II	4dr Sdn	$9,800	$15,600	$22,900	$29,800 -30% for RHD.
1991	Phantom VI	4dr Limo	$187,000	$232,000	$283,000	$329,000 -30% for RHD.
1992	Corniche IV	2dr DHC	$49,500	$63,400	$89,000	$112,000 -30% for RHD.
1992	Silver Spirit II	4dr Sdn	$9,400	$14,700	$21,700	$28,000 -30% for RHD.
1992	Silver Spur II	4dr Sdn	$9,800	$15,600	$22,900	$29,800 -30% for RHD.
1993	Corniche IV	2dr DHC	$54,000	$72,000	$99,000	$120,000 -30% for RHD.
1993	Silver Spur II	4dr Sdn	$11,300	$17,100	$24,600	$31,600 -30% for RHD.
1994	Corniche IV	2dr DHC	$60,000	$87,000	$118,000	$130,000 -30% for RHD.
1994	Silver Spur II	4dr Sdn	$11,300	$17,100	$24,600	$31,600 -30% for RHD.
1995	Corniche IV	2dr DHC	$60,000	$87,000	$118,000	$130,000 -30% for RHD.
1995	Silver Spur II	4dr Sdn	$11,300	$17,100	$24,600	$31,600 -30% for RHD.
1995	Flying Spur	4dr Sdn	$24,000	$31,700	$42,000	$49,500 -30% for RHD.

Rover

Year	Model	Body Style	4	3	2	1
1960	2000TC	4dr Sdn	$3,800	$7,600	$13,200	$18,200
1961	2000TC	4dr Sdn	$3,800	$7,600	$13,200	$18,200
1962	2000TC	4dr Sdn	$3,800	$7,600	$13,200	$18,200
1963	2000TC	4dr Sdn	$3,800	$7,600	$13,200	$18,200
1964	2000TC	4dr Sdn	$3,800	$7,600	$13,200	$18,200
1965	2000TC	4dr Sdn	$3,800	$7,600	$13,200	$18,200
1966	2000TC	4dr Sdn	$3,800	$7,600	$13,200	$18,200
1967	2000TC	4dr Sdn	$3,800	$7,600	$13,200	$18,200
1968	2000TC	4dr Sdn	$3,800	$7,600	$13,200	$18,200
1969	2000TC	4dr Sdn	$3,800	$7,600	$13,200	$18,200
1970	2000TC	4dr Sdn	$3,800	$7,600	$13,200	$18,200
1971	2000TC	2dr Sdn	$3,800	$7,600	$13,200	$18,200

Saab

Year	Model	Body Style	4	3	2	1
1950	92	2dr Cpe	$4,900	$7,800	$11,500	$18,800

Saab

Year	Model	Body Style	4	3	2	1
1951	92	2dr Cpe	$4,900	$7,800	$11,500	$18,800
1952	92	2dr Cpe	$4,900	$7,800	$11,500	$18,800
1953	92B	2dr Cpe	$4,800	$7,700	$11,500	$18,700
1954	92B	2dr Cpe	$4,800	$7,700	$11,500	$18,700
1955	92B	2dr Cpe	$4,800	$7,700	$11,500	$18,700
1956	92B	2dr Cpe	$4,800	$7,700	$11,500	$18,700
1956	93	2dr Cpe	$4,900	$8,900	$13,900	$23,200
1957	93	2dr Cpe	$4,900	$8,900	$13,900	$23,200
1958	93B	2dr Cpe	$4,700	$7,500	$11,200	$17,600
1958	GT 750	2dr Cpe	$8,400	$15,400	$25,000	$39,600
1959	93B	2dr Cpe	$4,700	$7,500	$11,200	$17,600
1959	95	2dr Bullnose Wgn	$9,000	$16,300	$20,100	$40,000
1959	GT 750	2dr Cpe	$8,600	$15,400	$25,000	$39,600
1960	95	2dr Bullnose Wgn	$5,600	$9,900	$18,700	$30,000
1960	96	2dr Bullnose Cpe	$3,900	$8,400	$14,400	$21,900
1961	95	2dr Bullnose Wgn	$5,600	$9,900	$18,800	$30,000
1961	96	2dr Bullnose Cpe	$3,900	$8,400	$14,400	$21,900
1961	GT 750	2dr Cpe	$6,600	$12,300	$20,100	$31,600
1962	95	2dr Bullnose Wgn	$5,600	$9,900	$18,800	$30,000
1962	96	2dr Bullnose Cpe	$3,900	$8,400	$14,600	$21,900
1962	GT 750	2dr Cpe	$6,600	$12,300	$20,100	$31,600
1963	95	2dr Bullnose Wgn	$5,600	$9,900	$18,800	$30,000
1963	96	2dr Bullnose Cpe	$3,900	$8,400	$14,400	$21,900
1963	GT 850	2dr Spt Cpe	$6,500	$13,400	$19,300	$29,600
1964	95	2dr Bullnose Wgn	$5,600	$9,900	$18,800	$30,000
1964	96	2dr Bullnose Cpe	$3,900	$8,400	$14,400	$21,900
1964	GT 850	2dr Spt Cpe	$6,500	$13,400	$19,300	$29,600
1965	95	2dr 3-cyl. Wgn	$3,300	$7,100	$12,900	$19,500
1965	96	2dr 3-cyl. Cpe	$3,100	$6,500	$10,000	$15,800
1965	Monte Carlo	2dr Cpe	$5,900	$13,000	$19,500	$30,000
1966	95	2dr Wgn	$3,300	$7,100	$12,900	$19,500
1966	96	2dr Cpe	$3,100	$6,500	$10,000	$15,800
1966	Sonett	2dr II Cpe	$8,400	$15,700	$24,100	$31,300
						-20% for later flat rear window.
1967	95	2dr 3-cyl. Wgn	$3,300	$7,100	$12,900	$19,500
		2dr V4 Wgn	$3,300	$9,000	$16,000	$24,800
1967	96	2dr 3-cyl. Cpe	$3,100	$6,500	$10,000	$15,800
		2dr V4 Cpe	$3,200	$6,700	$14,600	$20,500
1967	Monte Carlo	2dr Cpe	$5,900	$13,000	$19,500	$30,000
1967	Sonett	2dr II Cpe	$8,400	$15,700	$24,100	$31,300
						-20% for later flat rear window.
		2dr V4 Cpe	$4,900	$9,400	$17,600	$30,500
1968	95	2dr 3-cyl. Wgn	$3,000	$6,500	$11,700	$16,900
		2dr V4 Wgn	$3,300	$9,000	$16,000	$24,800
1968	96	2dr 3-cyl. Cpe	$3,100	$6,500	$10,000	$15,800
		2dr V4 Cpe	$3,200	$6,700	$14,600	$20,500
1968	Sonett	2dr V4 Cpe	$4,900	$9,400	$17,600	$30,500
1969	95	2dr V4 Wgn	$3,300	$9,000	$16,000	$24,800

Saab

Year	Model	Body Style	4	3	2	1
1969	96	2dr V4 Cpe	$3,200	$6,700	$14,600	$20,500
1969	Sonett	2dr V4 Cpe	$4,900	$9,400	$17,600	$30,500
1970	95	2dr V4 Wgn	$3,300	$9,000	$16,000	$24,800
1970	96	2dr V4 Cpe	$3,200	$6,700	$14,600	$20,500
1970	Sonett	2dr III Cpe	$3,000	$6,300	$11,100	$16,100
1971	95	2dr V4 Wgn	$3,300	$9,000	$16,000	$24,800
1971	96	2dr V4 Cpe	$3,200	$6,700	$14,600	$20,500
1971	Sonett	2dr III Cpe	$3,000	$6,300	$11,100	$16,100
1972	95	2dr V4 Wgn	$3,300	$9,000	$16,000	$24,800
1972	96	2dr V4 Cpe	$3,200	$6,700	$14,600	$20,500
1972	Sonett	2dr III Cpe	$3,000	$6,300	$11,100	$16,100
1973	99 EMS	2dr Cpe	$2,600	$5,000	$9,600	$16,000
1973	95	2dr V4 Wgn	$3,300	$9,000	$16,000	$24,800
1973	96	2dr V4 Cpe	$3,200	$6,700	$14,600	$20,500
1973	Sonett	2dr III Cpe	$3,000	$6,300	$11,100	$16,100
		2dr III Cpe (fed bump)	$2,600	$5,700	$10,500	$15,000
1974	99 EMS	2dr Sdn	$2,600	$5,000	$9,600	$16,000
1974	Sonett	2dr III Cpe	$2,600	$5,700	$10,500	$15,000
1975	95	2dr V4 Wgn	$3,300	$9,000	$16,000	$24,800
1975	96	2dr V4 Cpe	$3,200	$6,700	$14,600	$20,500
1975	99 EMS	2dr Sdn	$3,000	$5,700	$10,400	$17,300
1976	99 EMS	2dr Cpe	$3,000	$5,700	$10,400	$17,300
1977	99 EMS	2dr Cpe	$3,000	$5,700	$10,400	$17,300
1977	99 Turbo	2dr Cpe	$3,200	$6,000	$10,200	$17,200
		2dr Press Car Cpe	$3,800	$7,100	$12,100	$20,500
1978	99	2dr Turbo Cpe	$3,600	$6,400	$11,400	$23,900
1978	99 EMS	2dr Cpe	$3,600	$6,400	$11,400	$23,900
1981	99	2dr Turbo Cpe	$3,600	$6,400	$11,400	$23,900
2005	9-2X	4dr Aero Wgn	$5,100	$10,200	$14,300	$22,400
						-15% for auto trans.
2006	9-2X	4dr Aero Wgn	$5,100	$10,200	$14,300	$22,400
						-15% for auto trans.

Sabra

Year	Model	Body Style	4	3	2	1
1962	Sports	2dr GT Cpe	$14,600	$22,300	$39,100	$65,600
		2dr Rdstr	$18,700	$39,500	$54,800	$78,300
1962	Sussita	2dr Wgn	$4,600	$9,200	$14,000	$21,200
1963	Sports	2dr GT Cpe	$14,600	$22,300	$39,100	$65,600
		2dr Rdstr	$18,700	$39,500	$54,800	$78,300
1963	Sussita	2dr Wgn	$4,600	$9,200	$14,000	$21,200
1964	Sports	2dr GT Cpe	$14,600	$22,300	$39,100	$65,600
		2dr Rdstr	$18,700	$39,500	$54,800	$78,300
1964	Sussita	2dr Wgn	$4,600	$9,200	$14,000	$21,200

Saleen

Year	Model	Body Style	4	3	2	1
2002	S7	427/550 2dr Cpe	$235,000	$328,000	$411,000	$542,000
2003	S7	427/550 2dr Cpe	$235,000	$328,000	$411,000	$542,000
2004	S7	427/550 2dr Cpe	$235,000	$328,000	$411,000	$542,000
2005	S7	427/550 2dr Cpe	$235,000	$328,000	$411,000	$542,000
		427/750 2dr Twin Turbo Cpe	$454,000	$550,000	$645,000	$760,000
2006	S7	427/750 2dr Twin Turbo Cpe	$454,000	$550,000	$645,000	$760,000
2007	S7	427/750 2dr Twin Turbo Cpe	$454,000	$550,000	$645,000	$760,000
2008	S7	427/750 2dr Twin Turbo Cpe	$454,000	$550,000	$645,000	$760,000
2009	S7	427/750 2dr Twin Turbo Cpe	$454,000	$550,000	$645,000	$760,000

Saturn

Year	Model	Body Style	4	3	2	1
2007	Sky	145/177 2dr Conv	$5,100	$7,700	$13,300	$20,500
		122/260 2dr Redline Conv	$6,600	$11,000	$17,300	$27,000
						-5% for auto trans.
2008	Sky	122/260 2dr Redline Conv	$6,600	$11,000	$17,300	$27,000
		145/177 2dr Conv	$5,100	$7,700	$13,300	$20,500
						-5% for auto trans.
2009	Sky	122/260 2dr Redline Conv	$6,600	$11,000	$17,300	$27,000
		145/177 2dr Conv	$5,100	$7,700	$13,300	$20,500
						-5% for auto trans.
2010	Sky	2.4L 2dr Conv	$5,700	$8,400	$14,600	$22,600
		2.4L 2dr Preferred Conv	$6,700	$10,300	$16,400	$26,200
		122/260 2dr Redline Conv	$7,300	$12,100	$19,100	$29,700
						-5% for auto trans.

Shelby

Year	Model	Body Style	4	3	2	1
1962	Cobra	2dr 260 Rdstr	$660,000	$735,000	$875,000	$1 mil
			CSX2000-2010 factory competition cars should be valued separately according to race history.			
1963	Cobra	2dr 260 Rdstr	$660,000	$735,000	$875,000	$1 mil
			CSX2000-2010 factory competition cars should be valued separately according to race history.			
		2dr 289 W&S Rdstr	$660,000	$765,000	$900,000	$1.1 mil

Year	Model	Body Style	4	3	2	1
		2dr 289 R&P Rdstr	$875,000	$950,000	$1.25 mil	$1.5 mil
		2dr Dragonsnake Rdstr	$1.05 mil	$1.15 mil	$1.5 mil	$1.8 mil
		-20% for road cars converted to Dragonsnake specification, individual history and originality of chassis, body, and components dictate value more than condition.				
1964	Cobra	2dr 289 R&P Rdstr	$875,000	$950,000	$1.25 mil	$1.5 mil
		2dr Dragonsnake Rdstr	$1.05 mil	$1.15 mil	$1.5 mil	$1.8 mil
		-20% for road cars converted to Dragonsnake specification, individual history and originality of chassis, body, and components dictate value more than condition.				
1965	Cobra	2dr 289 R&P Rdstr	$875,000	$950,000	$1.25 mil	$1.5 mil
		2dr Dragonsnake Rdstr	$1.05 mil	$1.15 mil	$1.5 mil	$1.8 mil
		-20% for road cars converted to Dragonsnake specification, individual history and originality of chassis, body, and components dictate value more than condition.				
		2dr 427 (CSX3101 - CSX3200) Rdstr	$1 mil	$1.3 mil	$1.9 mil	$2.1 mil
		+15% for narrow hip cars (manufactured in the CSX3125-CSX3158 range).				
		2dr 427 S/C Rdstr	$1.5 mil	$1.9 mil	$2.2 mil	$2.5 mil
		2dr 427 Competition Rdstr	$1.75 mil	$1.9 mil	$2.4 mil	$3.3 mil
		2dr 428 Rdstr	$750,000	$850,000	$1.1 mil	$1.35 mil
		2dr COB/COX Rdstr	$414,000	$520,000	$607,000	$748,000
		Some COB and COX prefix cars were built in period, while others were finished later. Be mindful of completion date.				
		2dr 427 S/C Completion Rdstr	$167,000	$200,000	$248,000	$300,000
		2dr CSX 4000 Continuation Rdstr	$94,500	$122,000	$157,000	$190,000
		+$15,000 for aluminum body. Quality and correctness of this series Cobra vary greatly and can have a tremendous impact on value.				
1965	Cobra Daytona	2dr Cpe	$20.2 mil	$23.25 mil	$27.25 mil	$30.3 mil
1965	GT350	2dr Fstbk	$265,000	$368,000	$435,000	$520,000
1965	GT350R	2dr Fstbk	$685,000	$770,000	$898,000	$1.05 mil
1966	Cobra	2dr 427 (CSX3101 - CSX3200) Rdstr	$1 mil	$1.3 mil	$1.9 mil	$2.1 mil
		2dr 427 (CSX3300 - CSX3360) Rdstr	$925,000	$1.05 mil	$1.35 mil	$1.95 mil
		Some 428s exist in the CSX3300 S/N range (3300, 3301, 3305, 3306), and should be valued as 428 cars.				
		2dr 427 S/C Rdstr	$1.5 mil	$1.9 mil	$2.2 mil	$2.5 mil

Shelby

Year	Model	Body Style	4	3	2	1
		2dr 427 Competition Rdstr	$1.75 mil	$1.9 mil	$2.4 mil	$3.3 mil
		2dr 428 Rdstr	$750,000	$850,000	$1.1 mil	$1.35 mil
1966	GT350	2dr Fstbk	$120,000	$147,000	$196,000	$275,000
		For fastback: +35% for 1965 carry-over cars up to S/N 252.				
		Supercharged 2dr Fstbk	$264,000	$370,000	$435,000	$490,000
		2dr Conv	$681,000	$740,000	$856,000	$946,000
		2dr Hllywd Sports Cars Conv	$93,000	$114,000	$146,000	$176,000
		For fastback: +35% for 1965 carry-over cars up to S/N 252.				
1966	GT350H	2dr Fstbk	$97,000	$128,000	$171,000	$232,000
1967	Cobra	2dr 427 (CSX3300 - CSX3360) Rdstr	$925,000	$1.05 mil	$1.35 mil	$1.95 mil
		Some 428s exist in the CSX3300 S/N range (3300, 3301, 3305, 3306), and should be valued as 428 cars.				
		2dr 428 Rdstr	$750,000	$850,000	$1.1 mil	$1.35 mil
1967	GT350	2dr Fstbk	$94,500	$117,000	$145,000	$185,000
		+10% for factory a/c. -20% for auto.				
		Supercharged 2dr Fstbk	$234,000	$287,000	$325,000	$385,000
1967	GT500	2dr Fstbk	$111,000	$155,000	$220,000	$274,000
		+10% for factory a/c. -20% for auto.				
1968	GT350	2dr Fstbk	$58,200	$68,600	$87,000	$111,000
		2dr Conv	$88,000	$97,000	$127,000	$155,000
		+10% for factory a/c. -20% for auto.				
1968	GT500	2dr Fstbk	$82,100	$103,000	$136,000	$160,000
		2dr Conv	$89,600	$115,000	$147,000	$180,000
		+10% for factory a/c. -20% for auto.				
1968	GT500 KR	2dr Fstbk	$94,100	$120,000	$160,000	$205,000
		2dr Conv	$112,000	$136,000	$211,000	$269,000
		+10% for factory a/c. -20% for auto.				
1969	GT350	2dr SprtsRf	$50,200	$60,600	$74,500	$94,800
		2dr Conv	$87,000	$102,000	$143,000	$197,000
		+10% for factory a/c. -20% for auto.				
1969	GT500	2dr SprtsRf	$72,100	$91,000	$116,000	$146,000
		2dr Conv	$111,000	$147,000	$189,000	$228,000
		+20% for Drag Pak. +10% for factory a/c. -20% for auto.				
1970	GT350	2dr SprtsRf	$50,200	$60,600	$74,500	$94,800
		2dr Conv	$87,000	$102,000	$143,000	$197,000
		+10% for factory a/c. -20% for auto.				
1970	GT500	2dr SprtsRf	$72,100	$91,000	$116,000	$146,000
		2dr Conv	$111,000	$147,000	$189,000	$228,000
		+20% for Drag Pak. +10% for factory a/c. -20% for auto.				
1999	Series 1	2dr Conv	$82,600	$103,000	$120,000	$144,000

Siata

Year	Model	Body Style	4	3	2	1
1949	Amica	2dr Cpe	$17,500	$26,800	$38,000	$57,100
		2dr Spider	$23,200	$37,300	$49,500	$67,000
1950	Amica	2dr Cpe	$17,500	$26,800	$38,000	$57,100
		2dr Spider	$23,200	$37,300	$49,500	$67,000
1951	Amica	2dr Cpe	$17,500	$26,800	$38,000	$57,100
		2dr Spider	$23,200	$37,300	$49,500	$67,000
1951	300BC	2dr Spider	$132,000	$160,000	$212,000	$280,000
1951	Daina	2dr Cpe	$132,000	$153,000	$199,000	$278,000
		2dr Spider	$205,000	$220,000	$268,000	$361,000
1952	Daina	2dr Cpe	$132,000	$153,000	$199,000	$278,000
		2dr Spider	$205,000	$220,000	$268,000	$361,000
1952	200CS	2dr Cpe	$460,000	$541,000	$604,000	$685,000
1952	300BC	2dr Spider	$132,000	$160,000	$212,000	$280,000
1952	440L	2dr Spider	$398,000	$460,000	$588,000	$691,000
1953	Daina	2dr Cpe	$132,000	$153,000	$199,000	$278,000
		2dr Spider	$205,000	$220,000	$268,000	$361,000
1953	200CS	2dr Cpe	$460,000	$541,000	$601,000	$685,000
1953	300BC	2dr Spider	$132,000	$160,000	$212,000	$280,000
1953	208	2dr Cpe	$970,000	$1.2 mil	$1.5 mil	$1.75 mil
1953	208S	2dr Spider	$1.1 mil	$1.3 mil	$1.65 mil	$1.95 mil
1954	Daina	2dr Cpe	$132,000	$153,000	$199,000	$278,000
		2dr Spider	$205,000	$220,000	$268,000	$361,000
1954	200CS	2dr Cpe	$460,000	$541,000	$601,000	$685,000
1954	300BC	2dr Spider	$132,000	$160,000	$212,000	$280,000
1954	208	2dr Cpe	$970,000	$1.2 mil	$1.5 mil	$1.75 mil
1954	208S	2dr Spider	$1.1 mil	$1.3 mil	$1.65 mil	$1.95 mil
1955	Daina	2dr Cpe	$132,000	$153,000	$199,000	$278,000
		2dr Spider	$205,000	$220,000	$268,000	$361,000
1955	200CS	2dr Cpe	$460,000	$541,000	$601,000	$685,000
1956	200CS	2dr Cpe	$460,000	$541,000	$601,000	$685,000
1957	200CS	2dr Cpe	$460,000	$541,000	$601,000	$685,000
1958	200CS	2dr Cpe	$460,000	$541,000	$601,000	$685,000
1968	Spring	2dr Conv	$3,600	$7,200	$15,100	$20,200
1969	Spring	2dr Conv	$3,600	$7,200	$15,100	$20,200
1970	Spring	2dr Conv	$3,600	$7,200	$15,100	$20,200
1971	Spring	2dr Conv	$3,600	$7,200	$15,100	$20,200
1972	Spring	2dr Conv	$3,600	$7,200	$15,100	$20,200
1973	Spring	2dr Conv	$3,600	$7,200	$15,100	$20,200
1974	Spring	2dr Conv	$3,600	$7,200	$15,100	$20,200
1975	Spring	2dr Conv	$3,600	$7,200	$15,100	$20,200

Singer

Year	Model	Body Style	4	3	2	1
1951	SM	2dr 4AD Rdstr	$8,800	$13,800	$20,000	$30,000
1952	SM	2dr 4AD Rdstr	$8,800	$13,800	$20,000	$30,000
1953	SM	2dr 4AD Rdstr	$8,800	$13,800	$20,000	$30,000
1954	SM	2dr 4AD Rdstr	$8,800	$13,800	$20,000	$30,000
1955	SM	2dr 4AD Rdstr	$8,800	$13,800	$20,000	$30,000

Skorpion

Year	Model	Body Style	4	3	2	1
1952	Base	2dr Rdstr	$9,100	$12,500	$23,500	$37,200

Studebaker

Year	Model	Body Style	4	3	2	1
1947	Champion	169.6/80 2dr Dlx Cpe 3P	$3,200	$6,500	$12,300	$16,100
		169.6/80 2dr Rgl Dlx Cpe 3P	$3,400	$6,800	$12,600	$16,900
		169.6/80 2dr Dlx Cpe 5P	$2,700	$6,000	$11,900	$16,100
		169.6/80 2dr Rgl Dlx Cpe 5P	$2,800	$6,400	$12,300	$16,500
		169.6/80 2dr Dlx Sdn	$2,300	$5,700	$9,000	$14,200
		169.6/80 2dr Rgl Dlx Sdn	$3,200	$6,100	$9,700	$14,800
		169.6/80 4dr Dlx Sdn	$2,300	$4,700	$7,800	$13,000
		169.6/80 4dr Rgl Dlx Sdn	$2,900	$4,800	$8,300	$13,300
		169.6/80 2dr Rgl Dlx Conv	$14,100	$22,600	$33,000	$44,300
1947	Commander	226.2/94 2dr Dlx Cpe 3P	$4,300	$7,600	$14,400	$18,800
		226.2/94 2dr Rgl Dlx Cpe 3P	$4,400	$8,000	$14,500	$19,300
		226.2/94 2dr Dlx Cpe 5P	$3,500	$6,600	$13,500	$17,800
		226.2/94 2dr Rgl Dlx Cpe 5P	$3,600	$7,400	$14,000	$18,400
		226.2/94 2dr Dlx Sdn	$3,800	$7,100	$10,700	$16,300
		226.2/94 2dr Rgl Dlx Sdn	$4,200	$7,400	$11,200	$17,100
		226.2/94 4dr Dlx Sdn	$2,700	$5,200	$8,900	$14,800
		226.2/94 4dr Rgl Dlx Sdn	$3,300	$6,400	$9,500	$15,300
		226.2/94 4dr Land Cruiser Sdn	$5,000	$7,300	$13,300	$17,100
		226.2/94 2dr Rgl Dlx Conv	$17,800	$25,700	$37,000	$51,700
1948	Champion	169.6/80 2dr Dlx Cpe	$3,200	$6,500	$12,300	$16,100
		169.6/80 2dr Rgl Dlx Cpe	$2,500	$5,900	$12,600	$16,900
		169.6/80 2dr Dlx Cpe 5P	$2,700	$5,900	$11,500	$15,400
		169.6/80 2dr Rgl Dlx Cpe 5P	$2,800	$6,400	$12,500	$16,800

Year	Model	Body Style	4	3	2	1
		169.6/80 2dr Dlx Sdn	$2,300	$5,700	$9,000	$14,200
		169.6/80 2dr Rgl Dlx Sdn	$3,200	$6,100	$9,700	$14,800
		169.6/80 4dr Dlx Sdn	$2,300	$4,700	$7,800	$13,000
		169.6/80 4dr Rgl Dlx Sdn	$2,900	$4,800	$8,300	$13,300
		169.6/80 2dr Rgl Dlx Conv	$12,000	$19,200	$28,000	$37,600
1948	Commander	226.2/94 2dr Dlx Cpe	$4,300	$7,600	$14,400	$18,800
		226.2/94 2dr Rgl Dlx Cpe	$4,400	$8,000	$14,500	$19,300
		226.2/94 2dr Dlx Cpe 5P	$3,500	$6,600	$13,500	$17,800
		226.2/94 2dr Rgl Dlx Cpe 5P	$3,600	$7,400	$14,000	$18,400
		226.2/94 2dr Dlx Sdn	$3,800	$7,100	$10,700	$16,300
		226.2/94 2dr Rgl Dlx Sdn	$4,200	$7,400	$11,200	$17,100
		226.2/94 4dr Dlx Sdn	$2,700	$5,200	$8,900	$14,800
		226.2/94 4dr Rgl Dlx Sdn	$3,300	$6,400	$9,500	$15,300
		226.2/94 4dr Land Cruiser Sdn	$5,000	$7,300	$13,300	$17,100
		226.2/94 2dr Rgl Dlx Conv	$15,100	$21,800	$31,400	$43,900
1949	Champion	169.6/80 2dr Dlx Cpe 3P	$3,200	$6,500	$12,300	$16,100
		169.6/80 2dr Rgl Dlx Cpe 3P	$3,400	$6,800	$12,600	$16,900
		169.6/80 2dr Deluxe Starlight Cpe	$2,700	$5,900	$11,500	$15,400
		169.6/80 2dr Regal Deluxe Starlight Cpe	$2,800	$6,300	$12,000	$15,700
		169.6/80 2dr Dlx Sdn	$2,300	$5,700	$9,000	$14,200
		169.6/80 2dr Rgl Dlx Sdn	$3,200	$6,100	$9,700	$14,800
		169.6/80 4dr Dlx Sdn	$2,300	$4,700	$7,800	$13,000
		169.6/80 4dr Rgl Dlx Sdn	$2,900	$4,800	$8,300	$13,300
		169.6/80 2dr Rgl Dlx Conv	$12,000	$19,200	$28,000	$37,600
1949	Commander	245.6/100 2dr Dlx Starlight Cpe	$4,300	$7,600	$14,400	$18,800

Studebaker

Year	Model	Body Style	4	3	2	1
		245.6/100 2dr Regal Dlx Starlight Cpe	$3,600	$7,400	$14,000	$18,400
		245.6/100 2dr Dlx Sdn	$3,800	$7,100	$10,700	$16,300
		245.6/100 2dr Rgl Dlx Sdn	$4,200	$7,400	$11,200	$17,100
		245.6/100 4dr Dlx Sdn	$2,700	$5,200	$8,900	$14,800
		245.6/100 4dr Rgl Dlx Sdn	$3,300	$6,400	$9,500	$15,300
		245.6/100 4dr Land Cruiser Sdn	$5,000	$7,300	$13,300	$17,100
		245.6/100 2dr Rgl Dlx Conv	$15,100	$21,800	$31,400	$43,900
1950	Champion	169.6/85 2dr Cstm Cpe	$4,300	$9,600	$14,100	$18,200
		169.6/85 2dr Dlx Cpe	$4,600	$10,000	$14,500	$18,900
		169.6/85 2dr Rgl Dlx Cpe	$4,800	$10,300	$15,100	$19,400
		169.6/85 2dr Cstm Sdn	$3,300	$7,200	$11,800	$15,400
		169.6/85 2dr Dlx Sdn	$3,400	$7,300	$12,100	$15,800
		169.6/85 2dr Rgl Dlx Sdn	$3,600	$7,600	$12,500	$16,100
		169.6/85 4dr Cstm Sdn	$2,100	$5,600	$8,700	$12,600
		169.6/85 4dr Dlx Sdn	$2,300	$5,700	$9,200	$13,000
		169.6/85 4dr Rgl Dlx Sdn	$2,800	$6,000	$9,500	$13,300
		169.6/85 2dr Cstm Strlt Cpe	$5,300	$11,000	$15,800	$24,600
		169.6/85 2dr Dlx Strlt Cpe	$5,500	$11,500	$16,500	$26,400
		169.6/85 2dr Rgl Dlx Strlt Cpe	$5,700	$12,100	$17,000	$27,400
		169.6/85 2dr Rgl Dlx Conv	$11,100	$18,800	$27,100	$38,800
1950	Commander	245.6/102 2dr Dlx Sdn	$4,500	$9,100	$14,000	$18,200
		245.6/102 2dr Rgl Dlx Sdn	$4,900	$10,000	$15,000	$19,200
		245.6/102 4dr Dlx Sdn	$3,200	$7,200	$10,600	$15,100
		245.6/102 4dr Rgl Dlx Sdn	$3,600	$7,400	$11,300	$15,700
		245.6/102 2dr Dlx Strlt Cpe	$6,200	$13,100	$18,700	$29,500

Year	Model	Body Style	4	3	2	1
		245.6/102 2dr Rgl Dlx Strlt Cpe	$7,000	$13,800	$22,500	$31,300
		245.6/102 2dr Rgl Dlx Conv	$14,400	$22,900	$32,900	$47,100
1950	Land Cruiser	245.6/102 4dr Rgl Dlx Sdn	$5,700	$8,000	$14,600	$19,100
1951	Champion	170/85 2dr Cstm Bus Cpe	$4,300	$9,600	$14,000	$18,200
		170/85 2dr Dlx Bus Cpe	$4,600	$10,000	$14,500	$18,900
		170/85 2dr Rgl Bus Cpe	$4,800	$10,300	$15,300	$19,400
		170/85 2dr Cstm Sdn	$3,300	$7,200	$11,900	$15,400
		170/85 2dr Dlx Sdn	$3,400	$7,300	$12,100	$15,800
		170/85 2dr Rgl Sdn	$3,600	$7,600	$12,500	$16,100
		170/85 4dr Cstm Sdn	$2,100	$5,600	$8,700	$12,600
		170/85 4dr Dlx Sdn	$2,300	$5,700	$9,200	$13,000
		170/85 4dr Rgl Sdn	$2,800	$6,000	$9,500	$13,300
		170/85 2dr Cstm Strlt Cpe	$5,300	$11,000	$15,800	$24,600
		170/85 2dr Dlx Strlt Cpe	$5,400	$11,400	$16,100	$25,700
		170/85 2dr Rgl Strlt Cpe	$5,700	$12,100	$17,000	$27,400
		170/85 2dr Rgl Conv	$11,100	$18,800	$27,100	$38,800
1951	Commander	233/120 2dr Rgl Bus Cpe	$5,400	$11,500	$17,000	$22,000
		233/120 2dr Rgl Strlt Cpe	$7,500	$14,200	$24,600	$32,900
		233/120 2dr State Strlt Cpe	$7,800	$14,900	$24,800	$34,000
		233/120 2dr Rgl Sdn	$5,600	$10,900	$15,700	$20,200
		233/120 2dr State Sdn	$6,100	$11,500	$16,600	$22,100
		233/120 4dr Rgl Sdn	$3,800	$8,200	$11,900	$16,100
		233/120 4dr State Sdn	$4,200	$9,300	$13,000	$17,500
		233/120 4dr Land Cruiser Sdn	$5,300	$7,400	$13,700	$17,600
		233/120 2dr State Conv	$14,400	$22,900	$32,900	$47,100
1952	Champion	170/85 2dr Cstm Sdn	$3,100	$6,800	$11,100	$14,200

Studebaker

Year	Model	Body Style	4	3	2	1
		170/85 2dr Dlx Sdn	$3,300	$7,200	$11,400	$14,700
		170/85 2dr Rgl Sdn	$3,400	$7,300	$12,000	$15,000
		170/85 4dr Cstm Sdn	$1,900	$5,100	$8,100	$11,800
		170/85 4dr Dlx Sdn	$2,200	$5,400	$8,500	$12,300
		170/85 4dr Rgl Sdn	$2,300	$5,700	$9,100	$12,600
		170/85 2dr Cstm Strlt Cpe	$4,700	$9,900	$14,400	$21,800
		170/85 2dr Dlx Strlt Cpe	$4,800	$10,300	$14,600	$22,400
		170/85 2dr Rgl Strlt Cpe	$5,100	$10,900	$15,000	$24,300
		170/85 2dr Regal Starliner Hdtp	$5,300	$11,300	$15,400	$22,900
		170/85 2dr Rgl Conv	$11,100	$18,800	$27,100	$38,800
1952	Commander	233/120 2dr Rgl Sdn	$5,400	$10,500	$15,000	$18,800
		233/120 2dr State Sdn	$5,700	$11,000	$15,800	$20,600
		233/120 4dr Rgl Sdn	$3,700	$7,800	$11,300	$14,900
		233/120 4dr State Sdn	$4,000	$8,800	$12,400	$16,300
		233/120 2dr Rgl Strlt Cpe	$6,700	$13,000	$21,800	$29,200
		233/120 2dr State Strlt Cpe	$7,100	$13,600	$22,600	$30,200
		233/120 2dr State Starliner Hdtp	$6,800	$14,100	$23,400	$30,700
		233/120 2dr State Conv	$14,400	$22,900	$32,900	$47,100
1952	Land Cruiser	233/120 4dr Sdn	$5,600	$8,000	$14,300	$18,000
1953	Champion	170/85 2dr Cstm Sdn	$2,600	$6,300	$9,300	$11,800
		170/85 2dr Dlx Sdn	$3,100	$7,100	$10,100	$13,500
		170/85 2dr Rgl Sdn	$3,500	$7,800	$10,900	$14,400
		170/85 4dr Cstm Sdn	$2,100	$3,700	$5,700	$9,700
		170/85 4dr Dlx Sdn	$2,400	$4,100	$6,200	$10,600
		170/85 4dr Rgl Sdn	$2,500	$4,500	$6,400	$11,000
		170/85 2dr Rgl Strlt Cpe	$9,500	$14,700	$20,400	$26,700

Year	Model	Body Style	4	3	2	1
		170/85 2dr Dlx Strlt Cpe	$9,000	$13,900	$18,800	$24,700
		170/85 2dr Rgl Strlnr Hdtp	$9,700	$15,000	$20,500	$26,800
1953	Commander	233/120 2dr Dlx Sdn	$3,800	$8,500	$10,500	$14,000
		233/120 4dr Dlx Sdn	$2,700	$4,500	$6,800	$11,300
		233/120 4dr Rgl Sdn	$2,800	$4,700	$7,300	$12,000
		233/120 2dr Dlx Strlt Cpe	$10,400	$16,500	$24,300	$31,400
		233/120 2dr Rgl Strlt Cpe	$12,600	$17,200	$25,500	$33,000
		233/120 2dr Rgl Strlnr Hdtp	$14,300	$19,500	$27,900	$35,900
1953	Land Cruiser	233/120 4dr Sdn	$3,500	$5,800	$8,200	$13,800
1954	Champion	170/85 2dr Cstm Sdn	$2,600	$6,300	$9,300	$11,800
		170/85 2dr Dlx Sdn	$3,100	$7,100	$10,100	$13,500
		170/85 2dr Rgl Sdn	$3,500	$7,800	$10,900	$14,400
		170/85 4dr Cstm Sdn	$2,100	$3,700	$5,600	$9,700
		170/85 4dr Dlx Sdn	$2,400	$4,100	$6,200	$10,600
		170/85 4dr Rgl Sdn	$2,500	$4,500	$6,400	$11,000
		170/85 2dr Dlx Conestoga Wgn	$7,300	$12,100	$17,400	$22,400
		170/85 2dr Rgl Conestoga Wgn	$7,600	$12,600	$18,500	$23,700
		170/85 2dr Rgl Strlt Cpe	$9,000	$13,900	$19,400	$25,300
		170/85 2dr Dlx Strlt Cpe	$9,100	$13,900	$18,800	$24,700
		170/85 2dr Strlnr Hdtp Cpe	$10,200	$15,800	$21,600	$28,100
1954	Commander	233/120 2dr Dlx Sdn	$3,800	$8,500	$10,500	$14,000
		233/120 4dr Dlx Sdn	$2,700	$4,500	$6,800	$11,300
		233/120 4dr Rgl Sdn	$2,800	$4,700	$7,300	$12,000
		233/120 4dr Land Cruiser Sdn	$3,300	$5,500	$8,000	$13,600
		233/120 2dr Dlx Conestoga Wgn	$7,400	$13,200	$19,300	$23,400
		233/120 2dr Rgl Conestoga Wgn	$8,000	$13,200	$19,700	$24,600

Studebaker

Year	Model	Body Style	4	3	2	1
		233/120 2dr Dlx Strlt Cpe	$10,400	$16,500	$24,400	$31,400
		233/120 2dr Rgl Strlt Cpe	$12,600	$17,200	$25,600	$33,000
		233/120 2dr Rgl Strlnr Hdtp	$14,300	$19,500	$27,900	$35,900
1955	Champion	186/101 2dr Dlx Cpe	$10,500	$16,500	$23,300	$30,400
		186/101 2dr Cstm Sdn	$2,600	$6,300	$9,300	$11,800
		186/101 2dr Dlx Sdn	$3,100	$7,100	$10,100	$13,500
		186/101 4dr Cstm Sdn	$2,100	$3,700	$5,600	$9,700
		186/101 4dr Dlx Sdn	$2,400	$4,100	$6,200	$10,600
		186/101 4dr Rgl Sdn	$2,500	$4,500	$6,400	$11,000
		186/101 2dr Dlx Conestoga Wgn	$7,300	$12,100	$17,500	$22,400
		186/101 2dr Rgl Conestoga Wgn	$7,600	$12,600	$18,500	$23,700
		186/101 2dr Rgl Hdtp	$10,200	$15,800	$21,600	$28,100
		186/101 2dr Rgl Strlt Cpe	$9,000	$13,900	$20,300	$26,900
1955	Commander	259/162 2dr Cstm Sdn	$3,400	$7,500	$9,500	$12,400
		259/162 2dr Dlx Sdn	$3,800	$8,500	$10,500	$14,000
		259/162 4dr Cstm Sdn	$2,500	$4,200	$6,600	$10,300
		259/162 4dr Dlx Sdn	$2,700	$4,500	$6,800	$11,300
		259/162 4dr Rgl Sdn	$2,800	$4,700	$7,300	$12,000
		259/162 2dr Dlx Conestoga Wgn	$7,400	$13,200	$19,300	$23,400
		259/162 2dr Rgl Conestoga Wgn	$8,000	$13,200	$19,700	$24,600
		259/162 2dr Dlx Strlt Cpe	$10,400	$16,500	$24,300	$31,400
		259/162 2dr Rgl Strlt Cpe	$12,600	$17,200	$26,300	$34,800
		259/162 2dr Rgl Strlnr Hdtp	$14,300	$19,500	$27,900	$35,900
1955	President	259/175 2dr State Cpe	$9,300	$14,300	$16,900	$24,300
		259/175 4dr Dlx Sdn	$2,400	$4,200	$6,800	$12,300
		259/175 4dr State Sdn	$2,700	$4,400	$7,200	$12,500

Year	Model	Body Style	4	3	2	1
		259/175 2dr State Hdtp	$9,900	$16,600	$24,400	$31,800
		259/175 2dr Spdstr Hdtp	$18,400	$30,800	$50,400	$61,800
						+15% for factory a/c.
1956	Champion	185/101 4dr Sdn	$2,100	$3,400	$5,200	$9,400
		185/101 2dr Sdnt	$2,200	$5,300	$8,700	$11,600
		185/101 2dr Sdn	$2,600	$6,300	$9,400	$11,900
		185/101 4dr Rgl Sdn	$2,500	$4,500	$6,400	$11,100
		185/101 2dr Pelham Wgn	$6,800	$9,800	$16,100	$20,000
		185/101 2dr Flight Hawk Cpe	$7,700	$12,100	$22,000	$27,700
		185/101 2dr Flight Hawk Hdtp Cpe	$8,000	$12,800	$22,800	$30,300
1956	Commander	259/170 2dr Sdnt	$2,400	$5,400	$8,900	$11,800
		259/170 2dr Sdn	$2,900	$6,600	$9,600	$12,100
		259/170 4dr Sdn	$2,300	$3,400	$5,400	$9,800
		259/170 4dr Cstm Sdn	$2,400	$3,600	$5,700	$10,300
		259/170 2dr Parkview Wgn	$6,800	$10,700	$17,100	$21,400
		259/170 2dr Power Hawk Cpe	$9,000	$15,500	$28,800	$40,700
1956	President	289/210 2dr Sdn	$2,600	$5,900	$9,300	$12,300
		289/210 4dr Sdn	$1,900	$3,000	$5,400	$10,300
		289/210 4dr Classic Sdn	$2,100	$3,300	$5,800	$10,800
		289/210 2dr Pinehurst Wgn	$7,000	$10,800	$17,100	$21,900
		289/210 2dr Sky Hawk Hdtp Cpe	$10,700	$19,200	$32,400	$44,600
1956	Golden Hawk	352/275 2dr Hdtp Cpe	$16,100	$25,700	$40,300	$59,100
						+20% for factory a/c.
1957	Champion	185/101 2dr Silver Hawk Cpe	$11,400	$18,000	$26,000	$34,200
		185/101 2dr Scotsman Clb Sdn	$2,400	$6,000	$9,200	$11,200
		185/101 2dr Cstm Clb Sdn	$2,400	$6,200	$9,600	$11,600
		185/101 2dr Dlx Clb Sdn	$2,500	$6,500	$9,700	$12,300
		185/101 4dr Scotsman Sdn	$2,200	$3,500	$5,500	$10,600
		185/101 4dr Cstm Sdn	$2,100	$3,700	$5,600	$9,700
		185/101 4dr Dlx Sdn	$2,400	$3,900	$6,000	$10,300

Studebaker

Year	Model	Body Style	4	3	2	1
		185/101 4dr Rgl Sdn	$2,500	$4,500	$6,400	$11,100
		185/101 2dr Scotsman Wgn	$4,700	$7,600	$12,400	$15,600
		185/101 2dr Pelham Wgn	$6,800	$10,400	$16,300	$20,400
		185/101 4dr Cstm Wgn	$7,100	$10,700	$16,600	$20,700
		185/101 4dr Dlx Wgn	$7,300	$10,900	$16,800	$20,900
		185/101 2dr Silver Hawk Hdtp Cpe	$11,200	$18,400	$26,000	$31,800
1957	Commander	289/225 2dr Silver Hawk Cpe	$9,600	$17,000	$28,300	$38,600
		259/180 2dr Cstm Clb Sdn	$2,700	$6,400	$9,400	$11,900
		259/180 2dr Dlx Clb Sdn	$2,900	$6,600	$9,600	$12,300
		259/180 4dr Cstm Sdn	$2,300	$3,900	$6,000	$10,500
		259/180 4dr Dlx Sdn	$2,500	$4,000	$6,300	$10,800
		259/180 2dr Parkview Wgn	$6,200	$10,800	$17,100	$22,200
		259/180 4dr Provincial Wgn	$5,900	$10,400	$16,500	$20,000
		289/210 2dr Silver Hawk Cpe	$9,600	$17,000	$28,300	$38,600
		289/210 2dr Silver Hawk Hdtp Cpe	$9,800	$17,600	$30,900	$40,700
1957	President	289/225 2dr Clb Sdn	$2,800	$6,100	$9,700	$12,600
		289/225 2dr Cstm Sdn	$2,800	$6,300	$9,800	$12,900
		289/225 2dr Dlx Sdn	$3,000	$6,500	$10,000	$13,000
		289/225 4dr Sdn	$2,100	$3,200	$5,600	$10,400
		289/225 4dr Cstm Sdn	$2,200	$3,400	$5,800	$10,800
		289/225 4dr Dlx Sdn	$2,200	$3,600	$6,000	$11,100
		289/225 4dr Classic Sdn	$2,300	$3,500	$6,100	$11,100
		289/225 4dr Broadmoor Wgn	$6,500	$10,900	$16,600	$21,300
		289/225 4dr Cstm Wgn	$5,900	$10,400	$16,100	$19,500
		289/225 2dr Dlx Wgn	$5,700	$10,400	$16,300	$21,300
1957	Golden Hawk	289/275 2dr Hdtp Cpe	$17,400	$31,300	$45,100	$68,700

Year	Model	Body Style	4	3	2	1
						+15% for factory a/c.
1958	Champion	185/101 2dr Scotsman Sdn	$2,400	$6,000	$9,200	$11,200
		185/101 2dr Sdn	$2,400	$5,900	$8,500	$10,700
		185/101 4dr Scotsman Sdn	$2,200	$3,500	$5,500	$10,600
		185/101 4dr Sdn	$2,100	$3,400	$5,100	$9,500
		185/101 4dr Econ-O-Miler Sdn	$2,400	$3,700	$5,600	$11,300
		185/101 2dr Scotsman Wgn	$4,700	$7,600	$12,400	$15,800
		185/101 4dr Dlx Wgn	$7,200	$10,800	$16,300	$20,400
		185/101 2dr Silver Hawk Cpe	$11,400	$18,000	$25,700	$33,200
		185/101 2dr Hdtp Sdn	$2,400	$5,200	$8,400	$10,800
1958	Commander	259/180 2dr Scotsman Sdn	$3,500	$7,300	$9,900	$13,300
		259/180 4dr Scotsman Sdn	$2,300	$3,500	$5,500	$10,800
		259/180 4dr Sdn	$2,100	$3,300	$5,200	$9,900
		259/180 2dr Scotsman Wgn	$4,600	$7,900	$13,000	$15,800
		259/180 4dr Provincial Wgn	$5,900	$10,400	$16,500	$20,000
		259/180 2dr Strlt Cpe	$2,800	$5,700	$8,500	$12,400
		259/180 2dr Silver Hawk Cpe	$9,600	$17,000	$28,300	$38,600
		259/180 2dr Silver Hawk Hdtp Cpe	$9,800	$17,600	$30,500	$40,700
1958	President	289/225 2dr Silver Hawk Cpe	$11,500	$20,000	$33,900	$46,900
		289/225 4dr Sdn	$2,100	$3,200	$5,600	$10,400
		289/225 4dr Dlx Wgn	$8,300	$14,000	$18,000	$22,900
		289/225 2dr Strlt Cpe	$4,400	$7,800	$14,400	$17,900
						+$1,000 for Marshal (exc Silver Hawk)
1958	Golden Hawk	289/275 2dr Hdtp Cpe	$19,800	$35,700	$54,100	$73,900
						+15% for factory a/c.
1959	Silver Hawk	259/180 2dr Cpe	$12,000	$20,500	$34,300	$44,400
						-20% for 6-cyl.
1959	Lark	170/90 2dr Dlx Sdn	$1,900	$4,100	$8,500	$12,700
		170/90 4dr Dlx Sdn	$1,600	$3,800	$7,500	$11,700

Studebaker

Year	Model	Body Style	4	3	2	1
		259/180 4dr Rgl Sdn	$2,000	$4,200	$7,500	$12,300
		170/90 4dr Econ-O-Miler Sdn	$2,100	$5,200	$8,800	$12,700
		170/90 2dr Dlx Wgn	$2,800	$7,400	$14,000	$17,500
		259/180 2dr Rgl Wgn	$3,100	$7,900	$14,600	$17,900
		259/180 2dr Rgl Hdtp Sdn	$2,100	$4,800	$8,900	$13,600
						-20% for 6-cyl.
1960	Lark	259/180 2dr Dlx Sdn	$1,900	$4,100	$8,500	$12,700
		259/180 4dr Dlx Sdn	$1,600	$3,800	$7,500	$11,700
		259/180 4dr Rgl Sdn	$2,000	$4,200	$8,400	$12,300
		259/180 4dr Econ-O-Miler Sdn	$2,100	$5,200	$8,800	$12,700
		259/180 2dr Dlx Wgn	$2,800	$7,500	$14,000	$17,500
		259/180 4dr Dlx Wgn	$2,400	$5,800	$11,500	$14,700
		259/180 4dr Rgl Wgn	$2,500	$5,900	$11,800	$15,200
		259/180 2dr Rgl Hdtp Cpe	$1,800	$4,200	$7,800	$12,000
		259/180 2dr Rgl Conv	$4,900	$11,700	$19,100	$25,900
						-20% for 6-cyl.
1960	Hawk	289/210 2dr Cpe	$8,000	$13,400	$21,800	$28,500
1961	Lark	259/180 2dr Dlx Sdn	$1,900	$4,100	$8,500	$12,700
		259/180 4dr Dlx Sdn	$1,600	$3,800	$7,500	$11,700
		259/180 4dr Rgl Sdn	$2,000	$4,200	$8,400	$12,300
		259/180 2dr Dlx Wgn	$2,800	$7,500	$14,000	$17,500
		259/180 4dr Dlx Wgn	$2,400	$5,800	$11,500	$14,700
		259/180 4dr Rgl Wgn	$2,500	$5,800	$11,800	$15,200
		259/180 2dr Rgl Hdtp Cpe	$1,800	$4,200	$7,800	$12,000
		259/180 2dr Rgl Conv	$4,900	$11,700	$19,100	$25,900
						-20% for 6-cyl.
1961	Hawk	289/210 2dr Cpe	$7,900	$13,400	$21,800	$28,700
1962	Lark	170/112 2dr Dlx Sdn	$1,900	$3,900	$8,100	$13,200

Year	Model	Body Style	4	3	2	1
		170/112 2dr Rgl Hdtp Cpe	$2,200	$4,300	$8,500	$13,800
		170/112 4dr Dlx Sdn	$1,700	$4,000	$7,600	$12,000
		170/112 4dr Dlx Wgn	$2,400	$5,500	$11,000	$14,700
		170/112 4dr Rgl Sdn	$1,900	$4,100	$7,900	$13,600
		170/112 4dr Rgl Wgn	$2,600	$5,800	$11,300	$15,400
		259/180 2dr Dlx Sdn	$2,200	$4,500	$9,300	$15,200
		289/210 2dr Dlx Sdn	$2,400	$5,000	$10,300	$16,600
		259/180 4dr Dlx Sdn	$2,100	$4,600	$8,600	$13,900
		289/210 4dr Dlx Sdn	$2,300	$4,900	$9,700	$15,100
		259/180 4dr Rgl Sdn	$2,200	$5,000	$7,300	$15,700
		289/210 4dr Rgl Sdn	$2,400	$5,200	$10,000	$17,000
		259/180 4dr Dlx Wgn	$2,700	$6,400	$12,600	$17,100
		289/210 4dr Dlx Wgn	$3,000	$6,900	$13,700	$18,500
		259/180 4dr Rgl Wgn	$3,000	$6,700	$12,900	$17,700
		289/210 4dr Rgl Wgn	$3,200	$7,300	$14,100	$19,200
		259/180 2dr Rgl Hdtp Cpe	$2,400	$5,000	$9,800	$16,000
		289/210 2dr Rgl Hdtp Cpe	$2,800	$5,500	$10,600	$17,400
		259/195 2dr Daytona Hdtp Cpe	$8,900	$13,000	$17,600	$22,400
						-20% for 6-cyl.
		289/210 2dr Daytona Hdtp Cpe	$9,900	$14,100	$19,000	$24,600
						-20% for 6-cyl
		170/112 2dr Rgl Conv	$9,100	$14,100	$20,000	$31,300
		259/180 2dr Rgl Conv	$10,400	$15,800	$21,800	$34,900
		289/210 2dr Rgl Conv	$11,100	$17,100	$23,700	$38,500
		170/112 2dr Daytona Conv	$13,600	$19,700	$26,400	$41,600
		259/180 2dr Daytona Conv	$14,900	$21,500	$29,300	$45,600

Studebaker

Year	Model	Body Style	4	3	2	1
		289/210 2dr Daytona Conv	$16,200	$23,500	$31,900	$49,500
						-20% for 6-cyl.
1962	Gran Turismo Hawk	170/112 2dr Hdtp Cpe	$6,600	$10,100	$18,400	$23,800
		259/180 2dr Hdtp Cpe	$7,000	$10,600	$18,900	$25,300
1963	Lark	170/112 2dr Cstm Sdn	$2,600	$5,000	$9,100	$14,700
		170/112 2dr Rgl Sdn	$2,400	$4,700	$8,700	$14,100
		170/112 2dr Std Sdn	$2,100	$4,300	$8,600	$13,600
		170/112 4dr Cstm Sdn	$2,300	$4,700	$8,700	$14,400
		170/112 4dr Rgl Sdn	$2,200	$4,400	$8,200	$14,000
		170/112 4dr Rgl Wgn	$2,900	$6,100	$11,600	$15,700
		170/112 4dr Std Sdn	$2,000	$4,300	$7,900	$12,300
		170/112 4dr Std Wgn	$2,700	$5,800	$11,300	$15,000
		289/210 2dr Cstm Sdn	$3,200	$6,300	$11,400	$18,500
		289/210 2dr Rgl Sdn	$3,000	$5,800	$10,900	$17,700
		289/210 2dr Std Sdn	$2,800	$5,300	$10,700	$17,100
		289/210 4dr Cstm Sdn	$2,900	$5,800	$10,900	$17,300
		289/210 4dr Rgl Sdn	$2,800	$5,600	$10,400	$17,500
		289/210 4dr Rgl Wgn	$3,500	$7,600	$14,500	$19,700
		289/210 4dr Std Sdn	$2,600	$5,300	$10,000	$15,700
		289/210 4dr Std Wgn	$3,300	$7,300	$14,100	$18,900
		259/180 2dr Std Sdn	$2,500	$4,900	$9,900	$15,800
		259/180 2dr Rgl Sdn	$2,900	$5,300	$10,100	$16,400
		259/180 2dr Cstm Sdn	$2,900	$5,800	$10,500	$17,000
		259/180 4dr Std Sdn	$2,300	$4,900	$9,100	$14,300
		259/180 4dr Rgl Sdn	$2,500	$4,900	$9,400	$16,200
		259/180 4dr Cstm Sdn	$2,800	$5,300	$10,100	$16,700

Year	Model	Body Style	4	3	2	1
		259/180 4dr Std Wgn	$3,100	$6,700	$12,900	$17,500
		259/180 4dr Rgl Wgn	$3,200	$7,000	$13,400	$18,000
						-20% for 6-cyl.
1963	Daytona	170/112 2dr Conv	$14,200	$20,300	$27,800	$41,200
		170/112 2dr Hdtp Cpe	$8,700	$12,500	$18,100	$23,000
		170/112 4dr Wagonaire Wgn	$8,400	$13,700	$18,500	$23,600
		289/240 2dr Hdtp Cpe	$10,000	$14,200	$19,300	$23,800
		289/289 2dr Hdtp Cpe	$12,400	$17,900	$24,100	$29,400
		289/240 4dr Wagonaire Wgn	$10,000	$16,400	$22,100	$28,700
		289/289 4dr Wagonaire Wgn	$12,600	$20,400	$27,700	$35,500
		289/240 2dr Conv	$16,200	$23,100	$31,500	$47,100
		289/289 2dr Conv	$21,200	$29,500	$42,700	$66,500
						+15% for 4-spd. +25% for sunroof. -20% for 6-cyl.
1963	Gran Turismo Hawk	289/210 2dr Hdtp Cpe	$7,200	$10,600	$19,200	$24,800
		289/289 2dr Hdtp Cpe	$8,600	$12,800	$23,200	$31,700
						+15% for factory 4-spd.
1963	Avanti	289/240 2dr Cpe	$11,500	$19,700	$33,500	$58,700
		289/289 2dr Cpe	$16,000	$30,300	$49,500	$77,500
						+15% for factory 4-spd on R-1. +25% for factory 4-spd on R-2. -15% for 3-spd. -8% for Regal interior. +20% for factory a/c (N/A w/R-2).
1964	Cruiser	289/210 4dr Sdn	$3,000	$5,900	$8,500	$12,400
						-20% for 6-cyl.
1964	Challenger	259/180 2dr Sdn	$2,700	$5,300	$8,100	$12,700
		259/180 4dr Sdn	$2,400	$5,000	$7,100	$10,100
		259/180 4dr Wgn	$3,200	$6,100	$9,800	$15,600
						-20% for 6-cyl.
1964	Commander	259/195 4dr Wgn	$3,700	$6,500	$10,200	$16,700
		259/180 2dr Sdn	$3,000	$5,800	$9,000	$13,800
		259/180 4dr Sdn	$2,600	$5,200	$7,600	$11,200
						-20% for 6-cyl.
1964	Daytona	259/180 2dr Hdtp Cpe	$8,400	$12,000	$17,500	$22,200
		259/180 4dr Sdn	$4,200	$8,100	$10,400	$14,100
		259/180 4dr Wagonaire Wgn	$8,600	$14,000	$18,900	$24,200
		259/180 2dr Conv	$13,800	$19,700	$27,000	$40,000
						+15% for 4-spd. +25% for sunroof. -20% for 6-cyl.

Studebaker

Year	Model	Body Style	4	3	2	1
1964	Gran Turismo Hawk	289/289 2dr Hdtp Cpe	$9,000	$13,000	$23,800	$34,100
		289/210 2dr Hdtp Cpe	$7,400	$10,700	$19,500	$26,800

+15% for factory 4-spd.

Year	Model	Body Style	4	3	2	1
1964	Avanti	289/240 2dr Cpe	$11,500	$19,700	$33,500	$58,700
		289/289 2dr Cpe	$16,000	$30,300	$49,500	$77,500
		305/335 2dr Cpe	$46,400	$64,900	$91,500	$135,000

+15% for factory 4-spd on R-1 and R-3. +25% for factory 4-spd on R-2. -15% for 3-spd. -8% for Regal interior (N/A w/R-3). +20% for factory a/c (N/A w/R-2).

Year	Model	Body Style	4	3	2	1
1965	Commander	283/195 2dr Sdn	$3,100	$6,100	$9,100	$14,000
		283/195 4dr Sdn	$2,600	$5,000	$7,800	$11,500
		283/195 4dr Wgn	$3,700	$6,500	$10,200	$16,700

-20% for 6-cyl.

Year	Model	Body Style	4	3	2	1
1965	Daytona	283/195 2dr Spt Sdn	$6,500	$10,300	$17,000	$21,900
		283/195 4dr Wagonaire Wgn	$7,900	$12,100	$15,600	$21,100
1965	Cruiser	283/195 4dr Sdn	$3,000	$5,900	$8,500	$12,400

-20% for 6-cyl.

Year	Model	Body Style	4	3	2	1
1966	Commander	283/195 4dr Sdn	$2,800	$5,300	$7,900	$11,800

-20% for 6-cyl.

Year	Model	Body Style	4	3	2	1
1966	Daytona	283/195 2dr Spt Sdn	$6,500	$10,300	$17,000	$21,900
		283/195 4dr Wagonaire Wgn	$7,800	$11,900	$15,300	$20,700
1966	Cruiser	283/195 4dr Sdn	$3,200	$6,100	$8,800	$12,800

-20% for 6-cyl.

Stutz

Year	Model	Body Style	4	3	2	1
1971	Blackhawk	400/425 2dr Cpe	$105,000	$140,000	$165,000	$215,000
1972	Blackhawk	472/220 2dr Cpe	$14,700	$22,800	$45,900	$68,700
1973	Blackhawk	472/220 2dr Cpe	$14,700	$22,800	$45,900	$68,700
1974	Blackhawk	455/431 2dr Cpe	$14,700	$22,800	$45,900	$68,700
1975	Blackhawk	455/431 2dr Cpe	$14,700	$22,800	$45,900	$68,700
1976	Blackhawk	455/431 2dr Cpe	$14,700	$22,800	$45,900	$68,700
1976	D'Italia	2dr Cpe	$13,900	$20,000	$38,200	$50,400
1977	Blackhawk	455/431 2dr Cpe	$14,700	$22,800	$45,900	$68,700
1977	D'Italia	2dr Cpe	$13,900	$20,000	$38,200	$50,400
1978	Blackhawk	403/185 2dr Cpe	$14,700	$22,800	$45,900	$68,700
1978	D'Italia	2dr Cpe	$13,900	$20,000	$38,200	$50,400
1979	Blackhawk	403/185 2dr Cpe	$14,700	$22,800	$45,900	$68,700
1979	D'Italia	2dr Cpe	$13,900	$20,000	$38,200	$50,400

Stutz

Year	Model	Body Style	4	3	2	1
1979	Duplex/Iv-Porte/Victoria	403/185 4dr Sdn	$12,300	$17,700	$33,000	$50,300
1979	Royale	4dr Limo	$13,000	$19,200	$35,600	$43,400
1979	Bearcat	403/185 2dr Conv	$14,000	$19,400	$39,200	$55,300
1980	Blackhawk	403/185 2dr Cpe	$14,700	$22,800	$45,900	$68,700
1980	Duplex/Iv-Porte/Victoria	350/160 4dr Sdn	$12,300	$17,700	$33,000	$50,300
1980	Royale	425/180 4dr Limo	$13,000	$19,200	$35,600	$43,400
1980	Bearcat	403/185 2dr Conv	$14,000	$19,400	$39,200	$55,300
1981	Blackhawk	350/160 2dr Cpe	$14,700	$22,800	$45,900	$68,700
1981	IV-Porte	350/160 4dr Sdn	$12,300	$17,700	$33,000	$50,300
1981	Royale	425/180 4dr Limo	$13,000	$19,200	$35,600	$43,400
1981	Bearcat	350/160 2dr Conv	$14,000	$19,400	$39,200	$55,300
1982	Blackhawk	350/160 2dr Cpe	$14,700	$22,800	$45,900	$68,700
1982	IV-Porte	350/160 4dr Sdn	$12,300	$17,700	$33,000	$50,300
1982	Bearcat	350/160 2dr Conv	$14,000	$19,400	$39,200	$55,300
1983	Blackhawk	350/160 2dr Cpe	$14,700	$22,800	$45,900	$68,700
1983	Bearcat	350/160 2dr Conv	$14,000	$19,400	$39,200	$55,300
1983	IV-Porte	350/160 4dr Sdn	$12,300	$17,700	$33,000	$50,300
1984	Blackhawk	350/160 2dr Cpe	$14,700	$22,800	$45,900	$68,700
1984	IV-Porte	350/160 4dr Sdn	$13,100	$18,500	$35,800	$50,300
1984	Bearcat	350/160 2dr Conv	$13,800	$19,300	$37,400	$51,400
1985	Blackhawk	350/160 2dr Cpe	$14,700	$22,800	$45,900	$68,700
1985	Bearcat	350/160 2dr Conv	$13,800	$19,300	$37,400	$51,400
1986	Blackhawk	2dr Cpe	$14,700	$22,800	$45,900	$68,700
1986	Bearcat	2dr Conv	$13,900	$19,600	$38,600	$54,600
1987	Blackhawk	2dr Cpe	$14,700	$22,800	$45,900	$68,700
1987	Bearcat	2dr Conv	$13,900	$19,600	$38,600	$54,600
1988	Bearcat	2dr Conv	$13,900	$19,600	$38,600	$54,600
1989	Bearcat	2dr Conv	$13,900	$19,600	$38,600	$54,600
1990	Bearcat	2dr Conv	$13,900	$19,600	$38,600	$54,600
1991	Bearcat	2dr Conv	$13,900	$19,600	$38,600	$54,600
1992	Bearcat	2dr Conv	$13,900	$19,600	$38,600	$54,600

Subaru

Year	Model	Body Style	4	3	2	1
1968	360	2dr Sdn	$3,300	$7,000	$10,100	$14,900
		5dr Van	$2,800	$5,300	$8,900	$11,500
					+$700 for sunroof on cpe.	
1969	360	2dr Sdn	$3,300	$7,000	$10,100	$14,900
		5dr Van	$2,800	$5,300	$8,900	$11,500
					+$700 for sunroof on cpe.	
1970	360	2dr Sdn	$3,300	$7,000	$10,100	$14,900
		5dr Van	$2,800	$5,300	$8,900	$11,500
					+$700 for sunroof on cpe.	
1985	XT	2dr GL-10 AWD Turbo Cpe	$1,600	$3,500	$5,700	$8,200

Subaru

Year	Model	Body Style	4	3	2	1
		2dr GL-10 Turbo Cpe	$1,300	$2,900	$5,100	$7,600
		2dr DL Cpe	$1,600	$2,500	$5,000	$7,000
1986	XT	2dr GL-10 AWD Turbo Cpe	$1,600	$3,500	$5,700	$8,200
		2dr GL-10 Turbo Cpe	$1,300	$2,900	$5,100	$7,600
		2dr DL Cpe	$1,600	$2,500	$5,000	$7,000
1987	XT	2dr Turbo Cpe	$1,300	$2,900	$5,100	$7,600
		2dr GL-10 Turbo Cpe	$1,600	$3,500	$5,700	$8,200
		2dr DL Cpe	$1,600	$2,500	$5,000	$7,000
1988	XT	2dr DL Cpe	$2,000	$2,800	$5,200	$7,400
1988	XT6	2dr Cpe	$2,000	$3,500	$5,900	$7,100
1989	XT	2dr GL Cpe	$2,000	$2,800	$5,200	$7,400
1989	XT6	2dr Cpe	$2,000	$3,500	$5,900	$7,100
1990	XT	2dr GL Cpe	$2,000	$2,800	$5,200	$7,400
1990	XT6	2dr Cpe	$2,000	$3,500	$5,900	$7,100
1991	XT	2dr GL Cpe	$2,000	$2,800	$5,200	$7,400
1991	XT6	2dr Cpe	$2,000	$3,500	$5,900	$7,100
1992	SVX	2dr LS Cpe	$3,000	$5,300	$8,200	$12,100
1993	SVX	2dr LS-L AWD Cpe	$3,000	$5,300	$8,200	$12,100
1994	SVX	2dr L Cpe	$3,200	$5,600	$8,400	$12,200
		2dr LSI Cpe	$3,600	$6,900	$10,000	$14,200
1995	SVX	2dr L AWD Cpe	$3,100	$6,000	$9,200	$12,900
		2dr LSI Cpe	$3,600	$6,500	$10,100	$14,300
		2dr L FWD Cpe	$3,000	$5,500	$8,300	$12,200
1996	SVX	2dr L Cpe	$3,500	$6,200	$9,800	$14,200
		2dr LSI Cpe	$4,100	$7,000	$10,400	$14,800
1997	SVX	2dr L Cpe	$3,500	$6,200	$9,800	$14,200
		2dr LSI Cpe	$4,100	$6,900	$10,400	$14,800
2002	Impreza	4dr WRX Wgn	$5,800	$11,600	$16,500	$25,200
		4dr WRX Sdn	$6,100	$12,200	$17,300	$26,500
						-15% for auto trans.
2003	Impreza	4dr WRX Wgn	$5,800	$11,600	$16,500	$25,200
		4dr WRX Sdn	$6,100	$12,200	$17,300	$26,500
						-15% for auto trans.
2004	Impreza	4dr WRX Wgn	$5,300	$10,700	$15,300	$24,100
		4dr WRX Sdn	$5,600	$11,200	$15,800	$24,900
						-15% for auto trans.
		4dr WRX STI Sdn	$12,600	$21,000	$34,700	$50,800
2005	Impreza	4dr WRX Wgn	$5,300	$10,700	$15,300	$24,100
		4dr WRX Sdn	$5,600	$11,200	$15,800	$24,900
						-15% for auto trans.
		4dr WRX STI Sdn	$11,000	$19,000	$31,900	$47,300
2006	Impreza	4dr WRX Wgn	$5,300	$10,700	$15,300	$24,100
		4dr WRX Sdn	$5,600	$11,200	$15,800	$24,900
						-15% for auto trans.

Subaru

Year	Model	Body Style	4	3	2	1
		4dr WRX STI Sdn	$11,000	$19,000	$31,900	$47,300
2007	Impreza	4dr WRX Wgn	$5,300	$10,700	$15,300	$24,100
		4dr WRX Sdn	$5,600	$11,200	$15,800	$24,900
		4dr WRX TR Sdn	$5,900	$11,700	$16,300	$25,000
						-15% for auto trans.
		4dr WRX STI Sdn	$12,600	$21,000	$34,700	$50,800
		4dr WRX STI LTD Sdn	$13,000	$21,500	$35,900	$51,800

Sunbeam

Year	Model	Body Style	4	3	2	1
1953	Alpine	2dr Mk IIA Rdstr	$19,000	$34,000	$60,000	$79,000
1954	Alpine	2dr Mk IIA Rdstr	$19,000	$34,000	$60,000	$79,000
1955	Alpine	2dr Mk IIA Rdstr	$19,000	$34,000	$60,000	$79,000
1956	Alpine	2dr Mk IIA Rdstr	$19,000	$34,000	$60,000	$79,000
1958	Rapier	2dr II Conv	$4,000	$7,000	$12,600	$18,500
1959	Rapier	2dr II Conv	$4,000	$7,000	$12,600	$18,500
		2dr III Conv	$4,000	$7,000	$12,600	$18,500
1960	Alpine	2dr I Conv	$6,500	$11,000	$19,200	$29,000
1961	Rapier	2dr III Conv	$4,000	$7,000	$12,600	$18,500
		2dr IIIA Conv	$4,000	$7,000	$12,600	$18,500
1961	Alpine	2dr I Conv	$6,500	$11,000	$19,200	$29,000
1962	Rapier	2dr IIIA Conv	$4,000	$7,000	$12,600	$18,500
1962	Alpine	2dr I Conv	$6,500	$11,000	$19,200	$29,000
1963	Rapier	2dr IIIA Conv	$4,000	$7,000	$12,600	$18,500
1963	Alpine	2dr II LeMans Fstbk	$21,200	$30,300	$43,000	$50,900
		2dr II Conv	$5,600	$9,900	$16,500	$26,900
1964	Venezia	2dr Cpe	$13,700	$21,000	$30,000	$42,600
1964	Rapier	2dr IV Cpe	$4,000	$7,000	$12,600	$18,500
1964	Alpine	2dr II LeMans Fstbk	$21,200	$30,300	$43,000	$50,900
		2dr II Conv	$5,600	$9,900	$16,500	$26,900
1964	Tiger	2dr Mk I Conv	$35,200	$53,500	$78,500	$128,000
						+$5,000 for factory hard top.
1965	Venezia	2dr Cpe	$13,700	$21,000	$30,000	$42,600
1965	Alpine	2dr IV GT Cpe	$6,600	$12,200	$17,400	$30,300
		2dr IV Conv	$6,500	$10,700	$16,600	$26,200
1965	Tiger	2dr Mk IA Conv	$44,500	$66,800	$87,600	$134,000
						+$5,000 for factory hard top.
1966	Alpine	2dr V Conv	$7,200	$11,800	$17,800	$27,900
1966	Tiger	2dr Mk IA Conv	$44,500	$66,800	$87,600	$134,000
						+$5,000 for factory hard top.
1967	Alpine	2dr V Conv	$7,200	$11,800	$17,800	$27,900
1967	Tiger	2dr Mk IA Conv	$44,500	$66,800	$87,600	$134,000
		2dr Mk II Conv	$68,500	$105,000	$137,000	$189,000
						+$5,000 for factory hard top.
1968	Alpine	2dr V Conv	$7,200	$11,800	$17,800	$27,900
1969	Alpine	2dr Fstbk	$5,600	$8,500	$13,300	$17,300

Sunbeam

Year	Model	Body Style	4	3	2	1
		2dr GT Cpe	$5,700	$9,100	$14,600	$19,400

Sunbeam-Talbot

Year	Model	Body Style	4	3	2	1
1949	90	2dr Mk I DHC	$8,500	$14,800	$19,900	$31,500
1950	90	2dr Mk I DHC	$8,500	$14,800	$19,900	$31,500
1951	90	2dr Mk II DHC	$8,500	$14,800	$19,900	$31,500
1952	90	2dr Mk II DHC	$8,500	$14,800	$19,900	$31,500
1953	90	2dr Mk IIA DHC	$7,800	$13,100	$17,600	$30,300
1954	90	2dr Mk IIA DHC	$7,800	$13,100	$17,600	$30,300
1956	90	2dr Mk III DHC	$8,200	$14,000	$18,800	$30,300

Swallow

Year	Model	Body Style	4	3	2	1
1954	Doretti	2dr Conv	$35,000	$57,000	$115,000	$157,000
1955	Doretti	2dr Conv	$35,000	$57,000	$115,000	$157,000

TVR

Year	Model	Body Style	4	3	2	1
1958	Grantura	2dr Mk I Cpe	$14,600	$24,800	$34,600	$47,900
1959	Grantura	2dr Mk I Cpe	$14,600	$24,800	$34,600	$47,900
1961	Grantura	2dr Mk II Cpe	$14,600	$24,800	$34,600	$47,900
1962	Grantura	2dr Mk III Cpe	$16,100	$25,000	$38,800	$55,900
1964	Grantura	2dr Mk III Cpe	$16,100	$25,000	$38,800	$55,900
1965	Grantura	2dr Mk III Cpe	$16,100	$25,000	$38,800	$55,900
1967	Vixen	2dr II Cpe	$9,400	$17,800	$26,500	$31,500
1967	Tuscan	2dr Cpe	$55,300	$82,700	$98,500	$130,000
1968	Vixen	2dr II Cpe	$9,400	$17,800	$26,500	$31,500
1968	Tuscan	2dr Cpe	$55,300	$82,700	$98,500	$130,000
1969	Vixen	2dr II Cpe	$9,400	$17,800	$26,500	$31,500
1969	Tuscan	2dr Cpe	$55,300	$82,700	$98,500	$130,000
1970	Vixen	2dr II Cpe	$9,400	$17,800	$26,500	$31,500
1970	2500	2dr Cpe	$8,900	$14,300	$22,000	$30,800
				+10% for hybrid M chassis (90 built).		
1970	Tuscan V8	2dr Cpe	$55,300	$82,700	$98,500	$130,000
1971	2500	2dr Cpe	$8,900	$14,300	$22,000	$30,800
				+10% for hybrid M chassis (90 built).		
1972	2500	2dr Cpe	$8,900	$14,300	$22,000	$30,800
				+10% for hybrid M chassis (90 built).		
1973	2500M	2dr Cpe	$9,100	$15,300	$23,000	$33,400
1974	2500M	2dr Cpe	$9,100	$15,300	$23,000	$33,400
1975	2500M	2dr Cpe	$9,100	$15,300	$23,000	$33,400
1976	2500M	2dr Cpe	$9,100	$15,300	$23,000	$33,400
1976	Taimar	2dr Cpe	$9,300	$16,100	$24,400	$35,500
1977	2500M	2dr Cpe	$9,100	$15,300	$23,000	$33,400
1977	Taimar	2dr Cpe	$9,300	$16,100	$24,400	$35,500

TVR

Year	Model	Body Style	4	3	2	1
1978	2500M	2dr Cpe	$9,100	$15,300	$23,000	$33,400
1978	3000S	2dr Conv	$14,400	$20,000	$29,300	$39,400
1978	Taimar	2dr Cpe	$9,300	$16,100	$24,400	$35,500
1979	3000S	2dr Conv	$14,400	$20,000	$29,300	$39,400
1979	Taimar	2dr Cpe	$9,300	$16,100	$24,400	$35,500
1982	280i	2dr Cpe	$6,100	$8,100	$12,500	$15,600
		2dr Conv	$5,400	$7,900	$12,200	$15,000
						Note: Also known as the Tasmin.
1983	280i	2dr Cpe	$6,100	$8,100	$12,500	$15,600
		2dr Conv	$5,400	$7,900	$12,200	$15,000
						Note: Also known as the Tasmin.
1984	280i	2dr Cpe	$6,100	$8,100	$12,500	$15,600
		2dr Conv	$5,400	$7,900	$12,200	$15,000
						Note: Also known as the Tasmin.
1985	280i	2dr Cpe	$6,100	$8,100	$12,500	$15,600
		2dr Conv	$5,400	$7,900	$12,200	$15,000
						Note: Also known as the Tasmin.
1986	280i	2dr Cpe	$6,100	$8,100	$12,500	$15,600
		2dr Conv	$5,400	$7,900	$12,200	$15,000
						Note: Also known as the Tasmin.
1987	280i	2dr Cpe	$6,100	$8,100	$12,500	$15,600
		2dr Conv	$5,400	$7,900	$12,200	$15,000
						Note: Also known as the Tasmin.

Talbo

Year	Model	Body Style	4	3	2	1
1990	Series 1	2dr Cpe	$86,500	$111,000	$139,000	$181,000
1991	Series 1	2dr Cpe	$86,500	$111,000	$139,000	$181,000
1992	Series 1	2dr Cpe	$86,500	$111,000	$139,000	$181,000
1993	Series 1	2dr Cpe	$86,500	$111,000	$139,000	$181,000
1994	Series 1	2dr Cpe	$86,500	$111,000	$139,000	$181,000
1995	Series 1	2dr Cpe	$86,500	$111,000	$139,000	$181,000
1996	Series 1	2dr Cpe	$86,500	$111,000	$139,000	$181,000
1997	Series 1	2dr Cpe	$86,500	$111,000	$139,000	$181,000
1998	Series 1	2dr Cpe	$86,500	$111,000	$139,000	$181,000
1999	Series 1	2dr Cpe	$86,500	$111,000	$139,000	$181,000
2000	Series 1	2dr Cpe	$86,500	$111,000	$139,000	$181,000
2001	Series 1	2dr Cpe	$86,500	$111,000	$139,000	$181,000
2002	Series 2	2dr Cpe	$91,400	$123,000	$156,000	$200,000
2003	Series 2	2dr Cpe	$91,400	$123,000	$156,000	$200,000
2004	Series 2	2dr Cpe	$91,400	$123,000	$156,000	$200,000
2005	Series 2	2dr Cpe	$91,400	$123,000	$156,000	$200,000
2006	Series 2	2dr Cpe	$91,400	$123,000	$156,000	$200,000

Talbot-Lago

Year	Model	Body Style	4	3	2	1
			All Talbot-Lagos are valued by coachbuilder. Many will be worth less than these prices; many will exceed these prices.			
1947	Quinze-Luxe	2690/100 2dr Cpe	$210,000	$257,000	$321,000	$400,000
		2693/110 2dr Cpe	$99,900	$167,000	$256,000	$319,000
1947	Record	4dr Sdn	$160,000	$234,000	$313,000	$370,000
1947	Grand Sport	2dr Cpe	$540,000	$836,000	$1 mil	$1.25 mil
1948	Record T26	4dr Sdn	$160,000	$234,000	$313,000	$370,000
		2dr Grand Spt Cpe	$542,000	$839,000	$1 mil	$1.25 mil
		2dr Cab	$440,000	$590,000	$735,000	$985,000
		2dr Grand Sport Cab	$980,000	$1.25 mil	$1.5 mil	$1.9 mil
1949	Record T26	2dr Sdn	$150,000	$228,000	$305,000	$361,000
		2dr Grand Spt Cpe	$542,000	$839,000	$1 mil	$1.25 mil
		2dr Cab	$440,000	$590,000	$735,000	$985,000
		2dr Grand Sport Cab	$980,000	$1.25 mil	$1.5 mil	$1.9 mil
1950	Record T26	4dr Sdn	$160,000	$234,000	$313,000	$370,000
		2dr Grand Spt Cpe	$542,000	$839,000	$1 mil	$1.25 mil
		2dr Cab	$440,000	$590,000	$735,000	$985,000
		2dr Grand Sport Cab	$980,000	$1.25 mil	$1.5 mil	$1.9 mil
1951	Record T26	4dr Sdn	$160,000	$234,000	$313,000	$370,000
		2dr Grand Spt Cpe	$542,000	$839,000	$1 mil	$1.25 mil
		2dr Cab	$440,000	$590,000	$735,000	$985,000
		2dr Grand Sport Cab	$980,000	$1.25 mil	$1.5 mil	$1.9 mil
1952	Record T26	4dr Sdn	$160,000	$234,000	$313,000	$370,000
		2dr Grand Spt Cpe	$542,000	$839,000	$1 mil	$1.25 mil
		2dr Cab	$440,000	$590,000	$735,000	$985,000
		2dr Grand Sport Cab	$980,000	$1.25 mil	$1.5 mil	$1.9 mil
1953	Record T26	4dr Sdn	$160,000	$234,000	$313,000	$370,000
		2dr Grand Spt Cpe	$542,000	$839,000	$1 mil	$1.25 mil
		2dr Cab	$440,000	$590,000	$735,000	$985,000
		2dr Grand Sport Cab	$980,000	$1.25 mil	$1.5 mil	$1.9 mil
1954	Record T26	4dr Sdn	$160,000	$234,000	$313,000	$370,000
		2dr Grand Spt Cpe	$542,000	$839,000	$1 mil	$1.25 mil
		2dr Cab	$440,000	$590,000	$735,000	$985,000
		2dr Grand Sport Cab	$980,000	$1.25 mil	$1.5 mil	$1.9 mil
1955	T14 LS	2dr Cpe	$183,000	$269,000	$321,000	$370,000
1955	Record T26	4dr Sdn	$160,000	$234,000	$313,000	$370,000

Talbot-Lago

Year	Model	Body Style	4	3	2	1
		2dr Grand Spt Cpe	$542,000	$839,000	$1 mil	$1.25 mil
		2dr Cab	$440,000	$590,000	$735,000	$985,000
		2dr Grand Sport Cab	$980,000	$1.25 mil	$1.5 mil	$1.9 mil
1956	T14 LS	2dr Cpe	$183,000	$269,000	$321,000	$370,000
1956	Record T26	4dr Sdn	$160,000	$234,000	$313,000	$370,000
		2dr Grand Spt Cpe	$542,000	$839,000	$1 mil	$1.25 mil
		2dr Cab	$440,000	$590,000	$735,000	$985,000
		2dr Grand Sport Cab	$980,000	$1.25 mil	$1.5 mil	$1.9 mil
1957	America	2dr Cpe	$244,000	$322,000	$376,000	$421,000
1958	America	2dr Cpe	$244,000	$322,000	$376,000	$421,000
1959	America	2dr Cpe	$244,000	$322,000	$376,000	$421,000
1960	America	2dr Cpe	$244,000	$322,000	$376,000	$421,000

Tatra

Year	Model	Body Style	4	3	2	1
1948	T600 Tatraplan	4dr Sdn	$18,700	$28,700	$42,500	$71,100
1949	T600 Tatraplan	4dr Sdn	$18,700	$28,700	$42,500	$71,100
1950	T600 Tatraplan	4dr Sdn	$18,700	$28,700	$42,500	$71,100
1951	T600 Tatraplan	4dr Sdn	$18,700	$28,700	$42,500	$71,100
1952	T600 Tatraplan	4dr Sdn	$18,700	$28,700	$42,500	$71,100
1953	T600 Tatraplan	4dr Sdn	$18,700	$28,700	$42,500	$71,100
1954	T600 Tatraplan	4dr Sdn	$18,700	$28,700	$42,500	$71,100
1955	T600 Tatraplan	4dr Sdn	$18,700	$28,700	$42,500	$71,100
1956	T600 Tatraplan	4dr Sdn	$18,700	$28,700	$42,500	$71,100
1957	T603	4dr Sdn	$19,600	$32,800	$48,700	$74,800
1958	T603	4dr Sdn	$19,600	$32,800	$48,700	$74,800
1959	T603	4dr Sdn	$19,600	$32,800	$48,700	$74,800
1960	T603	4dr Sdn	$19,600	$32,800	$48,700	$74,800
1961	T603	4dr Sdn	$19,600	$32,800	$48,700	$74,800
1962	T603	4dr Sdn	$19,600	$32,800	$48,700	$74,800
1963	T603	4dr Sdn	$19,600	$32,800	$48,700	$74,800
1964	T603	4dr Sdn	$19,600	$32,800	$48,700	$74,800
1965	T603	4dr Sdn	$19,600	$32,800	$48,700	$74,800
1966	T603	4dr Sdn	$19,600	$32,800	$48,700	$74,800
1967	T603	4dr Sdn	$19,600	$32,800	$48,700	$74,800
1968	T603	4dr Sdn	$19,600	$32,800	$48,700	$74,800

Toyota

Year	Model	Body Style	4	3	2	1
1967	2000GT	2dr Cpe	$475,000	$550,000	$640,000	$790,000 *-15% for RHD.*
1968	2000GT	2dr Cpe	$475,000	$550,000	$640,000	$790,000 *-15% for RHD.*

Toyota

Year	Model	Body Style	4	3	2	1
1969	2000GT	2dr Cpe	$475,000	$550,000	$640,000	$790,000
						-15% for RHD.
		DOHC 2dr Cpe	$620,000	$682,000	$750,000	$855,000
1970	2000GT	2dr Cpe	$475,000	$550,000	$640,000	$790,000
						-15% for RHD.
		DOHC 2dr Cpe	$620,000	$682,000	$750,000	$855,000
1979	Celica	2dr Supra Cpe	$3,500	$7,800	$13,000	$19,900
1980	Celica	2dr Supra Cpe	$3,500	$7,800	$13,000	$19,900
1981	Celica	2dr Supra Lftbk	$3,500	$7,800	$13,000	$19,900
1982	Celica	2dr Supra Mk II Cpe	$4,600	$9,100	$15,300	$21,200
1983	Celica	2dr Supra Mk II Cpe	$4,600	$9,100	$15,300	$21,200
1984	MR2	2dr Mk I Cpe	$5,400	$9,200	$14,500	$20,800
1984	Supra	2dr Mk II Cpe	$4,700	$9,100	$15,800	$22,100
1985	MR2	2dr Mk I Cpe	$5,400	$9,200	$14,500	$20,800
1985	Supra	2dr Mk II Cpe	$4,700	$9,100	$15,800	$22,100
1986	MR2	2dr Mk I Cpe	$5,400	$9,200	$14,500	$20,800
1986	Supra	2dr Mk II Cpe	$4,700	$9,100	$15,800	$22,100
1987	MR2	2dr Mk I Cpe	$5,400	$9,200	$14,500	$20,800
1987	Supra	2dr Mk III Lftbk	$4,100	$7,300	$12,800	$19,700
						-15% for auto trans.
1988	MR2	2dr Mk I Cpe	$5,400	$9,200	$14,500	$20,800
		SC 2dr Mk I Cpe	$7,200	$11,500	$18,700	$24,200
1988	Supra	2dr Mk III Cpe	$4,100	$7,200	$12,500	$18,500
						-15% for auto trans.
1989	MR2	2dr Mk I Cpe	$5,400	$9,200	$14,500	$20,800
		SC 2dr Mk I Cpe	$7,200	$11,500	$18,700	$24,200
1989	Supra	2dr Mk III Cpe	$4,100	$7,200	$12,500	$18,500
		2dr Mk III Turbo Cpe	$9,200	$15,900	$25,200	$40,000
						-15% for auto trans.
1990	Supra	2dr Mk III Cpe	$4,100	$7,200	$12,500	$18,500
		2dr Mk III Turbo Cpe	$9,200	$15,900	$25,200	$40,000
						-15% for auto trans.
1991	Supra	2dr Mk III Cpe	$4,100	$7,200	$12,500	$18,500
		2dr Mk III Turbo Cpe	$9,200	$15,900	$25,200	$40,000
						-15% for auto trans.
1992	Supra	2dr Mk III Cpe	$4,100	$7,200	$12,500	$18,500
		2dr Mk III Turbo Cpe	$9,200	$15,900	$25,200	$40,000
						-15% for auto trans.
1993	Supra	2dr Mk IV Cpe	$15,400	$20,300	$32,600	$44,500
		2dr Mk IV Spt Rf	$14,900	$19,500	$31,200	$42,600
1994	Supra	2dr Mk IV Cpe	$15,400	$20,300	$32,600	$44,500
		2dr Mk IV Spt Rf	$14,900	$19,500	$31,200	$42,600
		2dr Mk IV Turbo Cpe	$40,000	$62,500	$95,000	$139,000

Toyota

Year	Model	Body Style	4	3	2	1
		2dr Mk IV Turbo Spt Rf	$35,200	$55,500	$88,000	$129,000
						-25% for auto.
1995	Supra	2dr Mk IV Cpe	$15,400	$20,300	$32,600	$44,500
		2dr Mk IV Spt Rf	$14,900	$19,500	$31,200	$42,600
						-15% for auto.
		2dr Mk IV Turbo Cpe	$40,000	$62,500	$95,000	$139,000
		2dr Mk IV Turbo Spt Rf	$35,200	$55,500	$88,000	$129,000
						-25% for auto.
1996	Supra	2dr Mk IV Cpe	$15,400	$20,300	$32,600	$44,500
		2dr Mk IV Spt Rf	$14,900	$19,500	$31,200	$42,600
						-15% for auto.
		2dr Mk IV Turbo Spt Rf	$35,200	$55,500	$88,000	$129,000
						-25% for auto.
1997	Supra	2dr Mk IV Ltd Ed Cpe	$18,600	$23,200	$35,500	$47,500
						-25% for auto.
		2dr Mk IV Ltd Ed Spt Rf	$17,700	$22,100	$34,000	$45,400
						-15% for auto.
		2dr Mk IV Ltd Ed Turbo Spt Rf	$37,800	$58,600	$95,000	$139,000
						-25% for auto.
1998	Supra	2dr Mk IV Cpe	$18,600	$23,200	$35,500	$47,500
		2dr Mk IV Spt Rf	$17,700	$22,100	$34,000	$45,400
						-15% for auto.
		2dr Mk IV Turbo Spt Rf	$35,200	$55,500	$88,000	$129,000
						-25% for auto.

Triumph

Year	Model	Body Style	4	3	2	1
1946	1800	4dr Sdn	$4,100	$6,900	$9,800	$14,300
		2dr Rdstr	$15,600	$23,800	$33,500	$46,500
1947	1800	4dr Sdn	$4,100	$6,900	$9,800	$14,300
		2dr Rdstr	$15,600	$23,800	$33,500	$46,500
1948	1800	4dr Sdn	$4,100	$6,900	$9,800	$14,300
		2dr Rdstr	$15,600	$23,800	$33,500	$46,500
1949	2000	4dr Sdn	$5,000	$8,300	$11,700	$15,000
		2dr Rdstr	$16,800	$27,900	$39,000	$54,300
1950	2000 Renown	4dr TDB Sdn	$5,000	$8,600	$10,800	$18,200
1951	2000 Renown	4dr TDB Sdn	$5,000	$8,600	$10,800	$18,200

Triumph

Year	Model	Body Style	4	3	2	1
1952	2000 Renown	4dr TDB Sdn	$5,000	$8,600	$10,800	$18,200
1953	Mayflower	2dr Cpe	$3,000	$4,500	$7,500	$14,400
1953	TR2	2dr Rdstr	$12,000	$22,500	$33,400	$48,500
1954	Mayflower	2dr Cpe	$3,000	$4,500	$7,500	$14,400
1954	TR2	2dr Rdstr	$12,000	$22,500	$33,400	$48,500
1955	Mayflower	2dr Cpe	$3,000	$4,500	$7,500	$14,400
1955	TR2	2dr Rdstr	$12,000	$22,500	$33,400	$48,500
1956	TR3	2dr Rdstr	$8,600	$17,000	$28,400	$46,000
					+$1,000 for factory hard top.	
1957	TR3	2dr Rdstr	$8,600	$17,000	$28,400	$46,000
					+$1,000 for factory hard top.	
1958	TR3A	2dr Rdstr	$9,100	$17,700	$30,400	$46,000
					+$1,000 for factory hard top.	
1959	TR3A	2dr Rdstr	$9,100	$17,700	$30,400	$46,000
					+$1,000 for factory hard top.	
1959	Italia 2000GT	2dr Cpe	$46,000	$62,000	$90,000	$120,000
1960	TR3A	2dr Rdstr	$9,600	$18,100	$32,400	$47,500
					+$1,000 for factory hard top.	
1960	Italia 2000GT	2dr Cpe	$46,000	$62,000	$90,000	$120,000
1961	Herald	2dr Cpe	$2,300	$4,600	$6,100	$9,500
		2dr Sdn	$1,600	$3,800	$5,200	$7,800
		2dr Conv	$3,900	$6,400	$10,100	$15,500
1961	TR3A	2dr Rdstr	$9,600	$18,100	$32,400	$47,500
					+$1,000 for factory hard top.	
1961	TR4	2dr Rdstr	$8,200	$17,100	$27,400	$45,800
1961	Italia 2000GT	2dr Cpe	$46,000	$62,000	$90,000	$120,000
1962	Spitfire	2dr Mk I Rdstr	$2,600	$5,700	$11,200	$16,000
1962	Herald	2dr Cpe	$2,300	$4,600	$6,100	$9,500
		2dr Sdn	$1,500	$3,800	$5,200	$7,800
		2dr Conv	$3,900	$6,400	$10,100	$15,500
1962	TR3A	2dr Rdstr	$9,600	$18,100	$32,400	$47,500
					+$1,000 for factory hard top.	
1962	TR3B	2dr Rdstr	$10,300	$20,400	$34,700	$50,500
1962	TR4	2dr Rdstr	$8,200	$17,100	$27,400	$45,800
1962	Italia 2000GT	2dr Cpe	$46,000	$62,000	$90,000	$120,000
1963	Spitfire	2dr Mk I Rdstr	$2,600	$5,700	$11,200	$16,000
1963	Herald	2dr 1200 Sdn	$1,800	$4,100	$5,700	$8,100
		2dr 1200 Conv	$4,100	$6,600	$10,300	$15,900
1963	TR3B	2dr Rdstr	$10,300	$20,400	$34,700	$50,500
1963	TR4	2dr Rdstr	$8,200	$17,100	$27,400	$45,800
1963	Italia 2000GT	2dr Cpe	$46,000	$62,000	$90,000	$120,000
1964	Spitfire	2dr Mk I Rdstr	$2,600	$5,700	$11,200	$16,000
1964	Herald	2dr 1200 Sdn	$1,800	$4,100	$5,700	$8,100
		2dr 1200 Conv	$4,100	$6,600	$10,300	$15,900
1964	TR4	2dr Rdstr	$8,200	$17,100	$27,400	$45,800
1965	Spitfire	2dr Mk II Rdstr	$3,000	$5,900	$11,300	$16,200

Year	Model	Body Style	4	3	2	1
						+$750 for factory hard top.
1965	Herald	2dr 1200 Sdn	$1,800	$4,100	$5,700	$8,100
		2dr 1200 Conv	$4,100	$6,600	$10,300	$15,900
1965	TR4	2dr Rdstr	$8,200	$17,100	$27,400	$45,800
1965	TR4A	2dr Rdstr	$11,500	$19,400	$31,800	$47,000
						-$1,000 for solid rear axle. +$1,000 for factory Surrey top.
1966	Spitfire	2dr Mk II Rdstr	$3,000	$5,900	$11,300	$16,200
						+$750 for factory hard top.
1966	Herald	2dr 1200 Sdn	$1,700	$4,100	$5,700	$8,100
		4dr 2000 Sdn	$1,900	$4,900	$7,600	$10,500
		2dr 1200 Conv	$4,100	$6,600	$10,300	$15,900
1966	TR4A	2dr Rdstr	$11,500	$19,400	$31,800	$47,000
						-$1,000 for solid rear axle. +$1,000 for factory Surrey top.
1967	GT6	2dr Mk I Fstbk Cpe	$5,400	$9,500	$19,500	$29,000
1967	Spitfire	2dr Mk II Rdstr	$3,100	$6,100	$11,400	$16,200
		2dr Mk III Rdstr	$3,000	$6,200	$11,700	$16,300
						+$750 for factory hard top.
1967	Herald	2dr 1200 Sdn	$1,700	$4,100	$5,700	$8,100
		4dr 2000 Sdn	$1,900	$4,900	$7,600	$10,500
		2dr 1200 Conv	$4,100	$6,600	$10,300	$15,900
1967	TR4A	2dr Rdstr	$11,500	$19,400	$31,800	$47,000
						-$1,000 for solid rear axle. +$1,000 for factory Surrey top.
1967	TR250	2dr Conv	$13,800	$21,600	$35,700	$52,300
1967	TR5	2dr Conv	$24,900	$35,600	$50,000	$75,400
1968	GT6	2dr Mk I Fstbk Cpe	$5,400	$10,200	$19,300	$29,000
1968	Spitfire	2dr Mk III Rdstr	$3,300	$6,200	$11,700	$16,300
						+$750 for factory hard top.
1968	Herald	2dr 1200 Sdn	$1,800	$4,100	$5,700	$8,100
		2dr 1200 Conv	$4,100	$6,600	$10,300	$15,900
1968	TR4A	2dr Rdstr	$11,500	$19,400	$31,800	$47,000
						-$1,000 for solid rear axle. +$1,000 for factory Surrey top.
1968	TR250	2dr Conv	$13,800	$21,600	$35,700	$52,300
1968	TR5	2dr Conv	$24,900	$35,600	$50,000	$75,400
1969	Spitfire	2dr Mk III Rdstr	$3,300	$6,200	$11,700	$16,300
						+$750 for factory hard top.
1969	TR6	2dr Conv	$7,500	$14,000	$24,000	$37,000
1970	Spitfire	2dr Mk III Rdstr	$3,300	$6,200	$11,700	$16,300
						+$750 for factory hard top.
1970	GT6+	2dr Fstbk Cpe	$4,900	$8,700	$17,300	$27,000
1970	TR6	2dr Conv	$7,000	$13,200	$23,400	$36,500
1971	Spitfire	2dr Mk IV Rdstr	$3,400	$6,200	$11,600	$16,300
						+$500 for factory hard top.
1971	GT6	2dr Mk III Cpe	$5,200	$10,500	$18,500	$26,500
1971	Stag	2dr Conv	$8,000	$15,000	$22,000	$30,000
1971	TR6	2dr Conv	$7,000	$13,200	$23,400	$36,500
1972	Spitfire	2dr Mk IV Rdstr	$3,400	$6,200	$11,600	$16,300

Triumph

Year	Model	Body Style	4	3	2	1
						+$500 for factory hard top.
1972	GT6	2dr Mk III Cpe	$5,200	$10,500	$18,500	$26,500
1972	Stag	2dr Conv	$8,000	$15,000	$22,000	$30,000
1972	TR6	2dr Conv	$7,000	$13,200	$23,400	$36,500
1973	Spitfire	2dr 1500 Conv	$3,100	$5,700	$11,100	$16,100
						+$500 for factory hard top.
1973	GT6	2dr Mk III Cpe	$5,200	$10,500	$18,500	$26,500
1973	Stag	2dr Conv	$8,000	$15,000	$22,000	$30,000
1973	TR6	2dr Conv	$7,000	$13,200	$23,400	$36,500
1974	Spitfire	2dr 1500 Conv	$3,100	$5,700	$11,100	$16,100
						+$500 for factory hard top.
1974	TR6	2dr Conv	$6,900	$12,800	$23,400	$35,500
1975	Spitfire	2dr 1500 Conv	$3,400	$6,200	$11,600	$17,000
						+$500 for factory hard top.
1975	TR6	2dr Conv	$6,900	$12,800	$23,400	$35,500
1975	TR7	2dr Cpe	$2,000	$3,800	$7,300	$11,300
1976	Spitfire	2dr 1500 Conv	$3,400	$6,200	$11,600	$16,900
						+$500 for factory hard top.
1976	TR6	2dr Conv	$7,000	$13,100	$23,600	$36,000
1976	TR7	2dr Cpe	$2,000	$3,800	$7,300	$11,300
1977	Spitfire	2dr 1500 Conv	$3,400	$6,200	$11,600	$16,900
						+$500 for factory hard top.
1977	TR7	2dr Cpe	$2,000	$3,800	$7,300	$11,300
1978	Spitfire	2dr 1500 Conv	$3,400	$6,200	$11,600	$16,900
						+$500 for factory hard top.
1978	TR7	2dr Cpe	$2,000	$3,800	$7,300	$11,300
1979	Spitfire	2dr 1500 Conv	$3,400	$6,200	$11,600	$16,900
						+$500 for factory hard top.
1979	TR7	2dr Cpe	$2,000	$3,800	$7,300	$11,300
		2dr Conv	$3,300	$4,300	$8,700	$14,200
1980	TR7	2dr Cpe	$2,000	$3,800	$7,300	$11,300
		2dr Conv	$3,300	$4,300	$8,700	$14,200
1980	TR8	2dr Cpe	$4,200	$7,200	$14,300	$19,000
		2dr Conv	$4,700	$9,700	$19,000	$24,600
1981	TR7	2dr Conv	$3,300	$4,300	$8,700	$14,200
1981	TR8	2dr Cpe	$4,200	$7,200	$14,300	$19,000
		2dr Conv	$4,700	$9,700	$19,000	$24,600

Tucker

Year	Model	Body Style	4	3	2	1
1948	48	335/166 4dr Sdn	$1.05 mil	$1.2 mil	$1.45 mil	$1.9 mil

Turner

Year	Model	Body Style	4	3	2	1
1958	950	2dr Rdstr	$14,600	$20,000	$29,400	$38,000
1959	950	2dr Rdstr	$14,600	$20,000	$29,400	$38,000

Turner

Year	Model	Body Style	4	3	2	1
1959	Sports Mk I	2dr Rdstr	$16,300	$22,500	$30,900	$40,000
1960	Sports Mk I	2dr Coventry Rdstr	$16,300	$22,500	$30,900	$40,000
1961	Sports Mk I	2dr Coventry Rdstr	$16,300	$22,500	$30,900	$40,000
1961	Sports Mk III	2dr Coventry Rdstr	$17,400	$23,000	$32,300	$43,000
1962	Sports Mk III	2dr Coventry Rdstr	$17,400	$23,000	$32,300	$43,000
1963	Sports Mk III	2dr Coventry Rdstr	$17,400	$23,000	$32,300	$43,000

Vector

Year	Model	Body Style	4	3	2	1
1991	W8	2dr Cpe	$550,000	$780,000	$990,000	$1.25 mil
1992	W8	2dr Cpe	$550,000	$780,000	$990,000	$1.25 mil
1993	W8	2dr Cpe	$550,000	$780,000	$990,000	$1.25 mil
1996	M12	2dr Cpe	$95,500	$116,000	$149,000	$210,000
1997	M12	2dr Cpe	$95,500	$116,000	$149,000	$210,000
1998	M12	2dr Cpe	$95,500	$116,000	$149,000	$210,000
1999	M12	2dr Cpe	$95,500	$116,000	$149,000	$210,000

Volkswagen

Year	Model	Body Style	4	3	2	1
1946	Beetle	2dr Splt-Wndw Sdn	$38,500	$58,700	$110,000	$143,000
1947	Beetle	2dr Splt-Wndw Sdn	$21,800	$39,100	$81,100	$121,000
1948	Beetle	2dr Splt-Wndw Sdn	$21,800	$39,100	$81,100	$121,000
1949	Beetle	2dr Splt-Wndw Sdn	$10,000	$18,100	$40,300	$61,800
1950	Beetle	2dr Splt-Wndw Sdn	$10,000	$18,100	$40,300	$61,800
		2dr Dlx Conv	$27,500	$43,400	$71,200	$103,000
1951	Beetle	2dr Splt-Wndw Sdn	$10,000	$18,100	$40,300	$61,800
		2dr Conv	$31,600	$49,900	$81,800	$119,000
1951	Transporter	4dr Microbus	$14,700	$26,500	$40,400	$77,100
		4dr Dlx 15W Microbus	$18,400	$29,800	$50,800	$88,700
		4dr Samba 23W Microbus	$39,000	$60,600	$111,000	$198,000
1952	Beetle	2dr Splt-Wndw Sdn	$10,000	$18,100	$40,300	$61,800
		2dr Conv	$31,600	$49,900	$81,800	$119,000
1952	Transporter	4dr Microbus	$14,700	$26,500	$40,400	$77,100
		4dr Dlx 15W Microbus	$18,400	$30,300	$48,700	$88,700
		4dr Samba 23W Microbus	$39,000	$60,600	$111,000	$198,000
1953	Beetle	2dr Splt-Wndw Sdn	$10,000	$16,000	$35,400	$52,600
		2dr Conv	$13,300	$25,600	$55,800	$85,300
1953	Transporter	4dr Microbus	$14,700	$26,500	$40,400	$77,100
		4dr Dlx 15W Microbus	$18,400	$30,300	$48,700	$88,700
		4dr Samba 23W Microbus	$39,000	$60,600	$111,000	$198,000

Volkswagen

Year	Model	Body Style	4	3	2	1
1954	Beetle	2dr Ovl-Wndw Sdn	$7,100	$15,000	$32,600	$48,000
		2dr Dlx Conv	$13,300	$25,600	$55,800	$85,300
1954	Transporter	4dr Microbus	$14,700	$26,500	$40,400	$77,100
		4dr Dlx 15W Microbus	$18,400	$29,800	$50,800	$88,700
		4dr Samba 23W Microbus	$39,000	$60,600	$111,000	$198,000
1955	Beetle	2dr Ovl-Wndw Sdn	$7,200	$15,200	$32,900	$49,500
		2dr Conv	$13,300	$25,600	$55,800	$85,300
1955	Transporter	4dr Dlx 15W Microbus	$18,400	$29,800	$50,800	$88,700
		4dr Samba 23W Microbus	$39,000	$60,600	$111,000	$198,000
1956	Beetle	2dr Ovl-Wndw Sdn	$7,200	$15,200	$32,900	$49,500
		2dr Conv	$13,300	$25,600	$55,800	$85,300
1956	Karmann Ghia	2dr Cpe	$9,700	$19,600	$34,900	$52,300
1956	Transporter	4dr Dlx 15W Microbus	$18,400	$29,800	$50,800	$88,700
		4dr Samba 23W Microbus	$39,000	$60,600	$111,000	$198,000
1957	Beetle	2dr Ovl-Wndw Sdn	$7,200	$15,200	$32,900	$49,500
		2dr Conv	$13,300	$25,600	$55,800	$85,300
1957	Karmann Ghia	2dr Cpe	$9,700	$19,600	$34,900	$52,300
1957	Transporter	4dr Dlx 15W Microbus	$18,400	$29,800	$50,800	$88,700
		4dr Samba 23W Microbus	$39,000	$60,600	$111,000	$198,000
1958	Beetle	2dr Sdn	$7,500	$15,000	$30,300	$50,000
		2dr Conv	$11,900	$23,900	$53,200	$79,500
1958	Karmann Ghia	2dr Cpe	$8,300	$16,700	$28,600	$44,000
		2dr Conv	$10,500	$22,000	$38,500	$60,500
1958	Transporter	4dr Dlx 15W Microbus	$18,400	$30,300	$48,700	$88,700
		4dr Samba 23W Microbus	$39,000	$60,600	$111,000	$198,000
1959	Beetle	2dr Sdn	$7,500	$15,000	$30,300	$50,000
		2dr Conv	$11,900	$23,900	$53,200	$79,500
1959	Karmann Ghia	2dr Cpe	$8,300	$16,700	$28,600	$44,000
		2dr Conv	$10,500	$22,000	$38,500	$60,500
1959	Transporter	4dr Dlx 15W Microbus	$18,400	$29,800	$50,800	$88,700
		4dr Samba 23W Microbus	$39,000	$60,600	$111,000	$198,000
1960	Beetle	2dr Sdn	$7,500	$15,000	$30,300	$50,000
		2dr Conv	$11,900	$24,900	$61,800	$94,800
1960	Karmann Ghia	2dr Cpe	$8,300	$16,700	$28,600	$44,000
		2dr Conv	$10,500	$22,000	$38,500	$60,500
1960	Transporter	4dr Dlx 15W Microbus	$18,400	$29,800	$50,800	$88,700
		4dr Samba 23W Microbus	$39,000	$60,600	$111,000	$198,000

Year	Model	Body Style	4	3	2	1
1961	Beetle	2dr Sdn	$6,300	$12,300	$24,900	$41,200
		2dr Conv	$11,200	$22,300	$54,600	$89,600
					+7% for sunroof on cpe.	
1961	Karmann Ghia	2dr Cpe	$8,300	$16,700	$28,600	$44,000
		2dr Conv	$10,500	$22,000	$38,500	$60,500
1961	Transporter	4dr Dlx 15W Microbus	$18,400	$29,800	$50,800	$88,700
		4dr Samba 23W Microbus	$39,000	$60,600	$111,000	$198,000
1962	Beetle	2dr Sdn	$5,900	$12,300	$26,400	$43,600
		2dr Conv	$11,200	$22,300	$54,600	$89,600
					+7% for sunroof on cpe.	
1962	Karmann Ghia	2dr Cpe	$8,300	$16,700	$28,600	$44,000
		2dr Conv	$10,500	$22,000	$38,500	$60,500
1962	Transporter	4dr Dlx 15W Microbus	$18,400	$29,800	$50,800	$88,700
		4dr Samba 23W Microbus	$39,000	$60,600	$111,000	$198,000
1963	Beetle	2dr Sdn	$5,900	$12,300	$26,400	$43,600
		2dr Conv	$11,200	$22,300	$54,600	$89,600
					+7% for sunroof on cpe.	
1963	Karmann Ghia	2dr Cpe	$8,300	$16,700	$28,600	$44,000
		2dr Conv	$10,500	$22,000	$38,500	$60,500
1963	Transporter	4dr Dlx 15W Microbus	$18,400	$29,800	$50,800	$88,700
		4dr Samba 23W Microbus	$39,000	$60,600	$111,000	$198,000
1964	Beetle	2dr Sdn	$5,900	$12,300	$26,400	$43,600
		2dr Conv	$10,200	$20,100	$51,200	$85,100
					+7% for sunroof on cpe.	
1964	Karmann Ghia	2dr Cpe	$7,200	$14,500	$24,800	$37,900
		2dr Conv	$11,000	$21,100	$37,900	$58,100
1964	Transporter	4dr Dlx 15W Microbus	$18,400	$29,800	$50,800	$88,700
		4dr Samba 21W Microbus	$32,300	$48,500	$101,000	$165,000
1965	Beetle	2dr Sdn	$5,700	$12,200	$24,900	$41,200
		2dr Conv	$10,200	$20,100	$51,200	$85,100
					+7% for sunroof on cpe.	
1965	Karmann Ghia	2dr Cpe	$7,200	$14,500	$24,800	$37,900
		2dr Conv	$11,000	$21,100	$37,900	$58,100
1965	Transporter	4dr Dlx 13W Microbus	$14,400	$25,700	$42,600	$69,800
		4dr Samba 21W Microbus	$32,300	$48,500	$101,000	$165,000
1966	Beetle	2dr Sdn	$5,700	$12,200	$24,900	$41,200
		2dr Conv	$10,200	$20,100	$51,200	$85,100
					+7% for sunroof on cpe.	
1966	Karmann Ghia	2dr Cpe	$7,200	$14,500	$24,800	$37,900

Volkswagen

Year	Model	Body Style	4	3	2	1
		2dr Conv	$11,000	$21,100	$37,900	$58,100
1966	Transporter	4dr Dlx 13W Microbus	$14,400	$25,700	$42,600	$69,800
		4dr Samba 21W Microbus	$32,300	$48,500	$101,000	$165,000
1967	Beetle	2dr Sdn	$7,600	$13,900	$31,300	$48,800
		2dr Conv	$10,400	$22,000	$51,300	$85,900
						+7% for sunroof on cpe.
1967	Karmann Ghia	2dr Cpe	$7,200	$14,500	$24,800	$37,900
		2dr Conv	$11,000	$21,100	$37,900	$58,100
1967	Transporter	4dr Samba 21W Microbus	$32,300	$48,500	$101,000	$165,000
		4dr Dlx 13W Microbus	$14,400	$25,700	$42,600	$69,800
1968	Beetle	2dr Sdn	$4,500	$8,600	$20,400	$37,000
		2dr Conv	$5,700	$11,300	$30,300	$40,400
1968	Karmann Ghia	2dr Conv	$8,700	$16,700	$28,800	$48,000
		2dr Cpe	$6,700	$12,900	$21,700	$34,100
1969	Beetle	2dr Sdn	$4,500	$8,600	$20,400	$37,000
		2dr Conv	$5,700	$11,300	$30,300	$40,400
1969	Karmann Ghia	2dr Cpe	$6,700	$12,900	$21,700	$34,100
		2dr Conv	$8,700	$16,700	$28,800	$48,000
1970	Beetle	2dr Sdn	$4,500	$8,600	$20,400	$37,000
		2dr Conv	$5,800	$10,300	$29,400	$39,300
1970	Karmann Ghia	2dr Cpe	$6,700	$12,900	$21,700	$34,100
		2dr Conv	$8,700	$16,700	$28,800	$48,000
1971	Beetle	2dr Conv	$5,200	$9,700	$24,800	$32,300
		2dr Sdn	$4,500	$8,600	$20,400	$37,000
1971	Super Beetle	2dr Sdn	$4,300	$8,300	$15,500	$20,900
		2dr Conv	$6,000	$11,300	$28,000	$36,800
1971	Karmann Ghia	2dr Cpe	$6,400	$12,600	$20,600	$33,100
		2dr Conv	$9,400	$16,900	$29,000	$49,100
1972	Beetle	2dr Sdn	$4,500	$8,600	$20,400	$37,000
		2dr Conv	$5,800	$10,400	$30,800	$40,500
1972	Super Beetle	2dr Sdn	$4,300	$8,300	$15,500	$20,900
		2dr Conv	$6,000	$11,300	$28,000	$36,800
1972	181 Thing	4dr Conv	$10,200	$17,600	$25,000	$36,900
		4dr Acapulco Ed Conv	$12,600	$20,300	$29,500	$39,600
1972	Karmann Ghia	2dr Cpe	$6,400	$12,600	$20,600	$33,100
		2dr Conv	$9,400	$16,900	$29,000	$49,100
1973	Beetle	2dr Sdn	$4,500	$8,600	$20,400	$37,000
		2dr Conv	$5,800	$10,400	$31,000	$40,500
1973	Super Beetle	2dr Sdn	$4,300	$8,300	$15,500	$20,900
		2dr Conv	$6,000	$11,300	$28,000	$36,800
1973	Karmann Ghia	2dr Cpe	$6,300	$11,800	$19,300	$31,700
		2dr Conv	$8,900	$15,300	$26,800	$43,800
1973	181 Thing	4dr Conv	$10,200	$17,600	$25,000	$36,900
		4dr Acapulco Ed Conv	$12,600	$20,300	$29,500	$39,600

Year	Model	Body Style	4	3	2	1
1974	Beetle	2dr Sdn	$4,500	$8,600	$20,400	$37,000
		2dr Conv	$5,800	$10,400	$31,000	$40,500
1974	Super Beetle	2dr Sdn	$4,300	$8,300	$15,500	$20,900
		2dr Conv	$6,000	$11,300	$28,000	$36,800
1974	Karmann Ghia	2dr Cpe	$6,300	$11,800	$19,300	$31,700
		2dr Conv	$8,900	$15,300	$26,800	$43,800
1974	181 Thing	4dr Conv	$10,200	$17,600	$25,000	$36,900
		4dr Acapulco Ed Conv	$12,600	$20,300	$29,500	$39,600
1975	Beetle	2dr Sdn	$4,500	$8,600	$20,400	$37,000
		2dr Conv	$6,400	$11,400	$36,900	$48,300
1975	Super Beetle	2dr Sdn	$3,500	$7,100	$13,200	$19,600
		2dr Conv	$6,000	$11,300	$28,000	$36,800
1975	181 Thing	4dr Conv	$10,200	$17,600	$25,000	$36,900
		4dr Acapulco Ed Conv	$12,600	$20,300	$29,500	$39,600
1976	Beetle	2dr Sdn	$4,500	$9,000	$21,100	$36,800
		2dr Conv	$5,800	$11,900	$38,000	$48,500
1977	Beetle	2dr Sdn	$4,800	$9,300	$21,900	$37,900
		2dr Conv	$5,900	$12,900	$37,600	$49,900
1978	Beetle	2dr Conv	$8,900	$14,100	$43,700	$60,800
1979	Beetle	2dr Conv	$9,700	$16,900	$51,700	$71,900
1983	GTI	2dr Cpe	$4,700	$7,100	$11,000	$20,600
1984	Golf	2dr GTI Mk II Htchbk	$4,300	$6,400	$8,600	$19,800
1985	Golf	2dr GTI Mk II Htchbk	$4,000	$5,400	$8,300	$18,000
1986	Golf	2dr GTI Mk II Htchbk	$4,000	$5,400	$8,300	$18,000
1987	GTI	2dr Htchbk	$3,600	$5,000	$7,200	$13,100
1987	Scirocco	2dr 16 Valve Cpe	$8,400	$13,000	$21,600	$33,300
1988	GTI	2dr 16V Htchbk	$3,700	$5,200	$8,000	$13,800
1988	Scirocco	2dr 16 Valve Cpe	$8,400	$13,000	$21,600	$33,300
1989	GTI	2dr 16V Htchbk	$3,700	$5,200	$8,000	$13,800
1990	Golf	2dr GTI Mk II Htchbk	$4,000	$5,200	$8,100	$15,700
1990	Corrado	2dr Cpe	$2,800	$3,900	$8,000	$13,900
1991	Golf	2dr GTI Cpe	$3,400	$5,000	$7,400	$13,100
		2dr GTI 16V Htchbk	$3,600	$6,200	$8,500	$16,600
1991	Corrado	2dr G60 Cpe	$2,800	$3,900	$8,000	$13,900
1992	Golf	2dr GTI Cpe	$3,400	$5,000	$7,400	$12,900
		2dr GTI 16V Cpe	$3,600	$6,200	$8,500	$16,600
1992	Corrado	2dr G60 Supercharged Cpe	$3,400	$4,600	$9,000	$15,000
		2dr SLC V6 Cpe	$4,100	$8,600	$19,500	$29,000
1993	Golf	2dr GTI Cpe	$3,400	$5,000	$7,400	$13,100
		2dr GTI 16V Cpe	$3,600	$6,100	$8,300	$16,600
1993	Corrado	2dr SLC V6 Cpe	$4,100	$8,600	$19,500	$29,000
1994	Corrado	2dr SLC V6 Cpe	$4,100	$8,600	$19,500	$29,000

Volvo

Year	Model	Body Style	4	3	2	1
1956	PV444	2dr Cpe	$6,100	$13,400	$18,900	$26,900
1956	PV445	2dr Wgn	$6,800	$14,500	$20,000	$29,700
1956	P1900	2dr Rdstr	$49,500	$67,300	$88,000	$122,000
1957	PV444	2dr Cpe	$6,100	$13,400	$18,900	$26,900
1957	PV445	2dr Wgn	$6,800	$14,500	$20,000	$29,700
1957	P1900	2dr Rdstr	$49,500	$67,300	$88,000	$122,000
1958	PV444	2dr Cpe	$6,100	$13,400	$18,900	$26,900
1958	PV445	2dr Wgn	$6,800	$14,500	$20,000	$29,700
1959	122	4dr Sdn	$4,000	$6,900	$9,800	$17,000
1959	PV445	2dr Wgn	$7,600	$15,800	$22,200	$31,900
1959	PV544	2dr Sdn	$7,000	$14,000	$21,000	$30,300
1960	PV445	2dr Wgn	$7,600	$15,800	$22,200	$31,900
1960	PV544	2dr Sdn	$7,000	$14,000	$21,000	$30,300
1961	122	4dr Sdn	$4,000	$6,900	$9,800	$17,000
1961	PV445	2dr Wgn	$7,600	$15,800	$22,200	$31,900
1961	PV544	2dr Sdn	$7,000	$14,000	$21,000	$30,300
1961	P1800	2dr Cpe	$10,900	$17,800	$35,400	$64,400
1962	122	4dr Sdn	$4,000	$6,900	$9,800	$17,000
1962	PV445	2dr Wgn	$7,600	$15,800	$22,200	$31,900
1962	PV544	2dr Sdn	$7,000	$14,000	$21,000	$30,300
1962	P1800	2dr Cpe	$10,900	$17,800	$35,400	$64,400
1963	122S	2dr Sdn	$4,700	$9,000	$14,700	$24,600
		4dr Sdn	$3,300	$6,300	$9,300	$16,800
		4dr Wgn	$3,700	$8,500	$12,200	$21,000
1963	PV445	2dr Wgn	$7,600	$16,000	$22,200	$31,900
1963	PV544	2dr Sdn	$7,000	$14,000	$21,000	$30,300
1963	1800S	2dr Cpe	$11,300	$19,800	$36,300	$66,100
1964	122S	2dr Sdn	$4,700	$9,000	$14,700	$24,600
		4dr Sdn	$3,300	$6,300	$9,300	$16,800
		4dr Wgn	$3,700	$8,500	$12,200	$21,000
1964	PV445	2dr Wgn	$7,600	$15,800	$22,200	$31,900
1964	PV544	2dr Sdn	$7,000	$14,000	$21,000	$30,300
1964	1800S	2dr Cpe	$11,300	$19,800	$36,300	$66,100
1965	122S	2dr Sdn	$4,700	$9,000	$14,700	$24,600
		4dr Sdn	$3,300	$6,300	$9,300	$16,800
		4dr Wgn	$3,700	$8,500	$12,200	$21,000
1965	PV445	2dr Wgn	$7,600	$15,800	$22,200	$31,900
1965	PV544	2dr Sdn	$7,000	$14,000	$21,000	$30,300
1965	1800S	2dr Cpe	$11,300	$19,800	$36,300	$66,100
1966	PV445	2dr Wgn	$7,600	$15,800	$22,200	$31,900
1966	1800S	2dr Cpe	$11,300	$19,800	$36,300	$66,100
1967	122S	2dr Sdn	$4,700	$9,000	$14,700	$24,600
		4dr Sdn	$3,300	$6,300	$9,300	$16,800
		4dr Wgn	$3,700	$8,500	$12,200	$21,000
1967	123GT	2dr Sdn	$14,100	$21,400	$30,100	$41,200
1967	144S	4dr Sdn	$2,800	$4,200	$6,900	$11,000
1967	1800S	2dr Cpe	$11,300	$19,800	$36,300	$66,100
1968	122S	2dr Sdn	$4,700	$9,000	$14,700	$22,600
		4dr Sdn	$3,300	$6,300	$9,300	$16,800

Year	Model	Body Style	4	3	2	1
		4dr Wgn	$3,700	$8,500	$12,200	$21,000
1968	1800S	2dr Cpe	$11,300	$19,800	$36,300	$66,100
1969	142S	2dr Cpe	$4,100	$6,100	$9,600	$16,400
1969	144S	4dr Sdn	$2,800	$4,200	$6,900	$11,000
1969	145S	4dr Wgn	$2,900	$4,400	$6,700	$11,500
1969	1800E	2dr Cpe	$10,300	$17,400	$30,900	$49,200
1970	142S	2dr Cpe	$4,100	$6,100	$9,600	$16,400
1970	144S	4dr Sdn	$2,800	$4,200	$6,900	$11,000
1970	145S	4dr Wgn	$2,900	$4,400	$6,700	$11,500
1970	164	2dr Sdn	$2,500	$4,800	$7,000	$12,000
1970	1800E	2dr Cpe	$10,300	$17,400	$30,900	$49,200
1971	142E	2dr Cpe	$4,300	$6,200	$9,000	$12,800
1971	142	2dr Cpe	$3,900	$5,600	$8,300	$11,800
1971	144	4dr Sdn	$2,900	$5,100	$7,800	$10,500
1971	145	4dr Wgn	$2,800	$4,800	$6,900	$9,800
1971	164	4dr Sdn	$2,500	$4,800	$7,000	$12,000
1971	1800E	2dr Cpe	$10,300	$17,400	$30,900	$49,200
1972	142	2dr Cpe	$3,900	$5,700	$8,300	$11,800
1972	144	4dr Sdn	$2,900	$5,200	$7,800	$10,500
1972	145	4dr Wgn	$2,800	$4,800	$7,100	$10,000
1972	164E	4dr Sdn	$2,500	$4,000	$5,300	$9,200
1972	1800E	2dr Cpe	$10,300	$17,400	$30,900	$49,200
1972	1800ES	2dr Wgn	$11,500	$21,100	$39,800	$72,000
						-25% for auto trans.
1973	142	2dr Cpe	$3,900	$5,700	$8,300	$11,800
1973	144	4dr Sdn	$2,900	$5,200	$7,800	$10,500
1973	145	4dr Wgn	$2,800	$4,800	$7,100	$10,000
1973	164E	4dr Sdn	$2,500	$4,000	$5,300	$9,200
1973	1800ES	2dr Wgn	$11,500	$21,100	$39,800	$72,000
						-25% for auto trans.
1974	142	2dr Cpe	$3,900	$5,700	$8,300	$11,800
1974	144	4dr Sdn	$2,900	$5,200	$7,800	$10,500
1974	145	4dr Wgn	$2,800	$4,800	$7,100	$10,000
1974	164E	4dr Sdn	$2,500	$4,000	$5,300	$9,200
1975	242	2dr Cpe	$3,100	$4,700	$6,900	$10,600
1975	242GT	2dr Cpe	$4,300	$6,600	$9,500	$15,800
1975	244	4dr Sdn	$2,000	$3,200	$4,300	$6,300
1975	245	4dr Wgn	$2,400	$4,000	$5,200	$7,600
1975	164E	4dr Sdn	$2,500	$4,000	$5,300	$9,200
1976	242	2dr Cpe	$3,100	$4,700	$6,900	$10,600
1976	242GT	2dr Cpe	$4,300	$6,600	$9,500	$15,800
1976	244	4dr Sdn	$2,000	$3,200	$4,300	$6,300
1976	245	4dr Wgn	$2,400	$4,000	$5,200	$7,600
1977	242	2dr Cpe	$3,100	$4,700	$6,900	$10,600
1977	242GT	2dr Cpe	$4,300	$6,600	$9,500	$15,800
1977	244	4dr Sdn	$2,000	$3,200	$4,300	$6,300
1977	245	4dr Wgn	$2,400	$4,000	$5,200	$7,600
1977	264	4dr Sdn	$2,300	$3,400	$4,600	$6,300

Volvo

Year	Model	Body Style	4	3	2	1
1977	265	4dr Wgn	$2,300	$3,600	$4,600	$6,500
1978	242	2dr Cpe	$3,100	$4,700	$6,900	$10,600
1978	242GT	2dr Cpe	$4,300	$6,600	$9,500	$15,800
1978	244	4dr Sdn	$2,000	$3,200	$4,300	$6,300
1978	245	4dr Wgn	$2,400	$4,000	$5,200	$7,600
1978	262C	2dr Bertone Cpe	$3,200	$5,200	$8,500	$16,700
1978	264	4dr Sdn	$2,300	$3,400	$4,600	$6,300
1978	265	4dr Wgn	$2,300	$3,600	$4,600	$6,500
1979	242	2dr Cpe	$3,100	$4,700	$6,900	$10,600
1979	242GT	2dr Cpe	$4,300	$6,600	$9,500	$15,800
1979	244	4dr Sdn	$2,000	$3,200	$4,300	$6,300
1979	245	4dr Wgn	$2,400	$4,000	$5,200	$7,600
1979	262C	2dr Bertone Cpe	$3,200	$5,200	$8,500	$16,700
1979	264	4dr Sdn	$2,300	$3,400	$4,600	$6,300
1979	265	4dr Wgn	$2,300	$3,600	$4,600	$6,500
1980	242	2dr Cpe	$3,100	$4,700	$6,900	$10,600
1980	242GT	2dr Cpe	$4,300	$6,600	$9,500	$15,800
1980	244	4dr Sdn	$2,000	$3,200	$4,300	$6,300
1980	245	4dr Wgn	$2,400	$4,000	$5,200	$7,600
1980	262C	2dr Bertone Cpe	$4,300	$7,800	$12,400	$18,700
1980	264	4dr Sdn	$2,300	$3,400	$4,600	$6,300
1980	265	4dr Wgn	$2,300	$3,600	$4,600	$6,500
1981	262C	2dr Bertone Cpe	$4,700	$9,100	$13,400	$20,400

Warwick

Year	Model	Body Style	4	3	2	1
1960	GT	2dr Cpe	$17,200	$28,700	$50,000	$56,400 *-25% for RHD.*
1961	GT	2dr Cpe	$17,200	$28,700	$50,000	$56,400 *-25% for RHD.*
1961	GT350	2dr Cpe	$18,100	$32,300	$51,000	$59,100 *-25% for RHD.*
1962	GT350	2dr Cpe	$18,100	$32,300	$51,000	$59,100 *-25% for RHD.*
1963	GT350	2dr Cpe	$18,100	$32,300	$51,000	$59,100 *-25% for RHD.*
1964	GT350	2dr Cpe	$18,100	$32,300	$51,000	$59,100 *-25% for RHD.*
1965	GT350	2dr Cpe	$18,100	$32,300	$51,000	$59,100 *-25% for RHD.*

Willys

Year	Model	Body Style	4	3	2	1
1949	Jeepster	134/63 2dr Phtn Conv	$8,100	$17,300	$26,200	$38,400

Willys

Year	Model	Body Style	4	3	2	1
1950	Jeepster	134/63 2dr Phtn Conv	$8,100	$17,100	$25,900	$37,600
		148/72 2dr Phtn Conv	$9,300	$19,100	$29,100	$40,200
1951	Jeepster	134/72 2dr Phtn Conv	$8,100	$17,100	$25,900	$37,600
		161/75 2dr Phtn Conv	$9,500	$19,400	$29,200	$40,500

Woodill

Year	Model	Body Style	4	3	2	1
1952	Wildfire	2dr Conv	$36,800	$68,900	$96,800	$131,000
1953	Wildfire	2dr Conv	$36,800	$68,900	$96,800	$131,000
1954	Wildfire	2dr Conv	$27,000	$54,200	$80,200	$111,000
1955	Wildfire	2dr Conv	$27,000	$54,200	$80,200	$111,000
1956	Wildfire	2dr Conv	$27,000	$54,200	$80,200	$111,000

Order your next issue or renew your subscription on the next page:

USA - single book - $23
1 yr subscription - 3 books - $40
2 yr subscription - 6 books - $65
3 yr subscription - 9 books - $85

Canada - single book - $30
1 yr subscription - 3 books - $60
2 yr subscription - 6 books - $95
3 yr subscription - 9 books - $135

International - single book - $35
1 yr subscription - 3 books - $75
2 yr subscription - 6 books - $115
3 yr subscription - 9 books - $165

Make U.S. Dollar checks payable to
Hagerty Media Properties, LLC.
or order by VISA/MC/AMEX

Hagerty Price Guide
Box 477
Great Falls, VA 22066-0477
(877) 872-7772
International (703) 759-9100

ORDER FORM

Select One:

USA - *US shipping address*

☐ Single Book-$23 ☐ 1yr-$40 ☐ 2yr-$65 ☐ 3yr-$85

Canada - *Canadian shipping address*

☐ Single Book-$30 ☐ 1yr-$60 ☐ 2yr-$95 ☐ 3yr-$135

International - *Shipping address outside of US/Canada*

☐ Single Book-$35 ☐ 1yr-$75 ☐ 2yr-$115 ☐ 3yr-$165

☐ Check enclosed ____________ ☐ Charge my VISA/MC/AMEX

Name ______________________________

Street ______________________________

City ______________ State ______________

Zip ______________________________

Phone ______________________________

Email ______________________________

Credit Card # ______________________________

SIC Code ______________ Exp. ______________

Signature ______________________________

Order your next issue or renew your subscription on the next page:

USA - single book - $23
1 yr subscription - 3 books - $40
2 yr subscription - 6 books - $65
3 yr subscription - 9 books - $85

Canada - single book - $30
1 yr subscription - 3 books - $60
2 yr subscription - 6 books - $95
3 yr subscription - 9 books - $135

International - single book - $35
1 yr subscription - 3 books - $75
2 yr subscription - 6 books - $115
3 yr subscription - 9 books - $165

Make U.S. Dollar checks payable to
Hagerty Media Properties, LLC.
or order by VISA/MC/AMEX

Hagerty Price Guide
Box 477
Great Falls, VA 22066-0477
(877) 872-7772
International (703) 759-9100

ORDER FORM

Select One:

USA - *US shipping address*

☐ Single Book-$23 ☐ 1yr-$40 ☐ 2yr-$65 ☐ 3yr-$85

Canada - *Canadian shipping address*

☐ Single Book-$30 ☐ 1yr-$60 ☐ 2yr-$95 ☐ 3yr-$135

International - *Shipping address outside of US/Canada*

☐ Single Book-$35 ☐ 1yr-$75 ☐ 2yr-$115 ☐ 3yr-$165

☐ Check enclosed ____________ ☐ Charge my VISA/MC/AMEX

Name ______________________________

Street ______________________________

City ______________ State ______________

Zip ______________________________

Phone ______________________________

Email ______________________________

Credit Card # ______________________________

SIC Code ______________ Exp. ______________

Signature ______________________________